# Organizing Black America

An Encyclopedia of
African American Associations

# Organizing Black America

## An Encyclopedia of African American Associations

*Edited by*

Nina Mjagkij

*Ball State University*

Garland Publishing, Inc.
*New York & London*

Published in 2001 by
Garland Publishing, Inc.
29 West 35th Street
New York, NY 10001

Garland is an imprint of the Taylor & Francis Group.

## Editorial Staff

Laura Kathleen Smid
*Project Editor*

Arlene Belzer
Edward Cone
Tim Roberts
*Copyeditors*

Martin A. Levick
*Art Researcher*

Jeanne Shu
*Production Editor*

Laura-Ann Robb
*Production Director*

Richard Steins
*Development Manager*

Sylvia K. Miller
*Publishing Director, Reference*

10   9   8   7   6   5   4   3   2   1

Organizing Black America: an encyclopedia of African American associations/edited
by Nina Mjagkij.
    p. cm.
  Includes bibliographical references and index.
  ISBN 0-8153-2309-3 (acid-free paper)
    1. Afro-Americans—Societies, etc.—Encyclopedias. I. Mjagkij, Nina, 1961–

E185.5 .O74 2001
305.896'073'06—dc21                                        00-061779

Printed on acid-free, 250-year-life paper
Manufactured in the United States of America

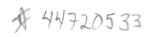

# Contents

# Introduction

In a 1944 article in the *American Historical Review,* historian Arthur M. Schlesinger traced the history of American voluntary organizations. Pointing to a profusion of associations that penetrated "nearly every aspect of American life," Schlesinger concluded that America was "a Nation of Joiners" ("Biography of a Nation of Joiners," vol. L, no. 1 [October 1944]: 1–25). While Schlesinger's study focussed on organizations with white memberships, his conclusion applies equally to African Americans.

Throughout American history, African Americans have established a multitude of religious, professional, business, political, recreational, educational, secret, social, cultural, and mutual aid associations. Frequently ignored by historians, these voluntary organizations served a variety of purposes and pursued diverse goals. Yet all of them provided important services to the black community and played a crucial role in the struggle for freedom, racial advancement, and equality.

Many black associations were the product of the racism that resulted in the exclusion of African Americans from the majority of the nation's white-controlled associations. In response, African Americans founded organizations that paralleled those of their white counterparts. Black medical practitioners, for example, launched the National Medical Association because the American Medical Association excluded them from membership. During the second half of the twentieth century, many of these black-initiated associations ceased to exist when white-dominated organizations started to desegregate and open their ranks to black members. While African Americans joined these previously all-white organizations, they often established black caucuses to assure the proper representation of their interests within the larger associations.

Although African Americans established numerous associations in response to racism, discrimination, and segregation, other organizations were the product of the black community's expression of racial solidarity and an assertion of self-determination. Providing services and programs that addressed the particular needs of the race in slavery and freedom, these associations furnished African Americans with opportunities for companionship, professional networking, intellectual stimulation, and educational advancement, as well as artistic, literary, and spiritual expression. Moreover, many of the organizations served as outlets for social, economic, religious, and political discussions and often generated activism and reform. Indeed, the associations created a racially autonomous world that shielded African Americans from racial abuse and humiliation, while enabling them to serve the needs of the black community with honor, dignity, and respect.

In addition to racially exclusive associations, many organizations united black and white members in the struggle to end slavery, segregation, and discrimination. Beginning in the first half of the nineteenth century, abolitionist societies, such as the American Anti-Slavery Society, attracted black and white members in the fight against slavery. Following the Civil War, joint organizational efforts on behalf of African Americans continued, as blacks and whites worked together in various freedmen's aid associations. By the early twentieth century, emerging civil rights organizations, such as the National Association for the Advancement of Colored People, provided yet another forum for interracial cooperation. The number of racially inclusive organizations further increased during and after World War II, when numerous local and state governments appointed interracial committees. Sparked by the eruption of urban race riots as well as wartime and cold war concerns about America's image abroad, these government agencies studied racial conditions and formulated policies to end discrimination and segregation. Finally, at the height of the postwar civil rights movement, large numbers of blacks and whites united in protest activities, culminating in legislation that signalled the beginning of the end of Jim Crow laws.

*Organizing Black America: An Encyclopedia of African American Associations* is the most comprehensive reference work illustrating the rich history of these associations and their leaders that has been published. Organized alphabetically, the encyclopedia seeks to provide easy access to information about associations established by African Americans, such as the National Negro Business League; interracial organizations that served a predominantly black constituency, such as the National Urban League; groups working in the interest of African Americans, such as the President's Committee on Civil Rights; and association activities in cities with a significant black population, such as Chicago and New York. Entries trace the origins, goals, founders, membership, staff, activities, achievements, failures, and demise of African American associations. Moreover, they assess the historical significance of black organizations and the contributions of individuals who assumed leadership positions within their respective associations.

A detailed index to the volume as well as cross-references provide easy access to information. For readers interested in pursuing further research, each entry contains a selective bibliography citing the most authoritative secondary literature. Since organizations frequently change headquarters, officers, and personnel, no mailing addresses or fax and phone numbers have been included.

While the encyclopedia is the most comprehensive reference work chronicling African American association activities, it is by no means complete. An attempt has been made to provide information about all large organizations and those of regional, national, or international importance. Short-lived organizations, small groups, and associations of predominantly local significance were not included.

Compiling the entry list and identifying authors as well as the research, writing, and editing of this volume took several years and involved the collaboration of 184 scholars from Europe and the United States. Without their expertise, completion of this volume would have been impossible. Thus, an expression of my gratitude for their assistance seems at best inadequate.

The 576 entries in this encyclopedia illustrate that African American associations helped to improve the quality of black life, fostered a sense of community, and played a crucial role in the struggle for racial advancement and civil rights. Moreover, they point to an abundance of opportunities for scholars to conduct further research that will illuminate the rich tradition of association building in the black community.

*Nina Mjagkij*
*Ball State University*

# List of Entries

# Contributors

**Saheed A. Adejumobi**
*University of Texas at Austin*
  Pan-African Congress

**Norm R. Allen Jr.**
*Council for Secular Humanism, Center for Inquiry*
  African Americans for Humanism

**Donald Altschiller**
*Boston University*
  A. Philip Randolph Institute
  Black Academy of Arts and Letters
  Hatza'ad Harishon
  National Dental Association
  National Optometric Association

**Karen Anderson**
*Georgia State University*
  National Council of Negro Women

**Felix L. Armfield**
*Western Illinois University*
  National Association of Black Social Workers
  Social Workers' Club

**Eric Arnesen**
*University of Illinois at Chicago*
  Negro Railway Labor Executives Committee
  Provisional Committee to Organize Colored
    Locomotive Firemen
  Railway Men's International Benevolent Industrial
    Association
  United Transport Service Employees of America

**Julius H. Bailey**
*University of North Carolina at Chapel Hill*
  Black Methodists for Church Renewal
  Fraternal Council of Negro Churches
  National Conference of Black Churchmen

  Women's Missionary Society, African Methodist
    Episcopal Church

**Robin B. Balthrope**
*Plattsburgh State University of New York*
  American Council on Race Relations
  Committee for Welfare, Education, and Legal Defense
  Eta Phi Beta
  Southern Society for the Promotion of the Study of
    Race Conditions and Problems in the South

**Alwyn Barr**
*Texas Tech University*
  Lone Star Medical, Dental, and Pharmaceutical
    Association

**Abel A. Bartley**
*University of Akron*
  Jacksonville, Florida: Civic, Literary, and Mutual Aid
    Associations
  Miami: Civic, Literary, and Mutual Aid Associations

**Amy Bass**
*State University of New York at Stony Brook*
  Black Coaches Association
  Black Entertainment and Sports Lawyers Association
  Central Intercollegiate Athletic Association
  National Interscholastic Basketball Tournament

**Loretta E. Bass**
*University of Oklahoma*
  Library Company of Colored Persons, Philadelphia
  National Alliance of Postal Employees

**Beth Tompkins Bates**
*Wayne State University*
  AFL-CIO Committee on Civil Rights
  Trade Union Leadership Council
  United Auto Workers: Fair Practices and Anti-
    Discrimination Department

**John F. Bauman**
*California University of Pennsylvania*
 National Committee Against Discrimination in
  Housing
 President's Committee on Equal Opportunity in
  Housing

**Colin A. Beckles**
*Washington State University*
 Oregon Fair Employment Practices Advisory
  Committee
 Seattle: Civic, Literary, and Mutual Aid Associations
 Washington State Board Against Discrimination in
  Employment
 Washington State Fair Employment Practices
  Committee

**Scott Beekman**
*Ohio University*
 African Blood Brotherhood for Liberation and
  Redemption
 Friends of Negro Freedom

**Jayne R. Beilke**
*Ball State University*
 General Education Board
 John F. Slater Fund
 Julius Rosenwald Fund
 Negro Rural School Fund
 Peabody Education Fund
 Phelps-Stokes Fund
 Southern Education Foundation

**Sybril M. Bennett**
*Vanderbilt University*
 Association of Black Admissions and Financial Aid
  Officers of the Ivy League and Sister Schools

**Samuel W. Black**
*Western Reserve Historical Society*
 Cleveland: Civic, Literary, and Mutual Aid
  Associations

**Richard Blackett**
*University of Houston*
 African Aid Society
 African Civilization Society
 American Colonization Society

**Kristine Boeke**
*University of Notre Dame*
 British and Foreign Anti-Slavery Society
 Freedmen's Aid Society, London
 London Emancipation Society

**Beverly Greene Bond**
*University of Memphis*
 Memphis: Civic, Literary, and Mutual Aid Associations
 Memphis Lyceum

**Nancy Bowman**
*University of Maryland*
 Black Women's Liberation Committee
 Delta Sigma Theta
 Ida B. Wells Social Club

**Anne Braden**
*Louisville, Kentucky*
 National Alliance Against Racist and Political Repression
 Southern Conference Educational Fund
 Southern Organizing Committee for Economic and
  Social Justice

**Linda Brown-Kubisch**
*State Historical Society of Missouri*
 St. Louis: Civic, Literary, and Mutual Aid Associations

**Barbara Buice**
*Penn State University at Monroeville*
 Black Emergency Cultural Coalition
 National Association for the Advancement of Black
  Americans in Vocational Education
 National Association of Black Storytellers
 National Association of Real Estate Brokers
 National Coalition of Black Meeting Planners
 Organization of Black Screenwriters, Inc.

**Ronald E. Butchart**
*University of Georgia*
 American Freedmen's Union Commission
 Baltimore Association for the Moral and Educational
  Improvement of the Colored People
 Bureau of Refugees, Freedmen, and Abandoned Lands
 Freedmen's Aid and Southern Education Society of the
  Methodist Episcopal Church
 National Freedmen's Relief Association
 Northwestern Freedmen's Aid Commission
 Pennsylvania Freedmen's Relief Association
 Savannah Education Association
 Western Freedmen's Aid Commission

**Dominic J. Capeci Jr.**
*Southwest Missouri State University*
  Detroit Interracial Committee
  National Advisory Commission on Civil Disorders
    (Kerner Commission)
  National Association for the Advancement of Colored
    People
  Sojourner Truth Citizens Committee

**Clayborne Carson**
*Stanford University*
  Student Nonviolent Coordinating Committee

**Derek C. Catsam**
*Ohio University*
  Colored Farmers' National Alliance and Cooperative
    Union
  New Negro Alliance

**Dennis W. Cheek**
*Rhode Island Department of Education*
  American Association of Blacks in Energy
  Minority Women in Science
  National Action Council for Minorities in
    Engineering
  National Association of Black Geologists and
    Geophysicists
  National Organization for the Professional
    Advancement of Black Chemists and Chemical
    Engineers
  National Society of Black Engineers
  National Society of Black Physicists
  National Technical Association

**Geoffrey Coats**
*Indiana University at Bloomington*
  American Society of African Culture

**Peter Cole**
*Western Illinois University*
  Office of Production Management, Minorities (or
    Minority Groups) Branch
  Trade Union Unity League
  War Manpower Commission, Negro Manpower
    Service
  War Production Board, Negro Employment and
    Training

**James L. Conyers Jr.**
*University of Nebraska at Omaha*
  National Afro-American League
  National Conference of Black Mayors
  National Conference of Black Political Scientists

**Daniel E. Crowe**
*Prescott College*
  HARYOU
  Louisville, Kentucky: Civic, Literary, and Mutual Aid
    Associations
  US

**Stephen Davenport**
*University of Illinois at Urbana-Champaign*
  Black Stuntmen's Association
  Malcolm X Society
  Negro Theatre Guild
  100 Black Men of America, Inc.
  Organization of Black Episcopal Seminarians
  Union of Black Episcopalians

**James J. Davis**
*Howard University*
  College Language Association

**Vanessa L. Davis**
*Southwestern University*
  Council of Federated Organizations
  Deacons for Defense
  Delta Ministry
  Mississippi Freedom Democratic Party
  Mississippi Progressive Voters' League

**Gary Daynes**
*Brigham Young University*
  Fellowship of Reconciliation
  Knights of Peter Claver
  National Equal Rights League
  Negro Fellowship League
  Oblate Sisters of Providence
  United Colored Democracy

**Lawrence B. de Graaf**
*California State University at Fullerton*
  Los Angeles: Civic, Literary, and Mutual Aid
    Associations
  San Francisco: Civic, Literary, and Mutual Aid
    Associations

**Sara Diamond**
*Rutgers University*
   African Academy of Arts and Research
   African Heritage Studies Association
   Afro-American Research Institute

**Katherine Kuntz Dill**
*Indianapolis*
   American Citizens' Equal Rights Association
   National Association of Human Rights Workers
   National Black MBA Association
   National Committee on Segregation in the Nation's
      Capital
   Negro Christian Student Conference

**Julie S. Doar**
*The Newport School*
   Big Eight Council on Black Student Governments
   Iota Phi Theta
   National Council of Negro Youth
   National Pan-Hellenic Council, Inc.
   Phi Beta Sigma
   Zeta Phi Beta

**L. Mara Dodge**
*Westfield State College*
   Phyllis Wheatley Women's Clubs and Homes

**Sherry Sherrod DuPree**
*Santa Fe Community College*
   Institute for Black Family Development
   Intercollegiate Pentecostal Conference International
   International Fellowship of Black Pentecostal Churches
   National Colored Spiritual Association of Churches, Inc.

**Joseph T. Durham**
*Community College of Baltimore, President Emeritus*
   Congressional Black Caucus
   National Association of African American Studies
   National Association of College Deans, Registrars, and
      Admissions Officers
   National Black Leadership Roundtable
   Sigma Pi Phi

**Gary R. Entz**
*McPherson College*
   American Negro Labor Congress
   Genesis Group, Church of Jesus Christ of Latter-Day
      Saints

   International Migration Society
   Kansas Human Rights Commission
   League of Struggle for Negro Rights
   Topeka, Kansas: Civic, Literary, and Mutual Aid
      Associations
   United Transatlantic Society

**Alexandra Epstein**
*University of California at Santa Barbara*
   American Tennis Association
   National Bowling Association
   United Golfers Association

**Michel Fabre**
*Sorbonne University of Paris*
   Comité des Citoyens
   French-American Fellowship

**David M. Fahey**
*Miami University*
   Colored Knights of Pythias
   Grand United Order of Moses
   Grand United Order of Odd Fellows
   Grand United Order of True Reformers
   Independent Order of Good Templars
   Independent Order of St. Luke
   United Brothers of Friendship and Sisters of the
      Mysterious Ten

**Adam Fairclough**
*University of East Anglia*
   Montgomery Improvement Association
   Southern Christian Leadership Conference

**Lynne Barbara Feldman**
*Toronto, Canada*
   Birmingham, Alabama: Civic, Literary, and Mutual Aid
      Associations

**Earline Rae Ferguson**
*University of Illinois at Urbana-Champaign*
   Indianapolis: Civic, Literary, and Mutual Aid
      Associations

**Phyllis Field**
*Ohio University*
   Bureau for Colored Troops
   Union League

**Vivian Njeri Fisher**
*Morgan State University*
  Anti-Slavery Convention of American Women
  National Association for the Relief of Destitute
    Colored Women and Children

**Oscar Flores**
*Moorhead State University*
  Blacks in Government
  Council for a Black Economic Agenda
  National Association of Black Real Estate Professionals
  National Association of Market-Developers
  National Association of Minority Architects
  National Association of Securities Professionals
  National Economic Association

**Catherine Fobes**
*Alma College*
  National Welfare Rights Organization

**Nishani Frazier**
*Columbia University*
  Association of Southern Women for the Prevention of
    Lynching
  MOVE
  President's Initiative on Race

**Karen Garner**
*Florida International University*
  Equal Suffrage League
  Julia Ward Howe Republican Women's Club
  Women Wage Earner's Association
  Women's Christian Temperance Union, Department of
    Colored Work
  Women's Day Workers and Industrial League
  Women's Volunteer Service League

**Sandra E. Gibbs**
*National Council of Teachers of English*
  Black Caucus of the National Council of Teachers of
    English and Conference on College Composition and
    Communication

**John M. Giggie**
*Princeton University*
  Mosaic Templars of America
  Twelve Knights of Tabor

**Stephanie Gilmore**
*Ohio State University*
  National Black Feminist Organization
  National Coalition of Black Lesbians and Gay Men
  National Hook-Up of Black Women

**Richlyn F. Goddard**
*Howard University*
  Association for the Study of Afro-American Life and
    History

**Fon Louise Gordon**
*University of Kentucky*
  Arkansas Commission on Race Relations
  Little Rock, Arkansas: Civic, Literary, and Mutual Aid
    Associations

**Barbara L. Green**
*Wright State University*
  Columbus, Ohio: Civic, Literary, and Mutual Aid
    Associations
  Commission for Multicultural Ministries, Evangelical
    Luthern Church in America
  Dayton, Ohio: Civic, Literary, and Mutual Aid
    Associations
  Gospel Music Workshop of America
  International Rhythm and Blues Association

**Cheryl Greenberg**
*Trinity College, Hartford, Connecticut*
  Citizens' League for Fair Play
  Negro Industrial and Clerical Alliance
  New York Mayor's Commission on Conditions in
    Harlem

**Peggy Hardman**
*Palo Alto Community College*
  American Academy of Medical Directors
  Association of Black Cardiologists
  Medical Committee for Human Rights
  National Association of Health Service
    Executives
  National Pharmaceutical Association
  Negro Medical Association of Virginia
  Palmetto State Medical Association
  Sickle Cell Disease Association of America, Inc.
  Tri-State Dental Association of DC, VA, MD

**Paul Harvey**
*University of Colorado at Colorado Springs*
American National Baptist Convention
Baptist Foreign Mission Convention of the United States
Consolidated American Baptist Missionary Convention
National Baptist Convention of America
National Baptist Convention, U.S.A., Inc.
National Baptist Educational Convention

**Leslie Heaphy**
*Kent State University, Stark Campus*
League of Colored Baseball Clubs
National Negro Baseball Leagues
Negro American League
Negro National League
Negro Southern League

**Gerald Horne**
*University of North Carolina at Chapel Hill*
Civil Rights Congress
National Conference of Black Laywers
National Negro Congress
Southern Negro Youth Congress

**Angela Hornsby**
*University of North Carolina at Chapel Hill*
National Association of Colored Girls
Order of the Eastern Star

**Dolan Hubbard**
*Morgan State University*
College Language Association
Langston Hughes Society

**John N. Ingham**
*University of Toronto*
Colored Merchants Association
National Business League

**Eric R. Jackson**
*Northern Kentucky University*
Black Rock Coalition
Cincinnati's Mayor's Friendly Relations Committee
Harmon Foundation
Indianapolis Community Relations Council

**Robert J. Jakeman**
*Auburn University*
National Airmen's Association of America

National Black Coalition of Federal Aviation
   Employees
Negro Airmen International
Organization of Black Airline Pilots

**Bryan Bartlett Jarmusch**
*University of Kentucky*
Community Relations Service
Freedom and Peace Party
Peace and Freedom Party

**Robert F. Jefferson**
*University of Iowa*
National Civil Rights Committee of the American
   Veterans Committee
Negro Service Committee of the United Service
   Organizations
United Negro and Allied Veterans of America, Inc.

**Joan Marie Johnson**
*University of Cincinnati*
Universal Association of Ethiopian Women

**J. Angus Johnston**
*City University of New York*
National Student Association
United States Student Association

**Rhett S. Jones**
*Brown University*
African-American Museums Association
Association of Black Anthropologists
Kappa Alpha Psi
National Council for Black Studies
Southern Conference on Afro-American Studies

**Faustine C. Jones-Wilson**
*Howard University, Emeritus*
American Teachers Association

**Mitchell Kachun**
*Grand Valley State University*
Afro-American Council
American Moral  Reform Society
American Negro Academy
American Negro Historical Society, Philadelphia
Negro Society for Historical Research
Society for the Collection of Negro Folk Lore,
   Boston

**Andrew E. Kersten**
*University of Wisconsin at Green Bay*
  Cincinnati: Civic, Literary, and Mutual Aid
    Associations
  Committee on Race and Caste in World Affairs
  Federal Council on Negro Affairs
  Joint Committee on National Recovery
  March on Washington Committee
  Ohio Commission for Fair Employment Practices
    Legislation
  State Council for a Pennsylvania Fair Employment
    Practices Commission

**William M. King**
*University of Colorado at Boulder*
  Colorado Anti-Discrimination Commission
  Denver Colored Civic Association
  Denver Interracial Commission
  Denver Unity Council
  Denver's Mayor's Interim Survey Committee on
    Human Relations
  National Institute of Science

**Jack Knight**
*Southwest Missouri State University*
  National Association for the Advancement of Colored
    People

**Anne Meis Knupfer**
*Purdue University*
  Chicago: Civic, Literary, and Mutual Aid Associations

**David F. Krugler**
*University of Wisconsin at Platteville*
  Chicago Mayor's Commission on Human Relations
  Hoover's Colored Advisory Commission
  President's Commission on Campus Unrest

**Angela Darlean LeBlanc-Ernest**
*Stanford University*
  All-African People's Revolutionary Party
  Black Panther Party (for Self-Defense)
  Black Women Organized for Action

**Charles Franklin Lee**
*Carnegie Mellon University*
  Afro-American Republican League of Pennsylvania
  Pittsburgh: Civic, Literary, and Mutual Aid
    Associations

**Anthony J. Lemelle Jr.**
*Purdue University*
  Association of Black Sociologists
  Nation of Islam

**Gretchen Lemke-Santangelo**
*Saint Mary's College of California*
  Bay Area Council Against Discrimination
  Council for Civic Unity, San Francisco

**Thomas Leuchtenmüller**
*University of Munich*
  Coordinating Council for Negro Performers,
    Inc.
  Negro Actors Guild of America
  Theater Owners Booking Association

**Bobby L. Lovett**
*Tennessee State University*
  Nashville: Civic, Literary, and Mutual Aid
    Associations

**Christine Lutz**
*Georgia State University*
  Center for Democratic Renewal
  National Domestic Workers Union
  Women's International League for Peace and Freedom

**Stuart McElderry**
*Doane College*
  American League of Colored Laborers
  Central Trades and Labor Assembly
  CIO Committee to Abolish Racial Discrimination
  Coalition of Black Trade Unionists
  International Working People's Association
  National Association for the Promotion of Trade
    Unionism Among Negroes
  National Brotherhood Workers of America

**Phillip McGuire**
*Fayetteville State University*
  Circle for Negro War Relief
  Committee Against Jim Crow in Military Service
    and Training
  Committee for the Participation of Negroes in the
    National Defense
  Lynn Committee to Abolish Segregation in the
    Armed Forces

**David MacLaren**
*Loyola University of Chicago*
  Blue Circle Nurses
  Committee on Negro Troop Policies
  Illinois Interracial Commission
  National Association of Colored Graduate Nurses
  National Committee of Negro Veteran Relief

**Norman C. McLeod Jr.**
*Hazard Community College*
  African American Women's Clergy Association
  Fellowship of Southern Churchmen
  General Commission on Religion and Race, United
    Methodist Church
  Lott Carey Baptist Foreign Mission Convention
  New York African Clarkson Association

**Virginia M. Matthews**
*University of South Carolina*
  National Committee to Abolish the Poll Tax
  South Carolina Council on Human Relations
  Southern Coalition for Educational Equity
  University Commission on Southern Race Questions
  Visions Foundation

**Jim Meriwether**
*California State University at Bakersfield*
  Africa Watch
  American Committee on Africa
  American Negro Leadership Conference on Africa
  Operation Crossroads Africa
  Universal African Nationalist Movement

**Dennis N. Mihelich**
*Creighton University*
  Omaha, Nebraska: Civic, Literary, and Mutual Aid
    Associations

**Nina Mjagkij**
*Ball State University*
  Young Men's Christian Association, Colored Work
    Department

**Jacqueline M. Moore**
*Austin College*
  Alley Improvement Association, Washington, D.C.
  Bethel Literary and Historical Association
  Medico-Chirurgical Society, Washington, D.C.
  Niagara Movement
  Washington, D.C.: Civic, Literary, and Mutual Aid
    Associations

**Jesse T. Moore Jr.**
*University of Rochester*
  National Urban League

**Shirley Ann Wilson Moore**
*California State University at Sacramento*
  California Council for Civic Unity
  East Bay Negro Historical Society
  Negro Equity League of San Francisco

**Paul D. Moreno**
*Hillsdale College*
  Fair Share Organization
  Office of Federal Contract Compliance Programs
  President's Committee on Equal Employment
    Opportunity
  President's Committee on Government Employment
    Policy

**Wilson J. Moses**
*Pennsylvania State University*
  Alpha Phi Alpha

**Derryn E. Moten**
*Alabama State University*
  New Orleans: Civic, Literary, and Mutual Aid
    Associations
  New Orleans Community Relations Council
  Savannah: Civic, Literary, and Mutual Aid
    Associations

**Earl F. Mulderink III**
*Southern Utah University*
  Massachusetts General Colored Association
  New England Anti-Slavery Society
  New England Freedmen's Aid Society

**Thalia M. Mulvihill**
*Ball State University*
  Association of Colleges and Secondary Schools for
    Negroes
  Black Women's Educational Alliance
  National Alliance of Black School Educators
  National Black Youth Leadership Council
  National Congress of Black Faculty

**Bernard C. Nalty**
*Air Force History Program, Emeritus*
  President's Committee on Equality of Opportunity in
    the Armed Forces (The Gesell Committee)
  President's Committee on Equality of Treatment and
    Opportunity in the Armed Forces (The Fahy
    Committee)

**Timothy B. Neary**
*Loyola University of Chicago*
  National Council of Churches, Commission on
    Religion and Race

**Cynthia Neverdon-Morton**
*Coppin State College*
  Atlanta Neighborhood Union
  Baltimore: Civic, Literary, and Mutual Aid Associations

**Cassandra Newby-Alexander**
*Norfolk State University*
  Norfolk, Virginia: Civic, Literary, and Mutual Aid
    Associations

**Debra Newman Ham**
*Morgan State University*
  Black Caucus of the American Library Association

**Kimberly E. Nichols**
*University of Memphis*
  Alabama Council on Human Relations
  Arkansas Council on Human Relations
  Atlanta Conferences for the Study of Negro Problems
  Commission on Interracial Cooperation
  Council of Social Agencies, Pasadena, California,
    Interracial Commission
  Florida Council on Human Relations
  Georgia Council on Human Relations
  Louisiana Council on Human Relations
  Mississippi Council on Human Relations
  National Women's Committee for Civil Rights
  Partners for Progress
  Potomac Institute
  Southern Regional Council
  Tennessee Council on Human Relations
  Virginia Council on Human Relations

**Dawn Nickel**
*University of Alberta*
  National Health Circle for Colored People
  National Hospital Association

**Betty Nyangoni**
*Washington, D.C.*
  Committee for Racial Justice, United Church of Christ
  National Association For Equal Opportunity in Higher
    Education
  Poor People's Campaign
  Sigma Gamma Rho

**Opolot Okia**
*West Virginia University*
  National Association of Black Accountants
  National Association of Minority Contractors
  National Black Media Coalition

**Sharon Parkinson**
*State University of New York at Albany*
  Minority Business Development Agency
  National Association of Black Women Entrepreneurs
  National Association of Minority Women in Business
  National Black Chambers of Commerce

**Tiffany Ruby Patterson**
*Binghamton University*
  United Negro College Fund

**Kurt W. Peterson**
*Judson College*
  African American Lutheran Association
  American Baptist Black Caucus
  Society for the Study of Black Religion

**Paula F. Pfeffer**
*Loyola University Chicago*
  National Council for a Permanent Fair Employment
    Practices Commission

**Julieanne Phillips**
*Baldwin-Wallace College*
  Alpha Kappa Alpha
  Jackie Robinson Foundation
  Liberian Development Association
  National Association of Negro Business and
    Professional Women's Clubs
  National Congress of Colored Parents and Teachers

**Lisa Phillips**
*Rutgers University*
  League of Revolutionary Black Workers
  National Negro Labor Council
  Negro American Labor Council
  Negro Labor Committee

**Michael Phillips**
*Univeristy of Texas at Austin*
  Coalition Against Blaxploitation
  Council for United Civil Rights Leadership
  Dallas: Civic, Literary, and Mutual Aid Associations
  Houston: Civic, Literary, and Mutual Aid Associations
  National Alliance of Black Organizations
  Southern Commission on the Study of Lynching
  Southern Organization for United Leadership

**Bill Stanford Pincheon**
*Washington State University*
  African American AIDS Associations
  African American Lesbian and Gay Associations

**Claudia Polley**
*Indianapolis, Indiana*
  National Association for African American Heritage
    Preservation

**Jill Quadagno**
*Florida State University*
  National Welfare Rights Organization

**Peter Rachleff**
*Macalester College*
  Readjusters
  Richmond, Virginia: Civic, Literary, and Mutual Aid
    Associations

**James Ralph**
*Middlebury College*
  Alabama Christian Movement for Human Rights
  Leadership Conference for Civil Rights
  Nashville Student Movement
  Northern Student Movement
  Voter Education Project

**Maria Elena Raymond**
*Robbins, California*
  National Bankers Association
  National Coalition on Black Voter Participation

**Merl E. Reed**
*Georgia State University, Emeritus*
  President's Committee on Fair Employment Practice

**Eric W. Rise**
*University of Delaware*
  National Association of Black Women Attorneys
  National Bar Association
  National Lawyers Guild

**Angel R. Rivera**
*Ball State University*
  Afro-American Police League
  Afro-American Press Association
  Guardians Association
  National Association of Black Journalists
  National Association of Black Scuba Divers
  National Association of Blacks in Criminal Justice
  National Black Police Association
  National Caucus and Center on Black Aged
  National Newspaper Publishers Association
  Organization of Afro-American Unity

**Jo Ann O. Robinson**
*Morgan State University*
  Congress of Racial Equality

**Mary G. Rolinson**
*Georgia State University*
  Atlanta Negro Voters League

**Nancy Jean Rose**
*Penn State University*
  Association of Black Psychologists
  Chi Eta Phi
  Iota Phi Lambda
  National Black McDonald's Operators Association
  National Forum for Black Public Administrators

**Nichole T. Rustin**
*New York University*
  Association for the Advancement of Creative Musicians
  Jazz Composers Guild
  Mutual Musicians' Foundation
  National Association of Negro Musicians
  Society of Black Composers

**Elizabeth D. Schafer**
*Loachapoka, Alabama*
  Afro-American Federation of Labor
  Alabama Share Croppers Union
  Association of Deans of Women and Advisers to Girls
    in Negro Schools
  Black Gold Star Mothers
  Black Public Relations Society of America
  Conference of Presidents of Negro Land-Grant
    Colleges
  Council of 1890 College Presidents
  International Association of African and American
    Black Business People
  International Association of Black Business Educators
  International Association of Black Professional Fire
    Fighters
  Liberty Party
  National Association of College Women
  National Association of Extension Home Economists
  National Association of Management Consultants
  National Association of Personnel Deans and Advisers
    of Men in Negro Institutions
  National Association of Personnel Workers
  National Black Music Caucus of the Music Educators
    National Conference
  National Conference of Editorial Writers
  National Democratic Party of Alabama
  Southern Tenant Farmers' Union
  Tuskegee Conference

**Mark R. Schneider**
*Weymouth, Massachusetts*
  Boston: Civic, Literary, and Mutual Aid Associations
  Boston Literary and Historical Association
  League of Women for Community Service, Boston
  Massachusetts Commission Against Discrimination

**Joel Schwartz**
*Montclair State University*
  Greater New York Coordinating Committee for
    Employment
  Harlem Tenant League
  New York City Commission on Human Rights
  New York State Commission Against Discrimination
  New York's Mayor's Committee on Unity

**A. J. Scopino Jr.**
*Central Connecticut State University*
  Association of Black Catholics Against Abortion
  Connecticut Commission on Human Rights and
    Opportunities
  Committee for the Advancement of Colored Catholics
  Episcopal Commission for Black Ministries
  Federated Colored Catholics of the United States
  Moorish Science Temple of America
  National Black Catholic Clergy Caucus
  National Black Catholic Congress
  National Black Catholic Lay Caucus
  National Black Catholic Seminarian Association
  National Black Sisters' Conference
  National Office for Black Catholics
  Secretariat for Black Catholics
  Sisters of the Blessed Sacrament for Indians and
    Colored People
  Society of the Divine Word

**Janet Harrison Shannon**
*Davidson College*
  Free African Societies
  Philadelphia: Civic, Literary, and Mutual Aid
    Associations

**Ruthe T. Sheffey**
*Morgan State University*
  Zora Neale Hurston Society

**Julie Shipe**
*Madison, Wisconsin*
  Black Affairs Council, Unitarian Universalist
  Governor's Human Rights Commission, Wisconsin

  Milwaukee's Mayor's Commission on Human Rights
  Ministers for Racial and Social Justice
  National Black Presbyterian Caucus

**Joel Shrock**
*Miami University at Hamilton*
  Ancient Egyptian Arabic Order Nobles of the Mystic
    Shrine
  Improved Benevolent and Protective Order of the Elks
    of the World

**Josh A. Sides**
*University of California at Los Angeles*
  Governor's Commission on the Los Angeles Riots

**Andrew Smallwood**
*University of Nebraska at Omaha*
  National Black Caucus of Local Elected Officials
  National Black Caucus of State Legislators
  National Citizens' Rights Association
  National Organization of Black County Officials

**Carol J. Smith**
*Washington, D.C.*
  National Advisory Committee on Black Higher
    Education and Black Colleges and Universities

**Elaine M. Smith**
*Alabama State University*
  International Council of Women of the Darker Races
  National Youth Administration, Office of Negro Affairs

**Susan L. Smith**
*University of Alberta*
  National Medical Association

**Isabel Soto**
*Universidad Autónoma of Madrid*
  American Association for Affirmative Action
  Black Filmmaker Foundation
  International Black Writers and Artists

**Allan H. Spear**
*University of Minnesota at the Twin Cities*
  Chicago Commission on Race Relations

**Mollie A. Spillman**
*Ramsey County Historical Society, Saint Paul, Minnesota*
  Governor's Interracial Commission, Minnesota
  Minneapolis' Mayor's Council on Human Relations
  Minnesota Fair Employment Practice Commission

**Margaret A. Spratt**
*California University of Pennsylvania*
  Young Women's Christian Association, Council on
    Colored Work

**Richard D. Starnes**
*Western Carolina University*
  Black and Tan Republicans
  Chattanooga, Tennessee: Civic, Literary, and Mutual
    Aid Associations
  North Carolina Council on Human Relations
  Old North State Medical, Dental, and Pharmaceutical
    Society

**Judith Stein**
*Graduate School of City University of New York*
  Universal Negro Improvement Association and African
    Communities League

**James Brewer Stewart**
*Macalester College*
  American and Foreign Anti-Slavery Society
  American Anti-Slavery Society

**Patricia Sullivan**
*Harvard University*
  Southern Conference for Human Welfare

**Rosalyn Terborg-Penn**
*Morgan State University*
  Association of Black Women Historians
  Jack and Jill of America, Inc.
  Sisters of the Holy Family

**Richard W. Thomas**
*Michigan State University*
  Detroit: Civic, Literary, and Mutual Aid Associations

**Timothy N. Thurber**
*State University of New York at Oswego*
  Equal Employment Opportunity Commission
  Government Contract Compliance Committee
  President's Committee on Civil Rights
  President's Committee on Government Contracts
  United States Commission on Civil Rights

**Joseph S. Townsend**
*Ball State University*
  National Political Congress of Black Women
  Southern Poverty Law Center
  Southern Sociological Congress

**Joe W. Trotter**
*Carnegie Mellon University*
  Milwaukee: Civic, Literary, and Mutual Aid
    Associations

**Harold Dean Trulear**
*Philadelpha, Pennsylvania*
  American Church Institute for Negroes, Episcopal
    Church
  Black Council, Reformed Church in America
  Conference of Church Workers Among Colored
    People, Episcopal Church
  Interreligious Foundation for Community
    Organization
  National Black Evangelical Association

**André D. Vann**
*North Carolina State University*
  The Links Incorporated
  National Funeral Directors and Morticians
    Association
  Progressive National Baptist Convention

**Penny M. Von Eschen**
*University of Michigan*
  Council on African Affairs

**Jill Watts**
*California State University, San Marcos*
  Peace Mission Movement

**Walter B. Weare**
*University of Wisconsin at Milwaukee*
  National Insurance Association

**Scott W. Webster**
*University of Maryland*
  Afro-American Party
  Association of Black American Ambassadors
  TransAfrica

**Robert E. Weir**
*Bay Path College*
  Brotherhood of Sleeping Car Porters
  Colored National Labor Union
  Prince Hall Masons

**Matthew C. Whitaker**
*Michigan State University*
  Committee on Negro Housing
  Michigan Commission on Civil Rights
  Michigan Committee for Intercultural Understanding
  Phoenix: Civic, Literary, and Mutual Aid Associations

**John White**
*University of Hull, United Kingdom*
  National Rainbow Coalition
  Operation Breadbasket
  People United to Save Humanity

**William H. Wiggins Jr.**
*Indiana University*
  Association of African and African-American
    Folklorists

**Craig Steven Wilder**
*Williams College*
  New York City: Civic, Literary, and Mutual Aid
    Associations

**Jimmy Elaine Wilkinson Meyer**
*Shreve, Ohio*
  National Black Women's Health Project
  National Black Women's Political Leadership
    Caucus
  National Coalition of 100 Black Women

**Lillian Serece Williams**
*State University of New York at Albany*
  National Association of Colored Women's Clubs,
    Inc.

**Maria Williams-Hawkins**
*Ball State University*
  Black Women Organized for Educational Development

**Carol Wilson**
*Washington College*
  Colored Conventions
  Manumission Societies
  Society for the Relief of Free Negroes Unlawfully Held
    in Bondage

**Lyle K. Wilson**
*Negro Leagues Committee, The Society for American
Baseball Research*
  Baseball Hall of Fame, Negro Leagues
  Eastern Colored League
  International League
  Middle States Baseball League
  West Coast Baseball Association

**Jennifer J. Wojcikowski**
*University of North Carolina at Chapel Hill*
  American Baptist Home Missionary Society
  American Missionary Association
  Presbyterian Church Committee on Missions to
    Freedmen
  Society for the Propagation of the Gospel in Foreign
    Parts

# Organizing Black America

An Encyclopedia of
African American Associations

## A. Philip Randolph Institute

Founded in the spring of 1965 by the labor leader A. Philip Randolph and the civil rights activist Bayard Rustin, the A. Philip Randolph Institute was organized to strengthen the alliances between African Americans and progressive organizations, especially labor unions. Supported by a $25,000 grant from the Industrial Union Department of the American Federation of Labor–Congress of Industrial Organizations (AFL-CIO), the institute established its headquarters in Harlem at 217 West 125th Street, in the same building occupied by Randolph's union, the Brotherhood of Sleeping Car Porters.

The Randolph Institute was involved in many labor and progressive causes, including the boycott of California grapes, support for the 1968 strike of Memphis sanitation workers, nationwide voter registration campaigns, and establishment of the national Citizens Committee to Support General Electric strikers in 1969. In the same year, in an action that created some controversy, the institute supported the United Federation of Teachers' strike of the New York City schools. Many civil rights organizations supported community control of the New York City public schools, but the institute viewed the strike as a labor conflict and supported the teachers union. In addition to its support of labor, national health care, and civil rights, the institute defended the rights of Soviet dissidents, aided the struggle against South African apartheid, and supported the State of Israel.

The A. Philip Randolph Educational Fund, a tax-exempt institute affiliate, organized the Joint Apprenticeship Program—later renamed the Recruitment and Training Program—which tutored more than 4,000 young African Americans and Hispanics for jobs in the building construction trades, which had historically barred minori-

ties. In 1967, the institute actively campaigned for the Freedom Budget, a highly ambitious economic plan to raise $18.5 billion to be spent toward the eradication of poverty in the United States within ten years. However, neither Congress nor Presidents Lyndon B. Johnson and Richard M. Nixon supported this social welfare plan.

In March 1970, the institute organized local affiliates to work with the trade union movement, to engage in voter education and registration and to support liberal social legislation. As of 2000, the institute had more than 150 chapters in thirty-six states. Randolph Institute publications include *Black Studies: Myths and Realities*, a collection of critical essays edited by Bayard Rustin. In 2000, Norman Hill was the president of the institute, which remains a constituency group of the AFL-CIO.

FURTHER READINGS

Anderson, Jervis B. *A. Philip Randolph: A Biographical Portrait*. New York: Harcourt Brace Jovanovich, 1972.

———. *Bayard Rustin: Troubles I've Seen: A Biography*. New York: HarperCollins, 1997.

Pfeffer, Paula F. *A. Philip Randolph: Pioneer of the Civil Rights Movement*. Baton Rouge: Louisiana State University Press, 1990.

Rustin, Bayard. "The History of the A. Philip Randolph Institute." *Debate and Understanding* 1, 1 (Winter 1976): 29–35.

*Donald Altschiller*

## AFL-CIO Committee on Civil Rights

When the Unions of the American Federation of Labor (AFL) and the Congress of Industrial Organizations (CIO) merged in 1955, the architects of the union wrote into the constitution a clause against discrimination, establishing a Committee on Civil Rights (CCR). The committee was "vested with the duty and the responsibility to assist the Executive Council [of the federation] to bring about at the earliest possible date the effective implementation of the principle stated in this constitution of non-discrimination in accordance with the provisions of this constitution." James B. Carey, president of the International Union of Electrical Workers (IUEW) and chairman of the CIO's equal rights committee before the merger, chaired the first meeting of the CCR on February 9, 1956. From its inception, the CCR was criticized because it included such members as George M. Harrison, president of the Brotherhood of Railway Clerks, an organization that had excluded black workers from its union for decades, had evaded court orders against discriminatory practices, and continued to circumvent the spirit and the letter of orders to remove color bars even as its president served on the CCR. During its first year, the committee criticized the formation of white citizens councils, which were supported by many white rank-and-file union members in the South. By December 1957, Carey resigned from the chairmanship of the committee because, as he told the *New York Times*, he had not "been given enough power or freedom to do an effective job of stamping out racial bias in unions." Although day-to-day administration of the CCR was supposed to be carried out with the assistance of a Department on Civil Rights, headed by Boris Shiskin, both the committee and the department had little power to discipline unions and largely relied on the power of moral persuasion.

At the AFL-CIO convention in 1959, A. Philip Randolph, president of the Brotherhood of Sleeping Car Porters and one of the two black vice presidents on the executive council, criticized the labor organization for its failure to prevent discriminatory practices within its unions. Randolph asked why the AFL-CIO had not supported the committee and the Department on Civil Rights with the same vigor that the federation had applied to eliminating communism. The question inspired repeated confrontations between Randolph and George Meany, president of the AFL-CIO, who countered: "Who the hell appointed you as guardian of all the Negroes in America?" In response, Randolph formed the Negro-American Labor Council (NALC) in 1960 as an alternative organization to work for equality within the AFL-CIO.

While the executive council of the AFL-CIO continued to applaud efforts of the federation in the area of civil rights, the National Association for the Advancement of Colored People (NAACP) in the early 1990s issued a detailed criticism of the AFL-CIO's record on civil rights. The CCR was cited as an obstacle to executing equal rights directives because it lacked enforcement power. Debate continued between racial advancement organizations and the labor federation over the gap between theory and practice on discrimination issues. Constitutional color bars, segregated locals, and exclusion of black workers from apprenticeship programs continued to define racial relations in many AFL-CIO unions in the early 1960s. By 1964, after adoption of the federal Civil Rights Act, the AFL-CIO joined with other civil rights groups to found the Leadership Conference on Civil Rights, a lobbying organization. The CCR was thus overshadowed after 1964 by larger efforts, with more teeth, initiated by the federal government. Nevertheless, a decade after the merger and formation of the CCR, little progress had been made in terms of changing patterns of racial discrimination in the major AFL-CIO affiliates. In numerous cases, unions removed racial exclusion clauses from their constitutions as a public relations gesture but continued to exclude or limit black membership to unions and apprenticeship programs through other means.

**FURTHER READINGS**

Boyle, Kevin. *The UAW and the Heyday of American Liberalism, 1945–1968.* Ithaca, N.Y.: Cornell University Press, 1995.

Foner, Philip S. *Organized Labor and the Black Worker, 1619–1981.* 2nd ed. New York: International Publishers, 1982.

Geschwender, James A. *Class, Race, and Worker Insurgency: The League of Revolutionary Black Workers.* New York: Cambridge University Press, 1977.

Jacobson, Julius, ed. *The Negro and the American Labor Movement.* New York: Anchor Books, 1968.

Lichtenstein, Nelson. *Walter Reuther: The Most Dangerous Man in Detroit.* New York: HarperCollins, 1995.

Ross, Arthur M., and Herbert Hill, eds. *Employment, Race, and Poverty.* New York: Harcourt, Brace & World, 1967.

UAW Fair Practices Department. United Auto Workers Papers. Walter Reuther Library. Archives of Labor and Urban Affairs. Wayne State University, Detroit, Michigan.

*Beth Tompkins Bates*

## Africa Watch

Established in 1988, Africa Watch is part of the broader Human Rights Watch organization. This liberal, interracial human rights group monitors and promotes the observance of human rights in sub-Saharan Africa. Its efforts include work to abolish summary executions, torture, arbitrary detention, and violations of due process; to stop restrictions on expression, assembly, association, and religion; and to end discrimination on racial, gender, ethnic, and religious grounds. Prominent African Americans, including the writers Toni Morrison and Randall Robinson, have served on the group's advisory committee.

In recent years, for example, Africa Watch has targeted repression in Nigeria, supported prosecution of those accused of genocide in Rwanda and Burundi, backed the abolition of the death penalty in South Africa, and urged the universal barring of children under age eighteen to serve in any military capacity. Africa Watch has funded fact-finding missions to interview both victims and witnesses of human rights abuses and has met with a wide range of local people, including government officials, opposition leaders, journalists, doctors, and church officials. It also supports local human rights activists in an effort to strengthen an international network of human rights proponents.

With a worldwide operating budget of millions of dollars, of which close to a million is earmarked for Africa, Human Rights Watch and its African operation stand as one of the leading human rights monitors and agencies active in Africa.

*Jim Meriwether*

## African Academy of Arts and Research

In 1943, three African students—Kingsley Mbadiwe, Mbonu Ojike, and A. A. Nwafor Orizu—founded the African Academy of Arts and Research (AAAR) while attending school in the United States. The AAAR's goal was to educate Americans about African culture and to promote African independence. The academy's first officers were Mbadiwe, the historian Ojike, Lawrence Reddick, South African D. Buyabuye Mdodana, and West Indian businessman A. A. Austin.

In 1945, the AAAR's Board of Directors was reorganized to provide it with "more dynamic leadership and promote collective responsibility for policy and decisions" (Lynch, 193). The Reverend James H. Robinson became chair, A. George Daly vice president, and Ojike executive director. Five new members joined the board, including the lawyer, judge, and politician Raymond Pace Alexander; Charles E. Seifert; and the Methodist minister Charles Y. Trigg. Although most board members were African or African American, three white liberals joined in 1946, including former First Lady Eleanor Roosevelt, Roger Baldwin, and Maurice P. Davidson. By December 1945, the group's membership had grown to one thousand.

To spark American interest in African culture, the academy sponsored critically acclaimed African Dance Festivals at Carnegie Hall in 1943, 1945, and 1946. Moreover, the academy published *Africa Today and Tomorrow* (1945), a collection of eighteen essays on African history, culture, and politics. The publication also announced the recipients of the 1945 and 1946 Wendell Wilkie Awards. First recipients were former Vice President Henry A. Wallace, who was honored as "an outspoken champion of civil rights in the United States and freedom for all colonial people" (Lynch, 194) and Ethiopian Emperor Haile Selassie, who was recognized in 1946 for his support of African independence and his patronage of the academy. During the winter of 1945–1946, the AAAR organized lectures on Africa at the American Museum of Natural History Washington, D.C. In 1946, the academy sponsored fund-raising events known as "Africa Days" at black churches in New York, and it produced *Greater Tomorrow*, a newsreel highlighting AAAR activities that became an important fund-raising tool. In 1947 the academy purchased Africa House, which became a meeting place for expatriate Africans in New York City.

To remedy Western inattention to Africa, the academy cultivated relationships with African American journalists and newspaper editors such as Claude Barnett and James Jones-Quartery. The academy used these connections to publicize and generate American support for Nigerian workers during a general wage strike in the summer of 1945.

In addition to educating Americans about African culture and politics, the AAAR also promoted African independence. In 1945, for example, Ojike lobbied the U.N. San Francisco Conference for the establishment of target dates for African independence, but his efforts to meet with American and British representatives were unsuccessful. At the Academy's first annual conference in October 1946, George W. Harrison, president of the Ethiopian World Federation, called for the establishment of a pan-African federation to support African decolonization and "foster vigorous commercial and cultural ties between Africans and blacks in the new World" (Lynch, 196). Academy members embraced capitalism as a beneficial force for African development and advocated pan-African entrepreneurship in Africa. To strengthen the ties between America and Africa, Mbadiwe opened AAAR branch offices in Sierra Leone, Gold Coast (Ghana), Nigeria, and Liberia when he returned to West Africa in 1947.

Before the academy ceased operating in 1957, it facilitated postwar ties between Africa and America by generating American awareness of and appreciation for African culture and politics, assisting African students in the United States, and encouraging African Americans to pursue pan-Africanism. The academy, for example, encouraged Barnett, who became a staunch supporter of African liberation, to make his first of fifteen visits to Africa in 1947, and it facilitated Horace Mann Bond's first visit to Nigeria in 1949. The AAAR also set an example for and inspired the formation of other American organizations focused on Africa, including the American Society for African Culture and Crossroads Africa, which was founded by James H. Robinson, former chair of the academy's board in 1958.

**FURTHER READING**

Lynch, Hollis. "K. O. Mbadiwe, 1939–1947: The American Years of A Nigerian Political Leader." *Journal of African Studies* 7, 4 (Winter 1980–1981): 184–203.

*Sara Diamond*

**SEE ALSO**   American Society for African Culture; Crossroads Africa

## African Aid Society

Reverend Theodore Bourne, corresponding secretary of the African Civilization Society (founded in 1858), launched the African Aid Society (AAS) in Great Britain in 1860. The AAS—made up of businessmen, philanthropists, and others eager to promote British interests in West Africa—was headed by Lord Randolph Churchill, a minor government official. The AAS aimed to develop African resources and to promote Christian civilization on the Continent through the establishment of colonies of free African Americans. It would assist all African Americans who wished to leave Canada and the United States for colonies in the tropics and would supply settlers with the means to establish themselves in their new homes.

The antislavery movement, from its inception, struggled to address a contradiction of its own making: How could one call logically for the emancipation of slaves and at the same time continue to consume slave-grown pro-

duce? Abolitionists resolved the dilemma in two ways: They boycotted goods produced by slave labor, and they promoted schemes to produce sugar and cotton by free labor. The first approach proved very effective in the years leading up to emancipation in the British West Indies. The second, while more problematic, and having less tangible results, remained an important feature of the transatlantic abolitionist movement in the years after 1834. Known generally as the Free-Produce Movement, it called for the boycotting of slave-grown goods, especially cotton from the United States, and searched for alternative sources of cotton particularly in the West Indies and Africa. These efforts won the support of such African Americans as the abolitionists Henry Highland Garnet and Samuel Ringgold Ward in the 1850s. Part of Garnet's responsibilities as a missionary of the United Presbyterian Church of Scotland in Sterling, Jamaica, was to encourage the cultivation of goods for export. Ward agreed to go to Jamaica in 1854 to put the movement's principles into practice.

Both of these efforts coincided with a rising concern among British textile manufacturers about their almost total reliance on American cotton. In 1857 their concerns found expression in the formation of the Cotton Supply Association, which aimed at encouraging the cultivation of cotton throughout the tropical world. Not surprisingly, Africa became an important field of operation. Not long after the formation of the association, African Americans and their supporters interested in establishing a colony in West Africa wrote to enquire about prospects in the area. British abolitionists were also aware of these developments. Colonies of the sort proposed by the abolitionist Martin Delany and the African Civilization Society in Yorubaland could answer both the needs of British textile manufacturers and free-produce advocates.

Even before Delany left for West Africa in 1859, the African Civilization Society had sent its corresponding secretary, the Reverend Theodore Bourne, to make contact with potential supporters in Britain. By the time Delany arrived in Britain in the summer of 1860, Bourne already had in place the nucleus of a support group that in July adopted the name, the African Aid Society. Over the next few months, Delany toured Britain promoting the work of the AAS. By the time of his return to Canada in early 1861 branches of the society had been formed in Glasgow and Birmingham with plans already in place for an auxiliary in Manchester.

While Delany and others tried to interest African Americans in the United States and in Canada in the proposed colony, the AAS lobbied the British government to support its plans. But the proposed colony faced a number of obstacles that in the end proved insurmountable. With the outbreak of civil war in the United States potential settlers turned their attention to a struggle that many believed would end in the destruction of slavery. In West Africa, British missionaries pressured local authorities to rescind their agreement with Delany. When Britain occupied Lagos in mid-1861 it effectively put an end to any efforts to introduce a colony of African Americans into the area. Before the Civil War was over in 1865, the AAS had abandoned any plans for encouraging settlement in the area and instead turned its attention to promoting British colonial interest in Lagos and other parts of Africa. For a time it supported William Craft's two missions to Dahomey in 1862 and 1863. Craft, a former slave from Georgia, had been living in England since 1851 and during that period had been very active in the abolitionist movement. Craft saw his missions as a way of persuading the king of Dahomey to abandon the practice of human sacrifices and to end participation in the slave trade. By the time Craft returned to England in 1867 the AAS had abandoned all efforts at philanthropy and turned its attention almost exclusively to the promotion of British business and colonial interest in West Africa.

Little is known of the society's activities in the closing decades of the nineteenth century, although it remained an active player using its newspaper, the *African Times*, to promote British colonial interests.

**FURTHER READINGS**

Blackett, R. J. M. *Building an Anti-Slavery Wall: Black Americans in the Atlantic Abolitionist Movement, 1830–1860.* Baton Rouge: Louisiana State University Press, 1983.

Miller, Floyd J. *The Search for a Black Nationality: Black Colonization and Emigration 1787–1863.* Urbana: University of Illinois Press, 1975.

Schor, Joel. *Henry Highland Garnet: A Voice of Black Radicalism in the Nineteenth Century.* Westport, Conn.: Greenwood Press, 1977.

*Richard Blackett*

## African American AIDS Associations

African American AIDS associations in cities across the United States provide urgent health education, counseling, housing, financial, and other types of support to people affected by HIV/AIDS. They offer AIDS education and prevention resources to groups, organizations, and individuals who would like information, outreach, and counseling on AIDS prevention, testing, and treatment. In 1991, HIV infection and AIDS was the sixth leading cause of death among African Americans and the seventh leading cause of death among Hispanics, while it ranked tenth among white Americans. Because many of the early AIDS organizations did not focus on minority health concerns, special interest groups—such as the National Minority AIDS Council—emerged to combat the rise of AIDS and the spread of the disease among African Americans and other minority groups in the United States. The Centers for Disease Control has worked to establish collaborative arrangements with national programs that involve business, labor, industry, religious institutions, youth agencies, the media, and voluntary, ethnic, and racial minority organizations.

In September 1994, the office of the assistant secretary for health and the United States Public Health Service sponsored the first National Congress on the State of HIV/AIDS in Racial and Ethnic Communities. The congress was the first of its kind to focus on public policy issues related to HIV/AIDS prevention programs and services in racial and ethnic communities in the United States. The congress, assisted by key nongovernmental organizations such as AIDS Project Los Angeles; Morehouse School of Medicine; Iris House; Riverside Church; Outreach, Inc.; Black Entertainment Television; and Inner City Aids Outreach developed workshops that placed special emphasis on promoting a greater understanding of the role of biomedical and behavioral research. With 935 community leaders in attendance, the congress met to reflect on the broad spectrum of racial and ethnic minorities involved in HIV/AIDS prevention, services, and research. In workshops and special institutes, representatives from African American, Asian, Pacific Islander, Hispanic/Latino, and Native American communities sought to identify opportunities to improve efforts to combat HIV/AIDS. The congress explored avenues of expanding the use of technology and computers to support HIV/AIDS services and enhancing new and existing opportunities for partnerships between governmental organizations.

Despite these efforts, African Americans are still disproportionately affected by HIV and AIDS. They account for about 34 percent of the total reported AIDS cases in the United States, while comprising only 11 percent of the American population. Racial and ethnic disparities of those infected with AIDS are much more striking for women and children than they are for men. In June 1996, the Centers for Disease Control reported that African American women accounted for 55 percent of AIDS cases reported among women and that 58 percent of all children reported with AIDS were African Americans. Likewise, African Americans accounted for over half of all AIDS cases reported among injection drug users (or IDUs). Clearly, there is an urgent need for health care professionals and other leaders within the African American community to be concerned about HIV and AIDS. While many organizations within the African American community offer AIDS awareness institutes and workshops, perhaps the greatest impact is often made by medical and biomedical research, direct-service providers, and AIDS educational organizations with a grass-roots focus.

In the African American community several factors have played a significant role in limiting proper AIDS education and awareness training. Workshops initiated and conducted by black groups have tried to reduce these barriers by promoting improved access to and the delivery of comprehensive AIDS-related services for people of color. Workshops, for example, identify public policies that respect the traditions and cultures of America's diverse racial and ethnic communities. Moreover, they identify components of effective programs that promote the development of culturally competent and linguistically appropriate service models.

Among African Americans, AIDS and HIV has been, and to some extent still is, often thought of as a disease that primarily affects gay males. Many black churches, for example, teach that homosexuality is a sin and blame the gay community for the spread of AIDS. Some black ministers such as the Reverend Yvette Flunder have tried to combat that perception, arguing that the characterization of homosexuality as a sin perpetuates denial and contributes to the spread of the disease among African Americans. Flunder, a former lead gospel singer with the Edwin Hawkins Love Center Choir of Oakland, California, now conducts an HIV/AIDS support agency in San Francisco. Her organization, the Ark of Refuge, provides housing, education, training, and care partners for HIV/AIDS clients. During the past years, she has conducted AIDS education seminars at esteemed venues such as the annual Gospel Music Workshop of America Convention, reaching many people through a combined effective ministry and advocacy that culminates in a supportive educational outreach program.

While HIV/AIDS is not primarily a "homosexual issue" among African Americans, black lesbians and gay men have often been at the forefront of providing financial, educational, and other types of assistance. They have worked through a variety of community organizations that serve African Americans, people of color, and gays, often volunteering or serving in key managerial roles within HIV/AIDS resource organizations. As a result of their involvement they are often able to demand more inclusive perspectives on health care delivery practices and the distribution of other types of assistance in HIV/AIDS prevention and management programming. New York City's Gay Men's Health Crisis (GHMC), for example, began to target minority populations after increased pressure to be more inclusive and has since endeavored to increase minority outreach. Another gay and lesbian organization involved in outreach work with the African American community is Washington, D.C.–based Black Lesbian and Gay Pride, Inc. (BLGP). The nonprofit organization was established as a direct fundraising provider for community-based organizations that offer HIV/AIDS services to African Americans. BLGP is committed to removing the barriers of homophobia, fear, denial, and alienation through fund-raising efforts and civic involvement. The group is dedicated to raising social consciousness through community action, unifying communities of color, and bridging the gap between heterosexual and homosexual communities. The group's "passion to action" is bred out of a desire to decrease the rate of HIV/AIDS infection among communities of color. BLGP offers support to community-based organizations that provide a wide array of HIV/AIDS services including health education, medical and mental health services, HIV testing, legal and financial support, volunteer training, and shelter and food support for African American children, teenagers, and adults affected by or infected with HIV/AIDS.

There are a number of similar organizations around the country that provide education, housing, resources, and other forms of assistance. Groups that have launched efforts to combat AIDS among African Americans include the Minority Task Force on AIDS in New York City; the Jefferson County AIDS in Minorities program in Birmingham, Alabama; the African-American AIDS Support Services and Survival Institute in Los Angeles; the San Francisco Black Coalition on AIDS; Black Gays and Lesbians United Against AIDS in Denver; the HIV Support Group for African-American Men and Women at the Whitman-Walker Clinic in Washington, D.C.; the AIDS Education and Services for Minorities program in Atlanta; the Minority Outreach Intervention Project in Chicago; Project Survival in Detroit; Men of Color Aids Prevention in the Office of Gay and Lesbian Health Issues in Manhattan; the Oregon Minority AIDS Coalition in Portland; Blacks Educating Blacks about Sexual Health Issues in Philadelphia; the Renaissance II, Brother2Brother Project in Dallas; and the People of Color Against AIDS Network in Seattle.

These groups provide a collective front against the rise of HIV/AIDS among African Americans and other minorities, disseminating vital health care information to a variety of clients on a year-round basis and keeping abreast of important developments in the war against AIDS. They help educate those who might not otherwise be reached by traditional health care networks, and they provide a valuable service to African Americans from all walks of life.

**FURTHER READINGS**

Graham, Rhonda. "And the Choir Sings On." *(Wilmington, Delaware) Sunday News Journal*, October 23, 1994.
————. "Special Report: AIDS in the Gospel Choir." *(Wilmington, Delaware) Sunday News Journal*, October 23, 1994.

*Bill Stanford Pincheon*

# African American Lesbian and Gay Associations

African American lesbian and gay associations create and provide supportive political, social, health, and educational networks that affirm the lives and identities of same-gender-loving and transgendered people of African descent. They also serve to provide a base of support to sustain networks of people actively committed to strengthening those structures that further their interests as black gay women and men. Most of these organizations have been founded in cities with large black and/or minority populations, such as Washington, D.C.; New York City; Oakland; California; Philadelphia; Atlanta; and New Orleans. Dating back to at least the 1920s, such organizations existed privately as informal social groups that hosted small weekly "rent" or house parties, staged elaborate dance balls and socials, and supported activist and political groups that emerged in the wake of the civil, women's and gay rights movements. Some multiracial groups such as Men of All Colors Together (formerly Black and White Men Together) and Black Lesbian and Gay Pride, Inc. (BLGP) are committed to combating racism and discrimination in the lesbian and gay male community and provide a supportive environment for less oppressive multiracial relations among gay men.

While some organizations provide social and political support, others are dedicated to exploring the cultural legacy and richness of their black and gay heritage. Groups such as the Lavender Light Black and People of All Colors Lesbian and Gay Choir keep alive the black gospel music

tradition in an environment supportive of lesbian and gay people. Lavender Light, which includes members of many ethnic groups, has a special ministry to black lesbians and gays who have been pressured historically by their communities to choose between their racial and their sexual identities. Founded in 1986, Other Countries, a black gay men's writing collective, was established by a group of black gay men who had worked as writers and organizers with the Blackheart Collective. The group provides a supportive environment for black gay male writers who are largely instrumental in publishing their own work and who wish to perform public readings and engage in self-critiques in weekly meetings. Circle of Voices, a non-profit organization that seeks to establish a creative arts environment where women of color can exchange information, herstories, knowledge, and skills with each other and the community at large, promotes an annual Womyn of Color Music Festival and other events for charitable and educational purposes.

Black lesbian and gay organizations generally seek to provide an increased awareness of the interlocking systems of oppression that endanger the lives of women and men who are both African American and gay. They seek to further public understanding of multiple forms of discriminatory oppression and provide support to their black lesbian and gay members who often encounter homophobia in the African American community, sexism in the male-dominated society, and racism in the gay community. Moreover, these organizations provide a political front for many issues that affect African Americans, gay people, and women and serve as a cultural voice to articulate a unified stance against a multiplicity of oppressions. Gay Men of African Descent, for example, promotes advocacy, health education, and consciousness-raising and fights racism, sexism, and homophobia while creating nurturing environments that affirm, celebrate, and empower gay people of African descent in all their diversity.

The largest and perhaps most well-known of these organizations is the Washington, D.C.–based National Coalition of Black Lesbians and Gay Men (NCBLGM), which was founded in 1979 by a core group of activists as the National Coalition of Black Gays. The NCBLGM functions as a lobbying group and seeks to provide a stronger cultural and political unity among lesbians and gay men. Another equally important group is the National Black Gay and Lesbian Leadership Forum, founded by Phil Wilson in Los Angeles in 1988. The forum recently opened a national office in Washington, D.C., headed by the newly appointed executive director Jubi D. Headley Jr. The forum is dedicated to empowering black lesbians, gays, bisexuals, and transgendered persons through advocacy, public education, increased visibility, developing strong leadership, and building bridges between communities. African Ancestral Lesbians United for Societal Change, Inc., or Salsa Soul, an eighteen-year-old organization serving lesbians of color, is committed to the spiritual, cultural, educational, economic, and social empowerment of "African Ancestral Lesbians and all Wimmin of Color."

In addition to these organizations that are national in scope, black gays and lesbians have launched numerous local support groups including Gay Men of African Descent in New York City; Black Gay Men United and the Nia Collective in Oakland, California; the Mosaic in Norwalk, Connecticut; the Delta Phi Upsilon Fraternity in Miami; Boyz of Distinction in Atlanta; Onyx in Chicago; Umoja in Baltimore; the James Baldwin–Pat Parker Society in Detroit; the African American Lesbians of Color Organization in Minneapolis; Kaleidoscope in Kansas City, Missouri; the Triangle Coalition of Black Lesbians and Gays in Carrboro, North Carolina; Cleveland Black Pride in Cleveland; the Black Gay and Lesbian Alliance for Dignity in Memphis; Ujima in Milwaukee; Adodi in Philadelphia; and the Sistah2Sistah and Brother2Brother groups that started to emerge in communities around the country in the late 1990s. While these organizations serve a local constituency, some of them have attracted a large following. Sisters of Something Special, for example, which began in the summer of 1990 when a group of thirty-five black lesbians met at Sheila's Restaurant in Brooklyn, is now more than 1,000 sisters strong.

A number of religious organizations exist that seek to affirm the spiritual needs of black lesbians and gay men, including the Metropolitan Community Church. Many branches of the predominantly black gay and lesbian Unity Fellowship Church exist around the country in cities such as Los Angeles; Washington, D.C.; Orlando; Detroit; Newark; New Jersey; Brooklyn; New York; and Philadelphia. These religious organizations not only promote the health and spiritual well-being of their members but also provide economic, educational, and housing assistance to those in need.

Some of these organizations have also produced or influenced a number of important creative works including books, periodicals, journals, dramas, films, and videos. On stage, Pomo Afro Homo, a black gay men's performing trio, has electrified audiences from coast to coast with searing monologues and other performances that high-light the nexus of race and sexual orientation with a decidedly Afro-Gay flair. Other Countries, the New York black gay male writing collective, for example, has produced *Other Countries Journal* and *Other Countries Journal II*, seminal volumes that celebrate and encourage black gay male writing. Kitchen Table: Women of Color Press, founded in the early 1980s by black lesbian Barbara Smith, has produced *Homegirls: A Black Feminist Anthology*. The men and women of black gay organizations have also provided support for collaborative works such as Marlon Rigg's award-winning video *Tongues Untied*. Riggs, a longtime member of Oakland's Black Gay Men United, utilized some of the consciousness-raising sessions that such a group offer to inform his experimental documentary. Members of the performing trio Pomo Afro Homo, who have also been involved in Black Gay Men United, participated in the various stages of the video's production.

African American lesbian and gay organizations serve an important role in fulfilling the health and spiritual needs and enriching the social life of their constituents. Moreover, they seek to empower black gays and lesbians, African Americans, gay people, and women. Their members often protest the exclusion of the voices and perspectives of black gay men and lesbians in a variety of contexts and seek to enlighten those who marginalize them. Black gays, for example, have participated in African American pride parades in Harlem, to achieve a greater level of visibility and to protest homophobia among African Americans. They sought with their presence to demonstrate that they are indeed a part of the African American community. Black gays have also protested homophobic and sexist remarks made by some leaders at the historic Million Man March on October 16, 1995.

These organizations have provided black gays and lesbians not only with a strong public voice and presence but have also created a nurturing environment for social support and activities. Moreover, they have established a political venue for black gay and lesbian organizing, activism, and coalition building. As Keith Boykin, former executive director of the Black Lesbian and Gay Leadership Forum, argues in his *One More River to Cross*, the shared experience of homosexuality is not so great as to eliminate all other differences between people of various races, genders, ethnicities, and backgrounds. The ability of black gay and lesbian groups to respond creatively to the needs of their constituents and to initiate social and political change will ensure their continued growth and leadership during the next millennium.

FURTHER READINGS

Beam, Joseph, ed. *In the Life: A Black Gay Anthology.* Boston: Alyson Press, 1986.

Boykin, Keith. *One More River to Cross: Black & Gay in America.* New York: Doubleday, 1996.

Hemphill, Essex. *Brother to Brother: New Writings by Black Gay Men.* Boston: Alyson Press, 1991.

Pincheon, Bill Stanford. "Framing Culture: Africanism, Sexuality and Performance in *Tongues Untied* and *Paris is Burning.*" Ph.D. diss., Indiana University, 1997.

Smith, Barbara, et al., eds. *Homegirls: A Black Feminist Anthology.* New York: Kitchen Table: Women of Color Press, 1983.

*Bill Stanford Pincheon*

# African-American Lutheran Association

The African American-Lutheran Association (AALA), established in 1987 as the United Lutherans for Black Concerns (ULBC), is a caucus of primarily African American clergy and laity who are members of the Evangelical Lutheran Church of America (ELCA). Through its Commission on Multicultural Ministries, the AALA works to unify African Americans and ensure their full participation in the life of the ELCA. It is working to develop partnerships between the ELCA and African American as well as African communities through worship, education, evangelism, stewardship, social ministry, and global awareness.

Although American Lutherans are predominantly white, the number of African Americans in Lutheran denominations has been rising steadily since Reconstruction. African American Lutheran history began in 1669, when an ordained Lutheran minister baptized a free black named Emmanuel in New York City. During the antebellum era, many African Americans became Lutherans largely because their white masters introduced them to their own faith. After a lull in the development of African American Lutheranism during the Civil War era, the number of black Lutherans began to rise in the late nineteenth century. During Reconstruction, several northern white synods established black churches and parish day schools in the South. While the white synods made an effort to train African American clergy to pastor the new black congregations, they espoused a model of middle-class respectability that worked in the North but failed to appeal to most southern blacks. In response, African American Lutherans formed the Alpha Synod, the first exclusively black Lutheran synod, in 1889.

In the twentieth century, when the number of African American Lutherans increased in the North and the Midwest, due to black migration and the arrival of black Lutherans from the West Indies, so did the need for organizations to meet and communicate their needs.

The AALA was the product of a merger between the Association of Black Lutherans of the Lutheran Church in America and the Coalition of Black Lutherans of the American Lutheran Church. Both groups formed in the 1960s in response to the assassination of Martin Luther King Jr. and the call for black power. They advocated an increased leadership role of African Americans in the Lutheran denominations and urged their churches to become more aware of racial issues and civil rights. In 1968, African American Lutheran pastors formed the Association of Black Lutheran Clergymen (or Churchmen), to unite black members of the three major Lutheran denominations, the American Lutheran Church, the Lutheran Church in America, and the Association of Evangelical Lutheran Churches. The organization lasted only three years, but it paved the way for other organizations and made white Lutherans increasingly aware of the needs of African Americans. In 1987, the Association of Black Lutherans and the Coalition of Black Lutherans joined to form the United Lutherans for Black Concerns (ULBC). When the nation's Lutheran denominations merged to establish the ELCA in 1988, the ULBC changed its name to AALA the following year.

The AALA, headquartered in the office of its incumbent president, represents the ELCA's 49,000 African American Lutherans as well as its 118 black male and thirty-five black female clergy. The AALA is organized into regional chapters, each holding monthly meetings. On the national level, the AALA meets biannually and publishes a monthly newsletter entitled *Ujamaa.* There are currently more than 200 ELCA congregations with a black membership of at least 20 percent.

FURTHER READINGS

Anderson, Hugh George. *Lutheranism in the Southeastern States, 1860–1886: A Social History.* The Hague, Netherlands: Mouton, 1996.

Johnson, Jeff G. *Black Christians: The Untold Lutheran Story.* St. Louis: Concordia, 1991.

Pero, Albert and Ambrose Moyo, eds. *Theology and the Black Experience: The Lutheran Heritage Interpreted by African and African-American Theologians.* Minneapolis: Augsburg Publishing House, 1988.

Stumme, Wayne C., ed. *Study of Black and Lutheran Congregations*. Columbus, Ohio: Institute for Mission in the U.S.A., 1987.

*Kurt W. Peterson*

## African-American Museum and Library at Oakland

*See* East Bay Negro Historical Society.

## African-American Museums Association

The African-American Museums Association (AAMA) originated in the late 1960s and was formally established in 1978. The AAMA is the voice of black museums in the United States. It serves African American museums, cultural institutions, universities, museum professionals, board members, scholars, and volunteers. The AAMA provides consultant services in marketing, conservation, personnel and collection management, exhibit design, visitor studies, program and audience enhancement, and trustee development. For this purpose the AAMA publishes a quarterly newsletter, *Scrip*, and an annual directory of black museums and their staffs. The AAMA is a frequent presenter of programs sponsored by the American Association of Museums, the American Association for State and Local History, and other scholarly and cultural organizations. The association has received support for its work from the National Endowment for the Arts, the National Endowment for the Humanities, the National Museums Act, and various private foundations, civic groups, and professional organizations.

In the late 1960s, Margaret Burroughs, founder of Chicago's DuSable Museum of African American History, and Charles Wright, founder of the Afro-American Museum of Detroit, called a series of conferences for black museums and their staffs, establishing an informal network in the process. In 1969, Wright invited representatives of six African American museums to Detroit to discuss the formation of a national association. Early in the 1970s, Tom Lloyd, director of the Storefront Museum in New York City, launched the first black museum organization when he established the National Association of Museums and Cultural Organizations. Lloyd's group did not survive, perhaps because most black museums had limited funds and were not able to support a national organization. Burroughs of Chicago's DuSable museum, however, persisted. In 1975 she sponsored a meeting of black museum professionals and scholars who gathered regularly and soon became known as the Black Seminar Group. While these informal meetings played an important role in the development of the fledgling black museum movement, participants believed that a formal organization was the best way to support black museums.

Thus, in 1978, a consortium of six black museums, with funding from the National Museum Act and the Smithsonian Institution, organized a series of conferences at participating African American museums. These meetings crystallized the need for a formal organization. Edmund Barry Gaither of the Museum of the National Center of Afro-American Artists in Boston chaired the group that prepared the AAMA's bylaws, which were ratified in Detroit in February 1978.

In the two years following its founding the AAMA was headquartered at the Museum of the National Center of Afro-American Artists. Jamiese Martin, the AAMA's first director, worked part-time and was the organization's sole staff member. In 1980, with the help of Betty Thomas, director of the Mary McLeod Bethune Museum and Archives, the AAMA relocated its office to Washington, D.C. In the same year the association hired its first full-time executive director, Joy Ford Austin, who managed the AAMA until Ronald L. Sharp replaced her in 1987. During the 1980s the AAMA was a vigorous force in the museum movement. It helped curators plan exhibits, aided administrators in the recruitment of staff, and assisted scholars in their research. Moreover, the AAMA advised collectors about making donations, aided museum trustees in meeting responsibilities, and counseled artists on planning exhibits. It also served as a valuable model as other people of color began to develop museums and cultural organizations.

By the end of the 1980s, however, the AAMA faced financial difficulties. White museums with far greater resources than their black counterparts experienced increasing public pressure to reflect in their exhibits America's racial diversity, and they began to compete with black museums for funds to support programs about African Americans. The lack of funding that resulted combined with organizational and financial problems of the underfunded AAMA created a crisis. Rowena Stewart, director of the African American Historical and Cultural Museum of Philadelphia, and AAMA president from 1981 to 1984, was named acting executive director in 1991. In the fall of that year the AAMA's Washington office closed and an Interim Governing Committee was formed to guide the organization through these difficult times. The AAMA reopened its office in February 1992 at the National Afro-American Museum and Cultural Center in Wilberforce, Ohio, with Jocelyn Robinson-Hubbuch as half-time executive director. Despite the financial hardships, the AAMA has resumed its central role in the African American museum movement, reorganizing in 1998 as the Association of African American Museums.

**FURTHER READING**

African-American Museums Association. *A Decade of Devotion: African-American Museums Association, 1978 to 1988*. Washington, D.C.: African-American Museums Association, 1988.

*Rhett S. Jones*

## African American Women's Clergy Association

Established in 1969 as the American Women's Clergy Association, the African American Women's Clergy Association (AAWCA) promotes the clergy as a profession for women. The organization strives to open all denominations to the idea of ordained female ministers and seeks to convince women of all faiths and races to heed "the call" to be religious leaders. The AAWCA is a national organization headquartered in Washington, D.C., with state and regional coordinators who call yearly meetings of local church and religious leaders. The group's founder, Bishop Imagene Bingham Stewart, is the guiding force and most visible manifestation of the organization, and the AAWCA's House of Imagene, a shelter for homeless and battered women in the District of Columbia, may be the association's most tangible and successful venture. Financial difficulties have troubled the shelter, but it has survived and served between 2,000 and 3,000 people since the early 1970s.

Bishop Stewart, the descendant of three generations of black Baptist ministers, grew up in Dublin, Georgia. Here she watched and heard her father and grandfather preach and "felt the call." Her formal training and ordination took place in Washington, D.C. Stewart was graduated and ordained by the Inter-Met Seminary in Washington, D.C., and is pastor of the Greater Pearly Gate Baptist Church in northwest Washington.

The struggle to open the clergy to women did not begin with the establishment of the AAWCA in 1969. Early in the nineteenth century women gained numerical superiority in American congregations, and their partici-pation in the benevolent and moral crusades of American Protestantism were crucial to whatever success those crusades enjoyed. For both black and white women, the church played a significant part in establishing social identity and broadening their social roles and influence. As women used the church to branch out in society, they also sought to gain more influence and power within the church. Not content to be lay leaders only, women from all denominations have sought roles in church governance, scriptural interpretation, and even ordination. Northern women in the African Methodist Episcopal Church were recognized for their spirituality and commitment and in the 1830s demanded their ordination. They, like others since in both black and white religious communities, however, met considerable opposition to such formal acknowledgment of their spiritual gifts. In 1853, Antoinette Brown Blackwell, sister-in-law of feminist Lucy Stone, became the first woman to be ordained by a mainstream Protestant church. By 1891, Anna Howard Shaw had succeeded in becoming an ordained Methodist minister as well as a physician and urged that other women be able to follow in her footsteps.

The arguments and examples of those nineteenth-century reformers failed to change public or church leaders' opinions of female ordination. In 1974, the illegal ordination of fourteen women in the Episcopal Church in Philadelphia threw that denomination into crisis, and two years passed before the issue was resolved in favor of the women. Stewart recognized a continued need to agitate for women's access to the clergy. The founding of her organization is another point of intersection between the resurgence of feminism and the cresting of the civil rights movement in the late 1960s. While the role of the AAWCA in opening the clergy to women may be small and even immeasurable, the profession increasingly attracts women. Between 1977 and 1987, the number of Master of Divinity degrees awarded to women rose 224 percent.

**FURTHER READINGS**

Brooks-Higginbotham, Evelyn. *Righteous Discontent: The Women's Movement in the Black Baptist Church, 1880–1920*. Cambridge, Mass.: Harvard University Press, 1993.

Evans, Sara. *Born for Liberty: A History of Women in America*. New York: The Free Press, 1989.

McKenzie, Vashti. *Not Without a Struggle: Leadership Development for African American Women in Ministry*. Cleveland: United Church Press, 1996.

Wheeler, Linda, and Ruben Castaneda. "House of Imagene Shelter May Have to Close the Door." *Washington Post*, June 29, 1997, B3.

Women's Action Coalition. *WAC Stats: Facts About Women.* New York: The New Press, 1993.

Woodward, Kenneth L. "Feminism and the Churches." *Newsweek*, February 13, 1989.

*Norman C. McLeod Jr.*

## African Americans for Humanism

The African Americans for Humanism (AAH) was founded in 1989 in Buffalo, New York, as a subcommittee of the Council for Democratic and Secular Humanism, now known as the Council for Secular Humanism. AAH is an interracial organization engaged in developing and promoting critical thinking and a rational and ethical approach to life, particularly among people of African descent. AAH is primarily an educational organization that provides speakers, debaters, and lecturers who explain and defend humanist values and who promote human-centered living as a rational and ethical approach to organized religion. AAH members have spoken on radio and television and at major universities. Writers who are members of the organization have published in numerous black-owned publications in the United States and Africa.

In 1990 shortly after the founding of the AAH, the organization's International Advisory Board issued an African American Humanist Declaration in the spring issue of *Free Inquiry* magazine, one of the world's leading humanist publications. News of the declaration was reported in several black-owned newspapers throughout the United States. The AAH declaration called on African Americans to rely less on organized religion and more on reason, ethical conduct, and concerted human action in dealing with problems such as poverty, white supremacy, unwanted pregnancy, and alcohol and substance abuse.

AAH Executive Director Norm R. Allen Jr. in Amsterdam for the 40th anniversary International Humanist and Ethical Union (IHEU) Congress. July 29, 1992. *Courtesy of Norm R. Allen Jr.*

In 1991 AAH produced the first issue of the *AAH Examiner*, the organization's international newsletter. The quarterly newsletter is distributed to the organization's 500 members who live in the United States, Europe, Africa, and the Caribbean, and to subscribers at libraries and institutions of higher learning. The AAH has received further public exposure as a result of the publication of *African-American Humanism: An Anthology* (1991), which demonstrates how humanism and free thought have helped to shape the history and ideals of black activism and intellectualism. In recent years AAH has played an active role in preventing the teaching of creationism in public schools.

FURTHER READING

Allen, Norm R. Jr. *African-American Humanism: An Anthology.* Buffalo, N.Y: Prometheus, 1991.

*Norm R. Allen Jr.*

## African Association

*See* Pan-African Congress.

## African Blood Brotherhood for Liberation and Redemption

The African Blood Brotherhood for Liberation and Redemption (ABB) was a Communist, nationalist, and anti–Marcus Garvey organization. Established by the Caribbean journalist Cyril V. Briggs in 1919, the ABB was one of the seminal black leftist groups in American history. The ABB launched a highly successful campaign against Marcus Garvey, leader of the Universal Negro Improvement Association (UNIA); promoted the creation of an independent black republic in the southern United States, which was later adopted by the Communist Party–USA (CPUSA); and became the first black wing of the nascent American Communist movement. Through the organization's official publication, the *Crusader*, and the Crusader News Service, the ABB provided articles for newspapers across the United States. This well-organized news service helped to publicize the ABB's campaign against Garvey and contributed to his arrest for mail fraud in 1922.

After coming to the United States in 1912, Briggs worked for various newspapers, including the *Amsterdam News* and the *Colored American Review*. During this period he began a political shift to the left that culminated in his adoption of communism by 1920. Initially, however, Briggs maintained a socialist stance while promoting African irredentism, which advocated the return of West-

ern hemisphere blacks to Africa and their participation in black-controlled governments.

In August-September 1918 Briggs launched his own magazine, the *Crusader*, with initial financial support from the basketball coach Robert "Bob" Douglas, the sports writer R. L. Dougherty, the merchant Anthony Crawford, and the journalists Hubert H. Harrison and Anselmo Jackson. The magazine's earliest issues advocated socialism, democracy, and support of black soldiers serving in World War I. Briggs and his followers hoped that the American government would grant African Americans civil rights as a reward for their support of the war effort. After all, President Woodrow Wilson's Fourteen Points advocated the protection of persecuted minorities. Moreover, Wilson's suggestion to redraw international boundaries, they hoped, might result in the creation of an independent black republic in the southern United States. Briggs, however, soon gave up those hopes and began promoting an international socialist commonwealth without racial distinctions.

While the first issues of the *Crusader* displayed no official organizational affiliation on its masthead, by early 1919, copies bore the legend "Publicity Organ of the Hamitic League of the World," an organization founded by *Children of the Sun* author George Wells Parker to promote African pride and black economic progress. The partnership between the Hamitic League and Briggs was primarily a financial relationship that lasted until December 1920. Briggs hoped to capitalize on Parker's acclaim as a writer and to increase circulation of the *Crusader* among members of the Hamitic League.

While the *Crusader*'s alliance with Parker's Hamitic League appears to have been the product of pragmatic considerations, Briggs's support of communism was sparked by his disillusionment with American socialism and his admiration for the Russian Bolsheviks. Angered by the lack of racial consciousness among American socialists and enthralled by the success of the Russian Revolution, Briggs embraced communism and openly proclaimed his support for the Bolsheviks in the October 1919 issue of the *Crusader*. The same issue also included the first reference to the ABB. Briggs joined the Communist Party at roughly the same time he formed the ABB. It is unclear, though, whether he formed the ABB independently or under instructions from the Communist Party.

The initial program and aims of the ABB, formulated primarily by Briggs, represented an amalgamation of race and class consciousness. The ABB's 1920 program urged blacks to oppose racist and capitalist oppression and promoted racial solidarity and equality. While ABB membership was open only to blacks, the program stressed the need to cooperate with class-conscious white workers. Briggs hoped that the ABB would grow into an international organization with numerous, semi-autonomous local chapters. The ultimate goal of the ABB was the establishment of a global socialist commonwealth that offered its citizens full racial equality.

By 1921, partly due to the urgings of the communist activists Robert Minor and Rose Pastor Stokes, the *Crusader*, now recognized as the official organ of the ABB, began a virulent campaign against Marcus Garvey. Concerned about the endemic corruption of the UNIA and afraid that Garvey's repatriation schemes would damage black class-consciousness in the United States, Briggs began to advocate Garvey's removal from power. He did so partly hoping that ABB officials would take control of the UNIA and move it toward the political left.

In addition to attacking Garvey in the *Crusader*, the ABB distributed leaflets at the UNIA's Second International Negro Convention in 1921 that characterized Garvey as dictatorial, undemocratic, and insufficiently class conscious. These activities infuriated Garvey and set off a series of verbal, written, and legal battles that continued until Garvey's arrest in 1922. Not content with attacking Garvey publicly, Briggs and the ABB members W. A. Domingo and Richard B. Moore initiated a private investigation into the financial operations of the UNIA. Determined to remove Garvey from his leadership position, they hoped to find evidence that the UNIA mailed fraudulent materials to solicit funds for its steamship corporation, the Black Star Line. Briggs, despite his knowledge of government investigations of the ABB, contacted the United States Post Office Department. In November 1921 Briggs presented the postal agent Mortimer Davis with the findings of his study of the UNIA's finances. The information proved invaluable in the government's mail fraud case against Garvey.

Having dedicated so much of its energies to defeating Garvey, the ABB floundered after Garvey's arrest. Following the January 1922 issue, the *Crusader* stopped publication and the Crusader News Service closed shortly afterward. By 1923, the Communist Party had fully absorbed the ABB and two years later the organization officially disbanded. Briggs, Domingo, Moore, and other former ABB leaders became central to the Communist Party's attempts to win black support during the 1930s.

Although the ABB was short-lived and established only a handful of local chapters, the organization represents an important chapter in the history of the American Left. While the organization's anti-Garvey campaign proved more successful than any attempts at radicalizing the black masses, the ABB stands as the first black communist organization in the United States. Moreover, the nationwide distribution of Crusader News Service wire articles to black newspapers demonstrates that the ABB was not only the Communist Party's first black vanguard organization, but also one of its most successful.

**FURTHER READINGS**

Beekman, Scott. "This Judas Iscariot: Cyril Briggs and the African Blood Brotherhood's Relationship with Marcus Garvey and the Universal Negro Improvement Association, 1918–1922." M.A. thesis, Ohio University, 1998.

Hill, Robert A., ed. *The Crusader*. 3 vols. New York: Garland Publishing, 1987.

Taylor, Theman R. "Cyril Briggs and the African Blood Brotherhood: Another Radical View of Race and Class During the 1920s." Ph.D. diss., University of California, Santa Barbara, 1981.

*Scott Beekman*

## African Civilization Society

African Americans interested in emigrating to Africa founded the African Civilization Society in New York in 1858. The aim of the American Colonization Society, established in 1816, critics insisted, was to settle free blacks and emancipated slaves in Africa to alleviate whites' fears about the rise in the number of free blacks. The objective of black emigration, on the other hand, was completely different: it was a movement inspired and led by African Americans that aimed to encourage the voluntary expatriation of select groups of skilled African Americans to countries where they could develop their talents free from the restrictions of American slavery and discrimination. Emigrationists insisted that the happiness and prosperity of African Americans could not be achieved in the United States; that their success elsewhere, in demonstrating their abilities, would help to bring down slavery; that their efforts would help to improve the conditions of the natives among whom they lived; and finally, that their colony would encourage trade and development. These were objectives with which no colonizationists would have argued. Yet the two movements remained at loggerheads; colonizationists continued to be a white-led movement dominated by a very visible national association, the American Colonization Society, while emigrationist activity was much more sporadic and diffuse and dominated by African Americans.

Ever since the 1780s, black Americans had proposed ways to improve their lot by leaving the United States. In 1794, for instance, African Americans in Providence, Rhode Island, had sent a mission to West Africa to explore the possibility of establishing a colony there. Others like Paul Cuffe, a black Massachusetts sea captain, had developed plans for increasing trade between Africa and the United States. The 1820s had seen an intense but shortlived movement to encourage emigration to Haiti, and over the next decade or so West Indian planters, eager to find replacements for the slaves freed by emancipation in 1834, tried to persuade black Americans to settle in the Caribbean.

The decade of the 1850s saw a dramatic increase in emigrationist activities sustained by a growing belief that African Americans had to take control of movements for their own improvement. Some suggested settlement in Africa, a few recommended Canada, and yet others Haiti. Emigrationist views may have found their fullest expression in the 1852 publication of Martin R. Delany's tract *The Condition, Elevation, Emigration and Destiny of the Colored People of the United States, Politically Considered*, which, among other things, denounced the American Colonization Society, insisted that blacks could not achieve full equality in the United States, and called on readers to take control of their destiny. Not surprisingly, because of his opposition to the American Colonization Society, Delany, a doctor, editor, and teacher from Pittsburgh, rejected Africa as the site of his proposed colony. The future of African Americans, he declared, would be best served if they settled in other parts of the Americas. Delany called a series of emigration conventions over the next few years in which he attempted to consolidate his leadership of the movement and determine the location of his proposed colony. Neither came easy. By the end of the decade Delany found himself at the head of a small and impoverished organization, the Niger Valley Exploration Party, which hoped to establish a colony in West Africa.

In New York, blacks interested in emigration held a series of three meetings during the spring and summer of 1858 which explored the merits of alternative sites. In the end, those in favor of Africa met in October to form the African Civilization Society. Africa had grown in popularity due in part to the activities of the British explorer, David Livingstone, and the work of the Southern Baptist missionary, the Reverend Thomas Bowen, who soon after his return to the United States had published an account of his activities in the Yoruba country. Interest in Africa was bolstered further by the 1858 publication of Benjamin Coates's *Cotton Cultivation in Africa*. Coates, a Philadelphia wool merchant and supporter of the American Colonization Society, aware of African American antipathy to the society, suggested the creation of an alternative interracial organization to promote emigration to Yorubaland. Coates's proposal was endorsed by a number of New York and Philadelphia colonizationists and emigrationists who named Henry Highland Garnet, a black Presbyterian minister, its president. Garnet had only recently returned from a two-year stint as a missionary of the Scottish United Presbyterian Church in Sterling, Jamaica where he had ministered to, and quite likely was influenced by, "recaptured Africans" settled in the island following their release from slave ships.

The formation of the African Civilization Society coincided with Delany's plans to visit West Africa. Over the next few months Delany and the society jostled for position as the dominant force in the African movement. While Delany insisted that he would only accept financial support for his mission from African Americans, his fellow commissioner, Robert Campbell, a Jamaican who had been teaching at the Institute for Colored Youth in Philadelphia, had fewer qualms, and Campbell accepted support from any source. By the time Delany and Campbell left for Africa it was unclear who were the sponsors of their mission. Delany insisted he was his own boss while Garnet and others declared that the mission had been commissioned by the society. After a brief visit to Liberia, Delany and Campbell signed what they called a "treaty" with the Alake of Abeokuta in which they agreed to settle a colony of skilled black Americans in the area. They left soon after for a visit to Britain where they hoped to win support for the proposed colony from British philanthropists and businessmen. By the time Delany returned to the United States in early 1860 he had won the endorsement of a group of prominent men in Britain who pledged to raise sufficient funds to finance the movement to and settlement of the colonists.

While Delany and Campbell were still in Africa, the society sent its corresponding secretary, the Reverend Theodore Bourne, grandson of the British abolitionist George Bourne, to Britain to win support for its effort. Always sensitive to attempts to circumvent his authority, and adamant that the movement had to be led by African Americans, Delany did everything he could to undermine Bourne's activities in Britain. By the time he left for home, Delany was master of the situation. Over the next few months he toured Canada and the United States trying to rally support for and to attract potential immigrants to the colony. Throughout, Delany managed to maintain strained relations with the society which continued to promote the colony. But the beginning of the Civil War in April 1861 effectively put an end to their efforts as African Americans turned their attention to the struggle to defeat slavery. Any chances of success finally evaporated when the Alake of Abeokuta, under pressure from British missionaries in the area, abrogated the "treaty."

Although Delany remained committed to emigrating to Africa until at least mid-1862, and Garnet toured Britain in support of the movement in late 1861, by early 1862 the society had shifted its focus away from a colony in Africa to supporting freedmen in the southern United States. To all intents and purposes, the society had been transformed into a freedmen aid society, raising funds to aid the newly freed slaves and providing teachers for schools in the South during and after the Civil War. Little is known of the society's activities during this period, and evidence suggests that it remained in existence at least until 1867.

### FURTHER READINGS

Miller, Floyd J. *The Search for a Black Nationality: Black Colonization and Emigration 1787–1863*. Urbana: University of Illinois Press, 1975.

Pease, Jane H., and William H. Pease. *They Who Would be Free: Blacks' Search for Freedom, 1830–1861*. New York: Atheneum, 1974.

Schor, Joel. *Henry Highland Garnet: A Voice of Black Radicalism in the Nineteenth Century*. Westport, Conn.: Greenwood Press, 1977.

*Richard Blackett*

## African Heritage Studies Association

The African Heritage Studies Association (AHSA) is an organization of scholars of African descent who study African history from an Afrocentric perspective. The AHSA emerged at the 1969 annual meeting of the African Studies Association (ASA), in response to agitation by several young black and white Africanists who protested the lack of organizational democracy within the ASA and rejected the traditional view that scholarship should or could achieve "objective" standards. They advocated instead that African studies be pursued from a politically engaged perspective that facilitates African interests.

Members of the ASA's Black Caucus who led the insurgents charged that the ASA was dominated by "the white

caste and . . . identified with a white posture." Insisting that "the study of African life be undertaken from a Pan-Africanist perspective . . . [which] defines that all black people are African people" (*African Studies Newsletter*, 7 and 11), the group demanded that half the seats on the ASA's Board of Directors be reserved for scholars of African descent. Led by John Henrik Clarke, the AHSA became an independent organization when its demands were rejected by the ASA in early 1970. Among the founding members of the AHSA were the historian Nell Painter; P. Chike Onwuachi, Director of the African Studies and Research Program at Howard University; and Leonard Jeffries Chair of City College of New York's Black Studies Department.

The AHSA's goals are to make the study of African life and history relevant to both African and African American communities, to "use African history to effect a world union of African people," and to encourage scholarship among "activist-scholars" committed to the "restoration of the cultural, economic and political life of African peoples everywhere" (Clarke, 9). For nearly thirty years, the AHSA has pursued its goals through various avenues. It organizes annual conferences, encourages African American youths to study Africa from an Afrocentric perspective, and publishes a biannual newsletter and the *International Journal of Africana Studies*. In 1995, for example, the ASHA sponsored a National Student/Youth Conference on Afrocentricity: From Rhetoric to Praxis, with panel discussions on Mental and Physical Health and Family, Relationships, and Children and a Special Community Forum on Politics and Economics. Beginning in 1996 the AHSA focused on the struggle to obtain reparations for those who had been brought involuntarily to America. This emphasis on reparations was also reflected at the AHSA's 1998 annual meeting in New Orleans, which was organized around the theme Reparations, Repatriation, and Reconstructions: African People in the 21st Century.

The AHSA operates on an annual budget of over $25,000 and has a membership of about two hundred individuals and affiliated organizations. It is governed by a twenty-person Board of Directors and headquartered at the Center for Black Studies at Northern Illinois University in DeKalb.

### FURTHER READINGS

*African Studies Newsletter* 2, 6–7 (November-December 1969).

Clarke, John Henrik. "The African Heritage Studies Association (AHSA): Some Notes on the Conflict with the African Studies Association (ASA) and the Fight to Reclaim African History." *Issue: A Journal of Africanist Opinion* 6, 2–3 (Summer/Fall 1976): 5–11.

Skinner, Elliot P. "African Studies, 1955–1975: An Afro-American Perspective." *Issue: A Journal of Africanist Opinion* 6, 2–3 (Summer/Fall 1976).

Sullivan Challenor, Herchelle. "No Longer at Ease: Confrontation at the 12th Annual African Studies Association Meeting at Montreal." *Africa Today* 16, 5–6 (October-December, 1969): 4–7.

*Sara Diamond*

# Afro-American Council

The Afro-American Council (AAC), like its predecessor, the National Afro-American League, was an organization formed in the late-nineteenth century to agitate for civil and political rights as anti-black violence, disfranchisement, and segregation became increasingly entrenched in American society. Both the league and the council established important precedents for black activists who were later involved in national rights organizations like the Niagara movement and the National Association for the Advancement of Colored People (NAACP).

By the 1880s, former political allies of African Americans in the Republican Party had abandoned black rights in the interest of pursuing sectional reconciliation and national economic and political stability. Disillusioned, many black activists turned away from the established political party structure and founded a variety of independent race organizations. One of the most militant and outspoken of these activists was the young New York journalist Timothy Thomas Fortune. Born a slave in Florida, Fortune is best known for editing the New York *Globe, Freeman,* and *Age* between 1883 and 1907. In an 1887 *Freeman* editorial, Fortune called for the creation of a National Afro-American League to address a series of issues confronting African Americans in the late nineteenth century. These included the suppression of black voting rights in the South, the increasing prevalence and toleration of lynchings, segregation in public transportation and accommodations, inequities in black school funding, and the southern penal system's use of chain gangs and convict lease programs. Fortune's call to action received enthusiastic support in the black press, and numerous state and local leagues formed across the country. In January 1890, 141 delegates from twenty-three states met in Chicago to form a permanent national organization. Emphasizing its focus on southern concerns and hoping to stimulate participation of southern blacks,

the league selected its officers primarily from the South. The North Carolina educator Joseph C. Price was elected president and William A. Pledger of Georgia, vice president, and Fortune was selected as the league's secretary.

The constitution adopted at the inaugural meeting called for the use of the press, churches, public speakers and meetings, and the courts to seek redress for the denial of black rights. It also stressed the league's independence from political parties and prohibited any political office-holder from simultaneously holding a league office. This policy kept the league free from the Republican Party's control, but it also discouraged the participation of most black politicians. Opposition from black political leaders, inadequate funds, and a lack of mass support combined to make the league a short-lived endeavor. It was disbanded formally in 1893.

As conditions among African Americans in the South continued to worsen during the 1890s, the African Methodist Episcopal Zion bishop Alexander Walters and other black leaders urged Fortune to revive the organization. Despite his pessimism regarding the league's ability to effectively address racial problems, Fortune lent his support and called for a national convention. In 1898 delegates met in Rochester, New York, and launched the new organization named the Afro-American Council. Walters was elected president. The council retained much of the league's agenda, but, unlike the league, permitted the active participation of black politicians. With the inclusion of a broader spectrum of black leaders, the council became a site of conflict between those favoring militant activism and those advocating a conservative policy of gradualism and accommodation.

The conservative position reflected the ideas of Booker T. Washington, who, after his conciliatory Atlanta Exposition address in 1895, had emerged as the nation's most influential black leader. Washington, principal of Alabama's Tuskegee Institute, stressed the importance of industrial training and economic self-help for blacks while rejecting public agitation for civil and political rights. Working behind the scenes and drawing on a network of allies, Washington attempted to steer the council away from militant positions. In 1900 he formed the Negro National Business League to serve as his national mouthpiece and to undermine the potential influence of the council. Through skillful political manipulations, Washington managed to overcome the influence of the militants and gain effective control of the council by 1902. By this time he had become well-connected with white philanthropists and politicians and wielded considerable control over African

Americans' access to their financial contributions and political appointments. Even Fortune, along with many black editors and politicos, found Fortune's militancy tempered by his need for Washington's financial and political favors. Despite the continued opposition of activist council members such as Reverdy C. Ransom, Ida B. Wells Barnett, and William Monroe Trotter, Washington and his allies prevented the council from effectively challenging the denial of civil and political rights for blacks.

With conflict over the council's leadership and direction dominating its activities, the masses of African Americans remained indifferent and membership in local councils declined. As Washington's gradualist and accommodationist position came to dominate the council, many militants withdrew from the organization. In 1905, disgruntled council members and other anti-Washington intellectuals, most notably W. E. B. Du Bois, founded the Niagara movement as a militant organization that would agitate for suffrage, civil rights, economic opportunity, and racial justice. Ironically, Fortune accused Du Bois of stealing language from the league's constitution in Du Bois's outline of the Niagara movement's platform. This incident suggests the extent to which the initial militancy of Fortune and the league had been lost when Washington gained influence over the council. Even moderate council members came to reject Washington's leadership. The most telling desertion was the resignation of Bishop Walters, who joined the Niagara movement in 1908. By then, however, the council existed in name only. The Niagara movement also proved ineffective in pursuing its agenda, but in 1909 a number of white Progressives joined with Walters, Du Bois, and others to form a new biracial organization. The NAACP concerned itself largely with the same issues Fortune had attempted to address with the founding of the league in 1890. Though the league and council could celebrate few successes, and were torn by factionalism throughout their existences, they provided important precedents for independent black action in an era of limited political alternatives for African American activists.

**FURTHER READINGS**

Goldstein, Michael L. "Preface to the Rise of Booker T. Washington: A View from New York City of the Demise of Independent Black Politics, 1889–1902." *Journal of Negro History* 62, 1 (1977); 81–99.

Meier, August. *Negro Thought in America: Racial Ideologies in the Age of Booker T. Washington, 1880–1915.* Ann Arbor: The University of Michigan Press, 1963.

Thornbrough, Emma Lou. "The National Afro-American League, 1887–1908." *Journal of Southern Education* 27, 4 (November 1961); 494–512.

———. *T. Thomas Fortune: Militant Journalist.* Chicago: The University of Chicago Press, 1972.

*Mitchell Kachun*

## Afro-American Federation of Labor

Established by Sufi Abdul Hamid in 1934, the Afro-American Federation of Labor (AAFL) attempted to secure picketing rights for African American workers. The AAFL emerged from the "Don't Buy Where You Can't Work" movement, which began in 1931 in Chicago, and from there spread to the East Coast. Advocates of the movement urged African Americans to picket and boycott white-owned stores in black communities, especially stores that hired few black employees.

Hamid was an African American who had participated in picketing demonstrations in Chicago before he moved to Harlem. Claiming that he was Sudanese, Hamid adopted a Muslim name and wore Oriental attire. During the summer of 1933, he spoke on 7th Avenue between 125th and 138th Streets in Harlem. At that time, several street orators complained about the socio-economic conditions in Harlem, especially poor housing, high rents, and limited employment opportunities for blacks. Some of their material tended to be more propagandistic than factual, and both whites and blacks considered many of these speakers, including Hamid, to be agitators.

Hamid stressed that African Americans were denied employment where they spent their money. He urged blacks to unite and demand better socio-economic conditions. Calling himself the "Black Hitler," Hamid encouraged racial conflict by pressuring blacks to use economic boycotts to drive white and Jewish landlords, businessmen, and employers out of Harlem. He organized the Negro Industrial and Clerical Alliance (NICA) to promote this purging and declared himself president. African American leaders such as Fred R. Moore, editor of the *New York Age*, perceived Hamid as a threat to public safety and interracial cooperation. Moore called Hamid a racketeer who "schemes for his own personal financial gain and in order to acquire for himself a following which would look to and follow his leadership."

Moore identified the NICA as one of Hamid's schemes. Hamid defended his alliance, stating that it "is an association with offices, a membership of hundreds and governing by-laws: the purpose of it is to, by lawful means, obtain better working conditions for its members, shorter working hours, higher pay and in general to improve the economic conditions of Negroes." The alliance's primary action was to promote picketing of stores to demand better working conditions. Hamid also sought to establish a legal basis for picketing because of an injunction preventing such protest.

In autumn 1934, the picket committee of the Citizens' League for Fair Play picketed in front of the A. S. Beck shoe store on 125th Street in Harlem. The league had demanded that African Americans account for 50 percent of the store's employees, but the manager refused to hire blacks. Protestors carried signs and distributed handbills, warning people not to patronize the store. When a picketer collided with a customer, attorneys for the store sought an injunction to prevent picketing and boycotting. New York County Supreme Court Justice Rosenman agreed, declaring that the protest was not a labor dispute because the defendants were not members of a labor union or organization. Rosenman stressed that this was a racial dispute because protestors' demands did not directly concern improving wages, hours, and working conditions. Instead, the protest was about how many whites and blacks worked in the store. Rosenman warned that if whites were fired to hire blacks that they in turn might protest such displacement and possible race riots could result, damaging the community.

Hamid interpreted this injunction as a need to organize a labor union and secure membership. He created the AAFL and drafted a certificate of incorporation application that he presented to the New York Department of Labor. Hamid declared that the AAFL had six objectives. His proposed union would "promote the principles of friendship, fraternity, and good fellowship among working men and working women including persons of African descent." He stated the union would "peaceably and by lawful suasion organize workers" to settle labor conflicts and demand higher wages, shorter hours, and better conditions "without regard to race or creed or branch of trade." Hamid wanted members of the AAFL to form locals that would provide volunteer aid to needy members; have club rooms where they could meet, eat, and sleep; and edit and distribute literature to educate and inform members and the public of the group's principles.

Hamid also requested the Department of Labor to permit auxiliary bodies such as labor unions to affiliate with the AAFL. While waiting for his application hearing before the Industrial Board of the Department of Labor, Hamid declared the NICA an affiliate of the AAFL and

recruited members in the 125th Street business section. AAFL members encouraged black store employees to join the union, promising better hours and wages, and threatened individuals who refused to join with physical harm. Although members were forced to join the union and pay a $5 initiation fee and weekly dues of a quarter, they generally benefited from wage increases. If employers complained about their activities, AAFL members picketed in front of their businesses, informing patrons that the store was unfair to union labor. In response, the employers usually agreed to meet AAFL demands to prevent boycotts.

The AAFL briefly ceased its activities during and after the Harlem race riot on March 19, 1935, in which thousands of black employees clashed with white owners of stores on Lenox and Seventh Avenues. After tensions eased, Hamid insisted that AAFL members resume their work. The AAFL, however, was soon stopped when an injunction was issued. A black salesgirl who worked for the Lerner shop refused to join the AAFL. As a result, members began picketing the store on May 31, 1935. They carried signs indicating their affiliation with the "AAF and L" and denouncing the business for its refusal to hire union labor. The Manhattan Lerner Company, Inc., filed suit against Hamid, and New York Supreme Court Justice Cotillo granted an injunction. "It does not appear that defendants are a labor union, but on the contrary are using a union name as a cloak for their activities," he ruled. "The use of the letters A.A.F.L. is an ingenious device to induce the belief that the defendants belong to the American Federation of Labor."

Although Hamid never managed to incorporate the AAFL as a labor union, his group helped some African Americans attain better employment opportunities. Moreover, the AAFL raised race and class consciousness in Harlem by illustrating the potential power of labor unions. Workers recognized the need for collective bargaining power to protest employment exploitation and discrimination and applied for membership in unions that also began addressing problems faced by black workers.

**FURTHER READINGS**

Bracey, John H., Jr., August Meier, and Elliott Rudwick, eds. *Black Nationalism in America*. Indianapolis and New York: The Bobbs-Merrill Company, Inc., 1970.

Cantor, Milton, comp. *Black Labor in America*. Intro. by Herbert G. Gutman. Westport, Conn.: Negro Universities Press, 1969.

Foner, Philip S. *Organized Labor and the Black Worker, 1619–1973*. New York: International Publishers, 1976.

Franklin, Charles. *The Negro Labor Unionist of New York: Problems and Conditions Among Negroes in the Labor Unions in Manhattan with Special Reference to the N.R.A. and Post–N.R.A. Situations.* New York: Columbia University Press, 1936; rpt., New York: AMS Press, 1968.

*Elizabeth D. Schafer*

SEE ALSO    Negro Industrial and Clerical Alliance

## Afro-American League

*See* National Afro-American League.

## Afro-American Party

The Afro-American Party (AAP), the first independent black political party in Alabama, was organized by Reverend Clennon King in 1960. King founded the AAP to improve black life and secure for blacks the rights they were guaranteed by law, but which they were so often denied in practice. In 1960 the AAP attracted 1,485 votes for its presidential and vice-presidential candidates that year and then faded from the political landscape. The AAP was unable either to attract an adequate following or raise enough money to support even a meager organizational apparatus. Unlike some third parties that maintain a modest affiliation with one of the two major national parties for purposes of economic viability, the AAP steadfastly held to its independence.

The AAP's search for distinctiveness led to its demise. But short-lived though it was, the AAP was an important organization because it suggested that in the coming decades blacks might constitute a powerful voting bloc in American politics, independent of white voters. Moreover, the AAP's existence raised the possibility that blacks might not remain loyal to either of the two major parties but rather seek to create their own party vehicle to induce political change. For nearly three decades, beginning with the elections of President Franklin D. Roosevelt, the majority of African Americans had deserted the Republican Party and began voting regularly for Democratic Party candidates. The AAP's brief appearance in 1960 suggested that the political landscape regarding black voting predictability might change yet again. Political parties like the Mississippi Freedom Democratic Party, the Freedom Now Party, and the Peace and Freedom Party—all of which emerged in the years after AAP's existence and all of which catered primarily, if not exclusively, to black political interests—undoubtedly learned valuable lessons from the AAP's short lifespan.

The AAP's appearance in 1960 was a logical consequence of ever-increasing efforts by blacks to secure their social, political, and economic equality alongside whites. Thousands of African Americans enlisted in the U.S. armed forces during World War II and were frustrated by the inconsistency and hypocrisy of fighting for the liberation of European peoples when African Americans did not enjoy such freedom at home. This consciousness and sense of common purpose among blacks was accented further by the increasing proximity of blacks to each other in American cities like Chicago, Detroit, New York, and Washington, D.C.

As the post–World War II period wore on, issues of racial segregation and discrimination were inciting protests and making headlines all across the United States. Events such as the 1955–1956 Montgomery, Alabama, bus boycott and the February 1960 Greensboro, North Carolina, sit-in convinced the Reverend Clennon King of Alabama that the creation of a black political party was necessary. By 1960 Reverend King and his supporters had concluded that blacks needed to agitate for their own issues because allying with whites was not producing satisfactory levels of change.

In 1960, the AAP ran the Reverend King as its presidential candidate and Reginald Carter as its vice presidential candidate. Both King and Carter were black, as were other candidates who ran for local offices under the AAP banner. No AAP candidates, however, were elected to office. By 1964, the AAP had breathed its last breath, partly because of renewed efforts by the national Democratic Party to win black votes.

**FURTHER READINGS**

Frye, Hardy T. *Black Parties and Political Power: A Case Study.* Boston: G. K. Hall & Co., 1980.

Walton, Hanes, Jr. *Black Political Parties: An Historical and Political Analysis.* New York: The Free Press, 1972.

*Scott W. Webster*

## Afro-American Patrolmen's League

*See* Afro-American Police League.

## Afro-American Police League

In 1967, five Chicago police officers organized the first chapter of the Afro-American Police League (AAPL), initially known as the Afro-American Patrolmen's League. Much like the National Association of Black Police, with which the AAPL became affiliated, the league changed its name to acknowledge the significant presence of women in the ranks. Thus, the league became the Afro-American Police League in 1979. The AAPL sought to improve relationships between police departments and their communities. To this end, the league worked to educate the public about police department procedures and operations and assisted police departments with implementing effective and fair law enforcement programs in black communities.

In Chicago, the league exemplified the rising militant stance of black police officers during the late 1960s and early 1970s. Its first president, Renault Robinson, firmly believed that Black Nationalism offered a way for disenfranchised blacks to solve their problems. In 1971, Robinson even made a controversial appearance on the *Phil Donahue Show* to discuss issues of concern to the black community. The appearance caused mixed reactions. While some people praised Robinson, others condemned his nationalist rhetoric. The AAPL in Chicago openly criticized the Chicago Police Department and other police organizations, such as the Fraternal Order of Police. Even though Chicago was the first northern city to hire black police officers and the first city outside of the Reconstruction South to appoint black sergeants, lieutenants, and captains to its police force, the Chicago Police Department and the white Fraternal Order of Police openly discriminated against black police officers. Black police officers were treated as token figures and often received poor assignments. The Chicago Police Department retaliated against the AAPL and its members by hindering their reform efforts and attempting to discredit the league. The AAPL appealed to the courts. In 1977, Robinson sued the Chicago Police Department for discrimination and won a settlement.

Two years after the founding of the AAPL's Chicago chapter, black police officers in Atlanta organized their own chapter in 1969. Similar to Chicago's black officers, Atlanta's black law enforcement officials constantly suffered racial discrimination. When they criticized their department, Atlanta's police chief, John Inman, retaliated with officer suspensions and demotions. Despite official attempts to stifle black criticism, Atlanta's AAPL continued its struggle. In 1974, the group achieved an important victory when newly elected black mayor, Maynard Jackson, stripped Inman of his power and provided some reforms for the black officers.

The AAPL's Chicago and Atlanta chapters illustrate the league's commitment to fight discrimination in the police

ranks. To this end, the AAPL has taken its battle to the courts, suing because of unfair treatment of black police officers. The AAPL hopes to deny police departments access to federal grant money, arguing that such grants would finance discriminatory practices in hiring, assignments, and promotions. Overall, the AAPL became an aggressive and vocal participant in the struggle against black oppression. In addition to fighting for the rights of black law enforcement officials, the AAPL has always emphasized its foundation as a community organization. AAPL chapters have been involved actively in their local communities. For example, chapters have established citizen complaint referral services and implemented voter registration drives. Also, the AAPL has maintained a speakers' bureau and has conducted professional training seminars for members and other interested parties. Furthermore, it has maintained a library focusing on police science and law enforcement and has conducted research on various subjects such as law and order legislation. To recognize individuals in public service who actively promote the AAPL's goal of improving police and community relations, the league awards the National Law and Social Leadership Award.

**FURTHER READINGS**

Dulaney, W. Marvin. *Black Police in America.* Bloomington: Indiana University Press, 1996.

Juris, Hervey A., and Peter Feuille. *Police Unionism.* Lexington, Mass.: Lexington Books, 1973.

Maurer, Christine, and Tara E. Sheets, eds. *Encyclopedia of Associations.* Detroit: Gale, 1999.

*Angel R. Rivera*

## Afro-American Presbyterian Council

*See* National Black Presbyterian Caucus.

## Afro-American Press Association

The Afro-American Press Association (AAPA) represented the various attempts to organize African American newspaper publishers during the later half of the nineteenth and the beginning of the twentieth centuries. The AAPA sought to improve the black press morally and materially and to increase the influence of black newspapers as effective tools for racial advancement. The association had varying degrees of success and different names during this time. On August 4, 1875, the Louisiana politician P. B. S. Pinchback brought together delegates from various African American newspapers in Cincinnati for the

National Convention of Colored Newspaper Men. The convention delegates discussed the possibility of forming a press organization and a business affiliate in order to assist each other with newspaper operations. The convention did not yield any concrete results, but it paved the way for a more durable organization to emerge.

There were various calls during the 1880s for a black press association. In 1882, the American Press Association, at the time known as the National Colored Press Association, emerged out of these calls. During the group's 1886 convention, members of the American Press Association addressed concerns about blacks' loss of rights in the South after Reconstruction. The convention also called for a national news bureau in Washington, D.C. In addition, the organization changed its name from American Press Association to Colored Press Association of the United States; during this year, it represented fourteen newspapers. The association soon embodied the crusading tradition of the black press. In 1894, Virginia's governor refused to address the group's convention in Richmond because the association supported the anti-lynching efforts of the journalist and activist Ida B. Wells. By 1894, the association was undergoing more change. It began to be known as the National Afro-American Press Association.

The association did not survive into the twentieth century. Its elder leaders, who had lived through Reconstruction and the advent of Jim Crow, began to retire or die. As a result, the association gave way to a new generation of black press leaders such as Robert S. Abbott of Chicago and Henry Allen Boyd of Nashville. These young enthusiastic men moved to form a new organization. In 1909, they formed the National Negro Press Association in Louisville, Kentucky, with Henry Allen Boyd as its corresponding secretary. This new organization continued to pursue the goals of the old Afro-American Press Association and in addition undertook recruitment efforts from the array of black periodicals existing at the time, planned fundraisers, and discussed forming a cooperative news service. It also worked on improving standards for advertising, circulation, and news agents. By 1921, the association was discussing the implementation of a National Negro Press Service, the enlargement of the central advertising office, and the appointment of standing committees. However, member dissatisfaction with the association's operational methods led to the group's decline in the 1940s. Meetings became infrequent during that decade, and by 1953, the organization had ceased to exist. By 1940, a new and stronger association had emerged— the National Newspaper Publishers' Association.

**FURTHER READING**

Pride, Armistead S., and Clinton C. Wilson II. *A History of the Black Press.* Washington, D.C.: Howard University Press, 1997.

*Angel R. Rivera*

## Afro-American Republican League of Pennsylvania

In 1895, leading blacks in Pennsylvania organized the Afro-American Republican League of Pennsylvania. The league endured until circa 1913. It provided an official political voice for black Pennsylvanians at a time when other minorities had none. Conceptualized as an adjunct to the Republican Party, the Afro-American Republican League represented the highest level of organized black political activity in the state. Political clubs from across Pennsylvania elected representatives to annual county conventions who in turn selected delegates to the state convention. Each year, the league's state convention met to consider civil rights actions and to pressure the Republican Party to award blacks patronage positions.

Peter C. Blackwell, publisher of the *Steelton Press*, dominated the league. He was its first president and a high-ranking officer until its demise. Blackwell, along with Robert J. Nelson of Reading, maintained a strong following among African Americans from eastern Pennsylvania. In 1899, league members from western Pennsylvania seceded and formed the Western Afro-American Republican League of Pennsylvania. Leaders of this group included William Maurice Randolph, a Pittsburgh attorney, and Captain William Catlin, a Civil War veteran from Monongahela, Pennsylvania.

Both groups continued to pressure Republican politicians for civil rights measures and patronage positions. In 1903, Nelson, president of the State League of Pennsylvania, successfully issued a call for a national suffrage convention to address southern disfranchisement. However, the league mainly acted in the State of Pennsylvania.

The decline of the Afro-American Republican League coincided with the resurgence of Democratic power in 1912 when Woodrow Wilson became president. Nevertheless, the league through its extensive organizational apparatus set the stage for the emergence and success of the National Association for the Advancement of Colored People (NAACP) in Pennsylvania.

**FURTHER READINGS**

Bodnar, John E. "Peter C. Blackwell and the Negro Community of Steelton, 1880–1920." *Pennsylvania Magazine of History and Biography* 17 (1973): 199–209.

Lee, Charles Franklin. "Race Men and the Republican Party: The Afro-American Republican League of Pennsylvania, 1895–1913." Unpublished Seminar Paper, Carnegie Mellon University, 1997.

Smith, Eric Ledell. "'Asking for Justice and Fair Play': African American State Legislators and Civil Rights in Early Twentieth-Century Pennsylvania." *Pennsylvania History* 63 (1996): 169–203.

*Charles Franklin Lee*

# Afro-American Research Institute

The Afro-American Research Institute (AARI) was founded as the Liberation Committee for Africa (LCA) in 1961. In 1963 the LCA changed its name to AARI while maintaining its membership and left-wing orientation. From 1961 to 1971, the organization published the *Liberator*, a monthly magazine that reported about the American civil rights and Black Power movements, the progress of liberation struggles in Africa, and other issues related to decolonization efforts of third world nations. During the first three years of publication, the majority of articles sympathetically examined Africa from a pro-revolutionary perspective. Fewer than half the articles were concerned with the American civil rights and Black Power movements. The *Liberator* was critical of the philosophy of non-violence and integration, and advocated militant self-defense and black solidarity. After 1963 the magazine devoted less space to African political or cultural concerns, and the majority of articles focused on African American issues. By 1967 less than one-third of the space was devoted to articles about Africa.

From 1961 to 1971, the *Liberator*'s editorial advisory board was composed of Lowell P. Beveridge, Evelyn Battle Kabilia, and Daniel H. Watts, who acted as editor in chief. Throughout its existence the advisory board also included various illustrious African American intellectuals and artists such as Ossie Davis, Paul Zuber, Len Holt, L. H. Michaux, Robert B. Moore, and James Baldwin. Others associated with the *Liberator* were the historian John Henrik Clarke, the writer Langston Hughes, and the poet and playwright LeRoi Jones (Amiri Baraka).

Even the *Liberator*'s most ardent critic, Harold Cruse, was a member of the magazine's editorial board for a number of years. Cruse asserted that "editorial elements in [the AARI] . . . were politically and ideologically incompatible" (Cruse, 405). White members of the AARI—both liberals and leftists—were ambivalent about and often hostile to the editor's pro-nationalist position. The all-black editorial board lacked intellectual and political unity and included anti-Marxist radicals like Cruse and pro-Marxists like Richard B. Moore. Significant tensions also existed between Black Power advocates like Watts and individuals willing to embrace integration. Cruse suggests that because these tensions remained unresolved, the *Liberator* "limped along" in an "inept, naive, and politically unimaginative" fashion until its demise in 1971 (Cruse, 405–406). Nevertheless, the *Liberator* enjoyed a sixfold increase in circulation in the years following 1963. While it might have displayed contradictory tendencies, its ardent and often antagonistic prose alternately delighted and disgusted its highly involved readers.

In 1966 the *Liberator* published a three-part exposé on "anti-Semitism in the Ghetto," which traced the historically contentious relationship between Jewish landowners and merchants to Harlem's black community, derided Jewish liberals involved in the civil rights movement, and portrayed blacks and Jews as naturally antagonistic. By accusing Jewish liberals of being a malevolent force within the black community, the *Liberator* simultaneously appeared to celebrate and foment black anti-Semitism, which precipitated a crisis in the AARI. In response, Ossie Davis and James Baldwin disassociated themselves from the *Liberator* and were subject to blistering editorial attacks by Watts. The AARI also suffered the withdrawal of significant financial support from liberal Jews and Jewish organizations like B'nai B'rith. Although the controversy imperiled the *Liberator*, it continued to be published until 1971.

**FURTHER READINGS**

Cruse, Harold. *Crisis of the Negro Intellectual: A Historical Analysis of the Failure of Black Leadership.* New York: Quill, 1984 [1967].

Liberation Committee for Africa. *Nationalism, Colonialism and the United States: One Minute to Twelve.* New York: Liberation Committee for Africa, 1961.

*Liberator* (New York, 1961–1971).

*Sara Diamond*

# Alabama Christian Movement for Human Rights

The Alabama Christian Movement for Human Rights (ACMHR) was a product of massive white resistance to the civil rights movement in Alabama. In the wake of the

Supreme Court's 1954 *Brown v. Board of Education* decision and the Montgomery bus boycott the following year, white Alabamians cracked down on the National Association for the Advancement of Colored People (NAACP), outlawing it in their state in 1956. In response, African Americans in Birmingham gathered for a mass meeting and founded the ACMHR in early June 1956.

For the next ten years, the ACMHR was one of the dominant local civil rights groups in Alabama. It not only helped undermine segregation in Birmingham and, ultimately, transform politics in a city that white supremacists had long governed, but it also played an important role in the creation of a successful national civil rights movement, first as a founding affiliate of the Southern Christian Leadership Conference (SCLC) and then as its local ally during the famous 1963 campaign in Birmingham.

The ACMHR was never intended simply to replace the local branch of the NAACP. Its organizers hoped that it would be more action oriented than the NAACP had been traditionally. The name of the ACMHR reflected its distinct spirit and mission. Local ministers were central to its formation, and they desired, as one leading organizer noted, a "Christian movement." That they sought "human rights," which meant "freedom and democracy and the removal from our society of any form of second-class citizenship," revealed their expansive goal.

From the start, the ACMHR was less an organization than a movement. Its opening mass meeting attracted over a thousand people. While an exact survey of its membership is impossible, its supporters tended to come from the black lower middle class. Women were as active as men, although men were more likely to be arrested during protests. Not all of Birmingham's African Americans rallied around the ACMHR. Many of the most influential black leaders questioned the value of such a militant organization.

Soon after its founding, the ACMHR turned to direct action. Segregation in the public arena was the enemy, and, as in other southern cities, segregated seating on the city's buses was the principal early target. The ACMHR combined protests with legal maneuvers to force Birmingham to desegregate.

The church orientation of the ACMHR was reflected in the commanding authority of its first president, Fred L. Shuttlesworth. A man of conviction, courage, and charisma, Shuttlesworth had returned to Birmingham in 1953 as the pastor of Bethel Baptist Church. Soon he was decrying racial injustice and laying the groundwork for the ACMHR. Shuttlesworth's boldness ensured the wrath of Birmingham's large contingent of white reactionaries. Eugene "Bull" Connor, the city's racist commissioner of public safety, had Shuttlesworth arrested several times, and white vigilantes, seemingly without fear of capture, also targeted him. On Christmas evening in 1956, they rolled sticks of dynamite under his house and nearly killed him. Shuttlesworth's bravery catapulted him to the front ranks of civil rights leadership. He was named one of the early vice presidents of the Southern Christian Leadership Conference (SCLC), and in 1957 he joined Martin Luther King Jr. as a speaker at the Prayer Pilgrimage in Washington, D.C.

The ACMHR continued its fight for racial justice into the early 1960s, despite few victories, constant intimidation, and criticism from segments of the black community. Realizing that the local struggle needed a lift, Shuttlesworth sought to persuade the SCLC to focus on Birmingham. In January 1963, King and the SCLC accepted the invitation of Shuttlesworth and the ACMHR.

Once the SCLC arrived in town, the Birmingham story assumed national importance. The joint ACMHR-SCLC effort sought to desegregate public facilities and to promote equal employment opportunities. A central committee composed of ACMHR and SCLC members, along with representatives from the traditional black leadership class, coordinated the campaign. Enlivened by the ACMHR choir, frequent mass meetings in black churches spread news of future activities and whipped up enthusiasm for the drive.

In early April 1963, ACMHR volunteers staged the first sit-ins of the campaign, whose fortunes fluctuated over the next five weeks. Later that month, the ACMHR-SCLC staff turned to local high school students to expand its nonviolent army. On May 2, "Bull" Connor ordered the arrest of marching teenagers. While momentarily clearing the streets, Connor energized the insurgency. By mid-May, Birmingham officials reluctantly agreed to meet some of the ACMHR-SCLC demands.

The negotiated truce revealed the inherent tensions of a campaign with both local and national missions. King's willingness to settle for a compromise agreement in order to guarantee a victory in Birmingham initially enraged Shuttlesworth. Though Shuttlesworth eventually embraced the accord, he recognized instinctively that its acceptance signaled that the high point for nonviolent grass-roots insurgency had passed. The ACMHR is still active, but its heyday ended almost forty years ago.

FURTHER READINGS

Branch, Taylor. *Parting the Waters: America in the King Years, 1954–1963.* New York: Simon Schuster, 1988.

Eskew, Glenn T. *But for Birmingham: The Local and National Movements in the Civil Rights Struggle.* Chapel Hill: The University of North Carolina Press, 1997.

Garrow, David, ed. *Birmingham, Alabama, 1956–1963: The Black Struggle for Civil Rights.* Brooklyn, N.Y.: Carlson Publishing, 1989.

Morris, Aldon D. *The Origins of the Civil Rights Movement: Black Communities Organizing for Change.* New York: The Free Press, 1984.

*James Ralph*

# Alabama Council on Human Relations

The Alabama Council on Human Relations (ACHR) was one of twelve state Councils on Human Relations established by the Southern Regional Council of Atlanta, Georgia. ACHR succeeded the Alabama Inter-Racial Committee and the Alabama Division of the Southern Regional Council in 1954. The ACHR was a non-political, non-denominational, interracial organization that worked for equal opportunities for all people of Alabama during the 1950s and 1960s. As an incorporated non-profit organization, the ACHR derived its financial support from membership dues, contributions, and grants from the Fund for the Republic.

Operating through fourteen local chapters in seven districts, the ACHR assisted in the establishment of local biracial programs to encourage the free exchange of ideas between members of the white and African American communities. Comprised of a cross-section of white and African American community leaders, these biracial committees mediated existing racial conflicts and worked to prevent the emergence of new racial problems. The ACHR also compiled statistics from fact-finding surveys conducted by local chapters on topics such as housing, health, education, recreation, law enforcement, and suffrage. Utilizing this information, the ACHR made recommendations to local, state, and federal government officials concerning improvements for African American citizens, and it made monthly reports to the United States Commission on Civil Rights.

The ACHR also worked to secure economic opportunities for African Americans. It exposed incidents of police brutality and Ku Klux Klan terrorism, supported various independent groups such as the Ecumenical Student Conference, and sponsored an educational and informa-tive project known as the "SAVE Movement" which worked to preserve democratic principles in Alabama race relations. The council ceased to function in the 1960s.

FURTHER READING

Southern Regional Council Papers. Series IV: State Councils on Human Relations, 1946–1968, Reels 140–141, Special Collections, Robert W. Woodruff Library, Atlanta University Center, Atlanta, Georgia.

*Kimberly E. Nichols*

# Alabama Share Croppers Union

The Alabama Share Croppers Union (ASCU) was established in 1931 by the Communist Party, which was organizing industrial workers in Birmingham. By 1930 the American Communist Party had opened its southern headquarters in Birmingham, a nucleus of the steel and iron industry, publishing the *Southern Worker* and running political candidates for local and state offices. A January 1931 sharecropper uprising in England, Arkansas, encouraged Birmingham party leaders to recruit members in rural Alabama for a similar protest against wealthy landowners.

Alabama's sharecroppers endured a submarginal existence. Displaced after the Civil War, black agricultural workers became sharecroppers. They farmed plots of landlords' plantations and bought supplies from local merchants on credit against their crop. Forced to plant cotton by landlords, the sharecroppers suffered crop losses from boll weevils and soil exhaustion and faced competition from foreign and western cotton growers. The 1920s agricultural depression continued into the next decade, lowering cotton prices and reducing the number of markets. Landlords demanded that sharecroppers accept non-cash wages, and merchants and bankers extended credit at unfair interest rates. Sharecroppers lived under constant threats from white landowners who evicted farmers who could not pay their debts. Some sharecroppers migrated north, seeking industrial opportunities to mitigate their agricultural misfortunes, but many farmers felt tied to the land despite its burdens. The Communist Party believed that impoverished Alabama sharecroppers could initiate a revolution against capitalism.

Printing letters in the *Southern Worker* allegedly written by sharecroppers detailing their plight and asking for help, the Communists sent Mack Coads, a steelworker, to Camp Hill in Tallapoosa County, Alabama, to recruit members for a sharecroppers' union. The Communists wanted to liberate exploited black farmers, confiscate land from owners to distribute to landless peasants, unify the Black Belt across state lines, and secure the self-determination of the African American majority in the Black Belt. Poor farmers, both black and white, were uninterested in the Communists' plans for an international struggle but were willing to organize to stay on the land and protect what they had to feed their families. The ASCU's immediate goals were to demand equal wages and decent working conditions, implement integration, secure voting rights for blacks, and abolish sharecropping.

Violence erupted when white landowners and officials tried to prevent sharecroppers from affiliating with the Communists. Angry that sharecroppers criticized the status quo, landowners feared economic losses if sharecroppers achieved their demands. Two major conflicts occurred at Camp Hill and Reeltown. The first fight was sparked when landowners and merchants ended food advances to farmers in midsummer in an effort to acquire cheap labor at area sawmills. ASCU recruits gathered at Wednesday night meetings to organize the union and outline their demands, especially food advances, the right to plant gardens, authority to sell their crops, cash wages, rest periods, and schools and school buses, as well as to protest the arrest of the Scottsboro prisoners (eight black teenagers who has been convicted of raping two white women). Brothers Ralph and Thomas Gray, the grandsons of Alfred Gray, a Reconstruction state legislator, led Camp Hill's ASCU.

On July 15, 1931, Tallapoosa County sheriff J. Kyle Young and seven deputies raided an ASCU meeting, confiscating literature and a membership list. On the following night, the sheriff approached an abandoned rural church where another ACSU meeting was scheduled. He encountered Ralph Gray, and a gunfight ensued. Primary accounts differ about who shot first and why. Gray was wounded but escaped to his home. The sheriff authorized a posse to storm Gray's house, killing Gray before burning his house down. His corpse was displayed on the courthouse steps where hundreds of residents viewed and abused it. Citizens were encouraged to hunt for ASCU members, and thirty-five blacks were arrested on a variety of charges but released by September because of insufficient evidence.

During the next year, Thomas Gray memorialized his martyred brother by encouraging sharecroppers to resist foreclosures and evictions and to demand equal payment for cotton. Gray expressed the sharecroppers' grievances, including victimization by landlords, merchants, and bankers who attempted to cheat them because they were illiterate and relied on verbal contracts or could not read the notes they signed. A new union organizer arrived in Tallapoosa County to charter local committees in surrounding counties and distribute leaflets. A second violent battle began when Reeltown farmer Clifford James was unable to pay his mortgage when cotton prices dropped. He and his creditor disagreed over how much James owed, and when the sheriff arrived to confiscate James's livestock in December 1932, ASCU members defended James. During the shootout, at least one sharecropper was killed, and both farmers and deputies were wounded. Lynch mobs searched for ASCU leaders in nearby swamps and woods. White liberals demanded that Alabama Governor Benjamin M. Miller investigate the situation, but he refused. Several ASCU members died in jail, and others were pressured to sign notes, deepening their debt. Six men were convicted at the trial of the Reeltown sharecroppers where prosecutor "Cotton Tom" Heflin decried communism and lauded segregation.

The ASCU executive board met quarterly. Harry Williams, a Tallapoosa County farmer, was president of the ASCU, and Thomas Gray's daughter Eula served as its secretary through May 1932 when Al Murphy was appointed to the position. He transferred the ASCU headquarters from Dadeville to Montgomery. The ASCU grew from several hundred to several thousand members, peaking at an estimated but probably inflated 10,000 in March 1935 when sharecroppers were evicted from lands because landlords plowed land under to receive Agricultural Adjustment Act funds. Each county hosted local committees, youth groups, and women's auxiliaries. Female members tended to be more literate and treated better than male sharecroppers, thus, women communicated with landlords and merchants and also taught African Americans reading and arithmetic to help them negotiate contracts. On July 4, 1935, the ASCU published the first issue of the *Union Leader: A Voice of the White and Negro Farm Toilers of the South*.

The ASCU directed wage strikers in Lowndes, Dallas, Montgomery, and several other Black Belt counties in August 1935. Racial tension heightened as laborers demanded that their wages increase from forty cents per hundred weight of picked cotton to one dollar. Vigilante citizen posses hunted organizers and strikers, shooting to kill. Sharecroppers' houses were raided and men, women, and children beaten and sometimes tortured as officials looked for ASCU membership cards and paraphernalia, arresting farmers who possessed such items. Attacks against

ASCU members in Lowndes County were especially violent, and bullet-riddled bodies were sighted frequently in the county's swamps. In September, ASCU wage strikes in Tallapoosa, Chambers, Lee, and Randolph counties were less hostile and more successful. Sharecroppers in east Alabama succeeded in receiving higher wages for cotton picking plus meals and transportation to and from work.

After this final wage strike, the ASCU sought alliances with other agricultural unions, particularly the Southern Tenant Farmers Union which did not encourage a Communist affiliation. At a 1936 convention, the ASCU outlined demands for civil rights, social welfare, liberation of political prisoners, crop insurance, and a farmer-labor third party for the working class. The ASCU's platform for tax and market reform resembled more traditional agrarian protests instead of a call to liberate the Black Belt. The ASCU found relief for farmers in liberal New Deal agencies. By late 1938, ASCU tenants transferred to the Farmers Union and wage laborers to the Agricultural Workers Union, which had been chartered by the American Federation of Labor as the Farm Laborers and Cotton Field Workers Union No. 20471 in 1937. Former ASCU members were not interested in Communist principles but instead sought survival and opportunities to earn a livelihood. They fought for security and subsistence and chose protection, not revolution. The ASCU briefly offered sharecroppers hope for a fair share in agricultural production and a voice in an environment traditionally deaf to the concerns of African Americans. World War II defense industries provided employment for some displaced agricultural workers, while those who chose to stay on the land were bolstered by increased production demands and federal funds.

**FURTHER READINGS**

Beecher, John. "The Share Croppers' Union in Alabama." *Social Forces* 13 (October 1, 1934): 124–132.

Kelley, Robin D. G. *Hammer and Hoe: Alabama Communists During the Great Depression.* Chapel Hill: University of North Carolina Press, 1990.

Rosen, Dale. "The Alabama Share Croppers Union." B.A. thesis, Radcliffe College, 1969.

Rosen, Dale, and Theodore Rosengarten. "Shoot-Out at Reeltown: The Narrative of Jess Hull, Alabama Tenant Farmer." *Radical America* 6 (November–December 1972): 65–84.

Rosengarten, Theodore. *All God's Dangers: The Life of Nate Shaw.* New York: Alfred A. Knopf, 1975.

*Elizabeth D. Schafer*

## All-African People's Revolutionary Party

Kwame Ture (1942–1998), formerly Stokely Carmichael, founded the All-African Peoples Revolutionary Party (AAPRP) in West Africa in 1971. The former Howard University student, chair of the Student Nonviolent Coordinating Committee (SNCC), and proponent of "Black Power," created the AAPRP to unite people of African descent throughout the world under the banner of socialism. The AAPRP argues that pan-Africanism in the cultural, economic, and political arena is the best approach to challenge inequalities and injustices in the world. By the early 1990s, the AAPRP had approximately twenty chapters in the United States. The major tenets of the AAPRP are opposition to Zionism, apartheid, racism, imperialism, and capitalism. To this end, the AAPRP has consistently been involved with other organizations that champion the same goals such as the American Indian movement, the Nation of Islam, and the Palestinian Liberation Front.

The AAPRP is founded on the principle that all Africans and descendants of Africa must focus their energies on improving the political, social, economic, and legal conditions in Africa as the foundation for any progress as a group throughout the world. Members advocate a reconnection with their African cultural identity as a first step to gain respect. For this purpose local chapters sponsor community events commemorating the anniversary of African Liberation Day, an international holiday created at the first conference of independent African states in 1958. The AAPRP's annual African Liberation Day celebration in Washington, D.C., at Meridian Hill Park, also known as Malcolm X Park, is visible evidence of the organization's pan-Africanist philosophy. The event features guest speakers who emphasize the need for people of African descent to collaborate in the struggle for political, economic, and cultural liberation, and AAPRP members distribute literature to raise the public's awareness of the organization's goal. In addition, vendors sell African clothing, food, and jewelry, while musicians and other artists provide entertainment.

The AAPRP has received a mixed reception in this country. In 1990, while Ture was on a lecture tour hundreds of Jewish students at the University of Maryland and Princeton charged him and his organization with anti-Semitism. The AAPRP continues to deny such charges, claiming that it distinguishes between anti-Semitism and anti-Zionism and opposes the establishment of Israel as a Jewish national state. Despite such criticism, Ture's message has been embraced by others. In 1996, Selma councilman

Yusuf Abdus-Salaam presented the AAPRP founder with a key to the Alabama city.

Prior to his death in November 1998, Ture traveled the world delivering the messages of socialism and pan-Africanism that are the ideological underpinning of the AAPRP. During his international recruiting tours, Ture consistently urged black people to join organizations, whether moderate or radical, or to form new groups that can address their needs. In the United States, AAPRP members have conducted workshops investigating the involvement of the Central Intelligence Agency in drug sales in America's inner cities. Moreover, the AAPRP has sponsored marches and rallies to protest poverty, prejudice, and violence. As of 1990, the AAPRP operated twenty chapters in various American cities, including Sacramento, Chicago, Cincinnati, Dallas, and New York.

**FURTHER READINGS**

Benn, Alvin. "Black Panther Party Organizer to Speak in Selma." *Montgomery Advertiser*, June 7, 1996, 1B.

Davis, Phillip. "Activist Kwame Ture: U.S. 'Ripe for Revolution.'" *Herald-Sun*, March 22, 1996, C1.

McCaslin, John. *Washington Times*, July 26, 1996, A7.

Magagnini, Stephen. "Hero is Honored, Agreed Over." *Sacramento Bee*, January 21, 1997, B1.

Rice, John. "Pan-African Crusader Still Ready for Revolution; Socialism: Activist Kwame Ture, the Former Stokely Carmichael, Remains Spirited Despite Battle with Cancer. He Says He Sees Progress for American Blacks But Also Growing Poverty." *Los Angeles Times*, May 26, 1996, A4.

*Angela Darlean LeBlanc-Ernest*

# Alley Improvement Association, Washington, D.C.

The Alley Improvement Association (AIA) of Washington, D.C., was organized in 1908 for the "industrial, moral and spiritual uplift of the people living in the alleys, courts, and back streets of Washington." The organization lobbied for alley clearance, cheap alternative housing, and improvement of sanitary conditions. Organized by an interdenominational group of ministers, including J. Milton Waldron and Francis J. Grimké, the group targeted the unique housing problems of African Americans in Washington.

Washington's population expanded rapidly in the years following the Civil War, including a significant influx of freedmen. Housing shortages led to the development of blind alley dwellings in the interior of city blocks. Often little more than shacks, these residences housed both blacks and whites of the lowest economic standing (in separate alleys) and provided a haven for disease. African Americans, denied housing elsewhere, were particularly drawn to the alleys.

The first investigations of alleys were conducted in the late 1890s and led to the creation of the white-owned Washington Sanitary Improvement Company, which aimed to provide low-cost housing. Although the corporation was a financial success, its rents were too high for alley dwellers. In the early 1900s articles began appearing in the press exposing the miserable conditions in the alleys, and in 1908 President Theodore Roosevelt ordered an investigation known as the President's Homes Commission. The AIA formed in the same year to investigate conditions in primarily black alleys because white organizations tended to concentrate on white alleys. A 1909 Associated Charities report, *Neglected Neighbors*, reported on alley conditions but focused on predominantly white alleys to counteract the prevailing opinion that alleys were an exclusively black problem.

The AIA held Sunday school meetings, Mother and Children's groups, and Temperance and Social Betterment Programs in the alleys to varied receptions. In cooperation with other organizations they demanded compulsory registration of all tuberculosis cases; provided free disinfection of homes; started an educational campaign with visiting nurses, leaflets, and lectures; and helped establish a public tuberculosis hospital.

In 1913 the AIA campaigned with Ellen Wilson, wife of President Woodrow Wilson, and white organizations for a congressional bill to abolish alleys as residences. In 1914 Waldron, one of the ministers who had founded the AIA, testified before Congress. He requested that no unnecessary hardship be placed on alley dwellers as a result of alley reclamation and that the process be completed with the least inconvenience and expense to the residents.

In 1917, following the passage of an act to abolish alley residences, AIA members, social service workers, and other interested parties formed the Emergency Housing Association (EHA), incorporated in 1918, to promote the erection of low-cost, sanitary housing for evicted alley residents. Members of EHA testified before the District Board of Commissioners requesting a $6 million bond issue to pay for the construction of these houses.

The AIA also conducted regular investigations into alley conditions and mediated tenant-landlord disputes. In 1934 Congress established the Alley Dwellers Authority to carry out a mandate of eliminating alley residences by 1944. This organization and other social agencies of the New Deal largely supplanted the AIA.

**FURTHER READINGS**

Borchert, James. *Alley Life In Washington: Family, Community, Religion, and Folklife in the City, 1850–1970.* Urbana: University of Illinois Press, 1980.

Green, Constance McLaughlin. *The Secret City: A History of Race Relations in the Nation's Capital.* Princeton: Princeton University Press, 1967.

Jones, William. *The Housing of Negroes in Washington, D.C.: A Study in Human Ecology.* Washington, D.C.: Howard University Press, 1929.

*Jacqueline M. Moore*

## Alpha Kappa Alpha

Founded in 1908, Alpha Kappa Alpha (AKA) is the first Greek-letter sorority established by and for African American women. AKA strives to improve social and economic conditions, provide educational and cultural opportunities, support social action imperatives, and foster economic ventures for African Americans.

AKA was launched by Ethel Hedgeman Lyle at Howard University in Washington, D.C., as a college-based sorority. In January 1908 sixteen female students under the leadership of Lyle organized AKA to contribute to Howard's academic and social life. In 1912, Nellie Quander, past president of AKA, suggested that the sorority broaden its constituency to a national level and include AKA alumni. AKA incorporated in January 1913 and established subchapters to promote its organization's motto, "Service To All Mankind."

AKA is headquartered in Chicago and led by the Supreme Basileus, or Directorate, who supervises the executive director and deputy director who oversee Fiscal Operations, Support Services, and Program Development. A network of volunteers implements programs initiated by the Board of Directors including endeavors in health care, education, and the social and political arenas. Between 1934 and 1942 the sorority supported the Mississippi Health Project, which provided the first mobile health clinic in the United States. The project funded diphtheria and smallpox vaccines and dispensed educational material on sound nutrition and improved oral hygiene. In 1958, AKA began funding sickle cell anemia research and disseminated educational literature about the disease.

AKA has also supported various educational projects. In 1934, AKA established a Summer School for Rural Teachers at Saints Industrial School in Lexington, Mississippi, to train teachers. AKA secured discarded library books and enrolled local teachers in classes such as child development, vocational education, English, mathematics, science, and music. The curriculum was approved by the Mississippi State Board of Education and teachers earned academic credits for their work. Another educational pursuit is AKA's support of excellence in lifelong learning. AKA awards scholarships to historically black colleges and universities and between 1974 and 1996 it contributed $789,000 to the United Negro College Fund. The priority of AKA's educational endeavors led the organization to create the Educational Advancement Fund in 1980 to direct the college fund donations.

To improve social and economic conditions in Africa, AKA initiated the African Village Development Program in 1984. AKA chapters adopt African partner villages and support them with contributions ranging from $300 to $5,000 annually. Africare distributes the funds that are used for health care, food production, child nutrition, livestock acquisition, and other areas of need. During the first two years of the project, eighty AKA chapters adopted villages in six African countries, including Niger, Chad, and Zimbabwe. For example, the Tau Omega Chapter in New York City donated over $5,000 for the building of a well to ensure a safe water supply and thus reduce infectious diseases. Similarly, an $8,000 gift from several AKA chapters was used to establish a fund for a health clinic in Kavalamanja, Rhodesia.

To confront discrimination and segregation in the United States, AKA organized the National Non-Partisan Council on Public Affairs in 1934. The council is a grass-roots civil rights lobby that aims to improve the social and economic conditions of African Americans. In conjunction with the National Association for the Advancement of Colored People (NAACP), the council has supported the creation of equal employment opportunities and decent housing for African Americans. The council has supported other campaigns such as voter registration and anti-lynching legislation and has censored discrimination in federal housing.

To overcome employment disadvantages in the United States, AKA opened a Job Corps Center for Women in Cleveland, Ohio, in 1965. Securing funds through the 1964 Economic Opportunity Act, AKA set up the center to provide academic and vocational training for women between the ages of sixteen and twenty-one. The center has trained more than 20,000 young women in over thirty occupations including the health care and service industries and clerical and sales work. The center boasts a 95 percent placement rate for women who complete its one- to two-year training program.

In 1997, the AKA membership was composed of 140,000 women in 860 undergraduate and graduate chapters in forty-two states and seven countries. Notable AKA members include author and educator Charlotte Hawkins Brown (1883–1961); civil rights advocate L. Pearl Mitchell (1883–1974); physician, Dorothy Ferebee (1898–1980); educator, singer, and actress Zelma George (1903–); first black woman commercial pilot, Willa B. Brown (1906–); and actresses Phylicia Rashad and Roxie Roker. Through its various programs, AKA maintains an ongoing commitment to the social, economic, and political advancement of African Americans.

### FURTHER READINGS

Alpha Kappa Alpha. "Building the Future: The Alpha Kappa Alpha Strategy—Making the Net Work." N.p.: Alpha Kappa Alpha, 1996.

"80 Years of Service and Sisterhood." *Ebony* 43 (October 1988).

Parker, Marjorie H. *Alpha Kappa Alpha Through the Years: 1908–1988.* Chicago: Mobium Press, 1990.

*Julieanne Phillips*

## Alpha Phi Alpha

Alpha Phi Alpha (APA), the first primarily undergraduate Greek letter fraternity organized by African Americans, was founded at Cornell University on December 4, 1906. It originated as a Social Study Club, which met in the rooms of a Mr. C. C. Pointdexter, a graduate student in agricultural sciences. For reasons that are unclear, several members decided to form a Greek letter association. Seven of the young men, who had worked in local white fraternity houses and knew of the customary rituals, decided to borrow the structure of these ceremonies and adapt them to an association of their own. Pointdexter, to whom Alpha Phi Alpha tradition refers as "the black Alpha," refused to go along with the plan and did not join with the seven. Apparently, Pointdexter did not believe that Greek letter associations were appropriate for African Americans. This seems likely, as Pointdexter was a protégé of the widely-respected leader Booker T. Washington and a firm believer in the sober, no-frills Tuskegee Institute philosophy of practical technological education.

Although the fraternity was founded as a Greek-letter association, with ritual forms putatively borrowed from white models, it had an "Afrocentric," or at least an "Egyptocentric" iconography and symbology from the beginning. The sphinx was displayed prominently on the fraternity crest, along with a symbol of European knighthood. Songs and poetry composed by first-generation members referred to African Americans as Ethiopians and alluded to the "Mighty Sphinx in Egypt." APA rhetoric also reflected a belief in the predominant ideals of Victorian manhood, including respect for the "chastity of women."

APA boasts a list of prominent members, including W. E. B. Du Bois, Paul Robeson, Max Yergan, and Martin Luther King Jr. While these distinguished APA members were known for their commitment to international class struggles and their interest in Marxist-influenced teachings, there appears to be little overlap between the ideology of the fraternity and that of its more radical members. Black social critics as different as Booker T. Washington, W. E. B. Du Bois, Carter G. Woodson, and E. Franklin Frazier have all suggested that black student associations have functioned perfunctorily, if at all, in discharging their professed mission of service to the laboring masses. APA is not a racially exclusive fraternity. White members have occasionally been pledged and have from time to time addressed the national convention. In practice, however, the association has been overwhelmingly African American.

APA suffers from some of the problems endemic to secret societies in the United States, such as the Freemasons, whose secret lore has been leaked to the larger society. It also suffers from an inability to maintain tradition over a number of generations. In the early days, pledges were identifiable by a small but elegant bronze emblem, the sphinx pin, which was worn discreetly on the lapel. In recent years, the sphinx pin has largely vanished, as undergraduates prefer to make their own emblems, usually taking the form of a "tiki," a wooden plaque suspended from a cord about the neck.

Few African American fraternities have been strong enough fiscally to provide housing for undergraduates. Their functions remain primarily social rather than economic. From time to time, the black fraternities, including APA, have taken an official stand against public hazing of pledges, but enforcement has been sporadic. Fraternity pledges are ordered frequently by their undergraduate superiors to march about campuses in single file, dressed in varying styles of uniform. They are seldom instructed that they must leave such behavior at the classroom door, and some professors have complained that the enforced conformity is destructive to the spirit of university life.

**FURTHER READING**

Wesley, Charles H. *The History of Alpha Phi Alpha: A Development in College Life, 1906–1979.* 14th ed. Chicago: Foundation Publishers, 1996.

*Wilson J. Moses*

## American Academy of Medical Directors

Founded in Falls Church, Virginia, in 1975, the American Academy of Medical Directors (AAMD) is the professional organization of black physician managers, those doctors working in management or administrative positions in hospitals, group practices, managed care, government, universities, the military, and industry. The AAMD provided educational forums designed to enhance administrative management skills and facilitate networking.

With the assistance of the University of Colorado in Durango and funding from the Robert Wood Johnson Foundation, the AAMD launched its first Physician in Management seminar at Durango in 1975. In the following year, the American Medical Association (AMA) recognized the AAMD and praised the integrity of its continuing medical education courses. That accolade encouraged an expanded venue, and by 1977, the AAMD offered seven training programs. Courses continued in Durango, but black physicians also took advantage of programs offered in several key national locations, including Washington, D.C. In 1979, the AAMD further broadened its scope when it offered its first National Institute on Health Care Leadership and Management. By 1980 the organization was able to fund its own programs, and by 1997 the number of AAMD-sponsored educational courses had risen to twenty-one.

The AAMD'S educational efforts were supplemented by the organization's bimonthly newsletter, *Medical Director*, which provided members with professional news and information about activities and programs. The newsletter, launched in 1976, became the organization's monthly journal, *Physician Executive,* in 1986.

In 1980, the AAMD's growth led to the formation of the American College of Physician Executives (ACPE), which worked to establish graduate training programs for black physician managers. The parent organization and its offspring continued to offer seminars focusing on developing trends and events in health care and health care management. In 1984, the AMA again praised the value of the AAMD seminars in training physicians for roles in professional medical management and awarded the AAMD a seat in the AMA House of Delegates. Formal academic training of physician managers was further enhanced when the ACPE, in conjunction with the University of Wisconsin, started to offer a Master's Degree in Administrative Medicine in 1987. By the end of the 1980s, the ACPE found itself involved in an extensive publishing operation, offering books, monographs, technical reports, and other medical management works to an international audience.

In 1989, the AAMD and the ACPE merged and continued to operate under the name of the latter group. Following the merger, the ACPE created the American Board of Medical Management, which assumed the duty of granting certification to qualified physician executives. In 1990, the organization joined with the University of South Florida to offer an MBA program for physicians, and three years later it began offering courses at the University of Wisconsin and Tulane University, leading to a Certificate in Medical Management. Tulane now recognizes the certificate courses for credit in its Master's Degree in Medical Management program.

The ACPE, built and nourished by the ideals and leadership of the AAMD, serves more than 10,000 physicians. Some twenty years after its founding, it offers twenty-six training programs and from its headquarters in Tampa, Florida, continues to serve the needs of physician managers through publications and an extensive Internet site that provides a myriad of services, including online courses and forums.

**FURTHER READINGS**

American College of Physician Executives. *Twenty Years of Growth: An Historical Overview of the American College of Physician Executives.* Tampa: American College of Physician Executives, ca. 1995.

Furtaw, Julia C., ed. *Black Americans Information Directory, 1992–1993.* Detroit: Gale, 1992.

*Peggy Hardman*

## American and Foreign Anti-Slavery Society

The American and Foreign Anti-Slavery Society (AFASS) was founded in May 1840 by abolitionists who had seceded from the American Anti-Slavery Society (AASS) because of doctrinal disagreements with William Lloyd

Garrison and his supporters as well as with a second faction of abolitionists that proposed the creation of an abolitionist political party. While Garrison and his followers argued that women's rights, religious anti-clericalism, and opposition to governmental institutions were fundamental parts of abolitionist doctrines, some of his prominent opponents such as James G. Birney and Elizur Wright Jr. argued that abolitionists must instead enter electoral politics by developing their own third party, the Liberty Party. Still other reformers such as Arthur Tappan and Lewis Tappan, Amos Phelps, and William Jay dissented vigorously against both of these alternatives, and these men became the originators of the AFASS.

After Garrison's faction had captured a majority of delegates to the 1840 annual meeting of the AASS, the Tappan brothers and their supporters seceded in order to form a new organization that more faithfully reflected their abolitionist principles. For this reason, the constitution of the AFASS upheld the literal truth of Scripture, denied women the right to vote in society proceedings, and embraced the doctrine that abolitionism could triumph only by appealing to the consciences of individuals by means of peaceful "moral suasion" and not by seeking their votes or attacking their religious denominations.

The organization never developed sufficient vitality to influence significantly the ongoing crusade against slavery. Many leading activists spurned its traditional emphasis on scripturalism for the more innovative approaches pursued by Garrisonians and Liberty Party organizers. It was also widely viewed by skeptical abolitionists as an organization dominated by the wealthy Tappan brothers who had created it as their personal vehicle for denouncing their abolitionist enemies, not only in the United States, but also in Great Britain, where quarreling American activists always competed for sponsorship and endorsements. Although the society did fund the occasional publication of tracts and pamphlets, it remained largely inactive in the periods between its annual meetings and never attracted significant new members. In 1855, Lewis Tappan finally decided that the society was, indeed, moribund, and disbanded it permanently.

**FURTHER READING**

Wyatt-Brown, Bertram. *Lewis Tappan* and *the Evangelical War Against Slavery*. Baton Rouge: Louisiana State University Press, 1997.

*James Brewer Stewart*

## American Anti-Slavery Society

The American Anti-Slavery Society (AASS), founded December 1833, signaled the emergence of an unprecedentedly radical religious movement to abolish slavery and white supremacy within the United States. The delegates who met in Philadelphia to found this organization demanded in their "Declaration of Sentiments" the "immediate abolition" of slavery in the United States and the "secur[ing] to the colored population all the rights and privileges that belong to them as men and as Americans." For the next thirty-seven years, until it dissolved in 1870, the AASS continued to serve as a significant agency for reformers opposed to slave holding and was committed to acting on behalf of the principles of racial equality. But during this long history, the AASS underwent several significant transformations.

In its earliest years, from 1833 to 1840, the AASS united abolitionists across the free states by sponsoring an unprecedented program of popular agitation against slavery and white bigotry. In the later 1830s, however, the organization fell prey to external repression from its enemies and to bitter internal divisions. Once abolitionist dissenters had withdrawn in 1840, the AASS became nearly synonymous with the doctrines of one particular leader, William Lloyd Garrison, who from 1840 until 1861 stressed pacifism, women's rights, boycotting elections, and the repeal of a presumably proslavery U.S. government.

Following the onset of the Civil War, from 1861 to 1865, the AASS transformed itself again, becoming a broad-based organization dedicated to promoting slave emancipation as a military measure and the recruitment of African American troops into the Union's war effort. But with peace and emancipation achieved in 1865, change overtook the AASS one last time when Garrison and his followers declared their crusade against slavery to be at an end, and retired from the organization. Those who dissented from Garrison's point of view, led by Wendell Phillips and Frederick Douglass, then took over the society's leadership and continued its work for another five years, campaigning for equal civil rights for African Americans, the franchisement of all African American men, and land redistribution within the defeated Confederacy in favor of the emancipated slaves. Finally, in 1870, Phillips and Douglass disbanded the society permanently, once the ratification of the Fourteenth and Fifteenth Amendments promised to secure equal citizenship for African Americans in every part of the Union.

The sixty-three men and women who founded the AASS in 1833 saw themselves joining a powerful world-

Anti-slavery meeting, Boston Common, 1851. © *Bettmann/Corbis*

wide movement. Only six months before, the British Parliament had legislated emancipation for all slaves throughout its empire, and these Yankee abolitionists anticipated similar success in the United States. They also represented the racially mixed, gender-inclusive constituency that always characterized the AASS and the abolitionist movement generally. Evangelically zealous Protestant whites such as Arthur Tappan, and Lewis Tappan, William Jay, William Lloyd Garrison, and Theodore Weld dominated the proceedings, but participants also included four Quaker women—Lucretia Mott, Sara Pugh, Lydia White, and Ester Moore—and three African American men—Robert Purvis, James McCrummell, and James G. Barbadoes.

Uniting this disparate fellowship were unshakable beliefs in slavery's inherent sinfulness and one's personal Christian duty to awaken the nation's repentance. The abolitionists' initial demand was therefore for "immediate emancipation"; slave holders and bigots must repent, seek God's forgiveness, and quickly begin to do justice to the oppressed. Their methods relied on the doctrine of "moral suasion," which meant peacefully spreading their message of sin and repentance by organizing antislavery societies all over the nation, circulating tracts, legislative petitions, and newspapers, "purifying" the doctrines of all-Christian denominations, and assisting free African American communities in their efforts to secure equality.

By the late 1830s, the Society's efforts had created an impressive network of antislavery societies across the North, had flooded the U.S. mail system with antislavery literature, had conveyed thousands of antislavery petitions to representatives in Congress, and had founded institutions supportive of African American education such as Oberlin College in Ohio and the Oneida Institute in Whiteboro, New York. The success of these initiatives, however, also provoked unprecedented violence and legislative repression in defense of white supremacy in all parts of the nation. Throughout the South slave holders united in angry protests, and in cities across the North whites of all social classes engaged in unprecedented mob violence against abolitionists and free African American communities. Congress forbade the presenting of anti-slavery petitions. Though no slaves had been emancipated as a result of the society's efforts, by the end of the 1830s the AASS had done much to ensure that slavery would henceforth be a subject that could not be ignored.

Anti-abolitionist repression, in turn, caused the AASS to shatter into warring factions. To Garrison and his supporters such as Wendell Phillips, Angelina and Sarah Grimké, and Abby Kelly, the mobs and legislative suppression proved that the nation's deepest values were mired fatally in sin. "True Christians" must therefore respond by cutting all ties with "corrupting" institutions such as churches and governments, embrace radical pacifism, and expand the crusade for equality to encompass women's rights. To Garrison's leading opponents, such as Arthur and Lewis Tappan, Joshua Leavitt, and Henry B. Stanton, these doctrines were anti-Christian delusions, repellent to potential converts to the cause, and subversive to the original intentions of immediate abolitionism. By 1840, these deep disagreements had driven Garrison's critics to abandon the AASS in favor of their own, newly created American and Foreign Anti-Slavery Society, which attempted to perpetuate the original spirit of "immediatism." Henceforth, until 1861, "Garrisonianism" and the AASS meant almost one and the same thing.

Until the outbreak of the Civil War, the AASS remained a small but highly vocal group of radicals who called incessantly for the boycotting of elections and the overthrow of the "proslavery" U.S. Constitution. At the same time the organization initially supported the lecturing careers of such noteworthy African American spokespersons as Frederick Douglass, Sojourner Truth, and Charles Lennox Remond, while its official newspaper, *The National Anti-Slavery Standard*, served as an important vehicle for circulating the political opinions of African American and women writers. Most important, however, was the impact of all these activists in deepening the secessionist impulses of southern slaveholders as the North-South political crisis deepened throughout the 1850s. To such planters, by 1861, there seemed to be little difference, if any, between zealots of the AASS and "black Republicans" like president-elect Abraham Lincoln.

With the onset of the Civil War, the AASS's membership suddenly expanded once again; its vigorous espousal of general slave emancipation as a military objective neces-

sary for winning the war was a position that abolitionists of nearly all varieties gladly supported. African American activists who had deplored the society's doctrines and had abandoned it in the 1840s, such as Douglass, Henry Highland Garnet, and James McCune Smith, now joined again with Garrison and Phillips to pressure Lincoln's administration for the issuance of an emancipation proclamation, support of abolitionist-minded Republicans in Congress, and the mobilization of African American regiments. In all these respects, the AASS played an absolutely vital role during the war years in mobilizing political opinion in favor of the destruction of slavery, as was finally guaranteed by the 1865 ratification of the Thirteenth Amendment.

With slavery's destruction assured, Garrison announced that the AASS should disband since its original mission had finally been accomplished. Though a substantial number of members agreed with Garrison, several of its most illustrious leaders—including Douglass, Phillips, and Elizabeth Cady Stanton—did not. Hotly contesting Garrison's recommendations, these individuals seized control of the society just as the politics of African American equality shifted to debates over the position of the emancipated slaves in the post-war reconstruction of the defeated Confederate states.

From 1865, when Reconstruction's legislative struggles opened, until 1870, when the Fifteenth Amendment was ratified finally, the AASS stood militantly in favor of the most radical formulations of racial equality developed during that era. Not content with the Fourteenth Amendment's general guarantees of equal national standing for African Americans before the law, its members pushed heavily for an explicit "equal suffrage amendment," which finally was embodied in the Fifteenth Amendment. This was accomplished only after alienating feminist abolitionists such as Elizabeth Cady Stanton who protested its applicability to males alone.

Beyond these constitutional struggles, the Society also served as a vocal pressure group that influenced congressional legislation that applied to the reconstruction South. From 1867 to 1865, society spokespersons pressed the Republican Congress as it passed a battery of civil rights legislation and enforcement bills designed to ensure the civil and political rights of southern freed people against restrictions sought by whites. When President Andrew Johnson, successor to the assassinated Lincoln, attempted to thwart such protective legislation, Phillips, Douglass, and other society leaders led the unsuccessful Republican attempt to impeach and try him while continuing to insist that the lands of former slaveholders be confiscated and distributed to the freed people.

In so proposing, the AASS had become in its final phase a direct extension of the Republican Party's radical wing, led in Congress by politicians such as Thaddeus Stevens, Charles Sumner, and Benjamin Wade. Hence, as the political spirit of radicalism began to wane in the late 1860s, the AASS's influence quickly faded. Once the Fifteenth Amendment had been ratified in 1870, Phillips and Douglass announced the Society's dissolution. Many of its members continued to crusade for a variety of causes such as those of the labor and women's movements, and for Phillips and Douglass problems of racial injustice always retained paramount concern. But until the founding of the National Association for the Advancement of Colored People (NAACP) in 1911, there was no organization to struggle, as the AASS had, for the achievement of racial justice in the United States.

**FURTHER READING**

Stewart, James Brewer. *Holy Warriors: The Abolitionists and American Slavery.* New York: Hill and Wang, 1996.

*James Brewer Stewart*

## American Association for Affirmative Action

The American Association for Affirmative Action (AAAA) was created in 1974 as a nonprofit organization to implement and advance affirmative action and equal opportunity employment, to establish and maintain ethical standards for working persons, and to promote professional growth and development of its members. The AAAA is dedicated to the elimination of discrimination on the basis of race, gender, ethnicity, and any other criterion that deprives Americans of the opportunity to live and work. It seeks to promote understanding and advocacy of affirmative action and enhance access and equity in employment, economic, and educational opportunities.

The AAAA's most important work focuses on Equal Employment Opportunity/Affirmative Action (EEO/AA) legal issues. Committed to the prompt communication of relevant information on proposed EEO/AA legislation, the AAAA seeks to promote among its members and the public a clear understanding of the importance and benefits of a firm EEO/AA legislative agenda and protective laws.

The AAAA has currently more than 1,000 members who enjoy a number of benefits, including the chance to belong to a national network of EEO/AA professionals who provide information, counseling, and support. Members are also able to interact with federal, state, and local organizations that oversee compliance with EEO professional and educational standards.

The AAAA's national headquarters are in Indianapolis. In addition, ten regional divisions sponsor meetings and seminars that provide members with opportunities for education and networking. To enhance its members' knowledge of EEO/AA, the AAAA offers a certification training program four times a year. The AAAA's certificate in EEO/AA Program Management is based on the following courses, each consisting of eighteen contact hours: "Affirmative Action and the Law," "Complaint Processing, Counseling and Resolution," and "Affirmative Action Plan Development." The certificate is awarded upon completion of the three required courses, a 90 percent attendance record, and a national certification exam.

The AAAA also educates its members about the status of EEO/AA during its annual conference. A variety of sessions on issues such as homophobia in the workplace, sexual harassment, health care, hate speech, racial and ethnic classifications, and disability law provide participants with up-to-date legal information.

*Isabel Soto*

## American Association of Blacks in Energy

A small group of black professionals in energy-related fields established the American Association of Blacks in Energy (AABE) in Washington, D.C., on July 25–26, 1977. That year President Jimmy Carter convened a special task force to study the growing energy shortages associated with events in the Middle East. No members of minority groups were on the task force. Concerned about the lack of African American representation, Clarke Watson, owner of Westland Company of Denver, organized a meeting of black economists, engineers, and managers employed in energy companies. The group formed the AABE, elected Clarke Watson as chairperson, and scheduled a follow-up meeting to coincide with the annual meeting of the Congressional Black Caucus in Washington, D.C., on September 23, 1977. In November the fledgling AABE played an important role in a conference organized by the National Association for the Advancement of Colored People (NAACP) to examine the energy crisis. The AABE drafted a critique of the Carter administration's energy policy that the NAACP released as its formal position paper on the topic in January 1978.

From its humble beginnings, the AABE has grown to an organization with 900 members organized into six regions. It continues "to ensure the input of African Americans and other minorities into the discussion and development of energy policies, regulations, R & D technologies [emerging energy production systems and processes such as solar energy, emission control technology, and alternative energy production], and environmental issues in the United States." The organization's national headquarters in Washington, D.C., produces a quarterly newsletter, occasional position papers, and a biannual report. John M. Bush is the AABE's current executive director.

*Dennis W. Cheek*

## American Baptist Black Caucus

Founded in 1968 as the Black American Baptist Churchmen, the American Baptist Black Caucus (ABBC) is an organization of black congregations within the American Baptist Churches, U.S.A. Adopting its current name in 1981, the ABBC seeks to reform the American Baptist Churches to bridge the gap between white and minority members. Its many projects include developing denominational support for scholarship aid for disadvantaged students, increasing resources for business and religious projects in the inner cities, encouraging black appointments to denominational posts, raising support for black colleges and universities, and establishing open hiring policies on local, state, and national levels. The ABBC also operates a placement service for pastors seeking positions and churches seeking pastors.

The caucus is one of several black church organizations formed by African Americans during the civil rights movement of the 1960s. Denominational advocacy groups like the ABBC followed the example of the National Committee of Negro Churchmen (now the National Conference of Black Churchmen), which attempted to implement some of the demands for racial justice promulgated by the proponents of black power. Many black church groups, for example, proposed black economic empowerment programs. Moreover, they sought to increase the awareness of white church members concerning African American congregations and black representation in the church hierarchy.

African Americans had been members of the Baptist church since its emergence in the United States. In the antebellum era, white Baptists in the North took an interest in the conversion and education of slaves and freedmen and often permitted African Americans to join their churches. Soon, however, African Americans began to form their own congregations within the existing Baptist structure. Eventually, these black churches formed separate associations as well as conducted separate state and regional conventions. Initially, white Baptists in the North cooperated with them; however, beginning in 1830 cooperative activities declined due to the conflict over slavery.

In the postbellum era, many northern Baptists renewed their commitment to African Americans in the South and, with the cooperation of black Baptist groups, opened several schools for freedmen. While African American Baptist groups united to form the National Baptist Convention, U.S.A. in 1895, the Northern Baptists (which became the American Baptist Churches in the U.S.A.) continued to house both white and black congregations.

By the middle of the twentieth century the American Baptists began to experience a significant decline in white and a rise in black membership. At that time, many black churches in other Baptist denominations began to affiliate with the American Baptists because their own organizations provided little or no retirement benefits for their clergy. Although the number and proportion of African American members were rapidly increasing among the American Baptists, black representation at the higher administrative levels and on denominational boards did not reflect this growth. Concern about this lack of black representation in the church hierarchy led to the formation of the ABBC, which urged the denomination to pursue a policy of racial inclusivity. By 1970, only two years after its founding, the ABBC scored its first victory when the American Baptists elected Thomas Kilgore Jr. as its first black president. Since Kilgore's election, several other African Americans have succeeded him. Currently, the American Baptist Church has a representative number of blacks in top leadership positions.

Today, the ABBC represents 480,000 black members of the American Baptist Church, constituting roughly 30 percent of the total denominational membership. The ABBC, headquartered in the office of the annually elected incumbent president, publishes the semiannual *Black Caucus Newsletter* and the monthly periodical *ABC TAB*.

**FURTHER READINGS**

Fitts, Leroy. *A History of Black Baptists*. Nashville: Broadman Press, 1985.

Lincoln, C. Eric, and Lawrence H. Mamiya, eds. *The Black Church in the African-American Experience*. Durham, N.C.: Duke University Press, 1990.

Washington, James M. *Frustrated Fellowship: The Black Baptist Quest for Social Power.* Macon, Ga.: Mercer University Press, 1986.

*Kurt W. Peterson*

## American Baptist Board of National Ministries

*See* American Baptist Home Missionary Society.

## American Baptist Home Missionary Society

In 1832, several prominent missionaries, concerned about the effects of America's increasing religious and social diversity, and the inability of local Baptist missionary societies to address this area of concern, founded the American Baptist Home Missionary Society (ABHMS). Driven by the belief that America's national preservation depended on the unity of its religious faith, the ABHMS targeted in its initial missions unchurched westerners and urban immigrants. While these missions continued throughout the nineteenth century, the society committed one-half of its money and manpower in 1862 toward missionizing America's newly freed slaves.

Compelled by its prewar anti-slavery stance, which split the society into northern and southern factions in 1845, the ABHMS commissioned white and black Baptists to work among the freedmen. Unlike many of their northern competitors, ABHMS missionaries came south not to gain black converts, but rather to aid and educate an already established black Baptist constituency. Working in tandem with local black and white Baptist missionary societies, the ABHMS successfully trained black ministers, established Sunday schools, visited homes, and rebuilt churches.

Beyond the church and home, the society also reached southern black Baptists by establishing mission schools. By 1892 the ABHMS had founded at least fifteen colleges, universities, and seminaries, including Shaw University in Raleigh, North Carolina, and Morehouse University in Atlanta, and financially supported over a dozen black-owned schools. These educational institutions served as training centers for black teachers, missionaries, and clergy and provided meeting grounds for southern blacks and African students.

In the latter half of the nineteenth century, the society's schools also served as seedbeds of racial unrest. Whereas the ABHMS granted local autonomy to black ministers and their churches, in the mission schools, control remained in the hands of white society officials. This inequity caused a rift among black Baptists. While "cooperationists" wanted to continue their work with ABHMS educational and missionary efforts, "separatists" demanded black-funded and black-operated missionary and educational societies. The division culminated in the 1890s and acted as one of a number of catalysts that brought about the founding of the all-black National Baptist Convention in 1895.

Though the ABHMS failed to redefine its paternalistic relationship with its southern black constituency to the satisfaction of many black Baptist leaders, the society did provide African Americans with more representation in its schools. In 1894, black and white representatives from the ABHMS, the Southern Baptist Convention, and the black Baptist state conventions drafted the "Fortress Monroe Agreement." The agreement provided resources for the assessment and improvement of black ministerial education and opened doors for black preachers and scholars to move into administrative and faculty positions in ABHMS schools. In 1934, responsibility for these schools was transferred from the ABHMS to the American Baptist Board of Education. Though no longer a part of the ABHMS's current work, the southern mission schools and their graduates are perhaps the greatest legacy of the ABHMS's work among African Americans.

Throughout the twentieth century, the ABHMS expanded its work among African Americans to address the needs of the growing black urban communities. Following the migration of African Americans into southern and northern cities, ABHMS missionaries and educators provided loans for church buildings and established educational centers for urban ministerial training. The first such center, run by Dr. Vernon Johns, opened in Harlem in 1925. Designed to help rural, black Baptist clergy meet the demands of an urban constituency, these centers spread throughout the nation's cities by the 1930s. The ABHMS also built Christian centers to minister to inner-city black youth, providing them with Sunday schools, youth fellowship, and recreational facilities. Today, the ABHMS, renamed the American Baptist Board of National Ministries in 1972, is headquartered in Valley Forge, Pennsylvania. It continues to update its missionary outreach to African Americans and other minorities through urban mission centers, bilingual churches, and a mission website.

**FURTHER READINGS**

Beers, G. Pitt. *Ministry to Turbulent America: A History of the American Baptist Home Mission Society Covering its Fifth Quarter Century, 1932–1957.* Philadelphia: The Judson Press, 1957.

Carlson, Beverly Clark. "Pursuit of the Promise: An Overview." *American Baptist Quarterly* 11 (December 1992): 1–4.

Davis, Lawrence B. *Immigrants, Baptists, and the Protestant Mind in America.* Urbana: University of Illinois Press, 1973.

McPherson, James M. *The Abolitionist Legacy: From Reconstruction to the NAACP.* Princeton: Princeton University Press, 1975.

Martin, Sandy D. "The American Baptist Home Missionary Society and Black Higher Education in the South, 1865–1920." *Foundations* 24 (October/December 1981): 310–27.

*Jennifer J. Wojcikowski*

## American Church Institute for Negroes, Episcopal Church

The American Church Institute for Negroes (ACIN) was charged with advancing the Episcopal Church's educational efforts among African Americans. Immediately after the Civil War, the Episcopal Church established a Freedman's Commission to the Colored People as a primary missionary agency to formerly enslaved African Americans. By 1904, after two name changes and some modest financial support from the Episcopal Church, the work of the now Commission on Negro Work faired poorly, whether compared to the efforts of other denominations in the United States or the successes of Episcopal missions abroad. The church disbanded the commission and developed a small group of churchmen called the ACIN to oversee church efforts among blacks. The ACIN quickly determined that its best method of missionary involvement was to strive for racial uplift through Christian education. Yet, by 1912, it was clear that the educational aims of gradualists such as Booker T. Washington held dominant sway in the ACIN's thinking. Their annual report deemed their mission to be the "religiously inspired education of practical workers in the world—farmers, industrial workers, homemakers, etc."

The institute's leadership was dominated by southern whites—clergy and lay—and could never move beyond a strongly accommodationist posture in its approach to black education. Indeed, enamored of the financial support given to Hampton Institute in Virginia and Tuskegee Institute in Alabama, the ACIN determined to establish or adopt institute-type schools in each southern state, both geographically accessible to its black population and philosophically committed to creating good black citizens and fostering better race relations. The ACIN put its commitment to Christian education in remission, opting for an industrial model accommodating to the times.

Despite its all-white leadership, the ACIN did employ black clergy and laity in its field work with its constituent schools. Schools such as the Bishop Payne Divinity School (named for Daniel Alexander Payne, the black Episcopal bishop of Liberia) educated the majority of Southern black clergy and came under the "adoption" of the ACIN, along with Voorhees College in Denmark South Carolina; Saint Paul's College, in Lawrenceville, Virginia; and Saint Augustine's College in Raleigh, North Carolina. These colleges, which at once drew more than half of their financial support from the ACIN, simultaneously struggled to place serious intellectual education alongside and even above the industrial and civic training espoused by the ACIN's leadership.

In 1940, the church, still dissatisfied with its work among African Americans, dissolved the ACIN and established the office of secretary for Negro Work. Ironically, it did so in accordance with the belief that "a greater share in the responsibility for the progress of the Negro Work must be placed upon the shoulders of the Negroes themselves." Such a sentiment had been voiced for years by black Episcopalians, chiefly through their organization, Conference of Church Workers Among the Colored People (CCWACP). The secretary for Negro Work began to function as the representative of the voice of the church, while the CCWACP operated as the voice of blacks within the denomination.

**FURTHER READING**

Lewis, Harold T. *Yet with a Steady Beat: The African American Struggle for Recognition in the Episcopal Church.* Valley Forge, Pa.: Trinity Press International, 1996.

*Harold Dean Trulear*

## American Citizens' Civil Rights Association

*See* American Citizens' Equal Rights Association.

## American Citizens' Equal Rights Association

Established in February 1890, the American Citizens' Equal Rights Association (ACERA), also known as the American Citizens' Civil Rights Association, advocated civil rights and voiced African American demands for equality. The founding of the ACERA was the product of African American demands for national conventions designed to address the concerns of the black community. Since 1830, free blacks had gathered frequently in so-called colored conventions to discuss their social and economic conditions and their legal status. The 445 black leaders and politicians who gathered in Washington, D.C. to found the ACERA hoped to revive the antebellum convention movement. Among those who attended the meeting were P. B. S. Pinchback, Joseph C. Price, John Mercer Langston, John E. Bruce, and John Mitchell. Price, founder of North Carolina's Livingstone College and a minister of the African Methodist Episcopal Zion Church, chaired the convention and became the ACERA's spokesman. Attendants elected Pinchback as the association's first president.

Like the antebellum convention movement, the ACERA met inconsistently and accomplished little. Among the association's projects was the publication of a pamphlet urging moral conduct, good education, and the acquisition of wealth as a means to achieve full citizenship. Similar to Booker T. Washington's accommodationist and gradualist philosophy, the ACERA placed the burden of racial advancement on the shoulders of African Americans.

From its inception, the ACERA competed with the Afro-American League (AAL), which weakened the support base of both groups. Price was heavily involved in both groups and, as president of the AAL, proposed a merger of the two organizations. Pinchback, however, neither supported the merger nor the AAL. Ideological differences and lack of mutual support between the two groups led to the demise of both groups by 1892. In the following year, A.M.E. bishop Henry Turner made an attempt to revive the ACERA but he failed to generate sufficient support.

The existence of the ACERA is significant despite its short-lived duration and its failure to launch a national black convention movement. The association represented the early effort of African Americans to establish a permanent civil rights organization with a national agenda.

**FURTHER READINGS**

Meier, August. *Negro Thought in America: Racial Ideologies in the Age of Booker T. Washington.* Ann Arbor: University of Michigan Press, 1963.

Thornbrough, Emma Lou. *Thomas Fortune: Militant Journalist.* Chicago: The University of Chicago Press, 1972.

Williams, Michael W. *African-American Encyclopedia,* vol. 2. New York: Marshall Cavendish, 1993.

*Katherine Kuntz Dill*

## American College of Physician Executives

*See* American Academy of Medical Directors.

## American Colonization Society

Robert Finley, a New Jersey Presbyterian minister, and a group of influential political figures including Henry Clay, Daniel Webster, John Calhoun, Francis Scott Key, and Bushrod Washington, met in December 1816 to form the American Society for Colonizing the Free People of Color in the United States, known commonly as the American Colonization Society (ACS).

At its founding, the question of what was to become of blacks had engaged the attention of some of the best minds in the United States. Thomas Jefferson thought he had a solution in 1781: They should be removed, he proposed in his *Notes on the State Of Virginia*, "beyond the reach of mixture." Jefferson was not willing to fly in the face of traditional Christian beliefs by suggesting that blacks and whites were originally distinct and that both races were not descended from Adam and Eve, but he felt confident that time and circumstances had made the blacks inferior in "the endowments of both body and mind." That and their distinctive color had produced a deep and abiding antipathy toward them by whites. As a result, emancipation had to be followed by expatriation to an area far removed from any possible contact with whites.

Some contemporaries questioned Jefferson's call for emancipation, seeing it as a direct assault on private property. What was needed, Ferdinando Fairfax, a fellow Virginian, insisted, was not emancipation but the removal of free blacks whose mere presence posed a threat to the system of slavery. Others suggested a more benevolent approach. The New England minister and theologian Samuel Hopkins called for the training of blacks as missionaries to take the message to benighted Africans. Finally, there were those like the eccentric William Thornton who proposed the establishment of economically viable settlements in Africa that would act as breaks on the slave trade by encouraging what was called legitimate trade.

African colonization came to embody one or more of these approaches in the years leading up to the Civil War. As slavery strengthened its influence on the American

ACS warehouse on Water Street, Monrovia, Liberia, ca. 1895. *Library of Congress*

economy and polity in the years after the Revolution, colonization emerged as a reasonable solution to an apparently intractable problem. Those interested in antislavery saw it as a way to increase the likelihood of emancipation by providing an escape hatch for those who wanted to free their slaves but who were concerned about the rise in the number of free blacks. Others who were more interested in consolidating the gains of slavery believed that the absence of free blacks would ensure the survival of the institution. In the early years of the nineteenth century colonization came to mean different things to different people.

Contemporaneously, there was an active emigrationist movement among African Americans who believed that their futures were best served outside of the United States. Unlike colonizationists, however, theirs was to be a voluntary movement of a select group of individuals. As early as 1783 plans were being made by a group of blacks in Newport, Rhode Island, to settle in Africa. Eleven years later a similar group in Providence sent one of its members on a fact-finding mission to Sierra Leone. None of these efforts bore fruit. But in January 1811, Paul Cuffe, a black Massachusetts sea captain, made the first of two voyages to west Africa to explore the possibilities of increased trade between Africa and black America and the establishment of a colony in the area. On his second trip in December 1815 Cuffe took thirty-eight settlers, pioneers in what he hoped would be a viable colony. But Cuffe died soon after his return to the United States.

While Cuffe was in Africa, Robert Finley began exploring plans for the establishment of a colonization organization that would be based in Washington, D.C., and would rely for much of its support on the federal government. While Finley argued the antislavery potential of colonization many of those who formed the nucleus of the organization saw things differently. From its inception the ACS attempted to straddle, and where it could not, to contain the conflicting interests of its renowned leaders. The prestige of the founding members could not, however, guarantee government financial support. The ACS would have to rely on the support of local societies and bequests from its members.

The ACS's first attempt to establish a colony on Sherbro Island, off Sierra Leone in 1820, ended in abject failure, with most of the colonists falling victim to the "African fever." The second expedition headed for Cape Masurado the following year and forced the local authorities to cede land on which the nucleus of a colony was established. The fledgling colony was named Liberia, and its capital was called Monrovia in honor of the support given the ACS by President James Monroe. Over the next few years the number of settlers increased largely due to an influx of manumitted slaves. In the mid-1820s a number of slaveholders freed their slaves with the expressed intention of sending them to Liberia. But these and emigrants from other parts of the United States, as well as recaptured Africans from the slave trade who were settled in Liberia, were never large enough in numbers to guarantee that the colony would be anything more than a ward of the ACS.

Neither commerce nor agriculture prospered appreciably over the next few decades. In fact, increases in the number of settlers tended to reflect crises in the United States. In the two years following the slave leader Nat Turner's rebellion in Virginia in 1831, for example, nearly 1,500 blacks chose to leave the United States for Liberia. And in the twelve years after the colony's independence in 1847, a period of rising restrictions on black freedom in the United States, epitomized by the Fugitive Slave Law of 1850 and the Dred Scott decision (a decision by the U.S. Supreme Court stating that slaves could not sue for their freedom in federal courts because slaves were not citizens) seven years later, almost 5,900 settlers moved to Liberia. That was just six hundred shy of the number who went to the colony in the previous twenty-seven years.

From its inception the ACS met with strenuous opposition from free blacks and later abolitionists. Finley's pleas to the contrary, many considered the ACS a mechanism devised by the slave system to forcefully remove the free black population. Although a number of prominent African Americans, among others Alexander Crummell, John B. Russwurm, and Thomas Morris Chester, chose to settle in Liberia because they saw it as the site of a vital "black nationality," by and large the ACS and its colony won the enmity of the free black population. "Here we were born," declared a group in Pittsburgh, "here bred— here are our earliest and most pleasant associations—here is all that binds man to earth, and makes life valuable. And we consider every colored man who allows himself to be colonized in Africa, or elsewhere a traitor to our cause." Martin R. Delany of Pittsburgh, one of Liberia's most vocal critics, dismissed the country as "a poor *miserable mockery*—a *burlesque* on government." While the ACS initially won the support of a number of individuals who would later emerge as prominent figures in the abolitionist movement (William Lloyd Garrison, Arthur Tappan, Gerrit Smith, and James Gillespie Birney), by the end of the 1820s they were all actively opposed to any form of colonization.

The ACS had its greatest success—as measured by the number of immigrants it attracted and the size of its treasury—in the decade of the 1850s. Many state and local societies that had atrophied since the 1830s were now reenergized. Annual receipts increased dramatically in a decade when the country faced increasing political turmoil. State legislatures in all sectors of the country voted to support colonization, and some states like Indiana (anxious to stop the settlement of free blacks in the state), hired commissioners to persuade blacks to move to Liberia. Liberia seemed the solution to the country's mounting problems. Even the clearest articulation of abolitionist sentiment in popular culture, Harriet Beecher Stowe's *Uncle Tom's Cabin* ended with the chief protagonist settling in Liberia. But the decade of the 1850s was the high point of the ACS's activities. Although there were brief spurts of colonizationist activity in the years immediately after the Civil War, the ACS never again attracted the kind of support it did in the 1850s.

While the ACS faced unrelenting opposition from blacks and abolitionists, much of its problems were of its own making. The alliance between those who saw the ACS as an antislavery instrument and those who considered it a protector of slavery was an uneasy one at best. At times of national tension over slavery as occurred during the 1850s, the alliance frayed. Many in the South who had supported its efforts now opposed the ACS for doing the work of abolitionists. In addition, Liberian independence in 1847 had a profound impact on the society: colonization, the prescription for solving the race problem, gave way increasingly to the more pragmatic concern of selecting and transporting immigrants across the Atlantic.

Yet the ACS continued to limp along well into the twentieth century with a drastically reduced treasury catering to fewer emigrants. As in the past, however, there were years of crisis, 1886 and 1887 typically, when the demand for its services increased. In the last year of the nineteenth century it sent just four settlers to Liberia. Although it survived into the twentieth century, the ACS had been moribund for a number of years.

**FURTHER READINGS**

Garrison, William Lloyd. *Thoughts on African Colonization*. New York: Arno Press, 1968.

Miller, Floyd J. *The Search for a Black Nationality: Black Colonization and Emigration 1787–1863*. Urbana: University of Illinois Press, 1975.

Staudenraus, Philip J. *The African Colonization Movement 1816–1865*. New York: Columbia University Press, 1961.

*Richard Blackett*

# American Committee on Africa

In 1953, the American Committee on Africa (ACOA) emerged from the Americans for South African Resistance (AFSAR), which had been founded in the previous year. In 1952, when nonwhite South Africans began their campaign of civil disobedience, a group of American pacifists, liberals, and religious leaders created AFSAR. These Americans with connections to organizations such as the Fellowship of Reconciliation, the War Resisters League, and the International League for the Rights of Man, were concerned about the lack of an institutional constituency for Africa in the United States.

Numerous black American activists such as Charles S. Johnson, Mordecai Johnson, Adam Clayton Powell Jr., A. Philip Randolph, and Bayard Rustin were involved in the efforts of AFSAR. For example, on the afternoon of April 6, 1952, AFSAR staged a rally at the Abyssinian Baptist Church in New York City. Speakers included congressman Reverend Adam Clayton Powell Jr., the actor Canada Lee, and the Reverends Donald Harrington and Charles Trigg, the co-chairmen of AFSAR. By the end of 1952 AFSAR had sent $1,500 to the South African resisters, and by April 1953 it had doubled that amount. By that time, however, the protest campaign was waning. Facing the campaign's demise, the leaders of AFSAR chose not to disband, but instead to broaden the organization's focus to all of Africa. In 1953 AFSAR transformed itself into a broader-scoped organization, when it became the

ACOA. A driving force behind the creation of AFSAR, and then its transformation into the ACOA, was the liberal clergyman George Houser, who subsequently managed the ACOA for several years. The ACOA's purpose was to help the emerging democratic self-governing states in colonial Africa and to free the African people from exploitation, poverty, and racial discrimination.

In the mid-1950s, African Americans had few organized routes through which they could act on their interest in Africa. Due to cold war repression, the Council on African Affairs dissolved in 1955, leaving the ACOA as the most prominent American organization involved in African freedom struggles. The ACOA offered African Americans an outlet for their concerns with Africa, and from the beginning it included African Americans such as the historian Rayford Logan and the civil rights activist James Farmer who served on the initial national board.

The ACOA, though, was dominated by white liberals, and generally targeted the more affluent white liberal community in the United States. Still, with few viable alternative organizations, black activists such as Martin Luther King Jr. and A. Philip Randolph supported the ACOA and utilized the organization to express their concern about Africa. King issued various appeals on behalf of the work of the ACOA, wrote introductions to its pamphlets, and acted as an honorary chairman of the ACOA-sponsored Africa Freedom Day in 1960. Randolph involved himself in numerous ACOA activities, and became co-Chairman of the ACOA in 1961. The interracial character of the ACOA has remained consistent to the present.

During the 1950s, many of the ACOA's efforts continued its founding tradition and targeted South Africa. For example, following the arrest of 156 South Africans in December 1956, which triggered a more than four-year–long treason trial, the ACOA coordinated the sending of protest letters and managed to raise tens of thousands of dollars for the legal defense of the defendants and for aid for their families. In the following year, the ACOA sponsored a campaign for a worldwide Day of Protest against apartheid, coinciding with Universal Human Rights Day on December 10, 1957. Former First Lady Eleanor Roosevelt acted as the international chair of the campaign, while King served as the U.S. National Vice Chairman. Both urged people to sign a "Declaration of Conscience" denouncing racial conditions in South Africa and calling on the South African government to honor its moral and legal obligations as a signatory to the United Nations

Charter and the Declaration of Human Rights. The Day of Protest became an annual event for several years.

Concern about human rights violations in South Africa continued to remain a prominent item on the ACOA's agenda in the 1960s. The ACOA, for example, raised funds to help the survivors of the Sharpeville shooting and those who had been victimized by police brutality during the subsequent state of emergency. In March 1960, South African police had killed sixty-seven African demonstrators in Sharpeville; most of them were shot in the back as they fled the scene of protest. The following week, to combat continuing racial unrest, the South African government declared a state of emergency, granting its police force broad powers to act against all forms of alleged subversion and resulting in further abuses of African residents. In the months after Sharpeville, the ACOA's Africa Defense and Aid Fund raised $15,000 to help the victims. Sponsors included the actor Harry Belafonte, the author Lorraine Hansberry, the educator Mordecai Johnson, the Reverend Martin Luther King Jr., the educator Benjamin Mays, the educator Frederick D. Patterson, the labor leader A. Philip Randolph, the baseball hero Jackie Robinson, the ACOA member Hope Stevens, and the civil rights activist Roy Wilkins.

While the ACOA held a special concern for South Africa, it consciously broadened its efforts to expose human rights abuses in all of Africa. The ACOA's involvement with liberation struggles and nationalist leaders was especially extensive in places such as Angola, the Congo, Guinea-Bissau, Kenya, Mozambique, Namibia, and Zimbabwe. While the ACOA concentrated its initial efforts on sub-Saharan Africa, the struggle in Algeria also became a concern of the committee.

In order to carry out its mission, the ACOA developed numerous contacts and lobbied extensively in the United Nations, regularly wrote and sold pamphlets articulating particular problems faced by Africans, and inaugurated the journal *Africa Today*. The efforts of the ACOA continue today, even as its early emphasis on helping to bring about black majority rule have necessarily shifted to helping resolve the dramatic problems facing independent Africa.

**FURTHER READING**

Houser, George. *No One Can Stop the Rain: Glimpses of Africa's Liberation Struggle.* New York: The Pilgrim Press, 1989.

*Jim Meriwether*

## American Council on Race Relations

In 1944, Edwin R. Embree, president of the Rosenwald Fund, established the American Council on Race Relations (ACRR) following the eruption of World War II race riots. Financed by the Rosenwald Fund and the Field Foundation, the interracial ACRR gathered information about racial and ethnic discrimination and provided educational and consulting services to local communities to ameliorate race and ethnic relations and prevent the eruption of further racial violence. Under the guidance of the ACRR, hundreds of American communities established interracial committees during the final war years and the immediate post-war period.

The ACRR's leadership was composed of men and women who were known nationally for their interest in promoting social and racial justice. The council's first chairman was Clarence Pickett, who worked with the American Friends Service Committee. The first executive director was A. A. "Sandy" Liveright, a member of the Liveright publishing family. Other well-known individuals who joined the ACRR included the educator and presidential advisor Mary McLeod Bethune, the future diplomat Ralph Bunche, the civil rights attorney Charles Hamilton Houston, the author Pearl Buck, Bishop William Scarlett, and Louis Adamic, director of the Common Council for American Unity.

Based in Chicago, the ACRR was a national organization that functioned mainly as a clearinghouse for information about the prevention of racial strife. It gathered data about the status of race relations in various American cities in order to foster better communication between white municipal government officials and black urban residents. To compile the data, the ACRR recruited the services of black and white scholars, including the prominent University of Chicago sociologist Louis Wirth. Between 1945 and 1948, the ACRR commissioned sixteen studies of various aspects of race relations, including the effects of discrimination, segregation, and racism on community relations. Among those studies were Robert Weaver's *Hemmed In: ABC's of Race Restrictive Housing Covenants* (1945) which exposed legal restrictions to fair housing and proposed new legislation to remedy the problem. In addition to housing, ACRR studies examined police harassment of minorities and lack of economic opportunities. The ACRR's San Francisco branch publication *Intergroup Relations in San Diego* (1946), for example, proposed improved training programs for police officers and increased community meetings to ease interracial tensions. In the same year, the ACRR, in conjunction with the California Department of Justice, sponsored publication of the *Police*

*Training Bulletin: A Guide to Race Relations for Police Officers.* In addition to this publication, the ACRR established race relations training courses for the police forces of Youngstown, Ohio; Richmond, California; Minneapolis; Detroit; and San Francisco.

While the ACRR primarily worked to educate white Americans in order to improve race relations, or "intergroup relations," it also collaborated with other civil rights groups to protest racially motivated violence. In August 1946, the organization joined forces with the National Association for the Advancement of Colored People (NAACP) to form the National Emergency Committee Against Mob Violence. On August 6, under the leadership of the ACRR and the NAACP, the leaders of over forty civil rights groups who had joined the National Emergency Committee met with President Truman to protest the increase in lynchings following World War II. In 1947, the ACRR also joined the efforts of other civil rights groups when it distributed a fifty-nine page pamphlet urging implementation of the recommendations of President Truman's Committee on Civil Rights, which were published earlier that year in the report *To Secure These Rights.*

In addition to public education campaigns and civil rights protests, the ACRR worked to dismantle legal discrimination, particularly in housing. For this purpose, the ACRR filed amicus curiae briefs with the U.S. Supreme Court to help overturn restrictive covenants. In the years following World War II, the ACRR's research on housing discrimination also provided civil rights attorney Charles Hamilton Houston with invaluable data for his briefs on behalf of the NAACP, which resulted in the Supreme Court's decision to overturn racially restrictive housing covenants in *Shelly v. Kraemer* (1948).

In 1948, Wirth assumed leadership of the ACRR and worked tirelessly to promote legislative reform in the area of civil rights. During his tenure as chairman, the ACRR launched an investigation into the desegregation of the armed forces and fair employment practices in American industries. These investigations formed the basis of the testimony of Wirth and other ACRR members before various legislative committees. Wirth also collaborated with Walter White of the NAACP and Roger Baldwin of the American Civil Liberties Union (ACLU), lobbying Congress to pass the civil rights and anti-lynching proposals of President Truman's Committee on Civil Rights. ACRR members were also active in several other organizations that promoted racial justice. Arnold Aronson, for example, was named secretary of the executive committee for the National Council for a Permanent Fair Employment

Practices Committee in 1946. In 1948, Aronson and other civil rights advocates sent Senator Robert Taft, Republican of Ohio, a memorandum about S.984, a pending Fair Employment Practices Committee bill sponsored by two Republican congressmen.

The ACRR ceased to operate in 1949, as no new postwar riots erupted and the fear of racial violence subsided.

**FURTHER READINGS**

Dykeman, Wilma, and James Stokely. *Seeds of Southern Change: The Life of Will Alexander.* Chicago: The University of Chicago Press, 1962.

Guzman, Jessie Parkhurst, ed. *Negro Yearbook: A Review of Events Affecting Negro Life, 1941–1946.* Atlanta: Foote and Davies, Inc., 1947.

Kellogg, Peter J. "Civil Rights Consciousness in the 1940s." *The Historian* 42 (November 1979): 18–41.

McCoy, Donald R., and Richard T. Ruetten. *Quest and Response: Minority Rights and the Truman Administration.* Lawrence: The University Press of Kansas, 1973.

Salerno, Roger A. *Louis Wirth: A Biobibliography.* New York: Greenwood Press, 1987.

Zangrando, Robert L. *The NAACP Crusade Against Lynching, 1909–1950.* Philadelphia: Temple University Press, 1980.

*Robin B. Balthrope*

# American Freedmen's Union Commission

The American Freedmen's Union Commission (AFUC) was an "umbrella" agency intended to coordinate the activities of the freedmen's aid societies during Reconstruction. Organized on January 31, 1866, the commission was the culmination of a series of efforts to bring together the many competing groups that were providing aid to the freed slaves of the American South. At its largest, nine state and regional secular aid societies, embracing scores of local auxiliaries, were affiliated with the AFUC. Riven from the beginning by disagreements, however, the organization began losing branch societies within its first year of existence. By 1869, after only three years of effort, the AFUC dissolved, leaving the work of secular freedmen's aid and education in the hands of the remaining secular aid societies. The history of the AFUC illustrates the bitter rivalry between ecclesiastical and secular aid organizations over control of freedmen's education, appropriate forms of schooling for former slaves, and notions of the place of African Americans in American society.

African American women sew at the Freedmen's Union Industrial School, Richmond, Virginia, 1866. *Library of Congress*

Within weeks of the beginning of the U.S. Civil War, missionary societies and voluntary secular groups organized relief efforts for southern freed slaves and white refugees. The American Missionary Association and various Quaker groups organized quickly, sending supplies and teachers into northern Virginia in late 1861. By March 1862, abolitionists and humanitarians had created independent organizations in Boston, New York, and Philadelphia to send plantation managers, teachers, and relief supplies to Port Royal, South Carolina. In the course of the next four years, some fifty organizations, primarily religious societies, entered the South to organize schools and churches, provide medical assistance and food, organize stores and distribution posts, and in other ways offer an outlet for northern benevolence among southern refugees.

Inevitably, dozens of organizations at work on the same problems resulted in conflict and rivalry. Though dedicated to good works, few of the organizations were above seeking a good name at the same time. Ecclesiastical groups vied with each other for advantage in the competition for expanded church membership among the four million freed slaves. And all, groups competed for limited financial resources from benefactors, tailoring their messages to the hopes and fears of northern audiences.

To gain recognition from governmental agencies and from the national media, most of the aid societies established schools and churches in Washington, D.C., and in the major cities of the South, competing for students and support in a handful of southern centers while neglecting the majority of the freedmen. Church building sometimes eclipsed education and was always foremost in the minds of missionary societies. Secular societies, certain that reconstructing the South required the creation of secular common schools separate from churches, competed for northern funds with agents of the churches who spoke darkly of the danger to the republic of four million former slaves whose education lacked the moral bulwark of "the Bible and the schoolbook together." By the end of the war, two distinct positions on freedmen's aid and education had emerged from the aid societies—a more liberal position roughly associated with the more secular groups along with the Quaker aid societies and a more conservative position taken by most of the missionary societies.

The mergers that eventually led to the AFUC were intended to bring together one wing of the freedmen's aid movement. In late 1863 the five major eastern secular aid groups—the New England Freedmen's Aid Society, the National Freedmen's Relief Association of New York, the Pennsylvania Freedmen's Relief Association, the Western Freedmen's Aid Commission (based in Cincinnati), and the Northwestern Freedmen's Aid Commission (based in Chicago)—created the United States Commission for the Relief of the National Freedmen. Its purpose was to give the secular freedmen's aid movement a stronger, more unified voice in national politics. It advocated grants of land to the freedmen, the creation of a governmental agency charged to guarantee the fruits of emancipation to the freedmen, and equal pay and provisions for black troops. It was, however, simply a paper organization with no officers and no coordinating authority; it existed simply as the voice of its constituent societies.

Without authority, the United States Commission could not gain cooperation in fund-raising among its members. Four of the five societies voluntarily limited their fund-raising to the geographical areas defined by their corporate titles. However, the New York group, insisting upon the prerogatives of its title as the National Freedmen's Relief Association, infringed on the territory of other societies, particularly in New England and Pennsylvania. That led, in February 1865, the Pennsylvania and New England societies, along with the new Baltimore Association for the Moral and Educational Improvement of the Colored People, to create the American Freedmen's Aid Union. According to the organizers of this union and its successors, a national merger would end competition for funds and students, would provide a single clearinghouse for benevolent funds operated by nationally known leaders, and would standardize the quality of education provided in the South. They hoped as well to limit the growth of denominational influences in freedmen's schooling, believing that education should remain a public, not a religious, institution.

Initially, the National Freedmen's Relief Association remained outside the American Freedmen's Aid Union. But in May 1865, after the resignations of officers who were also leaders in the rival American Missionary Association, the New York group withdrew its agents from other states and joined the union. Three western aid groups joined in August 1865—the Western Freedmen's Aid Commission, the Northwestern Freedmen's Aid Commission, and the Freedmen's Aid Commission of Western Pennsylvania. The expanded organization changed its name to the American Freedmen's Aid Commission, the direct predecessor to the AFUC.

Then, in an expression of the interracial beliefs of its eastern societies, the commission began negotiating with another organization, the American Union Commission (AUC). The AUC had been created in mid-1864 to provide relief to war refugees. Although its constitution claimed that it made no distinction on the basis of race, it served primarily white refugees. Leaders from the eastern aid societies and officers of the AUC sought to unite the two organizations in part to reaffirm their belief that Reconstruction would require integrated schools and interracial cooperation if emancipation was to free successfully African Americans from southern tyranny. The merger of the American Freedmen's Aid Commission and the American Union Commission in January 1866, created the American Freedmen's Union Commission.

No sooner was AFUC founded, however, than it began to crumble. Its weaknesses were clear months earlier. The American Freedmen's Aid Commission had been bedeviled from its founding in August 1865, by friction between the western and eastern branches. The western branches, particularly officers of the Western Freedmen's Aid Commission, sought to dominate the organization, declaring one of its members, the Reverend Jacob R. Shipherd, as general secretary of the new organization, and establishing him in an office at a handsome salary in Washington, D.C. More ominously, however, the western societies dissented from the eastern emphasis on interracialism and integrated schools for the South. Their donors, they feared, opposed any suggestion of racial equality. To complicate matters, ecclesiastical aid societies, sensing disaffection within the secular organizations, began raiding the western societies whose members tended to be more closely aligned philosophically with the missionary societies than with the liberal eastern societies.

The Western Freedmen's Aid Commission withdrew from national union even before the AFUC was fully formed. Within the next few months, one of its leaders, the Reverend John M. Walden, withdrew with many Methodist members to form the Methodist Episcopal Freedmen's Aid Society, taking with him a number of schools and teachers belonging to the western, the northwestern, and other freedmen's aid commissions in western states. What was left of the Western Freedmen's Aid Commission, under Shipherd's guidance, quickly fell into the orbit of the American Missionary Association where it retained its identity as the Western Department of the association for a few more years.

The AFUC survived for three years. By 1867, its western branches had defected, folded, or were in decline. The following year the National Freedmen's Relief Association dissolved, leaving its assets and teachers in the hands of trustees and ceding its schools to the New England Freedmen's Aid Society. The AFUC turned the work back to its remaining eastern branches on January 1, 1869. The Pennsylvania society discontinued its work in late 1869, though some of its auxiliary societies continued supporting teachers for a few more years. The Baltimore Association, always entirely dependent upon the larger branches for its life, closed its operations in 1870. Only the New England society, the first to organize in 1862, and the small Delaware Association, remained after 1870.

The destruction of the AFUC and its constituent societies silenced the organizations most committed to public education for all children in the South and muted a dissenting tradition within freedmen's aid that called for egalitarian human relationships and integrated education. On the other hand, like its rivals, the AFUC was ultimately committed to an improbable panacea. Where the greatest need was for southern economic reform and for forceful protection of the civil rights of the freedmen, the AFUC opted for schools. Essential as it was, schooling proved incapable of securing either economic change or civil rights.

**FURTHER READINGS**

Butchart, Ronald E. *Northern Schools, Southern Blacks, and Reconstruction: Freedmen's Education, 1862–1875.* Westport, Conn.: Greenwood Press, 1980.

Jones, Jacqueline. *Soldiers of Light and Love: Northern Teachers and Georgia Blacks, 1865–1873.* Chapel Hill: University of North Carolina Press, 1980.

McPherson, James M. *The Struggle for Equality: Abolitionists and the Negro in the Civil War and Reconstruction.* Princeton: Princeton University Press, 1964.

Morris, Robert C. *Reading, 'Riting, and Reconstruction: The Education of Freedmen in the South, 1861–1870.* Chicago: The University of Chicago Press, 1981.

Richardson, Joe M. *Christian Reconstruction: The American Missionary Association and Southern Blacks, 1861–1890.* Athens: University of Georgia Press, 1986.

*Ronald E. Butchart*

## American League of Colored Laborers

In July 1850, African American skilled workers in New York City organized the American League of Colored Laborers (ALCL). The league sought to encourage unity among African American mechanics and other tradespeople and to help them establish their own businesses. It also promoted the training of young African Americans in agriculture, commerce, and industrial crafts.

At its founding convention, ALCL members elected Samuel R. Ward as the organization's president. Frederick Douglass, the well-known former slave and abolitionist, agreed to serve as the league's vice president. Douglass's participation, and the presence of several newspaper editors among the organization's leadership, ensured it a significant degree of publicity in the African American press and contributed a measure of prestige. In addition to Ward and Douglass, the ALCL's leadership consisted of an executive committee of twenty-three officers who met each month to transact the group's business and plan its activities.

Although the ALCL was the product of an antebellum trade union movement, the league was concerned with more than labor issues. It was also intended as a mutual benefit society. At the organization's 1851 convention in New York City, members proposed the creation of a mutual savings bank whose purpose was not only to provide a source of credit for African American businesses, but also to encourage thrift and savings. The bank's dual purpose reflected the ALCL's membership and orientation. Governed by a small group of African American elites for the benefit of an equally small black artisan class, the ALCL purposely tied economic matters to social and cultural uplift. The organization believed that by increasing the number and visibility of black business people and skilled workers it could challenge racist notions of African American inferiority and efforts by white workers and proprietors to limit black economic activity to menial occupations and service industries.

The ALCL sought to live up to its name by establishing close ties with similar African American organizations throughout the United States. One of its activities was an industrial fair to showcase the accomplishments and skills of African American workers.

Despite its ambitious goals and prominent leadership, the ALCL suffered the same fate as nearly every other nineteenth-century African American labor organization. Although African Americans resisted the efforts of white workers to limit their economic pursuits to low-paying, unskilled activities, the relatively small number of blacks in American cities at this time made resistance through organization difficult. The growing strength of craft unions, which typically excluded African Americans, also cut into this kind of activity, as did increasing job competition from European immigrants. Finally, like white organized labor, black unions at this time suffered from poor leadership and internal disputes. The ALCL ceased to exist during the later half of the 1800s.

**FURTHER READINGS**

Foner, Philip S., and Ronald L. Lewis, eds. *The Black Worker: A Documentary History from Colonial Times to the Present. Vol. 1, The Black Worker to 1869.* Philadelphia: Temple University Press, 1978.

Franklin, Charles Lionel. *The Negro Labor Unionist of New York: Problems and Conditions among Negroes in the Labor Unions in Manhattan with Special Reference to the N.R.A. and Post–N.R.A. Situations.* New York: Columbia University Press, 1936; rpt., New York: AMS Press, 1968.

*Stuart McElderry*

## American Library Association, Black Caucus

*See* Black Caucus of the American Library Association.

## American Missionary Association

The American Missionary Association (AMA), founded in 1846, provided African Americans with physical, political, spiritual, and educational resources and opportunities. Working both for and with African Americans, the AMA fought for black citizenship, the Christianization of American society, and the abolition of slavery. The AMA's story is one of mixed success. Although the AMA often exhibited race prejudice and paternalism and fell short of its initial political and religious goals, it was the most successful benevolent association of its day, providing educational opportunities for African Americans that trained a generation of twentieth-century black leaders, including the reformer, educator, and lecturer Booker T. Washington and the educator and writer W. E. B. Du Bois.

In 1846, several northern abolitionist leaders including Lewis Tappan, Simeon Smith Jocelyn, Gerrit Smith, and James Pennington met in Syracuse, New York, to join forces against American slavery. Frustrated by the silence of the American Home Missionary Society and the American Board of Commissioners for Foreign Missions on the issue of slavery, these leaders combined four newer missionary bodies—the Amistad committee, the black Union Missionary Society, the Committee for West Indian Missions, and the Western Evangelical Missionary Society for Work among the American Indians—to create the AMA. Tappan, a New York merchant and New England Congregationalist, acted as the AMA's organizational genius and served as its treasurer for nineteen years. Committed to American evangelical ideals of political, religious, and racial equality, Tappan established a nondenominational and biracial executive committee to govern the AMA from its New York City headquarters. He and his evangelical compatriots dedicated their voluntary society and themselves to the promotion of abolitionism, Christian education, and Yankee industrialism.

In the antebellum period, the AMA used its funds and energies to assist fugitive slaves and free blacks while working to end the peculiar institution's southern stronghold and western expansion. The AMA commissioned black and white missionaries and teachers who established abolitionist churches and Christian schools. In its *American Missionary* magazine, the AMA reported mission successes in Canada, Jamaica, Africa, and among American Indian nations. In the United States the AMA worked with western settlers, inner-city blacks and immigrants, and southern whites. True to its original vision, the AMA's prewar mission work was both nondenominational and biracial. Black and white churches of thirteen separate denominations funded the association's activities, and several prominent African Americans, including the clergyman and abolitionist Henry Highland Garnet, served on the AMA's home missions board. Rallying around their mutual belief in the necessity of complete abolition—not just of slavery, but also of ignorance and sin—AMA supporters worked under the assumption that the end of the latter would result in the dissolution of the former.

For the AMA, the Civil War represented both an ending and a beginning; the culmination of its abolitionist efforts, and the inauguration of its southern mission. During the war AMA missionaries and teachers followed Union war successes, tending to the freedmen's immediate needs for relief and protection. What began as a means of temporary survival, however, became by the war's end a mission of permanent uplift. Shaded by northern, middle-class provincialism and by the evangelical belief in universal brotherhood, AMA postwar missions among the freedmen combined paternalism and prejudice with unprecedented efforts to transform the former slaves into an educated, moral, and industrious black citizenry.

Employing teachers, home visitors, and missionaries, the AMA sought to reconstruct the freedmen's religious and educational lives according to New England Protestant standards. Religiously, the AMA enjoyed little success among the freedmen due to a combination of factors. While the AMA's postwar mission began with the nonsectarian goal of Christianizing the freedmen, by the late 1860s its mostly Congregational supporters pushed for the establishment of Congregational churches among southern blacks. In 1869, the association stipulated that a church had to be built adjacent to any AMA educational facility and that black students were required to attend both. Compulsory church attendance, however, could not overcome African American frustration with AMA ministerial paternalism and prejudice, and it could not conquer black enthusiasm for African American preachers and churches. Comparing their students to New England Congregational bodies, northern, white ministers who ran AMA churches were critical of their black parishioners' emotional worship style. This, coupled with Congregationalism's sober intellectualism, led the majority of black converts to leave AMA churches and join black Baptist and Methodist bodies. By the century's end, no black AMA churches in the South were self-supporting.

While the AMA's churches gained few black converts, its postwar schools trained generations of African American teachers, ministers, and political leaders. Driven by their faith in the efficacy of Christian education, their fear of the danger of uneducated black masses, and their desire to recast southern society in New England's mold, AMA missionaries fought for and authored public school legislation, built schools for southern blacks and whites, and established African American universities throughout the South. The AMA today is best known for the educational legacy provided by its colleges. Southern schools such as Hampton University in Virginia, Fisk University in Tennessee, and Talladega College in Alabama offered the freedmen a curriculum of both classical education and industrial training, combined with Yankee values and Christian ideals. These schools not only trained the majority of black teachers and ministers who worked in the AMA's southern churches and secondary schools, they also produced a generation of African American artists,

intellectuals, and leaders who guided American blacks through the nadir of race relations and demonstrated in the twentieth century the power and potential of the African American community.

Following Reconstruction, the AMA experienced a period of marked conservatism and inaction. Faced with dwindling funding from northern contributors, the end of military Reconstruction, and the rise of New South industrialism, AMA leaders sought alliances with southern moderates, and encouraged southern blacks to adopt a strategy of self-help and gradualism. While AMA missionaries and teachers continued their efforts in the South, their tone became less celebratory of black achievement and more cautious regarding black potential. The AMA was frustrated by the limits of its mission efforts—the persistence of southern racial prejudice and what it considered to be the failure of black suffrage. In searching for answers, AMA officials decided that Reconstruction, with its responsibilities of full citizenship, had occurred before the freedmen were ready. And to the AMA, blacks were ready only to the degree that they became more like Christian, middle-class, northern whites. AMA leaders, therefore, placed their faith in the ability of the black middle class to raise the race, while hoping that the New South's rising economic prosperity would eliminate race prejudice.

With black disfranchisement and the rise of Jim Crow, however, AMA leaders discovered a renewed sense of purpose. Beginning in the 1890s, the AMA resumed its activistic agenda, fighting against scientific racism and segregation while lobbying for equal educational and economic opportunities for blacks. To assist in this battle, the AMA published in its monthly magazine columns featuring successful African Americans such as Booker T. Washington as examples of black potential and achievement. The AMA also supported African American movements such as the Niagara Movement in 1905. Led by W. E. B. Du Bois, one of the AMA's most well-known graduates, this movement hearkened back to the AMA's original mission statement, demanding voting rights and equal educational opportunities for African Americans, as well as the abolition of all caste distinctions. Five years later, several other AMA graduates played key roles in the founding of the National Association for the Advancement of Colored People (NAACP) in 1910. James G. Merrill, for example, left the presidency of Fisk University in 1908 to devote himself to the development of a national organization of equal rights for African Americans. Beyond serving as one of the NAACP's founding members, Merrill also worked to update the AMA's mission strategy for the twentieth century, calling for educational and spiritual outreach to inner-city blacks and immigrants.

In 1913, the AMA discontinued its sixty-three years of missionary service as a nondenominational, voluntary society. While its name, universities, and mission fields remain active today, the AMA ceased to exist when the National Council of Congregational Churches (NCCC) assumed control over its affairs. As a Congregational Home Missionary Society, the AMA continued to provide black Americans with educational and spiritual resources and opportunities. The NCCC immediately appointed black superintendents to oversee the AMA's southern mission field and established a southern headquarters in Atlanta, where it continues its work today. While the AMA ended in 1913, its historical legacy lives on, not only in the Congregational church agency that bears its name, but even more so in the millions of African American graduates of AMA universities.

### FURTHER READINGS

DeBoer, Clara M. *Be Jubilant My Feet: African American Abolitionists in the American Missionary Association, 1839–1861.* New York: Garland Publishing, Inc., 1994.

———. *His Truth is Marching On: African Americans Who Taught the Freedmen for the American Missionary Association, 1861–1877.* New York: Garland Publishing, Inc., 1995.

McPherson, James M. *The Abolitionist Legacy: From Reconstruction to the NAACP.* Princeton, N.J.: Princeton University Press, 1975.

Richardson, Joseph M. *Christian Reconstruction: The American Missionary Association and Southern Blacks, 1861–1890.* Athens: University of Georgia Press, 1986.

Stanley, A. Knighton. *The Children is Crying: Congregationalism Among Black People.* New York: The Pilgrim Press, 1979.

*Jennifer J. Wojcikowski*

## American Moral Reform Society

The American Moral Reform Society (AMRS) was an important focus of reform activity among free, northern African Americans in the late 1830s. Between 1830 and 1835 black leaders in the northeast met annually in either New York or Philadelphia, establishing the Negro Convention movement. The AMRS was founded at the 1835 meeting, when activists concerned with a broad program of reform called for a society whose goal was the moral elevation of the entire human race. Often referred to as the second phase of the Convention movement, the six annual meetings of the AMRS that convened between 1836 and 1841 represent the only concrete effort to maintain a national forum for African American activists during those years. The AMRS also brought into sharp focus some of the key issues dividing the northern black leadership during a period when both white racism and black activism were expanding.

Philadelphians William Whipper, James Forten Sr., and Robert Purvis were among the most prominent founders. Whipper in particular dominated the organization throughout its brief existence. These men were proponents of "moral suasion"—a tactic based on the idea that advertising the obvious evil of slavery would so deeply affect the consciences of slaveholders, legislators, and others that the institution would crumble under the weight of its own sinfulness. The society condemned slavery in the strongest terms, calling for the boycott of slave-produced goods and specifically aiming to have slavery abolished in the nation's capital. Furthermore, the AMRS roundly denounced both black and white churches for race prejudice and for failing to speak out against human bondage. The moral reformers planned at their first meeting to establish a newspaper, to petition Congress, and to appoint lecturers to pursue the society's goals.

To some degree then, the AMRS devoted considerable attention to concerns of particular importance to African Americans. For the most part, however, the society consciously attempted to distance itself from narrow racial issues. Its stated goals included the pursuit of liberty, education, temperance, and moral improvement for all humanity without regard to race or nationality. The AMRS also advocated equal participation for women reformers, although it was not until 1839 that women were permitted full membership rights. To a large extent this expansive program reflected the views of William Whipper. A wealthy businessman and reformer who had attended every National Negro Convention in the 1830s, Whipper served as the corresponding secretary for the AMRS and editor of its short-lived newspaper, the *National Reformer*. Whipper was especially controversial among black leaders because of his opposition to the formation of any racially exclusive organizations and his aversion to the use of racial appellations like "colored" or "African." Many African American leaders criticized the AMRS for its unrealistic goals, its lack of a concrete program of action, its refusal to concentrate specifically on the needs of African Americans, and its apparent disavowal of blacks' racial identity.

One of the most vocal critics of the society was Samuel Cornish, editor of the New York newspaper, the *Colored American*. Cornish was one of the Society's original vice presidents and, like many northern activists, had high hopes for the new organization's ability to provide a national focus for addressing the key issues facing blacks at the time: the abolition of slavery and the acquisition of equal citizenship rights. By 1837, however, it had become clear that the AMRS was not concentrating on these issues. Cornish began using his influential paper to criticize the society's program and leadership, arguing that racial unity and the assertion of a racial identity were essential for addressing race-specific concerns. Cornish's opposition also indicates the contention between cities for control of the expanding national networks of black activism. Leaders in New York and Philadelphia, in particular, competed for positions from which they could direct the goals and activities of free black activists across the North.

The AMRS increasingly became the mouthpiece for a small faction of black reformers in Philadelphia who clearly did not represent the majority of black activists even in their own city. By the time of its final meeting in 1841 the AMRS had lost virtually all of its influence. But for several crucial years it provided an important transitional vehicle for free black activists in the North. With the revival of the National Negro Convention movement in the 1840s many African Americans began to move toward a more militant stance with their abolitionist and civil rights activities.

**FURTHER READINGS**

Bell, Howard H. "The American Moral Reform Society, 1836–1841." *Journal of Negro Education* 27 (Winter 1958): 34–40.

———. *A Survey of the Negro Convention Movement, 1830–1861*. New York: Arno Press, 1969.

Winch, Julie. *Philadelphia's Black Elite: Activism, Accommodation, and the Struggle for Autonomy, 1787–1848*. Philadelphia: Temple University Press, 1988.

*Mitchell Kachun*

## American Muslim Mission

*See* Nation of Islam.

## American National Baptist Convention

The American National Baptist Convention (ANBC) was founded in Louisville, Kentucky, in 1886 to support black Baptist educational and missionary endeavors in the country. The founding force of the group was William J. Simmons, a minister, historian, and denominational organizer based in Louisville. As the editor and publisher of *Men of Mark: Eminent, Progressive Rising*, a biographical dictionary and paean to black progress put out in the 1880s, Simmons was part of a rising generation of black denominational leaders after Reconstruction who sought "uplift" of the race through hard work, respectability, education, and ceaseless extolling of the achievements of African Americans. Unlike many of his colleagues, however, Simmons was also sensitive to women's rights in black organizations. In the ANBC, Simmons afforded women such as Mary V. Parrish (nee Cook) and Lucy Wilmot Smith prominent positions. Parrish and Smith both gave addresses, published in the group's proceedings in the 1880s (of which only two years are extant), that outlined some of the ideas that historian Evelyn Brooks Higginbotham has labeled "black feminist theology." Simmons himself, and the women encouraged by him, promoted individual success, racial solidarity, and the cultivation of female virtues. Simmons also used the group as a forum for educational endeavors in the upper South, especially the black Baptist college, later to be named Simmons University, of which Simmons was president. Simmons's death in 1890, however, apparently ended further meetings of the organization. In 1895, the remnants of the ANBC eventually folded, along with two other denominational groups, into the National Baptist Convention, U.S.A., Inc., the largest black denomination in the country from its founding through the twentieth century.

**FURTHER READINGS**

Harvey, Paul. *Redeeming the South: Religious Cultures and Racial Identities Among Southern Baptists, 1865–1925*. Chapel Hill: University of North Carolina Press, 1997.

Higginbotham, Evelyn Brooks. *Righteous Discontent: The Women's Movement in the Black Baptist Church, 1880–1920*. Cambridge, Mass.: Harvard University Press, 1993.

Washington, James Melvin. *Frustrated Fellowship: The Black Baptist Quest for Social Power*. Macon, Ga.: Macon University Press, 1988.

*Paul Harvey*

## American Negro Academy

The American Negro Academy, founded in 1897, was the earliest national African American organization established explicitly for the promotion of black literature, science, art, and scholarship. The primary goals of the exclusive, all-male academy were to encourage and nurture the race's intellectual elite; to support scholarship that refuted racist arguments that proliferated both among mainstream academics and in the popular culture; and to expound the position that the uplift of the race depended on the leadership of its most intelligent and educated members. Until its dissolution in 1928 the academy played a major role in a broad social movement that sought to stimulate black cultural development through racial solidarity and cooperation.

The academy's founding in the 1890s was the product of important developments in the African American community and in American culture at large. The academy was an expression of a general American movement toward the formation of ethnic, academic, and professional societies. Such organizations began to appear in unprecedented numbers after the 1880s. Other motivating factors included an expansion of antiblack activities in American society and a crucial moment of transition among national black leaders. The most important founder and elder statesman of the academy was the eighty-year-old Episcopalian minister Alexander Crummell. The idea of forming such a society was suggested to Crummell as early as 1893, but he delayed action for a variety of reasons. At the time, the Bethel Literary and Historical Society in Washington, D.C., founded by the African Methodist Episcopal bishop Daniel A. Payne, was engaged in similar, though more local, activities. Upon the death of his close friend Payne in 1894, Crummell apparently felt more comfortable starting his own organization. Furthermore, the death of the ex-slave, abolitionist, and orator Frederick Douglass in 1895 and the rise of the reformer, educator, and lecturer Booker T. Washington with his Atlanta Exposition address in 1895 made it clear to Crummell that a strong voice was needed to oppose Washington's accommodationist stance on civil rights and his emphasis on the need for industrial training rather than academic education for blacks. While most of its members were staunch advocates and activists for black civil rights, the academy itself focused on race uplift through education, eschewing public agitation and protest activities.

At a December 1896 meeting of several black intellectuals at the Washington, D.C., home of the lawyer, editor, and politician John W. Cromwell, Crummell presented a thorough outline of the proposed organization. Eighteen black intellectuals attended the first annual meeting of the academy on March 5, 1897, a date specifically selected to honor the death of Crispus Attucks, a

former slave who was one of the first martyrs in the American Revolution. Booker T. Washington was invited, but declined to attend. Crummell, elected president by acclamation, delivered an inaugural address, entitled "Civilization: The Primal Need of the Race," that articulated his view that capable blacks needed to pursue higher education in order to provide a vanguard for the uplift of the entire race. Crummell maintained an enormous race pride, but his years living and studying in Africa and England (he had earned an A.B. from Queen's College, Cambridge University) also drew him toward European cultural ideals. His somewhat ironic position was that black intellectual attainments based largely on Eurocentric models of scholarship and civilization would allow the African American intellectual elite to make a distinctively Negro contribution that would earn the race the respect of the world.

Crummell's death in 1898 did not deter the academy. The other founders attempted to carry on the work of diffusing the knowledge of the few among the many so that the entire race could climb together. Most important among these were Cromwell; the poet Paul Laurence Dunbar; the young scholar William H. Ferris; the Howard University professor Kelly Miller; the African Methodist Episcopal Church leader Richard R. Wright; the professor and National Association for the Advancement of Colored People (NAACP) co-founder W. E. B. Du Bois; the classics professors William H. Crogman and William S. Scarborough; and the Presbyterian minister Francis J. Grimké. Later members of note included the bibliophile Arthur A. Schomburg; the historian Carter G. Woodson; the Rhodes scholar Alain L. Locke; the educator John Hope; and the writer, diplomat, and civil rights leader James Weldon Johnson. The high stature of this short list reflects the academy's discerning selectivity—membership was limited strictly to forty men with suitable academic and intellectual credentials whose work was deemed consistent with the goals of the organization.

This selectivity led to a narrow base of support that was at once the academy's strength and its weakness. The intellectual capability of its members and the quality of much of their scholarship were unarguable. But the academy's program was hindered in its early years by the opposition of Booker T. Washington—probably the most powerful African American in the United States until his death in 1915. By the 1920s numerous other vehicles for intelligent, educated black writers were available: the NAACP's magazine the *Crisis*; the radical monthly, the *Messenger*; Carter G. Woodson's *Journal of Negro History*;

the National Urban League's journal, *Opportunity*; and other publications were less exclusive and more accessible to a wider audience. Throughout its existence the academy proved unable to connect effectively with either the black masses or the growing black middle classes who were more concerned with day-to-day survival than with academic exercises.

Still, the academy played a crucial role for African American intellectuals during the first decades of the twentieth century. For thirty-one years the academy provided a vital source of stimulation and affirmation for an emerging, university-trained black male intelligentsia. It was a unique forum through which this intellectual elite could present, reflect upon, and debate its scholarly inquiries and arguments pertaining to the black experience in America. Through annual meetings, public exhibits, and the important publication of a series of twenty-two Occasional Papers in 1924, the academy articulated its distinctive perspective on black history and culture, race relations, and African American civil rights.

**FURTHER READINGS**

Meier, August. *Negro Thought in America, 1880–1915: Racial Ideologies in the Age of Booker T. Washington.* Ann Arbor: The University of Michigan Press, 1963.

Moses, Wilson Jeremiah. *Alexander Crummell: A Study of Civilization and Discontent.* Amherst: University of Massachusetts Press, 1989.

Moss, Alfred A. *The American Negro Academy, Voice of the Talented Tenth.* Baton Rouge: Louisiana State University Press, 1981.

*Mitchell Kachun*

# American Negro Historical Society, Philadelphia

The American Negro Historical Society (ANHS) was founded in 1897 by a group of black Philadelphians for the purpose of collecting and studying materials relating to the historical presence and experience of blacks in the United States. The society's activities and membership were largely centered in Philadelphia, but many items in the sizable collection of documents, institutional records, correspondences, clippings, photographs, and other miscellaneous materials have a broader relevance. The ANHS is indicative of the burgeoning desire among African Americans after the Civil War era to lay claim to their own history during a time when the demands of white sectional reconciliation threatened to erase their accom-

plishments and contributions from the historical record. As one of the earliest African American institutions established specifically to preserve and disseminate information on black history, the ANHS played an important role in the efforts of black Americans to assert both their American identity and their pride in a distinctive racial identity and history.

The most notable of the founders of the society were Robert M. Adger, Jacob C. White, William H. Dorsey, and William Carl Bolivar, all prominent activists and intellectuals in late nineteenth-century black Philadelphia. The ANHS initially excluded women from membership, but public protest by the poet and activist Frances E. W. Harper helped to remove this restriction. Membership lists from 1904 include the names of Harper, Gertrude Mossell, and several other women. Adger was the driving force behind the society's founding, but it was Bolivar who made its early years productive and successful. Bolivar was an avid collector who established ties with other African American bibliophiles in the early twentieth century, including Daniel Murray and Arthur A. Schomburg. After Bolivar's death in 1914 the care of the society's collection and the coordination of its declining public activities fell to Leon Gardiner, who worked vigorously to expand its holdings by encouraging members of old black Philadelphia families to scour their attics and basements in search of forgotten artifacts. The society's activities seem to have ceased around 1923, when many former members became involved with Carter G. Woodson's Association for the Study of Negro Life and History, which established a Philadelphia branch during the late 1920s.

The ANHS was most active in the public sphere during its first decade of existence, sponsoring public exhibits and lectures; presenting papers on black history at regular meetings; organizing public commemorations of signal events like Emancipation Days; and making its collection available to scholars and others interested in the African American past. The society's extensive collection remained in Leon Gardiner's possession until 1934, when he presented the material to the Historical Society of Pennsylvania, where it is housed today.

**FURTHER READINGS**

Lane, Roger. *William Dorsey's Philadelphia and Ours: On the Past and Future of the Black City in America.* New York: Oxford University Press, 1991.

Spady, James G. "The Afro-American Historical Society: The Nucleus of Black Bibliophiles (1897–1923)." *Negro History Bulletin* 37 (July 1974): 254–257.

Wesley, Charles H. "Racial Historical Societies and the American Heritage." *Journal of Negro History* 37 (January 1952): 11–35.

*Mitchell Kachun*

## American Negro Labor Congress

In the spring of 1925 the Central Committee of the American Communist Party (ACP) announced the formation of the American Negro Labor Congress (ANLC) as a vehicle to eliminate racial prejudice in labor unions and the workplace. The ACP invited representatives from black unions, racially integrated unions, agricultural organizations, and nonunionized African American workers to attend the ANLC's October 1925 organizational meeting in Chicago. Communist leaders hoped that the ANLC would build a party base among black workers and eventually challenge the National Association for the Advancement of Colored People (NAACP), the National Urban League (NUL), and Jamaican black rights activist Marcus Garvey's nationalist Universal Negro Improvement Association (UNIA) for leadership among African Americans.

Lovett Fort-Whiteman, who had been representing the ACP in the Soviet Union, returned to organize and head the ANLC. Fort-Whiteman was a graduate of the Tuskegee Institute in Alabama, had received some training as an actor, and had worked as a drama critic for the radical black newspapers the *Messenger* and the *Crusader*. As a black Communist who had spent time in Moscow, Fort-Whiteman enjoyed dressing like a Russian peasant and using his drama training and flamboyant persona to attract media attention to the Communist cause. During the summer of 1925 he promoted the ANLC by holding frequent press conferences and addressing black organizations in the North and South. Fort-Whiteman worked diligently to make the congress a reality, and by October he had generated considerable interest in the ANLC's organizational meeting.

Forty official delegates representing African American labor groups, fraternal societies, and local community benefit organizations arrived for the opening-day rally in Chicago on October 25, 1925. The congress organizers received telegrams of support from the South African Industrial and Commercial Union of Negro Miners, the Peasants' International, and the Defense League of Italian Peasants. A large crowd of about 500 black and white workers from the Chicago area came to the opening night mass meeting to hear Fort-Whiteman declare that the

ANLC's goal was to gather, mobilize, and coordinate into a fighting machine the most enlightened and militant of the class-conscious African American workers. United under the banner of the ANLC they would work to abolish lynching, Jim Crow laws, industrial and agricultural discrimination, political disfranchisement, and social segregation of black people. C. W. Fulp, president of the Primrose, Pennsylvania, local union of the United Mine Workers, and Norval Allen, southern organizer of the ANLC, told the crowd of the difficulties blacks experienced with trade unions and urged the delegates to turn the congress into a united labor front.

After the opening resolutions the delegates explicitly declared their solidarity with white workers and called for the removal of all barriers and discriminatory practices that prohibited blacks from joining labor unions. While they resolved that racism stemmed from capitalistic manipulation of the working classes, the conference participants clearly stated that race prejudice more than class oppression was the prevailing cause of black persecution. They rejected the accommodationist theories of the reformer and educator Booker T. Washington and demanded an immediate end to the racial caste system in America. During the summer of 1925 the ACP had circulated two editions of the periodical *Negro Champion* in Harlem to promote the upcoming congress. The paper became popular enough that during the October meeting in Chicago the delegates voted to make the *Negro Champion* the official publication of the ANLC and the medium through which they would enlighten the masses.

Despite the exuberance of the opening night ceremonies, members of the ANLC's organizing committee were sorely disappointed with the remainder of the conference. Only the official delegates came for the subsequent business meetings, and they were already members of the ACP or close party sympathizers. Congress organizers had expected to transcend the party's constituency, and their inability to attract interest from non-communist groups disheartened them. To make matters worse, national black labor leaders like A. Philip Randolph declared that the ANLC served no useful purpose and would only increase African American isolation from the mainstream labor movement. Randolph was trying to break down the color barrier in unions by getting his Brotherhood of Sleeping Car Porters (BSCP) admitted as a full member of the American Federation of Labor and saw radical groups like the ANLC as a hindrance to his efforts.

Although the ANLC failed to garner support from established African American labor groups, few could argue against the congress's racial program of desegregating schools and battling discrimination in housing and the workplace. This agenda of racial progression was what Fort-Whiteman highlighted during a multi-city speaking tour immediately following the ANLC's organizing convention. He believed strongly in the congress and shrugged off Randolph and other labor leaders' criticisms while downplaying the ANLC's Communist affiliation.

Fort-Whiteman was moderately successful, and while the ANLC remained small, by 1927 the group had established more than forty-five local chapters and a dozen more provisional committees across the United States. With seventy members, the Chicago local was the largest ANLC chapter. The rest remained less than half that size, but Fort-Whiteman doggedly insisted that the congress would grow once black workers learned the truth of its message.

The ANLC did not grow as Fort-Whiteman had predicted, and despite the seeming early success in establishing local chapters, by 1927 the organization was in trouble. Fort-Whiteman had done his best to minimize the ANLC's Communist connections, but in the pre-depression decade of the 1920s most black Americans saw no reason to invite white hostility by affiliating themselves with the ACP when respected groups like the NAACP offered similar programs of racial progress. The ACP itself dealt a crippling blow to the ANLC when an ill-advised edict came down ordering congress leaders to condemn African American churches and the faith black people placed in them. By alienating the black churches, the ANLC eliminated any chance it may have had of gaining widespread popular support among African Americans.

In 1927 Richard B. Moore and Cyril V. Briggs, both of whom had been part of the ANLC since its beginning, started to take a more active role and used their experience as grass-roots organizers in the African Blood Brotherhood for Liberation and Redemption (ABB) to help Fort-Whiteman save the congress from extinction. Moore was a fiery speaker who refused to downplay the ANLC's radical connections and proclaimed that whites would have to recognize that the rise of black workers was inescapable. Moore and Fort-Whiteman worked tirelessly, and in the election year of 1928 the ACP nominated Moore as a candidate for U.S. Congress from New York and Fort-Whiteman as a candidate from Harlem for the office of state comptroller. The effort highlighted the two leaders, but it did little to help the ANLC. The congress continued to wane, and in 1928 the ACP further devalued the organization by ordering its leaders to limit ANLC activities to recruiting African Americans for party membership.

In 1929 the congress experienced a brief revival when Moore and Briggs, who had become the ANLC's national secretary, championed the cause of black film projectionists during a strike at Harlem's Lafayette Theater. Moore and Briggs managed to convince the American Civil Liberties Union (ACLU), the UNIA, and the BSCP to join them in a public demonstration in support of the strikers. Police officers arrested Moore for his role in the protest, and the visibility he gained gave the ANLC a renewed voice. Briggs used that voice through editorials in his own periodical, the *Crusader*, to condemn the ongoing U.S. military occupation of the black Caribbean nation of Haiti. The ANLC followed with an anti-interventionist demonstration in New York, but it was the last gasp of the organization.

By the fall of 1929, ACP leaders decided that the ANLC should start closing down its operations. In early 1930 congress members participated with several other groups in a small rally in Charlotte, North Carolina, and in July the ANLC held its last convention in St. Louis. The delegates made an abortive attempt to save the organization by renaming it the League of Revolutionary Struggle, but without ACP support the effort was fruitless.

The ANLC ceased to exist in the summer of 1930. Fort-Whiteman and other congress leaders had formulated a program of racial uplift that was as solid as any in existence at the time. They could, however, never transcend their Communist roots and failed to convince black workers that the ANLC's approach offered anything that could improve substantially the programs of mainstream groups like the NAACP. This was particularly true after 1927 when the ACP made it clear that the Communists were less interested in advancing black civil rights than they were in recruiting new party members. The ANLC's African American leaders remained loyal to the party and most went on to become participants in the League of Struggle for Negro Rights, the ACP's next effort to organize and recruit African Americans.

## FURTHER READINGS

Du Bois, W. E. B. "Progress and Emancipation." *The Crisis* 37 (April 1930): 137.

Foner, Philip S., and James S. Allen, eds. *African Communism and Black Americans: A Documentary History, 1919–1929*. Philadelphia: Temple University Press, 1987.

Haywood, Harry. *Black Bolshevik: Autobiography of an Afro-American Communist*. Chicago: Liberator Press, 1978.

Hutchinson, Earl Ofari. *Blacks and Reds: Race and Class in Conflict, 1919–1990*. East Lansing: Michigan State University Press, 1995.

Record, Wilson. *Race and Radicalism: The NAACP and the Communist Party in Conflict*. Ithaca, N.Y.: Cornell University Press, 1964.

*Gary R. Entz*

**SEE ALSO**    League of Struggle for Negro Rights

## American Negro Leadership Conference on Africa

In the 1950s and early 1960s African Americans who felt frustrated by the fact that organized efforts vis-a-vis Africa fell beyond the scope of most contemporary African American organizations debated the idea of creating a new organization. Efforts to create an organization controlled and operated by black Americans, designed to raise interest in America about the situation in Africa, and with the intention of exerting African American influence on U.S. policy toward Africa, bore fruit with the establishment of the American Negro Leadership Conference on Africa (ANLCA).

In early 1962 a group of concerned individuals gathered to organize a conference of African American leaders to discuss Africa. The planning committee included John A. Davis of the American Society for African Culture (AMSAC); James Farmer of the Congress of Racial Equality (CORE); George Houser, David Jones, and Hope Stevens of the American Committee on Africa (ACOA); Clarence Jones of the Gandhi Society; Frank Montero of the African American Students Foundation; John Morsell of the National Association for the Advancement of Colored People (NAACP); Guichard Parris of the National Urban League (NUL); and A. Philip Randolph of the Brotherhood of Sleeping Car Porters (BSCP). Over the course of several months this committee organized a conference on "The Role of the American Negro Community in U.S. Policy Toward Africa." The planning committee arranged for a "Call Committee" to issue a call for organizations to sponsor and for individuals to attend the conference. Leaders of the established civil rights organizations constituted the Call Committee: James Farmer, Dorothy Height of the National Council of Negro Women (NCNW), Martin Luther King Jr. of the Southern Christian Leadership Conference (SCLC), A. Philip Randolph, Roy Wilkins of the NAACP, and Whitney Young of the NUL. These leaders argued that African Americans needed to take a greater role in the formation of U.S. foreign policy in sub-Saharan Africa and hoped that the conference would activate the masses and provide a channel through which their voices could be heard. The Call Committee invited approximately seventy-five organizations to sponsor the conference, about half of which responded. By November 1962, a broad range of African American business, civil rights, educational, fraternal, sorority, labor, professional, religious, and social organizations had contributed money in order to sponsor the conference.

The conference was held at the Arden House campus of Columbia University in November 1962. Ted Brown, formerly employed by the BSCP and the American Federation of Labor–Congress of Industrial Organizations, served as the conference director. The conference addressed those areas in Africa still under white rule, specifically Portuguese Africa, Kenya, the Central African Federation, South West Africa, and South Africa, as well as the ongoing crisis in the Congo. A few related topics were also on the agenda, including the employment of African Americans by the State Department.

In the weeks and months immediately following the Arden House conference, the ANLCA lobbied extensively on a series of issues relating to Africa and African Americans. For this purpose, the Call Committee leaders met with President John F. Kennedy, U.S. ambassador to the United Nations Adlai Stevenson, and Assistant Secretary of State for African Affairs G. Mennen Williams. The ANLCA and its sponsoring organizations lobbied these and other top officials on a variety of African-related U.S. foreign policy issues.

While the Arden House conference had not authorized the establishment of a permanent organization, it had recommended that the members of the Call Committee continue as an informal committee. They evaluated developments in areas the conference examined and consulted with the constituent organizations on further activity. This, then, formed the basis for the lobbying efforts, and for attempts to turn the ANLCA into a more permanent organization. The ANLCA continued its work and held a second conference in 1964 attended by Secretary of State Dean Rusk, Adlai Stevenson, and G. Mennen Williams.

But after its bright beginning, the ANLCA never firmly positioned itself as a long-term, powerful player in shaping U.S. policy toward Africa. Chronic difficulties stemmed from its inability to gain the full financial support it needed. A second basic problem arose from the competing commitments of its leadership. No member of the Call

Committee could devote sufficient time and energy to launching the ANLCA and nurturing it through its infancy. Further, an ever-increasing number of younger and more militant voices moved beyond political lobbying as a tactic. The ANLCA survived for several years as an interim organization, but these constraints undermined efforts to establish permanency.

In 1967, the ANLCA held a final conference and also tried to mediate a solution to the Biafran crisis. Unable to do so, and unable to transform itself into a permanent organization, the ANLCA slowly faded from the scene.

**FURTHER READINGS**

Erhagbe, Edward. "The American Negro Leadership Conference on Africa: A New African-American Voice for Africa in the United States, 1962–1970." *Working Papers in African Studies* 157. Boston: Boston University African Studies Center, 1991.

Fierce, Milfred. "Selected Black American Leaders and Organizations and South Africa, 1900–1977: Some Notes." *Journal of Black Studies* 17 (March 1987): 305–26.

Houser, George. "'Freedom's Struggle Crosses Oceans and Mountains': Martin Luther King, Jr., and the Liberation Struggles in Africa and America." In *We Shall Overcome: Martin Luther King, Jr., and the Black Freedom Struggle.* Ed. Peter J. Albert and Ronald Hoffmann. New York: Pantheon Books, 1990.

*Jim Meriwether*

## American Press Association

*See* Afro-American Press Association.

## American Society of African Culture

The American Society of African Culture (AMSAC) was founded by John A. Davis, Horace Mann Bond, Mercer Cook, William T. Fontaine, and James Ivy in June 1957. The society brought together African American scholars, writers, and artists interested in promoting an understanding of the cultural heritage of Africa and peoples of African descent. Headquartered in New York City, the society sponsored educational and cultural projects designed to foster global dialogues among "Negro Men of Culture" and to demonstrate to the world the cultural contributions of peoples of color. During its existence from 1957 to 1968, the organization promoted intellectual and cultural exchanges with African and African Diaspora intellectuals. Moreover, the society worked within

the United States to raise awareness of the cultural contributions of Africa and African Americans.

AMSAC emerged in 1956 in the aftermath of the First Congress of Black Artists and Writers held in Paris under the auspices of the African-run publishing house Présence Africaine. The Paris conference issued a call for an international organization of "Men of Culture of the Negro World" with branches in every country that had a population of African descent. Thus was born the international organization the Société Africaine de Culture (African Society of Culture) with AMSAC serving as the U.S. subsidiary. Membership in AMSAC was by invitation and limited to individuals of African descent who were deemed by the executive council to have contributed significantly to the advancement of black culture. Early members of the society included the writer, editor, and critic Arna Bontemps, the sociologist St. Clair Drake, the musician Edward "Duke" Ellington, the historian John Hope Franklin, the sociologist E. Franklin Frazier, the sociologist Adelaide Cromwell Hill, the novelist and poet Langston Hughes, Supreme Court justice Thurgood Marshall, the dancer and choreographer Pearl Primus, Calvin H. Raullerson, and the writer Joy Saunders Redding. In October 1958, the executive committee of the Société Africaine de Culture in Paris, at the request of AMSAC, created the category of "associate membership" for persons of non-African descent and Africans temporarily residing in the United States. Associate members could attend all society functions but were not permitted to vote. In the context of the civil rights movement, the question of full membership for persons of non-African descent remained a point of debate throughout the life of the organization.

AMSAC's goals and membership criteria ensured that the organization remained an elite group of well educated, predominantly male professionals. In June 1958, at the time of the society's First Annual Conference, AMSAC boasted 102 members; total membership, however, never surpassed 500. The society's academic and solidly middle-class bias explains its programs, most of which reflected a belief in the efficacy of intellectual exchange. Annual conferences with such themes as "The American Negro Writer and His Relationship to His Roots" demonstrate the group's emphasis. While a modern audience might question AMSAC's class and gender biases, few white cultural and intellectual organizations had any African American members during the late 1950s, much less annual conferences devoted to black culture.

In the United States, the annual conference brought together speakers from across the nation and the globe to discuss issues of importance for peoples of African descent. AMSAC convened conferences in New York, Washington, D.C., Philadelphia, Atlanta, Houston, and Los Angeles. The organization also sent delegates to the 1958 All Africa Peoples Conference in Accra, Ghana, the Second Congress of Negro Writers and Artists held in Rome in 1959, Nigeria's 1960 independence celebrations, the 1960 Conference for Women of Africa and African Descent held in Ghana, and the First World Festival of Black Arts held in Dakar, Senegal, in 1966. AMSAC worked in conjunction with the Société Africaine de Culture to organize the Dakar festival and chartered a plane to take African Americans to the celebration.

In October 1958 the society began publication of its newsletter and in January 1959 the first of its periodic supplements appeared. The supplements, usually written by members of AMSAC, discussed the work of the Society and/or African affairs. The newsletter achieved a wide distribution in the United States and abroad. For a short period in the early 1960s the newsletter appeared in English and French editions. In addition, the society published several important monographs including *Africa Seen by American Negro Scholars* (1958), *The American Negro Writer and His Roots* (1960), *West African Vignettes* (1960), *Pan Africanism Reconsidered* (1962), and *Southern Africa in Transition* (1965).

As part of its international project, AMSAC sent books by African American authors to governments and universities in Africa and to the offices of the Société Africaine de Culture in Europe. These "bookshelves" included works such as W. E. B. Du Bois's *Black Reconstruction*, Ralph Ellison's *Invisible Man*, E. Franklin Frazier's *Black Bourgeoisie*, Langston Hughes's *Tambourines to Glory*, Lorraine Hansberry's *Raisin in the Sun*, Claude McKay's *Selected Poems*, Saunders Redding's *Lonesome Road*, and Richard Wright's *Native Son* and *White Man, Listen!* Each bookshelf also contained the special volume by Présence Africaine published by the society entitled *Africa Seen by American Negroes*.

In addition to its literary work, AMSAC initiated other cultural projects. In 1959 it began producing a series of radio shows about African American life. The series, entitled "The Life and Culture of the Negro in America," was distributed free of charge to six broadcasting stations in West Africa and included segments on "The Negro Family Looks at Africa," "Brother John, Mississippi Delta Music," "The Cultural Implications of Integration," and African American music. In February 1960, the society also launched a lecture series featuring Africans visiting the United States and Americans with special knowledge of Africa. Finally, in 1965 AMSAC began publishing *African Forum*, a journal dedicated to African culture, which covered art, literature, politics, and economics in Africa and in the African Diaspora. The journal attained subscription levels of 1,800 in 1966. Many copies reached Africa through direct subscriptions or through U.S.–government sponsored libraries and reading rooms.

Hoping to breach the gap between Africans and African Americans, AMSAC opened an office in Lagos, Nigeria, in 1961. The Lagos office staged cultural events during which African American artists performed for African audiences, provided French language classes, and distributed information about African American culture and achievements. The office, however, enjoyed only minimal success. It closed in June 1966 due to AMSAC's growing financial problems and the desire of society members to shift the focus of the organization to the United States.

In September 1966 AMSAC confronted a financial crisis that would bring about the demise of the organization. The Committee on Race and Caste in World Affairs (CORAC), which had supported AMSAC for nearly a decade, announced its intention to end its funding. CORAC provided AMSAC with a substantial severance grant and transferred its remaining assets to the society in December 1966. Soon newspapers alleged that the CIA had funded AMSAC. While there were no direct links between the CIA and AMSAC, apparently several of the foundations that had provided financial support for the society over the previous decade had received funds from the CIA. The scandal destroyed any legitimacy that AMSAC had within the African American community.

Throughout 1967 the directors struggled to redefine the organization, but their efforts failed. The final edition of *African Forum* appeared in early 1968, and by the end of the year AMSAC had ceased operations. The cultural nationalism of the society proved uninspiring in the context of growing black nationalism in the United States in the 1960s. AMSAC never succeeded in expanding its appeal beyond a narrow academic stratum. Limited to this fragile elite and restricted, for all intents and purposes, to the Eastern seaboard, AMSAC remained an intellectual endeavor. Internationally, the society succeeded in initiating and expanding dialogues between African American intellectuals and their African and Diaspora counterparts. While certain aspects of the society's work were continued by the Black Studies Programs that emerged in American colleges and universities in the late 1960s and early 1970s, AMSAC disappeared leaving little visible legacy.

FURTHER READINGS

Davis, John A. "An Editorial Statement." *African Forum* 1, 1 (Summer 1965): 3–6.

———. "Editorial." *African Forum* 3, 4 and 4, 1 (Spring and Summer 1968): 2–4.

———. "Senghorian Thought in the United States." In *Hommage à Léopold Sédar Senghor: Homme de Culture.* Paris: Présence Africaine, 1976.

*Geoffrey Coats*

# American Teachers Association

The American Teachers Association (ATA) was founded in 1904 in Nashville, Tennessee, and operated continuously until June 28, 1966, when it merged with the National Education Association (NEA). Originally the ATA was known as the National Colored Teachers Association, and in 1907 its name was changed to become National Association of Teachers in Colored Schools (NATCS). It operated under this designation until the organization's 1937 Philadelphia meeting when, under the leadership of Dr. Willa Carter Burch, the name was changed to American Teachers Association.

The ATA's first president was Dr. J. R. E. Lee, who was then academic director at Tuskegee Institute in Alabama. Other founders and early leaders were Professor Nathan B. Young Sr., Dr. George Washington Trenholm, Clinton J. Calloway, and Dr. Frank G. Smith. The organization's first female president was Mary McLeod Bethune who headed the ATA in 1923.

The ATA was composed primarily of African American teachers, principals, supervisors, and academicians, but included some white educators who taught African American students and in its early years several whites who headed black colleges. The ATA received some white financial support. Initially its membership was concentrated in the southern states, which operated "separate-but-equal" schools for the races, but later the ATA expanded geographically to become a national organization composed of state and smaller units that included teachers of African American children across the nation.

The ATA's Certificate of Incorporation was registered in the District of Columbia because the organization intended to establish national headquarters in Washington. The organization had a dues structure that allowed participating states to collect dues from each member. Where there were no state organizations, dues were higher for individual members. Libraries, societies, and groups could join as organizations and pay annual membership fees. Life member-

ships for individuals also existed. NATCS, the predecessor of the ATA, was divided into the following departments: College Education, High School Education, Elementary Education, Rural Education, School Supervision, Health Education, Agricultural Education, and Vocational Education. These departments were to hold annual meetings concurrent with the annual convention of the NATCS.

During the first half of the twentieth century major concerns of the NATCS and later the ATA were the lack of public high schools for African Americans particularly in many southern locales and the length of the school year, which was shorter for blacks than for whites, especially in rural areas where black children were to attend school in-between planting and harvesting of crops. Other troublesome issues were the inequitable per pupil funding and spending for black and white schools, ill-prepared teachers, the lack of equipment, the shortage of black teachers, and the inequitable salaries black teachers received. Committed to equal opportunity in education, the organization discouraged the creation of racially segregated schools.

By the 1940s the ATA's specific goals were: "(1) to develop a national organization of American educators devoted to the realization of America's objective of EQUALITY OF EDUCATIONAL OPPORTUNITY for all children irrespective of sex, RACE, economic circumstance and place of residence; (2) associating those teachers of America's Negro children with other interested educational workers in an organization designed to give dramatic emphasis to the place of the Negro child and of the teachers of Negro children in this total program of education in America; (3) to offer opportunity for the teachers of America's Negro children throughout the nation to have beneficial professional contact and to rally their numbers and influence behind all efforts designed to improve the educational opportunities for America's children (particularly the disadvantaged and frequently separated Negro children) as well as to insist that there be equity of consideration for all teachers without regard to race" ("Souvenir Program").

Based on its goals the ATA developed a program consisting of several components. These were: "(1) to build a distributed membership to be proportionately drawn from the various states, and which will cause teachers of all levels and areas to be associates within the body; (2) to articulate with all national and professional bodies to the end of increasingly 'normal' and equitable participation of the interests of Negro schools and their teachers; (3) to provide channels for the expression of professional opinion and the stimulation of public opinion that may reflect itself in educational legislation at all levels; (4) to provide

Children seated in a classroom in Howard Orphanage and Industrial School, 1920s. *Photographer: Carl Kins Studios. Schomburg Center for Research in Black Culture*

professional outlet and professional stimulation for the maximum calibre of professional service which the Negro teachers of the U.S. may render in their respective areas of assignment and responsibility" ("Souvenir Program").

Throughout its existence, the ATA's general goals were to attain equity with its white counterparts in education and to instill racial and personal pride in African American youth. The ATA's leaders realized that although their concerns were educational, to effect changes necessary in that field it was essential to plan and interact with political and socioeconomic-based organizations to fight for the ultimate goal of "equality of opportunity" for African Americans. Education became the testing mechanism.

Members and friends of the ATA testified before the Education Committee of the U.S. House of Representa-

tives in an attempt to force the states to guarantee equitable distribution of funds to black and white schools. In 1937, for example, the ATA supported the Harrison-Black-Fletcher bill and sought to amend it so that it would provide federal appropriation for African American students proportionate to a state's total population. Moreover, the ATA tried to add to the bill a stipulation that required the U.S. commissioner of education to receive and publish a report of disbursement of state and federal funds by race. Finally, the ATA attempted to change the language of the bill so that it would read that "every school shall be kept open for 160 days." the ATA, however, failed to change the bill to include a clause that would have stipulated that funds be withheld from any state violating these provisions.

By 1957–58 the ATA annual membership roster had reached 20,954, and there were 757 life members. That year the ATA issued a five-part mission statement that included as first priority the realization of equality of educational opportunity for every child and equality of professional status for every teacher. Five ATA projects were initiated in 1958–59 and included teacher education for more effective human-relations education, a historically accurate treatment of African Americans in school encyclopedias, raising the professional welfare of black educators, and expanding the ATA's field service. Moreover, the ATA launched a cooperative project with the Association for the Study of Negro Life and History (ASNLH) designed to get schools to purchase books by and about African Americans and to support Negro History Week.

To reach its membership, other organizations, and the public the ATA published two newsletters, *The Bulletin*, begun in 1923, and *American Teachers Association Studies*. The ATA also worked closely with the ASNLH to advocate the teaching of black history in schools.

The all-white NEA had been working with the NATCS and the ATA since 1926 on resolving troublesome issues in black education. The ATA was instrumental in identifying problems such as the depiction of black people in textbooks and the unequal distribution of federal funds in education by racial classification. Moreover, the ATA urged the NEA to develop materials on race relations for teacher training and classroom use. In 1947 a joint NEA-ATA committee recommended the integration of African Americans into the NEA, and the organization started to accept black teachers as members.

In Boston in July 1949 another joint NEA-ATA meeting sought to solve membership problems of black teachers who had joined the NEA. African American NEA members were concerned about NEA meetings that took place in cities and hotels that practiced racial discrimination. Moreover, black NEA members complained that African American teachers were excluded from membership in NEA-affiliated state organizations in fourteen southern states and were not eligible for designation as state-level delegates to the annual NEA Representative Assembly. The NEA executive committee did not challenge its southern affiliates to accept black members on the basis of equality. Instead the NEA acquiesced and permitted black state teachers' associations to send their own delegates to the Representative Assembly.

Following the *Brown v. Board of Education* decisions of 1954 and 1955, and the Civil Rights Act of 1964 many southern black teachers were displaced from their jobs.

This caused a membership crisis in the ATA, which escalated. The ATA and the NEA had been communicating about a merger, and it was effected in 1966. At that time the ATA had 41,000 members; most of them, however, were also NEA members in the South's dual affiliates.

The ATA was an essential part of the educational history of the United States and a key player in the effort to remedy problems caused by racial discrimination in education.

**FURTHER READINGS**

American Teachers Association. "44th Annual Convention Souvenir Program." Tallahassee, Fla.: American Teachers Association, July 20–22, 1947.

———. Vertical file American Teachers Association, Moorland Spingarn Research Center, Howard University, Washington, D.C.

Lewis, Earl, and Victoria Wolcott. "American Teachers Association." In *Black Women in America: An Historical Encyclopedia*. Ed. Darlene Clark Hine. Brooklyn, N.Y: Carlson Publishing, Inc., 1993.

Perry, Thelma D. *History of the American Teachers Association*. Washington, D.C.: National Education Association, 1975.

*Faustine C. Jones-Wilson*

# American Tennis Association

The American Tennis Association (ATA) was founded shortly before World War I by the tennis players Henry Freeman, John F. N. Wilkinson, Talley Holmes, H. Stanton McCard, William Wright, B. M. Rhetta, and Ralph Cook. The group was the result of the exclusion of black tennis players from the United States National Lawn Tennis Association (USNLTA), the governing body of tennis in the United States, and a tennis tour conducted by some members of the black Young Men's Christian Association (YMCA) in Washington, D.C., in the 1910s. By the early twentieth century some of the public schools in the District of Columbia, as well as black colleges, offered the sport to its students. McCard was the ATA's original president and Gerald Norman its executive secretary. The ATA had four main goals: to promote the game of tennis among blacks in the United States, to stimulate the formation of tennis clubs and the construction of tennis courts throughout the nation, to promote local tennis groups, and to encourage young tennis players. In August 1917, the ATA held its first national competition in Baltimore,

Maryland, attracting thirty-nine players from twenty-three clubs. Talley Holmes won the men's singles that year. In 1924, the ATA started to organize women's championships, and Lucy Diggs Slowe won the women's singles that year, making her the first black female national sports champion.

In 1929, with the proliferation of black tennis talent, African Americans challenged the USNLTA's unwritten policy that barred African Americans from its sponsored competitions. That year, two black tennis players, Reginald Weir and Gerald Norman Jr., registered to play in the USNLTA's junior indoor tournament in New York City. When the men showed up to compete, USNLTA representatives told them that they would not be allowed to play. Norman's father complained to the National Association for the Advancement of Colored People (NAACP), which initiated an inquiry. The USNLTA responded that the group did not have anything against black players per se. Rather, the organization claimed, that it practiced racial segregation because it believed that it was the best policy for all involved in the tennis world.

This episode did not dampen tennis activity among African Americans. Instead, over the next decade, there was increasing interest in the game. For example, Ora Washington set an ATA record with eight tournament wins between 1929 and 1937. Roumania Peters and Margaret Peters won the ATA doubles title fourteen times—a record unsurpassed by any other tennis pair. On the men's side, Nathaniel McCampbell and Ernest McCampbell were the best doubles during the 1930s. When New Deal federal funds provided for the construction of numerous new tennis courts nationwide, ATA events became even more popular and many colleges initiated tennis programs. In 1937, the ATA sponsored an exhibition tour that showcased some of its best talent.

It was not until after World War II, however, that the racial barriers in tennis began to wane. The dominating presence of Althea Gibson and Oscar Johnson on the American tennis tour as well as the onset of massive civil rights protests eventually forced the United States Lawn Tennis Association, the USNLTA's successor organization, to discard its racial discrimination policy.

**FURTHER READING**

Ashe, Arthur R., Jr. *A Hard Road to Glory: A History of the African-American Athlete Since 1946*, vol. 2. New York: Amistad Press, Inc., 1988.

*Alexandra Epstein*

## Americans for South African Resistance

*See* American Committee on Africa.

## Ancient Egyptian Arabic Order Nobles of the Mystic Shrine

John George Jones, an ambitious Chicago lawyer and Prince Hall Mason, founded the Ancient Egyptian Arabic Order Nobles of the Mystic Shrine (AEAONMS), on June 3, 1893. The AEAONMS became part of an already extensive network of auxiliary orders of the Prince Hall Masons, which provided members with opportunities to assume leadership roles in community activism, civil rights efforts, and large-scale charitable fund-raising. In spite of early internal divisions and external threats the order survived and carved its own distinctive niche among African American fraternal organizations.

Jones devised the idea for the creation of the order during the 1893 Columbian Exposition in Chicago. As the first Imperial Potentate of the African American Shriners, Jones was the dynamic force who spread the order to cities such as St. Louis; New York; Indianapolis; Los Angeles; Washington, D.C.; and Kansas City. Jones's leadership, however, proved to be a mixed blessing due to his attempts to dominate the governance of the Shriners, Prince Hall Masons, and Scottish Rite Masons, which caused a great deal of dissension among these groups. In 1900 another faction took control of the AEAONMS. The group added the term "Egyptian" to the title of the order to distinguish it from white Shriners and decreed that only official Prince Hall Masons who were members of lodges that descended from Prince Hall's original African Lodge #459 could join the order.

Like most black fraternal organizations, the AEAONMS confronted the hostility of its white counterparts and endured long years of lawsuits that sought to deny the African American order the right to use the symbols, rituals, and names of the white groups. The coffers of the fraternity were drained by the costs of fighting legal battles in states like Arkansas, Louisiana, Texas, and Florida. Though the black Shriners lost important cases in Georgia and Texas, in 1928 the U.S. Supreme Court ruled in favor of the AEAONMS, ending decades of legal harassment.

Throughout its history the AEAONMS challenged discrimination and segregation and fought for racial equality. In 1913 Imperial Potentate John Murphy attacked Jim Crow laws and urged the order to support the National Association for the Advancement of Colored People

(NAACP) in its efforts to fight segregation in the courts. The AEAONMS, for example, supported the NAACP's legal battle on behalf of the black soldiers who had been imprisoned because of their participation in the Houston mutiny of 1917. That year, a race riot involving city residents and members of the all-black twenty-fourth infantry resulted in the largest court martial in U.S. history. Nineteen of the black soldiers were executed and sixty-one were sentenced to life imprisonment. The AEAONMS joined forces with the NAACP, working for eleven years to secure the release of the black troops. In 1931 the order also raised money for the defense of the eight black teenagers, known as the Scottsboro boys, who had been convicted of raping two white women in Alabama.

In the 1920s, as the order expanded to over 9,000 members, Imperial Potentate Caesar Blake Jr. urged the black Shriners to showcase their "racial consciousness." He encouraged members to support the black community, patronize African American businesses, and get involved in politics. Moreover, Blake urged African Americans to demand the enforcement of the Fourteenth and Fifteenth Amendments to the Constitution. By the 1960s, the AEAONMS worked to further the civil rights movement through its organized activism in politics and support of events such as the Freedom Rides.

The AEAONMS, however, is best known for its charity work. In 1948, for example, the order formed the Tuberculosis and Cancer Research Foundation in Washington, D.C., which changed its name to the Health and Medical Research Foundation in 1973. The foundation continues to offer financial support for medical research and remains one of the nation's few incorporated black charitable institutions. In addition, the AEAONMS has made contributions to Howard University, Meharry Medical College, Harlem Hospital, the National Jewish Hospital, the United Negro College Fund, and the NAACP Legal Defense Fund.

Members of the order have also supported a variety of local charities. In addition to financial contributions, imperial potentates and members of the imperial council have served on the Board of Directors of Howard University and the National Jewish Hospital. In the 1990s, the Shriners started to embrace new areas of community outreach. They are involved actively in crisis intervention in cities like Los Angeles by providing gang members with alternatives to crime and violence. The fraternal order also sponsors a National Scholarship Program for young women in higher education, annual education grants for underprivileged youths, voter education and registration

drives, and summer camp programs. The AEAONMS currently maintains a membership of 37,000 and is headquartered in Detroit, Michigan.

**FURTHER READINGS**

Muraskin, William A. *Middle-Class Blacks in a White Society: Prince Hall Freemasonry in America.* Berkeley: University of California Press, 1975.

Walkes, Joseph A. *History of the Shrine: Ancient Egyptian Arabic Order Nobles of the Mystic Shrine, Inc. (Prince Hall Affiliated): A Pillar of Black Society, 1893–1993.* Detroit: Ancient Egyptian Arabic Order Nobles of the Mystic Shrine of North and South America and Its Jurisdictions, Inc., 1993.

*Joel Shrock*

## Anna T. Jeanes Foundation
*See* Negro Rural School Fund.

## Anna T. Jeanes Fund
*See* Negro Rural School Fund.

## Anti-Discrimination Division of Colorado
*See* Colorado Anti-Discrimination Commission.

## Anti-Slavery Convention of American Women

On May 9, 1837, more than 200 women from ten states met in New York City for three days to form the first national female antislavery convention. This interracial organization, founded by several abolitionist women, including Lucretia Mott of Philadelphia, Sarah and Angelina Grimké of South Carolina, and Lydia Maria Child of Boston, condemned slavery and racial prejudice. As these women coordinated their national campaign against slavery, a consensus was reached to exclude men from their convention activities. The first public meeting and convention of American women was held at the Third Free Church at the corner of Huston and Thompson Streets. The convention was called to order that afternoon by Lucretia Mott. Sarah M. Grimké outlined the objectives of the convention. She noted that the convention was to "interest women in the subject of anti-slavery, and establish a system of operations throughout every town and village in the 'Free States,' that would exert a powerful influence in the abolition of American slavery."

Several African American women representing various associations, including the Rising Daughters of Abyssinia, the Colored Ladies Literary Society of New York, and the Female Anti-slavery Societies of Philadelphia and Boston, gathered at this historic convention. They along with their white sisters worked and sat side by side, passing resolutions in support of the antislavery movement, promoting the consumption of free labor goods, and condemning racial prejudice as "one of the chief pillars of American slavery." They formed committees to draft six pamphlets and "open letters" for publication and organized a campaign to collect a million signatures on abolition petitions to Congress. Several of the delegates were African American women, including Sarah M. Douglass, Grace Douglass, Maria Stewart, and Sarah L. Forten, and at least one black woman, Grace Douglass of Philadelphia, was appointed as one of the officers of the convention—vice president. Sarah L. Forten, of the prominent Forten family of Philadelphia, wrote a poem, "We Are Thy Sisters," that was published in the 1838 publication *An Appeal to the Women of the Nominally Free States*. The first convention ended with a commitment from these women to continue to push for the abolition of slavery.

The second antislavery convention held in Philadelphia on May 15–18, 1838, was overshadowed by the destruction of Pennsylvania Hall by a mob of angry whites. African American women continued to show their support by attending the convention and working in the hierarchy of the organization as elected officers. Susan Paul was chosen as one of the vice presidents and Sarah M. Douglass as treasurer. Grace Douglass and Harriet Purvis attended the convention, which held its final meeting at Sarah Pugh's school since other meeting places refused to host the women, fearing white mob violence.

For the third national convention the women returned to Philadelphia to demonstrate that they were not intimidated by the mob violence of the previous year. Between May 1 and 3, 1839, the women gathered at the Pennsylvania Riding School because other venues refused to rent their facilities to the interracial group. African American women continued to serve as elected officers. Sarah M. Douglass continued as treasurer and Grace Douglass served as vice president. Clarisa C. Lawrence, president of the Colored Female Religious and Moral Society of Salem, praised "the unity of women coming together for such an important cause" and noted that it was an event worth attending.

The majority of the 102 women who attended the meeting concluded that they should fight for equal participation in the various state and regional antislavery societies as well as the national American Anti-Slavery Society. The group's 1839 gathering was the last national convention that catered exclusively to women. Separate conventions were abandoned after the American Anti-Slavery Society admitted women on an equal basis. Though short-lived, the Anti-Slavery Convention of American Women helped forge lasting bonds between many black and white women and laid the foundations for a new generation of reformers who assumed influential roles in the various social movements of the nineteenth century.

**FURTHER READINGS**

Anti-Slavery Convention of American Women. *An Appeal to the Women of the Nominally Free States: Issued by an Anti-Slavery Convention of American Women*. Anti-Slavery Convention of American Women, 1837; New York; reprint, Freeport, N.Y.: Books for Libraries Press, 1971.

Brown, Ira V. "Am I Not a Woman and a Sister? The Anti-Slavery Convention of American Women, 1837–1839." *Pennsylvania History* 50 (January 1983): 1–19.

Nell, William C. *The Colored Patriots of the American Revolution*. Salem, N.H.: Ayer Company Publishers, Inc., 1986.

Quarles, Benjamin. *Black Abolitionists*. New York: Oxford University Press, 1969.

Sterling, Dorothy. "Introduction." In *Turning the World Upside Down: The Anti-Slavery Convention of American Women* (Held in New York City, May 9–12, 1837). New York: The Feminist Press at the City University of New York, 1987.

*Vivian Njeri Fisher*

# Arkansas Commission on Race Relations

The Arkansas Commission on Race Relations was organized as a biracial panel in the aftermath of the Elaine race riot in Phillips county in September 1919.

The rural Elaine riot was the product of economic conditions that reduced black sharecroppers and tenants to peonage. Black farmers in the county organized the Progressive Farmers and Household Union as a legal vehicle to redress their exploitation. The county's white residents, led by the Committee of Seven, a group of Helena business and civic leaders, and supported by the

*Arkansas Gazette,* county law enforcement authorities and Governor Charles H. Brough, charged that the Progressive Union was a planned black conspiracy to murder white landowners and appropriate their land. Within the context of white mob hysteria and the presence of the U.S. Army, the "race war" was suppressed, resulting in the death of large numbers of blacks; estimates range from 25 to 100 deaths. In addition, 5 whites were killed and over 100 blacks arrested. Within a short period after the riot, the all-white county grand jury indicted 122 blacks, 73 on charges of murder, while no whites were indicted. In the subsequent trials, in which deliberations took no longer than nine minutes, all-white juries convicted and sentenced to death 12 black men. Sixty-seven other men pleaded guilty to lesser charges and received prison terms ranging from one to twenty-one years.

The National Association for the Advancement of Colored People (NAACP) and the Citizens Defense Fund Commission (CDFC), comprised of black leaders in Little Rock, secured the release of the twelve men in 1923 and 1925 as well as the release of those charged with lesser offenses. The NAACP was also successful in blocking the extradition of Robert L. Hill to Arkansas. Hill, who had fled to Kansas, was indicted for murder and nightriding and accused of being the ringleader of the alleged insurrection.

In response to adverse national publicity generated by the severity and quickness of the Elaine verdicts, Governor Brough appointed a sixteen-member commission with eight white and eight black men in November 1919. The commission's black members were African Methodist Episcopal bishop J. M. Conner; Dr. J. A. Booker, president of Arkansas Baptist College; Dr. J. M. Cox, president of Philander Smith College (Methodist Episcopal Church, North); and Rev. S. L. Green, all of Little Rock; Professor H. C. Yerger of Hope; Scott Bond of Medicine; Dr. E. C. Morris of Helena; and S. J. Money of Hot Springs. The white members included Dr. John VanLiere; Colonel John M. Gracie; Professor J. A. Presson; Lewis Altheimer; Robert E. Wait; G. D. Henderson; and John L. Hunter, all of Little Rock; and John H. Reynolds, president of Hendrix College, Conway.

In February 1920, the white members of the commission and three black members (Conner, Booker, and Cox) endorsed a petition to Kansas governor Henry L. Allen urging him to return Hill to Arkansas to stand trial. The support of the three black members represented a break with the NAACP, local black leadership, and state and national black consensus which sought to block state and federal charges against Hill.

**FURTHER READINGS**

Cortner, Richard. *A Mob Intent on Death: The NAACP and the Arkansas Riot Cases.* Middletown, Conn.: Wesleyan University Press, 1988.

Gordon, Fon Louise. *Caste and Class: The Black Experience in Arkansas, 1880–1920.* Athens: University of Georgia Press, 1995.

J. H. Reynolds to D. Y. Thomas, December 24, 1919, Series 2, file 4, folder 1, David Yancey Thomas Papers, Special Collections Division, University of Arkansas Libraries, Fayetteville, Arkansas.

*Fon Louise Gordon*

## Arkansas Council on Human Relations

The Arkansas Council on Human Relations (ACHR) was one of twelve state Councils on Human Relations established by the Southern Regional Council of Atlanta, Georgia, in 1954. The ACHR was a nonpolitical, nondenominational, interracial organization, designed "to improve communication between the races, contribute to a better understanding of the principles of good human relations by the people of Arkansas, and to work through and between the white and African American communities toward the ultimate goal of the elimination of segregation and discrimination." As an incorporated nonprofit organization, the ACHR derived its financial support from membership dues, contributions, and grants from the Fund for the Republic.

Operating through fourteen local chapters, the ACHR initially focused most of its work on the desegregation of public schools. The ACHR aided local communities in actualizing the spirit and letter of the 1954 *Brown v. Board of Education* decision. Moreover, the ACHR's interracial committees that formed in schools, churches, women's organizations, and civic groups provided participants with biracial experiences. Broadening its focus during the 1960s, the ACHR sponsored activities aimed at the desegregation of public accommodations; the improvement of welfare programs, child care centers, voter education projects, housing, and urban renewal plans; increasing equal employment opportunities; and lessening poverty. Working as a service agency, the ACHR's state office became a clearinghouse for information that provided local groups with source material to educate citizens and officials about improving human relations in Arkansas. The council ceased to function in the 1960s.

FURTHER READING

Southern Regional Council Papers, Series IV: State Councils on Human Relations, 1946–1968, Reel 141, Special Collections, Robert W. Woodruff Library, Atlanta University Center, Atlanta, Georgia.

*Kimberly E. Nichols*

## Association for the Advancement of Creative Musicians

The Association for the Advancement of Creative Musicians (AACM), was established in 1965 under the aegis of Muhal Richard Abrams, founder of the free jazz ensemble, the Experimental Band. The AACM, based in the South Side of Chicago, provides space for musicians who share no particular style, other than what they term "creative" music, allowing them to experiment with compositions and various instruments. For a brief time in the late 1970s, the AACM relocated to New York City, but eventually returned to its home in Chicago. Early members of the AACM included Anthony Braxton, Malachai Favors, Lester Bowie, Maurice McIntyre, Leroy Jenkins, Leo Smith, Steve McCall, Joseph Jarman, and Roscoe Mitchell.

The AACM pursues a nine-point program designed to (1) cultivate young musicians and create music of a high artistic level; (2) provide an atmosphere conducive to artistic endeavors; (3) conduct free training for disadvantaged city youth; (4) increase employment opportunities for musicians; (5) set an example of high moral standards for musicians and improve their public image; (6) foster respect between creative musicians and music trade professionals; (7) uphold the tradition of cultured musicians handed down from the past; (8) stimulate spiritual growth in musicians; and (9) assist charitable organizations.

The musicians are concerned with keeping control of the production and dissemination of their music, as well as building community awareness of the variety of black music among the African American residents of Chicago's South Side. For this purpose the AACM stages free concerts, performed at a variety of venues; sponsors performance groups, like the Art Ensemble of Chicago; and offers free musical instruction.

FURTHER READING

Giddins, Gary. "Inside Free Jazz: The AACM in New York." *Village Voice*, May 30, 1977, 46–48.

*Nichole T. Rustin*

## Association for the Study of Afro-American Life and History

On September 9, 1915, the Association for the Study of Afro-American Life and History (ASALH) was organized at Chicago's Wabash Avenue Young Men's Christian Association (YMCA) as the Association for the Study of Negro Life and History (ASNLH). The founders of the association were Dr. Carter G. Woodson, author of numerous works on African American history; Chicago physician Dr. George Cleveland Hall; W. B. Hartgrove; J. E. Stamps; and YMCA secretary Alexander L. Jackson. The ASALH was incorporated as a non-profit educational organization under the laws of the District of Columbia one month later, with Hall serving as chairman, YMCA secretary Jesse E. Moorland as custodian of funds, and Woodson as editor of the association's publications. The purpose of the organization was to collect sociological and historical data on Africans and African Americans, to study the peoples of African descent, to publish books in the field, and to promote harmony between the races by acquainting one with the achievements of the other. Since its inception, the ASALH has promoted the study of black history through its membership and branches in schools, colleges, churches, sororities, fraternities, and community groups nationwide.

The ASALH is governed by its charter, constitution, by-laws, and executive council. A national organization with headquarters in Washington, D.C., the ASALH's structure is based on its membership, branches, executive council, and appointed officers. In 1955, the ASALH had fifty branches. By 1980, that number nearly tripled to 139 branches operating in thirty-seven states. ASALH members have voting privileges and receive a newsletter informing them of the organization's activities. Additional fees are required for subscriptions to the ASALH's quarterly *Journal of Negro History* (JNH) and its magazine the *Negro History Bulletin* (NHB).

The ASALH holds its annual meetings during the first week of October, bringing together scholars and graduate students from various disciplines and lay persons, librarians, and archivists to present papers that explore a variety of topics related to the African and African American experience. The ASALH also sponsors educational programs, defines the national theme for Black History Month, and publishes teaching resources. In 1998, for example, the ASALH's theme was "African Americans in Business: The Path Towards Empowerment." In 1997, the organization's Scholar-in-Residence program collaborated with Howard University in sponsoring a national summer institute for school teachers on "The Middle Passage: The Making of the Atlantic World," which was funded by the National Endowment for the Humanities.

The ASALH's "conception, inspiration, growth, and development" was largely the product of "Woodson's personal genius and energy." Woodson was convinced that if a race had no recorded history, its achievements would be forgotten or ignored and eventually claimed by others. He believed that an understanding of African American history promoted pride in the black community and ultimately fostered white society's respect for blacks. An entrepreneur, scholar, editor, administrator, and historian, Woodson pioneered the movement for the study and preservation of African American history and created the organizational structure of the ASALH. In January 1916, four months after the founding of the ASALH, he laid the cornerstone of the association by publishing the first volume of the *JNH*. In 1920, he established the ASALH's for-profit publishing house, the Associated Publishers, Inc. (API), to assist black scholars in the publication of their manuscripts. Six years later, in February 1926, he initiated Negro History Week, which was expanded to Black History Month in 1976, to celebrate African American achievements and to educate the public about black contributions to America's past. In 1937, Woodson created the final element of the ASALH's structure when he launched publication of the NHB, aimed at primary and secondary school teachers, children, and the general black reading public.

Since the ASALH's founding, women have played a significant role in virtually every aspect of the organization. In 1935, Lucy Harth-Smith, a school principal from Lexington, Kentucky, was the first woman named to the executive council; Mary McLeod Bethune, principal of Bethune-Cookman College and member of President Franklin D. Roosevelt's "Black Cabinet," served as national president of the ASALH from 1936 to 1951; Dr. Lorraine A. Williams, professor of history at Howard University, worked as editor-in-chief of the *JNH* between 1974 and 1976; Dr. Dorothy Porter Wesley, noted archivist and librarian of Howard University's Moorland-Spingarn Research Center, assisted Woodson; and Willie Leanna Miles served as the ASALH/API's managing director for approximately fifty years. Acknowledging the active role of women in the ASALH, the Association of Black Women Historians (ABWH) started to hold its annual meetings in conjunction with the ASALH convention beginning in 1979. In 1994, the ASALH recognized the important contributions of black women to the success of the organization when it

established the Mary McLeod Bethune Service Award at its seventy-ninth annual meeting in Atlanta. Inaugurated in 1995 at the ASAHL's eightieth annual meeting in Philadelphia, the award was named in honor of McLeod Bethune who served as the ASALH's first woman president and remained at the helm of the organization for fifteen years. The award recognizes her dynamic leadership and life-long dedication to education, women's history, and African American life and culture. The ASALH presents the annual award to an individual who has been a contributing member of the association for at least ten years and whose career, like that of McLeod Bethune, has been characterized by service to education, African American history, and the community.

While the ASALH's annual meetings serve the important purpose of honoring the achievements of association members, providing a forum for intellectual exchange, and fostering a sense of community, the centerpiece of the association has been the *JNH*. The quarterly journal provides a scholarly medium for the publication of articles that chronicle the black experience in the African Diaspora. To this date, the *JNH* remains one of the few scholarly magazines devoted exclusively to the scientific study of the history of African Americans. While *JNH* articles tend to emphasize the black experience in the southern states during the nineteenth century, the journal has published articles covering almost all geographic regions of North America from the sixteenth through the twentieth centuries. Articles on the slave trade, slave resistance and rebellion, and abolition as well as black culture, family, and religion, have appeared along with biographical accounts of the achievements and accomplishments of African American business owners, congressional delegates, educators, physicians, and inventors. Moreover, *JNH* articles have explored the experiences of black people in Great Britain, Canada, Africa, the Caribbean, and Latin America. In addition to scholarly articles, each *JNH* volume contains historical documents, book reviews, and notes by the editor. In 1937, Woodson organized the journal's first editorial board, including Sterling Brown, James B. Browning, Lorenzo Greene, Luther Porter Jackson, Lawrence Reddick, and Arthur A. Schomburg. Other noted scholars who have served on the fourteen-member editorial board include Benjamin Quarles, John Blassingame, Leon Litwack, Mary Frances Berry, Robert Harris Jr., Bettye Gardner, June O. Patton, Gloria Dickinson, and Darlene Clark Hine. Since the journal's inception six individuals have served as editors: Woodson (1916–1950), Rayford W. Logan (1950–1951), William M. Brewer (1952–1970), W. Augustus Low (1970–1974),

Lorraine A. Williams (1974–1976), and Alton Hornsby Jr. (1976–). When Hornsby assumed the editorship, the *JNH* was relocated from Howard University's Department of History to Atlanta's Morehouse College's Department of History, chaired by Hornsby.

During Woodson's thirty-four year tenure as editor of the *JNH*, the journal published over 500 articles on various aspects of the black experience and race relations. While Woodson advocated the scholarly study of black history, he also encouraged African Americans outside of the historical discipline to write about their experiences. Articles by black ministers, poets, attorneys, political scientists, and clubwomen appeared frequently in the *JNH*.

Through the editorial policy he formulated for the *JNH*, Woodson sought to combat racist historical interpretations and pursue his lifelong aim of advancing a positive self-image of peoples of African descent. He maintained that all aspects of the black experience needed reexamination. Woodson biographer, Jacqueline Goggin, concluded that he and other scholars publishing in the *JNH* were innovators not only in their interpretations of African American history, but in the methods they used to arrive at their conclusions. Using previously untapped census data, marriage registers, birth and death certificates, letters, diaries, and oral histories, these pioneering black scholars pointed to the positive achievements and contributions of African Americans during the adverse conditions of slavery. In the pages of the *JNH*, scholars challenged widely held beliefs of racial inferiority, emphasized black struggles against slavery, and uncovered the rich cultural traditions African Americans maintained in bondage.

In 1940, on the occasion of the twenty-fifth anniversary of the ASALH, Professor W. B. Hesseltine of the University of Wisconsin acknowledged that the association had made crucial contributions to the discipline of history. By doing scholarly research on African Americans, the ASALH had not only prompted a reconsideration and subsequent revision of the role of blacks in American history, but it had also illustrated the interrelationship between history and sociology. Thus, the ASALH's efforts to enrich the content of American history contributed to a more accurate assessment of the American past and improved the methods of scientific research.

Despite the ASAHL's long struggle to establish black history as a viable subject of scholarly inquiry, it was not until the 1970s that the majority of the historical profession acknowledged the important contributions of African Americans to American history and the centrality of race in America's past. This interpretative shift, sparked largely by the civil rights movement, resulted in the publication of numerous studies of African American history and race relations. Many scholars who had ignored African American history previously started to rely heavily on the research published in the *JNH*. Without Woodson's and the ASALH's effort to publish articles documenting the history of African Americans, contemporary scholars would have far fewer resources for the study of black contributions to America's past.

Woodson and the ASALH, however, not only published manuscripts illustrating African American life and history, but also collected primary source materials. Woodson knew that most libraries and archives showed little or no interest in collecting primary source materials dealing with black culture. The ASALH's dual effort to preserve documents of the African American past and to publish research based on these materials, made the association's work more expansive than that of other scholarly organizations. For the purpose of gathering records that documented the African American experience, the ASALH operated its own research bureau "to explore fields of Negro history hitherto neglected or unknown."

Impressed by Woodson's determination and recognizing the need to preserve black documents, J. Franklin Jameson, chief of the Manuscript Division of the Library of Congress during the late 1920s, assisted Woodson in his work. With only a small amount of funds, but a great deal of enthusiastic support from the black community, Woodson launched his effort to collect and preserve African American records. He initiated regular correspondence with scholars and asked blacks as well as whites from all walks of life to join in the effort. Woodson collected over 5,000 documents, which now comprise the Carter G. Woodson Collection of Negro Materials housed at the Library of Congress.

Recognizing the difficulties black scholars faced when trying to get their works published by mainstream publishers, Woodson organized a publishing company in 1920. The API, a business venture linked to the not-for-profit ASALH, is the oldest African American publishing company in the United States. Woodson had long been aware of the need for adequate teaching materials for a satisfactory presentation of African American history. His experiences as a teacher at the secondary school and college levels strengthened this conviction. The API's purposes were to nurture the African presence through publications, to promote historical research of and by African Americans, and to supply educational materials to teachers, organizations, and the general public.

The API's first board of trustees consisted of Woodson, who served as president; John W. Davis, who held the post of treasurer; and Louis R. Mehlinger, who became secretary. Davis was the president of West Virginia Collegiate Institute, where Woodson taught following his tenure as dean of literal arts at Howard University. Mehlinger, an attorney for the U.S. Department of Justice, with his stenographic skills, made a major contribution to the venture by reproducing on paper the thoughts of Woodson and other black historians. Mehlinger also served as the ASALH's first secretary, retiring in 1951.

Originally located at 1216 U Street, N.W. in Washington, D.C., the API was organized on November 18, 1920, and incorporated on June 10, 1921, under the laws of the District of Columbia. In the following year, Woodson purchased a three-story rowhouse at 1538 Ninth Street, N.W. The ASALH as well as the API maintained their headquarters at that location until September 1971, when a spacious building at 1407 Fourteenth Street N.W. was purchased and dedicated in honor of Woodson. During the 1980s, a Speakers Bureau was formed, the API initiated the Afro-American History Month Kickoff Workshops each January, and the ASALH sponsored the Afro-American History Month Luncheon, a major fundraiser in the Washington metropolitan area, held on the first Saturday each February.

The API sells its publications to bookstores, libraries, individuals, and boards of education through direct mail catalogs, at conferences, and during Black History Month exhibits. For the past decade, federal government agencies have been the API's largest customer base for thematic resource packets published for Black History Month. The API also sends inventory circulars, reviews, and publicity copies to churches, schools, professional organizations, and the media.

Prior to establishing the API, Woodson had published two books. The first work, *The Education of the Negro Prior to 1861* (1915), initiated a new field of research in American education. This volume has been regarded as a significant contribution to educational history and is still an essential reference work. In his second book, *A Century of Negro Migration* (1918), Woodson used census statistics to document black population movements during World War I. He showed that while there had been a large migration of African Americans from rural to urban areas, from South to North and from East to West during the war, there had also been continuous migrations as a result of the submarginal status imposed on African Americans. In 1922, the API published Woodson's *The Negro in Our History*, which remained in print for more than twenty-five years and went through nine editions, selling more than 50,000 copies. In 1928, the API published *The Story of the Negro Retold* for high school students and *Negro Makers of History* for students in the elementary schools. Woodson's most noted classic work, *The Mis-Education of the Negro* (1933) was reprinted in 1969 with the assistance of a grant from the United Supreme Council 330 Ancient and Accepted Scottish Rite of Freemasonry, Southern Jurisdiction. Due to continuing demand, API president Edgar Allan Toppin announced at the ASALH's seventy-fifth annual meeting in Chicago the reprint of 25,000 copies by 1992. Another Woodson classic, *The History of the Negro Church*, first published in 1921, and reprinted in 1945 and 1972, has been used both as a supplementary work and as a basic text for courses in church history in numerous black and white schools of theology.

The API also published rare first editions of works by many other scholars, including Beatrice Fleming's and Marion Pryde's *Distinguished Negroes Abroad*, Charles H. Wesley's *Richard Allen: An Apostle of Freedom*, W. Montague Cobb's *The First Negro Medical Society*, and James Dallas Parks's *Robert S. Duncanson: 19th Century Black Romantic Painter*.

In addition to advancing scholarly research of African American history, the ASALH sought to educate the public about black achievements. For this purpose, the ASALH initiated Negro History Week in 1926. Observance of the week began on the second Sunday in February to embrace both the birthdays of Abraham Lincoln and Frederick Douglass. Week-long public exercises emphasized the contributions of African Americans to American history and led to growing demands for books, literature, and pictures featuring African Americans. The celebration enlarged the scope of Woodson's work beyond the circle of scholars to include public school systems and curricula.

The ASALH's effort to involve school teachers in the promotion of African American life and history led to the creation of the *NHB* in 1937. For a number of years, McLeod Bethune, both as a member of the ASALH and as its president, had urged Woodson to devise new ways to reach primary and secondary school teachers, children, and the general black reading public. In response, Woodson launched the *NHB* to provide teachers at primary and secondary schools with easily accessible educational resources. Initially published monthly, the now quarterly *NHB* promotes appreciation of African Americans' life and history, encourages an understanding of the present status of race relations, and seeks to inspire black youth. According to the educator and civil rights activist Dr. W. E. B. Du Bois, who knew Woodson for some forty-odd years, "He wanted the youngsters to grow up with an appreciation of their own possibilities, gained through knowledge of the contributions black folk made to history." Only by rediscovering their past, Woodson thought, could they also find their true place in the present world.

Each *NHB* issue focuses on one theme and features a series of articles on a variety of topics, photographs of annual ASALH meetings or branch members, and announcements of black history activities throughout the country. In addition, the bulletin frequently contains articles about historically black colleges and universities, highlights of trips to African nations, particularly Ghana and Nigeria, and articles by African scholars. Moreover, each issue features "A Young People's Corner" with columns entitled "For Whom Is Your School Named?" and "Know Your History," and a "Poet's Corner." The *NHB* also serves as an advertising medium for ASALH fund-raising activities and events, API theme kits and books, and other publishers of black history textbooks and biographies.

The *NHB* continues to serve a broad audience and plays a significant role in providing teachers with educational resources. The demand for these resources has grown particularly since 1976 when the ASALH expanded Negro History Week to Black History Month, in commemoration of the nation's bicentennial. The month-long observance of African American history triggered an ever-growing demand for resource materials illustrating the black experience. The ASALH responded with the publication of theme kits and resource packages containing teaching materials such as theme posters, photos and biographical sketches suitable for display, a series of historical monographs in booklet or textbook form, and thematic calendars of historic events.

Today, more than forty ASALH chapters operate in the United States. Continuing Woodson's mission, they promote education, research, and publication of African American history and culture.

**FURTHER READINGS**

Cobb, W. Montague. "Carter Godwin Woodson, Ph.D., LL.D., 1875–1950: The Father of Negro History." *Journal of the National Medical Association* (September 1970).

———. "Carter Godwin Woodson." *Negro History Bulletin* 36, 7 (1973): 151–155.

———. *Paper #17.* Washington, D.C.: Associated Publishers, 1989.

Gardner, Bettye. "Association for the Study of Afro-American Life and History." In *Black Women in America: An Historical Encyclopedia.* Ed. Darlene Clark Hine. Brooklyn, N.Y.: Carlson Publishing, Inc., 1993.

Goddard, Richlyn F. "The Associated Publishers as an Entrepreneurial Enterprise: A Case Study of the First Black-Owned and Operated Academic Publisher." In *African Americans in Business—The Path Toward Empowerment.* Washington, D.C.: Associated Publishers, 1998.

Goggin, Jacqueline. "Countering White Racist Scholarship: Carter G. Woodson and the Journal of Negro History." *Journal of Negro History* 68, 4 (Autumn 1983): 355–375.

———. *Carter G. Woodson: A Life in Black History.* Baton Rouge: Louisiana State University Press, 1993.

———. "Association for the Study of Afro-American Life and History." In *Encyclopedia of African-American Culture and History.* Ed. Jack Salzman, David Lionel Smith, and Cornel West. New York: Macmillan Library Reference, 1996.

Woodson, Carter G. "Ten Years of Collecting and Publishing the Records of the Negro." *Journal of Negro History* 10, 4 (October 1925): 598–606.

———. "The Annual Report of the Director." *Journal of Negro History* 33, 4 (October 1948): 387–394.

*Richlyn F. Goddard*

## Association for the Study of Negro Life and History

*See* Association for the Study of Afro-American Life and History.

## Association of African and African-American Folklorists

A group of twenty-five African American university professors, graduate students, museum staff members, and community-based researchers founded the Association of African and African-American Folklorists (AAAAF) in 1974. Gathering on the campus of Washington, D.C.'s Howard University, the group sought to provide an international forum for black folklorists, anthropologists, historians, ethnomusicologists, sociologists, language scholars, writers, storytellers, staff members of museums, editors of popular and professional publications, cultural photographers, documentary filmmakers, college students, and the general public to study African Diaspora folklore.

In 1975, delegates to the first AAAAF conference, indicating their interest in exploring the folk expressions of African peoples around the world, adopted as their symbol: Nkonsonkonson, the Akan symbol meaning "Links of a Chain." In the following year, the group adopted a constitution, pledging "to foster and facilitate the definition, exploration, dissemination, presentation and preservation of folklore and folklife in the African Diaspora." The AAAAF offers individual, household, student, institutional, honorary, and life membership categories to persons of African descent who have "demonstrated any interest in the folklore and folklife of peoples of the African Diaspora." Participants of the second annual conference elected William H. Wiggins Jr. of Indiana University, Bloomington, president; Gladys-Marie Fry of the University of Maryland, College Park, vice-president; Gerald L. Davis of Rutgers University, secretary-treasurer; and Stephen E. Henderson of Howard University, Bernice Reagon of the Smithsonian Institution, Roland Freeman of the Mississippi Folklife Project, and James C. Early of Antioch College executive committee members.

Following its initial two meetings on the campus of Howard University, the AAAAF held its next two national conferences on the campuses of Indiana University and the University of Maryland at College Park. In October 1977 Indiana University hosted the AAAAF's third annual conference, which explored "The Role of Afro-American Folklore in the Teaching of the Arts and the Humanities." In November 1978, the University of Maryland at College Park was the site of the AAAAF's fourth annual conference, which centered on the theme "Folktalk: The Dynamics of African-American Expressive Culture." Beginning in 1979, the AAAAF has held its national conference in conjunction with the annual meetings of the American Folklore Society (AFS).

Since its inception, AAAAF members have actively promoted, albeit with uneven results, a series of publications whose primary purpose has been to encourage research and documentation of African Diaspora folklore. Patricia A. Turner of the University of California at Davis published an occasional newsletter informing members about upcoming events and current research projects. Lance A. Williams of California State at Northridge devoted an issue of his journal *Blackfolk: A Journal of Afro-American Folklore* to articles written by AAAAF members and produced *What Time is De Meeting*, a color video documentary of the AAAAF's 1977 conference. Adrienne Lanier Seward edited the papers presented at the AAAAF's third national conference and published them in *The Role*

*of Afro-American Folklore in the Teachings of the Arts and the Humanities.*

Under the leadership of John Roberts, the AAAAF's former president and the first African American president of the AFS, and Marilyn White, the current AAAAF president, the association continues to provide a collegial forum for the exchange of ideas. Often, issues discussed at AAAAF meetings have subsequently been published, including the works of Patricia A. Turner, Gerald L. Davis, Roland Freeman, Gladys-Marie Fry, Trudier Harris, Kathryn Morgan, John Roberts, and William H. Wiggins Jr. This creative flame of collegial research is kindled anew each year among the twenty-five or so African American folklorists who attend the annual conference of the AFS where they present papers and host an informal members-only dinner to remember past members and initiate new ones.

Despite its small membership, the AAAAF has wielded significant influence in increasing public awareness and appreciation of African American folklore. AAAAF members affiliated with universities have added African Diaspora folklore courses to their departments' curriculums; staff members of the Smithsonian Institution have initiated the African Diaspora Program division of the Smithsonian's Festival of American Folklife; cultural photographers have mounted exhibits of traditional rural and urban African Diaspora life in museums, libraries, and universities; and documentary filmmakers have produced cultural studies of the African Diaspora, including a nationally televised film about the blues.

*William H. Wiggins Jr.*

## Association of Black Admissions and Financial Aid Officers of the Ivy League and Sister Schools

Founded in 1970, the Association of Black Admissions and Financial Aid Officers of the Ivy League and Sister Schools assists students who have traditionally and historically been underrepresented at Ivy League and Sister School institutions. Initially, the association aided African American, Native American, Asian, and Hispanic students with their transition from high school to college. In addition, the organization interpolates issues of diversity into the admissions and financial process. Moreover, the organization systematically analyzes retention policies and practices as they pertain to students of color. Furthermore, the association challenges the Ivy Leage and Sister School institutions to be more sensitive to the needs of the changing minority population.

The organization is run by admissions and financial aid professionals from Brown University, Columbia University, Cornell University, Dartmouth College, Harvard University, Radcliffe College, Massachusetts Institute of Technology, University of Pennsylvania, Princeton University, Yale University, Vassar College, Barnard College, Bryn Mawr College, Mount Holyoke College, Smith College, and Wellesley College.

**FURTHER READING**

Maurer, C. and T. E. Sheets, *Encyclopedia of Associations: National Organizations of the U.S.*, vol. 1, pt. 1, 33d ed. Detroit: Gale, 1998, p. 775.

*Sybril M. Bennett*

## Association of Black American Ambassadors

The Association of Black American Ambassadors (ABAA) was founded to represent the interests of black American ambassadors. Based in Washington, D.C., the ABAA was incorporated in 1982 and currently boasts some fifty members. Only African Americans who presently serve or have served as U.S. ambassadors are eligible for membership.

The ABAA works to represent the interests of Black American ambassadors in various ways. It recognizes the roles African American ambassadors have played in the creation and implementation of U.S. foreign policy; promotes cohesion and fellowship among black American ambassadors; encourages young blacks and other minorities to join the U.S. foreign service; helps blacks and other minorities prepare for and enjoy upward mobility in the foreign service; offers blacks and other minorities insight on the purpose of American foreign policy in Third World nations; and advances Americans' understanding of the problems of developing nations in Africa and the Caribbean.

The ABAA was created when an increasing number of African Americans joined the ambassadorial ranks. Black ambassadors realized that they might constitute a positive force in the American foreign service if they organized. The ABAA's founding members included Horace Dawson, who served as U.S. ambassador to Botswana; Clyde Ferguson, former ambassador to Uganda; Ulric Haynes, former ambassador to Algeria; Elliott Skinner, former ambassador to Upper Volta; and Franklin Hall Williams, former ambassador to Ghana. The ABAA regularly supports African American candidates for ambassadorships, and ABAA members have met with various Secretaries of State to that end. In the mid-1980s, many ABAA members were involved in efforts to end apartheid in South Africa. Of late, the ABAA has been contemplating what, if any, action it should take regarding the human rights abuses by and anti-democratic practices of Nigerian dictator General Sani Abacha.

Every American president since Harry Truman has appointed at least one black ambassador. The first black American ambassador was Edward R. Dudley, appointed to Liberia in West Africa in 1949. Dudley's two immediate successors to Liberia, both appointed by President Dwight D. Eisenhower, were also African Americans: Jessie D. Locker in 1953 and Richard L. Jones in 1955. The ABAA's very existence honors the memory and pioneering work of these men.

An enduring concern of ABAA members has been ensuring that black Americans are offered ambassadorial posts in countries other than Africa or the Caribbean. Some ABAA members would like to see more black ambassadors follow in the footsteps of Clifton R. Wharton, who was the first African American to head a U.S. Embassy in Europe. President John F. Kennedy named Wharton the ambassador to Norway in 1961.

The ABAA holds regular meetings among its members. It is governed by a president, a vice-president for finance, a vice-president for programs, and a secretary-treasurer. Each of these officers serves a one-year term. In 2000, the ABAA's president is Theodore Britton Jr., former U.S. ambassador to Barbados and Grenada.

*Scott W. Webster*

## Association of Black Anthropologists

The Association of Black Anthropologists (ABA) originated in 1968 and was formally established in 1975. The ABA encourages the anthropological study of black people and supports the professional development of black anthropologists. For this purpose the association monitors the discipline and fosters communication among black anthropologists. Since 1989, the ABA has been affiliated with the American Anthropological Association (AAA).

In 1968 the AAA established a Minority Caucus at its annual meeting in Seattle. Following this meeting several black anthropologists, including Council Taylor, Delmos Jones, Diana Lewis, Johnetta Cole, and Oliver Osborne, concerned about the black curriculum in anthropology, agreed to meet regularly to examine the contributions of minority anthropologists and to increase their number. In 1970, the AAA established a Committee on Minority Participation in Anthropology from which emerged the

Caucus of Black Anthropologists. In 1973 the caucus began publication of a four-page newsletter, *Notes from the Natives*. The newsletter, started by Sheila Walker while a graduate student at the University of Chicago, explored the work of black anthropologists and carried book reviews, commentaries, paper abstracts, and job listings.

In the early 1970s, regular caucus participants, largely consisting of junior faculty and graduate students, agreed to launch a formal organization. Under the leadership of Anselme Remy, chair of the caucus, and the members of the steering committee, Jerry Wright, Delmos Jones, and Patricia Guthrie, the caucus reorganized as the ABA at the 1975 AAA meeting in San Francisco. The late Vera Green became the ABA's first president, succeeded by Anselme Remy, Johnnetta Cole, John Stewart, A. Lynn Bolles, Tony Whitehead, and Ira E. Harrison.

In 1978, the ABA expanded its newsletter, renamed it *Notes from the ABA*, and appointed Walker as editor. *Notes* continued to carry its regular features and in addition started publishing brief scholarly notes and regular contributions by John Gwaltney and Rhett S. Jones. In 1981, Glenn Jordan, a graduate student at the University of Illinois, and Willie Baber, assistant professor of Anthropology and African Studies at Purdue University, became co-editors of *Notes*. A year later Jordan also launched the ABA's *Occasional Paper* series. With the support of AAA and ABA members, *Notes* gradually evolved into *Transforming Anthropology*, a refereed journal committed to the study of "race, ethnicity, class, gender, and other invidious distinctions." In addition to these publications, the ABA has published a *Black Anthropologists Directory* and *The ABA Directory*.

While the ABA began as an informal organization of black anthropologists it is now open to all anthropologists and those in allied fields who are committed to the goals of the association.

**FURTHER READINGS**

Green, Vera, ed. *Black Anthropologists Directory*. N.p.: Association of Black Anthropologists, 1978–1979.

Harrison, Ira E., and Arthur K. Spears, eds. *The ABA Directory*. Washington, D.C.: The Association of Black Anthropologists, 1991.

*Rhett S. Jones*

## Association of Black Cardiologists

Dr. Richard Allen Williams founded the Association of Black Cardiologists, Inc. (ABC), at the annual meeting of the American Heart Association in Dallas, Texas, in 1974. The ABC, headquartered in Atlanta, is dedicated to prevention and reduction of cardiovascular disease among African Americans and other minority populations. Williams, a graduate of the State University of New York Downstate Medical Center, served as the first president of the ABC until 1986. He is the author of *Textbook of Black-Related Diseases* (1975), the seminal work on diseases affecting black Americans. The seventeen black men and women who joined Williams in creating the the ABC served as the organization's first board of directors.

Prominent African American physicians who followed Williams in serving two-year terms as presidents of the ABC include Daniel D. Savage, Elijah Saunders, Jay Brown, Augustus O. Grant, Paul L. Douglass, and Frank S. James, president in 2000. Committed to encouraging young blacks to achieve good health and educational excellence, the organization boasts numerous role models among its approximately 500 predominantly black members, including Dr. Edward S. Cooper who became the first African American to receive tenure as full professor at the University of Pennsylvania School of Medicine in 1972. Cooper also holds the distinction of becoming the first black physician to be elected president of the American Heart Association in 1992. Another renowned ABC member is Dr. Janice Electa Green Douglass, an internationally recognized physician and scientist in the field of cellular and molecular mechanisms of blood pressure regulation. Douglass was the first woman to be appointed professor of medicine as well as vice chair of medicine at Case Western Reserve University School of Medicine.

Cardiovascular disease afflicts African Americans in numbers greater than other population groups. Based in Atlanta, the ABC views its mission in global terms. Members affirm their commitment to conquering cardiovascular and related diseases among "minority and under served populations wherever the disease ravages those who through ignorance, or lack of access to resources, suffer and die needlessly."

Witnessing the tragedy of heart disease among its own membership, the ABC established an Outstanding Achievement in Cardiovascular Medicine Award. In 1999, the ABC awarded its Outstanding Achievement in Cardiovascular Medicine Award posthumously to Dr. David Bernard Todd Jr., who created the first cardiac surgical team at Meharry Medical College. Todd, who was a full professor of surgery at Meharry, headed the college's first open heart surgical team and served as chief of the Division of Thoracic and Cardiovascular Surgery. Todd died in 1987 at age forty-eight, a victim of sudden cardiac death.

The ABC also offers a Continuing Medical Education program that allows members to maintain and increase their skills and performance in cardiac medicine and related fields. Lectures, seminars, scientific meetings, publications, and the dissemination of medical education literature aimed at the lay public are other important ABC activities. The Community Health Risk Reduction Program (CHRRP) rounds out ABC initiatives. A joint professional-lay volunteer program, the CHRRP operates clinics at local churches and provides nutritional counseling and exercise classes to counter obesity and inactivity (which is more prevalent among black women than other population groups). The CHRRP, for example, offers a holistic exercise program, "Sweatin' With The Sisters," which seeks to educate black women and thereby reduce and prevent heart disease. Moreover, the CHRRP publishes a member-produced cookbook of heart healthy recipes. A mentor program for black youth promotes education and character building and encourages career choices in science and medicine. Finally, the CHRRP trains community volunteers to identify symptoms of hypertension. For example, it trains black barbers to screen their clients who are at risk of heart disease and refer them to physicians.

The ABC faces unique challenges. Stroke rates for African Americans have increased over the past years, affecting not only the general black population but also black physicians who die on average ten years younger than their white counterparts. Despite the alarming growth of heart disease among African Americans, only 2 percent of blacks entering the field of medicine have chosen cardiovascular training. The record is worse for minorities in other parts of the world.

For a quarter of a century, the ABC has led the fight against heart disease among African Americans and, more recently, it has extended its struggle to the Caribbean and Africa. In 1998, for example, the ABC sponsored an "International Conference on Update and Recent Advances in Cardiology" in South Africa. In the same year, the ABC, under the direction of its Chief Executive Officer, B. Waine Kong, Ph.D., J.D., started to establish computer links and websites with several African countries. Through its diverse agenda of national and international activities the ABC continues to battle the odds in its fight against heart disease.

**FURTHER READINGS**

Association of Black Cardiologists. *ABC Newsletter* 24, 3 (Fall 1998).

James, Frank S. *Pioneering African Americans in the Conquest of Heart Disease*. Atlanta: Association of Black Cardiologists, Inc., 1999.

Rodney, Roxanne A. "Noninvasive Evaluation of Coronary Artery Disease in Women." *The ABC Digest of Urban Cardiology* 5, 6 (November/December 1998): 22–23, 26.

*Peggy Hardman*

## Association of Black Catholics Against Abortion

Founded in New York City, in 1986, by Dr. Dolores Bernadette Grier, an occupational therapist, the Association of Black Catholics Against Abortion (ABCAA) seeks to eliminate the rising number of abortions within the black community through education, legislation, and prayer. In 1985, Grier was appointed Vice Chancellor of Community Relations for the Diocese of New York, the first woman, first African American, and first laywoman to serve in such a high post within the Roman Catholic Church in America. Shortly thereafter, she founded the ABCAA.

In addition to the high mortality rate among African Americans, due to drug and alcohol abuse, murder, and suicide, the Reverend Terry Steib, auxiliary bishop of St. Louis, Missouri, has recently charged that black women undergo twice as many abortions as their white counterparts. In response, the ABCAA seeks to inform African Americans that abortion is yet another attempt on the part of some segments in American society to wage "race genocide" within the black community. Abortion, legalized in 1973 in the landmark case of *Roe v. Wade*, according to the ABCAA, was thrust upon black women and serves to further destabilization within African American communities.

ABCAA advocates counter pro-choice advocates with the claim that blacks who support abortion, in essence, deny their African heritage whose respect for life extends from one's ancestors, to the living, and to those yet unborn. The group conducts conferences, workshops, and programs to promote alternatives to abortion.

**FURTHER READING**

Grier, Dolores Bernadette. *Death by Abortion*. New York: Rosemont Press, 1997.

*A. J. Scopino Jr.*

## Association of Black Psychologists

In 1968, sixteen black professional and student psychologists, concerned about the lack of black representation in the American Psychiatric Association and its failure to address mental health concerns of African Americans, established the Association of Black Psychologists (ABPsi). The organization's current membership of 1,400 includes psychologists and psychology students, as well as professionals in associated behavioral science disciplines. The nonprofit ABPsi operates exclusively for charitable and educational purposes.

The ABPsi seeks to enhance the professional development of its members and strengthen the provision of mental health care for African Americans. For this purpose the ABPsi provides its members with professional networking opportunities and a forum for the exchange of research. Moreover, the ABPsi conducts research and formulates "policies for local, state, and national decision making" that affect the mental health of the black community (King, 21).

Since the formation of the ABPsi, many black mental health care practitioners have joined the faculties of major universities, assuming new administrative and policy-making positions. This growing professional visibility in the educational arena has led to an increase in African American clinicians and stimulated new research on minority mental health. Currently there are approximately 14,000 black psychiatrists and 1,200 black psychologists practicing in America. As a result of the growing number of black professionals and research studies that explore the mental health of African Americans, white mental health care providers have become increasingly aware of and sensitive to the particular psychological needs of the black community. Many of the mental health care practitioners have begun to realize that the psychological problems of African Americans differ from those of whites because of their different life experiences. For example, until the early 1970s, black patients were twice as likely as whites to be diagnosed with schizophrenia. Through the use of racially sensitive evaluation and testing techniques, psychologists have found that the majority of black patients suffer not from schizophrenia but from other psychological problems, particularly clinical depression. Moreover, most African American patients tend to display more severe symptoms than whites because they often seek treatment late in their illness, avoiding white psychologists and psychiatrists whom they feel will not understand them.

Membership in the ABPsi is open to all individuals, professionals and students, who are interested in promoting the goals and objectives of the organization. The ABPsi operates through various committees including committees on AIDS, the black family, communications, ethics, research and development, social action, social work, liaison, student affairs, and testing. Moreover, the ABPsi sponsors Black Mental Health Month and publishes the *Association of Black Psychologists Publications Manual.*

FURTHER READINGS

King, R. E. G. "Highlights in the Development of ABPsi." *Journal of Black Psychology* 4 (1978): 9–23.

Poussaint, Alvin F. "Psychology and Psychiatry." In *Encyclopedia of African-American Culture and History*, vol. 4. Ed. Jack Salzman, David Lionel Smith, and Cornel West. New York: Simon and Schuster Macmillan, 1996.

*Nancy Jean Rose*

## Association of Black Sociologists

The Association of Black Sociologists (ABS) was founded as the Caucus of Black Sociologists at the 1970 meeting of the American Sociological Association (ASA) in Washington, D.C. The ABS represents the professional interests of black sociologists, seeks to enhance their academic opportunities, fosters recognition of their scholarly contributions, and provides them with a support system.

Black sociologists had joined the ASA since its founding in 1905, however, black membership remained small and never exceeded ten African Americans. Concerned about the small number of black ASA members, the lack of black representation on the organization's boards and committees, as well as the ASA's failure to appoint African Americans to national and regional executive leadership positions, black sociologists launched the ABS. Leading organizers of the ABS included James E. Blackwell, University of Massachusetts, Boston; James E. Conyers, Indiana State University; Jacquelyne J. Jackson, Duke University; and Joseph W. Scott, University of Notre Dame.

First efforts to organize the ABS emerged in 1968, when a group of black and white sociologists interested in civil rights and peace issues joined under the leadership of Tilman C. Cothran, chairman of Atlanta University's department of sociology. That year, Cothran and his supporters presented the ASA with several resolutions designed to increase black participation. They urged the ASA to ensure black representation on the organization's council and various committees and to invite black sociologists to present papers and serve as panel discussants and section chairs at annual meetings. Moreover, they demanded that ASA journals clearly state the criteria for the acceptance of papers for publication and secure black sociologists as readers and referees. While the ASA council approved the resolutions, black sociologists feared that the response was no more than a token concession of the white male-dominated organization.

Thus, Cothran's group launched the organization of the ABS at the ASA meeting in 1970. The founding group, consisting of seventy-six members, elected James E. Blackwell national chairman; Jacquelyne J. Jackson, secretary-treasurer; Ernest Works, program chairman; Edgar Epps, research chairman; Charles V. Willie and Charles King, chairmen for membership; and James E. Conyers, Tilman C. Cothran, Ralph Hines, Albert J. McQueen, Joseph W. Scott, Charles U. Smith, Alphonso Pickney, Walter L. Wallace, and William J. Wilson, executive committee members. The ABS Executive Committee consists of the organization's president, past president, president-elect, executive officer, secretary, treasurer, membership chair, newsletter editor, and two members-at-large as well as a student representative. Past presidents of the ABS include some of the most prestigious names in the discipline such as James E. Blackwell (1970–1972), Jacquelyne J. Jackson (1972–1973), James E. Conyers (1973–1974), Albert J. McQueen (1975–1976), La Francis Rodgers-Rose (1976–1977), Joan R. Harris (1977–1978), Albert W. Black (1978–1979), Wilbur H. Watson (1979–1980), John Sibley Butler (1980–1981), Rutledge M. Dennis (1981–1983), James Pitts (1983–1984), Lena Wright Myers (1984–1985), Essie Manuel Rutledge (1985–1986), Aldon D. Morris (1987–1989), Sandra V. Walker (1989–1990), Florence B. Bonner (1990–1991), Mareyjoyce Green (1991–1992), Walter R. Allen (1992–1993), Robert G. Newby (1993–1994), Cedric Herring (1994–1995), Robert Davis (1995–1996), Joseph Scott (1996–1997), Carole Marks (1997–1998), and Diane Brown (1998–1999). While the ABS is not restricted to scholars of African descent, their interests define the focus of the organization.

The ABS holds annual meetings that provide members with professional networking opportunities and scholarly forums to discuss their research. Encouraging student participation, the ABS has launched a Student Paper Competition to recognize the efforts of aspiring young scholars. Moreover, the organization recognizes the contributions of seasoned scholars with its Distinguished Career Award. In addition to its annual conference, the ABS sponsors joint sessions with other professional groups such as the Society for the Study of Social Problems and the Society of Women Sociologists. The ABS publishes the *Association of Black Sociologists Newsletter* and since 1998 the journal of *Race and Society*. In 1974 the ABS initiated the publication of *Black Sociologists: Historical and Contemporary Perspectives*, the most comprehensive book on black sociologists.

The ABS has also been effective in increasing the visibility and representing the interests of African Americans in the ASA. The ABS instituted an ASA Minority Fellowship Program, established the position of Executive Specialist for Minorities and Women within the ASA, appointed an ASA Committee on the Status of Racial and Ethnic Minorities in Sociology, initiated the ASA's DuBois–Johnson–Frazier Award Selection Committee, and supported the efforts of Charles U. Smith, Florida A & M University, to organize a Race Relations section within the ASA which remains the organization's largest standing committee on race relations. In 1997, 90 percent of the ABS's 150 members also held membership in the ASA.

**FURTHER READINGS**

Blackwell, James E., and Morris Janowitz, eds. *Black Sociologists: The First Half Century.* Belmont, Calif.: Wadsworth, 1974.

———. *Black Sociologists: Historical and Contemporary Perspectives.* Chicago: The University of Chicago Press, 1974.

Conyers, James E. "The Association of Black Sociologists: A Descriptive Account from an 'Insider.'" *The American Sociologist* (Spring 1992): 49–55.

*Anthony J. Lemelle Jr.*

## Association of Black Storytellers

*See* National Association of Black Storytellers.

## Association of Black Women Historians

The Association of Black Women Historians (ABWH) is the first and the only professional organization to provide a network and recognition for women of African descent who are historians or students of history, for scholars who research and write about black women's history, and for those who support the professional goals of the organization.

Rosalyn Terborg-Penn, Eleanor Smith, and Elizabeth Parker first conceived the ABWH during the 1977 annual meeting of the Association for the Study of Afro-American Life and History (ASALH). Following the convention the founders formed a steering committee called "Black Women United," to canvass the nation in search of interested black women academics. After the untimely death of Parker in 1978, Terborg-Penn and Smith continued the organizing effort, hosting interest meetings at the Berkshire Conference of Women Historians in South Hadley, Massachusetts, the ASALH convention in Los Angeles, and the American Historical Association Convention in San Francisco. Realizing that the majority of their constituency lived on the East Coast and attended the ASALH conventions, the steering committee, consisting of Gloria Dickinson, Darlene Clark Hine, Juanita Moore, Eleanor Smith, Janice Sumler-Lewis (later Sumler-Edmond), and Rosalyn Terborg-Penn, decided to affiliate with the ASALH. The steering committee agreed to hold annual meetings in conjunction with the ASALH convention and resolved to organize at least three sessions on Black Women's History. In addition, the ASALH launched a newsletter, *Truth*, which was initially published by Darlene Clark Hine. The ASALH's official organ is published at least three times a year.

The organization was officially named the Association of Black Women Historians in 1979. About fifty African American women attended the first meeting held during the ASALH convention in New York City. A nominations committee, chaired by Janet Sims-Wood, was elected at this meeting. The first elected officers began their two-year term in 1980 with the following executive council members: national director, Rosalyn Terborg-Penn; director-elect, Darlene Clark Hine; secretary, Janice Sumler-Lewis; treasurer, Bettye J. Gardner; director of publications, Sharon Harley; membership director, Cheryl Johnson (later Cheryl Johnson-Odom); Eastern regional director, Marquita L. James; Southern region director, Sylvia M. Jacobs; Midwestern regional director, Juanita Moore; Western regional director, Maria A. Brown; and parliamentarian, Cynthia Neverdon-Morton. In later years the constitution was amended to change the composition of the executive council. Past national directors have been Nell Irvin Painter, Sylvia M. Jacobs, Janice Sumler-Lewis (Edmond), Johnetta G. Richards, Jacqueline A. Rouse, and Barbara A. Woods.

In fostering the growth of black women's history, the ABWH started to collaborate with the Organization of American Historians (OAH) in 1980. Under the leadership of Darlene Clark Hine of the ABWH and Gerda Lerner of the OAH, the Fund to Improve Post-Secondary Education (FIPSE) funded a series of regional workshops for students and college teachers interested in developing the field.

The following year, the ABWH incorporated in the District of Columbia as a nonprofit association. The year 1981 also marked the first of the ABWH luncheons, held annually during the ASALH conventions. Mary Frances Berry was the first of many distinguished speakers to deliver the keynote address. Even presidential candidate Bill Clinton addressed the organization briefly during the 1992 luncheon held in Detroit. The luncheon serves as an opportunity to honor the many members of the organization and the profession.

In 1983 the ABWH's efforts to promote networks and scholarship in black women's history resulted in a National Endowment for the Humanities grant that provided funding for a research conference on "Women in the African Diaspora: An Interdisciplinary Perspective." Held at Howard University in the District of Columbia under the leadership of project director Rosalyn Terborg-Penn, this was the first scholarly conference of its kind. It drew an international audience of participants who shared their research and discussed the emerging field of African Diaspora women's history.

The ABWH administers four awards, three of which are sponsored by the membership. The publication prize award was created in 1983 by National Director Nell Painter to recognize excellence in scholarship. The prize was named to honor the late black woman historian Letitia Woods Brown. Other awards recognize books, anthologies, and articles written about black women's history or by black women historians. In 1987 National Director Sylvia Jacobs announced the creation of the Lorraine Anderson Williams Leadership Award, named for the late Howard University educator, to honor black women leaders who mentor and provide black women historians with role models. The Drusilla Dunjee Houston Scholarship was created in 1989 by Paul Coates, the publisher of Black Classic Press, during the tenure of Janice Sumler-Edmond as national director. The scholarship celebrates the life and work of Houston, a teacher, journalist, and lay historian. The award, presented to an outstanding black woman graduate student, is administered by the ABWH, which matched the grant in 1994, so that now two annual awards are given, one to a master's degree candidate and one to a Ph.D. candidate.

Through these various vehicles, the ABWH fosters its goal to advance the study of black women's history and to establish a network among the membership of men and women from various ethnic groups. Twenty years after the initial organizational effort in 1977, the ABWH serves several hundred members.

**FURTHER READINGS**

Sumler-Edmond, Janice. "Association of Black Women Historians, Inc." In *Black Women in America: An Historical Encyclopedia*. Ed. Darlene Clark Hine, et al. Bloomington: Indiana University Press, 1994.

Terborg-Penn, Rosalyn. "A History of the Association of Black Women Historians, 1977–1981." *Truth: Newsletter of the Association of Black Women Historians* (Special Issue 1981): 4–5.

*Rosalyn Terborg-Penn*

## Association of Colleges and Secondary Schools for Negroes

The Association of Colleges and Secondary Schools for Negroes (ACSSN) emerged in 1934 from the Association of Colleges for Negro Youth (ACNY), founded in 1913. The ACSSN served as an accreditation body for African American educational institutions from 1934 through 1964.

The ACSSN and its predecessor were established in response to the exclusion of African American schools from membership in the Southern Association of Colleges and Secondary Schools (Southern Association), organized in 1895. The ACSSN evaluated African American educational institutions using the same standards as the Southern Association. In 1948, the ACSSN formed a committee to seek membership in the all-white Southern Association. Yet it was not until 1957 that the Southern Association granted membership to black educational institutions. That year, fifteen African American colleges and three junior colleges joined the Southern Association. Fourteen additional black colleges were admitted in 1958. The Southern Association's decision to admit African American educational institutions was aided by the Supreme Court's 1954 *Brown* decision, which ruled that separate educational facilities were "inherently unequal," and a study conducted by the organization in 1955. The study, funded by the General Education Board (GEB), a philanthropic organization that provided funds for educational initiatives without discrimination based on race, sex, or creed, examined whether African American educational institutions

met the standards applied to other members of the Southern Association.

In 1964, encouraged by the passage of the Civil Rights Act, the ACSSN decided to disband because of the growing number of African American educational institutions with full membership in the Southern Association and the increasing number of African American students enrolled in predominantly "white" institutions.

**FURTHER READINGS**

Association of Colleges and Secondary Schools, Manuscript Collection, Atlanta University Library, Atlanta.

Cozart, Leland Stanford. *A History of the Association of Colleges and Secondary Schools, 1934–1965*. Charlotte, N.C.: Heritage Printers, 1967.

*Thalia M. Mulvihill*

## Association of Colleges for Negro Youth

*See* Association of Colleges and Secondary Schools for Negroes.

## Association of Deans of Women and Advisers to Girls in Negro Schools

The Association of Deans of Women and Advisers to Girls in Negro Schools (ADWAGNS) professionalized academic positions for women employed in African American colleges and high schools. For twenty-five years, the association promoted higher education for black women, especially for administrators. The office of dean of women was established in the 1920s, and most college leaders misunderstood the position's responsibilities.

Lucy Diggs Slowe (1885–1936), Howard University's first permanent dean of women, expressed her concern about the role of female African American faculty and students on campuses. She emphasized that women educators and staff members were not selected for influential administrative positions and that they endured poor pay and living conditions.

As founder of the National Association of College Women (NACW), Slowe arranged a conference of deans and advisers of girls in African American schools sponsored by the NACW committee on standards. Women from ten black colleges and schools gathered at Howard University on March 1 and 2, 1929, to establish what would eventually be called the ADWAGNS.

Initially, the women identified five problems on which they focused. They were primarily concerned that few

African American women were policy-making administrators or school trustees. They stressed the need for female deans and advisers to have professional academic credentials equivalent to those expected for men hired for similar positions and that the women must receive pay equal to their male colleagues and have professional autonomy.

Also, the women deplored the quality of college housing for female students and criticized the lack of equipment and the poor conditions of existing facilities. They protested the absence of wholesome recreational and extracurricular activities for college girls, especially in comparison to services provided for male students. Finally, they noted the need for separate housing, activities, and regulations for girls attending high schools located on college campuses.

From 1930 to 1934, the African American women deans and advisers met annually at the NACW conference, discussing mutual concerns. Slowe chaired all of these meetings, and in 1935, she arranged for a conference at Howard University where the women decided to create an independent organization. At the first official group conference in 1936, which was the women's seventh meeting, Slowe was elected president, serving until her death in 1937.

The association did not meet that year and almost ceased to exist without Slowe's leadership. Several of the women who had participated since the first meeting in 1929 urged the others to continue Slowe's work. Georgia Myrtle Teale was voted president, and an annual conference was scheduled in 1938 at Tuskegee Institute. At this meeting, the women approved a constitution and agreed on the name ADWAGNS.

The association's goals were to promote cooperation and unity amongst deans and advisers who sought to obtain professional recognition and status. All female African American deans, advisers, and counselors were welcomed to join. Together, the women debated how to counsel and provide for female students' educational needs.

In 1946, the women deans agreed to stage a joint conference with the National Association of Personnel Deans and Advisers of Men in Negro Institutions to discuss similar concerns. By 1954, members of both groups voted to merge, and the combined group ultimately was called the National Association of Personnel Workers.

During its twenty-five year history, the ADWAGNS provided professional encouragement to its members, teaching them how to deal with college politics and pursue their goals. Denied participation in white administrative associations, African American women obtained a voice in higher education through the ADWAGNS. The association aided them to battle conservative, restrictive attitudes toward women on campus. Through this organization, the position of dean metamorphosed from a matron concerned with students' moral and physical health to a professional administrator, specializing in women's education.

**FURTHER READINGS**

Davis, Hilda A., and Patricia Bell-Scott. "The Association of Deans of Women and Advisers to Girls in Negro Schools, 1929–1954: A Brief Oral History." *Sage* (Summer 1989).

Noble, Jeanne L. *The Negro Woman's College Education.* New York: Bureau of Publications Teachers College, Columbia University, 1956.

Pierce, Anna Eloise. *Deans and Advisers of Women and Girls.* New York: Professional & Technical Press, 1928.

Slowe, Lucy D. "What Is a Dean of Women?" *Journal of the National Association of College Women* (April 1926).

———. "Summary of the Conference of Deans and Advisers to Women in Colored Schools." *Journal of the National Association of College Women* (April 1928).

———. "The Dean of Women in a Modern University." *The Howard University Alumni Journal* (December 1933).

*Elizabeth D. Schafer*

# Association of Southern Women for the Prevention of Lynching

White southern women established the Association of Southern Women for the Prevention of Lynching (ASWPL) in 1930. That year, the Commission on Interracial Cooperation (CIC), concerned about the increase in lynchings, had created a Sub-Committee on the Study of Lynching. The CIC invited the leaders of southern white women's civic and religious organizations to discuss the prevention of lynchings at a meeting in Atlanta, Georgia. On November 1, 1930, twenty-six women gathered for a one-day seminar on the findings of the CIC's Sub-Committee. Twenty-five of the seminar participants signed a declaration proclaiming their intentions to challenge mob violence.

Following the Atlanta meeting, twelve of the women, Mrs. W. C. Winsborough, Mrs. W. A. Turner, Una Roberts Lawrence, Mrs. R. L. Harris, Mrs. W. A. Newell, Mrs. J. Morgan Stevens, Mrs. Ernest Moore, Louise Young, Maud Palmer, Mrs. J. H. McCoy, Mrs. Buford Boykin, and Jessie Daniel Ames, launched the ASWPL. Ames, an active member of the CIC, served as the ASWPL's executive director. The ASWPL consisted of a central council of ten to twelve members who formulated the organization's policies and an executive committee that implemented them on a day-to-day basis. State councils, composed of five members, were responsible for coordinating efforts at the state level.

The ASWPL relied largely on moral persuasion to convince white southerners to challenge lynchings. By undermining the belief that the defense of southern white womanhood was the basis for most lynchings, the organization sought to dispute one of the underpinnings for lynching across the South. The ASWPL's fixation on this strategy, however, eventually led to dissension among its members and supporters.

Most of the founders of the ASWPL were leaders of Protestant organizations and clubs. The ASWPL's largest support group was the Methodist Women's Missionary council, which consisted of hundreds of women's auxiliaries affiliated with Methodist churches across the South. The largest civic group supporting the ASWPL was the Young Women's Christian Association (YWCA). In addition to Christian-based organizations, the ASWPL received assistance from the Federation of Jewish Women as well as business and professional women's clubs.

Pleased that white southern women were taking an active role in the fight against lynchings, the black press as well as civil rights groups and African American leaders applauded the formation of the ASWPL. Tuskegee Institute, the National Association for the Advancement of Colored People (NAACP), and numerous small groups working for racial advancement announced their approval and support of the ASWPL. Most black women, although they were not allowed to join the all-white ASWPL, understood the need for white women to be at the forefront of their own organization and supported the ASWPL. Despite the ASWPL's policy of racial exclusion, members of the organization met sporadically with African American women in an effort to promote goodwill and understanding. While the ASWPL had a large and diverse support base, differences regarding leadership and policy often divided supporters and members of the organization.

Active members of the ASWPL came largely from the ranks of the white middle and upper class and the vast majority of them lived in the urban centers of the South. Approximately 72 percent of the organization's members lived in cities with more than 25,000 residents while 49 percent lived in urban areas with a population over 100,000. Following the ASWPL's formation, the organi-

zation's leadership recognized the need for the participation of rural southern women. Through the efforts of the ASWPL's Mississippi State Council, these women soon became the bulwark of the organization.

Members of the Mississippi State Council contacted leaders of the state's women's clubs and requested that they sign the ASWPL's anti-lynching resolutions. Club leaders were not only responsible for obtaining the signatures of their members but also those of other residents of their communities. Within a year, the Mississippi State Council collected 700 signatures in support of the ASWPL's efforts to prevent lynchings. The ASWPL also instructed local club leaders to contact the organization after lynchings occurred or if they believed that lynchings were eminent in their communities. In a few rare instances, some white women tried to prevent lynchings by contacting law enforcement officers or urging mob leaders to refrain from violence. More often, however, these women collected information about the causes and the events leading up to lynchings. This information provided the ASWPL with crucial data and enabled the organization to compile detailed statistics that it used in its struggle to prevent lynchings.

After mobilizing state residents, the Mississippi State Council set out to obtain the support of police officials. Concerned that many law enforcement officers either participated in lynchings or stood idly by during mob violence, ASWPL supporters asked sheriffs to sign a resolution affirming their support of law and order and their dedication to the prevention of vigilante justice. The ASWPL was convinced that proper criminal investigations would serve to clear those who were accused falsely of rape or murder and would lead to the conviction of those who were guilty.

When the Mississippi State Council presented its list of signatures in support of the ASWPL's efforts to prevent lynchings at the association's first annual convention, the ASWPL quickly applied the Mississippi plan to the states with the highest lynching rates. Following Mississippi's lead, ASWPL supporters in Florida, Georgia, and Texas soon gathered large numbers of signatures and built strong memberships in those states. An average of 6,000 individuals signed the ASWPL's anti-lynching resolutions each year, and at the time of the association's demise in 1942, the ASWPL had gathered the signatures of over four million individuals.

The ASWPL expanded the signature drive to include local and state elected officials as well as state governors. Thus, ASWPL members, at least indirectly, entered the domain of politics and government. ASWPL members, for example, wrote letters to governors, encouraging them to mobilize state troops to disperse lynch mobs and to call on district attorneys to prosecute lynchers. In addition to letters targeting political officials, the ASWPL attempted to exert influence on elected administrators. The ASWPL, for example, listed in its bulletin elected sheriffs who failed to prevent lynchings as participants in vigilante hostilities and threatened to remove them from office for failure to perform their duties.

While the ASWPL used the Mississippi plan to create a base of mass support, it also sought to thwart lynchings through public education. Informing the public was a crucial concern of ASWPL members who believed that they could end lynchings through moral persuasion. In an effort to educate the public and create a climate conducive to the eradication of lynchings, ASWPL members presented lectures at colleges and high schools, offered training institutes on lynchings, and wrote letters to newspaper editors criticizing them for publishing inaccurate reports. The ASWPL sent thousands of flyers, pamphlets, and articles containing statistics about lynchings and antilynching resolutions to its members and supporters. The ASWPL even sponsored contests soliciting fictional works on lynching and distributed them to the public.

The ASWPL's public education campaign and its political activities fostered moral persuasion as a strategy for ending lynchings. The ASWPL's efforts helped to change the opinions of many white southerners who regarded lynching as a viable and necessary tool for the protection of white womanhood. By educating the public about the underlying causes of lynchings, the ASWPL moved the focus from white women to white men. The organization, based on its investigations and interviews, found that lynchings were often instigated by southern planters and landowners as a form of economic control. It was an effort to gain and maintain cheap labor by limiting and preventing job competition between lower-class whites and blacks. The ASWPL argued that if white southerners were to rely on the judicial system to punish alleged black perpetrators, they would realize that lynchings did not serve to protect southern white womanhood but the economic interests and labor needs of the white landowning elite. In addition, allowing jurisprudence to run its course would assist in changing the dominant perception of the South as lagging behind the North in civility. In effect, the ASWPL hoped to end lynching by appealing to reason, logic, and fairness.

The 1933 Scottsboro case, however, shattered the ASWPL's unequivocal faith in the judicial system and di-

vided its membership. That year, two white women in Scottsboro, Alabama, accused nine black men of rape. While it was clear that the men had been accused falsely, the South was not prepared to deal with the issue of consensual sex between black men and white women and neither was the ASWPL. Some ASWPL members, appalled by the judicial process, called the Scottsboro case a legal lynching and demanded that the organization draft an official statement denouncing the obstruction of justice. ASWPL executive director Jessie Daniel Ames and her supporters, however, advocated continued support of the judicial system. While they agreed that the defendants did not receive a fair trial, they feared that the public would misconstrue any challenge of the Scottsboro case as support of the International Labor Defense (ILD), the communist organization that provided the defense attorneys for the nine black men. Ames and her followers, however, were determined to avoid any association with the ILD, afraid that it would alienate southern supporters of the ASWPL and aggravate the question of consensual sex between the accusers and defendants. Although the ASWPL did not officially support the defense in the Scottsboro case, the organization finally settled on writing a letter to Alabama's governor expressing concern about the due process in the case.

While the Scottsboro case shook the foundation of the ASWPL, it was the controversy generated by the NAACP-sponsored Costigan-Wagner Bill that inflicted irreparable damage on the organization. The 1933 Costigan-Wagner Bill empowered the federal government to prosecute participants of mob violence whenever local law enforcement officials failed to exercise their authority, to fine or jail officers who failed to discharge their duties, and to assess damage claims against counties where lynchings occurred. The NAACP garnered the support of the African American community, the CIC, the YWCA, the Women's Division of the Federal Council of Churches, the National Council of Jewish Women, and the Methodist Women's Missionary Council, the ASWPL's largest supporter. The ASWPL, however, did not support the Costigan-Wagner Bill.

Ames, convinced that cooperation between federal and local agencies was the key to the prevention of lynchings, feared that adoption of the bill would anger southerners who resented federal intervention in state affairs. Moreover, she worried that once the bill became law it would undermine the ASWPL's efforts to use moral persuasion to alter the attitudes of white southerners. Many ASWPL members did not agree with Ames's assessment and neither did many of the organization's major supporters in the

African American community, including the NAACP, the black press, and African American female members of the CIC, all of whom attacked Ames and her supporters.

Initial attempts to pass the Costigan-Wagner Bill failed; however, in 1938 the bill was reintroduced. This time, Ames exacerbated tensions in the ASWPL when she wrote Texas congressman and friend, Senator Tom Connaly, expressing her support of his efforts to abort the bill. Connaly released her letter to the press to support his claim that the southern public was opposed to the bill. By that time, black leaders and organizations had already begun to distance themselves from Ames and the ASWPL. The letter, however, caused the final break between the ASWPL and its African American supporters and created a rift among the organization's members. The YWCA and the National Council of Jewish Women withdrew their support of the ASWPL. The Methodist Women's Missionary Council continued to work with the ASWPL; however, many of its members were critical of Ames's opposition to the Costigan-Wagner Bill.

In 1942, the ASWPL officially ceased to function. Invoking the ASWPL's charter, which required that the organization disband two years after lynchings ended, Ames declared that the organization had fulfilled its mission. She announced that her decision to disband the ASWPL was based on the absence of newspaper reports of lynchings. African American organizations, however, questioned the reliability of her sources. Tuskegee Institute, in particular, which had gathered the most detailed statistics on lynchings and had provided the ASWPL with much of its information, challenged Ames' decision. Tuskegee Institute pointed out that newspapers often failed to print stories of lynchings and insisted that the existence of eye-witness reports documented the continued occurrence of lynchings in the South.

Although the ASWPL's charter influenced Ames's decision to disband the organization, other factors also played a role in the disintegration of the ASWPL. The outbreak of World War II certainly distracted many Americans from internal problems. More important though, the dissatisfaction with Ames and her management style initiated an internal and external struggle for control of the ASWPL. As the CIC began the process of reorganizing as the Southern Regional Council, opponents of Ames tried to prevent her from assuming a leadership role in the new organization and as a result phased out the ASWPL, which had been a CIC affiliate.

The ASWPL's effect on southern society remains vague at best. Convinced that the American justice system was essentially fair, the ASWPL served largely as an enforcer of law and order, rather than as an initiator of fundamental change. But perhaps the ASWPL's effort to use moral persuasion and education helped undermine popular perceptions of southern white women as helpless victims and indirectly challenged and redefined the role of southern white men as their protectors. Thus, the ASWPL's most important impact may have been its role in changing gender perceptions among southern white men and women.

**FURTHER READINGS**

Ames, Jessie Daniel. *Southern Women and Lynching*. Atlanta: Association of Southern Women for the Prevention of Lynching, 1936.

———. *Southern Women Look at Lynching*. Atlanta: Association of Southern Women for the Prevention of Lynching, 1937.

Dudley, Julius Wayne. "A History of the Association of Southern Women for the Prevention of Lynching, 1930–1942." Ph.D. diss., University of Cincinnati, 1979.

Hall, Jacquelyn Dowd. *Revolt Against Chivalry: Jessie Daniel Ames and the Women's Campaign Against Lynching*. New York: Columbia University Press, 1979.

*Nishani Frazier*

# Atlanta Conferences for the Study of Negro Problems

These annual conferences gathered at Atlanta University between 1896 and 1914 to conduct a systematic study of the "Negro and his development." Influenced by the annual conferences hosted by the Hampton and Tuskegee Institutes that began in the early 1890s, Boston philanthropist and Atlanta University trustee George C. Bradford proposed that the university sponsor a new series of conferences to investigate the condition of the urban black population. University president Horace Bumstead agreed, and in 1896 the Atlanta Conference of the Study of Negro Problems, also known as Atlanta University Studies, began. Bradford recruited the secretarial and research skills of three recent graduates and later race notables, James W. Johnson, Butler Wilson, and George A. Towns, to develop and distribute questionnaires concerning the general living conditions of African Americans in nine cities. The results of this research provided the foundation for the first two conferences, the 1896 Study on Morality and the 1897 Study on the Social and Physical Conditions of Urban Blacks. Couched in the biases of

Bradford and Bumstead, both reports suggested that the unfavorable conditions that plagued African Americans was due in large part to their ignorance and disregard for laws and not as a result of social and political ostracism they suffered at the hands of whites. The tone of the conferences would change dramatically after Bumstead recruited W. E. B. Du Bois to join Atlanta University and to take charge of the annual study series.

In late 1897, the series came under the direction of Du Bois who "without thought or consultation" broadened the focus of the conferences to include all possible topics in the field of race. He believed that the new focus would allow for a more comprehensive decennial study of the "American Negro" that would explore annually in each decade the important issues of education, employment, religion, morality, family, crime, mortality, etc., and repeat the same program in the succeeding decade making the necessary changes to the topics of study and methodology. Funded solely through philanthropy, the event would take place in late May of every year and feature the best minds in the world. The findings of each conference would be published in a report that would collectively form the most "current encyclopedia on the American Negro problems."

Du Bois's influence on the purpose and conclusions of the annual meetings were immediately apparent. The reports provocatively demonstrated the shackling effect of slavery and segregation on the advancements of African Americans. While boasting the remarkable achievements of blacks in such areas of business and education, the findings of conference participants underscored the disparate avenues of opportunities of white and black citizens and the need for American society to break down the barriers that race constructed. Endorsements for the conference were abundant not only from within the white and African American communities but also from abroad. The most notable of these praises came from Lymann Abbott's *Outlook* in 1903, which stated that "no student of the race problem, no person who would either think or speak upon it intelligently, can afford to be ignorant of the facts brought out in the Atlanta series."

Soon, Du Bois was overwhelmed by the task of conducting the study and organizing the conference in addition to maintaining a demanding public-speaking schedule while organizing the Niagara movement. In 1908, Du Bois solicited the help of one of his most successful and most able students, Augustus Dill, a notable sociologist. From 1908 until 1910, Dill collaborated on each Atlanta University study with his mentor, bringing his talent and enthusiasm to the project. When Du Bois decided to leave Atlanta in order to organize the National Association for the Advancement of Colored People (NAACP) in New York, Dill took over the reins, continuing the conference despite dwindling funds. The conference series ceased in 1914 when Du Bois asked Dill to join him in New York as the business manager of the NAACP's *The Crisis*. As Du Bois later noted, "These studies with all their imperfection were widely distributed in the libraries of the world and used by scholars. It may be said without undue boasting that between 1896 and 1920 there was no study of the race problem in America made which did not depend in some degree upon the investigation made at Atlanta University; often they were widely quoted and commended."

## FURTHER READINGS

Du Bois, W. E. B. *Dusk of Dawn: An Essay Toward an Autobiography of a Race Concept.* New York: Schocken Books,1968; rpt., New Brunswick, N.J.: Transaction Publishers, 1983.

Lewis, David Levering. *W. E. B. Du Bois: Biography of a Race, 1868–1919.* New York: Henry Holt and Company, 1993.

*Kimberly E. Nichols*

## Atlanta Negro Voters League

The Atlanta Negro Voters League (ANVL) organized the city's African American electorate and sought improvements for the black community from 1949 until the early 1960s. Founded on July 7, 1949, the ANVL was an umbrella organization of affiliated neighborhood, women's, church, and other local interest groups. A. T. Walden, president of the city's National Association for the Advancement of Colored People from 1924 to 1936 and a prominent civil rights attorney, and John Wesley Dobbs, a prominent Mason and retired federal postal employee, co-chaired the executive committee. Walden, a Democrat, and Dobbs, a Republican, established the bipartisan organization in order to harness the potential of the city's black electorate, which comprised 30 percent of Atlanta's registered voters in 1949.

The ANVL executive committee included the wealthiest and most influential African American professional men in Atlanta. Before the primaries, they screened candidates for various city posts, and shortly before election day, they advertized their slate from pulpits, in the black *Atlanta Daily World*, and over the city's black radio station,

WERD. The ANVL also arranged car pools to the polls and held mass meetings to rally the community and demonstrate mechanical voting booth procedures.

The executive committee endorsed candidates who were most sympathetic to the ANVL's goals, which included African American representation in all branches of city administration; increased employment opportunities for blacks in municipal jobs; hiring of black policemen and firemen; repeal of segregation ordinances; improvement of public services and facilities for black neighborhoods; and implementation of school integration.

During the ANVL's existence, Atlanta primaries consistently pitted an arch-segregationist against several white moderates. Because the black vote was not large enough to elect a black candidate who could win in the general election, the ANVL executive committee decided to support white moderates. Recognizing that African American voters represented the balance of power against a strong-running racist, white moderates competed for ANVL endorsement. The ANVL never picked a loser for Atlanta mayor. Its votes assured William B. Hartsfield his second, third, and fourth terms in 1949, 1953, and 1957, and Ivan Allen Jr. his first in 1961.

During the administrations of these racial moderates, conditions in Atlanta's African American community improved as they provided better housing and lighting in the black business district and moved to implement several other of the ANVL's goals. In 1953, with the help of moderate white voters, Atlanta University president Rufus Clement joined the Atlanta Board of Education to become the first black city-wide elected official. The druggist Miles Amos and A. T. Walden won bids to represent their heavily black districts on the city executive committee—the body responsible for conducting elections.

The ANVL did not vote as solidly in the primaries as in the general elections. Walden worked hard to maintain the appearance of a united black community, but in 1953, even the executive committee showed solidarity problems. Co-chairman Dobbs split with the ANVL over Hartsfield's endorsement, citing the mayor's foot dragging on promises he had made to the African American community. In 1954, the Reverend William M. Jackson of Bethlehem Baptist Church replaced Dobbs as the Republican leader, and he and Walden remained in charge through 1961.

In the early 1960s, Atlanta's African American community clearly split over the pace of civil rights reform. The city's students in particular resisted domination by older leaders who so thoroughly controlled the ANVL executive committee. This trend weakened the ANVL's influence during the early 1960s, and by the time of Walden's death in 1965, Atlanta's black leadership was more fractured than ever.

**FURTHER READINGS**

*Atlanta Daily World*, 1949–1965.

Austin T. Walden Papers, Atlanta Negro Voters League Files, Atlanta Historical Society, Atlanta, Georgia.

Stone, Clarence N. *Regime Politics: Governing Atlanta, 1946–1988*. Lawrence: University of Kansas Press, 1989.

*Mary G. Rolinson*

## Atlanta Neighborhood Union

The Atlanta Neighborhood Union (ANU), a prototype for self-help and social service organizations, was initiated by black women during the Progressive Era. In July 1908, Lugenia Burns Hope, wife of the president of Morehouse College, invited to her home eight middle-class women to discuss the need for settlement activities in Atlanta's underprivileged black neighborhoods. The meeting resulted in the formation of committees that collected demographic data to assess community concerns and to help plan ANU programs.

Adopting the motto "Thy Neighbor as Thyself," the ANU launched a variety of programs during its first year. It organized classes focusing on many facets of home and personal care, sponsored health clinics, visited the sick, provided entertainment for girls, and coordinated special after-school activities for children. In 1909 the ANU boldly began its political activism by circulating and submitting a petition to Atlanta's City Council to rid the community of "a house of questionable character." Throughout its existence, the ANU continued to rely on petitions as a strategy for effecting legislative change.

Increased attention to political and economic issues prompted the ANU to seek incorporation in March 1911. Within a year, the union extended its services to fourteen black neighborhoods in Atlanta. The organizational structure of the ANU ensured that the group's expansion did not weaken the quality of its programs. Hope, who served as ANU president during the early years, led a Board of Management, Board of Directors, neighborhood committees, and directors in charge of districts. No organizational component, however, was considered more important than the membership.

In September 1915, after outgrowing several sites, the ANU opened a Neighborhood House staffed with a paid director and several employees. Initially, the ANU financed its program goals through membership dues and fund-raisers. In 1920, the city provided some funds for health care programs for preschoolers. Improved educational facilities, community health campaigns, neighborhood beautification, and the replication of the ANU as a model in other states were key union objectives through 1925.

For more than six decades the women of the ANU helped to improve the quality of life for African Americans in Atlanta. The ANU disbanded during the 1970s.

FURTHER READINGS

Neverdon-Morton, Cynthia. *Afro-American Women of the South and the Advancement of the Race, 1895–1925*. Knoxville: University of Tennessee Press, 1989.

Record of the Neighborhood Union, Archives Department, Trevor Arnett Library, Atlanta University, Atlanta.

Rouse, Jacqueline. *Lugenia Burns Hope: Black Southern Reformer*. Athens: University of Georgia Press, 1989.

*Cynthia Neverdon-Morton*

## Atlanta University Studies

*See* Atlanta Conferences for the Study of Negro Problems.

# B

## Baltimore: Civic, Literary, and Mutual Aid Associations

In 1860, Maryland had a population of 83,922 "free people of color," the largest number of them residing in Baltimore. The city's free blacks had started to create numerous associations to address their myriad interests and needs in the early nineteenth century. At times, the programs and activities initiated by Baltimore's free African Americans also involved the city's slave population. Whites often perceived this interaction between slaves and free African Americans as a threat to the institution of slavery and enacted restrictive laws to limit the formation of black associations. Despite these repressive efforts, black associations blossomed in Baltimore.

As early as 1835 the city's free black population operated more than thirty mutual aid societies, each boasting a membership of 35 to 150 persons. The societies, some secret in nature, incorporated the concept of extended kinship while providing financial assistance, social programs, and various activities. The Baltimore Bethel Benevolent Society of the Young Men of Color, founded in 1821, was the first society of its kind in the city. Other early societies included the African Friendship Benevolent Society for Social Relief, Star in the East Association, Daughters of Jerusalem Association, and the Masonic Order-Friendship Lodge No. 6.

The majority of Baltimore's black societies had open membership policies; but some groups had specific requirements based on gender or occupation. The Baltimore's Caulkers' Association, founded in 1838 as a trade union and mutual aid society, for example, organized black shipyard workers and used its influence to become the collective bargaining agent with the city's shipyard owners. Funds accrued by Baltimore's black societies were largely deposited in the two savings banks that free African Americans had established by the 1840s.

The steady increase in the number of free African Americans and the proliferation of black societies troubled whites, who responded with restrictive legal measures. In 1842, the state of Maryland passed a law making the membership of free African Americans in secret societies a felony. The law imposed a fine of no less than fifty dollars on blacks and whites for attempting to form them or for trying to induce African Americans to join them. Half the fine was paid to the informer and the other half was placed in the state's coffers. Convicted offenders who failed to pay their fines faced the prospect of being sold for a term of service sufficient to pay the fine. In case of a second offence, the law stipulated that individuals be sold into slavery out of state or given fifty-nine lashes on the back.

Many of Baltimore's residents objected to the passage of the 1842 law, but they did not have enough votes in the Maryland General Assembly to defeat the bill. In 1845, based on the testimony of highly respected white citizens, a bill to modify the 1842 law passed the Maryland Senate. Proponents of the modification argued that the 1842 law prevented many honest and industrious African Americans from forming beneficial societies for the relief of the destitute members of their race, a responsibility that could fall upon the state if African Americans did not assume it. After considerable debate in both houses of the assembly, the 1845 bill passed, ruling that free African Americans of good character who paid at least five dollars in taxes could form charitable societies with written permission from the mayor of Baltimore. Permits were issued annually, with the provision that all black association meetings were subject to police inspection. Yet an 1846 Maryland Act prohibited the incorporation of black lyceums, Masonic and other lodges, fire companies, and literary, dramatic, social, moral, and charitable societies.

In spite of legal efforts to limit the freedom of Baltimore's free black community, the city's African American residents persisted in the development of mutual aid societies. Their determination to create black associations was a testament to their sense of community and their recognition that joint efforts would more readily assure the continuation of programs designed to ensure the survival of the members of their race.

While black societies attended to various needs of their members and the larger African American community, their paramount concern was educational programs. Recognized by a black Baptist minister in 1847 as "advanced in education, quite beyond what I had conceived of," Baltimore's free population established numerous church Sabbath schools and by 1860 had opened fifteen secular schools. Not surprisingly, the literacy rate among Baltimore's black residents was very high. Prior to the Civil War, 70 percent of the city's black population under the age of thirty and more than 40 percent of those older than thirty were literate.

Baltimore's black literary clubs, debating societies, and lyceums, however, not only tried to raise the educational level of African Americans but also hoped to provide "moral and mental uplift." The Young Men's Mental Improvement Society for the Discussion of Moral and Philosophical Questions of All Kinds and the Phoenix Society were two of the earliest. Through membership in debating and literary clubs, free blacks sought to develop skills essential for personal growth and community enhancement. Yet membership in literary societies more than in other associations was often based on social and occupational status, and at times those who claimed free-born status excluded recently freed slaves. Despite class differences, the very nature of urban life in a slave society promoted group cohesiveness and racial solidarity.

In the years following the Civil War, black residents of Baltimore made economic, social, and political gains, yet they still faced significant challenges fueled by racism. As racial discrimination persisted, the city's African American population expanded its self-help initiatives. A growing number of mutual aid societies assisted members who faced financial hardship and provided varied socialization opportunities. In 1884, at a joint meeting of many of the black societies, forty of them reported a combined membership of 2,100. The Friendly Beneficial Society, Union Star of the Rising Generation, and Barbers' Society reported more than

$290,000 in assets derived from membership dues of fifty cents a week.

By 1900, African Americans operated more than seventy mutual aid societies in Baltimore. Among the most popular groups were secret societies, such as the Samaritans, Nazarites, Galilean Fisherman, and Wise Men, all with a strong religious underpinning. These groups used their membership dues to provide funds to purchase buildings, bury members, and stage social activities. The work of these groups illustrates the interaction among black cultural, self-help, and religious institutions.

As the number and size of black mutual aid and benevolent societies expanded, so did their mission. The Independent Order of St. Luke, established by former slave Mary Prout in 1867, best symbolizes the transformation of black mutual aid societies from benevolence to community service. The order expanded its original mission of benevolent assistance to include youth programs and the development of savings institutions. Moreover, the order sought to represent a unified voice of protest against social ills. By 1920, African Americans established chapters of the order in other states, and soon the accomplishments of the Virginia chapter overshadowed the efforts of the Baltimore group. With a reported membership of over twenty thousand black men and women, the Virginia chapter founded the *St. Luke Herald Newspaper* and the St. Luke Bank and Trust Company in Richmond, Virginia.

In addition to mutual aid, benevolent, and community service groups, black residents of Baltimore also launched civil rights organizations. Following the end of Reconstruction, as white southerners tried to reverse many of the gains that African Americans had made in the immediate postwar years, black Baltimoreans founded the city's first civil rights organization. In 1885, a corps of Baptist preachers, led by Harvey Johnson, pastor of the Union Baptist Church, founded the Mutual United Brotherhood of Liberty "to use all legal means within our power to procure and maintain our rights as citizens of this common country." Among the organization's first actions was a frontal attack against the "Black Laws" that legalized racial inequality. In 1888, the Brotherhood of Liberty succeeded in gaining the admission of qualified black males to the Maryland Bar.

In the 1890s, perhaps emboldened by the successful activities of the Brotherhood of Liberty, many of Baltimore's black civic organizations started to embrace politics as a means for racial advancement. Involvement in the political process also sparked the formation of the Negro Suffrage League. Quickly, league chapters emerged throughout the state, and their members lobbied against discriminatory bills and threatened to boycott certain establishments and public transportation facilities if segregationist laws prevailed. League members rallied the public and private sectors of the larger community and sought the support of educators as well as business, fraternal, and religious leaders. The league kept the public abreast of its actions through the newspaper the *Afro-American*, which had been acquired by John H. Murphy, a former slave, in 1892. In 1902, the league led the movement that defeated the Poe amendment, which sought to disfranchise African Americans.

The franchise was a subject of discussion of many African American groups. The Du Bois Circle, founded in 1906 for "social uplift and higher literary attainment," championed not only the continuation of the vote for black males but in 1911 also started to support women's suffrage. The circle's membership consisted of thirty black women, most of whom were educators in the Baltimore public schools, who had served as hostesses at a public meeting at which W. E. B. Du Bois had explained the purpose of the Niagara Movement. The group often discussed topics of special interest to black women and in 1924 hosted a visit by the teacher, writer, and women's suffragist Alice Dunbar Nelson, who presented a lecture on the status of the colored woman in American politics. During the early years of its formation, circle meetings were held monthly between October and April in the homes of members. The May meeting was open to the public. Since its inception, the Du Bois Circle has accepted only professional women as members, and its membership number and format remain unchanged. Functioning principally as a literary society, members explore annual themes that enhance their intellectual development and empowerment. Most monthly topics are selected to illuminate some aspect of the annual theme. Although the circle expanded its mission in 1983 to "acquaint members with current academic, literary, political, and social issues and to urge participation in activities which enhance quality of life for others," it still remains true to its founding objective. Members remain committed to the idea that by becoming more informed citizens, they can provide service to others. The circle sponsors no organized outreach activities.

Just as the Du Bois Circle extended its intellectual interests to include discussions of contemporary affairs affecting the black community, so did other African American literary societies. In the 1890s, when a resurgence of the antebellum lyceum movement swept the United States, members of Baltimore's black middle class formed numerous literary societies. These groups, unlike their white counterparts, discussed not only literary works but also issues of concern to African Americans, such as "The Future of Our Boys and Girls," and "What Is the Cause of the Anti-Negro Spirit in the United States?" Some of the literary societies were affiliated with religious institutions; thus their membership was often not as exclusive and gender-based as the Du Bois Circle. For example, the Monumental Literary and Scientific Association, organized in 1885, was composed of men and women representing the city's various black churches.

Throughout the early twentieth century, Baltimore's African Americans joined the ranks of urban progressive reformers. They formed a large number of civic and social service organizations to remedy the many societal ills affecting the race. Black middle-class women were particularly active, establishing the Colored Empty Stocking and Fresh Air Circle, Day Nursery Association, and Women's Cooperative Civic League, which launched programs to improve the quality of life for African Americans of all ages. Generally operating with limited funds and an all-black membership, the civic and self-help groups accomplished much in spite of seemingly insurmountable opposition.

The Women's Cooperative Civic League, organized in 1913 at the invitation of the all-white Women's Civic League, had an all-black membership with an interracial advisory board. Under the leadership of Sarah Collins Fernandis, the league gave special attention to health, housing, and beautification issues affecting African Americans. The group was quite successful when it operated as an all-black organization but apparently lost its effectiveness when it merged with the all-white Women's Civic League during the throes of the civil rights movement. Following the merger, the league ceased to address concerns primarily affecting Baltimore's black community. Although the league is still in existence, its membership is predominantly white.

The civil rights movement, accelerated by the onset of World War II, politicized the programs and activities of many black civic associations in Baltimore. During the war, the city's veneer of racial harmony was stripped away to reveal a highly structured, segregated system enforced by Jim Crow laws. The *Afro-American* newspaper, accused by the FBI in its infamous *Survey of Racial Conditions in the United States* of agitating racial feelings by publishing militant articles, regularly printed studies of racial conditions that exposed inequities in employment, housing, education, and social justice.

Baltimore's black societies also challenged the city's discriminatory laws and practices when they staged a highly successful march on the state's capitol at Annapolis on April 23, 1942. Juanita J. Mitchell, the daughter of Lillie Carroll Jackson, who had helped to revitalize the Baltimore branch of the National Association for the Advancement of Colored People (NAACP), coordinated the march, which lobbied for civil rights and employment opportunities and protested against police brutality. Mitchell and Jackson's involvement thrust the NAACP branch into the national spotlight and left no doubt as to its pivotal role in the struggle to secure equity for Baltimore's black citizens.

In preparation for the march, Adam Clayton Powell Jr., the first African American to win election to the New York City Council, came to Baltimore the night before the thirty-five–mile trip to Annapolis to further energize an overflow audience at Sharp Street Methodist Church. Over two thousand individuals representing 150 black church, labor, business, political, and fraternal organizations filled both houses of the Maryland General Assembly as Jackson, Carl Murphy of the *Afro-American*, and other black leaders addressed legislators.

In response to the protest march, Governor Herbert R. O'Connor appointed the Commission on Problems Affecting the Negro Population. Jackson and Murphy were appointed to the commission, which presented its final report in March 1943. The commission submitted an extensive list of recommendations encouraging white employers to hire African Americans, urging the city to provide federal housing, and stressing the need for educational and vocational training programs for African Americans. Moreover, the commission appealed to Baltimoreans to prevent racial tensions as black migrants continued to flock to the city in search of employment in wartime defense industries.

As the end of the war neared, many African Americans remained optimistic that further gains could be made through participation in the political process. In March 1943, a group of black women, representing forty-nine of the state's most influential African American organizations and clubs, met to discuss ways to mobilize for postwar political activism. Concerned that the end of the war would increase racial tensions, raise segregation barriers, and limit job opportunities for blacks, the number one priority was to register as many African Americans as possible for the crucial national election of 1944.

By 1950 Baltimore's black community had undergone numerous changes stemming in part from wartime hiring initiatives. Many breakthroughs were the product of organizing and mediation efforts of black civic groups and Baltimore-based branches of national organizations such as the National Urban League and the NAACP.

Against the backdrop of the wartime gains was a profusion of problems compounded by the overwhelming numbers of migrants who continued to flock to Baltimore during the postwar years. Education, housing, and Jim Crow laws presented the most serious challenges. The overwhelming majority of African Americans, 92.6 percent, were confined to blighted spaces limited to a mere 9.5 percent of the city's area. Except for the Lyric Concert Hall, the Maryland Theater, public libraries, museums, and selected modes of public transportation, segregation was still the norm.

A plan of action, based on lessons learned during the war and dependent on continual involvement of African Americans from every economic and social stratum of the city, evolved in the 1950s. The plan called on black civic, fraternal, and special-interest organizations to demand racial progress and challenge segregation; to mobilize other minorities and interested whites to form a unified force against racism; to agitate for the passage of federal laws; to educate black workers about the benefits of affiliating with labor unions; and to inform citizens of the inherent power of bloc voting.

Since the 1970s, black churches, chapters of national sororities and fraternities, professional groups, and local branches of national organizations have undertaken numerous projects formerly spearheaded by civic and mutual aid societies. All too often, however, the new associations were not the product of grassroots efforts. Instead, they represented the efforts of affluent African Americans to elevate the less fortunate members of their race. Assisting in the funding of social service and self-help projects is the Associated Black Charities (ABC), one of two such organizations in the nation. Funded primarily by private donations, the ABC seeks to coordinate health and human services for African Americans residing in Maryland. Approximately 50 percent of its resources are allocated within Baltimore.

While economic and social stratifications have increasingly divided black residents of Baltimore during the last decades, many of the same issues that required concerted, unified action during the early twentieth century are still plaguing the city's black community. To address these problems, some city residents believe that components of past civic and mutual aid associations might serve as models for structuring strategies for community organizing and initiating a new self-help thrust.

FURTHER READINGS

Brackett, Jeffrey R. *The Negro in Maryland and Notes on the Progress of the Colored People of Maryland Since the War.* (Johns Hopkins University Studies in Historical and Political Science Eighth Series 7–9). Baltimore: Publication Agency of Johns Hopkins University, July-September, 1890.

Healy, Joseph P., chairman. *Report of the Governor's Commission on Problems Affecting the Negro Population.* Annapolis, Md.: State Publications Office, March 1943.

McConnell, Roland C. "The Black Experience in Maryland, 1634–1900." In *The Old Line State,* ed. Morris L. Writeoff. Annapolis, Md.: Hall of Records Commission, 1971, 405–432.

Neverdon-Morton, Cynthia. *Afro-American Women of the South and the Advancement of the Race, 1895–1925.* Knoxville: University of Tennessee Press, 1989.

Phillips, Christopher. *Freedom's Port: The African American Community of Baltimore, 1790–1860.* Urbana: University of Illinois Press, 1997.

*Cynthia Neverdon-Morton*

## Baltimore Association for the Moral and Educational Improvement of the Colored People

Responding to efforts of Baltimore Quakers to organize a freedmen's aid society for the state, white businessmen, philanthropists, and ministers launched the Baltimore Association for the Moral and Educational Improvement of the Colored People in November 1864. The association affiliated with major northern secular freedmen's aid societies to establish and support schools for African Americans in Maryland. Until its demise in 1870, the association established nearly one hundred schools throughout the state and a teacher training school in Baltimore for aspiring black teachers. Its goals were to meet the demand of the state's African American community for schools, while encouraging the state to assume public responsibility for black education.

Throughout its lifetime, the association received less than half its support from sources within Maryland; much of the funds it raised within the state came from the freedmen themselves, along with grants from the Baltimore city council. The majority of the association's monetary support came from northern aid societies, including the Pennsylvania Freedmen's Relief Commission, the New England Freedmen's Aid Society, and the American Freedmen's Union Commission, along with crucial

assistance from the Freedmen's Bureau. The bureau initially provided materials for new school buildings and subsidized the rent of existing schools. By the end of the decade, however, the bureau had assumed responsibility for many of the association's schools, particularly those in the state's southern counties, as the association's financial difficulties forced it to scale back its operations.

The year 1867 marked the high water mark for this Baltimore association. Its budget had more than quadrupled in two years. It supervised over eighty schools, with fifty more schools awaiting teachers. Although Baltimore took control of the schools within the city in that year, the association faced deficits by year's end. Northern aid societies, stretched to their limits and facing declining public interest in freedmen's education, retrenched. By 1869, the association supervised sixty schools but was deeply in debt. It ceased operations in June 1870.

The Baltimore association failed in its goal of encouraging the state of Maryland to accept responsibility for publicly supported African American education. It did, however, contribute significantly to black education. Many of the schools it relinquished in 1870 failed within two or three years, but many others continued to operate. Working together, the black teachers from the association's normal schools, the black trustees who had learned to supervise the schools, and the rural black communities managed to keep many of the schools in operation until years later, when the state of Maryland assumed responsibility for public education.

FURTHER READINGS

Butchart, Ronald E. *Northern Schools, Southern Blacks, and Reconstruction: Freedmen's Education, 1862–1875.* Westport, Conn.: Greenwood Press, 1980.

Fuke, Richard Paul. "The Baltimore Association for the Moral and Educational Improvement of the Colored People, 1864–1870." *Maryland Historical Magazine* 66 (Winter 1971): 369–404.

*Ronald E. Butchart*

## Baptist Foreign Mission Convention of the United States

The Baptist Foreign Mission Convention of the United States (BFMC), founded in Montgomery, Alabama, in 1880, supported black Baptist missionary endeavors in Africa. In the late 1870s, William W. Colley and Solomon Cosby, two black Baptists from Virginia, served in Africa under the joint auspices of the white Southern Baptist

Convention and their own black Virginia Baptist State Convention. Both felt constricted by the racism of the white missionaries under whom they served, most notably William J. David, head of Southern Baptist Convention mission efforts in Africa, and by their dependence on funding from white organizations. In 1879 Colley returned to America to organize support for a black Baptist convention specifically devoted to foreign missions, an effort that came to fruition with the creation of the BFMC in 1880.

The convention gradually drew support from Baptists nationwide, though Virginians always dominated the organization's leadership. In 1883–1884, the BFMC commissioned six missionaries to South Africa: Joseph H. and Hattie Presley, W. W. Colley and his wife, John J. Coles, and Henderson McKinney. In contrast to earlier generations of missionary emigrants such as Lott Carey, the six missionaries of the BFMC went as American Christians under a missionary board rather than as agents to prepare the way for a larger back-to-Africa movement. But like the earlier pioneers, the BFMC missionaries of the 1880s saw themselves as part of God's plan to bring the light of Christian civilization to darkest Africa. In 1886 Coles published a small volume entitled *Africa in Brief,* which provided a view of the African world for the black Baptist constituency at home.

Health problems, funding shortfalls, and conflicts with individual missionaries plagued the effort of the BFMC. The missionaries sent in 1883–1884 soon encountered health problems. Hattie Presley died within seven months of her arrival in West Africa, and McKinney perished probably in 1887. A founder of the BFMC, William W. Colley, was involved in the accidental shooting of a Liberian boy, and rumors of moral failings followed John J. Coles's career. The BFMC pressed on despite these difficulties. In 1890 the BFMC's executive board reported that since its founding the organization had employed eleven persons as African missionaries, supported three missionary stations, and expended $25,000 in its mission program. In 1893, however, it acknowledged that "tribal wars, disease, death, and furlough" hampered the black Baptist missionary enterprise. Without any missionaries to its name and after rejecting a variety of plans that called for cooperation with white organizations, BFMC leaders advocated forming a nationwide body to unify the diverse black Baptist entities that pursued separate forms of denominational work. In 1895 this advocacy came to fruition with the formation of the National Baptist Convention, whose Foreign Mission Board continued the work of the BFMC.

In its fifteen-year existence, the precedent set by the BFMC provided a staging ground for future generations to organize black mission endeavors in Africa.

**FURTHER READINGS**

Fitts, Leroy. *A History of Black Baptists.* Nashville: Broadman Press, 1985.

Jacobs, Sylvia, ed. *Black Americans and the Missionary Movement in Africa.* Westport, Conn.: Greenwood Press, 1982.

Martin, Sandy Dwayne. *Black Baptists and African Missions, 1880–1915.* Macon, Ga.: Mercer University Press, 1989.

Roth, Donald. "Grace Not Race: Southern Negro Church Leaders, Black Identity, and Missions to West Africa, 1865–1919." Ph.D. diss., University of Texas at Austin, 1975.

Williams, Walter. *Black Americans and the Missionary Movement in Africa, 1877–1900.* Madison: University of Wisconsin Press, 1982.

*Paul Harvey*

## Baseball Hall of Fame, Negro Leagues

In his Baseball Hall of Fame induction speech in 1966, Ted Williams stated that he hoped that "someday Satchel Paige and Josh Gibson will be voted into the Hall of Fame as symbols of the great Negro players who are not here only because they weren't given the chance."

Five years later, in 1971, the National Baseball Hall of Fame created a special committee to recognize players of the Negro Leagues. From its inception through 1977 when it was disbanded, the committee selected a token team of nine players: Satchel Paige, Josh Gibson, Buck Leonard, Martin Dihigo, Judy Johnson, Pop Lloyd, Cool Papa Bell, Oscar Charleston, and Monte Irvin.

Paige was the first inductee, followed the next year by Gibson and Leonard. Monte Irvin had told Leonard that the committee wanted him to attend a meeting to discuss placing the names of some more of the great Negro League players on a plaque in Cooperstown, New York. To Leonard's surprise, the Veterans Committee announced his selection to the Hall of Fame, along with Gibson. Leonard would later recount this as the greatest thrill of his life.

Over the eighteen years following 1977, the Veterans Committee voted only two Negro League players—Rube Foster and Ray Dandridge—into the Hall of Fame. Dandridge had been among the top candidates for induction when the committee was formed. He had to wait sixteen years before finally getting the call from the president of the Hall of Fame, who informed him, "From this moment on, your life will never be the same." Induction into the Hall of Fame was some measure of consolation for Dandridge. Still active when the color line was broken, he was never given the chance to play in the major leagues, in part perhaps because of his age, but more likely because he was such a great draw at the Triple A level. In the early years of integration in baseball, the major league teams were reluctant to have more than just a small number of blacks on their rosters.

Then, in 1995, a new plan was formulated to elect five more Negro League players to the Hall of Fame. Monte Irvin and Buck O'Neil, Chairman of the Negro Baseball Leagues Museum in Kansas City, were members of the committee making the selection of these additional players. The five selected players were Leon Day, Willie Foster, Willie Wells, Bullet Rogan, and Smokey Joe Williams. James Riley had written that Day's induction would be "as sweet as the smell of roses." Unfortunately, Day had only a few days to savor that wonderful fragrance. He died just six days after the announcement of his selection to the Hall of Fame.

Efforts are under way to convince the Veterans Committee of the Hall of Fame to extend the number of years in which at least one Negro League player would be added to the Hall of Fame. Certainly, there are many more who are deserving of this honor.

**FURTHER READINGS**

Clark, Dick, and Larry Lester. *The Negro Leagues Book.* Cleveland: The Society for American Baseball Research, 1994.

Riley, James A. *Dandy, Day, and the Devil.* Cocoa, Fla.: TK Publishers, 1987.

———. *Buck Leonard: The Black Lou Gehrig. The Hall of Famer's Story in His Own Words.* New York: Carroll & Graf, 1995.

Society for American Baseball Research. *Negro Leagues Newsletters.*

*Lyle K. Wilson*

## Bay Area Council Against Discrimination

The Bay Area Council Against Discrimination (BACAD), a multiethnic organization that promoted "sound, democratic racial relations," was founded in San Francisco in 1942. During World War II, thousands of African Americans migrated from the South to the Bay Area in response to the region's expanding defense economy and reputation for greater racial tolerance. Wartime migrants, however, soon discovered that the Bay Area was not the Promised Land. Discrimination in housing, employment, and public accommodations, widely practiced before the war, grew even worse during the 1940s.

The BACAD, established to address the racial hostility and discrimination associated with the expanding size and diversity of the region's population, drew its membership from several Bay Area cities and included representatives from over seventy local organizations ranging from the National Association for the Advancement of Colored People (NAACP) to the Jewish Survey Council. Until it ceased operation in 1944, the BACAD worked to document, publicize, and ameliorate discrimination against ethnic and religious minorities.

The BACAD housing subcommittee pressed local officials to formulate open housing policies and lobbied for state legislation banning restrictive housing covenants. Its labor subcommittee investigated union and employment discrimination and pressured state and federal agencies to enforce more aggressively equal hiring policies. Finally, the BACAD drafted "San Francisco's Plan for Democratic Race Relations." Unanimously passed by the Board of Supervisors in 1943, this proposal called on the city to ban all employment and housing discrimination, promote racial understanding in public schools, hire more minority teachers and police officers, and discourage police brutality and racial bias in newspaper reporting.

**FURTHER READINGS**

Broussard, Albert S. *Black San Francisco: The Struggle for Racial Equality in the West, 1900–1954.* Lawrence: University Press of Kansas, 1993.

*Gretchen Lemke-Santangelo*

## Bethel Literary and Historical Association

The Bethel Literary and Historical Association was the preeminent debating society and forum for racial issues in Washington, D.C., at the turn of the twentieth century. The organization was founded in 1881 by Bishop Daniel A. Payne under the auspices of Union Bethel African Methodist Episcopalian Church (now Metropolitan AME) after an 1859 attempt to create a similar organization had failed. Payne hoped to encourage an educated ministry and congregation and thought that literary associations were an important factor. In its early years the association consisted largely of church members, but after 1883 the group attracted a larger audience. Most of Washington's black elite attended meetings and participated in debates. The activities of the Bethel Literary were reported widely in the black press, both locally and nationally.

From its inception, meetings addressed clearly racial topics, emphasizing African heritage and the progress of blacks in the United States. By 1896 the organization had spawned models in the District of Columbia and nationwide. In 1903 the association debated the ideas of Booker T. Washington and W. E. B. Du Bois. During World War I the organization discussed black contributions and northern migration. In the 1920s the membership debated race leadership and education.

Not surprisingly, most of Washington's black leaders participated in the organization, including the diplomat and activist Archibald Henry Grimke, the historian and educator Carter G. Woodson, the historian and educator Kelly Miller, the philosopher and Rhodes scholar Alain Locke, and the black women's club organizer Mary Church Terrell. Ironically, by studying their past in an elite format, Bethel members rediscovered their common ancestry with all African Americans, which heightened their convictions that they had a responsibility toward their race. As such, the Bethel Literary provided an important alternative approach to racial uplift by promoting racial pride. The group ceased to meet sometime in the 1920s or 1930s.

### FURTHER READINGS

Cromwell, John Wesley, Sr. *History of the Bethel Literary and Historical Association*. Washington, D.C.: Press of R. L. Pendleton, 1896.

Gatewood, Willard B. *Aristocrats of Color: The Black Elite, 1880–1920*. Bloomington & Indianapolis: Indiana University Press, 1990.

Moore, Jacqueline M. *Leading the Race: The Transformation of Washington D.C.'s Black Elite, 1880–1920*. Charlottesville: University Press of Virginia, 1999.

*Jacqueline M. Moore*

## Big Eight Council on Black Student Governments

Founded in 1976, the Big Eight Council on Black Student Governments aims to unite African American student leaders nationwide. Until 1996, the council's member schools were referred to as the Big Eight schools, after their athletic conference name. These schools included Iowa State University, the University of Kansas, Kansas State University, Oklahoma State University, the University of Nebraska, Colorado State University, the University of Missouri, and the University of Oklahoma. As of July 1, 1996, the Big Eight became the Big Twelve with the addition of the University of Texas, Texas A & M, Baylor, and Texas Tech.

The council was formed originally to facilitate communication among African American students at member schools and to serve as a vehicle to address their common concerns, particularly those that arose from being black students on predominantly white college campuses. In 1976, the council held its first conference to provide the presidents of black student government organizations at the Big Eight Schools with the opportunity to network. In the following year the conference was opened up to rank-and-file members of black student government organizations in order to share information with a wider audience.

The responsibility for hosting annual conferences falls to one of the council member schools. Attendance at the conference now tops 1,000 students and attendees come from over fifty colleges and universities. Highlights of the conference include annual traditions such as a step-show (a popular African American fraternity and sorority tradition that includes dancing, singing, and/or skits) and a gospel extravaganza, both of which are open to the public. Workshops and speakers that address contemporary issues facing the African American community at large, as well as those facing black collegians, are the main focus of the conference. These include HIV/AIDS, alumni relationships, leadership, affirmative action and other civil rights policies, student activism, voting rights and electoral politics, and education. The council also produces several publications, the annual *Big Eight Update*, and the two semiannual *Harambee* and *New Renaissance*.

### FURTHER READINGS

"A Chance to be Open: This Weekend Brings an Opportunity to Learn from One Another. Show You Have Time to Learn What's Important." *Iowa State Daily*, February 19, 1997.

Adams, Kate. "Black Student Conference Is Coming to ISU." *Iowa State Daily*, February 6, 1997.

"Big Eight Council on Black Student Governments," in Burek, Deborah M., ed. *Encyclopedia of Associations*, vol. 1, part 1. Detroit: Gale, 1991.

Kopatich, Bill. "Big 12 to Benefit Iowa State." *Iowa State Daily*, July 23, 1996.

Ladd, Scott M. "BSU Big 8 Conference Begins Today." (Kansas State University) *Collegian*, February 15, 1996.

*Julie S. Doar*

## Big Twelve Council on Black Student Governments

*See* Big Eight Council on Black Student Governments.

## Birmingham, Alabama: Civic, Literary, and Mutual Aid Associations

Civic, literary, and mutual aid associations played a pivotal role in the growth and development of Birmingham, Alabama's African American community. These were multifaceted organizations that served to stimulate race consciousness, civic responsibility, and financial support among the city's burgeoning black population.

Birmingham was a city that experienced phenomenal growth in the late nineteenth and early twentieth centuries. The coal mining and iron and steel industries that developed in the area in response to the wealth of natural resources created unprecedented employment opportunities for those seeking economic improvement. Birmingham's population surged as blacks and whites flocked to the area from the surrounding region. In 1871, Birmingham's founding year, 3,086 people lived in the city. By 1910, through annexation and migration, Birmingham's population exceeded 130,000. At that time the African American community made up 39 percent of Birmingham's population, giving it the highest black percentage of any American city with a population of more than 100,000.

Before this population surge, the black community was relatively small. African Americans had exercised their political rights until 1890, when an all-white city Democratic primary successfully barred them from participating in municipal elections. Birmingham's blacks continued to vote in state and national elections until 1901 when the state of Alabama disfranchised them. African Americans were allowed to register, but of the 5,240 voters who registered in 1902 only seventy-six were black. Through the Colored Man's Suffrage Association, blacks unsuccessfully challenged the constitutionality of the disfranchising provision. Some prominent Birmingham residents also organized the Negro Republican party in opposition to the revitalization of the lily-white Republican party, which refused to seat any of the twenty-five black delegates present at the Republican convention in Birmingham. As their efforts were dashed at every turn, their enthusiasm waned. The Colored Citizens' League, founded in 1916, also failed to elicit change. When returning black World War I veterans sought to exercise their voting rights, African American men and women again took collective action. In 1919 they organized a local branch of the National Association for the Advancement of Colored People (NAACP) to dismantle discrimination, but they failed to garner the necessary support to effectively challenge the status quo. Throughout the decades, black leaders attempted to win voting rights, but it was not until 1966, when the U.S. Department of Justice sent federal examiners into Jefferson County under the provisions of the 1965 Voting Rights Act, that large numbers of blacks registered.

African Americans in Birmingham realized greater success when they coordinated their efforts and organized a variety of self-help organizations to improve conditions for the city's black residents. Although the city's racial policies in the late nineteenth and early twentieth centuries were not yet as comprehensive as they would become in later years, governmental support for welfare agencies discriminated in favor of the city's white communities. Largely, blacks relied on their own devices to serve the unique needs of their communities. In the 1880s, it was the black church that initiated and coordinated efforts to assist the indigent and infirm. Pastors throughout the city directed their congregants to reach out to the needy. Reverends William R. Pettiford and Thomas Walker were the most visible forces behind early mutual aid activities. Their churches' roles extended beyond their respective parishes as they worked to improve conditions in the black community. Pettiford's Christian Aid Society, founded in the early 1890s at his Sixteenth Street Baptist Church, was one of the earliest manifestations of benevolent societies among the city's black community. His Representative Council, established in the 1880s, served as an umbrella organization to coordinate diverse community services while his Penny Savings Bank, founded in the 1890s, supported several black institutions including Industrial High, the first high school for black children. Walker's Union Central Relief Association provided insurance benefits to the overlooked black community. Other mutual aid associations that offered burial services and sick and death benefits thrived, especially A(rthur) G(eorge) Gaston's Booker T. Washington Burial Insurance Company, established in 1923, which served the black community throughout the twentieth century.

Membership in the Knights of Pythias, Prince Hall Masons, and the Protective Order of Elks and other fraternal organizations ensured individuals and families financial assistance during personal crises, arranged for a proper burial, and frequently awarded educational scholarships to members' children. These lodges also reached out to nonmembers. In 1900, black fraternal organizations and secret societies offered financial assistance to the Alabama Colored Orphans and Old Folks Home, which provided shelter for the elderly and orphans and for a time operated a small hospital unit run by black physicians, a nurses training school, and a school for domestic workers. The Carrie Tuggle Institute, founded in 1902, also received support for its orphanage and its school from similar black organizations as well as from two local judges and a white merchant.

Black women's clubs and auxiliary lodges played a central role in the development of a network of mutual aid services. Women who worked to bring about social reform in the African American community drew from their experiences in the church, which served as the organizational base for their benevolent activities. Throughout Birmingham, there were numerous women's missionary societies that were involved in helping the poor, visiting homes of nonchurch-going individuals, as well as various fund-raising activities. Birmingham's black women also organized a Juvenile Court Association in the early twentieth century that was responsible for building the Mt. Meigs Reformatory. Church women also supported the war effort during World War I when they promoted and practiced food conservation and sponsored fund-raising rallies. Women who joined the women's auxiliaries of fraternal organizations as well as the members of the City Federation of Colored Women's Clubs exhibited their civic conscience when they supported numerous black institutions, including Tuggle Institute and the Old Folks' and Orphans' Home.

Beyond the church associations and the fraternal orders, leading members of the city's African American community founded independent civic organizations that sought to secure reform measures. The Four Minute Men Negro Organization of Birmingham was a World War I manifestation that organized men and women to work toward effecting change in employment, education, social services, and black suffrage. Local black men also organized the Birmingham Civic Association in 1924 to address the broader concerns of business and civic responsibility. During the late 1920s, African Americans established other self-help organizations, including the

Colored Welfare Council. They created a Colored Division of the Community Chest in an effort to receive allotments from the white-controlled county Chest, which had no black board members until 1942. They also created a black branch of the Young Men's Christian Association (YMCA) in 1916 and one year later, African American women organized a black Young Women's Christian Association (YWCA). Through these black-created and black-controlled chapters, men and women worked separately toward a common goal: improving conditions for the city's black population.

African American newspapers were instrumental in developing a literary tradition in black Birmingham, as they disseminated important information to their readers. Between 1880 and 1890, eleven black newspapers were published in the city and several others appeared around the turn of the century, including the *Weekly Pilot*, *Wide-Awake, Hot Shots*, and the *Truth*. No single paper served the entire black community; rather, economic differences among African Americans reflected their choice of publication. During these years, no paper in Birmingham could rival Oscar Adams's *Reporter*, a weekly publication that appealed to members of the black professional class who supported his role as social and civic activist. Adams used his position with the paper to rally support for the Birmingham Civic Association and the Colored Citizen's League, in which he held leadership roles. The *Reporter*, like other local black papers, failed during the early years of the Depression. It was not until several years after the 1930s Depression that another black paper emerged. The *Birmingham World*, under the capable guidance of Emory O. Jackson, had a broader appeal than earlier papers and experienced the greatest success of all local black papers. Jackson, the paper's editor from 1941 to 1975, launched fearless attacks on racial discrimination that struck a chord with the city's African American population. Jackson used the *World*, as did earlier editors of black papers, as a vehicle through which to challenge disfranchisement, promote self-help, and inspire racial uplift.

Literary clubs also served members of the black community. Primarily composed of middle-class women, these clubs gave members an opportunity to socialize and to discuss various contemporary topics. Although the membership in these elite clubs underlined the class divisions within the black community, the women members not only attended to their own needs, but they also reached out to the broader community. After the turn of the century, when health crises plagued blacks, and the city failed to offer adequate assistance, it was the club women who organized tuberculosis clinics and sponsored health and sanitation campaigns. These women recognized the responsibility they held as members of an elite class.

From the time they arrived in Birmingham, African Americans recognized the necessity of establishing a myriad of organizations to serve the specific needs of the black community. Despite the absence of adequate public aid and the persistence of racial discrimination, African Americans who had the ability to mobilize members of the community empowered residents to seek and elicit improvements for blacks living in Birmingham.

**FURTHER READINGS**

Eskew, Glenn T. *But for Birmingham: The Local and National Movements in the Civil Rights Struggle.* Chapel Hill: University of North Carolina Press, 1997.

Fallin, Wilson, Jr. "A Shelter in the Storm: The African-American Church in Birmingham, Alabama, 1815–1963." Ph.D. diss., University of Alabama, 1995.

Feldman, Lynne Barbara. *A Sense of Place: Birmingham's Black Middle-Class Community, 1890–1930.* Tuscaloosa: University of Alabama Press, 1999.

Kelley, Robin D. G. *Hammer and Hoe: Alabama Communists During the Great Depression.* Chapel Hill: University of North Carolina Press, 1990.

LaMonte, Edward S. *Politics & Welfare in Birmingham, 1900–1975.* Tuscaloosa: University of Alabama Press, 1995.

McKiven, Henry M. *Iron and Steel: Class, Race, and Community in Birmingham, Alabama, 1875–1920.* Chapel Hill: University of North Carolina Press, 1995.

Tarry, Ellen. *The Third Door: The Autobiography of an American Negro Woman.* Tuscaloosa: University of Alabama Press, 1955.

*Lynne Barbara Feldman*

# Black Academy of Arts and Letters

The Black Academy of Arts and Letters was organized in 1969 to recognize "notable" contributions to African American culture, literature, and the performing arts. Originally underwritten by the Twentieth Century Fund to provide financial support for three years, the purpose of the academy was both to provide African Americans with a sense of cultural pride and to increase awareness of black achievements among all Americans. The first academy president, religion professor C. Eric Lincoln, noted that "the organization obviously exists because the membership feels there does not exist in society an organization which is sufficiently colorblind to give due recognition and encouragement to black arts and letters."

Founded on March 27, 1969, at a New York dinner attended by twenty-three members, the academy originally comprised fifty members, including novelist John O. Killens, psychiatrist Dr. Alvin Poussaint, political science professor Charles V. Hamilton, former U.S. ambassador Carl Rowan, and historian John Hope Franklin. The academy's constitution stipulated that each year no more than ten persons were to be elected to join the group.

At its annual awards banquet, the Black Academy presented prizes to notable scholars, authors, and artists. Some of the recipients included anthropologist and dancer Katherine Dunham, jazz artist Duke Ellington, and novelist Ernest J. Gaines. More than 800 guests attended the second annual awards banquet. In July 1970, the academy established a Hall of Fame to honor deceased eminent individuals. The first inductees were Carter G. Woodson, founder of the Association for the Study of Negro Life and History, artist Henry O. Tanner, and historian and sociologist W. E. B. Du Bois. The Bureau of Immigration and Naturalization Service (INS) initially declined to grant a visa to Shirley Graham Du Bois, the widow of W. E. B. Du Bois, to attend the ceremony, claiming she was a member of "thirty subversive organizations which made her inadmissible under the law." After Lincoln sent a letter of protest, the INS reversed its earlier decision and granted her a visa. The Black Academy Hall of Fame later inducted abolitionist Frederick Douglass, actor Ira Aldridge, and historian George Washington Williams. Descendants of two of these distinguished nineteenth-century individuals attended the ceremony.

The academy is no longer in existence. The date and reasons for its demise are unknown.

**FURTHER READINGS**

"Black Academy of Arts and Letters." *Negro Digest* (July 1969): 91–94.

"Black Academy of Arts and Letters: Second Annual Awards Dinner." *Black World* 21, 1 (November 1971): 68–71.

Fraser, C. Gerald. "Black Academy Names 3 Leaders to Hall of Fame." *New York Times*, July 14, 1970, 34.

———. "Du Bois's Widow Granted U.S. Visa." *New York Times*, August 16, 1970, 23.

Reinhold, Robert. "Black Academy of Arts and Letters Is Founded." *New York Times*, March 28, 1969, 42.

*Donald Altschiller*

# Black Affairs Council, Unitarian Universalist

The Black Unitarian Universalist Caucus (BUUC), a group of Unitarian Universalist chapters composed of about 600 members, established the Black Affairs Council (BAC) in 1968. The BAC's goal was to raise money to assist African Americans in establishing leadership positions within the Unitarian Universalist Association (UUA) and to aid them in their struggle to gain economic, political, educational, and social equality.

By the 1960s, a couple of dozen black ministers served in the UUA; however, the majority of black ministers lacked official ordination or assignment to a church. In 1961, only five African Americans served black churches and four served white churches. The BUUC and the BAC blamed the UUA's paternal and patronizing practices for the small number of ordained African Americans. Insisting that the black experience differed from the white experience in the UUA, black Unitarian Universalists explained that African Americans often felt underrepresented, powerless, and misunderstood. They demanded that the UUA increase the number of black ministers, distribute educational materials describing black contributions, appoint African Americans to the UUA's governing boards, and adopt a black liturgical style. To accomplish these tasks, the BUUC developed proposals to empower blacks and the BAC implemented such proposals through various programs serving the black community. For instance, the BUUC asked the UUA to contribute $250,000 to the BAC for four years and allow blacks rather than an established white UUA organization to control these funds. The UUA Board of Trustees agreed to the proposal and made BAC an affiliate of the UUA in 1968.

The BAC was composed of nine to twelve individuals, including two black women, three nonblack members, five regionally elected representatives, and the BUUC chairman. The BAC established a policy committee to study and provide guidelines for its programs, an investment committee to determine ways to sustain funding, and a bond program for churches. Through such efforts, the BAC funded such programs as Young Afro-Americans of Philadelphia, "Soul Generation" of Syracuse, the Ghetto Training Center in Philadelphia, Black "P" Stone Nation in Chicago, the Center for Black Education in Washington, D.C., the Malcolm X Liberation University, and the National Association of Afro-American Educators. The BAC designed these programs to end political repression and economic exploitation and to foster educational and cultural development in black communities.

In 1970, when other initiatives demanded UUA support, the UUA Board of Trustees reduced the BAC's funding to $50,000. Upset about this reduction, the BAC separated from the UUA and raised its own funds. BAC programs, such as the May 25th Fund, which funded community building projects, and white support groups, such as FULLBAC (Full Funding for the Black Affairs Council), became the organization's main financial resources. Although the UUA continued to offer additional funding, the BAC refused to accept UUA money because the organization insisted on controlling those funds rather than allowing the BAC to allocate the money.

In 1972, however, the UUA allocated money to the Racial Justice Fund, which aided several organizations including the BAC. While the BAC accepted the UUA's financial support, the UUA continued to limit the BAC's control of these funds. This interplay between the BAC and the UUA illustrates the BAC's dependency on UUA funds. While each group shared similar goals of empowering blacks, their methods differed and neither welcomed submitting financial control to the other.

By the end of 1972, the BUUC grew frustrated with the strained relationship between the BAC and the UUA and suggested that the BAC and the BUUC merge as the Black Humanist Fellowship. Plans to merge the BUUC and the BAC resulted in a volatile meeting in 1973. As BUUC and BAC members discussed constitutional changes, they vehemently disagreed about disassociating from the UUA, where to seek funding, and how to reestablish an organizational purpose, identity, and structure. Following this meeting, the BAC and the BUUC eventually broke into factions and resorted to litigation to liquidate the remaining funds.

While the BAC and the BUUC dissolved, the groups heightened the UUA's awareness of its black membership. Many BAC programs merged into existing organizations within the UUA that continued to promote black empowerment in the UUA and the larger community.

**FURTHER READINGS**

Carpenter, Victor H. *Unitarian Universalism and the Quest for Racial Justice.* Boston: Unitarian Universalist Association, 1993.

Payne, Wardell J., ed. *Directory of African American Religious Bodies: A Compendium by the Howard University School of Divinity.* Washington, D.C.: Howard University Press, 1991; 2nd ed., 1995.

*Julie Shipe*

## Black American Baptist Churchmen

*See* American Baptist Black Caucus.

## Black and Tan Republicans

This interracial political coalition emerged during Reconstruction when the former Confederate states were required to draft new constitutions as a condition for their readmission to the Union. Beginning in 1867, southern states began to elect representatives to draft new constitutions. Due to the political restrictions placed on former Confederate military and civilian leaders, the constitutional conventions were dominated by Republican delegations composed of carpetbaggers, scalawags, and southern blacks. Carpetbaggers, motivated by various political, economic, and idealistic reasons, had come from the North to the South after the war. Scalawags, native white southerners, had opposed the Confederate government and joined the Republican party to express their support of the Union. Southern blacks, the third component of this coalition, joined the party of Lincoln to exercise their newly found political power and to help meet the needs of the black community. The label "Black and Tans" was a pejorative term given to these conventions by conservative native white southerners who opposed their social, political, and economic agendas, as well as their racial composition.

Convention demographics varied widely from state to state. Collectively, southern whites made up just over 50 percent of all convention delegates, while blacks constituted approximately one-quarter. Most southern white Republicans were wartime Unionists and came predominantly from the upcountry of Alabama, North Carolina, Arkansas, Virginia, and Georgia. Southern whites made up the majority of delegates to eight of the ten state conventions. African Americans were in the majority in the remaining two conventions that gathered in South Carolina and Louisiana. Most black delegates were clergymen, teachers, or artisans, and more than four-fifths were illiterate. Carpetbaggers represented significant minorities in Alabama, Arkansas, Mississippi, and Florida. Many of these northern-born delegates were Union army officers or Freedmen's Bureau agents who occupied key leadership positions in the state conventions and gave a liberal, progressive tenor to the constitutional debates. A significant number of conservative southern Democrats and former Whigs among the delegates forced Republicans to rely on interracial cooperation to maintain political power.

The post–Civil War constitutional conventions succeeded in bringing significant political reform to the former Confederate states. All states renounced the ordinance of secession and several banned whipping as a punishment for crimes, decreased the number of capital crimes, enacted some form of prison reform, and made the state government responsible for some aspects of social welfare. Some states increased property taxes to pay for these new public services, but they usually included homestead exemptions for real and personal property to protect landowners from foreclosure. Most important, all new constitutions guaranteed civil and political rights for African American men.

Another important innovation was the provision of public education. Before the Civil War, public schools barely existed in the South. Recognizing the role of education in economic development, the conventions in North Carolina, Virginia, Florida, Arkansas, Louisiana, and Mississippi included provisions for statewide public school systems. Black delegates, in particular, were vocal champions of public education, arguing that state-supported schools represented the best way of increasing social and economic opportunities for their children. However, despite pressure from black delegates, separate educational systems for black and white children were created.

To solidify their political position and to punish the leaders of the Confederacy, conventions in Mississippi, Alabama, Virginia, and Arkansas restricted the political power of former Confederate officials. The new state constitutions of Mississippi, Alabama, and Virginia disfranchised approximately 10 percent of the former Confederate leaders, while Arkansas stripped about 20 percent of their political rights. This was a contentious issue in all four states. The constitutions of Mississippi and Virginia were defeated in the initial referendum and were not passed until the controversial political restrictions were removed. Alabama and Arkansas repealed the disfranchisement clauses by 1872.

To varying degrees, each of these constitutional conventions took up the cause of African American civil rights. All constitutions guaranteed civil and political rights, but they did little to extend social equality. Black politicians were vocal champions of their race, and most white delegates recognized the importance of civil rights to southern blacks, but white contemporaries took advantage of the political inexperience of blacks to thwart efforts at social equality such as school integration. Convention delegates represented biracial electorates. Therefore, white politicians had an important stake in supporting civil rights legislation. However, white members of this faction were not racial egalitarians. While many truly believed in the principles of racial equality, others merely tolerated black social and political aspirations for political profit. Despite racial and sectional division, the "Black and Tan" conventions produced the most progressive state constitutions in the country.

During Reconstruction the Republican "Black and Tan" coalition continued to influence southern elections at all levels. African American members such as Robert Smalls, John R. Lynch, James T. Rapier, Hiram Revels, James O'Hara, and countless others subsequently were elected to Congress or high state offices. Large numbers of blacks sat in the state legislatures of South Carolina, Louisiana, and Mississippi, and smaller numbers were elected in the remaining states. At the local level, blacks were elected to municipal offices ranging from register of deeds to sheriff. White members of the "Black and Tan" coalition also continued to have great influence in the Republican party. More important, they continued to control political patronage.

Following the 1876 political compromise that placed Rutherford B. Hayes in the White House, the "Black and Tan" coalition began to erode slowly. White Republican politicians sought black votes, but found that any support of civil rights limited their appeal to white voters. Southern whites, reenfranchised by 1877, threw their support behind Democrats who promised to "redeem" the South from the supposed excesses of Republican rule. In certain areas of the South, such as the second congressional district of North Carolina, black and white Republicans continued to cooperate until the twentieth century. Attempts at fusion between Populists and Republicans, outbreaks of racial violence, and the disfranchisement of blacks dissolved the last vestiges of the interracial Reconstruction coalition. Soon after 1900, Republican party officials, attempting to appeal to the newly defined southern electorate, recognized only white candidates and "lily white" convention delegations.

The "Black and Tan" faction of the southern Republican party represented the first interracial political coalition in American history. Its existence demonstrates that whites and blacks could put aside racial differences to pursue a political agenda. Most important, the "Black and Tans" gave African Americans a political voice at all levels of government in the post–Civil War South. This group of southern politicians continued to wield significant influence until disfranchisement stripped them of their electorate.

**FURTHER READINGS**

Cripps, Thomas. "The Lily White Republicans, the Negro, the Party, and the South in the Progressive Period." Ph.D. diss., University of Maryland, 1967.

Foner, Eric. *Reconstruction: America's Unfinished Revolution.* New York: Harper & Row, 1988.

Hume, Richard L. "Carpetbaggers in the Reconstruction South: A Group Portrait of Whites in the 'Black and Tan' Constitutional Conventions." *Journal of American History* 64, 2 (September 1977): 313–30.

Rabinowitz, Howard M., ed. *Southern Black Leaders of the Reconstruction Era.* Urbana: University of Illinois Press, 1982.

*Richard D. Starnes*

## Black Caucus

*See* Congressional Black Caucus.

## Black Caucus of the American Library Association

In 1968, Effie Lee Morris proposed that the African American members of the American Library Association (ALA) meet to discuss mutual interests and complaints. The ALA, though open to blacks, rarely addressed the needs of its African American members and often met in segregated southern cities where black members were sometimes humiliated. African American librarians encountered racism and segregation in the use of libraries, as applicants to library schools, and as employment competitors for professional librarian positions. Consequently, African American members of the ALA formed the Black Caucus of the ALA in 1970. The purpose of the caucus was to monitor any aspect of librarianship as it related to African Americans as librarians and library users, including the selection of books relating to African American history and culture in local libraries, the admission of blacks to library schools, the hiring and promotion of black librarians, and ALA meeting places and agendas. The caucus's statement of purpose included provisions for analyzing, evaluating, and recommending to the ALA actions to address the needs of African American librarians and library users as well as methods for the improvement of black librarians' status in areas of recruitment, development, advancement, and general working conditions.

The caucus also decided to review the records and analyze the platform statements of candidates for ALA offices and monitor the composition and activities of governing boards of public libraries throughout the United States in order to improve library services to the black community. The caucus's first president, E. J. Josey, explained that the African American librarians were "especially concerned about the effects of institutional racism, poverty, and the continued lack of education, employment, and promotional" opportunities for African American librarians and other minorities. The activities of the caucus were eagerly encouraged and aided by African American and other sympathetic leaders in various communities in the United States and in several African nations.

**FURTHER READINGS**

Cunningham, William D. "The Black Caucus of the American Library Association: The First Four Years." In *Activism in American Librarianship, 1962–73.* Ed. Mary Lee Bundy and Frederick J. Stielow. New York: Greenwood Press, 1987.

Josey, E. J. "Black Caucus of the American Library Association." In *Handbook of Black Librarianship.* Comp. and ed. E. J. Josey and Ann Allen Shockley. Littleton, Colo.: Libraries Unlimited, Inc., 1977.

*Debra Newman Ham*

# Black Caucus of the National Council of Teachers of English and Conference on College Composition and Communication

The Black Caucus of the National Council of Teachers of English (NCTE) and Conference on College Composition and Communication (CCCC) was founded at the annual convention of CCCC in Seattle, Washington, in 1970. A group of black participants, dissatisfied with the convention's insensitive treatment of black literature and black studies as well as the small number of African American scholars presenting papers, launched the Black Caucus of the NCTE/CCCC. Marianna White Davis, then a professor of English at Benedict College in South Carolina, issued the call for the group's initial meeting. Participants drafted a statement and a list of recommendations, which they presented at the CCCC business meeting. The Black Caucus of the NCTE/CCCC demanded the inclusion of black scholarship and the submission of a "pool of names of competent Black scholars to be used for future programs of both CCCC and NCTE." From its beginning, the Black Caucus of the NCTE/CCCC moved to become "a formal viable component of NCTE and CCCC." Because many of its founders were members of the College Language Association (CLA), the caucus also sought the full support of the CLA.

The Black Caucus of the NCTE/CCCC functions as a special interest group of black English language arts teachers and scholars, from kindergarten teachers through educators of professionals, who are involved in the teaching and learning of communication skills, as well as others involved in the teaching of communication skills. Its membership includes kindergarten, elementary, secondary, college, and other professional educators. Committed to blacks experiencing success in teaching and learning, the caucus promotes positive images and meaningful status for black professional English language arts educators and seeks to enhance their professional status. For this purpose, the caucus maintains a network of black educators who advocate functional curricula, effective teacher training, balanced teaching materials, and equitable assessment measures for African American students.

The caucus has endorsed the CCCC's 1974 resolution *Students' Right to Their Own Language.* Moreover, it has initiated resolutions in the NCTE and the CCCC that have resulted in the growing involvement of African Americans in both organizations. The caucus has also been instrumental in the election of African Americans to key positions in the NCTE and the CCCC, including four African American NCTE and eight African American CCCC presidents.

The caucus is the founder and sponsor of the national African American Read-In, now in its eleventh year. The African American Read-In, held the first Sunday and first Monday following in February, is designed to have participants read works written by black writers on the specified dates. The Read-In also promotes the importance of literacy in the African American community. In addition, the caucus sponsors sessions at the annual NCTE and CCCC conventions and continues support of activities related to its founding purposes such as the African American Read-In. The caucus publishes a biannual newsletter, *Black Caucus Notes,* for its more than 300 members and holds biannual meetings in conjunction with the NCTE and CCCC conventions.

**FURTHER READINGS**

Black Caucus of NCTE/4Cs. *Tapping Potential: English and Language Arts for the Black Learner.* Urbana, Ill.: National Council of Teachers of English, 1985.

Conference on College Composition and Communication. *Students' Right to Their Own Language.* Special Issue, vol. 25. Urbana, Ill.: National Council of Teachers of English, Fall 1974.

Davis, Marianna White. *History of the Black Caucus.* Columbia, S.C.: Davis Associates, 1994.

*Sandra E. Gibbs*

## Black Coaches Association

A group of black assistant basketball and football coaches founded the Black Coaches Association (BCA) in 1988. The nonprofit organization is composed of coaches as well as administrators and corporate officials working in the sports industry. The BCA seeks to improve career opportunities for African Americans and other minorities within the world of sports and works to overcome barriers preventing their professional advancement. The organization seeks to resolve conflicts resulting from inequities, advocates uniform hiring practices for coaching and administrative positions in the sports industry, serves as an advocate for student athletes, and works to combat the stereotyping of minority coaches and administrators as well as poor media coverage of minorities in sports.

Emphasizing intercollegiate athletics, the BCA works to strengthen commitment to diversity within the National Collegiate Athletic Association (NCAA) and to create and enforce a series of policies to improve the professional mobility of minorities in the sports industry. Operating on the NCAA Division I level, the BCA encompasses the entire sports spectrum, ranging from the professional ranks to the lower divisions as well as representing those employed at high schools and junior colleges.

Dedicated to enlarging the number of qualified men and women holding high positions in the coaching profession, the association also maintains an online resume data bank and offers a series of career development seminars to its members.

*Amy Bass*

## Black Congressional Caucus

*See* Congressional Black Caucus.

## Black Conventions

*See* Colored Conventions.

## Black Council, Reformed Church in America

Formed in 1969, the Black Council was the organization of African American churches, clergy, and laity within the Reformed Church in America (RCA). The Reformed Church came to the United States from the Netherlands. While African American individuals and congregations of note dotted the church landscape during its growth in America, blacks joined the denomination in larger numbers during the 1950s when the RCA began to take interest in urban ministry. By the 1960s the denomination had formed a Commission on Race Relations. No formal organization of African Americans within the RCA existed until the formation of the Black Council.

On June 6, 1969, James Forman of the National Black Economic Development Conference led a "sit-in" at the RCA national offices in New York City to dramatize his presentation of the Black Manifesto to church organizations a month earlier. The RCA appointed an ad hoc committee to offer recommendations to the denomination in response to the manifesto. One recommendation called for the formation of a black leadership caucus to aid and sponsor program development and management for the denomination's black constituency. The initial council consisted of Elders Clyde Watts, John Ashley, and Edgar Dillard, with B. Moses James elected as the first chairperson. An implementation grant of $100,000 provided the base for the funding of proposals and programs.

When the Reverend M. William Howard became executive director in 1972, the council focused its attention on three key areas. First, the council sought to develop black leadership within and for the RCA, seeking especially to increase the number of black pastors in the denomination. Second, the council offered support for congregational development, encouraging churches to move away from dependence on the denomination for operating expenses and to move toward self-reliance. Third, the council provided guidance to the denomination in its relationship to the reformed churches in South Africa and helped the RCA to play a major role in American opposition to apartheid. This took on even greater significance when Howard was elected the first black president of the National Council of Churches of Christ in 1979.

The ongoing work of the Black Council continues in congregational and leadership development and social justice. It meets four times yearly and publishes a monthly newsletter entitled *Black Caucus, RCA*. Each year, the council sponsors a lectureship in honor of B. Moses James, designed to highlight important issues concerning church, society, and African Americans. The council's work has helped to create many new congregations, numbering some forty-five churches by 1991. It has also worked closely with the seminaries of the Reformed Church, notably the New Brunswick Theological Seminary, which holds evening classes in both New Brunswick, New Jersey, and on the campus of Saint John's University in Queens, New York, where significant numbers of African American students matriculate and a growing black faculty presence aids in leadership recruitment and development.

FURTHER READING

Erskine, Noel. *Black People and the Reformed Church in America*. New York: Reformed Church Press, 1978.

*Harold Dean Trulear*

## Black Emergency Cultural Coalition

The Black Emergency Cultural Coalition (BECC) was a New York–based organization of African American and white artists founded in the fall of 1968. The group sought to focus attention on the failure of New York's museums and galleries to exhibit the work of black artists. Instrumental in the founding were African American artists Benny Andrews, Cliff Joseph, Henri Ghent, and Edward Taylor. At the height of its activities during the late 1960s and early 1970s, the coalition had more than 150 active members.

In the fall of 1968, the group held its first public demonstration at New York City's Whitney Museum, protesting the absence of works by black artists from an exhibition on American paintings and sculptures from the 1930s. In the following year, an exhibit titled "Harlem on My Mind," a documentary photographic history of Harlem, sparked another BECC protest. The coalition charged that the Metropolitan Museum of Art's exhibition was so "full of distortions and misrepresentations that it should be closed down." In 1971, the coalition objected to another Whitney Museum exhibit, titled "Contemporary Black Artists in America," claiming that it demonstrated a lack of racial sensitivity. The BECC criticized the museum for selecting the works on display without the assistance of a black art specialist and claimed that the exhibit was distorted, irrelevant, and insulting to African Americans. In response, the BECC sponsored an alternative exhibit featuring the works of fifty black artists. The "Rebuttal to the Whitney Museum Exhibition" was displayed at New York's Acts of Art Galleries, owned by black painter Nigel Jackson. The BECC staged its last recorded rally in 1976, when members protested the Whitney Museum's exhibit in celebration of 200 years of American art. The bicentennial exhibit, BECC protestors pointed out, failed to display any works by African American artists and included the works of only one woman.

While the BECC discontinued its public protests in the mid-1970s, it remained active well into the 1980s. It conducted art workshops in prisons and worked as an advocacy group fostering the employment of African Americans in art-related fields.

FURTHER READINGS

"Black Emergency Cultural Coalition." In *Encyclopedia of Associations*, vol. 1, part 1. Ed. C. A. Fischer and C. A. Schwartz. New York: International Publishing Company, 1995.

Glueck, Grace. "Black Show Under Fire at the Whitney." *New York Times*, January 31, 1971, D25.

———. "Fifteen of Seventy-five Black Artists Leave as Whitney Exhibition Opens." *New York Times*, April 6, 1971, 50.

Handler, M. S. "Seventy-five Artists Urge Closing of Museum's Insulting Harlem Exhibit." *New York Times*, January 23, 1969, 14.

Russell, Thaddeus. "Black Emergency Cultural Coalition." In *Encyclopedia of African-American Culture and History*, vol. 1. Ed. Jack Salzman, David Lionel Smith, and Cornel West. New York: Simon and Schuster Macmillan, 1996.

Tapley, Marvin. "Racism Charged Against Museum." *New York Amsterdam News*, April 4, 1971, 1, 47.

*Barbara Buice*

## Black Entertainment and Sports Lawyers Association

The Black Entertainment and Sports Lawyers Association (BESLA), with approximately 400 members, is an organization of African American attorneys who specialize in entertainment and sports law.

The BESLA emerged in 1979, when a group of eighteen African American attorneys met in Philadelphia during the First Annual Black Music Association Conference. In the following year, the group established the Black Entertainment Lawyers Association as a nonprofit organization. In 1986, the association adopted the name BESLA to incorporate the growing number of attorneys working for black athletes.

The primary objective of the group is to provide African American entertainers and athletes with practical and efficacious legal representation. The BESLA also conducts educational seminars and provides resource materials for its members, associates, affiliated organizations, and law students. In addition, it maintains the role of industry "watchdog" in order to protect the rights of African Americans in the entertainment and sports industries.

In 1989, the group created a scholarship program to provide financial aid to law students interested in pursuing a career in entertainment or sports law. The BESLA Scholarship Fund annually provides assistance to such students enrolled at one of the four historically black law schools—Howard University, North Carolina Central, Southern University, and Texas Southern Thurgood Marshall. In 1990, the BESLA established the Sayde Gibson Scholarship for deserving student members of the National Black Law Students Association.

The BESLA, headquartered in Mitchellville, Maryland, publishes the proceedings of its annual conference, as well as a quarterly newsletter and a resource guide.

*Amy Bass*

## Black Entertainment Lawyers Association

*See* Black Entertainment and Sports Lawyers Association.

## Black Filmmaker Foundation

Warrington Hudlin, George Cunningham, and Al Emhart founded the Black Filmmaker Foundation (BFF) in 1978. A nonprofit organization, the BFF was created to establish a support system for independent black filmmakers, to showcase their work, and to generate audience support. The BFF, with national headquarters in New York City, has currently more than 2,500 members.

The BFF was launched in the wake of "blaxploitation" films that uncovered a previously untapped market for black films. Moreover, by the mid-1970s African Americans had increased their presence in the Hollywood guilds and academic film schools, and some black filmmakers had entered the television field. As a result, a growing number of African Americans started to produce a steady output of independent films.

The BFF does not fund, produce, or distribute films; instead it seeks to facilitate professional networking of black film and videomakers by providing a forum for the exchange of ideas and information. The BFF also offers introductory and advanced-level film and television courses and workshops for writers, actors, producers, and directors, as well as seminars and conferences that address issues related to black cinema. Proceeds from benefit film premieres and screenings, made possible by supportive filmmakers and Hollywood studios, partly underwrite BFF activities.

The BFF also promotes discussions between producers, directors, actors, and audiences. For this purpose the BFF's Film Society offers monthly screenings of new films as well as works-in-progress by filmmakers of African descent from around the world. The screenings are followed by question-and-answer sessions allowing the filmmaker to communicate with the audience. Film Society screenings, held in New York and Los Angeles, provide independent black filmmakers with a chance to showcase their works and also provide audiences with the opportunity to see films that may not be distributed through regular television and movie theater channels.

In the late 1990s the BFF introduced the works of black independent filmmakers to international audiences. In June 1997, the BFF co-sponsored with UniWorld Entertainment a six-day film festival in Acapulco. The event was a showcase for black artists and independent films that featured aspects of the black experience traditionally ignored by mainstream film festivals. Among the films shown were Peter Brat's *Follow Me Home,* starring Alfre Woodard, which explores aspects of African, American Indian, and Latino cultures. Another film exploring race relations in the United States was *Bleeding Heart,* the directorial debut of Tony–award-winning choreographer, dancer, and actor Gregory Hines.

In addition to publicizing black films, the BFF serves as a clearinghouse for information about the film industry. For this purpose the BFF publishes a monthly newsletter that contains information about the arts and entertainment industry such as job opportunities, funding sources, casting calls and auditions, internships, and special events.

*Isabel Soto*

## Black Gold Star Mothers

Black Gold Star Mothers offered a compassionate support group for women who lost children in military service. Affiliated with the American Gold Star Mothers, Incorporated, which did not restrict membership by race, the Black Gold Star Mothers began during World War I.

At that time, each soldier was represented symbolically by a blue star that the family displayed in windows and on flags. When a serviceman died, a black star covered the blue star. By 1917, family members demanded that soldiers' deaths be honored and glorified instead of mourned, suggesting that the color gold replace black. By May 1918, President Woodrow Wilson approved the Women's Committee of the Council of National Defense's plan to issue black bands to wear on the left arm, emblazoned with a star for each family member who had died in service.

On June 4, 1928, twenty-five Gold Star Mothers, living in the Washington, D.C., area, decided to establish a nondenominational, nonprofit, and nonpolitical group to honor deceased World War I veterans and their families. The group was incorporated in January 1929 with a national headquarters built in Washington, D.C., on Leroy Place, storing membership records, information, and supplies, and publishing the bimonthly *The Gold Star Mother*. Members could also affiliate with state chapters.

Both natural and adoptive mothers who had lost children in military service were invited to join. Husbands could become associate members but were unable to vote at the national convention. All members were considered equals. Several thousand women, both white and black, have participated in the American Gold Star Mothers since its creation. With each new war, more women qualified for inclusion if their sons or daughters died while on duty with the armed forces or from injuries suffered in service.

On September 14, 1940, President Franklin D. Roosevelt proclaimed the last Sunday in September as annual Gold Star Mothers Day to be celebrated by a ceremony at Arlington National Cemetery, where a wreath was placed in their honor at the Tomb of the Unknown Soldier. Similar services were staged by chapters across the country. The U.S. Postal Service recognized Gold Star Mothers in 1948 with a three-cent stamp.

The American Gold Star Home opened in January 1957. The U.S. Department of Housing and Urban Development (HUD) renovated the home in 1973. Members, regardless of race, qualified for residency in Gold Star Manor, an apartment complex located on Gold Star Drive in Long Beach, California.

By 1974, the U.S. Congress granted the American Gold Star Mothers a federal charter, proclaiming, "This is an organization of mothers whose sons or daughters served and died that this world might be a better place in which to live." The American Gold Star Mothers continues to function in 2000.

The group's primary purpose was to promote peace and patriotism and to develop educational materials about how to respect the United States, its flag, and the pledge of allegiance. Gold Star Mothers helped grieving families and offered assistance to Gold Star Mothers and their descendants, veterans, and dependents. Funding fellowships in memory of soldiers and relatives, the Gold Star Mothers also provided charitable services to individuals and communities, especially being responsible for aiding Veterans' Administration hospitals.

Despite efforts to include Black Gold Star Mothers, a 1930s incident enraged the African American community. The federal government offered to finance a trip to send Gold Star Mothers to France to see their sons' graves and tour battlefields. However, the War Department issued a statement that Black Gold Star Mothers would be transported on a separate ship. Fifty-five Black Gold Star Mothers petitioned President Herbert Hoover to cancel the order for a segregated voyage.

"As a Gold Star Mother who happens to be colored," one woman wrote, "I wish to protest against the gratuitous insult . . . in segregating colored Gold Star Mothers who are entitled to go to France to visit the graves where our loved ones are buried." In the petition, the Black Gold Star Mothers wrote that "our anguish and sorrow have been assuaged by the realization that our loved ones who rest in the soil of France gave their lives to the end that the world might be a better place in which to live for all men, of all races and colors."

They continued, "We who gave and who are colored are insulted by the implication that we are not fit persons to travel with other bereaved ones. Instead of making up parties of Gold Star Mothers on the basis of geographical location we are set aside in a separate group, Jim Crowed, separated and insulted." Headlines declared, "Negro Gold Star Mothers Resent Racial Distinction."

Poet Clarence L. Peaslee wrote: "God save a country/That ever turns back/A Gold Star Mother/Because she is black," and Claude T. Eastmond penned: "Black mothers', like white mothers' hearts are grieved./Their heroic sons have left them, too, bereaved."

Some women refused to travel, although a large group made the pilgrimage to Europe despite enduring inferior accommodations. Before they embarked, New York commissioner Ferdinand C. Morton, of the Municipal Civil Service, told the Black Gold Star Mothers that "mother love, courage and patriotism are peculiar to no race, creed or color." Each woman was given a gold star medal and certificate.

During World War II, African American author Ruby Berkley Goodwin, prepared *A Gold Star Mother Speaks*. She wrote: "But if in other years mothers still know/The agony of seeing strong young sons/Marched off to war, yet come back still enslaved/To old concepts and stifling bigotries,/The cause is lost."

After the war, African American newspapers, such as the *Pittsburgh Courier*, reported about Black Gold Star Mothers on Memorial Day. *Ebony* magazine chronicled the establishment of the interracial Gold Star Wives in 1945 for war widows to help them secure higher pensions and educational funds and send their children to the group's interracial camp. Marian F. Croson was that group's first black member.

FURTHER READINGS

American Gold Star Mothers, Inc. *American Gold Star Mothers Inc. History*. Washington, D.C.: American Gold Star Mothers, Inc., 1984.

"Gold Star Wives." *Ebony* 9 (January 1953): 60–62, 64–66.

Goodwin, Ruby Berkley. *A Gold Star Mother Speaks*. Fullerton, Calif.: Orange County Printing Co., 1944.

Johnson, Toki Schalk. "Gold Stars Glimmer in Crowns of These Mothers: Memorial Day and Memories." *Pittsburgh Courier* (New York edition), May 28, 1949, 8.

Schomburg Center for Research in Black Culture Clipping File.

U.S. Congress, House, Committee on the Judiciary, Subcommittee on Administrative Law and Governmental Relations. *American Gold Star Mothers, Inc.: Hearing Before the Subcommittee on Administrative Law and Governmental Relations of the Committee on the Judiciary, House of Representatives, Ninety-eighth Congress, Second Session, on H.R. 3811, March 21, 1984*. Washington, D.C.: Government Printing Office, 1984.

U.S. Congress, Senate, Committee on the Judiciary. *American Gold Star Mothers, Inc.: Report (To Accompany S. 2413)*. Washington, D.C.: Government Printing Office, 1984.

*Elizabeth D. Schafer*


## Black Humanist Fellowship

*See* Black Affairs Council, Unitarian Universalist.


## Black Leadership Caucus

*See* National Black Presbyterian Caucus.


## Black Leadership Forum

*See* Council for United Civil Rights Leadership.


## Black Leadership Roundtable

*See* National Black Leadership Roundtable.


## Black Methodists for Church Renewal

In 1967, black Methodists launched the formation of the Black Methodists for Church Renewal (BMCR) to ensure that the predominantly white Methodist Church would continue to meet the needs of its African American constituency. Black Methodists had created a similar advocacy group following the merger of the Methodist Episcopal Church, the Methodist Episcopal Church South, and the Methodist Protestant Church in 1939. That year, black methodists established the Central Jurisdiction that represented African American interests in the Methodist Church. In July 1967, however, the pending union of the Methodist Church and the Evangelical United Brethren Church provided for the creation of a new denomination, which would result in the elimination of the Central Jurisdiction and end the term of its last bishop, Dr. L. Scott Allen.

Concerned about the continued representation of black Methodists in the predominantly white denomination, thirty members of the Central Jurisdiction met in Detroit in the fall of 1967. At this initial meeting, the group decided to hold a National Conference of Negro Methodists in February 1968. Between February 6 and 9, 1968, 259 delegates from across the nation attended the conference in Cincinnati. Led by the ministers Negail Riley, Woodie White, Maceo Pembroke, and James M. Lawson Jr., the conference adjourned under the name BMCR and adopted the motto "Our time under God is now!" The BMCR formed committees to draft recommendations to the plenary session regarding the role of African American Methodists within the Methodist Church. Cain Felder served as the BMCR's first executive director and James M. Lawson Jr. as first chairman of its national board of directors. While developing the organization's governance structure, the BMCR sought to ensure the participation of men, women, clergy, lay members, and representatives of various age groups on the board of directors. The BMCR's constitution and bylaws, for example, mandated that if the group's executive director was a man, the associate director was to be a woman, and vice versa.

The BMCR's determination to secure continued black participation in the governance of the Methodist Church caused a turmoil at the 1968 General Conference. That year, the Methodist Church and the United Methodist Church gathered in Dallas to formalize their merger, resulting in the elimination of the Central Jurisdiction. In protest, BMCR members staged a walk-out during the opening communion service. Subsequently, however, the protestors returned to the convention floor to voice their grievances. They demanded that the church establish a Commission on Religion and Race, finance the development of black caucuses, and provide funds for African American Methodist colleges. While the General Conference had rejected a similar proposal in 1964, the 1968 motion was greeted by a standing ovation. Following the 1968 General Conference, the Methodist Church appointed Woodie White to serve as first General Secretary of the General Commission on Religion and Race.

The BMCR continued its efforts on behalf of black Methodists in the late 1960s. It picketed the Methodist Church's publishing house, United Methodist Publishing House, in Nashville and succeeded in improving the working conditions of black employees and enhancing job opportunities for African Americans. In response to the BMCR's pressure, the General Conference established a Minority Group Fund and a Black College Fund in 1970. Meeting annually, the BMCR continues to represent the spiritual needs of black Methodists.

### FURTHER READING

White, Woodie W. *Our Time Under God Is Now: Reflections on Black Methodists for Church Renewal.* Nashville: Abingdon Press, 1993.

*Julius H. Bailey*

## Black Muslims
*See* Nation of Islam.

## Black Panther Party (for Self-Defense)

On October 15, 1966, Huey P. Newton and Bobby Seale co-founded the Black Panther Party for Self-Defense in a small West Oakland Poverty Center office in northern California. Initially the Panthers addressed the needs of poor African Americans; however, through the years, they expanded their ideological scope to incorporate poor and oppressed people throughout the world. The Panthers provided services to disfranchised individuals and subsequently inspired them to define actively and serve their own needs through political organizations and community programs. Within three years of their creation, the Panthers had expanded into a national and international group with more than forty chapter and branch offices. Between 1974 and 1977, the group administered more than fifty programs. This tremendous membership and program growth is a testament to the appealing message of the Panthers to African Americans and other underprivileged

Black Panthers demonstrate in front of the courthouse during the 1970 trial of the Panther 21 in New York City. *Archive Photos*

population groups. Programmatically, the organization dissolved in 1982 when the 1971 Panther-initiated Oakland Community School closed.

Although Newton and Seale were the organization's co-founders, over the course of its history, the Panthers had a large number of national leaders. The first three years were most fraught with leadership turnover, resulting in numerous shifts in the rate of organizational growth, changing dynamics in community relations, and tensions between national chapters and branches. Some of the early Panther leaders included individuals such as Eldridge and Kathleen Cleaver, David Hilliard, Elaine Brown, Fred Hampton, Andrea Jones, Doug Miranda, and Malik Rahim.

The Panthers and their programs grew out of the group's 1966 Ten Point Platform. The most interesting part of the Panther programming history was the organic nature of its development. While Seale and Newton were aware of the black community's needs, such as after-school programs for youth and transportation for the elderly, they were unable initially to implement these programs. Instead, the co-founders organized police patrols, which served the dual purpose of addressing the black community's concerns with Oakland's unwillingness to establish a citizens' police review board while raising the black population's awareness of the Panthers. Six months after the Panthers initiated their police patrols, the group launched a news organ, *The Black Panther Black Community News Service*, to inform black residents of other Bay Area communities about their activities.

Another example of the Panthers's organic nature was their shifting ideology, which changed four times between 1966 and 1970. Initially, the organization was nationalist, focusing only on the needs of African Americans. As time passed, however, the leadership began incorporating socialism into the group's agenda, and the Panthers became revolutionary nationalists. The leaders began to analyze the American social system through a combination of race and class. The next theoretical phase was the shift to internationalism, characterized by the argument that African Americans shared common experiences with other non-white people throughout the world and consequently, should seek solidarity with those population groups. In August 1970, Newton urged the Panthers to embrace the concept of intercommunalism, arguing that "nations have been transformed into communities of the world." This was the Panthers's final ideological shift.

The years 1968 and 1969 were the best and the worst for the Panthers. The organization experienced its greatest growth during 1968 as a result of the Free Huey Campaigns that sought the release of Newton, who had been incarcerated on the charge of murdering an Oakland Police Department officer. Numerous individuals rallied to Newton's defense, generating unprecedented publicity for the Panthers and increasing the group's membership. Although no records document membership growth, some contemporaries claimed that the Panthers gained as many as 3,000 or 4,000 members. The Panthers, however, not only attracted a growing number of members but also the attention of law enforcement agencies, which infiltrated many of its chapters. In 1969, federal and local law enforcement agents attacked members in New York City, Chicago, and Los Angeles, and several Panther leaders were either imprisoned or killed during these ambushes. The national headquarters of the Panthers responded to the threats of law enforcement infiltration through a series of membership purges beginning in early 1969.

Between 1969 and 1971, highly publicized images of armed-and-dangerous Black Panthers overshadowed the group's social programming efforts, yet the organization managed to expand its indigenous base and increase its community programs. During this period, the Free Breakfast for Schoolchildren Program became the most widely known Panthers program. It was followed closely by Liberation Schools, offering summer and after-school programs for children, and free health clinics. The common link between these programs was that local communities were involved intimately in providing manpower and finances. Perhaps this community involvement helps explain why the Panther programs prospered despite federal law enforcement's incessant efforts to undermine them.

By August 1970, when Newton was released from prison after his murder conviction had been reversed on appeal, the Panthers had suffered tremendous setbacks. Law enforcement efforts to undermine Panther activities and the group's membership purges had taken their toll. In addition, internal conflicts generated by a breach between Newton and Cleaver threatened to weaken the Panthers. Newton claimed that during his prison term, Cleaver had alienated many community supporters through his use of violent and profane rhetoric in public speaking engagements and as editor of *The Black Panther* newspaper. While the public believed that Newton embraced nonviolence and Cleaver endorsed violence, the tensions between the two men were largely due to differences in leadership styles and disagreements over programming priorities. Panther chapters in different regions focused on the needs of local communities, and programs differed accordingly. The North Carolina chapter, for example, established a Free Ambulance Program while the New York chapter focused its initial efforts on improving low-income housing. East Coast and southern members accused the West Coast Panthers leaders of financial favoritism, claiming that they amassed funding and refused to pay bail for incarcerated members.

After Newton reassumed Panthers leadership in August 1970, he launched efforts to rebuild community support and sought to establish the organization as part of the political and economic structure of Oakland. He ordered numerous chapters and branches around the country to shut down and transfer their members to the national headquarters to begin the process of taking over Oakland's government. As a result, some of the group's most effective organizers were concentrated in the Bay Area between 1971 and 1974. During this time, numerous Panther members entered community and citywide elections, including Seale, who ran for mayor of Oakland in 1973, and Elaine Brown, who made a bid for city council in the same year. While both campaigns were unsuccessful, they initiated an organizing process that contributed to the 1977 election of Oakland's first black mayor, Lionel Wilson. Newton's efforts to concentrate Panthers leadership in Oakland ended in August 1974. That year, Newton fled to Cuba after being charged with assaulting his tailor, Prestin Collins, and murdering fourteen-year-old prostitute Kathleen Smith.

While tensions between Newton and Cleaver as well as constant police harassment had hampered Panthers growth and programming efforts in the early 1970s, the group's programs grew tremendously after Elaine Brown succeeded Newton as chair in August 1974. Prior to 1974, the Panthers had initiated approximately twenty community service programs including a Free Shoe Program, free health clinics, a Sickle Cell Anemia Foundation, and tutoring services for students. By the fall of 1974, the Panthers and their nonprofit entity, Educational Opportunities Corporation, Inc., had developed additional programs to serve the needs of the poor, homeless, ill, imprisoned and their family members, youth, senior citizens, and numerous other underprivileged groups. By July 1977, the number of Panther programs had grown to approximately fifty-eight nationwide. While the majority of Panther programs continued to provide services for black residents of Oakland, the group also expanded its activities to the national and international arena.

This tremendous growth was the result of several factors, most prominently Brown's chairmanship, which lasted from August 1974 to October 1977, and the subsequent rise of numerous women to leadership positions as well as their increased electoral and community networking. Brown's appointment of qualified women to high-level leadership positions at the national headquarters of the Panthers in Oakland had an overwhelmingly positive impact on the morale of those who wanted to focus the organization's energy on program development rather than revolutionary rhetoric and armed posturing. Finally, Panther involvement in electoral and grass-roots political activity during the group's early years and, especially as a result of Seale's and Brown's 1973 campaigns, paved the way for the development of new programs that served a broader constituency. Programs such as the Oakland Community School (OCS), Seniors Against a Fearful Environment (SAFE), and the Oakland Community Learning Center (OCLC) received the widest praise and largest amount of local and national attention between 1974 and 1977. Although Newton had developed the theoretical foundation for these programs, local coordinators and members implemented them.

In addition to the Educational Opportunities Corporation, Inc. (EOC), which operated the increasingly popular OCS, the Panthers and their supporters initiated another crucial nonprofit organization, the Educational Opportunities Corporation Service, Inc. (EOCS). The EOCS provided community service programs through the OCLC, the first nonprofit Panther program. The OCLC operated the OCS, which offered "general and vocational educational opportunities to individuals, both adults and minors, at the primary, secondary, and high school grade levels" as well as adult educational extension services. The goals of the EOCS were more wide-ranging than those of the OCS, encompassing community programs such as services for seniors, teens, children, and young adults.

During Brown's leadership, the Panthers started to professionalize their programs and tried to keep them free of public scandal. Yet, in mid-1977, after a routine audit by the City of Oakland, the EOC administration was forced to acknowledge publicly that its accounting practices were not on par with traditional methods. EOC administrators explained that their inability to account for all funding in their records was due to a lack of funds necessary to hire skilled personnel to keep the organization's records. Apparently the group's failure to keep proper financial records was also due to a tremendous amount of personnel turnover in the community programs between 1974 and 1977.

Leadership and membership changes had a direct impact on the programs that suffered from a loss of manpower and expertise. Moreover, several Panther members had been involved in illegal activities that generated negative publicity and contributed to the gradual erosion of community support. As a result, Panthers programs were significantly reduced in size. Only four chapters—those in Oakland, Chicago, Los Angeles, and Winston-Salem, North Carolina—were still active in July 1977 when Newton returned from his three-year Cuban exile.

Upon his return to the United States, Newton received a hero's welcome from his staunchest supporters and numerous individuals expressed hopes that he would reestablish himself as spokesperson of the Panthers. The media, fascinated with Newton's return, speculated whether he would replace Brown as the most influential Panther and whether his return would mark a retreat from the intensive community programming that the organization had conducted between 1974 and 1977. Initially, Newton claimed that he had no intention of replacing Brown. By November 1977, however, he had resumed his leadership and Brown had departed under a cloud of secrecy and rumors that Newton had beaten her.

After reclaiming his leadership position, Newton sought to rebuild the Panthers. He closed the Chicago and North Carolina chapters and centralized the organization's power base in California. Newton's leadership generated considerable criticism among some Panthers, who complained about financial inequalities and unwarranted physical punishments. Dissatisfied with the organization's new direction, many leading members of the national headquarters left the Panthers. By December 1978, only the Los Angeles and Oakland chapters remained open.

While Newton continued Panthers community programs, the departure of leading program coordinators at the national headquarters, such as Brown, Phyllis Jackson, and Norma Armour, spelled almost certain downsizing of the scale and scope of community programs. By 1979 the Panthers were embroiled in a financial crisis from which they never recovered. Most severely affected by the lack of funds were the OCLC and Panthers newspaper. Beginning in early 1979 and lasting through 1980, the organization explored creative ways to finance its work and recruit staff, such as assigning college students who received work study to work in the OCS. Lack of communication between Newton and the rank-and-file members was apparently responsible for the inability of the Panthers to recover from the financial crisis. Numerous members called for a reorganization of the group's structure and its affiliated programs. But few changes were made and the Panthers continued to decline.

The final years of the Oakland and Los Angeles chapters suggest that the organization's centralized structure, with Newton as the ultimate decision maker, left the group in a precarious position that led to its dissolution. The final years of the Panthers also reveal the daily rigor and intensity under which the membership worked. Those who remained until the end were passionate about their commitment to "serve the people" and the final years truly tested their commitment and stamina.

**FURTHER READINGS**

Brown, Angela. "Women and the Black Panther Party." *Socialist Review* 96, 1 & 2 (1997): 33–67.

Brown, Elaine. *A Taste of Power: A Black Woman's Story.* New York: Pantheon, 1993.

Brown LeBlanc, Angela D. "The Most Qualified Person to Handle the Job: Black Panther Party Women, 1966–1982." In *The Black Panther Party Reconsidered.* Ed. Charles E. Jones. Baltimore: Black Classic Press, 1998.

Dr. Huey P. Newton Foundation Records, Special Collections Department, Stanford University, Stanford, California.

Newton, Huey P. *Revolutionary Suicide.* New York: Ballantine, 1974.

Seale, Bobby. *Seize the Time: The Story of the Black Panther Party and Huey P. Newton.* New York: Random House, 1968.

*Angela Darlean LeBlanc-Ernest*

## Black Panthers

*See* Black Panther Party (for Self-Defense).

## Black Pilots of America

*See* Negro Airmen International.

## Black Presbyterians Concerned

*See* National Black Presbyterian Caucus.

## Black Presbyterians United

*See* National Black Presbyterian Caucus.

## Black Public Relations Society of America

Contradictory sources claim that the Black Public Relations Society of America (BPRS) was either established in 1982 in Chicago, Illinois, or in 1983 as the Black Public

Relations Society of Southern California. Public relations professionals Pat Tobin and Helen Goss recognized that the public relations field needed more African American practitioners. Hoping to encourage blacks to enter the profession, they started the BPRS to provide resources, support, and educational advice to people interested in public relations, media relations, advertising, and marketing. The society is affiliated with the National Association of Black Journalists.

Of the two co-founders, Tobin served as the society's first president and Goss as vice president. Paul Brock was the group's first recording secretary, Dr. George Hill was treasurer, and Paul Clark served as parliamentarian. The officers served on a steering committee with nine other charter members: Mike Anderson, Felicia Bragg, Richard Brooks, Cheryl Dixon, Yolanda Dodd, Sheila Eldridge, Fitzroy Hamilton, Pat Logan, and Valerie Shaw.

The BPRS, called "beepers" by its members, acts as a repository of information for public relations professionals. Expanding through chapters established in major metropolitan areas, including Atlanta, Los Angeles, New York, and Washington, D.C., BPRS members represent almost all public relations specialties. BPRS strives to inform members about current public relations techniques to acquire clients and disseminate news efficiently through the media. Educational forums sponsored by the BPRS and hosted by universities and television and radio stations educate both public relations professionals and citizens about the uses and benefits of public relations.

Striving to increase opportunities for minorities in public relations, BPRS encourages African American public relations professionals to network with each other and to serve as mentors to African American and other students interested in the field. BPRS members deliver lectures and programs and lead seminars, teaching others about opportunities in public relations, including jobs in government, entertainment, and charitable organizations. The BPRS publishes a student and professional career guide to aid individuals seeking employment in public relations and has a skills bank for public relations professionals to consult. The quarterly *BPRS Newsletter* provides current news to members.

As of 2000 BPRS's headquarters were based in Los Angeles, California. Tobin serves as national president with Morgan D. Carter as vice president and Paula Robinson as secretary. African American public relations professionals attend a variety of special events sponsored by the BPRS. Every April the association holds its Annual Professional Development Seminar in Los Angeles, and in June it spon-

sors an annual awards and scholarship luncheon. The BPRS also sponsors an Internet website that contains society news, public relations links, and a directory of members.

**FURTHER READING**
*Guide to Black Organizations.* New York: Philip Morris Company, 1995.

*Elizabeth D. Schafer*

## Black Rock Coalition

The Black Rock Coalition (BRC) was established in 1985 by Konda Mason, a New York City video and film producer; Greg Tate, a prominent literary and music critic for the *Village Voice*; and Vernon Reid, the founder of the black American rock group Living Colour. The BRC, headquartered in New York City, aims to provide financial support and musical assistance to African American rock groups and musicians. Moreover, the BRC seeks to challenge racial stereotypes in the music industry through public meetings, seminars, and various educational programs. At its inception the BRC had some twenty members. Over the years, membership has fluctuated; it has been as high as 150 and as low as 25 members.

The success of Reid's band Living Colour, which included vocalist Corey Glover, bassist Muzzy Skillings, and drummer Will Calhoun, illustrated by their million-selling debut album *Vivid* (1988), generated much-needed support for the coalition. Yet, financial problems, personnel changes, irregularly scheduled meetings, and the lack of member groups and performers signed by major record labels continued to trouble the BRC. Despite these obstacles the BRC continues to have an impact on the careers of many African American rock-and-roll performers as it expands the minds of the music industry and the American public. For example, in 1990, the BRC sponsored a series of free concerts in New York to promote local and regional black rock groups and musicians.

In late 1993, after the breakup of Reid's band, the coalition's impact on the music industry and its influence on the development of popular music declined. The organization, however, continued its quest to promote African American rock groups and musicians with the release of a twelve-song, twelve-band album titled *Blacker Than That.* Moreover, the BRC continues to provide financial and musical assistance to black rock bands and performers and remains committed to raising public awareness.

**FURTHER READINGS**

Fricke, David. "Back in Black: A Group of Musicians Unites to Reclaim the Right to Rock." *Rolling Stone*, September 24, 1987, 64–66, 149–150.

Hochman, Steve. "Black Rock Coalition Pushes for an End to Musical Apartheid." *Los Angeles Times*, June 14, 1989, Sec. 6, 6.

Kot, Greg. "Musical Apartheid: Black Rockers to Break Down Stereotypes." *Chicago Tribune*, October 27, 1991, Sec. 13, 6–7.

Mahon, Maureen Elizabeth. "The Black Rock Coalition and the Cultural Politics of Race in the United States." Ph.D. diss., New York University, 1997.

Smith, Danyel. "UNV Breaks Down Spiritual & Secular; Janet & The Tonys; Backing Black Rock." *Billboard*, September 11, 1993, 37, 21.

Watrous, Peter. "Black Rock Coalition Sunders Stereotypes." *New York Times*, January 19, 1990, Sec. C, 14.

*Eric R. Jackson*


# Black Star Line

*See* Universal Negro Improvement Association and African Communities League.


# Black Stuntmen's Association

In 1966, movie extra Eddie Smith founded the Black Stuntmen's Association (BSA) in response to the virtual exclusion of African Americans from the Hollywood's Stuntmen's Association (HSA). HSA guild rules, which stipulated that members earn at least $10,000 a year, made it impossible for black stuntmen to join the professional association. In the mid-1960s, Hollywood movies cast black actors only in a limited number of roles, few of them requiring the skills of stuntmen. When black actors did require stunt doubles, filmmakers were willing to use white stuntpeople in black face. Led by Smith, a group of black men and women began to acquire stunt skills by secretly observing white stuntpeople during their training in the Los Angeles area. The members of the black group then practiced the stunts in a neighborhood near Compton, California, until they were ready to showcase their skills and apply for jobs in the movie and television industries.

From the beginning in 1966, black stuntpeople sought to organize a racially integrated group and intended to call themselves the Stuntmen's Association. The threat of an HSA-initiated lawsuit over ownership of the name, however, forced the group to adopt its current name. The BSA, under the leadership of its first president, Ernie Robinson, provided crucial training for aspiring black stuntpeople and succeeded in casting several of its members in television shows and movies, including *Mission Impossible* (1966–1973), *Mod Squad* (1968–1973), *Halls of Anger* (1970), *Dirty Harry* (1971), *Across 110th Street* (1972), and *Live and Let Die* (1973). The BSA won a major victory in its struggle to secure work for black stuntpeople when the Hollywood branch of the National Association for the Advancement of Colored People (NAACP) pressured the studios to use black stunt doubles for African American actors in the acclaimed television miniseries *Roots* (1977).

Ironically, increasing employment opportunities for black stuntpeople also triggered the demise of the BSA. Beginning in the mid-1970s BSA membership declined, as the demand for black stuntpeople grew and the resulting increase in earnings started to qualify them for membership in the HSA and its affiliate, Stunts Unlimited. Smith knew all along that BSA members would leave the organization as they gained experience and acquired contacts in the film industry. When the color line in the stunt guilds was broken, the need for a separate association diminished. Nevertheless, the BSA continues to operate under the leadership of Smith, who is retired from stunt work but occasionally still finds jobs for BSA members. Most recently he helped place two stuntwomen in the film adaptation of Toni Morrison's *Beloved* (1998). Smith also maintains a small library at his Los Angeles home that provides a record of the historic achievements of the BSA.

**FURTHER READINGS**

"Black Stunt Men: Ex-Athletes Organize to Gain Film Roles." *Ebony* (December 1969): 114.

Pantovic, Stan. "Black Stuntmen of Hollywood." *Sepia* (December 1971): 39.

*Stephen Davenport*


# Black Unitarian Universalist Caucus

*See* Black Affairs Council, Unitarian Universalist.


# Black Women Historians

*See* Association of Black Women Historians.

## Black Women Organized for Action

Aileen Hernandez, renowned feminist and former chairperson of the National Organization for Women (NOW), along with Patsy G. Fulcher, Eleanor R. Spikes, Alma Jackson, and Maxine Ussery, founded Black Women Organized for Action (BWOA) in San Francisco in 1973. Until its demise in 1980, BWOA assisted African American women in the San Francisco Bay Area with employment, day care, and tax preparation and provided counseling for family violence. The group emerged in response to philosophical differences with the strategies of existing black women's organizations and the changing political climate of San Francisco. BWOA was a vehicle for developing a sense of common purpose among black women of different classes and backgrounds. The organization had a significant political and social impact, but it dissolved by December 1980, in the midst of an increasingly conservative political tenor and declining membership participation.

BWOA's formation signaled the inability of the black power and the feminist movements to address the needs of African American women. The black power movement of the 1960s largely focused on gaining respect for African American men, while the feminist movement emphasized the needs of middle-class white women. The BWOA's co-founders realized that black women needed an organization that combined both approaches and modified them to address issues of specific concern to African American women. Hence, BWOA members focused their efforts on increasing black women's participation in politics and improving their economic status. They sought to integrate black women into San Francisco's employment and political structure to provide them with opportunities to acquire leadership skills. BWOA also supported women in public positions formerly reserved for men. The BWOA, for example, campaigned for Black Panther party member Elaine Brown's bid for city council in 1975. Furthermore, BWOA members supported only those male political candidates who were responsive to black women's political and economic concerns. BWOA provided a forum for women to bond and develop leadership skills in addition to forming political coalitions with other women at the local, national, and international levels. BWOA's most important contribution was its ability to organize working- and middle-class women while raising their awareness of and involvement in community affairs.

FURTHER READINGS

Brown, Angela Darlean. "Crossroads: A History of Black Women Organized for Action." Unpublished paper, Stanford University, March 16, 1994.

Fulcher, Patsy G., Aileen Hernandez, and Eleanor R. Spikes. "Sharing the Power and the Glory." *Contact* (Fall 1974): 50.

Gilford, Flora. Personal interview, Daly City, California, February 14, 1994.

Hernandez, Aileen C. Personal interview, San Francisco, California, December 6, 1993.

"What It Is: A Newsletter for Black Women Organized for Action," May 1973–December 1980, Black Women Organized for Action Organizational Files, San Francisco, California, Office of Aileen Hernandez and Associates.

*Angela Darlean LeBlanc-Ernest*

## Black Women Organized for Educational Development

The nonprofit Black Women Organized for Educational Development (BWOED) was organized in Oakland, California, in 1984. BWOED promotes economic self-sufficiency and fosters efforts to empower socially or culturally disadvantaged women.

To meet the needs of women who had not yet realized their potential, the California-based organization established a mentoring program, support groups, and a resource center. BWOED's mentoring program educates young women on teen pregnancy, HIV infection, substance abuse, community violence, and the effects of dropping out of school. Women in the community provide career guidance, cultural and social exposure, and emotional support to mentees in the program. BWOED also provides workshops that help students improve academically while building self-esteem. The BWOED support group "Just Between Us Sis'tuhs" provides women with a forum to talk about and learn new techniques to cope with issues such as single parenting, male/female relationships, homelessness, women's health, women in violent relationships, and financial planning. The BWOED's resource center provides employment referral services for women and youths and teaches participants how to complete job applications, how to work with government agencies or businesses, and how to get involved in the community. In addition to helping women at the center, BWOED produces a women's resource guide entitled *emerge* that lists agencies and organizations helpful to black women in the areas of advocacy, education, health, law, politics, religion, and social and civic service.

As BWOED moves through its second decade, it continues to grow and ally itself with organizations sharing similar visions. BWOED leaders continue to meet the needs of California's black women, helping them to develop physically, emotional, socially, and professionally.

**FURTHER READINGS**

*BWOED Press Releases*, January 9, February 7, May 2, June 7, June 10, and August 1, 1997.
*Sistah to Sistah Newsletter* 1, 1 (June 1997): 3.

*Maria Williams-Hawkins*

## Black Women's Educational Alliance

Founded in 1976, the Black Women's Educational Alliance (BWEA) serves black women working in the field of education as well as those who have retired from it. The BWEA provides professional growth opportunities for its members, paying particular attention to career mobility, equal opportunity for women, political education issues, and leadership opportunity enhancement. The BWEA, currently headed by Deidre Farmbey, seeks to enhance educational standards and encourages community involvement in the schools. For this purpose, the organization offers seminars and forums to help communities talk about formal and informal school curricula and other forms of public education, such as medical and parenting education. The BWEA provides educational opportunities through scholarships and rewards educational excellence with an education and service awards program. To serve the BWEA's nearly three hundred members, the organization publishes a periodic bulletin and semiannual newsletter and holds biennial meetings.

*Thalia M. Mulvihill*

## Black Women's Liberation Committee

The Black Women's Liberation Committee (BWLC) originated within the Student Nonviolent Coordinating Committee (SNCC) in 1968. Its purpose was to expose and ameliorate the triple exploitation of black women in America: as blacks, as women, and as workers. BWLC members believed, as many in the civil rights movement did, that education was the best means of achieving their ends. Working from within SNCC, they established "heritage houses" in numerous communities to enable African American youth to obtain information about their black

heritage. By the summer of 1970, the BWLC had divorced itself from SNCC; expanded its mission to address the concerns of African, Asian, and Latin women, as well as African American women; and been rechristened the Third World Women's Alliance.

A separate group within and ultimately an organization completely outside SNCC appeared necessary to BWLC founders for a variety of reasons. In comparison to American society, SNCC and other civil rights groups were remarkably egalitarian in their treatment of women and men, and women had been important participants in the modern civil rights movement from its inception. As in the rest of society, however, men rather than women assumed leadership roles in the movement. Women often occupied local positions of power but rarely found equal status at the national level. Indeed, many women found themselves relegated to clerical and other support positions. In later years, both men and women who had been involved in the movement remarked on the subordination of women in SNCC, the civil rights movement, and the left wing organizations.

Though black and white women realized the imbalance of power between men and women who were active in the movement, cooperation between the two groups of women was difficult. The women of the BWLC believed that black and white women, even those who had been working side by side in the civil rights movement, shared little common interest. White feminists of the 1960s were mostly middle class and did not face the same sort of social, economic, and intellectual oppression or the struggle for survival that black women did.

Many black women recognized racism, not sexism, as their primary obstacle to success and survival in the United States. Yet, with the rise of the "Black Power" movement in 1966 and its emphasis on the pride and potential of black men, black women began to realize the need for their own organizations. Hence the creation of the BWLC and other black feminist organizations such as the National Black Feminist Organization, founded in 1973.

The BWLC believed in black liberation and black nationalism but not at women's expense. Defending themselves against charges of divisiveness, the BWLC and similar organizations reminded black men that progress must be judged by the position of the women of the race as well as its men. Liberation could come to half a race.

**FURTHER READINGS**

Evans, Sara. *Personal Politics: The Roots of Women's Liberation in the Civil Rights Movement and the New Left.* New York: Alfred A. Knopf, 1979.

Fleming, Cynthia Griggs. "Black Women Activists and the Student Nonviolent Coordinating Committee: The Case of Ruby Doris Smith Robinson." *Journal of Women's History* 4, 3 (winter 1993): 64–82.

Records of the Black Women's Liberation Committee. Mary McLeod Bethune Council House. Washington, D.C.

*Nancy Bowman*

## Blacks in Government

Blacks in Government (BIG), originally conceived by the Department of Health, Education, and Welfare federal workers in Rockville, Maryland, was founded as a non-profit organization in the District of Columbia in 1975. BIG is a network for African American civil servants as well as an advocacy group. While BIG was initially intended to serve black federal workers, soon the group decided to include African American state and local civil servants.

BIG's main objective is to represent the interests and to advance the status of black civil servants. For this purpose the organization monitors on-the-job discrimination, supports implementation of affirmative action laws, and sponsors legislative initiatives and court cases affecting equal employment opportunities. BIG's 1.2 million membership is organized in eleven regions and more than two hundred chapters. Each August, BIG holds its annual National Training Conference with over one hundred workshops and seminars. Headquartered in Washington, D.C., the organization informs its members through the quarterly newsletter *Blacks in Government—News.*

### FURTHER READINGS

"Blacks in Government hit federal job bias." *Jet* 76, 23 (1989): 26.

Maurer, Christine, and Tara Sheets, eds. *Encyclopedia of Associations: An Associations Unlimited Reference,* 33d ed. Detroit: Gale, 1998, p. 517.

*Oscar Flores*

## Blue Circle Nurses

Adah B. Thoms, a registered black nurse with New York's Lincoln Hospital and Home who had helped organize the National Association of Colored Graduate Nurses in 1908, founded the Blue Circle Nurses (BCN) in 1917. The BCN sought to provide health care and medical services for black troops and southern rural black communities, to advance the professional status of black nurses, and to challenge the exclusion of black nurses from the American Red Cross and the U.S. Army Nurse Corps.

Prior to World War I, public health care providers had largely neglected the physical and mental health care of African Americans. Moreover, professional medical organizations, such as the American Nurses' Association (ANA) and the American Medical Association (AMA), excluded African Americans. The BCN was one of many separate organizations that black health care providers established to serve the health and medical needs of African American communities, to foster racial solidarity, and to advance the professionalization of black nurses.

During World War I the BCN was affiliated with the Circle for Negro War Relief, a war relief organization that raised money among African Americans and used the funds to recruit black nurses for work in African American communities. The nurses not only provided health care services but also educated impoverished rural blacks about sanitation advances, promoted healthy nutrition, and advocated housing improvements. After the war, the circle continued its efforts and, in 1919, launched health care programs for the families of disabled black veterans. While Thoms hoped that the BCN would become the central organization that would standardize and coordinate black public health work nationwide, lack of funds proved to be an insurmountable obstacle.

In addition to providing much-needed health and medical care to black communities during World War I, the BCN also spearheaded a crusade to integrate the nursing profession. Thoms and Etnah R. Boutte, executive secretary of the Circle for Negro War Relief, challenged the Red Cross to end its exclusion of black nurses. Afraid of southern white opposition, white Red Cross leaders maintained that the exclusion was justified, claiming that black nurses were ill-prepared for the work because few of them had passed the nursing certification exam. In response, Thoms and Boutte insisted that all BCN nurses meet American Red Cross certification requirements. Moreover, they placed BCN nurses under the authority of the state health departments, allowing the Red Cross to monitor the work of the BCN nurses. In addition, Thoms and Boutte demanded that local Red Cross chapters help pay the salaries of black nurses, although without any success. During the war, the African American community raised funds to pay BCN nurses to serve with the Circle for Negro War Relief. The black nurses affiliated with the state health departments, but continued to wear BCN emblems and uniforms to demonstrate their autonomous identity.

Throughout the 1920s, the BCN continued its wartime efforts and tried to provide health care programs for black veterans and rural black communities in the South.

Moreover, the BCN tried to raise funds to offer scholarships to black nurses interested in pursuing postgraduate education courses in public health. Despite its noble efforts, the BCN was hampered by a chronic lack of funds. Without Red Cross affiliation or white philanthropic assistance, the BCN was forced to rely largely on donations from the black community, which did not have the financial means to support the venture. By 1934, the BCN ceased to exist as the larger and financially stronger National Association of Colored Graduate Nurses (NACGN) assumed much of its work. The NACGN continued the struggle to improve health and medical care for African Americans and to integrate the nursing profession.

**FURTHER READINGS**

Elmore, Joyce Ann. "Black Nurses: Their Service and Their Struggle." *American Journal of Nursing* 76 (March 1976): 435–437.

Hine, Darlene Clark. "The Call That Never Came." *Indiana Military History Journal* 8 (January 1983): 23–27.

———. *Black Women in White: Racial Conflict and Cooperation in the Nursing Profession, 1890–1950.* Bloomington: Indiana University Press, 1989.

Staupers, Mabel Keaton. *No Time for Prejudice: A Story of the Integration of Negroes in Nursing in the United States.* New York: Macmillan, 1961.

Thoms, Adah B. *Pathfinders: A History of the Progress of Colored Graduate Nurses.* New York: Kay Printing House, 1929; rpt., New York: Garland Publishing, 1985.

*David MacLaren*

**SEE ALSO** Circle for Negro War Relief; National Association of Colored Graduate Nurses

## Board of Missions to Freedmen

*See* Presbyterian Church Committee on Missions to Freedmen.

## Boston: Civic, Literary, and Mutual Aid Associations

The history of Boston's black civic associations is deeply rooted in the unique relations between African American and white residents of the city. Originally settled in 1630 as a Puritan enclave that strove to be a moral example to Europe as a "city on a hill," the idealistic English inhabitants held slaves, and their descendants participated in the slave trade. Later "Brahmin" descendants of the original settlers built cotton mills that relied upon a raw material produced by slave labor. Yet the abolitionist movement initiated by William Lloyd Garrison in the 1830s flowed out of the original Puritan ideas, the ideology of the American Revolution, and the synthesis of these free African Americans. The mass immigration by Irish Catholics during the famine of the 1840s brought a new ethnic group to Boston, hostile both to the Yankees and the small black community. From that time on, Boston's black associations had to negotiate the complex relations between antislavery activists and their descendants, ambivalent Brahmins, and largely antipathetic Irish Americans. Abolition and its aftermath made Boston's small African American community disproportionately influential in the national black community until the great migration of World War I to the North, which bypassed Boston.

Boston's first African American community of slaves and free people lived along the waterfront in what is today the city's North End, the men working as sailors, longshoremen, and shipbuilders. After the Revolution, they moved to the north slope of Beacon Hill and many became personal service workers. By 1790, 4,000 people of color lived in what became the West End, and about one hundred years later, when new European immigrants arrived, black people moved to the South End. After World War II, the next wave of southern migrants moved to the Roxbury, Mattapan, and Dorchester districts.

A lawsuit brought by Quock Walker, a slave who argued that his master's will had freed him, ended slavery in Massachusetts in 1781, the first state to do so. This favorable climate helped foster an early fraternal organization, the African Masonic Lodge, now named for its founder, Prince Hall. Hall, originally from Barbados, was a Methodist minister and patriot soldier. The Masons performed traditional fraternal services for members and the community as a whole, but they were also antislavery men. Hall used the rhetoric of the Bible and the American Revolution to show the contradiction between the nation's devotion to "liberty" and Christian values on the one hand and its toleration of slavery on the other.

The African Society, by contrast, focused on moral and spiritual uplift rather than economic mutual aid. Founded in 1796, it claimed about 200 supporters by 1808. Convening at the African Meeting House, the society encouraged moral familial relations, temperance, respect for law, and self-improvement. Two years later black Bostonians founded the African school, which moved in 1806 to a Baptist church.

As the question of slavery assumed more importance in American life, Boston's African Americans formed the General Colored Association in 1826 to oppose it. David Walker, a freedman from North Carolina, and John T. Hilton, a barber, were its guiding spirits. Walker issued a fiery pamphlet, the "Appeal," which justified slave rebellion, encouraged education, and condemned the colonization movement that sought to deport colored people to Africa.

The framework of the debate shifted, however, when William Lloyd Garrison of Newburyport, Massachusetts, launched the New England Antislavery Society and the *Liberator* newspaper in 1831. Garrison and his interracial colleagues met at the African Meeting House; black people at first were the main supporters of the newspaper. Garrison's group called for the immediate freedom of slaves without compensation to the slaveholders, citizenship rights for African Americans, and opposition to colonization. Leading black Garrisonians like William Cooper Nell, Charles Lenox Remond, and Frederick Douglass helped to end much legal discrimination against people of color. Nell led a successful crusade to desegregate the public schools; Remond secured thousands of signatures on an antislavery petition in Ireland; and Douglass effectively "sat-in" to end segregation on a railroad line.

This movement had a complex effect on black community institutional development. On the one hand, by boldly challenging race prejudice, Boston's antislavery activists created the atmosphere that led to the first regiment of free black troops in the Civil War. On the other hand, the Garrisonian argument that all black organizations represented a concession to racism (and their antipolitical stance) led some activists, like Frederick Douglass, to break with the movement, and in Douglass's case, to leave town. During the antebellum period, African Americans continued their community service groups and developed some new ones: the Daughters of Zion (1845), the Female Benevolent Firm (1850), and the Juvenile Garrison Independent Society.

After the Civil War, African American Bostonians participated in Republican politics, winning local elections and some patronage. By 1890 the city's black population stood at only 8,125, less than 2 percent of the total. Despite its small size, the community produced a weekly newspaper, the *Hub* in the 1880s and the *Courant* in the 1890s. Anxious about deteriorating race relations nationally, Bostonians joined the Colored National League and the Citizens' Equal Rights Association, to safeguard the Fourteenth and Fifteenth Amendments, known as the civil rights amendments.

The appearance of Booker T. Washington as spokesman for black America in 1895 divided the Boston community. Washington had powerful connections among the city's white and black elites, who funded his Tuskegee Institute and conferred an honorary Harvard degree upon him. In 1900, Washington launched his National Negro Business League in Boston and advanced funding for the *Colored American Magazine*.

Civic activity among Boston's African American women dates back at least to the days of Maria Stewart, a Garrisonian speaker of the early 1830s. During the 1890s Josephine St. Pierre Ruffin and Maria Baldwin started the Women's Era Club and its newspaper, *Women's Era*. Working with the militant Ida B. Wells of Chicago and Margaret Murray Washington, wife of the conservative Tuskegee principal, they straddled the emerging divide between militants and accommodationists. At an 1895 Boston convention they launched the National Federation of Afro-American Women, which merged with other groups to form the National Association of Colored Women's Clubs. The Boston chapter challenged lynching, conducted moral and educational programs in keeping with its "lifting as we climb" motto, and Ruffin tried but failed to integrate the General Federation of Women's Clubs.

As the nation's racial climate worsened in the new century, a small group of black Bostonians challenged Booker T. Washington's public acceptance of segregation and disfranchisement. In 1901 William Monroe Trotter launched the *Guardian* newspaper, and in 1903 he and his colleagues disrupted a speech by Washington. Trotter founded a series of organizations, which lasted until his death in 1934, that focused on using the black vote independently. Trotter's National Equal Rights League and similar groups often called for voting Democratic at a time when most African Americans voted Republican. Trotter was notoriously difficult to work with; he disrupted the Boston chapter of W. E. B. Du Bois's Niagara movement and remained aloof from the National Association for the Advancement of Colored People (NAACP).

Trotter's wariness toward the NAACP limited the early organizing efforts of the Boston branch, whose prime movers were the descendants of white abolitionists, such as Francis Jackson Garrison, and Moorfield Storey, a former secretary to Senator Charles Sumner and the NAACP's national president until Storey's death in 1929. Among the most influential early African American leaders of the

NAACP were Butler and Mary Wilson, who recruited black members during the post–World War I period in Boston and the northeast. The association aggressively combatted local discrimination, but faltered during the 1920s and acted only sporadically until the 1960s.

The wave of African American migration to Boston after World War II changed the shape of the city's ethnic geography. The new migrants inhabited a segregated community with separate and inferior schools, suffered limited job opportunities, and faced the hostility of entrenched Irish American political and union leaders, who took control of the city's patronage during the 1880s. Their attempts to break free of these limitations produced a host of new, mostly militant and integrationist organizations.

The first of the new groups in the civil rights era was Freedom House, founded in 1949 by social workers Muriel and Otto Snowden. Freedom House was a privately funded social service agency and early "think tank." Its moderate leaders worked in a collaborative way with white leaders to ease relations between the growing black community and a disinterested white power structure.

During the 1950s the all-white Boston School Committee engineered the de facto segregation of the schools by refusing to assign African American children to mainly white "neighborhood" schools. Around 1960, an interracial group called Citizens for Boston Public Schools ran a slate for school committee that included Mel King. King, the son of a militant Guyanese immigrant dockworker, became the most visible activist in black community politics for the next thirty years. He helped found, among other groups, the Boston People's Organization, which worked on a variety of issues and promoted King's two mayoral campaigns.

To combat job discrimination, King and co-worker Chuck Turner launched a series of organizations: the Boston Action Group, United Community Construction Workers, and the Third World Jobs Clearing House. These groups employed confrontational tactics of boycotts, picket lines, and community mobilizations to insist upon equal opportunity in employment. The Third World Jobs Clearing House was a coalition of minority groups that won significant concessions in construction and municipal hiring.

In the early 1950s, a young mother named Ruth Batson joined the NAACP and turned the organization's attention toward the public schools. Along with King, Paul Parks, Melnea Cass, Ellen Jackson, and others, she insisted that the all-white school committee face up to the inferior conditions in the segregated schools. By 1963 they hired Thomas Atkins as executive secretary for the NAACP,

and this team of activists led the movement to desegregate Boston's schools. After they won a federal court decision, these NAACP leaders mobilized the community and its allies to defend black students from violent racist mobs. One of their accomplishments was the creation of METCO, the Metropolitan Council for Educational Opportunity, which bused students to suburban schools.

The thrust of postwar civic organizations in Boston has been to ensure equal rights in the face of exclusion. Nationalist organizations have never been strong in Boston, but the city did help shape two of the most influential leaders of the Nation of Islam. Malcolm X was recruited to the organization while in a Charlestown, Massachusetts, prison, and Louis Farrakhan, the central leader of the Nation during the 1980s and 1990s, was born and raised in Boston.

One long-term institution in Boston's cultural life applauded by all groups was the Elma Lewis School of Fine Arts. Founded in 1950 by a dynamic teacher of music and dance, the school lasted until funds ran out in 1996. The building now houses the National Center of Afro-American Artists. Boston is also home to an Afro-American History Museum founded by Sue Bailey Thurman, and local historians Robert Hayden and Byron Rushing have contributed to the museum's success. The W. E. B. Du Bois Institute at Harvard University has attracted such outstanding scholars as Henry Louis Gates, Cornel West, and William Julius Wilson.

During the 1980s and 1990s, as many of Boston's industrial plants closed, unemployment, crime, and drugs became more prevalent. The Dudley Street Neighborhood Initiative united a wide range of interracial community activists and developers to build low-cost housing for those who were affected by the plant closings. The Ten Point Coalition, a ministerial alliance of small congregations led by Reverend Eugene Rivers III and similar to the African Society of 1796, worked with African American youth. In the tradition of the Prince Hall Masons, the Organization for a New Equality (ONE), founded by Reverend Charles Stith of the Union United Methodist Church, focuses on increasing employment opportunities for African Americans. The work and community dedication of the early leaders of Boston's African American associations continue to inspire the city's present leaders.

**FURTHER READINGS**

Hayden, Robert C. *African Americans in Boston: More than 350 Years.* Boston: Trustees of the Public Library of Boston, 1991.

Horton, James Oliver, and Lois E. Horton. *Black Bostonians: Family Life and Community Struggle in the Antebellum North.* New York: Holmes and Meier Publishers, Inc., 1979.

King, Mel. *Chain of Change: Struggles for Black Community Development.* Boston: South End Press, 1981.

Pleck, Elizabeth Hafkin. *Black Migration and Poverty: Boston 1865–1900.* New York: Academic Press, 1979.

Schneider, Mark R. *Boston Confronts Jim Crow, 1890–1920.* Boston: Northeastern University Press, 1997.

*Mark R. Schneider*

## Boston League of Women for Community Service

*See* League of Women for Community Service, Boston.

## Boston Literary and Historical Association

Militants opposed to Booker T. Washington's leadership founded the Boston Literary and Historical Association (BLHA) in March 1901. Its leading figures included the activists Archibald H. Grimké, William Monroe Trotter, Butler Wilson, Clement Morgan, and George W. Forbes. Modeled on Washington, D.C.'s Bethel Literary and Historical Association, the group served as a forum and discussion club for Bostonians worried about the worsening racial climate at the start of the twentieth century.

Washington, the principal of Tuskegee Institute, had powerful connections among Boston's African-American and white elites. After winning prominence with his 1895 Atlanta speech that accepted southern racial norms, he frequently spoke in Boston. His themes prompted a suspicious response from some black Bostonians, who protested racist outrages, such as the lynching of Sam Hose near Atlanta in 1899. The BLHA had its roots in this ferment.

The association met every two weeks for nine months of the year, adjourning during the summer, and in winter it met weekly. It convened at the Prince School in the Back Bay, a mostly white neighborhood accessible to the West and South End districts, where most black Bostonians then lived. Its stated purpose, "to promote the intellectual life of the community," was similar to that of the St. Mark's Literary Association, which met at a Congregational church. This group, however, was more conservative and less influential than the BLHA.

Grimké, the first president, and Trotter were the leading spirits of the BLHA. Grimké was the son of a Charleston slaveholder and his slave mistress. He escaped to freedom in Boston where his illustrious white aunts, Angelina Grimké Weld and Sarah Grimké, lived. His brother Francis became a minister in Washington, D.C., and Grimké may have imported the idea of a forum series from there. Trotter, the son of a prominent black Boston Civil War veteran, launched the crusading *Guardian* newspaper later in 1901.

According to John Daniels, a contemporary white observer, the BLHA attracted between 250 and 750 people to its meetings. Speakers included men and women of both races, and the discussion from the floor was learned, but contentious when the lecturer was conservative. Music was often on the program. Many leading African American intellectuals came from out of town to speak, including W. E. B. Du Bois, novelist Charles Chesnutt, and Kelly Miller of Howard University. Local activists spoke as well, such as Trotter, Grimké, educator Maria Baldwin, and Reverends Reverdy Ransom and James H. Henderson. The audience was not afraid to challenge sympathetic white speakers, such as William Lloyd Garrison Jr., Oswald Garrison Villard, Harvard professor Edward Cummings, and Thomas Wentworth Higginson, whose politics were often more conservative.

It is not clear how long the BLHA lasted, but its original purpose was superseded by the time the Boston chapter of the National Association for the Advancement of Colored People (NAACP) became a mostly African American group after World War I. Grimké by then was the NAACP leader in Washington, D.C., and Trotter's movement, which remained aloof from the NAACP, faltered in the 1920s.

**FURTHER READINGS**

Bruce, Dickson D., Jr. *Archibald H. Grimké: Portrait of a Black Independent.* Baton Rouge: Louisiana State University Press, 1993.

Cromwell, Adelaide M. *The Other Brahmins: Boston's Black Upper Class 1750–1950.* Fayetteville: University of Arkansas Press, 1994.

Daniels, John. *In Freedom's Birthplace: A Study of the Boston Negroes.* New York: Negro Universities Press, 1968.

Fox, Stephen R. *The Guardian of Boston: William Monroe Trotter.* New York: Atheneum, 1970.

Schneider, Mark R. *Boston Confronts Jim Crow, 1890–1920.* Boston: Northeastern University Press, 1997.

*Mark R. Schneider*

## British and Foreign Anti-Slavery Society

The British and Foreign Anti-Slavery Society (BFASS) operated from 1839 through the late 1860s, tackling issues such as the apprenticeship system in the West Indies, the Cuban slave trade, American slavery, the safety of fugitive slaves, and the role of the church in the struggle to end slavery. The society became the most influential British abolitionist organization of the nineteenth century as it helped mold British public opinion through a barrage of lectures, advertising and publishing campaigns, economic boycotts, and lobbying efforts.

Prior to the founding of the BFASS, the British antislavery movement had secured a series of crucial victories, including the abolition of slavery in England in 1772, the end of the British slave trade in 1807, and the abolition of slavery in the British colonies in 1833. Despite these significant achievements, British antislavery activists continued their struggle when they learned that slaveholders in the British colonies of the West Indies had instituted an apprenticeship system for former slaves that hardly differed from slavery. British abolitionist Joseph Sturge traveled to the West Indies to gather evidence and, with the formation of the Central Negro Emancipation Committee in 1837, he successfully lobbied Parliament to end the apprenticeship system by 1839.

Celebrating their victory, committee members then launched the BFASS on April 17, 1839, in order to fight slavery throughout the world. John Scoble, a dogmatic, unpopular conservative who served as the BFASS's secretary from 1839 through 1852, toured Britain along with Sturge that first year to raise support for auxiliary groups. By 1869, over one hundred local groups had emerged. Members of the society tended to be middle-class religious humanitarians, especially Quakers and Nonconformists. They appealed to distinguished aristocrats, scholars, ministers, and the working class to support their struggle and advocated traditional political tactics such as petitioning, voting, and parliamentary lobbying.

Although concern about the apprenticeship system in the West Indies had provided the impetus for the creation of the BFASS, the society quickly focused its efforts on ending slavery in the United States. In 1842, Great Britain and the United States signed the Anglo-American Treaty that required British citizens to return fugitive slaves who had sought refuge with them. The BFASS refused to comply, and many of its members aided fugitives who had escaped to Canada and Britain. In the following year, the society resolved to focus solely on abolishing slavery in America.

In 1844, the Free Church of Scotland sent delegates to the United States to raise money among southern Presbyterians, many of whom were slaveholders. But the purist Garrisonian abolitionists perceived any alliance with slaveholders as potentially corrupting and sinful. They initiated a "Send Back the Money" campaign to pressure the Free Church to return the funds it had raised among southern white Presbyterians. The BFASS joined the successful campaign, proclaiming the "excommunication" of religious slaveholders. In the 1840s, the society feared that the U.S. annexation of Texas would lead to the further extension of slavery and urged the British government to recognize the Republic of Texas on the condition that it abolish slavery.

While BFASS members sought to collaborate with American abolitionists, efforts at transatlantic cooperation were strained from the beginning. In 1840, shortly after the founding of the BFASS, the society invited American abolitionists to attend a World Convention in London. Unbeknownst to British antislavery activists, the American abolitionists movement had divided over the role of women in the antislavery struggle. When American radical William Lloyd Garrison, a champion of pacifism and women's rights, arrived at the convention with several women delegates, the BFASS refused to seat them on the grounds of "Evangelical custom." Protesting the exclusion of women, Garrison, Charles Remond, and other American delegates decided to sit in the women's section behind a curtain in the balcony. The incident generated bitter rivalry between the society and the Garrisonians until the 1850s, when a younger generation filled the membership ranks of the BFASS. Led by Louis Chamerovzow, who had replaced the conservative Scoble as BFASS secretary in 1853, the new generation attempted to heal divisive relations between the society and the Garrisonians by sponsoring another world convention in 1854. That year, the convention received two women delegates; however, their seating resulted only in a modest improvement of the relationship between the BFASS and American abolitionists.

Throughout the 1850s, the society continued to champion the abolition of slavery in the United States. It challenged American churches to support abolition and urged them to deny membership to slaveholders. Moreover, the BFASS advocated a boycott of slave-grown products and greater reliance on Indian cotton. Quaker and BFASS member Anna Richardson led the society's free-produce movement, and by 1851 helped establish at least thirty stores that carried goods produced exclusively by free labor. While many British women purchased only free-labor cotton, their efforts did not succeed in reducing the imports of American cotton, which tripled between 1840 and 1860. Yet, the free-produce movement had a curious side effect. Through the organization of fund-raising efforts and economic boycotts, women assumed a greater role in the BFASS. As a result, they joined the society in increasing numbers and soon women's local auxiliaries began to outnumber men.

The activities of the society diminished with the advent of the U.S. Civil War. Some BFASS members voiced support for the secessionist states on the condition that the Confederacy suppress illegal slave trading. Others joined abolitionists George Thompson and F. W. Chesson, who created the London Emancipation Society in 1859 to encourage support for the Union's cause. Meanwhile, the BFASS succeeded in pressuring the British government to end the illegal Cuban slave trade. In 1862, Great Britain and the United States signed the Treaty for the Suppression of the African Slave Trade, whereby both parties agreed to patrol and search for slaves on board American and British vessels leaving Cuba. In January 1863, when Abraham Lincoln announced the emancipation of the slaves and the abolition of slavery as one of the Union's war aims, BFASS and Garrisonian abolitionists united for the first time and launched the freedmen's aid movement. Both groups joined forces to distribute clothing items, religious materials, educational supplies, and financial aid to the newly freed slaves. The BFASS continued to support the former slaves until its demise in the late 1860s.

BFASS played a crucial role in shaping British public opinion of slavery and generating support for abolitionism in the 1840s and 1850s. Through lobbying efforts and public education campaigns, BFASS members succeeded in pressuring Parliament to end the Cuban slave trade and encouraging members of the clergy to view slavery as a sin. Moreover, the society's economic boycotts and free-produce movement helped usher in a new era of women's political involvement, in spite of its initial opposition to women. While the society's numerous and diverse campaigns against slavery stimulated the political activism of many British men and women, BFASS's greatest weakness was its inability to overcome its differences with the Garrisonians prior to the Civil War.

**FURTHER READINGS**

Coupland, R. *The British Anti-Slavery Movement.* London: Thornton Butterworth, Limited, 1933.
Midgley, Clare. *Women Against Slavery: The British Campaigns, 1780–1870.* New York: Routledge Press, 1992.
Temperley, Howard. *British Antislavery, 1833–1870.* Columbia: University of South Carolina Press, 1972.
Turley, David. *The Culture of English Antislavery, 1780–1860.* New York: Routledge Press, 1991.

*Kristine Boeke*

## Brotherhood of Sleeping Car Porters

The Brotherhood of Sleeping Car Porters (BSCP), was the first African American labor organization to affiliate with the American Federation of Labor (AFL). The BSCP, founded by the labor leader Asa Philip Randolph in 1925, organized black Pullman car porters. Far more than a labor union, the BSCP was also a pivotal organization in the twentieth-century civil rights movement.

The emancipation of slaves following the Civil War did little to resolve their precarious social and economic status. As late as 1910, 83.3 percent of African Americans resided in the South. The vast majority were engaged in agricultural work, with black artisanship suffering erosion when Reconstruction ended and Jim Crow systems became dominant. One of the few corporations to employ large numbers of African Americans was the Pullman Company, the maker and supplier of luxury cars for railroads.

Founder George Pullman hired ex-slaves as servants for his cars as early as 1870, and by the turn of the century, Pullman was the single largest employer of black labor. So synonymous with Pullman were black porters that patrons derisively addressed them as "George." Of the 12,000 porters employed by Pullman in 1925, all were black except for about 400 Mexicans and a handful of Asians. What emerged was a complex relationship between black employees, the Pullman Corporation, and rail passengers.

Pullman porters performed many tasks, ranging from taking tickets to making up berths, serving food, and shining shoes. Wages, though higher than those paid by most businesses employing African Americans, were very low. Porters were dependent upon tips to make a living wage, an economic reality that placed them in a servile relationship to white patrons. An affected smile became part of the porters' unofficial uniform, and Pullman demanded exacting standards of propriety and obedience. A single complaint from a white customer often resulted in dismissal; thus porters learned the arts of submissive manipulation and ignoring insults.

Nonetheless, porters commanded great respect within the African American community. Those wearing Pullman uniforms were afforded travel and cultural activities that were out of reach for most agrarian laborers, including the

Members of the Brotherhood of Sleeping Car Porters display their banner at a 1955 ceremony celebrating the organization's 30th anniversary. Asa Philip Randolph, Union president, holds the Brotherhood flag (left side from our view). *Corbis-Bettmann*

opportunity to visit northern cities where Jim Crow systems were less well developed. Company paternalism, including large contributions to black churches, further confirmed Pullman's status among African Americans.

By the 1920s an increasing number of porters were discontent with their wages and terms of employment. New employees earned only $67 per month, and the pay scale topped out at $94.50, after fifteen years of service. In addition, porters were on duty for 11,000 miles each month, the equivalent of 400 hours of travel time. They were not paid when the train was not in motion, thus time spent preparing berths and cleaning when the train was at the station was gratis labor. Porters were at the beck and call of both passengers and the company. On duty, they seldom got more than two hours uninterrupted sleep.

Organizing Pullman porters presented special challenges. Since Pullman jobs were coveted, the company easily replaced malcontents. The rapid decline of the Knights of Labor after 1890 removed one of the few labor organizations that might have assisted black porters. Railroad brotherhoods and the American Railway Union excluded blacks, as did most affiliates of the AFL. Moreover, there was little consensus among African American leaders as to how to address challenges facing post-Reconstruction black America. Options ranged from the nonconfrontational self-improvement philosophy of Booker T. Washington to the black separatist views of Marcus Garvey. In the early 1920s the Order of Sleeping Car Employees and the Sleeping Car Porters' Protective Union attempted to organize black porters but failed.

The genesis of the BSCP lay in the cultural milieu of the Harlem Renaissance and the strategic political agitations of leaders like Frederick Douglass and W. E. B. Du Bois. Heir to the political challenges of the latter was Asa Philip Randolph.

Early in the century, Florida-born Randolph moved to Harlem where he attended City College of New York. He was drawn to the political radicalism of the Harlem Renaissance. In 1917, Randolph and Chandler Owen started the *Messenger*, a newspaper of independent socialist thought. The paper was sympathetic to the Industrial Workers of the World (IWW) and critical of black involvement in World War I. Both men were arrested as suspected Bolsheviks in 1918 and jailed briefly for their antiwar views. They were released and drafted, but the war ended and their cases were dropped.

The *Messenger* was a major voice within the black community. It was highly critical of capitalism, even though many of its expenses were underwritten by Mrs. C. J. Walker, the cosmetics entrepreneur. The paper advocated that African Americans join unions, and it blasted the AFL's racist exclusion policies. The paper also criticized Du Bois and the National Association for the Advancement of Colored People (NAACP), which Randolph felt was elitist and overly cautious.

Randolph's efforts to form black unions predated the BSCP. In 1917, he set up the United Brotherhood of Elevator and Switchboard Operators, and in 1919, he served on the executive board of the National Brotherhood Workers of America. In 1920, he promoted tenant rights and the unionization of migrant workers in the Friends of Negro Freedom. After a stillborn attempt to create the National Association for the Promotion of Unionism among Negroes, Randolph launched the Brotherhood of Sleeping Car Porters in 1925. The National Urban League's Department of Industrial Relations gave important logistical support to the BSCP and pressured the AFL to reverse its racial policies.

Randolph was president of the BSCP from 1925 to 1968. Although he also held general organizer credentials, his role within the BSCP was largely that of public spokesperson and agitator, with practical matters being left in the hands of men like the BSCP organizers Milton Webster, Ashley Totten, and C. L. Dellums.

Black women were instrumental in advancing the brotherhood from its earliest days. A small number of black women employed as maids by the Pullman Company took out memberships in the BSCP, but women were most active in auxiliaries. Wives and other female relatives of Pullman employees started to establish local auxiliaries in 1926, and that same year several auxiliaries combined to form the Colored Women's Economic Council. Women's auxiliaries were instrumental in raising money for the brotherhood in the days before an AFL charter boosted the organizational treasury. They also performed important community functions such as offering financial assistance to families left destitute when the Pullman Company dismissed black wage earners.

It was not until twelve years after its founding that the BSCP successfully negotiated a contract with the Pullman Company. The corporation responded to the formation of the brotherhood with an aggressive, multipronged plan to crush it in its infancy. Black ministers and community leaders were enlisted to denounce the union, and many BSCP leaders, including Randolph, were red-baited (labeled as communists) when they rejected company bribes to discontinue their agitations. Pullman established a company union ostensibly to deal with grievances and made wide use of paid spies to apprise it of union activity. Stock options and pension plans, coupled with modest pay increases, deterred some from joining the BSCP, as did periodic firings of union agitators.

During this difficult period, the job of negotiating on behalf of individual porters often fell to women. Because many of the activities of the BSCP's ladies auxiliaries were shielded from Pullman observers, women were able to negotiate with company officials on an individual basis and help resolve labor disputes. The historical record is replete with cases of women successfully approaching Pullman management to improve the working conditions of porters and to rehire dismissed employees. Women were also unencumbered by codes of etiquette that required Pullman porters to be polite and subservient. Often, they did not shy away from haranguing Pullman officials when the women felt that they or their family members were treated with disrespect.

By 1928, increased militancy among workers and support from community and family members led Randolph to consider a strike against Pullman. He hoped that the National Mediation Board established by the 1926 Railway Labor Act would declare a transportation emergency and force both sides to the bargaining table. In the end, however, Randolph felt that the BSCP was not strong enough to endure a prolonged dispute, and he called off the strike. For the next few years, the BSCP was torn by internal disputes over strategy, with tensions especially high between Randolph and Milton Webster.

Randolph continued to press the AFL to charter the BSCP. This was especially important as AFL hotel and bartender unions both claimed jurisdiction over the porters and denounced the BSCP as dual unionism. In 1928, Randolph was able to get the AFL to recognize the BSCP as the representative of the porters. He did not obtain a charter because of low membership, but thirteen locals were placed under the inner council of AFL president William Green. Nonetheless, the BSCP had very little vitality when the Great Depression began.

The BSCP took advantage of President Franklin D. Roosevelt's election in 1932. New Deal legislation outlawed company unions and granted workers the right to bargain through their own elected units. In 1934, the Railway Labor Act was amended to include sleeping car employees. Women continued their feverish activity on behalf of the union, and women's auxiliaries became so numerous that a coordinated network of Ladies Auxiliaries of the Brotherhood of Sleeping Car Porters emerged in 1938. Increased political, legal, and organizational activity gave Randolph the necessary leverage to call for a union election. In June 1935, despite massive layoffs by Pullman, the BSCP won collective bargaining rights by a nearly eight-to-one margin.

One year later, the BSCP obtained its international charter from the AFL. By then, the AFL faced a challenge from the Congress of Industrial Organizations (CIO) that Randolph was able to exploit. He cast his lot with the AFL because the fate of the CIO was uncertain, and he did not wish to tie the brotherhood's twelve-year struggle to a nascent organization. Despite AFL recognition and sole bargaining rights, it took the BSCP over two years and a court challenge to win a contract from Pullman, a task accomplished on August 12, 1937. Pullman agreed to raise wages $12 per month, to cut hours from 400 to 240, and to change onerous work conditions concerning racial discrimination, rest periods, seniority rules, and job security.

Increasingly, the attention of both Randolph and the union was drawn to the broader context of civil rights. In 1936, Randolph and other brotherhood members founded the National Negro Congress (NNC) to promote black employment and workplace rights. Randolph subsequently quit the NNC when it fell under the control of John L. Davis, an avowed Communist.

As World War II approached, the BSCP protested racial discrimination in the defense industry. Randolph threatened to organize hundreds of thousands of African Americans to march on Washington, D.C., to protest discrimination. He called off the event when President Roosevelt signed Executive Order 8802 establishing the Fair Employment Practices Committee (FEPC) on June 25, 1941. Although Milton Webster disagreed with canceling the march, he served on the first FEPC board. The FEPC outlawed racial and ethnic discrimination on all government and defense industry jobs.

Randolph and others, such as the activist Bayard Rustin, kept the idea of a march on Washington alive. By 1942, Randolph contemplated the use of nonviolent protest, modeled after that of Mahatma Gandhi in India, as a tactic in the battle for civil rights. This thinking crystallized in 1944, when Randolph was a co-founder of the Congress of Racial Equality (CORE), which later used direct action techniques like sit-downs and mass picketing in the struggle for social justice. Randolph and the brotherhood also protested segregation in the U.S. military. The League for Non-Violent Civil Disobedience Against Military Segregation was formed and, on June 26, 1948, President Harry S. Truman's executive order ended Jim Crow in the armed forces.

By the end of World War II, Randolph and the brotherhood were major forces within American labor and society. When the AFL and the CIO merged in 1955, Randolph became vice president of the organization. At that time the AFL-CIO had approximately 1.5 million black members, roughly 10 percent of the total membership. Also in 1955, brotherhood member E. D. Nixon organized the Montgomery, Alabama, bus boycott to protest the arrest of Rosa Parks for refusing to vacate her bus seat for a white man. The campaign in Montgomery gave birth to the Southern Christian Leadership Conference (SCLC) and its subsequent victory heralded a severe challenge to the Jim Crow south. Like E. D. Nixon, many of the men and women who became involved in the civil rights movement had their roots in the BSCP.

In 1960, Randolph formed the Negro American Labor Council for black workers, with the BSCP becoming a charter member. Randolph continued to press the AFL-CIO to support the civil rights movement, despite stiff opposition from union president George Meaney.

On August 28, 1963, twenty-two years after Randolph first proposed a march on Washington, more than a quarter million Americans marched onto the nation's capital. The day is best remembered for the Reverend Martin Luther King Jr.'s "I Have a Dream" speech, but he was proceeded to the podium by Randolph, who spoke passionately of both social and workplace justice.

In 1963, the Brotherhood of Locomotive Firemen and Engineers ended its ban of black members, the last railway union to do so. One year later, President Lyndon B. Johnson signed the Civil Rights Act, which made public segregation illegal in the United States. Throughout the 1960s, Randolph and the BSCP freely mixed civil rights and labor organizing, though the latter was becoming less relevant within the railroad industry.

A. Philip Randolph retired as BSCP president in 1968. By then, American passenger railways were anemic, having been supplanted by airplanes and the private automobile. In 1978, the BSCP merged with a larger union, the Brotherhood of Railway and Airline Clerks. The demise of the BSCP confirmed what had been reality for several decades. As railroads declined, the BSCP's significance came from its involvement in the civil rights movement, and its focus shifted from the confines of Pullman cars to civil rights. The BSCP, which had since the 1930s demanded justice in society, not just the workplace, fought and won the right for black workers to be treated with respect and dignity.

**FURTHER READINGS**

Chateauvert, Melinda. *Marching Together: Women of the Brotherhood of Sleeping Car Porters.* Urbana: University of Illinois Press, 1997.

Harris, William. *Keeping the Faith: A. Philip Randolph, Milton P. Webster, and the Brotherhood of Sleeping Car Porters, 1925–37.* Urbana: University of Illinois Press, 1977.

Perata, David. *Those Pullman Blues: An Oral History of the African American Railroad Attendant.* New York: Twayne Publishers, 1996.

Pfeffer, Paula F. *A. Philip Randolph, Pioneer of the Civil Rights Movement.* Baton Rouge: Louisiana State University Press, 1990.

Santino, Jack. *Miles of Smiles, Years of Struggle: Stories of Black Pullman Porters.* Urbana: University of Illinois Press, 1991.

*Robert E. Weir*

## Bureau for Colored Troops

The Adjutant General's Office, U.S. War Department, created the Bureau of Colored Troops (BCT) in 1863 to recruit, organize, and oversee U.S. Colored Troops (USCT). Following the Civil War the BCT continued operating until it was absorbed by the Volunteer Service Division in 1888. The BCT eagerly accepted nearly 200,000 African American recruits during the war at a time when white enlistments were lagging. Its 135 infantry, 6 cavalry,

and 12 heavy artillery regiments plus 10 batteries of light artillery fought in 39 major and 410 minor engagements. During most of the post–Civil War period 4 regiments of African American "buffalo soldiers" served in the West. Although the troops had a lower desertion rate and comparable conduct to white troops, the BCT indulged white prejudices against African Americans. It discouraged the training of black officers and hence career possibilities for African Americans in the military. Nevertheless, African American soldiers won pay equality during the war and secured opportunities to serve in the Signal, Hospital, and other Corps by the 1880s.

At the beginning of the Civil War in 1861, existing army regulations required that soldiers be white as well as eighteen or over and in good health. The antislavery views of some white officers serving in the South, however, led them to experiment with arming and training escaped slaves, or "contraband." When President Abraham Lincoln issued the Emancipation Proclamation on January 1, 1863, such experiments received official sanction. Lincoln acknowledged African Americans as the most available but unused source of manpower for restoring the Union. Following the Emancipation Proclamation John Andrew, Republican governor of Massachusetts and antislavery proponent, led northern states in seeking permission to organize an African American regiment, the 54th Massachusetts. George L. Stearns, a manufacturer, abolitionist, and financial backer of John Brown's raid (the 1859 raid of the government arsenal at Harper's Ferry—an attempt at the violent overthrow of slavery), served as Andrew's advisor. Stearns suggested that Massachusetts, with its small black population, fill a black regiment by sending white and black paid agents to recruit volunteers in other northern states and in Canada. Stearns raised money among philanthropists and businessmen who were anxious to avoid conscription of their white employees and used it to pay for the travel of black recruits to enlistment locations and to aid their families. For the abolitionist recruiters, social transformation was the principal goal of military service. The war, they hoped, would end slavery, but it was also a way for African Americans to earn respect, exercise leadership, and perhaps receive government land grants. Governors in other states, fearing the loss of recruits necessary to fill their state quotas, began raising regiments as well and eagerly looked to the slave states, where 90 percent of the African American population resided, for future recruits.

In the spring of 1863, the War Department launched its own recruitment drive. Secretary of War Edwin Stanton

Recruiting poster for the enlistment of colored soldiers. Published in Philadelphia by the "Supervisory committee for recruiting colored regiments." Undated. *Corbis-Bettmann*

dispatched Adjutant General Lorenzo Thomas, a career staff officer, to the Mississippi Valley to engage army officers in enrolling contrabands. Aware that many whites in the army had enlisted to preserve the Union but were opposed to emancipation and resented the idea that black soldiers were needed to win the war, Thomas warned officers that they had to cooperate or resign with dishonorable discharges. Thomas's primary concern was the military efficiency of black units, a prerequisite in his view for their acceptance by whites. He did not care whether African American enlistees were impressed into service or volunteered; their performance would depend on their leaders, whom he insisted should be white and able to pass an oral examination given by other officers. Abolitionists, however, considered impressment little different from slavery and criticized it strongly. Thomas believed that recruiters from northern states were disruptive because their promises of money lured soldiers to desert the regiments he was organizing.

On May 22, 1863, Stanton sought to create a centralized recruitment system by issuing General Order No. 143,

which established the BCT. Its function was to create uniform rules and procedures for organizing and administering African American regiments and to provide them with officers. Centralized authority would eliminate competition for African American enlistments. While volunteer regiments bore the names of states, the USCT bore the name of the nation. Indeed, the BCT redesignated many regiments named earlier. While governors had appointed officers to command their state volunteer regiments, General Order No. 144 set up boards of officers who examined and approved individuals for appointment by the BCT. To head the BCT Stanton chose Captain and Assistant Adjutant General Charles W. Foster, a regular army officer and Massachusetts native, who had risen through the ranks. Practical and professional, Foster placed army needs first, always hoping they would coincide with justice and fairness. He was assisted by two staff officers and as many as forty-five clerks.

Senator Henry Wilson of Massachusetts, chair of the Senate's Military Affairs Committee, challenged the BCT's assumption of national authority and protected the right of northern states to recruit black volunteers. Thus, states continued to recruit African Americans in the South until March 1865, but, due to hostility, they managed to raise only 5,000 men. The BCT hired the most effective state recruiters and commissioned Major George L. Stearns, asking his advice on recruitment techniques. Stearns recommended ceasing all impressment and employing civilian agents to be paid through private funds raised in the North. While the BCT, with the support of Lincoln and Stanton, disavowed impressment, scattered reports continued. The BCT experimented with paid agents in Pennsylvania and Tennessee but feared their relative autonomy because many were political radicals unconcerned about creating dangerous confrontations with supporters of slavery. Stearns was equally dissatisfied with having to follow army orders rather than his conscience and resigned in early 1864.

The BCT ultimately adopted a variety of recruitment techniques. In the North it authorized governors to raise regiments and recommend officers. Some northern governors, usually Democrats, held back, and in those cases Union League Clubs assumed the organizing role. In the border slave states, the BCT promised loyal slaveowners bounties if their slaves enlisted and compensation of up to $300 for the emancipation of each slave who enlisted. Much of the paperwork handled by the BCT involved validating these claims, although on July 28, 1866, Congress suspended any payment by the Treasury. In occupied Confederate states, recruiting began in contraband camps. As these emptied of suitable men, partially filled USCT regiments sent "scouts" into the surrounding countryside to recruit volunteers.

Recruitment was neither simple nor easy. White residents of the border states were especially hostile, arresting or even killing some recruiters. If the army intervened to protect recruiters, it faced complaints that they were undermining civil authority that recognized slaves as property and regarded recruiters as thieves. The BCT typically ordered recruiters to be discreet and obey the laws. Acknowledging the danger of recruitment, the BCT authorized the enlistment of those found physically unfit for performance of light tasks to protect them from retaliation by angry whites. Recruiters also complained of interference by prejudiced U.S. officers. General William T. Sherman thought it foolish to turn contrabands from useful tasks like digging entrenchments to drilling as soldiers. For a period he even arrested recruiters. To get cooperation from Andrew Johnson, military governor of Tennessee, the BCT granted Johnson the right to appoint USCT officers and to assign black troops as he saw fit, including digging entrenchments.

The BCT acknowledged prejudice as inevitable and did nothing to challenge it. Indeed, the BCT ordered African American troops not to parade in Philadelphia because the mayor disliked the idea. It allowed General Nathaniel P. Banks to purge African American regiments, raised by radical Benjamin F. Butler in Louisiana in 1862, of most of their black officers. It reassigned the African American surgeon of the 54th Massachusetts to detached duty at a hospital because white surgeons felt "degraded" by his presence. It took the utmost persistence of African Americans and radical politicians for any black man to become an officer. Many of the eighty-seven black officers received their commissions near the end of the war and often served outside the line of command as surgeons, chaplains, and recruiters. Nonetheless, army service, whether as privates or officers, represented important new experiences for African American men; many future leaders recalled proudly their service in the USCT.

African American soldiers often paid the price for the limitation of officerships primarily to whites. Only by recruiting in medical schools in antislavery New England did the BCT begin to address the shortage of surgeons for USCT regiments. Although the war department demanded that white officer applicants have their "heart" in the work, the principal attraction of the USCT units remained the chance for promotion and higher pay. Because of the difficulty of getting good white officers, the BCT cooperated with a Free Military School, later continued as a tuition institution, in Philadelphia, which prepared white applicants for the officers' test. Since half of all applicants with no preparation failed, the school, 96 percent of whose graduates passed, was a godsend to the BCT, which permitted school enrollees extended leave from their regiments to attend. Still, to fill the need, many officers of black regiments had to be appointed without having passed certification examinations.

Discriminatory practices sometimes interfered with recruitment. At Stanton's instigation, the War Department's solicitor general ruled that laws specifying the pay and bounties due volunteers did not apply to African Americans. Regardless of rank, black soldiers were paid the army's laborer's wage of $7 per month, compared to the $13 dollars paid white privates. Apparently intended to mollify white recruits, not only did this discrimination raise protests from radicals and cause mutinies in some regiments but it also discouraged African American enlistments and made it especially difficult to secure black non-commissioned officers. Foster joined in protest and Congress remedied the situation through piecemeal legislation. By 1872 Congress equalized all bounties, wages, and pensions for all categories of the USCT.

Stereotyping and paternalistic attitudes permeated the BCT. Foster advised against paying lump sum monies due soldiers for fear they would lose it to con men. Statistical analysis of appointments indicates that the BCT preferred to appoint non-field workers and light-skinned individuals for leadership positions. While the USCT denied any discrimination, the BCT received reports that black troops were forced to use inferior weapons such as "twice-condemned flintlocks," which had been obsolete for decades, and cavalry mounted on mules. Moreover, black soldiers were assigned in disproportionate numbers to fatigue duty because of "their industry and docility."

The war's end radically changed priorities. While African American soldiers desired the steady employment at equal wages offered by the army, some whites wished to reinstitute an all-white military. The BCT demobilized all its volunteer regiments by 1867. An 1866 act, authored by radical Henry Wilson, kept four black infantry and two black cavalry regiments in the peacetime army, but the infantry regiments were reduced to two in 1869. In 1876 and 1878, Congress rejected proposals to remove the requirement that four regiments be African American. This was allegedly intended to integrate the army and implement the Fourteenth Amendment's pledge of equal protection. Yet, wary African Americans feared that it indicated the desire of army officers to recruit only among whites. In 1881 the army segregated its training facilities.

The BCT accommodated by assigning African American troops to remote spots in the West. Many white officers disliked such assignments because of the remoteness, and they had to perform more clerical work because their largely unskilled and illiterate recruits were unprepared for such tasks. Legislation authorized chaplains to provide schooling, but facilities were poor at most forts. The BCT continued to discourage the training of black officers and denied them assignments to service branches such as the Signal, Hospital, and Ordnance Corps. Not until 1884 and at the insistence of the secretary of war did W. Hallett Greene, a black college graduate, gain admission to the Signal Corps. The following year African Americans won entry to the Hospital Corps, Ordnance Corps, and Commissary and Quartermaster Departments. In a move for greater efficiency, the army consol-idated the BCT's functions into the Volunteer Service Division in 1888. One of the last tasks of the BCT was to gather documents detailing the military service of African Americans; Congress, however, never authorized publication of the data.

Under the BCT black men demonstrated their patriotism and competence as soldiers, but bowing to white prejudices, the bureau failed to increase military leadership opportunities for African Americans. Nevertheless, blacks and their white allies consistently protested injustices, such as unequal pay during the war and exclusion from the service branches, and had some successes.

**FURTHER READINGS**

Berlin, Ira, ed. *Freedom: A Documentary History of Emancipation, 1861–1867. Ser. II: The Black Military Experience.* Cambridge: Cambridge University Press, 1982.

Carroll, John M., ed. *The Black Military Experience in the American West.* New York: Liveright, 1971.

Cornish, Dudley Taylor. *The Sable Arm: Negro Troops in the Union Army, 1861–1865.* New York: Longman, Greens, 1956; 2nd ed., New York: W. W. Norton, 1966.

Gladstone, William A. *United States Colored Troops, 1863–1867.* Gettysburg, Pa.: Thomas Publications, 1990.

Glatthaar, Joseph T. *Forged in Battle: The Civil War Alliance of Black Soldiers and White Officers.* New York: Macmillan, 1990.

*Phyllis F. Field*

## Bureau of Refugees, Freedmen, and Abandoned Lands

On March 3, 1865, Congress created the Bureau of Refugees, Freedmen, and Abandoned Lands to resolve war-generated civil problems regarding black and white refugees, freed slaves, and abandoned property. Although commonly referred to as the "Freedmen's Bureau," the agency's charge embraced more than the pressing social, political, and legal issues faced by freed slaves. The bureau was expected to coordinate relief and resettlement efforts for all war refugees, to provide a modicum of protection for the freedpeople, and to rent or sell confiscated rebel and Confederate government property to finance its operations.

Congress created the "Freedmen's Bureau" more than four years after civilian groups and the military had initiated refugee aid. Northern humanitarian groups and missionary societies organized philanthropic freedmen's aid

Man representing the Freedmen's Bureau stands between armed groups of white Southerners and black Southerners. *American Stock/Archive Photos*

and refugee relief associations, beginning in late 1861. Black and white refugees fleeing to Union lines forced the Union Army to provide a modicum of relief in refugee camps.

Leaders of the freedmen's aid societies, aware that mere philanthropic responses were utterly inadequate to address the immense suffering in the South, lobbied for systematic governmental responses to the plight of the freed slaves. In 1863, Representative Thomas D. Eliot of Massachusetts introduced legislation to create a Bureau of Emancipation; in 1864, he pressed for a Bureau of Freedmen's Affairs. Both bills died in Congress. Meanwhile, the American Freedmen's Inquiry Commission, created by the War Department to study the problems faced by the freed slaves, also urged the creation of a freedmen's agency within the federal government.

When Congress finally created the Freedmen's Bureau it charged the agency with three tasks: caring for southern white refugees; providing for the freedpeople; and taking charge of all abandoned and confiscated southern property. A key provision of the original legislation was the redistribution of southern land in forty-acre plots to loyal refugees and freedmen—the fabled "forty-acre and a mule" provision. The 1865 legislation provided for only one year of operation.

Congress envisioned the Freedmen's Bureau as an extension of the military. It established the bureau within the War Department. The War Department, in turn, organized the bureau as a military bureaucracy, imposed military procedures, and subjected all agents, civilian as well as military, to military discipline. Congress appropriated no operating funds to the bureau, expecting it to rely upon the army for rations, supplies, transportation, buildings, medicine, and the salaries of its military employees; other operating revenues were to accrue from the sale and rental of abandoned and confiscated lands.

Abolitionists and many leaders in the freedmen's aid societies pressed President Lincoln to appoint someone with antislavery sentiments to head the bureau. However, the choice of bureau commissioner fell to General Oliver Otis Howard, a white career army officer. Howard assigned an assistant commissioner to each of the southern states under military jurisdiction and provided himself and the assistant commissioners with small staffs of subordinate officers. Each state office was responsible for inspections, protecting property and refugees, coordinating relief operations and education, adjudicating claims, managing disbursements, attending to medical issues, and in other ways overseeing the transition to peacetime. By May 1865, the bureau was operating throughout the South and making preliminary preparations to create forty-acre freeholds.

On May 29, 1865, however, President Andrew Johnson issued his Proclamation of Amnesty, ending any dream of land redistribution and gutting most of the bureau's expected source of revenue. The amnesty and generous pardons to Confederates restored nearly all confiscated lands to the former rebels. That left the bureau with a small fraction of the southern land previously under the control of Union forces. President Johnson moved more directly against the bureau in early 1866, vetoing legislation reauthorizing the agency, and thereby signaling the rift between the president and Congress over the contours of Reconstruction. Subsequent legislation, overriding a second veto, extended the bureau for two years and authorized $7 million for operating costs. Two years later, Congress began dismantling the Freedmen's Bureau, terminating all of its activity as of January 1869 except for its assistance to freedmen's education and its bounty offices. Those activities, inadequately funded, ended in 1872.

Six distinct activities and concerns dominated the work of the Freedmen's Bureau during its brief life: providing relief, dealing with land redistribution, regularizing labor, promoting justice, cultivating moral reform, and coordinating education. Chronically underfunded, staffed with personnel who were often indifferent, if not hostile, to the interests of the freedmen, and plagued by constant turnover as officers were mustered out of the army, the bureau's record in those six areas was checkered.

In its first year, relief for war refugees was the most pressing need. Masses of freed slaves had fled the plantations, crowding into freedmen's camps, towns, and cities, and traveling throughout the South in search of family members. Black and white refugees needed immediate aid in the form of food, clothing, shelter, and medical care. With the collapse of the southern economy, employment was scarce and destitution was common. Among its first tasks, the bureau assumed responsibility for the army's relief work and assisted northern philanthropic groups in their efforts to extend aid to the refugees.

Convinced that charity created dependency, particularly among freed slaves, and determined to reestablish the southern cotton economy as quickly as possible, the bureau endeavored from the beginning to terminate relief work quickly. Bureau agents used labor contracts, control of relief supplies, moral suasion, and promises of schools on plantations to break up the refugee camps and to move African Americans back into the plantation economy. However, disastrous floods, drought, and agricultural insect devastation conspired to savage the southern economy for three years after the conclusion of the war, forcing the bureau to continue its relief efforts until 1868.

The freedmen's greatest need after immediate relief was land ownership. Though not a guarantee of freedom without civil rights and protection, land ownership was certainly the essential condition of emancipation, a fact not lost upon the freedmen themselves. Redistribution of southern agriculture would have broken the power of the southern white elite while giving African Americans and poor southern whites greater independence and an economic stake in the region. Johnson's amnesty and pardon, however, left the bureau with no land to redistribute. By autumn 1865, Commissioner Howard and his subordinates began informing the freedmen that they would not receive the promised portions of plantations and urged them to return to work for their former masters. Thereafter, the bureau's land policy was reduced to promoting black settlement on homesteads provided by the Southern Homestead Act of 1866—a largely futile effort since the federal property in the South made available by the homestead bill was inaccessible and often of poor quality. In the following decade most would-be southern homesteaders, white and black, earned too little from the land to gain title to it.

Without a means to establish economic independence, and aware of business and planter demands to rebuild the plantation economy, the Freedmen's Bureau took up the task of regularizing new labor relations. Bureau officers encouraged the freedmen to return to the plantations, introducing labor contracts between planters and workers as the symbol of the freedmen's new free-labor status. In the cash-poor South, the contracts frequently called for remuneration in shares of the crop or in forms of tenantry. Without intending to do so, the bureau indirectly contributed to sharecropping becoming the dominant form of southern agricultural labor relations. Bureau agents found their time absorbed in devising, registering, and adjudicating labor contracts. Labor policy, including returning African Americans to their traditional position as the South's agricultural labor force, became the keystone of the bureau's effort in the South.

As the imposition of labor contracts revealed, legal relationships in the South were undergoing profound change. Yet, many white southerners resisted that change, intent on retaining traditional discriminatory forms of justice. The Black Codes of 1866 and the actions of courts throughout the South denied basic rights and privileges to the freedpeople. The North understood that the freedmen needed justice and protection.

To that end, the bureau inaugurated freedmen's courts under the protection of the Union Army. Those courts claimed jurisdiction over the local civil justice system when it appeared that the local courts would deny the legal equality of African American citizens. However, the bureau's efforts to promote justice were limited and short-lived. President Johnson managed to restrict the bureau's courts to a single issue: the acceptance of freedmen's testimony in local courts. Southern states quickly acquiesced on that point, and the bureau abolished its freedmen's courts in late 1866. The South regained control of the local administration of the law, accepting in principle the citizenship rights of its African American population, but changing little in the actual administration of justice.

The Freedmen's Bureau was half-hearted in its efforts to obtain land and justice for the freedmen, terminating both initiatives prematurely. Yet it was untiring in its zeal for the freedmen's moral reform. As part of the bureau's land and labor policies, its agents counseled the freedmen on the moral value of labor and fidelity to contracts and the moral horrors of vagrancy and intemperance. The bureau organized the Vanguard of Freedom, a temperance union for southern freedmen, and authorized bureau officers to sanctify slave marriage through a religious and civil ceremony. Moreover, the bureau promoted the Freedmen's Savings and Trust Company, a private enterprise with no connection to the bureau and destined to lose millions of dollars in freedmen's savings in the early 1870s, as part of its encouragement of thrift.

The primary means to moral reform, however, was freedmen's education. The bureau did not have schools of its own. Rather, it provided valuable services to the numerous northern aid organizations that were active in freedmen's education. It transported teachers and supplies to southern schools, provided government buildings for schoolhouses, coordinated and superintended schools and school efforts, and gathered and published data regarding freedmen's education. The bureau's general superintendent of freedmen's education, Reverend John W. Alvord, served the agency from 1865 to 1870, aided by assistant superintendents in each state.

The bureau was of great importance in the effort to establish southern African American education. It appropriated over $5 million to freedmen's education. Its assistance and coordination of the school work in the South allowed the freedmen's aid societies to work more efficiently and effectively. It was instrumental in establishing many of the early southern black colleges. Alvord's *Semi-Annual Reports on Schools for Freedmen* (1866–1870) publicized the educational work and provided the aid societies with valuable information. On the other hand, the bureau tended to favor the more conservative of the aid societies, contributing to a politically conservative tenor in freedmen's education. More aid went to those societies that emphasized moral reform, less to those that stressed civil rights. Like those aid societies, the bureau promoted schooling as the moral equivalent of landholding and economic independence for the freedmen, deflecting attention from concrete economic reforms.

Contrary to traditional interpretation, the Bureau of Refugees, Freedmen, and Abandoned Lands was neither radical nor a tool of congressional radicals. It was fully operational for less than four years. It contributed modestly to establishing minimal civil rights for the freedpeople and to easing their transition to freedom. Bureau regulations, carefully observed, banned partisan activity on the part of agents. Assistant commissioners who demonstrated strong sympathies for the freedmen were quietly removed and replaced with officials more solicitous of the interests of planters and other whites. The bureau's policies on land, labor, and education served to blunt the revolutionary implications and the ethical obligations of emancipation. In the final analysis, the Freedmen's Bureau softened in some measure the most jarring impacts of war and emancipation; it did little to address the nation's moral debt to its former bondsmen.

## FURTHER READINGS

Bentley, George R. *A History of the Freedmen's Bureau.* Philadelphia: University of Pennsylvania Press, 1955.

Butchart, Ronald E. *Northern Schools, Southern Blacks, and Reconstruction: Freedmen's Education, 1862–1875.* Westport, Conn.: Greenwood Press, 1980.

Cimbala, Paul A. "On the Front Line of Freedom: Freedmen's Bureau Officers and Agents in Reconstruction Georgia." *Georgia Historical Quarterly* 76 (Fall 1992): 577–611.

Crouch, Barry A. *The Freedmen's Bureau and Black Texans.* Austin: University of Texas Press, 1992.

Rapport, Sara. "The Freedmen's Bureau as a Legal Agent for Black Men and Women in Georgia: 1865–1868." *Georgia Historical Quarterly* 73 (Spring 1989): 26–53.

*Ronald E. Butchart*

# C

## California Council for Civic Unity

In 1946 an interracial group of social activists met in San Francisco, California, to organize a statewide federation of civil rights and civil liberties organizations. This federation was known as the California Council for Civic Unity (CCCU). Among the most notable of this group of activists were Joseph James, the shipyard worker whose fight against auxiliary unions resulted in the legal prohibition of segregated unions; Laurence J. Hewes, the Pacific Coast director of the American Council on Race Relations; and Ruth Kingman, community activist and wife of Harry L. Kingman, the West Coast regional director of the Fair Employment Practices Committee (FEPC).

They and other local leaders worked closely with the National Association for the Advancement of Colored People (NAACP), the Pacific Coast Committee on American Principles and Fair Play (Fair Play Committee), and the influential American Council on Race Relations (ACRR) to form an omnibus federation of interracial organizations. Ruth Kingman was elected the first president of the CCCU, the first of three women to hold that office. The CCCU became the most influential of the interracial coalitions to emerge in the San Francisco Bay Area. The Bay Area became the center of civil rights and interracial activism in the state and on the West Coast.

Benefiting from the climate of liberalism that briefly flowered in the aftermath of World War II, the CCCU enjoyed support from California's most influential community and business leaders and claimed a diverse membership of more than forty organizations including the NAACP, the Young Women's Christian Association (YWCA), the Jewish Survey, and the B'nai B'rith Committee. The CCCU board and staff—which included Lester Granger, executive director of the National Urban League (NUL), Walter

White of the NAACP, and renowned author Richard Wright—adopted an array of goals that demanded nothing less than an end to all segregation and discrimination. The CCCU targeted employment discrimination, segregation in public accommodations and services, and discrimination in private institutions.

From its inception the CCCU depended on financial, administrative, and technical support from the ACRR, whose prestigious staff and board included the acclaimed author Pearl S. Buck, the UN Secretariat member Ralph J. Bunche, and the sociologist and editor Charles S. Johnson. However, within a year of its founding, the fledgling CCCU left the protective wing of the ACRR when the older organization discontinued operations on the Pacific Coast. The break was not precipitated by ideological or personal conflicts. The ACRR continued to assist the CCCU with technical expertise and advice whenever called upon but severed its financial ties with the CCCU, passing the torch of social activism and financial autonomy to the CCCU.

After a brief bout of self-doubt and concern over the CCCU's stability, Ruth Kingman confidently committed the organization to an aggressive program of fund-raising and held the organization to its original goals. However traumatic the break with ACRR might have been initially, it had no impact on CCCU leadership or policy. Few outsiders detected any transition. The only visible change came in 1948 when the CCCU changed its name to the California Federation for Civic Unity (CFCU). The CFCU continued for a decade as a statewide coalition of interracial organizations whose agenda gave top priority to desegregation.

While the CCCU and CFCU were most effective as educational and fact-finding instruments, they achieved only modest success in attacking segregation and discrimination. Their efforts would be rewarded when the civil rights movement began to dismantle the barriers of legal segregation in the 1960s.

**FURTHER READINGS**

Broussard, Albert S. *Black San Francisco: The Struggle for Racial Equality in the West, 1900–1954.* Lawrence: University of Kansas Press, 1993.

Moore, Shirley Ann Wilson. *To Place Our Deeds: The African American Community in Richmond, California, 1910–1963.* Berkeley: University of California Press, 1999.

Taylor, Quintard. *The Forging of a Black Community: Seattle's Central District from 1870 through the Civil Rights Era.* Seattle: University of Washington Press, 1994.

*Shirley Ann Wilson Moore*

**SEE ALSO**   American Council on Race Relations

## California Federation for Civic Unity

*See* California Council for Civic Unity.

## California Governor's Commission on the Los Angeles Riots

*See* Governor's Commission on the Los Angeles Riots.

## Caucus of Black Sociologists

*See* Association of Black Sociologists.

## Center for Democratic Renewal

In 1979 civil rights movement veterans organized the Center for Democratic Renewal (CDR) in response to a national resurgence of right-wing "hate violence." The Reverend C. T. Vivian organized a board of directors and has remained chairman of the board. The group, initially known as the National Anti-Klan Network, established its headquarters in Atlanta, Georgia. Executive director Lyn Wells assembled an interracial staff from the ranks of those who had staged a march protesting the Ku Klux Klan's (KKK) involvement in the killing of five people in Greensboro, North Carolina, in early 1980.

The network's board and staff members, as well as affiliated civil liberties and labor groups, feared a reversal of the civil rights gains of the 1960s. Democracy itself, they claimed was endangered, should organized "hate groups" such as the KKK regain influence in national politics. They agreed that broad, nonsectarian education about hate groups and racial violence, especially among southern white workers, was key to discrediting the KKK. The staff and numerous volunteers successfully lobbied Congress for public hearings on the revived KKK violence; assisted victims of racial and religious attacks in the rural South; produced and widely distributed a guide to community action titled *When Hate Groups Come to Town*; monitored the far right's activities; and made their findings public through dozens of speeches and newspaper articles.

In 1985, the network's programs became more complex and far-reaching and the organization changed its name to the Center for Democratic Renewal. The CDR became the premier "think tank" to oppose the far right's ever-increasing violence and propaganda against African Americans, Jews, and other minority groups. The CDR combined sophisticated research with an extensive educational program. Staff members and supporters, for example, spoke to hundreds of farmers about the desires of spurious populists and racist "posses" to exploit the agricultural economic crisis for their own ends. Journalists and many law enforcement officers and politicians relied on the CDR for its exposés and pursuits of violent racist or anti-Semitic groups. Some CDR-produced pamphlets, such as Lenny Zeskind's *The "Christian Identity" Movement: A Theological Justification for Racist and Anti-Semitic Violence* and Chris Lutz's *They Don't All Wear Sheets: A Chronology of Racist and Far Right Violence, 1980–1986,* sold over 5,000 copies each. Board members such as Mab Segrest of North Carolina organized statewide movements against hate violence. Under Vivian's and Zeskind's direction, the research department produced what Jim Ridgeway of the *Village Voice* called "an extraordinary brand of independent journalism."

During the 1990s, the CDR again shifted its focus, embracing a more traditional civil rights program while arguing that far right racism and violence derived from an inherently racist society. The activists Loretta Ross, Rose Johnson, Beni Ivey, and others revived the "network" aspect of the CDR. The group launched and pursued a successful lawsuit challenging segregation as well as the KKK in Baxley, Georgia; served as a "friend of the court" in many legal cases involving racial violence; and helped to organize large-scale protests against the KKK. In the late 1990s, the CDR called attention to the racist undertones and dangers to democracy posed by militia groups and worked with the National Council of Churches and the Center for Constitutional Rights to raise money for black churches destroyed by arson.

**FURTHER READINGS**

Center for Democratic Renewal. "How to Fight the Right." In *Eyes Right! Challenging the Right Wing Backlash*. Ed. Chip Berlet. Boston: South End Press, 1995.

"Organizational History Collection." Center for Democratic Renewal Archives, Atlanta, Georgia.

Ridgeway, James. "The Invisible Empire's New Clothes." *Village Voice*, January 26, 1988.

———. "Lenny Zeskind." *Utne Reader* 53 (September 1992): 40.

Sobnosky, Matthew James. "A Critical Rhetorical Analysis of Three Responses to White Supremacy." Ph.D. diss., University of Nebraska, 1990.

*Christine Lutz*

# Central Intercollegiate Athletic Association

The Central Intercollegiate Athletic Association (CIAA) was founded as the Colored Intercollegiate Athletic Association at Hampton Institute, Virginia, in 1912. Still headquartered at Hampton, the CIAA is the oldest African American athletic conference in the United States. Historically black colleges and universities, barred from intercollegiate competition with southern white schools, launched the CIAA "to unite area colleges in a common effort for athletic elevation . . . to train students in self-reliance and stimulate race-pride through athletic attainment." The CIAA provided its member schools with strict rules and an organizational framework that helped to elevate the standards of intercollegiate African American athletic competition.

Although CIAA membership has changed since 1912, the organization continues to draw its member institutions from the historically black colleges and universities, spanning the East Coast from Maryland to North Carolina. The association is governed by a board of directors composed of the presidents or chancellors of its thirteen current member schools: Bowie State University (Maryland), Elizabeth City State University (North Carolina), Fayetteville State University (Arkansas), Johnson C. Smith University (North Carolina), Livingstone College (North Carolina), Norfolk State University (Virginia), North Carolina Central University, Saint Augustine's College (North Carolina), Saint Paul's College (Virginia), Shaw University (North Carolina), Virginia State University, Virginia Union University, and Winston-Salem University (North Carolina).

Prior to the CIAA's founding, historically black colleges and universities had enjoyed little success in creating all-black intercollegiate athletic leagues and conferences. Perhaps the CIAA's success was due to the fact that five prestigious black schools—Howard University (Washington, D.C.), Shaw University, Lincoln University (Missouri), Virginia Union University, and Hampton University (Virginia)—all within a six-hour train ride of each other, agreed to join the association. In addition, the CIAA's location in the mid-Atlantic region provided the conference with access to some of the strongest African American high school athletic programs in the country.

The CIAA offered its member schools, most of which had been created after the Civil War without much, if any, government assistance, a system of centralized athletic competition rules. Until the creation of the conference, for example, no rules existed that governed the length of an athlete's membership on a team. Perhaps more important, black colleges and universities had no minimum age requirements for their athletes. Thus, prior to the emergence of the CIAA, historically black colleges and universities often recruited high school athletes to play on college teams. The CIAA, under the direction of Howard University professor Ernest J. Marshall, limited athletic eligibility to four years.

The creation of the CIAA and its mission to foster self-reliance and race-pride attracted the attention of African Americans throughout the nation. Student enrollment at CIAA member schools increased and athletic rivalries between them soared to new heights. Moreover, the CIAA's founding inspired the creation of other black athletic conferences. In 1920, for example, several schools united to create the Southeastern Athletic Conference at Morehouse College in Atlanta and eight years later the Southern Intercollegiate Athletic Conference made its debut.

Despite the CIAA's influential role in black intercollegiate sports, the organization initially encountered numerous obstacles. One of the most peculiar problems facing the conference was its inability to maintain regular schedules for basketball and baseball games during the tourist season (spring), which provided lucrative employment opportunities for many African American students. Aware of the students' need to earn money, some CIAA member schools even tried to arrange class schedules to accommodate the vacation time of wealthy white tourists from the North.

Nevertheless, the CIAA was able to create athletic competitions for a multitude of intercollegiate sports, including some of the less popular ones. In 1924, for example, the CIAA launched track and field conference competitions despite the lack of solid track programs at black schools until the 1930s, when athletes such as Ralph Metcalfe and Jesse Owens made international headlines. The CIAA also fielded the strongest tennis conference, dominated by athletes from Smith, Morgan State, Howard, and St. Augustine during the 1930s and 1940s.

A far more popular intercollegiate sport, particularly in the spring, was baseball. Each baseball season, CIAA member schools played an initial schedule of twelve games. Baseball, unlike other sports, provided black college teams with the opportunity to compete occasionally against white schools. While baseball was a popular intercollegiate sport, football was central to the CIAA's effort to bolster athletic programs at black colleges and universities. African American intercollegiate football made its debut in 1892, when teams from Livingstone College and Biddle College (North Carolina, now Johnson C. Smith University), met for the first football game between two black colleges. In little time, rivalries developed between various black schools, and African American spectators started to flock to the games in increasing numbers. In 1919, for example, the game between Howard and Lincoln, resulting in a 0–0 tie, attracted 18,000 fans who arrived on trains decorated with banners and ribbons, known as "flapper specials." Those unable to attend the spectacle could read about it in the *Pittsburgh Courier*, which dispatched five reporters to cover the game. The growing popularity of the Howard-Lincoln football rivalry continued to attract ever-increasing numbers of fans. By 1922, Howard University had to move its game against Lincoln from the university stadium to Griffith Stadium, home of the Washington Senators, to accommodate the large number of spectators. The first heroic figure of CIAA football to emerge from the Howard-Lincoln rivalry was Franz Alfred "Jazz" Bird. The five foot seven, 145-pound Bird, was considered to be small for football, yet, Lincoln did not lose to Howard while Bird was on the team.

In the 1920s, CIAA football was plagued by a variety of problems, including rule infractions, the forfeiting of games, questions of player eligibility, and poor equipment. In 1924, for example, Howard University's Haywood "Speed" Johnson died at Freedman's Hospital in Washington, D.C., from injuries sustained during a game. That

same year, Howard withdrew from the conference because the CIAA censured the school for the illegal use of a player, and in the following year, Lincoln was censured. Both incidents, many observers felt, revealed the high level to which the rivalry between the two schools had escalated.

Despite the centrality of football, the CIAA had its largest impact on basketball. Following World War I, basketball gained in popularity when a number of poor African Americans from the North, where basketball was already well established as a winter sport, moved to the South and attempted to use their basketball skills to attain athletic scholarships and college degrees. The arrival of black athletes from the North spurred black southerners to get into the game and soon intercollegiate basketball began to gain a national African American audience. Between 1924 and 1927, Morgan State University (Maryland) dominated CIAA basketball with players like Ed "Lanky" Jones, Talmadge Hill, and Daniel "Pinky" Clark. Morgan State's team was coached by Charles Drew, who went on to lead an illustrious medical career and is known best for developing the use of blood plasma during World War II. Drew graduated from Dunbar High School in Washington, D.C., a basketball stronghold under the direction of Edwin Henderson, who promoted African American athletics throughout the capital region. At Amherst College, Drew lettered in basketball, track, and football, and was named outstanding all-around athlete in 1923. Following graduation, he coached the Morgan State team before enrolling at McGill University Medical School in 1928. Under Drew's direction, the Morgan State squad was undefeated in 1927, and many contemporaries considered the team the unofficial national champion of black college basketball. After Drew's departure, Eddie Hurt became the coach, leading the team to new heights. In 1928, under Hurt's tutelage, Morgan State beat the nation's top black professional basketball team, the Harlem Renaissance, in a 41–40 game in Baltimore. Until 1934, Morgan State's basketball team remained undefeated on its home court, and between 1931 and 1934 it won the CIAA title.

In its contemporary state, the CIAA is one of the largest Division II Conferences in the National Intercollegiate Athletic Association (NCAA). Attendance records indicate that the CIAA holds the third largest basketball tournament in the country, superseded only by the Atlantic Coast Conference (ACC) and the Big East Tournaments. The CIAA Basketball Tournament, initiated in 1946, provides the primary financial support for the CIAA. In addition to men's and women's basketball, the conference holds annual championships in cross country, volleyball, men's and women's indoor and outdoor track, tennis, golf, baseball, and softball.

**FURTHER READINGS**

Ashe, Arthur R., Jr. *A Hard Road to Glory: A History of the African-American Athlete.* New York: Amistad Press, 1988.

George, Nelson. *Elevating the Game: Black Men and Basketball.* New York: HarperCollins, 1992.

Henderson, Edwin B. "Physical Education and Athletics Among Negroes." *Proceedings of the Big Ten Symposium on the History of Physical Education and Sport.* Chicago: The Athletic Institute, 1971.

*Amy Bass*

## Central Jurisdiction of the Methodist Church

*See* Black Methodists for Church Renewal.

## Central Trades and Labor Assembly

In the summer of 1881, black and white workers in the city of New Orleans formed the Central Trades and Labor Assembly (CTLA). Following the economic depression of the 1870s, workers throughout the United States took advantage of a relatively strong economy to demand better pay and working conditions. In New Orleans, the new labor militancy was notable for its interracial character, at a time when Jim Crow laws provided for the complete segregation and disfranchisement of African Americans throughout the South. The CTLA grew out of a general movement toward biracial unionism among black and white New Orleans waterfront workers that developed in the early 1880s.

The CTLA was launched officially by the president of the New Orleans Typographical Union, the oldest union of skilled workers in the city. Its purpose was to organize all the city's labor unions, black and white, under a single banner in order to provide mutual assistance and to advance their collective-working class interests. Like its membership, the CTLA's leadership was integrated. Although the assembly's president was always white, African Americans served as vice president and recording secretary. In addition to its leadership structure, the ideal of interracial solidarity was evident in CTLA social and political events. Between 1882 and 1888 every CTLA parade featured black and white workers marching together.

The CTLA was a politically active organization even though it avoided ties with particular political parties. The assembly lobbied politicians for more stringent laws concerning child labor practices and maximum work hours. It also pushed for reforming the convict labor system and for the enforcement of all existing labor laws. In terms of tactics, the CTLA declared its support for arbitration between labor and capital whenever possible. However, in cases where capital refused to negotiate, the CTLA declared itself willing to use "all honorable means" at its disposal, including boycotts, to secure fair wages and working conditions.

By 1882, the CTLA consisted of more than twenty trade unions and roughly 15,000 workers. In addition to the typographical and cotton unions whose early support made the assembly possible, the organization represented boilermakers, bricklayers, coopers, foundry workers, and iron molders. Member unions granted the CTLA a significant degree of legislative and executive power. The assembly determined tactics and policies and supported strikes and other actions by its members only after CTLA leadership had approved of them.

Despite the unprecedented degree of biracial unionism and interracial class-based solidarity that the CTLA represented, it could not survive the economic and racial climate of the 1890s. As another depression hit the American economy, employers and their federal and state government allies suppressed labor activism. At the same time, the South's governing elite responded to the strength of interracial, class-based alliances such as the CTLA with racist appeals to white superiority and unity. As a result, groups like the CTLA disappeared.

**FURTHER READING**

Arnesen, Eric. *Waterfront Workers of New Orleans: Race, Class, and Politics, 1863–1923.* New York: Oxford University Press, 1991.

*Stuart McElderry*

## Chattanooga, Tennessee: Civic, Literary, and Mutual Aid Associations

After Reconstruction, African Americans across the South formed numerous associations to improve their social, economic, and political positions. Excluded from many aspects of southern life by both law and custom, these associations gave blacks the power to shape their own destiny and collectively improve the conditions of their race.

During Reconstruction, African Americans in Chattanooga were prominent in civic affairs. Blacks served on the police force, the board of education, and in the state legislature. They organized fire and militia companies and played an important role in Republican party politics. As Republican power waned, however, so did direct involvement by blacks in official city affairs. In response, black Chattanoogans, like other black contemporaries in cities across the South, formed various mutual aid societies. These black-controlled organizations were designed to aid individuals in need and to improve the social and economic conditions of the race.

One of the earliest mutual aid associations in Chattanooga was the Penny Savings Bank founded by Squire J. W. White and H. N. Willis in 1890. White and Willis tried to encourage thrift among their fellow blacks, and the bank attracted local black depositors as well as investors from Atlanta and elsewhere. The initial success of the Penny Savings Bank was largely due to White's excellent reputation among both races. Willis, however, who had arrived recently in Chattanooga, used the bank's holdings to support an extravagant lifestyle, including the construction of a large home. The panic that swept the nation in 1893 exposed embezzlement and the bank's weak financial position, and Willis apparently fled to Mexico. The failure of the Penny Savings Bank, however, was not illustrative of black Chattanoogan's efforts to establish mutual aid, social, and economic improvement associations.

The most influential and successful organization was the local chapter of the National Negro Business League (NNBL). Founded in 1900 by Booker T. Washington, this organization was designed to capitalize on the social and economic power of black entrepreneurs to improve the lives of African Americans. Formed in 1905, the Chattanooga chapter was second only to Nashville in its influence. The organization encouraged trade with black businesses in an effort to keep jobs and valuable capital under black control. Following the philosophy of Booker T. Washington, black business leaders advocated a gradualist approach to social equality. They did not challenge segregation but supported better educational opportunities for blacks and used their collective economic power to act as advocates of their race among the city's white leadership. The organization received important support from Randolph M. Miller, the editor of the Chattanooga *Blade*, the city's most important black newspaper. Despite wide support, white dominance of local businesses and industries limited the economic successes of this group.

Although the NNBL advocated accommodationism and racial harmony, some of its members supported a streetcar boycott in 1905. That year, Tennessee passed a new law segregating streetcars. African Americans were outraged and black Chattanoogans as well as black resi-

dents of Nashville, Memphis, and other cities in the state, initiated a boycott of the white-run streetcars. The boycott posed a serious problem for the city's black community. Without transportation to commute to and from their jobs, support from working-class blacks was likely to be short-lived. To sustain the boycott and demonstrate the resolve of the black community, Randolph M. Miller, who used his newspaper to voice the anger of black citizens, and several other prominent members of the NNBL began to operate a series of horse-drawn hack lines to provide blacks with transportation. This endeavor was so successful that in August the men organized the Transfer Omnibus Motor Car Company. Eventually, they hoped to use the proceeds from the hack lines and the capital of newly recruited investors to purchase motorized cars. However, pressure from white city officials and a withering of support of some black leaders weakened their efforts. In October, the boycott withered.

In addition to seeking social justice, Chattanooga's black businessmen were also concerned about social welfare. In 1912, in response to the high mortality rate among the city's black population, the local chapter of the NNBL petitioned municipal officials to investigate health conditions in black neighborhoods. White city leaders, however, took little action, and a 1916 report on public health in Chattanooga continued to show a much higher death rate among black city residents. To address this problem, George Edmund Haynes, a Fisk University professor and leader of the National Urban League (NUL) in Tennessee, approached local NNBL members. At Haynes's urging, the business leaders formed the Central Community Betterment League, which called for the enforcement of housing standards in black neighborhoods, better working conditions in local industries, and an end to lynching. This new organization was a vocal advocate for African Americans, but ultimately accomplished little. Nevertheless, its existence shows that black business leaders were interested in both economic development and mutual uplift.

Black Chattanoogans continued to have an interest in collective uplift. Chattanooga was the only city in the state where the ideas of Marcus Garvey and his Universal Negro Improvement Association (UNIA) found resonance. In 1923, Garvey visited the city, but his ideas did not become popular with working-class blacks until 1925 when Milton Minyard, an activist from Chicago, organized a local chapter of the UNIA. The organization, which emphasized black pride and nationalism, met regularly and attracted a large number of local blacks. During one of its 1927 meetings, a police raid left two blacks wounded. More important was the discovery of a large cache of weapons that fueled the rumor of a black uprising. Business leaders and other prominent blacks distanced themselves from the UNIA, and the organization ceased to function in Chattanooga.

Chattanooga's chapter of the National Association for the Advancement of Colored People (NAACP) also had a troubled history. It was formed after several false starts in late 1918 and attracted only a small membership. By 1921, the chapter had become ineffectual as an agent of the city's black population. The organization continued to exist in name only until the 1950s. Energized by the Supreme Court's 1954 *Brown* decision, the local NAACP, as in other southern cities, took the lead in registering voters, organizing protests, and acting as a liaison between city leaders and the black community. As a result of the NAACP's efforts, school integration, the extension of voting rights, and other issues that spawned violence in other southern communities were accomplished much more peacefully in Chattanooga.

African American women were heavily involved in mutual aid societies in Chattanooga. Many black women embraced Marcus Garvey's message in the 1920s and served in various capacities in the NAACP. Black women, however, made their most important civic contributions through church-affiliated organizations. As members of denominational groups, black women organized voter registration drives, planned strategy to achieve school integration, and served as liaisons between other organizations and the city's black community.

African American mutual aid associations had a troubled history in Chattanooga. While sometimes meeting with intense opposition from whites and blacks, these organizations played important roles in the local black community. They often led the fight for civil rights, economic development, and better living conditions. In short, they empowered African American Chattanoogans during a period of worsening race relations. That, more than anything else, is their greatest legacy.

**FURTHER READINGS**

Cartwright, Joseph H. *The Triumph of Jim Crow: Tennessee Race Relations in the 1880s.* Knoxville: University of Tennessee Press, 1976.

Lamon, Lester C. *Black Tennesseans, 1900–1930.* Knoxville: University of Tennessee Press, 1977.

———. *Blacks in Tennessee, 1791–1970.* Knoxville: University of Tennessee Press, 1981.

*Richard D. Starnes*

## Chi Eta Phi

Aliene C. Ewell, with the assistance of eleven other black nurses, founded Chi Eta Phi at Freedmen's Hospital in Washington, D.C., on October 16, 1932. The sorority was established to enhance the professional status of black nurses and to stimulate interest in the nursing profession among African Americans.

Excluded from white sororities, the founders chose the name Chi Eta Phi, symbolizing their commitment to character, education, and friendship, and adopted the motto "Service for Humanity." To fulfill this mission, the sorority participates in a variety of volunteer and community service projects and has collaborated with other professional, civic, and educational organizations such as the American Nurses' Association, the National Council of Negro Women, the United Negro College Fund, the National Association for the Advancement of Colored People (NAACP), the National Association for Sickle Cell Disease, the American Cancer Society, the National Cancer Institute, and the National Institute on Drug Abuse. Chi Eta Phi also participates in the Adolescent Pregnancy Child Watch program to prevent adolescent pregnancy, hosts food and clothing drives, and serves inner-city youths through its Student Nurses Tutorial Project. Moreover, the sorority sponsors a variety of disease prevention and health promotion programs, including consumer health education sessions, health screenings, and cancer and AIDS detection and awareness projects. Special outreach programs such as Chi Care Calls provide services and assistance to the elderly, while the CHI-TEEN program promotes healthy lifestyles among teenagers.

As a professional organization, Chi Eta Phi emphasizes scholarship. It presents awards to recognize the achievements of outstanding nurses and encourages its members to keep abreast of medical research and to pursue continuing education. Chi Eta Phi's national, regional, and local conferences as well as its workshops and leadership seminars provide members with professional networking and vocational enhancement opportunities. In addition, the sorority has launched various programs to foster the recruitment and retention of black nursing and health care professionals. Chi Eta Phi offers educational scholarships, and its campus chapters provide mentoring and workshops for nursing students.

Since its founding Chi Eta Phi has grown from an African American sorority to an international organization composed of male and female nurses and nursing students. Headquartered in Washington, D.C., Chi Eta Phi's more than 7,000 predominantly black members are organized in more than seventy graduate and twenty-three undergraduate chapters in twenty-six states, the District of Columbia, the U.S. Virgin Islands, and Liberia, West Africa. Providing a communication link for its geographically diverse membership, the sorority publishes the annual *Glowing Lamp* Journal, a biennial *Directory*, and the biannual newsletter *Chi Line*.

**FURTHER READINGS**

Jaszczak, S., and T. E. Sheets, eds. *Encyclopedia of Associations*, vol. 1, part 2. New York: Gale, 1997.

Miller, Helen S. *The History of Chi Eta Sorority, Inc., 1932–1967*. Durham, N.C.: Association for the Study of Negro Life and History, 1968.

———. *Mary Eliza Mahoney, 1845–1926. America's First Black Professional Nurse—A Historical Perspective*. Washington, D.C.: Chi Eta Phi Sorority, 1988.

Ploski, H. A., and J. Williams, eds. *The Negro Almanac*. New York: Gale, 1989.

*Nancy Jean Rose*

# Chicago: Civic, Literary, and Mutual Aid Associations

By 1843, there were already 500 African Americans living in Chicago, most of whom were freed slaves. The abolitionist John Jones and members of William Paul Quinn's A.M.E. Church assisted runaway slaves during the following two decades and by 1860 the city's black population had nearly doubled. In the 1880s, Chicago's black residents began to form fraternal societies, female church auxiliaries, and social clubs, two of which—the Old Settlers' Club and the Prudence Crandall Club—were reserved for the city's black elite. Despite class differentiation, all African Americans began to face exclusion from Chicago's mainstream social agencies during the 1890s. Although many of the first black settlers had opposed establishing segregated facilities, other African American leaders, most notably the journalist and activist Ida B. Wells, emphasized the need for health and educational facilities in the black community. Accordingly, African Americans established Provident Hospital (1891), a kindergarten (1893), and the Home for the Aged and Infirm Colored People (1898).

Between 1890 and 1920, African American women were particularly active in creating social clubs and mutual aid societies in Chicago. During this thirty-year period, they established nearly 160 clubs. Embracing the "lifting as we climb" motto of the National Association of Colored Women's Clubs, Inc. (NACW), which had been founded in 1896, these clubs created and sustained many community facilities, such as the Phillis Wheatley Working Girls' Home Association, the "Old Folks' Home," social settlements, day nurseries, homes for dependent and orphan children, employment bureaus, and reading rooms. Through fund-raising benefits and charities, black club women wedded their interest in racial uplift to their desire to enhance their own standing in the community. The focus of many of their clubs reflected this nexus, as the study of literature and fine arts was conjoined to issues of suffrage, child welfare, and community betterment.

Chicago's African American churches, too, continued their historic roles as educative and social institutions. The Institutional Church and Social Settlement, founded in 1900, offered newcomers many services, such as mothers' clubs, an employment bureau, a day nursery, and classes in cooking and sewing. The more prestigious black churches organized lyceums that sponsored prominent African American speakers such as the civil rights leader W. E. B. Du Bois, the reformer Booker T. Washington, the civil rights activist and clubwoman Mary Church Terrell, and the social scientist George E. Haynes. Leading church women, too, organized lyceums for youth who performed recitations, oratory, and music concerts. Like the women's clubs, the black churches often distinguished programs intended for their congregations from those designed for the general African American community.

Chicago, like other cities, also had chapters of the National Association for the Advancement of Colored People (NAACP), the National Urban League (NUL), the Equal Opportunity League (EOL), and the National Negro Business League. The EOL, although it ceased to exist by 1905, was perhaps the most active political organization in protesting segregation of public facilities. The Chicago NAACP, founded in 1911, took up the EOL's charge, although it focused mostly on discriminatory legislation. The Chicago Urban League (CUL) was the most pragmatic of these organizations. Established in 1917, it assisted migrants in locating employment and housing and helped them to adjust to northern urban life by dispensing information on schools, public transportation, and codes of behavior.

Chicago's African American men also created numerous clubs, many of them along political and professional lines, including the Appomatox Club (1900) and the Hyde Park Republican Colored Club (ca. 1906). Black postal workers, too, formed their own organization, the

Phalanx Forum (ca. 1910), to promote civic betterment through fundraisers and charity balls. Like the women's clubs, the men's clubs combined Washingtonian and Du Boisian ideologies. That is, they utilized their educational and professional leadership to improve the lives of those less fortunate. In employing such strategies, they also helped to build a formidable black voting bloc on Chicago's South Side.

African American women, excluded from voting in municipal elections until 1914, wielded a powerful pre-election influence. They educated other black residents on how to vote, discussed candidates' platforms, and raised funds for political parties. Anticipating the right to vote, black women formed suffrage clubs to discuss political and civic issues, to recommend candidates, and to sponsor speakers. In 1914, for example, the Alpha Suffrage Club (1913) and the Women's Second Ward Republican Club (1910), both founded by Ida B. Wells, worked in conjunction with other black women's clubs to ensure the election of the alderman of their choice in the predominantly African American Third Ward. These clubs were largely responsible for the 1915 victory of Chicago's first black alderman, Oscar de Priest.

During the early twentieth century, Chicago's Black Belt expanded and increasingly became segregated. In response, the black community established its own Young Men's Christian Association (YMCA) in 1913, a Young Women's Christian Association (YWCA) in the following year, and Red Cross units and Girl and Boy Scout troops during World War I. Moreover, African Americans made some attempts to foster interracial organizations. In 1905, for example, Celia Parker Woolley launched the Frederick Douglass Center and in 1907 Jenkins Lloyd Jones founded the Abraham Lincoln Center. But by and large, the World War I era was characterized by restrictive covenants, redlining tactics (housing discrimination by realtors), and white protective neighborhood associations. Racism and segregation culminated in the Chicago Race Riots of 1919, resulting in 38 deaths, 500 injuries, and mass destruction of homes and other property.

During the 1920s, Chicago's African Americans continued to combat racism as well as to assist black migrants. Many African American women remained active in the city's women's clubs. Indeed, by the mid-1920s, there were well over 3,000 women in sixty-three NACW-affiliated clubs. But others shifted their affiliations to the CUL and Chicago's NAACP. Few women, however, assumed administrative positions in these two organizations. Instead, they joined women's auxiliaries of the CUL, the Urbanaides and

the Westside Women's Group, and the NAACP's Flying Squadron, working largely as fundraisers.

While the CUL and NAACP chapters blossomed during the 1920s, Marcus Garvey's "Back to Africa" movement did not attract many followers in the city. This was in part due to the criticism prominent blacks such as Robert S. Abbott, publisher and editor of the *Chicago Defender*, levied against Garvey. Abbott, like many other members of the black-educated elite who advocated racial integration, disapproved of Garvey's escapist philosophy and his money-making schemes. Nevertheless, Garvey's movement, coupled with the Harlem Renaissance's celebration of African and African American art, did kindle an interest in the "Black Atlantic" during the 1920s and 1930s. In the late 1920s African Americans in Chicago celebrated their own Black Renaissance in the arts, literature, and letters. Accompanied by a renewed sense of solidarity and pride, residents of Chicago's Black Belt renamed their South Side community "Bronzeville," replete with its own mythical mayoral election, annual celebrations, and institutions. Many of these black institutions were staffed by women, including the Wabash YMCA, the Parkway YWCA, the George Cleveland Hall Branch of the Chicago Public Library (1932), Parkway Community House (1939), and the South Side Community Art Center (1941).

Parkway Community House, an expansion of Chicago's first African American Congregational Church's community center, provided particularly broad-ranging services for Bronzeville residents. It offered a day nursery; an after-school youth program; a dormitory for young working women; classes for children, youth, and adults; and a political forum that bridged pan-African issues to local ones. Its most experimental program was a community service project that required dormitory residents to engage in outreach in exchange for a reduction of their rent. A cadre of young working women taught literacy skills to young men interested in joining the army, helped retrieve birth certificates for young migrants eager to work in defense factories, and documented incidents of discrimination for Parkway's clearinghouse. Neither the city's Phillis Wheatley Working Girls' Home Association, established in 1907, nor the black Elam Home for Girls, founded in the 1920s, required their residents to participate in social outreach programs.

Although Parkway did not rely on federal funding, its director, Horace Cayton, was affiliated with the Works Progress Administration's (WPA) "Negro in Illinois" project during the 1930s. Consequently, he employed many African American writers, social workers, and unemployed professionals to complete his monumental sociological study of Bronzeville, *Black Metropolis* (1945). Some of the projects' writers and artists later became affiliated with the South Side Community Art Center (SSCAC), a Federal Arts' Project art center. Like Parkway, the SSCAC conducted many outreach programs, offered classes for children, youth, and adults, and nurtured a pan-African consciousness by sponsoring African-centered art discussions, talks, and exhibits.

Other black community institutions forged alliances with Parkway and the SSCAC. The George Cleveland Hall branch of the Chicago Public Library coordinated and co-sponsored book drives, discussions of black literature, and exhibits of African American art. The editors of the *Chicago Sunday Bee*, founded in 1927 by prominent businessman Anthony Overton, also co-sponsored programs with the community centers and libraries, including essay contests for youth, history forums, and celebrations of Negro History Week. Perhaps one of the newspaper's most impressive accomplishments was its creation of a repository of photographs documenting the contributions of African American men and women during World War II.

A number of storefront and independent churches, led by female ministers, also launched community betterment programs during the 1940s. To some extent, they continued the traditions of earlier churches. The Cosmopolitan Community Church, under the pastorship of Mary G. Evans, had started its own day nursery, free medical services, and recreational programs for youth in 1931. A decade later, its facilities expanded to include a kindergarten, a gymnasium, and a home for aged members of its congregation. The Commonwealth Community Church, founded in 1943 by Reverend Dorothy Sutton, a graduate of Northwestern University's Biblical Institute, served a younger, middle-class congregation through its art and drama guilds.

Although black migration to Chicago had subsided during the 1930s and 1940s, African American residents continued to suffer from a severe housing shortage, caused largely by the demolition of tenements in black neighborhoods. Federally funded housing projects, first constructed in the late 1930s, and other low-income housing did not alleviate this shortage because most of the new housing units were segregated and excluded black residents. The housing shortage worsened as Chicago's African American population increased by over 80 percent between 1940 and 1950. This population increase, caused largely by a growing number of black migrants, coupled with white resistance to integrated housing, sparked mob violence at

Trumbull Park Homes and Altgeld Gardens in the early 1950s. The city's African American organizations, including the NAACP, the Northern District Association of Colored Women's Clubs, and the National Urban League, were troubled by the eruption of racial violence and protested residential segregation. Between 1953 and 1958, African American organizations filed lawsuits against the Chicago Housing Authority in an attempt to integrate the Bridgeport and Lathrop Homes. White resistance to residential integration, however, succeeded in preventing blacks from moving into the Bridgeport and Lathrop Homes during the 1950s.

Despite racism, discrimination, and segregation, black and white Chicagoans formed fledgling interracial coalitions beginning in the 1940s. These included the Fellowship of Reconciliation; the Chicago Committee of Racial Equality, which in 1942 became known as the Congress of Racial Equality (CORE); the American Council of Race Relations (ACRR); and the South Side Community Committee (SCC). CORE, utilizing nonviolent direct action to challenge racial inequality in public accommodations, staged the city's first sit-ins during World War II. Meanwhile, the ACRR targeted housing discrimination, especially restrictive covenants and mob violence. The ACRR, working through local committees, recommended increased police protection of African Americans living in housing projects and in-service job training for black residents. Seeking to improve the quality of life of black residents of housing projects, the SCC, in conjunction with the University of Chicago–sponsored Chicago Area Project (CAP), set up a broad program of delinquency prevention for African American neighborhoods on the city's South Side.

During the 1950s and 1960s, segregation in housing, employment, and education intensified, despite landmark court cases and legislation. In response, African Americans in Chicago continued to form interracial coalitions. In 1962, the Coordinating Council of Community Organizations (CCCO), a predominantly black group, joined black parents and students to protest segregated and overcrowded schools on Chicago's South Side. CORE soon joined the CCCO and submitted to the Chicago Board of Education a list of demands designed to eliminate segregation and overcrowding in schools. Among the demands was a call for the resignation of Superintendent Benjamin Willis. The board, however, refused to consider CORE's demands and declined to accept Willis's resignation in 1963. CORE and CCCO responded with more school boycotts, yet their demands were never met.

In 1965, when Martin Luther King Jr. moved to Lawndale, one of Chicago's poorest and most segregated neighborhoods, he helped CORE and the CCCO build an even larger coalition. Along with the CUL, the Chicago NAACP, the Southern Christian Leadership Conference (SCLC), churches, labor organizations, and other civil rights organizations, CORE and the CCCO organized the Chicago Freedom movement, as an umbrella organization in 1966. The movement had three overarching goals: to promote equal opportunity; to procure better housing, employment, and education; and to empower the disfranchised. To implement its goals, the movement organized open housing marches and protested in front of real estate offices that practiced redlining tactics.

During the late 1960s, other nonviolent groups emerged, often working in cooperation with King. Perhaps the most well known was Operation Breadbasket, led by the Reverend Jesse Jackson, which boycotted food companies that refused to hire African Americans. In 1968, Jackson declared a "Black Christmas," urging African Americans to revitalize their cultural connections with their communities by patronizing black businesses. The holiday was followed by a "Black Easter," which also emphasized African American support of black businesses. To target the concerns of specific interest groups, Operation Breadbasket branched into various divisions for teachers, ministers, laborers, and political and cultural workers. This reorganization apparently splintered Operation Breadbasket's collective spirit, and in 1971 the organization ceased to exist.

A new organization, People United to Serve Humanity (PUSH), immediately arose from its ashes. PUSH, also headed by Jackson, continued much of Operation Breadbasket's agenda, especially its fight against employment discrimination. During the summer of 1988, PUSH threatened to block traffic on one Chicago expressway unless African American businesses received their fair share of contract work on state and city construction projects. During the 1980s, the CUL and the Chicago NAACP joined PUSH in promoting African American businesses. In addition to enhancing economic opportunities in the black community, CORE and the NAACP organized block clubs to curb drugs and violence in African American neighborhoods.

Perhaps the most successful effort of Chicago's African American organizations was their support of Harold Washington, who became the city's first black mayor in 1983. Prior to the primary election, black organizations had launched successfully a series of mass protests that prompted the formation of a black voting bloc. They organized demonstrations to protest poor health facilities and the lack of African American representation on Chicago's School Board. PUSH continued to protest high African American unemployment rates and organized a voter registration drive. Heightened protest activities mobilized the black community and ensured Washington's victory. When Washington unexpectedly died following his reelection in 1987, much of that momentum dissipated because of a lack of strong leadership in the black community.

The last decade of the twentieth century continued to witness black activism on Chicago's South Side, although it did not reached the magnitude or degree of success associated with the 1960s civil rights movement and Washington's mayoral campaign. Many community organizations, including Operation PUSH, 21st Century VOTE, and neighborhood and church groups as well as public housing tenant associations organized protest activities to rid their neighborhoods of gangs and drugs. But African American gang members, too, were activists in their own right. In 1993, for example, they helped to register new voters, marched in protests, and conducted voter education classes. The Nation of Islam, especially through its Million Man March, sought to appeal to a large constituency but has been criticized by ministers and advocates of integration for its anti-Jewish and separatist sentiments.

At the end of the twentieth century, African American activism remained localized and focused on specific neighborhood concerns. Unlike the first part of the century, when Chicago's middle-class clubs and organizations spoke collectively for African Americans, modern black community leaders come from all socioeconomic classes. Working-class and poor residents of the predominantly black neighborhood of Englewood, for example, have protested high crime rates and organized marches to "take back their streets" from gang members and drug dealers. And at Cabrini-Green and other public housing projects, presidents of resident advisory councils often wield more power in their neighborhoods than local alderpersons. Leaders of Cabrini-Green's resident advisory council, for example, have been negotiating with the Chicago Housing Authority to determine the council's share of ownership in new housing units. Perhaps no one umbrella organization can speak to the complex and diverse needs of Chicago's African Americans today.

## FURTHER READINGS

Drake, St. Clair, and Horace R. Cayton. *Black Metropolis: A Study of Negro Life in a Northern City*. New York: Harcourt, Brace, 1945; rpt., Chicago: University of Chicago Press, 1993.

Garrow, David J., ed. *Chicago 1966: Open Housing Marches, Summit Negotiations, and Operation Breadbasket.* Brooklyn, N.Y.: Carlson Publishing, Inc., 1989.

Knupfer, Anne Meis. *Toward a Tenderer Humanity and a Nobler Womanhood: African American Women's Clubs in Turn-of-the-Century Chicago.* New York: New York University Press, 1996.

Reed, Christopher Robert. *The Chicago NAACP and the Rise of Black Professional Leadership, 1910–1966.* Bloomington: Indiana University Press, 1997.

Spear, Allan H. *Black Chicago: The Making of a Ghetto, 1890–1920.* Chicago: The University of Chicago Press, 1967.

*Anne Meis Knupfer*

## Chicago Commission on Human Relations

*See* Chicago Mayor's Committee on Race Relations.

## Chicago Commission on Race Relations

The Chicago Commission on Race Relations, an interracial commission appointed by Illinois governor Frank Lowden in the wake of the 1919 Chicago race riot, spent eighteen months investigating race relations in Chicago. The result of its labors, a volume entitled *The Negro in Chicago*, became a classic in the study of twentieth-century American race relations.

The riot was in its fourth day when a committee assembled by the Chicago National Association for the Advancement of Colored People (NAACP) asked Governor Lowden to appoint a commission. Two days later, a second request came from a group of prominent Chicago business and community leaders. Lowden, who even before the riot had tried unsuccessfully to persuade the legislature to create a state commission on race relations, was sympathetic to these appeals and turned the task over to his cabinet member for education, Francis Shepardson. Because the commission was never authorized by the legislature, it received no public funding and throughout its short life relied entirely on private contributions.

Shepardson recommended the appointment of twelve members to the commission, six white and six African American. In deciding on the African American appointees he relied heavily on the advice of Julius Rosenwald, the head of Sears Roebuck, who had been involved deeply in philanthropy within the African American community.

The white members included Rosenwald, Edgar Bancroft, a prominent attorney, who became chairman, and Victor Lawson, editor of the *Chicago Daily News*. Among the African Americans were Robert S. Abbott, publisher and editor of the *Chicago Defender*, George Cleveland Hall, a leading physician, and Lacey Kirk Williams, pastor of Chicago's largest African American church.

The first tasks facing the commission were to define its mandate and to hire a staff. There was some question at first whether it was to be a study commission whose one goal was to determine the causes and impact of the riot or whether it would become an ongoing agency that would attempt to prevent future racial conflict in the city. The commission's unofficial status and lack of public funding virtually ruled out the latter role and determined that it would be a temporary body, disbanding after the study was completed. But the commission did hope that its findings would have an impact on the future course of race relations. After considerable discussion as to whether the executive secretary should be white or African American, the commission hired Graham Romeyn Taylor, a white social worker and journalist. An African American, Charles S. Johnson, a graduate student in sociology at The University of Chicago and a researcher for the Chicago Urban League (CUL), was named associate executive director. Johnson conceived the outline of the study and was clearly the more skilled researcher of the two.

Taylor and Johnson hired a research staff of eighteen—about equally divided between whites and African Americans—and later added seven persons to compile the data and write the report. Most of the investigators had backgrounds in social work; several were, like Johnson, students of the eminent sociologist Robert Park at The University of Chicago. Park's theories of urban development, migration patterns, and cultural interaction were clearly reflected in the staff's work. The staff conducted its research independently with only minimal supervision from members of the commission.

The research strategy included the analysis of data already compiled by scholars, journalists, and social agencies, and the collection of new data from court records, interviews, and personal observation. The work was organized around several specific areas—racial conflict, migration and population patterns, housing, racial contacts, crime, employment, and public opinion. The staff conducted door-to-door interviews, distributed questionnaires to community leaders, and held thirty conferences or informal hearings. Although the research was wide-ranging, it concentrated on leadership groups rather than randomly selected members of the public. Critics later charged that the investigators neglected one significant segment of the population—ordinary working-class whites, who were the source of much of the antagonism toward African Americans.

The research was completed substantially by September 1920, and the commission was presented with a text of the findings in January 1921. The recommendations were then drafted by Taylor, Johnson, and Shepardson and circulated among the commission members for final approval. The report was published as a 672-page book by The University of Chicago Press in September 1922.

*The Negro in Chicago* was a landmark in the emerging "liberal" view of race relations that would culminate in Gunnar Myrdal's massive 1944 study, *An American Dilemma.* Despite fears within the African American community that the commission would recommend southern-style racial segregation in Chicago, the make-up of both the commission and its staff precluded that outcome. Although it is never explicit, *The Negro in Chicago* clearly assumes the equality of African Americans and whites. It attributes the difficulties faced by African Americans in adjusting to an urban environment to economic and social conditions rather than innate racial differences. The riot is blamed on hostile white response to African American migration, not on the behavior of Chicago's African Americans. *The Negro in Chicago* is also clearly integrationist in its outlook. It rejects the notion that instinctual racial hostility makes an integrated society impossible and is sympathetic to neither the Jim Crow system nor the black nationalist vision of the Garvey movement. Its recommendations focus on inter-racial cooperation and understanding, more sensitive police work, integrated neighborhoods, better educational and employment opportunities for African Americans, and fairer and more positive press coverage of the African American community.

The Chicago Commission on Race Relations succeeded in providing a thorough analysis of the causes of the 1919 riot and a valuable compendium of information on race relations in an early twentieth-century American city. Its recommendations, though sensible and judicious, largely were ignored. Housing in Chicago remained segregated, job opportunities for African Americans limited, and racial prejudice widely prevalent. Arthur Waskow, an expert on the history of the commission, concludes that the fatal weakness in its recommendations was that it failed to indicate how those in power could be induced to make the changes it thought necessary.

**FURTHER READINGS**

The Chicago Commission on Race Relations. *The Negro in Chicago: A Study of Race Relations and a Race Riot.* Chicago: The University of Chicago Press, 1922.

Spear, Allan H. *Black Chicago: The Making of a Negro Ghetto, 1890–1920.* Chicago: The University of Chicago Press, 1967.

Waskow, Arthur I. *From Race Riot to Sit-In, 1919 and the 1960s.* Garden City, N.Y.: Doubleday & Company, 1966.

*Allan H. Spear*

## Chicago Mayor's Commission on Human Relations

*See* Chicago Mayor's Committee on Race Relations.

## Chicago Mayor's Committee on Race Relations

In July 1943, Chicago mayor Edward J. Kelly, prompted by the race riot that had erupted in Detroit in the previous month, appointed the Mayor's Committee on Race Relations. The purpose of the committee was to undertake a comprehensive study of social conditions of black Chicagoans, provide recommendations for improving these conditions, and suggest ways to ease racial tensions. Chaired by Edwin R. Embree, the president of the Julius Rosenwald Fund, the committee's other members included representatives from Chicago businesses and labor unions, a doctor, a pastor, and Robert R. Taylor, the chair of the Chicago Housing Authority. The director of Fisk University's Social Science Institute, Charles S. Johnson, served as the committee's consultant. In November 1945, the committee was renamed the Mayor's Commission on Human Relations, which in December 1947 became the Chicago Commission on Human Relations, a standing department in the city's government.

The first task of the mayor's committee was to organize a conference on city planning. Chicago's school system was singled out as a prime example of the discrimination suffered by the city's black residents. Overcrowding was such a problem that elementary schools on the South Side, where nearly all black Chicagoans lived, ran double shifts each school day. A representative of the Chicago Council of Negro Organizations accused the school system of racial gerrymandering, a charge that Board of Education president James B. McCahey denied. The committee ended the conference promising to work to equalize the city's school facilities.

In May 1945, the committee convened the Chicago Conference on Home Front Unity, held in conjunction with over seventy local and national organizations representing a diverse cross-section of society. Participants of the conference included the Boy Scouts of America, the Japanese American Citizens League, the Congress of Racial Equality (CORE), and the Polish National Alliance. The scope of the mayor's committee was ambitious, and its inclusion of diverse organizations demonstrated an effort to show that racial discrimination was a problem that all residents of Chicago, not just blacks and city officials, needed to confront. Drawing on the various participating organizations and local government officials, the conference organized six commissions to examine and make recommendations in the fields of employment, law, health, housing, education, and recreation. A steering committee under the direction of the mayor's committee coordinated the work of the commissions, which presented preliminary studies at the fall 1945 session of the conference.

The studies of the six commissions provided a comprehensive survey of racial discrimination in Chicago. Examples of racism included a quota system that greatly limited the availability of tuberculosis treatment, widespread failure to enforce laws prohibiting segregation in restaurants and hotels, and the use of restrictive covenants to deny blacks access to housing. Some of the commissions provided precise recommendations to end discrimination and improve living conditions for black Chicagoans. The Commission on Health and Welfare, for example, proposed that 2,400 beds be added to the city's tuberculosis sanitariums and recommended that 1,500 of the beds be set aside for black patients.

Many recommendations, however, simply proposed further study of the problems uncovered or else urged the city to begin enforcing existing laws. An underlying assumption of the conference and its participants was that the solution to racism was to equalize living and working conditions for blacks and whites. This was evident in the Chicago Charter on Human Relations, which the conference drafted and the mayor's committee adopted: "We desire to establish conditions in our city where all our children can walk without fear, where justice prevails, where all the facilities of our community life are open to all without restrictions." The renaming of the Mayor's Committee on Race Relations in late 1945 as the Mayor's Commission on Human Relations reflected this broader approach to racial conflict.

The Mayor's Committee on Race Relations and its successors, the Chicago Mayor's Commission on Human Relations and the Chicago Commission on Human Relations, achieved some success in improving conditions and opportunities for black Chicagoans. In November 1948, the Chicago conference evaluated the progress made toward meeting the recommendations of the 1945 conference. The findings were published in the 1949 Chicago Commission on Human Relations report, which observed a reduction of attacks on minorities at skating rinks, the construction of new recreation facilities, and the abolition of the quota system that limited availability of tuberculosis treatment for blacks.

The commission, however, made little headway in ending discrimination in education and housing. In 1948, double-shift school days, one of the first problems addressed by the mayor's committee, still existed at six elementary schools in black neighborhoods and black teachers continued to be assigned to schools with majority black student enrollments. Similarly, the efforts of the mayor's committee to end segregation in housing produced few results, even though the 1948 U.S. Supreme Court's decision in *Shelley v. Kraemer* held restrictive covenants unconstitutional. As the commission's report on housing recognized, the elimination of restrictive covenants did not "change traditional attitudes nor eliminate fears and resulting resistance" to the movement of blacks into white neighborhoods. The commission noted several instances of violence against blacks who had tried to move into white neighborhoods. Despite the efforts of the commission to work with school officials and real estate agents—both black and white—de facto school and housing segregation remained problems in Chicago for years to come.

**FURTHER READINGS**

Anderson, Alan B., and George W. Pickering. *Confronting the Color Line: The Broken Promise of the Civil Rights Movement in Chicago.* Athens: University of Georgia Press, 1986.

Chicago Conference on Civic Unity and Mayor's Commission on Human Relations. *Inventory in Human Relations, 1945–1948; Recommendations for the Future.* Chicago: Chicago Mayor's Commission on Human Relations, 1949.

Chicago Conference on Home Front Unity and Mayor's Commission on Human Relations. *Human Relations in Chicago, Reports of Commissions and Charter of Human Relations.* Chicago: Mayor's Committee on Race Relations, 1945.

*David F. Krugler*

## Christian Movement for Life

*See* MOVE.

## Church of Jesus Christ of Latter-day Saints, Genesis Group

*See* Genesis Group, Church of Jesus Christ of Latter-day Saints.

## Cincinnati: Civic, Literary, and Mutual Aid Associations

For most of its history, Cincinnati was a precarious place for African Americans. Antiblack attitudes were common by the early 1800s and occasionally flared into riots in which whites attacked blacks. Racism and prejudice were not only elements of the culture but of the law as well. In 1804 and 1807, the Ohio legislature passed a series of "Black Laws" to discourage African American migration and settlement in the state. Blacks or mulattos could not reside in Ohio permanently unless they had certificates of freedom issued by a U.S. court. African Americans had no voting rights, were excluded from jury service, were denied benefits of the Poor Law, were barred from the militia, and for many years had no access to public education. Since the early nineteenth century African Americans have challenged racism and prejudice in Cincinnati and Ohio and have fostered the growth of the black community through numerous literary, civic, and mutual aid associations.

Some of the first Cincinnati organizations to aid black residents centered on literary pursuits. In 1817, several white female philanthropists formed the Female Association for the Benefit of Africans to encourage the study of religious and secular texts. Despite the interest in books, most black educational societies in the nineteenth century focused their energies not on literature but on primary schooling for African Americans. In 1825, Cincinnati established a public school system that excluded the children of black, tax-paying citizens. Several groups such as the Colored Education Society, founded in 1839, raised money for schools for black Cincinnatians and for a campaign to pressure the Ohio state legislature to establish free schools for black children, which it did in 1849. These activities of African American educational organizations overshadowed the projects of literary associations. Only a handful of black literary groups are known, including perhaps the most famous formed by Peter H. Clark after the Civil War. Clark, one of Cincinnati's first

black public school teachers and a leading member of the Republican party in Ohio, encouraged the study of literature by establishing in 1869 Peter Clark's Literary Club, which existed until Clark moved to St. Louis in the late nineteenth century.

In addition to education, many of the black civic groups attacked vice, immorality, and especially intemperance among African Americans. In 1839, for example, Owen T. B. Nickens, a whitewasher and black teacher, established the Moral Reform Society. Nickens founded the society out of concern for the spiritual life of African American men and women. Members of the society pledged to uphold moral principles and to work for the suppression of intemperance, licentiousness, gambling, sabbath-breaking, and blasphemy. Many female civic associations such as the Daughters of Samaria and the Daughters of Temperance also concentrated on antidrinking campaigns. By the end of the 1850s, drunken blacks seldom appeared on Cincinnati's streets and black whiskey peddlers were forced to operate secretly.

Many of the nineteenth-century black civic associations had twin purposes. They attempted to make African Americans better citizens and sought to help them materially. For example, the Sons of Enterprise, established in 1852, promoted temperance and virtue while assisting African Americans in the purchase of real estate. Other mutual aid associations formed for a single purpose. The United Colored American Association, founded in 1844, organized to buy land for a black cemetery. The Colored Ladies' Anti-Slavery Sewing Circle of Cincinnati made clothes for runaway slaves who traveled through the city. Although evidence is sketchy, it seems clear that the city was a major hub on the Underground Railroad, since Levi Coffin, reputed president of the railroad, lived in antebellum Cincinnati. Most black mutual aid societies provided help to those in the black community who lacked financial and family support. In 1844, under the leadership of Lydia P. Mott, a white Quaker, a group of blacks and whites formed the Colored Orphans' Asylum because all other homes for children excluded blacks. African Americans also created associations to help the poor, sick, and the families of the dead such as the Dorcas Relief Society, established in 1866. Toward the end of the century, several organizations, such as the Cincinnati Protective and Industrial Association for Colored Women and Children, established homes for young black women and for the elderly.

African American associations for the young and elderly continued to thrive during the early twentieth century. Yet, black civic associations also focused their activities on racial advancement. For this purpose Cincinnati African Americans established a black branch of the Young Men's Christian Association (YMCA) in 1912 and a separate Young Women's Christian Association (YWCA) in 1916. The YMCA and YWCA devised programs for the intellectual, social, physical, and spiritual development of the young men and women of the race.

But the most influential mutual aid groups of the twentieth century have focused on ending de jure and de facto discrimination and on creating economic opportunities. In 1915, the Cincinnati branch of the National Association for the Advancement of Colored People (NAACP) formed under the leadership of Wendell P. Dabney, a black publisher, author, and leading city activist. Two years later, William Ware founded the Welfare Association for the Colored People of Cincinnati, which later became the Cincinnati chapter of the Universal Negro Improvement Association and African Communities League (UNIA). At its peak, Ware's UNIA branch enlisted 8,000 members and promoted racial pride and community improvement through education and commercial development. Also in 1917, James Hathaway Robinson established the Negro Civic Welfare Committee under the auspices of the Community Chest and Council of Social Agencies. Robinson used the committee, which was a National Urban League (NUL) affiliate, to work for better housing in black neighborhoods and the creation of more educational and job opportunities. In 1935, Robinson's committee was renamed the Negro Division of the Council of Social Agencies, and in 1949 the association became the Cincinnati Urban League, formalizing its three-decade relationship. Beginning in the 1930s the Cincinnati Urban League led efforts to eradicate all manifestations of Jim Crow.

During World War II, tensions between whites and blacks rose sufficiently to prompt the city government to establish in 1943 the Mayor's Friendly Relations Committee, which sought to reduce racial hostility. After the war, the committee became a permanent agency and still exists as the Cincinnati Human Relations Commission. Since the 1970s, however, both the Urban League's and NAACP's activities have waned and other mutual aid associations such as the entrepreneur-oriented Inroads Inc. have tried to provide the resources for the black community to challenge the vestiges of Jim Crow in Cincinnati.

**FURTHER READINGS**

Dabney, Wendell P. *Cincinnati's Colored Citizens: Historical, Sociological, and Biographical.* 1926; rpt., Cincinnati: Dabney Publishing Company, 1988.

Franklin, John Hope. *George Washington Williams: A Biography.* Chicago: The University of Chicago Press, 1985.

Kersten, Andrew E. "Fighting for Fair Employment: The FEPC in the Midwest, 1941–1946." Ph.D. diss., University of Cincinnati, 1997.

Koehler, Lyle. *Cincinnati's Black Peoples: A Chronology and Bibliography.* Cincinnati: University of Cincinnati, Institute for Policy Research, and the Center for Neighborhood and Community Studies,1986.

Taylor, Henry Louis, Jr., ed. *Race and the City: Work, Community, and Protest in Cincinnati.* Urbana: University of Illinois Press, 1993.

*Andrew E. Kersten*

## Cincinnati's Mayor's Friendly Relations Committee

The Cincinnati's Mayor's Friendly Relations Committee (MFRC), established in 1943, sought to ease racial tensions and prevent race riots in Cincinnati. Its goal was to solve the city's racial problems and promote community fellowship through the use of neighborhood meetings, community workshops, and school-related activities. Throughout its existence more than 120 individuals served as members of the committee.

The interracial committee was led initially by Robert Segal, executive director of the Cincinnati Jewish Community Council. In 1944, the MFRC appointed Marshall Bragdon, a native of Minneapolis and Wesleyan University graduate, as its executive secretary. Bragdon's appointment was largely due to his knowledge of the "Springfield Plan." Initiated in 1939, the "Springfield Plan" was an educational program used by the public schools in Springfield, Massachusetts, in an effort to eliminate racial conflicts and develop a harmonious learning environment for students, teachers, and parents from various backgrounds.

Under the guidance of Bradgon, the committee sponsored a variety of programs in hopes of improving the racial climate in Cincinnati. In 1965, the MFRC changed its name to the Cincinnati Human Relations Committee (CHRC) to broaden its appeal. However, the committee's lack of enforcement powers, constantly changing personnel, financial crises, and attempt to solve the city's racial problems without taking a public stance on controversial issues led to the organization's ineffectiveness during the 1970s, 1980s, and 1990s.

**FURTHER READINGS**

Burnham, Robert A. "The Mayor's Friendly Relations Committee: Cultural Pluralism and the Struggle for Black Advancement." In *Race and the City: Work, Community, and Protest in Cincinnati, 1820–1970.* Ed. Henry Louis Taylor, Jr. Urbana: University of Illinois Press, 1993.

———. "The New Interracialism: The Citizen's Committee for Human Rights and Restaurant Desegregation in Cincinnati." *Queen City Heritage* 52 (Fall 1994): 53–63.

Cincinnati Human Relations Committee Papers, Rare Books and Archives, University of Cincinnati Libraries, Cincinnati, Ohio.

*Eric R. Jackson*

# CIO Committee to Abolish Racial Discrimination

The Congress of Industrial Organizations (CIO) formed the Committee to Abolish Racial Discrimination (CARD) in November 1942. Although the CIO had long invoked egalitarian rhetoric concerning race, it was forced to act on these ideals during World War II, when members of its white rank-and-file launched a series of so-called hate strikes in response to the growing number of African American industrial workers. The CIO hoped that by quelling racism among its white members, it could bring into its ranks large numbers of increasingly militant black workers who were taking advantage of wartime labor shortages, federal fair employment strictures, and antifascist ideology to forge a place for themselves in the nation's manufacturing industries.

The CIO named George L. P. Weaver, an African American officer in the United Transport Service Employees union, to head the interracial committee, whose activities consisted primarily of education and propaganda. CARD organized interracial conferences, printed pamphlets and other literature stressing workers' common interest in developing and maintaining a democratic workplace, and rallied in support of President Franklin Roosevelt's Fair Employment Practices Committee. Although CARD supported the inclusion of antidiscriminatory clauses in union contracts, it left the actual hiring policies up to the local unions themselves. Through these activities, CARD developed close ties with national civil rights organizations such as the National Association for the Advancement of Colored People (NAACP) and strengthened the appeal of industrial unionism among the black working class.

After the war, CARD, which was renamed the Civil Rights Committee in 1952, handled all matters of race and rights in CIO unions until the organization's 1955 merger with the American Federation of Labor.

**FURTHER READING**

Zieger, Robert H. *The CIO: 1935–1955.* Chapel Hill: University of North Carolina Press, 1995.

*Stuart McElderry*

# Circle for Negro War Relief

The Circle for Negro War Relief promoted the psychological welfare of African American soldiers and provided material goods for them and their families during World War I. The circle was organized and incorporated in New York City in November 1917.

The officers and board of directors included several prominent black and white Americans. Mrs. Emile Bigelow Hapgood was the circle's honorary president and Charles Hanson Towne was its president. Dr. E. P. Roberts served as treasurer and Mrs. Etnah Rochon Boutte was selected executive secretary. The vice presidents were Harrison Rhodes, Dr. W. E. B. Du Bois, Dr. Robert R. Moton, and George Foster Peabody. Other directors included Colonel Charles Young, Charles S. Whitman, Ray Stannard Baker, Dr. J. D. Bushell, Mrs. James W. Johnson, Mrs. Egerton L. Winthrop, Lucy Frelinghuysen, Mary Vida Clark, Mrs. J. W. Rose, John Hope, Dora Cole Norman, Mrs. William Quick, Mrs. Salisbury Field, Mrs. Sewell Tappan Tyng, Dr. J. W. Brown, Lloyd Osbourne, Charles F. Wilcox, Fannie Hurst, Edna Ferber, Mrs. E. P. Roberts, and Arthur Spingarn.

This interracial group focused on activities designed to improve the treatment of black soldiers and enhance their chances for promotion in the segregated military establishment. The circle also provided foodstuffs and other kinds of sundry items and commodities for the families of black soldiers.

The circle was very successful. Within months of its incorporation, local branches were set up in other communities across the country. Each branch selected a "vital need" for relief in a particular community or a nearby army camp. The Circle in New York City, for example, raised $2,000 to purchase an ambulance for the use of black troops stationed at Camp Upton in New York City. In St. Helena, South Carolina, circle members knitted clothing, wrote letters to and for black soldiers, and worked with the American Red Cross during the influenza epidemic.

Throughout the country, the circle tried to provide for the needs of African American soldiers and their dependent families. The circle's varied activities ranged from supplying comfort kits and educational materials to purchasing victrolas and records for the black troops. Moreover, the circle advised white camp commanders to ensure that black soldiers were accorded the same treatment as white soldiers under which they trained to become effective fighting men of the U.S. military.

**FURTHER READINGS**

"The Circle for Negro Relief." *Crisis* (February 1918): 201.

The Circle for Negro War Relief. *Report* (1920). The Schomburg Center for Research in Black Culture, New York Public Library.

Paton, Gerald W. *War and Race: The Black Officer in the American Military, 1915–1941.* Westport, Conn.: Greenwood Press, 1981.

Scott, Emmett J. *Scott's Official History of The American Negro In The World War.* Chicago: Homewood Press, 1919.

*Phillip McGuire*

## Citizens' League for Fair Play

During the Great Depression African Americans in numerous cities launched "Don't Buy Where You Can't Work" or "Jobs for Negroes" campaigns to pressure local white storekeepers to hire African Americans for clerical and white-collar jobs. In New York City's Harlem, the Citizens' League for Fair Play spearheaded this jobs effort. Spurred by earlier local attempts by the Harlem Housewives League and the *Amsterdam News* to improve employment opportunities, and by successful campaigns in Chicago and elsewhere, Effa Manly called a meeting between a group of activist African American women and local ministers. Reverend John Johnson of St. Martin's Episcopal Church and Fred Moore, publisher of the newspaper the *New York Age*, responded and called for a mass meeting to form the Citizens' League for Fair Play in 1934.

The Citizens' League for Fair Play attracted widespread and diverse organizational support including African American churches, political, business, fraternal, women's, and social clubs. Members' politics ranged from the more traditional approaches of the local Democratic and Republican clubs to the nationalism of street corner orators Ira Kemp and Arthur Reid. Northern- and Southern-born blacks joined with West Indians in the coalition,

women with men, and the Cosmopolitan Social and Tennis Club with the Young West Indian Congress and the New York branch of the Universal Negro Improvement Association. Others, like black nationalist Sufi Abdul Hamid, who had been involved in Chicago's jobs campaign, and his Negro Industrial and Clerical Alliance, worked alongside the Citizens' League for Fair Play. Nevertheless, while across Harlem there was widespread agreement on the problem of employment discrimination, several African American groups opposed the "Don't Buy" campaign. Some socialists and trade unionists feared it would undercut their efforts to integrate African Americans into traditionally white unions and could, if there was a white backlash, ghettoize black employment generally. If only black people should work in Harlem, might employers argue only whites should be employed in white neighborhoods? Communists, who later reversed their position, argued that the campaign was disruptive to working-class unity across racial lines. The National Urban League (NUL) and the National Association for the Advancement of Colored People (NAACP) feared the public and possibly confrontational nature of the campaign, preferring quieter methods of persuasion. And some black businessmen preferred a more nationalist strategy of encouraging Harlem consumers to buy only at stores owned by black people.

The league's first campaign, against Blumstein's Department Store on 125th Street, Harlem's main business thoroughfare, brought hundreds to daily picket lines and demonstrations. Several weeks of protests and the resulting boycott proved successful, and Blumstein and several other local stores hired African American clerks, with the promise of more to come. Nevertheless, internal controversies between nationalists like Kemp and Reid and more traditional political activists slowed the league's momentum. Kemp and Reid first quarreled over the selection of African American clerks actually hired, arguing they were not dark-skinned enough. Ultimately, they broke from the Citizens' League for Fair Play to form their own organization, the Harlem Labor Union, and reinstated the picket lines at Blumstein's and elsewhere. Hamid's nationalist organization joined the controversy as well. Competing picket lines; demands that employees come from one organization or another; and allegations of threats, corruption, and anti-Semitism by the nationalist groups led to a state court injunction against picketing at the end of 1934. The ruling insisted that there could be no legal pickets because the grounds for protest did not constitute a labor dispute. Unwilling to resort to either illegal pickets or other, more confrontational forms of pressure, the Citizens' League for Fair Play was left without a strategy, and its gains quickly evaporated. Many of the promised jobs for African Americans never materialized, and few additional employees were hired after the pickets ceased. The campaign was revitalized in 1938 when the Supreme Court in *New Negro Alliance v. Sanitary Grocery Company* overturned the lower court injunction by ruling that since employment discrimination was based on racial restrictions, pickets also based on race were therefore acceptable. The Reverend Adam Clayton Powell Jr. of Harlem's Abyssinian Baptist Church then organized a new and even larger coalition, the Greater New York Coordinating Committee for Employment, which successfully negotiated employment for African Americans in a variety of local and citywide jobs.

**FURTHER READINGS**

Greenberg, Cheryl Lynn. "Or Does It Explode?" In *Black Harlem in the Great Depression*. New York: Oxford University Press, 1991.

Hunter, Gary. "Don't Buy From Where You Can't Work: Black Urban Boycott Movements During the Depression, 1929–1941." Ph.D. diss., University of Michigan, 1977.

Muraskin, William. "The Harlem Boycott of 1934 and its Aftermath." M.A. thesis, Columbia University, 1966.

Naison, Mark. *Communists in Harlem During the Depression*. Urbana: University of Illinois Press, 1983.

Weiss, Melville. "Don't Buy Where You Can't Work: An Analysis of Consumer Action Against Employment Discrimination in Harlem, 1934–1940." M.A. thesis, Columbia University, 1941.

*Cheryl Greenberg*

## Civic Unity Committee of Seattle

*See* Washington State Fair Employment Practices Committee.

## Civil Rights Commission

*See* United States Commission on Civil Rights.

## Civil Rights Congress

In 1946 the National Negro Congress (NNC), the National Federation for Constitutional Liberties (NFCL), and the International Labor Defense (ILD) merged to form the Civil Rights Congress (CRC).

Like the organizations from which it sprung, the CRC was viewed by many contemporaries as a "Communist front," that is, an organization that was a version of the Communist Party–USA in everything but name. Certainly, Communists—particularly African American Communists, like William Patterson—played a central role in the organization, but those not known to be Communists, for example, the singer, actor, and political activist Paul Robeson, also played crucial roles in this organization that specialized in coming to the aid of black defendants facing charges perceived to be motivated by racial or political animus.

During its ten-year history the CRC's multifaceted activities mirrored those of the organizations that helped bring it into existence. The ILD had been catapulted into prominence because of its militant defense of the "Scottsboro 9" (nine black men accused of raping two white women) and Angelo Herndon (arrested for leading a march in Fulton County, Georgia); the NNC was an early expression of an attempt to build a "Black United Front"; and the NCFL often brought cases to the U.S. Supreme Court concerning civil rights and civil liberties. The CRC encompassed all of these activities—and more.

One of its earliest cases involved Willie McGee, an African American truck driver from Mississippi whose white lover accused him of rape after her husband discovered their affair. It appeared that McGee, like so many black defendants before him, was on his way to a certain execution until the CRC intervened. The CRC highlighted the fact that spurious charges of rape had been used historically as a pretext to lynch black men. The CRC launched an international campaign to save McGee's life; it portrayed McGee as an example of the plight facing African Americans: persecuted and victimized by a pervasive bigotry. The organization, however, did not succeed and McGee was executed in 1951.

Indeed, a significant percentage of the CRC's campaigns resembled the McGee case. For example, there was the case of the "Martinsville 7" in Virginia, which also involved allegations of interracial rape. In its declining days the CRC helped to bring publicity to the case of Emmett Till, a youthful Chicago resident who was lynched during a visit to Mississippi in 1955 after supposedly "getting fresh" with a white woman.

To be sure, such cases were not the sole preoccupation of the CRC. The organization rallied to the defense of Rosa Lee Ingram, the black female sharecropper from Georgia who was accused of killing her white landlord, who in turn had been accused of molesting her. Such focused emphasis on the sensitive intersection of race and gender touched a raw nerve in the United States. Though the CRC subsequently has been criticized for disrupting potential interracial alliances, others have argued that their interventions—by embarrassing the United States in the global arena—hastened the disintegration of Jim Crow.

Due to its ties to an international left-wing movement, the CRC was able to bring sharp attention in the global arena to the question of Jim Crow. This was no small matter, for at the same time the United States was seeking to portray itself as the paragon of human rights virtue in the cold war competition with the Soviet Union.

The issue was joined in 1949 when the CRC chapter in New York sponsored a fund-raising concert in Peekskill, New York, featuring Paul Robeson, the well-known activist, actor, and singer. This was in the midst of concern expressed about comments allegedly made by him at a peace conference in Paris, where he was said to have cast doubt on whether African Americans would join in a war against the Soviet Union. As a result, protesters gathered en masse to raise their voices against Robeson and the supposed "Communist front" he was representing. They decided not only to raise their voices but also raised clubs and hurled stones at CRC supporters, who were routed. There were numerous injuries and the police, who were on the scene, decided not to intervene. Though the CRC's international supporters pointed to Peekskill as evidence of the hollowness of American pretensions to represent the zenith of civil liberties, this "riot" also suggested that the CRC was attracting adversaries who were becoming increasingly forceful.

The CRC's crusades on behalf of African Americans were epitomized by its petition filed at the United Nations charging the United States with "genocide" against African Americans. This petition, which was published in book form as *We Charge Genocide*, garnered global attention with its gruesome catalogue of lynchings, police murders, and other outrages perpetrated against African Americans with the—at least tacit—support of government.

Still, the CRC cases involving "reds" were probably more controversial than those involving "blacks." The CRC was the major organization fighting the Smith Act prosecutions of leading Communists like Ben Davis Jr. and Henry Winston; these two men were African Americans, but the CRC also defended numerous nonblack Communists against charges of teaching and advocating Marxism-Leninism. The CRC felt that a robust political atmosphere that stifled the free speech rights of unpopular political minorities like Communists eventually would lead to the repression of rights of unpopular racial minorities, like African Americans. This was not altogether inaccurate, for the authorities moved rapidly from requesting the membership lists of the Communist party to requesting the same from the National Association for the Advancement of Colored People (NAACP) in Alabama.

Nevertheless, there were repeated clashes between the CRC and the NAACP as the latter strained to distance itself from this "Communist front." Just as the CRC's predecessor, the ILD, had clashed with the NAACP in the 1930s over the defense of the "Scottsboro 9," the CRC clashed with the association over the defense of the "Martinsville 7," the "Trenton 6," and other leading cases of the era involving African Americans.

Though at its zenith the CRC may not have had more than 10,000 members, this was no small matter in the otherwise "silent" 1950s. Its strongest chapters were in cities with large African American populations, for example, Detroit, New York City, Chicago, and Los Angeles.

Ironically, the CRC's frequent target—the U.S. government—was no small factor in helping to bring the CRC to its knees. The Subversive Activities Control Board brought charges against the CRC alleging that it was no more than the Communist party in disguise. Fighting this legal battle, as well as constant surveillance and harassment by the FBI, finally convinced the CRC to liquidate the organization in 1956, just as a new civil rights movement was sprouting in Montgomery, Alabama. Though the CRC ceased to exist, its imprint was not erased as a new stage in the freedom struggle commenced. Many who had honed their skills with the CRC went on to play significant roles after 1956: This was the ultimate legacy of the Civil Rights Congress.

**FURTHER READINGS**

Horne, Gerald. *Communist Front? The Civil Rights Congress, 1946–56*. London: Associated University Presses, 1988.

Plummer, Brenda Gayle. *Rising Wind: Black Americans and U.S. Foreign Affairs, 1935–1960*. Chapel Hill: University of North Carolina Press, 1996.

Rise, Eric W. *The Martinsville Seven: Race, Rape, and Capital Punishment*. Charlottesville: University Press of Virginia, 1995.

*Gerald Horne*

## Cleveland: Civic, Literary, and Mutual Aid Associations

Cleveland's numerous black civic, literary, and mutual aid associations were manifestations of the social, cultural, educational, political, and economic activism of the city's African American residents.

Prior to the Civil War, Cleveland's black population was relatively small. Only twelve African Americans lived in the city in 1830, and by 1840 their number had risen to sixty-seven. Despite their small number, the city's black population, consisting of former slaves and free blacks, started to establish a variety of abolitionist, literary, debating, and mutual aid societies as well as schools in the 1830s. These early organizations were often the product of collaboration between white abolitionists and black city residents. In 1833, for example, black and white residents formed the Cleveland Anti-Slavery Society. Members included leading businessmen, physicians, and attorneys, as well as thirty women. Similar to other abolitionist societies that emerged during those years, the Cleveland Anti-Slavery Society used public forums to promote its mission and sponsored speeches and lectures on the evils of slavery. The Cuyahoga County Anti-Slavery Society, founded in 1837, succeeded the Cleveland organization. Former slave and community leader John Malvin was an active member in both societies. While the Cuyahoga County group included some of the same officers as the Cleveland organization, its formation may indicate a growth of abolitionist activities and an increase in membership.

In addition to these interracial groups, African Americans also established all-black organizations to fight for the abolition of slavery. In 1850, for example, Cleveland blacks founded the Ohio Colored American League, which reorganized in 1853 as the Ohio State Anti-Slavery Society. In 1859, Clevelanders organized the Cuyahoga Anti-Slavery Society as a branch of the state society and raised funds for its operations. The Ohio State Anti-Slavery Society wrote petitions that were circulated throughout the state, calling for the repeal of Ohio's "Black Laws" (laws that existed to keep blacks as a lower class than whites) and the elimination of racial distinctions from the state's constitution. Other petitions demanded that the state protect the rights of every resident and prohibit the kidnapping of blacks. Leading members of these abolitionist groups included the attorney John Mercer Langston, the Reverend S. T. Jones, the barber John L. Watson, the lecturer Charles Langston, and the printer and librarian William Howard Day. Opposition to the state's "Black Laws" also provided the impetus for the founding of the Colored Ladies Benevolent Sewing Society, which opposed slavery and advocated temperance.

In addition to supporting antislavery efforts, African Americans in Cleveland sought to provide the city's black residents with educational opportunities. In 1829 the state of Ohio passed a law prohibiting African Americans from attending public schools. In the 1830s African Americans founded the School Education Society and the School Fund Society to oversee the establishment of schools in Cleveland and throughout the state. Malvin, John Brown "the Barber," and Cleveland residents David Smith and Alexander Bowman headed this effort that resulted in the founding of the School Education Society and a school in 1832. Funding was met by subscription. Using the same methods, the School Fund Society, established in 1835, was able to open schools in Cincinnati, Columbus, and Springfield. The society's president, Malvin, and its secretary, R. D. Kennedy, used newspaper advertisements to solicit financial support.

Other pre–Civil War educational ventures included the founding of literary and debating clubs. Beginning in the 1830s, black churches launched these societies to foster intellectual stimulation through discussion of literature, historic events, and social, political, and economic issues of contemporary concern. Founded in 1839, the Young Men's Union Society, for example, sponsored a school, operated a library with nearly one hundred volumes, and hosted debates. Members of this group included the barbers John L. Watson and J. M. Whitfield as well as the carpenter Charles Freeman. The group's lively debates on subjects such as colonization and abolition also attracted many whites. Another early debating club, which attracted the members of the Young Men's Union Society, was the Colored Americans of Cleveland, which was organized in the 1840s. The club sponsored public debates and invited "Freemen of all classes who are friends of Freedom and genuine Republicanism."

Benevolence and mutual aid associations provided charitable and philanthropic support for the needy, assisted fugitive slaves, and established funds for schools. Founded in 1852, in response to the Fugitive Slave Law of 1850, the Colored Ladies Benevolent Sewing Society aided mainly fugitive slaves. Members of this organization took considerable risks since the state's "Black Laws" prohibited any aid to fugitives. The women solicited aid from Cleveland's citizens to "sustain them in this undertaking and further benevolent objects."

In addition, black men started to launch fraternal organizations, including the Masons, which were established in 1855. The Grand United Order of Odd Fellows, Ohio Lodge 1188, also established in 1855, was the first African American lodge west of New York City. Even after the onset of the Civil War, black men continued to establish fraternal organizations. During the war, for example, William T. Boyd founded Excelsior Lodge 11.

Due to natural increase and a steady influx of fugitive slaves, Cleveland's black population grew to 800 by 1860 and to 1,250 by 1870. While Cleveland's black population growth troubled many white residents, African Americans welcomed migrants to the city. In 1863, for example, the city's black residents organized a mass gathering to welcome Lucy Bagby Johnson, who just two years earlier had been returned to bondage from Cleveland as a fugitive slave.

When the Civil War started, the city's black residents were eager to fight for the freedom of those held in bondage. In 1861, they formed a militia and offered their services to Governor Dennison and his successor Brough. Both men, however, denied black requests for military service. Subsequently, many of those who had hoped to serve in the Cleveland militia, including John and Charles Brown, sons of John Brown the barber, joined the 54th and 55th Massachusetts regiments. Those who did not serve as soldiers became recruiters for the cause. Dr. Robert Boyd Leach, Cleveland's first African American physician, turned to recruiting after he was denied enlistment. In 1863, he traveled to Washington, D.C., and tried to enlist there, but he became ill and passed away in Philadelphia on July 29, 1863.

The Emancipation Proclamation and the passage of the 13th, 14th, and 15th Amendments changed the agendas of African American organizations. Beginning during the war, Cleveland blacks organized to secure political and civil rights. In 1864, the abolitionist Frederick Douglass convened a meeting of the National Convention of Colored Citizens of the United States in Syracuse, New York. The meeting resulted in the formation of the National Equal Rights League, under the leadership of President John Mercer Langston, which convened a meeting in Cleveland. The league pledged "to encourage Black self-improvement and to obtain full rights of citizens by appeals to the minds of Americans and by legal process when necessary." State auxiliaries formed in Ohio, Michigan, Pennsylvania, New York, North Carolina, Tennessee, and Louisiana. These auxiliaries welcomed members of both races and genders. The Cleveland branch of the league's Ohio auxiliary worked toward goals to abolish the state's "Black Laws."

Following the Civil War, Cleveland's black population continued to increase due to the influx of black migrants from the rural South. By 1900, approximately 6,000 African Americans resided in Cleveland, and by 1910 their number had grown to more than 8,400. The arrival of large numbers of rural southern blacks generated an increase in the number of civic, literary, and mutual aid associations. Moreover, it heightened existing class divisions, resulting in the formation of societies that catered exclusively to the city's black elites. The Social Circle, established in 1869, was composed of the city's light-skinned, middle-class elites. It organized outings and social gatherings at the homes of its members, including the families of the attorneys John P. Green and Leonidas Wilson, the writer Charles W. Chesnutt, and the businessman George A. Myers. By 1904, the circle was known as the Euchre Club.

Another exclusive domain of the city's black educated, cultured, and financial elite were the literary associations that emerged in the late nineteenth and early twentieth centuries. Groups such as the Cleveland Literary Society (1873), the Tawawa Literary Society (1874), the Ideal Literary Society (1886), and the Wide Awake Literary Society (ca. 1894) fostered literary appreciation and intellectual stimulation while promoting Christian values. Other literary groups included the Du Bois Literary Club (1912); the Alpha Reading Association (1915), which counted among its members the former *Cleveland Journal* newspaper publisher Nahum Brasher; and the Topaz Cluster Embroidery Club (1915), which consisted of ten African American women who gathered for weekly meetings to discuss literary topics and to work for charitable and social purposes.

While these groups provided their members with opportunities for social interaction and cultural refinement, they also stimulated social and political activism. In 1896, for example, the Tawawa Literary Society, under the leadership of the Reverend Reverdy C. Ransom and the military chaplain William T. Anderson, protested against the Supreme Court's ruling in *Plessy v. Ferguson*. Society members, appalled by the court's decision to uphold legal segregation, presented a resolution to Ohio congressman Theodore E. Button. Among the signers was the Mt. Zion Congregational Church minister Jesse Moorland, who in 1898 became one of two black men to supervise the nationwide growth of the black Young Men's Christian Association (YMCA).

The Du Bois Literary Club also involved itself in political issues. In 1913 it was one of several Cleveland organizations to appear before an Ohio House Committee to oppose a bill that outlawed interracial marriages. However, despite the group's efforts, the bill passed.

Another outlet for black political activism were the city's Republican party clubs. In 1900, George A. Myers founded the Central Colored League, which functioned as a Republican political action group that sought to increase the influence of leading black politicians. The Attucks Republican, founded in 1906 by Thomas W. Fleming, was headed by a new generation of professionals. The club sponsored an annual "Lincoln-Douglass Banquet," which featured political speeches by honored guests that included local politicians and activists.

The city's black elites also found an outlet for community activism in various temperance societies. Black women were active particularly in groups such as the Ladies Perseverance Society (1872), the Non-Partisan Christian Temperance Association (1889), and the Loyal Temperance Legion (1903), which held socials for young people, usually at the home of one its organizers. Dedicated to improving the morals of Cleveland's black population, these temperance societies worked to eliminate alcohol abuse and vice, particularly among the city's growing number of southern migrants.

Black women were also instrumental in the founding of institutions that catered to the elderly and young working women. In 1893, the dressmaker Rosa Johnson and the educator Mamie Walker founded the Home for Aged Colored People, which was incorporated in 1896. The Phillis Wheatley Association, founded in 1911 by Jane Edna Hunter as the "Working Girls Home Association," provided housing for young black women who had come to Cleveland in search of employment. Black women were also active in the Cleveland chapter of the Federation of Colored Women's Clubs (FCWC), founded in 1898. In 1912, the FCWC, led by Carrie Clifford, a well-known club woman and wife of state assemblyman William Clifford, Rosa Johnson, and Mamie Walker, established a short-lived settlement house. The settlement house planned to provide social services to African Americans, especially to migrants.

Likewise, African American men launched several associations to advance the interest of the city's black population. In 1908, the attorneys Thomas Fleming, Robert R. Cheeks, and Harry E. Davis; the inventor of the gas mask and traffic signal Garrett A. Morgan; and the businessman Samuel E. Woods, founded the Cleveland Association of Colored Men. Composed of the city's leading black business, political, social, and professional men, the group

organized a Sunday afternoon lecture course, launched large-scale celebrations to commemorate the Emancipation Proclamation, raised money for charitable institutions such as the Home for the Colored Aged and the Humane Society, and initiated a Christmas Inn Movement to collect clothes, food, and money for the poor. Moreover, the group protested against discrimination and met with city officials to resolve racial tensions. The reformer and educator Booker T. Washington and Judge Robert H. Terrell were honorary members of the group.

The influx of black migrants from the rural South grew dramatically as a result of the Great Migration of World War I, which increased Cleveland's black population by 300 percent. By 1920, more than 34,000 African Americans resided in the city, many of whom had come to Cleveland to find jobs in defense industries. Large numbers of the migrants settled on the city's east side, where a distinct African American community began to emerge.

In response to the black population increase, African Americans organized various associations to address the problems generated by the Great Migration, such as the lack of adequate housing, jobs, and education as well as the deterioration of social conditions in black neighborhoods. In 1915, black residents founded the Playhouse Settlement to serve as a social settlement house for the growing African American community. A significant part of its service consisted of theater and arts programs. Another product of the Great Migration was the 1917 founding of the Negro Welfare Association, an affiliate of the National Urban League (NUL), which addressed the lack of adequate housing, jobs, and education as well as the deterioration of social conditions in the black neighborhoods. In 1940, the group changed its name to the Cleveland Urban League.

Literary and debating societies continued to serve as outlets for cultural refinement, literature appreciation, and public debates. In 1927, St. James African Methodist Episcopal Church established a Literary Forum to facilitate public discussion of racial issues. The forum provided the community with an opportunity to listen to renowned national figures such as Mary McLeod Bethune, founder of Bethune Cookman College, and leading black intellectual W. E. B. Du Bois.

In 1930, a group of young literary artists, some of whom were affiliated with the Playhouse Settlement (Karamu House), founded the January Writers Club, which sought to stimulate young people's interest in creative writing. Its members included the artist Gwendolean

Mitchell, the educator Harvey Williamson, the world traveler Clarence F. Bryson, and James H. Robinson, founder of Crossroads Africa, an international student exchange program. Club members read and discussed the works of the artists of the Harlem Renaissance, including Countee Cullen, Jean Toomer, Claude McKay, and the Cleveland native, author, and poet Langston Hughes. Moreover, the group financed the publication of the writings of its members between 1930 and 1933.

The economic boom triggered by World War I gave way to despair during the Great Depression. Determined to ensure the economic survival of Cleveland's African American community, black residents launched several associations that aided black businesses, fought for equal access to federal relief and employment programs, and protested racism and unfair labor practices. The Progressive Business Alliance (PBA), founded by entrepreneur Herbert Chauncey as the Cleveland Business Association in 1925, promoted cooperation between black entrepreneurs and retailers. It hosted the "Negro Business Hour" radio show, sponsored an annual trade exhibit, and provided training and assistance to minority business enterprises. Beginning in 1935, the Future Outlook League (FOL) challenged unfair labor practices and worked to increase black employment opportunities. The FOL, founded by John O. Holly, an industrial laborer and political appointee, organized a "don't buy where you can't work" campaign and secured jobs for African Americans in the private sector and in government agencies. Between 1937 and the early 1940s, the FOL published the *Voice of the League,* and its employees union, with several hundred members, became one of the largest all-black unions in Ohio. Noted members of the FOL were the attorney Alexander H. Martin, the businessman M. Milton Lewis, the porter Robert S. Warren, and the clerk Linton Freeman. The FOL was successful in breaking down racial barriers to employment and helped to integrate Cleveland's work force.

The outbreak of World War II revived Cleveland's industry and sparked a new wave of black migration to the city. By 1948, as a result of the renewed influx of black migrants during the war, Cleveland's black population had increased to 147,000. A variety of African American associations, advocating mutual aid and racial solidarity, continued to serve the needs of the city's black residents. Yet, increasingly, black organizations started to attack racism and segregation and to demand political power and civil rights.

During the postwar decades, several groups emerged that worked to rid the community of racism while fostering economic self-sufficiency and political independence. The United Freedom Movement (UFM), initially called Freedom Fighters for the Cleveland NAACP, was established by Levi Foster and local activists in 1960. The group became the first Cleveland contact for the Congress of Racial Equality (CORE) and the Student Non-Violent Coordinating Committee (SNCC). Beginning in 1961, Lewis Robinson, a city housing inspector and community activist, headed the group. In 1963 the Cleveland United Freedom movement was formed, with the NAACP heading the umbrella group. The UFM picketed local retail businesses, launched efforts to desegregate Cleveland's public schools, and established freedom schools that taught black history, culture, and civil rights. UFM protests frequently resulted in violent confrontations with whites. In 1964, the Reverend Bruce Klunder, a white minister and member of the UFM, was run over by a bulldozer during demonstrations at the construction site of a segregated school. Perhaps in response to the growing violence, the UFM, under Robinson's direction, started a rifle club and entered into an alliance with the Afro-Set.

Founded by Harllel Jones in 1968, the Afro-Set advocated cultural nationalism and separate black-controlled institutions. It operated out of the Jomo Freedom Kenyatta House and provided numerous services to the black community, including a head start program and community crime patrols. Moreover, the group attacked police brutality in African American neighborhoods, which had resulted in riots in Hough (1966) and Glenville (1968). In 1971, the Afro-Set entered into another alliance when it formed a coalition with the National Committee to Combat Fascism (NCCF).

The NCCF was the local arm of the Black Panther party. It planned to operate a health center and a prison visitor bus service, but these two projects never developed fully. The NCCF gained notoriety when it charged the police with the bombing of its headquarters, and some of its members were arrested during an alleged shoot-out with the police. White liberals organized fundraisers for the defense of the arrested NCCF members, yet several NCCF members were convicted for their participation in the shoot-out as well as on charges of kidnapping and rape. By 1972 the NCCF was almost disbanded.

Another group attracting the attention of law enforcement officials was Operation Black Unity (OBU). Founded in 1969, OBU served as an umbrella organization for some twenty-five groups that sought to improve the conditions of Cleveland's black population. Its early leadership included the Reverend Dr. Donald G. Jacobs, the newspaper publisher W. O. Walker, and Rabbi David Hill of the Black House of Israel. Hill initiated the "McDonald's project," which supported the acquisition of a black-owned and -operated McDonald's fast-food franchise. Hill, who served as chairman of the OBU's negotiating committee, contacted the McDonald's corporation to initiate a peaceful settlement. However, when McDonald's refused to negotiate with him, the OBU launched boycotts and pickets of local restaurants. In 1969, Carl B. Stokes, the city's first black mayor, agreed to mediate between OBU and McDonald's. Despite Stokes's efforts, Hill and James Raplin, another OBU member, were arrested and indicted on blackmail charges. Both men were found guilty by twelve white jurors, but defense attorney Stanley Tolliver averted the verdict. In 1970, the city's first black-owned McDonald's restaurant was purchased by Charles E. Johnson and two other restaurants soon followed.

In addition to economic empowerment, Cleveland's black population also used its political power following passage of the 1965 Voting Rights Act. In 1967, African Americans helped elect Carl B. Stokes, the city's first black mayor. In the aftermath of the election, Cleveland's black residents launched a number of political action committees, including the 21st District Political Caucus. Stokes established the caucus in 1970 to ensure the continued political gains of African Americans and to support the congressional seat of his brother Louis. The caucus was named for Louis Stokes's congressional district, and its executive board was composed of black elected officials and ministers. The caucus became a powerful political body as black and white candidates sought its endorsement in order to gain the support of black political officials and the vote of their constituents. With support of the city's black residents, the caucus has managed to maintain significant political power. When the U.S. Congress redrew Cleveland's congressional districts, the 21st district became the 11th district, and the caucus became the 11th Congressional District Caucus.

During the 1980s, other groups sought to increase black political power, including the Black Women's Political Action Committee (BWPAC), founded in 1983, and the Black Men's Political Action Committee (BMPAC). Among the BWPAC's founding members were Judges Una Keenon, Patricia Blackmon, and state representative Barbara Boyd. The BWPAC is a nonpartisan organization that gives "financial, moral and physical support to Black women interested in or serving in political office." It provides voter education, promotes voter registration, and seeks to enhance the participation of black women in the governmental process. The BWPAC participates in communitywide activities that heighten political awareness, including the African American Family Picnic and the 11th Congressional District Caucus Labor Day Picnic. Moreover, the BWPAC collaborates with the National Council of Negro Women and the Cuyahoga Women's Caucus. As a result of these joint efforts, BWPAC-endorsed candidates were elected as local judges, state representatives, school board officials, and city councilpersons. The BMPAC serves a similar function. It seeks to increase the number of black-elected officials, endorses candidates for political office, and seeks to influence the campaign issues of candidates.

During the 1980s, black literary societies also continued their efforts, promoting the works of black authors and offering writers workshops to stimulate creativity and enhance the artistic skills of their members. Some of the literary societies were named for noted African American writers, such as the Charles W. Chesnutt Literary Society, which was founded by the antiquarian Nathan Oliver in 1985. Oliver succeeded Chesnutt as the second African American to join the Cleveland Rowfant Club, a men's literary organization. The Chesnutt Society worked to promote black literature through various programs, including public readings. Similarly, the Adrienne Kennedy Society sought to popularize the works of Cleveland playwright Adrienne Hawkins Kennedy, whom the Great Lakes Theatre Festival commissioned to write *The Ohio Murders* in 1990. In the same year, Louise Kent Hope, a lifelong friend of Kennedy, and other leading members of Cleveland's black community established the society to introduce Kennedy's work to the public. Between 1991 and 1996, the society organized annual fund-raiser balls that helped pay for a series of theatre luncheons. In 1993, the society, with a grant from the Lila Wallace Reader's Digest Fund, launched its Creative Writers Workshop Projects, which sponsored mentor and workshop programs in Cleveland's Public Schools. Since 1997, local agencies have contributed additional funding to the society's educational programs.

Since the early nineteenth century, Cleveland's numerous black associations have provided important social, cultural, educational, political, and economic services to the city's expanding African American community. Various societies sponsored educational and cultural enrichment programs, aided those in financial need, launched forums for public debates, and fostered community activism in order to improve the living and working conditions of the city's African American population. While black associations were the product of racism, discrimination, and segregation, they also provided a training ground for political leadership and laid the foundation for the civil rights struggle. Particularly after 1945, many of the city's black civic groups retreated from advocating racial advancement through self-help and mutual aid and started to demand political and legal equality.

**FURTHER READINGS**

Chatterjee, Prenab. *Local Leadership in Black Communities.* Cleveland: Case Western Reserve University, 1975.

Davis, Lenwood. "Nineteenth Century Blacks in Ohio: An Historical View." In *Blacks in Ohio History.* Ed. Rubin F. Weston. Columbus: Ohio Historical Society, 1976.

Davis, Russell H. *Black Americans in Cleveland from George Peake to Carl B. Stokes, 1796–1969.* Washington, D.C.: Associated Publishers, 1972.

Gerber, David A. *Black Ohio and the Color Line, 1860–1915.* Urbana: University of Illinois Press, 1976.

Kusmer, Kenneth L. *A Ghetto Takes Shape: Black Cleveland, 1870–1930.* Urbana: University of Illinois Press, 1976.

Loeb, Charles H. *The Future Is Yours: The History of the Future Outlook League, 1935–1946.* Cleveland: The Future Outlook League, 1947.

Malvin, John. *The Autobiography of John Malvin, Free Negro, 1795–1880.* Cleveland: Leader Print Co., 1879.

Phillips, Kimberly L. "Heaven Bound Black Migration: Community and Activism in Cleveland, 1915–1945." Ph.D. diss. Yale University, 1992.

Stokes, Carl B. *Promises of Power: Then and Now.* Cleveland: Friends of Carl B. Stokes, 1989.

Van Tassel, David D., and John J. Grabowski, eds. *The Encyclopedia of Cleveland History.* Bloomington: Indiana University Press, 1987; 2nd ed., 1996.

Women Celebrating the Bicentennial. *Cleveland Women's Groups: An Amazing Story.* Cleveland: Women Celebrating the Bicentennial, 1996.

*Samuel W. Black*

## Coalition Against Blaxploitation

Representatives of Los Angeles–area chapters of the National Association for the Advancement of Colored People (NAACP), the Congress of Racial Equality (CORE), and the Southern Christian Leadership Conference (SCLC) founded the Coalition Against Blaxploitation (CAB) in 1972. Composed of approximately 400 African American artists working in the Hollywood film industry, the CAB objected to the wave of black-oriented action films released in the early 1970s. The group attacked the demeaning stereotypes promoted by blaxploitation films such as *Shaft* (1971) and *Super Fly* (1972), which typically unfolded in African American ghettoes and centered on problems such as drug abuse, crime, and police brutality. Blaxploitation films depicted heroes and antiheroes alike as oppressed and exploited by white America. At best, they carried a nationalist message of independence and self-assertion. The characters, however, were primarily drug dealers, pimps, and prostitutes. Critics argued that blaxploitation films played on old negative racial stereotypes. The Harvard psychologist Alvin F. Poussaint condemned these movies for promoting the message that African Americans were violent, criminal, and imitative of whites.

The CAB promoted positive film characterizations of African Americans and sought to expand black employment opportunities in the movie industry. The CAB proposed creating its own rating system, classifying movies as superior, good, acceptable, objectionable, or thoroughly objectionable on the basis of their portrayals of black characters. In addition to the ratings, the CAB planned to use boycotts and grass-roots protests against objectionable films. African American stars such as actor and former professional football star Jim Brown objected to the proposed ratings, claiming that they would victimize black actors, who already faced great difficulties in obtaining Hollywood roles. Major studios, noting the enormous black audience for films with all-white casts, such as *The Exorcist,* soon abandoned blaxploitation films as troublesome and unnecessary to attract African American moviegoers.

**FURTHER READINGS**

Guerrero, Ed. *Framing Blackness: The African American Image in Film.* Philadelphia: Temple University Press, 1993.

Murray, James P. *To Find an Image: Black Films from Uncle Tom to Super Fly.* New York: The Bobbs-Merrill Company, 1973.

Patterson, Lindsay. *Black Films and Film-Makers: A Comprehensive Anthology from Stereotype to Superhero.* New York: Dodd, Mead Company, 1975.

*Michael Phillips*

## Coalition of Black Trade Unionists

Established in 1973, the Coalition of Black Trade Unionists (CBTU) was the product of growing discontent among African American workers over the policies and practices of the American Federation of Labor-Congress of Industrial Organizations (AFL-CIO). By 1972, African Americans represented approximately three million of the twenty million unionized workers in the United States, yet very few of them held leadership positions in organized labor. As a result, the AFL-CIO often ignored issues important to African Americans, ethnic minorities, and women. However, the growing number of African Americans in the union rank and file, combined with the impact of the civil rights and black power movements of the 1960s, altered the political culture of organized labor as much as it changed the AFL-CIO's demographic characteristics. The CBTU represents one way African American workers asserted themselves in the larger labor movement.

The catalyst for the CBTU's formation was the AFL-CIO's official position of neutrality in the 1972 presidential campaign between the incumbent Richard Nixon and the Democratic party nominee George McGovern. Although African American unionists were not necessarily enthusiastic McGovern supporters, they expected the AFL-CIO at least to protest Nixon's policies on civil rights, labor, and the war in Vietnam. When AFL-CIO president George Meany announced the organization's position, many blacks perceived it as further evidence of labor's refusal to take seriously the needs and views of its African American membership. In response, a small group of African American labor leaders, including William Lucy, the secretary-treasurer of the American Federation of State, County, and Municipal Employees; Jack Nelson, vice president of the United Auto Workers; Charles Hayes, vice president of the Amalgamated Meatcutters and Butcher Workmen of North America; Cleveland Robinson, president of the Distributive Workers of America; and William Simons, president of the American Federation of Teachers' Local 6 scheduled a meeting of African American workers for September 1972.

Approximately 1,200 workers, representing more than thirty unions, attended the conference in Chicago. Although the presidential campaign was the most popular issue at the meeting, those in attendance agreed that a permanent coalition was needed to voice the concerns of African American workers within the upper echelons of organized labor. In May 1973, 1,100 African American unionists, representing more than thirty organizations, gathered in Washington, D.C., to establish the CBTU. Delegates appointed an executive council whose statement, entitled "The Need for a Coalition of Black Trade Unionists," spelled out the new organization's purpose. In addition to increasing the number of African Americans

in union leadership positions, the CBTU sought to improve the image of organized labor in the African American community. Moreover, it addressed bread-and-butter issues such as pay inequalities between white male workers and their nonwhite and female counterparts and pledged itself to political activism aimed at improving conditions in African American communities around the country. Also on the CBTU's agenda were voter registration and voter education drives, efforts to increase job opportunities for poor people and minorities, and support for civil rights campaigns. The coalition established working ties with the Congressional Black Caucus (CBC) and other groups in order to influence federal labor legislation and to oppose the apartheid regime in South Africa. Despite its name, the CBTU did not limit membership to African Americans. Nor did it limit its activities specifically to black issues. Rather, the CBTU represented all workers previously ignored by the AFL-CIO's leadership.

The CBTU grew quickly and steadily throughout the 1970s. In 1974, only two years after its initial meeting, the coalition represented more than thirty unions and over one million workers. By 1980, seventy-two trade unions belonged to the CBTU, which maintained twenty-six local chapters throughout the United States. While the 1980s and 1990s have been a difficult time for organized labor, the CBTU has remained active and committed to its mission.

**FURTHER READINGS**

Foner, Philip S. *Organized Labor and the Black Worker, 1619–1981*. New York: Praeger Publishers, 1974; rpt., New York: International Publishers, 1982.

Foner, Philip S., and Ronald L. Lewis, eds. *Black Workers: A Documentary History from Colonial Time to the Present*. Philadelphia: Temple University Press, 1989.

*Stuart McElderry*

## College Language Association

On April 23, 1937, ten college teachers of English founded the College Language Association (CLA) as the Association of Teachers of English in Negro Colleges (ATENC) at LeMoyne College in Memphis, Tennessee. The ten scholars, nine black and one white, founded the CLA in response to the exclusion of blacks from membership in the Modern Language Association (MLA), the largest learned society in the humanities. The goal of the CLA was to further English proficiency among African American students, to serve the academic and professional interests of its members, and to help showcase the work of black scholars.

57th CLA Convention, April 17–19, 1999, Atlanta. Left to right: Dr. Herman Bostick, CLA president 1975–1977; Dr. Hugh M. Gloster, CLA founder and president 1937 and 1948–1950; Yvonne Gloster, Esq. *Archives and Special Collections, Atlanta University Center, Robert W. Woodruff Library*

Hugh Morris Gloster, a professor of English at LeMoyne College, organized the CLA's founding meeting. Gloster, who served as the CLA's first and fifth president, was joined by Stella B. Brooks (Clark College, Georgia), J. L. Cary (Knoxville College, Tennessee), Gladstone Lewis Chandler (Morehouse College, Georgia), V. C. Clinch (Morris Brown College, Georgia), Lydia Edgerly, the only white member (LeMoyne College), J. Randolph Fisher (Rust College, Mississippi), Valorie O. Justis and Carrie Pembroke (Lane College, Tennessee), and Elizabeth Pinkney (Philander Smith College, Arkansas). A year after its founding, the ATENC launched its first newsletter, the *News-Bulletin*. The newsletter ceased publication in 1941, perhaps due to the impact of the national emergency created by World War II, which also forced the organization to cancel its national meetings.

Following the war, the ATENC started to attract a growing number of scholars from historically black colleges and universities, including foreign language teachers. In 1949, in response to the groundswell of interest among foreign language teachers, the ATENC changed its name to CLA to reflect its broadening membership and scope. Many of the foreign language teachers made invaluable contributions to the CLA, including John F. Matheus of West Virginia State College, who served as treasurer between 1943 and 1975; Mercer Cook of Howard University, who spearheaded the recruitment of foreign language teachers in the 1940s; and Billie Geter Thomas of Spelman College, who served as the CLA's first female president in 1956.

In 1949, the organization, now renamed the CLA, revived its publishing efforts when it launched the *CLA*

*Bulletin*, which included digests of papers presented at the annual convention and, beginning in 1951, carried presidential addresses. In the 1970s, the *CLA Bulletin* was supplanted by the sporadic publication of the *CLA Notes*. In 1957, the organization launched *The College Language Association Journal*, which publishes scholarly articles on a variety of subjects and provides information about the CLA Job Placement Bureau. The CLA's publications provided many aspiring and seasoned authors with an opportunity to present their writings to a broad audience and helped to define black literary scholarship. The *CLA Journal* has been edited by Therman B. O'Daniel of Morgan State University (1957–1977), Edward A. Jones of Morehouse College (1978–1979), and Cason L. Hill of Morehouse College (1979–).

In addition to the CLA's newsletters and journal, the publications of association members have played a crucial role in establishing and defining black literary scholarship. In 1938, for example, CLA member Velaurez Spratlin published *Juan Latino, Slave and Humanist*, a groundbreaking work exploring the role of Africans in European culture. In 1941, the publication of the monumental *The Negro Caravan*, edited by association members Sterling A. Brown, Arthur P. Davis, and Ulysses Lee, ushered in a new era in American literary scholarship when it established the canon of African American literature. Three years later, the publication of Mercer Cook and Dantes Bellegarde's *The Haitian-American Anthology* prompted American scholars to investigate critically the comparative aspects of black literatures of the Americas.

Furthermore, the CLA has played an influential role in the creation of numerous scholarly organizations. With few exceptions, those who have founded other black American literary organizations and/or publications have been members of the CLA. In addition, CLA members provided much of the energy and muscle that led to the founding of black interest sections in the major professional organizations, including the National Council of Teachers of English (NCTE) (1970) and the MLA Division on Black American Literature and Culture (1981). The CLA was also a charter member of the influential English Coalition (1987), a consortium of eight professional associations that meets annually to discuss issues of mutual concern.

In addition, CLA members have taught thousands of students from the Americas, Africa, Asia, and Europe, including the civil rights activist Martin Luther King Jr.; the historian Lerone Bennett; King Kgosi Lebone Boikanyo MolotLegi II of the Royal Bafokeng Nation in Phokeng,

South Africa; the Nobel Prize–winning author Toni Morrison; the entrepreneur Earl Graves; the athlete Wilma Rudolph; the West Indian activist and political theorist Kwame Toure; the astronaut Ron McNair; the politician Kweisi Mfume; the television host and philanthropist Oprah Winfrey; the acclaimed filmmaker Spike Lee; and the scholars Trudier Harris, R. Baxter Miller, Emmanuel Nelson of India, and Houston A. Baker Jr., who became the MLA's first African American president in 1992.

The CLA traditionally holds its annual convention on the third weekend in April. The conference serves as a forum for the presentation of scholarly research and provides attendees with an opportunity to engage in professional networking. Moreover, the meetings have played an important role in the recruitment and training of black graduate students. CLA affiliates, including the Charles Chesnutt Society, the Langston Hughes Society, the Middle Atlantic Writers Association, the Richard Wright Circle, and the Zora Neale Hurston Society, are entitled to sponsor one program session at the annual convention. In addition to hosting its own convention, the CLA is an affiliated member of the MLA, entitling it to sponsor two sessions at the MLA's annual conference.

The CLA has never had official headquarters or an institutional sponsor. The longevity and continued success of the CLA is largely due to the invaluable support of historically black colleges and universities, which provided meeting spaces, occasional staff support, and in-kind services, as well as the assistance of predominantly white institutions such as Brooklyn College, University of Georgia, Indiana University of Pennsylvania, LaGuardia Community College, University of North Carolina at Chapel Hill, University of North Carolina at Charlotte, Ohio State University, Rutgers University at Camden, University of South Carolina at Spartanburg, University of Tennessee, and New York City Technical College.

In 1988, the CLA, under the leadership of Dr. Eleanor Q. Tignor of Long Island's LaGuardia Community College, designated the Robert W. Woodruff Library in the Atlanta University Center as its official archival repository. The CLA annually recognizes the service and achievements of its members with a Distinguished Service Award, a Book/Creative Project Award, and the Margaret A. Walker Creative Writing Prize. The CLA Study Abroad Scholarship, initiated in 1995, seeks to encourage future generations of teachers to study foreign languages and cultures.

Since its 1937 formation, the CLA has become the nation's preeminent organization of African American scholars of languages and literature. For more than sixty years, the CLA has played a crucial role in establishing and defining black literary scholarship, laying the foundations for the emergence of new generations of black intellectuals and training black leaders. Its nearly 1,000 members continue to work as a unified intellectual community to break the chains of white cultural hegemony, to desegregate the academy, and to advocate the democratization of knowledge.

**FURTHER READINGS**

Brooks, A. Russell. "The *CLA Journal* as a Mirror of Changing Ethnic and Academic Perspectives." *CLA Journal* 26, 3 (March 1983): 265–276.

Fowler, Carolyn. *The College Association: A Social History.* Ann Arbor: University Microfilm Inc., 1988.

Hubbard, Dolan. "Slipping into Darkness: CLA and Black Intellectual Formation." President's Address Delivered at the Fifty-sixth Annual CLA Convention. Winston-Salem, North Carolina, April 11, 1996. *CLA Journal* 40, 1 (September 1996): 120.

O'Daniel, Therman B. *A Twenty-Five-Year Author-Title Cumulative Index to the CLA Journal (1957–1982).* Baltimore: J. H. Furst, 1985.

Parker, John W. "The Origin and Development of the College Language Association." *The Quarterly Review of Higher Education Among Negroes* 27 (1959): 35–37.

*James J. Davis and Dolan Hubbard*

## Colorado Anti-Discrimination Commission

In 1951, the General Assembly of the State of Colorado passed an Anti-Discrimination Act that created the Industrial Commission of Colorado, an Anti-Discrimination Division, and a Governor's Human Relations Commission (GHRC). Although it had advisory powers only, the "GHRC was authorized to prepare and plan education programs aimed at the elimination of discrimination in employment; to advise the Governor and the Director of Fair Employment Practices upon matters of policy; to recommend to public employers ways to eliminate discrimination in public employment; and . . . to submit to the General Assembly changes in the law which it deemed necessary for the successful accomplishment of the Act."

In 1955, the General Assembly amended the law upon the recommendation of the GHRC, creating an Anti-Discrimination Commission to oversee the work of the Anti-Discrimination Division and allowing it to function more effectively in addressing the problems created by prejudice and discrimination. The commission, whose seven members are appointed by the governor to four-year overlapping terms with the "consent and approval of the Senate . . . is empowered to initiate complaints of alleged discriminatory or unfair employment practices against public employers . . . hold hearings, . . . issue cease and desist orders, order employment or reinstatement either with or without back-pay, and . . . order such other affirmative actions as it deems proper. [It may also] resort to the Courts for the enforcement of its orders." Further, the commission may receive and investigate complaints of alleged discrimination and initiate studies to ascertain "the existence, causes, character, and extent of discrimination in employment and to carry out educational programs aimed at the elimination of racial and religious discrimination in employment." Finally, the commission may also "cooperate with both public and private agencies and organizations whose aims are consistent with those of the Commission." In 1957, the state legislature added private employers to the scope of the commission's concerns and empowered it to enforce Colorado's first civil rights statute, passed in 1895. The nineteenth-century law sought to prohibit discrimination in public accommodations; however, it had not been enforced because no government agency was charged with its implementation. In 1959, the commission's power further increased when a "state fair housing law to cover both publicly assisted and privately financed housing" was added to its jurisdiction.

In 1979 the commission's name changed to the Colorado Civil Rights Division/Commission following its first sunset review (a study of the organization's quality of performance). At that time it was relocated from the Industrial Commission, the forerunner of the Colorado Department of Labor and Employment, to the State Department of Regulatory Agencies, its current location. The Division/Commission has the authority to issue subpoenas in cases of housing and employment discrimination and it can "award back pay in employment cases and actual costs of obtaining comparable housing in housing cases." During the last two decades, the responsibility of the Division/Commission has increased as new categories, such as "mental impairments," have been added to its list of responsibilities. A review of cases covering the period from 1991 through 1996 shows a slight overall increase in the number of charges filed in the areas of employment, housing, and public accommodations, whereas charges alleging race/color and sexual discrimination have decreased. At the same time, charges filed in the retaliation category in the employment area have doubled. As new categories of offenses are added, complainants have more avenues to explore in the search for remedies, as is evident by the addition of the "Multiple and Other" category in the early 1990s. The future of the Colorado Civil Rights Division/Commission will be determined by its next sunset review, which is scheduled for the year 2002.

*William M. King*

## Colorado Civil Rights Division/Commission

*See* Colorado Anti-Discrimination Commission.

## Colorado Governor's Commission on Human Relations

*See* Colorado Anti-Discrimination Commission.

## Colored Conventions

The first National Negro Convention met in Philadelphia in September 1830. While almost half of the forty delegates were from Pennsylvania, other states were represented, including New York, Rhode Island, Maryland, Virginia, and Ohio. Richard Allen, bishop of the African Methodist Episcopal (AME) Church, was the dominant leader. Also present were the businessman and abolitionist James Forten, the businessmen and activist John B. Vashon, the used-furniture dealer John T. Hilton, and the minister Samuel Cornish.

The immediate cause for convening the convention was the forced exodus of over 1,000 blacks from Ohio. State law required free blacks moving into the state of Ohio to post a $500 bond guaranteeing good behavior. In 1829, this part of the state's Black Codes (laws that existed to keep blacks as a lower class than whites) was enforced in response to white Cincinnati's fear of the growing black population in that city. As impatient white mobs roamed the city, blacks fled for Canada, having

Colored National Convention, Nashville, Tennessee, 1876. *Archive Photos*

received indications from the governor of Upper Canada that they would be welcomed there.

Those fleeing from Ohio joined earlier fugitives in communities in what is today southern Ontario. When emigrés (formerly included in the Ohio or Western Synod of the AME Church) called for a preacher, Bishop Allen did much more than just meet their simple request; he convened the first meeting of what would become the first National Negro Convention to consider the plight of the Canadian refugees.

The body elected Allen president and adopted the name American Society of Free Persons of Color, for Improving their Condition in the United States; for Purchasing Lands; and For Establishing of a Settlement in Upper Canada. "An Address to the Free People of Color" was composed, which recommended that the proceedings be published through local chapters that would continue to act as auxiliaries of the National Convention. They also planned to collect funds to purchase land in Canada.

William Hamilton's 1834 presidential address stated the organization's purpose in the broadest terms: "Under the present circumstances, it is highly necessary [that] the free people of color should combine, and closely attend to their own particular interest." Emigration remained the major focus for the early years, but mismanagement of the Wilberforce community in Canada resulted in a shift of interest.

While the conventions concentrated on emigration as a solution to racist treatments, they also focused on ameliorating the condition of those who remained in the United States and fostering racial pride. Thus, the conventions condemned segregation and discriminatory legislation and stressed economy, temperance, and education. They also set aside July 4 as a day of fasting and prayer for blacks to ask God's intervention in bringing about an end to slavery. The formation of temperance and improvement societies was encouraged regularly, as was the formation of benevolent associations and educational institutions.

White abolitionists exerted strong influence; some, like William Lloyd Garrison and Arthur Tappan, attended the conventions. This influence resulted in the formation of the American Moral Reform Society, which temporarily replaced the convention movement and deflected members away from their original purpose—the development of race pride and unity. Instead, the Reform Society urged blacks to integrate into society and avoid separate black organizations.

The parent body lost focus; there was much discussion of ideals, such as nonresistance, women's rights, and temperance, and little in the way of a practical program of action. Largely dominated by Philadelphia blacks, the Reform Society received little support outside the Garrisonian strongholds of Philadelphia and Boston. Other black leaders upheld the need for independent action.

In the 1840s, the conventions shifted focus, working primarily toward acquiring suffrage and participating in political action, including working with the antislavery Liberty party. Through this, the national convention movement was revitalized and enjoyed considerable growth. In addition to the state and national meetings, local and regional gatherings were held, furnishing numerous leadership opportunities for rising black leaders.

It was at the 1843 meeting in Buffalo that the clergymen and abolitionist Henry Highland Garnet delivered his militant "Address to the Slaves of the United States." In it, Garnet called for insurrection: "Brethren, arise, arise! . . . Let every slave throughout the land do this, and the days of slavery are numbered." They should, according to Garnet, "RATHER DIE FREEMEN THAN LIVE TO BE SLAVES." Members of the convention failed by a single vote to endorse Garnet's call to action, preferring the orator and abolitionist Frederick Douglass's more moderate emphasis on "moralsuasion."

Also noteworthy was the 1853 convention, held in Rochester, New York. There, a stirring memorial addressed to the American people asserted that "with the exception of the Jews, under the whole heavens, there is not to be found a people pursued with a more restless prejudice and persecution, than are the free colored people of the United States." But in spite of this, the memorial declared that blacks had made significant progress: "In view of our circumstances, we can, without boasting, thank God, and take courage, having placed ourselves where we may fairly challenge comparison with more highly favored men." Members of this convention included Frederick Douglass, the physician and abolitionist James McCune Smith, the minister and abolitionist J. W. C. Pennington, the politician John Mercer Langston, the historian and abolitionist William C. Nell, the abolitionist and lecturer Charles L. Remond, and the reformer and businessman William Whipper.

The 1850s saw increased tension over competing visions of black nationalism, highlighted by the 1854 National Emigration Convention of Colored People in Cleveland. Emigration outside the country was endorsed by the political reformer Martin Delany. Proponents of the scheme to create colonies in Central and South America argued that continued discrimination was the black future in the United States. But most blacks supported the view of Frederick Douglass, who advocated the creation of separate race institutions within the United States while working toward eventual equality and integration. The national body almost paralyzed again over the dissension, state and local meetings once more took up the burden of organized action.

Between 1830 and 1864, there were twelve National Negro Conventions. Meetings were held yearly from 1830 to 1835, four times in Philadelphia and twice in New York City. Six more meetings occurred over the next nearly thirty years, held mainly in cities in New York State and once in Cleveland. Some conventions were attended by large numbers of delegates: 140 were present at the Rochester meeting in 1853 and 144 at the Syracuse convention in 1864.

**FURTHER READINGS**

Bell, Howard H. *A Survey of the Negro Convention Movement, 1830–1861.* New York: Arno Press, 1969.

———. ed. *Minutes of the Proceedings of the National Negro Conventions, 1830–1864.* New York: Arno Press, 1969.

Foner, Philip S., and George E. Walker, eds. *Proceedings of the Black State Conventions, 1840–1865.* 2 vols. Philadelphia: Temple University Press, 1979–1980.

Gross, Bella. *Clarion Call: The History and Development of the Negro Convention Movement in the United States from 1817 to 1840.* New York: n.p., 1947.

Pease, William H., and Jane H. Pease. "The Negro Convention Movement." In *Key Issues in the Afro-American Experience.* Ed. Nathan Huggins, Martin Kilson, and Daniel M. Fox. New York: Harcourt Brace Jovanovich, 1971.

*Carol Wilson*

## Colored Farmers' National Alliance and Cooperative Union

Established in 1888, the Colored Farmers' National Alliance and Cooperative Union, more commonly known as the Colored Farmers' Alliance (CFA), was the largest predominantly black agricultural self-help organization in the late nineteenth century.

Following the end of Reconstruction, black farmers in the South were especially vulnerable in the agrarian marketplace, as they rarely possessed the holdings of many of their white counterparts. A sizable majority of black farmers were either sharecroppers or tenant farmers, and many others were hired hands on white-owned farms. These black farmers were excluded from the Southern Farmers' Alliance (SFA), one of the most important agricultural interest groups to emerge in the South after Reconstruction.

Yet, not all white farmers endorsed the SFA's exclusion of African Americans. Some whites believed that it was in their best interest to collaborate with black farmers, many of them convinced that it would prevent economic competition or the rise of black radicalism. The support of whites who favored interracial agricultural cooperation and the desire of many black farmers to promote their own interests led to the formation of the CFA.

First efforts to organize black southern farmers date back to 1876. That year, black farmers in Texas attempted to create the Colored State Grange to help African Americans purchase land. In 1882, in Prairie County, Arkansas, Milton George, the leader of the Northern Farmers' Alliance, had chartered a black alliance group based loosely on his own organization. Other scattered state and local organizations emerged but did not make much headway in gaining concessions for black farmers. It was not until December 11, 1886, when black farmers and several whites met in Houston County, Texas, that the CFA started to emerge. In the wake of the Houston meeting, a number of CFA chapters sprang up across Texas. Later that month, representatives from these groups met at the Good Hope Baptist Church in Weldon, Texas, where they announced the consolidation of all local groups into The Alliance of Colored Farmers of Texas. Within a few months, CFA chapters emerged in every state in the South and, in 1888, they established a national organization. By 1891, the CFA claimed more than 1.2 million members, making it one of the largest African American organizations in U.S. history.

The CFA emphasized self-help and mutual aid. It encouraged its members to learn new and more efficient farming techniques, to obtain ownership of their farms, and to improve their level of education. The organization also championed both black- and white-run cooperative stores and exchanges where members could buy goods at cheaper prices and where they could obtain loans at reasonable rates to allow them to pay off mortgages. Alliance affiliates published newspapers, many of them managed by black editors and staffs, and in some cases they even raised funds to promote longer school years. In sum, the CFA advocated the uplift of the rural black masses in the region of the country hit hardest by economic instability and racism.

The difficulties a large-scale predominantly black organization faced in the South in the 1880s and 1890s were numerous. In the summer of 1889, for example, Oliver Cromwell, a black CFA organizer, tried to organize alliance chapters in Mississippi. Visiting plantations in Leflore County, Cromwell urged black farmers to conduct their business at an SFA cooperative in Durant, thirty miles south of Greenwood, the largest town in the county. Although the cooperative was an SFA store, it recognized the CFA and allowed its black members to trade there. Cromwell evidently made several trips to the Durant store on behalf of his customers, and the white Leflore County merchants grew worried. Many of them relied on black business to remain solvent; furthermore, Cromwell's incipient radicalism alarmed them. Whites worked to undermine Cromwell's efforts through a calculated smear campaign followed by threats of violence. When blacks showed their support of Cromwell, many whites grew fearful of the heightened black militancy. The county sheriff, fearing escalating black violence, appealed to Mississippi governor Robert Lowry, who mobilized three National Guard companies. Meanwhile, a local white posse committed to vigilantism joined the troops in attempting to crush what they feared was an imminent black rebellion. In September 1889, the posse and the Guardsmen apparently killed approximately twenty-five African Americans in an indiscriminate orgy of violence that lasted five days. Cromwell, however, escaped from the state unscathed.

The incident reveals the tenuous relations between the CFA and the society it hoped to change. Many white southerners had been uneasy with the CFA but were willing to accept its existence as long as it pursued the same goals as the SFA or did not otherwise attempt to challenge white racial and economic supremacy. If black farmers, however, started to threaten the racial status quo or white economic domination, retribution could be swift and in many cases deadly.

One of the main leaders of the CFA was Richard Manning Humphrey, a white native South Carolinian who was a Baptist minister and missionary in Lovelady, Texas. Humphrey headed the 1886 Texas state meeting and was given the role of that CFA's general superintendent—the alliance's main organizing position. When the leaders of alliance chapters from various southern states met at Lovelady in March 1888 to form the Colored Farmers' National Alliance, Humphrey continued in his leadership role. Although many blacks were among the CFA's national and local leadership, most notably J. J. Shuffer, the first president of the alliance, and H. J. Spencer, the first

secretary, Humphrey was the most visible and influential CFA leader. Humphrey was a committed champion of black economic advancement and had been active in radical politics for many years. Yet, his racial liberalism was sometimes marred by paternalism. Furthermore, while Humphrey's ability and willingness to cultivate important contacts with the white community, particularly the SFA, occasionally proved beneficial to the CFA, at times he seemed willing to appease white leaders, which undermined the efforts of black farmers. Moreover, he often ignored the opinions of local black leaders and their constituents and tended to force his own views on the policy formulations of the CFA. For all of his good intentions, Humphrey was not always cognizant of the double bonds of class and race that plagued the black farmers whom he purported to represent.

Humphrey's limitations as leader of a black mass movement as well as the schisms between black and white would eventually hasten the decline of the CFA. Although the SFA excluded blacks, a position that had served as an impetus for the formation of the CFA, many white alliance leaders supported the organization of a separate black farmers' alliance, as long as both groups pursued common goals. On issues such as cooperative stores and opposition to lotteries, the CFA worked together easily with the SFA. Nonetheless, when conflict arose between the two organizations, the SFA maintained white-supremacist dogma and worked to uphold the racial hierarchy and social order. In 1890, the two organizations met concurrently in Ocala, Florida. One of the issues raised was the Lodge election bill, a proposal that guaranteed federal protection for black voting rights. The SFA unanimously condemned the bill. Humphrey concurred with the SFA, maintaining that the black farmers were not concerned about voting rights. His constituents in the CFA, however, strongly supported passage of the Lodge bill and continued to do so for the duration of the alliance. Humphrey, who was likely aware of the black farmers' position, was committed to maintaining the support of the white alliance and thus willing to overlook the demands of his constituency.

Despite Humphrey's desire to avoid alienating whites in the SFA, he was at times willing to resort to radical measures that challenged white supremacy. In 1891, Humphrey and some CFA members proposed a cotton pickers' strike—a radical initiative that was not in keeping with the SFA's usually cautious approach. The strike never materialized, largely because many of the black cotton pickers feared economic and violent physical retaliation by their white employers. Furthermore, black farmers who were not sharecroppers but owned their land and either picked their own cotton or hired hands showed little inclination to support the strike. Poorly coordinated and lacking support among black farmers, the strike made little headway. While the strike's failure reveals that the majority of CFA members were not prepared to support radical action, it also demonstrates that Humphrey and at least a small number of his supporters were willing to challenge the power of white plantation owners.

Ultimately, the CFA failed due to a number of factors. The demise of the Populist movement, which had provided much of the impetus for the formation of agrarian-based social movements, accounts in part for the decline of the CFA. Increased racial hostilities that characterized the last decade of the nineteenth century further limited black collective action, as did the inability of competing farm associations to work together for common goals and interests. White racial animosity, which had made the CFA's efforts to mobilize black farmers difficult in the best of times, ultimately proved to be a major handicap. The CFA also failed because many of its economic programs, such as cooperative stores and exchange networks, remained unsuccessful because they were based solely on self-help and racial solidarity. Lacking money as well as political and legal rights, poverty-stricken black farmers were unable to rely on their meager financial resources to improve their economic plight. Another important factor contributing to the demise of the CFA was the depression of 1893–1897, which affected many sectors of the economy but was particularly devastating for farmers. In response to the depression, many farmers started to turn away from coalitions that seemed to be failing them. By 1892, the CFA, as well as most of its white counterparts, ceased to exist.

The CFA was a brief but important phenomenon in U.S. history that revealed both the limitations and the possibilities of racially centered reform movements as the nineteenth century came to a close. Working within the confines of racism and segregation, the CFA was unable to provide long-term solutions for poverty-stricken southern black farmers. Moreover, the CFA's advocacy of financial self-help, while designed to empower black farmers, placed the burden of economic reform on the shoulders of the most impoverished segment of the black southern population. Despite the CFA's failure to improve the economic conditions of black farmers, the organization served an important function. It emboldened the dispossessed black farmers and provided them with the opportunity to challenge and defy the racial and economic hierarchy of the South.

**FURTHER READINGS**

Dann, Martin. "Black Populism: A Study of the Colored Farmers' Alliance Through 1891." *Journal of Ethnic Studies* 2 (1974), 58–71.

Gaither, Gerald H. *Blacks and the Populist Revolt: Ballots and Bigotry in the "New South."* Tuscaloosa: University of Alabama Press, 1977.

Holmes, William F. "The Leflore County Massacre and the Demise of the Colored Farmers' Alliance." *Phylon* 4 (1973), 267–274.

———. "The Demise of the Colored Farmers' Alliance." *Journal of Southern History* 41 (1975), 187–200.

———. "The Southern Farmers' Alliance: The Georgia Experience." *Journal of Southern History* 72 (1988), 627–652.

McMath, Robert C. *Populist Vanguard: A History of the Southern Farmers' Alliance.* Chapel Hill: University of North Carolina Press, 1976.

Miller, Floyd J. "Black Protest and White Leadership: A Note on the Colored Farmers' Alliance." *Phylon* 3 (1972) 169–174.

*Derek C. Catsam*

## Colored Golfers Association

*See* United Golfers Association.

## Colored Intercollegiate Athletic Association

*See* Central Intercollegiate Athletic Association.

## Colored Knights of Pythias

The Knights of Pythias of North America, South America, Europe, Asia, Africa, and Australia (or Colored Knights of Pythias) was one of the three major African American fraternal organizations of the late nineteenth and early twentieth centuries. The black Knights derived their original rituals and organizational structure from a white Pythian organization, one of the many new societies that sprang up during the 1860s fraternal revival. The white Pythian society had its beginning in 1863, when the founders, mostly government clerks in the District of Columbia, devised a ritual, and in 1864, when they organized the first lodge. The name that they chose for the new brotherhood refers to the story in classical mythology in which Damon pledged his life to guarantee the return of his friend Pythias. The Pythian ritual evoked medieval chivalry. Knights wore elaborate regalia, staged ceremonies rich in mythic symbolism, addressed each other as "sir," and described their lodges as "castles." The Pythian order provided opportunities for fellowship among men who might disagree about religion and politics. Moreover, it offered practical assistance in burying the dead and caring for widows and orphans.

Like virtually all white-organized fraternal societies, the original Knights of Pythias restricted membership to white males. In 1870, the order rejected a membership petition from black men residing in Philadelphia. Few white Pythians favored opening membership to African Americans; the postmaster of New Orleans, a native of Massachusetts, was expelled for advocating a change in the whites-only policy.

In Mississippi, several light-skinned African Americans who managed to join as white men acquired the Pythian rituals and constitutions. These individuals included Dr. Thomas W. Stringer (1815–1893), a prominent Mason and African Methodist Episcopal (AME) minister. He had spent most of his life in Ohio and Canada prior to Reconstruction, when he relocated to Mississippi and was elected to the state Senate. In 1880, Stringer organized the first black Pythian lodge in Vicksburg, the grand lodge for Mississippi, and the Supreme Council. He was elected the first supreme chancellor and served in that capacity from 1880 to 1887. The order next spread to Louisiana, where Stringer won over several Masonic and Good Samaritan leaders, and then to other parts of the United States, Canada, and the Caribbean region. In 1883, the black Pythians created a women's auxiliary, the Independent Order or Courts of Calanthe. In the same year, the order added another degree in its internal hierarchy of honors, the uniform degree. More than twenty thousand degree holders dressed in uniforms and took part in military drills under leaders who assumed the titles of military officers. Early in the twentieth century, the Pythians established a sanitarium in Arkansas, apparently a hospital and rest home for ailing members.

From its earliest years, the black Pythian society offered insurance known as the "endowment" for the support of the families of deceased members. Fearful of competition from the Knights, rival African American orders denounced the endowment scheme as "a farce and a fraud." It also was controversial within the Pythian order itself. The cost of the insurance and doubt about whether the benefits would be paid kept many members from subscribing, and, in a struggle with the supreme council over control of the insurance money, some grand lodges insisted on managing the endowment in their own states. Despite such frictions, as a result of fraternal insurance offered by the Knights of Pythias and their competitors, African Americans apparently were more likely than whites to have insurance policies in the first part of the twentieth century.

To distinguish themselves from the white Knights of Pythias of the World, the black Pythians officially styled themselves the Knights of Pythias of North America, South America, Europe, Asia, Africa, and Australia. They were sometimes called the Colored Knights of Pythias or, to distinguish themselves from rival black Pythian organizations, the "alphabetical jurisdiction" because the lengthy official name was abbreviated as the Knights of Pythias of N.A., S.A., E., A., A., and A. Whites disputed the right of the "Negro Knights" to call themselves Pythians since they had not obtained charters from the white Pythian order. For instance, in 1909 the Georgia Legislature made it illegal for African Americans to use the names, rituals, and emblems of white societies. In 1912, after litigation that cost the black Pythians $25,000 in legal fees, the United States Supreme Court ruled in their favor.

The black Knights had other problems. Like most fraternal societies, they suffered from bitter internal quarrels that brought about resignations and schisms. A split that began in 1888 over the question of the endowment produced a splinter group called the Knights of Pythias of the Eastern and Western Hemispheres. In 1907, an attempt to unify the two organizations failed, but more than half of the membership of the secessionist society, which had lodges in Maryland and Connecticut, joined the main black order. In addition to the Eastern and Western Hemispheres group, grand lodges that seceded or were expelled sometimes operated independently.

The strength of the Knights of Pythias in the various African American communities depended largely on the support of established local leaders who belonged to the small black middle class. For instance, one of the co-authors of the Pythias's official history, Joseph. L. Jones (1868–1923), taught in Kentucky, Texas, and Ohio, worked for thirteen years in the country recorder's and county clerk's offices of Hamilton County, Ohio, founded the Central Regalia Company, edited a Pythian paper in Cincinnati called the *Fraternal Monitor*, and served as the first president of a Federation of African American Fraternal Societies. Newspaper editors were important in the Pythian order, including John Mitchell Jr., the editor of the *Rich-*

mond *Planet;* George P. Stewart, the editor of the *Indianapolis Recorder;* and Oscar W. Adams, the editor of the *Birmingham Reporter.* Many Pythians were also active in competing fraternal societies. E. A. Williams of Louisiana, who succeeded Stringer as supreme chancellor and who helped write the official history, was a prominent Mason, devised a ritual for the women's auxiliary of the Elks, and was elected supreme dictator of the Knights of Honor of the World.

Probably most black Pythians were unskilled laborers, but collectively they built a prosperous fraternal order with large numbers of members, particularly during their early-twentieth-century heyday. In 1909, the Knights of Pythias reached its greatest membership for the years covered by its official history. That year, 124,569 members had joined 3,158 lodges. In 1912, the *Negro Year Book* reported that the Knights of Pythias had collected more than $1 million for the endowment, had more than $40,000 cash in the supreme council treasury, and owned buildings in Chicago, Indianapolis, and New Orleans valued at from $30,000 to $100,000, part of its $1.5 million in property. The 1916–1917 edition of the *Negro Year Book* claimed that the Knights had more than a quarter-million members, a figure that, straining belief, it repeated for many years. The peak membership probably came in the early 1920s, as, for instance, it did in West Virginia, which counted 7,515 Knights of Pythias and Sisters of Calanthe in 1921–1922. Like most black fraternal societies, the Pythians lost membership during the Great Depression and World War II. During the years of decline, the black Knights of Pythias fared best in parts of the Deep South such as Alabama, but by the 1990s few lodges survived anywhere. In 1998, the supreme chancellor was Benjamin L. Hooks.

**FURTHER READINGS**

Foner, Eric. *Freedom's Lawmakers: A Directory of Black Officeholders during Reconstruction.* New York: Oxford University Press 1993.

Morgan, Joseph H. *History of Knights of Pythias, Supreme Jurisdiction North America, South America, Europe, Asia, Africa and Australia, State of New Jersey.* Nashville: AME Sunday School Union, 1913.

Trotter, Joe William, Jr. *Coal, Class, and Color: Blacks in Southern West Virginia, 1915–32.* Urbana: University of Illinois Press, 1990.

Williams, Ephie Augustus, Smith Wendell Green, and Joseph Lawrence Jones. *History and Manual of the Colored Knights of Pythias.* Nashville: National Baptist Publication Board, 1917.

Work, Monroe, ed. *The Negro Year Book and Annual Encyclopedia of the Negro.* Tuskegee, Ala.: Monroe N. Work, 1912–1952.

*David M. Fahey*

## Colored Merchants Association

The Colored Merchants Association (CMA) was established in August 1929, just prior to the stock market crash that launched the Great Depression. Sponsored by the National Negro Business League (NNBL), the CMA tried to create an African American buyers cooperative to allow black grocers to pool their buying power to secure the best possible wholesale prices. The initiative originated in Montgomery, Alabama, where black businessmen had established a local CMA in August 1928. In the early 1930s, efforts shifted to New York City, where the CMA backed a widely publicized but largely unsuccessful campaign to boycott white merchants, organize the black mercantile community, and create a chain of black-owned stores with a central office and a series of franchised outlets.

The genesis of the CMA came when Albon Holsey of Tuskegee Institute in Alabama and the NNBL decided that African American grocers, who controlled 50 percent of the trade of their own racial group, were the key to building a strong retail infrastructure for black business. Holsey assumed sponsorship of the group of black business leaders who had formed the CMA in Montgomery in 1928.

He took the model provided by the Montgomery group and developed a national plan to organize black grocers into cooperative buying units, establish standardized store service policies for the chain, and promote business through cooperative advertising and the efforts of local NNBL chapters.

Although Holsey first envisioned a nationwide chain of 350 African American stores, he ultimately scaled down his plans to a single city—a chain of black-owned grocery stores in Harlem, the "Capital of Black America." The permanent central office of the CMA was established in Harlem in 1930 and incorporated in that state with capital of $100,000. To raise this capital, ten thousand shares of preferred stock were offered at $10 a share, and later one thousand shares of common stock were issued. To secure a CMA franchise, a retailer had to agree to alter the appearance of his store to conform to a uniform standard, purchase CMA products, allow supervision of bookkeeping policies, pay a weekly fee, and purchase a prescribed number of shares in the CMA. Once a member, the grocer had to abide by the weekly procedures of the association.

The CMA took over a bankrupt African American grocery as its first store and commenced business with the slogan, "Quality, Service, Price." New York City's black newspapers enthusiastically supported the opening. In 1931, Holsey was named president of the corporation; John E. Nail, a Harlem realtor, served as its vice president; and Frederick R. Moore became secretary-treasurer. Other African American stores soon joined, bringing the total number of stores to more than 250 in the city of New York. Despite the CMA's successful start, the organization was plagued by problems from the beginning. Some of these were internal, relating to staff and management, but most complaints came from African American consumers, who claimed that they could get better bargains in white-owned stores. The CMA, despite great publicity and noble dreams, never succeeded and limped along until July 1934, when the offices were permanently closed.

**FURTHER READINGS**

Burroughs, John Howard. "The Necessity of Myth: A History of the National Negro Business League, 1900–1945." Ph.D. diss., Auburn University, 1977.

Holsey, Albon L. "Meeting Chain Store Competition through Cooperation." *Southern Workman* 58 (July 1929), 298–301.

Oak, Vishnu V. *The Negro Adventure in General Business.* Yellow Springs, Ohio: Antioch University Press, 1949.

*John N. Ingham*

## Colored National Labor Union

The Colored National Labor Union (CNLU) was a stillborn attempt to create a central body to coordinate the activities of African American unions between 1869 and 1871.

The years immediately following the Civil War were uncertain ones for organized labor and the African American community. A series of labor congresses convened to explore the possibilities of trades union federation and to discuss broader issues of political and social reform. In 1866, seventy-seven white delegates gathered in Baltimore, Maryland, to announce the formation of the National Labor Union (NLU). The NLU styled itself an umbrella organization for reformers and unions. Each affiliated organization received one delegate for every five hundred members, and annual congresses were held to determine common goals. An executive board coordinated policy

during the remainder of the year. John C. Whalley, a government office proofreader, was the NLU's first president, though the organization was largely the brainchild of William Sylvis, an iron molder.

The NLU's agenda was typical of mid-nineteenth-century political reform groups. It combined vague rhetoric with calls for land reform, an end to convict labor, the substitution of mandatory arbitration for strikes, and the establishment of cooperative industries and distribution networks. Moreover, the NLU advocated a reduction of work hours, as seven of its delegates hailed from the various eight-hour leagues that had emerged throughout the country.

From the beginning, NLU delegates split over two important questions: organizing black workers and politics. Andrew Cameron, the editor of the *Workingman's Advocate*, recommended organizing black workers. Both Whalley and Sylvis concurred. Although the latter opposed Radical Reconstruction and had little personal sympathy for African Americans, he feared that black workers would be employed as strikebreakers if the NLU turned its back. A committee was appointed to study the issue. In addition, NLU delegates debated politics, with a large faction favoring the creation of a labor party.

These disputes had profound effects on black workers. At the 1867 NLU convention, another committee was set up to explore cooperation with black unions. The three-man Committee on Colored Labor was headed by A. W. Phelps, a New Haven, Connecticut, carpenter whose union excluded African Americans. The committee's 1868 report did not recommend organizing African Americans, declaring the issue steeped in too much "mystery" to resolve. Sylvis, Cameron, and Detroit activist Richard Trevellick spoke out against the report and warned of dire consequences should the organization of African Americans be postponed. In the end, the 1868 congress passed a vague call for unity but split over whether African Americans should be incorporated into existing NLU structures or enrolled in a separate order.

Editorials and debates over the issue raged after the congress adjourned, and matters came to a head at the 1869 convention. Nine black delegates attended that meeting, including five from Philadelphia's United Hod Carriers Association. The most vocal delegates were Issac Myers of the Colored Caulkers' Trade Union Society, Robert H. Butler of the Colored Engineers' Association of Maryland, and Peter P. Brown of the Hod Carriers. Ultimately, white delegate Horace Day introduced a successful resolution that removed the NLU's color barrier.

The presence of so many African American delegates at the NLU's 1869 congress is indicative of the resurgence of black unionism in the half-decade following the end of the Civil War. In 1867, black longshoremen in Charleston, South Carolina, won a strike to preserve their jobs from returning white Confederate soldiers. Between 1867 and 1870, there were also successful job actions among black levee workers in Mobile, Alabama; dock workers in Savannah, Georgia; and ship caulkers in Baltimore. Overall organization among black workers in the South was far in advance of that among white workers. In Richmond, Virginia, black plasterers, building tradesmen, ironworkers, tobacco workers, and shoemakers all had unions, and great strides were made to connect newly freed slaves with the part of the city's black population that had long been free.

The passage in 1868 of the Fifteenth Amendment to the United States Constitution made it illegal for federal or state governments to restrict the right to vote on the basis of "race, color, or previous condition of servitude." This galvanized hopes that African Americans could participate as equals in American society. While the NLU dragged its heels on the question of black labor, African Americans held their own labor congresses in 1868 and 1869. The July 20, 1869, State Labor Convention of the Colored Men of Maryland issued a call for a national convention of black laborers. In December, Issac Myers convened 214 Negro Labor Congress delegates in Washington, D.C., who launched the Colored National Labor Union (CNLU). Among those assembled were engineers, basketmakers, tobacco workers, waiters, barbers, carpenters, ministers, smelters, printers, reformers, and Prince Hall Freemasons.

The CNLU was consciously patterned after the NLU, with whom it voted to affiliate. Myers was appointed its first president, and a Washington-based National Bureau of Labor was created to exercise executive board functions whenever the Negro Labor Congress was not in session. Much of the CNLU's agenda was identical to that of the NLU, which delegates initially regarded as a parent organization. It even adopted the NLU's antistrike policy and its xenophobic call to exclude Chinese immigrants. In addition, the CNLU advocated free public education, the establishment of black cooperative institutions, and the removal of racial and gender employment restrictions. Myers was sent to organize workers in the South, and Sella Martin was chosen to represent the CNLU at the Congress of the First International in Paris.

On the issue of politics, however, the CNLU parted company with the NLU. The CNLU was overtly partisan, identifying with the Republican party as the agent of emancipation, the Freedmen's Bureau, Radical Reconstruction, and future promises of land reform. The congress nearly bogged down over whether or not to admit delegates from the Massachusetts Labor Reform Party, with J. M. Langston, a lawyer, accusing them of trying to sabotage the Republican Party. The delegates were seated, but Langston and his followers were not appeased.

Moreover, the composition of the CNLU differed from that of its white counterpart. The NLU was more overtly class oriented than the CNLU, the latter containing larger percentages of ministers, secret-society members, professionals, and political reformers. The CNLU's more reform-minded members were given a boost in 1870, when the Sixteenth Amendment to the United States Constitution was passed, pledging congressional enforcement of citizenship rights.

The Sixteenth Amendment served also to highlight the gap between white rhetoric and action within the NLU. Despite calls for racial unity, few of the NLU's constituent unions removed color barriers. At the 1870 Negro Labor Congress, J. M. Langston introduced a resolution to bar white members to the congress and the CNLU. The resolution boomeranged on Langston, who was denied a seat at the NLU's own convention later that year.

The year 1870 was a critical one within the CNLU. When the NLU decided to explore the creation of a third party, Issac Myers spoke out against it. The Negro Labor Congress subsequently voted to disaffiliate with the NLU and intensify partisanship efforts on behalf of the Republican Party. Myers was replaced as CNLU president by Frederick Douglass, who had deep ties to the Republicans. The CNLU's official organ, *New National Era*, reflected the organization's increased political focus. Douglass proved to have little pull with the NLU, however; his own son, Lewis, was denied membership in the all-white typographers union.

By 1871, activists within the CNLU began to question the sincerity of Republican commitment to African Americans. In Richmond, six thousand spectators witnessed a mile-long parade to celebrate the passage of the Sixteenth Amendment in 1870; one year later, the city's black leaders expressed their frustration over the Republicans' failure to advance land reform and to curtail emergent Jim Crow systems. Throughout the South, the Democratic Party quickly reclaimed political power, and black activists like James Rapier of the Labor Union of Alabama advocated more forceful action. Although his attempt to organize black and white farmworkers was unsuccessful, it foreshadowed future efforts by the Knights of Labor and the Populists.

The CNLU held its last congress in 1871. By then, Radical Reconstruction was on the wane and Frederick Douglass's more political focus had borne little fruit. The white NLU was itself on its last legs. In 1872, its political wing, the National Labor Reform Party, crashed at the polls, and the NLU quickly faded away.

The Panic of 1873 dealt a horrible financial blow to those hoping to revive either the CNLU or the NLU. Several industrial congresses were held between 1873 and 1875, but there were no black delegates at any of them. Instead, many African Americans threw their support to the emergent Knights of Labor, an organization that contained no racial restrictions for membership.

Although the CNLU was more noteworthy for its rhetorical bluster than its concrete accomplishments, many of its constituent bodies did impressive organizing work among black workers, especially in the ex-Confederate South. The ambivalence, and in some cases hostility, of the white NLU, the abandonment of Radical Reconstruction, political debates, and the Panic of 1873 combined to doom the CNLU. These same forces also retarded the growth of a black industrial proletariat that emerged immediately after the Civil War. Although the Knights of Labor and the Populist Party delayed further erosion, African American integration into white-led labor organizations remained slight until the 1930s.

**FURTHER READINGS**

Foner, Philip S., and Ronald Lewis, eds. *Black Workers: A Documentary History from Colonial Times to the Present*. Philadelphia: Temple University Press, 1989.

Grossman, Jonathan. "William Sylvis, Pioneer of American Labor." Ph.D. diss., Columbia University, 1945.

Matison, Sumner E. "The Labor Movement and the Negro During Reconstruction." *Journal of Negro History* 33, 4 (October 1948), 426–468.

Rachleff, Peter. *Black Labor in Richmond, 1865–1890*. Urbana: University of Illinois Press, 1989.

Spero, Sterling D., and Abram L. Harris. *The Black Worker: The Negro and the Labor Movement*. New York: Atheneum, 1968.

*Robert E. Weir*

# Colored Press Association of the United States

*See* Afro-American Press Association.

# Columbus, Ohio: Civic, Literary, and Mutual Aid Associations

Columbus, founded in 1816 as the capital of the state of Ohio, was considered a relatively secure place for African American settlements prior to the Fugitive Slave Act of 1850. Between 1820 and 1850, the city's African American population grew in spite of the state's comprehensive racial proscription and because of its central location, as well as the significant settlement of antislavery New Englanders in Columbus. In 1820, the city was home to sixty-three African Americans. By 1850, that number had grown to 1,277 African Americans, representing 7.1 percent of Columbus's total population. Following the passage of the 1850 Fugitive Slave Act, which resulted in mass exodus to Canada, the number of black residents dropped. By 1860, Columbus recorded 997 African Americans, who constituted 5.4 percent of the city's total population.

In the decades following the Civil War, Columbus again attracted African American migrants from Ohio's rural communities and the South. By 1890, the black population in Columbus reached 5,547, constituting 6.3 percent of the total population. This growth continued throughout the early twentieth century due to the great migration that brought large numbers of rural southern blacks to the urban North. Between 1910 and 1920, the number of African Americans residing in Columbus grew from 12,739 to 22,181, constituting a 75 percent black population increase. By that time, African Americans represented 9.4 percent of the total population of Columbus. Throughout the twentieth century, African Americans continued to migrate to the city, and by 1990 they numbered 143,038, or 22.6 percent of the total population.

As early as the 1830s, blacks in Columbus took the lead in providing education for their children. In 1836, they formed the School Society, which, four years later, operated a school enrolling sixty-three black students. In 1906, black Columbus native Pearl Chavers, an admirer of Booker T. Washington, organized the self-help Ohio Colored Educational and Agricultural Association and held an exposition to promote and advertise black economic advancement and boost black enterprise. A year later, Chavers founded the Lincoln-Ohio Industrial Training School, which trained poor and unskilled African American girls in domestic and industrial fields until 1916.

While African Americans tried to provide educational opportunities for the black community, the city of Columbus did not exclude black students from its schools. Between 1887 and 1916, Columbus had one of three racially integrated school systems in Ohio. Some of the public schools employed a small number of African American teachers, but a serious movement for resegregation prevailed until the 1960s.

During the 1890s, several African American fraternal organizations appeared in Columbus. At one point, the city had four Prince Hall Mason lodges, eleven Knights of Pythias lodges, and two Odd Fellows lodges. By 1900, these lodges and their sororal affiliates provided their members with social, economic, and recreational benefits, but they offered very little to the black community at large. One Columbus Odd Fellows Lodge was the exception. It raised $15,000 to launch a business enterprise, bought property, built a meeting hall, and erected stores and an auditorium that was available for rent to the community.

A branch of T. Thomas Fortune's Afro-American League (founded in 1895), later known as the Afro-American Council, existed briefly in Columbus. In 1899, led by Everett J. Waring, an attorney, this group enabled black Republican voters to have a significant, though not conclusively influential, role in politics. The Afro-American Council (ca. 1900) also assisted the Columbus Civic Betterment and Protective Association (ca. 1910), which had been created to improve relations between the white police and the black community. Both groups cooperated and pressured the city to appoint black officers to the Columbus police force.

The Ministers' Association of Columbus (1907) also attempted to improve relations between African Americans and the city's police force, and it addressed issues of social justice across denominational lines. The Ministers' Association served the African American community as a unifying moral force on such issues as law and order in black neighborhoods. Moreover, it proposed that churches serve as social and recreational alternatives to keep African Americans off the streets and out of the bars.

As a result of the city's black population increase during the early twentieth century and the simultaneous deterioration of race relations in Columbus, as elsewhere in the United States, African Americans organized numerous self-help programs and associations. Several benevolent, fraternal, and sororal organizations emerged during these years. Very few of these groups, however, have attracted scholarly attention or left public records of their activities.

Between 1900 and 1920, membership in all of Ohio's black churches increased. This increase was especially apparent in the Baptist and African Methodist Episcopal (AME) churches. As a result of the membership growth, the value of black church property increased. During those years, property values of African American Baptists churches in Columbus rose from $76,000 to $106,700. The city's AME Mt. Vernon Church, for example, saw its value increase from $9,000 to $20,000. In addition to the black churches, the city's Young Men's Christian Association (YMCA) sought to serve as a social center for young black men, as well as other members of the African American community. Three prominent black men, attorney Robert Barcus, physician W. J. Woodlin, and businessman Pearl Chavers, spearheaded the committee that raised funds to build the black YMCA branch that opened its doors in 1911. The establishment of the YMCA in Columbus also led to the hiring of black social workers and other professionals. Nimrod B. Allen, for instance, was hired to develop a comprehensive program of activities for the YMCA.

Barcus and Woodlin were also instrumental in establishing branches of the National Association for the Advancement of Colored People (NAACP) and the National Urban League in Columbus. Founded in 1915, the city's NAACP branch initially met with indifference by African Americans, perhaps because Chavers charged that the organization was opposed to Booker T. Washington. However, gradually the city's black population embraced the NAACP and its fight against discrimination in Columbus, laying the foundation for future campaigns and litigation for equality and full citizenship.

In 1917, Woodlin founded the Welfare League of Columbus to address the problems many African American newcomers to the city encountered (including poor housing, unemployment, and juvenile delinquency) and to promote recreation and social welfare. In 1918, the group reorganized as the Columbus Urban League. One of its ongoing programs was a food bank for African Americans in Columbus. Working with the Godman Guild of Columbus, which had been established in 1917, the Urban League responded to wartime food shortages by starting community-garden projects. These community-garden projects were also implemented during the Depression and World War II. The Columbus Urban League has an extensive history of serving the African American community and remains one of the most important black organizations in Columbus.

**FURTHER READINGS**

Davis, Lenwood. "Nineteenth Century Blacks in Ohio: An Historical View." In *Blacks in Ohio History*. Ed. Rubin F. Weston. Columbus: Ohio Historical Society, 1976, 8–10.

Dulaney, W. Marvin. "Blacks as Policemen in Columbus, Ohio, 1895–1945." In *Blacks in Ohio History*. Ed. Rubin F. Weston. Columbus: Ohio Historical Society, 1976, 11–13.

Gerber, David A. *Black Ohio and the Color Line, 1860–1915*. Urbana: University of Illinois Press, 1976.

James, Felix. *The American Addition: History of a Black Community*. Washington, D.C.: University Press of America, 1979.

*Barbara L. Green*

## Comité des Citoyens

Le comité des citoyens, or Citizens' Committee, was formed by New Orleans Creoles of color on September 1, 1891. Alarmed by the growing number of segregation laws, the group offered legal resistance to the separate public transportation law enacted by the Louisiana Legislature of 1890. Rodolphe Desdunes had already envisioned assertive civil rights action in the courts, and the *Crusader*, founded by the pro-Republican Union Louisianaise, served as an organ of this campaign. In early 1890, the editors had helped gather African American and white progressive leaders throughout the South to form the American Citizens' Equal Rights Association (ACERA) in Washington, D.C. But the black Protestant ministers involved in ACERA backed away after the Methodist Church removed Reverend A. Albert from the editorship of the *Southwestern Christian Advocate*. The Creoles of color of New Orleans now stood virtually alone. Old Reconstruction radical Aristide Mary wanted to give a dignified appearance to the resistance, which had to be implemented by long judicial procedure, and he provided most of the financial support ($3,000) needed by the committee.

The committee's board was composed of Arthur Esteves, president; C. Antoine, vice president; Firmin Christophe, secretary; and fifteen other leading men of color, including Louis Martinet, the founder of the *Daily Crusader;* A. J. Giuranovitch; Numa Mansion; Alcee Labat; and E. A. Williams. The committee's initial address, published in the *Crusader*, stated its purpose: to protest the adoption and enforcement of the statutes that established discrimination against African Americans. The committee received support from various parts of the United States and from such well-known men as Supreme Court Justice John M. Harlan and the white activist lawyer Albion Tourgee, who was retained, with three others, as the committee's legal adviser.

In March 1892, the committee went to court. In the case brought against Act 111 of 1890, Daniel Desdunes, a son of Rodolphe Desdunes, was the plaintiff. Daniel Desdunes, while traveling on the Louisville & Nashville Railroad to Mobile, Alabama, had been arrested for riding in a coach reserved for white passengers. The committee obtained from Judge John H. Ferguson an annulment of segregation involving traffic between several states. But the law, which established discrimination in transportation within the state of Louisiana, was upheld. The committee challenged it again. In June 1892, the committee engaged Homer A. Plessy to travel in a "white" car of the East Louisiana railroad. The case eventually went to the United States Supreme Court. When the *Plessy v. Ferguson* case reached the Supreme Court, it resulted in the famous "separate but equal" decision of 1896, which sanctioned segregation.

The group intervened when the committee's treasurer, Paul Bonseigneur, and his family were forced to flee their recently purchased and renovated home in Mandeville, Louisiana, in 1893. Bonseigneur had enjoyed a rental in the summer resort of Mandeville for several years; however, when he acquired property, leading white residents reacted with hostility and drove him out of town. The committee organized a large protest meeting at the Friends of Hope hall.

The committee also pursued legal action against the exclusion of African Americans from juries, and directed its efforts against the proposed law prohibiting racial intermarriage, which was defeated in the state Senate in 1892. Shortly after the 1896 "separate but equal" decision, the committee disbanded at a public meeting.

**FURTHER READINGS**

Desdunes, Rodolphe L. *Our People and Our History*. Trans. and ed., Sister Dorothea Olga McCants. Baton Rouge: Louisiana State University Press, 1973.

Hirsch, Arnold R., and Joseph Logsdon, eds. *Creole New Orleans*. Baton Rouge: Louisiana State University Press, 1992.

Martinet, L.A., ed. *The Violation of a Constitutional Right*. New Orleans: Crusader Print, 1893.

*Michel Fabre*

## Commission for Multicultural Ministries, Evangelical Lutheran Church in America

In 1987, the Evangelical Lutheran Church in America (ELCA), at its Constituting Convention, decided to increase its membership of African American, Asian, Hispanic, and Native American Lutherans by 10 percent over a ten-year period. For this purpose, the ELCA established a Commission for Multicultural Ministries (CMM) in

1989. By 1991, the CMM developed a comprehensive multicultural strategy for outreach and proclamation of the gospel to persons of color and those whose primary language is not English. This strategy, designed to increase the ELCA's membership by 440,000, proposes to create an attitude and climate within the church for an intentional outreach ministry to all people; to help all members understand the evangelical roots of multicultural ministries in ways that are biblically, confessionally, and pastorally sound; to provide language- and culture-specific resources for its congregation; to develop curriculum and worship material that emphasizes social justice; to recruit and prepare African American, Asian, Hispanic, Native America, and white individuals, lay and ordained, for multicultural ministry in the ELCA; and to expand advocacy, health, education, and social services for African American, Asian, Hispanic, and Native American people.

More than 5.2 million members from more than eleven thousand congregations in sixty-five synods across America, along with numerous churchwide agencies, institutions, and programs, serve as resources in the ELCA's efforts to become an inclusive, multicultural body. Each congregation is encouraged to work with the CMM to develop a local strategy for increasing the membership of racial and ethnic groups living in the community.

The CMM is governed by a steering committee of twenty members elected by the ELCA Church Council. The commission's members represent the diverse white, African American, Asian, Hispanic, and Native American communities active in the Evangelical Lutheran Church in America. The commission seeks to be representative of the diverse communities that the ELCA serves, since the ELCA is an immigrant church and has a history of serving immigrant people.

In the late 1990s, the Reverend Frederick Rajan was the director of the CMM, ELCA. The commission's headquarters are in Chicago.

### FURTHER READINGS

Christiansen, Lia. "Steering Committee Report." *CMM Messenger* 1, 3 (Winter 1995–1996), 4–5.

*Multicultural Mission Strategy: A Strategy for Proclamation of the Gospel.* Chicago: Commission for Multicultural Ministries, Evangelical Lutheran Church in America, 1991, 1–8.

*Multicultural Mission Strategy: Congregational Study Guide.* Chicago: Commission for Multicultural Ministries, Evangelical Lutheran Church in America, 1992, 5–6.

*Barbara L. Green*

## Commission for the Presidential Appointment of African American Women
*See* National Political Congress of Black Women.

## Commission of the Study of the Participation of the Negro in Southern Life
*See* Commission on Interracial Cooperation.

## Commission on Interracial Cooperation

Following World War I, African American soldiers returning from the European battlefields were painfully aware that the democratic principles they had fought to preserve abroad still eluded them at home. Heightened black expectations for a change in the racial status quo collided with white assumptions that African Americans would resume their prewar role. The resulting racial tensions erupted in 1919 with a series of race riots that engulfed cities throughout the country. In the wake of these racial tensions, a number of white southerners began to reevaluate race relations in the United States, hoping to create racial harmony among blacks and whites in the South. The culmination of this effort was the Commission on Interracial Cooperation (CIC), an interracial group that worked until the early 1940s to foster democracy, racial justice, and economic opportunity for African Americans in the South.

The CIC grew out of a series of meetings among southern whites and blacks who were reacting to postwar racial tensions. The first of these meetings was held in March 1919 in Atlanta's Georgian Terrace Hotel where a small number of white middle-class ministers, educators, and businessmen gathered to discuss ways in which white southerners could guarantee African Americans justice in the courts, equal travel accommodations, school provisions, and housing. Among those in attendance were Will W. Alexander, a Methodist minister from Nashville; John J. Eagan, an Atlanta banker; and M. Ashby Jones, a Baptist minister from Atlanta. Taking a paternalistic approach, this charter group had no desire to form an interracial committee; instead, it argued for the need to mobilize members of the white community to make great strides in improving race relations. Naming themselves the Committee on After-the-War Cooperation, this group of white men posited that others of their race, class, education, and religious commitment would support their endeavors because they believed that "the great bulk of the best [white] people of the South" were ready to be led into "service for the Negro."

Meeting in July 1919, the Committee on After-the-War Cooperation received a $50,000 grant from the War Works Council of the Young Men's Christian Association (YMCA) to continue the work of an interracial program that had been established by the YMCA at the conclusion of the war. Pioneered by Willis Duke Weatherford, head of the YMCA's war work personnel training school and close personal friend of Will Alexander, this interracial program had established two training schools—one for whites and one for blacks—to gather information concerning southern racial conditions and to educate conference participants on how to cope with racial conflicts in their communities. Finding this program to be amenable to the committee's purpose, the group accepted the grant and changed its name to the Interracial Committee.

At that same time, the committee considered the inclusion of African Americans. Will Alexander shared his belief with other committee members that there were a great number of "radical African Americans" who distrusted the intentions of whites and, therefore, posed a threat to their work. Agreeing with Alexander, committee members decided their best course of action would be to foster close cooperation among whites and blacks in southern communities in order to demonstrate that they were, indeed, "Southerners of Good Will." Therefore, the committee proposed the establishment of local interracial committees to foster mutual understanding by leading discussions on issues such as equalizing schools, recreational facilities, housing, and public transportation for African Americans. By early 1920, approximately five hundred state, county, and local interracial groups were affiliated with the committee. Despite such affiliation, however, the groups retained their autonomy, allowing each community to set its own reform agenda according to its racial environment and availability of community support.

Despite the success in fostering these interracial coalitions at the grassroots level, the role of African Americans within the committee remained unclear. Many members, particularly Ashby Jones, believed that it was not necessary for the committee to include African Americans to ensure that the organization was fulfilling its responsibilities in improving race relations. However, other members, including Will Alexander and University of South Carolina Professor Josiah Morse, believed that it was essential to give African Americans the opportunity to participate in order to stifle black aspirations of ending segregation.

According to Alexander, the intent of the committee was not to challenge but to improve segregation by making separate truly "equal." Allowing African Americans to work toward any other goal, he believed, would be detrimental to the organization and the South. Most committee members agreed with Alexander and Morse, convinced that the majority of "educated and developed" African Americans espoused the doctrines of Booker T. Washington, which held that it was in the best interest of race relations to work within the boundaries of segregation. Therefore, committee members reached a consensus to include blacks in their efforts to make separate truly equal.

Initially, many African Americans viewed the efforts of the committee with suspicion and bitterness, in part due to the organization's reluctance to expand its membership to blacks. After years of experiencing legal segregation, as well as the horrors of southern lynch mobs and urban race riots, African Americans were skeptical of the group's intentions and its commitment to racial reform. Seeking to overcome this skepticism, the committee admitted its first black members, Robert R. Moton, president of Tuskegee Institute, and Robert Elijah Jones, publisher of the *Southwest Christian Advocate*, in March 1920. By the end of the summer, other black leaders had joined the organization, including John Hope, president of Morehouse College; John Manuel Gandy, president of Virginia Normal School; and Isaac Fisher, publisher of *Fisk University News*. Accepting the committee's position on segregation, black members hoped that, by working within the confines of the southern racial system, they could reduce racial violence, gain access to equal justice before the law, and foster improvements in housing and public education, transportation, and other services—the rights and amenities that southerners routinely denied them.

In early 1921, after gaining further financial assistance from the YMCA's War Work Council, as well as a number of northern philanthropic foundations, such as the Phelps Stokes, Laura Spelman Memorial, Carnegie, and Rosenwald Funds, the committee decided to establish a permanent organization, calling itself the CIC. Headquartered in Atlanta and governed by an elected board of directors, the CIC sought to coordinate the work of the vast number of interracial committees that had emerged throughout the South. CIC members elected Alexander as the group's first executive director, whose responsibilities included handling the day-to-day business of the organization and administering its programs. As outlined in *A Realistic Approach to the Race Problem*, a 1936 CIC pamphlet produced to explain the organization's origin and mission, the commission's goals were twofold: (1) the correction of interracial injustice and the betterment of conditions affecting African Americans; and (2) the improvement of those interracial attitudes out of which unfavorable conditions grow.

Women also played a vital role in the formation of the CIC. Working through church-sponsored organizations like the Woman's Missionary Council of the Methodist Episcopal Church and the Women's Missionary Union of the Southern Baptist Convention, southern white women had taken an interest in improving race relations. In early 1920, several white women active in these church-sponsored organizations established their own separate Interracial Committee for women, headed by Carrie Parks Johnson, a member of the Woman's Missionary Council. Sponsoring a conference in Memphis, Tennessee, in October 1920, these women called for the improvement of working conditions of black domestic servants, the establishment of day-care facilities and kindergartens for black children, a campaign against lynching, and the creation of a Continuation Committee of seven women. At a 1921 meeting of the CIC, the Continuation Committee became the Woman's Committee of the CIC and was administratively placed in the CIC's Division of Women's Work. In 1923, black women were invited to join the CIC, forging an interracial coalition under the leadership of Woman's Work directors Mrs. Luke Johnson (1921–1925), Maud Henderson (1925–1928), and Jessie Daniel Ames (1929–1937), who also became the executive director of the Association of Southern Women for the Prevention of Lynching (ASWPL) in 1930. Among the CIC's prominent female reformers were Mary McLeod Bethune, president of the Southeastern Federation of Colored Women's Clubs; Lugenia Burns Hope, wife of John Hope, president of Morehouse College, and founder of Atlanta's Neighborhood Union; Nannie Helen Burroughs, founder of the Women's Convention Auxiliary of the National Baptist Convention and the National League of Republican Colored Women; and Charlotte Hawkins Brown, president of the North Carolina Federation of Colored Women.

By 1921, the CIC employed twenty-six black and sixty-one white field-workers to continue its mission of establishing local interracial committees. Traveling in biracial teams, CIC field-workers interviewed leaders of the black and white communities in each southern locale they visited. After coordinating a meeting between the two groups, the field-workers asked that they conduct a survey of issues of racial concern in their community. Following the completion of the survey, field-workers encouraged communities to create a permanent interracial committee and inaugurate projects to address the ills their study identified. Using this method, the CIC persuaded seven thousand southerners in more than eight hundred communities to become involved in interracial work. Recognizing that such interracial work would undoubtedly draw negative attention from organizations such as the Ku Klux Klan, the CIC urged communities to work behind the scenes and "say as little as possible" about their group's work. Throughout the 1920s, CIC affiliates embarked on such programs as establishing a scholarship program for blacks to attend college, providing legal aid for many poor African Americans, launching health campaigns in southern blacks communities, supporting efforts to pave streets and build libraries in black neighborhoods, and rallying support against lynching.

In 1924, after successfully initiating and coordinating the work of local interracial committees, the CIC shifted its emphasis to research, publicity, and education. Aiming its work at community leaders—the press, church representatives, educators, and students—who shaped public policy and opinion, the CIC planned programs that reflected its new emphasis. It encouraged the press to examine its poor coverage of the black community and sensationalist approach to race relations; planned lectures, conferences, and pamphlets to educate southern church leaders about race relations; and sponsored summer schools and conferences for teachers to discuss race relations and ways of integrating the study of African Americans into the general curriculum of southern schools.

The work of the CIC's staff also resulted in the formation of several other organizations committed to interracial cooperation and the CIC's emphasis on research, publicity, and education. These organizations include the Conference on Education and Race Relations (CERR), the Commission of the Study of the Participation of the Negro in Southern Life (CSPN), and the Special Committee on Negroes and Economic Reconstruction (SCNER). The CERR, established ca. 1929, was largely active in southern universities, bringing black speakers such as George Washington Carver to white campuses, publishing educational materials, and organizing conferences and annual seminars on race relations for black and white educators. The SCNER, organized in 1934, investigated farm tenancy in the South and the CSPN, established in 1933, published some of the CIC's most famous books and pamphlets, including Arthur Raper's *The Tragedy of Lynching* (1933), Raper and Ira De A. Reid's *Sharecroppers All* (1941), and Charles Johnson's *The Collapse of Cotton Tenancy* (1935).

One of the CIC's most important functions was to publicize the extent of lynchings, through its Southern Commission on the Study of Lynching (SCSL). Organized in 1930, the SCSL recorded 3,703 lynchings, mostly of African Americans, for the period between 1889 and 1929. While many of the lynchings were triggered by charges of rape, the CIC found that most lynch mobs were motivated by "vengeance" and economic competition. In addition to publicizing the nation's lynching record, CIC supporters and affiliates also tried to prevent lynchings and, in a few cases, succeeded in prosecuting members of lynch mobs. The CIC took partial credit for the gradual decline in lynchings from eighty-three in 1919 to eight in 1932 to zero between May 1939 and May 1940.

By the mid-1930s, it appeared as though the CIC was on the verge of collapsing as it suffered from a lack of ideas, energy, and leadership. In 1935, the CIC's executive director, Will Alexander, left the organization, dividing his time between serving in the federal Farm Security Administration in Washington, D.C., and the Rosenwald Fund in Chicago. The CIC's research director, Arthur Raper, moved to Washington, D.C., to work for the United States Department of Agriculture, and the CIC's information director, Robert B. Eleazer, was on the verge of retiring after serving the organization for twenty years. Finally, CIC President Howard Odum stopped coming to the organization's headquarters, claiming that there was nothing more for him to do.

Steadily losing ground, the CIC would begin to turn the tide when Jessie Daniel Ames assumed the position of executive director in 1935. Firmly committed to seeing the CIC survive, Ames began a program of reinvigorating and coordinating the state and local interracial committees. Virtually abandoning its focus on research, the CIC put its full force behind its fieldwork by initiating conferences on race relations, creating uniform methods to govern state bodies and their programs, and publishing a monthly publication, *Southern Frontier*, to keep CIC members informed about the organization's activities.

Despite Ames's efforts, the CIC continued to decline in popularity and support into the early 1940s. Fisk University President Charles S. Johnson, Morehouse College President Benjamin Mays, and other African American CIC leaders were dismayed at the organization's failure to call for an end of segregation and its lack of response to the changing racial climate triggered by World War II. However, white CIC leaders, afraid of a white conservative backlash, were reluctant to endorse an equal rights agenda.

While not heeding black demands, Ames wanted to regain the confidence of black leaders from both within and outside the organization in the hope of reasserting the CIC as an interracial body committed to remedying the ills of southern society through gradual yet steady social change. Therefore, with the help of Gordon Hancock, a sociologist at Virginia Union University, Ames set forth a plan to reconcile the different demands of southern blacks and whites in order to revitalize the CIC.

After two separate conferences were held—one for blacks in Durham, North Carolina, in December 1942 and one for whites in Atlanta in April 1943—the demands for racial reform were laid out on the table. The agenda each conference put forth emphasized the hope to create an atmosphere of cooperation, good will, and mutual understanding among the races of the South. Yet, the "Durham Statement," as it came to be known, advocated the gradual elimination of segregation, while the "Atlanta Statement" barely broached the subject. The next step was a collaborative meeting of the Durham and Atlanta delegations in which members of each group could work out "methods and practical means of approach" for achieving their goals. Meeting in Richmond, Virginia, in June 1943, approximately thirty-three whites and an equal number of blacks initiated what would become a heated discussion about white paternalism and black demands for the abolition of segregation. As calm voices turned into fierce shouts, it seemed as though the delegates were unable to reach a compromise. However, level heads prevailed as Howard Odum seized control of the meeting and outlined his vision of a new biracial organization that would work to alleviate the South's suffering by extending economic, political, and educational opportunities to African Americans. Operating as a regional research and development council, this new organization could defuse the issue of race under the aegis of economic, political, and educational development by gathering a broader base of support among business and labor leaders to end racial discrimination and, eventually, segregation. The majority of those in attendance agreed to the formation of such an organization, and, by the end of the year, the Southern Regional Council (SRC) was created to replace the CIC.

At its final meeting in February 1944, the CIC formally merged with the newly formed SRC. Successful in reducing racial tensions and racial violence, the CIC did help establish a productive dialogue on various racial issues that would provide a strong foundation for the work of the SRC in generations to come.

## FURTHER READINGS

Ducey, Mitchell F., ed. *The Commission on Interracial Cooperation Papers, 1919–1944, and The Association of Southern Women for the Prevention of Lynching Papers, 1930–1942: A Guide to the Microfilm Editions.* Ann Arbor: University Microfilm International, 1984.

Egerton, John. *Speak Now Against the Day: The Generation Before the Civil Rights Movement in the South.* New York: Knopf, 1994.

Eleazer, Robert B. *A Realistic Approach to the Race Problem: Origin and Work of the Commission of Interracial Cooperation.* Atlanta: Commission on Interracial Cooperation, 1936.

Hall, Jacqueline Dowd. *Revolt Against Chivalry: Jessie Daniel Ames and the Women's Campaign against Lynching.* Rev. ed. New York: Columbia University Press, 1993.

McDonough, Julia Anne. "Men and Women of Good Will: A History of the Commission on Interracial Cooperation and the Southern Regional Council, 1919–1954." Ph.D. diss., University of Virginia, 1993.

Moton, Robert R. *Finding a Way Out.* Garden City: Doubleday, Page 1920.

Rouse, Jacqueline. *Lugenia Burns Hope: Black Southern Reformer.* Athens: University of Georgia Press, 1989.

*Southern Frontier* 1–6 (1940–1945). New York: Negro Universities Press, 1969.

*Kimberly E. Nichols*

**SEE ALSO**    Southern Commission on the Study of Lynching; Southern Regional Council

## Committee Against Jim Crow in Military Service and Training

The Committee Against Jim Crow in Military Service and Training advocated equal treatment of African Americans in the U.S. armed forces. Founded in 1947, the committee protested discrimination and segregation in the armed forces and launched various lobbying efforts to end Jim Crow practices in the military. Committee members appealed to government representatives, organized and addressed mass rallies, conducted citizens hearings with elected officials, consulted civil rights leaders and retired army personnel, and testified before the Senate Committee on Armed Services.

Grant Reynolds, a former World War II army captain, and A. Philip Randolph, president of the Brotherhood of Sleeping Car Porters, founded the committee. Reynolds and Randolph were cochairmen; B. F. McLaurin was treasurer; William Worthy Jr., executive secretary; Lynn Seitter Kirk, field secretary; and Albert Black, Washington, D.C., chairman. Its legal committee consisted of Raymond Pace Alexander, Matthew W. Bullock Jr., Robert L. Carter, Earl B. Dickerson, Charles H. Houston, Belford V. Lawson Jr., and James M. Nabrit Jr.

After World War II, *United States Board of Officers on Utilization of Negro Manpower in the Post-War Army* (1946) concluded that black manpower had been poorly utilized during the war. The so-called Gillem Report recommended that such manpower be utilized more efficiently in the postwar army, primarily on the basis of an increase in the education, skills, and economic attainment of African Americans since World War II. The report also recommended that remedial steps be taken to eliminate deficiencies in the military training of both black officers and black enlistees in future wars; that more black officers and enlisted personnel be added to the army to provide cadres and leaders for future national emergencies; that black female components be added to the military as African American manpower increased; that preference be given to black combat units as the military expanded its base of black personnel; that the United States War Department and major military posts create standing committees of military officers to devote full-time efforts to solving problems that black troops were experiencing in the military; and that all forms of segregation and racial discrimination against black officers be eliminated.

When the War Department published the Gillem Report, African American leaders, civil rights organizations, and the black press rejected the new policy because it recommended desegregation of only the officers rank. Reynolds and Randolph were among the black leaders who vociferously protested the absence of a specific statement in the Gillem Report recommending the abolition of racial segregation in all ranks and units of the armed services.

Randolph and Reynolds were particularly distressed when they learned that the legislation proposing the establishment of universal military training did not specifically ban racial segregation. As cochairs of the Committee Against Jim Crow in Military Service and Training, they clashed with President Harry S. Truman and others over civil rights for African Americans both in and out of uniform. Randolph, in particular, reminded the president that the Committee on Civil Rights, which Truman had appointed in December 1946, strongly condemned segregation and racial discrimination in the armed forces. In its 1947 report, the committee recommended that segregation be barred from all military programs enacted by Congress.

These developments spurred Randolph and Reynolds to push even harder for integration. On March 22, 1948, along with several other prominent black leaders, they met with President Truman to solicit his support for the antidiscrimination amendment to the proposed peacetime draft bill. Randolph, in particular, told the president: "I found Negroes not wanting to shoulder a gun for democracy abroad unless they get democracy at home" (*New York Times*, March 23, 1948). Randolph then informed Truman that if the president did not exercise his authority as commander in chief to end segregation in the armed services, he (Randolph) would counsel civil disobedience.

Meanwhile, Randolph and Reynolds asked their Legal Committee to translate into legal terminology several amendments for incorporation into H.R. 4278—the bill proposing universal military training (UMT). The amendments called for (1) prohibition of segregation and racial discrimination in all UMT programs; (2) a ban of discrimination and all racial segregation "in interstate travel for trainees in the UMT uniforms or any other military uniform"; (3) "making attacks on, or lynching of, a trainee in UMT uniform or a person in any other military uniform a federal offense"; (4) "banning the poll tax in federal elections for any trainee otherwise eligible to vote" (Committee against Jim Crow in Military Service and Training, *Memo to Legal Committee*, October 30, 1947).

These amendments became a crucial part of the committee's struggle to integrate universal military training, and Randolph and Reynolds presented them in their testimony at the Senate hearings on UMT on March 30, 1948. There, Randolph and Reynolds repeated their threats to encourage young African Americans to boycott the peacetime draft unless segregation and racial discrimination were abolished in all units of the armed services.

Meanwhile, at a New York City meeting on March 27, 1948, the National Association for the Advancement of Colored People (NAACP) and several other black organizations also called for the immediate end to segregation in the armed forces. By this time, however, presidential politics had become a major topic of discussion among the conferees. Subsequently, they passed resolutions and released a public statement declaring black support in exchange for the elimination of segregation and racial discrimination in the armed services.

By mid-1948, President Truman had joined the forces for integration. He was determined to carry on the principle, solidified with Franklin D. Roosevelt's New Deal administration, of positive government action to rehabilitate and preserve the dignity and human resources of the United States. Yet, Secretary of the Army Kenneth Royall; his successor, Gordon Gray; and advocates of segregation continued to maintain that integration would impair military efficiency and damage the morale of American troops. But the forces of integration were too strong to be overlooked. Secretary of Defense James V. Forrestal, Secretary of the Navy John L. Sullivan, Secretary of the Air Force W. Stuart Symington, black and white political and civic leaders, powerful civil rights organizations, and the black press increasingly pressured the White House to end segregation in the military. On July 26, 1948, President Truman acted. He issued Executive Order 9981, which called for "equality of treatment and opportunity for all persons in the armed services, without regard to race, color, religion, or national origin."

The order established the President's Committee on Equality of Treatment and Opportunity in the Armed Services. The committee was authorized to examine race relations in the armed services and determine how best to implement the new policy. It was named the Fahy Committee after its white liberal chair, Charles Fahy. In 1950, after having worked with all branches of the military, the committee issued its report, which recommended an end to segregation in the armed services.

By 1950, Randolph and Reynolds, convinced that they had achieved their objectives, ended the nonviolent civil disobedience campaign against Jim Crow in military service and training.

**FURTHER READINGS**

Dalfiume, Richard M. *Desegregation of the U.S. Armed Forces: Fighting on Two Fronts, 1939–1953*. Columbia: University of Missouri Press, 1969.

McGuire, Phillip. *He, Too, Spoke for Democracy: Judge Hastie, World War II, and the Black Soldier*. Westport, Conn.: Greenwood, 1988.

Moore, Jesse T. A *Search for Equality: The National Urban League, 1910–1961*. University Park: Pennsylvania State University Press, 1981.

U.S. Senate. Committee on Armed Services. *Hearings on Universal Military Training*. Washington, D.C.: GPO, 1948.

Committee Against Jim Crow in Military Service and Training. Records, 1947–1950. Manuscript, Archives, and Rare Books Division. Schomburg Center for Research in Black Culture, the New York Public Library.

*Phillip McGuire*

SEE ALSO    Committee for the Participation of Negroes in the National Defense; President's Committee on Equality of Treatment and Opportunity in the Armed Services (The Fahy Committee)

## Committee for Racial Justice Now, United Church of Christ

*See* Committee for Racial Justice, United Church of Christ.

## Committee for Racial Justice, United Church of Christ

In 1963, the United Church of Christ (UCC) established the Committee for Racial Justice as the Committee for Racial Justice Now at its Fourth General Synod in Denver. The UCC launched the committee in response to the heightened racial tensions that followed the assassination of Medgar Evers, president of the Mississippi National Association for the Advancement of Colored People (NAACP), and the bombing deaths of five African American schoolgirls who were killed while attending Sunday school in a Birmingham, Alabama, church. Authorized to work for a two-year period, the committee was charged with eliminating "racial segregation and discrimination in the life of our churches; and in securing justice for Blacks and other minorities in our society." Dr. Gary Oniki of the Council of Christian and Social Action and the Board for Homeland Ministries served as the committee's first executive coordinator. Until 1966, several interim executives succeeded him, including the Reverends Dr. Truman Douglas, Dr. Ray Gibbons, Dr. W. Sterling Cary, and Dr. Charles Cobb. Under their leadership, the organization worked through and with existing UCC boards and agencies.

The committee was reconstituted in 1965 for an additional two-year period at the Fifth General Synod in Chicago. Moreover, a UCC subcommittee recommended:

1. That the mandate to the Committee for Racial Justice Now be addressed to the entire United Church of Christ, including all its instrumentalities, conferences, associations, and churches.

2. That the Committee for Racial Justice Now be reconstituted by the Sixth General Synod, 1967, as a four-year committee, with smaller membership, to be appointed by the president; and that the committee advise and support the executive coordinator and that he be responsible to it.

3. That the Committee for Racial Justice Now renegotiate and communicate with various conferences, instrumentalities, and associations with the aim that its executive coordinator will have access to, and hopefully influence upon, the decision-making process of the United Church of Christ.

4. That the Committee for Racial Justice Now continually analyze and seek to change the structure, policies, and practices of the United Church of Christ toward the establishment of racial justice within the United Church of Christ and its work in the world.

On January 25, 1967, the above recommendations were accepted at the regular meeting of the committee.

Meanwhile, the thrust of the civil rights movement had shifted from nonviolent protest marches to militant black-power rhetoric. In an effort to remain abreast of these changes, the committee decided to broaden its focus and started to advocate economic, political, and educational improvements among African Americans. Explaining its decision, the committee stated that racial justice could be achieved only if the black community gained "enough political power to effect change whereby racial justice could be demanded." Acknowledging that the depth of the U.S. racial problem was so severe that any hopes for an immediate solution were unrealistic, the committee dropped the appendage "Now" from its name following the Fifth Synod.

The most decisive turning point in the committee's history occurred at the Seventh Synod, which convened in Boston on June 25, 1969. In response to an appeal from the Ministers for Racial and Social Justice, the synod decided that the UCC president would appoint committee members based on the recommendations of the church's black constituency. Following this decision, African Americans represented a majority on the fifteen-member committee. Moreover, the UCC agreed to change the status of the committee, providing for guaranteed funding. The committee became a commission and held its first meeting on December 11, 1969. The Reverend Albert Cleage Jr., minister of the Shrine of the Black Madonna of Detroit, Michigan, became the first elected chairman of the newly empowered commission.

As the national civil rights agency of the UCC's 1.5 million members, the commission has been involved in various efforts. In the 1970s, the commission addressed injustices in the judicial and prison system and led a successful campaign to free the Wilmington Ten, political activists for African-American rights whose arrest was the first official case of political prisoners in the United States cited by Amnesty International. In the 1980s, the commission supported the fight against apartheid in South Africa and challenges to voting rights in Alabama and Chicago, and it led a fact-finding mission to Angola and brought children from that nation to the United States for medical treatment. During the 1990s, the commission helped disseminate the UCC's *Pastoral Letter on Contemporary Racism and the Role of the Church.* In October 1991, it helped organize the First National People of Color Environmental Leadership Summit and published the proceedings to heighten public awareness and to increase the interest and involvement of minorities in environmental issues. The commission sponsored its first Annual National Racial Justice Awards Dinner, which honored those who have made an outstanding contribution to the progress of racial justice.

In addition, commission programs have embraced a wide range of issues, including African American family life, capital punishment, racially motivated violence, child abuse, displaced homemakers, battered wives, teenage pregnancy, welfare hotels, homelessness, persons with disabilities, computer literacy, and African American, Hispanic American, and Native American church empowerment. Headquartered in Cleveland, Ohio, the commission also operates offices in Enfield, North Carolina, Washington, D.C., and New York City. Since its founding, the commission has published books, conference proceedings, reports, and the weekly *Civil Rights Journal.*

## FURTHER READINGS

Cobb, Charles E. *History of C.R.J.* Cleveland: United Church of Christ, n.d.

United Church of Christ. *Racism and the Role of the Church.* Cleveland: United Church of Christ, 1991.

———. *Commission for Racial Justice.* Cleveland: United Church of Christ, 1993.

*Betty Nyangoni*

## Committee for the Advancement of Colored Catholics

The Committee for the Advancement of Colored Catholics was founded between 1916 and 1917 by a Catholic layman and Howard University professor, Thomas Wyatt Turner (1877–1976), to challenge the discriminatory practices of the Catholic Church in the United States. The committee was composed of Catholic laymen and women and initially targeted the failure of the Church to provide adequate educational opportunities

for its African American communicants. Gaining momentum, the committee began to promote more extensive demands that included the need for an indigenous clergy, better race relations, and a voice in the decision-making process within the Church.

The committee demonstrated a growing black solidarity and, by 1924, had evolved into the Federated Colored Catholics in the United States, with Turner serving as president. The Federated Colored Catholics helped lay the foundation for interracial efforts that began to emerge in the 1930s under the direction of Jesuit John LaFarge, who became the Church's most articulate spokesperson on race relations. Other lay-oriented groups, such as the Catholic Laymen's Union (1927), the Catholic Student Mission Crusade (1931), and the Catholic Interracial Council (1934), emerged and started to displace the Federated Catholics, who nevertheless continued to lobby for African Americans until the mid-1950s.

Despite the committee's brief existence, the organization and its vocal membership created the forum through which the laity could voice its spiritual concerns to the Catholic Church in the United States.

## FURTHER READINGS

Davis, Cyprian, O. S. B. *The History of Black Catholics in the United States.* New York: Crossroad, 1991.

Nickels, Marilyn. *Black Catholic Protest and the Federated Colored Catholics, 1917–1933: Three Perspectives on Racial Justice.* New York: Garland, 1988.

Ochs, Stephen J. *Desegregating the Altar: The Josephites and the Struggle for Black Priests, 1871–1960.* Baton Rouge: Louisiana State University Press, 1990.

*A. J. Scopino Jr.*

## Committee for the Participation of Negroes in the National Defense

The Committee for the Participation of Negroes in the National Defense was organized in 1938 to pressure the federal government and the War Department to increase the number of African Americans in the military and to open all branches of the armed forces and the defense industries to African Americans on an integrated and nondiscriminatory basis. The committee specifically lobbied and pressured the military to include a nondiscriminatory clause in the pending Selective Service Act. Robert L. Vann, publisher of the influential black newspaper the *Pittsburgh Courier* financed the committee and invited World War I veterans to join the organization. The historian Rayford W. Logan of Howard University headed the committee; Louis Lautier, a Washington-based correspondent for the *Courier*, the *Baltimore Afro-American*, and the *Chicago Defender*, was its secretary; P. L. Prattis, correspondent for the *Courier*, was in charge of publicity; and the attorney Charles H. Houston, chief counsel for the Legal Defense Fund of the National Association for the Advancement of Colored People (NAACP), was its legal adviser. Houston, Lautier, Logan, and Louis R. Mehlinger, who had been a captain in the famed black 369th Infantry Regiment during World War I, were the committee's chief lobbyists in Washington, D.C. Other members of the committee included West A. Hamilton, James E. Scott, Ralph E. Mizelle, Henry Lincoln Johnson Jr., and Campbell C. Johnson.

As early as 1938, Vann had described the purpose of the group in an open letter to President Franklin D. Roosevelt: "I feel, and my people feel, that this is the psychological moment to strike for our rightful place in our National Defense. I need not tell you that we are expecting a more dignified place in our armed forces during the next war than we occupied during the World War" (Buni 1974, 310). Vann's letter was published in the *Courier*, along with an invitation asking other national organizations and the black press to join the committee. A number of black and white organizations—such as the National Bar Association, the National Negro Insurance Association, the black press, the Brotherhood of Sleeping Car Porters, the Federal Council of Churches of Christ in America, the Interracial Commission, the Council for Democracy and Fight for Freedom, and the Citizens' Non-Partisan Committee for Equal Rights and Defense— sent letters, telegrams, and various delegations to Congress with the hope of forcing the military to open its doors to African American troops on a nondiscriminatory basis. The committee also coordinated testimony before congressional committees, conferences with the president and congressional bodies, appeals for local protests, and meetings with War Department officials. Moreover, the committee waged a campaign to pressure the Democratic and Republican National Conventions to include in their platforms nondiscriminatory language with regard to African American participation in the armed services.

Although the committee had marshaled an impressive group of support, the NAACP initially refused to back the *Courier* and the committee because they were willing to accept segregated army units. The objective of the committee was integration of the military; however, the committee determined that, if integration was unattainable,

then the group would, at least temporarily, accept segregated units in order to increase the number of African Americans in the armed forces. For example, Logan, spokesman for the committee, advocated proportional racial quotas as a means to achieve the group's objective. The NAACP, advocating integration of the armed services, refused to support the committee's quota proposal.

By 1939, the committee had achieved modest successes. The War Department had promised to train more black combat troops and officers. But hopes that Congress would pass a law abolishing segregation in the military were dashed when the army blocked the legislation, claiming that "racially mixed units would demoralize the white soldiers" (Buni 1974, 311). Subsequently, a June 1950 amendment to An Act to Expedite the Strengthening of the National Defense maintained the status quo but indicated "that no Negro because of race shall be excluded from enlistment in the army for service with colored military units now organized or to be organized for such service" (Lee 1966, 69).

Nevertheless, Logan continued to demand that "Negro citizens be given equal opportunity to participate in the National-Defense Program, civil as well as military; to be trained for work in national-defense industries and to serve in the naval and military services of this country in proportion to their numerical strength in the whole population" (Nalty and MacGregor 1977, 136).

On September 16, 1940, President Roosevelt signed the Selective Service Act into law. The committee was pleased because the act included a nondiscrimination clause. The War Department also indicated that the army was planning to create additional all-black units and increase the number of African Americans in the military to equal their proportion in the population.

Although the committee had achieved its goal of increasing the number of African Americans in the military, it was disappointed when the War Department issued a statement a month after the Selective Service Act became law. The statement of October 9, 1940, insisted that "the policy of the War Department is not to intermingle colored and white enlisted personnel in the same regimental organizations." Shortly after the release of the War Department's policy statement, the committee ceased much of its activities, and its members joined forces with the NAACP; William H. Hastie, the civilian aide to the secretary of war; the black press; and other black and white national organizations in an all-out assault on segregation in the armed forces. It was, however, not until after the war that President Harry S. Truman abolished segregation in the armed services when he signed Executive Order 9981 on July 26, 1948.

**FURTHER READINGS**

Buni, Andrew. *Robert L. Vann of the Pittsburgh Courier: Politics and Black Journalism*. Pittsburgh: University of Pittsburgh Press, 1974.

Finkle, Lee. *Forum for Protest: The Black Press During World War II*. Cranbury, N.J.: Associated University Presses, 1975.

Lee, Ulysses. *United States Army in World War II: Special Studies: The Employment of Negro Troops*. Washington, D.C.:, 1966.

Nalty, Bernard C., and Morris J. MacGregor, eds. *Blacks in the United States Armed Forces: Basic Documents*. Vol. 4. Wilmington: Scholarly Resources, 1977.

Osur, Alan M. *Blacks in the Army Air Forces During World War II: The Problem of Race Relations*. Washington, D.C.: GPO, 1977.

Wynn, Neil A. *The Afro-American and the Second World War*. New York: Holmes and Meier, 1993.

*Phillip McGuire*

**SEE ALSO** Committee Against Jim Crow in Military Service and Training; President's Committee on Equality of Treatment and Opportunity in the Armed Forces (The Fahy Committee); President's Committee on Equal Opportunity in the Armed Forces (The Gesell Committee)

## Committee for Welfare, Education, and Legal Defense

Philanthropist Stephen R. Currier established the Committee for Welfare, Education, and Legal Defense, also known as WELD, in the summer of 1963. Headquartered in New York City, the nonprofit WELD coordinated fund-raising efforts for various tax-exempt civil rights groups, including the National Urban League, the Legal Defense and Education Fund of the National Association for the Advancement of Colored People (NAACP), and the National Council for Negro Women.

In June 1963, Currier met with white executives of several corporations and foundations to discuss the financial needs of the civil rights movement and persuaded them to pledge more than $500,000. The single largest amount of the money came from the Taconic Foundation, which Currier and his wife, Audrey Bruce Currier, had founded in 1958 to assist disadvantaged people. The money was used to support WELD and the Council for United Civil Rights Leadership (CUCRL), which coordinated funds for the NAACP, the Southern Christian Leadership Conference (SCLC), the Student Nonviolent Coordinating Committee (SNCC), and the Congress of Racial Equality (CORE). Civil rights leaders who participated in joint WELD-CUCRL meetings included Whitney M. Young of the Urban League, Roy Wilkins of the NAACP, and James Forman of SNCC, who allocated the funds among the various civil rights groups. In addition, the Reverend Martin Luther King Jr. donated the royalties from his "I Have a Dream" record to WELD in the mid-1960s.

Between 1963 and 1967, WELD received approximately $200,000 of the pledged money, half of which came from the Field Foundation, which supported child-welfare causes. Both WELD and CUCRL became defunct before the end of 1967 as a result of tensions within the civil rights movement. More important, though, WELD lost its leadership due to the disappearance of Stephen and Audrey Bruce Currier, whose plane was lost at sea in January 1967.

While WELD was in existence, it helped sustain the activities of many civil rights groups and provided a forum for meetings between the civil rights community and politicians, such as President Lyndon B. Johnson and Vice President Hubert Humphrey.

**FURTHER READINGS**

Blumberg, Rhoda Lois. *Civil Rights: The 1960s Freedom Struggle*. Boston: Twayne, 1991.

Brauer, Carl M. *John F. Kennedy and the Second Reconstruction*. New York: Columbia University Press, 1977.

Cleghorn, Reese. "The Angels Are White: Who Pays the Bills for Civil Rights?" *New Republic* (August 17, 1963), 12–14.

Greenberg, Jack. *Crusaders in the Courts: How a Dedicated Band of Lawyers Fought for the Civil Rights Revolution*. New York: Basic Books, 1994.

Weiss, Nancy J. "Creative Tensions in the Leadership of the Civil Rights Movement." In *The Civil Rights Movement in America*. Ed. Charles W. Eagles. Jackson: University Press of Mississippi, 1986, 39–55.

*Robin B. Balthrope*

**SEE ALSO** Council for United Civil Rights Leadership

## Committee on After-the-War Cooperation

*See* Commission on Interracial Cooperation.

## Committee on Negro Housing

In 1928, President Herbert Hoover created the Committee on Negro Housing (CNH) to advise his Conference on Home Building and Home Ownership on the housing needs of the African American community.

The CNH was the product of the Great Migration that brought millions of African Americans from the rural South to the urban North during and after World War I. African Americans migrated in large numbers to cities in the North in the hope of finding employment and less racially oppressive living conditions. One of the most daunting problems facing many of the black migrants and African Americans already living in urban areas was the shortage of adequate housing. African Americans, regardless of their economic status, were forced to live in segregated neighborhoods by restrictive covenants and discriminatory real-estate agents and mortgage companies. The boom in black migration, the resulting housing shortage, and the racially volatile conditions created by the black population influx prompted the federal government to establish the President's Conference on Home Building and Home Ownership and the CNH.

Nannie Helen Burroughs, a charismatic leader and skilled orator, served as the CNH's chair. Burroughs, who had played a pivotal role in the women's movement in the Black Baptist Church, was also a member of the National Association of Colored Women and the National Association for the Advancement of Colored People (NAACP). Chosen to serve on the fact-finding committee were Charles S. Johnson, a renowned writer and sociologist of Fisk University; the architect Moses McKissick of Nashville; and the clubwoman and political activist Daisy Lampkin of Pittsburgh. Johnson, a leading member of the National Urban League, understood the unique needs of urban blacks and called the government's attention to the interrelated nature of education, unemployment, discrimination, segregation, and housing shortages. Johnson routinely voiced his views in *Opportunity*, the official organ of the National Urban League.

After four years of research, the CNH organized and analyzed its data and published its findings in *Negro Housing: Report of the Committee on Negro Housing* (1932). The report called for the construction of low-income housing, the elimination of restrictive covenants, and an end to discriminatory actions on the part of real-estate agents and private lenders. Though the work of the committee was extensive and prescriptive, the body had no enforcement powers, and, consequently, its recommendations fell upon deaf ears.

FURTHER READINGS

Higginbotham, Evelyn Brooks. "Burroughs, Nannie Helen (1879–1961)." In *Black Women in America: An Historical Encyclopedia*. Ed. Darlene Clark Hine, Elsa Barkley Brown, and Rosalyn Terborg-Penn. Bloomington: University of Indiana Press, 1993, 201–205.

Lisio, Donald J. *Hoover, Blacks, and Lily-Whites: A Study of Southern Strategies*. Chapel Hill: University of North Carolina Press, 1985.

Nannie Helen Burroughs Papers. Library of Congress, Washington, D.C.

President's Conference on Home Building and Home Ownership. *Negro Housing: Report of the Committee on Negro Housing*. Ed. Charles S. Johnson, John M. Gries, and James Ford. Washington, D.C.: President's Conference on Home Building and Home Ownership, 1932.

*Matthew C. Whitaker*

## Committee on Negro Troop Policies

On August 27, 1942, the United States War Department created the Committee on Negro Troop Policies (CNTP) to formulate racial policies for the segregated armed forces and to issue information on race relations to white officers commanding black troops. Assistant Secretary of War John J. McCloy chaired the committee of seven, which was appointed by the War Department. With the exception of Benjamin O. Davis Sr., the highest-ranking African American officer during World War II, the committee was composed of white officers from the United States Army's General Staff.

Notably absent from the CNTP was William H. Hastie, former dean of Howard University's law school and black civilian aide to the secretary of war. Apparently, Hastie was passed over because he had criticized military segregation. McCloy disapproved of Hastie's campaign to end segregation in the armed forces, fearing it would undermine homefront unity. Frustrated with his omission from the CNTP and the military's intransigence on racial matters, Hastie resigned from the War Department in January 1943. He was succeeded by his former assistant, Truman K. Gibson, who became acting civilian aide. Gibson apparently had better rapport with McCloy than Hastie; however, like his predecessor, he was also not asked to join the CNTP.

Throughout the war, the CNTP sought to increase combat opportunities for black soldiers, provide equitable housing and transportation for African American troops, and eliminate racial designations of military facilities in an attempt to ease racial tensions. The War Department initially ignored the committee's proposals until widespread racial violence erupted on the homefront in the summer of 1943. Fearing a detrimental effect on the morale of black troops as well as military efficiency, Secretary of War Henry L. Stimson agreed to mobilize the all-black Ninety-Third and Ninety-Second combat divisions in March 1944.

In addition to increasing combat opportunities for African American troops, the CNTP helped publicize black contributions to the war effort through the release of the propaganda film *The Negro Soldier* (1944). The CNTP also produced *Leadership and the Negro Soldier* (1944), a pamphlet for use by white officers commanding black troops, in cooperation with the army's research branch, and it published the navy's *Guide to Command of Negro Personnel* (1944). Both publications urged white officers to maximize their use of black soldiers in order to meet military manpower needs.

While the war was still raging, the CNTP also started to discuss the role of blacks in the postwar army. As early as February 1944, McCloy suggested the preparation of a study documenting the performance of black troops in World War II. Gibson welcomed McCloy's recommendation and, in July 1944, suggested that the army General Staff also initiate a study, detailing plans for the postwar use of African American soldiers. The CNTP supported Gibson's suggestion and, in May 1945, adopted a resolution requesting the U.S. armed forces to conduct the study. Following the war, as military personnel demobilized, the CNTP was disbanded; the Gillem Board assumed its responsibilities in October 1945.

While the CNTP did not challenge military segregation, it was instrumental in increasing combat opportunities for black soldiers, publicizing the contributions of African American troops to the war effort, and laying the foundations for the postwar work of the Gillem Board, which resulted in the desegregation of the armed forces in 1948.

**FURTHER READINGS**

Dalfiume, Richard M. *Desegregation of the U.S. Armed Forces: Fighting on Two Fronts, 1939–1953.* Columbia: University of Missouri Press, 1969.

Lee, Ulysses. *The United States Army in World War II: Special Studies: The Employment of Negro Troops.* Washington, D.C.: Office of Chief of Military History, 1966.

MacGregor, Morris J. *Defense Studies: Integration of the Armed Forces.* Washington, D.C.: Center of Military History, 1981.

McGuire, Phillip. *He, Too, Spoke for Democracy: Judge Hastie, World War II, and the Black Soldier.* New York: Greenwood, 1988.

Nalty, Bernard C. *Strength for the Fight: A History of Black Americans in the Military.* New York: Free Press, 1986.

*David MacLaren*

**SEE ALSO**    Committee Against Jim Crow in Military Service and Training

## Committee on Race and Caste in World Affairs

Originally known as the American Information Committee on Race and Caste, the Committee on Race and Caste in World Affairs (CORAC) was organized in 1957. Among its founding and most influential members were Horace Mann Bond, a well-known black educator and president of Pennsylvania's Lincoln University from 1945 to 1957, and John A. Davis, a black political scientist and civil rights activist. Davis, after receiving a Ph.D. from Columbia University, joined the political science faculty at Lincoln University and later taught at Brooklyn College. During World War II, Davis worked for President Franklin D. Roosevelt's wartime Fair Employment Practice Committee (FEPC), the most controversial civil rights agency of its time. During the 1950s, both Bond and Davis shared an interest in the development of the new post-colonial African states. CORAC was one of their organizational instruments to support their anti-Communist and pro-democracy activities in Africa.

CORAC's main purpose was to fund and publicly support the American Society for African Culture (AMSAC), which Bond and Davis had helped establish in 1956. AMSAC, which began as an affiliate of the Society for African Culture, sought "to defend the great cultural contributions of man against the perversions of political, economic, and national movements" (Urban 1992, 162). The founders of AMSAC were particularly troubled by the threat that Communism posed to African cultures. Because of AMSAC's overt anti-Communist bent and its all-black organizational structure, several black intellectuals, including John Hope Franklin and W. E. B. Du Bois, shunned the organization. To garner public support, AMSAC tried to appear politically neutral and relied on CORAC to issue pro-American and pro-democracy statements and to seek funding.

CORAC received its operating budget from the United States Central Intelligence Agency (CIA), which hoped to use the organization to counter the activities of the Council for African Affairs (CAA), a group run by Du Bois and other Left-leaning blacks such as Paul Robeson. Bond always defended AMSAC and, by extension, CORAC against charges of imperialism, and it is not clear that he knew of the financial ties among the CIA, CORAC, and AMSAC. As Bond's biographer has written: "the record cannot definitively answer that question, yet there is ample evidence for concluding that, if he did not know, he did not want to know" (Urban 1992, 164).

In addition to maintaining AMSAC, CORAC promoted and supported Bond. It provided him with money to travel to Africa to present lectures, visit with government and educational officials, and pursue his own economic interests, as well as those of U.S. corporations such as Republic Steel and Firestone. To be fair, as Bond's biographer points out, Bond also wanted his trips to enhance the image of Africa in the minds of black Americans. Nevertheless, as scholars eventually turn their attention to CORAC, they will no doubt place more weight on the organization's materialistic and political goals than its intellectual ones.

**FURTHER READINGS**

Horace Mann Bond Papers. University of Massachusetts, Amherst, Massachusetts.

Lynch, Hollis R. *Black American Radicals and the Liberation of Africa: The Council on African Affairs, 1937–1955.* Ithaca: Cornell University Press, 1978.

Marable, Manning. *W.E.B. Du Bois: Black Radical Democrat.* Boston: Twayne, 1988.

Urban, Wayne J. *Black Scholar: Horace Mann Bond, 1904–1972.* Athens: University of Georgia Press, 1992.

*Andrew E. Kersten*

# Community Fellows for Public School Change

*See* Southern Regional Council.

# Community Organization for Urban Politics

*See* Southern Organization for United Leadership.

# Community Relations Service

The Community Relations Service (CRS) was established by Title X of the Civil Rights Act of 1964. Its original mission was to find peaceful resolutions to disputes based on color and to identify means to avoid mass demonstrations and riots. As envisioned by President Lyndon B. Johnson and Attorney General Robert Kennedy, the CRS was to serve as a mediator.

Roger Wilkins was the CRS director from its inception in 1964 until 1969, when Benjamin Holman succeeded him. Holman served as the organization's second director until 1976. Originally part of the Commerce Department, the CRS became part of the Justice Department in 1966. The CRS hired specialists in justice, education, community development, and human relations. Originally the CRS focused on the South but quickly had to deal with urban areas outside that region when riots erupted in the Watts ghetto of Los Angeles in 1965 and in Newark, Detroit, Cleveland, and other American cities in 1967. Hoping to prevent racial conflicts, the CRS moved from crisis resolution to seeking long-term solutions for the underlying causes of racial strife. Thus its mission expanded and it sought to ameliorate urban poverty, improve poor neighborhoods, and encourage black employment.

After 1974, the CRS's mission changed drastically. The Nixon administration out the office's budget by two-thirds and forced a restructuring of its mission. With the waning of civil rights protests and ghetto riots, the CRS worked increasingly with local communities to ensure a fair division of funds from federal programs. Its mission then became an effort to ease the process of integration in the nation's schools. To this end, the Nixon administration sought for the office to become a liaison among local communities, the attorney general's office, the Civil Rights Division of the Justice Department, and the Office of Civil Rights in the Health, Education, and Welfare Department.

Perhaps the CRS's greatest successes came with the Supreme Court's *Swann v. Charlotte-Mecklenburg Board of Education* (1971) ruling that endorsed busing to improvement desegregation in public schools. In the school year 1970–1971, the CRS was involved in 268 communities to ensure the peaceful integration of schools. Particularly in the South, the CRS frequently served as a third-party observer during school desegregation efforts. Throughout the desegregation process, the CRS focused on mediation and conciliation to ease tensions and to secure binding agreements. Moreover, it offered technical assistance to local governments and businesses coping with desegregation and provided them with training and materials. Throughout its existence, however, the CRS was limited by a lack of authority because it had no enforcement power and could not initiate litigation. Its ability to provide assistance further waned after the 1974 budget cut.

The CRS not only served the interests of African Americans but also assisted other population groups. Native Americans worked through the CRS to negotiate land claims and to address other concerns. The growing Hispanic American communities also required its services, as did prison administrators who used it to resolve racial disputes and prevent litigation. Law enforcement agencies asked for help to quell tensions in minority communities, businesses sought guidance to avert workplace disputes, and government officials at all levels used CRS training materials and programs to prevent disruptions. In the 1980s the CRS helped refugees from Cuba, Haiti, and Asia to resettle and locate jobs in the United States.

**FURTHER READINGS**

Community Relations Service. *Examples of Community Relations Service Aid to Communities.* Washington, D.C.: Government Printing Office, 1977.

———. *A National Review.* Washington, D.C.: Government Printing Office, 1978.

———. *A Synopsis: Community Relations Service.* Washington, D.C.: Government Printing Office, 1978.

*Bryan Bartlett Jarmusch*

## Conference of Church Workers Among Colored People, Episcopal Church

The Conference of Church Workers among Colored People was the primary caucus of African Americans in the Episcopal Church from the late nineteenth into the twentieth century. Organized in 1883 by the Reverend Father Alexander Crummell, rector of St. Luke's Church of Washington, D.C., the conference dedicated itself to work for justice for African Americans in the Episcopal Church and the larger society. Initially called the Convocation of Colored Clergy, the association changed its name when, under pressure, it began to admit black laity and, even more controversial, white clergy serving black congregations. Yet, the organization managed to remain at the forefront of issues of racial justice in its denomination, and it maintains a strong commitment to the evangelization and social uplift of the race. Indeed, Anna Julia Cooper, a member of St. Luke's Church, made her signal speech, "Womanhood: A Vital Element in the Regeneration and Progress of a Race" (in which she uttered the oft-quoted "When and where I enter, then and there the whole Negro race enters with me"), at the 1886 gathering of the conference. George Freeman Bragg of St. James Church, Baltimore, served the conference as general sec-

retary during most of the early twentieth century, publishing the *Church Advocate* as the primary voice of black Episcopalians. There, Bragg issued a regular call for black self-determination, reasoning that the passivity of too many black Episcopalians was rooted in the financial dependency of their congregations on white denominational benevolence. Under the leadership of Thomas Logan, the conference began significant discussion concerning its mission in light of the emerging civil rights movement. Also, historic divisions between nationalist and integrationist sentiments arose. Finally, in 1968, self-determination forces formed the Union of Black Clergy and Laity (later the Union of Black Episcopalians) while more moderate persons joined with the Episcopal Society for Cultural and Racial Unity.

**FURTHER READINGS**

Bragg, George Freeman. *The History of the Afro-American Group of the Protestant Episcopal Church.* Baltimore: Church Advocate Press, 1922.

Burgess, John, ed. *Black Gospel/White Church.* New York: Seabury, 1982.

Lewis, Harold. *Yet with a Steady Beat: The African American Struggle for Recognition in the Episcopal Church.* Valley Forge: Trinity Press International, 1996.

*Harold Dean Trulear*

## Conference of Presidents of Negro Land-Grant Colleges

The Conference of Presidents of Negro Land-Grant Colleges (CPNLGC) was established in 1923 for administrators of historically black land-grant colleges. The second Morrill Act, passed by the United States Congress in 1890, allocated funds for African American land-grant colleges and provided for a division of monies between white and black land-grant institutions. Initially, seventeen states, primarily in the South, had colleges that received the 1890 designation. Prior to organizing, African American land-grant-college presidents met informally, often simultaneously with conferences of white college officials where they were sometimes invited to attend sessions.

At the Southern Conference on Education in Negro Land-Grant Colleges held at Tuskegee Institute in Alabama on January 15–16, 1923, the CPNLGC was created as a means to address and resolve mutual problems unique to black colleges, such as racial barriers to scholarship and jobs. The group's purpose was also to act as an intermediary with the federal government and to improve education and employment opportunities for African Americans. Members included presidents of black land-grant colleges, as well as federal officials who represented governmental departments that oversaw land-grant policies and activities. The presidents and administrators of non-land-grant black colleges, including Tuskegee Institute, were welcomed as associate members.

The CPNLGC's first slate of officers included President John N. Gandy of Virginia Normal and Industrial Institute, Vice President Nathan B. Young of Florida Agricultural and Mechanical College for Negroes, and Executive Committee members John W. Davis, J. B. Dudley, and Thomas H. Kish. Selected at the organizational meeting in Hampton, Virginia, these leaders asked their colleagues for suggestions for cooperative educational planning. The organization initially was informal, with no constitution or bylaws, and was considered a means to exchange ideas and information about academic and administrative issues specific to black colleges.

During the first week of March 1924, the members met at Hampton Institute, where they formally named the organization the CPNLGC. They agreed to seek cooperation from white land-grant colleges, hoping to meet at the same time as the Association of Land-Grant Colleges. Among some of their early decisions was the resolution of administrators not to hire teachers under contract with other land-grant schools. The members also initiated a survey to assess the achievements and needs of black land-grant colleges. By 1926, the survey's findings were available for discussion. The survey revealed that the black land-grant colleges experienced similar concerns, such as limited access to governmental services traditionally granted to white land-grant schools.

The CPNLGC decided to tell the federal government's Office of Education and Department of Agriculture about the needs of black land-grant institutions and to demand an equitable distribution of land-grant funds to eligible schools based on enrollment, not race. Members agreed to convince each state's governor and education board of the value of their colleges. They advised administrators to keep careful records of college operations and budgets, to seek qualified employees, and to visit other colleges and view successful programs in an attempt to improve their schools. The conference also sought support for government-funded faculty experimental work to advance individuals and schools, seeking the cooperation of extension-service administrators.

During the 1930s, the organization focused on Depression employment, securing the first cooperative contracts with the Tennessee Valley Authority for black workers. Members also discussed their concerns for enhancing communities near their colleges by educating citizens. Guest speakers included secretaries of agriculture and notable African American leaders such as W. E. B. Du Bois, who endorsed the organization's social-studies projects in which faculty members collected, analyzed, and published data about the role of African Americans in their college's state. The conference identified vocational and military training opportunities, supporting World War II technical projects as sources for engineering education for postwar employment. Members sought equal opportunities for veterans enrolling in college, and the organization encouraged black students to apply to white graduate schools, promoting their social acceptance in integrated education and employment. Educator Clyde L. Orr considered the successful acceptance of black students in southern graduate schools to be the group's greatest accomplishment.

In 1933, Isaac Fisher wrote a ten-year history of the association. The group distributed bound copies of the *Proceedings of the Annual Conference of the Presidents of Negro Land-Grant Colleges*, which included minutes from 1923 to 1954, to each college's library. United States Supreme Court decisions in the mid-1950s held that the segregation of public schools was unconstitutional, and black land-grant schools continued operating as integrated institutions. The CPNLGC ceased on December 31, 1955, when it merged with the Association of Land-Grant Colleges and State Universities. In 1955, many of the conference's projects were transferred to its successor organization, the Council on Cooperative College Projects, which was renamed the Council of 1890 College Presidents in 1979.

**FURTHER READINGS**

Atwood, Rufus B. "The Future of the Negro Land-Grant College." *Journal of Negro Education* 19 (Summer 1958), 81–91.

Fisher, Isaac, ed. *Proceedings of the Annual Conferences of the Presidents of Negro Land-Grant Colleges, 1932–33, 1935–38: Including Ten-Year History, 1923–33.* Published by the Office of the Secretary. Frankfort: Kentucky State College, 1938.

Humphries, Frederick S. "1890 Land-Grant Institutions: The Struggle for Survival and Equality." *Agricultural History* 65 (Spring 1991), 3–11.

Orr, Clyde L. "An Analytical Study of the Conference of Presidents of Negro Land-Grant Colleges." Ed.D. diss., University of Kentucky, 1959.

*Proceedings of the Annual Conferences of the Presidents of*

*Negro Land-Grant Colleges.* Published by the Office of the Secretary. Frankfort: Kentucky State College, 1923–1954.

*Elizabeth D. Schafer*

SEE ALSO    Council of 1890 College Presidents

## Conference on Education and Race Relations

*See* Commission on Interracial Cooperation.

## Congress of Industrial Organizations

*See* CIO Committee to Abolish Racial Discrimination.

## Congress of Racial Equality

The Congress of Racial Equality (CORE) emerged during World War II as a nonviolent direct-action group that challenged racial injustices. CORE played an influential role in the nonviolent civil rights movement of the 1960s and became a focal point for black nationalism and separatism after 1968.

An interracial band of Gandhians composed of five men and one woman joined forces in Chicago in 1941 and in June 1942 adopted the name Committee of Racial Equality. The following year a loose federation of similar committees throughout the country took the name Congress of Racial Equality. From the 1940s to the 1960s, CORE evolved from an interracial group that advocated nonviolent protest against segregation and discrimination to a racially exclusive organization that proclaimed black separatism. Changes in leadership accompanied changes in strategy and philosophy. George Houser served as executive secretary from 1945 until 1954. In September 1957, when James Robinson assumed the executive position, CORE chapters and programs still centered on Gandhian tactics but were not always interracial. James Farmer replaced Robinson in February 1961, assuming the title of national director. Five years later, members elected nationalist Floyd McKissick as leader. His successor in 1968, Roy Innis, declared that CORE was a black nationalist organization "once and for all" (Meier and Rudwick 1975, 424).

All but one founder of CORE were students at the University of Chicago and members of a race-relations "cell" of the New York-based pacifist Fellowship of Reconciliation (FOR). Two of the founders, Joe Guinn and James Farmer, were African American, and the remaining four—Bernice Fisher, Homer Jack, James R. Robinson, and George Houser—were white. Houser and Farmer were employed by FOR. Accounts of early FOR-CORE connections are ambiguous. Farmer had submitted a proposal for a "Brotherhood Mobilization" to FOR's national director, A. J. Muste. According to Farmer's autobiography, the FOR national council authorized him "to start an organization along the lines he envisioned in one city, in Chicago" (Farmer 1985, 103). The Chicago cell thus was "authorized," but not "sponsored," by the FOR. George Houser insisted that "CORE was never a pilot project within FOR" (George Houser, letter to the editor, *Fellowship Magazine*, May/June 1996, p. 19). Historians August Meier and Elliott Rudwick concluded that "Farmer's memorandum and the cell's activities were parallel and converging, rather than causally related" (Meier and Rudwick 1975, 7). Throughout Houser's directorship, FOR subsidized CORE, permitting him, Farmer, and another FOR field secretary, Bayard Rustin, to spend considerable time on CORE projects. FOR also co-sponsored and helped fund CORE programs.

The early CORE used nonviolent techniques to challenge racial injustices. Following steps outlined by Indian nationalist leader Mohandes Gandhi (1869–1948), CORE groups, including chapters in Los Angeles, Denver, Detroit, Cleveland, St. Louis, Baltimore, Syracuse, and State College, Pennsylvania, conducted forays against discrimination in housing, public accommodations, and employment. Two major projects undertaken by national CORE were the 1947 Journey of Reconciliation and summer workshops that began in Chicago in 1945.

The Journey of Reconciliation sent eight black and eight white men on a bus trip through the Upper South. At least one woman, Juanita Nelson, had volunteered for the journey, but the wisdom of the time, that dangerous missions were inappropriate for women, prevailed. The purpose of the trip was to test implementation of the United States Supreme Court ruling in *Morgan v. Virginia* (1946) that segregation on interstate buses was unconstitutional. Traveling through Virginia, North Carolina, and Kentucky, the men experienced arrests and brief jailings and encountered situations that threatened their physical safety. These incidents, however, received only moderate media attention. Of most consequence were the arrests of four riders in a mill town outside Chapel Hill, North Carolina. The Chapel Hill Recorder's Court, oblivious to the federal ruling, found them guilty of violating state law. That judgment was upheld by an appeals

Members of a CORE-sponsored "Freedom Riders" group sit outside the gutted hulk of their Greyhound bus after it was burned by a mob of whites. Anniston, Alabama, May 14, 1961. *Library of Congress*

court and by the state's Supreme Court, leaving the four sentenced to thirty days on a chain gang. One defendant paid a fine while the others served twenty-two days before they were released with time reduced for good behavior. The Journey of Reconciliation team, disappointed that lawyers from the National Association for the Advancement of Colored People (NAACP) declined to carry their cases to the Supreme Court, had let the word go forth that "you don't have to ride Jim Crow," the title of a song Bayard Rustin wrote during their trip. In response, CORE pioneered a direct-action strategy that would have much greater impact fourteen years later.

Between 1945 and 1954, CORE also sponsored summer workshops, all but two conducted in Washington, D.C. Workshop recruits studied nonviolent action by seeking, with some successes, to integrate restaurants, playgrounds, theaters, and other public places. By 1954,

CORE was declining; it had no field staff and was beset by unresolved questions regarding structure. Between March 1955 and September 1957, it operated without a national director. When James Robinson assumed that position, he hired two field secretaries: James McCain, who was African American, and Gordon Carey, who was white. Moreover, Robinson encouraged new affiliates and prepared CORE for the high tide of civil rights activism that swept across the South in the 1960s.

Both secretaries became involved in the student sit-in movement, which began at the Woolworth lunch counter in Greensboro, North Carolina, on February 1, 1960. As the sit-ins spread to other cities, McCain and Carey provided guidance in nonviolent direct action and established new CORE chapters. In Tallahassee, Florida, CORE activists embellished nonviolent protest with a "jail-in" in March 1960. Five of the numerous students arrested, convicted, and fined for sitting in at the Tallahassee Woolworth refused to pay the fine, choosing to serve sixty-day sentences and inspiring a community boycott. CORE also led negotiations with the national corporate management of the five-and-dime stores, setting up picket lines in front of their northern stores and organizing boycotts when the corporation remained intransigent. By the spring of 1960, dime stores were desegregated in 140 cities, an accomplishment for which CORE could take substantial credit.

In 1961, three months after James Farmer succeeded James Robinson at the helm of CORE, the organization embarked on the Freedom Rides. Patterned after the Journey of Reconciliation, the Freedom Rides were a series of bus journeys into the Deep South that tested the Supreme Court's ruling in *Boynton v. Virginia* (1960) that segregation in bus and train terminals was unconstitutional. The fact that the Freedom Riders were interracial teams provoked vicious reprisals. When the original CORE riders were mobbed and beaten and one of their buses firebombed outside Anniston, Alabama, activists from the Student Nonviolent Coordinating Committee (SNCC) continued the ride into Mississippi. Freedom Riders descended on public travel terminals throughout the South, braving violence, filling jails, and pressuring the administration of Democratic President John F. Kennedy. In September 1961, the federal Interstate Commerce Commission issued an order that forced the Kennedy administration to implement the *Boynton* decision.

Following the Freedom Rides, CORE workers in the border states focused on desegregation of public transportation and accommodations, while those in the North centered their activities on public education, employment, and housing, and CORE chapters in the South concentrated on voter registration.

In Maryland in 1961–1962, the national CORE launched a project to desegregate all restaurants on Highway 40 between Washington, D.C., and New York City. The project was sparked by the arrest and fourteen-day jailing of Juanita and Wallace Nelson for protesting the refusal of a Highway 40 restaurant to serve them. The campaign mobilized several hundred college students to picket Baltimore restaurants and conduct a Route 40 Freedom Ride. The political objective was realized with passage of city and state public-accommodation laws in Maryland.

In 1962, in Illinois, New Jersey, and New York, CORE chapters organized boycotts against school systems that were avoiding integration. In 1963–1964, CORE chapters in the North and the Midwest entered coalitions with

other human rights groups and launched similar boycotts in Chicago, Boston, New York, Cincinnati, Kansas City, Cleveland, and Milwaukee. CORE activists also applied the boycott technique to employment issues, as in the case of the boycott of the Sealtest company in the New York area in 1962–1963. Sealtest capitulated by establishing a preferential-hiring agreement that presaged the concept of "affirmative action." As Gordon Carey explained: "We are approaching employers with the proposition that they have effectively excluded Negroes from their work force for a long time and that they now have a responsibility and obligation to make up for their past sins" (Meier and Rudwick 1975, 191–192). Several CORE chapters also pressured banks to hire African Americans. In St. Louis in 1963, demonstrators obstructed bank entrances and teller windows, went to jail en masse, and claimed credit when eighty-four African Americans were hired in white-collar positions. The following year, CORE chapters in California used similar tactics to gain 240 jobs for blacks with the Bank of America, while, through negotiation and picketing, Boston CORE won bank jobs for nearly two hundred African Americans.

CORE's housing initiatives included both opening middle-class housing to black home-buyers and empowering the residents of slum dwellings. In 1962, CORE demonstrators secured a measure of integration in a new housing development in Ann Arbor, Michigan. In 1963 and 1964, landlords and city hall representatives in New Haven, Connecticut; Boston; New York City; and Philadelphia found slum refuse dumped on their doorsteps as CORE organizers urged the victims of substandard dwellings to revolt. In New York City, CORE engineered a surge of rent strikes. According to some accounts, CORE's initiatives in community organizing in the urban North were absorbed, along with many CORE workers, by President Lyndon B. Johnson's War on Poverty in the mid-1960s.

Meanwhile, CORE chapters in South Carolina, Florida, and Louisiana helped hundreds of African Americans negotiate arcane and threatening registration practices to claim their rights as voters. In Mississippi, beginning in 1962, organizing around the vote took a different turn as CORE joined with SNCC and the NAACP in the Council of Federated Organizations (COFO) and helped mobilize support for the Mississippi Freedom Democratic Party (MFDP). The MFDP presented an alternative to the exclusionary regular Democratic Party. Holding "freedom votes" and affirming grassroots democracy in "freedom conventions," the MFDP geared up to unseat regular representatives at the 1964 Democratic National Convention in Atlantic City, New Jersey. Several weeks before the convention, COFO augmented its Mississippi organizing force with roughly one thousand northern, mostly white, volunteers. The murders by Ku Klux Klansmen of one African American and two white volunteers, the machinations of Lyndon Johnson by which the Atlantic City challenge was turned back, and the interorganizational and intra-CORE frictions all contributed to disillusionment after 1964.

With an exhausted staff, having lost faith in traditional political methods, and beginning to apprehend the limits of even the most courageous and well-planned direct action, CORE transformed. Resolutions passed at the 1965 national CORE convention repudiated nonviolence and limited the roles whites would be permitted to play. In 1967, the membership voted to remove the term "multiracial" from CORE's constitution, and, in the following year, the organization ceased to accept white members.

CORE chapters that valued local autonomy and espoused revolutionary violence walked out of the 1968 convention when Roy Innis, who was committed to centralized management and a program that emphasized separatism and economic development, succeeded Floyd McKissick as national director. The following year, *Ebony* reported that Innis faced "massive losses of membership and money" and was presiding over an organization that was "a shadow of its former self as a civil rights giant" (Poinsett 1969, 170). Nonetheless, as the end of the twentieth century approached, CORE was still operating, with a reported one hundred chapters. Innis was still its chief, having survived internal efforts to oust him, legal action for alleged misuse of CORE funds, including a lawsuit initiated by James Farmer and supported by Floyd McKissick, and media accusations of demagoguery. As Innis promoted leadership training, economic self-determination, and community control for African Americans, he evolved toward the right of the political spectrum. In 1996, the *New York Times* identified him as "one of the leading voices" among black conservatives, opposing such measures as school busing, affirmative action, and gun control (O'Connor 1996, 1). While critics regarded Innis's stance as a reversal of the founding principles and historical thrust of CORE, it was not inconsistent with his definition of black identity, which he explained in a 1969 interview with *Ebony*. "Brothers want you to declare yourself on one side or the other," Innis observed, adding emphatically: "I say to them, 'Look! I ain't no damn capitalist. I ain't no damn Marxist either . . .' I assume that black folks can devise their own style, their own philosophy . . . that . . . maximizes what we want to do" (Poinsett 169, p. 176).

**FURTHER READINGS**

Farmer, James. *Lay Bare the Heart: An Autobiography of the Civil Rights Movement.* New York: Arbor House, 1985.

Houser, George. *CORE: A Brief History.* New York: Fellowship Publications, 1949.

———. *Erasing the Color Line.* 3rd ed. New York: Fellowship Publications, 1951.

Meier, August, and Elliott Rudwick. *CORE: A Study in the Civil Rights Movement, 1942–1968.* Urbana: University of Illinois Press, 1975.

O'Connor, James V. "Roy Innis Defines Himself and Politics." *New York Times*, September 22, 1996, sec. 13WC, 1.

Poinsett, Alex. "Roy Innis: Nation-Builder." *Ebony* (October 1969), 170–176.

*You Don't Have to Ride Jim Crow.* Videocassette, Prod. Robin Washington. New Hampshire Public Television, 1996.

*Jo Ann O. Robinson*

## Congressional Black Caucus

The Congressional Black Caucus originated in 1971. That year, Michigan Congressman Charles C. Diggs Jr. organized fourteen black members of Congress into a loose confederation, known as the Democratic Select Committee. The goal of this group was to communicate the concerns of African Americans in Congress and their constituents to the Democratic leadership in the House of Representatives and thereby "promote the public welfare of . . . millions of neglected citizens." Diggs became the first chairman of the caucus, and Howard Robinson, an administrator who worked for the U.S. Embassy in Tokyo, served as the group's first executive director.

African Americans had entered Congress in the decades following the Civil War. In 1870, Hiram Rhoades Revels of Mississippi was elected to fill the unexpired term of Jefferson Davis, who had resigned to become president of the Confederate states. Revels, who served in the United States Senate for only thirteen months, was succeeded by Blanche Kelso Bruce of Mississippi, who served a full six-year term from 1875 to 1881. Ultimately, twenty-two African Americans served in Congress between 1870 and 1901, when George H. White of North Carolina left the

House of Representatives. It took more than a quarter-century before another African American sat in the Congress of the United States. In 1929, Oscar Stanton DePriest of Chicago was elected to the House of Representatives and served in that capacity until 1935. Between 1929 and 1970, with the exception of the leadership of a few black congressmen, notably William L. Dawson of Chicago and Adam Clayton Powell of New York City, African Americans had no organized congressional presence to represent their many-faceted interests.

In 1971, this lack of organization prompted Diggs to form the Congressional Black Caucus. The birth of the caucus was aided by a series of events that sparked a rising tide of militancy among African Americans during the late 1960s and the 1970s. Among these momentous events were the 1969 publication of James Forman's *Black Manifesto*, charges of military discrimination against African American soldiers, the December 1969 killings of two Black Panther leaders, and the May 1970 riot at Jackson State College in Mississippi that left two black students dead and twelve others wounded. These events frustrated and angered many African Americans, galvanized the black members of Congress, and hastened the formation of the caucus.

In the wake of these events, black congressmen approached Republican President Richard M. Nixon. In late 1970, Congressman Diggs formally requested that Nixon meet with the black congressmen. Two months later, the White House responded, not through the president but through a low-level staff member. For more than a year, Nixon refused to meet with the black congressmen. Incensed over the intransigence of the president, they decided to boycott the session at which Nixon was to give the State of the Union address. The boycott was successful. Senator Edward Brooke of Massachusetts was the lone black member present when the president gave his speech in January 1971.

Amid the unfavorable publicity following the boycott, Nixon finally agreed to meet with the Congressional Black Caucus on March 25, 1971. At this meeting, the caucus presented the president with sixty recommendations dealing with numerous concerns, including federal aid to minority businesses, home rule for the District of Columbia, an end to the Vietnam conflict, prevention of entry of drugs into the United States, grants instead of student loans for black college students, and justice for black soldiers. The May 18 response of the president was half-hearted and vague, and the members of the caucus

were left dissatisfied. On May 23, Congressmen Diggs and Augustus Hawkins of California appeared on national television to express the concerns of the caucus and to criticize Nixon's inadequate response.

Over the next two years, the relationship between Nixon and the caucus showed little improvement. On January 31, 1973, the Congressional Black Caucus presented a "True State of the Union" address before the House of Representatives. The address expressed the views of black congressmen on domestic issues such as poverty, welfare, health, reform, housing, education, civil rights, employment, revenue sharing, and the status of minorities in the military and the criminal justice system, as well as on America's foreign policy in Africa and other Third World countries. Vice President Spiro T. Agnew, responding for the White House, criticized the address. Agnew claimed that the American public was tired of the constant complaining of the caucus and informed the black congressmen that "more constructive action" was expected of them.

Nixon was not the only president who was aloof in his dealings with the Black Caucus. President Jimmy Carter often opposed the efforts of caucus members. Most notable was his opposition to the Full Employment and Balanced Growth Act, known as the Humphrey-Hawkins bill. Even though Carter signed the bill on October 27, 1978, he was lethargic in his support of it. Carter also opposed the efforts of black congressmen to designate Martin Luther King Jr.'s birthday as a legal holiday. Representative John Conyers of Michigan had first introduced such a bill in the United States House in 1968, and in 1971 he tried again while Senator Brooke did the same in the Senate. Both attempts failed.

Perhaps President Carter was not supportive of black congressmen because he was angered by events surrounding the Congressional Black Caucus Legislative Dinner of 1978. The turnout for the dinner was so overwhelming that two hotels in Washington, D.C., to be booked. The Washington Hilton was to be the main hotel, and the Shoreham was to be the backup site. Carter was scheduled to make his appearance at the Shoreham and was given fifteen minutes to address the audience. At first, he refused to speak at the Shoreham, demanding to address the guests at the main hotel. The caucus changed the arrangements and permitted Carter to speak at the Hilton; however, the fifteen-minute time limit was to remain the same. Carter ignored the time limit and spoke for one hour and fifteen minutes, thus throwing the entire schedule of the event out of kilter. Relations with

President Carter grew progressively worse after the dinner episode and reached their nadir in 1979. That year, Carter fired former caucus member Andrew Young as ambassador to the United Nations.

Relations with other presidents, particularly Republicans, were stressful, perhaps because almost all of the members of the Caucus served in the House of Representatives, which was often dominated by Democrats. Caucus members, for example, were opposed to President Ronald Reagan's concept of New Federalism, which they perceived as the states-rights concept in new garb and one that was inimical to the best interests of African Americans and other minorities. Reagan did meet with caucus members early in his first term, but eight years passed before the caucus was again invited to the White House by President George Bush. During this meeting on May 23, 1989, caucus members told Bush that, if he wanted to be known as the education president, he would have to stop the decline of inner cities.

One of the most visible activities of the Congressional Black Caucus is the annual dinner held during the Legislative Weekend in Washington, D.C. The first dinner, held in June 1971, attracted more than twenty-five hundred prominent political leaders and politically active citizens to the nation's capital. The popularity of the $100-a-plate dinner gala and the weekend has grown tremendously so that reservations must be made early to guarantee seating. In recent years, criticisms of the dinner have surfaced. Critics charge that the gala has degenerated into a social extravaganza characterized by frivolity. Nevertheless, proceeds from the dinner underwrite the costs of caucus activities. While the caucus does not have a staff, it provides funding for the Congressional Black Caucus Political Action Committee (PAC), which supports the political campaigns of caucus members, and the Congressional Black Caucus Foundation, which administers charitable funds received from individuals, corporations, and organizations.

For the development of policy and position papers, caucus leaders have relied on the support and resources of the Joint Center for Political Studies (renamed Joint Center for Political and Economic Studies in 1990), founded in 1970. Aided by a grant from the Ford Foundation, the operation of the Center involved an arrangement with Howard University and the Metropolitan Applied Research Corporation (MARC) of New York City, headed by Dr. Kenneth Clark. This tripartite partnership, which ceased in 1972, allowed Howard University and MARC to receive the funds and helped preserve the tax-exempt status of the caucus. The Joint Center became the clearinghouse to receive and disseminate information. It publishes a series of monographs on issues of concern to African Americans and also provides internships for political-science students.

In addition to the publications of the Joint Center for Political Studies, the caucus holds conferences on current issues. Between July 1971 and September 1972, the caucus sponsored seven national conferences and held three public hearings. The conferences dealt with such issues as racism in the military, the health of black Americans, careers for minorities in communication, racism in the media, education, black politics, and the legislative process. The conferences and hearings were conducted in various parts of the country to help caucus members determine a national agenda. Drawing on the conferences and hearings, caucus members opposed budget cuts to programs such as Aid to Families with Dependent Children and Small Business Administration funding, and they succeeded in restoring funding for minority educational institutions.

By the end of the first decade of its existence, the caucus had come of age. Not only had its membership increased, from fourteen to nineteen, but so had its influence. The caucus challenged the budget-slashing initiatives of Presidents Gerald Ford, Carter, Reagan, and Bush, and it waged constant warfare to save domestic programs from being gutted or eliminated.

Nevertheless, throughout the years, the caucus also has experienced difficulties due to internal dissensions and external attacks. Internal squabbles, for example, arose when the group discussed the purchase of a building as its permanent home. In 1983, the troublesome issue was finally resolved with the acquisition of a building on Pennsylvania Avenue. Other problems dividing the membership surfaced when U.S. Representative Shirley Chisholm declared her candidacy for president in 1972. Chisholm, a Democrat from New York City and a member of the Black Caucus, expected to receive the support of the caucus but instead was criticized for taking this unprecedented step for a black woman. During her campaign, Chisholm received hardly any support from the caucus, which she charged was due to male chauvinism. There were other occasions when sharp political differences caused some members to threaten resignation from the group. A particularly strange episode involved Representative Gary Franks of Connecticut, the first black Republican to serve in the House of Representatives since 1935. In 1993 caucus members denied Franks full membership because of his affiliation with the Republican

Party. Several caucus members accused Franks of having views that were not in the interest of African Americans, and, at one time, the group voted not to transact any business in his presence. After considerable wrangling, the move to oust Franks was reversed. In 1995, Franks became a member of the caucus, and, in the same year, a second black Republican, J. C. Watts of Oklahoma, joined him.

In addition to internal dissensions, the caucus was weakened by external assaults. Some caucus members became targets of criminal investigations and alleged activities such as wiretapping and office burglaries. In more than one instance, alleged criminal charges proved to be without foundation and were subsequently withdrawn. In addition, the caucus suffered a severe setback when it lost two of its most influential members to death: Congressmen George Collins (Dem.) of Illinois and Mickey Leland (Dem.) of Texas both perished in fatal air tragedies.

Since its founding in 1971, the Congressional Black Caucus has had more than sixty members. For more than two decades, in spite of internecine battles, severe financial problems, harsh criticism, and attempts to tarnish its leadership, the caucus has succeeded in becoming a powerful political voice for African Americans. In recent years, female members of the caucus have played a prominent role. During the 105th Congress, twelve African American women, most of them representing majority white districts, joined the caucus. In 1997, U.S. Representative Maxine Waters, a Democrat from California, became chairperson of the caucus.

**FURTHER READINGS**

Bostic, David A. *The Congressional Black Caucus in the 103rd Congress, 1994.* Lanham, Md.: University Press, 1994.

Clay, William L. *Just Permanent Interests: Black Americans in Congress, 1871–1991.* New York: Amistad, 1992.

Gill, LaVerne M. *African American Women in Congress.* New Brunswick, N.J.: Rutgers University Press, 1997.

Ross-Barnett, Marguerite. "The Congressional Black Caucus: Ten Years Later." *Crisis* (April 1981), 116–131.

Singh, Robert. *The Congressional Black Caucus.* Thousand Oaks, Calif.: Sage, 1997.

*Joseph T. Durham*

# Connecticut Commission on Human Rights and Opportunities

The Connecticut Commission on Human Rights and Opportunities was begun in January 1944 in Hartford, Connecticut. First known as the Connecticut Inter-Racial Commission, the body was among the first civil rights enforcement agencies in the United States and served as a model for other agencies. The commission's first executive director was Dr. Frank T. Simpson, a black graduate of Alabama's Tougaloo College, who had moved to Connecticut in 1929. The commission's purpose is to fight against discrimination by enforcing existing civil and human rights laws, and to establish equal opportunity and justice for all residents of Connecticut through educational and community outreach activities. The commission maintains offices in Waterbury, Hartford, Norwich, and Bridgeport.

In the past, the commission has fought against discrimination in education, housing, labor unions, and employment. Today, the commission's main areas include combating discrimination in employment, housing, public accommodations, and credit transactions. The overwhelming majority of complaints, some 95 percent, involve unfair employment practices. Connecticut law forbids discrimination in eighteen areas, including race, gender, age, religion, marital status, sexual orientation, ancestry, national origin, learning disabilities, familial status, mental retardation and illness, and guide-dog access.

The commission's instructional and outreach programs include educating the public about civil and human rights; investigating complaints of discrimination against any targeted group; developing systemic enforcement strategies; monitoring the affirmative action plans of state agencies; and reviewing and monitoring contract compliance, especially the employment of minority business enterprises in state public works contracts.

The commission's statutory provisions are inclusive and provide clear definitions for various forms of discrimination. The commission interprets and enforces state law, provides counsel, appoints investigators, fixes compensation rates according to law, recommends policies, conducts hearings, and subpoenas witnesses. The commission holds yearly meetings with the governor to make recommendations and to monitor state contracts.

**FURTHER READINGS**

Connecticut Commission on Human Rights and Opportunities. *Human Rights and Opportunities: Statutory Provisions Enforced and Administered by the Connecticut Commission on Human Rights and Opportunities.* Hartford: Connecticut Commission on Human Rights and Opportunities, 1993.

*A. J. Scopino Jr.*

# Consolidated American Baptist Missionary Convention

The Consolidated American Baptist Missionary Convention (CABMC) served as one of the first national conventions of African American Baptists after the Civil War. In 1866, representatives from several small regionally based black Baptist groups met in Nashville to form the CABMC. During its existence from 1866 to 1879, it represented a significant attempt to centralize the various regional associations that free black Baptists had formed before the war, along with the associations created by the newly independent churches of the freedpeople. Several of the leading members of the new group came from the ranks of the abolitionist American Baptist Free Mission Society, a splinter group of the American Baptist Home Mission Society, the largest group of white northern Baptists.

Delegates to the CABMC stressed their readiness to manage missionary work among the freedpeople. Rufus Perry, an early CABMC leader, argued that white northern control of missionary funds fostered paternalism rather than independence. When Perry requested funds from white northern Baptists to be administered by blacks in the CABMC, the white northerners responded negatively. To Perry, this episode exemplified how whites deliberately steered the development of free black institutions away from self-reliance. The very existence of the CABMC, he argued, was "our proclamation to the world that we are able to do this work and that we ought to do it." The CABMC also took inspiration from the historic developments of Reconstruction, seeing in Radical Republicanism the hand of God leading the people out of slavery.

By 1870, the organization claimed thirteen affiliated associations and groups and supported a theological training school in Richmond, Virginia. A number of CABMC leaders were politically active, creating a division between those who insisted that the politics of Reconstruction in both religious and political life were necessarily connected, and those who warned that black Baptists who became "more or less contaminated with political corruption" would thereby be "inefficient and depreciated as ministers of the gospel." The CABMC also attracted more urban, northern, and Upper South churches than the burgeoning rank-and-file congregations of the South, where the numbers of black Baptists increased dramatically after the Civil War. CABMC men were early advocates of the gospel of respectable spirituality. They had received their religious training primarily from northern missionaries and distrusted the enthusiasm of the southern congregations, which they viewed as evidence of primitiveness and backwardness. Yet, it was the very energy of these congregations that sustained many African American believers during the difficult transition to freedom. The division between free black Baptists and the freedpeople thus translated into delicate situations and difficulties for early organizations such as the CABMC. The CABMC placed great faith in the Republican Party as the savior of embattled black people. As Reconstruction faltered, however, convention spokesmen blasted the party for betraying their faith. Convention minutes from the 1860s and 1870s speak eloquently to the impassioned political hopes, and then bitter disappointment, experienced by the faithful black Christians and Republicans in the CABMC.

The CABMC became increasingly dependent on northern funding for its survival, as it failed to cultivate a broad enough funding base to establish financial independence. But its northern bases of funding gradually declined. The original benefactor of the organization, the abolitionist American Baptist Free Mission Society, disbanded after the war. The schools run by the CABMC for the Freedmen's Bureau ended after the demise of the bureau in 1869. In the 1870s, white northern Baptists increasingly concentrated their monies in black higher education and moved away from funding direct missionary work among the freedpeople. This created another hole in funding salaries for CABMC workers. Unable to withstand this series of setbacks, the CABMC went into decline and disbanded in the late 1870s. The last year for which convention minutes are extant is 1879. The CABMC provided a model of national black Baptist unity that would later be used by the National Baptist Convention, and, during its existence, it provided a strong voice for the independent religious life of African Americans after the Civil War.

**FURTHER READINGS**

Fitts, Leroy. *A History of Black Baptists*. Nashville: Broadman, 1985.

Montgomery, William. *Under Their Own Vine and Fig Tree: The African-American Church in the South, 1865–1900*. Baton Rouge: Louisiana State University Press, 1992.

Washington, James Melvin. *Frustrated Fellowship: The Black Baptist Quest for Social Power*. Macon, Ga.: Mercer University Press, 1986.

*Paul Harvey*

## Coordinating Council for Negro Performers, Inc.

A group of black actors and laymen founded the Coordinating Council for Negro Performers, Inc., in 1952. Among the council's founders and early officers were Lester A. Walton, Dick Campbell, John D. Silvera, P. J. Sidney, Bessie Williams, Leroy Butler, the actress and theater executive Rosetta Olive Burton LeNoire, and Frederick O'Neill, who in 1964 became the first black performer to be elected to the presidency of Actors Equity.

The New York City–based council worked to increase employment opportunities for black actors and to improve the portrayal of African Americans on television. The council's aims were to establish contacts with television networks, especially for liaisons between the casting departments and black performers; to consult with producers on script material in an effort to integrate African Americans into television programs; and to join church affiliates and civil rights groups, such as the New York chapter of the National Association for the Advancement of Colored People (NAACP), which urged citizens to write television stations to protest the exclusion of black performers and to express their approval of realistic and fair representations of African Americans.

A 1953 survey conducted by the council found that black actors constituted less than 0.5 percent of the total number of performers shown on the four television networks in a single week. At the same time, there were between 350,000 and 400,000 black owners of television sets in the New York City area alone. The council criticized network executives for their refusal to consider black actors simply as actors rather than "black" actors. This, the council claimed, resulted in casting decisions that contributed to racial stereotyping. The council was short-lived; the dates and reasons for its demise are unknown.

### FURTHER READINGS

Dewsberry, Jonathan. "Black Actors Unite: The Negro Actors Guild of America." Ph.D. diss., New York University, 1988.

Hay, Samuel A. *African American Theatre: A Historical and Critical Analysis.* Cambridge: Cambridge University Press, 1992.

*Thomas Leuchtenmüller*

## Council for a Black Economic Agenda

Founded in 1984, the Council for a Black Economic Agenda was a neoconservative group whose goal was to advance the self-sufficiency of black Americans. To reverse the black community's dependence on government programs, the council advocated free-enterprise policies such as the establishment of enterprise zones, which would provide tax write-offs for investments in small businesses located in distressed areas, ownership and management of public housing by residents organizations, increases in income-tax credits and income-tax exemptions for dependents, and expansion of educational choices. The council also advocated the provision of affordable day care for children of working parents and the use of government payments, such as unemployment benefits, for education, self-employment, and training.

The council was a twenty-member group composed of scholars, business people, community leaders, and former members of the Reagan and Nixon administrations. The council's leader was Robert Woodson, also chairman of the National Center for Neighborhood Enterprise. The membership included Arthur Fletcher, an assistant secretary of labor in the Nixon administration, and Dr. Glenn Loury, then a professor at Harvard University.

The council attracted public attention when it became the first black group to meet with President Ronald Reagan on January 15, 1984. Leaders of other black organizations and members of the media criticized the meeting, arguing that it was "staged." Critics charged that the council had no affiliation with traditional black organizations, that Reagan had refused to meet with other African American organizations to discuss the administration's policy toward South Africa, and that the meeting was held the day before the release of the National Urban League's *State of Black America* report. The council's leadership denied any White House involvement in the group's formation. The Council for a Black Economic Agenda is now defunct.

### FURTHER READINGS

Alpern, David, and Diane Weather. "Report on Black America." *Newsweek* (January 28, 1984), 30.

Barnes, Fred. "Inventanegro, Inc." *New Republic* (April 1984), 9–10.

Boyd, Gerald. "President Meets with 20 Blacks; Intent Disputed." *New York Times*, January 16, 1984, 1 and D21.

"Council for a Black Economic Agenda." In *The African American Almanac.* Ed. Kenneth Estell. Detroit: Gale, 1994, 465–466.

Jones, Kenneth. "A 'New' Black Agenda." *Black Enterprise* (April 1985), 20.

*Oscar Flores*

## Council for Civic Unity, San Francisco

The Council for Civic Unity (CCU) was established in San Francisco in 1944 to "promote equality of right and opportunity free from racial or religious discrimination" and to "improve intergroup relations with special attention to the main sources of misunderstanding and injustice."

Like its predecessor, the Bay Area Council Against Discrimination, the CCU drew its interracial membership from throughout the Bay Area and included representatives from local civil rights, service, and labor organizations. During its twenty-five-year history, the CCU supported its varied activities with membership dues and grants from the Columbia, San Francisco, and Rosenberg Foundations. Between 1952 and 1958, the CCU aired a weekly radio program, *Dateline Freedom*, focusing on racial concerns. Its newsletter, the *Bay Area Reporter*, highlighted local civil rights initiatives and publicized cases of racial discrimination.

The CCU also spearheaded the fight to establish a permanent state Fair Employment Commission; joined with other civil rights groups to form the California Council for Civic Unity, a statewide federation of interracial organizations established in 1946; published a comprehensive *Civil Rights Inventory of San Francisco* in 1958; and lobbied local governments to integrate schools, enforce fair-housing laws, and adopt affirmative-hiring practices in the private and public sectors.

By the mid-1960s, the CCU shifted its focus to "providing office, clerical, and professional services for a marshaling of many non-governmental groups in unified action and planning for advancement of equal opportunity." In the early 1970s, following several years of declining membership, the CCU quietly faded from public view.

FURTHER READING

Broussard, Albert S. *Black San Francisco: The Struggle for Racial Equality in the West, 1900–1954.* Lawrence: University Press of Kansas, 1993.

*Gretchen Lemke-Santangelo*

## Council for United Civil Rights Leadership

Founded in 1963 in New York City, the Council for United Civil Rights Leadership (CUCRL) was an umbrella organization that sought to coordinate the fund-raising efforts of the country's major civil rights organizations and minimize disagreements over tactics in the struggle against segregation.

The CUCRL was formed at the behest of the philanthropic Taconic Foundation (New York City), which had already contributed more than $1 million to civil rights causes by August 1963. Press reports of rivalry among the National Association for the Advancement of Colored People (NAACP), Martin Luther King Jr.'s Southern Christian Leadership Council (SCLC), and the Student Nonviolent Coordinating Committee (SNCC) in the weeks prior to the 1963 March on Washington, D.C., sparked the Taconic Foundation's move. The groups accused one another of "headline grabbing" as they competed for financial support. The competition for funds and each group's claim of leadership of the civil rights movement threatened to drive a wedge among civil rights advocates. In response, Taconic Foundation President Stephen R. Currier suggested creation of the CUCRL to ensure unity of the movement. The CUCRL channeled funds into the NAACP's Legal Defense and Education Fund, the SCLC, SNCC, the Congress of Racial Equality (CORE), the National Urban League, and the Educational Foundation of the National Council of Negro Women.

On June 19, 1963, Currier, a friend of President John F. Kennedy's family, arranged a meeting of the leaders of the seven civil rights organizations and ninety-six corporate executives and foundation leaders in New York City. The meeting raised nearly $800,000, which was distributed among the seven civil rights groups. Established organizations such as the NAACP and the Urban League, which usually did not engage in public protests, received the bulk of the funds, while only $15,000 was distributed to the SNCC activists. The CUCRL tried to mute controversy over the disbursement of funds, but SNCC leaders soon chafed at what they saw as the organization's attempt to push a more conservative agenda on the entire civil rights movement.

Tactical disagreements continued to divide the civil rights movement in the mid-1960s. The NAACP continued to fight discrimination through laborious legal battles in the courts. King's SCLC preferred drawing middle-class support for quick, scattered demonstrations in carefully selected cities with the goal of winning maximum media attention for individual campaigns. King hoped that such media events would highlight to a national and international audience the moral difference between nonviolent civil rights protesters and the often violent proponents of segregation in the South. Meanwhile, SNCC sought to build permanent grassroots organizations among the poorest of African American communities. Rather than focus on short-term protest campaigns like those conducted by the SCLC, SNCC sought to register voters, mobilize black voter turnout, and open Freedom Schools. These schools promoted literacy among rural blacks and, by emphasizing black history and art, sought to enhance the self-esteem of students. SNCC also questioned the moral efficacy of King's nonviolent approach and began to advocate self-defense and black nationalism, which stressed independence from the patronage of white liberals in the civil rights movement. By 1965, the CUCRL could no longer conceal the deep philosophical disagreements among the various civil rights groups. SNCC leader James Forman later dismissed the group as a "jungle of civil rights hyenas, each distrustful of the other, each with personal grievances against the other" (Forman 1972, 366). After the eruption of racial violence in Chicago in 1964 and in the Watts neighborhood of Los Angeles in 1965, contributions to the CUCRL fell off sharply. With fewer funds to distribute, many civil rights activists felt that the CUCRL had outlived its purpose, and they "were no longer trying to maintain any facade of unity" (Forman 1972, 370). Shortly after the summer of 1966, the CUCRL disbanded.

In 1977, Vernon Jordan of the National Urban League attempted to create the CUCRL's successor when he launched the Black Leadership Forum (BLF), an informal group that was still active in the 1990s. Unlike the CUCRL, the BLF does not involve itself in distribution of donations, but, like its predecessor, it seeks to coordinate the tactics of the nation's civil rights organizations, such as the Urban League, the NAACP, and Reverend Jesse Jackson's Operation PUSH.

**FURTHER READINGS**

Forman, James. *The Making of Black Revolutionaries.* New York:, 1972.

Garrow, David J. *Bearing the Cross: Martin Luther King, Jr., and the Southern Christian Leadership Conference.* New York: Vintage Books, 1988.

Meier, August, and Elliott Rudwick. *CORE: A Study in the Civil Rights Movement, 1942–1968.* New York: Oxford University Press, 1973.

Pfeffer, Paula F. *A. Philip Randolph: Pioneer of the Civil Rights Movement.* Baton Rouge: Louisiana State University Press, 1990.

Weiss, Nancy J. *Whitney M. Young, Jr., and the Struggle for Civil Rights.* Princeton, N.J.: Princeton University Press, 1989.

*Michael Phillips*

**SEE ALSO**    Committee for Welfare, Education, and Legal Defense

# Council of 1890 College Presidents

The Council of 1890 College Presidents was an administrative educational organization. Founded in 1923 at Tuskegee Institute in Alabama as the Conference of Presidents of Negro Land-Grant Colleges, it was renamed the Council on Cooperative College Projects in 1955. By 1979, it was called the Council of 1890 College Presidents to reflect its historical origins and membership composition. The original Conference of Presidents of Negro Land-Grant Colleges was established for administrators of seventeen African American land-grant colleges funded through provisions of the second Morrill Act, passed by the United States Congress in 1890. Leaders of historically black campuses were also invited to attend. The organization provided college and government officials with a forum to discuss and resolve issues unique to black land-grant colleges, such as overcoming racial barriers, securing employment opportunities for graduates, and assisting black students to enter traditionally white graduate schools.

The Council of 1890 College Presidents continued this practice, enabling presidents and chancellors of land-grant colleges attended mainly by African American students to discuss academic concerns. In the 1990s, Dr. William B. DeLauder served as the group's chairman, and Dr. Ernest L. Holloway acted as secretary-treasurer; both men were affiliated with Langston University, a historically black land-grant college in Langston, Oklahoma, where the association's records are maintained in the university's archives. In 1995, Dr. Delores Spikes of Southern University and A&M College System in Baton Rouge, Louisiana, was chairman of the council. By 1998, leadership of the Council of 1890 College Presidents had returned to Langston University.

Seeking to improve education and employment opportunities for African Americans, the Council of 1890 College Presidents continued its predecessor's programs to assess and enhance college academics. The group also contemplated new issues, such as the role of historically black colleges, specifically the necessity to fund land-grant schools in southern states following the desegregation of education in 1954. The Council of 1890 College Presidents meets annually in November at the Association of Land-Grant Colleges and State Universities conference.

**FURTHER READINGS**

Bunkley, Crawford B. *The African American Network.* New York: Plume, 1996.

Humphries, Frederick S. "1890 Land-Grant Institutions: The Struggle for Survival and Equality." *Agricultural History* 65 (Spring 1991), 3–11.

Rasmussen, Wayne D. "The 1890 Land-Grant Colleges and Universities: A Centennial Overview." *Agricultural History* 65 (Spring 1991), 168–172.

*Elizabeth D. Schafer*

SEE ALSO   Conference of Presidents of Negro Land-Grant Colleges

## Council of Federated Organizations

Established in Jackson, Mississippi, in 1962 by Bob Moses of the Student Nonviolent Coordinating Committee (SNCC), Tom Gaither of the Congress of Racial Equality (CORE), and Aaron Henry of the National Association for the Advancement of Colored People (NAACP), the Council of Federated Organizations (COFO) was an umbrella agency that coordinated the activities of the numerous national civil rights organizations operating in Mississippi. The COFO was created to unite representatives from the various voter-registration projects in order to improve communication between civil rights activists and Mississippi's Governor Ross Barnett. In 1962, Aaron Henry, president of the state's NAACP, reorganized COFO to assist in coordinating the increasing number of Mississippi voter-registration and civil rights campaigns. By bringing together representatives from the NAACP, SNCC, CORE, and smaller local organizations, Henry and other community activists hoped to maximize the efficiency of the state's civil rights campaigns, as well as reassert local control over the direction and scope of the freedom struggle. Led by a cadre of COFO members, including the NAACP's Henry, Medgar Evers, and Amzie Moore; SNCC's Robert Moses and James Forman; and CORE's Dave Dennis and Tom Gaither, the organization soon began to operate its own voter-registration campaigns funded by the Southern Regional Council's Voter Education Project. Under the direction of COFO President Henry, Director Moses, and Assistant Director Dennis, the organization struggled to stretch its meager funds to support a statewide registration and education project, hoping that increased black voter registration might result in greater political and social freedom for black Mississippians.

Much like those in the earlier Mississippi voter-registration projects spearheaded by the Mississippi Progressive Voters League and the Regional Council of Negro Leadership, COFO members believed that the ballot box provided the key to social and political equality. Unlike earlier organizations, however, the COFO showed a willingness to search for other solutions when the ballot box appeared closed. Perhaps one of the most creative solutions that

COFO proposed was the 1963 mock election. That year, COFO activists, frustrated in their attempts to register large numbers of black voters and disgusted by the claims of local whites that blacks were not interested in voting, organized the Freedom Vote. They urged local blacks to fill out mock voter-registration forms in order to register for the upcoming Freedom Election. COFO activists hoped that their efforts would not only promote voter education and literacy training, but also demonstrate to white critics that Mississippi blacks were willing to vote if only given the opportunity. The highlight of the mock election was the campaign of Henry and white Tougaloo chaplain Ed King for governor and lieutenant governor. By the end of the summer, eighty-three thousand mostly black Mississippians cast ballots in this mock election. One reason for the remarkable voter turnout was the utilization of white volunteers from Stanford University. Although small in numbers, they attracted significant national media attention.

The success of the 1963 Freedom Election created the impetus for a much larger civil rights campaign in the following year. In 1964, COFO and SNCC collaborated to launch the Mississippi Freedom Summer Project, which incorporated a variety of political and social programs, as well as utilization of hundreds of white college volunteers. Some COFO members feared that the use of white volunteers would result in black passivity, deflect deserved attention from local black activists, and increase local white violence. Most COFO members, however, believed that the national media attention white workers brought to Mississippi outweighed these concerns. Furthermore, the large numbers of volunteers meant that a broader variety of programs could be administered as part of Freedom Summer. In addition to door-to-door canvassing and voter registration, COFO also administered the Freedom School project to supplement the poor education most black Mississippians received. It initiated public health programs staffed by volunteer doctors and nurses and launched the creation of the Mississippi Freedom Democratic Party (MFDP) as an interracial third political party open to all Mississippians. Within the first month of the campaign, critics' fears were realized when black volunteer James Earl Chaney and his two white coworkers, Andrew Goodman and Michael Henry Schwerner, disappeared. After an extensive search, the bodies of the three activists were found in a small earthen dam.

Perhaps the most important of the Freedom Summer programs was the creation of the MFDP. Originally envisioned as an extension of the 1963 Freedom Vote and a hook to draw in potential black voters, organizers soon hit upon the idea of using the MFDP as a legitimate third-party challenger for political power within the state. To claim legitimacy as a third party and an alternative to the state's lily-white Democratic Party, the MFDP organized local precinct meetings, held county conventions, and eventually staged its own state convention and elected delegates to attend that summer's Democratic National Convention in Atlantic City, New Jersey. MFDP leaders and organizers hoped that the party would not only serve as a tool to increase black voter registration but might also win national approval to function as the official Democratic Party of Mississippi. Freedom Democrats reasoned that, if the state of Mississippi was unwilling to reform election laws and practices, perhaps pressure from the national party would change the hearts and minds of local leaders. COFO and MFDP organizers placed much faith in the national party's ability and willingness to engage in local civil rights campaigns. Their hopes, however, were shattered. In an effort to maintain party unity, President Lyndon B. Johnson ordered that the MFDP challenge be dismissed and that a compromise solution be offered. Under the compromise, two representatives from the MFDP would be seated as at-large delegates and only regular Mississippi delegates willing to swear their allegiance to the national Democratic ticket would be permitted to take their places as delegates on the convention floor. Both groups refused to accept the compromise, and, after staging a sit-in on the convention floor, MFDP delegates returned to Mississippi.

The MFDP's actions in Atlantic City precipitated a major argument among COFO members. Increasingly displeased with the radical nature of the Freedom Democrats and other COFO members, the NAACP decided to withdraw its membership in early 1965. At the same time, COFO was faced with the increasingly worrisome question of how it could sustain civil rights activities after the majority of white volunteers had returned to their college campuses and homes in the fall. The question of direction was especially troublesome because Moses, COFO's director and spiritual leader, had resigned from his post at the end of 1964. Faced with a weakening organizational structure and almost nonexistent financial resources, SNCC leaders suggested that COFO had outlived its usefulness and should be disbanded. By the end of 1965, COFO ceased to operate.

During its four-year existence, COFO had provided organization and direction to the myriad civil rights projects and campaigns in Mississippi. Perhaps COFO's most significant contribution to the Mississippi freedom struggle was its early insistence that Mississippians, rather than activists and field secretaries from outside the state, should be able to control the local civil rights campaigns. By pooling resources and efforts, COFO was able to coordinate the 1964 Mississippi Freedom Summer, which was the largest campaign of the civil rights movement. Despite this success, interorganizational bickering over limited funds and power provided for COFO's demise and left a void in its wake that no other Mississippi civil rights organization could fill.

**FURTHER READINGS**

Davis, Vanessa L. "'Sisters and Brothers All': The Mississippi Freedom Democratic Party and the Struggle for Political Equality." Ph.D. diss., Vanderbilt University, 1996.

Dittmer, John. *Local People: The Struggle for Civil Rights in Mississippi.* Urbana: University of Illinois Press, 1994.

Forman, James. *The Making of Black Revolutionaries.* Washington, D.C.: Open Hand, 1985.

Holt, Len. *The Summer That Didn't End: The Story of the Mississippi Civil Rights Project of 1964.* New York: DeCapo, 1965.

McAdam, Doug. *Freedom Summer.* New York: Oxford University Press, 1988.

Mills, Nicholas. *Like a Holy Crusade: Mississippi 1964: The Turning Point of the Civil Rights Movement in America.* Chicago: Dees, 1992.

*Vanessa L. Davis*

# Council of Social Agencies, Pasadena, California, Interracial Commission

The Council of Social Agencies was a national organization with chapters in several major cities including Washington, D.C., Boston, and Baltimore. It served as an umbrella organization, conducting needs studies and coordinating activities of societies on the local level that provided assistance directly to individuals. The Interracial Commission was appointed in 1943 by the Pasadena, California, branch to devise recommendations that would relieve existing racial tensions in that city. The commission, headed by Dr. Eugene Carson Blake, was composed of representatives from various ethnic groups, religious organizations, and business associations from within the community, as well as members of the women's civic league. After its first organizational meeting, the members agreed to operate the commission under a few basic ground rules: be open and frank with each other, respect one another's points of view, remain unswayed by private and political interest groups, and seek no publicity in their work.

Within the first two years, the commission organized three subcommittees to address what it viewed as the three major areas of racial tension in Pasadena: recreational facilities and programs, housing, and economic opportunity for members of minority groups. Subcommittees were to study these problems, make reports that included recommendations for action, and submit their reports to the entire commission for approval. After being approved by the commission, the reports were passed on to the Council of Social Agencies, which found the appropriate methods to implement the recommendations.

In an attempt to reduce racial tensions among the city's youth, the Subcommittee on Recreation recommended the building of new recreational areas that would be strategically situated throughout the city. These plans were accepted by the Council of Social Agencies, which passed them along to the city government, which, in turn, adopted the plan as part of the city's postwar development program. The Subcommittee on Economic Opportunities studied racial barriers within the business community that blocked members of minority groups from obtaining high-paying jobs and from advancing within their profession. Recognizing the difficulty in standardizing employment practices throughout the city, the subcommittee recommended that minority children be encouraged to continue their education to enhance their employment opportunities. For this purpose, the Council of Social Agencies funded a scholarship program. Despite efforts of the Subcommittee on Housing to enforce building and health codes in substandard housing, war-induced overcrowding and the close proximity of diverse peoples in low-income-housing areas complicated the already dangerous situation. Little was accomplished in the field of housing until the postwar years. In 1945, two additional subcommittees were appointed to deal with minority employment opportunities and inadequate hospital facilities for minorities.

Paralleling its effort to improve opportunities for minorities in the city, the commission also sought to promote racial harmony. In a *Thorndike Report* released in the early 1940s, Pasadena was named the best community in the country in which to live. The commission amended the tribute to read as follows: "That Pasadena may continue to be the best city in America in which to live and that it shall become that best community for all its citizens of whatever color or race." To accomplish this, the commission promoted open discussion about racial attitudes

to increase understanding and tolerance. The culmination of this work was the creation of an official commission within city government to work on race relations.

**FURTHER READING**

Blake, Eugene. *Racial Tension and What To Do About It!: The Story of the Interracial Commission, Council of Social Agencies, Pasadena-Altadena.* Pasadena, Calif.: The Commission, 1945.

*Kimberly E. Nichols*

## Council on African Affairs

In 1937, Max Yergan and the actor Paul Robeson founded the New York City–based organization that became the Council on African Affairs (CAA). Over the next fifteen years, black American anticolonial activists in the CAA helped keep the issue of colonial liberation on the U.S. agenda and provided links to international anticolonial networks and African liberation groups. With the onset of Cold War hostilities after World War II, splits in the CAA exposed tensions endemic to many of the late-1940s alliances of Leftists and liberals. Finally, in the early 1950s, the CAA was at the center of anticolonialist activists' dramatic confrontation with the government as the United States sought to stifle internal opposition and make itself the undisputed leader of the "free world."

Robeson, a major donor, fund-raiser and chief policymaker of the CAA, served as chair of the council for most of its life. Other leaders included W. Alphaeus Hunton, who joined the organization in 1943 as its educational director and later became executive director; and W. E. B. Du Bois, who served as vice chair and, after 1948, chaired the CAA's Africa Aid Committee.

The CAA began as the International Committee on African Affairs (ICAA) under Yergan, an African American who had spent fifteen years working for the YMCA in South Africa, but its 1942 reorganization as the CAA made it distinctly different from its predecessor. The ICAA, representing a cross-section of interwar Left and liberal politics, had included social-gospel Christians and corporate philanthropists and had sought to educate the American public about Africa. When the ICAA was reorganized in 1942 as the CAA, with Paul Robeson as chairman, it retained its emphasis on educating the American public about Africa but also adopted more expressly political goals, including the political liberation of colonized African nations and improved economic and social conditions on the African continent. Its leadership sought to achieve these goals not only through education, but also by organizing broad political support for decolonization and lobbying the U.S. government on issues pertaining to Africa.

Most important, the new CAA embodied an explicit and militant diaspora consciousness, accompanied by a distinct shift to autonomous black leadership. Embracing anti-imperialist and anticapitalist politics, the CAA insisted that "our fight for Negro rights here is inseparably linked with the liberation movements of the people of the Caribbean and Africa and the colonial world in general." Hunton's appointment to the staff in 1943 marked a major turning point in his life and in the life of the organization. The day-to-day work and policy was now carried out by Hunton, with the much greater involvement than before of Paul and Eslanda Goode Robeson. Other newly active members included the educator Mary McLeod Bethune and the sociologist E. Franklin Frazier. They were joined by Charlotta Bass, a participant in the 1919 Pan-African Congress in Paris, a civil rights activist, a promoter of West Coast "Don't Buy Where You Can't Work" campaigns, and editor and publisher of the *California Eagle*, the state's oldest black newspaper.

The broad political and cultural connections of Yergan, the intellectual leadership of Hunton and Du Bois, and the cultural and political influence of Robeson made the CAA a strong and credible organization among black Americans, steeped in a rich world of black culture. In its heyday, its rallies and fund-raisers featured not only Robeson, but also major American artists such as Marian Anderson, Lena Horne, the jazz composer and pianist Mary Lou Williams, the Golden Gate Quartet, John Latouche, and Duke Ellington.

The addition of Hunton to the staff inaugurated the period of the CAA's greatest influence. Hunton developed widespread African contacts. As editor of *New Africa*, he enabled the CAA to publish extensive coverage of trade union and political organizing throughout Africa, with an emphasis on southern Africa, Nigeria, and the Gold Coast, and the organization lent its support to the 1946 Nigerian general strike. The most significant work of the CAA involved South Africa, culminating in the widely publicized CAA support of the South African miners' strike in 1946. Besides supporting the miners' strike, the CAA coordinated a highly visible campaign for famine relief in South Africa's Ciskei region. A rally of nineteen thousand in Madison Square Garden in New York City at the height of these campaigns was preceded by a week of radio broadcasts on South Africa, featuring Broadway stars such as Betty Garret, Canada Lee, Judy Holliday, and Kenneth

Spencer, along with Robeson and Hunton. Also drawing the support of such luminaries as the boxer Joe Louis, this campaign strikingly illustrates the extent to which attention to culture and political economy went hand in hand, as well as the importance and visibility of South Africa in 1946. Work on South Africa reached its climax later in that year and in 1947, when, through the United Nations, the CAA joined South African Indians and the African National Congress to challenge the South African government's attempt to annex South-West Africa and to restrict further the rights of Indians in the Union of South Africa.

After losing this battle in the United Nations, the CAA and its anticolonial allies increasingly saw the U.S. government as an adversary. With the beginning of the Cold War, the CAA's opposition to President Harry S. Truman's foreign policy, its emphasis on the growing U.S. involvement in Africa and U.S. uranium interests in the Belgian Congo and South Africa, and its support for African liberation groups placed the CAA outside mainstream opinion and increasingly at odds with the Truman administration. In 1947, the United States attorney general included the CAA on his official list of subversive organizations. By that time, the CAA was exhibiting the tensions endemic to Left and liberal politics in this period, and many members began to fall away.

In 1948, the organization underwent a major split when its founder, Yergan, took a sharp turn to the Right in perhaps the most pronounced political about-face among African American activists and intellectuals of the Cold War era. Paul and Eslanda Robeson and Hunton organized to save the CAA from a Yergan takeover. Much of the significant work of the CAA was yet to come. Du Bois had joined the CAA in 1947 and had moved his office to its headquarters when he left the National Association for the Advancement of Colored People (NAACP) in 1948. As the Robeson-Du Bois-Hunton alliance solidified, the organization's contact with African groups continued to deepen. But with Yergan's departure, such prominent civil rights leaders as Hubert T. Delany, Adam Clayton Powell Jr., Rayford W. Logan, and Channing Tobias resigned from the organization, and others—among them Mary McLeod Bethune—stopped attending its functions. Over the following four years, several former members, most notably Yergan and Tobias, cooperated fully with the Federal Bureau of Investigation (FBI) and the U.S. Attorney General's Office in prosecuting the CAA. The CAA increasingly found its support among the Left rather than the broad cross-section of black American institutions and leadership that had sustained it through its first decade.

Despite the fragmentation of anticolonial alliances and the split of the CAA in 1948, remaining council leaders such as Hunton, Robeson, and Du Bois continued to support African liberation movements and to monitor U.S. corporate initiatives in Africa. The CAA's Africa Aid Committee, chaired by Du Bois, raised money in 1950 for striking coal miners at Enugu, Nigeria, and the Nigerian National Federation of Labor. Hunton followed the activities of Edward R. Stettinius, the former U.S. secretary of state who, Hunton contended, controlled virtually the entire economy of Liberia through his Liberia Company. Alarmed by these activities, colonial powers sought to undermine the CAA's visibility in Africa. By 1950, the CAA's *New Africa* was banned from the mails of the Union of South Africa, Kenya, and the Belgian Congo.

In the United States, the CAA and its leaders increasingly faced government prosecution and harassment. In 1950, the federal government revoked Paul Robeson's passport. The rejection of Robeson's subsequent appeal plainly revealed that the government regarded anticolonialism and civil rights as interlocking issues that threatened national security. In the three years following the revocation of Robeson's passport, the CAA faced two sets of charges by the U.S. attorney general: first, as a Communist-front organization, according to the Subversive Activities Control Board; second, as a foreign agent under the Foreign Registration Act. Evidence for the second case rested on the CAA's relationship with the African National Congress, the South African Indian Congress, the Kenyan Africa Union, and the Nigerian mine workers. Evidence and testimony used against the CAA in the first case seldom related specifically to links with the Communist Party but, rather, simply assumed that support of African liberation groups was Communist and, therefore, treasonous. CAA proponents of the politics of the African diaspora had seen no conflict between the status of black Americans as Americans and the view that their struggles were linked to those of Africans and other colonized peoples. They believed that independent African and Asian states would help black Americans win their rights as Americans. But in the 1950s, the prosecution and its witnesses viewed these formulations of solidarity as incompatible with American citizenship.

As the case against the CAA wore on, the council struggled to continue its support of African liberation groups. In a bittersweet chapter closing this era of anticolonial politics, the weakening of the CAA in the United States came at precisely the moment when its ties to the African National Congress (ANC) had deepened. Through the South African Campaign for the Defiance of Unjust Laws, Hunton, Du Bois, and Robeson corresponded with ANC activists R. T. Bokwe, Walter Sissulu, Z. K. Matthews, and Oliver Tambo. During this era, Sisulu, who attempted unsuccessfully to organize a Pan-African Congress in 1953 and 1954, was in especially close contact with black Americans and other African activists.

The Attorney General's Office closely followed the CAA's support of these African liberation groups and renewed its aggressive prosecution. In the midst of the first case, another line of investigation emerged. In a 1953 memo to FBI Director J. Edgar Hoover, Assistant Attorney General Warren Olney III argued that information previously submitted by the FBI for the case before the Subversive Activities Control Board—namely, the CAA's support of the striking Nigerian workers and the South African defiance campaign—revealed that the council may have been acting as a publicity agent for a foreign principal and may have raised solicited contributions for a foreign principal.

The government's case against the CAA never reached a resolution because in 1955, financially crippled by defense costs and further weakened by the restrictions put on its leaders, the organization disbanded. Having made an enormous contribution to the definition of black American politics and its relation to Africa, the CAA was quickly forgotten, and there was no longer a home in the United States for this generation of anticolonial activists. Du Bois died in Ghana on August 27, 1963, one day before the historic civil rights March on Washington. Paul Robeson remained throughout the 1950s a political pariah in his own country and died in obscurity in 1976. Alphaeus Hunton, a Howard, Harvard, and New York University–educated Ph.D., was unable to find work in the United States. He died in Lusaka, Zambia, in 1970.

**FURTHER READINGS**

Lynch, Hollis R. *Black American Radicals and the Liberation of Africa: The Council on African Affairs, 1937–1955.* Ithaca, N.Y.: Africana Studies and Research Center, Cornell University, 1978.

Von Eschen, Penny M. *Race Against Empire: Black Americans and Anticolonialism, 1937–1957.* Ithaca, N.Y.: Cornell University Press, 1997.

*Penny M. Von Eschen*

## Council on Cooperative College Projects

*See* Conference of Presidents of Negro Land-Grant Colleges; Council of 1890 College Presidents.

## Dallas: Civic, Literary, and Mutual Aid Associations

With the second-largest African American population in Texas, Dallas became a regional center for black political and cultural activism. African Americans made up a significant percentage of the population and even under segregation wielded clout. In 1900, African Americans accounted for 21 percent of Dallas's residents. In the 1920s, the black population dropped to 11 percent due to increasing white migration into Dallas. It was not until the 1970s that African Americans again made up more than 20 percent of the city's population. During that decade, black residents accounted for nearly 30 percent of the population, largely due to white suburban flight.

Women provided leadership for some of the earliest African American civic organizations, which often aimed at racial uplift and promoted cultural refinement rather than explicit political activism. In 1911, black women organized the Priscilla Art Club under the slogan "Art and Beauty, Home and Duty." Leaders of such clubs typically were the wives of political, religious, or business leaders who brought a well-educated, middle-class sensibility to their volunteer work. Sometimes condescending, the membership acted as cultural missionaries to the poor. Nevertheless, they served as a bridge between economic classes and helped build a more unified African American community during the civil rights struggle between the 1930s and the 1970s.

Active church members, such as Barbara M. James, played key roles in bringing the Young Women's Christian Association (YWCA) to African American neighborhoods. Founded in 1928, Dallas's segregated YWCA chapter provided classes in domestic engineering, English, home nursing, and sex education. The YWCA served as a social hub, one of the few places black girls could hold meetings or social events. The segregated Young Men's Christian Association (YMCA), founded in 1930, offered similar programs for the city's black men and boys and, during the Great Depression, provided job registration and employment services.

More explicit political activism was needed, however, by the early and mid-1920s, when a revived Ku Klux Klan took over city and county government. A Dallas branch of the National Association for the Advancement of Colored People (NAACP) formed at the end of World War I but declined in the 1920s from an enrollment of one thousand in 1919. Black political activism revived during the late 1930s, largely due to the efforts of the Dallas Negro Chamber of Commerce.

The Negro Chamber of Commerce was founded in November 1926, after the Dallas chapter of Booker T. Washington's National Negro Business League (NNBL), originally formed in 1904, split from the national organization. Criticizing the NNBL for lack of leadership, one hundred black Dallasites launched the Chamber of Commerce. By the late 1930s, the Chamber evolved into a major force in municipal politics.

A. Maceo Smith, a Texarkana, Texas, native who moved to Dallas in 1933, led this transformation. Between 1933 and 1939, Smith served as executive secretary of the Negro Chamber of Commerce, expanding the group's membership. Smith urged African American voters to pay poll taxes and supported voter registration to increase black influence in local elections.

Under the leadership of Smith, the Negro Chamber of Commerce organized an "Education for Citizenship" week that resulted in the formation of the Progressive Citizens' League (PCL) in 1934. The PCL mobilized the city's African American population into an influential voting bloc. State election laws allowed black participation in nonpartisan municipal, school, and special elections. In 1935, African Americans demonstrated their political strength when they supported Ammon S. Wells, a black candidate, in a special election for the state's Fourteenth District Court. Wells lost the race but finished sixth of sixty-five candidates.

Yet, African Americans remained politically vulnerable. When the city of Dallas won a state bid to host the 1936 Texas Centennial Exposition, Smith gained $100,000 in state funding for a Hall of Negro Life, which was subsequently withdrawn in retaliation for Smith's support of Wells. Although Smith won federal funding for the project, the near-cancellation of the Hall of Negro Life underscored the African American community's precarious political status.

In the fall of 1936, Smith created the Progressive Voters' League (PVL), a successor to the PCL, which united the voter-registration and poll-tax-payment drives of fifty-two different African American organizations. By the following year, black voters in Dallas made up an estimated 20 percent of the city's electorate, and Dallas's white political elite began to court the PVL. In 1937, the PVL won concessions from city officials, including construction of a second black high school.

Other civil rights organizations emerged in the 1940s and 1950s. The Council of Negro Organizations lobbied for equal pay for black teachers. In the 1960s and 1970s, when the city proposed to level a black neighborhood near Fair Park to construct a parking lot, African American residents of South Dallas joined with a white neighborhood group, the Fair Park Block Partnership, to protest the proposed construction. One member, Elsie Faye Heggins, won a City Council seat in 1980.

In Dallas, the political world often merged with black social and artistic life. The Hall of Negro Life at the Texas Centennial Exposition represented not only a successful political struggle with white Dallas, but also a celebration of a black past ignored by the city's schools. When the Dallas art teacher Rezolia C. Grisham Thrash received an invitation as the only black artist to participate in the seventh annual Dallas Allied Arts Exhibition in 1935, many in the community perceived her inclusion as a civil rights triumph. The Dallas Black Arts Theatre, active in the late 1970s, reflected a 1960s desire for cultural autonomy. In the 1980s and 1990s, the Museum of African American Life and Culture, which established a Friends of the Texas Black Women's History Archives, represented a continua-

tion of that tradition of culture as political statement. The museum seeks to afford African Americans and women a more central place in history. Today's black artistic and political leadership in many ways still promotes the vision of earlier groups like the Priscilla Club who sought to uplift through the appreciation of art, education, and the African American past.

**FURTHER READINGS**

Dulaney, W. Marvin. "The Progressive Voters' League: A Political Voice for African Americans in Dallas." *Legacies* (Spring 1991), 27–35.

Gillette, Michael Lowrey. "The NAACP in Texas, 1937–1957." Ph.D. diss., University of Texas at Austin, 1984.

Payne, Darwin. *Big D: Triumphs and Troubles of an American Supercity in the Twentieth Century*. Dallas: Three Forks, 1994.

Schutze, Jim. *The Accommodation: The Politics of Race in an American City*. Secaucus: Citadel Press, 1986.

Winegarten, Ruthe. *Black Texas Women: 150 Years of Trial and Triumph*. Austin: University of Texas Press, 1995.

*Michael Phillips*

# Dayton, Ohio: Civic, Literary, and Mutual Aid Associations

Ohio, despite its comprehensive racial proscription, slowly yet steadily attracted African American migrants who established black communities throughout the state by the end of the nineteenth century. In major cities like Dayton, African Americans recognized the need to establish their own social, fraternal, sororal, benevolent, and religious organizations to assist black communities in their efforts to achieve economic stability and independence. Held in high esteem, many of these organizations were short lived or replaced by other associations. Still, some of these organizations persisted well into the twentieth century and continue to carry out effective programs.

In 1800, the African American population in Ohio numbered 337. By 1830, that number had increased to 9,568, and, in 1860, the 36,673 black residents of Ohio represented 1.6 percent of the state's total population. The black population continued to increase during the twentieth century; by 1990, the state's African American population of 1,154,826 represented a little over 10.6 percent of the total population of Ohio.

The first African American in Dayton appeared in 1798 on a Dayton Township tax list. "William Maxwell and his negro," a male, was joined in 1802 by the first black woman of record in Dayton, identified as a "colored girl" brought to the city by Daniel Cooper to be a servant to his family. By 1820, Dayton had a total population of 1,139, including 141 African American residents. Over the next fifty years, Dayton's black population grew slowly. By 1870, the Dayton black community barely quadrupled to 548.

Between 1820 and 1890, only a few but significant African American organizations emerged in Dayton. An antislavery society organized in 1839 and headed by Luther Bruen was joined in 1840 by the United Daughters of Zion, a church-based group, known to engage in antislavery activities, including providing refuge for runaway slaves.

In 1849, Dayton African Americans, led by Joseph J. Wheeler, formed their first mutual aid society, the American Sons of Protection. The organization was created when the city denied black residents benefits from tax-collected money. During the early twentieth century, the American Sons of Protection was also instrumental in aiding black Daytonians who were victims of the great flood of 1913.

The sons of Joseph J. Wheeler, the founder of the American Sons of Protection, were also community activists. William and George Wheeler organized the Colored First Voters in 1870 and a chapter of the Prince Hall Masons in the following year. Both organizations promoted education for African American children and successfully petitioned the Dayton school board to operate schools in the black neighborhoods.

During the last two decades of the nineteenth century and the first two decades of the twentieth century, Dayton's African American community benefited tremendously from the migration of southern blacks to the North. By 1920, the city's African American population increased to 9,052. As a result of the population growth, Dayton's black community established numerous new organizations. In 1889, black women of Dayton launched Young Women's Christian Association (YWCA) programs. Louise Troy, Jessie Hathcock, and Jennie Cox formed the Women's Christian Association No. 2, which is now the country's oldest continuous existing black YWCA. This group was one of several women's organizations established in Dayton over the next century.

In 1900, black women in Dayton, interested in reading the works of African American writers as well as promoting women's suffrage, organized the Unique Study Club. This literary club, still in existence, encourages reading the works of black authors and promotes human rights.

Other civic, social, and mutual aid groups organized by African American women in Dayton include the Dayton League of Colored Women Voters (1921) as well as chapters of the Eastern Star (1931), Alpha Kappa Alpha (1934), Delta Sigma Theta (1936), the National Council of Negro Women (1957), the National Association of Negro Women (1960), and the Links, Inc. (1949).

Predominantly male associations formed in Dayton during the twentieth century include the American Woodmen (1915), a fraternal insurance club; the Young Men's Christian Association (1924); and chapters of Alpha Phi Alpha (1921), Kappa Alpha Psi Fraternity (1946), and Omega Psi Phi (ca. 1930s). Of the numerous leisure and sports clubs organized in Dayton's black community, the Dayton Marcos is one of the oldest and best known. The Dayton Marcos were one of the eight baseball teams in the Negro National League that formed in 1920. Before joining the Negro National League, the Marcos, who started playing in the early 1900s, were the only black team in the Ohio-Indiana League.

Many organizations that promote the advancement of the African American community still exist in Dayton, including the city's chapters of the National Association for the Advancement of Colored People (1915) and the National Urban League (1947). These two civic groups continue to struggle to secure civil rights and economic stability for black Daytonians. They also work very closely with the West Dayton Area Council (1951) to promote physical and social improvements in the area and to conduct voter-registration drives.

**FURTHER READINGS**

Allbarger, David B. "Blacks in Dayton, 1798–1870." Unpublished paper, Wright State University, 1980. Wright State University Special Collection and Archives. Paul Laurence Dunbar Library, Detroit, Michigan.

Davis, Lenwood G. "Nineteenth Century Blacks in Ohio: An Historical View." In *Blacks in Ohio History*. Ed. Rubin F. Weston. Columbus: Ohio Historical Society, 1976, 4–10.

Gerber, David A. *Black Ohio and the Color Line, 1860–1915*. Urbana: University of Illinois Press, 1976.

Peters, Margaret E. *Dayton's African American Heritage: A Pictorial History*. Virginia Beach: Donning, 1995.

*Barbara L. Green*

## Deacons for Defense

Organized in July 1964 in Jonesboro, Louisiana, the Deacons for Defense was an African American armed self-defense group charged with protecting local black communities and civil rights volunteers, especially those working for the Congress of Racial Equality (CORE). After observing a Ku Klux Klan parade accompanied by the local police march through Jonesboro's black neighborhoods, about a dozen black residents banded together to form the Deacons. The group admitted men over the age of twenty-one who could supply their own weapons. Yet, the Deacons were not nearly as radical as the media portrayed them to be. In a 1965 interview, the vice president of the Deacons, Charles R. Sims, expressed his support of nonviolence and peaceful negotiations "providing the policemen [sic] do their job." For the most part, the Deacons saw their role as complementary to that of other civil rights organizations, particularly the local CORE field-workers who benefited from the protection the Deacons provided.

In 1964, African Americans in Bogulasa, Louisiana, founded the Deacons' second chapter, when police released from custody a group of six local whites who had beaten two civil rights workers. Charles R. Sims, the president of the Bogulasa Deacons, claimed that, at its height, the organization consisted of fifty-three local chapters with thousands of members. It is not likely, however, that the Deacons' membership was ever that large. Rather than a large membership, the organization relied upon public posturing, the fears of local whites, and the threat of black violence. In addition to protecting local civil rights activists, the Deacons' most public campaign was to provide armed security for James Meredith's 1966 March Against Fear. After Meredith was shot shortly into his march across Mississippi, a coalition of civil rights activists, including Martin Luther King Jr.'s Southern Christian Leadership Conference (SCLC) and the younger, more radical Student Nonviolent Coordinating Committee (SNCC), continued Meredith's journey. Although the presence of armed guards was frowned upon by King, the Deacons were allowed to protect the marchers in an effort to reduce violence and show organizational unity.

Ironically, the Meredith march also signaled the Deacons' demise. Not nearly as radical as the Black Power movement that emerged from the march, the Deacons for Defense faded into the civil rights woodwork. By 1967, the organization was defunct. Instead of creating the guerrilla warfare and armed counterinsurgency actions that many whites had feared, the Deacons quietly slipped out of existence.

**FURTHER READINGS**

Fairclough, Adam. *Race and Democracy: The Civil Rights Struggle in Louisiana, 1915–1972*. Athens: University of Georgia Press, 1995.

Raines, Howell. *My Soul Is Rested: The Story of the Civil Rights Movement in the Deep South*. New York: Penguin, 1977.

Sims, Charles R. "Armed Defense." In *Black Protest: History, Documents, and Analyses, 1619 to the Present*. Ed. Joanne Grant. New York: Fawcett, 1968, 357–365.

*Vanessa L. Davis*

## Delta Ministry

Founded in September 1964 in Mississippi, the Delta Ministry was an interracial outgrowth of the National Council of Churches' (NCC) involvement in the 1964 Mississippi Freedom Summer campaign. During Freedom Summer, the NCC, an ecumenical organization dedicated to bringing the social-gospel movement into the 1960s, assisted in training hundreds of young civil rights volunteers who staffed the Mississippi Freedom Summer projects. In addition to providing training and monetary support for the campaign, the NCC also provided a small army of ministers who served as spiritual advisers to the volunteers and attempted to bring about religious and social reconciliation between black and white Mississippians.

After the summer campaign ended, the NCC established a permanent residency in Mississippi. With offices throughout the Mississippi Delta, the Delta Ministry sought to address the growing economic, social, and health problems of black farmworkers, as well as reconcile Mississippi's black and white communities. Under the direction of its first director, the Reverend Art Thomas, a white North Carolinian, the ministry established its first permanent office in Greenville, Mississippi, and launched health-education programs, as well as citizenship, voter-registration, and literacy classes.

In 1966, responding to concerns that Greenville's white city officials were inhibiting the distribution of federal surplus food assistance, the Delta Ministry played a central role in the sit-ins at Greenville Air Base and the establishment of Strike City. The Delta Ministry also supported Mississippi's first Head Start agency, the predominantly black Child Development Group of Mississippi (CDGM). At one point, the CDGM even shared office space with the Delta Ministry, and ministry director Thomas served on the CDGM's board of directors.

In addition to the Delta Ministry's involvement in poverty campaigns, the organization also participated in political action. Considered by some to be the "spiritual successor" to the Student Nonviolent Coordinating Committee, the Delta Ministry became closely allied with the Mississippi Freedom Democratic Party (MFDP) and its various political campaigns. In 1966, for example, the ministry assisted in the MFDP's statewide election campaign and helped the Freedom Democrats make local arrangements for the James Meredith March Against Fear. By 1967, the ministry had offices throughout the Delta and a full-time staff of twenty-six.

By the end of the 1960s, with the demise of the MFDP, its closest political ally in Mississippi, the Delta Ministry began to focus much of its efforts on local economic and training programs. After twenty years of service, the Delta Ministry ceased to operate in the mid-1980s.

**FURTHER READINGS**

Davis, Vanessa L. "'Sisters and Brothers All': The Mississippi Freedom Democratic Party and the Struggle for Political Equality." Ph.D. diss., Vanderbilt University, 1996.

Dittmer, John. *Local People: The Struggles for Civil Rights in Mississippi*. Urbana: University of Illinois Press, 1994.

Findlay, James F., Jr. *Church People in Struggle: The National Council of Churches and the Black Freedom Movement, 1950–1970*. New York: Oxford University Press, 1993.

Hilton, Bruce. *The Delta Ministry*. New York: Macmillan, 1969.

*Vanessa L. Davis*

## Delta Sigma Theta

Delta Sigma Theta sorority (DST) was founded in 1913 on the campus of Howard University by twenty-two young women. From that single, small, campus-based sisterhood, DST has grown to become one of the largest associations of black women in the world. It is an international organization of some 850 chapters with 200,000 members whose ties to the sorority far outlast their four years of college and whose concerns extend far beyond the campus. Unlike conventional Greek societies, DST has evolved from a social sorority to an important public-service organization that can and does rely on the significant efforts and support of alumnae chapters as it addresses major social issues of contempory America.

DST was founded by members of another sorority on Howard's campus, Alpha Kappa Alpha (AKA), who wanted to expand the scope of the group's efforts. AKA was founded in 1908 as a social society, although, as in other African American women's associations, there was a strong sense of obligation to work for the uplift of the race. Five years later, however, AKA had no clear agenda and no national organization to allow members to cooperate with other women's and African American organizations. DST was founded by women who were stymied by AKA policies in their desire to reach beyond the bounds of Howard University and be part of the transformation of American society. The Alpha chapter of DST was founded in January 1913. In February 1914, the Beta chapter was formed at Wilberforce University. A third chapter was established at the University of Pennsylvania, Philadelphia, in 1918. By 1919, there were five chapters of DST, and the members of the Alpha chapter at Howard called a meeting of all chapters in Washington, D.C., to nationalize the society, draft a constitution for national sisterhood, establish a governing body, and determine a national agenda.

Education has been a primary cause for the sorority since 1913. Many of the early members became teachers as a means of serving their communities. Founded by some of the privileged few who could attend college, DST has since worked to persuade young people of every age of the importance of education and offers assistance in the form of loans and scholarships to young black women who have chosen to pursue a college degree. In 1937, the national convention initiated the National Library Project, with the purpose of establishing traveling libraries to offer rural southern blacks resources otherwise unavailable to them. Realizing the importance of a good education for racial progress as well as personal advancement, the sorority was an early supporter of school desegregation efforts.

The sorority did not shrink from other controversial issues. In March 1913, just two months after its founding, the Alpha chapter participated in a woman-suffrage parade in the nation's capital. Greater even than the interest in woman suffrage and women's rights has been the abiding interest of the sorority in racial uplift. In 1927, black fraternities and sororities from across the nation came together to discuss coordinating their efforts for racial advancement. In 1929, the Deltas established a Vigilance Committee "that would keep in touch with the political activities of the country as they affected our group." In the 1930s, members of DST worked alongside the National Association for the Advancement of Colored People (NAACP), the National Urban League, the Association for the Study of Negro Life and History, and the National Negro Congress. In that decade, the sorority supported Marian Anderson's fight to sing in Constitution

Hall and, at the request of the NAACP, was a key lobbyist in 1938 for the Costigan-Wagner federal antilynching bill. In the 1950s and 1960s, the sorority worked to raise money and consciousness for school desegregation and voter registration. In the post–civil rights era, DST has continued to address its efforts to the particular concerns of African Americans, such as maintaining affirmative action programs. In addition, DST has turned to issues of general concern in American society by encouraging breast cancer awareness and research and working closely with Habitat for Humanity to help the homeless.

Many of DST's sorors have attained positions of importance, power, and fame. It has been a training ground for public leaders, such as Barbara Jordan, and a source of support for black women in the arts, such as Leontyne Price and Lena Horne. The real significance of the organization, though, lies in the efforts of its more anonymous membership. As the twenty-first century dawns, DST continues to grow and offer black women all over the globe a sense of sisterhood and a means of directing their efforts for the improvement of their world.

**FURTHER READINGS**

Delta Sigma Theta Sorority, Inc. Archives. Washington, D.C.

Giddings, Paula. *In Search of Sisterhood: Delta Sigma Theta and the Challenge of the Black Sorority Movement*. New York: Morrow, 1988.

*Nancy Bowman*

## Denver Colored Civic Association

The Denver Colored Civic Association (DCCA) emerged on October 11, 1919, when Major Thomas Campbell, a veteran of the Spanish-American War, hosted a dinner meeting in the banquet hall of Denver's People's Tabernacle. The purpose of the meeting was to effect "a civic association of [Negroes] in Denver in order to bring the Colored citizens [in the city] in closer touch with one another and the better and higher element of the white citizens and business element of Denver." The DCCA operated until late 1946, when it was merged into the then newly created Denver Urban League.

Six months after the association's founding, an editorial in the black-owned *Colorado Statesman* observed that the purpose of the new organization, like most community-development efforts of the past, was to instill a sense of civic pride. However, unlike other Denver organizations, which were made up mostly of white men, the DCCA gathered the city's intelligent black men and women to harness their resources for the welfare and advancement of the black community.

In 1921, the DCCA became an affiliate organization of the Denver Civic and Commercial Association. Despite their affiliation with this predominantly white association, DCCA members insisted "that they neither claimed nor asked for social equality." Assuring whites that they were not challenging the racial status quo but willing to accommodate, DCCA members explained that "their work lies with their own people and that what they most earnestly desire[d was] the benefit of the advice and assistance of the Civic and Commercial Association upon matters of civic improvements, community welfare and other public problems of special concern to them and of general importance to all the city." Not surprisingly, black and white business and community leaders established friendly relations, as each group continued to work separately while agreeing to "act together in the future upon any problems that concern the two of them."

One of the DCCA's first and, for a while, most successful activities was the annual Lincoln-Douglass Banquet, usually held in the second week of February. Following the dinner, speakers presented talks on a variety of topics, including the status of Denver's black community and the significance of Abraham Lincoln, Frederick Douglass, and John Brown. Yet, as economic conditions worsened in the latter part of the 1920s and throughout the 1930s, attendance at the banquets decreased until they were stopped altogether.

Economic decline was not the only problem the DCCA faced as a result of the Great Depression. Another source of friction was the large number of black women who joined the DCCA in the 1930s. As the membership of the DCCA shifted and became predominantly female, the organization faced a dilemma when it sought a new executive secretary in 1941. While women held the majority of the votes, many DCCA members favored an "aggressive male who would help integrate the Negro" into the national defense. Several candidates ran for the position. John M. Williamson, who had been an active member for several years and was seen by many in the community as a "progressive Negro," emerged victorious. He became the DCCA's first male executive director and remained with the association until it disbanded in 1946.

In addition to internal frictions, there appeared to be some competition between the DCCA and the newly formed Negro Coordinating Council for Defense Jobs. Some Denver blacks charged that the latter was dominated by those interested in seeking power for themselves rather than helping black residents get off New Deal relief programs and into the growing number of defense-industry plants. In spite, or perhaps because, of this competition, Williamson was quite successful in getting black workers placed at the Remington Small Arms plants, which became the Denver Federal Center after World War II.

In 1946, the DCCA merged with the recently formed Denver Urban League. Apparently, DCCA members believed that a new organization with a broader scope and greater resources was necessary to meet the challenges of the postwar world.

**FURTHER READING**
*Colorado Statesman.*

*William M. King*

## Denver Interracial Commission

The Denver Interracial Commission was founded by black and white residents, including W. W. Grant Jr., Dr. T. T. McKinney, L. H. Lightner, Plat Louton, Ira Lute, and Fritz Cansler, in 1925. Its founding was likely catalyzed by the Tulsa, Oklahoma, race riot of 1921, which had received significant coverage in Denver's black press, and the rise and growing influence of the Ku Klux Klan in Colorado. The commission, composed of ten leading white and ten leading black citizens, was the local manifestation of the Commission on Interracial Co-operation that had been established by southern whites, ostensibly to address the rise of interracial violence during the infamous "Red Summer" of 1919. Once the commission had addressed the emergency that had called it into existence, it set out to develop "a constructive program of interracial adjustment, including the correction of oppressive conditions affecting Negroes and the improvement of those interracial attitudes out of which unfavorable conditions grow." Beginning in 1926, the commission initiated a series of "race relations Sundays" that lasted well into the 1930s. During race relations Sundays, members of the black and white clergy exchanged pulpits and spoke about the role of religion in altering attitudes and cultivating tolerance and respect for others. The commission was also responsible for a 1929 study conducted by Ira De A. Reid of the National Urban League that resulted in the publication of *The Negro Population of Denver, Colorado.* What little evidence remains of the commission's existence suggests that its attempts at moral suasion met with the same results as those of the abolitionist, activist, and journalist William Lloyd Garrison in the nineteenth century.

**FURTHER READINGS**
*Colorado Statesman.*
Denver Interracial Commission. "Tenth Annual Observance of Race Relations Sunday." Western History Department. Denver Public Library, Denver, Colorado.

*William M. King*

## Denver Unity Council

The Denver Unity Council was organized in January 1944 by a number of prominent black and white Denver citizens "conscious that bigotry and discrimination were not trademarks of Hitler's world alone" (Denver Unity Council, *Pamphlet* (1947), 2). The council's purpose was "to further the principle that Americanism [was] a matter of the mind and the heart, and not a matter of race, ancestry, or religion" (*Bulletin*, 2). Its chief concern was to safeguard and extend to all Denver residents the rights and immunities set forth in the Declaration of Independence. The council's first president, Dean Paul Roberts, of St. John's Cathedral, observed subsequently that "[t]he Unity Council feels that racial and religious antagonisms cannot exist where there is understanding and appreciation of the contributions all groups have to make to the American scene" (*Rocky Mountain News*, January 13, 1946, 34). Thus, the council sought to "integrate the efforts of all groups in the community with similar purposes in a program of (1) education; (2) action to meet situations demanding attention; and (3) studies of conditions of housing, health, employment, recreation, and education with a view to improving undesirable conditions" (*Bulletin*, 2). By 1948, the council comprised ninety-three organizations and eight hundred individual members. It had sponsored several conferences and established a speakers bureau and a publications and film division to combat prejudice and improve race relations. Moreover, the council had launched investigations of the city's slums, restrictive-covenant practices, and employment discrimination. Finally, it had explored complaints of police brutality and presented supporting evidence to a grand jury. The council's efforts to curb police brutality resulted in a race-relations training program for the city's police force, conducted by the former head of Milwaukee's police department. The council continued to operate until sometime in the 1950s, when it ceased to exist after having supplied the impetus for change in the community.

FURTHER READINGS
*Denver Post.*
Denver Unity Council. *Bulletin* 1, n.d.
"Race Relations Materials." Omer Stewart Archive. Western History Collection, Norlin Library, University of Colorado, Boulder, Colorado.
*Rocky Mountain News.*

*William M. King*

## Denver's Mayor's Interim Survey Committee on Human Relations

On June 19, 1947, shortly after his election as mayor of Denver, Quigg Newton appointed a committee "to report to him on the unity, or disunity, among the people of [the] city." Newton asked the committee "to point out to him those areas where barriers have been erected between neighbor and neighbor" and "to recommend to him ways of breaking down those barriers so that the lives of all . . . citizens might flow more freely into the mainstream of community life." The committee studied the experiences of Denver's black, Spanish, Japanese, and Jewish population. Its report, dated 1947, presented an overview of race relations in the city. It documented discrimination by government and community-service agencies and in employment, housing, education, recreation, public accommodations, health, and hospitals, as well as the presence of "hate" groups. Reporting to the mayor, the committee sought to estimate the cost and the consequences of prejudice in the city. In summarizing its findings, the committee concluded that "[p]rejudice [was] an expensive luxury. The cost in dollar and cents [was] staggering. The cost in human misery [was] enormous. Either way, the whole community [paid] the bill." Its principal recommendation was the establishment of a permanent commission on human relations whose authority would flow from an ordinance and whose scope would be defined by law. Furthermore, the committee recommended that the commission should be funded through annual appropriations from the City Council and that, while it "should touch all phases of City life . . . [it] should be divided into practical, compact working units." It also called for a full-time, paid professional staff and recommended that the commission focus on information and education rather than politics or advocacy. In 1948, in response to these recommendations, the mayor

established the Mayor's Commission on Human Relations. The commission continues to operate as the Mayor's Commission on Community Relations.

*William M. King*

## Department of Work for Colored People, Presbyterian Church

*See* Presbyterian Church Committee on Missions to Freedmen.

## Detroit: Civic, Literary, and Mutual Aid Associations

The African American community in Detroit has a long and proud tradition of civic, literary, and mutual aid associations. As in other black communities, the church was the first mutual aid association. In the 1830s, African Americans established schools in the basements of churches to educate black children who had been barred from public schools. Detroit's free blacks also extended their mutual aid activities to the Underground Railroad by providing assistance to their slave brethren who were escaping across the river to Canada. During the 1840s and 1850s, the city's black mutual aid and cultural organizations continued to increase. This was due, in part, to black Detroit's involvement in the Negro Convention movement. In October 1843, Detroit blacks hosted the Michigan State Colored Convention that brought African Americans from across the state to the city to discuss their political and economic conditions.

Between 1914 and 1924, thousands of rural southern blacks migrated to the Detroit area, creating a demand for larger and more effective civic and mutual aid associations. The sudden expansion of the African American community forced some black churches to increase their mutual aid functions. In 1924, for example, Second Baptist Church set up special programs to cater to the needs of black migrants. Ten years later, the church established a Big Sister's Auxiliary to build a home for homeless African American girls, and, in 1936, Second Baptist opened a social-service educational institution staffed with eighteen teachers.

During the Great Depression, two African American mutual aid associations emerged in Detroit that soon became models for economic self-help in the community. In 1930, Reverend William H. Peck and his wife, Fannie, founded the Booker T. Washington Trade Association (BTWTA) and the Housewives League of Detroit

(HWLD). The Pecks, who had arrived in Detroit in 1930 just after the reverend had assumed the pastorate of Bethel AME Church, found the city's black masses struggling to survive and black businesses and professionals in competition with whites. In April of that year, Reverend Peck called a meeting of black business leaders and professionals and organized the BTWTA. The HWLD was established several months later after A. L. Holsey, secretary of the National Negro Business League, spoke at Bethel AME Church about how Harlem's black housewives used their economic power to help the African American community. Mrs. Peck discussed the idea with her husband, called a meeting of fifty women, and set up the HWLD.

In a joint statement of their declaration of principles, the BTWTA and the HWLD explained their purposes: "We emphasize and declare it to be the most desirable to own our own business and manage it ourselves; while we recognize as an act of fairness, the employment of Negroes in businesses owned and operated by other racial groups, yet we feel that the solution of our economic problem is the ownership [of] business, and to this end we shall confine our efforts." In the following years, both organizations engaged in activities designed to develop a strong African American business and professional class.

However, this was not the first time that the African American community in Detroit was exposed to such ideas. The Detroit Negro Business League (DNBL), founded on July 14, 1926, by sixty charter members, had similar objectives. The DNBL worked for the development of a sense of unity of interest among African Americans. It advised black merchants on how to improve their business practices and educated African American consumers about the special advantages the league could offer.

Between World War I and the Great Depression, Detroit's black hospitals were among the best examples of mutual aid associations in the African American community. They were established to meet the rising medical needs of the expanding African American community and provided employment opportunities for black physicians and nurses, who were excluded from work in white hospitals. African American doctors, in particular, were having a difficult time obtaining internships in white hospitals. In 1917, Dr. David Northcross founded Mercy Hospital, which became Detroit's first black hospital. By 1918, Mercy Hospital had been approved by both the American Hospital Association and the American College of Surgeons, and the hospital reported thirty-seven beds and space for an operating room. In the same year, a group of black doctors incorporated the Dunbar Hospital Association, which later changed its name to Parkside Hospital. Members of the association studied sanitation, hygiene, and related sciences and treated advanced diseases and performed surgical operations.

During the Depression, African Americans founded two additional hospitals. In 1933, Trinity Hospital was established; two years later, the Edyth K. Thomas Memorial Hospital opened its gates. Both hospitals flourished. Between 1933 and 1943, Trinity grew from a thirty-five-bed facility to a one hundred-bed institution. Likewise, Thomas Memorial, which initially housed one hundred beds, expanded to become the Thomas Medical Center. By 1937, Thomas Medical Center had become the largest privately owned African American hospital in the United States. Other black hospitals established between the Depression and the early 1940s included Fairview Sanitarium, Bethesda Hospital, Good Samaritan, Wayne Sanitarium, St. Aubin General, and Kirwood Hospitals.

African American hospitals in Detroit provided jobs for the community as few other mutual aid associations were able to do. In 1943, these hospitals provided employment for more than five hundred African Americans. Although hospital jobs were relatively few, particularly when compared to employment sources outside the African American community, they had a much broader impact than their small number indicates. Not only did the jobs at the hospitals generate incomes for black employees and their families, they also helped ensure that African Americans would continue to operate and run their own hospitals for several more decades.

African American women played a key role in the formation of the civic and mutual aid tradition in Detroit. In the 1890s, African American women throughout Michigan began forming mutual aid associations to address black community problems such as homelessness, juvenile delinquency, and the plight of "deprived" young mothers. The In As Much Circle of King's Daughters and Sons Clubs, founded in Detroit in 1895, was one of the earliest of these black women's mutual aid associations. Mary McCoy, the wife of the famous black inventor Elijah McCoy, contributed to the establishment of this club. Mrs. McCoy, often called the "Mother of Clubs," became a leading figure in the establishment of African American women's mutual aid associations. She played a role in the founding of the Phyllis Wheatley Home for the Aged, the McCoy Home for Colored Children, the Lydian Association of Detroit, the Guiding Star Chapter Order of the Eastern Star, and the Willing Workers.

In 1989, African American club women in Detroit demonstrated their leadership in the field of mutual aid by hosting the first meeting to organize African American club women into a statewide organization. By the 1920s, the city's African American women had organized eight clubs. In April 1921, under the leadership of Veronica Lucas, these clubs combined to form the Detroit Association of Colored Women Clubs (DACWC). Members of the DACWC were models of the best mutual aid tradition in the African American community. The Entre Nous Club was founded in 1924 to raise funds to enable African American girls to attend the YWCA camp and to establish a separate black YWCA branch on Detroit's west side.

In 1938, black women's club work received a further boost when the Detroit Chamber of Commerce asked Dr. Violet T. Lewis, who had founded Indianapolis's Lewis College of Business in 1929, to open a branch of her college in Detroit. At that time, African Americans were excluded from attending most vocational schools in the city. Dr. Lewis accepted the invitation and opened her school in September of 1939.

African American women continue to play a leading role in mutual aid associations in Detroit. One of many impressive contemporary examples is the work of Clementine Barfield, who founded Save Our Sons and Daughters (SOSAD). Barfield launched SOSAD to prevent violence among black youths after her sixteen-year-old son was shot and killed in 1987. That year, more than three hundred African American youths had been shot by other black youths in Detroit. While most of the youths were injured, forty-one of them died. Barfield, along with other African American parents, "decided to go beyond mourning and began working together to create positive alternatives to violence throughout the community."

The premiere civic organization of Detroit's black community was the city's branch of the National Association for the Advancement of Colored People (NAACP), founded in 1911. Between 1911 and 1918, the Detroit NAACP focused primarily on national issues, such as lynchings, and local cases of racial discrimination. In 1914, for example, the NAACP took fourteen cases of racial discrimination in theaters to court and won four of them. Several years later, the NAACP protested racism in the United States Civil Service. The organization succeeded in placing a black woman as postal clerk, a job for which she had passed an exam, but which had been denied her because of racism. In 1925 and 1926, the De-troit NAACP came into the national and international spotlight when it marshaled support for the Sweet case. Black physician Dr. Henry O. Sweet and his relatives had been arrested for killing a member of a white mob that had surrounded their home. The famous lawyer Clarence Darrow was brought in to defend the Sweets, who were acquitted in May 1926. During the 1930s and 1940s, the Detroit NAACP also protested police brutality. By the 1960s, the Detroit branch of the NAACP had a membership of twenty-four thousand, making it the largest branch in the United States. The NAACP continues its work and remains one of the most active civic associations in Detroit's African American community.

Although the NAACP rendered important services to Detroit's black community, the association also attracted the criticism of some African Americans. Snow F. Grigsby, a member of the NAACP, was dissatisfied with the association's approach to racial discrimination and launched the Detroit Civic Rights Committee (CRC) in December 1933. Grigsby and the CRC took a more aggressive approach, particularly in the field of employment discrimination, and demanded that qualified African Americans be given jobs in municipal departments. Between 1933 and 1945, the CRC developed into the most effective protest organization in the community. The CRC far surpassed the NAACP in raising the consciousness of the African American community about employment discrimination and in achieving results.

African American newspapers in Detroit, as in other cities, represented the main literary association of the community. The *Western Excelsior*, Detroit's first African American newspaper, began operation on March 28, 1848. The *Plain Dealer* was established on May 19, 1883. Frederick Douglass once wrote for this paper. Most of the Detroit African American newspapers were weeklies and rarely lasted longer than fifteen years. Unlike most African American newspapers, which collapsed during the Great Depression, the *Detroit Tribune* was established during that period and served the African American community until 1966. In 1936, John H. Sengstacke, the publisher of the *Chicago Defender*, changed the Detroit edition to a full-scale local newspaper, the *Michigan Chronicle*, which is still operating.

The African American community in Detroit has a long tradition of civic, literary, and mutual aid associations. These associations formed the heart of the community-building process. They were the means by which Detroit's black community survived racism and poverty and made its mark on African American and American history.

**FURTHER READINGS**

Boykin, Ulysses W. *A Handbook on the Detroit Negro.* Detroit: Minority Study Associate, 1943.

Dancy, John C. *Sands Against the Winds: The Memoirs of John C. Dancy.* Detroit: Wayne State University Press, 1966.

Katzman, David. *Before the Ghetto: Black Detroit in the Nineteenth Century.* Chicago: University of Illinois Press, 1973.

Thomas, Richard W. *The State of Black Detroit: Building from Strength.* Detroit: Detroit Urban League, 1987.

———. *Life for Us Is What We Make It: Building Black Community in Detroit, 1915–1945.* Bloomington: Indiana University Press, 1992.

*Richard W. Thomas*

# Detroit Interracial Committee

In the wake of the worst race riot in U.S. urban history to that date, Detroit Mayor Edward J. Jeffries Jr., appointed a Peace Committee on June 25, 1943. It consisted of six white and six black members and was headed by William J. Norton, vice president of the Children's Fund of Michigan. The Peace Committee concentrated on tension-reducing programs involving residents and officials rather than assigning blame for the outburst that claimed thirty-four lives and resulted in 765 reported injuries, $2 million in property damage, and the loss of more than one million hours in war production. The Peace Committee was a temporary body that quit meeting three-and-a-half months later amid the racially intense mayoral campaign between Jeffries and Circuit Court Commissioner Frank FitzGerald.

Upon winning his third consecutive term despite the opposition of black voters, union leaders, and white liberals critical of his handling the riot and its aftermath, Jeffries created the Detroit Interracial Committee. With Common Council approval in January 1944, he appointed an eleven-person body, allotted it a budget of $15,000, and empowered it with quasi-official status. He returned Norton as chairman, named four prominent residents, including three blacks, and six municipal department heads. He instructed committee members to promote better race relations in Detroit and improve those municipal social services most affecting race rela-

tions, such as education, housing, health, recreation, safety, and welfare. In part, he drew his ideas from the Peace Committee and Reverend Horace A. White, Detroit housing commissioner.

Within weeks, the Detroit Interracial Committee hired a full-time director, assistant director, and senior stenographer. It selected Harold Thompson, public relations officer of the Detroit Trust Company, as director and social worker Beulah T. Whitby as assistant director. Both provided leadership and coordinated activities. Following a year of conferences with government officials and citizens and the establishment of volunteer subcommittees on education, health, and trends, Thompson was replaced by the more experienced George Schermer of the Federal Public Housing Authority.

Schermer prompted the committee to fashion a policy statement and restructure the program. He reorganized existing operations into areas of research, information, education, and action. In the following eight years, he expanded the staff to nine and, save for his last year, increased the budget steadily. Schermer also maximized the use of subcommittees, for instance on Popular Education. Over time, he advanced the committee through four phases of race relations: (1) reducing tension (rumor control); (2) educating residents and officials (speakers and workshops); (3) advocating democratic positions (policy recommendations and legislation endorsements); and (4) developing community action (field investigations and group meetings). Under Schermer, the committee involved itself in issues ranging from segregation in public housing to citizen complaints of police brutality.

Schermer resigned in March 1953 to become director of the better-financed and, he thought, more committed Philadelphia Commission on Human Relations. Shortly after his departure, Common Council replaced the Detroit Interracial Committee with the Detroit Commission on Community Relations, which operated until 1973. City charter voters later elevated that agency to the Human Rights Department, indicating both its institutional evolution and the original committee's significance as a model for race relations in municipal government.

**FURTHER READINGS**

Schermer, George. "Human Relations in Detroit in the Twentieth Century." Paper presented at the Association for the Study of Negro Life and History Conference, Detroit, Michigan, October 24, 1952.

Tillery, Tyrone. *The Conscience of a City: A Commemorative History of the Detroit Human Rights Commission and Department, 1943–1983.* Detroit: Wayne State University Center for Urban Studies, 1983.

Whitby, Beulah T. "Transfer Summary from the Mayor's Interracial Committee to the Commission on Community Relations." May 14, 1953. George Schermer Collection. Archives of Labor and Urban Affairs, Detroit, Michigan.

White, Horace A. "The City of Detroit Interracial Committee: A Case Study: A Survey of the Objectives, Program, and Methods of an Official Committee Established by the Mayor and Common Council of the City of Detroit." MPA thesis, Institute of Public Administration, Horace H. Rackham School of Graduate Studies, University of Michigan, 1945.

*Dominic J. Capeci Jr.*

## East Bay Negro Historical Society

On July 2, 1965, Eugene and Ruth Lasartemay, Jesse and Marcella Ford, Madison Harvey, and cartoonist Morrie Turner established the East Bay Negro Historical Society (EBNHS) in Berkeley, California. They founded the organization to house black historical materials that previously had been held in family and individual collections. Until the rapidly growing collection compelled the EBNHS to move to a west Oakland storefront within a few years, the Lasartemays stored the artifacts under their bed in their home.

The EBNHS grew out of the Carter G. Woodson Negro history study groups that proliferated earlier in the twentieth century. Its mission to collect, record, present, and disseminate information about the history and culture of African Americans and people of African descent in the East Bay, California, and the western United States also included teaching and community outreach. In 1966, educator Marcella Ford became the first person to teach African American history in night classes in the East Bay public schools.

During the first two decades of its founding, the EBNHS developed and presented black history exhibits, lectures, and programs in schools and institutions throughout the Bay Area. In the early 1970s, it published the *Newsletter*, which later changed its name to *Chronicle of Black History*.

In 1987, the EBNHS became the Northern California Center for Afro-American History and Life (NCCAAHL). Under Executive Director Dr. Lawrence P. Crouchett, the NCCAAHL received a grant from the state of California for the Visions Project. Crouchett, Lonnie G. Bunch, III, and Martha Kendall Winnacker authored the first book about the African American community in the East Bay, *Visions toward Tomorrow: The History of the East Bay Afro-American Community, 1852–1977*, which was published by the NCCAAHL in 1989. That same year, the NCCAAHL mounted an exhibition, *Visions toward Tomorrow: The East Bay Afro-American Community, 1852–1977*, at the Oakland Museum of California. This represented the museum's first black exhibit developed and curated by a black organization. The Visions Project and the 1990 debut of the *From the Archives* newsletter, edited by Crouchett, announced a more scholarly direction for the NCCAAHL. Crouchett died in 1993.

In 1994, the NCCAAHL merged with the Oakland Public Library and became the African American Museum and Library at Oakland (AAMLO). Senior curator Robert L. Haynes served as interim executive director of AAMLO from 1994 to 1995; Hope Hayes served as administrative director from 1995 to 1998; and in July 1998 Mae Bolton became AAMLO's administrative director.

AAMLO, a regional resource center for scholars, the media, and the general public, houses materials by and about African Americans in California and the West. Federal, state, and local funding enabled AAMLO to relocate to expanded facilities in the refurbished Charles Green Library in Oakland's civic center. The site houses a permanent exhibit on California's black history and is the repository for the organization's manuscript, photographic, and material-culture collection. Under the curatorship of Robert L. Haynes, this collection has expanded to include the papers of U.S. Representative Ronald Dellums, U.S. Representative Barbara Lee, Oakland Mayor and former state legislator Elihu Harris, and journalist Belva Davis, the first African American female television journalist in California.

The evolution of the East Bay Negro Historical Society reflects demographic, economic, educational, and social changes in the black and general population of California. Its transformation from a "family-run" organization to its present status as AAMLO illustrates the growing partnership between public and private institutions. However, the organization's essential mission of preserving and sharing western African American history has remained.

**FURTHER READINGS**

Crouchett, Lawrence P., Lonnie G. Bunch, III, and Martha Kendall Winnacker. *Visions toward Tomorrow: The History of the East Bay Afro-American Community, 1852–1977*. Oakland: Northern California Center for Afro-American History and Life, 1989.

East Bay Negro Historical Society. *Chronicle of Black History* 1, 1 (October, 1978).

———. *Newsletter* 1 (September 14, 1971).

———. *Newsletter* 2 (February 14, 1972).

*Shirley Ann Wilson Moore*

# Eastern Colored League

The Mutual Association of Eastern Colored Baseball Clubs, or Eastern Colored League (ECL), was formed in 1923, with five original teams: Brooklyn Royal Giants, Lincoln Giants of New York, Atlantic City Bacharach Giants, Baltimore Black Sox, and Hilldale. Before the season started, a sixth team, Alex Pompez's Cuban Stars, joined the ECL. During the league's early years, Hilldale was the best team, winning pennants in each of the first three years.

The league was governed by six commissioners, one from each team. Ed Bolden from Philadelphia and Nat Strong from Brooklyn, New York, were the two most powerful commissioners. Strong's authority stemmed from the fact that he controlled the bookings for all black teams and many white teams in New York City. Strong's control would remain a controversial issue throughout the history of the league, because he was white, and he often ignored the league schedule for his own profit and convenience.

The Negro National League (NNL), founded in 1920 by Rube Foster, was the rival of the Eastern League. Many players left their NNL teams for the ECL, enticed by better pay and shorter travel. A war of words broke out between league officials. Peaceful coexistence began to prevail in 1924, when the two leagues agreed to a world series and to honor the contracts of each other's players.

The Kansas City Monarchs, behind their star, Hall of Famer Bullet Rogan, prevailed over Hilldale in the first world series. Two of Hilldale's stars were Hall of Famer Judy Johnson and Biz Mackey, one of the many Negro League stars who is deserving of being inducted into the Hall of Fame. The following year, the same teams met again. Only this time Hilldale brought home the world championship to the ECL.

Most of the ECL seasons were designed to include seventy league games. Many dates were left open for playing independent teams, especially local or touring white teams. The league's schedule was sometimes ignored or not precisely kept by some of the teams, and this, along with poor umpiring and disputes over statistics, plagued the otherwise successful operation.

Bad weather and poor attendance added to the league's difficulties in 1926. A relatively new franchise, Newark, disbanded, and Strong's Royal Giants continued their sporadic observance of the schedule. The downward spiral continued in 1927, as the Lincoln Giants dropped out of the league, the Bacharach team went bankrupt, and Bolden experienced some serious health problems.

The year 1928 was the league's last. Strong removed his team from the league, and, though Bolden was again in good health, he pulled out Hilldale, pointing out persistent scheduling and money problems. Both men believed that their teams would be better off playing as independents, an approach that had been successful for them prior to the formation of the league.

The league had lasted six years, had produced some great teams, like the 1925 Hilldale World Champions, and spotlighted some of the great players of that era, including Johnson, Mackey, Pop Lloyd, Jud Wilson, Oscar Charleston, Louis Santop, and Martin Dihigo.

**FURTHER READINGS**

Lanctot, Neil. *Fair Dealing and Clean Playing: The Hilldale Club and the Development of Black Professional Baseball, 1910–1932*. Jefferson, N.C.: McFarland, 1994.

Peterson, Robert. *Only the Ball Was White: A History of Legendary Black Players and All-Black Professional Teams*. New York: Oxford University Press, 1970.

Rogosin, Donn. *Invisible Men: Life in Baseball's Negro Leagues*. New York: Kodansha International, 1995.

*Lyle K. Wilson*

SEE ALSO Baseball Hall of Fame–Negro Leagues; International League; Middle States Baseball League; National Negro Baseball Leagues; Negro American League; Negro National League; Negro Southern League; West Coast Baseball Association

## Episcopal Church, Conference of Church Workers Among Colored People

*See* Conference of Church Workers Among Colored People, Episcopal Church.

## Episcopal Commission for Black Ministries

In 1973, the Episcopal General Convention created the Episcopal Commission for Black Ministries (ECBM) in response to pressure from the Union of Black Clergy and Laity (UBE).

During the first four decades of the twentieth century, the Episcopal Church had made only sporadic attempts at administering to the needs of black Episcopalians. In 1940, presiding Bishop Henry Knox Sherrill appointed Reverend Bravid Washington Harris executive secretary for negro work. The work was discontinued in 1967 and replaced with the General Convention's Special Programs Department the following year. Black Episcopalians, concerned about the absence of an office devoted exclusively to their needs, protested their abandonment. Their protest, however, was unsuccessful. Undaunted by their initial failure and inspired by the mounting civil rights movement, the UBE successfully petitioned the 1973 General Convention, which created the ECBM.

The ECBM seeks to make the church more responsive to the needs of its black communicants, to promote greater black self-determination, and to enable African American Episcopalians to share their culture and traditions with the greater church community. More recently, the ECBM has been responsible for the publication of two black hymnals, *Lift Every Voice and Sing I* (1981) and the revised *Lift Every Voice and Sing II* (1992). Both volumes reflect the rich musical tradition of African Americans and the black historical experience. The ECBM also publishes a newsletter, *Linkage,* and a *Black Clergy Directory.*

Today, under the leadership of coordinator Reverend Lynn A. Collins, the ECBM concentrates on the recruit-ment, training, and deployment of black clergy and seminarians and offers financial aid and training to small black rural and urban congregations.

**FURTHER READINGS**

Collins, Lynn A. *"Let My People Go": The History of the Office for Black Ministries.* New York: Episcopal Church Center, 1995.

Sheridan, Sharon. "Black Ministries Office Builds Up Local Leaders." *Episcopal Life* (March 1997), 34.

Sumner, David E. *The Episcopal Church's History, 1945–1985.* Wilton, Conn.: Moorhouse, 1987.

*A. J. Scopino Jr.*

## Equal Employment Opportunity Commission

Created under the 1964 Civil Rights Act, the Equal Employment Opportunity Commission (EEOC) has been the chief federal agency for enforcing laws against employment discrimination by businesses, unions, employment agencies, and state and local governments. By the late 1990s, the agency, with more than twenty-five hundred full-time employees and a budget of $242 million, received approximately eighty thousand complaints annually in a wide array of areas that included race, gender, sexual harassment, and disability status.

The EEOC emerged out of the dramatic legislative struggle of 1963–1964. Direct-action protests across the South during the early 1960s, especially the confrontation in Birmingham, Alabama, in May 1963 between Reverend Martin Luther King, Jr. and Police Commissioner Bull Connor's police dogs, intensified pressure on President John F. Kennedy to back a strong civil rights measure. Kennedy did so in June, but his plan, which centered on ending segregation in public accommodations, did not contain an employment section because the president feared that including one would doom the bill. Civil rights proponents in the United States House of Representatives however, added Title VII, an antiemployment-discrimination provision that would be enforced by the EEOC, a five-member body appointed by the president and confirmed by the United States Senate. The new body, proponents hoped, would not stir the bitter opposition that had blocked legislation to create a Fair Employment Practices Committee (FEPC) during the 1940s and 1950s. Under the House plan, the EEOC would have the power to receive and investigate complaints, subpoena witnesses, require firms under its jurisdiction to

Clarence Thomas, chairman of the EEOC, 1985.
© *Bettmann/Corbis*

keep employment records, and file suit. The power to file suit proved especially controversial in the Senate, where Republican Everett Dirksen of Illinois led a successful effort to strip the EEOC of this authority. Under the final compromise, only the United States Justice Department could sue where a "pattern or practice" of employment discrimination existed. Thus, the EEOC would be an information-gathering organization that could rely only on persuasion in trying to prod employers to change their ways. The lack of enforcement powers greatly alarmed liberals in Congress and leaders from numerous civil rights organizations. Jack Greenberg of the National Association for the Advancement of Colored People (NAACP) Legal Defense and Education Fund dismissed Title VII as "weak, cumbersome, probably unworkable." Similarly, James Farmer of the Congress of Racial Equality (CORE) lamented that "before an aggrieved person can get a remedy, he may have found another job or starved to death."

A lack of enthusiasm among civil rights proponents was not the only difficulty the EEOC faced during the administration of President Lyndon B. Johnson. A month before it was to begin operation in July 1965, the EEOC had no leadership, staff or office. Johnson finally named Franklin D. Roosevelt, Jr., to head the agency, but Roosevelt showed his commitment to his new job by immediately setting off for a week of yachting before getting down to work. Roosevelt's predilection for the sea was apparent two months later, for, as Congress debated the EEOC's budget, he once again could be found on his boat. Johnson had counted on Roosevelt to give the EEOC instant credibility and power, but the former president's son resigned in April 1966. Indeed, four different individuals headed the agency during its first five years. The agency had no leader for three months during the summer of 1966, and for a time in 1967 there were two open seats. A measure of stability finally arrived in August 1967 when Clifford Alexander, Jr., an African American attorney, assumed the reigns.

A scarcity of resources compounded the leadership problem. The EEOC budget for fiscal year 1967 was a paltry $5.2 million, less than the Office of Coal Research. The budget increased only slightly over the next two years, but, in fact, the EEOC was losing ground because its jurisdiction expanded enormously. Initially covering organizations with one hundred or more employees, the EEOC by 1968 was responsible for enforcing equal employment opportunity at firms and unions with twenty-five or more workers. This represented an increase of nearly six million workers. The Federal Crop Insurance Program had a larger staff than the EEOC. A study by the Brookings Institution in 1967 observed that the EEOC was "very new, very weak, and very small." Urban League Director Whitney Young told Congress: "The actual agency experience . . . has given rise to disillusionment and a lack of confidence." Sources as diverse as the *Nation,* the *Wall Street Journal,* and the Budget Bureau offered similar pessimistic assessments.

It was thus no surprise that the EEOC had enormous difficulty processing cases. Budgetary, leadership, and technical difficulties, however, were not the only sources of the mounting caseload. Congress had mandated that the EEOC resolve complaints within sixty days of receipt, but by 1968 the agency faced a backlog of two years. Greater reliance on computers did little to solve the problem. Civil rights agencies, in an effort to prod Congress to give the EEOC more power, had flooded the agency with complaints. "We think the best way to get it amended," Jack Greenberg noted, "is to show that it doesn't work."

Problems within the leadership of the EEOC and the backlog of cases created an opportunity for staff to redefine the agency's role and place it at the fore of a quiet but dramatic shift in the conceptualization of employment law by the early 1970s. Traditional models of employment discrimination, embodied in state and local FEPCs across the North and then the EEOC, saw discrimination as an isolated matter remedied by the filing of complaints by individuals who believed they had been discriminated against. The standard of proof was showing that an employer had intended to discriminate. Employment decisions were to be color blind. By the mid-1960s, however, many civil rights leaders had concluded that discrimination was more subtle, and more widespread, than the traditional model assumed. The case-by-case approach was too slow and cumbersome to solve the massive problem of black unemployment and underemployment, while intent was almost impossible to prove. According to the new theory of institutional racism, meanwhile, discrimination could exist without a deliberate policy to exclude minorities. Rutgers University Professor Alfred Blumrosen, a strong critic of the traditional approach, helped propel the EEOC in a different direction when, in the summer of 1965, he discovered "Form 40," which the President's Committee on Equal Employment Opportunity (PCEEO) had sent to federal contractors. "Form 40" asked employers to indicate the number of African Americans they employed, making it easy for the EEOC to determine which employers had few or no African American workers. By March 1966, the EEOC was sending to every organization in its jurisdiction form EEO-1, which required employers to keep track of the race of every employee. Areas with low numbers of African Americans would be presumed to be areas with a great deal of discrimination. The EEOC need not wait for a complaint followed by a lengthy and difficult investigation to combat discrimination. Proof of commitment to equal opportunity would lie not in an employer's intent but rather in the effects of its employment practices on minority workers. The goal was no longer equal opportunity for employment but rather for African Americans to be hired and promoted in accordance with their numbers in the population. The agency also implemented this approach in attacking the use of employment tests and the seniority systems in many unions. Given the backlog of cases, pressures from the civil rights movement on the federal government in the wake of urban violence, and growing attention to African American poverty, it is not surprising that the EEOC was looking for a new method. In adopting this statistically driven, equal-results model, the EEOC directly contradicted several provisions of the 1964 Civil Rights Act. The changes were justified, EEOC administrators argued, because improving economic opportunity for African Americans, not creating rigid bureaucratic guidelines, was Congress's primary concern in drafting Title VII. The EEOC worked quickly to build a record of case law supporting the new standards, and this effort reached a culmination in 1971, when the United States Supreme Court endorsed the results-driven model in *Griggs v. Duke Power*. In just six years, the agency had overcome much of its early troubles and was revolutionizing how the nation thought about and enforced equal employment opportunity. Begun as a conciliatory agency that was to mediate between the accused and the accuser, the EEOC was now aggressively advocating on behalf of those who had suffered from discrimination.

The EEOC's influence broadened in other ways during the 1970s. Efforts to grant it cease-and-desist powers, which had been underway since the mid-1960s, ran into strong opposition from conservatives, who saw the agency as harassing businesses. As a compromise, Congress and the administration of President Richard M. Nixon agreed to allow the EEOC to sue employers in court and expand the agency's jurisdiction to firms and unions with fifteen or more employees. In 1978, the EEOC gained responsibility for coordinating the equal opportunity efforts of other federal agencies. That year was also notable for the fact that Eleanor Holmes Norton became the first African American woman to head the EEOC.

The EEOC became a center of controversy during the 1980s. President Ronald Reagan appointed a black lawyer, Clarence Thomas, who would later be named by President George Bush to the Supreme Court, to head the agency. Civil rights groups protested vociferously, for Thomas opposed the equal-results, statistically based, group-centered standard developed during the late 1960s and believed that African Americans should rely less heavily on the federal government. The Reagan years were notable for budgetary difficulties and a decline in the number of staff, but Thomas's chief legacy was moving the agency away from broad class-action suits against major companies and more toward individual complaints.

The EEOC underwent some notable changes during the 1990s. Alarmed by the agency's direction under

Thomas, Chair Gilbert Casellas vowed to return to stressing broad "pattern or practice" cases over individual complaints. During fiscal year 1997, the EEOC won $111 million in benefits for victims of discrimination, a record high. After swelling during the early 1990s, the number of cases pending dropped by more than 50 percent between 1995 and 1998, and the agency resolved cases faster than new charges were filed. Critics, however, complained that these numbers merely indicated that the agency had simply chosen to concentrate on cases that were easier to win. Meanwhile, in 1996 the EEOC implemented a mediation program as an alternative to traditional dispute resolution. The 1990s were also notable for increased educational efforts by the agency.

**FURTHER READINGS**

Gillon, Steve. *Laws of Unintended Consequences.* New York: Norton, 2000.

Graham, Hugh. *The Civil Rights Era: Origins and Development of National Policy, 1960–1972.* New York: Oxford University Press, 1990.

Moreno, Paul. *From Direct Action to Affirmative Action: Fair Employment Law and Policy in America, 1939–1972.* Baton Rouge: Louisiana State University Press, 1997.

Skrentny, John David. *The Ironies of Affirmative Action: Politics, Culture, and Justice in America.* Chicago: University of Chicago Press, 1996.

*Timothy N. Thurber*

## Equal Suffrage League

The Equal Suffrage League was organized in Brooklyn, New York, in the late 1880s to advocate black women's suffrage. It remained a small but active force until the death of its founder, Sarah Garnet, in 1911. The league insisted that women had the same human intellectual and spiritual capabilities as men and that denial of women's right to vote in a nation that was founded on the ideal of the people's right to rule was unjust.

In the late nineteenth and early twentieth centuries, few African American women supported women's suffrage. Many black women accepted prevalent gender roles that relegated women to the "private sphere" of the home and family. Even though many black wives and mothers worked outside the home, many believed that women's involvement in public, political activities would compromise their femininity. When African American women supported women's suffrage, they did so with the twin goals of promoting gender justice and racial progress. The ballot, black women hoped, would enable them to protect their economic interests as workers, improve educational opportunities for themselves and their children, safeguard against sexual exploitation perpetrated by white males, and protest black male disenfranchisement, which, by the turn of the century, had been implemented by nearly all southern states and was common practice in many of the northern states.

The league was the brainchild of Sarah J. Smith Tompkins Garnet, a pioneering New York City educator of African American and Native American Indian descent. Garnet, who began teaching in 1846 at age fourteen, continued to adopt new pedagogical methods throughout her teaching and administrative career. In 1863, her efforts were recognized when she became the first African American woman to be appointed principal in the New York City public school system, where she worked to abolish race-based discrimination against all colored teachers. Throughout her life, she championed equal rights for women, supporting suffrage and equal pay for equal work performed by women, as well as other causes that promoted social justice.

When Garnet founded the league, its initial numbers were so small that it met in the back of her Brooklyn seamstress shop. Later the league met in the homes of its wealthy members. In the early 1900s, Garnet became superintendent of the Suffrage Department of the National Association of Colored Women (NACW), and the league affiliated with the NACW. Dr. Verina Harris Morton-Jones was another leading member, and president, of the league. She was one of the first African American women to receive a medical degree. In the 1880s, she first practiced medicine in Mississippi; beginning in the 1890s she practiced in Brooklyn and Long Island. Actively involved in a variety of women's clubs, Morton-Jones promoted women's suffrage, the protection of black males' right to vote, education, community uplift, and civil rights. Like Garnet, Morton-Jones joined the NACW and became director of its Mother's Club in Brooklyn in the early 1900s.

In 1905, Morton-Jones and Garnet supported the formation of the radical Niagara Movement that aggressively and unconditionally demanded equal rights for all Americans. In 1907, the league and the NACW passed a joint resolution supporting the principles on which the Niagara Movement was founded and praised its uncompromising pursuit of racial justice. This resolution put the league and the NACW on the side of the radical Niagara

Movement led by W. E. B. Du Bois, and in opposition to Booker T. Washington and his more popular accommodationist racial uplift strategies.

FURTHER READINGS

Brown, Hallie Q. *Homespun Heroines and Other Women of Distinction.* New York: Oxford University Press, 1988.

Cott, Nancy F. *The Grounding of Modern Feminism.* New Haven: Yale University Press, 1987.

Salem, Dorothy. *To Better Our World: Black Women in Organized Reform, 1890–1920.* Brooklyn, N.Y.: Carlson, 1990.

Wesley, Charles Harris. *The History of the National Association of Colored Women's Clubs: A Legacy of Service.* Washington D.C.: National Association of Colored Women's Clubs, 1984.

*Karen Garner*

## Eta Phi Beta

In October 1942, eleven black women—Dorothy Sylvers Brown, Ivy Burt, Earline B. Carter, Mae Edwards Curry, Katherine F. Douglas, Merry Green Hubbard, Ethel Madison, Ann Porter, Mattie Rankin, Lena Reed, and Atheline Shelton—founded Eta Phi Beta at the predominantly black Lewis College of Business in Detroit. The founders of Eta Phi Beta sought to encourage black women to enter business careers and provide them with a support network and financial assistance through scholarships. The sorority fosters high scholastic standards, personal growth, career awareness and enhancement, and community service.

Eta Phi Beta provides its members with opportunities for personal fellowship, professional networking, and career enhancement. It sponsors business management seminars for black women across the country, hosts social and informational events at black churches to acquaint the community with the sorority, and promotes scholarship among young black women. Local chapters send speakers to high schools during "Career Day" and pro-

vide high school graduates with scholarships to attend college. Eta Phi Beta also sponsors youth auxiliaries for black children age twelve to eighteen: Senords for boys, and Bee-ettes for girls. These youth groups meet at Eta Phi Beta's biennial national convention. Husbands of Eta Phi Beta sorors have formed their own auxiliary, the National Auxiliary of Shad Clubs, Inc., which provides assistance for the sorority's activities.

Eta Phi Beta contributes to various charities and supports educational programs for developmentally disabled citizens. Eta Phi Beta has financially supported institutions such as the Shelly School Development Center in Raleigh, North Carolina, and the Dorothy Sylvers-Brown Developmental School in Los Angeles, California. Since the mid-1980s, Eta Phi Beta has contributed more than $500,000 to the United Negro College Fund in support of scholarships for disadvantaged black students. Meanwhile, local chapters continue to raise funds and award scholarships to individuals attending college.

Headquartered in Detroit, Eta Phi Beta has approximately five thousand members in ninety-one chapters in the United States and the Virgin Islands. Members gather every two years for a national convention.

FURTHER READINGS

Eta Phi Beta. *Not for Ourselves but for Others.* np., nd.

———. Gamma Omega Chapter Cultural Committee. *Tea Time in the South: A Southern Tradition.* February 23, 1997.

*Robin B. Balthrope*

## Evangelical Lutheran Church in America, Commission for Multicultural Ministries

*See* Commission for Multicultural Ministries, Evangelical Lutheran Church in America.

## Experts-in-Training

*See* Southern Regional Council.

## Fahy Committee

*See* President's Committee on Equality of Treatment and Opportunity in the Armed Forces.

## Fair Employment Practice Committee

*See* President's Committee on Fair Employment Practice.

## Fair Share Organization

The Fair Share Organization (FSO) was a direct-action protest group active in northern Indiana, including Gary, Michigan City, and East Chicago, in the 1950s and 1960s. The leaders of the FSO included local activists Hilbert L. Bradley, Julius James, Willie Byrd Jr., David C. Mitchell, and Maurice Preston. The FSO was one of many organizations that were part of the move of the civil rights movement from the South to the urban North. Instead of fighting legal segregation, as southern groups had done, northern activists focused on problems such as equal access to housing and employment.

The FSO began picketing local businesses in the late 1950s. It identified employers with few or no African American employees and demanded that they hire a certain number of blacks. If employers refused to implement the FSO's demands, the organization launched boycotts and pickets.

The FSO began its picketing campaign in an uncertain legal setting. Direct-action campaigns for jobs had been popular in black neighborhoods during the Great Depression; however, state courts had often issued injunctions against them. In 1938, the United States Supreme Court curbed the power of states to prevent direct action campaigns when it ruled in *New Negro Alliance v. Sanitary Grocery Company* that the federal courts could not issue injunctions stopping boycotts or pickets under the Norris-LaGuardia anti-injunction act of 1932. In 1950, however, the Supreme Court's ruling in *Hughes v. Superior Court* allowed state courts to continue to issue such injunctions to prohibit picketing for illegal purposes, including quota hiring demands.

When the FSO made racial-quota hiring demands on local retail establishments, business owners appealed to the Indiana courts for injunctions. The courts agreed and enjoined the FSO, ordering it to pay $10,000 in damages to the Philip Nagdeman and Sons clothing store in East Chicago. Appellate courts sustained the judgment, and in 1964 the U.S. Supreme Court declined to review the case. These injunctions effectively ended the FSO's efforts.

Like the FSO, the Congress of Racial Equality (CORE) and other civil rights groups participated in direct-action campaigns in border states and northern cities. Some of the groups negotiated with employers and won immediate concessions; others picketed successfully; and others were enjoined and chastised by local courts. The legal status of such direct-action campaigns remains unsettled but became less important after national fair-employment legislation was passed by the United States Congress and signed into law by President Lyndon B. Johnson as part of the Civil Rights Act of 1964.

**FURTHER READINGS**

Gelber, Steven. *Black Men and Businessmen: The Growing Awareness of a Social Responsibility.* Port Washington, N.Y.: Kennikat, 1974.

Rosen, Sanford Jay. "The Law and Racial Discrimination in Employment." *California Law Review* 53 (1965), 729–799.

Weiner, Harold M. "Negro Picketing for Employment Equality." *Howard Law Journal* 13 (1967), 271–302.

*Paul D. Moreno*

## Federal Council on Negro Affairs

Formed in 1936 in Washington, D.C., the Federal Council on Negro Affairs, popularly known as the Black Brain Trust or the Black Cabinet, was an informal group of black government officials. The council was composed of more than two dozen so-called Negro advisers who had been appointed by President Franklin D. Roosevelt to advise federal agencies and departments on racial matters. Key appointments included Mary McLeod Bethune (National Youth Administration), Edgar Brown (Civilian Conservation Corps), Joseph H. Evans (Farm Security Administration), Crystal Bird Fauset (Office of Civil Defense), William H. Hastie (Interior Department), Frank Horne (Housing Authority), Campbell C. Johnson (Selective Service), Eugene K. Jones (Department of Commerce), Edward H. Lawson Jr. (Works Project Administration), Lawrence A. Oxley (Department of Labor), William J. Trent (Federal Works Agency), Robert L. Vann (assistant to the attorney general), and Robert C. Weaver (Public Works Administration).

Council members met frequently at the house of Mary McLeod Bethune and sometimes at the home of Robert Weaver to discuss the problems facing black Americans, share information, and coordinate strategies to advance civil rights. During the Roosevelt years, the Black Cabinet served as a vital conduit between black leaders such as A. Philip Randolph and Walter White and policymakers in the White House. They gathered complaints, discussed solutions to problems, and presented them to the president's closest advisers, including Eleanor Roosevelt. Council members also affected public policy. Robert C. Weaver, for instance, helped shape Public Works Administration employment programs by instituting quotas to ensure a fair level of black representation on New Deal work projects. Furthermore, as one historian has pointed out, the Black Brain Trust altered the federal bureaucracy by stopping many of the"overt racial indignities previously accepted as routine" (Sitkoff 1978, 79). Harvard Sitkoff tells the story of Mary Bethune's first trip to the White House to meet President Roosevelt. As she crossed the White House lawn, the white gardener called out to her: "Hey, there, Auntie, where y'all think your goin'?" Bethune wheeled around and replied: "For a moment I didn't recognize you. Which one of my sister's children are you?"

(Sitkoff 1978, 80). The gardener never attempted to stop Bethune again. More powerful New Deal appointees also learned to respect members of the Black Cabinet.

There is a debate among historians about the impact of the council. Some scholars claim that it is another example of Roosevelt's unwillingness to make meaningful civil rights reforms and was no more than a symbolic gesture. Black Cabinet members never had the political power necessary to eliminate discrimination and racial prejudice in American society, let alone in the U.S. government. Nevertheless, the Black Brain Trust was a highly publicized example of what the New Deal meant to black Americans. For the first time since Reconstruction, a president was at the very least attentive to the problems and aspirations of African Americans.

Roosevelt's efforts on behalf of blacks such as these administrative appointments contributed to a voting shift as African Americans abandoned the party of Lincoln for the party of Roosevelt. Moreover, council members left their mark on federal policies, especially in the area of fair employment and what has become known as affirmative action. They helped end discriminatory practices in several federal agencies. Finally, after the New Deal, some of the Black Brain Trusters continued to serve the federal government. Perhaps the best illustration is the career of Robert Weaver, who, in 1965, became the first black cabinet official, heading the newly created Department of Housing and Urban Development. In short, these Roosevelt appointees, their informal organization, and its accomplishments are another aspect of what some have labeled as "the seedtime for the modern civil rights era."

**FURTHER READINGS**

Kirby, John B. *Black Americans in the Roosevelt Era: Liberalism and Race.* Knoxville: University of Tennessee Press, 1980.

Reed, Merl E. *Seedtime for the Modern Civil Rights Movement: The President's Committee on Fair Employment Practice, 1941–1946.* Baton Rouge: Louisiana State University Press, 1991.

Sitkoff, Harvard. *A New Deal for Blacks: The Emergence of Civil Rights as a National Issue: The Depression Decade.* New York: Oxford University Press, 1978.

Sternsher, Bernard, ed. *The Negro in Depression and War.* Chicago: Quadrangle Books, 1969.

Weiss, Nancy J. *Farewell to the Party of Lincoln: Black Politics in the Age of FDR.* Princeton, N.J.: Princeton University Press, 1983.

*Andrew E. Kersten*

# Federated Colored Catholics of the United States

In 1924, Thomas Wyatt Turner (1877–1976) founded the Federated Colored Catholics of the United States to combat racism and discrimination in the U.S. Catholic Church. Turner was born in Hughesville, Maryland, on March 16, 1877, the son of black Catholic sharecropper parents. Eager to learn at an early age, Turner enrolled in Charlotte Hall, an Episcopal school in St. Mary's County in 1892. Graduating in 1894, Turner attended the Howard University Preparatory School between 1895 and 1897 and graduated from Howard University four years later.

Pursuing graduate studies at Catholic University in Washington, D.C., shortly thereafter, he was forced to withdraw due to lack of funds. Following his departure, he taught at various schools, including Tuskegee Institute in Alabama and Baltimore High and Training School in Maryland, both institutions for black students. He returned to Howard to earn a master's degree in biology in 1905. He continued his graduate studies at Cornell University, where he earned a doctorate in botany in 1921. He later returned to Howard as an instructor in the sciences.

When Turner returned to Howard University and Washington, D.C., the black community was disturbed over the increasing discrimination confronting African Americans in federal agencies that accompanied the election of Democrat Woodrow Wilson in 1912. At about the same time, Catholic University, under heavy southern influence, reversed its admissions policy and started to exclude black students. Outraged about these incidents of racial discrimination, Turner became a secretary for the Washington branch of the National Association for the Advancement of Colored People (NAACP). His experience in that position provided him with the opportunity to study contemporary institutional racism.

Of all the grievances involving discrimination at that time, Turner was disturbed most by the lack of educational opportunities for black children in the Catholic school system. Black Catholic parents were encouraged to provide a Catholic education for their children, but these same children were denied further advancement at Catholic institutions of higher learning.

Frustrated, Turner founded the Committee for the Advancement of Colored Catholics in 1916–1917. The group was composed of black lay men and women who called upon Church officials to improve relations between black and white Catholics, provide better educational opportunities for black Catholics, and improve the spiritual and temporal conditions of the church's African American communicants. By 1919, the committee added the need for a native black clergy to its demands.

In 1924, the committee was renamed the Federated Colored Catholics of the United States, and Turner was elected president. Shortly after 1925, two white Jesuits, John LaFarge and William Markoe, lent their support to the Federated Catholics and urged the organization to work for justice through biracial means. Turner, however, defended the group's racial exclusivity. This appealed to many black Catholics, and, by the early 1930s, the organization boasted 100,000 members. In 1934, Turner and the Jesuits parted ways, which ultimately diminished the influence of the Federated Catholics. The growing interest in interracial activism among black and white Catholics, as a means of combating racism, replaced Turner's all-black federation. Nevertheless, the Federated Catholics continued to lobby for African Americans until the mid-1950s.

Although Turner and the Federated Catholics were unable to end discriminatory practices in the Church, they were able to focus attention on the subject of race. Ultimately, this generated greater participation of white Catholics in addressing racial issues.

**FURTHER READINGS**

Coakley, Jay J., and Richard A. Lammana. "The Catholic Church and the Negro." In *Contemporary Catholicism in the United States*. Ed. Philip Gleason. Notre Dame, Ind.: University of Notre Dame Press, 1969, 147–196.

Davis, Cyprian, O.S.B. *The History of Black Catholics in the United States*. New York: Crossroad, 1991.

Ochs, Stephen J. *Desegregating the Altar: The Josephites and the Struggle for Black Priests, 1871–1960*. Baton Rouge: Louisiana State University Press, 1990.

Raboteau, Albert J. *A Fire in the Bones: Reflections on African-American Religious History*. Boston: Beacon, 1995.

*A. J. Scopino Jr.*

# Federated Council of Churches, Department of Race Relations

*See* National Council of Churches, Commission on Religion and Race.

# Federated Council of Churches, Department of Racial and Cultural Relations

*See* National Council of Churches, Commission on Religion and Race.

## Federation of Southern Cooperatives

*See* Southern Regional Council.

## Fellowship of Reconciliation

The Fellowship of Reconciliation (FOR), a Christian pacifist organization, played a vital role in the movement for African American civil rights in the 1940s and 1950s. Though FOR's primary goal has always been the eradication of war, during the mid-twentieth century it broadened its mission to support the use of nonviolent tactics to challenge racism and segregation in the United States. The Congress of Racial Equality (CORE) and the American Committee on Africa were born with FOR's help. Civil rights activists James Farmer and Bayard Rustin spent the formative portions of their careers on FOR's payroll. During World War II, FOR led the fight to desegregate federal prisons. In 1947, it sponsored the Journey of Reconciliation, a model for the later Freedom Rides. And in 1956, FOR activists advised the Reverend Martin Luther King Jr. and the Montgomery Improvement Association on the use of nonviolence in their crusade to desegregate the Montgomery, Alabama, bus system.

FOR began in late 1914, at a meeting of European Christian Socialists in Cambridge, England. The outbreak of World War I served as the backdrop for FOR's rejection of violent solutions to conflict. One of FOR's original British members, Henry T. Hodgkin, founded the first U.S. branch in 1915. By the end of 1918, FOR counted more than one thousand members in the United States.

Though the vast majority of FOR's membership was white, the organization was always open to African American pacifists. One of them, Howard University theologian Howard Thurman, served as vice chairman of FOR in the late 1920s. But it was not until 1940 that FOR took an active interest in U.S. race relations. That year, A. J. Muste became FOR's executive secretary. Muste's meandering career had led him through the Presbyterian ministry twice, the leadership of a Quaker meeting, and union organizing. He had at various times been a Christian pacifist, a Marxist, and a Trotskyite, until a spiritual experience led him to disavow violence and return to his pacifist roots.

Muste's tenure at FOR coincided with the organization's most important work for African American rights. He penned FOR's first civil rights tract—"What the Bible Teaches about Freedom: A Message to the Negro Churches," which argued that Jim Crow laws and violence were inimical to true Christianity. Out of concern for the well-being of jailed conscientious objectors, he led FOR's campaign against segregation in federal prisons. Moreover, he hired two young African American pacifists, James Farmer (a student of Howard Thurman at Howard University) and Bayard Rustin, who became the leaders of FOR's new Department of Race Relations.

Wartime persecution of pacifists had led FOR to organize its members into local "cells." Farmer, as FOR field secretary in Chicago, took an active role in the Chicago cell. That cell, largely made up of black and white students from the University of Chicago, dedicated itself both to pacifism and desegregation. The cell's success, albeit limited, in desegregating Chicago's Hyde Park neighborhood and a skating rink called White City inspired Farmer to propose to Muste a "brotherhood mobilization" that would apply Gandhian nonviolence to American racism.

The leadership of FOR was divided on the wisdom of accepting Farmer's proposal. Opponents argued that an increased focus on race relations would distract FOR from the more pressing job of opposing the violence of World War II. As a compromise, FOR allowed Farmer to devote his time to the creation of a semiautonomous civil rights organization while remaining on FOR's payroll. The result was the first branch of CORE, founded in 1942. By the summer of 1943, CORE had become a national organization, with Farmer, George Houser, and Bernice Fisher, all members of the Chicago FOR cell, among its leadership.

The relationship between FOR and CORE was never easy. In return for bankrolling CORE, FOR's board of directors expected to have some control over CORE's direction. Muste moved Farmer from Chicago to New York City in 1943 to make sure he devoted enough time to FOR work. Farmer could not countenance the restrictions and left FOR in 1945. Muste also limited CORE's fund-raising attempts, arguing that fund-raising was FOR's responsibility. Still, Muste was CORE's strongest supporter among FOR's leaders; when he left FOR in 1953, the fellowship severed its ties with CORE.

While Farmer and his Chicago cellmates were founding CORE, FOR strove to promote racial equality on a national level. Bayard Rustin was FOR's point man on much of this work. Rustin, raised a Quaker, had already been an organizer for the Young Communist League and for A. Philip Randolph's March on Washington movement when he joined FOR's staff in September 1941. As the head of FOR's Youth Division, Rustin spoke on college campuses across the nation, urging students to abandon violence and segregation. He represented FOR in Randolph's planned summer of civil disobedience in 1943. Randolph called off the campaign after riots in Detroit and Harlem made provocative protest too dangerous. And after a two-year stint in federal prison for refusing to enter a civilian work camp for conscientious objectors, Rustin led FOR's Journey of Reconciliation.

In the 1946 case *Morgan v. Virginia*, the United States Supreme Court had ruled segregation on interstate transit unconstitutional. Rustin and George Houser, a FOR employee and a member of CORE's leadership, organized the Journey of Reconciliation, a bus ride through the Upper South to test compliance. Sixteen men, eight black and eight white, boarded two buses in Washington, D.C. The journey was peaceful until they reached the outskirts of Chapel Hill, North Carolina. There, several riders were arrested for breaching local segregation laws, and one, James Peck, was beaten by onlookers. The judge, claiming he had never heard of *Morgan v. Virginia*, sentenced four of the riders to thirty days on a chain gang. The decision was upheld by the North Carolina Supreme Court, and the National Association for the Advancement of Colored People (NAACP), citing inadequate court records, decided against further appeals. Three of the four riders, including Rustin, were released for good behavior after serving twenty-two days of the thirty-day sentence.

After his time on the chain gang, Rustin returned to FOR headquarters. There, he continued to lead FOR's race-relations work. In 1948, he again joined with A. Philip Randolph, this time to organize the protest effort that led President Harry S. Truman to issue Executive Order 9981, banning segregation in the military. In 1952, after an appeal from the African National Congress for help in organizing nonviolent civil disobedience against apartheid, Rustin and Houser helped FOR found Americans for South African Resistance, later to become the American Committee on Africa, the first U.S.-based organization opposing racism in Africa.

The year 1952 marked the high point of FOR's efforts to improve race relations. By the end of 1953, those efforts were almost dead. In January 1953, Rustin gave a speech to the American Association of University Women in Pasadena, California. Later that night, he was arrested for having sex with two other men. The arrest drew national attention and linked Rustin to FOR. In the aftermath, Muste fired Rustin. Later that year, Muste himself left FOR, and with him went much of the board's support for CORE. George Houser remained with FOR until 1954, when he took over the full-time leadership of the American Committee for Africa.

FOR's final foray into the national civil rights spotlight came in 1956 in Montgomery, Alabama. As soon as he heard of the Montgomery bus boycott, Rustin, now a field secretary for the War Resister's League, raced to Montgomery. Rustin provided advice on nonviolence to the Montgomery Improvement Association, which, early in the protest, had allowed protesters to carry handguns for self-defense, until the Alabama media raised his links with Communism and homosexuality. Rustin left for Birmingham. From there, he contacted FOR. The fellowship dispatched Glenn Smiley, a Methodist minister and friend of Rustin's, to take his place. Smiley stayed in Montgomery until the boycott was won. When the first desegregated bus rolled through Montgomery, Smiley sat at Martin Luther King Jr.'s side, symbolizing the important role that FOR and its vision of nonviolence had played in the success of the boycott.

Since 1956, FOR has maintained consistent support for racial equality, but its most important role is historical. As an important source of Gandhian nonviolence, FOR contributed a powerful method in America's battle for racial equality. And, as the launching point for James Farmer and Bayard Rustin, as the parent of CORE and the American Committee on Africa, FOR provided the organizational basis for some of the most creative activists and organizations in the history of the civil rights movement.

**FURTHER READINGS**

Anderson, Jervis. *Bayard Rustin: Troubles I've Seen*. New York: HarperCollins, 1997.

Farmer, James. *Lay Bare the Heart: An Autobiography of the Civil Rights Movement*. New York: Arbor House, 1985.

Meier, August, and Elliott Rudwick. *CORE: A Study in the Civil Rights Movement, 1942–1968*. New York: Oxford University Press, 1973.

Robinson, Jo Ann O. *Abraham Went Out: A Biography of A. J. Muste*. Philadelphia: Temple University Press, 1981.

*Gary Daynes*

## Fellowship of Southern Churchmen

The Fellowship of Southern Churchmen (FSC) grew out of a meeting of the Conference of Younger Churchmen of the South held in Monteagle, Tennessee, in 1934. By late 1936, this interracial, interdenominational group had adopted the name FSC and elected Christian activist Howard Anderson Kester as its first secretary general. The

FSC offered a far-reaching and radical Christian critique of twentieth-century southern society. The organization labored to bring about a social and economic reorganization of the South that encompassed most of the region's working people and that was strongly rooted in Protestant Christian principles.

Believing that the organization would be more effective if membership were restricted to southerners, the FSC did not encourage those from outside the region to join but gladly accepted contributions from, and maintained ties with, other areas of the nation. The FSC cooperated closely with other groups sharing the same interests and goals, among them the Anti-Defamation League of B'nai B'rith, the National Association for the Advancement of Colored People (NAACP), and the Congress of Racial Equality (CORE). Still, membership never exceeded more than about five hundred, a number that included numerous women and African Americans in the broad belt of southern states stretching from Virginia to Texas.

The FSC's principles likewise seemed to ensure that its membership would be confined to a small number of earnest reformers. Heavily influenced by Reinhold Niebuhr's neoorthodoxy, a new Calvinism that emphasizes the need to atone for flaws in man's social behavior more so than those exhibited in individual behavior, and the tenets of Christian socialism, Churchmen became dedicated participants in the southern struggle for social and economic justice. An important part of the FSC ideology involved what it referred to as prophetic evangelism, a direct approach to people by way of tent meetings and similar gatherings. FSC volunteers went into the countryside in but one of their many efforts to rouse people into action by bringing the resources of the Christian faith to bear on the economic, social, political, and racial problems of the South. Such luminaries as Niebuhr, James Weldon Johnson, and Lillian Smith addressed the group's annual conferences. The FSC's sporadically published journal, *Prophetic Religion*, expressed the Churchmen's ideas and concerns.

The FSC viewed its brand of applied Christianity as a comprehensive solution to the ills of the South, one that addressed the needs of the rural poor, industrial laborers, and disinherited African Americans. Churchmen focused on the plight of tenants, sharecroppers, and small farmers, blaming many of the South's agricultural woes on the Roosevelt administration's mishandling of farm policy. The FSC chastised urban middle-class churches for ignoring the spiritual needs of rural folk. Meanwhile, Howard Kester hoped to establish a rural seminary to combine theological training with instruction in improved methods of soil conservation, crop production, and marketing. As America's economic picture brightened in the 1940s, the FSC pressed less enthusiastically its Christian-socialist model for society. Remaining activists at heart, however, Churchmen continued entreating organized labor and the Church to be more socially responsible.

Although the FSC had always been concerned with the problems of African Americans in the South, changing conditions in the region in the late 1940s prompted it to redouble its fight against racial injustice. By the 1950s, this had become the chief focus of the organization's work. While the FSC labored for racial equality, its ultimate goal remained Christian fellowship free of racial and class distinctions. Toward this end, the FSC challenged Jim Crow legislation, endorsed federal antilynching bills, and advocated the abolition of the poll tax. It lobbied as well for the equalization of health, housing, and educational facilities and for the institution of regular biracial religious services.

Faced with the racist backlash resulting from the United States Supreme Court's decision in *Brown v. the Board of Education* (1954), Churchmen by the mid-1950s found themselves in a tactical quandary. While older members of the FSC never abandoned the hope that they might transform society through the steady application of Christian fellowship and love, numerous younger activists in the South, the rising generation of African Americans in particular, preferred pursuing change through lawsuits, confrontation, and force. In 1957, the FSC convened its last major conference in Nashville, Tennessee, a poorly attended affair at best. By the early 1960s, this minuscule group of Christian reformers, their generation's most ardent proponents of radical Christian-based socioeconomic reform in the South, had all but disappeared.

## FURTHER READINGS

Dunbar, Anthony P. *Against the Grain: Southern Radicals and Prophets, 1929–1959.* Charlottesville: University Press of Virginia, 1981.

Fellowship of Southern Churchmen Papers Southern Historical Collection. University of North Carolina at Chapel Hill.

Martin, Robert F. "Critique of Southern Society and Vision of a New Order: The Fellowship of Southern Churchmen, 1934–1957." *Church History* 52 (March 1983), 66–80.

———. *Howard Kester and the Struggle for Social Justice in the South, 1904–1977.* Charlottesville: University Press of Virginia, 1991.

*Norman C. McLeod Jr.*

## Florida Council on Human Relations

The Florida Council on Human Relations (FCHR) was one of twelve state Councils on Human Relations established by the Southern Regional Council of Atlanta, Georgia. The FCHR was launched in 1955 to succeed the Florida Division of the Southern Regional Council. The FCHR was a nonpolitical, nondenominational, interracial organization working to achieve better race relations in the South by appealing to the "interracial conscience" of southerners who were committed to solving the region's racial problems. The FCHR used the tools of education, mediation, consultation, and research to eliminate prejudice and discrimination. For this purpose, it launched a wide variety of programs concerned with broadening democracy through legal, economic, legislative, religious, and educational means. As an incorporated nonprofit organization, the FCHR derived its financial support from membership dues, contributions, and grants from the Fund for the Republic.

The FCHR, operating through twelve local councils, was particularly committed to the desegregation of schools and initiated a Save Our Schools project in the late 1950s. Foiling the efforts of White Citizens' Councils (WCC) to infiltrate local Parent-Teacher Associations and influence school board decisions, the FCHR attacked the WCC's campaign to maintain segregated schools and urged parent participation in public education and civil rights. In addition to school desegregation, the FCHR also assisted Governor LeRoy Collins's Race Relations Commission in establishing biracial government committees in fourteen of Florida's major cities. The FCHR continued its work throughout the 1960s, focusing on issues such as poverty, housing, public accommodation, and equal employment opportunity.

**FURTHER READING**

Southern Regional Council Papers, Series IV: State Council on Human Relations, 1946–1968, Reels 141–142. Special Collections. Robert W. Woodruff Library, Atlanta University Center, Atlanta, Georgia.

*Kimberly E. Nichols*

## Fraternal Council of Negro Churches

Founded in 1934, the Fraternal Council of Negro Churches of America (FCNC) was the first national ecumenical organization established by African Americans. African Methodist Episcopal (AME) Church Bishop Reverdy C. Ransom, attempting to unite the black churches,

began a movement to create a federal council of black churches in 1933. On January 5, 1934, under the leadership of Ransom, several denominational representatives gathered at Mount Carmel Baptist Church in Washington, D.C., to establish the Voluntary Committee on the Federation of Negro Religious Denominations in the United States of America. A second meeting was held on June 27 in Cincinnati, Ohio, and on August 22 and 23, 1934, 152 delegates met at Chicago's Bethesda Baptist Church to create the FCNC, draft a constitution, and select officers. The FCNC accepted no financial assistance from white churches or organizations and was funded entirely by membership dues. Nevertheless, the organization managed to survive the harsh Depression years.

Between August 21 and 23, 1935, the FCNC convened at Cleveland's Saint Paul AME Zion Church. The group issued "A Message to the Churches and to the Public," discussing its ecumenical goals and theological stance and criticizing America's white churches. Moreover, conference participants debated the exclusion of farm and domestic workers from the Social Security Act and the conditions of black sharecroppers. Finally, the FCNC endorsed the creation of the National Negro Congress, which worked to improve the socioeconomic status of African Americans. In 1936, the FCNC issued an "Address to the Country," calling on blacks to increase their political and economic power.

The FCNC met annually from 1934 through 1950, while the executive committee met twice a year. In 1938, Baptist Minister William H. Jernagin, who had served as president of the National Sunday School and Baptist Training Union of the National Baptist Convention, U.S.A., Inc., for thirty years, succeeded Ransom as FCNC president. From 1940 to 1946, Jernagin also served as chair of the FCNC's executive committee and during this time established the Washington Bureau. In 1947, Reverend J. Stalnaker replaced Bishop R. R. Wright Jr. as executive secretary for a three-year term. In 1950, G. W. Lucas succeeded Stalnaker. In the same year, the organization reduced its fifteen standing committees to seven: Evangelism and Worship, Education, Human Relations, Public Relations, Washington Bureau, Social Welfare, and African Affairs. In 1957, AME Bishop S. L. Greene assumed the FCNC presidency; a year later, after the death of Jernagin, he also became chair of the executive committee.

Largely due to Jernagin's efforts, the FCNC's Washington Bureau, for more than twenty years, pressed for civil rights for African Americans. From 1943 to 1964, Washington Bureau representatives met with presidents of the

United States and lobbied House and Senate committees on issues such as antilynching bills, desegregation of interstate travel, fairness in housing, education aid, civil rights for the District of Columbia, and the 1957 and 1964 Civil Rights Acts. In 1948, the FCNC organized a National Prayer Meeting March in Washington, D.C., and, during the following decade, Jernagin worked with Mary Church Terrell to end segregation in public accommodations in the nation's capital. The FCNC also organized the Committees of One Hundred, which consisted of ministers in metropolitan areas who lobbied their representatives for changes in legislation. In 1963, the FCNC participated in the March on Washington; however, by that time, the Washington Bureau focused primarily on issues facing the District of Columbia.

The FCNC embraced Reverend Martin Luther King Jr.'s nonviolent philosophies and his work toward integration, which was demonstrated in 1949 when the FCNC voted to change its name to the National Fraternal Council of Churches U.S.A., Inc., eliminating the word Negro. Throughout its existence, the FCNC provided black clergy with an arena to discuss race relations and civil rights. It was the first African American national interdenominational organization that sought to improve the conditions of African Americans and is representative of the enduring legacy of activism in the Black Church. As the civil rights movement gained momentum, however, the FCNC lost many of its members to other organizations.

**FURTHER READINGS**

Crayton, Spurgeon E. "The History and Theology of the National Fraternal Council of Negro Churches." Thesis. Union Theological Seminary, 1979.

Sawyer, Mary R. "The Fraternal Council of Negro Churches, 1934–1964." *Church History* 59, 1 (1990), 51–64.

———. *Black Ecumenism: Implementing the Demands of Justice.* Valley Forge, Penn.: Trinity Press International, 1994.

*Julius H. Bailey*

## Free African Societies

Free African societies formed as a result of the desire of Africans and their descendants to establish and control their own institutions, care for themselves in times of personal distress, provide proper burials and burial sites, educate themselves and their children, and set guidelines for the moral, intellectual and economic improvement of people of color. Societies thus were not only engaged in charitable endeavors, but also addressed political and economic issues that directly and indirectly concerned African Americans. The societies were established by free men and women of color, and, in many instances, the names of some of the early organizations included either one or both of the adjectives *free* and *African.* So critical were the descriptors that they were used in naming many other black institutions, including churches (First African Baptist, African Union, First African Presbyterian); schools (African Free School); beneficial associations (Sons and Daughters of Africa, African Humane Society, Free Daughters of Shipley, Free Dark Men of Color); and other organizations (African Insurance Company and African Fire Company).

It is significant that African Americans began to identify themselves as an ethnic group and members of a class as early as the 1700s. Not only were they exhibiting communal behavior by forming organizations and displaying other acts of collective conduct, but their group identification set them apart from whites and blacks who were not free. Using the term *free* denoted recognition of their status and the rights and privileges that should be accorded to them. Designating themselves as *free* also separated them and their societies from those groups formed by slaves. Unknown to white owners, slaves formed and operated a number of mutual aid societies, especially in Virginia. The totality of these actions initially represented ethnic community identification and formation, stratification by class and often gender, and a desire for autonomy. Moreover, it represented a collective response to the exclusion of free blacks from the benefits of citizenship and white institutions.

The term *society* is problematic when trying to locate and describe the first African societies because, in the antebellum period, the term *society* was often used to indicate groups of people who came together for religious worship. Especially in areas where there were Quakers and Methodists, *society* also referred to small religious groups. In other regions, these small groups were referred to as *bands* or *classes.* Moreover, by the 1780s, some societies might have been the early beginnings of Masonic lodges. In 1775, fourteen black men were initiated as Masons in Boston and thereafter, black Masonic lodges were organized in other cities. Thus, those multiple meanings of *society* cause some difficulty when trying to determine the first free African society.

Historical records indicate the early organization of societies by people of color in America and attribute these initial beginnings to the Second Great Awakening of the late eighteenth century. While there was apparently a relationship between religion and the formation of free African societies, in some areas a few societies predated black churches. Other societies formed as a result of African Americans establishing religious organizations, and still others formed some time after a church had been established.

A few scholars suggest that, as early as 1780, free blacks of Newport, Rhode Island, founded the African Union Society. In the South, the Perseverance Benevolent and Mutual Aid Association was organized in New Orleans, Louisiana, in 1783. One year later in Boston, Prince Hall, a Methodist minister who pastored a church in Cambridge, Massachusetts, and other black men received a charter from England that established the Masons. Some scholars suggest that the first black society in America was the Free African Society organized in Philadelphia in 1787 by Richard Allen, Absalom Jones, and others. In its preamble, dated April 12, 1787, Jones and Allen were referred to as "two men of the African Race."

Originally, the Free African Society of Philadelphia was organized to establish a religious society because of the need of African Americans to have their own place of worship. However, even though members of the Free African Society could not agree on religious affiliation, they did agree to continue their association as a mutual aid society "in order to support one another in sickness and for the benefit of their widows and fatherless children." In 1789, Richard Allen and several others withdrew from the society. Fortunately, their withdrawal did not deter those who remained, and the society continued to function as a mutual aid organization. In 1794, the members of the Free African Society formed the St. Thomas's African Episcopal Church. From this emerged another free African society, which was incorporated in 1796. Called by some The First Black Society for Mutual Assistance, the Friendly Society of St. Thomas's African Church of Philadelphia was composed of members of the African Episcopal Church. For many years, St. Thomas's was directly and indirectly linked to a multiplicity of mutual aid, secret, literary, and beneficial societies. At St. Thomas's on January 1, 1812, Russell Parrott, a member of the Benezet Philanthropic Society, spoke on the "Abolition of the Slave Trade." Four years later on the same date, he delivered a similar address "before the different African Benevolent Societies."

The second black church established in Philadelphia, Bethel Methodist Church, pastored by Richard Allen, was also crucial to subsequent associational formation. For example, the Augustine Education Society of Pennsylvania was organized in 1818 for the purpose of establishing a school for black children. Some of its members and officers were members of various black churches. In 1818 at Bethel Church, Prince Saunders addressed the Augustine Society on the importance of Christian education.

Members of the early free African societies in Philadelphia, Newport, and Boston were in contact with one another because of their mutual interests in religion, the abolition of slavery, colonization, the general welfare of African Americans in their respective cities, and their Masonic bonds, and they communicated on issues such as emigration and the condition of the black population in their respective cities. On one occasion, the Boston and Newport societies wrote a letter to the Philadelphia society. The Newport society indicated that at the time that it had forty members and that the situation of Africans in Newport, Rhode Island, was so burdensome that the society was advocating a return to Africa. The Philadelphia society's response was vague and not encouraging. Yet, there was financial help between and among the societies. When African Americans in Philadelphia were soliciting funds to construct a church, other black societies contributed.

In the last decade of the eighteenth century and the beginning of the nineteenth century, there was a proliferation of various organizations that sought to improve the overall condition of people of color. In 1796 in Boston, the African Society, a mutual aid and charity association, was organized. Unlike the Boston Masons, it was specifically a mutual aid and charity association. Members defined themselves as "African members" who organized "for the mutual benefit of each other." In 1808, the African Benevolent Society was organized in Newport, Rhode Island. A year later in Charleston, South Carolina, the Brown Fellowship Society, a mutual aid society, was formed. Wherever there were free blacks, there was usually some form of organization for mutual aid and self-help. Pennsylvania, Louisiana, New York, Massachusetts, Michigan, Maryland, South Carolina, and Virginia are a few states where free African societies emerged. Extant records of those societies and of one in the District of Columbia indicate that officers were elected, dues assessed, and the goals and objectives were clearly stated. Regular meetings were established, and guidelines were clear as to the conduct required of members.

While several small societies, which cared for the sick and handled the burial of the dead, were connected with churches and formed as a result of their mutual religious affiliation, many of these groups existed without direct church supervision. The Bonneau Literary Society, for example, was founded in Charleston, South Carolina, to help members become more literate, thereby improving "our mental faculties." In 1832, black women in Boston launched the African-American Female Intelligence Society to spread knowledge, to combat vice and immorality, and to appreciate those things that would bring them happiness and make them useful to society. In Detroit the Colored Vigilant Committee surveyed institutions in its community. Among the many organizations there existed a society of young men, a debating society, and a temperance society, all housed along with a library and a reading room in two black churches, the Colored American Baptist Church (1837) and Bethel Church (1839). There were at least twenty associations in Detroit in the 1840s, and more formed in the 1850s.

Many other cities also witnessed this dramatic increase in African-American societies. By 1862, Washington, D.C., had become home to thirty free African societies that provided care for the sick and burial of the dead. Free blacks boasted at that time that never had a black person been interred at public expense in the District.

After Emancipation, the need to include *free* in the organization's name was no longer necessary, and *African* was not prevalent in a number of the organizational names formed later, although there were still nominal references to occupation and religion. For example, in 1883 in the District of Columbia, the Hod Carriers Union, the Brick Machine Union Association, and the Paper Hanger's Union paraded along with the Fourth Ward Ethiopian Minstrels, the Knights of Moses, and the Galilean Fishermen. And, although care for the indigent was still required, new organizations adopted new names as the century closed. These included the Ladies' Relief Union Auxiliary (1897), Elder Men's Immediate Relief (1898), and Elder Ladies' Immediate Relief (1900).

Wherever there were free blacks, there were forms of organizations that cared for the sick, provided for proper burials, and generally sought, through their own means, to improve the general condition of their members and the wider black community. Early in the history of Africans and their descendants in the United States, there were concerted efforts to improve their condition by various means of self-help and mutual aid. That this help came in the form of various societies is a testament to the diversity and unity of African Americans.

**FURTHER READINGS**

Borchert, James. *Alley Life in Washington: Family, Community, Religion, and Folklife in the City, 1850–1970.* Urbana: University of Illinois Press, 1980.

Cromwell, Adelaide M. *The Other Brahmins: Boston's Black Upper Class, 1750–1950.* Fayetteville: University of Arkansas Press, 1994.

Du Bois, W. E. B. *The Philadelphia Negro: A Social Study.* New York: Schocken Books, 1967. (Originally published in 1899.)

Jacobs, Claude F. "Benevolent Societies of New Orleans Blacks during the Late Nineteenth and Early Twentieth Centuries." *Louisiana History* 29 (1988), 21–34.

Shannon, Janet H. "Community Formation: Blacks in Northern Liberties, 1790–1850." Ph.D. diss., Temple University, 1991.

*Janet Harrison Shannon*

# Freedmen's Aid and Southern Education Society of the Methodist Episcopal Church

The Freedmen's Aid and Southern Education Society of the Methodist Episcopal Church, initially known as the Freedmen's Aid Society of the Methodist Episcopal Church, was the northern Methodist Church's agency responsible for coordinating educational work among the freed people. The Methodist Church, North, was the last of the major Protestant denominations to create a separate, ecclesiastical freedmen's aid organization, founding the society on August 7, 1866 in Cincinnati. The church had earlier supported the nonsectarian educational efforts of the secular freedmen's aid societies. By the end of the Civil War, however, many Methodists were convinced that rival denominations were using freedmen's education as a means to proselytize among the freedmen. As a result, the Methodist Church joined the movement toward ecclesiastical coordination of educational efforts.

The Freedmen's Aid Society (FAS) of the Methodist Episcopal Church quickly became the second largest of the freedmen's aid societies, after the American Missionary Association. By 1870, it was supporting 110 teachers in sixty southern schools. As support began to wither among northern donors in the 1870s, the FAS shifted its focus from elementary education to forms of higher education, as did all the missionary societies. Teacher training and ministerial preparation took precedence in the numerous colleges, universities, normal schools, and other institutes and seminaries founded throughout the South. By 1878, the FAS of the Methodist Episcopal Church had established sixteen schools of higher grade, including such venerable historically black colleges and universities as Bennett College, Cookman Institute (later Bethune-Cookman College), Claflin College, New Orleans University (later Dillard University), Clark College, Central Tennessee College, Meharry Medical College, Walden Seminary (later Philander Smith College), Shaw University (later Rust College), and Wiley University. In total, the society founded more than two dozen black institutions of higher learning, many of which still exist.

In the 1870s, the FAS began providing schools for southern white youths in addition to freedmen's education. To more accurately reflect the realities of its work, the society changed its name in 1888 to the Freedmen's Aid and Southern Education Society of the Methodist Episcopal Church. In 1908, the schools for southern white students were put under the Board of Education of the Methodist Episcopal Church, and the society reverted to its original name. In 1920, the society was reorganized as the Board of Education for Negroes, then it was reorganized again in 1928 to become the Department of Education for Negroes within the General Board of Education of the Methodist Episcopal Church. With the reunification of the Methodist Episcopal Church in 1939, schools for African Americans fell to the Department of Educational Institutions for Negroes; after 1968, the colleges were administered by the Board of Higher Education and Ministry.

Four Protestant denominations stand out for their work in African American higher education: the Methodists, the Congregationalists (through the American Missionary Association), the American Baptists, and the Quakers. Under the leadership of the FAS, the Methodists were second only to the Congregationalists in founding institutions that have served African American students throughout the twentieth century.

**FURTHER READINGS**

Brawley, James P. *Two Centuries of Methodist Concern: Bondage, Freedom, and Education of Black People.* New York: Vantage, 1974.

Butchart, Ronald E. *Northern Schools, Southern Blacks, and Reconstruction: Freedmen's Education, 1862–1875.* Westport, Conn.: Greenwood, 1980.

Morrow, Ralph E. *Northern Methodism and Reconstruction.* East Lansing: Michigan State University Press, 1956.

Richardson, Harry V. *Dark Salvation: The Story of Methodism as It Developed among Blacks in America.* Garden City, N.Y.: Doubleday, 1976.

*Ronald E. Butchart*

## Freedmen's Aid Society, London

Between 1863 and 1868, the Freedmen's Aid Society (FAS) in London provided aid for the educational, religious, and material needs of newly freed slaves in the United States and Jamaica. British abolitionists formed the FAS on April 24, 1863, shortly after President Abraham Lincoln issued the Emancipation Proclamation on January 1, 1863. FAS members sent monetary donations, clothing items, and educational and religious materials to the former slaves. Afraid that Americans would resent foreign interference, the society did not send British missionaries or educators to the South but instead provided funds for the training of black teachers. The society disbanded in 1868 in order to encourage independence and self-help among the freedpeople.

The FAS was the first freedmen's aid organization to emerge in Britain. Its membership consisted mainly of upper-middle-class former abolitionists, both men and women. Yet, the society also appealed to the working class, arguing that aiding freedpeople in the South would ensure a cheap cotton supply for British consumers. Quakers, mostly drawn from the ranks of the British and Foreign Anti Slavery Society, constituted a majority of the FAS's all-male executive committee. The Birmingham Quaker Arthur Albright became one of the society's most active members, tirelessly lecturing, raising funds, recruiting speakers, and even traveling to the United States during the Civil War. Members of the American Society of Friends supported the efforts of their British brethren to provide assistance to the former slaves. In 1864, for example, Levi Coffin, renowned Indiana Quaker and abolitionist, traveled to London to help raise funds and generate support for the FAS.

The society's mission also reflected the strong influence of Quakers. FAS members insisted that it was their Christian duty to lift the former slaves from their degrading living conditions and to spread a "civilizing" influence among them. To elevate the freedpeople, the FAS provided religious materials, educational supplies, and clothing; awarded grants to schools and churches; and funded U.S. missionaries who trained black teachers in the South. British women, not all of them FAS members, made many of the garments that the society shipped to the former slaves. Large numbers of women, including those who had never before been involved in any political or social reform movement, as well as members of the working class, launched numerous sewing circles throughout Great Britain. Some women joined these circles, making a conscious decision to assist the freedpeople, while others remained unaware of the philanthropic cause their work supported. The sewing circles labored prolifically. Between 1863 and 1868, the city of Bristol alone sent an average of ten thousand to twelve thousand garments per month to American freedmen's aid groups. American officials agreed to ship the garments and other donated items duty free, saving the FAS untold amounts of money. The society also raised a significant amount of money, mainly among Quakers and Congregationalists. One historian estimates that, between 1863 and 1868, the British raised more money for freedmen's aid than they did for the entire antislavery cause in the decades prior to the Civil War.

In 1868, the FAS disbanded, claiming that it wanted to encourage independence and self-help among the freedpeople. Yet, another reason for the demise of the society was a divisive debate generated by a black revolt in the British colony of Jamaica. In October 1865, black workers in Jamaica revolted against harsh living conditions under the leadership of British Governor Edward Eyre. The governor ordered a brutal repression of the rioters, resulting in the death of five hundred blacks. While the British public generally supported Eyre's measures, FAS members were divided. Some members insisted that FAS extend aid to the former Jamaican slaves, while others demanded that the organization focus on assisting only the former slaves in the United States. Eventually, the society agreed to support former slaves in both Jamaica and the United States.

In addition to the financial and material aid that the FAS provided for former slaves, the society's work also helped foster cooperation between British and American abolitionists. Prior to the Civil War, ideological disputes had often hampered joint abolitionist ventures. These differences, however, started to fade as the FAS relied on American freedmen's aid groups to receive and distribute its funds and goods. Moreover, the work of the FAS helped redefine gender roles. Many British women who had previously confined themselves to the domestic sphere became involved in the society's efforts and started to question traditional notions about the types of political activities deemed appropriate for women.

### FURTHER READINGS

Bolt, Christine. *The Anti-Slavery Movement and Reconstruction: A Study in Anglo-American Co-operation, 1833–1877.* New York: Oxford University Press, 1969.

Midgley, Clare. *Women against Slavery: The British Campaigns, 1780–1870.* New York: Routledge, 1992.

Temperley, Howard. *British Antislavery, 1833–1870.* Columbia: University of South Carolina Press, 1972.

*Kristine Boeke*

## Freedmen's Aid Society of the Methodist Episcopal Church

*See* Freedmen's Aid and Southern Education Society of the Methodist Episcopal Church.

## Freedom and Peace Party

The Freedom and Peace Party (FPP) was established by a faction of the Peace and Freedom Party (PFP) in Chicago in 1968. That year the PFP nominated Black Panther leader Elridge Cleaver as its presidential candidate. In protest, supporters of activist and comedian Dick Gregory broke with the group, founded the FPP, and nominated Gregory as their presidential candidate, who accepted despite his desire for unanimity.

Gregory's campaign consisted of his regular college lecture tour. Along the way, he touted the party's platform, which included demands for an end to the Vietnam War and recognition of the National Liberation Front (South Vietnamese Communists) and territorial realities in Southeast Asia. Most of the platform, however, focused on domestic urban and economic issues. The party advocated adoption of the recommendations of the Kerner Commission on Civil Disorder; an increase in welfare payments, vocational training, and job opportunities; an end to racial discrimination in labor unions; creation of a commission to investigate rural disorders, corporate farming, and control of the nation's food supply; and an around-the-clock government television network to provide adult education. Other party demands included the prohibition of the sale and manufacture of handguns; mandatory registration of rifles and shotguns; creation of a commission to study youth issues; and a lowering of the voting age to eighteen years. Finally, the party insisted that the national government provide for the basic needs and education of the families of dead or disabled soldiers. After the party lost its bid for the presidency, Gregory promised to establish an administration in exile across the street from the White House.

### FURTHER READING

Gregory, Dick, and James R. McGraw. *Up From Nigger.* New York: Stein and Day, 1976.

*Bryan Bartlett Jarmusch*

SEE ALSO    Black Panther Party (for Self-Defense); National Advisory Commission on Civil Disorders (Kerner Commission); Peace and Freedom Party

## French American Fellowship

Self-exiled African American author Richard Wright's aims in initiating the French American Fellowship in Paris in December 1950 were political and cultural. Among the most active of some sixty mostly African American members were Samuel Allen Ligon Buford, the journalists William Rutherford and Ollie Stewart, and Leroy Haynes, who succeeded Wright as president. The group wanted to "combat the extension of racist ideas and practices" and "lend encouragement and support to all minorities and exploited groups in their aspirations and struggles for freedom." They also focussed on "the relation of the arts, literary, plastic and musical, to contemporary consciousness," thus continuing the liberal tradition of the progressive magazines *Seven Arts* and *Twice a Year*. By presenting a more accurate picture of the United States than embassy propaganda supplied, these good-willed Americans hoped to establish a more workable relationship between France and their country.

A committee was organized to fight job discrimination in certain U.S. businesses operating in France, for example, the refusal of the American Hospital in Paris to hire nurse Margaret McCleveland. In 1951, some thirty intellectuals protested the refusal of a U.S. visa to Marxist historian Daniel Guerin. The group also petitioned on behalf of the Martinsville Seven (seven black men executed for the rape of a white woman in Virginia) and soon-to-be executed Willie McGhee (convicted of raping a white woman in Mississippi); sent a message to the Peoples' Congress against Imperialism in Rome; and joined Josephine Baker's public call for justice concerning the Grand Bassam, Ivory Coast, trials.

Cultural activities included visits to painters' studios, an art exhibition, and a series of lectures. The fellowship ceased to function in 1952.

*Michel Fabre*

## Friends of Negro Freedom

In May 1920, A. Philip Randolph and Chandler Owen of *Messenger* magazine organized the Friends of Negro Freedom (FNF) to foster support for black-owned businesses and cooperatives and to provide blacks with training in labor union organization techniques and assistance in establishing and operating businesses. Randolph and Owen envisioned the creation of a series of local branches across the United States to promote the FNF's educational endeavors and to provide forums for speakers advocating the organization's ideas.

Founded by the *Messenger* editors in the wake of their break with T. J. Pree's National Brotherhood Workers of America (NBWA), the FNF differed from other national organizations that worked on behalf of African Americans. Unlike the National Association for the Advancement of Colored People (NAACP) and the National Urban League, the FNF was black led and financed, advocated economic reform, and recruited a predominantly black working-class constituency. Randolph and Owen excluded whites from membership, claiming that white participation in the NAACP and the National Urban League had diluted the fervor of these organizations. Moreover, they criticized both organizations for their failure to advocate a reorganization of the nation's economy, which they hoped would occur along socialist lines. Finally, they insisted that the FNF recruit its membership from the ranks of the black working class as opposed to the NAACP, which largely attracted the black educated elite, or "Talented Tenth."

The March 1920 issue of the *Messenger* announced the creation of the FNF and included a list of individuals who had agreed to participate in the organization, including Cyril Briggs, W. A. Domingo, Carter G. Woodson, the Reverend Robert W. Bagnall, Archibald Grimké, and C. Francis Stradford. While the roll of founding members was impressive, many of those who initially supported the FNF never played an active role in the organization.

Chaired by Bagnall, the founding convention met in Washington, D.C., in 1920. The resolutions adopted at this meeting revealed Owen's and Randolph's twin preoccupations with economic exploitation and concerns about the spread of Marcus Garvey's Universal Negro Improvement Association (UNIA). The FNF's initial program included plans to negotiate with white employers to increase employment opportunities for blacks, to assist migrants from the rural South and emigrants from the Caribbean who had recently arrived in the urban North, and to adopt an FNF union label to denote goods manufactured by firms that complied with the organization's program. The FNF also envisioned the establishment of protective services for those victimized by price gouging and inflated rents and the creation of a national black holiday in honor of John Brown's birthday. Moreover, the convention made plans for the FNF's educational-forum program, which was to involve a series of speaking tours by politicians, civil rights activists, and prominent black scholars and businessmen. This forum program proved to be one of the organization's most successful ventures.

While economic issues dominated the FNF's founding convention, the organization soon focused on the "Garvey Must Go" campaign. Chandler and Owen, convinced that Marcus Garvey posed a dangerous threat to the economic advancement of blacks, charged that the UNIA was corrupt and that its financial schemes deprived more deserving organizations of necessary funds. Furthermore, they criticized Garvey for his failure to demonstrate zeal for real economic reform. Not surprisingly, the educational forums of the FNF's New York City branch, for example, were almost solely devoted to attacking the UNIA leader.

During the UNIA's August 1922 convention, the FNF sponsored four widely publicized forums and numerous street meetings to combat Garvey. In January 1923, the FNF's anti-Garvey campaign culminated when the organization sent a public letter to United States Attorney General Harry Daugherty. The letter, signed by Owen, Randolph, and six others, called for the rapid prosecution of Garvey on mail-fraud charges, claiming that Garvey had solicited funds for his organization by mail and then used the funds to support his own lavish lifestyle.

After Garvey's conviction, the organization failed to establish a broad base of support, and the FNF lost much of its focus. By November 1923, the FNF apparently ceased to function, as most of its widely scattered local chapters disbanded. Yet, Randolph continued to use the FNF's name for informal, private chat sessions that he held at the *Messenger*'s New York City office.

**FURTHER READINGS**

Kornweibel, Theodore Jr. *No Crystal Stair: Black Life and the Messenger, 1917–1928*. Westport, Conn.: Greenwood, 1975.

Wintz, Cary D., ed. *African American Political Thought, 1890–1930: Washington, Du Bois, Garvey, and Randolph*. Armonk, N.Y.: Sharpe, 1996.

*Scott Beekman*

# Fruit of Islam

*See* Nation of Islam.

## General Commission on Religion and Race, United Methodist Church

In response to the social ferment of the 1960s, the United Methodist Church (UMC) sought to bridge the racial and ethnic divides within American Protestantism and make American religion part of the solution, rather than part of the problem, for African Americans and others seeking civil rights. In 1968, the same year in which the UMC was established, the Uniting Conference of that body provided for the creation of a General Commission on Religion and Race (GCRR). The commission's goal was to guarantee that UMC assistance and membership were open to persons of any race, color, ethnicity, or class. In 1970, the Uniting Conference, or General Conference, established the Minority Group Self-Determination Fund to support projects designed and administered by members of racial and ethnic minorities within and outside the church. The conference envisioned the fund as a tool of empowerment for minorities and entrusted its management to the GCRR. In addition to managing the fund, the GCRR has sponsored encounter sessions, racial workshops, and organizational counseling to alert people to the ways in which racism—subtle and overt—manifests itself in the church as well as in the larger society.

The creation of the UMC, and the GCRR within that body, was another in a series of efforts to remove racial and regional divisions among Methodists. The Methodists, like most other American Protestant denominations, had divided along sectional and racial lines over the issue of slavery in the mid-1840s. At the time of the schism, the northern Methodist Episcopal Church was a largely white organization with only 145,000 members of African descent; however, it was committed to antislavery. The Methodist Episcopal Church, South, was originally home to both whites and blacks but gradually succeeded in pushing black members into separate religious organizations, most notably the African Methodist Episcopal Church (AME) and the African Methodist Episcopal Church Zion (AME Zion). Before and during the Civil War, the Methodist Episcopal Church, South, defended slaveholding and the Confederacy. After the war, it was committed to advancing the welfare of white southerners at the expense of social reform generally and of millions of ex-slaves in particular.

In 1939, the northern and southern Methodist branches came together but maintained racial separation within the newly united body. White congregations were divided into five regional jurisdictions, while all black members of the Methodist Episcopal Church—whether from Maine or California—became part of a single "central jurisdiction." Some church members, notably white southerners who resented emancipation and resisted interaction with African Americans, argued that these separate governing bodies for blacks and whites permitted blacks a larger measure of power than they would have had in a racially integrated church. In reality, however, the church was acceding to, if not promoting, Jim Crowism.

Responding to the fervor of the civil rights movement, the Methodist Episcopal and the Evangelical United Brethren Churches combined in 1968 to establish the UMC. The five regional jurisdictions were maintained, but the central jurisdiction to which black congregants had been relegated was eliminated. The GCRR supplanted the old Commission on Inter-Jurisdictional Relations and took as its mission advocacy for African Americans and other racial and ethnic minorities within the church. From the beginning, the membership and leadership of the GCRR was inter-racial and inter-ethnic. But it took longer to transform the racial makeup of church leadership. In 1972, GCRR members lamented that minorities rarely appeared on board and agency staffs, much less in the capacity of chief executive of any board or agency. Since the 1970s, the GCRR has sensitized church membership to white racism and worked hard—through counseling, annual conferences, cooperation with theological schools, and regional monitoring—to combat racism and make the church more inclusive. The GCRR admits that while "some progress" has been made in the UMC, a "truly inclusive church is [still] in the process of becoming."

However inclusive the UMC may become, it is not destined to be the church of most African Americans. In 1991, fewer than 500,000 African Americans belonged to the UMC. In contrast, 3,500,000 African Americans belonged to the AME Church, and 1,200,000 to the AME Zion Church. Those denominations, established in the late eighteenth century, have remained independent of the larger white organizations. The successes of the GCRR, though real and admirable, have not been sufficient to draw members away from these historically black churches.

**FURTHER READINGS**

Marty, Martin. *Pilgrims in Their Own Land: 500 Years of Religion in America*. Boston: Little, Brown, 1984.

Norwood, Frederick A. *The Story of American Methodism: A History of the United Methodists and Their Relations*. Nashville, Tenn.: Abingdon Press, 1974.

Richardson, Harry V. *Dark Salvation: The Story of Methodism as It Developed Among Blacks in America*. n.p.: Doubleday Anchor Press, 1976.

*Norman C. McLeod Jr.*

# General Education Board

In 1902, John D. Rockefeller Sr. founded the General Education Board (GEB) for "the promotion of education within the United States of America, without distinction of race, sex, or creed." Incorporated by a congressional act in 1903 and backed by an initial gift of $1 million from Rockefeller, the GEB had a wide-ranging philanthropic agenda until it ceased to operate in 1964. Rockefeller envisioned the GEB as a clearinghouse for monetary gifts made not only by the Rockefeller family, but also by others who shared the fund's interests. Over the course of its existence, the GEB expended $325 million for the promotion of education in the United States, focusing particularly on the educational needs of the South.

During the fund's formative period between 1902 and 1923, its activities were dominated by Wallace Buttrick, who served as the board's first secretary and executive officer (1902–1917) and later president (1917–1923), and Frederick T. Gates, who was the board's first chairperson (1907–1917). Other GEB presidents included Wickliffe Rose (1923–1928), Trevor Arnett (1928–1936), Raymond B. Fosdick (1936–1948), Chester I. Barnard (1948–1952), Dean Rusk (1952–1961), and J. George Harrat (1961–1964). Since 1936, the president of the GEB has always been the president of the Rockefeller Foundation.

During the early years of its existence, the GEB emphasized the promotion of elementary education in the nation's rural districts, particularly in the South. To overcome southern opposition to tax-supported public education, Buttrick formed the Southern Education Board (SEB) in 1901. The SEB mobilized southern support for public education until 1914. That year, Buttrick, convinced that the SEB had accomplished its task, ordered its absorption by the GEB. While southern opposition to tax-supported education may have diminished, the GEB faced other obstacles. Its efforts to create a system of public elementary schools in the South were hampered by the lack of trained teachers and the absence of a secondary-school system in the South. To overcome these problems, the GEB carefully selected well-trained specialists, who traveled throughout the South to promote the establishment of secondary schools, assist in their organization, and marshal support for them. Occasionally, they also dispensed pedagogical advice. GEB agents were attached to the Office of the State Superintendent of Instruction and worked for both elementary- and secondary-school reform until 1952, when the fund's diminishing resources generated a policy shift.

In an effort to provide secondary schooling in the South, the GEB utilized county training schools under the auspices of the John F. Slater Fund to train teachers. Beginning in 1925, the GEB made grants to normal schools and state colleges and universities for the provision and improvement of teacher training. Coordinating and controlling philanthropic educational efforts in the South, GEB personnel were directly involved in the administration of other funds, including the Anna T. Jeanes Fund, also known as the Negro Rural School Fund, and the Phelps-Stokes Fund. The Jeanes Fund provided financial support to rural black schools and subsidized the salaries of industrial teachers, while the Phelps-Stokes Fund concentrated on improving secondary education in the South. Both funds, however, were too small to accomplish their agenda without financial support from the GEB.

Working with various state agencies in the South, the GEB tried to avoid antagonizing white southerners and often supported the Hampton-Tuskegee model of vocational education. The GEB, however, was not exclusively concerned with providing industrial training for southern blacks. In cooperation with the Julius Rosenwald Fund, the GEB also supported the creation of four national black university centers in Washington, D.C., Nashville, New Orleans, and Atlanta. In those cities, the Rosenwald Fund and the GEB supported ill-funded and poorly equipped black colleges, universities, and hospitals, enabling them to improve their graduate and medical training programs. A few black colleges, such as Fisk and Howard, offered graduate courses but only at the level of the master's degree. No black college awarded the doctorate at this time. Black educational institutions and medical facilities targeted by the national university centers plan included Howard, Fisk, Atlanta, Dillard, Clark, Morris Brown, Straight, and New Orleans Universities, Morehouse and Spelman Colleges, Gammon Theological Seminary, and Meharry Medical College and Flint-Goodridge Hospital.

In 1921, the GEB further addressed the lack of competent educational leadership in the South when it established a fellowship program for graduate and professional study at northern universities. Initially, the fellowships were limited to whites, but in 1924 the program was extended to black students, who were barred from white southern graduate schools. The GEB awarded more than one thousand fellowships to African Americans pursuing graduate training in the North, and approximately 85 percent of the fellows returned to the South to teach or work as educational administrators.

GEB support for medical education further increased as a result of the influence of Abraham Flexner, who joined the GEB as assistant secretary in 1913 and became the fund's secretary in 1917. Prior to his work with the GEB, Flexner had conducted a study of medical training in the United States and Canada on behalf of the Carnegie Foundation for the Advancement of Teaching. In 1910, the Carnegie Corporation published Flexner's highly critical report of 155 medical schools, citing severe deficiencies in most of them. Flexner's concern about the quality of medical training facilities affected the GEB's philanthropic efforts when he became the fund's director of studies and medical education. As a result, the GEB devoted an estimated $600 million to the reform of medical education between 1922 and 1933.

The GEB's activities in the area of higher education included support for the improvement of academic salaries, medical education to combat disease, hospitals and scientific research, and endowment funds for black colleges. Conditional giving, whereby a gift was contingent on its being matched by an equal or large amount from another source, was the hallmark of the GEB's approach to improving higher education.

In 1940, its capital diminished, the GEB restricted its activities to the southern states, making library and endowment grants to historically black colleges. In 1964, the GEB ceased to operate when it made its last appropriation, to Berea College, Kentucky. Overall, 20 percent of the total $325 million expended by the fund was appropriated for the education of African Americans. The most powerful of the philanthropic funds, the GEB largely controlled the educational destiny of southern African Americans during the first half of the twentieth century. The GEB continues as a legal corporation, holding an annual board meeting, even though it has no program.

**FURTHER READINGS**

Anderson, James D. *The Education of Blacks in the South, 1860–1935.* Chapel Hill: University of North Carolina Press, 1988.

Carbaugh, James Christopher. "The Philanthropic Confluence of the General Education Board and the Jeanes, Slater, and Rosenwald Funds: African-American Education in South Carolina, 1900–1930." Ph.D. diss., Clemson University, 1997.

Fosdick, Raymond G. *Adventure in Giving: The Story of the General Education Board.* New York: Harper and Row, 1962.

———. *General Education Board: Review and Final Report, 1902–1964.* New York: General Education Board, 1964.

*General Education Board Archives.* Wilmington, Del.: Scholarly Resources, 1993, 1996.

Smith, S. L. *Builders of Goodwill: The Story of the State Agents of Negro Education in the South, 1910–1950.* Nashville: Tennessee Book, 1950.

*Jayne R. Beilke*

**SEE ALSO**    John F. Slater Fund; Julius Rosenwald Fund; Negro Rural School Fund; Phelps-Stokes Fund

## Genesis Group, Church of Jesus Christ of Latter-Day Saints

In October 1971, the first cultural organization for African American members of the Church of Jesus Christ of Latter-Day Saints (LDS) formed in Salt Lake City, Utah, under the leadership of Ruffin Bridgeforth Jr., Darius Gray, and Eugene Orr. Approximately two hundred black Mormons lived in the Salt Lake area at that time, but they resided in various parts of the city and were either active or inactive members of different, largely all-white ward congregations. To offset feelings of isolation and to strengthen the role of African Americans in the Church, the three leaders originally proposed that the group be an independent branch for black fellowship and mutual support. The LDS Quorum of Twelve Apostles declined to sponsor a separate all-black branch of the Church but instead authorized Bridgeforth and his partners to form an auxiliary organization called the Genesis Group. The group's unwritten objectives were to promote missionary work among black people and to help bring inactive African American members back to the Church.

Although Mormon missionaries did not actively proselytize among blacks prior to the late 1970s, African Americans have been members of the LDS Church since its founding in the early nineteenth century. Early Mormon leaders organized the Church so that all male communicants over the age of twelve could become members of the lay priesthood and assume leadership positions within ward congregations. Discriminatory practices, started during the 1840s, however, denied the priesthood to black Mormons. Though it was not until 1949 that Church leaders issued a formal statement banning African Americans from holding the priesthood, the policy relegating black Saints to subordinate positions within the organization had deep historical roots.

During the early years of the civil rights movement, the Church's decision to ban African Americans from the priesthood elicited few protests. The Salt Lake City chapter of the National Association for the Advancement of Colored People (NAACP) led protests and worked to enact civil rights legislation in Utah, which in 1963 compelled the LDS Church to issue a statement supporting equal rights in housing, education, and employment. Nevertheless, the priesthood restriction continued, and, as the NAACP began to suspect the Mormon Church of working to block civil rights legislation, its leaders started drawing attention to the causes of prejudice and the Church's doctrinal beliefs. The publicity inspired student activists to join the protests, which turned the focus of the demonstrations toward the LDS-owned Brigham Young University and the school's athletic program. Pickets during sporting events and the refusal of black athletes to par-

ticipate in games involving Brigham Young teams led some universities to drop the LDS school from their athletic schedules. Negative press coverage of these protests forced Church leaders to reaffirm their support for black civil rights in 1969. However, they also made a point to separate religious tenets from civil rights issues and sustained the priesthood ban.

Although the protests against Brigham Young University abated after 1970, other demonstrations against Mormon racial beliefs continued, and it was in this context that the Genesis Group evolved. While Bridgeforth, Gray, and Orr did not form Genesis to protest the Church's racial policies, they did want the group to act as an independent branch enabling African Americans to gain ordination into the priesthood on a trial basis. By 1971, LDS Church leaders were growing more sympathetic toward black concerns, but they were unprepared to ease priesthood restrictions and did not want the appearance of a segregated branch to be the focus of additional protests. Thus, while the organizers believed that Genesis represented a new beginning and a positive step toward gaining full equality in the Church, the group confined its efforts to mutual aid and fellowship activities, including a women's auxiliary relief society, a mutual improvement association for black youth, and a choir.

Bridgeforth served as president of the organization throughout its existence, while Gray and Orr served as counselors. Under their leadership, Genesis members met monthly on Sunday evenings and started to familiarize the LDS Church with the feelings and concerns of its African American constituency. The group gave black Mormons an informal outlet for airing grievances and expressing hopes that otherwise would have gone unheard. Moreover, it offered counseling services on issues unique to African Americans. A few dissenters wanted a more structured means of effecting change in the Church, but Bridgeforth held fast to his faith and did not allow Genesis to become a radical pressure group.

In June 1978, the LDS Church finally lifted its restrictions and affirmed the right of the priesthood to black Mormon males. While questions arose concerning the continued need for Genesis after the priesthood ban was lifted, Bridgeforth held that the importance of maintaining social contacts among African American Saints remained unchanged. Therefore, Genesis persevered, and, though attendance fell in Salt Lake City, the group expanded its efforts to offer mail and telephone counseling for new black converts from across the nation. In 1985, a second Genesis Group formed in Oakland, California, and in 1986 a third group organized in Washington, D.C. In Utah, however, attendance continued to decline, and in 1987 the original organization stopped holding meetings.

The Genesis Group never officially disbanded, and in 1989 Bridgeforth joined the organization's remnants to the newly formed LDS African American Cultural Awareness Group (AACAG). Although Bridgeforth served as an officer in the AACAG, the group had no official sanction from the LDS Church and worked as an independent, nonprofit organization. Nevertheless, it continued the Genesis Group's goals into the twenty-first century and worked to maintain an appreciation for black culture in the Mormon Church.

**FURTHER READINGS**

Bringhurst, Newell G. *Saints, Slaves, and Blacks: the Changing Place of Black People Within Mormonism.* Westport, Conn.: Greenwood, 1981.

Embry, Jessie I. "Separate but Equal? Black Branches, Genesis Groups, or Integrated Wards?" *Dialogue: A Journal of Mormon Thought* 23 (Spring 1990), 11–37.

———. *Black Saints in a White Church: Contemporary African American Mormons.* Salt Lake City: Signature Books, 1994.

Mauss, Armand L. "The Fading of the Pharaoh's Curse: The Decline and Fall of the Priesthood Ban against Blacks in the Mormon Church." *Dialogue: A Journal of Mormon Thought* 14 (Autumn 1981), 10–45.

Olsen, Peggy. "Ruffin Bridgeforth: Leader and Father to Mormon Blacks." *This People* 1 (Winter 1980), 11–17.

*Gary R. Entz*

## George Peabody Education Fund

*See* Peabody Education Fund.

## George Peabody Fund

*See* Peabody Education Fund.

## Georgia Council on Human Relations

The Georgia Council on Human Relations (GCHR) succeeded the Georgia Committee on Interracial Cooperation in 1956. It was one of twelve state Councils on Human Relations established by the Southern Regional Council of Atlanta, Georgia. The GCHR was a nonpolitical, nondenominational, interracial organization that advocated

better race relations during the 1950s and 1960s. Devising, developing, and publicizing techniques and programs for youth and adult education, the GCHR worked to counteract prejudice and discrimination based on racial, religious, national, or ethnic group membership. As an incorporated nonprofit organization, the GCHR derived its financial support from membership dues, contributions, and grants from the Fund for the Republic.

Operating through ten local chapters, the GCHR initially focused on school desegregation. Following the United States Supreme Court's 1954 *Brown v. Board of Education* decision, southern whites mounted increasing pressure to close Georgia's public schools in an attempt to evade implementation of the desegregation ruling. The GCHR fought to keep public schools open, supported HOPE, Inc. (Help Our Public Education), and established a tutorial program for African American students who transferred to all-white schools. Often allying itself with other organizations to awaken interest in the problems of race relations, the GCHR cooperated with the Student Nonviolent Coordinating Committee (SNCC), the Congress of Racial Equality (CORE), the America Friends Service Committee, and the Young Men's and Young Women's Christian Associations (YMCA and YWCA). The GCHR initiated discussion groups, forums, conferences, institutes, workshops, and adult education programs concerned with economic, civic, and racial conditions in the state. It also initiated local interracial committees and devoted time and effort to voter education, desegregation of public accommodations, equal employment opportunities, and urban renewal projects. The organization ceased to function in the 1960s.

**FURTHER READING**

Southern Regional Council Papers, Series IV: State Councils on Human Relations, 1946–1968, Reels 142–143. Special Collections. Robert W. Woodruff Library, Atlanta University Center, Atlanta, Georgia.

*Kimberly E. Nichols*

## Gesell Committee

*See* President's Committee on Equality of Treatment and Opportunity in the Armed Forces.

## Gospel Music Workshop of America

In 1967, Reverend James Cleveland founded and became the first president of the Gospel Music Workshop of America (GMWA). The organization was established to convert people to Christianity through gospel music; to promote, edify, and encourage respect for traditional black gospel music; to increase knowledge of gospel music; and to introduce and teach new material to singers and musicians.

The GMWA held its first convention in 1968 in Detroit, attracting more than three thousand registrants. The following year, almost five thousand people attended the Philadelphia convention, and, in 1970, more than five thousand participants gathered for the annual meeting in St. Louis. At subsequent conventions in Dallas, Chicago, Los Angeles, Kansas City, and New York City, more classes and seminars were added to assist choir members and directors as well as radio announcers. While GMWA conventions foster appreciation, knowledge, and performance of gospel music, the meeting's slogan, "Where Everybody Is Somebody," also serves as a spiritual affirmation of participants.

Much of the early success of the GMWA conventions was due to the work and popularity of James Cleveland, the "crown prince" and "king" of traditional black gospel music of the 1960s and 1970s. Cleveland began his career singing in Thomas A. Dorsey's choir at Chicago's Pilgrim Baptist Church and later joined the Roberta Martin Singers, another renowned gospel music group.

In 1932, Dorsey, the "Father of Gospel Music," and Sallie Martin, the "Mother of Gospel Music," organized the National Association of Gospel Choirs and Choruses. Using this organization, Dorsey established a national network for gospel music, a term he coined. Dorsey, who had been greatly influenced by the progenitor of African American gospel song, Charles Albert Tindley, also operated his own publishing company in Chicago.

Inspired by and following his mentor's lead, Cleveland brought the next generation of gospel music and its performers into national and international prominence and gained commercial success with the GMWA conventions. While Cleveland did not own a publishing company, he composed more than three hundred gospel songs. Copies of only seventy-five songs are in existence.

In the 1980s and 1990s, the GMWA remained committed to spreading the gospel through music, utilizing gospel music as an alternative outlet for frustrated young people who are confronting negative peer pressure and social ills. The music of Kirk Franklin and God's Property speak specifically to that goal.

The GMWA is the largest gospel music convention in the world. Each year during the second week in August, the GMWA holds its seven-day meeting. In recent years, more than twenty thousand members and delegates from the United States and other countries have attended GMWA workshops covering topics that range from piano playing to radio announcing. Many auxiliary groups attend this meeting, the largest of which is the National Gospel Announcers Guild, which comprises more than six hundred gospel announcers from all over the world. There are fifteen hundred members in the GMWA Youth Choir, and more than two thousand members in its adult National Mass Choir. A highlight of the convention is the GMWA Mass Choir Concert recording, which give performers and writers an opportunity to display their talents. Each night of the convention, groups, choirs, and soloists perform concerts. MALACO Records is the official recording company of GMWA sound-tracks.

Many of those who attend the GMWA conventions have careers in the music industry, including musicians, singers, writers, technicians, business owners, corporate executives, and radio announcers. Performers like Andrae Crouch, the Edwin Hawkins Singers, the Winans, and Take Six have appealed to a wider audience and enjoyed commercial success as a result of the GMWA's promotion of gospel music. The 300,000 GMWA members come from various Christian denominations, and, while the majority of the membership is African American, an increasing number represents other races.

**FURTHER READINGS**

Cusic, Don. *The Sound of Light: A History of Gospel Music.* Bowling Green: Bowling Green University Popular Press, 1990.

DuPree, Sherry S., and Herbert C. DuPree. *African-American Good News (Gospel) Music.* Washington, D.C.: Middle Atlantic Regional Press, 1993.

"Gospel Music Workshop of America." *Gospel International* [electronic magazine] 1, 3 (August 10, 1997), 1–2. [cited 8/7/97]. Available at http://www.gospelweb.com/html/gmwa.htm.

Reagon, Bernice Johnson, ed. *We'll Understand It Better By and By.* Washington, D.C.: Smithsonian Institution Press, 1992.

Roach, Hildred. *Black American Music: Past and Present.* 2nd ed. Malabar, Fla.: Krieger, 1992.

*Barbara L. Green*

# Government Contract Compliance Committee

On December 3, 1951, President Harry S. Truman signed an executive order creating a Government Contract Compliance Committee (GCCC). An eleven-member body of six individuals from the broader public and five from various federal agencies, the committee was to ensure that various contracting agencies within the government held firms working on government business to equal employment opportunity standards. Government contracts had contained a nondiscrimination clause for several years, but Truman stressed that the new agency was needed to bring consistent implementation to the federal effort to ensure fair labor practices. The committee was also to advise the president in this area.

The GCCC was created primarily in response to demands from civil rights organizations that had been fighting for a federal Fair Employment Practices Committee (FEPC) since the end of World War II. Congressional opposition from southern Democrats had blocked FEPC legislation, and so civil rights proponents looked to the White House for assistance. Truman initially responded in 1948 with an executive order against discrimination in federal employment. The outbreak of the Korean War in 1950 brought pressure from A. Philip Randolph and other civil rights proponents for the creation of a committee similar to the FEPC that had existed during World War II, but the administration, likely out of concern over the midterm elections and preoccupied with developments in Korea, was slow to move in this area. That December, however, the United States Labor Department recommended to Truman that he establish an equal employment body with enforcement powers. Eager to preserve national unity amidst a wartime crisis and worried about his legislative agenda in other areas, the president continued to minimize his involvement in civil rights matters by refusing to meet with African American leaders and issuing a series of mild executive orders over a seven-month period declaring that nondiscrimination was federal policy for firms with government contracts. Troubled by the lack of enforcement powers in these orders, civil rights proponents favored more vigorous action and began an intensive lobbying campaign throughout the summer to mark the tenth anniversary of Franklin D. Roosevelt's wartime FEPC. Truman finally agreed to the committee later that year, but, much to the dismay of most civil rights leaders, the new body had no enforcement powers. Randolph and the National Association for the Advancement of Colored People's (NAACP) Walter White were so disturbed by this feature that they tried to stop the order from being issued. Other African American leaders shared their view but welcomed the new agency as the best that could be achieved

under difficult political circumstances. Under the administration's plan, federal agencies themselves were to be responsible for enforcement. The GCCC would operate through friendly exhortations to employers to change their ways. Pointing out that such an approach had helped desegregate the armed forces, several administration officials optimistically looked forward to substantial results in employment matters. The administration also hoped that this strategy would lessen fears of FEPC opponents, who had charged the wartime agency with running roughshod over business, but southern Democrats and conservative Republicans routinely denounced the GCCC.

The committee, which included two African Americans and two Jews, commenced operation in January 1952 under the leadership of Dwight Palmer, who had been a member of Truman's committee on integrating the armed services. The GCCC convened approximately once a month for the remainder of the president's term. During that time, it gathered information from dozens of private, local, and federal organizations working in this area. Members also traveled across the country to meet with leading firms doing government business.

Clearly, the committee could not expect to accomplish much in the last year of Truman's term, but its problems went far deeper than a shortage of time. Most of the workers it was designed to protect had either no knowledge of its existence or no faith in its ability to make a difference in their lives. During an eleven-month period in 1952, the GCCC received just 318 complaints. The decentralized system ensured that enforcement was wildly uneven. Some agency heads took the issue of discrimination seriously, while others gave it little attention. A GCCC study of twenty-eight federal agencies concluded that only two had made substantial efforts at enforcing nondiscrimination. Three had not even included nondiscrimination clauses in their contracts. During the Truman administration, no agency canceled a contract. More important, the inability of the GCCC to compel changes in behavior meant that firms determined to discriminate had little to fear. Efforts aimed at educating and persuading employers represented an improvement over past practices of ignoring the problem, but this was a small step forward indeed. A lack of money circumscribed GCCC activity in several ways. Members served part-time and without pay, the staff consisted of just ten individuals, and operating funds were obtained from the budgets of five governmental agencies. In the end, the chief legacy of the GCCC was to establish fair employment as a concern of the federal government and stir awareness of an ongoing problem. Presidents Dwight

D. Eisenhower and John F. Kennedy would create similar bodies, with the function of contract compliance eventually becoming permanently lodged in the Office of Federal Contract Compliance Program (OFCCP).

**FURTHER READINGS**

Berman, William. *The Politics of Civil Rights in the Truman Administration.* Columbus: Ohio State University Press, 1970.

McCoy, Donald, and Richard Ruetten. *Quest and Response: Minority Rights and the Truman Administration.* Lawrence: University Press of Kansas, 1973.

*Timothy N. Thurber*

SEE ALSO    National Council for a Permanent FEPC; President's Committee on Fair Employment Practice

## Governor's Board of Discrimination, Washington

*See* Washington State Board Against Discrimination in Employment.

## Governor's Commission on Human Relations, Colorado

*See* Colorado Anti-Discrimination Commission.

## Governor's Commission on the Los Angeles Riots

The Governor's Commission on the Los Angeles Riots sought to present an objective report on the causes of the Watts Riots of 1965, one of the most destructive civil disturbances in American history. Sparked by the unexceptional arrest of an intoxicated African American motorist on August 11, 1965, the Watts Riots lasted six days and resulted in thirty-four deaths, one thousand injuries, and more than $40 million in property damage. Several days after the rioting was quelled by the National Guard, California Governor Edmund G. Brown appointed a commission consisting of eight members—six white and two black—headed by prominent industrialist and former CIA Director John A. McCone. Also known as the McCone Commission, the governor's commission held sixty-four meetings and conducted more than eighty interviews

with Watts residents, police officers, teachers, local politicians, and several prominent social scientists. After three months of testimony, the commission published its findings in a brief report entitled *Violence in the City: An End or a Beginning?*

The immediate cause of the Watts Riots, the commission suggested, was a very small but "violent fraction" of the black community that was caught up in an "insensate rage of destruction." Reiterating some of the key assumptions of the highly contentious Moynihan Report, the governor's commission found the roots of this violent behavior in the African American "home life." Raised in environments inhospitable to education, some black children, the commission asserted, developed discipline problems that hindered their ability to secure steady employment. Trapped by this "devastating spiral of failure," black juvenile delinquents often lashed out in irrational "spasms" of violence. The commission's analysis of the long-term causes of the riots was more thorough and generally more sympathetic toward Los Angeles's beleaguered African American community. The commission rightly identified employment discrimination and chronic unemployment as the most influential long-term causes of dissatisfaction among African Americans and proposed that the California Fair Employment Practices Commission require employers to file annual reports listing the proportion of African Americans in their workforce. Nor would African Americans continue to tolerate racially motivated violence by the police department. Virtually every African American interviewed by the commission cited police abuse as a leading cause of black anger. The commission proposed that the police department appoint a departmental inspector who would report to the chief of police while remaining outside the department's chain of command. Finally, the commission recommended dramatically improving educational opportunities for black students by reducing class sizes, repairing deteriorating buildings, and increasing library staffs at schools in black neighborhoods.

Shortly after release of *Violence in the City*, the governor's commission came under attack by the United States Civil Rights Commission and several prominent liberal scholars. Critics argued that the commission mischaracterized the immediate causes of the Watts Riots and suggested that, in fact, a broad stratum of the black community either participated in or supported the riots. Second, they argued, the riots were not the product of "insensate rage" but of legitimate protest against rampant discrimination. Finally, critics charged that the commission, by virtue of its leadership, was ill equipped to understand the problems of the ghetto. In addition to John McCone, a principal at the multimillion-dollar Bechtel Corporation, the white leadership consisted of a prominent attorney, the chairman of a major life insurance company, the president of Loyola University, the dean of UCLA medical school, and the former president of the California League of Women Voters. While all were sympathetic to the underlying causes of the Watts Riots, these were not the profiles, critics argued, of individuals qualified to deliberate about life in Watts. Reverend James Edward Jones, one of only two African American committee members, offered his criticism of the commission's findings in an addendum to the report, in which he argued that rioting was a legitimate response to life in Los Angeles's ghetto.

Meeting on the first and second anniversaries of the riots in 1966 and 1967, the commission reported on the implementation of its original recommendations. The commission was "encouraged but by no means satisfied" with the steps that had been taken to ameliorate conditions in the ghetto. To be sure, there had been some improvements. In the wake of the riots, voters overwhelmingly passed a school-bond issue that improved classrooms in Watts; an inspector general was appointed to monitor the Los Angeles Police Department; and the California State Employment Service expanded job training programs in predominantly black neighborhoods. However, employment discrimination persisted; the number of welfare recipients increased; public transportation remained expensive and inaccessible; and health facilities remained sparse. Overall, the impact of the governor's commission on the daily life of Los Angeles's African Americans was minimal. Ultimately, however, this failure was not the commission's but the city's.

**FURTHER READINGS**

Governor's Commission on the Los Angeles Riots. *Violence in the City: An End or a Beginning? A Report by the Governor's Commission on the Los Angeles Riots.* Los Angeles: the Commission, 1965.

————. *Staff Report of Actions Taken to Implement the Recommendations in the Commission's Report.* Los Angeles: the Commission, 1966.

————. *Staff Report of Actions Taken to Implement the Recommendations in the Commission's Report, Status Report II.* Los Angeles: the Commission, 1967.

*The Los Angeles Riots.* Comp. Robert M. Fogelson. New York: Arno, 1969.

*Josh A. Sides*

## Governor's Human Rights Commission, Minnesota

*See* Governor's Interracial Commission, Minnesota.

## Governor's Human Rights Commission, Wisconsin

In 1949, the Wisconsin Legislature appropriated funds for a Governor's Human Rights Commission (GHRC) to research human rights violations in Wisconsin. The commission publicized its findings in various pamphlets and reports, such as the *Handbook on Wisconsin Indians*, and in weekly radio programs such as *Segregation in Wisconsin, Then and Now*. Moreover, the commission conducted public education campaigns, participated in Human Rights Day celebrations, sought to improve health and recreational facilities for the state's minority population, organized protest marches in support of equal housing and employment rights, and sponsored public conferences such as the Governor's Conference on Human Rights and Indian Leadership. The GHRC, composed of several committees, including the Committee on Affiliated Groups, the Interracial and Interfaith Activities Committee, the Committee on Intercultural Education, and the Committee on Survey of Laws, coordinated its efforts with other agencies such as the Wisconsin Committee on Children and Youth, the Wisconsin Welfare Council, and the State Board of Health.

Perhaps one of the commission's most controversial investigations was a study of discriminatory practices of Wisconsin's resorts. A field study in the late 1940s of the Baraboo–Devil's Lake area indicated that the majority of the state's resorts refused to accommodate Jews and African Americans. Resort owners, fearing a decline in business, criticized the GHRC's work, charging that the study was unfair and offensive to long-term customers. Following this investigation, the commission participated in a tristate conference to discuss similar discriminatory practices in Illinois and Minnesota. In 1950, the GHRC published the results of its investigation and the conference deliberations in *The Uninvited: A Study of the Resort Discrimination Problem in Wisconsin*. While the report documented that Wisconsin's resorts violated the state's human rights statute 340.75 (1949), which prohibited discriminatory policies, it also demonstrated that hotel owners and operators failed to implement the law without any legal repercussions. Based on its findings, the GHRC recommended strict enforcement of the state's human rights statute and the adoption of additional legislation designed to discourage discrimination. The GHRC particularly emphasized the need for legislation prohibiting discriminatory advertisement, increasing public education, and providing special training for law enforcement officers and officials of other government agencies. Moreover, the GHRC urged increased communication with resort owners and utilization of other local resources to promote human rights.

The GHRC also assisted Spanish-speaking and Native American residents of Wisconsin. To help raise public awareness of discrimination, the commission worked with local communities, particularly youth and children's groups, to open avenues of communication and understanding. The town of Waupun, for example, formed its own human rights commission in 1949 and, with the help of the GHRC, launched a pilot project that provided teachers to the children of Spanish-speaking migrants.

Discrimination in housing was another important focus of the GHRC. In 1954, the commission published a *Report on State Laws and Agencies of Civil Rights: A Comparative Study of Twenty-Eight States* and *Nonwhite Housing in Wisconsin* stating the need for affordable housing. The report also analyzed the factors preventing nonwhites from obtaining adequate housing, including whether home builders, contractors, realtors, and lenders practiced discrimination.

During its existence from 1945 to the late 1960s, the commission succeeded in proposing legislation governing housing (Statute Chapter 66), employment (Chapter 111), education (Chapter 40), and discrimination (Chapter 340). The commission also supported educational programs for migrants and established Indian scholarships. In the mid-1960s, the GHRC won another state legislative victory, when it adopted a fair-housing law that prohibited the use of discriminatory language in advertisements announcing the sale of a house.

The commission faded in the late 1960s, as its functions were absorbed by various government departments such as the Affirmative Action Division of the Health and Family Services Department, the Minority Business Division of the Department of Commerce, and the Department of Equal Rights.

### FURTHER READINGS

Governor's Commission on Human Rights. *Newsletters* (1949–1967). Madison, Wisc.

———. *Nonwhite Housing in Wisconsin*. Madison, Wisc. 1954.

———. *We Hold These Rights. Newsletters* 1–18 (1963–1967). Madison, Wisc.

Recknagel, K. C. *The Uninvited: A Study of the Resort Discrimination Problem in Wisconsin*. Madison, Wisc.: Governor's Commission on Human Rights, 1954.

*Julie Shipe*

## Governor's Interracial Commission, Minnesota

The Governor's Interracial Commission was established in 1943 by executive order of Governor Edward J. Thye. In 1956, when Minnesota enacted a Fair Employment Practices Law, the commission's name changed to the Governor's Human Rights Commission (GHRC). The GHRC's mission was to stimulate educational activities to develop respect for human rights and to direct government and public attention to racial injustices that might result in serious social disorder. Although the GHRC was not set up by statute, it was recognized as an official state body by the Minnesota Legislature, which appropriated money for its operation and functioning.

The governor appointed the commission's thirty members from diverse religious, socioeconomic, and political backgrounds. Initially, they served indefinite terms; however, in 1961, their terms were changed to coincide with the governor's tenure in office. The GHRC's chairs were the Reverend Francis J. Gilligan (1943–1955), Earl R. Larson (1955–1960), Gladys Brooks (1961–1965), the Reverend Thomas Basich (1965–1966), Katie McWatt (1967), and Raymond Plank (1967); its executive directors were Clifford Rucker (1947–1962), Calvin Watson (1962–1965), Lawrence Borom (1965–1966), and Beverly Bergman Wickstrom (1967). Throughout its existence, the GHRC retained three governor-appointed ex-officio members: a representative from the governor's office, the deputy attorney general, and the commission's executive director.

The commission conducted general education programs in human relations, engaged in research, and worked closely with the State Commission against Discrimination (SCAD) in areas of concern to both groups. Moreover, it supported the efforts of private organizations, churches, and labor and business groups. The GHRC also organized a biennial governor's conference on human rights, human relations institutes for law enforcement officers, and conferences and workshops to develop state plans to meet the commission's responsibilities. The GHRC tried to exert influence in areas untouched by other programs, in order to confront issues and problems on a statewide basis. African Americans,

Native Americans, Asians, and migrant workers remained the commission's core groups of interest.

In 1967, the state of Minnesota created the Department of Human Rights when the legislature broadened the scope of SCAD. The department absorbed the duties of the Governor's Human Rights Commission, the Minneapolis Mayor's Council on Human Relations, and the Governor's Commission on the Status of Women, which had been created by executive order in 1963.

**FURTHER READINGS**

Governor's Interracial Commission, Minnesota. *The Negro Worker in Minnesota: A Report to Governor Edward J. Thye, 1945*. Minnesota State Archives, Saint Paul, Minnesota.

———. *The Negro Worker's Progress in Minnesota: A Report to Governor Luther W. Youngdahl, 1949*. Human Rights Department Papers. Minnesota State Archives, Saint Paul, Minnesota.

———. *Race Relations in Minnesota, Reports to Commission, 1948*. Minnesota State Archives, Saint Paul, Minnesota.

*Mollie A. Spillman*

## Grand United Order of Moses

The Grand United Order of Moses, Inc., was a small fraternal insurance society for black men and women based in rural south-central Virginia. The founder and lifelong leader of the Order of Moses was James Murray Jeffress (or Jeffries) (1873–1951), who organized the society in 1904 at his birthplace, the village of Charlotte Court House. Jeffress graduated from Hampton Institute in 1894 and the Howard University divinity school in 1901. He was ordained a Baptist minister and served as principal of a public school in Charlotte County.

By 1900, white Virginians had disenfranchised blacks and had segregated schooling and public transportation. Jeffress, sometimes called "the Booker Washington of Charlotte County," was an accommodationist who tried to make life tolerable for his fellow blacks without challenging white racists directly. Fraternal societies such as the Order of Moses offered a modicum of economic security through medical and funeral insurance. They also supplemented the churches as black organizations that whites were willing to tolerate. They were organizations in which African Americans could vote, hold office, and brighten their drab lives with the color and spectacle of regalia and ritual, impressive titles and fancy-dress parades, lodge meetings and funerals.

Even more than in other fraternal societies, a charismatic oligarch dominated the Order of Moses: Murray Jeffress. He depicted the origins of his society in quasi-prophetic language. "It was in 1901 that I began having visions repeatedly. These visions consisted of a single blackboard in which was chalked the words: The Grand United Order of Moses. After the third vision, I decided that I would do something about it." In 1904, the Order of Moses recruited 203 members, and the society received a state charter. A few years later, it acquired Moses Hall as its headquarters. Jeffress took the title right worshipful grand leader.

A crisis in the society occurred when a black man, presumably instigated by whites, alleged that the Order of Moses had been organized to keep African Americans from working for white people. A prominent white man squelched this rumor by offering $150 for evidence in its support, evidence that never materialized. For his efforts, the Order of Moses made him an honorary member.

Jeffress resented the injustice of segregation and disenfranchisement, but he considered small economic advances the only realistic goals. "Let us teach every boy and girl to build and not tear down. Teach them that being God-fearing, property owning and debt paying citizens is greater than being a voter or being on social equality with [a] king" (speech, August 1942, quoted in Kreusler 1952, p. 21). He encouraged his followers to buy farmland or learn a vocational trade.

Although Jeffress opposed urban migration, many rural black Virginians moved to northern cities. As a result, Order of Moses lodges appeared outside Virginia, mostly in Pennsylvania and New Jersey. Northern lodges unsuccessfully asked for the headquarters to be moved to Philadelphia, which they regarded as more convenient than Charlotte Court House, a village that at the time of Jeffress's death had only 250 residents and neither a railroad station nor a bus stop.

The strength and the weakness of the Order of Moses was its identification with Charlotte Court House and Charlotte County. The order helped establish a high school there for black youth, provided bus transportation for the students, constructed and equipped a hospital building, and provided electrical service for the village. The order owned an auditorium that could accommodate four hundred people, an office building, and apartments for black schoolteachers. The society also owned three hundred acres of farmland worked by black sharecroppers.

As leader of the Order of Moses, Murray Jeffress became a respected figure in African American life. He was elected first vice president of the Negro Organization Society and president of the Federation of Negro Fraternal Organizations. He served a number of Baptist churches as pastor.

At the time of Jeffress's death in 1951, the Order of Moses claimed a little more than five thousand members. Apparently, his son Wilson became the society's new leader. How long it continued to operate is unknown. In any event, the little Order of Moses had survived into the post–World War II era, an achievement that few better-known African American fraternal societies equaled.

The organization created by Jeffress was distinct from the Grand United Order of Brothers and Sisters, Sons and Daughters of Moses, founded in 1868.

**FURTHER READINGS**

Kreusler, Lucy Felicia. "The Grand United Order of Moses, Inc.: A Case Study of a Social Institution, Its Growth and Decline." M.A. thesis, University of Virginia, 1952.

[James Murray Jeffress Obituary in Norfolk, Virginia]. *Journal and Guide*, April 14, 1951, 2.

*David M. Fahey*

# Grand United Order of Odd Fellows

The Grand United Order of Odd Fellows had the largest membership of any African American fraternal society in the late nineteenth and early twentieth centuries. Only the Elks and the Masons enrolled more black members in the late twentieth century. Like a few other black fraternal lodges that shared a name with a white organization, the black Odd Fellows obtained their initial charters from a white fraternal society located in England. Since their beginnings in the mid–eighteenth century, the Odd Fellows of England had undergone many splits, the major one taking place in 1813. At that time, the Independent Order (Manchester Unity), soon to become the numerically predominant Odd Fellow organization, broke away from the Grand United Order. Nearly all the white Odd Fellows in the United States identified themselves with the Independent Order of Odd Fellows. In the early 1840s, after the white Odd Fellow lodges in the United States refused to charter black lodges, African Americans living in New York City turned to the older organization, the Grand United Order in England.

In this attempt to become Odd Fellows, the Philomathean (or Philomethean) Institute, a literary club led by Patrick H. Reason and James Fields, received help from a black man who had joined the Grand United Order in the English seaport of Liverpool. He was Peter Ogden, a steward on the ship *Patrick Henry*. In the course of his work, he traveled to England, where he obtained a charter on March 1, 1843. In addition, England's Committee of Management commissioned Ogden as its agent in the United States. Predictably, the few white American lodges that had claimed affiliation with the Grand United Lodge in England refused to recognize the leadership of a black man. In the United States, the Grand United Lodge became identified as a segregated society for African American Odd Fellows. The Subcommittee of Management of the Grand United Order established for America kept loyally to the rules and practices of the parent English organization. Whites were eligible for membership, but over the years at best a handful joined.

In later years, Ogden was honored as the founder of black Odd Fellowship in America and consequently as one of the most influential African Americans of the mid-nineteenth century. Unfortunately, there is little information about Ogden, and nobody has attempted to write his biography. Ironically, Ogden's relationship with the black lodges was sometimes troubled. When Fields was elected the first grand master of Philomathean lodge, Ogden was honored with the title past grand master. In contrast, America's first Annual Moveable Committee, or general meeting, of the Odd Fellows challenged Ogden's authority in 1845. The English Board of Management stood by him. Ogden died in 1852. A year earlier, the American Grand Lodge claimed twenty-five mostly northeastern lodges with a combined membership of nearly fifteen hundred men.

In 1857, the Grand United Order of Odd Fellows created the Households of Ruth. The first Household was organized in Harrisburg, Pennsylvania. Originally, membership in the Households of Ruth was restricted to males who held the fifth, or scarlet, Odd Fellow degree and the wives, daughters, and widows of Odd Fellows who held that degree. A pioneer of black Odd Fellowship, Patrick H. Reason (1816–1898), had proposed the Ruth degree, and he was the first person to receive it. By the end of the nineteenth century, the Households of Ruth had become the women's auxiliary of the Grand United Order. Any woman sponsored by five inmates of a Household of Ruth could join.

Odd Fellow membership exploded after the Civil War when African Americans in the South were able to organize lodges. Members tended to be younger and better off financially than the black population in general. The

Odd Fellows adhered to a strict code of moral conduct, provided financial and fraternal assistance to members at times of illness and burial, and offered the diversion of regalia, ritual, and parades. In some states, the Odd Fellows pursued more ambitious programs of collective self-help. Before the Georgia organization dominated by Benjamin Davis went bankrupt in 1916, it had created a fund that provided members with loans with which to purchase homes, farms, and businesses. Often Odd Fellows belonged to other societies, too. For instance, in 1921, 75 percent of the Odd Fellows in Oklahoma also were Knights of Pythias.

Although as individuals the black Masons probably were more prosperous than the Odd Fellows, the Odd Fellows was the most visible African American fraternal society during their early-twentieth-century heyday. In 1912, the *Negro Year Book* stated that the Odd Fellows owned $2 million in property, including a building in New Orleans that had cost $36,000 and one in Philadelphia valued at $100,000. In 1925, the *Proceedings* of the Ohio District Grand Lodge stated that the various branches of the Grand United Order owned property valued at $3.9 million. In addition to owning physical assets, the order published a half-dozen newspapers.

The 1916–1917 *Negro Year Book* credited the order with what appears to have been its greatest membership: 304,557 in 7,562 financial lodges, supplemented with some overlap by 197,654 in 4,993 financial Households of Ruth and 6,875 in 275 Past Grand Master Councils. Shortly afterward, the Grand United Order broke into the Morris and Davis factions, the former named after Edward H. Morris of Chicago, the long-serving national grand master. Apparently, the schism made it impossible to collect meaningful statistics because the 1918–1919 and 1921–1922 editions of the *Negro Year Book* challenge probability by repeating the old figures exactly. Presumably, the editor copied the old statistics because he could get no new ones. The schism did not last. From its 1925–1926 through 1937–1938 editions, the *Negro Year Book* lists only Morris as grand master. There was no longer an attempt to report exact statistics, merely vague claims in 1925–1926 and 1931–1932 that the Odd Fellows had more than 300,000 members, a rounding off of the 1916–1917 membership. In West Virginia, for which statistics are available, 1925–1926 appears to have been the peak year: 8,471 as the combined membership of the Odd Fellows and Households of Ruth, nearly double the total for the reporting year 1921–1922. Like most African American fraternal societies, the Odd Fellows presumably declined in membership after the mid-1920s, a decline that became devastating during and following the Great Depression. Despite such losses, the Grand United Order in the late 1990s reported a membership of 108,000. At that time, the order's headquarters was in Philadelphia.

**FURTHER READINGS**

Beito, David T. "Mutual Aid, State Welfare, and Organized Charity: Fraternal Societies and the 'Deserving' and 'Undeserving' Poor, 1900–1930. *Journal of Policy History* 5 (1993), 419–431.

Brooks, Charles H. *The Official History and Manual of the Grand United Order of Odd Fellows in America.* 1902. Reprint, Freeport, N.Y.: Books for Libraries, 1971.

Salvatore, Nick. *We All Got History: The Memory Books of Amos Webber.* New York: Times Books, 1996.

Trotter, Joe William, Jr. *Coal, Class, and Color: Blacks in Southern West Virginia, 1915–32.* Urbana: University of Illinois Press, 1990.

Work, Monroe, ed. *Negro Year Book.*

*David M. Fahey*

## Grand United Order of True Reformers

The Grand United Order of True Reformers was a black fraternal society for men and women that began as a Jim Crow temperance organization set up by whites but that later became an African American insurance society headquartered in Virginia. In the early 1870s, white southern Good Templars who did not want blacks in their own order created the True Reformers, an organization for blacks. The initiative came from John J. Hickman of Kentucky. Another white man, English-born James G. Thrower of Georgia, was important in promoting the new order. In the mid-1870s, there were Grand Fountains in such southern states as Georgia, Alabama, and Virginia but no central organization other than Thrower, who was styled grand superintendent. Supposedly, at its height of popularity, the True Reformer order had forty thousand members. After a schism divided the Good Templar order in 1876, blacks were admitted to the two rival Templar factions; many True Reformers became Good Templars.

The survival of the True Reformers was the result of the work of William Washington Browne (1849–1897), who had been born into slavery in Georgia and fled north from slavery during the Civil War. Afterward, he settled in Alabama, where he became a Methodist minister and an active True Reformer. Eventually, he was elected grand master for Alabama. In Virginia, the True Reformers had lost most of their members to the Good Templars. At the request of the remnant of True Reformers there, Browne moved to Virginia, where he was elected head of the Grand Fountain in 1881. Browne reconstructed Virginia's True Reformers as a fraternal insurance society that eventually also owned a bank in Richmond Virginia, a weekly newspaper called the *Reformer*, and a number of retail businesses as well as farmland. Browne extended what had been a Virginian organization to northern cities and parts of the Upper South.

Browne's True Reformers became the model for many other black fraternal and nonfraternal insurance organizations. It was the True Reformer order that popularized among African Americans the notion of insurance for the support of family survivors and not just burial. Many True Reformers started their own insurance organizations, including Samuel Wilson Rutherford (National Benefit Life Insurance Company), John Merrick (North Carolina Mutual Life Insurance Company), A. W. Holmes (National Ideal Benefit Society), W. F. Graham (Richmond Beneficial and Insurance Company, later the American Beneficial Insurance Company), and Booker Lawrence Jordan (Southern Aid Society). Before Maggie Lena Walker became celebrated as the leader of the Independent Order of St. Luke, she had been a paid member of the True Reformer headquarters staff.

In 1897, within a few years after Browne's death, the order attracted about half of its members from outside Virginia. Browne's successor as head of the Grand Fountain was a Baptist minister, William Lee Taylor. The secretary, William Patrick Burrell, was also a major figure. In 1910, the bank failed, and many members—once about a hundred thousand strong—quit out of doubt over the safety of their insurance policies. Much shrunken, the organization lived on until the Great Depression. Apparently, it ceased to exist in the mid-1930s.

**FURTHER READINGS**

Burrell, W. P., and D. E. Johnson Sr. *Twenty-Five Years History of the Grand Fountain of the United Order of True Reformers, 1881–1905.* Richmond, Va.: [Grand Fountain, United Order of True Reformers,] 1909. Rpt. Westport, Conn.: Negro Universities Press, 1970.

Fahey, David M. ed. *The Black Lodge in White America: "True Reformer" Browne and His Economic Strategy.* Dayton: Wright University Press, 1994.

———. *Temperance and Racism: John Bull, Johnny Reb, and the Good Templars.* Lexington: University Press of Kentucky, 1996.

Watkinson, James D. "William Washington Browne and the True Reformers of Richmond, Virginia." *Virginia Magazine of History and Biography* 97 (July 1989), 275–298.

*David M. Fahey*

## Greater New York Coordinating Committee for Employment

The Greater New York Coordinating Committee for Employment was largely Reverend Adam Clayton Powell Jr.'s organization devoted to mass agitation for the employment of African Americans during the Depression in New York City. Founded in 1938 by Powell with the cooperation of Harlem minister the Reverend Dr. Williams Lloyd Imes and A. Philip Randolph, president of the Brotherhood of Sleeping Car Porters, it pressured 125th Street stores like Chock Full O'Nuts, Grant's, and Woolworth's with "Don't Buy Where You Can't Work" demonstrations, pickets, and leafletting. Victories were marked by blue-and-orange signs that store managers posted to signal compliance with the campaign. Inspired by Depression-born collective action in Spring 1938, Powell led a Tuesday evenings "Black Out Boycott" of Consolidated Edison electric service to force the utility company to hire blacks in positions above menials. He also staged a billpayers parade to the company's Harlem office, where customers insisted on paying their utility bills in nickels and pennies.

Nothing worked as well—or dramatized the cause as effectively—as persistent and targeted picketing, which had a negative effect on store owners and aroused the sympathies of downtown liberal whites. During 1938 and 1939, Powell's committee achieved breakthroughs with the white-dominated Harlem Chamber of Commerce, which set up employment quotas for 125th Street stores, and with Consolidated Edison and New York Telephone, both of which agreed to employ African Americans for the first time in white-collar positions. In Spring 1939, the Coordinating Committee picketed the New York World's Fair Corporation at its Empire State Building headquarters. When that action resulted in the employment of only a few token blacks in menial positions, Powell's group staged opening-day pickets at the fair, which led to the employment of seven hundred African Americans, representing 10 percent of the fair's workforce. In 1941, the Coordinating Committee cooperated with Michael Quill's Transport Workers' Union for a boycott that helped the white union organize the city's major bus companies. This solidarity aided Powell's adjunct group, the United Negro

Bus Strike Committee, a September 1941 victory that set up a quota system for hiring African American bus drivers and other skilled personnel. That same year, the Coordinating Committee scored breakthroughs in hiring at Silvercup Bread and at Macy's and Gimbels department stores. The Coordinating Committee became the nucleus of the People's Committee, which supported Powell's move into politics with his successful campaign for a New York City Council seat in 1941.

**FURTHER READINGS**

Hamilton, Charles V. *Adam Clayton Powell, Jr.: The Political Biography of an American Dilemma*. New York: Atheneum, 1991.

Ottley, Roi. "*New World A-Coming*." Cleveland: World, 1945.

*Joel Schwartz*

## Guardians Association

During World War II, black New York City police officers launched the Guardians Association to advance the interests of black law enforcement officials. The organization played a crucial role in pressuring the New York City Police Department to end discriminatory practices and implement fair and equitable hiring practices. In 1943, black officers in New York City, led by Robert Mangum, attempted to establish the association by recruiting members from Harlem's Twenty-Eighth District. However, first attempts to organize the association failed, due to opposition from city officials and the police department, which refused to recognize the association. Moreover, the association was inhibited by World War II, which interrupted its growth, and by other police members who urged black officers to abandon it and to stop segregating themselves. Finally, the Guardians Association was officially chartered in 1949. It soon became the primary representative of black police officers in the New York City Police Department.

Since its inception, the association has been interested in community service. Members worked to recruit young people in their communities to become police officers and supported community protests against unfair police practices, acting as mediators between community complaints and the department. During the 1963 March on Washington, D.C., Guardian members provided security for the protestors, and, in the following year, they tried unsuccessfully to resolve the conflicts that led to the 1964 Harlem riot. The Guardians also fought against police brutality. In 1966, the association supported a New York

City referendum that provided for the creation of a civilian review board. The measure, however, was defeated at the polls. In 1970, the organization challenged the police department and the city to halt brutality against African American and Hispanic suspects in custody. Association members bravely broke the wall of silence by providing specific dates and times of incidents to substantiate their claims. In 1974, they pressured the New York City Police Department to address the issue of "mistaken identity shootings," which involved the shootings of black plainclothes officers by white law enforcement officials. When the Guardians threatened to pull all black plainclothes officers out of their assignments, the police department began to train all officers in identification procedures.

Furthermore, the Guardians have been active in recruiting a growing number of minority police officers and in working to eliminate bias in hiring. In 1972, the Guardians Association sued the New York City Police Department in federal court, charging that the police entrance exams were racially biased and served to limit the number of black recruits. These efforts to improve black police recruitment resulted in a quota system that became operational in 1980 and that mandates the hiring of one black out of every four recruits. As a result of the quota system, the proportion of blacks in the force has grown to more than 10 percent. The Guardians Association has also pushed the department to establish a police cadet program, and its members have tutored cadets to help them pass the Civil Service entrance exams. The association also played a crucial role in the establishment of a candidate review board, which reviews cases of rejected applicants, most of them black.

Guardian chapters also emerged in other cities in the 1950s and 1960s. For example, black police officers in Philadelphia formed the Guardians Civic League in 1956. Similar to the New York City association, Philadelphia's Guardians Civic League also faced departmental opposition. However, the group managed to survive, perhaps because it initially served primarily a social function. When the Philadelphia league elected Alphonso Deal as its president, the group took a more active stance on black police labor issues, especially since the local chapter of the Fraternal Order of Police ignored the needs of black officers. In 1978, Deal criticized his department for the brutal treatment of a local black movement. Frank Rizzo, mayor of Philadelphia, threatened violence against Deal unless he retired. The Philadelphia branch of the Fraternal Order of Police supported the mayor and suspended and fined Deal. Inspired by Renault Robinson's legal success in

Chicago, Deal and the Guardians sued. The Fraternal Order of Police was ordered to remove Deal's suspension, and the city of Philadelphia was ordered to implement equality with whites in the hiring and promotion of black police officers.

The Guardians Association continues to fight for the rights of black police officers in the United States, but it has also moved beyond national boundaries. In its struggle for racial justice, it has supported political protests and has sent representatives to international meetings of police officers in foreign countries.

**FURTHER READINGS**

Alexander, James I. *Blue Coats: Black Skin*. Hicksville, N.Y.: Exposition, 1978.

Dulaney, W. Marvin. *Black Police in America*. Bloomington: Indiana University Press, 1996.

Juris, Hervey A., and Peter Feuille. *Police Unionism*. Lexington, Mass.: Lexington Books, 1973.

Leinen, Stephen. *Black Police, White Society*. New York: New York University Press, 1984.

*Angel R. Rivera*

## Harlem Tenant League

The Harlem Tenant League, organized in uptown Manhattan during World War I, began as a white organization committed to combating rent increases and organizing grassroots support for the Socialist Party. With never more than a handful of dues-paying members, it engaged in rent bargaining with landlords, signed more than four hundred leases with apartment owners, and, during the Left-wing upsurge in 1919–1920, led rent strikes among a handful of buildings.

The league faded away during the 1920s, when New York City rents remained reasonably stable, but resurfaced amid Harlem's segregated housing market later in the decade. In February 1928, black Communist leader Richard Moore led a protest against the State Legislature's decision to allow the lapse of emergency rent laws that mandated rent controls. The league held protest meetings and agitated at the New York City Board of Aldermen for renewal of the laws. In the *Daily Worker*, Moore attacked the "capitalist caste system," which, he claimed, segregated blacks in Harlem and made them "the special prey of rent gougers." Dominated by Communists, the league held protest meetings, sponsored marches, and helped force the enactment of Harlem Assemblyman Lamar Perkins' bill for partial control of the low-rent housing market. When the rent law was nullified by the courts in Fall 1929, the league organized a "Harlem-wide rent strike," although the results proved spasmodic, limited to a handful of tenants.

Despite its limited success, the Harlem Tenant League was a bridge to Harlem's mass mobilization in the early 1930s. It vied with Garveyite and African nationalist groups for street-corner attention, particularly after evictions mounted with the onset of the Depression. The league often worked with the Communists' Unemployed Councils in anti-eviction protests and staged a celebrated rent strike in September 1934. Tenant movement historian Mark Naison argues that it was "an important step in implanting a culture of collective protest among Harlem tenants." The league was phased out after 1935, when the Communists' united front emphasized mainstream tenant activity.

### FURTHER READINGS

Greene, Larry A. "Harlem in the Great Depression, 1928–1936." Ph.D. diss., Columbia University, 1979.

Lawson, Ronald. *The New York City Tenants Movement, 1904–1984.* New Brunswick, N.J.: Rutgers University Press, 1986.

Naison, Mark. *Communists in Harlem During the Depression.* New York: Grove, 1985.

———. *The Tenant Movement in New York City, 1904–1984.* New Brunswick, N.J.: Rutgers University Press, 1986.

*Joel Schwartz*

## Harlem Youth Opportunities Unlimited, Inc.

*See* HARYOU.

## Harmon Foundation

The Harmon Foundation, founded in 1922, provided philanthropic and educational support for many African American artists from the zenith of the Harlem Renaissance to the early 1930s. Moreover, the Harmon Foundation supported the development of urban playgrounds, extended educational loans to disadvantaged students, and stimulated the growth of African American art.

Harlem Art Workshop children's class, 1930s. *Library of Congress*

The foundation, located in New York City, was established by William Elmer Harmon (1862–1928), a white midwestern financier who made his fortune in the development of real estate in Boston, Cincinnati, and New York. Little is known about the philanthropic activities of Harmon before the creation of his foundation. Apparently, he developed an interest in African American art when he encountered a black artist who could not sell his works at a fair price because of his race. Harmon's philanthropy was also influenced by the 1920s dominant intellectual white liberal philosophy that sought to maintain social order and racial harmony. His philanthropy also rested in a religious ethos. In 1925, for example, Harmon gave $50,000 to the Religious Motion Picture Foundation.

Harmon was assisted by Mary Bettie Brady, a white Vassar College graduate, who was the only director of the foundation until it dissolved in 1967. Under the leader-

ship of Brady, the Harmon Foundation sponsored various programs that were administered by four divisions: Playgrounds, Student Loans, Research and Experimentation, and Awards for Constructive and Creative Achievements. Brady was particularly interested in the work of the Division of Playgrounds because she believed that certain aspects of juvenile delinquency in America could be traced to the lack of publicly operated urban playgrounds.

In 1925, the Harmon Foundation began to present awards to African Americans for their distinguished achievements; recipients included Countee Cullen, James Weldon Johnson, Arthur Schomburg, and C. C. Spaulding. But the organization became best known for its visual-arts awards and the exhibitions it sponsored in conjunction with the award presentation. Starting in 1928, most of the award ceremonies took place in Harlem, where many obscure African American artists, such as Edward J.

Brandford, Palmer Hayden, William H. Johnson, and Hale A. Woodruff, received public exposure and gained prestige as a result of their participation in Harmon Foundation exhibitions.

In 1933, after some financial difficulties and personnel changes, the foundation ended its sponsorship of art exhibits and achievement awards. But the organization continued to educate the American public about the achievements of African American artists and the importance of black American artwork. For this purpose, the foundation developed traveling art displays and created a series of educational films titled *A Study of Negro Artists* (1934).

Despite criticisms of several art critics, who questioned the quality of work and the selection of exhibit judges, the Harmon Foundation continued to have an enormous impact on the careers of many African American artists until it was dissolved in 1967. The foundation increased the participation and visibility of African Americans in American art.

**FURTHER READINGS**

Lewis, David Levering, David Driskell, and Deborah Wills Ryan, eds. *Harlem Renaissance Art of Black America*. New York: Studio Museum in Harlem, 1987.

Reynolds, Gary A., and Beryl J. Wright, eds. *Against the Odds: African-American Artists and the Harmon Foundation*. Newark, N.J.: Newark Museum, 1989.

*Eric R. Jackson*

# HARYOU

HARYOU (Harlem Youth Opportunities Unlimited, Inc.), was an innovative antipoverty program designed by social scientists and ghetto residents to combat the high unemployment, poor school facilities, and low self-esteem that plagued black youths in New York City's Harlem. Founded in 1962 and supported by planning grants from the city of New York and the President's Committee on Juvenile Delinquency, HARYOU quickly became a center of controversy, generating conflict between black politicians and social scientists. Negative publicity ultimately destroyed the program by 1968.

In the 1960s, HARYOU represented a dramatic break from traditional welfare agencies that operated in America's ghettos. Designed to stimulate "social action" in the poverty-ridden neighborhoods of black Harlem, HARYOU began as a unique social experiment in June 1962. The architects of HARYOU sought to organize job

training centers, improve Harlem's ghetto schools, and instill African American inner-city youths with a sense of self-worth and real social, economic, and political power.

HARYOU grew out of a protest movement created by the Harlem Neighborhood Association (HANA) in 1961, after the city announced funding for a youth-services program for ghetto areas that had been designed without the participation of Harlem residents. HANA appealed to Mayor Robert F. Wagner, and the following year HARYOU began an extensive study of the African American communities of central Harlem. Dr. Kenneth B. Clark, the noted African American scholar, was the chief project consultant and chairman of the board of directors of HARYOU, and his team of social scientists, community organizers, and local residents presented their massive study, *Youth in the Ghetto*, in 1964. Clark argued that the direct-action tactics of the civil rights movement should act as a blueprint for future efforts to fight against conditions in black ghettos across the country. Embracing the notion that youths were the spearhead of the recent sit-ins and demonstrations, Clark focused on black teens as the key to breaking the cycle of poverty in African American ghettos.

Shortly after the publication of *Youth in the Ghetto*, however, a struggle between Clark and Adam Clayton Powell Jr., the famous and flamboyant New York City congressman, erupted over control of HARYOU. Frustrated with Powell's vision of HARYOU as a vehicle for providing services to his constituents in Harlem, Clark resigned from the HARYOU project in July 1964. Powell then took control of the organization and merged it with his own project, Associated Community Teams (ACT). The combined HARYOU–ACT program successfully applied for funds from the newly created federal Office of Economic Opportunity, the main agency of President Lyndon B. Johnson's Great Society, and it quickly shifted from the path-breaking ideal of social action and returned to the more traditional approach of providing social services for the poor.

Unfortunately, the new executive director of HARYOU–ACT, Livingston Wingate, proved to be a poor administrator, and the specter of scandal haunted HARYOU–ACT throughout the rest of its brief history. Wingate failed to get many of the programs operating; critics complained of high staff salaries; and the project was $400,000 over budget by 1965. Public officials protested when young black militants gained control of HARYOU–ACT's Project Up-Lift and sponsored revolutionary playwright LeRoi Jones's Black Arts Theater. Wingate resigned under heavy criticism in November 1966, and HARYOU–ACT deteriorated until a tumultuous board meeting in 1968, when a pistol shot and the explosion of a teargas canister signaled the death knell of what had been perhaps the most innovative and promising community-action program of the early 1960s.

**FURTHER READINGS**

Clark, Kenneth B. *Dark Ghetto: Dilemmas of Social Power.* New York: Harper and Row, 1965.

Day, Mary W. "Harlem Youth Opportunities Unlimited." In *Advocacy in America: Case Studies in Social Change.* Ed. Gladys Walton Hall, Grace C. Clark, and Michael A. Creedon. Lanham, Md.: University Press of America, 1987, 11–25.

Harlem Youth Opportunities Unlimited, Inc. *Youth in the Ghetto: A Study of the Consequences of Powerlessness and a Blueprint for Change.* New York: HARYOU, 1964.

Matusow, Allan J. *The Unraveling of America: A History of Liberalism in the 1960s.* New York: Harper and Row, 1984.

*Daniel E. Crowe*

## Hatza'ad Harishon

Founded in July 1964 in New York City, Hatza'ad Harishon (Hebrew phrase meaning "the first step") was a national organization of African American Jews, serving black Jewish individuals and communities throughout the United States and abroad, including New York City; Hammonton, New Jersey; Philadelphia; Boston; Chicago; Venice, California; Nigeria; Cambridge, England; Kingston, Jamaica; Ethiopia; and Israel. The organizational objectives included creating unity among all Jews, black and white, and bringing religious and cultural knowledge to black Jews who were not raised with a Jewish education. The Scholarship Fund for Jewish Education assisted young people to pursue Jewish religious studies. In cooperation with the Jewish Association of College Youth and the American Zionist Youth Foundation (AZYF), Hatza'ad Harishon sent young people to take part in the 1971 Israel Summer Program.

The organization had headquarters in Manhattan and published a quarterly newsletter, *Am Echad* (Hebrew phrase for "one people"). While no organizational statistics are available, Robert Coleman, the black Jewish director of the Department of Social Justice of the Synagogue Council of America, estimated the number of African American Jews in the United States at around ten thousand in the early 1970s. Partly supported by a grant from the Federation of Jewish Philanthropies, Hatza'ad Harishon also raised funds from membership dues and contributions. Mordecai Joseph was president and James H. Benjamin served as executive director. The organization reportedly disbanded during the 1970s.

**FURTHER READINGS**

Benjamin, James H. *About Hatza'ad Harishon.* n.p., n.d.

Goodman, Irving. "El Pasoan Visits Black Jews in NY." *El Paso Times*, Sunday, July 25, 1971.

*Donald Altschiller*

## Help Our Public Education
*See* Southern Regional Council.

## Hoosier Minority Chamber of Commerce
*See* National Black Chambers of Commerce.

## Hoover's Colored Advisory Commission

In May 1927, then-Secretary of Commerce Herbert Hoover appointed a Colored Advisory Commission to investigate the mistreatment of black victims of the Mississippi flood. During the spring of that year, the Mississippi River overran its banks in parts of Arkansas, Mississippi, and Louisiana. Among the flood's victims were thousands of black and white tenant farmers who were driven from the land they worked as sharecroppers. Though President Calvin Coolidge refused to provide government relief for the flood victims, he asked Hoover to head a cabinet committee to assist the Red Cross and other agencies with their aid efforts. Such a committee was consistent with Hoover's philosophy that the federal government aided or advised but did not direct the efforts of private organizations in matters of charity, business, and economics.

Hoover appointed the Colored Advisory Commission to assist his cabinet committee after reports of mistreatment of black flood victims became public. The reports came from many sources, including Associated Negro Press head Claude Barnett, black constituents of Kansas Senator Arthur Capper, and the National Association for the Advancement of Colored People (NAACP). On May 9, 1927, the NAACP asked Walter White to conduct an investigation of the conditions of black flood victims. White found numerous examples of abuse and discrimination. Black tenant farmers were detained in separate camps and could leave only to work for their landlords or nearby businesses, which contracted for the detainees' labor. Furthermore, while the Red Cross was distributing aid to landlords, some of them sold rather than gave the supplies to their tenants. White published his findings in the *Nation* in June 1927.

Hoover, upset that the NAACP was acting on its own, appointed the Colored Advisory Commission to conduct a separate investigation. The commission, headed by Dr. Robert Moton of Tuskegee Institute, included no NAACP representatives. In its survey of the relief camps, the commission confirmed the findings of White and made recommendations to Hoover in its first report on June 11, 1927. The commission urged the removal of white National Guardsmen from black camps, direct distribution of relief supplies to the flood victims, provision of recreational activities in the camps, and appointment of black advisers to the Red Cross. Hoover responded by increasing recreational opportunities in the black camps and asking the Red Cross to place blacks on its state rehabilitation committees. Though local white representatives on the Red Cross committees resisted the appointment of blacks, Hoover insisted that they be placed on the committees, and eventually the Red Cross complied. Hoover also started to demobilize white National Guard units but was slow to remove them from the black camps.

In September 1927, Moton informed Hoover that conditions in the camps were still inadequate. The commission conducted another survey in November and presented its report the next month. Its findings were not encouraging. Blacks were still forcibly prevented from leaving the camps, sometimes under the threat of death, and landlords were still keeping relief provisions from their tenants, despite the Red Cross's policy requiring direct distribution. As the commission noted, most problems stemmed from white-controlled local chapters that failed to implement the Red Cross's national policy.

The gap between national Red Cross policy and local practice helps explain the commission's limited success in remedying the inequities existing in the flood-relief camps. There were other causes as well. In keeping with his philosophy of associationalism, Hoover was reluctant to interfere with the workings of a private relief agency such as the Red Cross. As Hoover noted in a letter to Walter White, the mistreatment of blacks was partly a result of the sharecropping system, and the "Red Cross cannot undertake

either social or economic reforms." Finally, Hoover's view of blacks must be taken into account. Hoover accepted the inherent superiority of whites over blacks, a point he made clear in his 1909 book, *The Principles of Mining*, and black contemporaries such as W. E. B. Du Bois and Walter White considered him a racist.

**FURTHER READINGS**

Garcia, George F. "Herbert Hoover and the Issue of Race." *Annals of Iowa* 44, 7 (Winter 1979), 507–515.

Grothaus, Larry. "Herbert Hoover and Black Americans." In *Herbert Hoover and the Republican Era: A Reconsideration.* Ed. Carl E. Kroge and William R. Tanner. Lanham, Md.: University Press of America, 1984, 120–156.

Lisio, Donald J. *Hoover, Blacks, and Lily-Whites: A Study of Southern Strategies.* Chapel Hill: University of North Carolina Press, 1985.

Sherman, Richard B. *The Republican Party and Black America from McKinley to Hoover, 1896–1933.* Charlottesville: University Press of Virginia, 1973.

White, Walter. *A Man Called White: The Autobiography of Walter White.* New York: Viking, 1948.

*David F. Krugler*

## Houston: Civic, Literary, and Mutual Aid Associations

African American slaves lived in the Houston area under Spanish and Mexican rule before the city's 1836 founding following the Texas Revolution. Slaves, toiling as teamsters, dockworkers, and railroadmen, accounted for 22 percent of the city's population by 1860. After emancipation in 1865, Houston attracted freedmen drawn by the city's already large black population and the availability of nonagricultural jobs. By 1870, blacks accounted for 40 percent of the city's 9,382 residents. The percentage of the black population dropped between 1900 and 1930, when large numbers of white migrants came to Houston after the discovery of oil and the completion of a ship channel enhanced the city's position as a regional trade center. Following desegregation and white flight to the suburbs in the 1960s, however, blacks accounted for 28 percent of the 1.6 million population in 1990, making Houston the largest black metropolis in the old Confederacy.

The African American population concentrated southwest of downtown in the Fourth Ward, called "Freedmantown" after the Civil War, and southeast of downtown in the Third and Fifth Wards. There, a tradition of mutual aid developed. Black congregations, such as Antioch Baptist Church, founded in 1866, served as community centers, schools, and political-action committees. When the city refused to provide activities for black youths, Antioch Baptist Church, along with Trinity Methodist Church, purchased land in 1872 that became Emancipation Park. Discrimination also politicized the city's black women's clubs. One of the earliest black women's organizations in Houston, the Grant and Colfax Club, backed the 1868 Republican presidential ticket and supported the political party credited for emancipation.

Blacks in late-nineteenth-century Houston created a self-contained community with its own newspapers, restaurants, and parks. African American lodges such as the Grand United Order of Odd Fellows, formed in 1881, often provided the only available death and burial benefits for their members. Fraternal lodges, however, suffered from shaky finances, and many proved short lived.

The Married Ladies Social, Art, and Charity Club, founded in 1906, advocated cultural refinement and self-help while fighting stereotypes of African American women as sexually promiscuous. Black women helped found Houston's National Association for the Advancement of Colored People (NAACP) in 1912 and, after women achieved suffrage in Texas primaries in 1917, led voter drives in Harris County.

World War I marked a nadir in Houston race relations, culminating in an August 23, 1917, riot involving black soldiers stationed at nearby Fort Logan. The soldiers marched on downtown Houston after weeks of police harassment, discrimination on streetcars, and an incident in which a black soldier was shot at by a Houston police officer. Fifteen whites and four blacks died in subsequent violence. The riot intensified the black community's isolation. Nevertheless, many African Americans hoped that support of the war would reduce discrimination. After the riot, women's groups battled racism through political participation and the formation of alliances with liberal whites.

With the advent of female suffrage in Texas in 1917, candidates emerged from the black women's club scene. Three women from the Harris County Republican Party's Black and Tan wing, Mrs. G. B. M. Turner, Mrs. R. L. Yocome, and Mrs. F. L. Long, ran unsuccessfully for public office in 1920. B. J. Covington sought to repair race relations through the Texas Commission on Interracial Cooperation (TCIC), which was active in the 1920s and 1930s. Covington, who founded Houston's Blue Triangle

Young Women's Christian Association in 1918, became the first chair of the TCIC's Negro Women's Division. The TCIC lobbied against lynching and the influence of the Ku Klux Klan, which dominated Texas politics in the 1920s.

Amid this turbulence, black leaders sought to stabilize African American-owned businesses. The Houston Colored Commercial Club (HCCC), founded in 1923, waged a "buy Black" campaign and encouraged business owners to promote community pride by keeping their buildings physically attractive.

The Great Depression of the 1930s proved relatively mild in Houston, but African Americans suffered disproportionately. Monthly government relief payments to blacks averaged 25 percent less than those to whites. Women's literary and arts clubs filled a philanthropic void, doubling as social agencies. Starting in 1927, the still-active Ethel Ransom Club provided embroidery lessons, discussed books by black authors, raised funds for playgrounds, and supported destitute families.

The growth of the shipping, natural gas, and chemistry industries sparked an economic boom in Houston during World War II, which also helped create jobs for black men and women. Club activities shifted from relief work to supporting the troops. As the draft reduced the male labor force, black women in the United Service Organization (USO) staffed the Southern Pacific train station to replace male workers.

Black soldiers returning from the war fought to complete the "double victory" by ending racism at home. The United States Supreme Court in 1944 ruled the state's whites-only Democratic primaries unconstitutional. The Harris County Council of Organizations (HCCO), established in 1949, launched voter registration and education programs aimed at increasing black participation in local politics.

In 1945, Houston's NAACP sponsored the case of Heman Sweatt, a black mail carrier denied admission to the University of Texas law school. The case resulted in the 1950 Supreme Court decision *Sweatt v. Painter*, which required the university to admit Sweatt and set a precedent for the *Brown v. Board of Education* ruling four years later.

Following the passage of the Civil Rights and Voting Rights Acts of 1964–1965, Houston organizations focused on economic discrimination. In 1966, the local chapter of Operation Breadbasket launched a boycott against Burger King, successfully pressuring the corporation to award franchises to black businessmen. Until 1978, when Operation

Breadbasket ran out of money, the group used boycotts and media pressure to force white-run businesses to hire and promote African Americans.

Civic groups continue to fill the gaps left by inadequate government services in African American neighborhoods. With an invitation-only membership of elite black women, The Links Incorporated, founded in 1946, supports local youth arts programs, sponsors alcohol and drug education, provides equipment and volunteers for public schools, and promotes voter registration. Jack and Jill of America, Inc., launched its educational and recreational children's programs in 1952 and sees its mission as reinforcing the black family. For nearly 140 years, such civic clubs have broken down class and gender barriers in the black community. These associations, like their predecessors during Reconstruction, simultaneously emphasize black institution building and reform of the larger society.

**FURTHER READINGS**

Beeth, Howard, and Cary D. Wintz, eds. *Black Dixie: Afro-Texas History and Culture in Houston.* College Station: Texas A&M University Press, 1992.

Bullard, Robert D. *Invisible Houston: The Black Experience in Boom and Bust.* College Station: Texas A&M University Press, 1987.

Davidson, Chandler. *Biracial Politics: Conflict and Coalition in the Metropolitan South.* Baton Rouge: Louisiana State University Press, 1972.

McComb, David G. *Houston: A History.* Austin: University of Texas Press, 1981.

Winegarten, Ruthe. *Black Texas Women: 150 Years of Trial and Triumph.* Austin: University of Texas Press, 1995.

*Michael Phillips*

**SEE ALSO**    Jack and Jill of America, Inc.; The Links Incorporated

## Ida B. Wells Social Club

The Ida B. Wells Social Club was founded in Chicago in 1893 and, like so many of Wells's activities, was a manifestation of her commitment to exposing and outlawing the evils of the lynch law. A testimonial meeting on October 5, 1892, sponsored by New York City's black women in honor of her antilynching efforts provided a catalyst for club formation among black women in all parts of the nation. The Ida B. Wells Social Club, though, did not limit itself to antilynching efforts but engaged in a wide variety of activities on behalf of the social uplift of the race. Like many women's clubs, the Ida B. Wells Social Club engaged in charity work, extolled the virtues of literacy and education, opened nurseries, trained mothers in child care and hygiene, operated a kindergarten in one of Chicago's African American neighborhoods, and worked on behalf of blacks' political and economic advancement.

Historically, black women in the United States had formed clubs and organizations for the benefit of their race. Most of the organizations of the early nineteenth century, however, were based in the African American church rather than in the secular community. Their foundation in community churches meant that most of the early-nineteenth-century organizations were very small and local in nature, without the capacity to effect change on a large scale. Only in the 1890s did African American women begin to form civic clubs and national networks that operated on many fronts to lift the race and to reform American society.

The 1892 New York testimonial was no doubt important in spurring black women to organize. Wells worked from that point on to encourage club formation. Her efforts redoubled after a visit to the United Kingdom in 1893 allowed her to observe the expansive and effective reform efforts of English women. Wells founded what its members would name the Ida B. Wells Social Club in 1893. Twenty years later, she maintained her beliefs in women's organization as a means of social uplift for all African Americans. She founded the Ideal Woman's Club in 1910 and the Alpha Suffrage Club of Chicago in 1913—her commitment to universal suffrage having grown even stronger.

By 1895, the club movement among African American women was sufficiently large and strong to necessitate the creation of an umbrella organization—the National Association of Colored Women (NACW). The NACW operated parallel to the larger but racially exclusive General Federation of Women's Clubs (GFWC) that formed in 1890. Ida Wells fought to break down the "color line" and succeeded in getting the Ida B. Wells Social Club—the only African American women's civic club in Chicago—voted into the umbrella League of Cook County Clubs. She was less successful in getting national organizations like the GFWC and the Women's Christian Temperance Union (WCTU) to embrace the idea of African American membership and participation.

Wells served as president of the Ida B. Wells Social Club for five years after its founding (1893–1898) and returned to that office in 1920. The Ida B. Wells Social Club of Chicago survived her death in 1931, and, indeed, Ida Wells Clubs were established in several large cities across the nation, extant in the late twentieth century.

**FURTHER READINGS**

Duster, Alfreda, ed. *Crusade for Justice: The Autobiography of Ida B. Wells.* Chicago: University of Chicago Press, 1970.

Harris, Trudier, ed. *Selected Works of Ida B. Wells-Barnett.* New York: Oxford University Press, 1991.

Knupfer, Anne Meis. *Toward a Tenderer Humanity and a Nobler Womanhood: African American Women's Clubs in Turn-of-the-Century Chicago.* New York: New York University Press, 1996.

*Nancy Bowman*

## Illinois Commission on Human Relations

*See* Illinois Interracial Commission.

## Illinois Department of Human Rights

*See* Illinois Interracial Commission.

## Illinois Equal Employment Opportunity Commission

*See* Illinois Interracial Commission.

## Illinois Interracial Commission

In July 1943, the Illinois General Assembly enacted House Bill 771, creating the Illinois Interracial Commission (IIC), the nation's first statewide human relations committee supported by public funds. The agency worked with local human relations commissions to identify and alleviate racial tensions, particularly in housing. The creation of the IIC was the product of numerous race riots that swept the nation during World War II. At least thirty-one cities across the nation formed municipal interracial commissions during the summers of 1943 and 1944. In addition to preventing racial violence at the local level, eleven states launched similar state commissions.

In the aftermath of the June 1943 Detroit race riot, black leaders and white political officials met in the offices of Chicago's leading black newspaper, the *Defender.* During this Emergency Citizens Conference, participants discussed local race relations and sought solutions for the prevention of racial violence. The group joined the chorus of various civic organizations who asked Mayor Edward J. Kelly and Governor Dwight Green to form an interracial commission similar to the Mayor's Committee on Race Relations that had been established in Chicago after that city's 1919 race riot. Their intent was to study statewide racial tensions and prevent the eruption of racial violence. The July 1943 creation of the IIC was a direct response to these demands.

The IIC was composed of twenty individuals, appointed by the governor to two-year terms. IIC members, with the exception of the commission's chair, who was also appointed by the governor, served without compensation. Among those who served on the ICC were Dr. Martin Bickhem, Roger Nathan, and William Graham Cole, president of Lake Forest College. The IIC met officially in meetings called by its chair or at regular meetings determined by resolution of the IIC as adopted by majority vote. The IIC's powers and duties were to investigate the most effective means of securing employment opportunities for all qualified persons; to cooperate with civic, religious, and educational organizations to combat discrimination; and to report its findings biennially to the governor and the State Legislature. The IIC employed a professional staff of three to four secretaries, stenographers, and clerks and submitted its budget to the Illinois state director of finance.

The IIC presented its first report in 1947. At that time, the commission had become known as the Illinois Commission on Human Relations. It continued to gather information about race relations and organized public forums, enabling white and black state residents to discuss discrimination and segregation in employment, housing, and education. The commission also urged the formation of municipal commissions to cope with local race relations problems. Considering the commission's recommendation, Illinois Governor Dwight Green asked mayors and community leaders throughout the state to form municipal commissions. By the early 1960s, at least twenty-nine such local organizations were in existence in Alton, Champaign, Chicago, East St. Louis, Elgin, Galesburg, Joliet, Moline, Park Forest, Peoria, Rockford, and Springfield. Other groups emerged in Beverly Hills-Morgan Park, Bloomington Normal, Champaign-Urbana, Evanston, Lombard, Monmouth, Niles Township, the Quad Cities (including Davenport, Iowa), Quincy, Decatur, LaGrange, and in south suburban, north suburban, west suburban, and North Shore Chicago, as well as the northwest Chicago suburbs. These local commissions galvanized civic activism and cooperated with the IIC.

With the assistance of the IIC and the collaboration of other public and private agencies, these local commissions initiated various education and research action projects, while serving as a "watchdog" in upholding state and local human rights statutes and ordinances. The Chicago Commission on Human Relations, the oldest of these groups in the state and the first city agency to establish a special program designed to assist newcomers to the city, had a full-time staff of specialists in community services, employment, education, and research. The Champaign Commission on Human Relations, with the aid of a group of faculty and students from the University of Illinois, completed a comprehensive survey of nonwhite employment in that city that served as a basis for its employment-opportunity program. The Peoria commission took the lead in the integration of a segregated public-housing project. It collected data about housing and housing needs in Peoria and gathered information about integrated housing in other locales, in order to convince city housing authorities that integration could be successful. The Rockford commission, through systematic enlistment of public support, secured positions for qualified black teachers in the city's school system. Several commissions, including the Joliet commission, created job training programs for minorities. Suburban human relations groups in the metropolitan Chicago area launched educational programs to analyze how human and property values could be maintained when nonwhite families moved into previously all-white communities. They held a number of home meetings during which small groups of white suburban residents met potential black homeowners. The IIC also added a youth-participation component to its human relations program. By the early 1960s, youth groups were established in Alton and Quincy. Other local commissions took advantage of this statewide program, such as Chicago, Evanston, Joliet, Lombard, and Rockford.

In 1980, the State Legislature combined the IIC with the Illinois Equal Employment Opportunity Commission to form the Illinois Department of Human Rights, which continued its work. Throughout its existence, the IIC sponsored interracial educational conferences, encouraged interracial cooperation, and escorted black home owners who penetrated all-white residential areas. The IIC received complaints of segregation, investigated violations of the state's Public Accommodation Act, and usually succeeded in enforcing compliance.

### FURTHER READINGS

Hirsch, Arnold R. *Making the Second Ghetto: Race and Housing in Chicago, 1940–1960.* Chicago: University of Chicago Press, 1998.

"Human Relations Progress in Illinois: The Role of the Illinois Commission on Human Relations, 1943–1960."

Chicago: Illinois Commission on Human Relations, April 1960.

"Special Report on Employment Opportunities in Illinois." Chicago: Illinois Interracial Commission, 1948.

*David MacLaren*

## Improved Benevolent and Protective Order of the Elks of the World

Arthur J. Riggs and Benjamin Franklin Howard initiated the Improved Benevolent and Protective Order of the Elks of the World (IBPOEW) in 1897 and organized the first meeting in Cincinnati, Ohio, in October 1898. Riggs had obtained a copy of the ritual of the whites-only Benevolent and Protective Order of Elks (BPOE), which the group had failed to copyright. Riggs copyrighted the ritual, but the white Elks put so much pressure on him that he was forced to flee Cincinnati, and Howard became the driving force during the organization's early years. The legal battles that erupted between the IBPOEW and the BPOE over the use of the name "Elk" and the ritual continued well into the 1920s and consumed a great deal of money, time, and legal expertise of the IBPOEW.

The IBPOEW provided its black members with the same type of opportunities and experiences that whites enjoyed in their racially exclusive secret fraternal organizations. It offered leadership training, professional networking opportunities, social fellowship, and community service. In addition, black Elks actively promoted racial uplift. They fought to eradicate African American illiteracy, challenged segregation, and advocated integration, political rights, and equal economic opportunities.

Capable and ambitious men accepted the challenge of first organizing and then leading the IBPOEW. They hoped that the fraternal order could provide them and their fellow members with the economic and political clout necessary to combat entrenched white racism. Although there were already a few similar organizations, the chance to create a new society with new leadership opportunities appealed to many ambitious black lawyers, doctors, businessmen, and politicians. Indeed, these men dominated the leadership ranks of the IBPOEW, particularly the high office of the grand exalted ruler. As the organization matured in the early decades of the twentieth century, many prominent black leaders joined the secret fraternity, such as Booker T. Washington, W. E. B. Du Bois, and later Thurgood Marshall. Harry Pace, who served as grand exalted ruler from 1911 to 1913, exemplified the type of dynamic leader the organization attracted. Not only did Pace help Du Bois establish the order's national magazine, the *Moon*, he also launched insurance companies like Standard Life, Northeastern, and Supreme Liberty Life and was a cofounder of the Black Swan Record Company. Businessmen such as Pace and professionals of all kinds benefited from their membership. The IBPOEW needed skilled lawyers to fight its many legal battles, accountants to manage the hundreds of thousands of dollars that poured into its coffers, and doctors to administer physical examinations required for membership. Businessmen used the order to network and attract new clients, and politicians found grassroots support among their Elk brothers. As Charles Edward Dickerson II has noted, the IBPOEW operated as a "shadow government" that provided black men with leadership opportunities and training that white society denied them.

During the 1920s, J. Finley Wilson provided the dynamic leadership for the phenomenal growth of the IBPOEW into an organization of national power. In 1922, when Wilson became the grand exalted ruler, the order had approximately 36,000 members. By 1927, as result of his leadership, the IBPOEW boasted 250,000 members. Much of Wilson's success was due to his ability to recruit large numbers of working-class blacks, and it was this massive constituency that attracted many businessmen and politicians to the organization. An indication of the mass appeal of the Elks were the annual Grand Lodge parades that were attended by thousands of delegates and drew even larger crowds. The 1927 Grand Lodge parade in Harlem, for example, had thirty thousand participants and attracted 100,000 spectators. Wilson continued as grand exalted ruler until his death in 1952 and helped expand the organization to international locales such as Liberia, Cuba, Haiti, Bermuda, Honduras, and many other nations.

Under Wilson's guidance, the IBPOEW also embraced community work, particularly in the areas of education, civil rights, and politics. In 1926, the black Elks created the Department of Education headed by Judge William C. Hueston, who was well known as a judge and president of the National Negro Baseball League. In subsequent years, the Elks provided thousands of young African American men and women with college scholarships, sponsored national oratory contests, and promoted literacy through the Elk's study clubs. Perhaps even more impressive was the IBPOEW's commitment to civil rights. In 1926, the Elks started a Civil Liberties Department and made it a permanent fixture in the following year. The department,

along with the staff of lawyers the Elks maintained, fought to end Jim Crow, lynching, and segregation in housing and the armed forces. The Elks fearlessly supported antilynching bills, published detailed pamphlets illustrating lynch victims, and called on African Americans to take action against those who supported or tolerated mob justice. The sheer size of the IBPOEW made the Elks an important political force. In 1928, Wilson's support of Democratic presidential candidate Al Smith foreshadowed the shift of African Americans voters from the Republican to the Democratic Party that occurred in 1936.

Throughout its history, the IBPOEW has defined itself as a patriotic American organization promoting the citizenship of African Americans. In spite of segregation, lynching, and racial injustices, the black Elks patriotically supported World War I and World War II, raising more than $30 million in war bonds during the latter. Using tactics of accommodation and resistance, they fought for racial unity, civil rights, and equality of educational and economic opportunity. The IBPOEW, headquartered in Winton, North Carolina, maintains a membership of 450,000.

**FURTHER READINGS**

Dickerson, Charles Edward, II. "The Benevolent and Protective Order of Elks and the Improved Benevolent and Protective Order of Elks of the World: A Comparative Study of Euro-American and Afro-American Secret Societies." Ph.D. diss., University of Rochester, 1981.

Harris, Theodore H. H. *The History of Afro-American Elkdom and Benjamin Franklin Howard in Covington, Kentucky, 1889–1918*. Covington: T. H. H. Harris, 1991.

Wesley, Charles. *History of the Improved Benevolent and Protective Order of Elks of the World*. Washington, D.C.: Association for the Study of Negro Life and History, 1955.

*Joel Shrock*

## Independent National Funeral Directors Association

*See* National Funeral Directors and Morticians Association.

## Independent Order of Good Templars

The Independent Order of Good Templars, a predominantly white fraternal temperance organization, founded in 1852, had a large black membership in the late 1870s and the 1880s. Unlike most fraternal societies organized by white men, the Good Templar order always welcomed women and never had a rule that barred African Americans. Local lodges decided whether to admit or reject individual blacks, and state Grand Lodges decided whether or not to charter de facto segregated black lodges. As early as 1853, a black man represented a New York State lodge at the convention of the Good Templar's ruling body, and a year later William Howard Day of Ohio, black editor of the *Aliened American*, joined the order.

After the Civil War, the order regarded the black population of the former slave states as possible recruits. In 1867–1868, a Yankee organizer set up several black lodges in North Carolina. In 1873, African Americans announced the organization of a Colored Grand Lodge of North Carolina, which the Good Templars did not recognize because there already was a "whites only" Grand Lodge of North Carolina. Many of North Carolina's black Templars, such as John Dancy and Bishop J. W. Hood, were active in the Zion AME Church.

In the 1870s, the order was torn by controversy over whether blacks had a right to join even if local whites did not want them. Many English and Scottish reformers who had joined the Good Templars believed that brotherhood was as fundamental a principle of the order as was total abstinence. Thus, they supported the membership of all teetotalers regardless of race. Yet, at the same time, the Good Templars had recruited many whites in the American South who strongly opposed the membership of African Americans. In an unsuccessful compromise, white southerners organized a separate fraternal temperance society for blacks, the United Order of True Reformers.

The controversy over black membership led to a schism in the Templar order in the years 1876–1887. A predominantly British faction seceded to protest the exclusion of blacks in the former slave states. Its supporters were called Malinites after Joseph Malins, an English leader. Supporters of the original Good Templar organization, headed by John Hickman of Kentucky, were called Hickmanites. During the schism, thousands of black southerners were recruited into the Independent Order of Good Templars, nearly always in segregated Grand Lodges and local lodges. Some of these black Templars belonged to the Malinite faction, which could not find any white members in the American South, while others joined segregated Dual Grand Lodges that white southern Hickmanites reluctantly allowed in their region to appease the conscience of Templars in the North and

overseas. The British faction elected the well-known writer and onetime fugitive slave William Wells Brown to its second-highest office. Brown also served as a paid organizer in Virginia, West Virginia, and Tennessee. W. B. Derrick, an AME minister born in the West Indies, headed the pro-British Grand Lodge of Virginia. William Pledger, a Republican politician in Georgia, successively headed Malinite and Hickmanite black Grand Lodges in his state. Nova Scotia–born S.C. Goosley, an AME minister, organized a brief-lived five-thousand-member Malinite Grand Lodge in South Carolina. In Florida, a more durable Malinite Grand Lodge was organized by Joseph E. Lee, born in Pennsylvania, and W. M. Artrell, born in the Bahamas. The Malinite Independent Order of the Good Templars used white northerners who taught in black southern schools as paid organizers. The major white organizer in the rival Hickmanite organization was J. G. Thrower of Georgia, who had been born in England. Sometimes, for instance in Kentucky, the Hickmanite section of the Good Templars paid African Americans to organize other blacks.

Although most of the black Templar organizations collapsed almost as soon as they were established, there were pockets of enduring strength, such as Norfolk, Virginia; Wilmington, North Carolina; and Key West and Jacksonville in Florida. Women made up a large proportion of the African American membership, perhaps nearly 50 percent. Probably the Good Templars were handicapped among African Americans by the lack of a fraternal insurance program. Outside the South, there were integrated lodges in Massachusetts and segregated ones scattered from New Jersey to Kansas and beyond. After the schism ended in 1887 on a compromise basis that offended both white southerners and black southerners, the appeal of the Good Templars to African Americans faded. Only in Florida did a small black Grand Lodge limp into the twentieth century. As late as 1908, a black Baptist minister from Florida was appointed to a minor office in the international Order of Good Templars.

Outside the United States, there were black Templars in the British Empire from Ontario and Nova Scotia to Trinidad and the Gold Coast (Ghana), as well as in Britain itself. A Good Templar–related organization in South Africa, the True Templars, attracted thousands of African and mixed-race people.

**FURTHER READINGS**

David M. Fahey, ed. *The Collected Writings of Jessie Forsyth, 1847–1937: The Good Templars and Temperance Reform on Three Continents.* Lewiston, N.Y.: Edwin Mellen, 1988.

————. "Blacks, Good Templars, and Universal Membership." In *The Changing Face of Drink: Substance, Imagery, Behaviour.* Ed. Jack S. Blocker Jr. and Cheryl Krasnick Warsh. Toronto: University of Toronto Press, 1997.

————. *Temperance and Racism: John Bull, Johnny Reb, and the Good Templars.* Lexington: University Press of Kentucky, 1996.

*David M. Fahey*

## Independent Order of St. Luke

The Independent Order of St. Luke entered the ranks of the major fraternal societies in the twentieth century. Open to both male and female members, it was unique in having a woman as leader and becoming identified with women. The first St. Luke organization was founded by ex-slave Mary Prout as a women's mutual insurance society in Baltimore in 1867. It provided for the care of the ill and the burial of the dead. Renamed the Grand United Order of St. Luke, it then admitted men. Almost immediately, the Virginian lodges broke away from the Independent Order of St. Luke, which then spread to other states. From 1869 to 1899, the Virginia St. Luke society was dominated by its secretary, William M. T. Forrester. He abandoned it when the order seemed on the verge of collapse and chose to identify himself instead with the Odd Fellows. His successor at the St. Lukes, Maggie Lena Walker (c. 1867–1934) of Richmond, turned a minor society into one of the best-known African American fraternal organizations of the first half of the twentieth century. As the daughter of a widowed washerwoman, she had been born, not with a silver spoon in her mouth, but, as she put it, "with a clothes basket almost upon my head."

Walker had joined the Independent Order of St. Luke when she was fourteen. Although she quickly occupied minor offices, her career in the order is best dated from her marriage in 1886, which, under the regulations of the time, forced her resignation as a schoolteacher. By 1889, she headed a "council," the name used for St. Luke lodges. She soon was appointed a national deputy, organizing new councils in Virginia and West Virginia. In 1895, she proposed the formation of a juvenile department, an initiative that gave St. Luke women a new status. Each local council was directed to create a juvenile "circle," headed by a woman bearing the title of "matron." Walker was elected grand matron in charge of a new council of matrons. In 1897, she was elected secretary of the endowment, or insurance, department.

In 1899, when Forrester withdrew, Walker became right worthy grand secretary, a post that she retained until her death in 1934. In 1899, the order had only fifty-seven chapters with 1,080 members. The treasury that Walker inherited contained $31.61 cash, offset by $400 in debts. At first, Walker was paid $100 per year, a third of her predecessor's salary.

At least through the mid-1920s, the Walker years would be ones of almost uninterrupted successes. During the Walker era, women made up at least half of the senior St. Luke officials, something that no other society that admitted men could match. In Walker's first year, membership grew to 3,830 financial members in eighty-nine councils, figures supplemented by 1,205 children in thirty-five circles. In 1902, she created a printing department and a newspaper, the *St. Luke Herald.* By the mid-1920s, it claimed six thousand subscribers. Outside the order, she organized a joint-stock association that purchased property in Richmond and erected a three-story building that served as the order's headquarters. In 1903, she started the St. Luke Penny Savings Bank. It began with deposits of $8,000, which rose by the mid-1920s to nearly $500,000 and provided mortgages that empowered many black families to purchase homes. Probably Walker was the first woman bank president in the country other than a few in the western states who had inherited the job in a family bank. In 1904, she started a regalia and supply department. In a rare failure, a department store called the St. Luke Emporium, organized by twenty-two St. Luke women in 1905, was forced to close at the beginning of 1912. It had been undermined by the systematic obstruction mounted by white merchants. Walker had hoped, among other things, that the Emporium would provide employment for black women. When the failure of another Richmond black fraternal society bank in 1910, that of the True Reformers, persuaded the state of Virginia to require that fraternal societies and financial institutions be separate, the St. Luke bank became officially independent of the order. The St. Lukes remained the principal depositor. The True Reformer scandal also induced the St. Luke order to install a new bookkeeping system in 1911. Increased government inspection made Walker joke that the "only secret we have left is our password." It was nervous insurance regulators that forced the closure of the Emporium. In 1929, the St. Luke bank merged with other black Richmond banks, with Walker as chairman of the board.

The membership and finances of the St. Luke order peaked in the 1920s, when at least 20 percent of Richmond's black adults were members of the order. The *Negro Year Book* of 1921–1922 credited the order with 82,687 members. By the mid-1920s, the membership appears to have been more than 100,000. By the end of 1925, there was more than $8 million of St. Luke insurance in force in more than twenty states. The order employed fifty-five clerks in the home office, most of them women, and 145 field-workers. In 1927, the order created an educational loan fund. After years of decline, the Independent Order of St. Luke ceased to exist in the late 1980s.

**FURTHER READINGS**

Brown, Elsa Barkley. "Uncle Ned's Children: Negotiating Community and Freedom in Postemancipation Richmond, Virginia." Ph.D. diss., Kent State University, 1994.

Dabney, Wendell Phillips. *Maggie L. Walker and the I.O. of Saint Luke: The Woman and Her Work.* Cincinnati: Dabney, 1927.

Duckworth, Margaret. "Maggie L. Walker (1867–1934)." In *Notable Black American Women.* Ed. Jessie Carney Smith. Detroit: Gale, 1992, 1188–1193.

Kuyk, Betty M. "The African Derivation of Black Fraternal Orders in the United States." *Comparative Studies in Society and History* 25 (1983), 559–592.

Marlowe, Gertrude W. "Maggie Lena Walker (c. 1867–1934)." In *Black Women in America: An Historical Encyclopedia.* Ed. Darlene Clark Hine. New York: Carlson, 1993, 1214–1219.

Work, Monroe, ed. *Negro Year Book.*

*David M. Fahey*

## Indianapolis: Civic, Literary, and Mutual Aid Associations

The African American community in Indianapolis has a rich history of civic, literary, and mutual aid associations that dates back to antebellum days. Black Indianapolitans did not make up a large part of the city's population. An 1840 counting indicated 122 black residents, or 0.5 percent of the city's population. By 1860, the number of black residents had increased to 498; however, blacks' percentage of the city's total population had decreased to 0.3 percent. By 1900, the city had 15,931 black residents, accounting for more than 9 percent of the total population. The number of African Americans continued to grow in the early twentieth century, largely due to the influx of rural black southerners who migrated to the city during World War I. During that time, the number of black Indianapolitans increased from 21,816 in 1910 to 34,678 in 1920, when African Americans made up 11 percent of the total population. During the interwar years, the city's black population increased by roughly 20 percent. By 1940, almost 52,000 African Americans lived in Indianapolis.

Facing racism, discrimination, and segregation throughout the nineteenth and much of the twentieth century, African Americans in Indianapolis founded their own literary societies, lodges, mutual aid and benevolent associations, women's clubs, and political organizations. While these groups provided black city residents with opportunities to socialize, they also offered educational and recreational programs and facilitated employment, housing, health care, and insurance. Promoting self-help and racial advancement, black-controlled organizations played a crucial role in fostering community survival, as well as civil rights. Social welfare and political goals were inextricably linked since community survival and racial advancement were critical to the success of subsequent political agendas.

Indianapolis's churches were among the earliest recorded black social organizations. Bethel African Methodist Episcopal (AME) Church, founded in 1836; Second Baptist, organized in 1846; and Allen Chapel AME, established in 1866, were centers not only of religious instruction, but also of education. In the nineteenth century, church Sunday Schools taught students the rudiments of Bible reading, and some of the ministers, including Joseph J. Fitzgerald of Second Baptist Church, gave private lessons to black students. In the 1840s, Bethel AME Church organized the town's first school for black children.

The black churches also hosted public meetings to discuss issues of importance to the African American community. In the 1840s and 1850s, for example, the churches hosted gatherings that were part of the Black Convention Movement. In January 1842, local barber John Britton called a meeting at Bethel AME for the purpose of planning a state convention in May of that year in Terre Haute, where delegates would discuss the educational needs of the black community, African colonization, temperance, and racial and moral uplift. In 1847, another convention met at Bethel to petition the State Legislature for money to create schools for black children who had been prohibited from attending classes with whites by an 1843 law. The petitions of both conventions fell on deaf ears, and in 1851 the State Legislature adopted a new constitution that prohibited African Americans from moving to Indiana while providing that fines collected from illegal black migrants would be used to colonize those already living in the state. Article 13 of the State Constitution set the tone for post–Civil War Jim Crowism in Indiana.

By the 1890s and early 1900s, Indianapolis's black churches had become community centers that provided a broad spectrum of services. Bethel AME (1836), Second Baptist (1846), Ninth Presbyterian (1872), and Waymon and Allen Chapel AME (1866) hosted chatauquas, fairs, and exchanges that informed black city residents about health and child care, sanitation, and education. Moreover, as centers of the African American community's social life, Indianapolis's black churches often provided nonreligious, social, political, and business organizations with meeting spaces. Some of the diverse groups that met at the city's black churches included the Indiana Negro Welfare League, the city's chapter of the National Negro Business League (1906), the Indiana Association of Colored Men (1916), and the Colored Speedway Association.

By the 1960s and 1970s, the city's black churches became the headquarters for a variety of programs aimed at easing the effects of urban poverty. Churches like People's Temple Christian, New Bethel Baptist, and St. John's Baptist started to offer breakfast programs for school-age children and supplied food for needy African American families.

The prominence of black churches in the city's black community was largely due to the work of thousands of African American women. The largest of the church-based women's groups was the Sisters of Charity, an independent interdenominational lodge that began as a mutual aid and insurance society in 1879. By the turn of the twentieth century, the lodge had almost five hundred members in various chapters affiliated with the city's black churches. In 1911, the group broadened its mission of self-reliance and self-help and launched a community hospital. In addition to the Sisters of Charity, women's auxiliaries of fraternal orders also provided an outlet for social services. In 1847, the Masons had organized the city's first black lodge, and within three years they operated three Masonic chapters: the Pythagorus, Central, and Gleaves lodges. In 1888, the Masons organized their female counterpart, the Order of the Eastern Star. By 1900, the United Brotherhood of Friendship and its women's auxiliary, the Sisters of the Mysterious Ten, were the largest black lodge in the city and state, with more than three thousand members. By 1930, black Indianapolis also boasted chapters of the Grand United Order of True Reformers, the Independent Order of St. Luke,

the Grand Army of the Republic, the Grand and United Order of Odd Fellows, the Knights and Daughters of Tabor, and the Knights of Pythias, as well as women's auxiliaries such as the Order of Calanthe and the Household of Ruth, in addition to the Sisters of the Mysterious Ten. Besides providing opportunities for socializing, the groups offered their members insurance benefits and banking facilities. They also created junior auxiliaries to educate and train black youngsters.

In addition to their work in the lodges, African American women also found an outlet for community activism in the women's club movement, especially during the first two decades of the twentieth century. Between 1880 and 1920, Indianapolis's black club women created more than five hundred clubs that addressed a wide range of social welfare issues and laid the foundation for political activism. Building coalitions across class and gender lines, black club women founded organizations such as the Norwood Citizens League (1906), which sought "to better conditions morally in the suburbs," and the Woman's Civic Club (1907), which emerged from the Idle Hands Needle Club, a late-nineteenth-century black women's philanthropic association whose purpose was to provide winter fuel, food, and clothes for the city's poor neighborhoods. In 1912, the Women's Civic Club organized Indiana's first chapter of the National Association for the Advancement of Colored People (NAACP), which functioned as a woman's club for the first fourteen months of its charter. Moreover, black club women were responsible for the creation of health-care institutions, including the Oak Hill Tuberculosis Camp (1905) and the Sisters of Charity State Hospital (1911); child-care facilities and rescue homes for young black women, such as the Rosa Parks' (1909) and Annie Woodford's (1910) Boarding Homes for Infants, the Door of Hope and Rescue Home (1907), and the Young Women's Protective Association (1907); educational and self-improvement ventures, such as the Colored Rescue Training School for Girls (1907) and the Norwood Library and Boys Gymnasium (1908); business training programs, such as Ada Harris's joint venture with the local tailor H. L. Sanders to train young black women for factory work in 1908; and neighborhood cooperatives, such as the Glencoe Progressive Aid Club (1907) and Vaughan & Company (1909).

Many of the women's clubs that were founded at the turn of the century, including the Woman's Improvement Club, the Sojourner Truth Club, the Fortnightly Literary Club, the Thursday Coterie Club, and the Sisters of Charity clubs, have continued their philanthropic work into the twenty-first century. Indeed, several of the institutions that the women's clubs initiated continue to be viable community organizations, including the Alpha Home and the Flanner Guild. Established in 1886, the Alpha Home provided care for elderly black women who found themselves alone and impoverished in their declining years. Today, the Alpha Home is part of Methodist Hospital and caters to both women and men. The Flanner Guild, founded in 1898, conducted settlement-house work in two frame buildings that Frank Flanner, a local white mortician and philanthropist, had donated to the Charity Organization Society to create a social-service center in the black community. Initially, black club women carried out much of the work, until the Flanner Guild hired a staff of black and white professional social workers in the 1920s. Following World War II, Flanner Guild became Flanner House, one of the city's premier black social welfare agencies. In the decades after the 1940s, under the superintendency of black social worker Cleo Blackburn, Flanner House sponsored a home-building program and provided health care and health education to community residents.

Between the mid-1960s and the mid-1980s, the Citizens Forum, a neighborhood self-help organization, joined Flanner House in its efforts to improve living conditions for black Indianapolitans. The Citizens Forum designed programs to promote better race relations and to facilitate implementation of the 1964 Civil Rights Act and Indianapolis's Open Occupancy Ordinance, which was passed in the same year. Under the leadership of Mattie Rice Coney, the Citizens Forum created block clubs that helped clean up and beautify black neighborhoods, conducted community education programs to prevent the physical deterioration of black residential areas, and initiated the Helping Hand Program to provide a network of emergency safe houses for children on their way to and from school.

Coney and her husband, Elmo, also carried on work that was begun in the first two decades of the twentieth century by the Senate Avenue Young Men's Christian Association (YMCA) and the Phyllis Wheatley Young Women's Christian Association (YWCA). Both of these black-controlled institutions had hosted a variety of neighborhood programs, clubs, training classes, "quiet hours," and recreational events aimed at improving neighborhood conditions, keeping children safe, and training them for success in life. Additionally, the Senate Avenue YMCA had a long history of challenging Indianapolis's racial codes. For decades, the Senate Avenue YMCA had pushed for racial reform, sponsoring so-called monster meetings. These political and educational forums brought renowned black speakers to Indianapolis, including W. E. B. Du Bois, actor Paul Robeson, and Walter White of the national office of the NAACP.

Indianapolis's black organizational life reflected a diversity of political and social welfare agendas. Although most groups focused on a particular cause, they shared a common goal aimed at improving the life of black residents and reforming the city's race agenda. In their struggle for racial advancement, many of the city's black organizations joined regional and national federations. In 1907, for example, Indianapolis's black women's clubs sent representatives to the Elizabeth Carter Council, the local federation of black women's clubs. The council joined the Indiana State Federation of Colored Women's Clubs and sent state representatives to the conference of the National Association of Colored Women (NACW). Through membership in local, state, and national federations, women's clubs consolidated their financial and other resources in pursuit of their goals. In 1937, local businessman Starling James, in an attempt to unite and coordinate the work of the city's many black men's and women's social clubs, organized the Federation of Associated Clubs (FAC). The FAC was composed of many different groups that pursued varied goals, including improvement of education and health care, economic and moral uplift, self-determination, and business and community development. While these splintered interests contributed to the FAC's inability to create a united political agenda, the federation provided the city's black clubs with a forum to assess the varied problems of black Indianapolitans.

After passage of the 1964 federal Civil Rights Act, the number of separate black social institutions in Indianapolis declined, as a new generation of African Americans put their energies into joining mainstream social and professional organizations that previously denied them entry on account of race.

## FURTHER READINGS

Bell, Howard Holman. *Minutes of the Proceedings of the National Negro Conventions, 1830–1864.* New York: Arno, 1969.

Ferguson, Earline Rae. "A Community Affair: African-American Women's Club Work in Indianapolis, 1879–1917." Ph.D. diss., Indiana University, 1997.

Foner, Philip S., and George E. Walker, eds. *Proceedings of the Black State Conventions, 1840–1865.* Philadelphia: Temple University Press, 1978.

Gibbs, Wilma L., ed. *Indiana's African-American Heritage: Essays from Black History News and Notes.* Indianapolis: Indiana Historical Society, 1993.

Jacobi, Lori B. "More Than a Church: The Educational Role of the African Methodist Episcopal Church in Indiana, 1844–1861." *Black History News and Notes* 31 (February 1988), 4–8.

Pierce, Richard. "Beneath the Surface: African-American Community Life in Indianapolis, 1945–1970." Ph.D. diss., Indiana University, 1996.

———. "Self-Help in Indianapolis." *Black History News and Notes* 60 (May 1995), 3–7.

Thornbrough, Emma Lou. *The Negro in Indiana before 1900: A Study of a Minority.* Bloomington: Indiana University Press, 1957.

*Earline Rae Ferguson*

**SEE ALSO** Colored Knights of Pythias; Grand United Order of Odd Fellows; Grand United Order of True Reformers; Independent Order of St. Luke; Order of the Eastern Star; United Brothers of Friendship & Sisters of the Mysterious Ten

# Indianapolis Community Relations Council

Established in 1946, the Indianapolis Community Relations Council (ICRC) was a short-lived interracial group that challenged the city's policy of racial segregation, particularly in public education. Throughout the late 1940s, the ICRC tried to end segregation and achieve racial harmony through the use of public pressure, educational forums, town meetings, and community workshops.

The ICRC, led by Cyrus E. Wood, emerged during a conference organized by the Indianapolis Church Federation to discuss the creation of programs to ease racial tensions and achieve social justice in the city. More than twenty individuals were members of the council at one time or another. In 1948, the ICRC appointed Charles Posner, a prominent member of the Jewish Community Relations Council, as its executive director. Posner was appointed, at least partly, for his ability to articulate the goals and objectives of the organization to a broader audience. Under his leadership, the ICRC, assisted by the National Community Relations Advisory Council, held a citywide conference and published a study of the negative impact of segregated schools in 1948. Although Posner's appointment generated much-needed public support for the council, in the end the ICRC's constantly changing personnel, financial problems, controversial policy decisions, and lack of widespread political support accounted for its inability to make any real changes and its demise.

**FURTHER READINGS**

"Drive Mapped against Bigots: Community Relations Council Established." *Indianapolis Star*, December 10, 1946, sec. 1, 5.

"For a Better Home City." *Indianapolis Times*, December 10, 1946, sec. 1, 16.

"New Community Group Formed: Council Represents All Faiths, Races." *Indianapolis Times*, December 10, 1946, sec. 1, 6.

"Stout Gets Post in Harmony Group." *Indianapolis Times*, December 23, 1947, sec. 2, 18.

*Eric R. Jackson*

# Institute for Black Family Development

In 1969, the Rev. Matthew Parker founded the Institute for Black Family Development (IBFD) to provide black families with nondenominational religious programs. Parker was inspired to launch the IBFD when he heard the late Evangelist Tom Skinner at the chapel of the Grand Rapids School of the Bible and Music in Grand Rapids, Michigan. The IBFD, headquartered in Southfield, Michigan, provides a prison ministry, educational programs, and books and other reading materials and conducts seminars and workshops in the interest of strengthening black families. In spring 1991, the National Coalition of Urban Youth Ministries was formed as a division of the IBFD to launch a national campaign challenging teenagers in cities to live in moral purity. In the same year, the group hosted the National Conference on the Family in Chicago. The organization has strong ties with Zondervan Publishing, which has resulted in the publication of forty titles by African America authors. The IBFD has received over $3,000,000 from foundations, churches, Christian agencies, and individuals for its work with black families.

**FURTHER READING**

DuPree, Sherry Sherrod. *African-American Holiness Pentecostal Movement: An Annotated Bibliography.* New York: Garland, 1996.

*Sherry Sherrod DuPree*

## Intercollegiate Pentecostal Conference International

The Intercollegiate Pentecostal Conference International (IPCI) was founded in 1965 by the ministers James O. Lewis, Leon Wright, and Monroe Saunders as the United Pentecostal Association of Howard University. It was the first African American Pentecostal center on any university campus in the United States. Its initial purpose was to unite the Pentecostal students on Howard University's campus and to promote spiritual awareness among the school's student body. In November 1969, the IPCI became a national campus ministry, and in the following year the group held its first conference. In 1975, the IPCI was incorporated as a national Pentecostal information research center that serves as a training agency for Pentecostal campus ministers and promotes unity between Pentecostal and other religious groups.

The IPCI has been active on more than thirty-five college campuses throughout the United States, where it seeks to establish a network of collegiate Christians dedicated to the nurturing and spiritual development of students, faculty, and staff. IPCI activities vary from campus to campus. At Howard University, for example, the group maintains an emergency pantry to assist students. Regular activities consist of Bible study, referrals, and fellowship. Headquartered in Washington, D.C., the IPCI is assisted by the Reverend Stephen N. Short and Betty Lancaster Short (husband and wife).

### FURTHER READING

DuPree, Sherry Sherrod. *African-American Holiness Pentecostal Movement: An Annotated Bibliography*. New York: Garland, 1996.

*Sherry Sherrod DuPree*

## International Association of African and American Black Business People

The International Association of African and American Black Business People (IAAABBP) was founded in 1965. William Bert Johnson served as president, and the association was located at several Detroit addresses. Established to encourage entrepreneurial education and activities in the African business community in the United States, Africa, and internationally, the group had a membership of eighty-four thousand African and American entrepreneurs, including forty-six state groups in the United States and 170 regional groups in Africa. Approximately 130 staff members assisted Johnson in publication of a bimonthly bulletin and a quarterly journal, both published in English.

The IAAABBP collected and compiled statistics about businesses on both continents, sponsored educational seminars about the creation and management of businesses, and presented awards to notable business owners and managers in the African American economic community. The group sponsored annual meetings, including the 1988 conference in Tanzania and a 1988 program in Ghana. The IAAABBP became defunct sometime after those conferences.

### FURTHER READINGS

*Encyclopedia of Associations*. 33rd ed. Detroit: Gale, 1998.
Van de Sande, Wendy S., ed. *Black Americans Information Directory, 1994–95*. 3rd ed. Detroit: Gale, 1995.

*Elizabeth D. Schafer*

## International Association of Black Business Educators

The International Association of Black Business Educators (IABBE) was founded in 1978 to improve and expand business education for minorities. Deans and directors of business schools on historically black campuses met to develop and distribute academic business curricula and to launch educational activities to increase the participation of minorities in business in the United States and internationally. Dr. Percy J. Vaughn Jr., dean of the School of Business at Alabama State University, served as president of the association, which he called the "flagship" for entrepreneurial education in traditionally black colleges. Funded by the Small Business Association for the purpose of encouraging entrepreneurship in the African American community, the IABBE gathered once a year during other academic and business conferences.

Establishing a foundation for business education in black colleges, the association's goal was to upgrade entrepreneurship and business teaching. According to Vaughn, the IABBE successfully elevated the quality of business education in African American colleges to a standard traditionally equated with Ivy League business schools such as Harvard and Yale. One of the group's major achievements was incorporating technology in business education by donating computers to historically black campuses. Other programs implemented included aspects of marketing such as analyzing consumer behavior, business research and strategy, advertising, and promotion, as well as education about computer information systems.

In 1994, Paul A. Young of Silver Spring, Maryland, was project director of the association, which at that time had a membership of fifty-five institutions of higher education and one hundred individuals. The association published the quarterly *IABBE Newsletter* and produced the Strategic Business Development Network video series about business education and other videotapes that explained how to start, own, and manage businesses. The IABBE sought to improve communications and relationships with American and international business and to stimulate cooperation with community businesses to provide students with practical business education experiences. The group also evaluated new business opportunities for minorities, while increasing the involvement of academia in enhancing entrepreneurial education in the classroom and the workplace.

By 1998, the membership of the IABBE had dwindled due to retirements and deaths, although remaining members kept the group from being defunct. At the Alabama State University campus, the theme of February 1998 Black History Month, "African-Americans in Business: The Path to Empowerment," reflected the association's mission.

### FURTHER READINGS

Green, Shelley, and Paul Pryde. *Black Entrepreneurship in America*. New Brunswick, N.J., and London: Transaction, 1990.

Van de Sande, Wendy S., ed. *Black Americans Information Directory, 1994–95*. 3rd ed. Detroit: Gale, 1995.

Vaughn, Percy. "The Black Business: What Is It Now?" *Proceedings of the Small Business Institute Directors' Association Annual Meeting*, February 1983.

Vaughn, Percy, with Richard H. Buskirk. *Managing New Enterprise*. St. Paul, Minn.: West, 1976.

*Elizabeth D. Schafer*

## International Association of Black Professional Fire Fighters

The International Association of Black Professional Fire Fighters (IABPFF) was founded in 1970, in Hartford, Connecticut. The association was established during a combined meeting of five groups of African American firefighters who wanted a central organization to focus on the special needs and concerns of black firefighters in the United States. Organizers also sought to increase the number of minority firefighters across the country and wanted to educate African American communities about fire prevention and safety, especially in inner cities.

The role of African Americans in the history of firefighting has been paradoxical. Colonial Americans both blamed blacks for setting fires and also expected slaves to risk their lives fighting fires. Throughout the seventeenth century, incidents were reported in the Colonies in which blacks were accused of arson, often falsely, although some fires were set to protest enslavement. Punishments were ironic and macabre. In 1679, a Massachusetts farmhand was forced to work twenty-one years for the man whose barn he allegedly burned down. Maria, a black servant, was convicted of burning the Joshua Lamb home in 1681, and she was "burnt to Ashes" on the Boston Common. Twenty-seven slaves were arrested as suspects in a building fire in New York City in 1712; twenty-one of the blacks were executed, and several were burned at the stake. Colonists constantly feared that blacks would set fires as a rebellious conspiracy to overthrow slavery.

Firefighting was rudimentary until the turn of the twentieth century. Primitive dousing of flames with bucket brigades and carriages with hoses were limited by the quantity of water supplies and volunteers. Entire cities often were inevitably razed because of ineffective firefighting techniques, and fire prevention methods were unknown. Although African Americans were expected to labor in efforts to fight fires, they were excluded when firefighting was professionalized. Scientific principles were incorporated in firefighting to control fires and protect people, property, and natural resources such as forests.

The National Fire Protection Association (NFPA) was created in 1896 to set professional firefighting standards. This group consisted only of white males, rejecting women and African American firefighters. The NFPA promoted fire prevention and protection through the development of more efficient technology and better methods of fire control. Distributing a variety of fire-safety publications written for children and adults, this association stressed community education and personal safety primarily for white neighborhoods. The NFPA cooperated with major insurance companies to establish building codes and fire-safety inspections to minimize monetary losses from fires and embraced technological advances such as computerized services to report and respond to emergency calls.

While white firefighters advanced fire prevention, black firefighters worked in segregated fire stations, protecting black neighborhoods. Denied access to white firefighting groups at both local and national levels, black firefighters established groups to address their concerns, educate their communities, and provide a social outlet. In New York City, Chief Williams encouraged black firemen to form the Vulcan Society in 1940. The first black firemen to integrate traditionally white fire stations experienced isolation and harassment. The San Francisco Fire Department hired its first black fireman in 1955 and its second in 1967. By 1972, only five African Americans were firemen in the department, which employed fifteen hundred firefighters.

Fire stations hired a few African Americans during the 1960s, but integration was slowly achieved. Throughout the United States, African Americans represented a small proportion of the firefighting labor force. By 1990, only 9 percent of firefighters were African Americans, and 1 percent were black women. In Oakland, California, the first black firefighters were hired in 1920, but they worked in segregated stations through the 1950s, limiting their professional opportunities. When stations were integrated, white firefighters created miserable conditions for black professionals and excluded them from firehouse life. Because teamwork was necessary in firefighting, black firefighters were often at risk when white firefighters did not support them at critical moments.

In response to this discrimination, the Oakland Black Fire Fighters Association (OBFFA) was created in 1973 to support black firefighters and encourage other African Americans to join the profession. This group legally challenged the city's fire department for discriminating against blacks and other minorities, filing a successful lawsuit in 1985 that required the department to hire qualified employees proportionate to the city's ethnic and gender workforce composition. When the OBFFA began, forty-seven of Oakland's 658 firefighters were black, but not all African American firefighters in that city joined the group. The association encouraged women and other minorities, especially Hispanics and Asians, to attend training sessions to aid them in securing employment.

The IABPFF coordinated local efforts designed to fight hiring discrimination into a national program. Black men and women joined the national organization and participated in local chapters to secure employment opportunities and respect for African American firefighters. The association also promoted fund-raisers for civil rights groups. Publishing the semiannual newsletter *Smoke* and the monthly bulletin *National Express,*

the IABPFF sponsored special events such as biennial conventions the last week in August of even-numbered years.

Chapters interacted with their communities, providing positive role models for youths and educating citizens about fire safety and prevention. African American firefighters also made appearances at celebrations such as Juneteenth, hosted annual community picnics, and raised funds for burn centers. Involvement with community groups strengthened relations between firefighters and residents. Membership increased as more African Americans decided to become firefighters, and the association attempted to improve communication between departments and related unions and administrators. Promoting professionalism, members of the IABPFF valued the organization's effort to facilitate exchanges with African American firefighters in other cities, encouraging interracial cooperation and networking and improving firefighting techniques and working conditions for blacks throughout the United States.

In 1983, the IABPFF was based in Philadelphia, Pennsylvania, with Charles Hendricks as president. By 1997, the association had relocated to Landover, Maryland, and its president, Romeo O. Spaulding, and treasurer, Arnold Hyacinthe, oversaw the activities of almost ten thousand members, representing firefighters, dispatchers, and related professionals, in 125 chapters in major cities such as Minneapolis and groups representing six geographic regions. The IABPFF also affiliated with the Southern Christian Leadership Conference (SCLC) and the National Association for the Advancement of Colored People (NAACP).

**FURTHER READINGS**

Bugbee, Percy. *Men against Fire: The Story of the National Fire Protection Association, 1896–1971.* Boston: National Fire Protection Association, 1971.

Cannon, Donald J., ed. *Heritage of Flames: The Illustrated History of Early American Firefighting.* Garden City, N.Y.: Doubleday, 1977.

Chetkovich, Carol. *Real Heat: Gender and Race in the Urban Fire Service.* New Brunswick, N.J., and London: Rutgers University Press, 1997.

Griffin, James S. *Blacks in the St. Paul Police and Fire Departments, 1885–1976.* Minneapolis: E & J, 1973.

"Vulcan Society for Black Firemen." *New York Amsterdam News,* February 13, 1971, 47.

*Elizabeth D. Schafer*

## International Baseball League

*See* International League.

## International Black Writers and Artists

International Black Writers and Artists (IBWA) was founded in 1974 as a nonprofit organization and has approximately five hundred members. Its headquarters are in Los Angeles, California. IBWA's mission is to provide "inspiration, support, information and resources as well as cultural opportunities to those who value our unique contributions to the literary and artistic genres."

IBWA accepts membership without regard to ethnic or racial origin or level of artistic or professional achievement. Membership provides the newsletter *Black Expressions*, discount admission to IBWA's Annual July Conference, and free or reduced admission to IBWA and sister-organization workshops and regular activities. Members are also offered priority for UCLA Extension scholarships and optional listing in the annually published *IBWA Directory*.

The IBWA's Annual July Conference provides a forum for aspiring as well as established writers and artists to network and share information. Past participants have included Octavia Butler, Michelle T. Clinton, Mildred Dumas, and John Ridley. Sponsors of the event have included the American Black Book Writers Association, the Organization of Black Screenwriters, the PEN Center USA West, and the UCLA Extension Writers Program. The conference also bestows artistic achievement awards. Past recipients have been Lula Washington (Phyllis Wheatley Community Service Vision Award), Mildred Dumas (Paul Lawrence Dunbar Performance Arts Award) and Eric Dickey (Founders Award for Literary Achievement). The conferences feature a variety of workshops on topics such as independent and self-publishing, children's books, the writer as entrepreneur, oral histories, and biographies.

In addition to the Annual July Conference, IBWA organizes numerous events and programs, such as the African American Youth Arts Association, which is dedicated to encouraging and developing talent in young people by introducing them to an artistic lifestyle through mentoring, field study, leadership, and recognition. IBWA also organizes Poetry on the Move, in association with POMP (Performance Opportunities Matching Program), which brings cultural programming to schools, colleges, churches, government, and community groups, and provides forums for performing and spoken-word artists. Moreover, IBWA sponsors a poetry and short story contest, conducts critique workshops to educate and motivate artists, and provides a manuscript evaluation service for new as well as seasoned writers. Finally, IBWA organizes community art exhibits, book signings, and retreats and promotes partnering opportunities to foster creative commercial enterprises.

In addition to the organization's newsletter, IBWA has also published monographs and anthologies, such as *A Black View of the Bicentennial, 76 and San Pedro*, and *River Crossings: Voices of the Diaspora* (1994), which contains the writings of more than fifty contemporary authors.

*Isabel Soto*

## International Brotherhood of Red Caps

*See* United Transport Service Employees of America.

## International Council of Women of the Darker Races

Between 1922 and 1940, the International Council of Women of the Darker Races (ICWDR) institutionalized for a small group of African American women a sense of global citizenship. It heightened their awareness of the collective conditions of some darker nationalities and led a few members to participate in projects that enhanced the worldview and self-concept of other nonwhites. The ICWDR shared ideological affinities with other international associations. Some were overwhelmingly white women's groups, including the International Council of Women (ICW) and the Women's International League for Peace and Freedom (WILPF). Others were black, notably the Universal Negro Improvement Association and the Pan African Congresses. Black women created the ICWDR because race prejudices militated against their leadership of predominantly white organizations while gender prejudices prevented them from assuming influential roles in gender-mixed groups. No other group focused primarily on their target population, nor, they believed, had their capacities to identify with it.

In August 1922, in Washington, D.C., educator Margaret Murray Washington, widow of Booker T. Washington, assembled eighteen women who organized the ICWDR. The gender-bifucation of society tended to preordain that women's organizations would focus on women and children regardless of more inclusive purposes. Therefore, the ICWDR was to facilitate "mutual international cooperation and sympathetic understanding in every

At a ceremony commemorating the freeing of the slaves, Philadelphia Mayor S. Davis Wilson presents Addie W. Dickerson, president of the national Council of Women of Darker Races, with the gavel he used to strike the Liberty Bell. Independence Hall, Philadelphia, 1940. *Library of Congress*

forward movement among women and children of the darker races of the world." More specifically, the ICWDR was to disseminate "knowledge of peoples of color the world over that there may be a larger appreciation of their history and accomplishments and further that they may have a greater degree of respect for their own achievements and a greater pride in themselves." Originally, organizational work was to be implemented through Committees on International Relations, Social and Economic Conditions, and Education.

Throughout its existence, well-known individuals led the ICWDR. Washington was president from 1922 until her death in 1925. She was succeeded by Vice President Addie W. Hunton, a New York City social worker, who served until Addie W. Dickerson, a Philadelphia real estate broker, assumed the ICWDR's presidency in 1928. Dickerson remained in the office until her death and the subsequent demise of the ICWDR in 1940. All three

women had traveled to Europe prior to their tenures, and they were extremely active in the National Association of Colored Women's Clubs (NACW), the forum through which virtually all ICWDR members had continuously related to one another in public service. Most officers and committee chairs serving in 1922 and 1923 retained leadership responsibilities until the council's demise in 1940. They included Mary Church Terrell and Nannie Helen Burroughs of Washington, D.C.; Lugenia Hope of Atlanta; Elizabeth Carter of New Bedford, Massachusetts; Marion Wilkerson of Columbia, South Carolina; Mary S. Josenberger of Ft. Smith, Arkansas; Charlotte Hawkins Brown of Sedalia and Mary McCorvey of Charlotte, North Carolina; and Emily Williams of Tuskegee, Alabama.

Counting as members at one time or another eight NACW presidents, the ICWDR functioned as an honor society. While Washington endeavored to recruit "women of standing, prominence, energy, and worth" in their own right, she also targeted women whose husbands had achieved distinction. Among the latter were the wife of the president of Liberia, the U.S. consul to Senegal, and the principal of Tuskegee Institute. In press releases and articles, the ICWDR consciously used the good names of member luminaries. In January 1923, for example, when Washington discussed the ICWDR in the *Southern Workman*, the first individual mentioned in the article was Mary B. Talbert, former president of the NACW and president of the Douglass Memorial and Historical Association. Similarly, the *Pittsburgh Courier*'s report on an ICWDR meeting a decade later emphasized members' distinguished accomplishments and listed notables who were present, beginning with Terrell, the first NACW president and everybody's favorite club woman.

Like typical honor societies, the ICWDR counted relatively few members. The constitution allowed for two hundred members, of which three-fourths were to come from the United States. The council's stationery in the late 1920s named forty American members. Hailing from California to New York, they represented eighteen states plus the District of Columbia. New York had the largest contingent with eight, followed by North Carolina and Washington, D.C., with four each.

The sustained membership of foreigners in the ICWDR was problematic, despite the efforts of President Washington. She contacted prospective members representing Puerto Rico, Haiti, Brazil, India, Ceylon, the Philippines, Sierra Leone, Liberia, South Africa, and perhaps other countries. She succeeded in getting some women from these countries to participate in the founding meeting and in the first public meeting two years later. Moreover, in 1922, she backed the successful election of Adelaide Casely-Hayford, an educator from Sierra Leone, to fourth vice-president, or "vice–president for Africa." Modeling the organization somewhat after the ICW, Washington announced that "each foreign country to be represented in the International Council [of Women of the Darker Races] will be honored with its own vice–president." Yet, after a year, no foreigners held office.

Beyond obvious considerations of expenses and juggling schedules to attend meetings, several factors militated against an international membership. Whether in the United States or in their home countries, foreigners gave the ICWDR a low priority. The ICWDR could not demonstrate an exportable, prototype program actively involving most of its members. Its activities were those that foreigners could develop without the organization's imprimatur. Convening, as it often did, in conjunction with the NACW, the council had to appear mostly as an aside to that foremost forum of African American women. Moreover, during the 1930s, the ICWDR's president scheduled council meetings with little advance notice, which virtually prevented the presence of foreign members. She understood that if the NACW, which offered foreigners more than the ICWDR, reaped only a tepid response to its bid for affiliating organizations of foreign women, the ICWDR could not expect to do better.

Although lacking a visible international membership, the ICWDR engaged in a broad range of activities, particularly under the leadership of Washington, who focused on educational initiatives. The ICWDR contributed $100 to Casely-Hayford's school in Sierra Leone, a respectable sum considering the NACW's contribution of $154. At the 1924 public meeting in Chicago, Washington presided when council members and visitors presented a series of knowledgeable reports on the living conditions of darker women in Cuba, Haiti, the Virgin Islands, West Africa, and India. Additionally, she organized a Committee of Seven at Tuskegee Institute that studied nonwhites in East and West Africa, India, and the United States. "This committee met weekly, and no visitor from foreign parts ever came to Tuskegee," one friend reported, "who was not invited into this meeting." While Washington claimed that the creation of Committees of Seven was the priority of the ICWDR in 1924, the council launched few, if any, of these committees outside Tuskegee. Probably more members participated in the ICWDR's black history course. Education Committee

members Dickerson, Burroughs, and Terrell designed it for schools, clubs, and community leaders. Washington distributed it energetically, and by January 1923 groups in several communities used it. However, it is doubtful that the ICWDR's black history course would have enjoyed ever-increasing adoption since the course was not updated.

During the presidency of Hunton and Dickerson, the ICWDR became less functional. Both presidents were frequently preoccupied. They were active officers in other organizations and demonstrated their international concerns in other forums, including the WILPF, through which they visited foreign lands. Hunton's ICWDR activity is unknown, but she may have convened only one meeting. Aside from token monetary contributions to worthy causes, Dickerson presided over little activity. On June 22, 1929, Dickerson lamented to Executive Committee Chair Burroughs: "Almost a year has elapsed [since I was elected president] and we have given to the women nothing." More than five years later, she told member Mary McLeod Bethune that the "one hue and cry against the organization has been its seeming inactivity, and yet whenever something is undertaken, instead of its meeting the interest and cooperation of the members, there is always some reason for its delay or abandonment." Regular meetings were erratic, and public meetings uncertain. In July 1935, Dickerson determined that the council would assemble only briefly, following the NACW Sunday afternoon mass meeting in Cleveland. She wrote members: "I shall try to cover a number of matters, and yet adjourn early enough so that any having evening engagements may keep them." Other meetings were similar.

Nevertheless, Dickerson endeavored to make the organization viable. A Pan-Africanist, she desired to advance "the cause of internationalism among women the world over." She wanted black women represented in white women's arenas such as a Goodwill Tour of Latin America, Conferences on the Cause and Cure of War, and gatherings of the WILPF. On some occasions they were. But in cases of international travel, the ICWDR could only appoint an individual already attending the meeting as its representative and then offer her a token donation. Such sums came from a diminishing treasury, for, in the Depression, the council reduced annual dues from $25 to $5. In March 1940, Dickerson had planned for selected members, herself included, to contribute to a series of articles highlighting the roles of British and French colored troops in World War II and other areas of special interest to blacks. She died before accomplishing this task.

With Dickerson's death, the ICWDR had run its course. Its exclusiveness and nonactivity had ensured the absence of loyal, energetic younger individuals to inherit the council's leadership. Its original intent of promoting mutual cooperation among women of color everywhere had been beyond its capabilities, as Washington recognized in 1924 when she omitted it in a descriptive statement of the council. Its educational activities were too general and short lived to attain a unique status. And during the Depression, its desire to represent black women in international venues required not only more money, but also a larger pool of well-heeled, knowledgeable, and relatively unencumbered individuals. Yet, after 1930, even the NACW failed to send representatives to the three European meetings of the ICW, of which it was a member.

Regardless of meager achievements, the ICWDR was significant. Its very existence symbolized black women's sensitivity to global racial and gender perspectives. These perspectives were grounded in Pan-Africanism, for ICWDR leaders subscribed to the 1920s "New Negro" thought of "re-establishing links with the scattered people of African descent" and accepting "advance-guard responsibility for African peoples in their contact with Twentieth Century civilization." Moreover, the ICWDR reinforced internationalism among NACW leaders, and its idealism and aspiration to represent African American women in international venues found expression in the National Council of Negro Women, which was established in 1935. In the post–World War II era, the internationalism of organized black female leaders surged higher than ever before.

**FURTHER READINGS**

Hoytt, Eleanor Hinton. "International Council of Women of the Darker Races: Historical Notes from Margaret Murray Washington." *Sage* 3 (Fall 1986), 54–55.

Locke, Alain, ed. *The New Negro*. New York: Albert and Charles Boni, 1925.

Rouse, Jacqueline Anne. "Out of the Shadow of Tuskegee: Margaret Murray Washington, Social Activism, and Race Vindication." *Journal of Negro History* 81 (Spring, Summer, Winter, Fall 1996), 31–46.

Shehee, Lena Cheeks. "Mrs. Margaret Murray Washington." *National Notes* [Periodical of the National Association of Colored Women] (April 1928), 9.

Washington, Margaret Murray. "Colored Women's International Council." *Southern Workman* 52 (January 1923), 7–10.

*Elaine M. Smith*

# International Fellowship of Black Pentecostal Churches, Intercollegiate Pentecostal Conference International

In 1984, Bishop J. O. Patterson of the Church of God in Christ, Bishop J. T. Bowen of the United Holly Church of America, and Bishop Amy Bell Stevens of the Mount Sinai Holy Church of America founded the International Fellowship of Black Pentecostal Churches (IFBPC) in Memphis. Initially, the organization was called the Conference of Bishops and Leaders of Black Pentecostal-Holiness Churches in the United States. The purpose of the IFBPC is to "spread the gospel of the New Testament and the teachings and practices thereof and the Christian religion. To preserve and secure the history of The Black Holiness Pentecostal movement. To preserve the liberties and maintain the identity inherent to each individual national body in this organization with respect to our relation to other churches of similar faith. To promote and provide excellence in education for all people. To spread the Gospel of Salvation to all the world." The membership consists of well-established Pentecostal denominations with ten or more affiliated churches.

Headquartered in Portsmouth, Virginia, the IBPC holds its annual assembly in May. Bishop Bowen, leader Emeritus of the United Holy Church of America, has served as president of the IFBPC since 1990.

**FURTHER READING**

DuPree, Sherry Sherrod. *African-American Holiness Pentecostal Movement: An Annotated Bibliography*. New York: Garland, 1996.

*Sherry Sherrod DuPree*

# International League

Established in 1906, the International (Baseball) League, composed of black, Cuban, and white teams, initially included the Cuban X Giants, the Quaker Giants, the Cuban Stars, the Havanas of Cuba, the Philadelphia Professionals, and the Riverton-Palmyra Athletics. As the season progressed, one of the Cuban teams and the Quaker Giants dropped out and were replaced by the Wilmington Giants and the Philadelphia Giants. The league lasted for two years and showcased the most talented black teams and athletes of the early twentieth century.

Despite their late-season start, the Philadelphia Giants won the league championship, and the team was awarded a beautiful cup by the league's president. The Philadelphia Giants also prevailed over Brooklyn's Royal Giants, a new black team formed by Royal Cafe owner J. W. Connor, and the Chicago Unions and Leland Giants of Chicago to claim the title World's Colored Champion. On September 30, 1906, the Philadelphia Giants won three games: 6–1 over the Royal Giants in the morning, 5–2 over the Cuban X Giants in the afternoon, and 6–2 over the Brighton Athletic Club later that day. Sol White, black professional baseball player, author of *Sol White's History of Colored Baseball*, and in subsequent years officer, manager, and coach of the Negro National League, recalled the day as the culmination of twenty years of professional black baseball and an indication of the "brightest prospects for great advancement in the future." Having conquered all other black teams, the Philadelphia Giants challenged the champions of the all-white National and American League. The challenge, however, remained unanswered.

Among the most acclaimed players of the International (Baseball) League were John Henry Lloyd and Rube Foster. Many baseball fans consider Lloyd, a shortstop for the Cuban X Giants, the greatest shortstop in American history. Fellow Hall of Fame inductee Rube Foster, one of the stars of the Philadelphia Giants, founded the Negro National League in 1920 and is rightly called the "Father of Black Baseball."

In its second season, the International League was composed entirely of black and Cuban teams, including the Philadelphia Giants, the New York Cuban Giants, the Brooklyn Royal Giants, and the Havana Cuban Stars. The teams played five games each against one another, and the Philadelphia Giants were crowned again as the champions, the Cuban Giants were in second place, the Royal Giants third, and the Cuban Stars fourth. It is unclear whether the International League continued beyond the 1907 season, but it is doubtful since neither of the Cuban teams that gave the league its international flavor appeared in 1908.

**FURTHER READINGS**

Clark, Dick, and Larry Lester. *The Negro Leagues Book.* Cleveland: Society for American Baseball Research, 1994.

Dixon, Phil. *The Negro Baseball Leagues: A Photographic History.* Mattituck, N.Y.: Amereon House, 1992.

Malloy, Jerry. *Sol White's History of Colored Baseball, with Other Documents on the Early Black Game, 1886–1936.* Lincoln: University of Nebraska Press, 1995.

Riley, James A. *The Biographical Encyclopedia of the Negro Baseball Leagues.* New York: Carroll and Graf, 1994.

*Lyle K. Wilson*

# International Migration Society

The International Migration Society (IMS) was founded in 1894 by a group of white Birmingham, Alabama, businessmen who acted on the advice of Henry McNeal Turner (1834–1915), a bishop in the African Methodist Episcopal (AME) Church. Turner had long dreamed of an African American transatlantic society that would provide affordable transportation between the United States and Africa. Turner had served as a chaplain in the Union army during the Civil War and as an agent of the Georgia Freedmen's Bureau during Reconstruction. Postwar racism led Turner, a lifelong proponent of black racial pride, to lose faith in the United States as a viable home for black Americans. He saw Africa as a place of refuge from prejudice and, through his editorials in the AME's *Christian Recorder*, became the leading advocate for a nationalist African migration movement.

Increased European competition for African colonies in the 1880s and 1890s alarmed Turner as much as the state of race relations in America. He made the first of four trips to West Africa in 1891 and returned to the United States convinced that the migration of black Americans to Africa would solve both problems. It would remove blacks from racism, discrimination, and segregation in the United States and allow them to help native Africans build a united Africa, modeled on the American system, to stand as a bulwark against European imperialism. Turner was a fiery speaker and arrogantly preached that slavery had been a providential institution that Christianized blacks and taught them the industrial skills necessary to redeem and uplift Africa. In 1893, after a second visit to Sierra Leone and Liberia, Turner intensified his Pan-African rhetoric in his widely read editorials in the AME's *Voice of the Missions*. His immediate goal was to establish regular steamship services between the United States and West Africa to facilitate emigration and to strengthen the African economy through trade.

Turner's editorials, expounding on the profits that enterprising businessmen could make by trading with Africa, caught the attention of a cadre of white businessmen from Birmingham. In 1894, J. L. Daniels, Jeremiah R. McMullen, Edwin B. Cottingham, and Daniel J. Flummer, convinced that a West African shipping line could be profitable, organized the IMS to recruit interested emigrants and launched a subsidiary enterprise, the African Steamship Company, to make shipping arrangements. Turner, who served on the society's board of advisers, would have preferred an exclusively black operation; however, economic difficulties forced him to rely upon white organizers for transportation. Although the African Steamship Company sold stock to investors for $50 a share, the organization never operated a single ship and collapsed early in 1895. Nevertheless, the IMS continued through the encouragement of the Liberian government and monetary support from thousands of poor blacks willing to emigrate to Africa. At its peak, the IMS attracted thousands of subscribers from throughout the South and at least as far west as Denver. African Americans desirous of emigrating had to invest a dollar per month in the IMS until they accumulated a total of $40, which qualified them for emigration. Dues were non-refundable, and most people who started paying into the society were extremely poor and never completed their payments. The IMS counted on the literally thousands of dollars left by delinquent members to subsidize the entire operation. After a prospective emigrant accumulated $40, the society agreed to provide steamship passage to Liberia and provisions for three months.

Between 1894 and 1896, the IMS provided transportation for three groups of African Americans to establish colonies in Liberia. In November 1894, intense public pressure forced the society to prove its sincerity by transporting a small group of thirteen fully paid members on a regularly scheduled New York-to-Liverpool passenger liner. In England, the emigrants transferred to a steamer bound for Liberia. When they arrived in Africa, an agent of the Liberian government took over, providing temporary housing until the assignment of twenty-five-acre homesteads in the country's interior. The Liberian government was eager to settle African American colonists in the country's interior regions as a buffer to French imperial encroachment.

The departure of the first group electrified the movement, and in January 1895 the society claimed it had seven thousand paying members. Soon a sufficient number of African Americans had completed the $40 requirement, enabling the society to charter the *Horsa* and the *Laurada*, two older cargo ships notorious for running illegal guns to rebels in Spanish-held Cuba. The second group of 197 colonists sailed on the *Horsa* in March 1895, and the third colony of 321 settlers left on the *Laurada* in March 1896.

While the IMS was the product of genuine concern, the organizational inexperience of its leaders combined with problems in Liberia left the colonists ill prepared and with inadequate provisions. The IMS had no representative in Liberia, and poor communication between organizers in America and Robert T. Sherman, the immi-

gration agent of the Liberian government, meant that Liberian officials were unprepared for the arrival of the settlers. Thus, African American colonists had to wait in Monrovia, consuming their meager provisions while awaiting their land assignment. The Liberian government made little effort to maintain the groups as cohesive colonies and sent individual families to different townships. Assistance stopped after settlement, and colonists had to endure a number of years as subsistence farmers before transforming undeveloped lands into profitable farms. Disease ravaged all three groups, and many settlers saw their homesteads fail before they could develop them. Many embittered survivors eventually worked their way back to the United States to speak against the society organizers. Although the society planned to transport a fourth colony group in 1897, news of the failure and suffering of the earlier colonists led African Americans to withdraw their backing. The society dissolved in 1899 without ever sending another emigrant.

Bishop Turner never relented on his Pan-African nationalism. He continued to endorse transatlantic proposals but never again participated in a successful emigration movement. He died in Canada in 1915.

**FURTHER READINGS**

Ponton, Mungo M. *The Life and Times of Bishop Henry M. Turner.* Atlanta, 1917. 2nd ed., New York: Negro Universities Press, 1970.

Redkey, Edwin S. *Black Exodus: Black Nationalist and Back-to-Africa Movements, 1890–1910.* New Haven, Conn.: Yale University Press, 1969.

———, ed. *Respect Black: The Writings and Speeches of Henry McNeal Turner.* New York: Arno, 1971.

Williams, Gilbert Anthony. *The Role of the Christian Recorder in the African Emigration Movement, 1854–1902.* Columbia, S.C.: Association for Education in Journalism and Mass Communication, 1989.

*Gary R. Entz*

# International Rhythm and Blues Association

In 1966, the International Rhythm and Blues Association was founded in Chicago to preserve and promote rhythm and blues music. The organization's membership is composed of musicians, record companies, songwriters, and fans of this genre of music.

Although a small organization maintained by only five staff members and a modest budget of $127,000, this association gathers material on rhythm and blues and maintains a library. It also is involved in fund-raising for scholarships for students pursuing a career in rhythm and blues music.

The association annually presents the International Jimmy Reed Blues Award in recognition of an outstanding musician in this genre of music. The award is named in honor of an outstanding musician of the Chicago blues sound during the 1940s and 1950s.

### FURTHER READINGS

Berry, Jason, Jonathan Foose, and Tad Jones. *Up from the Cradle of Jazz: New Orleans Music since World War II.* Athens: University of Georgia Press, 1986, 19–20.
"International Rhythm and Blues Association." *Encyclopedia of Associations.* Detroit: Gale, 1961–.

*Barbara L. Green*

## International Working People's Association

Founded in London in 1881, the International Working People's Association (IWPA), also known as the Black International, was a loose-knit federation of revolutionary anarchist and socialist groups that sought to mobilize the working people of the world in an effort to overthrow the capitalist system. Although European in origin, the IWPA acquired a significant following in the United States between 1883 and 1886, particularly among German and other European immigrant groups and native-born Americans of European ancestry.

In the United States, the IWPA was launched at a meeting in Pittsburgh in October 1883. The association reached a peak of approximately five thousand members in 1885 and represented nearly one hundred local organizations from every region in the United States. While the IWPA insisted that all member groups support its official declaration of principles, commonly known as the *Pittsburgh Manifesto*, it otherwise encouraged group autonomy. The manifesto championed "equal rights for all without distinction of sex or race" and called on workers to destroy the existing class structure and to replace it with a "free" and "cooperative" society.

Although historians disagree over the extent to which the IWPA concerned itself with racial justice, individual members, most notably Albert and Lucy Parsons, regularly spoke out in support of the rights of African Americans and other people of color. Albert was a white southerner, born in Alabama and raised in Texas, who had served in the Confederate army during the Civil War. During Reconstruction, he became a Radical Republican and an ardent supporter of African American civil rights. Lucy Parsons was a light-skinned woman of part African ancestry who was most likely born a slave in Texas, where she and Albert met and married. In 1873, the Parsonses moved to Chicago where they became active in the labor struggle. Both Albert and Lucy joined the IWPA in 1883. The following year, Albert accepted the position of editor of the IWPA's weekly English-language newspaper, the *Alarm*, to which Lucy regularly contributed articles.

Chicago provided the IWPA's strongest local following and eventually became the site of its greatest tragedy. In 1886, following police violence against workers engaged in a general strike in support of the eight-hour day, the IWPA scheduled a rally for May 4 at Haymarket Square. When nearly two hundred Chicago police arrived to break up the rally, a bomb exploded. The police responded by firing into the crowd, injuring and killing many people, including several of their fellow officers. Although investigators never found the person who threw the bomb, eight IWPA activists were convicted of the crime, and four of them, including Albert Parsons, were hanged. By the end of the decade, the IWPA had dissolved.

### FURTHER READINGS

Ashbaugh, Carolyn. *Lucy Parsons: American Revolutionary.* Chicago: Charles H. Kerr, 1976.
Avrich, Paul. *The Haymarket Tragedy.* Princeton, N.J.: Princeton University Press, 1984.
Nelson, Bruce C. *Beyond the Martyrs: A Social History of Chicago's Anarchists, 1870–1900.* New Brunswick, N.J.: Rutgers University Press, 1988.

*Stuart McElderry*

## Interreligious Foundation for Community Organization

The Interreligious Foundation for Community Organization (IFCO) is an ecumenical group that supports community organizing among the poor and marginalized. IFCO was founded in 1967 by a coalition of persons representing nine national religious organizations and one civic foundation. Soon, thirteen additional religious organizations, representing Protestant, Catholic, and Jewish denominations and constituencies, joined the effort.

Controlled by persons of color, IFCO has provided major funding support for a number of community-based projects dealing with issues such as unemployment, economic development, HIV/AIDS, and support for inner-city youth. IFCO has given financial support to such movements as the American Indian Movement and the Farm Labor Organizing Committee. It served as the driving force behind the organization of the Black United Fund and the Ecumenical Minority Bail Bond Fund and constitutes a significant presence in the institutional development of the National Anti-Klan Network, now called the Center for Democratic Renewal. In the international arena, IFCO has sponsored Nicaragua/Honduras study tours, Central America Information Week campaigns, and Pastors for Peace. The latter program serves to provide education and action strategies concerning American foreign policy, including the distribution of humanitarian aid to Nicaragua, Guatemala, Honduras, and Cuba. Longtime Executive Director Lucious Walker, a Brooklyn pastor, not only leads caravans into these countries to provide aid such as food, pharmaceutical supplies, eyeglasses, wheelchairs, school supplies, schoolbuses, musical instruments, bicycles, and Bibles, but also involves the foundation and its members in lobbying efforts on key American legislation on foreign policy. The foundation's *IFCO News* is published quarterly.

**FURTHER READINGS**

"IFCO Celebrates Thirty Years of Support for Justice and Self-Determination." *IFCO News* (Summer 1997).

"Manifest(o) Destiny and the Churches." *Christianity Today* 13, 18 (June 6, 1969), 42–43.

*Harold Dean Trulear*

## Interscholastic Athletic Association

*See* National Interscholastic Basketball Tournament.

## Interstate Dental Association

*See* Tri-State Dental Association of DC, VA, MD.

## Iota Phi Lambda

On June 1, 1929, Lola Mercedes Parker and a group of six other black women founded Iota Phi Lambda as a sorority for business and professional women in Chicago. Six of the women were graduates of the Chicago Business College and one had graduated from Kansas State College. At a time when black women found few opportunities in white-collar professions, Iota Phi Lambda served the needs of and assisted minority women in business.

Since its founding, Iota Phi Lambda has a become an international sorority boasting approximately five thousand members active in more than one hundred chapters in cities throughout the United States and the Virgin Islands. Iota Phi Lambda is affiliated with the National Council of Negro Women, the Leadership Conference on Civil Rights, and the National Committee for Children and Youth, and is accredited as a nongovernmental organization at the United Nations. It supports the National Association for the Advancement of Colored People, the National Urban League, the United Negro College Fund, the Black Woman's Agenda, and the Assault on Illiteracy. Moreover, the Iota Phi Lambda Sorority, Inc., sponsors educational programs and scholarships to raise interest in business education among female high school and college students.

Iota Phi Lambda Sorority imports its kente (ceremonial cloth) scarves and wood carvings from Ghana and its papyrus prints from Egypt. The sorority also raises funds to support the Africare's Women's Empowerment Program for a New South Africa. The program's goal is to raise the economic and social status of black women in the Republic of South Africa by expanding their participation in health care and education. Along with Africare, the sorority conducts several other national programs, including a Tutorial Program that assists students; a Career Exploration Program that seeks to broaden black youths' awareness of career opportunities; a Toys "U" Can't Return Program that assists in the prevention of childhood pregnancies; and a "Mothers' Career Assistance Program" that assists teens and disadvantaged mothers. Other programs designed to inspire and guide youths are the Future Iota Girls (FIGS) for young women ages sixteen to twenty; the Future Intellectual Leaders (FIL) for male preteens and teenagers; and GEMS for girls ages ten to fifteen.

Each year, the sorority celebrates the Iota Business Week in April and Founder's Day in June. At Iota Phi Lambda's annual national conference, the sorority recognizes outstanding commitment to and involvement in community service with the Lola M. Parker Achievement Award. Headquartered in Savannah, Georgia, the sorority publishes the annual *Iota Journal* and several newsletters throughout the year. The sorority also maintains an auxiliary for male spouses of members.

**FURTHER READING**

Ploski, H. A., and J. Williams, eds. *The Negro Almanac.* New York: Gale, 1989.

*Nancy Jean Rose*

# Iota Phi Theta

Iota Phi Theta Fraternity, Inc., is a national social-service organization. Founded in 1963 at Morgan State University in Baltimore, Maryland, it follows a long tradition of African American Greek-lettered organizations whose individual membership is based upon access to postsecondary education. Between 1906 and 1922, eight predominantly black Greek-lettered organizations were founded on American college campuses. Until the creation of Iota, virtually no additional organizations were chartered.

The 1963 founding of Iota was the product of several demographic trends of the late 1950s and 1960s. During those years, civil rights legislation and increased federal funding for higher education, including the G.I. Bill, resulted in larger numbers of African American college students. The larger numbers of African Americans on college campuses inevitably reflected a broader range of interests and experiences that sparked an increase in the formation of fraternal and sororital organizations. Iota took advantage of this dramatic demographic shift by creating an organization that met the needs of a new generation of black college students.

The founders of Iota set forth as their mission to develop and perpetuate scholarship, leadership, citizenship, fidelity, and brotherhood. Unlike the founders of many of the other predominantly African American fraternal and sororital organizations, the founders of Iota tended to be older than the average college population. Some were veterans, others were part-time students, and several were married. In seeking brotherhood from a more mature position, they came together to form a new organization that they believed would best serve their needs and interests. At latest count, Iota's membership included more than one hundred undergraduate and graduate chapters and approximately fifteen thousand members in twenty-five states and the District of Columbia.

Founded as a social-service organization, it has supported and become involved in programs sponsored by other organizations, including the National Association for the Advancement of Colored People (NAACP), the Southern Christian Leadership Conference (SCLC), the National Federation of the Blind, Big Brothers of America, the United Negro College Fund, and the National Sickle Cell Foundation. The fraternity motto is "Building a Tradition. . . not Resting on One," and its colors are charcoal brown and gilded gold.

In addition to forging a clear identity and a set of goals apart from other existing organizations, the membership of Iota also recognizes the need for interfraternity networking. Thus, in 1996, Iota joined the National Pan-Hellenic Council (NPHC), the umbrella organization for the nine largest, predominantly African American fraternities and sororities. The NPHC has yet to rule on membership criteria for organizations seeking to join. Since 1987, however, Iota has maintained membership in the National Interfraternity Conference (NIC). The NIC is an organization whose membership includes more than sixty national fraternities.

Fraternal and sororital organizations play an essential role in providing safe spaces for African American college students. Moreover, they serve as vehicles for networking between recent graduates and established black professionals who also serve as role models. In many black communities, their tradition of community uplift and volunteerism provides important social services that would otherwise be lacking.

**FURTHER READINGS**

Ploski, Harry A., and James Williams. *The Negro Almanac: A Reference Work on the African American.* 5th ed. Detroit: Gale, 1989, 1350.

Riley, Marc C. "Phi Beta Sigma and the National Interfraternity Conference (NIC): Should We Join?" *Crescent: The Official Publication of Phi Beta Sigma Fraternity, Inc.* 76, 1 (Winter 1995–1996), 30–31.

Talbert, Charles H. "NPHC Expansion! The Debate Continues. . . ." *Crescent: The Official Publication of Phi Beta Sigma Fraternity, Inc.* 76, 1 (Winter 1995–1996), 42–45.

*Julie S. Doar*

# J

## Jack and Jill of America, Inc.

Jack and Jill of America, Inc., began as a play group for children of African American professional women and the wives of black professional men. The goal of the founders, who started the group in Philadelphia in 1938, was to provide their children with social, cultural, and educational programs in a time of de facto segregation in northern cities. By the 1950s Jack and Jill had grown from a local mothers club to a national organization, and by the late 1980s there were nearly two hundred chapters serving children and families in black communities.

Miriam Stubbs Thomas called the first meeting of sixteen women to her Philadelphia home in January 1938. Thomas, who was a concert pianist, taught piano in her own studio while her children were young. Along with several others of Philadelphia's African American elite, she argued that the women in her social and professional circles had children who did not know one another but should. Developing a mothers' club for children ages two to twenty-two, the women sponsored cultural events and opportunities for their children to meet and mingle.

The club provided a local network for parents and children. Soon the network of Philadelphia's black elite extended to networks of African American professionals in other cities, where plans to organize similar clubs were in the making. In 1939, the New York chapter was founded. Like their Philadelphia friends, a group of New York City African American mothers had been meeting and bringing their children together for activities. When Philadelphia named its group Jack and Jill, the New Yorkers also decided to adopt the name.

Less than a decade after its founding, the Jack and Jill concept had spread so quickly that a national organization became essential. The first national officers were elected in 1946. Dorothy B. Wright of Philadelphia was selected president; Emily B. Pickens of Brooklyn, New York, was designated vice president; Edna Seay of Buffalo, New York, was elected secretary-treasurer; Constance Bruce of Columbus, Ohio, was chosen corresponding secretary; and Ida Murphy Smith (later Peters) of Baltimore became editor of *Up the Hill*, the organization's national journal. Local chapters were organized into eight regions, and emphasis was placed on building leadership opportunities for the children. Teen groups met with mothers at the yearly regional meetings and at the biannual national conventions. In later years, mothers remained in the club until their children graduated from high school and then became Jack and Jill alumni. Fifty years after its founding, Jack and Jill of America had expanded to 187 chapters across the nation.

During its thirtieth anniversary, Jack and Jill became one of the first national organizations of African American women to establish an endowment. In 1968, Jacqueline J. Robinson of the District of Columbia chaired the foundation's steering committee and became its first president. Articles of incorporation were drafted, and the foundation announced its purpose as a self-help organization that was to eliminate some of the obstacles that confront contemporary African American youth. Many of the projects sponsored by the foundation are centered at historically black colleges and universities around the nation. From 1968 to 1988, the foundation awarded $600,000 in grants to communities, serving thousands of black youth from preschool to college.

Founder Thomas, reflecting upon the legacy of Jack and Jill, believed that the organization had become an important link for contemporary black leaders. Many Jack and Jill alumni became professionals who then joined Jack and Jill chapters to promote the social and cultural development of their children. This process has continued for three generations. Like the Greek organizations that were founded by African American college students for social reasons in the early 1900s, Jack and Jill goals by the 1990s had expanded to provide services to the larger black community.

**FURTHER READINGS**
*Philadelphia Inquirer*, April 29, 1979.
Terborg-Penn, Rosalyn. "Jack and Jill of America, Inc." In *Black Women in America: An Historical Encyclopedia.* Ed. Darlene Clark Hine et al. Bloomington: Indiana University Press, 1994, 1: 619–620.
*Up the Hill: Journal of Jack and Jill of America* 39 (1988), 19–21.

*Rosalyn Terborg-Penn*

# Jackie Robinson Foundation

The Jackie Robinson Foundation (JRF) is a public, non-profit, educational foundation organized in 1973 in memory of Jackie Robinson, the first African American to break the color barrier in major-league baseball. The JRF serves as an advocate and resource center for young minority adults who have great potential but limited financial opportunities. Its programs support education, scholarships, and the development of leadership skills. The foundation was organized by Rachel Isum Robinson, widow of Jackie Robinson and JRF chairperson until 1996 when Leonard S. Coleman Jr., president of the National League of Professional Baseball Clubs, succeeded her.

Rachel Robinson, who was married to Jackie for thirty-two years, faithfully supported his endeavor to desegregate baseball. In 1947, Jackie Robinson became the first black player to join a major league baseball team when he signed with the Brooklyn Dodgers. Throughout his career with the Dodgers, Robinson suffered verbal and physical abuse from teammates, opposing team players, and fans. He endured these hardships by ignoring his attackers and avoiding confrontations. Despite this adversity, Robinson achieved greatness and received the Rookie of the Year Award during his first year with the Dodgers. In 1949, he was honored as the Most Valuable Player.

After his retirement from baseball in 1956, Robinson became active in the civil rights movement. From 1957 to 1964, he served as chairman of the Freedom Fund Drive of the National Association for the Advancement of Colored People (NAACP). Later he founded the Jackie Robinson Construction Company to build low- and moderate-income housing. He died in 1972 at the age of fifty-three from a heart attack.

In his autobiography, *I Never Had It Made* (1972), published posthumously, Jackie Robinson explained that he tried to provide all African American youths with the opportunity to succeed. To carry on his desire to uplift disadvantaged minority youths, the foundation awards scholarships of up to $5,000 per year for four years of college. Additional support services are provided to scholars during and after college, including counseling, networking, mentoring, summer jobs, leadership development seminars, and postgraduate placement. Between 1973 and 1996, the foundation supported nearly four hundred university and college students, aiding them in realizing their full potential. In 1997, the foundation funded 128 JRF Scholars at sixty-two educational institutions in twenty states and the District of Columbia. Foundation scholarship winners achieve a college graduation rate of 92 percent.

Besides supporting disadvantaged youths, each year the foundation recognizes two outstanding individuals for their dedication to improving the quality of life in America. The recipients personify the qualities that Jackie Robinson possessed—professional excellence, competitiveness, and a lifelong commitment to helping others. Past recipients of the Robie Award include Dionne Warwick, singer and humanitarian, for organizing fund-raising events to help AIDS patients and their families; August A. Busch III, chairman of the board and president of Anheuser-Busch Companies, Inc., for sponsoring each year more than four hundred community-based activities in urban areas; Chi Chi Rodriguez, professional golfer, for his Chi Chi Rodriguez Youth Foundation home for troubled and abused youths; and Marian Wright Edelman, founder and president of the Children's Defense Fund, for her dedication to children's rights.

**FURTHER READINGS**
Chace, Susan. "The True Color of Heroism." *Good Housekeeping* 223 (October 1996), 18–19.
Jackie Robinson Foundation; "Fact Sheet." (September 24, 1996), 1–2.
"Leonard S. Coleman Jr. Named Chairman of Jackie Robinson Foundation; Kenneth I. Chenault Receives Robie Award." *Jet* 89 (April 1, 1996), 59–61.
McManis, Sam. "A Lesson in Dignity." *Sporting News* 220 (October 21, 1996), 7.

Robinson, Jackie, as told to Alfred Duckett. *I Never Had It Made*. New York: Putnam, 1972.

Robinson, Rachel. *Jackie Robinson: An Intimate Portrait*. New York: Abrams, 1996.

*Julieanne Phillips*

## Jacksonville, Florida: Civic, Literary, and Mutual Aid Associations

Immediately after the Civil War, many African Americans flooded into urban areas of the South to find ways to exercise their freedom. With the end of hostilities, millions of newly freed blacks found themselves trying to carve out a niche in a radically changed society. To ensure their protection and provide for their needs, these emancipated people migrated to coastal urban areas where federal troops protected them and they could find employment, companionship, and group association. In Florida, Jacksonville immediately became an attractive area for those seeking a new start. Since its founding in 1822, Jacksonville had been home to African Americans. But for most of the antebellum period, blacks were relegated to the laboring class, made up primarily of slaves with fewer than 100 freedmen.

Once freedom came, African Americans immediately tried to establish the social, educational, economic, and political institutions necessary for group survival and racial progress. One of the first institutions established by African Americans was a school. In 1868 Stanton Normal school opened, providing eight grades of education for blacks in Jacksonville. Stanton was the product of Freedman's Bureau money, as well as the fund-raising efforts of local residents. In 1882, black efforts to obtain education were further enhanced when African Methodist Episcopal (AME) clergymen founded Edward Waters College and AME school. Black women were actively involved in institution building and helped found some of the city's oldest mutual aid societies. In 1868, for example, a group of African American women founded the Daughters of Israel, a burial society.

As Jacksonville's black population steadily increased, the economic fortunes of its African American residents improved. After a yellow fever epidemic hit the city in the 1880s, blacks gained a numerical advantage over the city when frightened whites fled to the suburbs. By the turn of the twentieth century, Jacksonville had become Florida's largest city with 29,429 residents, 16,236 of which were black. At this time, Jacsonville's black community reached its institutional maturity as African Americans founded various religious, civic, fraternal, economic, and athletic organizations. Abraham Lincoln Lewis's Afro-American Insurance Company served as the foundation of black Jacksonville's economic development. Lewis served as secretary of the Negro Business League, which had an affiliate in Jacksonville.

Black women also continued their efforts. Eartha M. M. White, one of the nation's best-known black philanthropists, founded a number of organizations to aid the poor. Her most impressive work was the founding of the Clara White Mission in 1902. Despite the economic hardship caused by the Depression of the 1930s and the banks' refusal to lend her money, White managed to solicit funds from generous friends and raised $15,000 to erect a building. Located on notorious Ashley Street, the mission operated in the heart of Jacksonville's crime belt and provided invaluable services to the city's poor. When a fire destroyed the mission in 1944, White replaced it with a modern structure valued at $65,000. By 1965 she had paid off the building, then worth $150,000, and greatly expanded its services. In addition to aiding the poor, the mission served as a community center for Jacksonville's African American residents. The building housed many black businesses as well as the offices of labor and political organizations. Moreover, the *Pittsburgh Courier*, one of the nation's leading black newspapers, published its Florida edition in a room in the Clara White Mission.

The economic prosperity associated with Jacksonville's growing African American community supported new and exciting social opportunities. Ashley, Davis, and Broad Streets formed the boundaries of the African American community. Within these streets resided a prosperous and vibrant society. In 1927, the Wilder Park Branch Library opened as the city's first library for black patrons. Within a decade, the Wilder Park branch "had one of the highest volumes of circulations" of any of the city's library branches. Blacks also had access to three parks in La Villa, the oldest part of downtown Jacksonville.

In addition, there were several African American professional and social clubs such as the Knights of Pythias Hall and the Black Masons. A group of black men, led by Grand Master John R. Scott, had established the Most Honorable Fraternity of Free and Accepted Masons of Florida in Jacksonville in 1870. The city's Most Worshipful Grand Lodge was Florida's first black masonic organization. In 1912, under the leadership of Grand Master

John D. Powell, the group launched a building project completed in the following year. The brick building at the corner of Broad and Duval Streets also served as the headquarters of the Florida Masons. By 1942, David D. Powell, a 33rd Degree Mason and one of the most respected men in Jacksonville, managed the state organization. He oversaw the group's property, then worth $100,000, making the lodge Florida's wealthiest black institution. The Masons remain an important organization, providing opportunities for social activities and professional networking in Jacksonville's black community.

Other national organizations that operate branches in Jacksonville include the National Association for the Advancement of Colored People (NAACP) and the National Urban League (NUL). The city's NAACP branch, established in 1918, has played a vital role in the struggle for integration in Jacksonville as well the state. During the Second World War, Jacksonville's NAACP chapter was influential in desegregating the Democratic Party and equalizing teachers' pay. Since 1947, Jacksonville has also had a very effective Urban League branch that emerged from the city's Negro Welfare League. Founded in 1925, the Negro Welfare League was a nonprofit organization that provided advice and help in meeting the educational, economic, social, and political needs of the city's black residents. Representatives of the National Urban League and local leaders of Jacksonville's Negro Welfare League formed the city's Urban Leage on November 17, 1947. The new Urban League branch had a biracial board, its own charter, and an office with an executive secretary at 704 Broad Street. Dr. I. E. Williams was a leading figure in Jacksonville's Urban League.

In 1995, Jacksonville's population topped the one million mark. By then African Americans made up about 28 percent of the city's population. Jacksonville still has the largest concentration of blacks in Florida.

**FURTHER READINGS**

Colburn, David R., and Jane L. Landers. *The African American Heritage of Florida.* Gainesville: University of Florida Press, 1995.

Crooks, James B. *Jacksonville After the Fire, 1901–1919: A New South City.* Jacksonville: University of North Florida Press, 1991.

Phets, Marsha D. *An American Beach for African Americans.* Gainesville: University of Florida Press, 1997.

Sessions, B. J. *A Woman from Charleston: The Life of Arnolta Johnston Williams (Moma Williams).* Jacksonville, Fla.: Jean-Aubrey, Ideas, Inc., 1991.

Walch, Barbara H. *New Black Voices: The Growth and Contributions of Sallye Mathis and Mary Singleton in Florida Government.* Jacksonville, Fla.: Barbara H. Walch, 1990.

*Abel A. Bartley*

## Jazz Composers Guild

Trumpeter, composer, and painter Bill Dixon founded the Jazz Composers Guild (JCG) in 1964 in the wake of a jazz festival at the Cellar Cafe on West Ninety-Sixth Street and Broadway in New York City. Known as the "October Revolution in Jazz," the six-day festival highlighted the work of more than twenty new jazz groups and solo performers and offered panels on topics like "The Rise of Folk Music and the Decline of Jazz" and "The Economics of Jazz." Dixon was dissatisfied with the efforts of Local 802 of the Musician Mutual Protective Association (MMPA). The MMPA, he believed, failed to address the working conditions of jazz musicians, who were often underpaid, did not receive royalties for their recordings, and lacked adequate performance spaces and recording opportunities. Jazz musicians saw the festival as an opportunity to create a cooperative.

The group of JCG charter members was composed of black and white Americans as well as European and Canadian musicians working in the United States, including Roswell Rudd, Jon Winter, Burton Green, Cecil Taylor, Archie Shepp, Sun Ra, Carla Bley, Paul Bley from Canada, Mike Mantler from Austria, and John Tchicai from Denmark.

The guild sought to establish jazz music, which many contemporaries regarded as a "primitive" form of music, in its "rightful place in society." The JCG hoped that awareness of the musicians' poor working conditions would spur the public to agitate on their behalf. Moreover, the guild hoped to secure and "provide facilities for the proper creation, rehearsal, performance, and dissemination of the music" (Levin 1965, 18). Dixon invited black and white jazz musicians to join the JCG, which provided legal counsel, monitored record companies to ensure that musicians received their due royalties, and negotiated equitable compensation for those involved in recordings and live musical performances.

The guild folded in 1965 for several reasons, including Dixon's disillusionment with the commitment of the members to the ideals of the guild; the incompatible temperaments of its members; and, perhaps most dire, the scabbing of musicians who ignored the cooperative vision of the guild and made their own contracts with producers, record companies, and clubs.

Though short lived, the guild was able to book a number of concerts featuring its ensemble, the Jazz Composers Guild orchestra, led by Carla Bley and Mike Mantler. The orchestra formed alternating performance groups (one of which featured Sun Ra's Arkestra) that performed weekly concerts at the Contemporary Center, a landmark jazz club in New York City's Greenwich Village, and four concerts at Judson Church opposite Carnegie Hall in December 1964.

**FURTHER READINGS**

Kernfeld, Barry, ed. *New Grove Dictionary of Jazz.* London: Macmillan 1988.

Levin, Robert. "The Jazz Composers Guild: An Assertion of Dignity." *Down Beat* May 6, 1965, 17–18.

Spellman, A. B. *Four Lives in the Bebop Business.* New York: Pantheon Books, 1966. 4th ed., New York: Limelight Editions, 1994.

Wilmer, Valerie. *As Serious As Your Life: The Story of the New Jazz.* London: Allison and Busby 1977. 2nd ed., London and New York: Serpent's Tail, 1992.

*Nichole T. Rustin*

## Jeanes Fund

*See* Negro Rural School Fund.

## John F. Slater Fund

In 1882, John Fox Slater, a textile manufacturer from Connecticut, established the fund that bears his name with a gift of $1 million "for the uplifting of the lately-emancipated population of Southern States." Slater had been encouraged to establish the fund by his neighbor Moses Pierce, a trustee of Hampton Institute. From the outset, the Slater Fund focused exclusively on educational opportunities for blacks. Between 1882 and 1911, the fund supported historically black colleges primarily through the provision of salary supplements for teachers employed in the fields of teacher training and industrial education. The fund consistently emphasized the latter field, and more than half of its aid was given to support the industrial education and teacher training programs of Hampton and Tuskegee Institutes and the initiation of similar programs at black normal schools and colleges.

In 1911, in cooperation with the General Education Board and the Anna T. Jeanes Fund, the Slater Fund embarked on its most noteworthy contribution to black education, the county training schools. The county-training-school model was developed by James H. Dillard, former president of the Jeanes Fund, who became general agent of the Slater Fund in 1910. The trustees of the fund envisioned a network of county training schools throughout the South, aimed at providing high school education, teacher training, and courses in "the basic industries of the community." The curriculum included training for domestic service for girls and manual training for boys. The first county training school established with the assistance of the fund was the Tangipahoa Parish Training School for Colored Children, organized in Louisiana in the year 1911–1912. Conditions under which the fund assisted state authorities in the establishment of county training schools required that schools be recognized as part of the local public school system; that an annual teacher's salary appropriation of no less than $750 be made from public funds; and that the coursework extend at least through the eighth grade. As an incentive, the fund awarded to each school during the first three years of its existence an annual grant of $500 and in the subsequent two years $250 annually for the employment of an industrial teacher. Following the initial five-year support, the fund allocated annually $100 for equipment. It was the fund's intention that the public school boards assume the responsibility for support of the county training schools and incorporate them into the public educational system, at which point the fund discontinued its support.

The provision of secondary education for blacks drew interest from other philanthropic entities such as the George Peabody Fund and the General Education Board, whose financial contributions were administered by the Slater Fund. The combined efforts of these educational philanthropic funds significantly aided the creation of county training schools for African Americans in the South. Between 1914 and 1930, 384 county training schools were established in thirteen southern states, more than half of them located in Virginia, North Carolina, South Carolina, Alabama, and Georgia. Many of these schools, which were founded to provide education for the rural black population, later evolved into secondary schools.

In 1937, the Slater, Peabody Education, Jeanes, and Virginia Randolph Funds were consolidated into the Southern Education Foundation, Inc. (SEF). Headquartered in Atlanta, Georgia, the SEF continues to support minority education.

**FURTHER READINGS**

Brawley, Benjamin. *Dr. Dillard of the Jeanes Fund.* New York: Fleming H. Revell, 1930.

Finkenbine, Roy E. "'Our Little Circle': Benevolent Reformers, the Slater Fund, and the Arguments for Black Industrial Education, 1882–1908." *Hayes Historical Journal* 6 (1986), 6–22.

Fisher, John E. *The John F. Slater Fund: A Nineteenth Century Affirmative Action for Negro Education.* Lanham, Md.: University Press of America, 1986.

John F. Slater Fund Papers. Rockefeller Archive Center, Pocantico Hills, New York.

John F. Slater Fund Papers. Southern Education Foundation Inc., Atlanta, Georgia.

Jones, Lance G. E. *The Jeanes Teacher in the United States, 1908–1933.* Chapel Hill: University of North Carolina Press, 1937.

Redcay, Edward E. *County Training Schools and Public Secondary Education for Negroes in the South.* Washington, D.C.: John F. Slater Fund, 1935.

*Jayne R. Beilke*

**SEE ALSO**    Southern Education Foundation

## Joint Committee on National Recovery

In July 1933, John P. Davis and Robert C. Weaver created the short-lived Joint Committee on National Recovery (JCNR) to fill a void in black political organizing. By the time of the Great Depression, there were several national black associations devoted to advancing civil rights. None, however, had effective lobbyists in Washington, D.C. Moreover, national reform efforts were largely uncoordinated. The Joint Committee sought to unite black lobbying and watchdog activities at the national level. As Davis put it, the JCNR was to "speak with authority for the major organized forces among Negroes."

Such a committee was desperately needed. During President Franklin D. Roosevelt's "hundred days," New Dealers were rapidly reforming the American economy. Groups such as labor unions and employers who utilized lobbyists had the opportunity to affect New Deal policies. Those who were poorly organized, such as the black community, were left out of the decision-making process. As a result, several New Deal policies and programs were designed without consideration of their effect on black workers. The National Recovery Administration did not prevent employers from discriminating against African Americans. Black farmers did not share equally in the benefits of the Agricultural Adjustment Administration, the Farm Credit Administration, or the Resettlement Administration.

The Joint Committee attacked the shortcomings of the New Deal in two ways. First, Davis and Weaver lobbied the White House and Congress for better treatment of African Americans. Second, they reported the abuses of Roosevelt's alphabet agencies to inform and sway political and public opinion. In their scathing critiques, Weaver and Davis pulled no punches, referring to the New Deal as the "raw deal."

Although the Joint Committee on National Recovery publicized the failures of the New Deal and influenced some federal policies, it made few substantial contributions. This was not the fault of either Davis or Weaver, who worked tirelessly to advance civil rights. The JCNR never had a paid staff or money to conduct an effective lobbying campaign. The committee also lacked the wholehearted support of the major African American associations. The National Association for the Advancement of Colored People (NAACP) and the National Urban League, as well as large granting institutions such as the Rosenwald Fund, saw the JCNR as a threat to their lobbying and investigative activities and, in response, redoubled their own efforts to shape the New Deal. Finding these conditions intolerable, Weaver left the Joint Committee in November 1933 to join the federal Public Works Administration. Although Davis continued on his own for two years, in 1935 he, too, quit the moribund JCNR and joined a more radical group, the National Negro Congress.

**FURTHER READINGS**

Kirby, John B. *Black Americans in the Roosevelt Era: Liberalism and Race.* Knoxville: University of Tennessee Press, 1980.

Mark, Elizabeth Chadwick. "The Joint Committee for National Recovery: Negro Lobby During the New Deal." M.A. Thesis, University of Maryland, 1971.

Sitkoff, Harvard. *A New Deal for Blacks: The Emergence of Civil Rights as a National Issue: The Depression Decade.* New York: Oxford University Press, 1978.

*Andrew E. Kersten*

## Julia Ward Howe Republican Women's Club

The Julia Ward Howe Republican Women's Club was founded by suffragist Bertha G. Higgins in 1920 to facilitate African American women's involvement in Republican Party politics after the passage of the Nineteenth Amendment to the United States Constitution. The club sought the Republican Party's recognition of, and support for, issues that were of particular concern to black constituents in exchange for votes in support of Republican Party candidates.

Most African American women who had fought for female suffrage since the late nineteenth century supported political equality of the sexes in order to promote the social and political equality of all races in the United States. Rather than advocate a radical feminist agenda that rejected the major Republican and Democratic political parties, they supported a reformist agenda that reflected their desire to work within the established political system. Concerned with promoting social policies that would improve living conditions in black communities and increase economic and educational opportunities for African Americans, black women who remained politically active after the passage of the Nineteenth Amendment did not focus on issues that concerned white feminist women, such as the Equal Rights Amendment. Nor did large numbers of black women join the exclusively female National Women's Party headed by Alice Paul. Instead, many politically active African American women chose to work within the Republican Party—the party that had fought for the emancipation of the black slaves and for black male suffrage during and after the Civil War. To honor the memory of Julia Ward Howe, a white author and reformer who had supported the Republican Party's position during the Civil War and had written the lyrics for the patriotic "Battle Hymn of the Republic," black Republican Party women named their special-interest association after Howe.

By 1920, many African Americans had become critical of the racism of the southern states' "lily-white" constituency within the Republican Party. Yet, party member Bertha Higgins, who founded and led the Julia Ward Howe Republican Women's Club, remained active within the Republican Party throughout the 1920s. She supported the candidacy and subsequent presidency of Warren G. Harding, who had asserted a bold antilynching and pro–civil rights position in his speech at the 1920 Republican Party national convention. After winning his party's presidential nomination, Harding had included African American political advisers among his campaign staff who had facilitated the organization of African American "clubs" within the Republican Party, such as Higgins's Julia Ward Howe Republican Women's Club.

Ironically, political analysts determined that the 1920 victory of the Republican Party was due to an increased southern vote and to the rise of a "new Republicanism"

that deemphasized the importance of black voters and emphasized the party's economic policies and its "return to normalcy" after the economic, political, and social disruptions caused by World War I. When leading Republican senators refused to support the passage of an antilynching bill proposed by Missouri Congressman Leonidas C. Dyer in the early 1920s, the party further lost credibility with black voters. Throughout the 1920s, during the Republican presidencies of Harding, Calvin Coolidge, and Herbert Hoover, the Republican Party refused to make commitments in support of African American voters that would have compromised its position among white southern voters. Frustrated by the Republican Party's failure to address issues that concerned African Americans, many black voters, including Bertha Higgins, turned to the Democratic Party in 1932. Leading her organization of black women voters, Higgins re-formed the Julia Ward Howe Democratic Women's Club in 1932 in support of the Democratic Party presidential candidate, Franklin D. Roosevelt.

**FURTHER READINGS**

Sherman, Richard B. *The Republican Party in Black America from McKinley to Hoover, 1896–1933*. Charlottesville: University of Virginia Press, 1973.

Terborg-Penn, Rosalyn. "Discontented Black Feminists: Prelude and Postscript to the Passage of the Nineteenth Amendment." In *We Specialize in the Wholly Impossible: A Reader in Black Women's History*. Ed. Darlene Clark Hine and Linda Reed. Brooklyn, N.Y.: Carlson, 1995, 487–503.

*Karen Garner*

## Julius Rosenwald Fund

Julius Rosenwald, who became president of Sears, Roebuck and Company in 1906, established the Julius Rosenwald Fund for "the well-being of mankind" in 1917. The fund was incorporated in 1928, capitalized by 200,000 shares of Sears stock worth approximately $20 million. Edwin Rogers Embree, who had served as a director and vice president of the Rockefeller Foundation, was named president of the fund and served in that capacity until the fund closed in 1948. Rosenwald's interest in black education stemmed from his affinity for the self-help philosophy of Booker T. Washington. Rosenwald served as a trustee and patron of Tuskegee Institute and supported the Hampton-Tuskegee program of industrial training for blacks.

Between 1928 and 1948, the fund's activities concentrated on four major areas: education, health, fellowships, and race relations. The best-known initiative of the fund, however, was the Rosenwald school-building program. In 1914, Rosenwald initiated the building of schoolhouses for rural southern blacks, following the philanthropic precedent set by the John F. Slater and Anna T. Jeanes Funds. The Rosenwald Fund offered to provide southern communities with approximately one-third of the funds necessary to construct school buildings. Emphasizing rugged individualism and self-help, the fund asked that local communities raise the remaining funds. States and counties were to contribute money or labor toward the construction of the buildings and agree to maintain them as part of the public school system. Interested in fostering interracial cooperation, Rosenwald stipulated that white citizens make financial contributions and that blacks contribute either money, labor, or both. When the school-building program ended in 1932, a total of 4,977 public schoolhouses, 163 shops, and 217 teachers' homes had been built in 883 counties in fifteen southern states at a cost of $28.4 million. The Rosenwald Fund had contributed $4.4 million to the overall cost.

Beginning in 1928, the fund, in cooperation with the General Education Board, attempted to develop four "university centers" for the education of black professionals. For this purpose, the fund supported Howard, Atlanta, Clark, New Orleans, and Fisk Universities; Morehouse, Straight, Spelman, and Meharry Medical Colleges; Gammon Theological Seminary; and Flint-Goodridge Hospital. Other educational ventures included the provision of books to black and white schools and colleges; the institution of a county library services program that provided rural schools with reading materials; the creation of branch libraries in schools, churches, and stores; and the support of teacher training programs at Tuskegee Institute and West Georgia, Fort Valley State, and Jackson Colleges.

In the area of health and medical services, the fund concentrated on the improvement of health-care facilities and personnel for blacks; the provision of affordable medical services to persons of moderate means; advanced training for physicians, nurses, and hospital administrators; and salary supplements for black health officers. The fund's fellowship program enabled blacks and white southerners to pursue graduate and professional training at northern universities or at schools abroad. In the area of race relations, the fund generated policy studies and publications that drew attention to discriminatory practices in employment, housing, and civil liberties. To this end, the fund supported the Commission on Interracial Cooperation and, in 1942, organized its own race relations division, codirected by Will W. Alexander and Charles S. Johnson.

The Rosenwald board of trustees used the fund's principal as well as the interest on it to effect its aims. Heeding Rosenwald's desire that its resources be used to benefit the current generation, the fund closed in 1948, having expended most of its capital.

**FURTHER READINGS**

Beilke, Jayne R. "To Render Better Service: The Role of the Julius Rosenwald Fund Fellowship Program in the Development of Graduate and Professional Educational Opportunities for African Americans." Ph.D. diss., Indiana University, 1994.

Bullock, Henry Allen. *A History of Negro Education in the South: From 1619 to the Present.* Cambridge, Mass.: Harvard University Press, 1967.

Embree, Edwin Rogers, and Julia Waxman. *Investment in People: The Story of the Julius Rosenwald Fund.* New York: Harper and Brothers, 1949.

Julius Rosenwald Fund Papers. Fisk University Special Collections, Nashville, Tennessee.

Julius Rosenwald Papers. University of Chicago, Chicago, Illinois.

*Jayne R. Beilke*

## Kansas Commission on Civil Rights

*See* Kansas Human Rights Commission.

## Kansas Human Rights Commission

The Kansas Human Rights Commission is a seven-member state agency empowered to investigate complaints of race, age, sex, religious, and disability discrimination and retaliation in employment, housing, and public accommodations. Providing impartial assistance to help mediate disputes is one of the commission's responsibilities. In addition, the commission has enforcement powers to prosecute violations of civil and human rights laws through public hearings. It also provides services to help educate Kansas citizens about state and federal harassment and discrimination laws.

The Kansas Human Rights Commission originated with the civil rights movement of the 1950s and 1960s. In the late 1940s, the Kansas Clearing House on Civil Rights began to press the State Legislature to end racial discrimination in Kansas businesses and labor unions. In 1949, lawmakers began to study the question, and in April 1953 Kansas became the twelfth state in the nation to enact fair-employment legislation when legislators passed a bill establishing the Kansas Anti-Discrimination Commission. The commission was a compromise between conservatives and civil rights advocates and had the power to investigate but not prosecute civil rights violations. Commission members noted this in their annual reports and insisted that, to be effective, they needed the ability to enforce Kansas civil rights laws.

By 1959, the commission's educational programs had made little difference, and Chairman Charles Arthur's 1960 study of other civil rights bodies across the nation strongly recommended that enforceable legislation in Kansas was the only way to eliminate prejudicial policies in the workplace. In 1961, legislators renamed the agency the Kansas Commission on Civil Rights and authorized it to enforce state laws prohibiting discriminatory employment practices based upon race, religion, or national origin. Although the commission now had enforcement powers, it could not initiate complaints of discrimination, and the statute of limitations for citizens to file a grievance was six months. Therefore, the commission had to rely on outside assistance, and this came from the Kansas Advisory Council on Civil Rights. Founded in 1962, the advisory council was a grassroots association that organized public support for the commission's activities and helped guide victims of discrimination through the system.

The commission's responsibilities have continued to increase throughout the ensuing decades. In 1963, the Legislature extended the commission's jurisdiction to investigate discrimination in restaurants, hotels, and other public accommodations. Legislators broadened this in 1965 and 1970 to include any business offering goods, facilities, accommodations, and personal services to the public. In 1967, the commission gained subpoena power and the authority to initiate complaints of discrimination. Its mission expanded again in 1970 to inquire into allegations of housing discrimination.

In the post–civil rights decades of the 1970s and 1980s, the commission broadened its scope to include complaints of physical and mental disability, gender, and age discrimination. In 1991, the Kansas Commission on Civil Rights reflected this growth when it became the Kansas Human Rights Commission. The commission remains an active force in Kansas and continues its mission to prevent and eliminate discrimination and segregation in employment relations, public accommodations, and housing.

**FURTHER READINGS**

Doherty, Joseph P. *Civil Rights in Kansas: Past, Present, and Future.* Topeka: Kansas Commission on Civil Rights, 1972.

Kansas Human Rights Commission. *Rules and Regulations.* Topeka: The Commission, 1993.

*Gary R. Entz*

## Kappa Alpha Psi

In 1911, Kappa Alpha Psi was established as Kappa Alpha Nu at Indiana University. The name of the fraternity was changed in 1915. The fraternity encourages African American men to improve themselves, their communities, and mankind by means of unity, education, and loyalty to one another and to the race. Along with the four black sororities and three other black fraternities established in the early years of the twentieth century, Kappa Alpha Psi resembles its white counterparts in organization and the use of Greek letters, but it differs from them in history and purpose. Kappa has never had a racial exclusionary clause and is proud of a record of initiating nonblacks into the fraternity. Kappa is an international organization with chapters in Africa, Asia, Europe, and the Caribbean, as well as in the United States.

Kappa was established by Indiana University undergraduates Ezra Alexander, Byron Armstrong, Henry Asher, Marcus Blakemore, Paul Caine, Elder Watson Diggs, George Edmonds, Guy Grant, Edward Irvin, and John Lee. Diggs was the leading force in the organization of the fraternity, served for six years as grand polemarch, or national president, and helped see Kappa through its early, difficult times. In 1911, Indiana University, like most other universities in the Midwest, was segregated. Black students were permitted to attend the school but could not live in the dormitories, participate in most extracurricular activities such as fraternities and sororities, or join cocurricular groups such as language clubs. As a source of support for black men, the young fraternity spread rapidly to other campuses in the Midwest. The Beta Chapter, established at the University of Illinois in 1913, had as the core of its membership the Illi Club, black men who faced problems similar to blacks at Indiana University. Other early chapters were established at the University of Iowa, Ohio State University, and the University of Nebraska.

In 1915, the first chapter at a historically black college was founded at Wilberforce University. It was soon followed by chapters at Lincoln University in Pennsylvania and Meharry Medical College in Tennessee. At these black colleges, members of the faculty as well as undergraduates were initiated. The Chicago Alumni Chapter, chartered in 1919, was Kappa's first chapter of men who had completed college.

Throughout its history, Kappa has been concerned with issues of human justice and has encouraged its members to be active in political, cultural, economic, educational, and religious organizations committed to fair play and equality. In 1921, for example, Kappa established the Guide Right movement, which called on members to help black high school seniors make career choices. Guide Right has since expanded to serve African American youth of all ages. The 1940 annual meeting of the fraternity indicates Kappa's broad range of interests as it called for the appointment of an African American to the Civil Service Commission, discussed the formation of a Washington lobby for blacks, and urged coverage of domestics, laborers, and farmworkers under the Social Security Act. Moreover, Kappa supported the Association for the Study of Negro Life and History, the Commission on Education, the federal antilynching bill, and the efforts of black teachers in the South who were struggling to receive the same pay as white teachers. Finally, it opposed the poll tax and condemned the oppression of all people of color.

When in the 1960s white fraternities, led by Jewish organizations, began to admit African Americans, many contemporaries predicted the demise of black fraternities. The onset of the counterculture movement of the 1970s, others presumed, would sound their death knell. But the black power and black pride movements, as well as the white backlash to black nationalism, stimulated the growth of black fraternities. When black men began to enroll in large numbers in Ivy League and other elite universities, they took their fraternities with them.

Kappa continues its long-standing commitment to Guide Right, established the Kappa Alpha Psi Foundation to further the work of the fraternity, and now has standing committees on leadership, undergraduate loans, senior citizens, publications, music, religion, persons with disabilities, and social action. Like other Greek-letter organizations, Kappa fought against hazing and outlawed the practice early in its history. After years of trying to stop hazing by fining, suspending, and expelling participants and by reporting incidents to the authorities, the fraternity eliminated pledging in the early 1990s. In its place, Kappa established a program that allows all eligible men to join the organization after they have studied the history, culture, and achievements of the fraternity. Kappa's pledge club, the Scroller's Club, established in 1919, was terminated. In 1990, Kappa members operated 302 undergraduate and 285 graduate student chapters on campuses throughout the United States.

### FURTHER READINGS

Crump, William L. *The Story of Kappa Alpha Psi: A History of the Beginning and Development of a College Greek Letter Organization, 1911–1983.* Philadelphia: Kappa Alpha Psi Fraternity, 1983.

Kappa Alpha Psi. *The Confidential Bulletin.*

———. *Directory.*

———. *The Journal of Kappa Alpha Psi.*

*Rhett S. Jones*

## Kerner Commission

*See* National Advisory Commission on Civil Disorders (Kerner Commission).

## Knights of Peter Claver

The Knights of Peter Claver is a fraternal organization of black Catholics, founded in Mobile, Alabama, in 1909. The impetus for the organization came from the Josephites, a Catholic order dedicated to expanding the Church's efforts among African Americans. Leaders of the Josephites, especially Conrad Rebesher, a priest in Mobile, worried that the Church was losing black men to fraternal organizations like the Masons and the Elks who had black lodges. Rebesher hoped that the Knights of Peter Claver would do for black Catholics what the Knights of Columbus did for their white counterparts—provide social opportunities and sponsor community service. At the founding meeting, John Henry Dorsey, the second black priest ordained by the Josephites, was named the national chaplain of the Knights.

The Knights spread quickly through the American South. Within a year of their founding, branches existed in Mobile, Alabama; Norfolk, Virginia; Richmond, Virginia; Nashville, Tennessee; and several small towns in Mississippi. The Knights soon developed a full complement of auxiliary organizations—the junior auxiliary opened in 1917, and the ladies auxiliary started in 1922. The Knights held their first national convention outside the South in 1930. By their second nonsouthern convention, in Chicago in 1946, they had become a national organization.

Early in their history, the Knights focused on providing social opportunities and support for members. The Knights sponsored brass bands that played at community functions and a life insurance program. They were less active in the effort to gain equality for blacks, in and out of the Church. In 1923, they expelled Marcellus Dorsey, brother of their chaplain, for writing articles critical of racial segregation in Catholicism. Through the 1920s the Knights supported the creation of segregated seminaries and parishes.

By 1939, though, the Knights had begun to oppose segregation in the Church. That year they rejected the efforts of the Catholic hierarchy to send black priests to Africa, for fear that it would diminish the effectiveness of religious work among black Americans. To make their position known, the national convention created a committee charged with raising the level of support for black priests among all Catholics. During the civil rights movement, their activism extended to the secular sphere, as the Knights worked with the National Association for the Advancement of Colored People (NAACP) and the National Urban League to end legal segregation in the United States. The organization remained active into the twenty-first century, with its headquarters in New Orleans.

### FURTHER READINGS

Abston, Emanuel J. "Catholicism and African Americans: A Study of Claverism, 1909–1959" Ph.D. diss., Florida State University, 1998.

Davis, Cyprian. *The History of Black Catholics in America.* New York: Crossroads, 1990.

Ochs, Stephen J. *Desegregating the Altar: The Josephites and the Struggle for Black Priests, 1871–1960.* Baton Rouge: Louisiana State University Press, 1990.

*Gary Daynes*

## Knights of Pythias of N.A., S.A., E., A., A. and A.

*See* Colored Knights of Pythias.

## Labor Education Program

*See* Southern Regional Council.

## Ladies' London Emancipation Society

*See* London Emancipation Society.

## Langston Hughes Society

Founded in 1981, the Langston Hughes Society (LHS) was the first scholarly association named in honor of an African American writer. The LHS is a national association of scholars, teachers, creative and performing artists, students, and lay persons who seek to increase awareness and appreciation of Langston Hughes (1902–1967), the first African American to make his living solely by his pen. Throughout his four decades of literary creativity that is virtually unrivaled in American letters, Hughes wrote fifty books, including poetry, drama, autobiography, history, fiction, prose comedy, juvenile literature, librettos, and black gospel song-plays. He was the recipient of numerous honors and awards, including the 1925 *Opportunity* magazine poetry prize, the 1925 *Crisis* magazine Amy Spingarn Contest poetry and essay prizes, the 1931 Harmon Gold Medal, the 1946 National Institute and American Academy of Arts and Letters Award in Literature, the 1953 Anisfield-Wolf Award, and the 1960 National Association for the Advancement of Colored People Spingarn Medal. Moreover, he was the recipient of Rosenwald Fellowships in 1931 and 1941 and a Guggenheim Fellowship in 1935. He received honorary doctorates from Lincoln University in 1943, Howard University in 1963, and Western Reserve University in 1964 and was the unofficial U.S. ambassador to the First World Festival of Negro Arts in Dakar, Senegal, in 1966.

The LHS emerged during the Langston Hughes Study conference held in Joplin, Missouri, Hughes's birthplace, March 13–14, 1981. Sponsored by Missouri Southern State College and funded by the Missouri Committee for the Humanities, the conference attempted to assess the status of Hughes in contemporary American literature and attracted scholars from across the country, as well as students and the general public. Featured speakers included prominent African Americanists such as Therman B. O'Daniel from Morgan State University, Richard K. Barksdale from the University of Illinois, Arnold Rampersad from Stanford University, George H. Bass from Brown University, Charles Nilon from the University of Colorado, Delitta L. Martin from the University of Alabama at Birmigham, Walter C. Daniel from the University of Missouri at Columbia, Leslie Sanders from York University in Toronto, and Eva Jessye, visiting professor at nearby Pittsburg State University and director of Hughes's play *Tambourines of Glory* (1958).

The LHS founding meeting was held in the Baltimore home of Therman and Lillian O'Daniel on June 26, 1981, the anniversary of the date that Hughes received the Spingarn Medal in 1960. O'Daniel, who had edited *Langston Hughes: Black Genius* (1971), a widely read collection of essays, initiated the LHS. Other founding members included the aforementioned George H. Bass; Faith D. Berry, an independent scholar from McLean, Virginia; Alice A. Deck, Grinnell College, Iowa; Akiba Sullivan Harper, Spelman College, Atlanta, Georgia; and Eloise Y. Spicer, Woodrow Wilson High School, Washington, D.C.

In October 1981, the six founding members met in Atlanta, Georgia, at the home of Millicent Dobbs Jordan from Spelman College, who had known Langston Hughes while he was a visiting teacher at the Atlanta University

Center. The group discussed a statement on the purpose and membership of the society. Initial LHS officers were Barksdale (president); Jordan (vice president); Deck (secretary-treasurer); O'Daniel (editor); and Bass (executor/trustee of the Langston Hughes estate and executive editor). Succeeding Barksdale as president have been R. Baxter Miller, University of Tennessee (1984–1990); Ruthe T. Sheffey, Morgan State University (1990–1992); Akiba Sullivan Harper (1992–1998); Leonard A. Slade Jr., State University of New York at Albany (1998–); and Dolan Hubbard, Morgan State University (2000–).

On April 22, 1982, the LHS held its first annual meeting in conjunction with the forty-second annual convention of the College Language Association (CLA) in Charlotte, North Carolina. Special guests included the officers of the CLA, acclaimed author Maya Angelou, poet laureate Gwendolyn Brooks, and illustrator and writer Richard Bruce Nugent, who offered personal reminiscences of his friendship with Hughes. Thirty-two new members joined the LHS, increasing its membership to eighty-nine. In the same year, the LHS launched publication of the *Langston Hughes Review*, which publishes scholarly articles, research notes, book reviews, and announcements. Editors of the *Review* have included Therman B. O'Daniel (1982–1983); Charles H. Nichols and Berry Beckman, Brown University (1984); George H. Bass (1985–1989); Amrijit Singh, Rhode Island College (1990–1991); Thadious Davis, Brown University (1992); Dorothy Denniston, Michael S. Harper, Michael E. Dyson, and Elmo Terry Morgan, Brown University (1994); R. Baxter Miller, University of Georgia (1994–1995); and Dolan Hubbard, University of Georgia (1995–1998).

With an active membership of more than three hundred, the LHS organizes panels at learned societies such as the CLA, the American Literature Association, the Modern Language Association, and the Association for the Study of Afro-American Life and History. The group often holds it executive meeting at the annual convention of the CLA. In 1998, the LHS presented Akiba Sullivan Harper with its first Langston Hughes Prize for scholarship and service. The LHS welcomes scholars and lay persons who are interested in promoting the legacy of Langston Hughes.

**FURTHER READINGS**

Berry, Faith. "The Universality of Langston Hughes." *Langston Hughes Review* 1, 2 (Fall 1982), 1–10.

Deck, Alice A. "The Langston Hughes Society: Its Inaugural Year." *Langston Hughes Review* 1, 2 (Fall 1982), 27–28.

Miller, R. Baxter. "Langston Hughes." *Dictionary of Literary Biography*. Vol. 51. Ed. Trudier Harris and Thadious M. Davis. Detroit: Gale 1987, 112–133.

*Dolan Hubbard*

## Leadership Conference for Civil Rights

Since 1950, the Leadership Conference for Civil Rights (LCCR) has fought for equal opportunity and social justice. It was founded just as civil rights for African Americans became a national issue, and over the years it has extended its scope to lobby on behalf of women, Hispanics, Asian Americans, gays, individuals with disabilities, and other minority groups.

The LCCR emerged out of the long-running battle for fair employment during the 1940s. With the threat of a march on Washington, D.C., the labor leader and civil rights activist A. Philip Randolph pressured President Franklin D. Roosevelt to create a temporary Committee on Fair Employment Practices (FEPC) in 1941. The March on Washington movement continued to agitate for black advancement and helped spawn the National Council for a Permanent FEPC in 1944. Roy Wilkins of the National Association for the Advancement of Colored People (NAACP) teamed up with Arnold Aronson, who represented the National Jewish Community Relations Advisory Council, to become the leading figures in the national council.

To overcome congressional resistance to President Harry S. Truman's civil rights proposals, the NAACP called for the observance of a two-month National Emergency Civil Rights Mobilization in late 1949. The nucleus of the LCCR cohered in planning sessions for a large gathering in Washington in mid-January 1950, which attracted more than four thousand delegates from national civil rights, religious, and labor groups. With Wilkins as its chairman and Aronson as its secretary, the LCCR became a permanent lobbying and coordinating vehicle for the interests of a broad, interracial coalition of roughly twenty organizations. Randolph, Wilkins, and Aronson can rightly be claimed as the cofounders of this organization of organizations.

Not surprisingly, the New York City–based LCCR, buoyed by funding from organized labor, initially lobbied for the creation of a permanent FEPC. Though its exertions in this battle were in vain, the conference was more successful in its efforts on behalf of the federal Civil Rights Acts of 1957 and 1960.

The high point for the LCCR came during the long struggle for a much more important civil rights measure in 1963 and 1964. By this time, a growing number of Americans believed that decisive federal action was necessary to ensure equal rights for blacks. Aware of the changing national mood, President John F. Kennedy in mid-June 1963 sent a civil rights bill to Congress. Wilkins, still chairman of the LCCR, promptly called a meeting in early July in New York City for representatives of the fifty or so organizations that now composed the coalition, including the NAACP, the National Urban League, the Southern Christian Leadership Conference (SCLC), the Industrial Union Department of the AFL-CIO, and the Americans for Democratic Action (ADA). In search of greater leverage, Wilkins also invited other groups, many of which represented America's churches, to participate. An expanded conference endorsed Kennedy's bill but also called for extension of coverage of public accommodations, federal protection of civil rights protestors, and a fair-employment provision.

The establishment of a permanent office in Washington in 1963 boosted the lobbying effectiveness of the LCCR. Walter Reuther of the United Auto Workers offered office space, and Aronson oversaw the Washington staff, which included Marvin Caplan, a reporter with labor ties and race-relations experience, and Violet Gunther, a former executive director of the ADA.

But the most important LCCR figures on the Washington scene were Clarence Mitchell of the NAACP and Joseph Rauh of the ADA. The cool-headed and courtly Mitchell, who had grown up in segregated Baltimore and served as the NAACP labor secretary, was a veteran of the Washington scene. He had directed the NAACP's Washington bureau since 1950 and had become such a familiar face in the nation's capital that he would later earn the title of the "101st Senator." Mitchell had worked closely with the LCCR since its founding, but he became its legislative chairman only when it became a more formal lobby in 1963. Rauh, a well-known white liberal, was much more combative than Mitchell. A graduate of Harvard Law School and a founder of the ADA in 1947, he, too, had labored for the LCCR since the 1950s, and in 1963 he became its official legal counsel.

While Mitchell and Rauh made the case for a stronger civil rights bill, the LCCR sponsored weekly strategy sessions and issued a steady barrage of newsletters and press releases. It also created an elaborate watchdog system to monitor proceedings in Congress, to keep track of the votes of congressmen, and to persuade wavering legislators. Starting in April, the LCCR organized the arrival in Washington of delegations of citizens to crowd congressional offices and demand the passage of civil rights legislation. The Civil Rights Act of 1964, when finally passed in July 1964, was the most comprehensive civil rights measure in the nation's history. While the LCCR cannot claim exclusive credit for this achievement, it did expedite its enactment.

The LCCR also fought for the passage of the Voting Rights Act of 1965 and the Civil Rights Act of 1968. Moreover, it never renounced its faith in integration or the legislative process. When the black-power impulse intensified in the late 1960s, the LCCR adopted a statement of purpose and bylaws that endorsed the goal of integration.

As the legal barriers to full citizenship for African Americans fell, the nonviolent wing of the civil rights movement faded, and new issues seized the nation's attention, the LCCR only intermittently occupied the central stage of national affairs. Nevertheless, in the ensuing years its membership has grown. By the early 1980s, more than 150 groups were affiliated with it. By the late 1990s, its membership consisted of more than 180 organizations representing more than 50 million Americans. This growth has stemmed in part from the expansion of rights consciousness among Americans since the 1960s. And, not surprisingly, a greater potential for intramural disputes has accompanied this growth. While the LCCR helped build an unexpectedly broad coalition in support of an extension of the Voting Rights Act early during the Ronald Reagan presidency, it has tended to sidestep controversial issues like affirmative action that are likely to divide its membership. Still, in an age of evanescent civil rights organizations, the durability of the LCCR—especially with the passing of its first generation of leaders—is impressive.

**FURTHER READINGS**

Findlay, James F., Jr. *Church People in the Struggle: The National Council of Churches and the Black Freedom Movement, 1950–1970.* New York: Oxford University Press, 1993.

Gellman, Barton. "The New Old Movement." *New Republic* (September 6, 1982), 10–13.

Graham, Hugh Davis. *The Civil Rights Era: Origins and Development of National Policy, 1960–1972.* New York: Oxford University Press, 1990.

Rauh, Joseph L., Jr. "The Role of the Leadership Conference on Civil Rights in the Civil Rights Struggle of 1963–1964." In *The Civil Rights Act of 1964: The Passage of the Law That Ended Racial Segregation.* Ed. Robert D. Loevy. Albany: State University of New York, 1997, 49–76.

Watson, Denton L. *Lion in the Lobby: Clarence Mitchell, Jr.'s Struggle for the Passage of Civil Rights Laws.* New York: William Morrow, 1990.

*James Ralph*

## League of Colored Baseball Clubs

In 1886, an effort began to create a colored baseball league for the following season. One of the leading figures in this venture was Walter S. Brown, reporter for the *Cleveland Gazette*, who served the league as president and secretary. In its inaugural season, the league included eight clubs. The clubs split all gate receipts for league games, which paid for stadium rental, equipment, publicity, travel, food, salaries, and umpires.

Only thirteen games were played before the league folded due to weak leadership and financial difficulties. Brown was unable to secure enough financial backing to help support the league. In addition, travel expenses were high because the entrants were spread from the East to the Midwest. For example, the Boston Resolutes had to travel nearly a thousand miles to play the Falls City Club in Louisville, Kentucky. Each team was expected to play two games in each city before moving on, but, when expenses were not met, most clubs did not honor that second competition. Most of the clubs' rosters consisted of local players who did not attract much attention when they traveled to other cities. Thus, league games failed to draw large crowds.

Though the league did not last, some of the teams continued to play independently with varied degrees of success. Louisville's Falls City club owners constructed a new ballpark for the 1887 season, hoping to build on their success of 1885. By compiling a 22–1 record in 1885, the Falls City team won the black championship in Kentucky. Unfortunately, the team ran into immediate trouble in the new league, losing its opening game to the Boston Resolutes, 10–3.

The Resolutes were a well-known local club, but they did not draw large audiences outside their own neighborhood. In addition to Boston and Louisville, the other founding members of the league were the New York Gorhams, the Philadelphia Pythians, the Lord Baltimores, the Washington Capital Citys, the Pittsburgh Keystones, and the Cincinnati Browns. The key team missing from this lineup was the Cuban Giants, which may have hurt the league's chances of success since many spectators wanted to see this famous team play.

The league opened its 1887 season with great fanfare in Pittsburgh. A parade and a band concert led off the festivities before the Gorhams beat the Keystones, 11–8. The Keystones also played in the league's final game, losing to the Lord Baltimores, 6–2. When ticket receipts dwindled, teams folded, leaving many of their players without money to pay for their return home. Despite the league's failure, Sol White, historian of early black baseball and a member of the Pittsburgh Keystones, believed that the existence of the league indicated a bright future for African American baseball.

**FURTHER READINGS**

*Sol White's History of Colored Baseball, with Other Documents on the Early Black Game, 1886–1936.* Introduction by Jerry Malloy. Lincoln: University of Nebraska Press, 1995.

*Sporting Life* (April–May 1887).

Sullivan, Dean Alan. "The Growth of Sport in a Southern City: A Study of the Evolution of Baseball in Louisville, Kentucky, as an Urban Phenomenon, 1860–1900." M.A. Thesis, George Mason University, 1989.

Wheeler, Lonnie, and John Baskin. "In the Shadows: Cincinnati's Black Baseball Players." *Queen City Heritage* (Summer 1988), 13–19.

*Leslie Heaphy*

## League of Revolutionary Black Workers

Organized in Detroit in 1969, the League of Revolutionary Black Workers (LRBW) functioned as a central coordinating body of the numerous Revolutionary Union Movements (RUMs) that formed in the auto plants, at United Parcel Service, and in the health-care industry in the Detroit area in 1968. The RUMs and the centralized LRBW provided a voice for the large number of black workers in Detroit and other areas of the country. The LRBW led a high-profile existence during the two years it remained active, gaining national and international attention for its dedication to combating racial and class-based oppression. Its eventual demise in 1971 resulted more from internal disagreements over how to sustain the organization than from dwindling interest in the LRBW's message.

The impetus for the creation of the LRBW was a wildcat strike staged by the Dodge Revolutionary Union Movement (DRUM) at Chrysler's Dodge Main plant in 1968. DRUM called the strike to protest the discrimination black workers experienced both on the job and within their union, the United Automobile Workers (UAW). The wildcatters had obtained relatively high-paying auto-plant jobs and had the benefit of union representation, but by 1968 they were working the lowest-paid and most dangerous jobs in the plant, and the UAW was doing nothing to change these conditions. To make matters worse, developments within the auto industry indicated that job conditions were liable to get worse. Dodge exerted constant pressure on its employees to make as many cars as possible with the fewest people. The burden of that dictate fell most heavily on black workers who endured the speed-up of the production line. The UAW, meanwhile, made pay increases rather than improved job conditions its bargaining priority.

In May 1968, four thousand workers, led by DRUM, shut down the Dodge Main plant. The strike and workers' grievances were publicized in papers across the country. Soon after, DRUM called for another shutdown. This time, more than three thousand black workers and some whites walked off the job and picketed both the company's and the UAW's headquarters. Although arrests were made and injunctions filed against individual workers and DRUM, the success of DRUM in publicizing the grievances of black workers inspired the formation of numerous RUMs throughout the country, including ELRUM (Chrysler's Eldon Avenue plant), FRUM (Ford at River Rouge), CADRUM (Cadillac), UPRUM (United Parcel Service), and HRUM (health workers). To coordinate the activities of the RUMs, seven black activists organized the LRBW in 1969.

According to Ernie Allen, the LRBW's director of political education, the organization's vision differed from that of other civil rights organizations. While other civil rights groups concentrated on eliminating what Allen called "the effects of Afroamerican oppression," (Allen 1979, 75) the LRBW focused its energies on eliminating the roots of that oppression. For example, the LRBW viewed police brutality as part of a larger system of class rule. Instead of embroiling the LRBW in an endless battle with brutal police officers, the organization worked toward creating what Allen described as a socialist society "in which all forms of exploitation of human beings by one another would be eliminated forever" (Allen 1979, 75).

The LRBW organized within the community as well as the auto plants, ran a small printing plant and bookstore, produced a film entitled *Finally Got the News*, and provided its members with legal defense. In 1971, seemingly at the height of its influence, the LRBW disbanded. Allen argues that the organization's demise was due, in part, to the inability of the LRBW's leaders to agree on a long-term agenda. Two factions developed among the seven-member executive board. One took a Marxist approach and argued that the oppression black Americans experienced was rooted in class-based inequality. Led by Mike Hamrel, Ken Cockrel, John Watson, Luke Tripp, and John Williams, this faction was more amenable to working with whites. The other faction, led by General Baker and Chuck Wooten, took more of a black nationalist approach and distrusted "black and white unite" strategies. Leaders of the LRBW also disagreed over how to expand the organization. The LRBW's primary constituency was auto workers; thus, the initial goals of the organization involved organizing auto workers and improving job conditions. By 1970, however, that membership declined. General Motors had hired a number of black foremen and had, as a result, weakened the LRBW's criticism that had initially attracted members. Numerous philosophical and practical disagreements among LRBW executive-board members resulted in a lack of responsiveness. This made it difficult for the LRBW to recruit new members, keep old ones, and sustain the financial base necessary to keep its press, bookstore, and organizing activities going.

By December 1970, tensions resulted in a call for reorganization of the LRBW. After heated debates, a meeting to lay out plans for restructuring was set for January 1971. The LRBW's executive board, however, canceled the meeting, and confusion abounded. Eventually, LRBW members stopped supporting the executive board and the LRBW was practically defunct by June 1971. Some members formed splinter groups while others joined the Black Worker's Congress or the Communist League, which later became the Communist Labor Party.

**FURTHER READINGS**

Allen, Ernie. "Dying from the Inside: The Decline of the League of Revolutionary Black Workers." In *They Should Have Served That Cup of Coffee*. Ed. Dick Cluster. Boston: South End, 1979, pp. 71–109.

Georgakas, Dan, and Marvin Surkin. *Detroit I Do Mind Dying*. New York: St. Martin's, 1975.

Geshwender, James. *Class, Race, and Worker Insurgency: The LRBW*. Cambridge: Cambridge University Press, 1977.

*Lisa Phillips*

## League of Revolutionary Struggle

*See* American Negro Labor Congress.

## League of Struggle for Negro Rights

The Central Committee of the American Communist Party (ACP) founded the League of Struggle for Negro Rights (LSNR) in 1930 to replace the defunct American Negro Labor Congress and to organize African American nurses, farmers, laborers, tradesmen, soldiers, small-business people, students, and women along class rather than racial lines. Primarily, the ACP wanted the league to steer black Americans away from nationalist movements, which it believed only divided black and white workers in their common struggle against capitalist oppression. The LSNR adopted a comprehensive platform that demanded complete political equality and an end to racial oppression and lynching. The league recognized the existence of a black nation in the American South and called for the confiscation without compensation of all large capitalist landholdings in the South and their redistribution between African Americans and landless white farmers. Moreover, the LSNR called for a nationwide trade-union movement to include workers of all races, the elimination of Jim Crow laws, the banning of the Ku Klux Klan, and the death penalty for lynchers.

Despite its radical platform and good intentions, the LSNR remained small and largely inactive for the first three years of its existence. The author Langston Hughes served as president of the league, though his was a largely symbolic position. In the summer of 1933, however, things changed dramatically. At a July conference in New York City, the ACP decided to make the LSNR a centerpiece in its drive to recruit African Americans. The league became a militant organization designed to fight for the complete liberation of black people in the United States and to aid African peoples around the world in the global struggle for freedom. James W. Ford, William L. Patterson, and Benjamin Davis Jr. came on board as vice presidents. Richard B. Moore became the league's general secretary, and Harry Haywood sat on the LSNR's National Council.

Cyril Briggs joined to edit the *Negro Liberator*, which became the primary means for the league to spread its doctrine. Under Ford's guidance, the LSNR started organizing at the local level and canvassed neighborhoods to find issues around which it could coordinate community struggles. Within a year, the league leapt from a single branch with thirty-five members to fifteen branches across the country with more than 625 members.

While the LSNR recruited members around local issues, it gained a national reputation through its outspoken stance against lynching violence. In November 1933, the league convened in Baltimore for a two-day anti-lynching conference. Two hundred delegates participated in the Baltimore conference to hear black farmers and sharecroppers tell the world about the grinding poverty and racial violence in the South. In the following year, the LSNR drafted a "Bill for Negro Rights" and promised to fight for congressional passage and enforcement of the bill. The bill reiterated the league's demand that lynchers receive the death penalty and added a section calling for mandatory jail terms for perpetrators of racial discrimination.

The LSNR had added its voice to that of the International Labor Defense and the National Association for the Advancement of Colored People (NAACP) in defense of the nine young men accused of rape in the famous Scottsboro case, and in 1935 it participated in a New York City May Day parade with members of Father Divine's Harlem Peace Mission. Marchers in the parade called for support of the Scottsboro Nine, denounced the spread of fascism around the world, and demanded federal workers' unemployment compensation. The LSNR was becoming an influential force in American cities, and league leaders had high hopes for future growth. In the fall of 1935, however, circumstances beyond the league's control dashed those aspirations.

In September 1935, the *New York Times* revealed that the Soviet Union had been supporting Fascist Italy's war effort against the African nation of Ethiopia with supplies of food and fuel. American Communists, and especially African American Communists, had been denouncing Italian imperialism in Africa. As news of Joseph Stalin's support of Benito Mussolini's Fascist adventurism on the African continent leaked out, the Communists seemed like hypocrites. Black members who had put their faith in the ACP felt betrayed, and many of them abandoned the LSNR. Internal purging of dissenters had sent enough others away that, by the end of 1935, the league had fallen apart. James Ford tried his best to keep the organization going, but by January 1936 he and other

Communist leaders admitted defeat. The LSNR ceased all operations, and the ACP quietly shut down the organization in early 1936.

**FURTHER READINGS**

Haywood, Harry. *Black Bolshevik: Autobiography of an Afro-American Communist.* Chicago: Liberator 1978.

Hutchinson, Earl Ofari. *Blacks and Reds: Race and Class in Conflict, 1919–1990.* East Lansing: Michigan State University Press, 1995.

League of Struggle for Negro Rights. *Equality, Land, and Freedom: A Program for Negro Liberation.* New York: League of Struggle for Negro Rights, 1933.

Record, Wilson. *Race and Radicalism: The NAACP and the Communist Party in Conflict.* Ithaca, N.Y.: Cornell University Press, 1964.

*Gary R. Entz*

## League of Women for Community Service, Boston

In 1918, the League of Women for Community Service (LWCS) was founded in Boston as the Soldiers' Comfort Unit. The group was composed of mostly upper-class black women who provided warm clothes, food baskets, and entertainment for African American troops stationed at nearby Fort Devens during World War I. The women raised money through functions that mobilized the resources of the wider African American community, including bazaars, art shows, and concerts.

After the war, in May 1919, the members decided to continue their work by aiding recent women migrants to Boston. For them and other needy people, the women raised money for coal, rent, holiday dinners, and medical emergencies. The LWCS provided lessons in "mothercraft," helped these women locate work as domestics, nurses, or civil servants, and scheduled social events for them. During the 1920s, the group established a handsome headquarters at 558 Massachusetts Avenue, which served as a meeting hall, temporary residence for recent migrants, library, and social center.

The league's rival, the Women's Service Club, performed similar functions from a nearby office. The two groups represented antagonistic cliques, the origins of which remain obscure. Prominent, older-line women with established roots in the community, including Maria Baldwin, Mrs. J. H. Lewis, Elizabeth Harley Forbes, and Mrs. [Florida?] Ridley, founded the LWCS. Baldwin was the principal of a mostly white Cambridge school. Along

with Josephine St. Pierre Ruffin, she had earlier founded the Women's Era Club, which helped launch the National Association of Colored Women. Lewis was the wife of the wealthiest African American man in Boston, who ran a tailoring establishment. Forbes's husband was a librarian at the West End Library. The group as a whole probably represented the older West End African American community.

These women may have resented leaders of the Women's Service Club, because they largely represented the residents of the newer South End community, which had become the larger area of African American concentration by 1915. The principal leader of the rival group was Mary Evans Wilson. Originally from Atlanta, Wilson was active in the National Association for the Advancement of Colored People (NAACP) whereas none of the LWCS women were members of that group. The LWCS continues to operate but generally keeps a low profile in the city. At its headquarters on Massachusetts Avenue, the LWCS offers classes for new mothers, maintains a library, and holds community forums.

**FURTHER READINGS**

*Black Women's Oral History Project.* Interviews: Melnea Cass, vol. II; Mary Thompson, vol. IX; Muriel Snowden, vol. IX. Westport, Conn.: Meckler, 1991.

Cromwell, Adelaide M. *The Other Brahmins: Boston's Black Upper Class, 1750–1950.* Fayetteville: University of Arkansas Press, 1994.

Minutes, League of Women for Community Service. Schlesinger Library, Radcliffe College, Cambridge, Massachusetts.

Schneider, Mark R. *Boston Confronts Jim Crow, 1890–1920.* Boston: Northeastern University Press, 1997.

*Mark R. Schneider*

## Liberation Committee for Africa

*See* Afro-American Research Institute.

## Liberian Development Association

The Liberian Development Association (LDA) promoted the colonization of African Americans to an area southeast of Liberia, Africa, from November 1907 to August 1908. Organized by prominent middle-class African Americans, the LDA was part of the larger African Emigration Movement that emerged between 1890 and 1910.

The nineteenth century saw repeated attempts to relocate African Americans to Africa because of the discouraging economic, social, and political conditions they faced in the United States. The LDA endorsed progressive emigration of African Americans to Liberia for economic and social betterment of their race. Ultimately, the LDA failed—in part, because of unfavorable living conditions in Liberia.

Inspiration for the LDA came from three sources: Sir Harry H. Johnston's book *Liberia* (1906), which lauded the country as an idyllic retreat; Bishop Henry M. Turner, editor of the *Voice of the People* and a vigorous advocate of African colonization; and Booker T. Washington, founder and president of the Tuskegee Institute in Alabama, who encouraged African Americans to establish a solid footing in technical and industrial training. While Washington argued against emigration, his ideas for racial uplift through education and economic self-sufficiency inspired the LDA, which hoped to attract skilled and educated African Americans to Liberia to make it a utopia for their race.

The idea for the LDA was first formulated in 1901 by Francis H. Warren, president of the Michigan Co-Operative League and editor of the *Detroit Informer*. Warren chose an area three hundred miles southeast of Liberia for colonization and advocated a rational, systematic, and progressive emigration of African Americans to Liberia to make it an independent state with a single-tax constitution. Most African Americans cared little about Warren's single-tax scheme, but some desired to emigrate to escape the poor legal and economic conditions in America. Warren envisioned a great African American republic in Liberia to solve the race problem of the United States.

Charles Alexander, editor and publisher of *Alexander's Magazine*, and Walter F. Walker, writer for that magazine, allied with Warren in November 1907 to arrange colonization of one thousand African Americans. While Warren attempted to find funding for the trip, Walker went to Liberia in March 1908 to gain an accurate picture of conditions there for the African American colonists.

In August 1908, Walker's report on Liberia appeared in *Alexander's Magazine* and sealed the LDA's fate. Walker found a virulent climate, hostile natives, rugged terrain, uncooperative governmental officials, and lack of survival resources in Liberia. He calculated that it would take fifteen years in Liberia for African Americans to gain a lifestyle equivalent to the one they had at the present time in the United States. Walker concluded that it was foolish to go to Liberia expecting to improve one's life. His article was the last one on African emigration to appear in *Alexander's Magazine*. Walker's findings destroyed any hopes that the LDA could succeed in attracting African Americans to Liberia. The LDA disbanded, and Walker remained in Liberia as a missionary while Warren sought other economic reforms in the United States.

**FURTHER READINGS**

Moses, Wilson J. *The Golden Age of Black Nationalism, 1850–1925.* New York and Oxford: Oxford University Press, 1988.

Redkey, Edwin S. *Black Exodus: Black Nationalist and Back-to-Africa Movements, 1890–1910.* New Haven, Conn., and London: Yale University Press, 1969.

*Julieanne Phillips*

## Liberty Party

Established on November 13, 1839, in Warsaw, New York, the Liberty Party was America's first anti-slavery political party. During its eight years of existence, the Liberty Party advocated the abolition of slavery, equality for African Americans, and religious reform through politics. Abolitionists Gerrit Smith and Lewis Tappan, staunch believers in egalitarianism, led the party's creation.

Tappan had previously formed the American and Foreign Anti-Slavery Society to counter William Lloyd Garrison's American Anti-Slavery Society. Critical of Garrison's non-political tactics, Tappan wanted to remove constitutional and legal obstacles preventing emancipation of African Americans. Working through churches and promoting the use of moral suasion to end slavery, members of Tappan's society formed the early membership of the Liberty Party. Black abolitionists, including Samuel Ringgold Ward and Henry Highland Garnet, supported the Liberty Party's efforts.

The Liberty Party's membership consisted primarily of religious proponents who utilized their ballots to protest slavery. Considered the first American political party based on religious principles, the Liberty Party sought to free congregations across the country of the sin of slavery by using biblical scriptures to outline political and social reforms grounded in morality and hoped to achieve a blending of Christianity with government. Liberty Party leaders sought social and political equality for blacks, protesting the deprivation of rights based on race and using such tactics as boycotting southern crops.

Nominating James G. Birney, a former slaveholder turned abolitionist, for president, and his running mate Thomas Morris, the Liberty Party was unsuccessful in the 1840 federal election. Birney received seven thousand votes, approximately 3 percent of the electorate. After the election, the party was split by a faction that argued that the Constitution empowered the federal government to abolish slavery. At the 1843 National Liberty Convention, party members officially objected to the Constitution's fugitive-slave provision. Renominating Birney and Morris, the party peaked in 1844 with sixty thousand votes cast for Birney.

State and local candidates secured some political offices, from which they promoted the Liberty Party's platform. Editors who were members of the party published newspapers, including *Signal of Liberty* and *Clarion of Freedom*, to disseminate party news and attract new members. Prominent people such as Salmon P. Chase affiliated with the party but also split its membership. Chase believed in abolition but stressed that the Liberty Party's goals were unobtainable. He thought that the party should focus on preventing slavery in the territories and encouraged merging with antislavery groups, including the secular Democrats and the Whigs, to form a powerful political coalition.

In 1848, the Liberty Party presidential nominee, New Hampshire Senator John Parker Hale, withdrew from the race when the Free Soil Party emerged as a competitor. Created and controlled by politicians, the Free Soil Party sought specific, achievable political goals unaffected by religious fervor, enabling a larger, more permanent, successful antislavery party. Historians disagree whether the Liberty Party died in 1848 or was incorporated within the Free Soil and Republican parties. Some historians even credit the Liberty Party with providing the political foundation for Abraham Lincoln's election.

The Liberty Party failed for several reasons. Primarily, the party needed more than an anti-slavery platform to gain the support of voters opposed to slavery. Political opponents were powerful, and the major parties were hostile toward the Liberty Party. Voters were apathetic toward third parties, especially an abolition party. The Liberty Party's narrow focus on a religious mission alienated voters who, although antislavery advocates, did not consider slavery a priority issue over socioeconomic and cultural concerns promoted by other parties. The Liberty Party lacked unity, being split by religious and ideological disputes that rendered leaders powerless. Party policy chose

principles and accompanying demise over politics and popularity.

## FURTHER READINGS

Bretz, Julian P. "The Economic Background of the Liberty Party." *American Historical Review* 34 (January 1929), 250–264.

Fladeland, Betty L. *James Gillespie Birney: Slaveholder to Abolitionist.* Ithaca, N.Y.: Cornell University Press, 1955. Rpt., Westport, Conn.: Greenwood, 1969.

Kraut, Alan Morton. "Partisanship and Principles: The Liberty Party in Antebellum Political Culture." In *Crusaders and Compromisers: Essays on the Relationship of the Antislavery Struggle to the Antebellum Party System.* Ed. Alan M. Kraut. Westport, Conn.: Greenwood, 1983, pp. 71–99.

Sewell, Richard H. *Ballots for Freedom: Antislavery Politics in the United States, 1837–1860.* New York: Oxford University Press, 1976. Rpt., New York: Norton, 1980.

Volpe, Vernon L. *Forlorn Hope of Freedom: The Liberty Party in the Old Northwest, 1838–1848.* Kent, Ohio, and London: Kent State University Press, 1990.

*Elizabeth D. Schafer*

## Library Company of Colored Persons, Philadelphia

On January 1, 1833, ten African Americans established the Philadelphia Library Company of Colored Persons. The company was the first successful literary institution established by and for African Americans in the United States. The Library Company collected a wide variety of literary works for the benefit of its members, who paid a one-time membership fee of $1 and monthly dues of twenty-five cents thereafter. By 1836, the Library Company was incorporated; by 1838, its collection contained six hundred volumes, pamphlets, and periodicals largely obtained through donations. In addition to providing African Americans with access to literature, the Library Company also introduced a series of debates to expose its members to historical and other research and to provide practice in public speaking. Discussions of diverse subjects were held on Tuesday of each week. The Library Company was housed in the basement of the St. Thomas African Episcopal Church, where its minister, Right Reverend Bishop White, took an interest in, and contributed to, the collection.

By 1841, the company had approximately one hundred members, and its library contained valuable historical, scientific, and encyclopedic volumes. The library continued to operate through the 1860s. In 1862, Thomas Morris Chester, an outspoken black activist, addressed the twenty-ninth-anniversary celebration of the Philadelphia Library Company. In his talk, Chester emphasized the importance of literary contributions in the development of "self-respect and pride of race."

The Library Company provided a place of learning and intellectual exchange for Philadelphia's black community and was the first library established for the benefit of African Americans.

**FURTHER READINGS**

Sinnette, Elinor Des Verney, W. Paul Coates, and Thomas C. Battle, eds. *Black Bibliophiles and Collectors: Preserves of Black History.* Washington, D.C.: Howard University Press, 1990.

Willson, Joseph. *Sketches of the Higher Classes of Colored Society in Philadelphia,* rpt. By a Southerner. 1841 Philadelphia: Historic Publications, 1969.

*Loretta E. Bass*

## The Links Incorporated

On November 9, 1946, Margaret Hawkins, Sarah Scott, Frances Atkinson, Katie Green, Marion Minton, Lillian Stanford, Myrtle Manigault Stratton, Lillian Wall, and Dorothy Wright gathered in Philadelphia to form The Links Incorporated. The group's purpose was to link women in a chain of friendship, to provide social and charitable services, and to foster intercultural activities. The name "Links" was suggested by Lillian Wall, one of the original charter members, as a symbol of the women's enduring and lasting friendship. The club soon expanded to other cities and states, including Atlantic City, New Jersey (1947); Washington, D.C. (1948); Baltimore (1948); Pittsburgh (1948); Petersburg, Virginia (1948); St. Louis (1948); Wilmington, Delaware (1948); Wilson, Rocky Mount, and Tarboro, North Carolina (1948); Dayton, Ohio (1949); Central Jersey (1949); Greater New York (1949); North Jersey (1949); and Raleigh, North Carolina (1949). The chapters promote and engage in educational, civic, and cultural activities to improve the quality of life in each community.

Incorporated in 1951 in Trenton, New Jersey, The Links supports a variety of educational and social programs, such as Service to Youth, the Arts, National Trends and Service, and International Trends and Service. All local chapters participate in programs that address particular needs in their communities and areas. The group's membership comprises teachers, principals, homemakers, lawyers, judges, morticians, editors, beauty consultants, independent entrepreneurs, and professionals in various health professions. The Links characteristically has been guided by an array of talented, educated, socially well connected middle-class black women. The national presidents of The Links have included Sarah S. Scott, Margaret R. Hawkins, Pauline Weeden Maloney, Vivian J. Beamon, Helen G. Edmonds, Pauline A. Ellison, Julia B. Purnell, Dolly D. Adams, Regina J. Frazier, Marion Sutherland, and Patricia Russell McLoud.

The Links has made substantial contributions to the following organizations: the National Association for the Advancement of Colored People (NAACP), the NAACP Legal Defense and Educational Fund, the National Urban League, the United Negro College Fund, Sickle Cell Disease Research, and Project Lead.

The Links Incorporated is a national nonpartisan volunteer public-service organization with a membership of more than ten thousand women in 270 chapters in forty states, the District of Columbia, the Bahamas, and Germany. The Links Incorporated and The Links Foundation dedicated its national headquarters on November 16, 1985, at 1200 Massachusetts Avenue, N. W., in Washington, D.C. The Links Incorporated has made a profound contribution to philanthropic causes, working on behalf of minorities—and youth especially—in America.

**FURTHER READINGS**

Bowen, Nancy T. *Southern Area History: The Links, Incorporated, 1949–1989.* Chapel Hill, N.C.: Colonial, 1989.

Parker, Marjorie H. *A History of The Links, Incorporated.* Washington, D.C.: The Links, Incorporated, 1982.

Yancy, Dorothy Cowser. "The Links, Inc." In *Black Women in America: An Historical Encyclopedia.* Ed. Darlene Clark-Hine, Elsa Barkley-Brown, and Rosalyn Terborg-Penn. New York: Carlson, 1993.

*André D. Vann*

## Little Rock, Arkansas: Civic, Literary, and Mutual Aid Associations

By the turn of the twentieth century, black Arkansans were nearly 30 percent of the state's population and almost half of the population of the capital city of Little

Rock. Pine Bluff, in adjacent Pulaski County, was home to Arkansas Agricultural, Mechanical, and Normal College (AM&N), land-grant institution opened in 1875 and the site of black public higher education in the state. The black community of Little Rock comprised a stable working class employed in domestic service and unskilled labor and a diverse middle-class leadership concentrated in religious, women's, educational, and fraternal community building.

An important segment of Little Rock's black middle class had origins in the antebellum history of the city. William Wallace Andrews, owned by the Chester Ashley family, opened the first black school in the city in 1863. The school was incorporated into the city school system in 1869 and Andrews's daughter, Charlotte Andrews Stephens, became its first black teacher in the same year. Stephens and her mother, Caroline Andrews, were also charter members of the Benevolent Society of United Sisters, No. 1. The society was the women's auxiliary of Wesley Chapel M.E. Church, also established by William Wallace Andrews. The membership of sixty women provided nursing care, sick and death benefits, and funeral expenses.

The largest denomination in the state, the Arkansas Baptist Convention, organized the *Baptist Vanguard*, a weekly newspaper in 1882, and founded Arkansas Baptist College in 1884, both in Little Rock. The publication of the paper was transferred to the college in 1887. The Reverend J. A. Booker, appointed president of the college in the same year, also served as editor of the newspaper. The Arkansas Baptist Convention also endorsed the statewide Emancipation celebration that African Americans staged in Little Rock's West End Park in 1897. Attended by Governor Dan Jones, Mifflin W. Gibbs, and the Reverend E. C. Morris, the event marked the recognition of the sixty-fourth anniversary of the liberation of slaves in the British West Indies and the thirty-fourth anniversary of Abraham Lincoln's Emancipation Proclamation.

The Women's Baptist Missionary Association of the state Baptist Convention established an Old Ladies' Home in the city in the 1890s. A nine-member board of guardians supervised management of the home and included the president of the state women's association, Darthula W. Thompson, member of Mt. Pleasant Baptist Church and the wife of Green W. Thompson, a black Republican; and Mattie P. Gaines, wife of Dr. D. B. Gaines, pastor of Mt. Pleasant in Little Rock. During the first decade of the twentieth century, Mifflin W. Gibbs, a black Republican businessman and Baptist, donated a new site for the

home, and it was renamed the Gibbs Home for Elderly Women.

The Baptist Young People's Union (BYPU), also part of the state convention, sponsored the Sunshine Band in Little Rock. The children's choir, with its members drawn from local congregations, frequently sang for the Old Ladies' Home.

Middle-class black women also grouped themselves according to profession and class in providing services for the community and themselves. Carrie Still Shepperson, the mother of William Grant Still, the composer and musician, was from Georgia and graduated from Atlanta University in 1886. In 1896, after the death of her husband, Carrie Fambro Still moved to Little Rock, where her mother and sister were living. In 1904, she married Charles B. Shepperson, a railway postal clerk, and continued her teaching career at Little Union School (1877). She taught English at Capital Hill School (1902) and Gibbs High School (1907).

At the turn of the century, the Little Rock public library did not admit African Americans, and Capital Hill School lacked a library. Shepperson initiated a school extravaganza that was so successful that it became an annual school event. The spring shows were held at the school until 1917, when Shepperson secured the downtown Kempner Theater for two nights. The desire of the black community to contest normal space arrangements of the Kempner, which restricted African Americans to the balcony, and to support the acquisition of school assets, in opposition to the racial status quo, combined to account for the success of the 1917 show.

Educated black women who were teachers formed literary societies. Carrie Still Shepperson was a member of the Lotus Club, a literary forum. A group of twelve city public school teachers organized the Bay View Reading Club. The first National Association of Colored Women's (NACW) club in the state was organized in Little Rock in 1897. Charlotte Andrews Stephens was a charter member. The NACW City Federation of Little Rock clubs, formed in 1905, included the Frances Harper Club, established in 1907. The founding group included Lothaire Scott Green, the mother of Ernest Green, who integrated Central High School in 1957 as one of the Little Rock Nine. Mattie P. Gaines formed the Provident Relief Club in 1914. The federation also included the Sunshine Charity Club (1910) and the Rosa Morris Club. The city federation assumed full support for the Gibbs Home for Elderly Women beginning in 1908. The home had ten rooms and was valued at $2,000 in 1909.

John E. Bush, Chester W. Keatts, and twelve other black men organized the Grand Mosaic Templars of America in 1882. Incorporated the next year, the fraternal and benevolent order promoted good character, education, employment, and health among black men and provided life insurance for them. The order also established a women's auxiliary. In 1884, Bush and Keatts organized the Mosaic Building and Loan Association as a subsidiary of the order, to assist members in financing homes and providing secured loans. The association was dissolved in 1895, when the order assumed its responsibilities. The order published the *Mosaic Guide*, the official newspaper, for more than thirty years. By 1920, the Templars had affiliate temples in twenty-one states, nearly forty thousand members, and assets of almost $200,000. The national headquarters in Little Rock consisted of two adjoining buildings: a four-story office building and a two-story annex.

In January 1920, Drs. J. G. Thornton and J. W. Suggs, and J. H. McConico, president of the Little Rock branch of the National Association for the Advancement of Colored People (NAACP), organized the Citizens Defense Fund Committee (CDFC) to raise funds for a legal defense of the twelve black men sentenced to death and the sixty-three others sentenced to lesser terms in connection with the 1919 Elaine riot. The CDFC raised and contributed more money toward the legal defense of the black men than the NAACP.

Amelia Bradford Ives, graduate of Little Rock Union High School in 1898 and of Fisk University and a colleague of Carrie Still Shepperson at Gibbs High School, established a branch of the National Urban League in 1937.

During World War II, the United States Army assigned the all-black 92nd Engineers Battalion to Camp Robinson, near Little Rock. In March 1942, city police shot and killed a member of the battalion, Sergeant Thomas B. Foster. Little Rock officials, including the chief of police and the county coroner, ruled the shooting justifiable homicide. A group of black citizens, the Negro Citizens Committee of Little Rock (NCCLR), initiated an independent investigation of the shooting. The NCCLR report concluded that the shooting was unlawful and called for a federal inquiry. Although no indictments resulted from the federal investigation, the Little Rock Police Department hired eight black policemen.

**FURTHER READINGS**

Cortner, Richard C. *A Mob Intent on Death: The NAACP and the Arkansas Riot Cases.* Middletown, Conn.: Wesleyan University Press, 1988.

Gordon, Fon Louise. *Caste and Class: The Black Experience in Arkansas, 1880–1920.* Athens: University of Georgia Press, 1995.

Smith, C. Calvin. *War and Wartime Changes: The Transformation of Arkansas, 1940–1945.* Fayetteville: University of Arkansas Press, 1986.

*Fon Louise Gordon*

## London Emancipation Committee

*See* London Emancipation Society.

## London Emancipation Society

British abolitionists F. W. Chesson and George Thompson founded the London Emancipation Society (LES) as the London Emancipation Committee (LEC) in June 1859. Initially, the LEC worked to advance the cause of American abolitionists; however, the group's goal changed following the announcement of Abraham Lincoln's preliminary Emancipation Proclamation on September 22, 1862. After President Lincoln made the emancipation of slaves an official war aim, the LEC adopted the name LES on November 11, 1862, and worked to counteract pro-Confederate sympathies in Britain and to drum up support for the Union. British abolitionists rallied behind Lincoln by sponsoring lectures and publishing pamphlets that explained the connection between the war and slavery. Women formed the Ladies' London Emancipation Society, which independently undertook similar activities.

When the LEC emerged, it served as a national organization for British supporters of American abolitionist William Lloyd Garrison's faction, which promoted equal leadership opportunities for women, nonviolent tactics such as moral suasion, and voluntary abstention from politics to protest political corruption. LEC's rival, the British and Foreign Anti Slavery Society (BFASS), denied women leadership roles in the abolitionist movement and urged its members to rely on voting, petitioning, and lobbying to effect change. Decrying BFASS's exclusion of women and its growing inactivity in the late 1850s, Chesson and Thompson formed the LEC in June 1859. The LEC attracted a diverse membership, including white Parliament member John Stuart Mill; leading black abolitionists such as William Craft, Ellen Craft, and Sarah Parker Remond; women's rights activist Elizabeth Reid; and white abolitionists such as Dennis McDonnell.

When the American Civil War started in 1861, the British government declared its neutrality and refused to recognize the Confederacy. Although most Britons opposed slavery, a large number initially favored the South. Some Britons expressed concern about the kingdom's dependence on Confederate cotton, and particularly the Irish championed the South's right to self-determination. British abolitionists, disappointed that Lincoln failed to include the abolition of slavery among the Union's war aims, favored the North but initially withheld unconditional support of the Union.

After Lincoln announced his preliminary Emancipation Proclamation on November 11, 1862, many British abolitionists who had previously been lukewarm in their support of the Union declared their unreserved allegiance to the North. Troubled by British press reports that favored the South and a growing number of pro-Confederate discussion groups that sprang up in virtually every British city, the LES tried to counteract pro-Confederate sentiments in Britain. In an effort to educate the British public, the society dispatched lecturers and published pamphlets that identified the cause of the Civil War as "Southern aggression" and explained the relationship between slavery and the war.

The LES worked closely with the Ladies' London Emancipation Society, Britain's first national, exclusively female, abolitionist organization. In March 1863, Mentia Taylor, a leader in the British women's suffrage movement, had established the Ladies' Society in response to an open letter from Harriet Beecher Stowe. In her 1862 letter, the author of *Uncle Tom's Cabin* had implored British women to take an interest in American slavery and to support the Union. While the Ladies' Society collaborated with the LES, it remained autonomous, insisting that slavery was "a question especially and deeply interesting to women." Executive committee members of the Ladies' Society included veteran abolitionists such as Mary Estlin, LES board members Sarah Parker Remond and Ellen Craft, George Thompson's daughter and F. W. Chesson's wife, Amelia Chesson, and Harriet Martineau, as well as less experienced antislavery activists. Most of the members of the Ladies' Society were committed to the women's rights movement and specifically emphasized the degrading effects of slavery on black women. The Ladies' Society also contributed funds to the London Freedmen's Aid Society, which emerged on April 24, 1863, to assist the freedpeople of the American South.

It is difficult to determine the effect LES and the Ladies' Society pamphlets and lecturers had on transforming British public opinion. Yet, the large number of auxiliary organizations that sprang up in virtually every city in Great Britain may indicate the groups' success. The efforts of these groups were also noticed by the U.S. minister in London, who informed Secretary of State William Seward that 114 pro-Union meetings had been held throughout Great Britain. Acknowledging the work of the LES, Garrisonians invited activist George Thompson to a speaking tour of the United States following the war. During his 1865 tour, Thompson visited the White House and accompanied Garrison to the raising of the Union flag over Fort Sumter, which symbolically ended the Civil War where it had started.

The LES thus completed its mission of countering pro-Confederate sympathies in Great Britain and disbanded shortly after the end of the Civil War in 1865. The Ladies' Society opened its membership to men, joined the freedmen's aid movement, and changed its name to the London Negro Aid Society.

### FURTHER READINGS

Midgley, Clare. *Women Against Slavery: The British Campaigns, 1780–1870.* New York: Routledge, 1992.

Temperley, Howard. *British Antislavery, 1833–1870.* Columbia: University of South Carolina Press, 1972.

*Kristine Boeke*

## London Negro Aid Society
*See* London Emancipation Society.

## Lone Star Medical, Dental, and Pharmaceutical Association

Established in Galveston, Texas, in 1866, the Lone Star Medical, Dental, and Pharmaceutical Association (LSMDPA) provided leadership and professional organization for African Americans in health-care professions in the state of Texas for almost a century.

The association was initiated by two Galveston physicians, J. H. Wilkins and L. M. Wilkins. The Wilkins brothers, joined by pharmacist J. S. Cameron of San Antonio, invited the state's other black health-care professionals to an organizational meeting. In August 1886, twelve black men representing nine communities in the eastern half of Texas gathered in Galveston and formed the first state medical association for African Americans. The LSMDPA attempted to join the all-white Texas Medical Association (TMA), but the organization rejected the request. During the 1880s, membership in the LSMDPA grew slowly, and the group met only occasionally in the 1890s.

In 1901, J. H. Wilkins, who had moved to Houston, cooperated with five men from other towns across East Texas to reorganize and revive the association during a gathering in Austin. As a result of their efforts, the LSMDPA experienced considerable growth and counted close to three hundred members by the late 1920s, making it perhaps the largest state medical organization for African Americans in the United States. Members included physicians, dentists, pharmacists, and nurses, with a woman, A. E. Hughes, serving as president in 1934–1935.

In the twentieth century, members of the LSMDPA met regularly to exchange information about new trends in medical methods and to draw public attention to African American health concerns. In the 1920s, the organization sought to improve medical care and training standards at hospitals and nursing schools open to African Americans by conducting visits and offering guidance. Moreover, Presidents L. G. Pinkston, T. L. Hunter, and J. R. Moore worked with LSMDPA members to gather information and joined with antituberculosis and interracial groups to lobby the Texas Legislature to provide funding for a tuberculosis sanitorium for black patients. In 1937, their efforts were successful, and the state authorized funding for such an institution, which also provided some staff positions for African Americans. During the 1930s and 1940s, the association cooperated with Prairie View College to hold post-graduate assemblies for black doctors.

Throughout the twentieth century, the LSMDPA invited white doctors to make presentations at the association's meetings. In 1939, as a result of increased contacts between black and white medical professionals, the TMA recognized the LSMDPA. In 1950, the year the United States Supreme Court's decision in the *Sweatt v. Painter* court case desegregated higher education in Texas, the TMA moved to increase cooperation with the Lone Star association. By 1955, after the U.S. Supreme Court's *Brown v. Board of Education* decision began to desegregate public schools, the TMA started to accept black doctors as members. The TMA's admission of African Americans did not bring about the demise of the LSMDPA but gradually reduced its membership to about 250 by the end of the 1950s. Membership continued to decline as dentists and pharmacists left the LSMDPA to establish separate professional organizations in the 1960s. Membership in the LSMDPA dropped below a hundred in the 1980s.

**FURTHER READINGS**

Chatman, Joseph A. *The Lone Star State Medical, Dental and Pharmaceutical History.* n.p. 1959.

Hardman, Peggy. "The Anti-Tuberculosis Crusade and the Texas African American Community, 1900–1950." Ph.D. diss., Texas Tech University, 1997.

*Alwyn Barr*

## Los Angeles: Civic, Literary, and Mutual Aid Associations

More than half of the founders of Los Angeles in 1781 had African ancestry, yet it took a century before the town had significant black organizations. Among the earliest black groups were the First African Methodist Episcopal and the Second Baptist Churches, formed in the mid-1880s. Before the end of that decade, black Republicans and Democrats established political committees, suggesting that the city's black residents were as interested in joining activities of the general population as they were in creating separate "race organizations."

By the turn of the century, however, a variety of associations emerged that were uniquely intended for African Americans. The major cause of this shift was their exclusion from white clubs or their segregation into separate branches. In 1896, black women set up the National Association of Colored Women (NACW), which by the early 1900s had a Los Angeles branch. Until the 1960s, the NACW remained the premier African American women's organization, spawning a variety of social-service, cultural, and charitable associations. Black residents of Los Angeles also established a "Colored" Young Men's Christian Association (YMCA) in 1906 and a separate black Young Women's Christian Association (YWCA) a few years later. Black churches grew to twelve by 1909, some of which had benevolent associations and literary societies. Churches facilitated the start of black social-service groups such as the Sojourner Truth Industrial Club (1904), a home for orphaned girls and a training school for domestic servants, and the Women's Day Nursery Association (1907).

Los Angeles African Americans also formed associations not tied to the church. An early political and civic organization was the Afro-American League, formed in 1893. Renamed the "Afro-American Council," it continued until 1915, but after 1903 it was overshadowed by the Los Angeles Forum. This association was a "model lyceum" that provided its members with the opportunity to explore ideas for racial advancement. Though led by community elites, the forum was open to all classes and functioned until 1942. Also spreading rapidly were black fraternal lodges. By 1914, Los Angeles had five orders and twenty-nine lodges. The fraternal organizations promoted black business enterprises, an interest they shared with the Businessmen's Association, a branch of the National Negro Business League (NNBL), formed in 1902. This era also saw the emergence of state clubs that reunited blacks from southern places of origin. Most of these groups emphasized self-help and socializing recent migrants.

In the early twentieth century, black residents of Los Angeles also formed several protest organizations. The longest lasting was the Los Angeles branch of the National Association for the Advancement of Colored People (NAACP), created in 1913 as a nearly all-black group. The NAACP became the most rapidly growing black association, setting up branches in eleven Southern California cities by 1940. More militant in rhetoric but short-lived were the All-American League, formed in 1915, and the Progressive Business League. Their campaign to "Get Together" and promote race enterprise was continued by Marcus Garvey's Universal Negro Improvement Association (UNIA), which established a Los Angeles chapter in 1921. Led by "second-level" community figures, the chapter soon split with Garvey's national office in New York City, but it continued to function until 1930. During the 1920s, a group of Tuskegee Institute alumni established a National Urban League branch. Focusing initially on character building and delinquency prevention, its paid staff paved the way for African Americans to join the ranks of human-service professionals.

During the 1920s, Los Angeles blacks formed several political associations, including a Lincoln League and a Republican Protective League to organize GOP voters and a Colored Democratic League. At the end of the decade, the Los Angeles Civic League was the first African American group to promote interracial work, while Republicans formed the Women's Political Study Group, which became one of the most active black political organizations of the 1930s and 1940s. Most of these associations were composed of community elites and located along Central Avenue, traits that carried over to 120 social groups, including tennis clubs, musical associations, lyceums and dramatic groups, and dance clubs. The last type reflected the blossoming of Central Avenue as a place of evolving jazz and nightclubs. During the 1920s, college fraternities and sororities also arrived in Los Angeles, growing to ten affiliates by 1929.

The Great Depression shifted the activities of African American associations, and they increasingly addressed the problems of the unemployed. The Urban League became prominent for training and placing African Americans in relief programs. Local churches helped by setting up welfare departments and providing assistance for black migrants, who continued coming to Southern California. Relief programs often slighted African Americans, insisting that black workers be used only on "Negro projects" and segregating them from whites. The local NAACP devoted much of its attention and energy protesting such incidents throughout the 1930s. It resisted the influence of Communists and labor groups, but in 1935 the National Negro Congress (NNC) introduced a platform that promoted trade unionism and attracted black community leaders.

The World War II influx of African Americans contributed to the growth of the city's black organizations, especially the NAACP, which enjoyed huge increases in membership. Yet, black employment in defense plants accentuated job and housing discrimination, which led to the formation of the Negro Victory Committee in 1942. Using mass marches and negotiations, the committee opened job training and key employment sectors to African Americans. Its efforts were supplemented by a worker-based Shipyard Workers Committee for Equal Participation (SWCEP), which forced the Boilermakers Union to grant blacks full membership and skilled jobs.

The involvement of African American workers led to political coalitions of labor, white liberals, and minority groups. A leading figure in this movement was the editor of the *California Eagle*, Charlotta Bass. The 1943 Zoot Suit riots led local authorities to push for the improvement of interracial relations, resulting in the creation of the Council for Civic Unity and the L.A. County Commission for Human Relations (LACCHR). Labor-Left groups, epitomized by the Civil Rights Congress, pushed for fair-employment laws and open housing, but anti-Communist investigations after the war led to the demise of that organization as well as the NNC and a marked decline in membership in the NAACP. The Urban League and the LACCHR continued to engage in educational work in the field of race relations throughout the 1950s.

The postwar civil rights movement revived activist organizations, particularly the Congress of Racial Equality (CORE). By the late 1950s, the Nation of Islam had established local mosques. Black nationalism also received a great boost from the 1965 Watts Uprising. In the aftermath of the riot, Ron Karenga founded United Slaves (US), a cultural nationalist group that set up Kwanzaa; the Black Panther Party established a branch in the city; and African Americans launched the Watts Summer Festival. But efforts at African American unity failed because of ideological differences. This was best epitomized by a shootout between US and the Panthers in 1969. The most lasting associations in South Central proved to be gangs, whose numbers grew steadily to about 100,000 by 1990.

The popularity of nationalist organizations declined in the late 1970s, and African American associations in Los Angeles increasingly mirrored the growing gap between impoverished South Central, the middle-class West Side, and growing affluent suburban communities. In the latter, organizations such as 100 Black Men encouraged future business and professional leaders, while social organizations like The Links Incorporated and Jack and Jill of America, Inc., met the yearning for community among a dispersed population. The 1992 riot, sparked by the acquital of police officers who had been charged with assaulting the black motorist Rodney King, led to the formation of the Brotherhood Crusade and the Black United Fund, which pressured for African-American employment in the rebuilding of neighborhoods destroyed during the riot. The Black Business Association of Los Angeles and the African-American Entertainment Coalition raised funds for new businesses and community-based programs. These are but the latest evidence that African Americans in Los Angeles have no lack of associations. Their historic problem has been forging a unified and consistent plan of activities for them.

## FURTHER READINGS

Anderson, E. Frederick. *The Development of Leadership and Organization Building in the Black Community of Los Angeles from 1900 through World War II*. Saratoga, Calif.: Century Twenty One, 1980.

Bond, J. Max. *The Negro in Los Angeles*. San Francisco: R and E Research Associates, 1972.

de Graaf, Lawrence B., and Quintard Taylor. "African Americans in California History, California in African American History: An Overview." In *Seeking El Dorado: African Americans in California, 1769–1997*. Ed. Lawrence B. de Graaf, Kevin Mulroy, and Quintard Taylor. Urbana: University of Illinois Press, forthcoming.

Los Angeles Urban League. *On the Move for Seven Decades and Still Going Strong*. Los Angeles: Urban League, 1991.

Tolbert, Emory J. *The UNIA and Black Los Angeles: Ideology and Community in the American Garvey Movement*. Los Angeles: Center for Afro-American Studies, 1980.

*Lawrence B. de Graaf*

## Lost Found Nation of Islam

*See* Nation of Islam.

## Lost-Found Nation of Islam in the Wilderness of North America

*See* Nation of Islam.

## Lott Carey Baptist Foreign Mission Convention

In 1897, twenty-eight black Baptist ministers founded the Lott Carey Baptist Foreign Mission Convention, at Shiloh Baptist Church in Washington, D.C. The convention derives its name and spiritual legacy from an enterprising former slave. Born ca. 1780 in Charles City County, Virginia, Lott Carey later found himself laboring in a Richmond tobacco factory, where he rose through the ranks to become a shipping clerk, a position that allowed him to purchase his freedom and that of his family. Listening to sermons from the gallery of Richmond's First Baptist Church awakened in Carey the desire for clearer religious understanding and literacy. Self-instruction and night school aided him in both these quests. Licensed as a minister by the First Baptist Church, Carey preached all over central and eastern Virginia. In 1821, his desire to do missionary work took him to the newly organized West African colony of Liberia, where a small group of black Baptists had decided to settle. The first American missionary to Africa, Carey remained Liberia's spiritual leader until his death in 1828.

In 1840, African American Baptists in New England and the Middle Atlantic states created the American Baptist Missionary Convention (ABMC) in response to African requests for missionaries and resources to continue the work of Lott Carey. This began an era that witnessed the rise and decline of various black Baptist missionary groups such as the Western and Southern Missionary Baptist Convention (1864), organized to serve areas of the nation not served by the ABMC. In 1866, these two groups merged to form the Consolidated American Baptist Missionary Convention, which disintegrated in 1878 due to competition from other regional missionary organizations. The Baptist Foreign Mission Convention (1880) and the Baptist National Educational Convention (1893) were two more short-lived efforts to unite the work of black Baptists in the United States. Subsequent to 1893, missionary work among black Baptists declined, falling into what some have characterized as the "Dark Age" of foreign evangelical efforts.

By 1897, however, the stage was set for a new organization. When disagreements among prominent black Baptist clergymen splintered old alliances, some of the disaffected ministers decided to hold a meeting at the Shiloh Baptist Church in Washington, D.C. Those who gathered there in December 1897 desired a convention that focused primarily on foreign missionary work and that sought cooperation with any and all Baptist organizations, including white Baptist congregations. Out of this meeting emerged the Lott Carey Baptist Foreign Mission Convention, established by twenty-eight clergymen to reflect the spirit of Reverend Lott Carey.

Celebrating its centennial in 1997, the Lott Carey Convention remains headquartered in Washington, D.C., and dedicated to foreign missionary work as well as local outreach programs. Its principal objectives are evangelizing foreign non-Christians and educating them for leadership roles in their own societies. The convention consists of local and state Baptist groups representing sixteen states and the District of Columbia. It conducts an annual meeting each September and publishes quarterly the *Lott Carey Herald*, the official organ of the convention. It has ministered to people in Haiti, Russia, and South Africa and continues its labors with more than one hundred missionaries serving in areas such as Guyana, India, Kenya, Liberia, and Nigeria.

## FURTHER READINGS

Fitts, Leroy. *The Lott Carey Legacy of African American Missions*. Baltimore: Gateway, 1993.

*Lott Carey Herald*. Washington, D.C.: Lott Carey Baptist Foreign Mission Society.

*Norman C. McLeod Jr.*

## Louisiana Council on Human Relations

The Louisiana Council on Human Relations (LCHR), one of twelve state Councils on Human Relations established by the Southern Regional Council, succeeded the Louisiana Division of the Southern Regional Council in 1955.

The LCHR was a nonpolitical, nondenominational, interracial organization that worked to improve economic, civic, and racial conditions in Louisiana. As an incorporated nonprofit organization, the LCHR derived its financial support from membership dues, contributions, and grants from the Fund for the Republic.

Operating through seven district chapters, the LCHR conducted research projects to secure information and statistics about the state's standard of living, education, government, economy, employment, housing, health, law enforcement, voting, poverty, labor relations, and trans-

portation. The LCHR then publicized its findings through lecturers, radio, and television and the publication of pamphlets, newspapers, periodicals, and its monthly newsletter, *Research in Action*. Meanwhile, local chapters evaluated community problems and worked with civic, business, religious, and public officials to improve human relations. In 1960, the LCHR initiated the organization of Save Our Schools, Inc., which worked to prevent the closing of the state's public schools despite pressures from segregationists. The LCHR also championed equal access to public accommodations, equal employment opportunities, and admission of African Americans to schools of higher education. The LCHR experienced organizational difficulties that led to its demise in the early 1960s; however, the council was reinstated in 1968. It continues to operate, though in slightly altered form, remaining true to its initial purpose of working for better human relations in the state.

## FURTHER READING

Southern Regional Council Papers, Series IV: State Councils on Human Relations, 1946–1968, Reels 143–144. Special Collections. Robert W. Woodruff Library, Atlanta University Center, Atlanta, Georgia.

*Kimberly E. Nichols*

## Louisville, Kentucky: Civic, Literary, and Mutual Aid Associations

Civic, literary, and mutual aid associations were the key to the everyday survival and growth of the black community in Louisville, Kentucky. As black residents became more active in local politics through the local chapter of the National Association for the Advancement of Colored People (NAACP) and other organizations, they also built an impressive collection of social-service agencies and mutual aid associations. These organizations, along with a robust black press, helped African Americans in Louisville traverse the terrain of the Jim Crow South and demonstrate their community's basic strengths and their own human dignity.

A gateway to the Midwest, Louisville stood as both a beacon of hope for African Americans seeking to escape the oppression of the South and as a frontier outpost of the society they were trying to leave behind. The city's dual nature as both a place of reported civility and a bulwark of segregation shaped the evolution of African American community organizations throughout the nineteenth and twentieth centuries. Beneath a façade of "polite racism" lay a brutal reality of interracial conflict and the economic, political, and social subordination of African Americans. Isolated from whites-only political clubs, schools, hospitals, community centers, and neighborhoods, black Louisvillians created their own web of civic, literary, and mutual aid associations to combat the evils of Jim Crow and the doctrine of black inferiority.

Following the Civil War, Louisville's black population increased and became politically more active. In December 1891, the city's black residents launched the Anti-Separate Coach Movement (ASCM) to challenge segregation laws. Protesting a state law that created separate accommodations for blacks and whites on trains, the ASCM and the Reverend W. H. Anderson of Evansville, Indiana, sued the Louisville and Nashville Railroad for $15,000 and eventually pleaded their case before the United States Supreme Court. Although the ASCM's efforts to overturn the law were unsuccessful, the group's actions set a precedent for later reform efforts.

In the realm of party politics, the most significant black challenge to the hegemony of the white-dominated Democratic and Republican parties came in the form of the Lincoln Independent Party (LIP) in 1921. Organized by young leaders including A. D. Porter, Wilson Lovett, Willis Cole, and William Warley, the LIP attacked the Democrats and the Republicans for failing to address the issues and concerns of Louisville's African Americans. In November 1921, the LIP ran a full slate of candidates for local offices; however, none of the candidates won. Yet, following the election, Louisville's Republican administration started to hire blacks in clerical positions and as police officers and firefighters.

Bolstered by the gains created by LIP pressure, young leaders like Warley helped strengthen the most important civic organization in Louisville's black community, the NAACP. The Louisville branch of the NAACP was an all-black organization that agitated against segregation in the courts and demonstrated against Jim Crow statutes in the streets. Founded in 1914, the Louisville chapter of the NAACP quickly won victories against residential segregation with the U.S. Supreme Court's *Buchanan v. Warley* decision in 1917, and it stopped the showing of the controversial film *The Birth of a Nation* in 1918. More militant and confrontational than the black leaders of Louisville's Urban League and the Commission on Interracial Cooperation, the members of the NAACP protested Ku Klux Klan activities, racial violence, and employment discrimination. Following World War II, African Americans made further progress on the political front in Louisville, and, by the late 1960s, most of the

local discrimination statutes crumbled before black protest. African Americans also proved to be an important political force, and black Louisvillians voted several black political leaders into local and state offices, including Mae Street Kidd, who served in the Kentucky Assembly from 1968 until 1985.

African American literary achievements in Louisville were most evident in the numerous newspapers founded and operated by blacks. Denouncing racial discrimination and segregation, as well as offering a vehicle for black artistic expression, the local black newspapers were an important voice for African Americans in Louisville. The first major black paper was the *Louisville Leader*, which was founded and run by Willis Cole from 1917 until 1950. The *Leader* contained features and columns on current events, education, black history, and community news. The Stanley family joined the ranks of Louisville's black publishing elite with its *Louisville Defender* in the early 1930s. This weekly paper soon gained national attention and fame, and President Harry S. Truman presented its publishers with the Wendell Wilkie Award for Public Service. The paper also won the President's Special Service Award of the National Newspaper Publisher's Association in 1971 and the prestigious Russwurm Award in 1974. Both of these papers and many other short-lived black weeklies kept Louisville's African American population abreast of important issues that affected their lives and, through the publication of poetry, essays, and stories by black authors, provided them with a rare outlet for self-expression.

Locked out of lily-white community centers, health facilities, and clubs, blacks in Louisville met their daily needs for cooperation, respect, and involvement through a wide variety of organizations and mutual aid societies. Women's clubs were an important vehicle that allowed black women to participate in civic affairs and support African American schools, hospitals, and shelters for orphans, the homeless, and the elderly. The Baptist Women's Missionary Convention and the Baptist Women's Education Convention supported education by raising scholarship money for girls, paying teacher salaries, and building dormitories for women at Kentucky State University, the only black college in the commonwealth. Women's clubs also donated beds, sheets, and funds to the Colored Orphan Home, the St. James Old Folks Home, and the Red Cross Hospital. These facilities were the only social-service agencies available to blacks in Louisville in the early 1900s. Other Progressive-era community organizations founded to help black children, the poor, and the elderly included the Georgia A. Nugent Improvement

Club, the Loyalty Charity Club, the Booker T. Washington Community Center, the Newsboys Improvement Club, the Colored Orphan Home, the Louisville chapter of the Young Men's Christian Association (YMCA), the Hope Mission Station and the Grace Mission Station settlement houses, and the Kentucky Home Finding Society for Colored Children.

Likewise, black men's lodges and their women's auxiliaries provided recreation, business training, and insurance for their members. By 1900, there were more than sixty-seven African American lodges in Louisville serving 7,535 members. The leading lodges included the Masons, the Odd Fellows, and the Colored Knights of Pythias. The most remarkable black lodge in Louisville was the United Brothers of Friendship and the Sisters of the Mysterious Ten. Founded by the Reverend Marshall W. Taylor and William N. Hazelton in 1861, the United Brothers of Friendship quickly spread its roots from Louisville to more than ten states by the turn of the century. African American social organizations remained an important component of black community life and black protest throughout the twentieth century, and future political leaders like Mae Street Kidd often began their careers by organizing groups like the Business and Professional Club for African American Women and programs such as the Executive for a Day project for school-age black youths.

The city's African American civic, literary, and mutual aid associations were an important part of the struggle for black self-determination and self-sufficiency in Louisville. A memorial to African American agency, the organizations helped Louisville's black community endure and prosper.

**FURTHER READINGS**

Dunnigan, Alice Allison. *The Fascinating Story of Black Kentuckians: Their Heritage and Traditions.* Washington, D.C.: Association for the Study of Afro-American Life and History, 1982.

Gibson, William H. *History of the United Brothers of Friendship and Sisters of the Mysterious Ten.* Louisville: Bradley and Gilbert, 1897.

Hall, Wade H. *Passing for Black: The Life and Careers of Mae Street Kidd.* Lexington: University Press of Kentucky, 1997.

Lucas, Marion B. *A History of Blacks in Kentucky.* Vol. 1: *From Slavery to Segregation, 1760–1891.* Frankfort: Kentucky Historical Society, 1992.

Wright, George C. *Life Behind a Veil: Blacks in Louisville, Kentucky, 1865–1930.* Baton Rouge: Louisiana State University Press, 1985.

———. *A History of Blacks in Kentucky.* Vol. 2: *In Pursuit of Equality, 1890–1980.* Frankfort: Kentucky Historical Society, 1992.

*Daniel E. Crowe*

## Lynn Committee to Abolish Segregation in the Armed Forces

During World War II, the Lynn Committee waged a campaign to end segregation and racial discrimination in the armed forces of the United States. In *Winfred William Lynn v. Colonel John Downer*—Downer was the commanding officer at Camp Upton, New York—Lynn initiated the only World War II court case to test the legality of the Jim Crow method of selecting men for the armed forces. He argued that African Americans were illegally separated from white inductees and drafted on the basis of a quota system.

In June 1942, Local Draft Board 261 of Jamaica, New York, notified Lynn that he had been classified 1–A—physically qualified for military service without restrictions. He replied to the notice: "Gentlemen: I am in receipt of my draft reclassification notice. Please be informed that I am ready to serve in any unit of the armed forces of my country which is not segregated by race. Unless I am assured that I can serve in a mixed regiment and that I will not be compelled to serve in a unit undemocratically selected as a Negro group, I will refuse to report for induction" (*Nation*, February 20, 1943, 263).

A lower-court judge informed Lynn that, before his case could be heard, he had to submit to induction and then file suit against his superior officer. Lynn did so, but in June 1942 the federal district court in New York ruled against him by refusing to hear the case. Lynn appealed to the U.S. Circuit Court of Appeals, which upheld the lower court's decision. Finally, the case reached the U.S. Supreme Court in 1944. The court refused to hear the case on grounds that Lynn was on active duty overseas—and, therefore, outside the jurisdiction of the court—and that the military officer against whom he had originally brought the suit had retired from the service.

The case attracted national attention and led to the formation of the Lynn Committee. The New York City–based interracial committee had an impressive membership roster that included William Kerr (cochairman), A. Philip Randolph, Carey McWilliams, George S. Schuyler, Broadus Mitchell (cochairman), E. Pauline Myers, Horace R. Cayton, Alain Locke, Mable K. Staupers, and Oswald Garrison Villard. These men and women solicited funds for legal action, publicity, and educational

Ruth Isaacs, Katherine Horton, and Inez Patterson, the first African American WAVES (Women Accepted for Volunteer Emergency Service) to go to Hospital Corps school, at the National Naval Medical Center in Maryland. 1945. *Archive Photos*

programs. Moreover, the committee kept the American public informed through press releases, leaflets, newsletters, and political questionnaires until the Supreme Court declared the case a "moot suit" in 1944.

On at least one occasion the committee sent a questionnaire to candidates for the 1944 congressional election that asked the politicians to pledge themselves to the task of working to abolish discrimination in the armed forces. Committee Cochairman William Kerr responded to those who pledged: "The candidates will be closely watched by the millions of colored voters to see that their campaign promises are fulfilled." Kerr also condemned the congressional candidates who ignored the committee's questionnaire: "Silence on this vital question is equivalent to sanctioning the fighting of a man against Nazi racial dogma with a segregated, Jim Crow army. This is the basest type of hypocrisy" (Press Release 1944, Winfred W. Lynn Case).

A petition to rehear the Lynn case was denied in 1945. It was not until July 26, 1948, that President Harry S. Truman abolished legal segregation and racial discrimina-

tion of African Americans in the armed services when he signed Executive Order 9981.

**FURTHER READINGS**

Breckinridge, S. P. "The Winfred Lynn Case against Segregation in the Armed Forces." *Social Service Review* 18 (September 1944), 369–371.

Dalfiume, Richard M. *Desegregation of the U.S. Armed Forces: Fighting on Two Fronts, 1939–1953.* Columbia: University of Missouri Press, 1969.

Finkle, Lee. *Forum for Protest: The Black Press during World War II.* Rutherford, N.J.: Fairleigh Dickinson University Press, 1975, 150–154.

McGuire, Phillip. *He, Too, Spoke for Democracy: Judge Hastie, World War II, and the Black Soldier.* Westport, Conn.: Greenwood, 1988.

Winfred W. Lynn Case. Vertical Files. Schomburg Center for Research in Black Culture, the New York Public Library.

*Phillip McGuire*

# Malcolm X Society

Organized in 1967, the Malcolm X Society stepped into the national spotlight March 30–31, 1968, when it sponsored the National Black Government Conference at the Central United Christian Church in Detroit, Michigan. Attended by a few hundred people, the conference announced the formation of the Republic of New Africa (RNA), which was to be composed of Alabama, Georgia, Louisiana, Mississippi, and South Carolina. Conference participants also drafted a constitution and a declaration of independence. To fund the RNA, organizers planned to negotiate with the United States for reparations and for status under the Geneva Convention. Gaidi Obadele—formerly Milton Henry, an attorney whose politics were shaped by his travels with Malcolm X through Africa—reported that attendees voted to renounce their American citizenship and selected Robert F. Williams, an American fugitive living in China, as the RNA's president. Although there was no official government response to the RNA's call for negotiations, it soon became clear that federal agents were watching the group. In the meantime, RNA strategists planned for a key land purchase in Mississippi and the inevitability of armed struggle.

Over the next few years, a series of events brought the RNA fully into the American conscience. On March 29, 1969, police raided the Detroit New Bethel Baptist Church, site of the second annual RNA conference. According to an RNA report, when a police officer was killed and another wounded in an attempt to assassinate Gaidi Obadele, the Detroit police fired on conference participants with nearly a thousand rounds of ammunition. During the raid, four RNA members were wounded and well over a hundred arrested. Eventually, all RNA members were released from prison, and the three charged with mur-

dering the police officer were acquitted. Two years later, the RNA attempted to purchase twenty acres of land in Mississippi, which it planned to name El Malik in honor of Malcolm X and use as a base for its operations. The RNA's attempt failed, reportedly due to FBI interference. Despite its failure, the RNA gained public support from a variety of quarters, particularly proponents of black nationalism. On August 17, 1971, when police raided the RNA in Jackson, Mississippi, a police officer was killed, resulting in another well-publicized trial. Eleven RNA members were arrested and imprisoned on a variety of charges, ranging from murder to sedition against the state of Mississippi. Among the "RNA–11" was President Imari Obadele, the former Richard Henry, Gaidi Obadele's brother. Three other RNA members made the news when they hijacked a plane to Cuba after killing a New Mexico police officer who had pulled them over on their way to the Jackson debacle.

After leaving prison in 1980, Imari Obdale received a Ph.D. in political science from Temple University in 1985. Obadele has accepted a number of college teaching positions and continues to advocate black nationalism in his writings such as *Free the Land! The True Story of the RNA–11 in Mississippi and the Continuing Struggle to Establish an Independent Black Nation in Five States of the Deep South* (1984). Although the imprisonment and loss of many RNA leaders depleted the ranks and power of the Malcolm X Society, the group's work and the well-publicized RNA struggles it helped produce remain a potent historical symbol of black nationalism.

## FURTHER READINGS

Lumumba, Chokwe. "Short History of the U.S. War on the R.N.A." *Black Scholar* 12 (January/February 1981), 72–81.

"Militants Seeking 'Black Government.'" *New York Times* March 28, 1968, sec. 50, 4.

"Negro Now in China Chosen as President of Black 'Nation.'" *New York Times* April 1, 1968, sec. 22, 7.

Ripley, Anthony. "Negro Group Asks End of Ties to U.S.: Separatists Begin Drive for Own Nation in South." *New York Times* March 31, 1968, sec. 32, 3.

Van DeBurg, William L. *New Day in Babylon: The Black Power Movement and American Culture, 1965–1975.* Chicago: University of Chicago Press, 1992.

*Stephen Davenport*

## Manumission Societies

The nation's first abolition society, formed by Philadelphia Quakers in 1775, initially called itself the Society for the Relief of Free Negroes Unlawfully Held in Bondage. In 1787, it was reorganized as the Pennsylvania Society for Promoting the Abolition of Slavery, Relief of Free Negroes Unlawfully Held in Bondage, and for Improving the Condition of the African Race.

One of the initial goals of the Pennsylvania Abolition Society was the promotion of like-minded organizations, and these groups followed its naming pattern. In 1789, for example, the Maryland Society for Promoting the Abolition of Slavery and for the Relief of Free Negroes and Others Held Unlawfully in Bondage was formed. The Delaware Society for Gradual Abolition, founded in 1788, reorganized in 1800 as the Delaware Society for Promoting the Abolition of Slavery and the Relief and Protection of Free Blacks and People of Color Unlawfully Held in Bondage or Otherwise Oppressed.

Most abolition societies were ostensibly statewide bodies, but, in fact, their memberships and activities centered in the larger cities, where organization was most feasible. By 1792, state and local societies ranged from Massachusetts to Virginia. North Carolina and Tennessee joined the list in the 1810s.

Quakers played an important part in the founding of the Pennsylvania Abolition Society (PAS) and other similar groups. American Quakers had begun discussing the abolition of slavery within their own community as early as 1688. By 1776, the Philadelphia Yearly Meeting, which included Friends from Pennsylvania, New Jersey, Delaware, and Maryland, prohibited the ownership of slaves by Church members. The majority of early white abolitionists were Quakers, and they played an important role in the establishment of nearly all the early abolition societies except those in Connecticut and Kentucky.

The Quaker-controlled PAS was the largest and most active abolition society in the nation. Quakers likewise did much of the real work in the very active New York Manumission Society. Not all those involved were Quakers, however, and some members were respected leaders of society and government. Benjamin Franklin served as president of the PAS; Dr. Benjamin Rush was also a member. Alexander Hamilton, John Jay, and George Clinton took part in the New York Society. Joseph Bloomfield, who served as president of the New Jersey Abolition Society, later became that state's governor. A striking number of active Pennsylvania and New York members held public office. They included senators, congressmen, federal judges, diplomats, federal and state attorneys general, state legislators, constitutional convention delegates, and city councilmen. There were no black members.

The original objective of the PAS was the relief of free blacks who were kidnapped into slavery. To that end, the society kept manumission records, provided legal and financial assistance in court cases, and pleaded individual victims' cases before public officials. The PAS also pressed for more stringent state antikidnapping legislation while urging greater enforcement of existing laws, and petitioned the federal government for a national law opposing kidnapping. After 1787, the reorganized group also monitored the execution of the state's gradual emancipation law, petitioned the state and federal government for the complete abolition of slavery, distributed antislavery literature, and agitated against the slave trade. All abolition societies engaged in similar activities. In states in which gradual emancipation laws did not yet exist, abolition societies promoted them as well.

Other groups also duplicated the structure of the PAS. The officers included two secretaries, who conducted the group's correspondence, and four lawyers, who interpreted the state's constitution and legal code as they pertained to slaves and free blacks and took freedom suits to court. An executive committee conducted the day-to-day business of the society, with new committees forming for particular functions as needed. They investigated free-black living conditions, encouraged education, found employment, and placed black children in indentureships to learn trades.

The nation's abolition societies met informally in the American Convention of Abolition Societies, and the Quaker influence carried over to this national body. The pronouncements of that group were strongly Quakerish in tone and approach, and the vast majority of the nearly annual meetings were held in Philadelphia. Of the twenty-four conventions held between 1794 and 1829, twenty met there. The first meeting saw twenty-five delegates from nine organizations meet in Philadelphia in 1794. Though they pledged to meet annually, some years saw no meeting, and attending organizations came and went.

At the meetings, individual societies exchanged information about topics of common concern, such as the extent of kidnapping in their locales, as well as tactics for addressing these concerns. They repeatedly discussed the need for federal antikidnapping legislation to prevent a crime that frequently crossed state boundaries. But they admitted that kidnapping and the internal slave trade were crimes that would be eradicated only with the complete abolition of slavery itself. Until that happened, the convention concerned itself also with the moral behavior of the free black population, believing that proving their worth would help free blacks secure the freedom of their brothers and sisters still in slavery. Temperance, industry, frugality, piety, cleanliness, education (particularly in order to read the Bible) would help convince racists that they were wrong in their negative estimation of black people.

Perhaps the greatest service abolitionist societies provided free blacks was financial assistance in kidnapping cases. Once taken into slavery or held as suspected fugitives, free blacks faced not only the hazards of incarceration, but also payment for court costs and lawyers' fees, as well as transportation costs for witnesses. For impoverished blacks, this proved an awesome combination of impediments that often prevented their release even when they could prove their free status. The bulk of these debts usually fell on abolition societies, and the financial burden was extreme. As early as 1798, some organizations were reporting to the American Convention their difficulty in resolving cases because of lack of funds. Even when money was available, obstacles were often insurmountable. Racism and hostility toward free blacks made getting a fair hearing difficult at best. And the sheer number of kidnapping cases was daunting: at the 1799 American Convention, the Virginia Abolition Society reported that it was involved in lawsuits for nearly one hundred persons, too many to prosecute adequately.

The gradualist abolitionist approach dominated the convention. Though gradual abolitionists disagreed with slavery, they refused to break the law to further their goals, much less to do so violently, preferring instead to work within the system to free as many people as possible until total abolition was brought about. And they had

substantial success. Largely through their influence, gradual abolition laws were passed or slavery abolished outright in all states north of Maryland by 1804. Abolition of the slave trade in 1808 gave further hope that slavery was dwindling.

But their belief that gradual abolition would spread to the southern states was not realized. Instead, resistance to abolition grew in the South after the American Revolution. In 1791, the Maryland House of Delegates censured that state's abolition society for its memorial concerning two black criminals and came close to declaring the society inimical to the interests of the state. Likewise, a member of the North Carolina Manumission Society indicated the need for circumspection in his state, saying: "We are well aware of the delicacy of the subject and that it must be the work of time."

Gradual abolitionists failed to realize the depth to which slavery had become entwined with southern economic and cultural identity. Two developments around the turn of the nineteenth century served to reverse the growing sentiment in the nation that slavery's days were numbered. The invention of the cotton gin made production of cotton faster and more profitable, while the Louisiana Purchase opened rich lands in the Southwest for plantation expansion.

A new solution to the problem of slavery gained attention at this time. After the formation of the American Colonization Society in 1816, gradual abolitionist sentiment was rechanneled into colonization. By the 1820s, the hopes of the gradual abolitionists had proven false, and the stage was set for a new, militant antislavery movement.

**FURTHER READINGS**

"The Appeal of the American Convention of Abolition Societies to Anti-Slavery Groups." *Journal of Negro History* 6 (April 1921), 200–240.

"Reports of the American Convention of Abolition Societies on Negroes and Slavery, Their Appeals to Congress, and Their Addresses to the Citizens of the United States." *Journal of Negro History* 6 (July 1921), 310–374.

Wilson, Carol. "'The Legitimate Offspring of Slavery': Kidnapping of Free Blacks and Abolitionists' Response." *Mid-America* 74 (April/July 1992), 105–124.

Zilversmit, Arthur. *The First Emancipation: The Abolition of Slavery in the North.* Chicago: University of Chicago Press, 1967.

*Carol Wilson*

## March on Washington Committee

In January 1941, A. Philip Randolph, president of the Brotherhood of Sleeping Car Porters, established the March on Washington Committee (MOWC) to organize a march on the nation's capital. On January 25, 1941, he called on ten thousand African Americans to join him in Washington, D.C., and walk down Pennsylvania Avenue to protest discrimination in the defense industries and the armed forces. While coordinating this event, the MOWC also pressured President Franklin D. Roosevelt to issue Executive Order 8802, which established a nondiscrimination employment policy for civilian agencies and employers with defense contracts. The order also created the Fair Employment Practice Committee (FEPC) to investigate

President Lyndon Johnson presents A. Philip Randolph with the Presidential Medal of Freedom, 1964. *UPI/Bettman*

complaints of job discrimination. The establishment of the FEPC was the MOWC's greatest achievement. It never staged the protest march and failed to force the federal government to desegregate the military. Nevertheless, the committee's activities helped black workers make advances during the war years.

In the early 1940s, the American economy emerged from the Great Depression as defense contracts rejuvenated factories and unemployment virtually disappeared. African Americans, however, did not participate fully in this economic boom. While whites entered defense plants and the military in increasing numbers, many blacks remained jobless or on New Deal work projects. Several influential black leaders, such as Walter White, executive secretary of the National Association for the Advancement of Colored People (NAACP), and Robert C. Weaver, a federal official in the Office of Production Management, tried to ease the color barrier to the preparedness program. They appealed to government officials and lobbied politicians. When it became clear, however, that these efforts were not creating employment opportunities, some African Americans began to consider more radical actions. Thus, Randolph launched the MOWC to orchestrate an all-black march on Washington.

Within a few months of Randolph's call, many black communities and activists, such as Walter White and the National Urban League's Lester Granger, declared their support. By the spring of 1941, Randolph was confident that he could parade not ten thousand but 100,000 African Americans on Washington. In May 1941, he wrote President Roosevelt, formally announcing the protest, scheduled for July 1, 1941. In the intervening months, the MOWC began organizing transportation and lodging.

With the assistance of Walter White, Randolph also negotiated with the Roosevelt administration, which wanted to prevent the march. The president and his advisers feared that the march would be grist for the Axis propaganda mills and that it would incite a race riot in segregated Washington, D.C. On June 12, 1941, Roosevelt tried to dissuade Randolph by telling the Office of Production Management, the agency in charge of industrial conversion, to issue a memorandum, urging defense contractors to provide equal employment opportunities. When the memorandum failed to stop the march, Roosevelt set up a meeting between his racial advisers and the leadership of the MOWC.

On June 13, 1941, in New York City, Randolph and White conferred with Aubrey Williams, Mayor Fiorello LaGuardia, and Eleanor Roosevelt. The MOWC leaders brought a six-point list of demands, asking the president to issue five executive orders banning discrimination in defense industries and the armed services. Additionally, the MOWC requested that the president support a new law amending the National Labor Relations Act in order to deny the benefits of the National Labor Relations Board to labor unions that discriminated against black workers. No agreement was reached, and Roosevelt's advisers failed to stop the march.

After the conference, LaGuardia recommended that President Roosevelt meet personally with White and Randolph. On June 18, twelve days before the protest was to begin, the MOWC leaders conferred with Roosevelt. Following much discussion, they reached a compromise. Roosevelt promised to issue an executive order banning discrimination in defense industries and establishing an agency to handle complaints if the MOWC canceled its march on Washington. Although Roosevelt's promise represented only a partial victory, the leaders of the MOWC agreed to cancel the march. A week later, on June 25, 1941, President Roosevelt signed Executive Order 8802 establishing a nondiscriminatory employment policy for civilian agencies and employers with defense contracts and creating the Fair Employment Practice Committee (FEPC) to redress grievances. Not all members of the MOWC, particularly Richard Parrish, head of the MOWC Youth Division, were pleased with the compromise, especially since Executive Order 8802 did not mention discrimination in the armed forces. Nevertheless, the creation of the FEPC was an important achievement.

The MOWC itself did not survive the war. In December 1941, Randolph renamed and expanded the organization, and it became the March on Washington Movement (MOWM). During World War II, the MOWM aided the FEPC and acted as a watchdog, ensuring that the federal government maintained its commitment to fair employment. Randolph's dream of a march on Washington to protest discrimination and economic injustice did carry over into the postwar period and was finally realized in 1963.

### FURTHER READINGS

Garfinkel, Herbert. *When Negroes March: The March on Washington and the Organizational Politics for FEPC.* Glencoe, Ill.: Free Press, 1959.

Kersten, Andrew E. "Fighting for Fair Employment: The FEPC in the Midwest." Ph.D. diss., University of Cincinnati, 1997.

Pfeffer, Paula F. *A. Philip Randolph: Pioneer of the Civil Rights Movement.* Baton Rouge: Louisiana State University Press, 1990.

Reed, Merl E. *Seedtime for the Modern Civil Rights Movement: The President's Committee on Fair Employment Practice, 1941–1946.* Baton Rouge: Louisiana State University Press, 1991.

*Andrew E. Kersten*

## Maryland Dental Society

*See* Tri-State Dental Association of DC, VA, MD.

## Massachusetts Anti-Slavery Society

*See* New England Anti-Slavery Society.

## Massachusetts Commission Against Discrimination

Massachusetts formed a Commission against Discrimination during the last year of World War II. African American participation in the war effort, the openly racist nature of Germany and Japan, and the emerging anticolonial struggles in Asia and Africa called attention to the contradiction between the promise of America and its reality. Massachusetts, once the most liberal state on race relations, had only a small black population by the end of World War II, which faced *de facto* segregation in many areas of life.

In 1944, the State Legislature established a special commission to investigate discrimination. The Commission found that the state had a problem, and Governor Maurice Tobin appointed a new committee to recommend methods of combating it. The committee proposed a permanent commission to enforce antidiscrimination laws, and Governor Tobin signed a bill forming a Fair Employment Practices Commission (FEPC) in 1946.

Understaffed and underfunded, the FEPC was ill equipped to implement the state's fair-employment mandate. African Americans were effectively barred from better-paying union jobs in most areas of the economy. Hiring in public education, transportation, fire and police departments, and public utilities was largely restricted to whites and heavily influenced by nepotism. In the private sector, the construction industry was similarly unionized, and, as new manufacturing enterprises moved to the suburbs along Route 128, the FEPC dubbed it "The Highway to Segregation." The new agency at first had only two full-time employees and handled only ninety-six complaints in its first year.

In 1950, the FEPC's mandate was broadened to include all aspects of race-based discrimination, and its name was changed to the Massachusetts Commission against Discrimination (MACD). Under the impact of the modern civil rights movement, the state expanded budget and staffing for the MACD. During the 1960s, the commission responded positively to complaints brought by black workers seeking jobs at government-funded and university construction sites. In the early 1970s, the commission sued the Boston School Committee on behalf of a black student denied admission to a mostly white, neighborhood school.

Gradually, the state expanded the budget, staffing, and mission of the MCAD. As women, gays, the handicapped, and elderly realized how employers, landlords, banks, and public institutions had limited their opportunities, the MCAD was charged with answering their complaints as well. By the 1970s, the MCAD handled more than fifteen hundred cases annually. In 1996, it fielded more than five thousand complaints and held 110 public hearings.

The MCAD maintains two offices, one in Boston and another in Springfield. In addition, it works with fourteen municipal human rights councils. Three commissioners, one of whom serves as chairman, oversee the work of five departments, which handle complaints at varying procedural levels.

In 1996, the commission celebrated its fiftieth anniversary in a racial climate that had improved from the time of its founding. Yet, while African Americans and other minorities have made significant employment gains since the end of World War II, they continue to face obstacles to further advancement. By 1996, race-based complaints made up only 20 percent of the MCAD's docket. Perhaps the commission's public profile prevailed upon many would-be violators to comply with the state's antidiscrimination laws.

**FURTHER READINGS**

Formisano, Ronald P. *Boston against Busing: Race, Class, and Ethnicity in the 1960s and 1970s.* Chapel Hill: University of North Carolina Press, 1991.

King, Mel. *Chain of Change: Struggles for Black Community Development.* Boston: South End, 1981.

Massachusetts Commission against Discrimination. *Annual Report of the Massachusetts Commission Against Discrimination, 1996.* Boston: The Commission, 1996.

*Mark R. Schneider*

## Massachusetts Fair Employment Practices Commission

*See* Massachusetts Commission Against Discrimination.

## Massachusetts General Colored Association

A group of black tailors and owners of clothing businesses founded the Massachusetts General Colored Association (MGCA) in Boston in 1826. The MGCA provided a public forum for black Bostonians committed to equality for all African Americans, including those nominally free in the North. Although the all-black association was short lived, its members helped create a new era of militant antislavery agitation that shook the nation before the Civil War.

Key founders of the MGCA included Thomas Dalton, William G. Nell, David Walker, Walker Lewis, John Hilton, John Scarlett, and James Barbadoes. These men protested discriminatory laws in Massachusetts, such as those that prohibited intermarriage of blacks and whites and those that permitted segregated public accommodations. MGCA members were also staunchly committed to the abolition of slavery, and they supported the New York-based *Freedom's Journal*, the nation's first black newspaper. African American men who joined the MGCA were also active in the city's other black community organizations, including those committed to self-help (the African Society), to religious uplift (the African Baptist Church), and to education (the African School).

Among the MGCA's founders, David Walker emerged as its most outspoken individual. A clothier by trade, Walker settled in the heart of Boston's black community in the mid-1820s and joined the African Masonic Lodge and the African Methodist Episcopal Church. He also served as an agent for *Freedom's Journal*, which published Walker's business advertisements and one of his speeches delivered before the MGCA in the winter of 1828. Walker gained national notoriety in 1829 when he published *Walker's Appeal*, an incendiary tract that called for an immediate end to slavery while urging slaves to actively resist their oppression, if necessary with violence. Walker's impassioned pleas circulated widely among free blacks in the North but fell upon hostile ears in the South. His suspicious death on June 28, 1830, led to charges that he had been poisoned.

*Walker's Appeal* and the MGCA played a significant role in shaping the subsequent national antislavery movement that emanated from Boston. Walker and Boston's African Americans influenced the foremost white apostle of abolitionism, William Lloyd Garrison, as well as the black female abolitionist Maria W. Stewart. In 1832, when Garrison and others established the New England Anti-Slavery Society (NEASS) they convened first in Boston's African Meeting House, and at least one-fourth of the signatories to the NEASS's constitution were black. One year later, the all-black MGCA merged with the NEASS, and several erstwhile MGCA stalwarts, including Reverend Samuel Snowden and John Hilton, emerged as leaders of the new, racially integrated organization. Former MGCA members also contributed significantly to the American Anti-Slavery Society (AASS), which was founded by Garrisonians in 1833. James Barbadoes, for example, was elected one of three black delegates to the first AASS convention in 1833 and was later elected to the society's board of managers.

By 1834, the MGCA had officially disbanded, and its members had been fully and formally incorporated into the integrated NEASS. During its short but vibrant life, the MGCA protested racial discrimination in the North and slavery in the South. Through its leadership, community support, and militancy, this small, all-black Boston association galvanized the larger crusade against slavery.

**FURTHER READINGS**

Horton, James Oliver, and Lois E. Horton. *Black Bostonians, Family Life and Community Struggle in the Antebellum North.* New York and London: Holmes and Meier, 1979.

———. *In Hope of Liberty, Culture, Community, and Protest among Northern Free Blacks, 1700–1860.* New York: Oxford University Press, 1997.

Jacobs, Donald M., ed. *Courage and Conscience: Black and White Abolitionists in Boston.* Bloomington: Published for the Boston Atheneum by Indiana University Press, 1993.

Quarles, Benjamin. *Black Abolitionists.* New York: Oxford University Press, 1969.

*Earl F. Mulderink III*

## McCone Commission

*See* Governor's Commission on the Los Angeles Riots.

## Med-Chi

*See* Medico-Chirurgical Society, Washington, D.C.

## Medical Committee for Human Rights

In 1964, led by physicians in New York City, various medical groups, dedicated to civil rights activism, combined to create the Medical Committee for Human Rights (MCHR). Inspired by the southern civil rights movement, medical practitioners in the North organized to attack discriminatory practices affecting the quality of health care in their local communities. Yet, MCHR members also played an active role in the southern civil rights movement. They participated in voter-registration drives in the Deep South and established a medical presence at civil rights demonstrations and marches. MCHR physicians, nurses, and medical students traveled to Mississippi to provide medical assistance to local black communities and civil rights groups involved in the Freedom Summer campaign (1964). Moreover, the MCHR raised money for civil rights activities and organizations and encouraged other medical practitioners to support the civil rights movement.

The 1964 discovery of the bodies of James Chaney, Andrew Goodman, and Michael Schwerner, northern students involved in Freedom Summer activities, outraged MCHR members. They sponsored the autopsies of the young men to keep the world aware of the virulent racism in Mississippi. Offering their services as medics, members of MCHR also joined the Selma to Montgomery, Alabama, march in the spring of 1965.

By 1965, the MCHR boasted local chapters in eight major cities and drew to its ranks dentists and psychologists. Membership reflected the interracial nature of the organization. Prominent MCHR leaders included its national chairman, Aaron O. Wells, a black physician in New York City, and renowned pediatrician Dr. Benjamin Spock.

Civil rights legislation passed in 1964 and 1965 resulted in the dismantling of Jim Crow in the South and allowed the MCHR to redirect its energies. Returning to its roots, the group addressed the needs of northern minority communities. It started health programs for children of poor neighborhoods, protested discrimination at health-care facilities, and created programs designed to attract young people from minority communities to medical work.

By the end of the 1970s, in the wake of the creation of numerous government programs aimed at enhancing the health and welfare of the poor, the MCHR declined. The significance of the organization cannot be overstated as an example of medical activism. Members of the MCHR recognized civil rights as a national concern transcending both class and the color line.

FURTHER READINGS

Falk, L. A. "The Negro American's Health and the Medical Committee for Human Rights." In *National Health Care: Issues and Problems in Socialized Medicine.* Ed. Ray H. Ellling. Chicago: Aldine-Atherton, 1971.

Kotelchk, B., and H. Levy. "The Medical Committee for Human Rights." In *Race, Politics, and Culture: Critical Essays on the Radicalism of the 1960s.* Ed. A. Reed, Jr. Westport, Conn.: Greenwood, 1986.

Morais, Herbert. *The History of the Negro in Medicine.* New York: Publishers Company, 1970.

Salzman, Jack, David Lionel Smith, and Cornel West, eds. *Encyclopedia of African-American Culture and History.* Vol. 3. New York: Simon and Schuster Macmillan, 1996.

*Peggy Hardman*

## Medico-Chirurgical Society, Washington, D.C.

The Medico-Chirurgical Society of Washington, D.C., is arguably the oldest local African American medical society in the United States. It was organized in 1884 by a biracial group of physicians associated with Freedmen's Hospital, including Robert W. Reyburn, S. L. Loomis, John R. Francis, and Daniel Smith Lamb. The stimulus for the formation was the rejection of black physicians from membership in the District of Columbia Medical Society. Without membership in the local medical association, black doctors could not gain membership in the American Medical Association (AMA), could not consult with local members, and frequently had patients taken away by member doctors who had the confidence of the community. The Medico-Chirurgical Society attempted unsuccessfully to gain recognition from the AMA and ceased meeting for a few years due to lack of interest.

In the 1890s, Francis and Furman J. Shadd applied to the District Medical Society but were again refused. Shadd, Francis, Reyburn, Daniel H. Williams, Arthur W. Tancil, and Thomas B. Hood, among others, revived Med-Chi in 1895, incorporating the organization for twenty years. They announced that their purpose was to provide opportunities for exchange and promotion of information relating to medicine and public health. William Montague Cobb, Howard University professor of anatomy and later president of Med-Chi, nonetheless described the segregated organization's founding as "a loser's best alternative after prolonged and angry strife."

Med-Chi members helped establish the Nineteenth Street Baptist Free Dispensary in 1907 and hosted several annual conferences of the National Medical Association, the black counterpart of the AMA. As white founding members passed away, none took their place, and, by the time the organization was reincorporated in 1917 on a permanent basis, the membership was entirely African American. By 1920, most of the District's prominent black physicians were members. The society sponsored reading groups and provided members with a sense of fraternity within their profession. Lack of funds, however, made it difficult to achieve much more in the early years.

In 1934, Med-Chi experienced a renaissance of activity. President Elmo C. Wiggins worked toward the creation of the annual banquet and two annual lectures named for the founders and Senator Charles Sumner. Wiggins also tried unsuccessfully again to get the AMA to recognize Med-Chi. By 1939, the organization's membership represented 84.7 percent of all black physicians in Washington. Some states required membership in Med-Chi as evidence of ethical acceptability before granting reciprocity to black doctors practicing outside the District.

The organization tried to establish a minimum fee schedule based on that of white doctors but was thwarted in these attempts by the lower economic condition of black patients. In the 1930s, the group worked with the Public Works Administration to investigate the need for a federal tuberculosis hospital. Med-Chi members conducted annual free health examinations for students and wrote a series of articles on disease, health, and nutrition for the *Washington Tribune*. They attempted to have black doctors admitted to practice at the District public hospital, purchased an organizational membership in the National Association for the Advancement of Colored People (NAACP), and raised money for Howard University medical school and scholarships for outstanding students.

In 1937, Med-Chi wives Nellie P. Stevens and Minnie L. Johnson formed a Ladies Auxiliary, comprising wives of black physicians and dentists, aimed at educating the public on health issues, aiding in the relief of problems related to health, and providing financial support to medical and other health fields. They began an annual fund-raiser banquet and, since 1937, have awarded more than $100,000 in scholarships to Howard University medical students.

During World War II, Med-Chi lobbied to have black physicians and dentists included in the Selective Service Examination process and ultimately evaluated 64,500 registrants. The group also established an in-house *Bulletin* in 1941. In the late 1940s, the organization focused on racial-discrimination issues and sponsored national-health-insurance bills.

The society continued its pressure on the District Medical Society to accept black members, a feat achieved in 1951, when Med-Chi President Edward C. Mazique became the first black applicant since the 1890s. In the 1950s, when many separate black professional organizations were disbanding as a result of desegregation, Med-Chi maintained its separate status to fight for equal treatment and to ensure that the dismantling of Jim Crow would continue. The organization held annual banquets and lectures throughout the 1960s and 1970s, and, with a brief hiatus in the 1980s, continued to publish the *Bulletin*. Since 1992, the group also publishes *Imhotep*. The organization now meets every other month, with monthly business meetings, and remains a forum for discussion of racial issues in the medical profession.

**FURTHER READINGS**

Cobb, William Montague. *The First Negro Medical Society: A History of the Medico-Chirurgical Society of the District of Columbia, 1884–1939*. Washington, D.C.: Associated Publishers, 1939.

———. "Medico-Chi and the National Selective Service." *Journal of the National Medical Association* 37, 6 (November 1945), 192–197.

———. "The Future of Negro Medical Organizations." *Journal of the National Medical Association* 43, 5 (September 1951), 323–328.

*Jacqueline M. Moore*

# Memphis: Civic, Literary, and Mutual Aid Associations

The earliest African American association in Memphis, the Social and Benevolent Society, was established by the city's small free black population in 1854. Between 1861 and the end of the nineteenth century, an extensive network of civic, literary, and mutual aid associations emerged in the city's black communities. The first lodge of the United Brothers of Friendship and Sisters of the Mystic Ten was organized in 1861, and, by the early 1900s, various lodges were active in the city, including the Independent Order of Odd Fellows, the Independent Order of Immaculates, the Knights of Tabor, the Seven Stars Grand Assembly of the United States, the Ancient Knights of the Crusades of the United States, the Mosaics, the Masons, and the Elks. These associations collected dues, distributed death benefits, marched in fraternal regalia in parades and funerals, and sponsored community celebrations on Emancipation Day and the Fourth of July.

Other organizations focused on providing community rather than individual assistance. The Sons and Daughters of Ham, the Sons and Daughters of Zion, the Daughters of Zion, the United Sons and Daughters of Zion, the Sons and Daughters of Canaan, and other men's and women's groups associated with African American churches raised funds for specific community needs and activities. In the late 1860s, the Daughters of Zion of Avery Chapel AME Church raised funds to pay a physician to care for members of the congregation. In the 1870s, the United Sons and Daughters of Zion purchased approximately fifteen acres of land outside the city limits on the Grand Municipal Parkway, where they established Zion Cemetery. Members and leaders of organizations like the United Sons and Daughters of Zion and the Daughters of Zion came primarily from the working class. Through their membership in these associations, less-affluent African Americans were able to pool their limited financial resources to provide important social services.

Poor African Americans, however, were not the only ones who established mutual aid associations. In the early twentieth century, prestigious national secret societies and fraternal orders started to organize chapters in Memphis and attracted large numbers of the black elite. The Memphis lodge of the Improved Benevolent and Protective Order of Elks of the World was organized in 1906. Its membership was made up of social and economic leaders like millionaire Robert R. Church Jr., Harry H. Pace, and George W. Lee. In 1910, Pace, attorney Josiah T. Settle, the Reverend Dr. E. Thomas Demby, and doctors A. L. Thompson, Ernest Irving, and E. E. Nebitts also established a chapter of Delta Boule of Sigma Pi Phi Fraternity, the first African American Greek-letter organization. The Memphis chapter was the fraternity's first expansion into the South. By the 1940s, nine other national fraternities and sororities had established chapters in the city.

In the late nineteenth and early twentieth centuries, black Memphians also established numerous civic associations to address particular community needs. The Old Folks and Orphans Home Club, for example, established a home for indigent elderly and orphans. The Negro Reform Association sought county approval for a reform school for young black offenders while it urged the city's government to admit these youths to the existing county industrial school.

African American women were active in these civic organizations as well as in women's clubs. From the 1860s through the twentieth century, women organized groups like the Daughters of Zion and the Baptist Sewing Circle, the Coterie Migratory Assembly, branches of the Women's Christian Temperance Union, the Phyllis Wheatley Union, the National League on Urban Conditions among Negroes, the YWCA, and the Free Kindergarten Association to foster women's suffrage, temperance, child and maternal welfare, education, and the development of a settlement house and a home for young female migrants. These groups sponsored lectures, raised funds, and publicized community problems to gather support for their causes. Two Memphis women represented their organizations at the first national meeting of the National Association of Colored Women (NACW) in Nashville in 1896; and in 1905 representatives of local black women's clubs established the City Federation of Colored Women's Clubs.

Black literary and culture clubs have been active in Memphis since the late nineteenth century. Among the earliest of these was the Lyceum, an association of students from LeMoyne Normal Institute and teachers who worked in Memphis's public schools. A similar group, the Shakespeare Club, was sponsored by Howe Institute, a local Baptist college. Organizations like the Coterie Migratory Assembly, the Listz-Mullard Club, the Music Club, the Sojourner Truth Club, the Phyllis Wheatley Literary and Social Club, and the Hiawatha Club sponsored lectures, public meetings, and travel tours, held literary discussions, and participated in charitable and civic activities.

Black Memphians also organized military groups, such as the Independent Order of the Pole Bearers, the McClellan Guards, the Zoave Guards, and the Tennessee Rifles. The last of these groups, the Tennessee Rifles, was forced to surrender its weapons after the 1892 lynchings of three prominent black businessmen, at least one of whom had been a member of a military organization.

Mutual aid associations, secret societies, and military organizations played an important role in the political life of the black community in the nineteenth century. After the passage of the Fourteenth Amendment to the United States Constitution, many of these associations worked with the Republican Loyal League. Their militant political activity in the 1860s and 1870s resulted in the election of several African Americans to public offices. Black political influence, however, waned in the late 1870s when some of the more powerful associations encouraged cooperation with southern Democrats. In 1875, Hezekiah Henley, president of the Independent Order of Pole Bearers and a leading advocate of racial reconciliation, organized an Independence Day celebration at the City Fair Grounds and invited Nathan Bedford Forrest, an antebellum slave trader, Civil War general, and a founder of the Ku Klux Klan, to address a crowd of black Memphians. Forrest accepted a bouquet of flowers from Lou Lewis, a black woman, as a "token of reconciliation between the white and colored races of the South" and assured the crowd that "every man who was in the Confederate Army is your friend." In the 1876 municipal election, African American voters, encouraged by Henley, supported southern white candidates rather than black and white Republicans. The election marked the beginning of the erosion of African American influence and involvement in city government. Although political disfranchisement reduced the African American electorate in other parts of Tennessee, blacks continued to vote in Memphis in the late nineteenth century.

In the twentieth century, civic associations rather than mutual aid societies were at the center of African American political activity. The Lincoln League was organized in 1916 to register black voters and to protest and monitor a conservative movement to place more suffrage restrictions in the Tennessee Constitution. The organization registered ten thousand voters, paid poll taxes for some black voters, held voting schools, and placed a Lincoln League ticket on the ballot. Lincoln League member Robert R. Church Jr. helped establish the National Lincoln League in 1919. The Republican Party under Robert R. Church and George W. Lee continued its strong influence until the 1930s, when many African Americans switched to the Democratic Party. Organizations like the National Association for the Advancement of Colored People (NAACP), the Urban League, and Reverend Sutton E. Griggs's Public Welfare League and interracial groups like the West Tennessee Civil and Political League also found supporters in the black community.

The organizational life of black Memphis in the twentieth century differed significantly from that of the late nineteenth century. African American burial associations and insurance companies like Universal Life, Supreme Life, Atlanta Life, and North Carolina Mutual replaced many of the secret societies and mutual aid associations that had once provided death benefits. Many African American neighborhoods and housing projects now sponsored civic clubs or tenant associations. Parent Teacher Associations were established in most of the city's segregated schools, and labor unions started to organize the city's black workers. Professional groups like the Bluff City Medical Association, the Colored Cosmetologists, Inc.,

the Colored Merchants Associations, the Colored Nurses, the Colored Women's Business and Professional Club, and the Colored Funeral Directors Association became active in Memphis as the number of black professionals increased. The Memphis Negro Chamber of Commerce, organized in 1934 by Dr. J. E. Walker, promoted African American business and professional interests and biracial cooperation. Social welfare agencies like Family Service of Memphis, the Children's Bureau, the Travelers Aid Society, and the City Beautiful Commission offered services in the black community through segregated divisions, special racial advisory committees, and black caseworkers. African American community groups also organized separate fairs such as the Tri-State Fair and the Cotton Makers' Jubilee to counter the segregated Mid-South Fair and Cotton Carnival until the latter activities were integrated.

During the 1960s, civic associations, labor unions, local chapters of national groups like the NAACP and the Urban League, as well as supporters of the Southern Christian Leadership Conference (SCLC) and the Congress of Racial Equality (CORE), joined with newly formed interracial organizations like the Saturday Lunch Group to promote integration. Although integration provided opportunities for black Memphians to participate in interracial organizations, African American literary, civic, social, and fraternal groups continue to be active and influential.

**FURTHER READINGS**

Berkeley, Kathleen C. "Colored Ladies also Contributed: Black Women's Activities from Benevolence to Social Welfare, 1866–1896." In *The Web of Southern Social Relations: Women, Family, and Education.* Ed. Walter J. Fraser Jr., R. Frank Saunders Jr., and Jon Wakelyn. Athens: University of Georgia Press, 1985.

Bond, Beverly Greene. "'Till Fair Aurora Rise': African American Women in Memphis, Tennessee, 1840–1915." Ph.D. diss., University of Memphis, 1996.

Hamilton, G. P. *The Bright Side of Memphis.* Memphis: G. P. Hamilton, 1908.

Robinson, Armstead L. "Plans Dat Comed from God: Institution Building and the Emergence of Black Leadership in Reconstruction Memphis." In *Toward a New South? Studies in Post–Civil War Southern Communities.* Ed. Robert McMath and Orville Burton. Westport, Conn.: Greenwood Press, 1982, 71–102.

Tucker, David. *Black Pastors and Leaders.* Memphis: Memphis State University Press, 1975.

———. *Lieutenant Lee of Beale Street.* Nashville: Vanderbilt University Press, 1971.

*Beverly Greene Bond*

## Memphis Lyceum

The Memphis Lyceum, a literary society established in the 1880s, met on Friday evenings at the city's LeMoyne Normal Institute. Membership in the group was open to LeMoyne's students and teachers at the city's African American schools. Meeting activities included dramatic readings and performances, musical presentations, book discussions, poetry readings, and lectures. Participation in the Lyceum provided members with opportunities to practice public speaking and debating skills.

The society published a newsletter, the *Evening Star*, which was edited in the 1880s by Ida B. Wells, who was teaching in the public schools at that time. The newsletter contained information about local events, critiques of selections presented at earlier meetings, poetry, literary notes, and a "They Say" column about Memphis's black personalities.

Wells described some Lyceum meetings in her diary entries as well as in her autobiography. She noted that members listened to lectures on race topics and the problems of Africa, readings from *Macbeth*, and a speech by P. B. S. Pinchback, former acting governor of Louisiana. In 1886, Wells presented a paper on "What Lack We Yet" to the group.

The Lyceum continued meeting as the LeMoyne Literary Society until the early 1900s and was one of several cultural organizations developed by black Memphians during this period.

### FURTHER READINGS

*Catalogue of the LeMoyne Normal Institute, 1907–1908.* Memphis: LeMoyne Institute Press, 1908.

DeCosta-Willis, Miriam, ed. *The Memphis Diary of Ida B. Wells.* Boston: Beacon, 1995.

Duster, Alfreda M., ed. *Crusade for Justice: The Autobiography of Ida B. Wells.* Chicago: University of Chicago Press, 1970.

*Beverly Greene Bond*

## Miami: Civic, Literary, and Mutual Aid Associations

In April 1896, Henry Morrison Flagler extended his Florida East Coast Railroad into Miami. Following completion of the railroad, Flagler built the Royal Palm Hotel, which led to rapid population growth in the south Florida area. On July 28, 1896, Miami was incorporated as a city, after 368 voters, 162 of whom were African Americans, voted for the incorporation charter. Ironically, the African American voters were disfranchised soon afterward through local and state action.

From the beginning of the city's settlement, African Americans played an important role in Miami's development. Labor shortages forced employers to depend on African Americans as the primary labor force. Coconut Grove was the first black settlement in south Florida. It was made up principally of Bahamians who resided in the Peacock Inn, the first hotel on south Florida's mainland. Segregation and racially restrictive codes locked African Americans into "Colored Town," a small northwestern section of the city initially settled by black employees of the Flagler system. City officials later changed the community's name to Overtown. Like African Americans in other southern cities, blacks in Overtown established a variety of social, economic, religious, and educational institutions that served the needs of black residents.

Churches and businesses were among the city's first black institutions. Flagler, Miami's leading developer, donated land for the building of black churches. Among the first black churches built in the Overtown area were the Mount Zion Baptist Church, Greater Bethel African Methodist Episcopal Church, and St. Agnes Episcopal Church. Not surprisingly, ministers were among the first leaders of the community. By 1904, the Reverend S. W. Brown had turned the Colored Town Bargain Store into a prosperous business. Another minister, the Reverend W. P. Pickens, edited the city's first black newspaper, the *Industrial Reporter*. These businesses were supplemented by grocery and drug stores as well as boarding houses and the Cola Nip Company, the only black-owned manufacturing company in the area. The Colored Board of Trade, which was run by Kelsey Leroy Pharr, a funeral director and owner of the first black cemetery, coordinated the African American commercial district. In 1905, the Miami Industrial Mutual Benefit Insurance Company was opened as part of the Colored Board of Trade. Dana Dorsey was Overtown's most successful entrepreneur. He built the area's first hotel and donated money to build the first park, library, and school in Liberty City, Florida's first public housing project. By 1915, Miami's black community was thriving. Its business district, located along Avenue G, was home to several establishments including barbers, cabdrivers, butchers, entrepreneurs, and manufacturers.

Despite the success of black businesses, the Overtown area also suffered from high poverty rates and overcrowding. In the 1920s, the Negro Civic League led the fight to build Liberty Square, Florida's first public housing project. Floyd Davis, a developer, convinced black families to move into the area to alleviate overcrowding.

In addition to business ventures, Miami's black population also pursued educational activities. In the 1890s, Marshall Williams started to operate the first school in his home, and in 1914 Arthur and Polly Mays opened another school. The Booker T. Washington Junior/Senior High School, the first public school offering twelve grades of instruction to the city's black residents, did not open until 1927. While the school served as a center for intellectual training, it also provided African Americans with public spaces for social gatherings. The school's auditorium was host to movies, art shows, concerts, and recitals.

Other efforts to foster education and provide intellectual stimulation for the city's African American residents were provided by the Literary Guild and the Friendship Garden and Civic Club. The Literary Guild, organized by a group of women and staffed by volunteers, encouraged the study of history and literature. The Friendship Garden and Civic Club, founded by Annie Coleman in 1936, operated Miami's first black public library. The Paul Lawrence Dunbar Library, established in Coleman's backyard, provided books, a Black History week celebration, and other educational material for children.

During the first four decades of the twentieth century, Overtown grew rapidly. By 1940, thirty-eight beauty shops, eighteen barber shops, eighteen grocers, twenty-six dry cleaners, thirty-two confectionery stands and ice cream parlors, thirty-one restaurants, three funeral parlors, and one florist operated in the black community. In addition, Overtown residents had access to their own hospital, staffed by ten doctors, three dentists, four pharmacists, three druggists, and several nurses, most of whom had been trained at Meharry Medical School in Nashville, Tennessee. Two black lawyers also served the community. African Americans in Miami maintained their own library, businesses, schools, and social organizations, and published five newspapers at various times, among them the *Miami Metropolis*, later renamed the *Miami News*.

The heart of the black community was N. W. 2nd Avenue, also known as "Little Broadway," where most of the hotels and night clubs were located. Overtown had several fine hotels for prominent black visitors performing at white-owned clubs near Miami Beach. Among the community's most reputable hotels were the Dorsey, Marsha Ann, and Lord Calvary. Perhaps the best of the hotels was the Mary Elizabeth, which had three floors, operated the first hotel elevator in the community, and was the tallest building in Overtown. Several prominent African Americans such as Thurgood Marshall, W. E. B. Du Bois, Mary Bethune, Adam Clayton Powell, and A. Phillip Randolph stayed there.

Miami's black residents also established several fraternal and social organizations. These included Masonic fraternities, lodges of F. and A. M., several courts of Heroines, three Prince Hall Grand Lodges, and one Most Worshipful Grand Lodge. The Masons owned and operated a three-story building in Overtown. There were also women's auxiliaries, such as the Queen of the South, the Ladies Court, the Household of Ruth, and the CWEST club, which provided welfare and relief services to African Americans.

Like black residents of other cities, Miami's African Americans launched a variety of social, economic, religious, and educational organizations that provided important services to the black community.

**FURTHER READINGS**

Colburn, David, and Jane Landers, eds. *The African American Heritage of Florida*. Gainesville: University of Florida Press, 1995.

Dunn, Marvin. *Black Miami in the Twentieth Century*. Gainesville: University of Florida Press, 1997.

Goings, Kenneth, and Raymond Mohl, eds. *The New African American Urban History*. Thousand Oaks, Calif.: Sage, 1996.

Hirsch, Arnold, and Raymond Mohl, eds. *Urban Policy in 20th Century America*. New Brunswick, N.J.: Rutgers University Press, 1993.

Mohl, Raymond, ed. *The Making of Urban America*. Wilmington, Del.: Scholarly Resources, 1993.

Smiley, Nixon. *Yesterdays Florida*. Miami: E. A. Seeman, 1974.

*Abel A. Bartley*

## Michigan Commission on Civil Rights

Established on January 1, 1964, the Michigan Commission on Civil Rights (MCCR) was a constitutional body that monitored abuses of civil rights by private corporations and government agencies while working to create governmental mechanisms to improve the socioeconomic status of historically marginalized groups, particularly African Americans.

The MCCR was the product of the 1961 State Constitutional Convention, which sought to append an anti-discrimination charter to the Michigan Constitution. For three years, opponents of the proposal tried to stall adoption of the new constitution, but ultimately they failed. On April 1, 1963, Michigan voters approved the new constitution on the heels of a well-organized campaign waged by a coalition of progressive social, economic, and political groups.

The new state constitution also provided for the creation of the MCCR. Initial members of the MCCR were Albert Wheeler, associate professor of bacteriology at the University of Michigan and leader of the Ann Arbor–Ypsilanti National Association for the Advancement of Colored People (NAACP); Daisy Elliott, legislator, president of the Michigan Federal Democratic Clubs, and representative to the 1961 Michigan Constitutional Convention; and Detroit delegates Lillian Hatcher, Sidney Barthwell, Richard Austin, and Coleman Young, future mayor of Detroit. Lending organizational support in the campaign to create the MCCR was the Michigan Coordinating Council on Civil Rights, a nonpartisan federation of Michigan organizations composed of various Christian and Jewish associations, the NAACP, the Michigan State American Federation of Labor–Congress of Industrial Organizations, and the United Automobile Workers Fair Practices and Anti-Discrimination Department. Other supporters included John A. Hannah, chairman of the United States Commission on Civil Rights, Republican delegate to the 1961 Michigan Constitutional Convention, and president of Michigan State University; and George Romney, governor of Michigan in 1964.

The MCCR monitored implementation of Michigan's antidiscrimination provision and notified the state's executive and legislative branches if it suspected businesses or government offices of violating the charter. The state then conducted hearings to determine the validity of the MCCR's claims and reprimanded violators and/or subjected them to economic sanctions, such as the refusal to grant or renew government contracts. Violators were also subjected to scrutiny by the MCCR, which made suggestions for diversifying work forces and administering resources on an equitable basis. The MCCR, however, had no enforcement powers, and the state of Michigan rarely went so far as to impose economic penalties on negligent groups.

**FURTHER READINGS**

"Civil Rights Commission Turns 25." *Detroit Free Press* November 27, 1989.

Dykes, De Witt, Jr. "Elliott, Daisy (1919– )." In *Black Women in America: An Historical Encyclopedia*. Ed. Darlene Clark Hine, Elsa Barkeley Brown, and Rosalyn Terborg-Penn. Bloomington: University of Indiana Press, 1993, 390–391.

Fine, Sidney. *Civil Rights and the Michigan Constitution of 1963*. Ann Arbor: Michigan Historical Collections, Bentley Historical Library, University of Michigan, 1996.

John A. Hannah Papers. University Archives and Historical Collections. Michigan State University, East Lansing, Michigan.

Pollock, James K. *Making Michigan's Constitution, 1961–1962*. Ann Arbor: George Wahr, 1962.

*Matthew C. Whitaker*

# Michigan Committee for Intercultural Understanding

The Michigan Committee for Intercultural Understanding (MCIU) was formed by black and white activists following the Detroit race riot of 1943. The MCIU worked to improve race relations and achieve racial equality. For this purpose, it picketed, marched, wrote letters of protest that were printed primarily in black newspapers, and lobbied the state government for political and economic support. Moreover, it helped organize interracial coalitions that addressed institutional racism and police brutality. The development of the MCIU and similar associations formed the cornerstone of a movement that blossomed into the civil rights movement during the 1950s and 1960s.

The MCIU emerged as Michigan's black urban population grew rapidly due to the influx of migrants attracted by the state's expanding World War II industry. As a result of the growing diversification of the state's population, as well as competition for jobs and housing, racial antagonisms and confrontations escalated to the point of rebellion in 1943. The committee was organized to deal with these problems and devise methods for improving race relations.

The MCIU demanded the complete desegregation of public places, including schools; the creation of a black residential housing project; a study of sewer and sidewalk needs in African American communities; an end to police brutality; and appointment of black officials to local and state government positions. Moreover, the MCIU insisted on equal employment opportunities, demanding that employers ensure that African Americans represented 10 percent of their work force.

African American women played key roles in creating and sustaining the MCIU, often working long hours, under stressful conditions, with few resources and no compensation. Pauline Byrd Taylor, a schoolteacher from Kalamazoo, for example, worked to improve the socioeconomic status of African Americans and race relations in Michigan with the help of local churches, the National Association for the Advancement of Colored People (NAACP), and several interracial coalitions. Taylor led protest marches and organized direct spending campaigns, fund-raisers, and other efforts to secure jobs and housing for blacks.

Ultimately, the MCIU's work helped pave the way for the 1961 Michigan State Constitutional Convention, out of which was born the Michigan Commission on Civil Rights (MCCR) on January 1, 1964. The MCCR was charged with monitoring civil rights abuses while working to create governmental mechanisms to improve the socioeconomic status of historically marginalized groups, particularly African Americans. The MCIU ceased to exist after 1963, most likely forming the cornerstone of the MCCR.

**FURTHER READINGS**

Fine, Sidney. *Civil Rights and the Michigan Constitution of 1963.* Ann Arbor: Michigan Historical Collections, Bentley Historical Library, University of Michigan, 1996.

Pollock, James K. *Making Michigan's Constitution, 1961–1962.* Ann Arbor: George Wahr, 1962, 68.

Rosenwald Fund Foundation Papers. Special Collections. Fisk University Library, Nashville, Tennessee.

Shaw, Stephanie. *What a Woman Ought to Be and Do: Black Professional Women Workers during the Jim Crow Era.* Chicago: University of Chicago Press, 1996.

Thompson, Kathleen. "Richardson, Gloria St. Clair Hayes (1922–)." In *Black Women in America: An Historical Encyclopedia.* Ed. Darlene Clark Hine, Elsa Barkeley Brown, and Rosalyn Terborg-Penn. Bloomington: University of Indiana Press, 1993, 980–982.

*Matthew C. Whitaker*

## Middle States Baseball League

Established in 1889, the Middle States Baseball League included two African American teams, the New York Gorhams and the Cuban Giants, and white teams from Harrisburg, Norristown, Lebanon, Lancaster, York, and Hazelton (all in Pennsylvania). Each team represented a city, the Gorhams Easton, Pennsylvania, and the Cuban Giants Trenton, New Jersey. The league lasted for one year.

The Gorhams, early rivals of the Cuban Giants as the best black team in the East, were owned by Ambrose Davis, who had been the first black owner of a salaried baseball team. The tenure of the Gorhams in the Middle States League, however, was short lived because the team fared poorly and dropped out early in the season. One of the Gorhams players was Sol White, who, at age nineteen, began to play baseball in 1887. White continued to play professional baseball for twenty-five years and then went on to a career as an officer, manager, and coach of the Negro National League. After his retirement from baseball, White wrote a column for the New York City *Amsterdam News* newspaper. His greatest contribution to African American baseball, however, was his *History of Colored Baseball.* Written in 1907, the book is the most significant source of information about the black teams and players of the late nineteenth and early twentieth centuries.

The Cuban Giants fared much better than the Gorhams, apparently winning the league's title. They edged out Harrisburg in winning percentage, .780 to .753. A series of rulings, however, resulted in a reversal of the order and the crowning of Harrisburg as the "official" champion. The Cuban Giants included Frank Grant and George Stovey on their roster. Grant played for nineteen years, with various teams, and is recognized as one of the outstanding baseball players of the nineteenth century. He was spiked so often by racist team opponents that he began wearing wooden shinguards and was eventually moved from second base to the outfield for his own protection. Stovey was the best black pitcher in the 1890s and may be best known as the player whom Cap Anson refused to play against in an exhibition game on July 16, 1887—an event that triggered the exclusion of African Americans from the major and minor leagues.

The Middle States League lasted one year and was replaced in 1890 by the Eastern Interstate League in which the Cuban Giants represented York, Pennsylvania, as the York Monarchs.

**FURTHER READINGS**

Clark, Dick, and Larry Lester. *The Negro Leagues Book.* Cleveland: Society for American Baseball Research, 1994.

Dixon, Phil. *The Negro Baseball Leagues: A Photographic History.* Mattituck, N.Y.: Amereon House, 1992.

Malloy, Jerry. *Sol White's History of Colored Baseball, with Other Documents on the Early Black Game, 1886–1936.* Lincoln: University of Nebraska Press, 1995.

Riley, James A. *The Biographical Encyclopedia of the Negro Baseball Leagues.* New York: Carroll and Graf, 1994.

*Lyle K. Wilson*

## Milwaukee: Civic, Literary, and Mutual Aid Associations

Although the late nineteenth and early twentieth centuries witnessed the gradual migration of southern blacks to northern industrial centers, Milwaukee failed to attract large numbers of African Americans. As late as 1900, the city claimed fewer than one thousand blacks. Even under the impact of the Great Migration of World War I, the city's black population made up just 0.2 percent of the total number of residents. Still, in absolute numbers, Milwaukee's African American population expanded from only about five hundred people in 1890 to seventy-five hundred in 1930. Although Milwaukee had one of the smallest black populations among the twenty-five largest U.S. cities, class, ethnic, and racial conflict soon undercut the position of African Americans in the urban political economy and precipitated the growth of all-black civic, literary, and mutual aid associations.

Next to churches, lodges and fraternal organizations were the most significant pre–World War I black institutions. Formed in 1891, the oldest of these was the Prince Hall Masonic Widows Son Lodge, Number 25. Blacks also organized a Colored Knights of Pythias in 1892 and an African American branch of the United Order of Odd Fellows in 1903. The number of black secret organizations reached a prewar peak of eight in 1905. Most of these orders soon established female auxiliaries, which helped mitigate social divisions along gender lines. These organizations also helped bridge emerging class and status distinctions within the small black community. Nonetheless, an old elite of professional and business people, catering mainly to a white clientele, took the principal leadership positions in these fraternal orders. The Prince Hall Lodge emerged under the leadership of Lucien Palmer, insurance agent and first black elected to the Wisconsin legislature. Attorney William T. Green and well-known waiter and grocer John J. Miles also held offices in as many as four or more of these organizations by the early 1900s. Black fraternal organizations provided members sickness, disability, and burial benefits, as well as social, cultural, and entertainment activities.

By the onset of World War I, several social-service, literary, self-improvement, and women's clubs rounded out the institutional life of Milwaukee blacks. Some of the women's clubs survived through various parts of the migration, the Depression, and World War II. In order of their formation, these included the Cream City Social and Literary Society (1880s), the Silver Leaf Charity Club (1890s), the Woman's Improvement Club (1908), and the Phyllis Wheatley Club (1912). These clubs sponsored fund-raising socials, balls, picnics, and entertainments of various types. Like their fraternal counterparts, however, they also both bridged and reflected social cleavages within the black community. The Cream City Social and Literary Society was made up primarily of wives of Milwaukee's oldest black residents. On the other hand, the Woman's Improvement Club and others formed just before World War I represented the distinct influence of an emerging middle class.

Under the impact of World War I, black civic, social, and fraternal orders underwent substantial change. As southern blacks entered the city in rising numbers, organizations like the Milwaukee Urban League emerged to address their employment, social-welfare, and housing needs. The rise of black professional social-service organizations accented the inadequate, though helpful, material-aid functions of black fraternal orders and social clubs. Still, the persistence of old prewar orders and the rise of new ones underscored the continuing and even expanded significance of black self-help organizations. Three major lodges established by the prewar elite persisted into the 1920s: the Masonic Widows Son Lodge, the Colored Knights of Pythias (Pride of Milwaukee), and the United Order of Odd Fellows. These organizations continued to provide mediums for cultural expression and social interactions. Their material and mutual-aid functions also continued, but they now increasingly emphasized fund-raising for such organizations as the Milwaukee branches of the National Association for the Advancement of Colored People (NAACP), the Milwaukee Urban League, and the churches.

In the wake of World War I and its early aftermath, as elsewhere in urban America, Milwaukee's fraternal organizations, lodges, and social-service clubs also mirrored the growing stratification of the black community. Lawrence E. Miller, a resident of Milwaukee since 1921 and later member of Widows Son, has described how, because of the stringent membership rules and practices governing old organizations, new lodges emerged to meet the needs of the changing class structure. In 1925, several newcomers banded together and formed the Blazing Star Chapter of the Prince Hall Masons. "New elite" in its leadership, membership, and orientation, Blazing Star was nevertheless more receptive to blacks from the expanding industrial working class than Widows Son. Elks Lodge Number 423, established around the same time, was even more decidedly working class in its membership and orientation.

Black women's organizations were particularly sensitive to changes in the African American class structure, as well as to changes in the functions of black institutions. More than male organizations, middle-class black women's groups conducted supportive "charity work" for social-welfare, civil rights, and religious organizations. Like male lodges, though, they continued to function as instruments of cultural expression and entertainment for members, a goal vividly reflected in the name of the most important new club to emerge by the mid-1920s: the Pleasant Company Needle Craft Club. The founding women of this club were the spouses of such men as P. Jay Gilmer, a physician; J. H. Kerns, head of the Milwaukee Urban League; J. A. Josey, editor of the Wisconsin Enterprise Blade; and the wives of ministers of leading congregations like St. Mark Methodist Episcopal Church and Calvary Baptist Church. The activities of black working-class women, though more casual and informal, complemented the civic and social-welfare services of Milwaukee's small black community. Material or economic aid weighed heavily among their primary activities. A glimpse of their work is revealed in Idella Blakely's description of her mother's role in the Church of God in Christ:

"My father started first in the ministry, and my mother thru his consistent urging and his hard work, was drawn into the ministry. She was a great gospel singer and great expounder of God's word. She helped many people, those that had no homes to live in, those that had no food, those that had no clothes. She went around the street gathering up wayward children. We reared two children that, she adopted them, two, we didn't adopt, we just raised them. My mother's home was always open to all strangers. . . . when my father would be at work, these people would come to the home . . . and she really pushed, when my father would come home, she would have a house full, we would go from home to home, and sing and pray and administer the word of God. We'd wash dirty clothes. We'd take food and feed them, and every day every evening we'd bring like 6, 7, 8 souls into God."

Black institutions within Milwaukee's small African American community nonetheless developed in marked contrast to those in larger centers of African American population. With fewer institutions at the outset of the period, Milwaukee blacks also moved less rapidly toward greater institutional diversity than blacks in Cleveland, Chicago, and other cities. As a consequence, class divisions in Milwaukee—themselves less prominent than elsewhere—found less institutional expression. Social stratification in the city's black institutional life usually involved one or two major institutions rather than distinct clusters of several middle- and working-class orders that prevailed among African Americans elsewhere in the urban north.

### FURTHER READINGS

Buchanan, Thomas R. "Black Milwaukee, 1890–1915." M.A. thesis, University of Wisconsin, 1967.

Trotter, Joe William, Jr. *Black Milwaukee: The Making of an Industrial Proletariat, 1915–1945*. Urbana: University of Illinois Press, 1985.

*Joe W. Trotter*

## Milwaukee Commission

*See* Milwaukee's Mayor's Commission on Human Rights.

## Milwaukee's Mayor's Commission on Human Rights

In 1944, Mayor John L. Bohn initiated the Mayor's Commission on Human Rights (MCHR) to assist in eliminating discriminatory policies and practices in Milwaukee. The Commission consisted of thirty citizens appointed by the mayor from the ranks of various religious, civic, racial, labor, and business organizations, as well as government agencies. MCHR members investigated human rights violations and advised the municipal government of its agencies' discriminatory practices. Moreover, the MCHR provided public education programs, sought to increase employment opportunities and housing availability, and stimulated interaction between different ethnic and racial groups. In 1954, the commission changed its name to the Milwaukee Commission on Human Rights and gained statutory authority.

Initially, the commission attempted to create understanding among various ethnic groups. By the mid-1950s, however, the commission realized the special needs of Milwaukee's African American and Spanish-speaking residents. During the mid- to late-1950s, the commission addressed discrimination complaints from Hispanics and blacks, especially in the areas of health, employment, and housing. As early as the 1920s, health care rarely incorporated nonwhite staff.

As whites moved to Milwaukee's suburbs in the 1950s, the commission also addressed discriminatory practices in the newly emerging residential communities. The commission asked the state to adopt nonsegregation statutes and urged suburban communities to pass similar ordinances. It supported programs provided by the 1954 Federal Housing Act, such as the voluntary home mortgage credit that diverted the flow of mortgage money from prosperous areas to less wealthy regions, the fair appraisal of property, and a builders warranty to ensure the quality of home constructions.

In addition to the lack of affordable housing, the 1950s also saw a shift in the city's employment opportunities from manufacturing to nonmanufacturing, construction, service, and trade employment. Employment opportunities for unskilled labor declined as employers looked for employees with more education, appropriate physical qualifications, skills, and good work habits. Because of these increasing standards, a more competitive market, and unfair hiring practices by employers, more people filed discrimination complaints. As the complaints grew, many social organizations supported fair-employment practices, such as the Wisconsin Industrial Commission, even though these agencies often lacked authority to order employers to cease discriminatory practices.

The Milwaukee Commission on Human Rights tackled community problems in a variety of ways. The commission sponsored meetings with local ministers, bar owners, and the National Association for the Advancement of Colored People (NAACP) to encourage understanding among white, blacks, and other ethic groups. It also sought assistance from scholars to study the effects of urban congestion on family life and community interaction. The commission challenged churches to extend full membership to all races and suggested that teachers and police officers receive inter-group-relations training and recognize the problems and cultural differences affecting disadvantaged children.

Beginning in 1953, the commission published a bimonthly newsletter to inform citizens of its activities and other local and national human rights trends. It also sponsored activities such as educational foreign exchange programs, fair election campaigns, and police-community conferences to improve relations between city residents and the police force. Commission members served as consultants and resource leaders for human-relations institutes

such as the Vocational Guidance Institute, which sought to assist teachers counseling black students. Commission members also appeared on television programs and made radio announcements, worked with other local and state organizations and agencies, and attended communitywide meetings with representatives from government, labor, industry, education, churches, and civic organizations.

The commission ceased to exist in the 1960s, when other municipal agencies incorporated its agenda. During its existence, the Commission successfully assessed Milwaukee's social and economic conditions, recommended solutions, and actively engaged the community in its mission.

**FURTHER READINGS**

Milwaukee Commission on Human Rights. *United in Diversity*. Milwaukee, Commission on Human Rights, 195?. Historical Library Pamphlet Collection. University of Wisconsin, Madison.

———. *These Are the People of Milwaukee*. Milwaukee, Commission on Human Rights, 1955. Historical Library Pamphlet Collection. University of Wisconsin, Madison, Wisconsin.

*Julie Shipe*

## Ministers for Racial and Social Justice

In 1967, a group of black clergy of the United Church of Christ (UCC) founded the Ministers for Racial and Social Justice (MRSJ) to enlighten the Church about racial and social concerns of African Americans.

The MRSJ emerged in response to the UCC's growing support for racial justice during the early 1960s. In 1963, for example, the Church Synod called on it members to support the civil rights movement, to end segregation within the Church, and to tackle unemployment, education, housing, and other community concerns of African Americans. Synod delegates encouraged members of their churches to welcome all people regardless of race, to exchange pastors between white and black churches, to contract with and buy from businesses that practiced fair employment, and to hold public schools accountable for desegregation. A year later, several church delegates visited Washington, D.C., to lobby congressional support for pending civil rights legislation. Moreover, the Church petitioned the Federal Communications Commission to deny license renewal to two television stations in Jackson, Mississippi, that had broadcast racists' announcements and given only minimal air time to minorities.

Emboldened by the Church's efforts on behalf of racial justice, the MRSJ challenged the General Synod in 1969 to seek new ways to minister to minorities and other nontraditional members of the Church. The MRSJ invited James Forman to the Synod's meeting. Foreman, a black militant leader, wrote an essay called the *Black Manifesto*, urging the UCC Synod and other predominantly white denominations to raise $130 million in support of a black university and $10 million to establish a United Black Appeal organization. In response to Forman's demands, the Synod agreed to investigate the feasibility of funding a black university in the South, supporting black publishers and printing businesses, creating a southern land bank, assisting missionaries to Africa, and conducting business with black financial institutions.

Despite the church's decision to study Forman's demands, many white-dominated Church organizations that had previously rallied for social and racial justice were alienated by the public criticism that the MRSJ voiced at the Synod's 1969 meeting. As a result, the MRSJ decided to reorganize and charter the United Black Churchmen (UBC) in 1970. In 1976, the group changed its name to the United Black Christians to include women.

United Black Christians represents more than fifty thousand African American clergy and laity within the UCC. The organization has challenged the Church to increase its efforts in reaching minority church members, launched several programs to promote black leadership within the UCC, and provided opportunities for black fellowship. UBC programs include a Black Youth Caucus, a Black Women's Caucus, Regional Leadership Workshops, a Regional Black Church Development Program, and a Black Seminary Student Network.

Located in Chesapeake, Virginia, the UBC also publishes newsletters and Synod briefings to provide its members with information about the organization's activities. The organization meets for a national convention every two years.

**FURTHER READINGS**

Braun, Theodore A. "United Church of Christ General Synod." *Christian Century* 86 (1969), 1000–1002.

Parker, Everett G. "For Civil Rights Legislation." *Christian Century* 81 (1964), 467–468.

Payne, Wardell J. ed. *Directory of African American Religious Bodies: A Compendium by the Howard University School of Divinity*. 2nd ed. Washington, D.C.: Howard University Press, 1995.

Wineke, William R. "A New F.C.C. Order—but Will It Work?" *Christian Century* 85 (1968), 1448–1450.

*Julie Shipe*

## Minneapolis' Mayor's Council on Human Relations

The Minneapolis' Mayor's Council on Human Relations was formed in 1946 by Mayor Hubert Humphrey and continued under Mayors Hoyer and Peterson. The council was an official agency of the city government, although it operated without government funds, raising money through public subscription. Operating under the authority of the Mayor's Office, the council had no office, staff, or legal status.

The mayor appointed twenty-seven citizens to serve on the council for three-year terms. Their mission was to reduce prejudice and discrimination through research, education, and social action. The council launched public education programs to improve community relations and monitored discrimination in employment, housing, and law enforcement. Through involvement with similarly oriented agencies and organizations, the council provided a base of resources for coordinating and planning in the field of civil rights.

Over the years, the council gained membership and public support, and it started to operate independently of the Mayor's Office, filling its own vacancies and determining its own program. As the council evolved and expanded, so did its mission. It sought to provide equality of opportunity and prohibit discriminatory practices based on race, color, creed, religion, ancestry, or national origin in employment, labor union membership, housing accommodations, property rights, education, public accommodations, and public services. In 1967, the council was absorbed by the newly created State Department of Human Rights.

**FURTHER READINGS**

Human Rights Department Papers. Minnesota State Archives, Saint Paul, Minnesota.

Minneapolis Civil Rights Papers. Minnesota State Archives, Saint Paul, Minnesota.

*Mollie A. Spillman*

## Minnesota Fair Employment Practice Commission

Created in 1955, the Minnesota Fair Employment Practice Commission (MNFEPC) was responsible for monitoring implementation of the state's Fair Employment

Practices Law. Section One of the law mandated the state "to foster the employment of all individuals in accordance with their fullest capacities, regardless of their race, color, creed, religion, or national origin, and to safeguard their rights to obtain and hold employment without discrimination."

The commission consisted of nine members, each representing a congressional district. The governor appointed the members with the approval of the Senate and empowered the commission to employ a small staff. The governor designated the commission's chairman, and the commissioners, who served a five-year term, chose the executive director. Eugenie Anderson (1955–1961), William Cratic (1961–1965), and Kennon V. Rothchild (1965–1967) chaired the MNFEPC, while Wilfred C. Leland (1955–1963), James C. McDonald (1963–1965), Walter S. Warfield (1965), and Viola May Kanatz (1965–1967) served as executive directors.

The function of the commission was to resolve complaints of discrimination and to promote fair-employment practices through education and public information, such as conferences and speeches directed at major employers, labor organizers, employment agencies, and community leaders. During the first seven years of operation, the commission received 205 charges of discrimination. The staff investigated complaints and provided summary reports to the commission members, who, based on the evidence, determined probable or no probable cause in the dispute. In cases in which evidence supported the allegations, the commission and its staff attempted to resolve the complaints through conciliation. If the commission's attempts at conciliation were unsuccessful, a hearing before a board of review was scheduled. This board consisted of three individuals, at least one of whom was an attorney, drawn from a twelve-person panel appointed by the governor. Members of the commission could not serve on the board of review.

In April 1961, the Minnesota Legislature amended the state's Fair Employment Practices Law to include a fair-housing provision. The MNFEPC, charged with monitoring housing complaints, changed its name and became the State Commission against Discrimination (SCAD). The commission enforced the State Act against Discrimination from the time it became effective in December 31, 1962, until 1967. The SCAD was responsible for eliminating discrimination based on race, color, creed, religion, or national origin in areas of employment and housing. Since the most frequent allegation in housing

complaints was refusal to rent, SCAD workers visited owners of rental property in the Twin Cities and explained the stipulations of the law to them. The SCAD also studied the equal-opportunity policies of businesses that employed fifty or more workers in order to recommend more effective affirmative action practices. In early 1964, the commission opened a part-time branch office in Duluth to facilitate processing complaints in the northern part of the state.

In 1967, the Department of Human Rights was created when the Legislature further broadened the scope of the SCAD. The department absorbed the duties of the Governor's Human Rights Commission and the Governor's Commission on the Status of Women, which had been created by executive order in 1963. Minnesota was the first state in the nation to establish an executive agency with departmental status to administer its equal-opportunity law.

**FURTHER READING**

Human Rights Department Papers. Minnesota State Archives, Saint Paul, Minnesota.

*Mollie A. Spillman*

# Minnesota State Commission Against Discrimination

*See* Minnesota Fair Employment Practice Commission.

# Minnesota's Governor's Human Rights Commission

*See* Governor's Interracial Commission, Minnesota.

# Minnesota's Governor's Interracial Commission

*See* Governor's Interracial Commission, Minnesota.

# Minority Business Development Agency

On November 1, 1979, United States secretary of commerce established the Minority Business Development Agency (MBDA), formerly known as the Office of Minority Business Development. The agency's national headquarters is located in Washington, D.C. It maintains regional offices in Atlanta, Chicago, Dallas, New York City, and San Francisco.

The MBDA was created to address inequalities resulting from certain business practices, such as lending discrimination of financial institutions. The agency serves the minority business community by providing developmental assistance nationwide, working to implement policies that will enable minority groups to start and operate successful businesses. It does so by coordinating efforts among business and government leaders. For instance, the MBDA works with minority associations like the National Minority Suppliers Development Council to provide minority vendors with opportunities to do business with government agencies and corporations. This might include the sale of cleaning supplies, food services, and a variety of other products and services. Each year, the MBDA hosts a Minority Enterprise Development Week that is designed to promote awareness of the resources available for minority business startup and operation.

Technical assistance is available through the Minority Business Development Centers (MBDC). There are approximately one hundred such centers, along with Native American Business Development Centers (NABDC), across the nation. In addition, the Minority Business Development Agency operates two Minority Enterprise Growth Assistance (MEGA) Centers, serving the Midwest and western regions of the United States. The MEGA Centers offer assistance geared to the specific needs and interests of potential entrepreneurs. For example, each houses a Franchise Profiles database that lists more than 450 franchise businesses available to prospective business owners.

One of the main objectives of the MBDA has been to provide minority entrepreneurs with opportunities to expand into global markets. In 1992, the agency began a partnership with the International Trade Administration (ITA) to provide minority businesses with export, marketing, and trade information designed to enable them to launch their products and services overseas. Together, both agencies sponsor the Matchmaker Trade Delegations Program through which minority businesses in the United States are connected with foreign partners that have been screened by the Commerce Department's staff.

Since December 1993, more than 170 minority business owners have participated in trade missions to Canada, Mexico, South Africa, Brazil, the Dominican Republic, Haiti, and Jamaica, where they have received information about doing business in those nations. The delegates meet with their international counterparts to make preliminary arrangements for joint business efforts. As a result of participation in the program, many minority firms have greatly increased their export sales.

**FURTHER READINGS**

"MBDA's National Franchise Initiative." *Franchising World* 26, 2 (March/April 1994), 40.

Rendineau, Judy. "Matchmaker Events Planned for Minority Companies." *Business America* 115, 6 (1994), 19.

Richardson, Linda L. "Minority Business Development Agency Helps Minority-Owned Firms Overcome Export Hurdles and Compete in the International Marketplace." *Business America* 116, 9 (1995), 25–26.

*Sharon Parkinson*

## Minority Women in Science

Minority Women in Science (MWIS), established in 1979, is a national network group of the American Association for the Advancement of Science (AAAS). The MWIS began its work as a special-interest group concerned with advancing equity among minorities and women in the scientific community. The group identifies and shares resources, strengthens communication among its members, and mentors young people. The benefits of membership are information sharing and developing contacts with other women and minorities working in science and engineering. The network comprises volunteers who establish informal local chapters to advance common objectives. Particularly active chapters are operating in Washington, D.C., Greensboro, North Carolina, and Selma, Alabama.

Members of all local network groups meet occasionally to share ideas about activities, programs, and materials that have been used successfully to spark interest in careers in science and engineering fields. Individuals or organizations contact the AAAS to identify minority women scientists who can serve as role models in print and broadcast materials, as grant-proposal reviewers, and as prospective board members or committee appointees. The MWIS presents individuals who conduct science programs in their local communities with a Certificate of Recognition at the AAAS annual convention. Members receive a yearly newsletter and special updates on fellowships and scholarships. Other MWIS publications include *Girls and Science, In Touch with Girls and Science, Status of African Americans in Science and Engineering in the United States,* and *Status of Women Scientists and Engineers in the United States.*

*Dennis W. Cheek*

## Mississippi Council on Human Relations

The Mississippi Council on Human Relations (MCHR) was one of twelve state Councils on Human Relations founded by the Southern Regional Council of Atlanta, Georgia, to succeed its Mississippi Division in 1955. Established as a private, nonpolitical, nonsectarian, interracial organization, the MCHR carried out educational programs designed to expand economic, civic, and cultural opportunities for Mississippians, regardless of racial, religious, or national origins. As an incorporated nonprofit organization, the MCHR derived its financial support from membership dues, contributions, and grants from the Fund for the Republic and the Field Foundation.

The MCHR, operating through eight local councils, advocated the elimination of discrimination and segregation in Mississippi. It adopted the motto "Overcoming Evil with Good" and worked in direct opposition to the White Citizens' Councils and the Sovereignty Commission of Mississippi. The MCHR supported voter-registration campaigns, equal access to public accommodations, equal employment opportunities, Head Start, black higher education through scholarship funds, the federal Office of Equal Opportunity's surplus-food distribution program, the Mississippians for Public Education, and the Mississippi Freedom Democratic Party's challenge at the 1968 National Democratic Convention. Based on data gathered by its local chapters on issues such as education, health, federal programs, law enforcement, and housing, the MCHR presented its findings on the status of Mississippi's human relations to state and federal government officials, as well as the United States Commission on Civil Rights. The council ceased to function by the early 1970s.

### FURTHER READING

Southern Regional Council Papers, Series IV: State Councils on Human Relations, 1946–1968, Reels 144–145. Special Collections. Robert W. Woodruff Library, Atlanta University Center, Atlanta, Georgia.

*Kimberly E. Nichols*

## Mississippi Delta Principals Institute

*See* Southern Regional Council.

## Mississippi Freedom Democratic Party

Created in 1964, the Mississippi Freedom Democratic Party (MFDP) was an interracial political party that challenged the regular Mississippi Democratic Party at that year's Democratic National Convention in Atlantic City, New Jersey. Formed as part of the 1964 Mississippi Freedom Summer campaign organized by the Council of Federated Organizations (COFO), the MFDP was an attempt to create an alternative political organization for Mississippi blacks.

Originally, COFO organizers merely planned to use the MFDP as an extension of their 1963 Freedom Vote, which featured the mock election campaign of Aaron Henry, president of the Mississippi National Association for the Advancement of Colored People (NAACP), for state governor and white Tougaloo chaplain Ed King for lieutenant governor. By the end of the summer of 1963, eighty-three thousand mostly black Mississippians had cast ballots in this mock election. COFO organizers hoped that the MFDP could capitalize on the success of the Freedom Vote campaign and continue to cultivate grassroots political activism.

Shortly into the planning sessions for the 1964 Freedom Summer, organizers realized that the MFDP might be able to play a national role. Increasingly frustrated by the systematic exclusion of African Americans from Mississippi's Democratic Party, organizers hoped that national Democratic leaders might recognize the MFDP as a legitimate alternative to the state's Democratic Party. Such a move would not only repudiate the lily-white regular Mississippi Democrats, it would also place the MFDP in a position to control federal assistance to the state. Freedom Democrats, fearing that regular Mississippi Democrats might never eradicate racial segregation if left to their own devices, thus sought federal and national assistance to further civil rights within the state.

To claim legitimacy as a third party and an alternative to the state's lily-white Democratic Party, the MFDP held local precinct meetings and county conventions and eventually staged a state convention to elect delegates to attend that summer's Democratic National Convention in Atlantic City. Although the Freedom Democrats initially received a large amount of support from liberal Democrats throughout the country, they encountered difficulty in Atlantic City. President Lyndon B. Johnson, in an effort to maintain party unity and secure his election as president, ordered vice presidential candidate Hubert Humphrey to develop a compromise that would allow the seating of the regular Mississippi delegates and,

Martin Luther King Jr. speaks to members of CORE and SNCC in Atlantic City, New Jersey. August 1964. *Library of Congress*

at the same time, recognize the growing racial tensions in Mississippi. Under the Humphrey compromise, two MFDP representatives were to be seated as at-large delegates and only Mississippi Democrats who were willing to swear their allegiance to the national Democratic ticket would be permitted to take their places on the convention floor. Much to the dismay of national civil rights leaders and liberal Democrats, both groups refused to compromise. Claiming that they had not journeyed to Mississippi to accept anything less than full political recognition, Freedom Democrats staged a sit-in on the convention floor and then returned to Mississippi.

In 1965, the MFDP attempted to unseat Mississippi's congressional delegates, claiming that they had been elected in violation of the Fourteenth and Fifteenth Amendments of the United States Constitution. Freeedom Democrats demanded that the election be invalidated, insisting that, until black Mississippians could participate in state elections, no elected official truly represented the state. The United States House of Representatives, assuring Freedom

Democrats that the 1965 Voting Rights Act would provide for fair elections, voted to allow the five white Mississippi congressmen to remain seated. Although MFDP members expressed disappointment and displeasure at this congressional decision, they also hoped that the Voting Rights Act would empower them to elect African Americans to local, state, and federal offices. By 1967, in the wake of only limited federal enforcement of the Voting Rights Act in Mississippi, Freedom Democrats wondered if the federal government would ever give them any real political assistance.

Any doubts about the federal government's and the Democratic Party's ambivalence toward the Freedom Democratic Party disappeared in 1968. Frustrated by the MFDP's unwillingness to enter into political compromises that were likely to harm black Mississippians, the national Democratic Party was in a quandary. It could not cooperate with the regular Mississippi Democratic Party because of the group's overt racism and growing hostility toward the national party. Yet, the MFDP's refusal to participate in political compromises also made the Freedom Democrats unattractive to the national party. To avoid the dilemma of choosing between two unappealing groups, the national party assisted in the creation of a third Democratic organization in the state—the Loyal Democrats of Mississippi.

Composed almost entirely of moderate black and white Mississippians, the Loyalists solidly supported Hubert Humphrey's presidential bid. The interracial group appealed to desperate national Democratic leaders because its moderation stood in sharp contrast to the vicious racist diatribes of some regular state Democrats and the radical cries for black power that some Freedom Democrats emitted. At the 1968 Democratic National Convention in Chicago, the Loyal Democrats of Mississippi sought and won seating as the official Mississippi delegation. The group returned home triumphant, possessing the blessings of the national Democratic Party.

One of the reasons why the MFDP had such difficulty working with the national Democratic Party was the MFDP's philosophy of participatory democracy. Many Freedom Democrats had been influenced by the Student Nonviolent Coordinating Committee's practice of nurturing and training local residents for community leadership and involving the largest possible number of people in the decision-making process. Freedom Democrats believed that local residents recognized and understood the needs of their community better than anybody else and should, therefore, be in charge of local politics. Implicit in this conceptualization of community dynamics was the belief that "experts" and politicians should not tell local community members what to do. Thus, Freedom Democrats took their cues and organizational leadership from their local constituency. During the MFDP's most active years, from 1964 to 1968, the party's state elected offices were filled with a wide variety of local activists, including Aaron Henry, Fannie Lou Hamer, Leslie McLemore, Merrill Lindsey, J. W. Brown, Annie Devine, Percy Chapman, Charles Robinson, R. L. T. Smith, Eddie Thomas, Evelyn Wright, Samuel Glover, Ed King, Victoria Jackson Gray, and Pinky Hall. The MFDP's emphasis on community participation also enabled a number of women and poor African Americans to assume leadership positions, something seldom seen in many of the larger national civil rights organizations such as the Southern Christian Leadership Conference (SCLC) or the National Association for the Advancement of Colored People (NAACP).

Despite the MFDP's ability to generate community involvement, it slowly faded out of existence in the late 1960s. The death knell for the MFDP was sounded in 1968. That year, the Democratic National Convention recognized the interracial Loyal Democrats of Mississippi as the state's official party delegation, depriving the MFDP of much of its national and local support base. Although the state organization ceased to function after 1969, local chapters continued to exist into the 1970s. While the MFDP was unable to sustain itself as an organization and failed to gain recognition as an official affiliate of the Democratic Party, it provided large numbers of dispossessed Mississippians with leadership training and an outlet for political activism.

**FURTHER READINGS**

Davis, Vanessa L. "'Sisters and Brothers All': The Mississippi Freedom Democratic Party and the Struggle for Political Equality." Ph.D. diss., Vanderbilt University, 1996.

Dittmer, John. *Local People: The Struggle for Civil Rights in Mississippi.* Urbana: University of Illinois Press, 1994.

Forman, James. *The Making of Black Revolutionaries.* Washington: Open Hand, 1985.

Holt, Len. *The Summer That Didn't End: The Story of the Mississippi Civil Rights Project of 1964.* New York: DeCapo, 1965.

McAdam, Doug. *Freedom Summer.* New York: Oxford University Press, 1988.

Mills, Nicholas. *Like a Holy Crusade: Mississippi 1964: The Turning Point of the Civil Rights Movement in America.* Chicago: Dees, 1992.

*Vanessa L. Davis*

# Mississippi Progressive Voters' League

Begun in 1947, one year after the United States Senate campaign of Democrat James Eastland, Chair of the Senate Judiciary Committee and an opponent of civil rights, the Mississippi Progressive Voters' League (MPVL) was the state's first African American voter-registration organization. The MPVL attempted to register black voters independent of the National Association for the Advancement of Colored People (NAACP), which had operated in Mississippi since 1918. MPVL President and founder T. B. Wilson, disgusted by what he considered to be the radical and counterproductive tactics employed by the NAACP, had launched the league to create a moderate alternative. The MPVL, Wilson hoped, would appeal to moderate black lodges and churches without attracting the wrath of Mississippi whites or the state's government. Under Wilson's direction, the MPVL focused exclusively on voter registration and legal education. The majority of the league's programs were aimed at middle-class, educated African Americans who had the money to pay Mississippi's poll tax and the formal education necessary to pass voter-registration literacy exams.

At its height, the MPVL had five thousand members and maintained offices in Jackson, Clarksdale, and Hattiesburg. By 1952, the MPVL, with the cooperation of the NAACP and the Mississippi State Democratic Association, raised the number of registered black voters in the state to a post–Reconstruction high of twenty thousand. Despite this impressive number, black registered voters represented a scant 6 percent of Mississippi's eligible black voting population, and black voter turnout in local, state, and national elections never equaled the number of black registered voters. By focusing exclusively on the registration and education of potential black voters, the MPVL neglected to tackle the larger issues of voter intimidation and unconstitutional election laws. Moreover, because the league largely addressed middle-class, educated African Americans, it failed to mobilize rural blacks, who remained ignorant of their citizenship rights.

As the 1950s progressed and massive white opposition to black political participation reached new heights, the league found its strategy increasingly difficult to implement, and gradually the organization began to diminish. As late as 1962, there were still some local chapters in existence, but the statewide organization had ceased to be a major factor in Mississippi politics. Other civil rights organizations, such as the Student Nonviolent Coordinating Committee and the Mississippi Freedom Democratic Party, continued the league's strategy of registering African American voters in the 1960s.

**FURTHER READING**

Dittmer, John. *Local People: The Struggles for Civil Rights in Mississippi.* Urbana: University of Illinois Press, 1994.

*Vanessa L. Davis*

## Montgomery Improvement Association

The Montgomery Improvement Association (MIA) was the organizational vehicle of the Montgomery bus boycott (December 5, 1955–December 20, 1956). The MIA not only prosecuted the bus boycott to a successful conclusion, but also propelled Reverend Martin Luther King Jr., to national and international prominence. Furthermore, it provided an organizational model that was widely imitated by other black communities. Finally, the MIA, together with the organizations that it inspired, formed the basis for the Southern Christian Leadership Conference (SCLC), which, under King's leadership, provided crucial direction to the civil rights movement between 1957 and 1968.

The MIA did not instigate the Montgomery bus boycott. The protest was precipitated by Rosa Parks, who was arrested on December 1, 1955, for refusing to yield her bus seat to a white man when ordered to do so by the driver. The idea for a boycott of the buses had been discussed for many months, and after Parks's arrest and conviction it received ready support from National Association for the Advancement of Colored People (NAACP) leader E. D. Nixon, lawyer and minister Fred Gray, college teacher Jo Ann Robinson, and from Parks herself. Robinson, assisted by fellow members of the Women's Political Council, took the decisive step of announcing and publicizing the boycott. When the MIA came into being on December 5—Reverend Ralph D. Abernathy suggested the name—the boycott was already underway.

The most important fact about the MIA was its local, independent character. Although Parks was a longtime NAACP activist, as was Nixon, blacks in Montgomery chose to create a new organization to coordinate the boycott. They wished to counter the white assertion that opposition to segregation derived from "outside agitators" and "Communists" rather than from southern blacks themselves. By distancing itself from the NAACP, with its headquarters in New York City, the MIA stressed the indigenous and autonomous nature of the bus boycott.

The MIA founders also believed that the best way to harness the enthusiasm and energy of Montgomery's black population was to create a local "umbrella organization" that would involve every section of the community. NAACP direction, they feared, would make mass involvement impossible: the organization was too bureaucratic, too legalistic, and too centralized. In addition, the intense white hostility toward the NAACP made many blacks fearful of associating with it. Finally, the MIA initially demanded only the fair treatment of blacks without challenging segregation; this goal was unacceptable to the NAACP, which in 1950 had abandoned the goal of "separate but equal" in favor of complete integration.

Rosa Parks (center) on her way to jail after being arrested on charges of violating segregation laws. February 22, 1956. *Library of Congress*

Broad-based ministerial leadership also distinguished the MIA from the NAACP. Although many NAACP branches in the South were led by ministers, it was rare for most of the black ministers in a community to unite across denominational lines in support of a militant protest. The formation of the MIA, however, thrust black ministers into a new position of leadership. That a clergyman, King, led the MIA and that other clergymen dominated, numerically at least, the MIA's executive board reflected the fact that lay people were often vulnerable to economic retaliation from whites, whereas ministers were relatively independent. It also testified to the enthusiasm of the ordinary people (which put pressure on the ministers to lead), a desire to accord the boycott moral respectability, and a recognition that the black church was the strongest and most widely rooted institution within the black community.

The MIA's most important tasks were to organize an alternative transportation system and to maintain the community's morale. It achieved the first by organizing a car pool and by purchasing a fleet of station wagons. It achieved the second by instituting regular mass meetings, always held in churches, that featured hymns, prayers, and inspirational speeches. The MIA looked to the example of the earlier Baton Rouge bus boycott, which took place in 1953, for lessons in organization. Led by the Reverend T. J. Jemison and organized by an ad hoc group calling itself the United Defense League, that protest had failed to integrate buses in Baton Rouge, but it did unite the black community for a week. Jemison's advice on forming a car pool proved especially useful.

The MIA at first tried to operate in a clandestine manner, so as to prevent the white authorities from identifying, and thereby persecuting, the leaders. Indeed, the fact that King, a relative newcomer to Montgomery, was selected to head the MIA was telling evidence of the timidity of other ministers and of the factional and personal divisions that plagued the black community.

Secrecy, however, proved impossible to maintain. Once King had been identified as the MIA's president, the authorities singled him out for harassment; they then indicted and prosecuted virtually the entire MIA leadership. These oppressive actions backfired on the whites, merely strengthening the resolve and unity of the black community. They also enhanced King's reputation, causing him quickly to eclipse the other MIA leaders. The local and national news media began to focus on King, as did outside activists such as Glenn Smiley, white field secretary of the Fellowship of Reconciliation, and Bayard Rustin, black executive director of the War Resisters League. These two veteran pacifists came to Montgomery to advise and assist the boycott. They immediately appraised King as a man of high intelligence, strong character, great charisma, and enormous leadership potential. They played a key role in orienting King, and the MIA, toward the philosophy of Gandhian nonviolence. Rustin, in particular, helped connect the MIA, through King, to labor, pacifist, and civil rights organizations in the North. While accepting outside help, however, King scrupulously maintained the MIA's independence.

As negotiations with the city and the bus company failed, and the Montgomery bus boycott continued into 1956, other functions, such as the raising of money, the nurturing of outside support, and the formulation of legal strategy, became increasingly important to the MIA. The MIA's broad base enhanced its effectiveness. Its executive board embraced most of the leading ministers, civic activists, and community leaders. Smaller committees dealt with specific tasks, such as negotiation, fund-raising, and transportation. The negotiating committee operated, in effect, as a strategy committee.

In 1956, with the help of NAACP lawyers, the MIA decided to directly challenge the principle of bus segregation. Affirmed by the United States Supreme Court, the decision of a three-judge federal panel in the case of *Browder v. Gayle* voided Alabama's bus segregation laws. When blacks in Montgomery returned to the buses on December 21, 1956, they could sit wherever they pleased.

The MIA had weathered harassment, threats, and prosecution from whites, as well as the defection of the Reverend U. J. Fields, one of its officers. Flexible and inclusive, it had pioneered an alternative method of organization to that of the NAACP. Above all, the MIA demonstrated that an entire black community could unite in a determined struggle against segregation, in the heart of the Deep South, and press on to victory.

Inspired by the boycott's success, blacks in other southern communities formed similar "umbrella organizations," most of them also led by ministers. They included the Inter-Civic Council of Tallahassee, Florida; the Baton Rouge Christian Movement; the United Christian Movement of Shreveport, Louisiana; the Petersburg Improvement Association of Virginia; the Nashville Christian Leadership Council; and the Birmingham-based Alabama Christian Movement for Human Rights. Like the MIA, they adopted loose structures and eschewed formal membership so as to minimize their vulnerability to state harassment. In Shreveport, Birmingham, Tallahassee, and elsewhere, they also copied the MIA in organizing bus boycotts, although none of them achieved the kind of clear-cut victory attained in Montgomery.

The persecution of the NAACP by state authorities throughout the South—the NAACP was outlawed in Alabama and decimated in Louisiana—provided a further stimulus to the formation of independent, church-based organizations. In January 1957, representatives of these and other groups joined MIA leaders King and Abernathy in forming the SCLC.

Despite King's prominence within the MIA, it is important to stress that the Montgomery bus boycott was a grassroots protest and that the MIA provided a collective leadership. Ministers like Abernathy, S. S. Seay, H. H. Hubbard, R. J. Glasco, B. J. Sims, B. D. Lambert, and Robert Graetz (a white man) ably supported King. Lawyer Fred Gray, businessman Rufus Lewis, and community leader E. D. Nixon also made vital contributions to the boycott. So did women such as Rosa Parks, Jo Ann Robinson, A. W. West, and Erna Dungee.

It was nonetheless true that, during 1956, decision-making in the MIA became increasingly centralized and King became the most important voice. King's dominance created some jealousy and dissension, and it anticipated the autocratic leadership style that he later exercised as president of the SCLC. On the other hand, the spontaneous acclaim that he received from ordinary people convinced King that blacks needed an individual leader, a symbol, around whom they could rally. There was also a very real sense in which King believed that God had chosen him for leadership.

King's active involvement with the MIA ceased upon his move to Atlanta in 1960. The MIA stayed in existence, engaging in voter-registration drives and playing a role in the student sit-in movement of 1960, the Freedom Rides of 1961, and other civil rights campaigns. It still functions today as a civic and civil rights organization. Its principal significance, however, lies in its coordination and leadership of the Montgomery bus boycott, a seminal event in the history of the civil rights movement.

**FURTHER READINGS**

Branch, Taylor. *Parting the Waters: America in the King Years, 1954–1963*. New York: Simon and Schuster, 1987.

Burns, Stewart, ed. *Daybreak of Freedom: The Montgomery Bus Boycott*. Chapel Hill: University of North Carolina Press, 1997.

Garrow, David J. *Bearing the Cross: Martin Luther King, Jr., and the Southern Christian Leadership Conference*. New York: William Morrow, 1986.

King, Martin Luther, Jr. *Stride Toward Freedom: The Montgomery Story*. New York: Harper and Brothers, 1958.

Robinson, Jo Ann Gibson. *The Montgomery Bus Boycott and the Women Who Started It*. Ed. David J. Garrow. Knoxville: University of Tennessee Press, 1987.

*Adam Fairclough*

# Moorish Science Temple of America

In 1913, Timothy Drew, the son of former slaves from North Carolina, established the Moorish Science Temple of the United States in Newark, New Jersey. Embodying a variety of Islam, the movement quickly spread through African American communities in urban centers across the United States, especially in the Midwest.

While mystery surrounds the origins of Drew's association with, and knowledge of, Islam, he apparently came into contact with various belief systems while traveling abroad. Convinced that Christianity was the white man's religion, Drew offered a brand of Islam that blended traditional Islamic beliefs, biblical teachings, Orientalism, racial pride, Masonic influences, and mythology. He proclaimed that blacks were the descendants of "Moors," who had originally migrated from Asia and eventually settled in Africa, specifically Morocco.

Declaring himself a prophet, he assumed the name Noble Drew Ali and wrote the *Circle Seven Koran*, an esoteric work, not to be confused with the Koran of orthodox Islam. Ali conferred "El" or "Bey" to the surnames of his followers, encouraged the adoption of Oriental garb, and directed his fellow "Moors" to follow strict moral and dietary guidelines. The temple also issued "Moors" identification cards, or passports, proclaiming their new identity.

As Moorish Science expanded, the organization became infiltrated with unscrupulous opportunists. In Chicago in 1929, internal rivalry led to the death of one of Ali's rivals. When police intervened, further violence erupted and Ali was arrested. Released on bond, the prophet died under mysterious circumstances several weeks later. Some suspect that he met his death at the hands of rival "Moors," others believe he died as a result of a police beating, while at least one historian posits that Ali died of pneumonia.

The most significant contribution of the Moorish Science Temple movement was that it offered meaning and identity to a people marginalized by greater American society. Today, several factions of "Moors" claiming to be the heirs of Noble Drew Ali continue to preach his brand of Islam.

**FURTHER READINGS**

Haddad, Yvonne, and Jane Idleman Smith. *Mission to America: Five Islamic Sectarian Communities in North America*. Gainesville: University Press of Florida, 1993.

McCloud, Aminah Beverly. *African American Islam*. New York: Routledge, 1995.

Wilson, Peter Lamborn. *Sacred Drift: Essays on the Margins of Islam*. San Francisco: City Lights Books, 1993.

*A. J. Scopino Jr.*

# Mosaic Templars of America

The Mosaic Templars of America was an all-black fraternal organization founded in 1882 in Little Rock, Arkansas, by two local black Republican politicians, Chester W. Keatts and John E. Bush. Keatts and Bush, joined by several friends, sought to create a male benevolent institution that would help its members pay for the care of ill family members and the burial of their dead. They chose the name Mosaic Templars to reflect their religious motivations: they sought to provide leadership and succor for African Americans in the years after Reconstruction just as Moses had done for the Children of Israel during their escape from Egypt in the biblical story of Exodus. The society grew rapidly in Arkansas and developed small chapters throughout the South; by the 1920s, it claimed more than twenty-five thousand members. Soon after its inception, the Mosaic Templars added auxiliary branches for women, a savings and loan association, and a training program for members interested in owning and operating small businesses. The organization eventually waned in public appeal in the decades after World War I, when it competed with new black-run banks and insurance companies to meet the financial needs of southern blacks.

Chester Keatts and John Bush probably first crossed paths in the late 1870s, but their lives up until that time ran a similar course. Keatts was born in 1854 to slave parents outside of Little Rock, Arkansas. He worked as a sharecropper for most of his early life, securing a common school education in the decade following the end of the Civil War. Active in Republican politics from an early age, Keatts secured a number of federal patronage positions, including posts as a railway mail clerk with the Postal Service and as a U.S. deputy marshal for the Eastern District of Arkansas in 1876. He served as a trustee of First Baptist Church in Little Rock and as a member of the black Masons, Odd Fellows, and Colored Knights of Pythias. Like Keatts, Bush was active in politics and black organizational life. Born in 1856 in Moscow, Tennessee, to slave parents, Bush moved to Little Rock after Appomattox. He earned a certificate of completion from the Little Rock public schools and trained as a brick mason. He also worked in local Republican politics, earning appointments as a railway mail clerk with the Postal Service and as a receiver of the land office at Little Rock in 1898. He was a charter member of the National Negro Business Men's League along with Booker T. Washington.

Keatts and Bush, by starting the Mosaic Templars, sought to help African Americans advance materially when many of the opportunities and civil rights won in the Civil War fell victim to the politics of sectional reconciliation in the 1870s and 1880s. They aimed to furnish ex-slaves and their families with an organization to help them save money, plan for the future, learn basic business skills, and keep alive the hope for full participation in American society.

**FURTHER READINGS**

Bush, A. E., and P. L. Dorman, eds. *History of the Mosaic Templars of America: Its Founders and Officials*. Little Rock: Central Printing, 1924.

Dillard, Tom W. "'Golden Prospects and Fraternal Amenities': Mifflin W. Gibbs' Arkansas Years." *Arkansas Historical Review* 35 (Winter 1976), 307–333.

Gatewood, Willard B. Jr., ed. "Arkansas Negroes in the 1890s: Documents." *Arkansas Historical Review* 33 (Winter 1974), 293–325.

*John M. Giggie*

# MOVE

Vincent Leaphart founded the Philadelphia-based Christian Movement for Life, which first shortened its name to The Movement and later to MOVE, in the early 1970s. MOVE is an interracial organization that advocates a natural lifestyle free of technology and the corruption of so-

ciety. Much of the organization's life, however, was characterized by violent confrontations with the Federal Bureau of Investigations (FBI) and Philadelphia city police and political officials.

Leaphart, who later took the name John Africa, formulated MOVE's philosophy in a three-hundred-page work titled *The Guidelines* or *The Book*, which serves as the organization's ideological blueprint. During MOVE's early years, John Africa conducted discussion sessions of *The Book* in his home, where he recruited many of the organization's original constituents, including various members of his family, homeless people, college students, business people, and political activists. Individuals who joined MOVE changed their last names to Africa to symbolize their connection as one family and their identification with African culture. The members of MOVE, both black and white, are also characterized by their dreadlocks, indicating their desire for natural living.

Described as a utopian organization, MOVE embraced natural living and advocated appreciation of all forms of life as well as access to pure air, clean water, and fertile soil. Rejecting modern technology as the antithesis of natural living, members banned the use of running water and electricity. MOVE also used political and social activism to convince others to adopt the organization's philosophy. MOVE members assisted the elderly with home repairs, attempted to rehabilitate and teach convicts the philosophy of MOVE, and helped the homeless find shelter. The organization also launched protests and rallies against city policies, specifically targeting the Philadelphia board of education, animal abuse, and police harassment in the black community.

These protests eventually led to an increase in violent confrontations with Philadelphia police and city officials. Originally a nonviolent organization, MOVE responded to these violent encounters by changing its philosophy and adopting self-defense as a legitimate tool in the fight against corrupt society. During the 1970s, violence between MOVE and Philadelphia city police continued to escalate and resulted in two deadly incidents.

In 1978, Philadelphia police attempted to remove MOVE members from their Powelton Village home by cutting their access to water, food, and other supplies between March 16 and May 5. Negotiations ended the blockade, and MOVE members agreed to turn over their weapons, permit an inspection of their property to determine code violations, remove all animals from the premises, desist from placing garbage in the backyard, and vacate their home by August 2, 1978. In return, the city released recently arrested and jailed MOVE members on their own recognizance. When the organization failed to vacate its property, the court issued arrest warrants for those MOVE members who had been released from prison but failed to appear at their bail hearings. The police again surrounded the Powelton Village home of MOVE, and a shootout ensued that left one officer dead and four officers, three MOVE supporters, two MOVE members, and six firefighters wounded. Nine MOVE members were arrested, tried, and convicted for the murder of police officer James Ramp. Although it was unclear who had killed the officer, MOVE members convicted of the crime received sentences ranging from thirty to one hundred years in prison.

The second violent encounter between MOVE and Philadelphia police and city officials occurred on May 13, 1985, when police tried to serve arrest warrants for Ramona, Conrad, Frank, and Teresa Africa on charges of disorderly conduct. On the morning of May 13, police surrounded the 6221 Osage Avenue home of MOVE after evacuating neighbors living within several blocks of the organization. When Ramona, Conrad, Frank, and Teresa Africa refused to comply with police orders and leave their house, violence erupted. The police propelled tear gas and fired more than ten thousand bullets into the MOVE home. Finally, city police bombed the roof of the MOVE house, which created a fire that spread to adjoining homes, burning two square blocks on both sides of Osage Avenue. Six MOVE adults, including John Africa, and five children were killed. Another 250 residents were left homeless as a result of the fire. One adult, Ramona Africa, and one child, Birdie Africa, survived the incident.

Following the Osage Avenue incident, Ramona Africa was imprisoned for seven years on disorderly conduct and conspiracy charges. After her incarceration, she and the relatives of John Africa, including his nephew Frank Africa, launched a successful lawsuit against the city of Philadelphia, former Mayor Wilson W. Goode, former Police Commissioner Gregore Sambor, and former Fire Commissioner William Richmond. Although Goode was exempt from charges, both Sambor and Richmond were forced to pay $1 a week for eleven years. The city of Philadelphia awarded the three plaintiffs $1.5 million. Relatives of the murdered adults each received $90,000. The city settled lawsuits filed by the parents of the five children killed in the fire for $25 million, while Birdie Africa, the only surviving child, received $1.7 million.

Although the organization had branched out of Philadelphia into Rochester, New York, and Richmond, Virginia, confrontations with the FBI and Philadelphia police and city officials eventually led MOVE to shut down most of its operations. Some of MOVE's New York and Virginia members who had returned to Philadelphia were killed in the Osage Avenue massacre, while others were convicted on various charges of weapon violations or disorderly conduct. The organization remains based in Philadelphia and continues to have conflicts with the police and city officials. The most recent of these controversies involved the suspicious death of Merle Africa on March 13, 1998. Merle, one of the nine MOVE members convicted of the murder of officer Ramp, died at Cambridge Springs prison at the age of forty-one. Although she was believed to be in perfect health, she became unconscious during a visit by another MOVE member. Medical services, though located ten minutes away from Merle, arrived on the scene forty minutes later. MOVE demanded an investigation into the sudden death of Merle Africa, but, as late as April 2000 (as this is written), correctional officials had not responded to the group's request. In the meantime, MOVE increased its efforts to obtain the release of the remaining eight imprisoned members.

**FURTHER READINGS**

Anderson, John. *Burning Down the House: MOVE and the Tragedy of Philadelphia.* New York: Norton, 1987.

Assefa, Hizkias. *Extremist Groups and Conflict Resolution: The MOVE Crisis in Philadelphia.* New York: Praeger, 1988.

Harry, Margot. *Attention, MOVE! This is America!* Chicago: Banner, 1987.

*Twenty-Five Years on the MOVE.* Philadelphia: MOVE, 1996.

Wagner-Pacifici, Robin Erica. *Discourse and Destruction: The City of Philadelphia Versus MOVE.* Chicago: University of Chicago Press, 1994.

*Nishani Frazier*

## Movement
*See* MOVE.

## Mutual Association of Eastern Colored Baseball Clubs
*See* Eastern Colored League.

## Mutual Musicians' Foundation

Founded in 1928 as the Musician's Protective Union, Local 627 of Kansas City, Kansas, the Mutual Musicians' Foundation (MMF) provided an artistic home for the area's many musicians. The segregated black local grew gradually and, by 1938, had 174 members. In its early years, the local sponsored an annual battle of the bands that often included as many as six bands. In 1930, the MMF moved into its current home, a bright pink stucco building with a neon treble clef painted above the door. The building, constructed in 1904, was named a Federal Historic Landmark in 1979. The site continues to serve as a rehearsal space during the day and as a space for musicians to gather for impromptu all-night jam sessions in the evening. Musicians who have played there include Benny Moten, Count Basie, Ben Webster, Walter Page, Lester Young, Mary Lou Williams, Joe Turner, and Charlie Parker.

*Nichole T. Rustin*

**FURTHER READINGS**

Haddix, Chuck. "Eighteenth and Vine: Streets of Dreams." *Artlog* 13 (1992), 1, 5.

"Kansas City Revives Jazz Landmark." *New York Times* May 2, 1985.

## Nashville: Civic, Literary, and Mutual Aid Associations

Persons of African descent were involved in the establishment of Nashville in 1780 and made up 20 percent of the city's original settlers. Free blacks constituted 21 percent of the city's African American population; however, the vast majority were slaves. Whether slave or free, Nashville's African Americans created numerous associations that catered to their religious, educational, and social needs. The number of associations, particularly prior to the Civil War, is difficult to discern because the institution of slavery and a set of laws, known as slave or black codes, limited the mobility and social interaction of Nashville's black population.

Slaves, who in their homeland had created secret societies and associations, were forced either to end their social activities or to go underground. In Nashville, slaves continued to gather secretly. They met for social gatherings in the homes of free blacks and conducted religious meetings in the woods that became their "invisible churches." Recent archaeological discoveries at the Hermitage plantation near Nashville in Davidson County indicate that many slaves wore lucky charms, such as clenched hands, carved of wood or stone, and other symbols of their secret societies and associations.

Similarly, free blacks quietly formed associations and organized clandestine schools prior to the Civil War. Between 1833 and 1837 Alphonso Sumner, a black barber, operated the first of these schools until he was accused of writing letters to fugitive slaves, whipped, and exiled. Sumner relocated to Cincinnati, where he became an abolitionist and publisher of that city's first black newspaper. Daniel Wadkins and other free blacks carried on Sumner's work in Nashville and continued to teach African American children until December 1856. That month working-class whites started a "race riot" and forced the black schools to close. Despite restrictions on educational activities, Nashville's free blacks were allowed to operate an "African Bazaar" and maintain four quasi-independent church congregations. By 1860 Nashville's black population numbered 3,945, constituting 26 percent of the city's total population.

The Civil War and the Union army's occupation of Nashville in February 1862 served as a social catalyst and provided a fertile and protective environment for the development of black institutions. During the war, the city's African American population increased to more than twelve thousand persons, not including some thirteen thousand U.S. Colored Troops who served with the Union army in middle Tennessee. The black population explosion was largely the result of the influx of fugitive slaves who were housed in contraband camps in and near the city, which now had five black residential areas.

In the immediate aftermath of the Civil War, Nashville's black population launched numerous social, religious, benevolent, and mutual aid societies. Prewar free blacks organized the Rock City Lodge F. and A. M., for those "who belonged to the more intelligent [elite] portion of their race" (*Republican Banner*, July 17, 1867). On August 17, 1865, Cincinnati's William G. Goff officially inaugurated the lodge, which had thirty-seven charter members, including John B. Hadley, Nelson Walker, James H. Sumner, John J. Cary, and James C. Napier. By 1866, almost all the black church congregations had declared their independence from the white churches and started to establish not only religious associations but also temperance and benevolent societies. Other postwar associations included the Colored Barbers' Association, established by Frank Parrish in 1866, and the Sons of Ham Benevolent Society.

A host of benevolent societies provided aid for destitute freedmen and organized institutions for their uplift. In 1866, Nelson Walker, a black businessman, established the Annual Agricultural and Mechanical Association Fair. The fair encouraged freedmen to focus on occupational assets such as trades, crafts, and mechanical and agricultural skills to "uplift the race." In 1872, Frederick Douglass, a former abolitionist and proponent of black Reconstruction, spoke at the fair, attracting thousands of freedmen. Another association that assisted freedmen was the Colored Benevolent Society No. 1, which collected funds and, in 1869, opened Mount Ararat Cemetery, the oldest black cemetery in Nashville.

Black efforts to assist the freedmen were supported by white northern missionaries, who flooded Nashville after the emancipation of the slaves in 1863. These whites helped establish schools for the black population, including the city's four freedmen's colleges—Tennessee Manual Labor University (1867–1874), Roger Williams University (1864–1929), Fisk University (1866–), Walden University (1868–1924), and Meharry Medical College (1875–). Moreover, they helped launch several churches and the Colored Temperance Society to stop immorality and alcohol abuse among freedmen.

During the 1870s, when African Americans formed 30 percent of Nashville's population, some of the city's black associations shifted their problem-solving focus to the acquisition of land and the removal of freedmen from impoverishment. In September 1869 the Black Exodus movement began in Nashville. In the following decade the movement attracted large numbers of disillusioned African Americans, and by the early 1880s, Benjamin "Pap" Singleton, a former slave and cabinet and coffin maker, led some twenty-five thousand area blacks to Kansas to acquire federal lands. Singleton, William A. Sizemore, and others formed the Edgefield Real Estate Association and the Colored Emigration Club and published three emigration newspapers.

After the 1896 Supreme Court ruling in *Plessy v. Ferguson*, when African Americans were forced to create a "World-Within-a-World," Nashville's black population, now some 40 percent of the city's residents, launched numerous new organizations to address the needs of the black community. Intellectual, cultural, and civic activities started to flourish, sparked in part by Nashville's four freedmen's colleges. Among the city's most prominent

black literary associations was the Nashville Colored Debating Society. In 1892 the society hosted a visit by Frederick Douglass, who talked about the terrible tide of racial lynchings in Nashville and elsewhere in the South. Another important source for stimulating debates was the black fraternal organizations. In the late nineteenth century Nashville was home to seven black lodges, including the Knights of Templar, which met either at the Pythian Temple on 5th and Capitol or Burrus Hall on Cedar and McLemore. All lodges had elaborate parade banners printed by the National Baptist Publishing Board (1896–), founded by Richard H. Boyd, a former slave. As black businesses started to boom, African American businessmen established professional and commercial organizations. Under the leadership of James C. Napier, they formed a chapter of the National Negro Business League in 1902 and founded the Negro Board of Trade in 1912.

Nashville's black women were particularly active in providing mutual aid and relief work at the turn of the century. They established numerous associations including the Nashville Federation of Colored Women's Clubs under Frankie S. Pierce; the Colored Prohibition Club under John and Sarah Woodson Early; the Nashville Provident Association; Mrs. A. Sumner's Colored Relief Society; the Ladies Relief Society, headed by Mary J. Marshall and Mary Nunnelly; the Colored Home Mission and Temperance Society of East Nashville; the Colored Women's Christian Temperance Union, headed by Mrs. C. H. Phillips; and the Women's Relief Auxiliary of the Grand Army of the Republic's Lincoln Chapter No. 1, an association for black veterans of the Union army, headed by Preston Taylor, a local minister and businessman. Moreover, Nashville's black women, under the leadership of Mrs. M. A. Dowling, established the old Colored Women's Home in 1894. Two years later they founded the Phyllis Wheatley Club, headed by Mrs. Evans Tyree, which operated a hospitality room in Mercy Hospital by 1907.

Black women also took a great interest in the plight of the city's black children. In 1897, for example, the Colored Orphans' Society established a Colored Orphanage. Similarly, the elite (in terms of wealth and education) women's Day Home Club, under the leadership of Nettie Langston Napier, assisted black children in need. The objective of the Day Home Club was "gathering the children from the streets, protecting them from harm, elevating them above crime, and helping the mother who has to leave them alone and go out to make a living for them."

In addition, black women held "Parents' Conferences and Mothers' Meetings" to mobilize the community behind a campaign designed to "Save the Children" and improve the local schools.

In the twentieth century the major objectives of black associations and their leaders was to initiate social reform, improve morality, and provide leisure facilities and wholesome recreation. In 1911, George E. Haynes, head of Fisk University's social science department, launched efforts to improve health and social conditions in Nashville's black neighborhoods. He collaborated with the Rock City Medical Academy and presented the city government with a list of critical social and health service needs of the black community. In 1912 African American doctors formed the Hubbard Hospital Association and raised funds to open Meharry's Hubbard Hospital. In the following year, Bethlehem Center, a product of the white Methodists' social activism among southern blacks, began to offer kindergarten services, classes in sewing and home economics, and clubs for children and mothers. The Bethlehem Center continues to operate in several modern buildings on Charlotte Avenue.

From 1894 until 1915, Joanna P. Moore, a white northern Baptist missionary, and several black women, including Ada F. Morgan and Mary Flowers, operated the Fireside School on Gay Street. The women taught black families how to use the Bible and teach Sunday school lessons within their homes to improve morality and spirituality. After Moore's death in 1916, Grace M. Eaton, another white northern Baptist missionary, headed the Fireside School and published its *Hope* magazine. In 1923 Eaton and black female colleagues started the Grace M. Eaton Day Home on Gay Street to provide child-care services for working black mothers. The Home continues to operate in a modern facility on 18th Avenue North under the supervision of a black female board of directors. In 1933 Eaton also organized the Joanna P. Moore Women's Christian Temperance Union, which remained active until her death in 1946.

Civil rights organizations had been active in Nashville since the end of the Civil War. These included the State Colored Men's Conventions (1865–1867, 1870–1885) and a state chapter of the Equal Rights League (1864–1867), both headquartered in Nashville. In the early twentieth century the city's black population also established chapters of the National Urban League and the National Association for the Advancement of Colored People (NAACP). By 1911 the National Urban League was operating in the city, trying to eradicate the awful slums and poor socioeconomic conditions that plagued the majority of black Nashvillians. Responding to a new wave of lynchings and the failure of the accommodationist strategy of the late Booker T. Washington, African Americans formed the Nashville chapter of the NAACP in January 1919. That year, James C. Napier, member of the NAACP, and other black residents staged a huge protest march on the governor's office in downtown Nashville to petition for protection from lynchers and the rights of black men as Tennessee citizens.

Baseball clubs fit prominently into the social life of Nashville's black population, and various clubs sponsored receptions and parties to honor the black baseball players cherished by the black population. African American civic leaders opened four recreational parks, including Preston Taylor's thirty-seven-acre Greenwood Park (1905–1951), which offered rides and provided a bandstand, buildings filled with attractions, and a large baseball stadium. Hadley Park, probably the country's first public park for African Americans, was opened on July 4, 1912.

Those who sought more intellectual stimulation could find it at the library. In 1916, Nashville's black community dedicated its first public literary facility, the Negro Carnegie Library on 12th Avenue South. To stimulate body, mind, and spirit African American men and boys could join the city's black branch of the Young Men's Christian Association (YMCA). Beginning in 1912, William N. Sanders, Henry A. Boyd, and others had launched efforts to organize the "Colored YMCA," and in 1917 they purchased a building on Cedar Street to provide spiritual, athletic, educational, recreational, and social services for Nashville's black boys and men.

Nashville's black women, particularly middle-class and professional women, continued to play an active role in the city's numerous associations. The YMCA's Women's Auxiliary, for example, carried out activities for "young ladies and young gentlemen." During World War I the Colored Girls Emergency Club entertained black soldiers at the Cedar Street YMCA, and under the leadership of Dr. Josie Wells, Nashville's first black female physician, African American women formed a state Colored Women's chapter of the National Council of Defense. Following the war black women organized the Blue Triangle, which was associated with the white Young Women's Christian Association (YWCA). On June 1, 1919, the Blue Triangle started operating at 436 5th Avenue North.

By the early twentieth century Nashville's African American population had created a network of associations and clubs that provided a broad spectrum of activities and services. By 1925, when the city had 39,154 African American residents constituting 28.7 percent of the population, black Nashville was home to eighty-nine churches and thirty-five literary and social clubs. In 1929 the city's black population boasted eight Greek organizations, twelve secret lodges, and forty social clubs. The "club season," a time when the civic and social clubs of black Nashville conducted their major activities, began in spring and lasted into winter. Black neighborhoods organized civic and social clubs that fostered art, gardening, embroidery, sewing, entertainment, discussion of community issues, and civic projects.

Black Nashville's social and civic clubs continued to remain active during the 1930s and 1940s, although dues-paying membership declined as a result of the Great Depression and the World War II draft. During the war the city's African American associations mobilized in support of America's war effort and the black troops. The City Federation of Colored Women's Clubs, for example, provided free lunches and distributed flags, cigarettes, matches, and Bibles donated by the National Baptist Publishing Board to black draftees and volunteers as they marched down Broad Street to the train stations. During the war the YMCA building on Cedar Street became a center for economic and social activities for black soldiers and the black community.

The war and postwar economic boom helped expand Nashville's black middle class and boosted the number of black social organizations. To accommodate the "club explosion," Greenwood Park opened a five-hundred-seat "Country Club Forrest" in May 1944. The country club provided a venue for performances by black artists and orchestras and furnished black associations with spaces for dinners, dances, parties, and meetings. The facilities were used by fraternities and sororities including Kappa Alpha Psi, Alpha Phi Alpha, Omega Psi Phi, Phi Beta Sigma, Alpha Kappa Alpha, Delta Sigma Theta, and Sigma Gamma Rho, whose alumni chapters held annual balls and fund-raisers for members of the African American middle class and elite.

Since 1960 Nashville's African Americans have extended their social, literary, and civic activities into the larger society. Although Nashville's black "club season" has ceased to exist, African Americans continue to stage some of their exclusive balls and organize fund-raisers and associations, such as Jack and Jill, and the Links. In recent years the balls of Nashville's black civic and social associations have become racially inclusive, and some whites who have attended them have invited African American guests to the prestigious Swan Ball, a fund-raiser for the Nashville Symphony. Despite more frequent social interaction between blacks and whites, Nashville's African Americans continue to establish racially exclusive organizations that serve the needs of the city's black residents. In the 1990s, for example, members of the black business and professional elite founded the 100 Black Men of Middle Tennessee to confront the problem of declining success among black children in the public schools.

**FURTHER READINGS**

Jones, Yollette T. "The Black Community, Politics, and Race Relations in the 'Iris City': Nashville, Tennessee, 1870–1954." Ph.D. diss., University of Arkansas, 1985.

Lovett, Bobby L. "The Negro in Tennessee, 1861–1866: A Socio-Military History of the Civil War Era." Ph.D. diss., University of Arkansas, 1978.

———. *The African-American History of Nashville, Tennessee, 1780–1930: Elites and Dilemmas.* Fayetteville: University of Arkansas Press, 1999.

Nashville *Globe*, 1906–1960.

Ridley, May Alice. "The Black Community of Nashville and Davidson County, 1860–1870." Ph.D. diss., University of Pittsburgh, 1982.

Robbins, Faye Wellborn. "A-World-Within-A-World: Black Nashville, 1880–1915." Ph.D. diss., University of Arkansas, 1980.

Taylor, Alrutheus A. *The Negro in Tennessee, 1865–1880.* New York: Negro Universities Press, 1941.

*Bobby L. Lovett*

## Nashville Student Movement

Like any movement, the Nashville Student Movement (NSM) is difficult to describe. It lacked a precise date of origin and conclusion. Its membership was fluid and shifting. But for a time in the early 1960s, it was the most influential student civil rights movement in the country.

The NSM emerged out of the seminars on nonviolence led by James Lawson. Lawson came to Nashville, Tennessee, in 1958 as the first southern secretary of the Fellowship of Reconciliation, a pacifist organization devoted to social change. By 1959, his nonviolent workshops had attracted future leaders of the civil rights movement like John Lewis, a student at the American Baptist

Theological Seminary, and Diane Nash, a student at Fisk University.

In 1959, the nonviolent group put its training into practice with test sit-ins against segregation. But it was the news of the Greensboro, North Carolina, sit-ins in early February 1960 and the cascading wave of supportive demonstrations elsewhere in the South that spurred Nashville activists to launch a bold campaign against Jim Crow practices in their city.

On February 12, 1960, over five hundred supporters packed the First Baptist Church for the first mass meeting of the sit-in project. There they received instruction from Lawson and other veterans of the nonviolent workshops. The next morning Lawson led over one hundred demonstrators, many of whom were recruited from Nashville's four black colleges—Fisk, Tennessee State, Meharry Medical, and the American Baptist Theological Seminary—to stage sit-ins at lunch counters in downtown department stores.

At the end of the second week of the sit-ins, word spread that future demonstrators would be arrested by the police. The Nashville activists prepared themselves for the new consequences. John Lewis composed a list of instructions that concluded with the admonition, "Remember the teachings of Jesus, Gandhi, Thoreau, and Martin Luther King, Jr." The next day the police arrested the demonstrators, many of whom were also beaten by angry whites. Once in court, Diane Nash, John Lewis, and fourteen others refused to pay fines, and their example inspired another sixty students to follow them to jail.

The courage of the students' nonviolent witness heartened Nashville's black community. Unlike in other southern cities such as Birmingham, Alabama, there was little public criticism of the demonstrators by local black leaders. The Nashville Christian Leadership Council, an affiliate of the Southern Christian Leadership Conference, in particular, supported the students. The Reverend Kelly Miller Smith opened his First Baptist Church to the movement and threw his substantial influence behind the cause.

The tenacity of the demonstrators troubled white Nashvillians, especially racial moderates like Mayor Ben West. Nashville prided itself on its progressive approach to race relations. The city's buses and public schools had been desegregated. West feared that more demonstrations would threaten racial progress and tarnish the city's reputation as the "Athens of the South." To resolve the crisis, he appointed a biracial committee to investigate discriminatory practices at downtown stores.

But the mass meetings and sit-ins continued. And when the home of Z. Alexander Looby, a prominent black attorney, was dynamited on April 19, the movement reached an even higher level of intensity. The next day, thousands of demonstrators marched on city hall, where Diane Nash and C. T. Vivian, a minister and an adviser to the students, confronted Mayor West, who publicly spoke about the immorality of segregation. The fate of Jim Crow in downtown Nashville was sealed.

The influence of the Nashville activists extended well beyond their city. Their firm theoretical and lived commitment to nonviolence shaped the founding of a new regional organization, the Student Nonviolent Coordinating Committee (SNCC), in April 1960. James Lawson helped give SNCC its original vision, and Lewis, Nash, Marion Barry, James Bevel, and Bernard LaFayette, all Nashville students, numbered among SNCC's early members.

In May 1961, the Nashville students again influenced the national scene when they rallied to rescue the Freedom Ride campaign. The Freedom Riders, who had left Washington, D.C., by bus bound for New Orleans, had been forced to end their ride when they met with violence in Alabama. Nash arranged for Nashville students to continue the stalled Freedom Ride out of Birmingham, Alabama. Ultimately, Lewis, Bevel, LaFayette, and other Nashville insurgents ended up in jail in Mississippi, but the Freedom Riders succeeded in spotlighting the injustice and brutality of the segregationist South.

In Nashville, activists continued to pressure the white community to open all realms of the city to blacks. Over time, original student leaders like Lewis and Nash moved away from Nashville. A new series of protests in 1964 aimed at the remaining segregationist restaurants were less disciplined and less focused than early rounds. And by 1967, when Stokely Carmichael came to Nashville to speak at Fisk, Tennessee State, and Vanderbilt, the old protest universe had clearly faded.

**FURTHER READINGS**

Branch, Taylor. *Parting the Waters: America in the King Years, 1954–1963*. New York: Simon and Schuster, 1988.

Carson, Clayborne. *In Struggle: SNCC and the Black Awakening of the 1960s*. Cambridge, Mass.: Harvard University Press, 1981.

Doyle, Don H. *Nashville Since the 1920s*. Knoxville: University Press of Tennessee, 1985.

Halberstam, David. *The Children*. New York: Random House, 1998.

*James Ralph*

## Nation of Islam

The Nation of Islam, whose followers are known as Black Muslims, originated in Detroit in 1930. Shrouded in secrecy, the organization advocates a separatist religious, economic, and political ideology based on black nationalism. It seeks to instill self-esteem and pride and promotes racial solidarity, economic self-sufficiency, and political and cultural self-determination. Despite the Nation's radical posturing, its members subscribe to a lifestyle frequently associated with conservative values. They emphasize the importance of traditional, family-centered life and advocate monogamous relationships, conventional gender roles, proper public deportment, and abstinence from alcohol, drugs, premarital sex, and crime.

The religious doctrine of the Black Muslims modifies and combines teachings from several sources including the Qur'an, the Bible, and the writings of Joseph F. Rutherford, leader of Jehovah's Witnesses; Hendrik Willem Van Loon's *The Story of Mankind* (New York: Boni and Liveright,

Elijah Muhammad, ca. 1964. *Library of Congress*

1921); and James Henry Breasted's *The Conquest of Civilization* (New York: Harper, 1938). The Nation of Islam's central theological doctrine claims that the human race originated with blacks and that whites were created by Yakub, a black mad scientist who rebelled against Allah. While Yakub created the white race as a genetically inferior hybrid group that lacked true humanity, whites used trickery and deceit to achieve power and subject the black race. According to the Black Muslims, an apocalyptic day, called the "Battle of Armageddon," will end white dominance and restore the power of the black race. Until blacks are once again the ruling race, Black Muslims rename their members. They adopt "original" African names to symbolize their rejection of the "slave" names given to them by their white oppressors.

The founder of the Black Muslims was a black peddler known by a number of names, including Farrad Mohammad, F. Mohammad Ali, Professor Ford, Wali Farrad, and W. D. Fard. The origins of Fard are obscure, but he claimed to have come from the Holy City of Mecca. In the summer of 1930, Fard arrived in Detroit and traveled from door to door selling raincoats and silks to the city's black residents. During his visits he made nutritional suggestions to his customers, claiming to improve their physical health, and discussed with them their history and race relations in America. Fard also used the opportunity to promulgate his religious philosophy. He proclaimed that the human race originated from blacks and that whites, whom he called "the blue-eyed devils," had distorted history and perverted "true Christianity" to oppress blacks and achieve world dominance. African Americans belonged to a powerful black nation, Fard insisted, claiming that he was divinely sent to help them reclaim their nationhood.

Fard's message, similar to that of other black charismatic, militant, and separatist leaders such as Marcus Garvey, Father Divine, and Daddy Grace, struck a chord with many disillusioned blacks during the Great Depression of the 1930s. Providing an organizational basis for his growing number of followers, Fard recorded his dogma in two manuals: *The Secret Ritual of the Nation of Islam*, which is transmitted orally, and the *Teaching for the Lost Found Nation of Islam in a Mathematical Way*, which requires complex interpretation. Both these documents laid the foundation for the creation of the institutional structure of the Nation of Islam. In 1933, Fard founded the first Black Muslim temple in Detroit; the University of Islam, an elementary school designed to socialize students in becoming Black Muslims; the Muslim Girls Training Class;

and the Fruit of Islam, a highly organized paramilitary unit that trains boys and men in the use of firearms, military drills, and defense strategy. Within a year, the Nation of Islam attracted approximately eight thousand black followers in Detroit.

The tremendous growth of the Nation of Islam was accompanied by internal dissension that threatened to tear the organization apart. Soon after the founding of the first temple, several men who had obtained high-ranking positions in the organization challenged Fard's doctrine and leadership. One faction, led by Abdul Muhammad, questioned Fard's teaching that Black Muslims should not pledge allegiance to the flag of the United States. Blacks, Abdul Muhammad insisted, were American citizens, and he urged Black Muslims to demonstrate their loyalty to the U.S. Constitution. Another group, apparently intrigued by Japan's expansion in Asia during the 1930s, wanted the Nation of Islam to build an alliance with other nonwhite people and advocated support of the Japanese government. Yet another faction, led by the Ethiopian Wyxzewixard S. J. Challouehliczilczese, advocated economic schemes, while other Black Muslims resented the appointment of Elijah Muhammad as minister of Islam. Adding to the turmoil was a group of Communists who tried to infiltrate the Nation of Islam, hoping to align it with the U.S. Communist Party. As a result, a number of factions broke away from the organization shortly after its founding.

In June 1934, in the midst of this turmoil, Fard disappeared as mysteriously as he had appeared and was never heard from again. Elijah Muhammad, who had been one of Fard's earliest followers, assumed leadership of the Nation of Islam. Born Elijah Poole, Elijah Muhammad had migrated with his family from Georgia to Detroit in the 1920s. He and several of his relatives became associated with Fard in 1930. That year, Elijah adopted the name Muhammad and became the chief minister of Islam and the autocratic leader of the organization.

In 1934, following Fard's disappearance, Elijah Muhammad moved to Chicago, established Temple No. 2, which became the Black Muslims' national headquarters, and launched the newspaper the *Final Call*. He quickly moved to deify Fard, referring to him as the "prophet," and worked to institute his early teachings. Weakened by Fard's disappearance and the factionalism that had divided the Black Muslims, the Nation of Islam grew only slowly after its move to Chicago.

Not until after World War II did the movement start to attract large numbers of followers throughout the United States and establish temples in all larger cities with sizable black populations. The group's growing popularity during the postwar years may have been the result of increasing African American awareness of global decolonization efforts and the emergence of independent African nations.

Between 1950 and 1964, the Nation of Islam experienced its greatest growth, attracting fifty thousand to one hundred thousand members. Undoubtedly, the Nation's effort to instill pride in black heritage and self-respect appealed largely to the black inner-city poor and members of the African American working class. Elijah Muhammad also tried to induce others to join the movement, however, and used charismatic speakers and celebrities, including Malcolm X and the boxing champion Muhammad Ali, to increase the attractiveness of the organization.

Malcolm X was probably the Nation's most acclaimed and notorious spokesman. Born Malcolm Little in Omaha, Nebraska, in 1925, he dropped out of school and entered a life of drug abuse, pimping, and small crimes at an early age. In 1946, he was sent to prison, where one of his brothers and a friend he met in jail introduced him to the teachings of the Nation of Islam. In 1952, after his release from prison, Malcolm X joined Elijah Muhammad and soon became one of the most effective organizers of the Nation.

Malcolm X, who embraced the group's rigorous asceticism, was a charismatic speaker. Aware of Malcolm's powerful rhetorical ability, the Nation sent him on speaking tours around the country, where he attracted large followings. Malcolm helped establish numerous temples across the United States and became a major force in the growth of the Nation during the late 1950s and early 1960s. In May 1960, he was appointed minister of Temple No. 7 in New York City's Harlem, and in the following year he helped launch the Nation's official newspaper, *Muhammad Speaks*, which replaced the *Final Call*. Acknowledging Malcolm's success as a speaker and organizer, Elijah Muhammad appointed him national minister of the Nation of Islam in 1963.

But soon tensions developed between the two men, generated at least in part by Elijah Muhammad's extramarital indiscretions. In November 1963, Elijah Muhammad suspended Malcolm X from the Nation, allegedly for referring to President John F. Kennedy's assassination as "the Kennedy chickens coming home to roost." In March 1964, Malcolm X stopped associating with the Nation of Islam and formed the independent Muslim Mosque, Inc. In the same year, he visited Mecca, converted to orthodox Islam, and founded the secular

Organization of Afro-American Unity on June 28, 1964. Following Malcolm X's departure from the Nation of Islam, Elijah Muhammad appointed Louis Farrakhan to assume Malcolm's post as minister of Harlem's Temple No. 7 and to serve as his personal representative and national spokesman. When Malcolm X was assassinated on February 21, 1965, members of the Nation of Islam were suspected of having committed the crime, and Elijah Muhammad and Farrakhan were rumored to have ordered his death.

Malcolm X was not the only Black Muslim who challenged Elijah Muhammad's leadership in the 1960s. In 1964, Clarence 13X, who had joined the Nation as Clarence Jowars Smith in 1961, was expelled from the organization when he started to teach that all black people are Allah. After leaving, he founded the Nation of the Five Percent, headquartered in New York City.

Despite the controversy generated by Malcolm X's dismissal and his subsequent assassination, as well as the expulsion of Clarence 13X, the Nation of Islam experienced tremendous growth during the 1960s. This was due in part to the decade's protest spirit that increased black interest in the Nation's emphasis on economic self-sufficiency and political and cultural self-determination. By the early 1970s, the Nation of Islam operated approximately 150 temples and 14 University of Islam schools in cities across the nation and by 1975 claimed a total membership exceeding one hundred thousand.

The Nation's growing popularity in the late 1960s and early 1970s gave way to heightened factionalism following the death of Elijah Muhammad on February 25, 1975. Divisions within the Nation surfaced when the ailing Elijah appointed one of his sons, Wallace Deen Muhammad, to assume leadership of the Black Muslims. As son of the Nation's leader, he had been raised in the movement, exposed to its rituals and traditions, and steeped in its dogma. Educated at the Nation's University of Islam in Chicago, he had served as a minister of Islam in Philadelphia and several other cities. Yet, Wallace Deen Muhammad was invariably at odds with the Nation's doctrine. He had been a close friend of Malcolm X and engaged in independent study of Islamic law, history, and theology. His freethinking personality led him to defy his father's authority and challenge the Nation's dogma, particularly the deification of Fard. As a result, he had been suspended from the Nation on numerous occasions, his final suspension ensuing in 1964 and lasting for four years. His lay privileges were not restored until 1974.

Not surprisingly, Wallace Deen Muhammad initiated a series of reforms when he assumed leadership of the Nation in 1975. He decentralized the organization, sold most of its businesses, and disbanded the controversial paramilitary Fruit of Islam. In an effort to lead the Nation toward orthodox Islam, he renamed its newspaper, *Muhammad Speaks*, the *Bilalian News*, in reference to a black companion of the prophet Muhammad; proclaimed the mortality of Fard; purged all racial considerations from the Nation's theological dogma, including the racial rhetoric of "blue-eyed devils"; and changed the organization's name to the World Community of Al-Islam in the West. Following another restructuring effort in 1980, Wallace adopted the Muslim name Warith Deen Muhammad and changed the organization's name to American Muslim Mission.

Warith Deen Muhammad's reforms sparked considerable opposition among many Black Muslims and led to a secessionist movement. The schism resulted in the formation of at least one dozen competing factions and four distinct groups using the name Nation of Islam. These included the Nation of Islam of Detroit, headed by Elijah Muhammad's younger brother John; the Nation of Islam of Baltimore and Chicago, under the leadership of Caliph Emmanual A. Muhammad; the Nation of Islam of Atlanta, led by Silis Muhammad; and the Lost-Found Nation of Islam in the Wilderness of North America, headed by Louis Farrakhan.

Farrakhan, confidant of Elijah Muhammad, captured the largest secessionist following. Born Louis Eugene Walcott in New York City, on May 11, 1933, Farrakhan graduated from Boston Latin School with honors, was recruited by Malcolm X into the Nation of Islam in the early 1950s, and was appointed minister of Boston's Temple No. 11 on March 18, 1954. In 1964, when Malcolm X left the Nation, Farrakhan succeeded him as minister of Harlem's Temple No. 7 and personal representative and national spokesman of Elijah Muhammad.

When Warith Deen Muhammad assumed leadership of the Nation of Islam, he recalled Farrakhan from the Harlem ministry and assigned him to the West Side of Chicago. Initially, Farrakhan accepted the reassignment that placed him under the close scrutiny of Warith Deen. Farrakhan remained a fervent believer in the Nation's original doctrine, however, including its teachings about the origins of humankind, the impending racial "Battle of Armageddon," and Elijah Muhammad's deification of Fard. Resenting Warith Deen's reforms, Farrakhan peacefully parted with Elijah's son and organized the

Lost-Found Nation of Islam in the Wilderness of North America in 1977.

Farrakhan's organization, built unequivocally on the foundations laid by Fard and Elijah Muhammad, emerged as the most popular of the secessionist Black Muslim movements. Farrakhan resurrected the publication of the Nation's original newspaper, the *Final Call*, retaining the columns "What the Muslims Believe" and "What the Muslims Want," and continued to stress the organization's dedication to racial solidarity, economic self-sufficiency, and political and cultural self-determination.

While Farrakhan remains wedded to the original teachings of the Nation of Islam, he has in recent years tried to broaden the involvement of black women. Traditionally, the Nation has been a male-dominated organization, subscribing to conventional gender roles and confining women to the roles of family nurturer and educator of children. Seeking to address charges of sexism, Farrakhan has included women speakers at all major events such as Savior's Day, the annual celebration of the birth of Fard on February 26, 1877, and the Million Men March in Washington, D.C., on October 16, 1995.

By the mid-1980s, Farrakhan's organization, headquartered in Chicago, operated approximately two hundred temples in the United States, the Bahamas, Barbados, Belize, Bermuda, Canada, Guyana, Jamaica, St. Thomas Island, and Trinidad. The group has accrued nearly $15 million in property including a small string of bakeries and cleaners, approximately forty rental units, a controlling interest in the Guaranty Bank and Trust in Chicago, a newspaper, a supermarket, a $22 million fish import business, and twenty thousand acres of farmland in Alabama, Georgia, and Michigan. By 1990, the organization had also established a trucking firm, a $5 million food-service complex (Salaam Restaurant) in Chicago with restaurant outlets in four American cities, and a two-thousand-seat auditorium.

Farrakhan's organization currently claims twenty thousand followers, while Warith Deen Muhammad's American Muslim Mission has an estimated one hundred thousand members. Despite the relatively small size of Farrakhan's group, it has attracted considerable publicity, owing largely to its controversial demands for reparations for slavery and repeated anti-Semitic statements. While the Nation of Islam continues to propagate its conservative, nationalist, self-help, and separatist ideology, it has failed to recapture the large number of followers it boasted when Malcolm X was its preeminent spokesperson. Yet, the organization appears to have struck an enduring chord particularly with lower- and working-class blacks, and it has garnered considerable sympathy among many African Americans. Even black critics of Farrakhan praise the group's rehabilitation programs for prisoners, drug addicts, alcoholics, and street gang members, as well as its efforts to improve the quality of life in black inner-city neighborhoods by exposing and preventing police brutality, closing crack houses, and patrolling low-income black housing projects. Despite the factionalism that continues to trouble the organization, the Nation of Islam has endured as the most long-lasting black separatist movement, and its essential message has remained remarkably consistent.

**FURTHER READINGS**

Blyden, Edward W. *Christianity, Islam and the Negro Race.* 1888. Baltimore: Black Classic Press, 1994.

Clegg, Claude Andrew. *An Original Man: The Life and Times of Elijah Muhammad.* New York: St. Martin's Press, 1997.

Gardell, Mattias. *In the Name of Elijah Muhammad: Louis Farrakhan and the Nation of Islam.* Chapel Hill: University of North Carolina Press, 1996.

Lee, Martha F. *The Nation of Islam: An American Millenarian Movement.* Lewiston, N.Y.: Edwin Mellen Press, 1988.

Lincoln, C. Eric. *The Black Muslims in America.* Trenton, N.J.: Africa World Press, 1994.

McCloud, Aminah Beverly. *African American Islam.* New York: Routledge, 1995.

Turner, Richard Brent. *Islam in the African-American Experience.* Bloomington: Indiana University Press, 1997.

*Anthony J. Lemelle Jr.*

## Nation of the Five Percent

*See* Nation of Islam.

## National Action Council for Minorities in Engineering

Established in 1974, the National Action Council for Minorities in Engineering (NACME) works to increase minority access to careers in engineering and other science-based disciplines. The NACME, a nonprofit corporation, was the product of a merger of four groups: the National Academy of Engineering's Council on Minorities in Engineering, an advisory panel that sought to increase minority participation and success in engineering education and research; the Minority Engineering Education Effort, a national organization that offered educational programs and career guidance to precollege students; the National Fund for Minority Engineering Students, a group that provided scholarships and loans to minority students majoring in engineering; and the National Advisory Council for Minorities in Engineering, an august panel of corporate leaders and professors of engineering.

Today, this $6 million corporation conducts research and public policy analyses; provides funding for scholarships, educational programs, and training; and disseminates information about minorities in engineering. The NACME publishes regularly reports on the status of minorities in engineering and other science-related disciplines in its *NACME Research Letter* and on its website at www.nacme.org. The organization has perhaps the largest database of longitudinal trends in minority enrollment, graduation, retention, and precollege education. The NACME also provides analyses of its data to various private and government groups such as the Office of Science and Technology Policy, the National Science Foundation, the U.S. Congress, the Supreme Court, the Department of Education, the Department of Energy, state legislatures, and major corporations.

Over 6,500 African Americans, Latinos, and Native Americans—more than 10 percent of all minority graduates in engineering—have completed undergraduate or graduate-level degrees with the support of NACME scholarships. Since NACME's founding, total minority college and university graduation rates in engineering have increased over 300 percent. This increase is due at least in part to the substantial financial assistance and programming that the NACME has either directly provided or helped instigate. Recent years, however, have witnessed a 12 percent drop in minority engineering enrollment (17 percent among African Americans) and increasing attrition rates, due largely to the escalating cost of higher education and changes in financial aid policies of academic institutions.

Nationwide over one million students, teachers, and faculty members have benefited from the NACME's precollege and university education and training programs. These have included a series of Spider Man comic books for young children, video kits for engineers who visit schools, and brochures for high school students. An additional five million or more children and parents have been exposed to the NACME's "Math is Power" media campaign, during which actor and comedian Sinbad urges high school students to enroll in mathematics and science

courses. For many years, the NACME has conducted Diversity Seminars, based on models long employed by the corporate sector. These seminars facilitate cross-cultural communication by allowing faculty and students on college and university campuses to examine attitudes about race, class, and gender. In 1995, the NACME, with funding from the Alfred P. Sloan Foundation, convened a national Research and Policy Conference to draft a national research and policy agenda. A volume delineating the outcomes of this conference, edited by George Campbell Jr., Ronni Denes, and Catherine Morrison, will be published by Oxford University Press.

The NACME's membership extends only to individuals and corporations who make substantial financial contributions to the organization. Its approximately two hundred members include companies such as DuPont, IBM, AT & T, Texaco, Raytheon, and Chase Manhattan Bank; philanthropic organizations such as the Alfred P. Sloan, Philip Reed, and Betz Foundations; and government agencies such as the National Science Foundation. George Campbell Jr. is president and chief executive officer of the NACME, which maintains a national office in New York City.

**FURTHER READINGS**

Campbell, George Jr., et al. *Measurable Performance: National Action Council for Minorities in Engineering Annual Report, 1995.* New York: National Action Council for Minorities in Engineering, 1995.

"Hawkins Undergraduate Fellowship Established." *Chemical & Engineering News* 71, 6 (February 8, 1993): 60–62.

Jones, J. Sydney. "W. Lincoln Hawkins." *Notable Twentieth-Century Scientists.* Ed. E. J. McMurray, J. K. Kosek, and R. M. Valade III. New York: Gale, 1995, vol. 2, 879–881.

*Dennis W. Cheek*

## National Advisory Commission on Civil Disorders (Kerner Commission)

On July 28, 1967, while Detroit still smoldered as a result of the most recent and the most destructive of over 130 urban disorders recorded during the first seven months of that year, President Lyndon B. Johnson established the National Advisory Commission on Civil Disorders (Kerner Commission) under the chairmanship of Illinois governor and fellow Democrat Otto Kerner. He instructed the Kerner Commission to determine the following: What happened? Why did it happen? What can be done to prevent it from happening again?

Thus Johnson named the first presidential race riot commission, though neither collective violence nor its official investigation was without precedent in twentieth-century U.S. history. Previous inquiries from local, state, and congressional bodies dated back to the 1917 East St. Louis upheaval and focused on communal bloodshed in which whites assaulted black newcomers. Perhaps Johnson knew of the shift to commodity upheavals of black attacks on white-owned property and widespread looting during the Great Depression and World War II. The latter characterized the violence of the 1960s and its worst manifestation in Detroit. The 1967 Detroit riot claimed forty-three mostly black lives, over six hundred injuries, and $40 million worth of property, and prompted the turning point in federal policy.

Johnson felt the political pressure of both civil rights leaders seeking peace with justice and conservative critics looking to reestablish law and order. He acted to preempt congressional investigations of the violence, allay public fear, buy time for further action, and regain leadership in less volatile circumstances. Thus, amid rumblings from senators and representatives—Left and Right—for legislative inquiries, Johnson moved demonstratively and set the commission to work with more publicity than that given any previous riot body.

Predictably, Johnson appointed eleven elites, whose statuses and racial views brought legitimacy to the commission and assured its moderate perspective. He balanced Kerner with Vice Chairman John Lindsay, Republican mayor of New York City; Edward W. Brooke, Republican senator from Massachusetts; and William M. McCulloch, Republican representative from Ohio, with Fred R. Harris, Democratic senator from Oklahoma, and James C. Corman, Democratic Representative from California; I. W. Abel, United Steel Workers president, with Charles B. Thornton, Litton Industries head; and Herbert Jenkins, Atlanta Police Chief, with Roy Wilkins of the National Association for the Advancement of Colored People. Thus, the Kerner Commission was composed of representatives of both political parties, various government levels, business, labor, and diverse regions. Moreover, Johnson provided black and female representation, respectively, in Brooke and Wilkins and in Kentucky Commerce Commissioner Katherine Graham Pede. The commissioners were in their early fifties and adhered to varying levels of liberal democracy and social justice. Socioeconomically and ideologically, they were very unlike those who rioted. The rioters were predominantly single, under- and unemployed, young black males, with little education and less political clout but great hostility toward whites and middle-class blacks; they identified themselves more closely with black power and community control.

The commissioners were served by executive and research staffs. Well-connected Washington, D.C., attorney David Ginsburg, Johnson's choice for executive director, became both presidential liaison and commission manager. He, in turn, appointed Janss Corporation president Victor H. Palmieri as deputy executive director in charge of administration and staffing. Palmieri, who, like seven of the commissioners, was a lawyer, employed many counselors on a full-time basis, which promoted the "advocacy" approach of establishing a position and then gathering evidence to support it. He also recruited social scientists, many as consultants, and expanded the staff to nearly two hundred within four months.

Shortly after their appointments, commission members became active. Originally scheduled to deliver an interim document in March 1968 and a final report later that August, they began a series of public hearings in Washington, D.C., examining 130 witnesses behind closed doors over the next several months. In the process, they released portions of the testimonies and educated themselves about the problems confronting black citizens. They also divided into teams and visited eight of the twenty-three riot cities under study, including Newark and Detroit, where they gathered firsthand information from several sources, including ghetto residents.

Also during the first month of meetings, commissioners moved the date of the interim document forward to mid-December. Their purpose was to influence Johnson's State of the Union message and, subsequently, Congress's legislative agenda before the expected long, hot summer of 1968. However, one week before issuing the analysis of what caused the riots, commissioners scrapped the timetable, fired the research director, released 120 staff members, and announced plans to issue a single report, complete with recommendations, on March 1. They accepted the action of Ginsburg and Palmieri, who deemed the interim document "The Harvest of American Racism: The Political Meaning of Violence in the Summer of 1967" unsubstantiated and out of line with the commission's and the president's thinking.

Like executive staff directors, commission members never could accept the interpretation of the 172-page working document of the social scientist staff researchers David Boesel, Louis Goldberg, Gary T. Marx, and David Sears. The social scientists considered the riots as political rebellions against racist institutions, whereas commissioners viewed them as nonideological upheavals over abject living conditions. This section of the report was rewritten, first by Hans Mattick of the University of Chicago Law School, who also recognized some riots as political protests, and consequently by Deputy Director of Operations Stephen Kurzman.

The commission was divided into liberal and conservative camps on specific issues, but it shared an overall riot theory that shaped its report. Riots, commissioners believed, were the products of deprivation and neglect, rather than conspirators, criminals, and riffraff. They bore no underlying political meaning, though racism, broadly conceived, created the misery that triggered spontaneous violence. As such, riots required quelling and a return to law and order, followed by government programs to improve conditions in the ghetto without questioning the basic socioeconomic structure of the larger society.

Commissioners, in sum, embraced the control and reform philosophy initially announced by President Johnson. In condemning the violence and calling for improvements, they indicated their commitment to the existing order and their belief that social change could come only through peaceful means. They did not implicate officials or government agencies in the riot conditions, thereby protecting public institutions and presidential social welfare programs. The commissioners understood the role of both if future bloodshed was to be averted and racial advances made through federal initiatives. Like Johnson, they endeavored to manage the outbursts rather than see in them the need for large-scale socioeconomic transformations.

Despite these limitations, the commission emerged as more historically significant than any of its predecessors. Its *Report* sparked hundreds of media stories and sales of 1,600,000 paperback copies over the next three months. It disproved conspiracy and riffraff theories. Indeed, a supplemental study by Robert M. Fogelson and Robert Hill found the rioters to be fairly representative of their neighbors. It promoted federal assistance to police and National Guard officials, enabling them to curtail disorders quickly and with less loss of life. It suggested more accurate media coverage of racial upheavals and everyday black life. Moreover, as a result of Mayor Lindsay's

far-reaching summary, the *Report* identified white racism as "deeply implicated" in the ghetto and called for a new will, national action, and additional resources in the struggle for racial equality, including funding for federal employment, housing, and education programs, and welfare reform. Otherwise, the *Report* implied, the nation, already moving toward two societies, would become separate and unequal, "one black, one white."

Surprising to some, President Johnson distanced himself from the Kerner Commission. He canceled plans to receive the commission at the White House and for a week withheld comment on the *Report*. Johnson seemed piqued by the commission's apparent disregard for his civil rights efforts, objected to its divided-societies contention, and disagreed with its costly recommendations as he fought for passage of the surcharge tax bill, which was designed to reduce the federal deficit. With his attention on the Vietnam War, which the commissioners ignored as a riot-related factor in deference to him, Johnson had already decided not to seek reelection. Concerned about his health and disliking conflict, he dedicated the final months of his presidency to trying to end the war.

Essentially, the Kerner Commission's 654-page report supplanted Gunnar Myrdal's *American Dilemma* (1944) as the source for future discussions, if not policy decisions, on race relations. The *Report* and the riots sparked short-term action in the Office of Economic Opportunity and the Departments of Housing and Urban Development, Justice, and Defense that carried through Richard M. Nixon's administrations. Although the *Report* was upended by shifting political climates, economic developments, and war expenditures, it nonetheless represented in scope and significance a major break with the past and epitomized the liberal reform effort of the 1960s. Ironically, it sought to extend Johnson's civil rights commitment and welfare state programs, only to mark the demise of both. Twenty years later the *Report* served as the centerpiece of the Commission on the Cities' endeavor to raise public awareness on race, poverty, and isolation among the urban "underclass," but with little success. When that issue receives official priority, the Kerner Commission *Report* doubtless will be resurrected anew.

**FURTHER READINGS**

Button, James W. *Black Violence: Political Impact of the 1960s Riots.* Princeton, N.J.: Princeton University Press, 1978.

Harris, Fred R., and Roger W. Wilkins, eds. *Quiet Riots: Race and Poverty in the United States.* New York: Pantheon, 1988.

Lipsky, Michael, and David J. Olson. *Commission Politics: The Process of Racial Crisis in America.* New Brunswick, N.J.: Transaction, 1977.

National Advisory Commission on Civil Disorders. *Kerner Report: The 1968 Report of the National Advisory Commission on Civil Disorders.* Foreword by Fred R. Harris, introduction by Tom Wicker. New York: Bantam, 1968; rpt., New York: Pantheon, 1988.

Platt, Anthony, ed. *The Politics of Riot Commissions, 1917–1970.* New York: Collier Books, 1971.

*Dominic J. Capeci Jr.*

## National Advisory Committee on Black Higher Education and Black Colleges and Universities

President Gerald R. Ford chartered the National Advisory Committee on Black Higher Education and Black Colleges and Universities in December 1976. The Notice of Establishment was not published in the Federal Register until June 21, 1977, however, and the committee did not convene for its initial meeting until September 1977. Although the committee was initially chartered for a two-year period, its charter was extended three times because of difficulties in obtaining resources commensurate with its extensive functions. During this time, the charter underwent several minor changes, but the committee's overall charge remained the same: to assess the status of higher education of black Americans as well as the needs of historically black colleges and universities. Drawing on its findings, the committee was to recommend to the U.S. Secretary of Education and the U.S. Assistant Secretary of Postsecondary Education how to raise the participation of blacks in postsecondary education; to aid in the development of educational alternatives sensitive to the needs of black youths; to ensure the continued operation of historically black colleges and universities; to support research on equity; to stimulate increased scholarship and research by African Americans on public policy and educational needs; to evaluate and monitor the impact of federal, regional, or state efforts designed to equalize educational opportunities; to help provide funding for students in need and institutions with the heaviest concentration of blacks; to increase access, retention, and graduation of blacks from institutions of higher education; to increase the number of blacks entering and completing graduate and professional degree programs; to increase the quality of black higher education; and to assess the implementation of the committee's policy recommendations.

The establishment of the committee was the culmination of long advocacy of persons and groups interested in achieving equity in higher education for African Americans and historically black colleges and universities. Among those instrumental in the committee's creation were Joffre T. Whisenton, who had been special assistant to David Mathews, former Secretary of Health, Education, and Welfare; and the National Association for Equal Opportunity in Higher Education (NAFEO).

The fifteen-member committee consisted of individuals with expertise in black higher education, historically black colleges and universities, and public policy. Members included college presidents; state university chancellors; and representatives from foundations, businesses, and the community; as well as one student. When the charter was renewed, first until December 22, 1979, then again until June 30, 1980, the original committee was reappointed almost intact. When the charter was extended to June 30, 1982, then U.S. Secretary of Education Shirley M. Hufstedler appointed a new committee, retaining the services of five members of the original body. Each person was appointed to serve a term of two and then three years. The chairperson, Elias Blake Jr., who served as the committee's chair from its inception to its demise, was appointed by the U.S. Secretary of Education.

Notices of all meetings were published in the *Federal Register* and sent to groups historically associated with black aspirations as well as organizations with a history of involvement on behalf of African Americans. The committee was required to meet no fewer than four times each year with the advance approval of the commissioner (later the U.S. Secretary of Education) or his or her designee. The twenty-two public meetings of the committee were well attended and provided interested individuals with a forum to express their concerns about the status of black higher education. Although the vast majority of these meetings were held in Washington, D.C., seven were held on campuses of historically black colleges and universities.

In addition to public forums, the committee reviewed Department of Education policies, plans, program regulations, and legislative initiatives to determine their potential and actual impact on equity for black Americans and historically black colleges and universities. Moreover, the committee commissioned nineteen studies and called on the expertise and advice of well-known administrators, faculty, and researchers, before issuing its recommendations. The vast majority of the more than two hundred recommendations were contained in ten detailed research reports, five substantive annual reports, and eleven fact sheets.

Despite the committee's efforts, it faced numerous problems. In addition to intermittent problems with securing personnel and financial resources, the committee's work was limited by a lack of cooperation with the U.S. Department of Education. In its final report, the committee lamented that "perhaps the most common characteristic of the Committee's relationship with the Department has been the complete absence of direct, systematic response to the Committee's advisement from either the Secretaries or any Federal policymaker." Indeed, the Reagan administration never published the committee's final report, which was issued in June 1982. Unlike all previous committee reports, which had been published, the final report was available only on request.

**FURTHER READINGS**

National Advisory Committee on Black Higher Education and Black Colleges and Universities. *First Annual Report—Higher Education Equity: The Crisis of Appearance Versus Reality*. Washington, D.C.: Government Printing Office, 1977.

———. *Second Annual Report*. Washington, D.C.: Government Printing Office, 1978.

———. *Third Annual Report—Overview of Committee Research*. Washington, D.C.: Government Printing Office, 1979.

———. *Fourth Annual Report—Overview of Committee Findings and Recommendations*. Washington, D.C.: Government Printing Office, 1980.

———. *Fifth Annual Report*. Washington, D.C.: Government Printing Office, 1981.

———. *Higher Education Equity: The Crisis of Appearance Versus Reality—Revisited, Final Report of the National Advisory Committee on Black Higher Education and Black Colleges and Universities*. June 1982.

*Carol J. Smith*

**SEE ALSO**    National Association for Equal Opportunity in Higher Education

## National Afro-American League

Thomas Fortune, the editor of *New York Age* and a civil rights leader, organized the National Afro-American League (NAAL) as the Afro-American League (AAL) in 1887. He established the organization to obtain full citizenship and equality for African Americans. By 1889, the AAL had changed its name to NAAL, and in December of that year organization delegates from twenty-three states convened for their first national meeting in Chicago, where they discussed the vision and direction of the organization. The NAAL, dominated by Fortune and Bishop Alexander Walters of the African Methodist Episcopal Zion Church, was plagued by a lack of funding throughout its existence. In 1898, the organization experienced another name change and became the Afro-American Council. In 1904, Fortune resigned as president and Walters continued to provide leadership for the organization. But Walters became increasingly involved in the formation of other civil rights groups. By 1908, he had joined a group of black civil rights advocates who had organized the Niagara Movement in 1905, and by 1910 he was one of six African Americans who helped establish the National Association for the Advancement of Colored People (NAACP).

During its brief existence, the nonpartisan NAAL used lobbying to improve the social, political, and economic conditions of African Americans. Its members attacked the suppression of black voting rights in the South, lynchings, mob law, inequality in the allocation and distribution of funding of black and white schools, the disproportionate amount of African American prisoners, and segregation in public and interstate transportation as well as housing. NAAL chapters apparently served different purposes, depending on their location. Southern chapters focused on fostering coalitions among blacks, while northern chapters tried to influence public opinion and lobbied for the passage of civil rights laws.

The NAAL's goal to defend, protect, and advance the civil rights of African Americans influenced the formation and agenda of the Niagara Movement and the NAACP.

**FURTHER READINGS**

Harlan, Louis, ed. *The Booker T. Washington Papers*, vol. 2, 1860–1889. Urbana: University of Illinois Press, 1972.

Thornbrough, Emma Lou. "The National Afro-American League, 1887–1908." *Journal of Southern History* 27 (November 1961): 494–512.

———. Thomas Fortune: A Militant Editor in the Age of Accommodationism." In *Black Leaders of the Twentieth Century*, eds. August Meier and John Hope Franklin. Urbana: University of Illinois Press, 1982, 19–36.

*James L. Conyers Jr.*

SEE ALSO   Afro-American Council; National Association for the Advancement of Colored People; Niagara Movement

# National Afro-American Press Association

*See* Afro-American Press Association.

# National Agricultural Workers Union

*See* Southern Tenant Farmers' Union.

# National Airmen's Association of America

The National Airmen's Association of America (NAAA) was organized in Chicago in 1936 by a group of African American aviators and aviation enthusiasts. The organization applied for incorporation in Illinois on August 16, 1939. The founding members included many key figures in Chicago's black aviation community such as Cornelius R. Coffey, Dale L. White, Harold Hurd, Willa B. Brown, Marie St. Clair, Charles Johnson, Chauncey E. Spencer, Grover C. Nash, Edward H. Johnson, Janet Waterford, and George Williams. Although not a pilot, another founding member—Enoch P. Waters, city editor of the *Chicago Defender*—took a keen interest in the NAAA and promoted it with feature stories and publicity in the pages of his influential newspaper.

During the 1930s a growing number of African Americans learned to fly and struggled to enter the burgeoning field of aviation in the face of racism and discrimination. Although black pilots and flying enthusiasts could be found scattered across the nation, by the mid-1930s Chicago was emerging as the center of African American aviation. Under the leadership of John C. Robinson and Coffey, Chicago's black pilots organized in the early 1930s as the Challenger Aero Club, later known as the Challenger Air Pilots Association. In 1935, following the Italian invasion of Ethiopia under Benito Mussolini, Robinson went to Ethiopia to fly for Emperor Haile Selassie. In his absence, Coffey and Brown began to plan for a national organization of black aviation supporters, with headquarters in Chicago. In 1936 Brown enlisted the support of Waters, who helped Chicago's black fliers organize the NAAA and promote its activities.

In the words of founding member Janet Waterford Bragg, the purpose of the NAAA "was to stimulate inter-est in aviation" and improve the knowledge of "the entire field of aeronautics for blacks." In its early years, the NAAA sought to stimulate interest by organizing air shows in Chicago. As secretary of the NAAA, Brown also launched an aggressive program to contact black pilots in other locales, recruit them as NAAA members, and help them form NAAA chapters in their cities. By the end of the 1930s, the NAAA letterhead listed vice presidents in eighteen cities across the nation.

As the threat of war loomed in the late 1930s, the federal government began to expand opportunities for aviation training under the auspices of both the Air Corps and the Civil Aeronautics Authority (CAA). NAAA leaders recognized that these new initiatives held great promise for expanding black participation in aviation. Consequently, in May 1939 they sponsored a cross-country flight to Washington, D.C., by two of their members—Chauncey Spencer and Dale White—to lobby for black participation in the new federally sponsored aviation training programs. Under the guiding hand of the black lobbyist Edgar G. Brown, Spencer and White met with Illinois congressman Everett M. Dirksen, who subsequently sponsored a nondiscrimination amendment to the act that established the CAA's Civilian Pilot Training Program (CPTP). Scores of young African Americans subsequently earned their pilot's licenses through CPTP courses offered at black schools such as Tuskegee Institute and Howard University. By 1940 the NAAA offered "non-college" CPTP courses in Chicago and trained a number of individuals who went on to become military pilots or flight instructors.

By the end of World War II in 1945, the NAAA was no longer a functioning organization, but it had nevertheless played an important role in focusing attention on black interest in aviation and insuring that African Americans were included in wartime aviation programs.

**FURTHER READINGS**

Bragg, Janet Harmon. *Soaring Above Setbacks: The Autobiography of Janet Harmon Bragg, African American Aviator.* As told to Marjorie M. Kriz. Washington, D.C.: Smithsonian Institution Press, 1996.

Hardesty, Von, and Dominick Pisano. *Black Wings: The American Black in Aviation.* Washington, D.C.: Smithsonian Institution Press, 1983.

Jakeman, Robert J. *The Divided Skies: The Establishment of Segregated Flight Training at Tuskegee, Alabama, 1934–1942.* Tuscaloosa: University of Alabama Press, 1992.

Spencer, Chauncey E. *Who Is Chauncey Spencer?* Detroit: Broadside Press, 1975.

Waters, Enoch P. *American Diary: A Personal History of the Black Press.* Chicago: Path Press, 1987.

*Robert J. Jakeman*

## National Alliance Against Racist and Political Repression

In May 1973, more than eight hundred individuals, representing nearly one hundred religious, political, and local community activist groups as well as labor unions, gathered in Chicago to form the National Alliance Against Racist and Political Repression. The goal of the alliance was to mount counteroffensives against the massive late 1960s and early 1970s attacks on individuals fighting for racial justice, especially activists of color. At its height in the late 1970s and 1980s, the alliance had thirty branches across the country and active members in forty-six states.

The organization was an outgrowth of the Free Angela Davis campaign that emerged in response to Davis's arrest on charges of kidnapping and murder. Davis, an African American activist and former Black Panther, was a philosophy teacher, an avowed member of the Communist Party, and a leader of the campaign for prisoner rights in California. In 1970, after a shoot-out in a California courtroom, during which she was not present, Davis became the target of a nationwide police search that resulted in her arrest. In 1972, a jury acquitted her of all charges.

After her acquittal, Davis was determined to use the huge network that had defended her to help other political activists imprisoned in the United States. For the next year, she and other activists traveled the country mobilizing civil rights organizations and local defense committees. Among the others who took part in the work were Charlene Mitchell, who had led the campaign to free Davis; the southern civil rights activist Carl Braden; and the Reverend Ben Chavis, who along with nine other African Americans faced criminal charges of firebombing a Wilmington, North Carolina, grocery store during a struggle against racism in public schools. This intense nationwide work resulted in the 1973 Chicago conference that led to the founding of the alliance. The conference, attended by African Americans, Latinos, Native Americans, Asian Americans, and whites, united activists across racial, ethnic, ideological, and religious lines. Most notably, the conference and the subsequent alliance included representatives of the Communist Party, making it the first civil rights coalition since the anti-Communist crusades of the 1950s to include Communists. Although the alliance was formed to defend the right of individuals to organize and struggle against racial oppression in the United States, conference participants also sought to aid the antiapartheid struggle in South Africa. Thus, the alliance launched a petition drive to free Nelson Mandela (who later became president of South Africa), initiating the first concerted American effort to free the South African activist.

Over the next two decades, the alliance provided legal support, launched petition drives and mass demonstrations, sent delegations to public officials, and mounted letter-writing campaigns on behalf of such well-known prisoners as the Wilmington Ten, the Charlotte Three, Joanne Little of North Carolina, the San Quentin Six of California, the Wounded Knee activists, and the Attica Brothers. In all these cases, people of color faced criminal charges that their supporters maintained were the result of their activity in defense of human rights. Moreover, the alliance worked to expose police brutality against citizens of color and for this purpose organized public hearings in several cities. The alliance also mounted demonstrations, public hearings, petition drives, and publicity initiatives in defense of African American elected officials and voting-rights organizers who were targets of character assassination and sometimes criminal charges.

For its first ten years, Charlene Mitchell served as the alliance's executive secretary. In 1983, Mitchell was succeeded by Frank Chapman, an African American who had spent seventeen years in a Missouri prison on a murder charge. While in prison, Chapman had educated himself and become a political activist. In the late 1980s, Mike Welch, a young white southern activist, assumed the executive secretary's post. He was succeeded in the mid-1990s by James Tate, an African American. For most of its organizational life, the headquarters of the alliance was in New York City. In the 1990s, the office was moved to Las Vegas, Nevada, where Tate lived.

By 1996, financial difficulties made it impossible for the alliance to maintain a national office or staff, and it became a loose network of local activists who continued to wage similar battles and maintained contact. At the end of the century, active branches continued to operate in Detroit, Chicago, Louisville, Birmingham, and Las Vegas. In addition, several hundred members scattered in other communities across the country kept in intermittent touch.

FURTHER READING

Papers of the National Alliance Against Racist and Political Repression, Schomburg Center for Research in Black Culture, New York, New York.

*Anne Braden*

# National Alliance of Black Organizations

In 1976, M. J. Anderson, an African American entrepreneur from Austin, Texas, founded the National Alliance of Black Organizations (NABO) to coordinate the efforts of African American civil rights, political, business, and social organizations. Anderson, who founded a real estate agency in Austin in the early 1930s, served as NABO's first president until 1978, and his office doubled as the group's headquarters until 1991. The NABO presidency rotated every two years. Small and loosely organized, the group operated on an annual budget of less than $25,000. Membership in the group consisted of the presidents of black associations, including civil rights groups and African American fraternities and sororities. As Anderson envisioned it, the NABO primarily served as a forum for black leaders to share ideas. The NABO also coordinated logistics, such as hotel contracts for conventions held by African American associations. At one point more than one hundred organizations, mostly clustered in the southern states, participated in the NABO, which also coordinated voter registration drives conducted by its member groups. In an interview, Anderson cited voter registration efforts, which included drives in his native Austin, as the most important work the National Alliance has conducted. The group closed its Austin office after 1991 following Anderson's retirement from the group.

FURTHER READINGS

Anderson, M. J. Telephone interview with author, August 29, 1997.

Van de Sande, Wendy S., ed. *Black Americans Information Directory, 1994–95.* 3d ed. "National Alliance on Black Organizations." Detroit: Gale, 1993.

*Michael Phillips*

# National Alliance of Black School Educators

Founded in 1971, the National Alliance of Black School Educators (NABSE) emerged from a meeting of fifteen of the nation's black school district superintendents in Chicago in 1970. Charles D. Moody Sr. provided the ini-
tial leadership for the National Alliance of Black School Superintendents (NABSS). In 1973, the alliance renamed itself NABSE and Ulysses Byas, from Macon County, Alabama, was named president. The NABSE has over five thousand members, including African American teachers and administrators.

The NABSE serves African American educators in three primary areas: professional development programs, intended to strengthen the skills of teachers, principals, specialists, superintendents, and school board members; information sharing, which fosters the exchange of ideas about practices, instructional innovations, and learning strategies that have been successful with African American youth; and policy advocacy, which seeks to secure high standards in public and private education systems.

The organization fosters improvement of educational opportunities through five primary objectives. It seeks to "promote and facilitate the education of all students, especially those of African descent; [to] establish a coalition of African American educators and others directly and indirectly involved in the educational process; [to] create a forum for the exchange of ideas and strategies to improve opportunities for people of African descent; [to] identify and develop African American professionals who will assume leadership positions in education; and to influence public policy concerning the education of African Americans."

To enhance professional development opportunities for its members, the NABSE sponsors an annual conference, and its 130 affiliates in the United States, Canada, and the Caribbean host local and regional conferences. Moreover, the NABSE sponsors the National Education Policy Institute (NEPI), a two-day conference that addresses critical issues in education that affect African American educators and students.

The NABSE also forms partnerships with corporations and institutions interested in investing in educational projects. For this purpose, the NABSE has established a foundation to provide funding for educational initiatives, including the Charles D. Moody Research and Development Institute on African American Education. Moreover, the NABSE has nine policy commissions that conduct research about special issues in education: district administration, higher education, instruction and instructional support, local school administration, policy development in public education program development, research and evaluation, retired educators special project administration, and superintendents' commission.

The organization publishes the newsletter *NABSE News Briefs*, the *NABSE Journal*, and the electronic *NABSE Net*. A 1995 NABSE report affirmed the organization's belief that "equity, most of all, concerns justice," and members pledged that "we must never leave the total education of our children in the hands of others." The report identified the lack of financial resources and inadequate government support and commitment to all children as major obstacles to African American education.

To achieve its goals, the organization is taking a proactive role in supporting federal legislation meant to assist school districts with building repairs and modernization. Moreover, it opposes any choice or voucher program that uses public tax dollars for private or parochial school education, even when funds are targeted for poor children, and supports locally governed public charter schools.

**FURTHER READING**

Task Force for Black Academic and Cultural Excellence of the National Alliance of Black School Educators, Inc. "Saving African American Children: A Statement of Belief and Expectation." *Education Digest* 50 (April 1995): 26.

*Thalia M. Mulvihill*

## National Alliance of Black School Superintendents

*See* National Alliance of Black School Educators.

## National Alliance of Postal and Federal Employees

*See* National Alliance of Postal Employees.

## National Alliance of Postal Employees

In 1913, black mail clerks representing thirteen states founded the National Alliance of Postal Employees (NAPE) in Chattanooga, Tennessee. The NAPE organized black railway clerks to protect their jobs from elimination and to combat discrimination and hazardous working conditions. African Americans made up the majority of mail clerks aboard trains from 1890 until 1913. During that time dangerous wooden railcars were used in the Railway Mail Service. In 1913, however, with the advent of steel railcars, mail clerk jobs on trains became safer and more attractive to white workers, who made a concerted effort to eliminate black railway mail workers. In 1923, the NAPE opened its membership to all postal employees.

Throughout its history, the NAPE has represented its members in equal employment opportunity cases and other grievances. The NAPE, for example, protested the early use of photographs to identify civil service applicants. Photographs, the NAPE recognized, revealed the racial identify of applicants and could be utilized to discriminate against African Americans. Following World War II, the NAPE campaigned for women's rights in the workplace, and during the McCarthy era it fought on behalf of its members who had been unjustly accused of Communist affiliation and suspended from their jobs. The NAPE also helped pressure the Post Office Department to create the Board of Appeals and Review as an objective and impartial body acting as the final adjudicator of grievances.

In 1965, the NAPE broadened its membership requirements to include federal employees, and its name became the National Alliance of Postal and Federal Employees (NAPFE). Today the organization has 70,000 members, organized into 143 local chapters and 10 regional districts, and a budget of $2 million. The NAPFE lobbies for legislation, monitors the Federal Service Equal Employment Opportunity Program, and informs and organizes members through meetings and publications. The NAPFE holds biennial conventions and is affiliated with the World Confederation of Labor. It publishes the monthly *National Alliance* and the labor union newsletter covering the postal and other branches of the federal government. The NAPFE provides affordable health and dental plans for its members, and for the past three years it has distributed annually $20,000 in scholarships to worthy dependent children of regular members in good standing.

Although the union was organized for the immediate purpose of preventing the elimination of African Americans from the railway mail service, the NAPFE remains open to all eligible persons regardless of race, sex, creed, or religion and continues to protect the work-related interests of federal employees.

**FURTHER READINGS**

Jaszczak, Sandra. *Encyclopedia of Associations*, 32d ed. Detroit: Gale, 1997.

*The Kaiser Index of Black Resources, 1948–1986*. Brooklyn, N.Y.: Carlson, 1992.

Moore, Jacquelyne C., ed. *Public Information Kit*. Washington, D.C.: National Alliance of Postal & Federal Employees, 1996.

Ploski, Harry A., and James Williams, eds. *The Negro Almanac: A Reference Work on the African American*, 5th ed. Detroit: Gale, 1989.

Smith, Darren L., ed. *Black Americans Information Directory, 1990–1991.* Detroit: Gale, 1990.

*Loretta E. Bass*

## National Association for African American Heritage Preservation

The National Association for African American Heritage Preservation (NAAAHP) is a national service organization dedicated to the identification, protection, and promotion of the contributions of African Americans to the history and culture of the Americas. The organization was cofounded by Claudia Polley and incorporated as a nonprofit organization in the state of Indiana in January 1995. Its national headquarters is located in Indianapolis at the Historic Ransom Place Museum in Indiana's first black neighborhood listed on the National Register of Historic Places. Additional offices are located in New York City, Washington, D.C., and San Francisco. The NAAAHP also has chapter affiliates in Houston, Los Angeles, Missouri, and Florida.

The NAAAHP quickly established itself as the leader of the African American heritage preservation movement. Born of efforts initiated by the National Trust for Historic Preservation to preserve the built history of all Americans, the NAAAHP is one of the trust's grateful offspring. Since the NAAAHP's inception, African American communities have become increasingly aware that preservation is a key tool for community rebirth. By using traditional and nontraditional strategies for overcoming neglect of history and historic resources, African Americans are participating in ever greater numbers in the world preservation movement. Through its programs, conferences, and publications the NAAAHP is spearheading campaigns to launch cohesive cultural and heritage preservation efforts throughout the United States. Of utmost importance is the African American Heritage Tourism Initiative that the NAAAHP inaugurated with its corporate partners, American Express and Alamo Rent A Car. The NAAAHP and its membership are allied with other countries of the African diaspora to identify and protect sites important to the history of African peoples around the world.

As of January 1999, the NAAAHP had approximately 1,500 individual and institutional/corporate members. Particularly the latter membership category has provided the NAAAHP with access to large numbers of individuals. The NAAAHP estimates that the information it disseminates to its members reaches more than one million people.

*Claudia Polley*

## National Association for Equal Opportunity in Higher Education

Founded in 1969, the National Association for Equal Opportunity in Higher Education (NAFEO) is the premier membership organization of the 117 historically and predominantly black colleges and universities in the United States. These institutions have produced approximately 70 percent of the nation's African American college and university graduates, more than 50 percent of the country's black business executives and elected officials, 75 percent of African American Ph.D.s, 80 percent of America's black judges, and 85 percent of all African American physicians. NAFEO's member colleges, consisting of public, private, two- and four-year, and professional institutions, enroll over 350,000 students. Annually, these institutions graduate close to forty thousand students—one-third of all black students enrolled in the United States—in a wide range of professional fields of study.

NAFEO's objectives are to serve as a strong, unified voice of its members in addressing the needs of the institutions and constituencies it represents; to act as a clearinghouse for the collection, analysis, and interpretation of information relative to issues and concerns of historically and predominantly black colleges and universities; to coordinate efforts and activities among organizations, agencies, and other entities interested in advancing higher education for African Americans; and to provide resources to presidents and chancellors of member institutions and assist them in communicating their concerns to policymakers and a wider community. NAFEO prides itself in being the "voice" of historically black colleges.

Leadership of NAFEO has been relatively stable since its founding in 1969. The organization's first executive director was Myles Fisher. Prior to his tenure at NAFEO, Fisher had served with the Institute of Services to Education. In 1977, Fisher was succeeded by Samuel Meyers from Bowie State College (now University), who remained NAFEO's executive director until 1995. Wilma Roscoe of Fayetteville State College (now University), who had for twenty-two years served NAFEO in various posts, served in an interim capacity until 1996. That year Henry Ponder, former president of Fisk University, assumed NAFEO's leadership.

NAFEO'S annual conference, held in Washington, D.C., each spring, is widely recognized as the single most important national forum in America for the discussion of issues relating to African Americans in higher education.

NAFEO publishes a bimonthly magazine, *Black Excellence*, maintains biographical data of member colleges and universities and their presidents or chancellors, compiles statistics on black graduates, and presents annually a Distinguished Alumni Award of the Year. Formerly based in Washington, D.C., NAFEO is now located in Silver Spring, Maryland. Ponder continues to lead NAFEO as president and chief executive officer.

**FURTHER READINGS**
*Black Excellence* 9, 31 (January/February): 1997.
Jaszczak, Sandra, ed. *Encyclopedia of Associations: An Associations Unlimited Reference.* Detroit: Gale, 1996, 991.
National Association for Equal Opportunity in Higher Education. *E Plus O Equals NAFEO.* Washington, D.C.: National Association for Equal Opportunity in Higher Education, 1995.

*Betty Nyangoni*

## National Association for Sickle Cell Disease

*See* Sickle Cell Disease Association of America, Inc.

## National Association for the Advancement of Black Americans in Vocational Education

Founded in 1977, the National Association for the Advancement of Black Americans in Vocational Education (NAABAVE) seeks to increase the participation of black Americans in all areas of vocational and technical education. Its membership consists of educational institutions, teachers, administrators, students, and government employees committed to increasing the number of black Americans in vocational and technical education.

While the organization fosters training in family life management, it is also engaged in developing specialized curricula and training models in the vocational and technical arena. For this purpose the NAABAVE assesses critical social and economic issues that affect black participation in vocational and technical education. Furthermore, the NAABAVE promotes recruitment and retention of black Americans employed in vocational and technical education, and recommends to member institutions strategies for the improvement of organizational motivation and support services. The NAABAVE also maintains a career placement service for blacks and other minorities.

The NAABAVE's quarterly newsletter, with a circulation of six hundred, discusses equity issues, highlights successful programs in vocational education, and provides chapter news and employment listings. The NAABAVE, headquartered in Detroit, conducts annual business meetings and holds its annual conference in conjunction with the American Vocational Association. The NAABAVE's nine hundred members are active in six state groups. The NAABAVE is affiliated with the National Association for the Advancement of Colored People and the National Urban League.

**FURTHER READING**
"National Association for the Advancement of Black Americans in Vocational Education." C. A. Fischer and C. A. Schwartz, eds. *Encyclopedia of Associations*, vol. 1, part 2, New York: International Publishing Company, 1995, 1127.

*Barbara Buice*

## National Association for the Advancement of Colored People

The National Association for the Advancement of Colored People (NAACP) formed in 1910 to obtain public safety and first-class citizenship for African Americans. Over the next eighty years the NAACP evolved from a neo-abolitionist, impromptu, white-led body into a moderate, institutionalized, black-dominated organization, signified by both internal rivalry and historic achievements. The NAACP's changing leadership and strategies emanated from the impact of personalities and social, economic, and political developments in periods of major change, which in turn boosted its reputation as the most long-standing and, until 1960, influential champion of racial equality. Thereafter the NAACP both competed with more direct-action groups and contributed to the civil rights movement, surviving its demise to consolidate gains and prepare for issues confronting an increasingly politically conservative and racially diverse society.

Spurred to action by the 1908 race riot in Springfield, Illinois, northern white progressives and socialists joined with black radicals to lay plans for what became the organizational meeting of the NAACP. Conferees combined the spirit of the nineteenth-century abolitionist William Lloyd Garrison with the Niagara Movement strategy of the civil rights activist W. E. B. Du Bois and the newspaper editor and civil rights activist William M. Trotter to protest black disfranchisement, social segregation, and

Marchers protest segregation in education at the college and secondary school levels. Houston, Texas, 1947. *Library of Congress*

educational inequalities. Like the Niagarans, they sought to improve race relations through agitation, court action, and federal legislation; like them, they envisioned a comprehensive organization with local chapters throughout the United States, including the South, designed to remedy "national wrongs" through agitation. Where the Niagara Movement failed because of disagreement among its founders, pressure from the accommodationist Booker T. Washington, and the eruption of racial violence in Atlanta, Georgia, the NAACP thrived on its biracial support, northern base, and reform appeal.

Unlike Trotter and other black radicals who considered the association dominated by moderate whites, Du Bois embraced its founders, including Oswald Garrison Villard, Moorfield Storey, Joel L. Spingarn, and Mary White

Ovington. Progressives in search of pragmatic solutions, social order, and moral uplift in a chaotic and harsh industrial society, they tried to assist African Americans. They opposed segregation for philosophical reasons and recognized the practical necessity of relying on white lawyers in the courts at a time when black attorneys were few.

With little money or grassroots support, NAACP founders used personal influence, established a central board, and formed chapters. The latter were to press local concerns, alert New York City headquarters of significant issues, and subsidize its operation. Within a year of its formation, the association reported fewer than 200 members, and its national office relied heavily on white philanthropy. Following the slow growth from 1,100 to 8,266 members between 1912 and 1915, however, the membership mushroomed to 91,203 in 310 branches by 1920, and the NAACP emerged as the major civil rights organization in the United States.

In part this growth reflected early successes in direct-action and first-name approach tactics, such as boycotting the New York City screening of the D. W. Griffith film *The Birth of a Nation* (1915), which portrayed African Americans in vicious, racist stereotypes, and pressuring President Woodrow Wilson to publicly condemn lynching. Early on, the NAACP also established a volunteer legal department that assisted black murder suspects in several states and created a division of labor. Most significant, it persuaded the U.S. solicitor general to challenge Oklahoma's "grandfather clause," which violated the Fifteenth Amendment by enfranchising only those black males whose ancestors had voted in 1866. While hardly increasing the number of black voters, *Guinn v. United States* (1915) signaled the beginning of the association's fifty-year attack on the separate-but-equal doctrine of *Plessy v. Ferguson* (1896) that underpinned Jim Crow. And as the United States fought to save the world for democracy in World War I, the NAACP assisted black victims and defended participants in the bloody 1917 race riot at East St. Louis, Illinois. It also protested by organizing the century's first mass demonstration of African Americans against racial violence, a silent parade of ten thousand in New York City. More violence occurred in the "Red Summer of 1919," which recorded twenty-five race riots nationwide. Clearly, the most dramatic membership gains came in response to white-initiated rioting.

Less obvious, but significant, NAACP membership expanded because of the efforts of James Weldon Johnson. Hired as the association's first black field secretary in 1916, he established thirteen southern branches comprising 738 members. By the decade's end, a majority of NAACP members lived in the South and prompted association leaders to schedule its annual convention in Atlanta, thereby adopting a beachhead in the heart of Dixie—where most blacks still lived—as Du Bois himself had done with the Niagara Movement fifteen years earlier. The NAACP's largest branch, in Washington, D.C., had seven thousand members, including government staffers who tracked discriminatory legislation.

Du Bois assisted membership growth. As director of publicity and research, he molded public opinion through the association's official magazine, *The Crisis: A Record of the Darker Races*, which was first published on November 1, 1910. Du Bois included news about local branches,

yet stressed "the great problem of interracial relations." He exercised near autonomy over the publication, a policy Ovington and Spingarn defended because of his stature as both a black intellectual and an opponent of Washington's accommodationism. Under Du Bois's editorship, *Crisis* subscriptions increased from ten thousand at the end of its first year of publication to one hundred thousand in 1920.

The NAACP entered its second decade as a truly national organization, growing fastest in the Far West. It had become increasingly centralized and bureaucratic, stressing litigation and agitation directed by the national office, though some branches pressed direct-action campaigns. It had become more fiscally self-sustaining, adding black membership contributions to white philanthropy. Perhaps most important, in 1920, it drew more African Americans into positions of influence, such as Johnson, who served as the NAACP's first black secretary. Despite these changes and the NAACP's efforts to extend assistance to ordinary citizens, the association still failed to attract large numbers of the black masses.

In the 1920s, the NAACP increased its efforts to curb racial violence, establish civil rights, and promote the Harlem Renaissance. As early as 1918, Republican congressman Leonidas Dyer from St. Louis sought NAACP support for legislation making lynching a capital offense liable to federal prosecution. Initially, NAACP board members debated the constitutionality of encroaching on states rights and acted independently of Dyer. In early 1919, they published *Thirty Years of Lynching in the United States, 1889–1918,* secured President Wilson's condemnation of mob violence, and sponsored an Anti-Lynching Conference. Only after white NAACP secretary John R. Shillady was savagely beaten in Austin, Texas, did they actively support Dyer's bill. Its passage fell to Johnson, Shillady's successor, assistant Walter White, and board member Arthur Spingarn. In 1922, their lobbying efforts succeeded in the House of Representatives but failed in the Senate before a southern Democrat–led filibuster.

Although an antilynching bill never became law, the NAACP had entered the national legislative arena, exposed the crime of lynching, and pressured the South to curtail its mob violence. The effort also accelerated an internal shift of power from white founders, like Storey, who had questioned the legality of the Dyer bill, to the black secretariat and his staff.

The NAACP also continued to represent black victims of racial violence. In 1919, when sharecroppers met in Elaine, Arkansas, to consider legal recourse to their peonage, they were rousted by a posse. During the confrontation a deputy sheriff's death sparked a reign of terror that took two hundred black lives. Subsequently seventy-nine African Americans were tried without adequate defense, summarily convicted of killing the lawman, and sentenced—in twelve instances—to death. Their verdict was reversed three-and-a-half years later by the U.S. Supreme Court, following White's investigation and NAACP expenditures of $50,000. *Moore v. Dempsey* (1923) set precedent for future civil rights litigation, declaring mob-dominated trials inherently unfair.

In 1925, the association received even greater publicity for defending Dr. Ossian Sweet and several relatives and friends, who shot into a crowd of whites seeking to oust him from his home in an all-white neighborhood of Detroit. Recognizing the case's significance, Johnson secured as counsel Clarence Darrow, who had gained notoriety that year for defending John Thomas Scopes against charges of teaching evolutionary theory in Dayton, Tennessee. NAACP stalwarts raised a $50,000 legal defense fund. In celebrated local trials, Sweet and his party were acquitted of murder as Darrow established the right of African Americans to protect their homes and kill in self-defense.

Beyond highlighting the antilynching crusade and the need to end mob rule, Du Bois opened the *Crisis* to black literary works. He became a promoter of the poetry and prose of the Harlem Renaissance, and the *Crisis* became the first magazine to print Langston Hughes's *The Negro Speaks of Rivers*. While not all "New Negro[es]"—so named by writer Alain Locke—agreed with what was being produced, they—Du Bois included—understood the need for fostering racial pride and celebrating accomplishment in the struggle for equality.

Even association critics would have agreed with that premise, but little else. Indeed, despite the impressive legislative and legal efforts by the NAACP during the 1920s, Marcus Garvey of the Universal Negro Improvement Association lambasted its bourgeois legalism and gradualistic approach. He considered the organization too elite and too white, calling it "The National Association for the Advancement of (Certain) Colored People." Garvey attracted thousands of lower-class Harlemites and recently arrived, slum-shocked rural southerners of the Great Migration (1916–1920) by preaching separatism, racial purity, and African repatriation. He recognized the alienation, race consciousness, and militancy wrought by their collective experience in the ever-expanding black community. Filling

the leadership void, Garvey admonished: "Be Black, Buy Black, Build Black." In time, he mocked Du Bois as a light-skinned lackey of white men and in response drew the *Crisis* editor's counterattack—as most prominent blacks questioned Garvey's philosophy, motives, and success (as NAACP rolls declined). Ultimately, black leaders nationally, including NAACP field secretary William Pickens, joined federal government efforts to undercut Garvey. In 1923 Garvey was found guilty of mail fraud and sentenced to prison, and in 1927 Garvey, a native Jamaican, was pardoned and deported.

Others in the 1920s questioned the NAACP's lack of an economic agenda, which the Great Depression magnified. In 1929, Walter White succeeded Johnson as acting secretary, and in 1931 he became permanent secretary. White took over an organization struggling to survive amid a declining membership and depleted treasury; even the *Crisis* required a subsidy from the board of directors.

Turned off by the Republican Party and Herbert Hoover's leadership, White helped deliver the black vote to Franklin D. Roosevelt in 1932 and, thereafter, set out to acquire assistance for African Americans as part of Roosevelt's New Deal program. He befriended the president's wife, Eleanor Roosevelt, and opened a path to the Oval Office, a first-name approach that characterized presidential access for blacks into the 1970s. He became one of the architects of an alliance between established black leaders and the liberal wing of the Democratic Party, which brought the NAACP more directly into the political process.

With association members radicalized by exclusion from early federal recovery efforts and quick to cite racism, spout Marxist dogma, and seek labor ties, White proceeded cautiously. He allied with the Joint Committee on National Economic Recovery in 1933, an umbrella organization created to ensure black influence and inclusion in New Deal policies and programs, but limited his involvement when the committee evolved into the National Negro Congress three years later. Increasingly controlled by labor and Communist delegates, the congress pressed black citizenship rights and occasionally undertook joint activities with NAACP branches, while promoting the Communist Party of the United States. By 1938, this effort chased away many early backers and failed to win support among the masses, but it did pressure the NAACP to take a more militant stand against discrimination.

White also opposed Du Bois's alternative of forming a separate black cooperative economy, which was unrealistic in conception. Those seeking alliance with the Congress of Industrial Organizations snubbed it and NAACP leaders committed to integration suppressed it. Citing mounting indebtedness, White wrested control of the *Crisis* and isolated Du Bois's influence, leading to his resignation in 1934.

White's ouster of Du Bois ended an era in NAACP history. He shed symbolic ties with the radical tradition, steering the NAACP toward a centrist position and setting its future direction. He consolidated power that previous secretaries would never have imagined; and when Louis T. Wright became the first black board chair in 1935, White accrued even more authority since the surgeon Wright deferred to him. Thus, his leadership was accompanied by the organizational shift toward greater structure and black control; African Americans now made up the majority of the NAACP's board members, while black staff lawyers continued to make up the largest number of association attorneys.

Originally, absorbed by the Depression and internal politics, White was slow to arrange counsel for nine black youths held in Scottsboro, Alabama, for allegedly having raped two white women aboard a freight train in the spring of 1931. He interceded only after the Communist front International Labor Defense (ILD) had wrested the case from the moribund NAACP branch at Chattanooga. In time the association played an important role as the case twice reached the U.S. Supreme Court, though not all the defendants were released until 1950. Yet the success of the ILD reinforced the NAACP's need to establish a permanent legal department of qualified black attorneys. Thus, in 1935, White and the board created the NAACP's legal department and selected the dean of Howard University Law School, Charles H. Houston, as the association's first permanent special counsel. Four years later, they appointed Thurgood Marshall to succeed Houston and formed the tax-exempt Legal Defense and Education Fund under William H. Hastie. By 1939, the organization had completed the move from retaining independent lawyers to relying on its own legal infrastructure and stepped up the assault on segregation before a reconstituted Supreme Court appointed by President Roosevelt.

Failure to pass antilynching legislation in the late 1930s, the end of the economic Depression, and the onset of World War II focused attention directly on Roosevelt. As the nation prepared for conflict during the spring of 1941, the black labor leader A. Philip Randolph threatened a march on Washington to protest discrimination in defense industries and segregation in the armed services. Randolph's protest ultimately attracted White's personal, if not official NAACP, support. White helped broker an end to the "march" in exchange for the first major presidential action in behalf of black citizens since Reconstruction. In June 1941 President Roosevelt issued Executive Order 8802 creating the President's Committee on Fair Employment Practice (FEPC). Though the order was limited to defense industries, ignoring discrimination in the military, and the committee was weak, it publicized the issue of racism in employment and urged federal responsibility to curb it, while spawning several effective state committees in the postwar era. It also demonstrated the effectiveness of black protest and power politics.

From the Japanese bombing of Pearl Harbor on December 7, 1941, until the eruption of race riots in several U.S. cities in 1943, NAACP officials joined black journalists to call for a "Double V" strategy: combining democratic war aims with black demands for victories over racism at home and abroad. Accordingly, White pressured federal officials and worked with local chapters and their allies on an array of issues, including the prosecution of lynchers in Sikeston, Missouri, and the occupation by blacks of defense housing in Detroit. Some of these efforts employed direct-action tactics that produced the unprecedented result of bolstering association membership. By mid-1943 the Detroit branch alone had twenty thousand members, prompting White to organize a mammoth Emergency War Conference. Within two weeks of having advanced "The Status of the Negro in the War for Freedom in Detroit," he cringed as that city exploded in the worst race riot of the war and one of several that dotted the nation that spring and summer. Thereafter, NAACP leaders and most of their counterparts backed away from direct action, fearing both charges of hindering the war effort and further racial violence.

In the wake of wartime victory, White brought the association even closer to liberal Democrats. Having toured the European and Pacific war zones, he understood the importance of postwar international affairs for race relations and, in 1944, hired Du Bois to assist in that area. Both men served the following year as consultants to the U.S. delegation at the founding of the United Nations, only to have their relationship soured again as Du Bois became increasingly critical of Western imperialism and supportive of the Soviet Union. White tolerated Du Bois's concern for colonial people until criticized himself for accepting a second appointment to the United Nations, which, Du Bois claimed, would tie the NAACP to President Harry S. Truman's "war-mongering colonial administration." This charge came in the 1948 presidential election campaign as White promoted Truman's candidacy and Du Bois fronted for Henry Wallace of the Progressive Party. White fired Du Bois and aligned the NAACP to the anti-Communist, Cold War wing of the Democratic Party, which ultimately indicted but failed to convict Du Bois as a foreign agent for supposed pro-Communist activities as chairman of the Peace Information Center.

White's dismissal of Du Bois dramatized the extent to which the association had been transformed from protest outsider—as was Du Bois himself—to political insider. Such had been done because White believed in the democratic-capitalistic system and because Truman, its most influential liberal exponent, advanced civil rights further than any previous executive. He had created the President's Committee on Civil Rights in 1946, supported its conclusions before the NAACP Convention of 1947, and issued Executive Order 9981 desegregating the armed forces in 1948.

White also had cast the die for his successors to peddle influence on Capitol Hill. Entering the postwar era with a record membership of 520,000 generally well-educated, middle-class black urbanites striving for true first-class citizenship, as well as lower-class, rural blacks seeking basic protection, White shored up the NAACP's Washington Bureau, which had been created during the war. In 1946, he hired Clarence M. Mitchell as its labor secretary to cement union ties and lobby for civil rights legislation. Within three years, Mitchell headed the bureau and, in 1950, called together sixty nonpartisan organizations committed to advancing civil rights legislation—such as the NAACP and the Americans for Democratic Action—to form the Leadership Conference on Civil Rights (LCCR). Mitchell represented the NAACP in this independent group, becoming its legislative chairman and chief lobbyist for the next twenty-eight years.

Meanwhile, the NAACP continued its courtroom assault on Jim Crow education, begun in 1938. Staff attorneys had plotted a strategy that demanded strict adherence to the separate-but-equal doctrine of *Plessy*, demonstrating its financial burden and preparing for its complete reversal. Thus they won law school concessions for Lloyd Gaines in Missouri (1938), Ada Sipuel and George W. McLaurin in Oklahoma (1950), and Marion Sweatt in Texas (1950) on the respective grounds that equal meant in-state schooling, identical curriculum, and elimination of Jim Crow restrictions. Other states followed suit or

yielded to judicial pressure. Having established equality in graduate education before the U.S. Supreme Court—and buttressed by victories prohibiting all-white primaries (1944), restrictive housing covenants (1948), and segregated interstate dining-car facilities (1950)—Legal Defense Fund lawyers undertook Oliver Brown's suit against the Board of Education in Topeka, Kansas, for refusing his daughter admission to a nearby white elementary school. The case was argued in 1952 and twice in 1953; Thurgood Marshall and his staff featured experts who testified that involuntary segregation damaged one's personality and, in effect, demonstrated that separate—even if equal—was inherently unequal. Owing in part to the judicial activism that emanated from the 1930s and was personified by Chief Justice Earl Warren, the court unanimously ruled segregated public school education unconstitutional.

Because *Brown v. Board of Education of Topeka* (1954) set no timetable for desegregation, white southerners stonewalled the verdict and offered massive resistance, including the formation of white citizens councils. Southern states also targeted the NAACP; for example, the attorney generals of Louisiana, Alabama, and Texas obtained injunctions against the association, and legislators in Virginia, South Carolina, and Florida enacted laws to thwart or terminate branch operations. Association members were harassed, organization records confiscated, and charges of Communist involvement leveled. NAACP lawyers fought back in the courts, but the organization lost ground: 226 branches closed between 1955 and 1957, and membership declined by 40 percent. Ironically, on the heels of unprecedented legal victory, the NAACP was distracted into a fight for its survival.

The South's stubbornness, coupled with President Dwight D. Eisenhower's indifference, prompted southern blacks to direct action. Beginning in 1955 at Montgomery, Alabama, they drew their ministers into a successful bus boycott that brought civil rights and the Reverend Martin Luther King Jr. to national attention. Their efforts also led to the formation of the Southern Christian Leadership Conference (SCLC) and benefited from the NAACP's behind-the-scenes litigation that deemed unconstitutional Montgomery's Jim Crow transportation policy. Nonetheless, neither the boycott victory nor limited civil rights acts in 1957 and 1960 stemmed black assertiveness. In 1960 student sit-ins in Greensboro, North Carolina, sparked mass demonstrations throughout the South and formation of the Student Nonviolent Coordinating Committee (SNCC) by black and white college students. In the following year they also inspired the

Congress of Racial Equality (CORE)–sponsored "Freedom Rides," which energized what rapidly became the civil rights movement.

As membership spiraled, the NAACP no longer monopolized black power and formed an uneasy alliance with rival civil rights organizations. Ministers who had been local branch stalwarts saw no disloyalty in joining the activist SCLC; King himself believed direct action supported the legal initiatives of the NAACP, and he relied on association lawyers to defend demonstrators and solidify gains. The SNCC, too, drew from disgruntled radicals within the NAACP to expand its ranks.

Despite the participation of many branches historically and in present-day sit-ins, NAACP secretary Roy O. Wilkins, who succeeded White in 1955, initially opposed the tactics of mass demonstration. He, his staff, and many local officers were not inclined, nor was their organization equipped, to head such a movement. After chiding black demonstrators in Jackson, Mississippi, in 1961, however, Wilkins returned two years later to join them and be arrested for picketing a Woolworth store. That year, he also challenged the association's peak membership of 534,710 to "accelerate, accelerate" civil rights agitation and expediently supported such chapter activities for the first time.

In this heady atmosphere, the NAACP, CORE, SCLC, SNCC, and the National Urban League competed for donations, members, and prestige, goading one another to score greater gains. They also cooperated with one another in major undertakings like the Voter Education Project, which was launched in 1962 with white financing. The next year, they pooled their efforts to organize a massive march on Washington to influence passage of President John F. Kennedy's civil rights bill. Their effort stalled in the face of bloodshed, including the church-bombing murder of four young black girls in Birmingham, Alabama, and Kennedy's assassination before year's end. Soon enough black leaders, Wilkins included, praised President Lyndon B. Johnson for having strengthened and brokered his predecessor's bill as the paramount Civil Rights Act (1964) in U.S. history and, in response to the 1965 voting rights march that departed from Selma, Alabama, having delivered on the Voting Rights Act (1965). Wilkins knew that the Mitchell-led LCCR lobbying efforts contributed significantly to the passage of these acts, which marked a transition from the segregation of black society to recognition of its first-class citizenship.

Through it all Wilkins walked a fine line, practicing momentum politics while endeavoring to preserve one-on-one influence with Kennedy and especially Johnson. His dilemma intensified in 1966 as the civil rights coalition divided over ways to advance the movement to another level. Following the shooting of James Meredith, who had been marching from Memphis to Jackson to encourage Mississippi blacks to vote, Wilkins joined others at the scene and suggested a nonviolent, biracial demonstration for additional civil rights legislation. Wilkins quickly departed with Whitney Young of the National Urban League, however, when SNCC and CORE leaders advocated that African Americans alone complete the march protected by the paramilitary Deacons of Defense and condemn the president for laxity in enforcing existing laws. King proved unable either to hold the coalition together or to temper the militancy of Stokely Carmichael, chairman of the Student Nonviolent Coordinating Committee (SNCC), who promoted "Black Power" as a slogan for an ambiguously defined radical nationalism. Within a year, King himself broke with the Johnson administration by denouncing the Vietnam War as imperialist and racist. Wilkins and Young, in turn, challenged black power and defended Johnson's policies, continuing to advocate integration, coalition politics, and Cold War strategies.

Wilkins and the NAACP were also out of step with many urban dwellers, who increasingly identified with the militancy of Malcolm X and whose own frustration with the direction and pace of change by both government officials and civil rights advocates exploded into riots between 1964 and King's assassination three years later. Even as he praised King's memory to dissidents who dismissed him as an "Uncle Tom," Wilkins's approach and Mitchell's lobbying resulted in passage of the landmark Fair Housing Act (1968), which prohibited discrimination in the sale or rental of about 80 percent of all housing and ratification of the Twenty-Fourth Amendment, which outlawed the poll tax as a voting requirement in national elections.

Civil rights activism collapsed by the end of the decade, yet its liberalizing influence continued on the legal front. Bolstered by Johnson's appointment of Thurgood Marshall to the U.S. Supreme Court and the remnants of the president's own liberal commitment, the NAACP achieved modest legal gains. In 1968, the Supreme Court demanded timely desegregation and the Department of Health, Education and Welfare (HEW) issued guidelines that cut off federal aid to schools that did not comply with them. Two years later in *Swann v. Charlotte-Mecklenburg*, Supreme Court justices unanimously approved mandated busing as a means to achieve integrated classrooms.

The NAACP enjoyed much less influence in the 1970s and concentrated on consolidating recent civil rights gains in the face of an increasingly conservative presidency and electorate. Association lawyers filed suit against Richard M. Nixon's Justice Department to enforce HEW guidelines calling for "terminal segregation." And NAACP lobbyists led the 1970 opposition to Nixon's U.S. Supreme Court nominations of Clement Haynsworth and Harold Carswell, whose pro-segregation and anti-labor philosophies advanced Nixon's strategy to win votes in the Democratic South. Saving existing legislation and staving off racist appointments—a strategy the NAACP used to prevent the seating of southerner John J. Parker in 1930—the association was once again on the outside looking in. The NAACP found Gerald Ford even more insensitive to the concerns of black society, as he ignored the Congressional Black Caucus—a reminder of the previous decade's political breakthrough—and opposed virtually every bill that would have assisted the black poor.

The election of James Earl Carter in 1976 on the strength of near unanimous black support raised NAACP hopes for the return of a presidential agenda on civil rights, which were soon dashed. Carter appointed several veterans of the civil rights movement, most notably former King confidant Andrew Young as U.N. ambassador, and opened the federal bureaucracy to unprecedented numbers of African Americans and women. Yet programs designed to employ black youths were underfunded, and executive plans for related areas like welfare reform languished in Congress.

In effect, NAACP and other reform efforts were checked throughout the decade by the political drift to the right and the upturned economy. Significantly, volatile "wedge" issues, particularly busing and affirmative action, sparked racial backlash and factionalism within the black community. The latter subject, which emanated from the Kennedy-Johnson era, fostered a color-conscious activism that stressed group rather than individual grievances. Affirmative action became standard employment practice for government jobs but faced opposition elsewhere. In *Regents of the University of California v. Bakke* (1978), the NAACP joined other civil liberties organizations to preserve the concept that race, as opposed to specific racial

quotas, could be a factor in admission considerations. The association defended the decision against backdoor assaults the following year and joined in its extension to union training programs and federal contracts. Essentially the NAACP preserved affirmative action in narrower legal parameters but deepened its rift with former allies in organized labor and the Jewish community, while also alienating white support and even blacks in its own ranks. By the time Wilkins retired in 1976, the NAACP was also facing costly lawsuits in Mississippi, filed by a state highway patrolman whom branch officials accused of brutality and by Jackson businessmen whose stores suffered as a result of local boycotts. Although the NAACP ultimately won both lawsuits, the association struggled with enormous debt.

Predictably, newly appointed executive secretary Benjamin L. Hooks sought realistic goals and new beginnings in a period that required a shift from consolidation in the 1970s to rearguard action in the 1980s. Thus he initially pressed for home rule in Washington, D.C., and mobilized support for the Humphrey-Hawkins full-employment bill before fighting to save past gains from the assaults of President Ronald Reagan, who rendered ineffective federal bodies created to check racial discrimination, including the U.S. Civil Rights Commission; eliminated or cut many social welfare programs; and instituted an economic agenda that benefited mainly the wealthy. As blacks registered poverty levels reminiscent of the pre-Johnson years as well as middle-class achievements wrought by the civil rights movement, Hooks struggled to establish economic opportunity programs with corporate leaders while also dissuading them from doing business with apartheid-practicing South Africa. He also feuded with Margaret Bush Wilson, the first black woman to chair the NAACP board beginning in 1975, over management issues that resulted in her ouster. At the same time, Hooks fought to save the association from fiscal ruin by moving the NAACP's headquarters from New York City to Baltimore in 1986.

Still, like that of Wilkins and White before him, Hook's leadership became an issue among some board members as the racial situation improved little during the presidency of George Bush. In 1993, Hooks stepped down as secretary, and the board appointed Benjamin F. Chavis Jr. to rejuvenate the NAACP's mission and expand its membership. Chavis's tenure was short-lived, however, as he became involved in controversy regarding his association with Nation of Islam leader Louis Farrakhan and his use of organization funds to settle a sexual harassment charge against him by a female staff member. With the association deeper in debt and board members divided over his secretariat, Myrlie Evers Williams won the chair and led the 1994 fight that expelled Chavis.

The board appointed Congressman Kweisi Mfume to lead the association's restoration and resurgence. He has moved to achieve economic solvency through fund-raising and fiscal responsibility, while reasserting the NAACP's long-standing commitment to establish an integrated society. Preparing to enter the twenty-first century, Mfume and his 600,000-member, 2,200-branch association faced an increasingly diverse and segmented citizenry stalled on its commitment to racial equality and indicated, since the association's heyday, the need for new strategies.

From 1910 to the present, the NAACP has played an historic role in the struggle to desegregate society, advance civil rights, and include women—for example, the organizers Ella Baker and Daisy E. Lampkin—in important positions. Yet the NAACP's inability to address the concerns of lower-and working-class blacks effectively remains its greatest challenge in an era whose technologically driven economy, right-of-center politics, and scarce resources accentuate the gap between all classes, but especially the underclass in black communities.

**FURTHER READINGS**

Kellogg, Charles Flint. *NAACP: A History of the National Association for the Advancement of Colored People, vol. 1, 1909–1920.* Baltimore: Johns Hopkins University Press, 1967.

Levy, Eugene. *James Weldon Johnson: Black Leader, Black Voice.* Chicago: University of Chicago Press, 1973.

Meier, August, and Elliott M. Rudwick. "The Rise of the Black Secretariat in the NAACP, 1909–35." In *Along the Color Line: Explorations in the Black Experience.* Eds. August Meier and Elliot M. Rudwick. Urbana: University of Illinois Press, 1976, 94–127.

Morris, Aldon D. *The Origins of the Civil Rights Movement: Black Communities Organizing for Change.* New York: Free Press, 1984.

Ross, Joyce B. *J. E. Spingarn and the Rise of the NAACP, 1911–1939.* New York: Atheneum, 1972.

Sitkoff, Harvard. *A New Deal for Blacks: The Emergence of Civil Rights as a National Issue, vol. 1, The Depression Decade.* New York: Oxford University Press, 1978.

Tushnet, Mark V. *The NAACP's Legal Strategy Against Segregated Education, 1925–1950.* Chapel Hill: University of North Carolina Press, 1987.

Watson, Denton L. "National Association for the Advancement of Colored People." In *Encyclopedia of African-American Culture and History.* Eds. Jack Salzman, David Lionel Smith, and Cornel West. New York: Simon and Schuster, 1996, vol. 4, 1932–1951.

Weisbrot, Robert. *Freedom Bound: A History of America's Civil Rights Movement.* New York: Norton, 1990.

Zangrando, Robert L. *The NAACP Against Lynching, 1909–1950.* Philadelphia: Temple University Press, 1980.

*Dominic J. Capeci Jr. and Jack Knight*

**SEE ALSO** Niagara Movement

# National Association for the Promotion of Trade Unionism Among Negroes

A. Philip Randolph and Chandler Owen established the National Association for the Promotion of Trade Unionism among Negroes (NAPTUN) in 1919. Randolph and Owen, the editors and publishers of the socialist magazine the *Messenger*, had recently left the National Brotherhood Workers of America, an organization that they helped to found, amid charges that they were more interested in personal gain than collective advance. Undaunted by these allegations, Randolph and Owen demonstrated their dedication to the cause of African American labor organizing by founding the new group.

The association was interracial, and its membership included several prominent socialists and union activists, including Charles W. Ervin, the editor of the New York *Call*; Julius Gerber of the New York Socialists and the Metal Workers Union; Max Prine of the United Hebrew Trades; and Rose Schneidermann of the International Ladies' Garment Workers' Union. These activists sought to bring more African Americans into the labor movement through education and organizing activity. This, they believed, was a crucial first step in building a strong interracial coalition capable of challenging the capitalist economic and political system.

Despite its lofty goals and impressive leadership, the association was never more than a paper organization. Randolph and Owen found it difficult to appeal to African American workers whose daily concerns did not involve discussions of political ideology and who were never recruited or otherwise welcomed into those unions in which the association's leadership had influence, such as the New York needle trades. In 1920, only a year after launching the association, Randolph and Owen considered it a failure and moved on to other organizing activities.

**FURTHER READINGS**

Foner, Philip S. *Organized Labor and the Black Worker, 1619–1981*. New York: Praeger, 1974; rpt., New York: International Publishers, 1982.

Harris, William H. *Keeping the Faith: A. Philip Randolph, Milton P. Webster, and the Brotherhood of Sleeping Car Porters, 1925–1937*. Urbana: University of Illinois Press, 1977.

Pfeffer, Paula F. *A. Philip Randolph: Pioneer of the Civil Rights Movement*. Baton Rouge: Louisiana State University Press, 1990.

*Stuart McElderry*

# National Association for the Relief of Destitute Colored Women and Children

On January 31, 1863, a group of women organized a national charity dedicated to the "relief, uplift, and salvation" of the freed orphans and destitute aged women left to the care of various benevolent societies. One of the founders of this organization was Elizabeth Keckley, a former seamstress and companion to Mary Lincoln. Keckley was listed as a member and financial donor of the association's home in the 1870 annual report.

The association was incorporated by an act of Congress on February 14, 1863, to assist the aged or indigent colored women and children who did not have a suitable home, board, clothing, and education. Initially, the organization depended on the philanthropy of the wealthiest and most cultured women of Washington, D.C., as well as contributions from friends. The Executive Committee was dominated by white women. In spite of this, African American women who worked for the association were considered the most refined and held leadership positions in political and social circles within their community. Helen Appo Cook was the first African American woman to become secretary of the association in 1880. She continued to serve in that important position for ten years. Gradually, African American women and men increased their representation on the Executive Board of the association.

African American men contributed to and supported the association in a number of capacities. In 1866, Frederick Douglass, the distinguished orator, became a life member and contributor. In 1872, two of the first African American men elected to the Board of Trustees were Dr. Charles B. Purvis and James Wormely, the owner of Wormley's Hotel in Washington, D.C. By 1879 John F. Cook, a prominent African American citizen of Washington, D.C., gave of his money, influence, and labor to the association. He influenced Congress more than any other man to provide appropriations in support of the association. Cook was elected a trustee of the association in 1885.

The association's first home was located in Georgetown Heights on eighty acres of land. These extensive grounds provided recreation for the "inmates" and also allowed the older children to obtain instruction in agriculture. The home's mission was to rescue the young and the destitute from demoralizing conditions of camp or street life. Lessons in housekeeping, Christianity, and industrial instruction were provided by the home as well as food, clothing, and medicines. Many of the home's residents were in poor health and nearly in a dying state. The annual report for 1863 listed 2 aged women and 62 children as residents of the home. By 1869 the home had a total of 153 residents in its care. The association also provided homes in the North for a few orphans.

Congress initially appropriated $9,900 annually to finance the work of the association's home. Several years later, however, Congress passed a law mandating that all institutions receiving congressional aid had to disperse it through the Board of Children's Guardians. Eventually, Congress withdrew all funding for child-caring institutions. Despite this setback, the association's home continued to provide for destitute black women and children. In 1883, Congress reappropriated funds to the association, increasing the amount to $20,000 in order to provide for a new location of the home on 8th Street.

The home's most famous resident was Elizabeth Keckley, confidante of First Lady Mary Todd Lincoln, who paid for her room and board for the short period that she resided at the home. Upon her death in 1907, her will stated that she bequeathed all her property, the sum of $179.11, to the Home for Destitute Women and Children. The home continued to provide services for African American women and children during the first two decades of the twentieth century.

**FURTHER READINGS**

*The Association for the Relief of Destitute Colored Women and Children Annual Reports, 1863, 1864, 1866, 1869, 1870, 1878, 1883, 1885*. Washington, D.C.

Garrett, Marie. "Elizabeth Keckley." In Jessie Carney Smith, ed. *Notable Black American Women*. Detroit: Gale, 1992, 616–621.

Green, Constance McLaughlin. *The Secret City: A History of Race Relations in the Nation's Capital*. Princeton, N.J.: Princeton University Press, 1967.

Montgomery, Winfield S. *Fifty Years of Good Works.* Washington, D.C.: Smith Brothers, 1914.

Quarles, Benjamin. "Keckley, Elizabeth." In Edward T. James, ed. *Notable American Women, 1607–1950: A Biographical Dictionary.* vol. 2. Cambridge, Mass.: Belknap Press of Harvard University Press, 1971, 310–311.

Washington, John E. *They Knew Lincoln.* New York: Dutton, 1942.

*Vivian Njeri Fisher*

# National Association of African American Studies

The National Association of African American Studies (NAAS) was founded by Lemuel Berry Jr. in 1993. NAAS is a scholarly organization that provides a forum for those who conduct research in black history and culture. It also serves as a medium for celebrating the achievements of African Americans. For these purposes the association publishes a newsletter and holds annual conventions at which students and scholars present their research. The annual meetings also feature several days of exhibits and programs celebrating African American life, culture, and history. In addition to fostering scholarly research, the NAAS also aims to stimulate public interest in African American studies and encourages the preservation of African American history in archives.

Each year the association honors an outstanding African American humanist or social scientist, presenting the honoree with a special medallion. The medallion, designed by a professional artist who was a founding member of NAAS, symbolizes the scholar's ceaseless search for truth and wisdom. The first recipient was L. Douglas Wilder, the first African American governor of Virginia.

The association has five classes of members: student, individual, sustaining donor, life, and honorary. In 1997 NAAS had more than four hundred members. The association is headed by an executive director with offices at Morehead State University, Morehead, Kentucky. The organization maintains a database of African American history and culture, and has electronic publishing capabilities. In the future, NAAS plans to expand membership on the editorial board of the newsletter.

**FURTHER READINGS**

National Association of African American Studies. *The Constitution.* Morehead, Ky.: National Association of African American Studies, n.d.

———. *Fact Sheet.* Morehead, Ky.: National Association of African American Studies, n.d.

———. "The Dream Becomes a Reality." National Association of African American Studies, n.d.

———. *Proceedings.* National Association of African American Studies, 1993–.

*Joseph T. Durham*

# National Association of Black Accountants

The National Association of Black Accountants (NABA) serves as a resource center for and seeks to increase the number of African Americans and other minorities in the accounting profession. The organization promotes professional development of its members and encourages and assists minority students in entering the accounting profession.

Nine African American professionals, concerned about the limited number of minorities in the field of accounting, established the NABA in New York in 1969. At the time of the organization's founding, approximately ten thousand African Americans were employed as accountants, and only one hundred of them were Certified Public Accountants (CPAs). Since the NABA's formation, the organization has grown to a network of over 130 professional and student chapters with a membership of approximately five thousand. Membership occupation in the organization is diverse, representing different fields such as accounting, auditing, finance, and general management. Members join at the general, student, or associate level or as members at large level, according to their background and experience in the industry.

The organization, with national headquarters in Greenbelt, Maryland, is composed of four geographic regions representing members in the East, North, South, and West. The NABA is governed by an Executive Council, composed of the organization's president, treasurer, and secretary, four national vice presidents, and eight national directors, and a National Board of Directors, consisting of members of the Executive Council and the presidents of each professional chapter.

The activities and programs sponsored by the NABA are designed to enhance the accounting careers of students and professionals. NABA programs include education seminars on topics relevant to the accounting profession, scholarship programs for outstanding minority accounting students, and recruitment services to place members with participating firms. In addition, the organization provides regional student conferences and national conventions to encourage networking while enhancing the professional growth and education of its members. The quarterly *News-Plus Newsletter* and the annual *Spectrum Magazine* provide further means of communication and education, keeping members abreast of changes in the field of accounting, finance, and business professions. The scholarship program for minority students has provided over $2 million in financial aid for top students. The NABA finances its various programs through membership fees and corporate sponsors, including Aetna Life and Casualty Company, Allstate Insurance Company, Bank of America, Boeing, Coca-Cola Company, and numerous other corporate contributors.

The work of the NABA has had a considerable impact on increasing the number of African Americans in the accounting profession. By the 1990s, the number of African American accountants had increased to over one hundred thousand, of whom five thousand were CPAs. The NABA's motto, Lifting As We Climb, illustrates the organization's commitment to foster economic empowerment and business formation in the minority community.

**FURTHER READINGS**

Collins, Stephen. "Blacks in the Profession." *Journal of Accountancy* (February 1988): 38–44.

Mitchel, Bert, and Virginia Flintall. "The Status of the Black CPA: Twenty Year Update." *Journal of Accountancy* (August 1990): 59–68.

National Association of Black Accountants. *Accounting: A Career Choice.* Greenbelt, Md.: National Association of Black Accountants, n.d.

*Opolot Okia*

## National Association of Black Geologists and Geophysicists

A group of black geoscientists in the Houston-Dallas area established the National Association of Black Geologists and Geophysicists (NABGG) in June 1981. The organization promotes professional relationships among black geoscientists, encourages and supports African American students of the geosciences, and provides financial assistance. The NABGG is a member of the American Geological Institute, an associate of the Geological Society of America, and a member of the National Petroleum Council. The NABGG convenes symposia during the annual meetings of each of these organizations. The association also sponsors an annual national conference, generally held

in the Southwest, and monthly meetings. Members conduct regular programs in high schools, colleges, universities, and churches in the greater Houston-Dallas area, focusing on career opportunities in geology and geophysics. NABGG members also offer some school-based programs that introduce students to hands-on activities in the geosciences.

In recent years the association has taken a particular interest in environmental justice. For that purpose the NABGG, in collaboration with other organizations, has participated in national forums that discuss issues related to environmental problems disproportionately associated with poor and minority communities. Major corporate supporters of the association include Amoco, Conoco, Exxon, Arco, and British Petroleum. The U.S. Geological Survey has underwritten a number of seminars and contributes human resources on a regular basis to advance the mission of the association. The current president of the NABGG and its 150 members is A. Wesley Ward Jr. of the U.S Geological Survey in Flagstaff, Arizona. The national headquarters of the NABGG is in New Orleans.

*Dennis W. Cheek*

## National Association of Black Journalists

The National Association of Black Journalists (NABJ) is a professional association that focuses on equal employment of black journalists in the media and on balanced coverage of the black community by the media. The association provides a forum for black journalists to discuss issues of common concern and to set high standards in their profession. Membership includes reporters, editors, photographers, and newsroom managers in newspapers, magazines, television, radio, and wire services, as well as part-time freelancers, journalism educators, and college students.

Black press coverage of black communities often declined as the civil rights movement surged during the 1960s. Even with the passing of the 1964 Civil Rights Act, the white media largely continued to ignore black communities, and many mainstream newsrooms remained segregated. During the civil rights decade, white newspapers often sent black reporters to cover dangerous assignments like demonstrations. These reporters were often inexperienced clerks, messengers, and porters, who were expendable after they completed their tasks. The unequitable coverage of the black community, newsroom segregation, and the lack of job security for black journalists prompted efforts to organize black journalists during the 1960s. Some local organizations emerged, but a national organization was not launched until 1975. On December 12, 1975, forty-four black journalists founded the NABJ in Washington, D.C., and elected Charles Sumner as its first president.

The NABJ held its first national conference in Houston on October 2, 1976. Even though Texas Southern University hosted the conference, the NABJ decided to exclude public relations professionals and journalism college professors, instead limiting its membership to full-time journalists. The NABJ's first national meeting was held during the 1976 presidential election, and the new organization sought recognition from both the Republican and the Democratic Party. However, presidential candidates Jimmy Carter and Gerald Ford ignored the organization. Carter acknowledged the organization during his presidency, when the NABJ met in conjunction with the National Organization of Black-Owned Broadcasting on February 16, 1978.

From 1979 to 1981, the NABJ, led by Robert Reid, expanded its membership base and began a trend of assisting minority students to pursue a career in journalism. First, the NABJ established rules for local black journalist organizations to become NABJ affiliate chapters. The fifty-five members of the Louisville Association of Black Communicators became the NABJ's first affiliate. Second, the NABJ established its first newsletter, the *NABJ News*. In March 1981, the NABJ agreed to cosponsor the Ida B. Wells Award with the National Conference of Editorial Writers and the National Broadcast Editorial Association. The award, which recognizes an editor, publisher, or broadcast owner for leadership in providing job opportunities for minorities, provided for the creation of two, $10,000 scholarships donated to the award winners' college of choice.

Initially, the NABJ experienced only a limited membership growth, owing to its lack of a national office; however, this changed in 1983. That year, the Louisville *Courier-Journal* provided the organization with office space and granted its reporter Mervin Auberspin, then NABJ president, permission to devote half his time on the job to represent the association. In 1985, the NABJ set up temporary headquarters in Miami at Knight-Ridder. A few months later, a site in Reston, Virginia, was chosen. Today, the NABJ has a permanent national office in Adelphi, Maryland.

During the 1980s, the NABJ began to take an active interest in African affairs, seeking to provide increased news coverage of the African continent. In 1985, for example, the NABJ sponsored a fact-finding trip to Africa. Fourteen black reporters traveled to Africa, reporting on drought areas and meeting with Organization of African Unity leaders. In 1988, the NABJ established the Percy Qoboza Award for Foreign Journalists to recognize excellence in African news reporting and to strengthen ties with African nations. The award was named in honor of Percy Qoboza, a South African journalist and editor of the black *City Press*. The award's first recipient was Zwalakhe Sisulu of *The New Nation,* a Catholic newspaper in Johannesburg. The NABJ's interest in South Africa was particularly strong because the country boasted a democratic image, unlike other African nations struggling with military dictators. Many blacks at the time, including members of the NABJ, saw a parallel between the struggle to end apartheid in South Africa and the efforts to obtain civil rights in the United States. In subsequent years, Qoboza Prize winners came from other African nations. In 1989, the NABJ annual conference included a session at the United Nations to foster closer ties with Africa. In addition, the NABJ awarded the first Ethel Payne Fellowships in 1993. These fellowships allowed two journalists to obtain international journalistic experience through assignments in Africa. The fellowships were named in honor of Ethel Payne, the Washington and foreign correspondent for the *Chicago Defender*, whose assignments have included black soldiers in Vietnam and Ghana's independence.

The NABJ has also been interested in collaborating with other minority organizations. In 1986, the NABJ participated in the first Unity Board Meeting with the National Association of Hispanic Journalists. During the meeting, the groups addressed concerns about job competition and divisive hiring practices. They agreed on sharing scholarships, a job bank, and internship opportunities. The Unity Board Meetings continue annually to this day. By 1988, the meetings included minority organizations representing Asian Americans and Native Americans.

Today, the NABJ continues to strengthen the journalistic profession. It assists young people desiring to pursue a journalism degree and provides job assistance for college graduates through recruiting and networking activities. The NABJ actively promotes diversity in the news media and balanced coverage of the black community and its concerns. Three thousand members in seventy-four professional and fifty-seven student chapters are active in a variety of programs, including scholarships and internships at selected news organizations as well as seminars and workshops on topics ranging from professional concerns to news coverage.

**FURTHER READING**

Dawkins, Wayne. *The Black Press: The NABJ Story.* Merrillville, Ind.: August Press, 1997.

*Angel R. Rivera*

## National Association of Black Real Estate Professionals

Under the leadership of Sherman L. Ragland II, five MBA students at the University of Pennsylvania's Wharton School of Business founded the National Association of Black Real Estate Professionals (NABREP) in 1984. The organization's membership comprised African American professionals working in the real estate industry, including design, development, law, engineering, management, and investment.

The NABREP's goals were to help companies identify qualified minority employees, provide African Americans with information related to the industry, assist black entrepreneurs to start their own businesses, encourage individuals to attend graduate school to enter the real estate profession, and provide network opportunities. By 1989 the NABREP had approximately one hundred members drawn mostly from Washington, D.C., New York City, and Atlanta. Ragland, a project manager for the Oliver T. Carr Company of Washington, served as the NABREP's president.

**FURTHER READINGS**

Estell, Kenneth, ed. *The African American Almanac*, 6th ed. Detroit: Gale, 1998, 474.

Maurer, Christine, and Tara E. Sheets, eds. *Encyclopedia of Associations: An Associations Unlimited Reference*, 33rd ed. Detroit: Gale, 1998, 319.

Wyman, Stephen H. "A Helping Hand for Blacks in Starting Careers." *Washington Post*, January 16, 1989, 11–12.

*Oscar Flores*

## National Association of Black Social Workers

In 1966, a group of black social work students at Columbia University in New York City began discussions of an association to unify black social workers. Concerned about the mounting racism of the National Association of Social Workers (NASW) and the slow progress of racial integration, they sought to address concerns peculiar to the black community.

Although there were loosely organized black social work groups in some major American cities, including Chicago, Detroit, Los Angeles, Philadelphia, and Pittsburgh, black social workers lacked a centralized organization prior to the formation of the National Association of Black Social Workers (NABSW). Efforts to organize a national body began in earnest at the 1968 National Conference of Social Workers in San Francisco. Some five hundred black social workers and social work students attending the conference openly criticized the racist social welfare system and the conference's failure to address the needs of black people. The group also criticized the conference for its failure to counter myths and misconceptions about black people and its lack of any official position on controversial issues. Moreover, the group was critical of the underrepresentation of racial and ethnic minorities on the conference's board and its planning, executive, and nominating committees, as well as a recent award presented to Wilbur Cohen, the secretary of the U.S. Department of Health, Education, and Welfare. Finally, the group requested a repeal of Public Law 90-248, which increased Social Security benefits but set new restrictions on welfare payments; insisted on support of the National Welfare Rights Organization; and stated that white racism was the major mental health problem in America.

Following the San Francisco convention, black social workers launched the NABSW and gathered for their first national conference in Philadelphia in February 1969. The theme of the conference was "The Black Family: Basic Unit of Survival; Toward a Theory of Liberation." While the organization represents the professional interests of black social workers, it also promotes the welfare, survival, and liberation of communities of African ancestry. It advocates black community control and works to empower black social workers and African diaspora communities. The NABSW fulfills its mission through a host of activities. It hosts national and international education conferences and provides professional leadership to local, national, and global communities.

The NABSW, headquartered in Detroit, is a nonprofit organization with chapters in Alabama, California, Connecticut, the District of Columbia, Florida, Georgia, Illinois, Indiana, Kansas, Maryland, Massachusetts, Michigan, Mississippi, Missouri, New Jersey, New York, North Carolina, Ohio, Oklahoma, Pennsylvania, and South Carolina. Each chapter has representation on the National Steering Committee.

*Felix L. Armfield*

# National Association of Black Storytellers

The National Association of Black Storytellers (NABS) began with a 1983 festival at the McKeldin Center, Morgan State University, Baltimore. The festival was organized by Mary Carter Smith (Mama Mary) and Linda Goss, who, in 1984, became founders and members of the permanent board of the organization that was originally known as the Association of Black Storytellers (ABS). The group changed its name to the National Association of Black Storytellers (NABS) in 1990. The NABS is a nationwide organization with more than four hundred individual members and eight affiliate organizations. The membership includes scholars, historians, authors, and storytellers dedicated to the preservation and publication of African and African American folk stories as well as the creation of new stories.

The enslavement of African people separated them not only from their homeland and families but also from their oral heritage and culture. By reintroducing contemporary audiences to the myths and legends of the African peoples, the NABS is working to reclaim the story of the African spirit. The NABS's mission is to enlighten listening audiences and to "preserve and perpetuate the African Oral Tradition in support of the values that comprise the unique character of the African American community specifically and the African people generally." Storytelling, NABS members believe, serves a multitude of purposes. Based on the African oral tradition, storytelling increases contemporary knowledge and appreciation of the history of the struggle of Africans to survive their removal and isolation from homeland and families. Recounting and commemorating African and African American folk stories fosters respect for the past, reverence for the achievements of Africans, spiritual empowerment, and racial cooperation.

An annual National Black Storytelling Festival and Conference draws an average of four hundred professionals and spectators. Each year the Festival and Conference, having the perpetual theme "In the Tradition," visits a different African American community. In 1998 the festivities were held in Eatonville, the oldest black township in Florida, and Orlando, Florida. The conference title, "Where Zora walked—reclaiming our stories—speaking our words," provided the basis for stories from "all stages for all ages, by oral sages." At each annual festival, the coveted "Zora Neal Hurston Award" is bestowed on a person or persons who have made outstanding contributions to the African/African American tradition. Some previous winners include Mary Carter Smith, Linda Goss, and Paul Keens-Douglass.

Zora Neale Hurston, whose name the award commemorates, was a cultural anthropologist. Born in Eatonville, Florida, she was a member of the Harlem Renaissance, authoring many books, among which are *Tell My Horse, Their Eyes Were Watching God*, and *Mule Bones*. Hurston was a strong proponent of folktales as a means for the spiritual and cultural revitalization of the African peoples. The NABS believes the oral tradition of storytelling to be the original art and literary form of the African peoples. Therefore, the Zora Neale Hurston Award is presented to the person or persons who have made a significant contribution to the promotion of the African heritage through the oral tradition.

Through the NABS's outreach program "Adopt-A-Teller," an additional twelve thousand students and teachers have heard the NABS's message. The NABS associate organizations sponsor six additional presentations each year, drawing an average of 125 listeners per event. The storytellers present the oral tradition in libraries, museums, festivals, and theaters. Moreover, they respond to invitations from corporations, associations, and government agencies. Professional appearances of NABS members have also been requested by the White House to entertain foreign dignitaries.

The NABS's vision is "to enchant the land and bring on the rapture of living to our people and all others whom we as a people encounter through the expert rendering of our stories." To fulfill this vision, the NABS works to preserve and perpetuate the oral tradition. Not only is this accomplished through the gift and art of storytelling but also through the publication of books and tapes containing stories and traditions. These items are sold by NABS members, many of whom have individual web pages, at organization festivals and special events. The NABS sells only articles that have been contributed to the organization as fund-raiser items. NABS membership is open to individuals as well as organization that wish to further the art of storytelling. The NABS, headquartered in Baltimore, publishes a newsletter and a souvenir journal available at the association's annual November festival.

## FURTHER READINGS

Fischer, C. A., and Schwartz, C. A., eds. "National Association of Black Storytellers." *Encyclopedia of Associations*, vol. 1, part 2. New York: International Publishing Company, 1995.

Grimmette, Bill (1999). Internet interview. billygriot@ prodigy.net

Neka, Kudzi. "NABS walked where Zora walked! It was an experience!" *The Act of Storytelling* 1, (1999): 1.

*Barbara Buice*

Withers, Wendy Renee. "Getting Together to Exercise Power: A Case Study of the National Association of Black Women Attorneys." M.A. thesis, Cornell University, 1989.

*Eric W. Rise*

# National Association of Black Women Attorneys

The National Association of Black Women Attorneys (NABWA) was founded in 1972 by Wilhelmina Jackson Rolark, a District of Columbia attorney and city council member. During the early 1970s black and female enrollment in law schools increased appreciably, yet both groups still faced discrimination in hiring, particularly at large law firms. This situation placed black women lawyers, who made up less than 1 percent of American lawyers in 1970, at a dual disadvantage when seeking employment or promotions. To make matters worse, they felt that black bar organizations, especially the largest one, the National Bar Association (NBA), had not taken their problems seriously. In 1972 the NBA responded by establishing a Women Lawyers Division. However, Rolark and others, including the black women attorneys Barbara Sims, Gwendolyn Cherry, and Jean Capers, believed that a separate organization could advocate most effectively for the particular needs of African American women who practiced law. Thus, they launched the NABWA.

Since then the organization has actively promoted the professional advancement of its constituency. It endorses affirmative action for minorities and women, encourages the appointment of black women as judges, and supports recruitment programs for black women prelaw and law students. In addition to professional concerns, it encourages litigation and legislation on issues that affect black women generally, including welfare rights, employment discrimination, and laws affecting families. It does not cooperate formally with other bar associations, but virtually all its members belong to other groups and several, including Rolark, have held leadership positions in the NBA and other lawyers' organizations. At the end of the 1990s NABWA had about five hundred members.

## FURTHER READINGS

"The Politics of Alertness: A Tribute to Wilhelmina Jackson Rolark and the National Association of Black Women Attorneys." *National Black Monitor* (January 1978): 4.

# National Association of Black Women Entrepreneurs

In 1978, Marilyn French-Hubbard founded the National Association of Black Women Entrepreneurs (NABWE) as an advocacy organization for female business owners. Its membership includes aspiring and established business owners, as well as women who head corporate entrepreneurial programs. While NABWE membership is largely made up of African American women, the association supports all women interested in small business enterprise. By the 1990s NABWE's membership had grown to approximately three thousand members in twenty-eight states. The association is currently based in Detroit, Michigan.

The association's main objective has been to provide African American and other female entrepreneurs with the knowledge necessary to build successful businesses. NABWE's leadership monitors trends in business ownership, particularly the steadily increasing number of women-owned businesses. Despite this growth, black women continue to start businesses at a lower rate than other groups of women, owing in part to a lack of business information and access to financial resources. NABWE attempts to address these needs by providing technical support and professional development opportunities through its workshops, forums, and symposia. The association publishes a bimonthly newsletter, *Making Success Happen*, to keep its membership informed. NABWE also coordinates a speaker's bureau, a national networking program, and placement services.

Each year the organization sponsors an annual conference. In 1996, the NABWE sponsored the Entrepreneurial Leadership Summit and Conference to encourage women to learn about business investments and to provide them with opportunities to form alliances with others interested in creating wealth for themselves and their families. Each year the association recognizes the achievement of black women in business with the presentation of the Black Woman Entrepreneur of the Year Award. In the future, NABWE's leadership will focus on creating alliances with other male- and female-owned majority businesses.

FURTHER READINGS

Johnson, Bill. "Black Women Take Care of Business." *Detroit News*, October 11, 1996.

Serju, Tricia. "Black Firms Unite to Get Work." *Detroit News*, October 18, 1996, 1B.

*Sharon Parkinson*

## National Association of Blacks in Criminal Justice

The National Association of Blacks in Criminal Justice (NABCJ) is a professional organization concerned about the effects of justice policies and practices on minority communities. The association is interested in improving the administration of justice at the local, state, and federal levels. To this end, it focuses attention on such issues as crime prevention, legislation, law enforcement, court systems, and corrections. It also advocates increased minority recruitment and career mobility in criminal justice agencies.

The NABCJ was founded at the 1974 Blacks and the Criminal Justice System Conference hosted by Charles Owen of the University of Alabama. Bennett Cooper, director of the Ohio Department of Rehabilitation and Correction, recommended to conference participants the formation of a permanent national association to work toward accomplishing an equitable administration of justice for minorities. Since its 1974 founding, the NABCJ has grown consistently, with local and state chapters organized into six national regions.

The association brings together a broad range of the criminal justice community with representatives from law enforcement, institutional and community corrections, courts, social service agencies, academia, religious institutions, and community interests. Furthermore, the NABCJ invites ex-offenders to join the association to share their views and experiences with members and the community. To keep its members informed about issues and developments in the criminal justice field, the NABCJ publishes the newsletter *Commitment*. This official publication covers many aspects of African American involvement in criminal justice and highlights African American achievements in the field. Moreover, the NABCJ is an active community service organization. Its members provide thousands of volunteer hours to local communities in local and state chapters through programs such as Adopt-A-School. The NABCJ implements educational programs that give community members a better understanding of the nature and workings of criminal justice at the local, state, and federal levels.

The NABCJ is also dedicated to enhancing and increasing criminal justice professionalism. A variety of conferences, seminars, and workshops provide many in-service training opportunities for members and address numerous issues such as prison management, at-risk youths, and child abuse. In addition, members are actively involved in academia through research and support of students seeking a career in criminal justice. Annually, the NABCJ awards the Thurgood Marshall Scholarship to a student in criminal justice. The NABCJ also recognizes excellence and professionalism in the criminal justice field through various awards. The William H. Hastie Award, named after the first black appointee to the federal bench, recognizes leadership in the criminal justice field at the national level. The Mary Church Terrell Award, named after the community leader and church reformer, recognizes activism and positive accomplishments in the field. As a whole, the NABCJ continues to be an active advocate of a better and more equitable criminal justice system.

FURTHER READING

Mabunda, L. Mpho. *Reference Library of Black America*. Detroit: Gale, 1997.

*Angel R. Rivera*

## National Association of Boys Clubs

*See* National Association of Colored Girls.

## National Association of College Deans, Registrars, and Admissions Officers

The National Association of College Deans, Registrars, and Admissions Officers, originally known as the Association of College Deans and Registrars, was founded in 1925. The National Association was the black counterpart to the white Association of College Deans and Admissions Officers, which did not admit black institutions as full-fledged members of its regional accrediting associations. The National Association was established to provide a forum for deans and registrars of historically black colleges to discuss mutual problems, set standards for accreditation, improve higher education, and help strengthen the efforts of minority institutions to gain full regional accreditation.

The National Association was conceived by Theophilus E. McKinney, dean of Johnson C. Smith University in Charlotte, North Carolina. McKinney recognized that black administrators needed a professional organization congenial to their unique needs and problems. Thus conceived, the National Association became a professional organization through which officers of black institutions could exchange information, discuss common problems, and learn about the latest developments in the field of education. When college admissions officers were invited to join the National Association, its name was changed to reflect their inclusion.

Membership in the National Association is open to all professionals who administer college curricula, are responsible for students' entrance credentials, or are in charge of recording academic standings of students. There are three classes of membership: regular, emeritus, and associate. Regular membership is open to institutions, entitling them to send five representatives to the National Association's Assembly. Emeritus status grants membership to individuals who no longer hold qualifying positions in educational institutions but remain interested in the work of the National Association. Associate membership is extended to persons or agencies interested in promoting the work of the group. Individuals employed at member colleges or universities but not designated as official representatives are eligible for associate membership. Institutional members pay annual fees based on their school's total enrollment. Membership runs from July 1 to June 30. The National Association maintains executive offices at Albany State College in Georgia. In 1997 its executive secretary was Arna Albritten, the registrar of the college.

**FURTHER READINGS**

McKenney, Theophilus. *A History of the Founding and Development of the National Association of Collegiate Deans and Registrars.* N.p.: The Association, 1951.

National Association of College Deans, Registrars, and Admissions Officers. *Directory: 1996–1997.* N.p.: The Association, 1997.

———. *Historical Highlights.* N.p.: The Association, n.d.

———. *National Association of College Deans and Registrars in Negro Schools.* N.p.: The Association, 1949.

———. *National Association of College Deans and Registrars.* N.p.: The Association, 1970.

———. *Proceedings.* N.p.: The Association, 1925–.

*Joseph T. Durham*

# National Association of College Women

The National Association of College Women (NACW) was established to promote higher education for African American females. Founded by Howard University Dean of Women Lucy Diggs Slowe (1885–1936) in 1923, the NACW was an organization of African American women who graduated from accredited liberal arts colleges and universities. Slowe served as the group's first president. In her inaugural speech, she emphasized the NACW's uniqueness and stressed that the group's purpose was to raise the standards of colleges that black women attended. Slowe sought to inspire advanced scholarship and improve professional conditions for black female faculty and students. She wanted the NACW to provide a "center of guidance, encouragement and information."

Through the NACW, Slowe conducted a study investigating the status of women on African American college campuses. She published the results in a 1933 *Journal of Negro Education* article, claiming that colleges did not prepare black women for leadership roles. This failure, Slowe explained, was due to the lack of mentors and adequate courses and activities. She urged presidents of historically black colleges to make such improvements a priority, especially the appointment of qualified deans of women to advise female students. In 1929, the NACW Committee on Standards had hosted a conference of deans and advisers of girls in African American schools. This group met annually at the NACW convention, becoming an independent organization called the Association of Deans of Women and Advisers to Girls in Negro Schools in 1935.

The NACW continued its efforts to elevate black women to academic and professional positions equivalent to those held by white and black men. Members wanted to empower African American women to thrive not only as leaders in their local communities but in national and international spheres. By 1974, the NACW adopted the name National Association of University Women (NAUW) to reflect the changing status of the educational institutions that many of its members had attended. The group's headquarters moves annually to the location of its president.

In the 1990s, the NAUW served approximately four thousand members in five regional and ninety-two local groups and coordinated local groups of college women in a national network. Members are encouraged to participate in community outreach services and extend assistance to young people, such as tutoring in local schools. The NAUW sponsors the "After High School—What?" youth development program. The organization attempts to enhance education at all levels, particularly exploring conditions and problems that affect female students, staff, and faculty. Publicizing the group's theme—"Women of Action: Reaching, Rising, Responding"—the

NAUW rewards high educational standards and intellectual achievements of women by presenting annual fellowship and scholarship awards.

The NAUW strives to develop civic activities and attain better human relations through committees focusing on literacy, national and international affairs, and political awareness. The organization is affiliated with the Leadership Conference on Civil Rights and the United Negro College Fund. Sponsoring a placement service, the NAUW publishes the annual *Directory of Branch Presidents and Members*, the biennial *Journal of the National Association of University Women*, and a *Bulletin*. The NAUW's biennial convention is usually held the week of July 30–August 4 on a historically black college campus.

**FURTHER READINGS**

Davis, Hilda A., and Patricia Bell-Scott. "The Association of Deans of Women and Advisers to Girls in Negro Schools, 1929–1954: A Brief Oral History." *Sage* (Summer 1989).

Noble, Jeanne L. *The Negro Woman's College Education.* New York: Bureau of Publications Teachers College, Columbia University, 1956.

Slowe, Lucy Diggs. "The Higher Education of Negro Women." *Journal of Negro Education* 2 (July 1933): 352–358.

Slowe Papers, Moorland-Spingarn Research Center, Howard University, Washington, D.C.

*Elizabeth D. Schafer*

# National Association of Colored Girls

In 1930, the National Association of Colored Women (NACW), under the leadership of its president, Sallie W. Stewart, founded the National Association of Colored Girls (NACG) to promote the moral, mental, and material development of black girls. The NACW, which sought to elevate black women in the interest of racial advancement, tried to instill in African American girls the virtues and values of its predominantly middle-class membership. Girls who joined the NACG were to be industrious, pious, artistic, and gracious. They were to be trained to be good mothers who in turn would maintain good homes. Through the NACG black club women sought to teach black girls how to lead moral lives and make their homes a bulwark in the defense of black womanhood. This, the NACW hoped, would enable them to vindicate their honor in the face of vitriolic white attacks

that characterized them as wanton, immoral, and socially inferior.

While the NACW sought to elevate black womanhood, it did so without challenging traditional gender roles. The NACW did not question black women's social position in the domestic sphere but instead tried to make them better wives and mothers. Black women's moral purity, the NACW maintained, was the key to social improvement and racial advancement.

Through the NACG, the NACW aimed to promote a commitment to service and philanthropy and to instill cultural and social interests among black girls. The girls were to seek a fuller and happier life through worship, recreation, education, industry, thrift, citizenship, racial solidarity, interracial relations, and social service. For this purpose, the NACG launched a variety of activities including arts and crafts programs, instruction in proper hygiene for home and school, religious education, and community service projects such as assisting the disabled.

Girls interested in joining one of the NACG clubs had to be members of a Sunday school, pledge to avoid "questionable" places, and promise to conform to the rules and regulations of the NACG. Each club operated autonomously, assessing dues and setting age limits for its members. Most clubs admitted girls between the ages of five and twenty-five. State branches were responsible for funding the work of their local clubs, while the national organization provided general guidance, handbooks, outlines, buttons, and pins that were used by both the NACW and the NACG.

In 1933, Stewart, ninth president of the NACW and a member of the NACG's scholarship board, initiated the *Girls' Guide.* This guide was revised several times in the 1930s and 1940s to unify the work of the girls' clubs. During Stewart's tenure girls' uniforms, tokens, and pens were also standardized.

In 1962, under the leadership of NACW president Rosa L. Gragg, the NACG changed its name to the National Association of Girls' Clubs to avoid any reference to race. In 1983, more than fifty years after the founding of the NACG, black women established a similar organization for boys. The National Association of Boys Clubs, under the presidency of Otelia Champion, fostered the moral and intellectual development of at-risk black males. In 1990, both organizations merged to form the National Association of Youth Clubs (NAYC). Open to black boys and girls ages six to eighteen, the organization promotes positive attitudes toward health, love, home, spirituality, and service among its members. Group activities include

March of Dimes drives, African American history and community revitalization projects, senior citizen days, scholarship fund-raisers, and HIV/AIDS awareness campaigns. Headquartered in Washington, D.C., the NAYC has currently forty chapters nationwide.

**FURTHER READINGS**

Davis-Lindsay, Elizabeth. *Lifting As They Climb*. New York: G.K. Hall & Co., 1996.

Wesley, Charles Harris. *The History of the National Association of Colored Women's Clubs: A Legacy of Service*. Washington, D.C.: Mercury Press, 1984.

*Angela Hornsby*

**SEE ALSO**    National Association of Colored Women's Clubs, Inc.

## National Association of Colored Graduate Nurses

A group of black women who championed the professional development of African American nurses founded the National Association of Colored Graduate Nurses (NACGN) in 1908. The formation of the NACGN was largely a response to the exclusion of black nurses from professional associations operated by whites, the lack of access to training schools, and restrictive state licensing legislation. The NACGN sought to represent the professional interests of black nurses and to combat racial segregation in nursing. Fighting Jim Crow barriers, the NACGN achieved its ultimate objective with the integration of American nursing in 1951. That year, the NACGN disbanded, and its members voted to merge with the American Nurses' Association (ANA).

The NACGN originated in 1906, when Martha Minerva Franklin (1870–1968), a black graduate of Philadelphia's Woman's Hospital Training School for Nurses, mailed over 1,500 letters to black graduate nurses, superintendents of nursing schools, and nursing alumni associations. Franklin inquired whether there was interest in creating a separate black nurses organization. Her letters stimulated the interest of Adah Belle Thoms (1870–1943), a 1905 graduate of New York City's Lincoln School for Nurses and president of the school's alumni association. Thoms was born in Virginia and taught school in Richmond before migrating to New York in the 1890s, where she entered the Women's Infirmary and School of Therapeutic Massage. She worked for a time as head

Group portrait of 1918 nursing class at Lincoln School for Nurses, Bronx, New York. *Schomburg Center for Research in Black Culture*

nurse at St. Agnes Hospital in Raleigh, North Carolina, but she soon returned to New York to earn her nursing diploma at Lincoln Hospital. Thoms and Franklin collaborated in an effort to launch a separate black nurses association.

In August 1908, fifty-two black nurses convened at New York City's St. Mark's Episcopal Church and founded the NACGN, electing Franklin as its president. While the group decided to organize all black nurses, it limited full membership privileges to registered nurses who had graduated from three-year hospital-based nursing schools. The NACGN granted associate memberships to nurses who had not completed their training at registered schools, lay persons who were interested in the promotion of nursing and black nurses, and honorary members recommended by the NACGN's board of directors. In 1912, the NACGN had 125 members, and by 1920 the number had risen to 500.

The NACGN sought to increase the number of professional black nurses as well as the quality of their training. It advocated elevated education standards, urged schools to raise admission rates, and encouraged black nurses to seek advanced training to qualify them for positions in public-health nursing. Moreover, the NACGN asked local affiliates to develop "coaching classes" to help black nurses prepare for board examinations. In addition, the NACGN promoted interracial cooperation with white nursing groups, attacked the racial exclusion of white professional nursing organizations, and challenged the policies of most southern states, which either barred black nurses from taking registration examinations or administered separate exams for them.

During the early years, the organization did not have an official organ or permanent headquarters. To communicate with its members, the NACGN used the black press to disseminate information about its activities and to raise its members' awareness of state board examinations. Under the leadership of Thoms, who served as NACGN president between 1915 and 1920, the association established temporary headquarters at New York City's 37th Street Young Women's Christian Association. By 1920, Thoms filed the NACGN's incorporation papers and established a national job registry for black graduate nurses to assist them in finding employment. Petra A. Pinn, a charter member of the NACGN, served as the organization's president from 1923 to 1926, and as its treasurer from 1929 to 1946. Pinn, a 1906 graduate of Tuskegee Institute's John Andrew Memorial Hospital School of Nursing, had served as head nurse at Mont-gomery's Hale Infirmary and as superintendent of nurses at the Red Cross Sanitarium and Training School in Louisville, Kentucky. As NACGN president, Pinn continued to support the job registry program initiated by Thoms, while trying to establish a national headquarters for the organization.

Carrie E. Bullock, who served as NACGN president from 1927 until 1930, further expanded the organizational structure of the association. Bullock studied for two years at the Presbyterian Missionary School at Aiken, South Carolina, before graduating from Scotia Seminary in Concord, North Carolina, in 1904. She taught school in South Carolina before entering the nurses' training school at Dixie Hospital in Hampton, Virginia, in 1906. A few months after entering Dixie, Bullock transferred to Provident Hospital in Chicago, where she completed her nursing training in 1909. She joined the staff of the Chicago Visiting Nurses Association in 1909 and ten years later was promoted to supervisor of black nurses. Bullock focused on two key issues during her presidency: increasing communication between black nurses and fostering a greater sense of professional and organizational involvement among them. In 1928, she founded and edited the NACGN's official organ, the *National News Bulletin*. To persuade black women to pursue postgraduate education, she initiated contacts with managers of the Julius Rosenwald Fund, leading to the establishment of a fellowship program for black graduate nurses.

While the NACGN struggled to increase the number and improve the quality of training of black nurses, black women interested in entering the profession continued to face numerous racial barriers. Most white nursing schools in the South refused to admit African Americans, and black women who managed to obtain professional training despite racial restrictions often encountered limited employment opportunities. Few white-run hospitals and settlement houses employed black nurses and usually paid them less than white nurses. The leading white-controlled professional organizations, the American Nurses' Association (ANA), the National League of Nursing Education (NLNE), and the National Organization for Public Health Nursing (NOPHN), continued their virtual exclusion of black nurses. Beginning in 1916, the ANA accepted new members only if they belonged to state affiliates. Indeed, sixteen southern states and the District of Columbia excluded black women nurses from joining local associations, thereby denying them access to most professional employment opportunities.

During its first two decades, the NACGN accomplished little, largely owing to its lack of permanent headquarters, low membership, and insufficient funds, which prevented the employment of a full-time salaried executive. In addition, the onset of the Depression in the late 1920s severely hampered the NACGN. Black nurses faced high unemployment rates, limited professional opportunities, and a reduction in wages. During this period the median salary for African American nurses was approximately $1,200 per year. Economic fluctuations particularly hurt black nurses, who often worked in private practice in black neighborhoods and earned significantly less than white nurses.

Despite the economic crisis sparked by the Depression, the NACGN made considerable advances during the 1930s. In 1934, Estell Massey Riddle assumed the NACGN's presidency. Riddle had attended nursing school at Homer G. Phillips Hospital and Nurses Training School in St. Louis, Missouri, in 1920. By 1927, she had moved to New York City, where she enrolled in Columbia University's Teachers College, becoming the first black recipient of a Rosenwald Fund Fellowship for nurses and the first black woman nurse to earn a master of arts. Under Riddle's leadership, the NACGN held its first regional conference at New York City's Lincoln School for Nurses in 1934. In the same year, Riddle secured white philanthropic support for the NACGN from Frances Payns Bolton of Cleveland, Ohio, the Julius Rosenwald Fund, and the General Education Board. With the help of these philanthropic funds, the organization moved into permanent headquarters at New York City's 50 West 50th Street, which also housed the national headquarters of the leading white professional organizations—the ANA, the NLNE, and the NOPHN.

Moreover, the funding enabled the organization to employ a full-time salaried officer. In 1934, Riddle hired Mabel Keaton Staupers as the organization's first executive secretary. Staupers, born in the West Indies, had graduated from Washington, D.C.'s Freedmen's Hospital nursing school in 1917 and worked in New York City as a private nurse. While in New York, she played a key role in organizing the Booker T. Washington Sanitarium, the first facility in the Harlem area where black physicians could treat their patients. She also served for twelve years as the executive secretary of the Harlem Committee of the New York Tuberculosis and Health Association.

Serving as the NACGN's executive secretary from 1934 to 1946, Staupers gained notoriety when she sought to secure the right for black nurses to serve in the segregated armed forces during World War II. Throughout the nation's history, African American soldiers had served in the military in every major conflict; however, the armed forces had excluded black nurses in World War I. During World War II, the military recruited black nurses to serve on a limited and segregated basis. The War Department established a quota of 56 black nurses, 120 black physicians, and 44 black dentists to work in the wards designated for black troops. While Staupers knew that the establishment of quotas was an advance over the total exclusion of black nurses, she was determined to fight for the complete integration of the Armed Forces Nurse Corps. Thus, Staupers and the NACGN launched increased agitation against the military's racial quotas, particularly after government officials informed the country's major nursing organizations of the growing need for nurses. Staupers informed William H. Hastie, the black civilian aide to the secretary of war, of the NACGN's campaign to force the integration of the Armed Forces Nurse Corps. She also sought allies among white civic groups, particularly nursing organizations, hoping to persuade them that black nurses could play an important role in the nation's war effort. Telegrams from wartime civil rights organizations pressured the War Department to declare an end to the quotas and racial segregation. On January 20, 1945, Staupers scored a major victory when Surgeon General Norman T. Kirk announced that all nurses regardless of race would be accepted into the Army Nurse Corps.

The integration of the ANA, however, was not achieved until 1948. That year, the ANA's House of Delegates authorized black nurses to apply for membership and elected Estelle Massey Riddle Osborne to the board of directors. When black nurses began to gain entry into white nursing organizations, they voted to disband the NACGN, assuming that its services were no longer needed. However, their optimism soon faded. Very few black women reached leadership positions in the ANA, and soon black members complained that the previously all-white association failed to recognize the contributions of black nurses. Thus, despite the ANA's racial inclusion, black nurses decided to establish a separate organization to address their professional needs and the health care problems of the African American community. In 1971, they launched the National Black Nurses Association.

**FURTHER READINGS**

Carnegie, M. Elizabeth. *The Path We Tread: Blacks in Nursing Worldwide, 1854–1994*. 3d ed. New York: National League for Nursing Press, 1995.

Hine, Darlene Clark. "Mabel K. Staupers and the Integration of Black Nurses into the Armed Forces." In John Hope Franklin and August Meier, eds. *Black Leaders of the Twentieth Century.* Urbana: University of Illinois Press, 1982, 241–258.

——. *Black Women in White: Racial Conflict and Cooperation in the Nursing Profession, 1890–1950.* Bloomington: Indiana University Press, 1989.

Staupers, Mabel Keaton. *No Time for Prejudice: A Story of the Integration of Negroes in Nursing in the United States.* New York: Macmillan, 1961.

Thoms, Adah B. *Pathfinders: A History of the Progress of Colored Graduate Nurses.* New York: Kay Printing House, 1929; rpt., New York: Garland, 1985.

*David MacLaren*

## National Association of Colored Women's Clubs, Inc.

Founded in 1896, the National Association of Colored Women's Clubs, Inc. (NACW) was the product of a merger of the National Federation of Afro-American Women (NFAAW) and the National League of Colored Women (NLCW). In the previous year, predominantly middle- and upper-middle-class African American women established the NFAAW and the NLCW to challenge racism, discrimination, and segregation and to foster racial advancement and community uplift. The creation of the NACW represented the culmination of their organizational activities and was a manifestation of the reform efforts occurring among African Americans and in the nation at the turn of the century.

The NFAAW emerged when the New Era Club of Boston invited black women from across the country to a national meeting in 1895. Organizers claimed that Boston, which had been a hotbed of abolitionist activities, could provide an atmosphere conducive to "interpreting and representing our position, our needs, and our aims." While black women had discussed the efficacy of meeting in a national conference for some time, a letter that John W. Jacks, president of the Missouri Press Association, sent to Florence Balgarnie of England acted as a catalyst in hastening their meeting. In the letter Jacks had impugned the character of African American women in an attempt to undermine the black journalist Ida B. Wells's antilynching activities in Britain. England was the largest importer of southern cotton, and Jacks feared that negative publicity about race relations in the United States would imperil the South's economy. While Jacks's letter may have served as a catalyst, black women insisted that long before "the base slanders, born in the vile mind of a common Missouri white man," they were actively working among their people to promote racial progress.

In July 1895, in response to the New Era Club's invitation, one hundred delegates gathered in Boston for the first national conference of black women. During the three-day conference delegates issued several resolutions that reiterated their commitment to improving the lives of African Americans. Conferees determined that they could best implement their mandate through a national organization. They founded the NFAAW and chose the New Era Club's *Woman's Era* as their official newsletter. Prominent club woman Margaret Murray Washington, dean of women at Alabama's Tuskegee Institute, became the NFAAW's first president. Victoria Earle Matthews of New York City, founder of the Woman's Loyal Union of New York and Brooklyn, chaired the Executive Committee. Matthews, who also founded New York City's White Rose Mission for migrant women and girls, brought a wealth of experience and skills to the position. These administrative choices highlighted the significance of black women's social and political activism in Boston and New York, as well as the influence of Tuskegee intellectuals.

Like Boston and New York, Washington, D.C., was also a major center of black women's activism at the turn of the century. It was the home of many educated black elites who either worked for the federal government or found professional positions in the segregated job market. In 1895, female members of Washington's black elite under the leadership of Mary Church Terrell—educator, lecturer, and politician—and the educator Anna Julia Cooper founded the National League of Colored Women (NLCW). The NLCW resolved "to collect all facts obtainable to show the moral, intellectual, industrial and social growth and attainments of our people, to foster unity of purpose, to consider and determine methods which will promote the interests of colored people." Specifically, the NLCW sought to redress black grievances such as lynchings, exploitation of women and children, educational and economic disparities, disfranchisement, and other Jim Crow laws that threatened to place African Americans in a permanent caste at the bottom of society.

In July 1896 both the NFAAW and the NLCW held their annual conventions in Washington, D.C. Realizing that their goals were the same, representatives from the two federations met to determine their fates. It was on this occasion that the two competing national organizations concluded that they could best implement their programs by joining forces. In a joint session held at Washington's 19th Street Baptist Church, the seventy-two delegates, representing a membership of about five thousand, founded the National Association of Colored Women's Clubs (NACW) to launch and sustain a program that employed contemporary scientific and professional techniques in the interest of protecting and advancing their status and that of their communities. The NACW's motto, "Lifting as We Climb," reflected the organization's goals of fostering racial solidarity and community uplift.

The delegates elected Terrell as the NACW's first president. Terrell was an excellent choice because she epitomized the type of black women who had been active in the club movement. She was intelligent, articulate, and committed to social change, and she had a successful track record of involvement in reform efforts. Born to wealthy, entrepreneurial parents, she earned bachelor and master's degrees from Oberlin College. Moreover, she studied in Germany and spoke French, Spanish, and German fluently. The NACW elected Josephine Silone Yates, a chemistry professor at Lincoln Institute in Jefferson City, Missouri, as its second president. Yates had completed her high school and normal school education in Rhode Island and had been educated at the Institute for Colored Youth in Philadelphia, a renowned preparatory school. Yates, who helped organize the Kansas City Women's League in 1893, was highly visible in the state federated clubs before assuming national office in the NACW. Other key leaders in the organization included Ida B. Wells, Mary Burnett Talbert, Hallie Q. Brown, Mary Waring, Mary McLeod Bethune, and the Reverend Florence Randolph.

The NACW operated through a federation of state and local clubs. The NACW's powerful Executive Cabinet, dominated by prominent national figures, ran the organization's day-to-day activities. The NACW established several departments to address contemporary concerns of African Americans including kindergarten, domestics, employment, temperance, suffrage, and education divisions. The newsletter *National Notes* served as the NACW's official organ that sought to educate black women about reform efforts, apprise them of the activities of local and state affiliates, and forge a national identity.

Committed to improving the lives of African Americans, NACW women were involved in a wide variety of social, educational, civic, and political activities. They sponsored clubs for single and married women that addressed the specific concerns of these women. They offered education programs for working women and skills-building courses for married women that included nutrition, sewing, and child care. They provided a forum for women to gather and hence created a nationwide network. While they probably had a "community mission," national records do not indicate specific activities. They also sponsored musical and literary groups and supported hospitals, orphanages, and clubs devoted to "doing slub work"—a term the women used to describe hard, monotonous work necessary to the success of the organization. Club women also worked to redress the crisis in black education, which had reached critical proportions, particularly in the Jim Crow South, where black students frequently received as little as one-third of the appropriations allocated to white youngsters in public schools. NACW affiliates raised money and, through direct appropriations, scholarships, and donations of land and equipment, sought to improve the educational opportunities of many black children. NACW affiliates also provided compensatory educational programs for African Americans through their literary and civic clubs. Moreover, they founded settlement houses and black branches of the Young Women's Christian Association (YWCA) that offered black women and girls training programs and affordable housing.

In 1916, when the NACW met for its tenth biennial meeting in Baltimore, the organization had grown to more than one hundred thousand members. Its work encompassed thirty-five departments devoted to legislation, social science, young women's work, business, industrial and social conditions, suffrage, civics, juvenile court, rural conditions, railroad conditions, and health and hygiene. The broad spectrum of these departments indicates that the NACW not only engaged in activities that had been a mainstay for black club women, such as education programs and support for single women and mothers, but that it was cognizant of the grave social, economic, legal, and political conditions of African Americans in the Progressive Era.

The NACW's sophisticated level of political development was also reflected in the organization's effort to build alliances with other women and activist groups. In 1915, for example, Talbert and Terrell participated in the national forum "Votes for Women: A Symposium by Leading Thinkers of Colored Women" in Washington, D.C. To implement its agenda of racial advancement, the NACW collaborated with the National League on Urban Conditions, the National Association for the Advancement of Colored People (NAACP), the Women's Christian Temperance Union, and the YWCA.

In 1916 Mary Burnett Talbert of Buffalo, New York, succeeded Margaret Murray Washington as president of the NACW; she served for two terms from 1916 to 1920. During Talbert's administration the NACW continued to grow and increase its visibility. In 1916, the NACW embarked for the first time on a national project when it sought to purchase the Frederick Douglass estate in Anacostia, D.C., to preserve it as an historic site and to use it as the organization's national headquarters. To achieve its goal the NACW launched a successful, national fund-raising campaign. At the 1918 biennial conference in Denver, Talbert announced that the NACW had purchased the Douglass estate. Talbert also continued to foster alliances with other women's organizations. In 1920, the NACW became a full-fledged member of the International Council of Women (ICW) when Talbert, the NACW's first officially elected delegate to the ICW, attended its quinquennial conference in Christiana, Norway.

The NACW seized the opportunity presented by the U.S. entry into World War I and the subsequent reconstruction to expand its programs. During World War I, NACW members raised $5 million in war bonds and promoted government conservation programs in black communities. Under the auspices of the Young Men's Christian Association, NACW members, including Talbert and Addie W. Hunton, joined the American Expeditionary Forces to provide religious and educational programs for black soldiers stationed in France in 1919. These soldiers, in turn, contributed $1,000 to the NAACP's Anti-Lynching Campaign headed by Talbert. As a result of these wartime activities some white politicians, including President Woodrow Wilson, state governors, and other elected officials, recognized that the NACW was a force to be reckoned with if they sought to gain access to the black community.

Despite the NACW's wartime cooperation with the government, black club women took every opportunity to protest the atrocities inflicted on African Americans. Members highlighted the hypocrisy of a nation that was at war "to make the world safe for democracy," yet permitted the lynching of black men and women with impunity and generally failed to uphold their rights. Arguing that mob violence was detrimental to the war effort, the NACW called on Congress to pass an anti-lynching bill. The NACW also urged Congress to enact the Susan B. Anthony amendment, granting women the right to vote, for they believed that the combined efforts of black men and women could yield political gains. Like many contemporary feminist organizations, the NACW

perceived alcoholism as a threat to the family and the economic stability of the community. Hence, it also lobbied for passage of the Prohibition amendment. Once the Nineteenth Amendment, which granted suffrage to women, was ratified, the NACW proposed the establishment of citizenship schools to enable their members to make intelligent and informed political decisions. During these sessions they discussed and debated the political issues of the day and evaluated the records of candidates.

The economic slump of the 1930s posed new challenges for the NACW. Most of the organization's activities were conducted by a myriad of local groups that suffered economic hardships as a result of decreasing budgets. Yet despite the financial crisis of the Great Depression, the NACW continued to expand its activities and constituency, drawing on the resources of its substantial middle- and upper-middle-class membership, as well as community support. In 1930 the NACW established the National Association of Colored Girls Club to provide the next generation of black women with leadership training and the vision to fulfill its mandates.

During the 1930s the NACW also increasingly embraced interracial dialogue and invited whites, such as Jessie Ames of the Commission on Interracial Cooperation and the Association of Southern Women for the Prevention of Lynching, to address NACW conventions and participate in public forums. Throughout the Depression the NACW continued its political activism by supporting the National Recovery Act and the Costigan-Wagner Anti-lynching Bill and by raising money for the defense of the Scottsboro Boys. Communism, socialism, public housing, and health care were also major issues of concern discussed and debated at NACW conferences.

In World War II the NACW supported the U.S. war efforts by promoting the purchase of savings bonds and the federal Thrift Program. Yet, as with World War I, the NACW protested against government-condoned racism and challenged segregation in the army and employment discrimination in the defense industry. The NACW criticized the discrimination of black members of the Women Army Corps (WACS) and called on the president to appoint an African American to the U.S. Civil Service Commission to prevent such disparities in other government agencies and in defense industries. Throughout the war the NACW continued its lobbying efforts and registered its support of antilynching and anti–poll tax legislation.

In the years following World War II the civil rights movement and human rights issues took center stage on the NACW's agenda. The organization addressed the United Nations Declaration of Human Rights, especially the provisions that applied to women and such forums as "Women and World Peace." Moreover, the NACW lobbied the Republican and Democratic National Committees to gain their support for a civil rights platform. In 1954, NACW President Irene McCoy Gaines attended the national conference of the General Federation of Women's Clubs, informing the delegates that she had worked "to build a climate through the press and the radio for the Supreme Court decision of 1954 outlawing segregation in the public schools." She further noted that the one hundred thousand NACW members continued to work for the full realization of the Brown decision, "which will do much to counteract the threat of . . . communism." In 1957, the NACW provided financial assistance to the nine black students who were the first to enroll in Little Rock's Central High School. The NACW also supported the civil rights initiatives of organizations like the NAACP and the Student Nonviolent Coordinating Committee, financing many of their projects and sponsoring workshops to inform its constituents. In the 1960s the NACW became a member of the Leadership Council on Civil Rights, and its local affiliates raised funds and provided volunteers for voter registration campaigns. The NACW also forged closer ties with other organizations that supported its agenda, such as People United to Save Humanity (PUSH), Planned Parenthood, the American Federation of Labor, and the Congress of Industrial Organizations. It expanded its participation in the dialogue on domestic issues such as the desegregation of federal housing programs, slum clearance, and anticommunism, and it financed and supported nurseries and homes for working girls.

Since its inception the NACW has remained an outspoken critic of racial discriminatory practices and policies in the United States and in its foreign policy, especially as it affected Africa. Likewise, women's health issues, including rape and battering, remained issues of great concern. In the 1970s the NACW also went on record in support of an investigation of the impact of pesticides on migrant workers and in support of national health insurance. In recent years the NACW has expressed concern about AIDS, drug abuse, and teenage pregnancy and has financed clinics and educational programs to address these public health issues.

The federal government and many black and white political leaders have recognized the NACW not only as an important force in the African American community

but also as a powerful voting bloc. President Lyndon Johnson, for example, invited NACW President Rosa Gragg to the White House, and political figures like Secretary of Labor Arthur Goldberg, Attorney General Robert Kennedy, the minister and political activist Adam Clayton Powell, and former First Lady Eleanor Roosevelt addressed NACW conventions.

The NACW recognized the importance of history, from its purchase of the Douglass estate in 1918 to its commissioning of Charles Wesley to write the organization's history in 1959. Through the efforts of the NACW the National Park Service designated the Douglass home as a national historic site during the John F. Kennedy administration.

Throughout the twentieth century the NACW provided black women with opportunities for civic and political activism. It developed into a sophisticated political organization on the cutting edge of reform. The NACW employed a multifaceted approach to issues of contemporary concern and forged alliances with key players when it was expedient. In the 1970s it received government funding for its health initiatives, including AIDS education programs and projects designed to prevent teenage pregnancy, and collaborated with Howard University and government agencies to implement its health programs. The NACW also collaborated with Howard University to provide young adults with training programs in political action.

The NACW's membership has declined in recent years. In 1998 the organization had about thirty thousand members in forty states and significant representation on college campuses, including Howard University, Michigan State University, and Purdue University. The NACW continues to address contemporary social issues that affect women and children, such as education, child care, health, and housing, and it remains an important force in the African American community. It is the oldest secular African American organization still in existence today.

## FURTHER READINGS

Kendrick, Ruby. "'They Also Serve': The National Association of Colored Women, Inc." *Negro History Bulletin* 17 (March 1954): 171–174.

Salem, Dorothy. "National Association of Colored Women." In *Black Women in America: An Historical Encyclopedia*, ed. Darlene Clark-Hine et al. Brooklyn, N.Y.: Carlson, 1993, 834–851.

Shaw, Stephanie. "Black Club Women and the Creation of the National Association of Colored Women." In

'We Specialize in the Wholly Impossible': A Reader in Black Women's History, ed. Darlene Clark-Hine, Wilma King, and Linda Reed. Brooklyn, N.Y.: Carlson, 1995, 433–447.

Williams, Lillian Serece, ed. The Records of the National Association of Colored Women's Clubs, Inc., Part I. Bethesda, Md.: University Publications of America, 1994; Part II. Bethesda, Md.: University Publications of America, 1995.

*Lillian Serece Williams*

SEE ALSO    National Association of Colored Girls; National Council of Negro Women

## National Association of Extension Home Economists

The National Association of Extension Home Economists (NAEHE) provided a professional forum for home demonstration agents to seek fellowship, education, and advancement. Established on June 29, 1933, in Milwaukee, Wisconsin, at the annual meeting of the American Home Economics Association, the group that was later named the NAEHE initially consisted of twenty-one white agents representing thirteen states.

The NAEHE's official history does not document when the organization was integrated. Apparently the name NAEHE was first used in 1964 when the National Association of Negro Home Demonstration Agents and the National Home Demonstration Agents' Association united. African American members were probably first included in the NAEHE when the bylaws were changed in 1960, opening membership to "any regularly employed extension agent with a degree in home economics who is actively engaged in work in counties and cities."

When the Cooperative Extension Service was established in 1914, white land-grant colleges accepted funds to direct black extension agents. African American home demonstration agents showed rural women how to improve the quality of their homes through various projects. Only a few African American home demonstration agents worked in each state, and with the exception of Alabama, black agents were supervised by white home economists.

White agents professionalized during the Depression, and African American agents established a national organization that paralleled the white group. Extension agents of both races shared common concerns such as time management, program improvement, recruitment of new home economists, and changes in their field due to technological and cultural developments.

In 1996 the NAEHE changed its name to National Extension Association of Family and Consumer Sciences to reflect changes in home economics disciplines. Currently based in Phoenix, Arizona, the organization has three thousand members representing every state. The association hosts conferences and educational programs addressing child care and development, nutrition, and other domestic issues. Scholarships and awards are presented to members, and two newsletters, The Communique and The Reporter, document recent concerns among professionals.

FURTHER READINGS

Crosby, Earl William. "Building the Country Home: The Black County Agent System, 1906–1940." Ph.D. diss., Miami University, 1977.

Reeves, Maxine E. History of the National Association of Extension Home Economists 1933–1975. Phoenix: National Association of Extension Home Economists, 1976.

Rieff, Lynne Anderson. "'Rousing the People of the Land': Home Demonstration Work in the Deep South, 1914–1950." Ph.D. diss., Auburn University, 1995.

*Elizabeth D. Schafer*

## National Association of Girls' Clubs

*See* National Association of Colored Girls.

## National Association of Health Services Executives

Founded in 1968 in Atlantic City, N.J., the National Association of Health Services Executives (NAHSE) is a multifaceted nonprofit organization dedicated to promoting the advancement of black health-care providers and enhancing the quality of health-care services rendered to poor and disadvantaged communities.

The NAHSE has its roots in the black National Hospital Association (NHA), an affiliate of the National Medical Association (NMA), which was founded in Atlanta in 1895. At that time, black hospital executives united to promote professional development and to advocate the improvement of health care in the communities they served. They elected Albert W. Dent, the educator and president of Dillard University in New Orleans, to serve as chairman of the NHA. Despite an encouraging beginning, the organization apparently managed to do little more than hold annual meetings.

In 1968, the same idealism that led to the creation of the NHA generated the formation of the NAHSE. Everett W. Fox served as the group's first president. While remaining true to the historic mission of their association, NAHSE members also dedicated efforts to research in health care and to creating and nurturing economic development opportunities in the health-care industry for minority-owned businesses.

To achieve its long-range and far-reaching goals, the NAHSE offers education programs, mentoring, a job bank, and community service projects. The Albert W. Dent Scholarship is awarded each year to an outstanding graduate student enrolled in a program of health services administration. A student internship is also available to qualified young people planning a career in health services management. A quarterly newsletter, *NAHSE Notes*, keeps members abreast of upcoming events, job openings, and news pertinent to health-care services executives. The NAHSE operates a website to disseminate information about the association and its programs.

In the 1990s, the organization and its more than twenty chapters across the United States launched the National Health Policy Development Project. NAHSE leadership and members expect the project to influence public policy in the health-care industry to reflect the aims of their organization. The project, underwritten by the Kellogg Foundation, will emphasize the potential impact of public health-care policies on underserved and disadvantaged populations and the institutions serving them.

The NAHSE is the nation's largest organization of its kind. A variety of membership levels are open to those with professional training in health-care provision and administration, or to those with work experience in the fields of health and medical care administration and/or delivery. The NAHSE's headquarters is located in Silver Spring, Maryland. In 2000, the president was Robert Currie and the president-elect was Sandra R. Gould.

**FURTHER READINGS**

National Association of Health Services Executives. *NAHSE Notes*, 15, 2 (September 1997).

Ploski, Harry A., and James Williams, eds. *The Negro Almanac: A Reference Work on the African American*, 5th ed. Detroit: Gale, 1989.

*Peggy Hardman*

**SEE ALSO** National Hospital Association; National Medical Association

## National Association of Human Rights Workers

In 1947, the National Association of Human Rights Workers (NAHRW) was established as the National Association of Intergroup Relations Officials (NAIRO) in Chicago. The group was launched when the executives of human rights committees of six cities appealed to the American Council on Race Relations (ACRR) and proposed the establishment of a central body to facilitate communication and cooperation. The founding conference—attended by representatives of private and public human rights, civil liberty, educational, and intergroup agencies—pledged to raise human rights awareness and to foster intergroup relations. During the NAIRO's formative years, the ACRR was an important source of financial support. The ACRR supplied the association's first executive director, Louis E. Hosch, and provided essential funding between 1947 and 1950. Since 1950, membership dues and grants from other agencies have funded the NAIRO's activities. In 1957, the NAIRO hired its first paid executive director, John V. P. Lassoe. Lack of funding, however, led to the elimination of that position in 1969. In the following year, the NAIRO changed its name to NAHRW. Since then it has operated without a paid staff or permanent headquarters.

Annual conferences have played a crucial part in the organization's activities, providing members with a public forum and the opportunity to discuss contemporary human rights problems and strategies for their redress. NAHRW national and regional seminars and workshops supplement annual conferences and provide additional opportunities for skill development, networking, and discussion of national human rights policy. In addition to conferences, seminars, and workshops, the organization sponsored the first annual police-community relations conference in 1954.

Constrained by limited funds, the NAIRO often collaborated with other agencies. In 1952 and 1953, the NAIRO and the University of Chicago cosponsored conferences on research in intergroup relations. In 1962, the Ford Foundation helped fund a training conference on equal opportunity in housing for sixty-five NAIRO representatives at the University of Georgia. Between 1957 and 1975, the organization, with the aid of the National Internship Program, worked with over seventy-five agencies to train 110 human rights students.

In the 1970s, the group not only changed its name to NAHRW but also started to take an interest in international human rights. For this purpose, the NAHRW filed for nongovernment status in 1973, enabling its members to attend human rights sessions of the United Nations as official observers. In 1978, the NAHRW also helped to create the International Consultation of Selected Human Rights Professionals (ICSHRP). That year, fifty-one delegates from the United States, Canada, Europe, and the Caribbean gathered in Ottawa, Canada, to attend the ICSHRP's first meeting on November 15–17. The group continued to discuss international human rights concerns at a second meeting in Baltimore in 1980.

The NAHRW consistently advocates human rights awareness. In addition to a bimonthly newsletter and the quarterly *Journal of Intergroup Relations*, the NAHRW publishes special reports relevant to contemporary human rights issues. In the 1960s, the group's report on *Executive Responsibility in Intergroup Relations* motivated President John F. Kennedy to facilitate the development of intergroup relations among his staff.

**FURTHER READINGS**

*Background Information on NAIRO*. Amistad Research Center Archives, Tulane University, New Orleans, 1967.

Cloud, Fred. "A Brief History of the National Association of Human Rights Workers." *Journal of Intergroup Relations* 13, 3 (Fall 1985): 3–9.

Roye, Wendell, Jr. "Special Report: Equal Educational Opportunity Workshop for Human Rights Workers at the Annual Conference of the National Association of Human Rights Workers, Seattle, Washington. October, 3–7, 1971." *Journal of Intergroup Relations* 1, 5 (Spring 1972).

*Katherine Kuntz Dill*

## National Association of Intergroup Relations Officials

*See* National Association of Human Rights Workers.

## National Association of Management Consultants

The National Association of Management Consultants (NAMC) was founded in 1985 as a nonprofit organization to promote minority management consultants. The association was based in Cleveland, Ohio, with Hosiah Huggins Jr.

as president and Ingrid Smith as executive director. Approximately fifty members, who were full-time or independent minority management consultants, paid annual dues of one hundred dollars at the association's peak.

The NAMC's goal was to increase the quality and quantity of opportunities for minorities in the profession of management consulting. The association sought to enhance minority participation in the consulting industry by improving communications, stimulating collaborative projects, fostering professionalism of the individual and group, and striving to set and maintain high standards.

Acting as a liaison between consultants and businesses, the NAMC shared information about professional improvement by publishing an annual newsletter, *Consulting to Management*, as well as hosting a biennial conference in August. The last known address for the group was in Washington, D.C. Since 1997, the NAMC has apparently been defunct.

**FURTHER READINGS**

Bunkley, Crawford B. *The African American Network*. New York: Plume, 1996.

*Encyclopedia of Associations*, 33rd ed. Detroit: Gale, 1998.

Van de Sande, Wendy S., ed. *Black Americans Information Directory 1994–95*, 3rd ed. Detroit: Gale, 1995.

*Elizabeth D. Schafer*

## National Association of Market Developers

Founded in 1953 by Naylor Fitzhugh, the National Association of Market Developers (NAMD) was composed of African American professionals from such areas as public relations, marketing, advertising, personnel management, and product management. The NAMD had twenty chapters and approximately three hundred members. It conducted outreach activities to attract young African Americans to the business world, sponsored workshops for its members, and provided technical assistance to small black-owned businesses. Past presidents included Joel P. Martin (1986), of J.P. Martin and Associates, and Charles E. Morrison (1989). The NAMD appears to be defunct.

**FURTHER READINGS**

"Don't Ignore Impact of Ethnic Market on U.S. Economy: NAMD Prexy." *Jet* (June 26, 1989): 23.

Herbert, Salomon. "A Meeting of Marketers." *Black Enterprise*, September 1986, p. 18.

"National Association of Market Developers, Inc." *The Negro Almanac: A Reference Work on the African American*, ed. Henry A. Ploski and James Williams. Detroit: Gale, 1989, p. 1356.

————. *Encyclopedia of Associations: An Associations Unlimited Reference*, ed. Sandra Jaszczak. Detroit: Gale 1997, p. 3003.

*Oscar Flores*

## National Association of Minority Architects

In 1971, the National Association of Minority Architects (NOMA) was founded as the National Organization of Black Architects in Detroit. The organization adopted its current name in 1973.

The NOMA, a confederation of local membership groups, sought to enhance the careers of minority architects and increase their number. The NOMA conducted educational programs and maintained a speakers' bureau to encourage minority youth to study architecture. Moreover, the organization gathered statistics on practicing minority architects, spoke on their behalf on political matters, organized annual meetings for professional enhancement and networking, and presented honors awards to recognize the achievements of its members.

The NOMA's twenty-second annual meeting in Washington, D.C., in October 1992 was sponsored by Howard University and held in conjunction with the first biennial Congress of African American Architects. Past presidents of the NOMA included Harry Overstreet of San Francisco, William Stanley of Atlanta, and Robert Easter of Richmond, Virginia. By 1996, the NOMA claimed six hundred members and published a quarterly newsletter, *NOMA News*.

### FURTHER READINGS

Dixon, John Morris. "Recognition for Minority Architects." *Progressive Architecture* 71, 13 (1990): 7.
————. "Minority Architects Meet and Honor Members." *Progressive Architecture* 72, 13 (1992): 15.
Maurer, Christine, and Tara E. Sheets, eds. *Encyclopedia of Associations: An Associations Unlimited Reference*, 33d ed. Detroit: Gale, 1998, p. 612.
Ploski, Harry A., and James Williams, comps. and eds. *The Negro Almanac: A Reference Work on the African American*, 5th ed. Detroit: Gale, 1989, p. 1362.

*Oscar Flores*

## National Association of Minority Women in Business

Founded in 1972, the National Association of Minority Women in Business (NAMWIB) is located in Kansas City, Missouri. Its president, Inez Kaiser, founded the organization as a result of a study that she conducted on female business ownership while employed by the U.S. Department of Commerce. That study revealed that minority women often experienced difficulty in gaining access to much-needed capital for their businesses and lacked the advantage of higher education or training in business.

The association serves small-business owners, managers, and college students. Its members benefit from workshops, conferences, seminars, and research that the organization generates on subjects related to the manufacturing, service, and technical industries. The association provides women with concrete strategies for improving the operation of their businesses. The NAMWIB maintains a Hall of Fame designed to honor outstanding female entrepreneurs. It has a speaker's bureau, and a placement service, and publishes a bimonthly newsletter called *Today*. There are approximately five thousand members nationwide.

One of the benefits of NAMWIB membership is the opportunity it affords business owners of attending the semiannual and annual conferences where they can acquire new information and exhibit their products and services. In the future, some of the NAMWIB's objectives are to build partnerships with other associations and organizations, and to provide access to resources that will enable their members to expand into global markets.

### FURTHER READING

Kirrane, Diane E. "Valuing Diversity: The Role of Minority Associations." *Association Management*, 47 (6) (1995): 49–76.

*Sharon Parkinson*

## National Association of Negro Business and Professional Women's Clubs

The National Association of Negro Business and Professional Women's Clubs (NANBPW) is a nonprofit, community-based social service organization. Founded in 1935, the NANBPW seeks to promote and protect the interests of black business and professional women, create fellowship among them, support youths through educational assistance, and improve social and civic conditions for African American families. Specifically, the NANBPW addresses drug abuse, inadequate health care, illiteracy, inequality, quality education, teenage pregnancy, unemployment, violent crime, deterioration of the African American family, and the plight of the black male and other at-risk groups. The NANBPW implements its mission through volunteerism, guidance, and technical and financial support.

The NANBPW was founded by Emma Odessa Young, a New York City realtor and member of the New York Club of Business and Professional Women, who conceived the idea of a national organization to unite local clubs. Ollie Chin Porter, president of the New York Club, extended an invitation to the Philadelphia and Atlantic City Business and Professional Women's Clubs to federate. Joining Young and Porter as founders of the NANBPW were Effie Ditton of New York City; Bertha Perry Rhodes, Josephine Keen, and Adelaide Flemming of Philadelphia; and Pearl Flippen of Atlantic City. Founded during the Great Depression, the NANBPW promoted employment, economic opportunities, better housing, education, and social welfare for African Americans.

Headquartered in Washington, D.C., the NANBPW supports several ongoing educational, social, and economic community programs. Since the 1970s, the association has sustained "Adopt-A-School" and "Adopt-A-Dropout" programs that provide educational tutorial services and career counseling for teens. Starting in 1987, NANBPW launched social programs like Childcare Initiative, which recruits foster and adoptive parents among its own members to care for orphaned children. The association also created the Walking Tall Program, which provides services and educational programs to assist teenage parents and to guard youths against premature parenthood. Between 1991 and 1996, the NANBPW awarded college scholarships totaling over $136,000 to 279 students throughout the nation. Similarly, the NANBPW sponsors the Leontyne Price Vocal Arts Competition to award scholarships to young African American singers aspiring to careers in classical vocal music.

In business, the NANBPW honors African American women for their outstanding career accomplishments at its Corporate Women's Hall of Fame Annual Luncheon to encourage excellence and leadership in corporate America. Moreover, the NANBPW's Business Exchange sponsors workshops on entrepreneurship, management, financial planning, and income tax preparation designed to assist minority and women business owners.

The NANBPW also cooperates with businesses and other groups whose goals are compatible with those of the organization. In 1991, the NANBPW organized Leadership 2000, a program designed to prepare young African American women to assume leadership positions. Initially funded by the W. K. Kellogg Foundation with a grant of $450,000, the one-year professional training program develops leadership skills through volunteer projects. Candidates for Leadership 2000 are usually between the ages of twenty-one and thirty and must submit proposals that address a societal need in their local communities. Selected participants engage in intense work-study sessions, hands-on training, and role-playing exercises to master administrative and authoritative roles. Past projects included the establishment of a nonprofit home for crack-addicted babies in foster-care systems and educational programs for mothers on public assistance, as well as the improvement of existing literacy programs. Similarly, in 1995 in partnership with Philip Morris Companies, the NANBPW provided $20,000 in funding to local clubs to support their Feed the Hungry programs.

Since 1986, the association has also collaborated with the National Urban League, the National Association for the Advancement of Colored People (NAACP), and the Brown Williamson Tobacco Corporation to present the annual KOOL Achiever Award to disadvantaged high school students who are improving the quality of life in urban America. Annually five recipients receive $10,000 and forty-seven finalists receive $1,000 to contribute to a nonprofit inner-city organization of their choice. The NANBPW also works with the Sickle Cell Anemia Foundation, American Cancer Society, American Heart Association, U.S. Department of Minority Health, and Black Women's Health Project to provide medical screening sessions.

In 1997, the NANBPW membership consisted of 350 clubs in forty-two states, the District of Columbia, and Bermuda. The NANBPW vision statement for 1996 stressed its commitment to provide services of a global nature, support programs for youth development, and develop strong organizational corporate partnerships to ensure support of diverse community needs.

**FURTHER READINGS**

Bauchum, Rosalind. "The Black Business and Professional Woman: Selected References of Achievement." Unpublished report. Kansas City, Missouri, National Association of Negro Business and Professional Women's Clubs, 1985.

Freeman, Gregory. "Training Tomorrow's Leaders." *St. Louis Post-Dispatch*, February 15, 1991.

National Association of Negro Business and Professional Women's Clubs. *What Is NANBPW?* Washington, D.C.: National Association of Negro Business and Professional Women's Clubs, n.d.

*Julieanne Phillips*

## National Association of Negro Dentists

*See* Tri-State Dental Association of DC, VA, MD.

## National Association of Negro Home Demonstration Agents

*See* National Association of Extension Home Economists.

## National Association of Negro Music Teachers

*See* National Association of Negro Musicians.

## National Association of Negro Musicians

Classical violinist Clarence Cameron White laid the foundation for the creation of the National Association of Negro Musicians (NANM) when he invited black composers and musicians to create the National Association of Negro Music Teachers in 1918. Through the establishment of an alliance of black music professionals, White hoped to raise the standard of black music teachers and improve music instruction as well as the musical taste of the public. Musicians and artists were prepared to meet in Hampton, Virginia, at the fiftieth anniversary of Hampton Institute; however, the meeting was canceled because of the outbreak of the influenza pandemic.

Following World War I, the organization, now named the NANM, reemerged under the leadership of White; R. Nathaniel Dett, the director of music at Hampton; and Nora Holt, the music critic, composer, pianist, teacher, and radio host. At an initial meeting in early spring 1919 at Holt's Chicago home, a group of musicians, composers, and music teachers agreed to hold a preliminary Initial Conference of Negro Musicians and Artists. In May 1919, the preliminary conference, organized by Henry L. Grant of the Washington Conservatory of Music and director of the Afro-American Folk Song Singers, was held at the Paul Lawrence Dunbar High

School in Washington, D.C. Shortly thereafter, on July 29–30, the group gathered for its first national convention in Chicago. Word of the conference spread through personal correspondence, announcements in the *Chicago Defender*, and with help from the Chicago Music Association. Among the NANM's charter members were Cleota Collins, R. Nathaniel Dett, Henry L. Grant, Nora Holt, Clara Hutchinson, Edwin Hill, James A. Mundy, Lillian LeMon, J. Wesley Jones, Florence Cole Talbert, and T. Theodore Taylor. Past presidents of the organization include Henry L. Grant, Clarence Cameron White, R. Nathaniel Dett, Carl Rossini Diton, J. Wesley Jones, Lillian LeMon, Maude Roberts George, Camille Nickerson, Kemper Herrold, Mary Cardwell Dawson, Clarence Hayden Wilson, Roscoe R. Polin, Kenneth Billups, Theodore Charles Stone, Brazeal Wayne Dennard, and Betty Jackson King.

NANM's earliest conferences were held in New York City, Philadelphia, and Nashville. The association organized concerts, lectures, and workshops to promote the work of black musicians and composers. In addition, the NANM provided scholarships to aspiring young musicians; the first such recipient was Marian Anderson in 1921. In 1961, the NANM also began giving accomplished artists, composers, teachers, and music historians an Annual Award for outstanding achievement and contribution to black culture.

### FURTHER READINGS

Holt, Nora. "The Chronological History of the NANM." *Black Perspective in Music* 2 (Fall 1974): 234–235.

Southern, Eileen. *The Music of Black Americans: A History*, 3d ed. New York: Norton, 1997.

*Nichole T. Rustin*

## National Association of Personnel Deans and Advisers of Men in Negro Institutions

The National Association of Personnel Deans and Advisers of Men in Negro Institutions (NAPDAMNI) was established as a resource for individuals employed in professional positions at African American colleges and high schools. Little is known about the organization's early history. Similar white professional associations emerged during the 1920s, and organizations for African American women employed in academia were established in the 1930s. The NAPDAMNI was probably created during this time, in response to the exclusion of African Americans from white associations.

The group's primary purpose was to provide guidance and support for its members and promote cooperation of personnel who pursued professional recognition and status. All deans and advisers of male students enrolled in African American institutions were permitted to join. Members addressed how to counsel and provide for their students' educational needs. The NAPDAMNI encouraged administrators and advisers who were frustrated by rigid school systems and offered examples of how to deal with institutional politics to obtain individual goals. The association also provided its members with a professional network, a source of collegial support, and inspiring role models.

The NAPDAMNI promoted educational opportunities for its members and the students they supervised. Specifically, the organization guided members to achieve professional academic credentials equivalent to those expected of whites hired for similar positions. Members used the NAPDAMNI as a forum to document unfair salaries and living conditions and to protest prejudicial hiring practices that prevented qualified applicants from securing influential, policy-making positions and achieving professional autonomy. The organization also voiced concerns about the poor quality of educational facilities.

As early as 1939, members of the Association of Deans of Women and Advisers to Girls in Negro Schools (ADWAGNS) passed a resolution to contact the NAPDAMNI "for the purpose of having joint annual meetings, since their problems are so closely woven." Seven years later, the female and male deans agreed to attend a joint conference. They talked about issues of mutual concern and decided to meet together annually. Compared with the women, the men were disorganized and benefited from the meetings, suggesting that it might be mutually beneficial to unite the two groups. At the 1954 meeting at Howard University, a proposal to merge the groups was debated. Critics protested that the women's group was active and thriving while the men's organization was stagnant. Members of both groups voted to cease their groups and combined to form the National Association of Personnel Workers, which continued their work into the 1990s.

**FURTHER READING**

Davis, Hilda A., and Patricia Bell-Scott. "The Association of Deans of Women and Advisers to Girls in Negro Schools, 1929–1954: A Brief Oral History." *Sage* (Summer 1989).

*Elizabeth D. Schafer*

SEE ALSO    Association of Deans of Women and Advisers to Girls in Negro Schools; National Association of Personnel Workers

# National Association of Personnel Workers

The National Association of Personnel Workers (NAPW) promoted the professional interests of student affairs personnel workers in historically black colleges. The NAPW was established in 1954 when the Association of Deans of Women and Advisers to Girls in Negro Schools and the National Association of Personnel Deans and Advisers of Men in Negro Institutions voted to merge after meeting jointly for nine years. The women deans provided the NAPW's early leadership, and the first officers included Sadie M. Yancey of Howard University as president; Arlynne Jones from Grambling State University as recording secretary; Jean Spinner of North Carolina Agricultural and Technical College as assistant recording secretary; and Valleta H. Bell Linnette from Virginia State College as the first regional vice president.

Members of these founding groups discussed mutual concerns that were incorporated into the NAPW's platform. Declaring that the NAPW "seeks to foster a unified spirit" of personnel in African American institutions of higher education, the NAPW primarily strove to improve student services and provide for students' educational needs at these schools. Acting as a professional agency, the NAPW conducted scientific studies and gathered and analyzed data to resolve problems encountered by student services administrators. Professional development for student affairs personnel enabled NAPW members concerned with achieving academic credentials to obtain policy-making administrative positions. NAPW members also lobbied for professional autonomy and salaries equitable to those of their white colleagues.

NAPW members sought professional recognition and status and learned how to handle institutional politics to achieve their aims. They initiated projects according to trends in postsecondary education and monitored legislation influencing student affairs programs and services in colleges. NAPW committees included Governmental Relations, Regional Organization, Scholarship, and Time and Place. The NAPW published the quarterly *NAPW Newsletter and Journal*, and sponsored an annual conference to vote on business and educational matters.

In 1995, the last known address for the NAPW was in care of Thomas Palmer, vice president of student affairs, Norfolk State University, Norfolk, Virginia.

**FURTHER READING**

Davis, Hilda A., and Patricia Bell-Scott. "The Association of Deans of Women and Advisers to Girls in Negro Schools, 1929–1954: A Brief Oral History." *Sage* (Summer 1989).

*Elizabeth D. Schafer*

**SEE ALSO**   Association of Deans of Women and Advisers to Girls in Negro Schools; National Association of Personnel Deans and Advisers of Men in Negro Institutions

# National Association of Real Estate Brokers

In 1947, one black woman and eleven black men, representing Michigan, Mississippi, Alabama, Florida, Ohio, Oklahoma, and Texas, founded the National Association of Real Estate Brokers, Inc. (NAREB) in Tampa, Florida. The group sought to address the poor housing conditions and residential segregation that African Americans encountered following World War II.

Racial discrimination continued to limit the ability of African Americans to gain access to equal housing or to purchase real estate, even after the Supreme Court's *Shelley v. Kraemer* (1948) ruled racially restrictive housing covenants unconstitutional. The NAREB challenged illegal, racially discriminatory real estate practices and pledged to provide all citizens with equal housing opportunities. To "serve the underserved," NAREB members work to safeguard the public against unethical or unequal racial or fraudulent practices connected with the real estate business. For this purpose, the organization sponsors realtor education programs and engages in committee liaison work with institutions and government agencies, such as the Department of Housing and Urban Development (HUD) and the Veterans Administration. Headquartered in Washington, D.C., NAREB's Public Affairs Committee (PAC) was established to promote the welfare of minority housing needs nationwide. The PAC also keeps track of and evaluates laws, codes, and regulations of governmental agencies that affect the nation's real estate industry. When the PAC confirms that pending legislation warrants intervention, it develops an action plan. Once

the Board of Directors approves the plan, the NAREB takes steps to contact all pertinent parties in the appropriate regulatory agencies.

The NAREB has recently linked forces with Chase Manhattan Mortgage Corporation and the Fannie Mae mortgage foundation in an experiment in offering minorities and immigrants affordable housing and mortgage interest rates. Under the terms of the agreement, borrowers can qualify for a down payment of 3 percent, with 1 percent coming from their own funds and 2 percent from a grant, gift, or seller contribution.

Founded by African Americans, the NAREB was originally an all-black organization. Today, however, it welcomes qualified real estate practitioners of all races who support its mission and ideals. The organization's recent "One America Initiative Program" agreement with HUD provides NAREB members with HUD-approved certification. This enables NAREB members to train and service other realtors. Moreover, the "One America Initiative Program" calls for educating home buyers about the social and economic importance of implementing the Fair Housing Act.

The NAREB currently represents 7,500 members organized in fifteen regional and six state groups, representing a total of thirty-nine states. Membership benefits encompass specialized training and education programs offered by NAREB and its eight professional affiliations, including the National Society of Real Estate Appraisers, Real Estate Management Brokers Institute, United Developers Council, Commercial Industrial Division, Sales Associates Division, Women's Council, Investment Division, and Contractors Division. In addition, the NAREB offers its members accreditation in areas such as real estate appraisal, brokerage, investment, sales, and contracting. The NAREB University of Real Estate also sponsors real estate licensing classes, and local chapters conduct classes, workshops, and seminars.

The NAREB produces a number of educational publications that keep its members updated on the activities of its sixty-two local housing boards and state associations. These publications include the *Communicator*, the official publication of NAREB, which provides a platform for the exchange and dissemination of technical and professional information; the *Realtist Flyer*, a bimonthly newsletter; a catalog of *NAREB'S Real Estate* offerings; an annual *Realtist Membership Directory*, and the *Convention Journal*, which keeps members up-to-date on NAREB's annual convention activities. The annual convention and the annual national meeting—the nation's largest gatherings of minority professionals in the housing field—provide an opportunity for professional training and networking. Headquartered in Washington, D.C., the group maintains an agent-linked web page, established in conjunction with Property AMERICA and the National Association of Real Estate Brokers.

**FURTHER READINGS**

"Chase Manhattan, NAREB and Fannie Mae Join Forces to Increase Minority Home Ownership." *Jet,* May 19, 1997.

Jaszczak, S., and Sheets, T. E., eds. *Encyclopedia of Associations*, vol. 1, part 1, "National Association of Real Estate Brokers." New York: Gale, 1997.

Ploski, H. A., and Williams, J., eds. *The Negro Almanac— A Reference Work on the African American.* New York: Gale, 1989.

*Barbara Buice*

## National Association of Securities Professionals

The National Association of Securities Professionals (NASP) was founded in 1985 with the dual objective of improving the professionalism of minorities in the securities industry and of enhancing the opportunities of minorities in the securities business. The cofounders were Joyce Johnson, a stockbroker at A. G. Edwards & Sons in Chicago, and Maynard Jackson, a former mayor of Atlanta and an attorney at Chappman and Cutler in Atlanta. In 1987, the membership of the NASP included three hundred black stockbrokers, attorneys, securities analysts, traders, investment bankers, and money managers. The latest chairman of the NASP was Raymond J. McClendon.

**FURTHER READINGS**

"NASP: Blacks Should Buy Part of American Economy." *Jet* 72 (September 21, 1987): 33.

"Maynard Jackson, Others Establish Securities Group." *Jet* 68 (June 3, 1985): 26.

"National Association of Securities Professionals." *The Encyclopedia of Associations: An Associations Unlimited Reference*, ed. Sandra Jaszczak. Detroit: Gale, 1997, 3006.

*Oscar Flores*

## National Association of Teachers in Colored Schools

*See* American Teachers Association.

## National Association of University Women

*See* National Association of College Women.

## National Association of Youth Clubs

*See* National Association of Colored Girls.

## National Baptist Convention

*See* National Baptist Convention of America and National Baptist Convention, USA, Inc.

## National Baptist Convention of America

The National Baptist Convention of America (NBCA) was formed in 1915 because of a legal dispute within the National Baptist Convention (NBC), the largest organized body of African American Baptists in the country. From its 1895 beginnings the NBC was plagued by internal frictions and personality conflicts. The most consequential of these for the future of black Baptists was a legal entanglement concerning ownership and control of the National Baptist Publishing Board, the NBC's financially most successful venture. Managed by publishing and banking entrepreneur Richard Henry Boyd, the publishing board employed over 125 black men and women in its downtown business office in Nashville, Tennessee, and turned a consistent profit from selling its products to black churches throughout the country. In 1915, disputes concerning who exercised legal authority over the denominational publishing house resulted in the fracturing of the NBC and the formation of a body eventually known as the NBCA.

The first party in this battle, led by Elias Camp Morris, president of the National Baptist Convention, insisted that the NBC had created the publishing board, owned it, and should control its operations. But Richard H. Boyd, leader of the second faction, contended that the board was, in effect, his board, an independently chartered business enterprise that elected to service denominational needs but was neither owned nor controlled by the denomination at large. Boyd incorporated his publishing house separately from the larger denominational entity, installing a self-perpetuating, nine-member board as its governing authority. Boyd was also the president of the Home Mission Board of the NBC, which he used as an advertising agency for the didactic religious materials he published through his National Baptist Publishing Board.

After attempting, unsuccessfully, to reach a compromise on the legal questions, the issue came to a head when black Baptists met in Chicago in 1915. Boyd sought a court injunction to block the proceedings of the NBC and thwart the efforts of E. C. Morris to retain presidency of the organization. Boyd's attempt failed and his supporters reconvened at another Chicago church and declared themselves the true NBC, while their opponents referred to them as a "rump" convention. Legal proceedings in the following two years failed to clarify the matter, and attempts by white Baptists to mediate were also unsuccessful. By 1920, two separate conventions had come into being, each with its own set of denominational institutions. The first became known as the National Baptist Convention, USA, Inc. The second, led by Boyd and his family, was originally known as the National Baptist Convention, Unincorporated. In the 1930s, after convention leaders restructured and incorporated the convention, it became known as the NBCA.

From its inception, the NBCA has been associated closely with the Boyd family and with churches in Tennessee, Arkansas, Texas, and Mississippi. In 1921, after the death of founder Richard H. Boyd, his son, Henry Boyd, a man as skilled an entrepreneur as his father, took over running his father's enterprises. Concentrated in Nashville and the southwestern states, the NBCA focused its efforts on publishing Sunday school materials and hymnals. The convention's publishing house produced large volumes of religious literature, published important milestones in black hymnody, built church pews, made black dolls for children, and marketed a variety of other products to black churches in regions where it was strong. The convention engaged in cooperative endeavors with other black organizations, including the Lott Carey Baptist Foreign Mission Convention, with which it joined in supporting foreign missionaries. However, like the Lott Carey group, the NBCA failed to find a secure enough funding base to support the joint foreign mission program as well as the several home missions projects it initiated. An educational board established under convention auspices proved more successful in raising money for a number of black Baptist colleges and seminaries. Later in the century, after the termination of cooperation with the Lott Carey group, the NBCA reorganized itself and created its own Foreign Mission Board, which proved more successful than earlier endeavors. After a period of decline in the years between the world wars, the NBCA revived after World War II and remains today a major national black Baptist body.

In past years the bitterness created by the original rift between the two national Baptist conventions has subsided, and the two groups have cooperated in joint ventures and generally had an amicable relationship. The separate structures for denominational work created by the two conventions, however, remain difficult to merge. As a result, efforts to reunite the two major black Baptist conventions have failed. This is unfortunate, since for all practical purposes the two conventions are virtually indistinguishable, the original issues dividing them having long since either been resolved or forgotten. Both groups have operated under the leadership of long-tenured presidents who have pursued cautious and even accommodationist stances on questions of civil rights. Only Martin Luther King Jr. and the Progressive National Baptist Convention took a prophetic stance of leadership on the questions of civil rights that moved the country in the 1960s. Today, the NBCA is the smallest of the three major national black Baptist bodies but continues to claim a status as the original and true National Baptist Convention.

### FURTHER READINGS

Boyd, Rev. Richard Henry. *The Story of the National Baptist Publishing Board: The How, When, Why, and by Whom It Was Established.* Nashville: National Baptist Publishing Board, 1916.

Fitts, Leroy. *A History of Black Baptists.* Nashville: Broadman, 1985.

Harvey, Paul. *Redeeming the South: Religious Cultures and Racial Identities Among Southern Baptists, 1865–1925.* Chapel Hill: University of North Carolina Press, 1997.

Jordan, Lewis G. *Negro Baptist History, U.S.A.* Nashville: Sunday School Board of the National Baptist Convention, 1930.

*Paul Harvey*

## National Baptist Convention, USA, Inc.

The National Baptist Convention, USA, Inc., is the largest black religious organization in the United States, currently numbering over eight million African American Baptists. The denomination was founded in Atlanta in 1895, the same year as Booker T. Washington's famous Atlanta Compromise address. That year leaders of the American National Baptist Convention, the Baptist Foreign Mission Convention, and the National Baptist Educational Convention united to form the National Baptist

Convention (NBC). The new denomination became a large, multifaceted denominational body delegating specific kinds of religious work to various boards and agencies subsumed under it. It was then, and remains now, the largest African American organization in the country. Since approximately 60 percent of black Christians are Baptists, the convention has a large constituency on which to draw. Its ability to exercise influence on social and political issues, however, has never been commensurate with its size and potential.

Efforts to establish a national black Baptist denomination emerged in the antebellum era. In the 1860s, the Consolidated American Baptist Missionary Convention served as a national voice for black Baptists, but its funding was contingent on support from white northern Baptists, which dried up after Reconstruction, and from the Freedmen's Bureau, which disbanded in 1869. This first postwar effort at forming a national black Baptist denomination thus ended in about 1879. In 1890, renewed calls for a national black Baptist denomination received an unexpected spur from a controversy in the religious publishing world. The editors of the *Baptist Teacher,* a Sunday school quarterly published by the American Baptist Publication Society, asked three well-known black Baptist authors to write articles for the quarterly. After the white Southern Baptist Convention raised objections to the plan, worrying that the Publication Society had encouraged blacks who advocated "assassination and arson," the editor withdrew the offer. Angered by this rebuff, black Baptists discussed unifying their forces under one tent and succeeded in doing so in 1895. Elias Camp Morris was the first president, and remained in that office until his death in 1921. D. V. Jemison of Selma, Alabama, and the Rev. Joseph Harrison Jackson of Chicago later served similarly long terms as presidents of the denomination.

The NBC supported a variety of enterprises typical of American denominations. It sent foreign missionaries, mostly to Africa, collected funds for educational institutions, established newspapers and journals, and cooperated with other denominations in carrying out missionary activities among black Americans. At its initial meeting, the convention laid plans for its own publishing board, which, beginning in 1896, published hymnals and a national monthly newspaper, the *National Baptist Union-Review.* Convention leaders such as Lewis G. Jordan cooperated with black women such as Nannie Burroughs in forming the NBC's Woman's Auxiliary in 1901. The Woman's Auxiliary supported the National Training School for Women and Girls in Washington, D.C., which

trained young black women in home economics and in middle-class values.

The leadership of the denomination came largely from the South, where 90 percent of black Americans resided, and where over 90 percent of black Baptists lived. In the twentieth century, northern ministers increasingly took positions of authority in the denomination, signifying the transition of African Americans from a predominantly rural southern population to an increasingly northern and urban base. Leaders of the NBC saw its mission as part of a broad-based campaign to "uplift the race." They interpreted religious segregation as God's plan to compel the race to develop its own institutions and thus strengthen its place in American life. They also insisted on the centrality of their mission to teach their constituents the norms of bourgeois values. But their insistence on "intelligent worship" met with resistance from the rank-and-file constituency of the convention, the thousands of small local churches, in which traditional antiphonal call-and-response worship and chanted sermonizing remained the predominant modes of expression.

Eventually, convention leaders learned to respond to black Baptists' desires for traditional black sacred music and worship styles. In the 1920s and 1930s, black gospel music emerged as a powerful force among black Baptists, in part because of the unforgettable performances at annual NBC meetings of gospel music pioneers such as W. M. Nix, Lucie Campbell, and Thomas Dorsey. Later in the century, Mahalia Jackson and Aretha Franklin, daughter of the Reverend C. L. Franklin, a Baptist minister in Detroit well known for radio broadcasts of his preaching performances, carried on and commercialized the gospel music traditions pioneered by these earlier figures.

In 1915, a disastrous legal battle and schism split the NBC, leading to the formation of the National Baptist Convention, USA, Inc. (NBCUSA), and the National Baptist Convention of America (NBCA). The split arose, again, from a publishing controversy. In this case, the National Baptist Publishing Board proved to be so successful that it threatened to eclipse the very denomination that had spawned it. Convention leaders such as Elias Camp Morris, president of the denomination from 1895 to 1921, saw Richard H. Boyd's National Baptist Publishing Board as an agency subsumed within the larger denomination, while Boyd believed that his publishing enterprise was an independent entity affiliated with but not specifically controlled by the convention. When, in 1915, convention leaders tried to secure control of the Publishing Board, Boyd and his forces bolted from the meeting hall in Chicago and formed the NBCA. A battle for the future of the NBC raged through court battles and unsuccessful mediation attempts over the next several years. In 1921, after Boyd and his main combatant, Elias Camp Morris, died, the conventions settled into a dual existence, each claiming to speak for black Baptists of America.

Later in the twentieth century, controversies arising from the civil rights movement again split the NBCUSA. In the 1950s, convention president Joseph Harrison Jackson, a well-known minister in Chicago and powerful politico, sensed a threat to his leadership in the charismatic Martin Luther King Jr. At first tentative allies, King and Jackson were soon to be major contenders in a battle for the soul of the convention. Jackson advocated a conservative approach to civil rights, while King spoke eloquently in favor of nonviolent civil disobedience. While King did not wish to foment a schism in the convention, supporters of King pushed his name in yearly meetings to be president. In 1961, King and his allies eventually left to form the Progressive National Baptist Convention.

The NBCUSA has been a "frustrated fellowship" because its influence in providing a unified national voice for black Baptists has not matched its potential. The polity of Baptist churches—absolute congregational independence, with no higher authority above that of the individual congregation—has fostered an intense sense of democracy, leading to endless schisms, while also encouraging what one black Baptist author has called "one-man rule," typified in the presidency of Joseph Harrison Jackson. In few other instances in African American history has the conflict between democratic governance and the need for unity been as poignantly apparent.

Nevertheless, the NBCUSA has given a voice to tens of thousands of black Baptist congregations, predominantly made up of ordinary working people. These congregations provided part of the backbone of the civil rights movement, even when the official convention leadership maintained its distance from movement activities. Today, the biggest threat to the NBCUSA comes, ironically, from the white Southern Baptist Convention (SBC), which is increasingly coaxing, mostly through offers of low-interest loans for church projects, black congregations to affiliate with the SBC. The NBCUSA remains dependent on white donors to support its American Baptist Theological Seminary in Nashville and on wealthy patrons to support large capital projects. Lack of secure and solid funding appears the primary obstacle preventing the convention from realizing its potential as the largest organization of African Americans.

FURTHER READINGS

Brooks-Higginbotham, Evelyn. *Righteous Discontent: The Women's Movement in the Black Baptist Church, 1880–1920.* Cambridge, Mass.: Harvard University Press, 1993.

Harvey, Paul. *Redeeming the South: Religious Cultures and Racial Identities Among Southern Baptists, 1865–1925.* Chapel Hill: University of North Carolina Press, 1997.

Montgomery, William. *Under Their Own Vine and Fig Tree: The African-American Church in the South, 1865–1900.* Baton Rouge: Louisiana State University Press, 1994.

Washington, James Melvin. *Frustrated Fellowship: The Black Baptist Quest for Social Power.* Macon, Ga.: Mercer University Press, 1986.

*Paul Harvey*

SEE ALSO    National Baptist Convention of America

## National Baptist Educational Convention

The National Baptist Educational Convention (NBEC) was organized in 1893 to centralize support for the education of black Baptist ministers. The NBEC was the brainchild of W. Bishop Johnson, the pastor of the Second Baptist Church, Washington, D.C. In the 1880s, Johnson had helped to organize the Sunday School Lyceum movement. As a theologian, author, and editor of the short-lived but important *National Baptist Magazine*, Johnson was an outspoken critic of what he felt to be an overreliance on "folk" preaching characteristics of African American Baptist worship. He founded the NBEC to centralize support for schools owned or managed by black Baptists, especially for institutions with theological programs that trained ministers. He hoped that a central educational convention would produce efficient fund-raising operations for black Baptist educational institutions. Johnson also used the new convention to campaign for the establishment of a seminary for black Baptists that would have a national, rather than a state, constituency. Two years later, in 1895, the NBEC merged with the American National Baptist Convention and the Baptist Foreign Mission Convention to form the National Baptist Convention (NBC), which soon thereafter became the largest organization of African Americans. In 1924, Johnson's dream of a national seminary for black Baptists came to fruition when the NBC established the American Baptist Theological Seminary in Nashville, Tennessee.

FURTHER READINGS

Fitts, Leroy. *A History of Black Baptists.* Nashville: Broadman, 1985.

Washington, James Melvin. *Frustrated Fellowship: The Black Baptist Quest for Social Power.* Macon, Ga.: Mercer University Press, 1986.

*Paul Harvey*

# National Bar Association

The National Bar Association (NBA), founded in 1926, pursues the complementary goals of civil rights reform and the professional development of black attorneys. Created at a time when every nationally organized bar association excluded blacks, the NBA gave black lawyers a collective voice during a century of significant legal change affecting African Americans.

From 1890 to 1920 the number of black attorneys more than doubled, from 431 to 950, but they were prohibited from participating in the development of their profession because the American Bar Association (ABA) and most regional and local bar associations refused to admit black members. Consequently, almost all organized activity by the black bar occurred in segregated state and local associations. The only national organization was the National Negro Bar Association, an affiliation of black lawyers who represented business clients, which lasted from 1909 to 1922.

In 1925 black lawyers from seven states and the Virgin Islands met in Des Moines, Iowa, to explore ways to pool the resources of black bar groups across the country. The following year the National Bar Association (NBA) was incorporated with George H. Woodson of Des Moines as president. According to its charter, the organization existed to "advance the science of jurisprudence, uphold the honor of the legal profession, promote social intercourse among the members of the American Bar, and protect the civil and political rights of all citizens of the several states and the United States." Thus, the organization concerned itself with traditional bar association issues such as professional ethics, legal education, and uniform state laws, as well as civil rights issues such as transportation discrimination, residential segregation, and voting rights.

Not surprisingly, many active members of the NBA were also leading figures in the National Association for the Advancement of Colored People (NAACP), including Charles Hamilton Houston and Thurgood Marshall. Although the two groups occasionally quibbled over strategy and politics, for the most part the NBA endorsed the NAACP's positions on eliminating segregated institutions. Unlike the NAACP, the NBA did not directly participate in civil rights litigation, although its individual members certainly did. Instead, it attempted to influence the course of civil rights law in two ways. First, it submitted amicus curiae briefs to the U.S. Supreme Court in cases brought by other civil rights groups. Second, it sought to influence the composition of the judiciary by opposing nominees to the federal courts who were not committed to racial equality. During the 1940s the NBA expanded its legal mission beyond constitutional civil rights, establishing free legal clinics in twelve states to assist black criminal defendants and indigent African Americans who needed help with civil litigation.

As both a professional and a civil rights organization, the NBA paid particular attention to discriminatory policies that adversely affected black lawyers. From its inception the group continually challenged the ABA's exclusion of blacks. It pressured the federal government, particularly the Department of Justice, to hire more black attorneys, and it urged presidents to appoint blacks to the federal judiciary. During World War II, it coupled its general advocacy of the desegregation of the armed forces with a more specific goal of increasing the number of blacks in the Judge Advocate General Corps. In 1968 it helped to found the Council on Legal Education Opportunity (CLEO), which sought to increase black enrollment in law schools through scholarship assistance, summer institutes for entering minority law students, and other programs. In addition, the NBA has submitted amicus briefs in affirmative action cases involving admission to professional schools, most notably the 1978 *Bakke* case.

The NBA's commitment to equal rights extended to its encouragement of women members. Gertrude Rush of Iowa was an NBA charter member, and in 1928 Georgia Jones Ellis of Chicago became the association's first woman officer. The reasons for welcoming women attorneys were not only egalitarian but practical: with so few black attorneys practicing in the United States, the NBA could not afford to exclude anybody. Since 1928, women have served as the association's officers or board members nearly every year, and in 1981 Arnette Hubbard of Chicago was elected as the first woman president of the NBA.

In 1943 the ABA formally opened its doors to black members, prompting some black attorneys to question whether a separate organization was necessary. In practice, however, the NBA remained the primary vehicle for black lawyers to participate in bar association activity on a national level. For one thing, although blacks were eligible for admission to the ABA, they were not actively courted until the late 1960s. Moreover, the dues structure of the ABA made it too expensive for most attorneys, white or black, to join. Finally, the sheer number of white lawyers in the ABA made it unlikely that the concerns of black professionals would receive more than passing attention. As a result, black attorneys continued to be attracted to the NBA.

In 1968 the NBA faced the first serious challenge to its position as the preeminent organization for black legal professionals. As the civil rights movement became more polarized, many younger black attorneys felt that the NBA had given middle-class professional values a higher priority than the legal needs of impoverished and working-class African Americans. In December 1968, seventeen black lawyers established the National Conference of Black Lawyers (NCBL) as a more activist alternative to the NBA; it soon grew to more than one thousand members. Although the NBA continues to hold more moderate positions on civil rights issues than the NCBL, since the 1970s the two groups have worked cooperatively on several projects, including the CLEO program and affirmative action cases. Many black lawyers are members of both organizations. At the end of the twentieth century the NBA remained the largest black bar association in the country with seventeen thousand members representing two-thirds of all black attorneys.

**FURTHER READINGS**

Smith, J. Clay, Jr. "The Black Bar Association and Civil Rights." *Creighton Law Review* 15 (1981–1982): 651–679.

———. *Emancipation: The Making of the Black Lawyer, 1844–1944*. Philadelphia: University of Pennsylvania Press, 1993.

*Eric W. Rise*

## National Black Catholic Clergy Caucus

The National Black Catholic Clergy Caucus was initiated by African American priests in 1968. By the late 1960s black frustration with the passivity and indifference of white society flared into anger and urban unrest. "Black Power" became a rallying cry for many African Americans, and a distinct Black Theology that identified the suffering of black peoples with the crucified Christ had been articulated. Preparing to meet with the biracial Catholic Clergy Conference, a support group that ad-

ministered to black Catholics, African American priests Herman Porter, George Clements, and Rollins Lambert spearheaded a separate meeting for black priests on April 16, 1968. Their goal was to formulate a program dealing with the frustration, anger, and mounting urban violence in America's black communities.

The caucus issued a statement, proclaiming that the "Catholic Church in the United States is primarily a white racist institution, has addressed itself to white society and is definitely a part of that society." The statement went on to demand black leadership training, better utilization of black clergy, and more programs for African American Catholic communities.

By 1970 the caucus had been instrumental in the church's decision to establish the National Office for Black Catholics. Moreover, the caucus has provided a fellowship and fraternity for black priests and has served as a vehicle for change in the Catholic Church in America. It has sponsored the Black Theological Symposium, helped to establish the Institute for Black Catholic Studies at Xavier University in New Orleans, and has participated in the Black Catholic congresses of 1987 and 1992.

The caucus conducts its annual meeting jointly with the National Black Catholic Sisters' Conference and the National Black Seminarians Association, promoting solidarity, discussion, and mutual understanding within the black Catholic community.

**FURTHER READINGS**

Davis, Cyprian, O.S.B. "After Twenty Years: The National Black Clergy Caucus." Unpublished manuscript, 1988.

———. *The History of Black Catholics in the United States*. New York: Crossroad, 1991.

Raboteau, Albert, J. *A Fire in the Bones: Reflections on African-American Religious History*. Boston: Beacon Press, 1995.

*A. J. Scopino Jr.*

## National Black Catholic Congress

In the last decades of the nineteenth century as the shadow of Jim Crow fell over the South and any substantive measure of social or economic equity remained elusive throughout the North, black Catholics voiced their concerns through the church. Black Catholic laymen called the first Colored Catholic congresses that were held annually between 1889 and 1894. Discontinued thereafter, the congresses resumed as the National Black Catholic congresses (NBCC) of 1987 and 1992.

The first five congresses were orchestrated by Daniel Rudd, born in 1858, a son of slave parents from Kentucky. Following the Civil War Rudd migrated to Springfield, Ohio, where he pursued an education and went on to publish the *American Catholic Tribune*, the first black-owned paper published by black Catholics.

The Catholic assemblies Rudd organized between 1889 and 1894 were not concerned with doctrine nor did they attempt to determine the place of African Americans within the church. Rather, they were fundamentally concerned with education, most specifically with the urgent need for industrial schools for blacks to make African Americans economically competitive. In an eloquent speech at the first congress, Rudd proclaimed that the only duty of the delegates was to determine the "needs" of African American Catholics and to formulate ways to improve the "temporal interests of the race." Rudd went on to discuss the lack of blacks in the skilled trades and the difficulties African Americans experienced in attempting to join trade unions.

The later congresses of 1987 and 1992 addressed the modern needs of the African American community and called for a more comprehensive and systemic way of meeting those needs. Furthermore, they questioned the racism inherent within the church. Black Catholic delegates discussed, formalized, and politicized racial issues in an effort to raise the consciousness of the predominantly white leadership of the church. They also demanded the forging of an African American perspective in the church's liturgical calendar, rituals, and rites.

The public policy statements of the later assemblies were comprehensive, calling for minimum-wage increases and pay equity, higher education opportunities, affordable child care, and guaranteed health care. Delegates also supported advocacy for all homeless, marginal, and displaced peoples. Other demands included the creation and implementation of an Afrocentric curriculum K-12 and the availability of more minority scholarships. Moreover, the congresses called for programs that addressed the special needs of African Americans, the development of parish prison ministries, programs that fostered better communication between family members, marriage preparation and enrichment classes, at-risk youth programs, and lay leadership training. Resolutions adopted at the congresses also called on the NBCC to strengthen its connections with the peoples of Africa, increase its efforts in the adoption of children, and establish an African American Catholic Rite in addition to the African forms already in use. Finally, the congresses called for the elevation of black bishops to the position of diocesan bishops.

As Daniel Rudd called attention to the problems of the black Catholic community over a century ago, the NBCC continues to advance the cause of African Americans today. Recent congresses, however, have promoted more comprehensive action that touches virtually every aspect of black sacred and secular life.

**FURTHER READINGS**

Davis, Cyprian, O.S.B. *The History of Black Catholicism in the United States*. New York: Crossroad, 1991.

"National Black Catholic Pastoral Plan." National Black Catholic Congress, May 21–24, 1987. *In A Word*. Bay St. Louis, Miss.: Society of the Divine Word, 1987.

Ochs, Stephen J. *Desegregating the Altar: The Josephites and the Struggle for Black Priests 1870–1960*. Baton Rouge: Louisiana State University Press, 1990.

"Public Policy and Pastoral Statements." National Black Catholic Congress, July 9–12, 1992. *In A Word*. Bay St. Louis, Miss.: Society of the Divine Word, 1992.

*Three Catholic Afro-American Congresses*. Cincinnati: American Catholic Tribune, 1893; rpt., New York: Arno Press, 1978.

*A. J. Scopino Jr.*

## National Black Catholic Lay Caucus

Born out of the disillusionment of African American Catholics with the racism inherent in white society and in the Catholic Church, the National Black Catholic Lay Caucus (NBCLC) was founded in 1970. Along with a host of other similar organizations emerging at the same time, the NBCLC, working in concert with the National Black Catholic Clergy Caucus, the National Black Sisters' Conference, the National Black Seminarian Association, and the National Office for Black Catholics, applied pressure on the church to implement sweeping changes affecting the role of black Catholics.

The NBCLC, with James McNeil serving as its first executive director, held its first national convention in August 1970. At the meeting delegates drafted a resolution demanding from the Catholic Church the elevation of four black bishops to regional posts, the establishment of a black lay pastorale, greater decision making by lay representation at all levels of church administration, hierarchical support in developing an African American liturgy that reflects African American heritage, the development of youth programs, and inclusion of black youth groups in decision-making policies affecting them.

The NBCLC has sponsored workshops for white religious instruction teachers, white clergy, and others involved with work among African American Catholic youth. In 1987, in conjunction with the National Office for Black Catholics, the NBCLC helped administer the first Black Catholic Church Life Survey in an effort to document the participation of African Americans in the church.

**FURTHER READINGS**

Davis, Cyprian, O.S.B. *Catholics in the United States.* New York: Crossroad, 1991.

"The Resolutions of the National Convention of Black Lay Catholics." *Freeing the Spirit* 1 (Summer 1972): 41–42.

*A. J. Scopino Jr.*

# National Black Catholic Seminarian Association

Created in 1972, the National Black Catholic Seminarian Association was inspired by the actions of the National Black Catholic Clergy Caucus four years earlier. On April 16, 1968, a group of black Catholic priests met to discuss the Roman Catholic Church's indifference to African American Catholics and what they believed to be overt racism in the church's infrastructure. The caucus condemned racism in the Catholic Church and demanded increased black leadership training, better utilization of black clergy, and the creation of more programs for African American Catholic communities. In addition to the caucus, the National Black Catholic Office, the National Black Catholic Sisters' Conference, the National Black Catholic Lay Caucus, and the National Black Catholic Seminarians Association were formed within four years of the historic April meeting.

The Seminarian Association serves as a fraternity for black Catholic men preparing for the priesthood. It also seeks to enhance each seminarian's understanding of the needs, issues, and movements affecting the black community and it furthers the church's efforts to recruit black candidates for religious vocations. The association conducts conferences with other black Catholic groups and participates in a Summer Institute that focuses on the sociopsychological development of black Catholics.

In 1997, the association reported that of the five thousand seminarians enrolled in the nation's Catholic seminaries, fewer than 1 percent were of African descent. The association's headquarters is at Notre Dame Seminary in New Orleans.

**FURTHER READINGS**

Davis, Cyprian, O.S.B. *The History of Black Catholics in the Unites States.* New York: Crossroad, 1991.

Raboteau, Albert J. *A Fire in the Bones: Reflections on African-American Religious History.* Boston: Beacon Press, 1995.

*A. J. Scopino Jr.*

# National Black Caucus of Local Elected Officials

Black local officials launched the formation of the National Black Caucus of Local Elected Officials (NBC-LEO) following the 1968 National League of Cities (NLC) national conference in New Orleans. While black elected officials had been active in the NLC, they resented that their white colleagues treated them with disrespect and were insulted when whites who attended the New Orleans conference made negative remarks about African Americans. In response the black elected officials drafted a bipartisan proclamation condemning racist remarks of white conference participants.

In the following year, black elected officials gathered for a strategic planning meeting in San Diego and organized a caucus to represent the interests of minority communities. With the support of the Joint Center for Political and Economic Studies, caucus members examined their roles as black elected officials and discussed the potential influence they could have as a caucus within the NLC. Determined to assure adequate representation of black elected officials in the NLC, the caucus successfully placed blacks on all NLC standing committees, and its members assumed leadership roles in the organization.

In 1970, the caucus officially became the NBC-LEO. It goals were to increase the representation of African American interests in the development, implementation, and influence of public policies; to provide a forum for black elected officials that would aid in the enhancement of services provided to their constituencies; to serve as a clearinghouse for information that would assist local elected officials nationwide; to increase minority participation on the NLC Steering and Policy Committees to ensure that policy and program recommendations reflect minority concerns and benefit minority communities; to inform its members about issues affecting the African American community; to devise ways to achieve community objectives through legislation and direct action; and to promote legislation and economic development initiatives directed toward the needs of the African American community.

Among those instrumental in the growth of the NBC-LEO was Clarence Townes, vice president of the Joint Center for Economic and Political Studies. Townes believed that the NBC-LEO could play a powerful role in addressing the problems of black urban America, particularly as the number of black elected officials increased. Other leading figures in the NBC-LEO were Robert Blackwell, mayor of Highland Park, Michigan, who became the group's chairman and leader; Douglas F. Dollarhide, mayor of Compton, California, who served as its vice chairman; and Stanley Anderson, councilman from Washington, D.C., who was elected secretary-treasurer. In addition, the NBC-LEO elected eight regional members to serve on the organization's steering committee.

The NBC-LEO's founding members believed that political affiliation had little bearing on their vision for the caucus. Thus, a desire to increase local services to black constituencies, rather than the pursuit of partisan politics, became their operative criteria. Aware of the value of a coalition able to transcend party lines, the NBC-LEO's motto became "No permanent friends, no permanent enemies, just permanent interests."

The NBC-LEO, headquartered in Washington, D.C., has approximately four hundred members who attend yearly regional conferences and board of directors meetings hosted by those members interested in showcasing their cities. NBC-LEO officers are often called on to attend White House briefings or serve on national boards and commissions that address issues such as economic development, housing, affirmative action, health care, education, welfare reform, immigration, and political redistricting.

The organization is governed by a board of directors, and its executive committee consists of a president, president-elect, first vice president, secretary, assistant secretary, treasurer, chaplain, historian, parliamentarian, at least ten but not more than twenty regional directors representing at least eighteen regions throughout the country, all past presidents of the corporation, and six at-large members.

The NBC-LEO encourages its members to participate in the governance of the NLC to ensure that the organization's policies and programs accurately reflect African American interests and lead toward the development of community objectives. The NBC-LEO attends annual meetings with the NLC's Congress of Cities, the Congressional City Conference, and various other national and regional conferences. The organization also conducts seminars, workshops, and regional conferences that focus on particular policy and governance issues and engages in community outreach programs.

**FURTHER READINGS**

*A Guide to Black Organizations.* New York: Phillip Morris, 1997.

Jaszczak, Sandra, ed. *Encyclopedia of Associations.* Detroit: Gale, 1997.

Oakes, Elizabeth H., ed. *Minority Organizations.* Chicago: Ferguson, 1997.

*Andrew Smallwood*

# National Black Caucus of State Legislators

Ninety African American state legislators founded the National Black Caucus of State Legislators (NBCSL) in Nashville, Tennessee, in 1977. They wanted to play "a larger leadership role in National Civil Rights and governmental affairs" and sought parity for their constituents through state legislatures.

The mission of the NBCSL is to develop, conduct, and promote educational, research, and training programs designed to enhance the effectiveness of its members as they consider legislation and issues of public policy that affect, either directly or indirectly "the general welfare" of African American constituents within their respective jurisdictions. In support of its mission, the organization has adopted the following objectives: to serve as a national network and clearinghouse for the discussion, dissemination, and exchange of ideas and information among African American state legislators and their staffs; to provide research, training, and educational services to African American state legislators and their staffs; to improve the effectiveness and quality of African American state legislators; and to serve as a strong, united, and effective advocate for African American state legislators and their constituencies at the federal level.

Among the most influential individuals who helped launch the NBCSL were Matthew McNeely, a state representative from Michigan, and Eddie Williams, president of the Joint Center for Political Studies. McNeely was elected chairman of the NBCSL at its first national conference in November 1977. At the time of his election, McNeely expressed the need for the NBCSL, which, he explained, would help gather information in and about black communities and communicate the concerns of African Americans to Congress. The federal government, he complained, often failed to ask state legislators for input, "yet they are asked to implement the programs. Nobody is closer to the grassroots than the state people, and we want to feel the pulse of the grass roots." Likewise, Williams believed that state legislators serving on important committees were instrumental in determining the impact of state governments on national policies and the growth and development of communities throughout the United States.

The NBCSL has over six hundred members from forty-five states, the District of Columbia, and the U.S. Virgin Islands. Voting membership is open to African Americans elected to state legislatures. Corporate representatives, small businesses, nonprofit groups, and labor organizations can join the NBCSL in an advisory capacity. The organization also offers associate membership to corporations, former legislators, and the public at large.

With headquarters in the Hall of States building in Washington, D.C., the national office of the NBCSL serves as a central clearinghouse and distribution center. Its staff monitors the impact of national, state, and local legislation on the African American community. The National Executive Committee, composed of the organization's national officers, the chairpersons of its twelve regional caucuses, and twenty-one elected at-large members, determines the NBCSL's policies and governs all its activities. These include arranging meetings between all governmental groups representing black elected officials, conducting seminars, maintaining a speakers bureau and biographical archives, compiling statistics about NBCSL members and their respective districts and constituencies, and operation of a resource library.

According to Ivan Lanier, the NBCSL's current executive director, the organization has successfully linked black state legislators into a unified force and influenced national legislative policy. Moreover, the NBCSL was instrumental in facilitating the national dialogue that led to U.S. economic and political sanctions against South Africa's apartheid regime during the 1980s.

**FURTHER READINGS**

*A Guide to Black Organizations.* New York: Phillip Morris, 1997.

King, Wayne. "Caucus of Black State Legislators Seeks Role in National Affairs." *New York Times,* November 20, 1977, 24.

Oakes, Elizabeth, ed. *Minority Organizations.* Chicago: Ferguson, 1997.

*Andrew Smallwood*

## National Black Chambers of Commerce

The mission of the National Black Chambers of Commerce (NBCC) is to educate African Americans about the capitalist system and to promote the development of a strong economic base that will remedy some of the poor social conditions that exist in black communities such as lack of adequate health care and affordable housing. The NBCC encourages African American economic self-sufficiency and assists entrepreneurs in creating new businesses that will be supported by black consumers and provide job opportunities for black workers.

The organization is committed to developing all types of businesses but focuses on the creation of manufacturing and construction businesses that can provide large numbers of jobs for African Americans. The NBCC serves as an advocate for black entrepreneurs by working with local government agencies, churches, and corporations to provide its members with information and services designed to enhance black economic development. In the past, the NBCC has also assisted several major corporations and local government agencies in the development of their minority business development programs.

The NBCC grew out of the Hoosier Minority Chamber of Commerce in Indianapolis. The original coalition comprised fourteen black business organizations and local chambers of commerce. In March 1993, the organization was incorporated as the NBCC and relocated to Washington, D.C., in September of 1994. Although the central office of the NBCC is located in the District of Columbia, its affiliates can be found nationwide. The national office of the NBCC is under the direction of a chairman/CEO and a board of directors, and the local chapters are guided by seven regional vice presidents responsible for overseeing ninety-nine local chambers, trade associations, and business groups.

One of the main objectives of the NBCC is to conduct fund-raising activities on behalf of its local chapters and to provide the affiliates with funds to fulfill the organization's mission of increasing business participation of African Americans.

The NBCC supports five main programs. First, the Black Congress on Health, Law and Economics, a coalition that includes the National Medical Association, National Black Firefighters Association, National Dental

Association, National Black Nurses Association, and other national organizations. The NBCC serves as a source of economic information for this twenty-two–member group. Second, the National Black Chamber Foundation (NBCF) serves as a source of information on the economic concerns of African Americans. The research generated by the NBCF is made available to affiliated chapters and others interest groups via the Internet. Third, the Venture Capital Fund provides financing for growing businesses in need of capital. Fourth, Insurance Captives provides group insurance coverage for small black-owned businesses that have difficulty obtaining reasonably priced insurance on their own. Fifth, International Exchange provides opportunities for business owners in Africa, the Caribbean, and South America to network with those in the United States.

The NBCC hopes to sell produce, including fruits, coffee, and spices, directly to consumers through black-owned and -operated stores. This network will eventually provide people of African descent with opportunities to become involved in manufacturing, distribution, and retail sales internationally.

*Sharon Parkinson*

## National Black Coalition of Air Traffic Controllers

*See* National Black Coalition of Federal Aviation Employees.

## National Black Coalition of Federal Aviation Employees

The National Black Coalition of Federal Aviation Employees (NBCFAE) is an advocate for the interests of African American employees of the Federal Aviation Administration (FAA) and seeks to identify and prepare qualified blacks for FAA employment. Although the FAA hired its first African American air traffic controller in the early 1960s, blacks did not enter the professional ranks of the FAA in any significant numbers until after 1969. In 1976—the first year for which detailed figures on FAA minority employment are available—the FAA employed about four thousand African Americans, representing roughly 7 percent of all FAA employees. That year, 1,240 black air traffic controllers, constituting fewer than 5 percent of the total number of controllers, were among the approximately 27,000 controllers employed by the agency. By 1996 the percentage of African Americans in the total FAA workforce had risen to almost 9 percent, and the percentage of black controllers stood at just over 5 percent.

In 1976, six African American air traffic controllers established the NBCFAE as the National Black Coalition of Air Traffic Controllers (NBCATC). The NBCATC grew rapidly as the organization began to accept members who were FAA employees but not air traffic controllers. Consequently, the present name was adopted in 1978. In the following year the FAA provided its upper management with guidelines for working with representatives of the NBCFAE. During that time the NBCFAE asked the predominantly white Professional Air Traffic Controller's Association (PATCO) to support affirmative action and equal employment opportunity initiatives, but the results were disappointing. On the eve of the 1981 PATCO strike, the NBCFAE had grown to approximately five hundred members. In the wake of the strike membership fell to below two hundred, but since the mid-1990s the organization has grown steadily. By 1998 the number of members had stabilized at approximately 1,200.

As the first professional organization to focus on the concerns of minority FAA employees, the NBCFAE's constitution has served as a guide to other groups organized in support of issues important to minority FAA employees. The NBCFAE's goals include serving as a voice for its members; helping to recruit African American, female, and other minorities for FAA positions; and informing members of their rights as federal employees. Four officers and a national executive committee direct the affairs of the NBCFAE at the national level. The regional branches, each headed by a regional president, correspond to the regional structure of the FAA. Several local chapters have also been established. The NBCFAE, currently headquartered in Oklahoma City, publishes *Visions,* a quarterly newsletter for its members.

### FURTHER READINGS

Federal Aviation Administration. *Status of Equal Opportunity Employment Program, September 30, 1980.* Washington, D.C.: Government Printing Office, 1981.

———. *1996 Affirmative Employment Program Accomplishment Report & 1997 Update.* Washington, D.C.: Federal Aviation Administration, 1997.

Gardner, Cathy D. "Aviation Group Charts Course for Fairness in Workplace." *Chicago Defender,* September 19, 1995, 5.

National Black Coalition of Federal Aviation Employees. "National Black Coalition of Federal Aviation Employees." N.p., National Black Coalition of Federal Aviation Employees, September 1997.

Shostak, Arthur B., and David Skocik. *The Air Controllers' Controversy: Lessons from the PATCO Strike.* New York: Human Sciences Press, 1986.

*Robert J. Jakeman*

## National Black Evangelical Association

Founded in 1963 as the National Negro Evangelical Association, the National Black Evangelical Association (NBEA) is composed of theologically conservative African American individuals, churches, and organizations. It functions as the primary ecumenical association of African Americans within the American evangelical movement.

American evangelicalism, an offshoot of the fundamentalist movement, gained ascendancy in the 1940s, when leaders such as Billy Graham, Carl Henry, and E. J. Carnell opted for a coalition that would maintain fundamentalism's historically conservative doctrine but seek to be more cooperative with and less strident toward American culture at large. The formation of the National Association of Evangelicals (NAE) in 1942 signaled the organizational crystallization of this movement.

The black presence in the NAE remained small and marginal in its early years, consisting of some African Americans and a relatively significant number of Caribbean immigrants, most from predominantly white church groups. Throughout the 1950s, these numbers were supplemented with blacks from African American church traditions, notably Pentecostals, who shared the theological conservatism of white evangelicals but became increasingly uncomfortable with their failure to address adequately the concerns of blacks in this country. Many of these individuals were graduates of fundamentalist and evangelical schools and colleges, where they had matriculated because of the affinity between the institutions' conservative theology and the historic biblicism of black churches. The NBEA grew out of this black presence in the NAE.

In the 1960s, the NBEA developed its mission on two fronts. First, it saw the need for a doctrinally sound, evangelically defined church presence among African Americans, and to this end it focused on leadership development in the black community. Second, the NBEA served as a prophetic voice toward the white evangelical establishment, challenging the latter's seeming lack of concern for evangelism and outreach in the black community.

As the 1960s drew to a close, however, the challenge of the black power movement and its constituent attention to black nationalism dramatically affected the NBEA's sense of mission and purpose. Black theology made its appearance on the intellectual horizon and the annual meetings of the association including spirited debate on the merits of nationalistic theological perspectives in light of historic orthodox Christianity. The long-standing NBEA leader William Bentley, a Pentecostal who had been the first graduate of evangelical icon Fuller Seminary, was a leading mediatory voice, arguing for and publishing material that looked seriously at the issue of contextualization and theology. Drawing heavily from historical and missiological studies, Bentley argued that the Christian religion had always had a dynamic intersection with the host culture and that African American Christianity was no different. Indeed, black evangelicalism did not have its roots so much in the black wing of the fundamentalist movement as in persons in the black church who maintained a historic, literal interpretive approach to the Bible. Bentley called this group "Bible believers in the Black Community," and pressed for more efforts in the NBEA for linkages with that ongoing strain.

Activists within the movement sided with Bentley and took his call for contextualization as one that included a strong emphasis on social concern. The effects of racism and poverty within the black community required that any evangelistic efforts in those areas reflect consideration of the whole person and the social system in which persons must live and function. Therefore, reasoned activists, the NBEA should give attention to matters of social justice as part of its evangelistic work. Conservatives within the organization argued, however, that human society could be changed only by changing human hearts and therefore pressed for signal attention to be given to personal evangelism and soul winning. At the same time, citing the universality of the gospel message, these persons called for a more conciliatory approach to whites and race relations, and suggested that the NBEA spend more of its efforts in effecting racial reconciliation.

The decade of the 1980s witnessed a general downswing in attendance at NBEA conferences, as the debate between the twin foci of the association's mission continued. Yet the association persisted, in part owing precisely to its willingness to address the tough questions before it. At the 1990 meeting of the association in Chicago, the NBEA considered dropping the word "evangelical" from the association's title because of its popular association with a distinct brand of conservative politics not shared by the entire group.

With a mailing list of over five thousand and an estimated constituency of between thirty and forty thousand, the NBEA remains a primary venue for the various factions within black evangelicalism to hold direct, constructive dialogue over issues that confront its members. In the 1990s, it has been a major force in the racial reconciliation movement, signing a reconciliation accord with the NAE and becoming a cosponsor of the William Bentley Theological Institute for the development of black evangelical theology and ministry.

**FURTHER READINGS**

Bentley, William H. "Bible Believers in the Black Community." In *The Evangelicals: What They Believe, Who They Are and How They Are Changing*, eds. David Wells and John Woodbridge. Grand Rapids, Mich.: Baker House, 1977, 128–141.

———. *The National Black Evangelical Association: Evolution of a Concept of Ministry*. Chicago: National Black Evangelical Association, 1979.

Pannell, William. *My Friend the Enemy*. Waco, Tex.: Word, 1968.

Potter, Ronald. "The New Black Evangelicals." In *Black Theology: A Documentary History, 1966–1979*, eds. James Cone and Gayraud Wilmore. Maryknoll, N.Y.: Orbis, 1979, 233–309.

Skinner, Tom. *Black and Free*. Grand Rapids, Mich.: Zondervan, 1968.

*Harold Dean Trulear*

# National Black Feminist Organization

In May 1973, thirty African American women established the National Black Feminist Organization (NBFO) to address the concerns of black women who encountered sexism in the civil rights movement and racism in the women's liberation movement. Immediately after its founding the NBFO attracted more than two thousand members who organized ten chapters in cities across the nation. By 1976, however, the organization was defunct.

During the 1960s black women had been marginalized by civil rights organizations and women's liberation groups. Influential black leaders, such as Elijah Muhammad of the Nation of Islam and Stokely Carmichael of the Student Nonviolent Coordinating Committee (SNCC), insisted that African Americans had to be free from racial oppression before they could address the plight of black women. Frequently, black power and civil rights groups relegated black women to traditional female work, utilizing them as typists or asking them to prepare meals. Yet they largely excluded black women from voter registration drives in the South and from highly visible leadership positions such as public spokespersons. In part this marginalization was due to sexism. Yet many black activists also wanted to avoid the subject of women's liberation, fearing that it would be a divisive force and sap the energy from the civil rights movement.

Similarly, leaders of the women's liberation movement, most of whom were white and middle class, played down the issue of race, afraid to divide feminists along racial lines. The white leaders of the women's movement failed to recognize that women of color came from different cultures and communities and had different concerns. Thus, what was important to white middle-class women was not always of primary importance to African American women.

To address the marginalization of black women in both the civil rights and the women's liberation movements, Michele Wallace, Margaret Sloan, Flo Kennedy, Doris Wright, and other black women created the NBFO. They were convinced that feminism would strengthen, not divide, the civil rights movement because it encouraged the utilization of the creative talents of black women. Likewise, they argued that attending to issues of race would enhance and lend credibility to the women's liberation movement.

At their first meeting in May 1973, NBFO members gathered in New York City to explore what it meant to be black, female, and feminist. They discussed common concerns such as systemic racism and sexism, living on welfare, inadequate day-care facilities, salary and job discrimination, low self-esteem, forced sterilization, abortion, and the negative image of black women in the media. The members of this newly formed organization quickly realized that the liberation of African American women had to be different from that of white women because black women had to overcome racism in addition to sexism.

Following the initial meeting, Margaret Sloan, a founding editor of *Ms.* magazine, and Eleanor Holmes Norton, New York City's human rights commissioner, announced the formation of the NBFO on August 15, 1973. Sloan and Holmes urged black women to recognize their dual oppression and invited them to join their organization. Immediately after its founding, the NBFO was greeted by overwhelming public interest. On August 16, the day after the organization's formation, the NBFO received over four hundred phone calls from African American women interested in joining the group.

Taking advantage of the public interest, the NBFO organized its first regional conference. Between November 30 and December 2, 1973, NBFO members and those interested in the organization's work gathered at the Cathedral of St. John the Divine in New York City. The NBFO scheduled approximately twenty workshops for conference participants, including panels on politics, portrayals of black women in the media, lesbianism, women in prison, drug addiction, and women's liberation. An indication of the success of the conference was the attendant increase in membership. By February 1974, the NBFO's membership had surged from its initial thirty members to more than two thousand, and the organization boasted more than ten chapters, located largely in major metropolitan areas such as New York City, Chicago, Washington, D.C., and Los Angeles. Influential and prominent African American women, such as Representative Shirley Chisholm, supported the NBFO, which may account for its initial popular appeal.

Maintaining its initial momentum, however, proved impossible as both external and internal forces challenged the existence of the NBFO. Despite a membership explosion during the early months, the NBFO failed to attract significant numbers of African American women. This was due in part to the relatively small number of black women who actively participated in the women's liberation movement. Perhaps some black women were unsure of dividing their loyalties between black and feminist causes. Others, because of economic realities, simply did not have the time and energy of the white middle-class women who dominated the women's liberation movement. Another problem was the lack of support the NBFO received from other black women's groups. Black sororities, for example, did not promote or lend their backing to the NBFO because the organization moved outside the traditional African American mainstream. As a result, the NBFO lacked access to the extensive networks and membership lists of these groups. While some black women deemed the NBFO too radical, others broke away from the organization charging that it was too bourgeois and lacked a clear political focus. Moreover, the NBFO encountered difficulties reconciling the perspectives and opinions of its remarkably heterogeneous membership, which included lawyers, editors, homemakers, and students. While the NBFO wanted to hear and give equal weight to the experiences of all black women, often members found themselves suppressing differences for the common purpose of feminism. This alienated many women who became increasingly frustrated with the NBFO.

Ultimately, these internal and external forces weakened and split the NBFO. Conflicts soon began to erupt, and often dissensions were played out in the public arena. At the NBFO's 1975 regional conference, for example, some members objected to the leadership of the New York group. Differences in personalities and geographic perspectives further divided the NBFO. By the 1976 convention, tensions were so high that instead of penning a constitution and bylaws, the NBFO folded. Ten local chapters of the NBFO, though, continued to operate until 1980.

Although the NBFO was short-lived, it was significant for a number of reasons. Some of the NBFO's local branches successfully publicized the plight of black women. The Los Angeles chapter, for example, influenced producers of television shows that portrayed black characters to eliminate distasteful stereotypes of African American women. In New York, the NBFO chapter drew attention to the paltry wages of domestic workers, who were largely African American, and the sexual harassment and abuse that black women faced in disproportionate numbers. Most important, though, the NBFO was the first national organization that recognized the dual burden of racism and sexism. It called attention to the fact that neither the leaders of the civil rights movement nor those heading the women's movement sufficiently addressed the unique conditions and concerns of African American women. Moreover, during its brief existence the NBFO united black women of diverse educational and economic backgrounds and provided them with a forum to discover that they shared similar experiences. As a result, those women active in the NBFO were able to overcome their sense of isolation in both the civil rights and the women's liberation movements.

## FURTHER READINGS

"Black Feminism: A New Mandate." *Ms.* 11, 11 (May 1974): 97.

Combahee River Collective. "A Black Feminist Statement." In *This Bridge Called My Back: Writings by Radical Women of Color*, eds. Cherrie Moraga and Gloria Anzuldua. New York: Kitchen Table: Women of Color Press, 1981.

Davis, Beverly. "To Seize the Moment: A Retrospective on the National Black Feminist Organization." *Sage* 5, 2 (Fall 1988): 43–47.

Golden, Bernette. "Black Women's Liberation." *Essence* (February 1974): 35–36, 75–76, 86.

National Black Feminist Organization. "Statement of Purpose." In *Feminism in Our Time: Essential Writings from World War II to the Present*, ed. Miriam Schnier. New York: Vantage Books, 1994.

Wallace, Michele. "A More Personal View of Black Feminism." In *Modern American Women: A Documentary History*, ed. Susan Ware. New York, McGraw-Hill, 1997.

*Stephanie Gilmore*

## National Black Leadership Roundtable

The National Black Leadership Roundtable (NBLR), established in 1983, is composed of the heads or representatives of black organizations working under one umbrella to take control of the destiny of African Americans. The NBLR is closely aligned with the Congressional Black Caucus. The organization was conceived by Congressman Walter E. Fauntroy from the District of Columbia, who served in Congress from 1971 to 1990 and chaired the Congressional Black Caucus from 1981 to 1983. Fauntroy envisioned the NBLR as a "brain trust," a network of black political organizations that would gather data to enable African Americans to understand pending legislation and to influence congressional action favorable to African Americans. The Roundtable is composed of over three hundred black organizations representing more than 250,000 persons in diverse fields of interest such as government, international relations, civil rights, education, media, labor, science, health, women's, social, and fraternal organizations.

The NBLR works through the elected and appointed leaders of its constituent organizations. The NBLR membership is drawn from three sources: organizations, caucuses, and a limited number of individuals. To join the NBLR, organizations must have black leadership and at least two hundred predominantly black members residing in more than one state. A caucus must fulfill similar requirements for membership. No more than 85 percent of the NBLR membership may be composed of chief executive officers of constituent organizations, and no more than 10 percent of the membership may be drawn from caucuses. The remaining 5 percent of the membership is open to individuals who are either formerly elected or appointed officials or former heads of caucuses or nationally recognized leaders.

The headquarter of the NBLR is located in Washington, D.C., and staffed by a resident agent. The roundtable is governed by a twenty-seven-member Board of Directors drawn from churches, educational organizations, fraternal orders, social associations, and government agencies. The current chair of the Congressional Black Caucus is also a member of the board. Members of the Board of Directors are elected annually and may serve three successive terms. Elections are held so that terms are staggered. The roundtable holds two annual meetings, one in September of each year coinciding with the Congressional Black Caucus Weekend, and one in March at a location designated by the executive committee of the board.

The NBLR pursues a four-point plan: to prevent assaults on policies designed to improve the quality of life of African Americans; to initiate and shape policies that will improve the life of African Americans; to organize a communications network; and to form coalitions with other ethnic and minority groups that have similar purposes. To implement its plan, the NBLR has engaged in a wide range of programs. In the 1980s, the organization focused on increasing black representation in Congress. In 1986, it identified five congressional districts with large numbers of African American voters and mobilized support for black candidates; this effort resulted in the election of John Lewis (Georgia), Mike Espy (Mississippi), and Floyd Flake (New York). At the same time, the NBLR targeted ten Senate seats; however, this effort did not result in the election of African Americans. Nevertheless, the NBLR's campaign influenced the vote in seven of the Senate races and resulted in the election of liberal white candidates who took control from conservative Republicans. Other NBLR campaigns include efforts to oppose budget cuts that affect social programs for cities and antibusing legislation. Moreover, the NBLR has supported the liberation of Zimbabwe, the abolition of apartheid in South Africa, the cause of Haitian refugees in the United States, and the enactment of the Martin Luther King holiday bill.

A key component of the organization's program is known as "Rules for Black Unity, Survival, and Progress." The rules emphasize the importance of the black church and family, excellence in education, respect for the elderly, and support for black economic development. The organization believes that adherence to these rules will be the means by which African Americans achieve parity, equity, equality, and justice.

**FURTHER READINGS**

Clay, William L. *Just Permanent Interests: Black Americans in Congress, 1971–1991.* New York: Amistad Press, 1992.

National Black Leadership Roundtable. *Articles of Incorporation.* Washington, D.C.: The National Black Leadership Roundtable, 1983.

National Black Leadership Roundtable. *The Black Leadership Family Plan.* Washington, D.C.: The National Black Leadership Roundtable, n.d.

*Joseph T. Durham*

## National Black MBA Association

Incorporated in 1974, the National Black MBA Association (NBMBAA) is a nonprofit organization that provides business professionals, entrepreneurs, and burgeoning MBA students with information, professional support, and networking opportunities. Black professionals from the private and public sectors join forces in the NBMBAA to foster economic and intellectual development in their communities by encouraging high school and college students to pursue business-related degrees in higher education. A number of local and national workshops also offer career enhancement programs that assist black business professionals.

In 1970, several University of Chicago students, recognizing the need for professional mentors, launched the NBMBAA to create a support network. The group's first mission was to encourage African Americans to obtain postgraduate degrees, to advance up the corporate ladder, and to provide each other with networking opportunities.

The NBMBAA's annual convention is attended by hundreds of representatives from high-level firms and offers a career fair. A series of conference sessions, such as the Executive Development Institute and the Minority Entrepreneur Program, encourages educational and professional development among African Americans. At the local level, NBMBAA affiliates provide programs such as Leaders of Tomorrow, which brings business mentors and resources to inner-city high school students, and the Junior Achievement Partnership, which encourages entrepreneurial capabilities among young African Americans. In cooperation with the Graduate Management Admissions Council and National Society of Hispanic MBAs, the NBMBAA has launched Destination MBA, which organizes panel discussions in local chapters to reinforce the value of the MBA degree. Since 1974 the NBMBAA and its local chapters have also provided annual scholarships for college-bound students.

In 1993, the NBMBAA's ten-member staff reassessed the needs of its members and broadened its mission. NBMBAA programs continued to focus on assisting students in securing MBAs and employment in business, yet they also emphasized skill enhancement, career training, and business development. Moreover, new workshops such as the NBMBAA Case Competition and Target Market Power encouraged teamwork among participants. While some members praised the NBMBAA's broadened scope, others complained that the changes were not sufficient. They welcomed the NBMBAA's new programming initiatives but insisted that the organization had too many social gatherings and did not pay enough attention to the professional needs of its members.

Almost thirty years after its inception, the NBMBAA boasts three thousand members in over thirty-two chapters nationwide, including one international affiliate. Professionals who hold an MBA degree or have commensurate business or entrepreneurial experience are welcome to join, as are students pursuing graduate degrees. Roughly 74 percent of the NBMBAA membership is between the ages of twenty-six and forty.

Headquartered in Chicago, the association continues to provide valuable networking opportunities for burgeoning professionals, and community programs encourage academic success and business leadership among young African Americans. Development of professional alliances and information resources will guide the NBMBAA into the twenty-first century.

**FURTHER READINGS**

Baskerville, Dawn. "Meeting the Changing Needs of Black MBAs." *Black Enterprise* 24, 3 (October 1993): 120–126.

Morrow, David J. "Black MBAs Look to the 1990s." *Fortune* 120 (November 6, 1989): 10.

National Black MBA Association. *Join the Organization That Works as Hard as You Do to Achieve Success.* Chicago: The Association, n.d.

———. *The Silver Lining: Twenty-five Years, National Black MBA Association.* Chicago: The Association, 1995.

*Katherine Kuntz Dill*

## National Black McDonald's Operators Association

In 1968, the McDonald's Corporation decided that African Americans should operate McDonald's restaurants in predominantly black neighborhoods. This decision marked the beginning of the National Black McDonald's Operators Association (NBMOA). Headquartered in Los Angeles, the NBMOA is a support organization for the black owners and operators of McDonald's restaurants throughout the United States. It is one of the largest black franchise groups of McDonald's operators in the nation. Dedicated to the success of black McDonald's restaurant owners and operators, the NBMOA provides members with training seminars that include marketing, better sales practices, improved labor relations, and profit sharing.

In addition, the NBMOA seeks to improve community relations and assists the communities in which their members operate through a philanthropic program of in-store fund-raising, scholarship programs, regional cooperative projects, and individual donations. The NBMOA also encourages active participation in the exchange of ideas to improve the operation and management of black-operated McDonald's restaurants.

The NBMOA has currently 327 owner/operator members who own 750 stores throughout the United States. The combined franchises gross in excess of $1 billion annually. The NBMOA publishes a quarterly newsletter and holds biennial conventions and a biennial symposium.

**FURTHER READINGS**

Fischer, C. A., and C. A. Schwartz, eds. *Encyclopedia of Associations*, vol. 1, part 1. New York: International, 1995.

National Black McDonald's Operators Association. *NBMOA Association History*. N.p., n.d.

*Nancy Jean Rose*

## National Black Meeting Planners Coalition

*See* National Coalition of Black Meeting Planners.

## National Black Music Caucus of the Music Educators National Conference

The National Black Music Caucus of the Music Educators National Conference (MENC) was founded in 1972 to promote African American musicians and music teachers and encourage the development of music education programs in schools with predominantly African American student bodies. A division of the MENC, the National Black Music Caucus encourages the creation and study of African American music and provides educational resources for black students from preschool to college levels. The caucus also seeks to make the public aware of problems encountered by African American music students and teachers. For this purpose it distributes publications, including the quarterly newsletter *Con Brio*; sponsors

gospel choir competitions; honors outstanding teachers with awards; maintains a database of African American musicians, educators, music, and books; and hosts an annual retreat. Leadership of the caucus is shared by professionals in the field. As of 1997, the executive director of the National Black Music Caucus was Ted Mc-Daniel, a professor in the School of Music at Ohio State University.

Originally named the Music Supervisors National Conference when it was formed in 1907, the MENC was located in Chicago and sponsored geographic sections. By 1997, the MENC consisted of approximately seventy two thousand music educators "dedicated to providing a complete, balanced, sequential [music] education to every child in America." The conference's national headquarters was relocated to Reston, Virginia, and serves as a repository of resources for music educators. The MENC pursues specific goals, including informing legislators about the importance of music education for all children and developing national music education standards. The conference and its subgroups, such as the National Black Music Caucus, sponsor outreach programs, including "Music in our Schools Month," the World's Largest Concert, and the "Music Makes the Difference" campaign, and join national coalitions that promote arts in schools.

National members receive numerous benefits and have access to advocacy resources and awareness items that teachers can cite to gain support for music education programs in schools. All members can attend national conventions and are encouraged to affiliate with state and local music educator groups where they can network and share ideas with colleagues. The MENC issues several publications to inform and assist music educators and students. *Teaching Music* contains association news as well as interviews and lesson plans. *The Music Educators Journal* discusses music philosophies, trends, techniques, products, and services. The *Journal of Music Teacher Education* focuses on the training of music teachers, *General Music Today* provides lesson ideas, the *Journal of Research in Music Education* offers theoretical articles, and *Applications of Research in Music Education* explains how to utilize the results of research projects in classrooms.

The MENC maintains an Internet web page with information about the organization. The Internet site also has links to music resources, including books, videotapes, instruments, audiovisual aids, and uniforms for sale as well as publishers of music textbooks and music schools. Additional resources for African American musicians are available at the Center for Black Music Research at Columbia College in Chicago.

**FURTHER READINGS**

Arneson, Arne Jon. *The Music Educators Journal: Cumulative Index 1914–1987, Including the Music Supervisors' Bulletin and the Music Supervisors' Journal.* Stevens Point, Wisc.: Index House, 1987.

Colwell, Richard, ed. *Handbook of Research on Music Teaching and Learning: A Project of the Music Educators National Conference.* New York: Schirmer, 1992.

*Elizabeth D. Schafer*

## National Black Police Association

The National Black Police Association (NBPA), founded as the National Black Policemen's Association, protects the interests of minority police officers and works for police reform in police departments throughout the United States. It strives to increase the number of minority police officers through recruitment efforts and promotes professionalism within the officers' ranks. The organization investigates departmental discrimination against black police officers, seeks to improve working conditions for black police officers, and works to eliminate police corruption and racial discrimination. Moreover, the NBPA promotes fair, just, and effective law enforcement and evaluates the effects of criminal justice policies on minority communities. The NBPA is also a strong advocate of improving relations between police departments and their communities.

The NBPA was established in November 1972, following the First National Conference of Black Policemen at St. Louis in August 1972. Since its founding, the NBPA has held annual conferences that provide a forum for black police officers to address issues of concern. These include civil rights and law enforcement issues such as team policing, use of deadly force, and community relations. In addition to providing a forum for the discussion of professional issues, the NBPA has challenged the lack of reform in American police departments. In 1977, the NBPA changed its name from National Black Policemen's Association to National Black Police Association, recognizing that law enforcement was not an exclusively male occupation. Women were gaining ground as police officers during the 1970s. Nationwide, various police departments began to assign women to police patrol duties and to eliminate gender-specific tasks. In 1979, the NBPA elected its youngest national chairman, Wilbert K. Battle, of the San Francisco Police Department. During his one-

year tenure, Battle helped the association grow into a strong advocate of black police advancement. He promoted professionalism, called for an end to abusive police practices, advocated regulating police use of deadly force, and demanded improvement of police training in community relations. These issues continue to be an important aspect of the NBPA's agenda.

Nationally, the NBPA is divided into five regions. It represents about thirty-five thousand members in more than 140 chapters in thirty-four states and the District of Columbia. The association also welcomes college students through student chapters at historically black college campuses. It provides scholarship assistance to high school graduates interested in pursuing a career in criminal justice. The association maintains a national office in Washington, D.C., to coordinate and monitor its various projects and programs. In addition, the NBPA keeps its members informed through its publication *NBPA Advocate*. It further informs and educates its members and other interested parties with its Annual Education and Training Conference. This event includes workshops, discussion groups, and seminars and provides networking opportunities for NBPA members and representatives of law enforcement and criminal justice. Recently, the NBPA has developed the Community-Oriented Policing program in collaboration with the National Organization of Black Law Enforcement Executives (NOBLE). This program represents a comprehensive strategy for community policing and exemplifies the belief of the NBPA in the importance of good community relations with the police.

**FURTHER READING**

Dulaney, W. Marvin. *Black Police in America.* Bloomington: Indiana University Press, 1996.

*Angel R. Rivera*

## National Black Policemen's Association

*See* National Black Police Association.

## National Black Presbyterian Caucus

The National Black Presbyterian Caucus (NBPC) was founded in 1983; however, black activism in the church dates back to the founding of the First African Presbyterian Church in Philadelphia in 1807. Prior to the Civil War, black Presbyterians fought against slavery. In 1894 they formed the Afro-American Presbyterian Council to encourage integration of the church's membership. In 1947 the group changed its name to the Presbyterian Afro-American Council of the North and West. It continued to support the Presbyterian Church's commitment to desegregation and to end discriminatory practices that defy Christian values of love, charity, and compassion.

The Afro-American Council of the North and West was one of several Presbyterian groups that promoted desegregation. In 1964, for example, southern Presbyterians formed the Black Presbyterians Concerned to increase black presence in the Presbyterian Church. In 1968, the Afro-American Council of the North and West and Black Presbyterians Concerned formed the Black Presbyterians United.

During the 1960s, the members of the national Presbyterian General Assembly challenged the Presbyterian Church to encourage antidiscrimination efforts among its affiliates, yet not all members supported such efforts. When the *Presbyterian Survey*, the church's monthly publication, devoted its June 1968 issue to racism, stereotyping, and intermarriage, it generated considerable controversy. Subscriptions declined and angry readers, offended by the magazine's endorsement of racial intermarriage and tolerance, wrote numerous letters. However, other subscribers, convinced that racism contradicted Christian teachings, supported the magazine's plea for racial tolerance.

Despite the church's efforts to improve racial understanding, blacks remained underrepresented in the Presbyterian Church. In response, some southern black Presbyterians formed the Black Leadership Caucus in 1969. In 1983, when the two geographic factions of the national Presbyterian Church merged to form the Presbyterian Church (USA), the Black Presbyterians United and the Black Leadership Caucus formed the National Black Presbyterian Caucus.

The caucus continued to challenge the Presbyterian Church to acknowledge the importance of the church's black leadership and membership. Moreover, the group supported the secular Black Power movement and endorsed James Forman's "Black Manifesto." In 1969, Forman, a black militant leader and spokesman for the National Black Economic Development Conference (NBEDC), published his "Manifesto," which called on religious bodies to contribute $80 million, land, property, and 60 percent of the value of all church assets annually to the NBEDC. Forman argued that African Americans were entitled to these assets because many white Presbyterians had enslaved African Americans and continued to discriminate against them. Forman claimed that while the church professed Christian brotherly love, its members demonstrated hypocrisy by failing to support desegregation or welcome blacks into the Presbyterian Church.

Despite the Manifesto's harsh tone, the Presbyterian General Assembly acknowledged the validity of Forman's demand for reparations, yet it struggled to identify the fairness and feasibility of such demands. Committees within the church, including the NBPC, responded with fund-raising proposals to fight poverty and convert used or unused church property into affordable land to be sold to blacks.

Today, the NBPC continues to promote black participation in the Presbyterian Church and it strives to educate black and white church members about black history. Black Presbyterian women, particularly those married to ministers, provide essential services to the NBPC such as conference presentations on the black family, youth, and education.

The NBPC, located in Richmond, Virginia, conducts annual, regional, and chapter meetings for the 65,000 African Americans it represents. Active in 450 congregations, black Presbyterians represent only 2 percent of the United Presbyterian (USA) Church. As with many churches, Presbyterians struggle with declining membership, a limited supply of pastors for black churches, and black ordained female ministers without church assignments.

**FURTHER READINGS**

Payne, Wardell J., ed. *Directory of African American Religious Bodies: A Compendium by the Howard University School of Divinity*, 2d. ed. Washington, D.C.: Howard University Press, 1995.

Smylie, James H. "On Being Presbyterian in the South." *The Christian Century* 87 (1970): 936–940.

Stotts, Jack L. "U.P.U.S.A. Challenged in San Antonio." *Christian Century* 86 (1969): 853–856.

Wilmore, Gayraud S. *Black Presbyterian: The Heritage and the Hope*. Philadelphia: Geneva Press, 1983.

———. "Identity and Integration: Black Presbyterians and Their Allies in the Twentieth Century." In *The Presbyterian Predicament*, ed. Milton Coalter, John M. Mulder, and Louis B. Weeks. Louisville, Kentucky: Westminster/John Know Press, 1990.

*Julie Shipe*

## National Black Sisters' Conference

The National Black Sisters' Conference (NBSC), an organization of black Catholic women, was established in August 1968. The NBSC was the product of the civil rights movement and the rise of black consciousness, which in the same year sparked the formation of the National Black Catholic Clergy Caucus, the National Black Catholic Lay Caucus, and the National Black Catholic Seminarian Association.

In its 1969 position paper, the NBSC pledged to work for the "liberation of black people" by combating both individual and institutional racism. To reach its goal, the NBSC promotes solidarity among African American religious women; advocates studying, speaking, and acting on unjust social conditions; encourages the Roman Catholic Church to address the roots of institutional racism; fosters a positive self-image among African American women through knowledge and appreciation of their own rich heritage; promotes community action; initiates, organizes, and participates in self-help programs in the African American Catholic Church community; and establishes relationships with the National Conference of Catholic Bishops, the Secretariat for African American Catholics, and all national religious women's groups, black Catholic associations, and African American organizations working on behalf of the black community.

The NBSC also seeks to develop more effective ministry, education, and control over African American communities. For this purpose it conducts training seminars for men and women in community organization and development, provides religious education from an African American perspective, and fosters the development of an African American spirituality within the Roman Catholic Church. The NBSC's educational programs include "Educating the Black Child," which conducts workshops for educators of black children and provides them with African American resources; and the "Black Women's Project," which sponsors regional forums to develop a collective sense of heritage, identity, and purpose that reflects the experiences of black Catholic women in the church, and offers programs that support black women exploring a religious vocation.

In 1997, the organization had approximately seven hundred members. The NBSC publishes a newsletter called *Signs of Soul* and "Tell It Like It is," a catechesis booklet written from a black perspective. It meets annually in conjunction with the National Black Catholic Clergy Caucus and the National Black Catholic Seminarian Association and maintains headquarters in Washington, D.C.

**FURTHER READINGS**

Davis, Cyprian, O.S.B. *The History of Black Catholics.* New York: Crossroad, 1991.

Raboteau, Albert J. *A Fire in the Bones: Reflections on African-American Religious History.* Boston: Beacon Press, 1995.

*A. J. Scopino Jr.*

## National Black Women's Health Project

The National Black Women's Health Project (NBWHP), founded by Byllye Avery in 1981, empowers African American women to improve their physical and mental health through education and self-help. The nonprofit group advocates worldwide for better health and health care, especially addressing the particular needs of low-income black women.

The creation of the NBWHP was the product of Avery's involvement in two health-care centers in Gainesville, Florida. In 1974, she and Judith Leavy, Margaret Parrish, and Joan Edelson established the city's Women's Health Center, and in 1978 Avery founded Birthplace, an alternative birthing center. Avery's experiences in Gainesville and her work with college women convinced her of the need to shatter black women's "conspiracy of silence," especially regarding health issues. The U.S. health system of the 1970s did not effectively address African American women's specific health concerns, such as shorter life expectancies than white women; higher maternal and infant mortality rates; higher rates of death from cervical cancer; high teenage pregnancy rates; a high incidence of diabetes, hypertension, and cardiovascular disease; and injuries due to family violence. Some of these alarming statistics resulted from the extreme stress of living in low-income neighborhoods. To confront these issues frankly and constructively, Avery created the Black Women's Health Project (BWHP) in Atlanta as a pilot program of the National Women's Health Network of Washington, D.C., of which Avery was then a board member.

In 1983, the BWHP sponsored the National Conference on Black Women's Health Issues at Atlanta's Spelman College, which was attended by over 1,700 women. The next year the group incorporated as a nonprofit organization, the NBWHP. In the late 1980s, the NBWHP created the Center for Black Women's Wellness in an Atlanta housing project, in cooperation with the Southern Christian Leadership Conference; participated in a cancer-prevention program with the Morehouse School of Medicine and the National Cancer Institute; and established SisteReach, supported in part by the John D. and Catherine T. MacArthur Foundation. Focused on the health and reproductive needs of Third World women, SisteReach promotes intercultural exchange and networking in countries such as Nigeria, Cameroons, Barbados, and Brazil. The NBWHP has continued to sponsor the triennial Health Conference for Women. In 1992, at a walker's rally sponsored by *Prevention* magazine, the organization began its Walking for Wellness program.

The NBWHP asserts that clients should direct healthcare change, in conjunction with providers. The organization emphasizes communication, encourages awareness about health care resources, and works to minimize isolation and foster a sense of control. The NBWHP's motto, Empowerment Through Wellness, is based on a holistic model of health and advocates individual wellness as a means of achieving collective wellness. For this purpose the NBWHP employs self-help groups to facilitate communication and to build self-esteem. Determining their individual and collective health-care needs and learning health management skills, self-help group participants commit to lifestyle changes for prevention and early detection of illnesses. For example, participants learn to diminish hypertension by changing their diets and dealing effectively with stress. The NBWHP offers such groups for health-care providers as well as for clients.

In the policy arena, the NBWHP tries to effect systemwide change, to make the health-care establishment more responsive to the needs of black women. The organization deals mainly with the issues of violence, including sexual abuse and battering; low-birth-weight infants and infant mortality; and early and prolonged motherhood and other areas of reproductive health. The group supports pertinent legislation, such as the Family and Medical Leave Act, and occasionally informs and appears before Congress. For example, the NBWHP testified in the 1990s for access to mammography for lower-income women and other health issues, and supported the overturn of the gag rule on abortion in 1992. The organization also works to modify local policy, occasionally in partnership with public health programs. In New York City in 1989–1990, the NBWHP self-help group discussions sparked the formation of a citywide coalition—Women Against Violence Everywhere (WAVE).

The NBWHP has published the "Self-Help Group Development Manual" (1987); issues the quarterly newspaper *Vital Signs*, health fact sheets, and brochures; maintains a database and library; offers a toll-free telephone service to answer health questions (800-ASK-BWHP); and supports a speakers' bureau. In 1987 the NBWHP produced the documentary film *On Becoming a Woman* to

promote effective mother-daughter communication about puberty and sexuality, and developed an accompanying workshop.

National recognition of founder Byllye Avery demonstrates the importance of the NBWHP's unique approach. In July 1989, Avery personally received one of twenty-nine "genius" prizes awarded that year by the John D. and Catherine T. MacArthur Foundation. Later the same year, Essence Communications, Inc., publisher of the national magazine *Essence*, named Avery one of seven outstanding black women in the country. And in 1994, she received the Lienhard Award for efforts to improve women's health care.

With two thousand members, NBWHP maintains 175 self-help groups in twenty-six states and in Nigeria, Barbados, and Belize, and has offices in U.S. cities such as New York, Philadelphia, Pennsylvania, and Oakland, California. The national office moved to Washington, D.C., from Atlanta in 1996. In 1997, Avery held the office of NBWHP founding president, and Julia Scott served as executive director. Membership dues—both individual and organizational—contributions, and foundation grants support the organization.

**FURTHER READINGS**

Avery, Byllye Y. "Breathing Life into Ourselves: The Evolution of the National Black Women's Health Project." In *The Black Women's Health Book: Speaking for Ourselves*, ed. Evelyn C. White. Seattle: Seal Press, 1990, 4–11.

Bricklin, Mark. "Change Your Life With a Walk." *Prevention* 47, 5 (May 1995): 15.

Kashof, Ziba. "The Mammography Matter." *Essence* 28, 1 (May 1997): 45.

Naylor, Gloria. "Power: Rx for Good Health; Byllye Avery's Battle Cry for Black Women Is 'Sister, I'm Here to Support You.'" *Ms* 14 (May 1986): 56–59.

Wilkinson Meyer, Jimmy E. "National Black Women's Health Project." *U.S. Women's Interest Groups*. Westport, Conn.: Greenwood Press, 1995, 319–322.

*Jimmy Elaine Wilkinson Meyer*

## National Black Women's Political Leadership Caucus

The National Black Women's Political Leadership Caucus, a nonprofit group founded on December 4, 1971, promotes greater political participation of black women on local, state, and national levels. Through training, communication, and networking, the caucus strives to increase black women's awareness of political and economic issues and seeks to empower those women to act.

In fall 1971, Nelis James Saunders, Michigan state representative (1969–1972), gathered a group of black women leaders to discuss the creation of an organization to educate black women in the mechanics of the political system. Those present included Florine James, president of the Ohio Federation of Democratic Women; C. DeLores Tucker, Pennsylvania Secretary of State; Elizabeth Duncan Koontz, the director of the U.S. Department of Labor Women's Bureau; Hildagadais Boswell, Maryland state representative; Aileen Hernandez of California, a housing expert and former president of the National Organization for Women; and Verda Freeman Welcome, Maryland's first black and first woman state senator. These women and other supporters created a group, first called the National Black Women's Political Caucus. But the name was soon changed to the present one. Thirty-three individuals from eighteen states attended the organizational meeting, while people from fifteen other states expressed an interest. In January 1972, one hundred people from thirty-three states participated in the first Executive Council meeting of the caucus in Washington, D.C.

The caucus was the product of anger and frustration about having little voice in U.S. politics, even after passage of the Civil Rights Act of 1964. The founders realized the need for leadership training for public service, and through education and voter registration sought to raise the political participation of black women from all economic levels.

The caucus sponsored a four-day conference in December 1978 in Birmingham, Alabama. Directed by Juanita Kennedy-Morgan, then national executive secretary and convention coordinator for the caucus, the event spawned eighteen resolutions. The caucus called for the revitalization of black culture, the reorganization of the African American community, and federal, specifically presidential, attention to the needs of people of color. The caucus then suffered a period of inactivity until 1981. Restructured that year, the group appointed Kennedy-Morgan as organizational director and Velma McEwen-Strode of Ohio as national chairperson. Strode soon left to direct the U.S. Labor Department Equal Employment Opportunity Office, and attorney Ruth Harvey-Charity of Virginia was appointed chair.

In 1984, a schism resulted when Congresswoman Shirley Chisholm and caucus founder Tucker created an organization with a similar name, the National Black Women's Political Caucus. After the original caucus petitioned the court, the new group modified its name to National Political Congress of Black Women. Although crippled for a time by the controversy, the caucus emerged from the setback with stronger political goals.

The caucus provides opportunities for advocacy, networking, and consciousness raising, and offers access to policy information as well as representation to government officials. The group aims to increase the number of legislators who are women of color. In 1997, only thirteen of the thirty-seven women who served in Congress were members of a minority group. By arranging meetings with current state and federal legislators, the caucus provides role models for members aspiring to public office. This nonpartisan group actively promotes and participates in registering voters and publishes election tabloids featuring candidates and issues across party lines. In 1997, Juanita Kennedy-Morgan held the position of executive secretary and organizational director while Florence Pendleton of Washington, D.C., served as acting chairperson. The caucus publishes a semiannual *Newsletter*.

**FURTHER READINGS**

National Black Women's Political Leadership Caucus. *Program of Twentieth Legislative Conference, National Black Women's Political Leadership Caucus, May 17, 1991.*

Wilkinson Meyer, Jimmy E. "National Black Women's Political Leadership Caucus." *U.S. Women's Interest Groups.* Westport, Conn.: Greenwood, 1995, 323–325.

*Jimmy Elaine Wilkinson Meyer*

## National Bowling Association

The National Bowling Association (NBA) was founded as the National Negro Bowling Association in Detroit on August 20, 1939. The NBA sought to provide African Americans, who were excluded from the all-white American Bowling Congress (ABC) and the Women's International Bowling Congress (WIBC), with the opportunity to bowl recreationally and competitively, at a time when organized competition was not open to them. In 1944, the organization adopted its current name. Today, the NBA is open to all men and women regardless of race and strives to further the goals of American democracy and "the principles of sportsmanship, fellowship, and friendship."

The first officers of the NBA were Wynston T. Brown, president; L. Huntley, vice president; Richard Benton, secretary; Brownie Cain, treasurer; and Henry Harden, organizer. These founding members hoped to foster black bowling skills and to provide a means for African Americans to participate "actively in the fight for equality in bowling." In 1939, the same year as its founding, the NBA held its first tournament in Cleveland, Ohio, allowing only male bowlers to compete. However, a year later the group included female bowlers.

Many African Americans joined the new group, and as a result of its popularity, the NBA quickly became an integral part of black sporting culture. As membership grew and practice facilities became available as a result of the lessening of racial segregation, there was considerable improvement in the players' performances. The increasing numbers of bowlers and their success added to the strength and political muscle of the NBA. In 1948, for example, the National Committee for Fair Play in Bowling was formed to combat discrimination in the sport. Threatening court action, the group pressured the ABC and the WIBC to amend their constitutions and eliminate their "whites only" qualification in 1950. In the following year, some African American bowlers broke barriers by competing in the formerly all-white ABC national competition in St. Paul, Minnesota.

Since the group's inception, NBA players came primarily from Midwestern and Eastern cities and thus dominated the early tournaments. In 1971, however, Wanda Bruce from Los Angeles won the women's NBA title, and in 1984, the men's winner, Joe Calloway, came from Denver. The Midwestern and Eastern cities drew the bulk of participants until the mid-1980s. African American women found bowling attractive because of the sport's year-round availability and women's increased leisure time after the Second World War. Thus, by the 1950s, bowling had become extremely popular among African American families. During these years, the NBA continued to grow as African Americans flocked to the nation's cities in search of increased economic opportunities and better lives. As a result of this population shift, a growing number of working-class African Americans joined the group, and bowling became further separated from such "upper-class" sports as tennis and golf.

The NBA, headquartered in New York City, is currently one of the largest African American–operated organizations in the nation. It has ninety-one chapters in the United States and Bermuda. Approximately 80 percent of the group's current membership of more than 30,000 adults and 7,500 youth are African American. The group offers programs for all age groups and skill levels. Bowlers can join leagues or compete at the elite

national championship tournaments. Furthermore, the NBA serves as one of the three major governing bodies for amateur bowling in the United States. The organization's publications include the quarterly magazine *The Bowler*, the annual *NBA History Book*, and a newsletter. The current officers of the NBA are Anthony Fikes, president; Cornell M. Jackson, vice president; and Margaret S. Lee, executive secretary/treasurer.

Throughout its history, the NBA has provided a means for African Americans to learn the sport, perfect their skills, and participate in tournaments in an atmosphere of camaraderie and encouragement.

**FURTHER READINGS**

Ashe, Arthur R., Jr. *A Hard Road to Glory: A History of the African-American Athlete Since 1946*, vol. 3. New York: Amistad Press, 1988.

"The Other N.B.A." *Ebony* (December 1994): 102.

*Alexandra Epstein*

## National Brotherhood Workers of America

The National Brotherhood Workers of America (NBWA) was a short-lived federation of African American unions organized in 1919. African American workers representing unions from twelve states and the District of Columbia created the NBWA in response to persistent discrimination by white labor organizations and the conviction that only by establishing their own unions could blacks improve their conditions. Influenced by the success of ethnic organizations such as the Hebrew Trades Union, the NBWA sought to increase the strength and visibility of African Americans in the larger union movement and to promote labor organizing among both skilled and unskilled African American workers.

At the NBWA's founding meeting, delegates elected T. J. Pree as president and R. T. Sims, a former member and organizer of the Industrial Workers of the World, as vice president. A. Philip Randolph, who would one day head the Brotherhood of Sleeping Car Porters, and Chandler Owen were two of the most prominent members of the NBWA's board of directors. Randolph and Owen edited and published the *Messenger*, an independent socialist magazine that in 1919 became the official journal of the NBWA. However, the NBWA's relationship with the *Messenger* and its publishers lasted only about one year. Randolph and Owen left the group following allegations from some NBWA members that the two editors were more interested in personal gain and the promotion of their magazine than in African American labor organizing.

The NBWA achieved its greatest success among the African American shipyard and dockworkers of Newport, Norfolk, and Portsmouth, Virginia, many of whom belonged to American Federation of Labor (AFL) unions. As members of the AFL these workers provided the NBWA with a voice in the councils of the Virginia State Federation of Labor. Not only did NBWA members help select the federation's president, but they also won representation on its executive board.

The NBWA's success lasted only a short time. Pressure from the AFL, competition from the International Longshoremen's Association, and the post–World War I rise in unemployment among African American shipyard and dock workers all contributed to a rapid decline in the NBWA's membership. In one final attempt to survive, the NBWA published a new magazine, *National Brotherhood Worker*, in which it labeled its primary opponent, the AFL, as unfriendly to African American workers. The NBWA's effort to rekindle its earlier appeal failed, and by the end of 1921 the organization had dissolved.

**FURTHER READINGS**

Foner, Philip S. *Organized Labor and the Black Worker, 1619–1981*. New York: Praeger, 1974; rpt., New York: International, 1982.

Spero, Sterling D., and Abram L. Harris. *The Black Worker: The Negro and the Labor Movement*. New York: Columbia University Press, 1931; rpt., New York: Atheneum, 1968.

*Stuart McElderry*

## National Business League

The National Business League (NBL), founded by Booker T. Washington in 1900 as the National Negro Business League (NNBL), was a trade association for a variety of African American business ventures. It advertised and promoted the success of various black businesses, urged African Americans to patronize their racial cohorts, and provided a forum at which black business owners, most of whom were new to traditions of business enterprise, could come together to compare notes and receive advice and encouragement. The league continues to operate but has a much lower profile than earlier in the century.

Although the league was launched by Washington, the founder of Tuskegee Institute and the most eminent black leader at the turn of the century, the idea for a black business league came from his principal ideological enemy, W. E. B. Du Bois. Du Bois, while perusing the 1900 federal census, was struck by the lack of progress African Americans had made commercially and published a short article detailing this in the *Southern Workman*, the

Arkansas Business Men's League, 1905. *Library of Congress*

magazine of Hampton Institute. Washington, on reading the article, determined to rectify the situation. Long convinced that salvation of African Americans would come only by building a separate economy, he believed that the creation of a core of successful black businesses was essential. As a result, in early 1900 he began pushing for an organizational response to the problem.

In May 1900, Washington called on African Americans around the country to collect information on the value and amount of property they owned, which he then published. He asked Du Bois to provide him with a list of black businessmen and called for a meeting of them as soon as possible. The avowed purpose was "to organize what will be known as the National Negro Business League," Washington said, which would be designed "to secure information and inspiration from each other." He further stressed the importance of a national organization, out of which "will grow local business leagues that will tend to improve the Negro as a business factor."

Washington employed a top-down approach to business organization. Whereas many white trade associations were capstones of large-scale, successful business enterprises that linked existing local and state trade associations, the NNBL's mission was to shore up existing small and fragile African American businesses and to foster the creation of local and state business leagues. It was not a confederation of existing local leagues but an ambitious attempt by Washington both to create a sense of national order for black business and to provide encouragement for the creation of more local businesses by African Americans.

The first NNBL convention in Boston in August 1900 brought together a wide variety of black business owners who detailed their achievements in pharmacy, real estate, hairdressing, dressmaking, catering, barbering, undertaking, and newspaper publishing. Washington, unanimously elected president, gave the keynote address, a classic example of boosterism. The Committee on Resolutions outlined the most important goal of the NNBL: the creation of local business leagues. These two concepts—boosterism and facilitating the creation of local black business leagues—remained the principal focus of the NNBL for the next two decades. The annual conventions were largely exercises in boosterism, while Washington and his aide, Emmett J. Scott, encouraged the creation and development of local leagues during the rest of the year.

The NNBL, during its first fifteen years, quite naturally reflected the ideology and approach of Washington. This was both a source of strength and of controversy. Washington not only insisted on the value of economic enterprise but also preached that African Americans had to prove themselves worthy of full citizenship. This, he claimed, they could do best by demonstrating their prowess in business enterprise. These ideas represented Washington's "accommodationist" approach, which was vigorously opposed by Du Bois and other black leaders. Moreover, Washington's promotion of "race businesses" smacked of economic nationalism and tacit approval of segregation, which these same intellectuals strongly opposed. As long as Washington was president of the NNBL, it was a lightning rod for ideological debate.

The growth of the NNBL was most vigorous from 1900 to 1907, when Frederick R. Moore was national organizer. By 1910 there were some 208 chartered organizations affiliated with the NNBL. During the next five years growth was slow, rising to just 278 locals. The national organization was chronically short of cash for operating expenses during these years, since most local chapters did not pay their dues. From 1905 to 1913 much of the NNBL operating capital was supplied by the industrialist and philanthropist Andrew Carnegie. When Carnegie came to America in 1848 at age thirteen with his family from Scotland, he believed that slavery was the one unforgivable sin in an otherwise perfect democracy; therefore, he decided to devote a significant portion of his philanthropy to African American causes. Carnegie funds were largely funneled through Booker T. Washington, who made sure that the NNBL, as one of his vehicles, shared in the largesse. After Washington's death in 1915, the organization floundered. Scott had expected to succeed his mentor, but a power struggle developed within the organization, and C. C. Spaulding of North Carolina Mutual Insurance, who was named secretary-treasurer, became a major power broker in the NNBL. Robert R. Moton, who emerged as head of Tuskegee Institute, became president of the NNBL in the 1920s. Spaulding and Moton were the guiding lights of the organization for several years.

After 1915, the NNBL did not maintain the influence and importance that it had assumed during Washington's years of leadership. Ties with local chapters that he and Scott had so laboriously built began dissolving during the 1920s. What was successfully promoted by Moton and Spaulding, however, was a series of affiliates. The first of these was the National Negro Bankers Association (NNBA), which was first established in 1906. Moribund throughout most of its early existence, it was reestablished under the leadership of Richard R. Wright Sr. in 1924. The purpose of the organization was to promote the founding of new black-owned banks and to safeguard the economic stability of those already in existence. As the decade wore on, this latter goal became more urgent, while the number of black bank failures grew exponentially.

As part of this effort to stabilize black banking, the NNBL under Moton and Spaulding also tried to establish an organization to provide funding for African American businesses on a national basis. The plan fell victim to a power struggle with Scott, however, who had set up his own rival finance organization. The NNBL-sponsored organization, the National Negro Finance Corporation (NNFC), with the charismatic con man Wante Gomez as the driving force, failed spectacularly by the late 1920s. This was due in part to Gomez's fraudulent activities. Yet the NNFC also lacked proper financing, and other officials of the NNBL did not have sufficient grasp of the problems facing black business in the 1920s. The NNFC's failure was a devastating blow to the prestige and influence of the NNBL among African American businesses.

By 1928, the NNBL was largely a paper organization, and Moton was anxious to distance himself from its problems, but he was unable to convince Spaulding to assume control. The NNBL continued to stagnate, while Spaulding founded another affiliated organization in 1921 that was more successful—the National Negro Insurance Association (NNIA). Executives from black-owned insurance firms soon split off from the parent NNBL and began meeting separately with fellow insurance executives. Spaulding was elected president, and the NNIA published its own journal and established courses of study in insurance at African American colleges and universities. After 1925, Spaulding took no active part in the NNIA, but it continued to thrive and grow at its Durham headquarters.

Other affiliates emerged during these years. Although the NNIA represented well the needs of the large African American insurance firms, it did not address issues of interest to the smaller, fraternal insurance organizations. Therefore, in 1929 the Federation of Negro Fraternals was founded. An older affiliate was the National Negro Press Association (NNPA), established in 1909 and run in its early years by Ralph W. Thompson, a close associate of Washington. Functioning not only as a trade association for African American newspapers but also as the voice of the NNBL and of Washington's philosophy, it generated a good deal of controversy. The NNPA distributed most of the pro-Tuskegee, pro-NNBL materials that appeared in African American newspapers, and it

functioned as more of a political weapon than a true trade association. After Henry Boyd assumed control of the organization in 1912, however, he strove to turn it into a trade association and to bring it in line with those policies that governed other NNBL affiliates. The NNPA continued to operate as such throughout the 1920s.

Other NNBL affiliates had a lower profile. One of the earliest affiliates was the National Negro Funeral Director's Association, established in 1907. It always held its meetings in conjunction with the national NNBL meetings and attracted the membership of most of the prominent black funeral home owners in the country; otherwise it maintained low visibility. There was also the National Association of Negro Tailors, Designers and Dressmakers and a myriad of loosely connected groups, such as the Afro-American Film Company of New York City.

One affiliate that assumed increased importance over the years was the Negro Retail Merchants Association, formed in 1914. As the tide of discrimination and segregation intensified the development of the African American retail sector in the 1920s, this affiliate became the core of the NNBL's crusades that promoted support for African American merchants with its "Buy Black" campaigns. There were several campaigns of this type during the 1920s and 1930s, but the most significant was staged during the Great Depression, when the NNBL supported the Colored Merchants Association's attempt to establish a chain of African American grocers to pool the buying power of black merchants and secure the best wholesale prices. The campaign started in Montgomery, Alabama, but reached its peak in New York City's Harlem in the 1930s.

Between 1937 and 1945 the NNBL failed to provide effective leadership to the African American business community. In 1945, with the resignations of Albon Holsey and Frederick Patterson, the nearly century-long affiliation of the NNBL with Tuskegee Institute and the disciples of Washington was finally broken. In 1947, Arthur G. Gaston, a Birmingham business leader, was elected president, and he guided the association through its fiftieth anniversary celebration in 1950.

The decline of the NNBL after the mid-1950s was due to a number of factors. Probably the most significant was the great drive for integration and inclusion in the white mainstream during this period. As a result the idea of a separate national economy fell into disrepute. Similarly, Booker T. Washington's idea that economic success could prove black worth became outmoded. In the late 1960s, when black nationalism asserted itself, many of the leading theorists of the movement were anticapitalist, making any kind of business program anathema. Others, although willing to accept the reality of capitalism, believed that small business was retrograde and urged African Americans to gain access to large American corporations. Only in the late 1980s and 1990s did the concept of black-owned business gain new acceptance.

Although the NNBL continued to function into the twenty-first-century, it became more of a symbolic organization most notable for the awards it has given to prominent African American business leaders, but even this became sporadic. This did not reflect a lack of qualified candidates but rather a lack of direction and leadership for the league in its later years.

**FURTHER READINGS**

Burroughs, John Howard. "The Necessity of Myth: A History of the National Negro Business League, 1900–1945." Ph. D. diss., Auburn University, 1977.

Harlan, Louis R. "Booker T. Washington and the National Negro Business League." In *Seven on Black: Reflections on the Negro Experience in America*, eds. William B. Slade and Roy C. Herrenkohl. New York: Lippincott, 1969.

———. *Booker T. Washington: The Wizard of Tuskegee, 1901–1915*. New York: Oxford University Press, 1983.

Lee, J. R. E. "The Negro National Business League." *Voice of the Negro* (August 1904): 327–331.

Washington, Booker T. *The Story of My Life and Work: An Autobiography*. Naperville, Ill.: J. L. Nichols, 1901.

*John N. Ingham*

# National Citizens' Rights Association

The National Citizens' Rights Association (NCRA) was formed in 1891, at a time when racial violence reached epidemic proportions and African Americans lost most of the political and economic gains they had made during Reconstruction. The NCRA's goals were to create a large national organization with one million members, collect and publicize information about black oppression, lobby for legislation designed to alleviate black political and economic oppression, and eliminate segregation through the judicial system. The NCRA's white founder and provisional president, Albion W. Tourgee, envisioned an interracial organization composed with a two-thirds white membership from the North. Tourgee, a native of Williamsfield, Ohio, had attended Western Reserve College, fought for the Union during the Civil War, and,

after he was wounded in 1864, moved to North Carolina, where he became a journalist and literary writer advocating black rights and suffrage. Between 1881 and 1897 Tourgee "was the most militant, vocal, persistent, and widely heard advocate of Negro equality in the United States, White or Black" (Olsen, 184). Tourgee's forcefulness and energy made him the most dominant figure in the growth and evolution of the NCRA. By 1892, he claimed that the NCRA had two hundred thousand members. This figure was likely inflated, however, considering that the NCRA's staff consisted of only Tourgee and an executive committee composed of an unspecified number of members. As president, Tourgee monitored the executive commmittee, which apparently did not play an active role in formulating NCRA policies. The NCRA's publication output was minimal, given Tourgee's journalistic and literary expertise. The organization advanced its philosophy in only one pamphlet and several circulars.

Seeking allies among other organizations, the NCRA presented memorials to several church conventions and the National Republican Convention of 1892. In the same year, NCRA members secured the adoption of a "Militant Resolution" by the General Conference of the Methodist Episcopal Church. The resolution denounced black oppression and segregation while calling on the government, churches, and newspapers to search for remedies.

The NCRA attempted to attack legal segregation in the South, particularly Louisiana's law that required blacks to travel in Jim Crow cars. The NCRA's efforts resulted in the 1896 *Plessy v. Ferguson* case, in which the Supreme Court acknowledged the constitutionality of segregation. By the time the Court handed down its decision, however, the NCRA had ceased to exist. Nevertheless, Tourgee's legal brief apparently influenced Justice John Marshall Harlan's dissenting vote, which provided a basis for future challenges that resulted in the 1954 *Brown* decision. While the NCRA did not succeed in ending segregation in intrastate transportation, the organization was able to free Dudley Stuard, one of its black members jailed in Mississippi while attempting to organize for Tourgee.

The NCRA ceased to function as a formal organization in 1895. Yet Tourgee continued to address civil rights issues using the NCRA's name, even after its membership base eroded. Several factors contributed to the demise of the organization. Tourgee lacked the financial resources to maintain a national organization with such sweeping goals. Moreover, his busy schedule left him with little time to manage the NCRA's day-to-day operations, and his autocratic rule may have alienated many supporters. In addition, the organization's failure to attract supporters in the Northeast or among northern blacks, who may have been skeptical of Tourgee's mandatory two-thirds white membership requirement, weakened the NCRA's appeal. Finally, the NCRA's demise coincided with Booker T. Washington's rise to fame and his advocacy of racial accommodationism, which stifled any discourse about civil, political, and economic justice for African Americans.

**FURTHER READINGS**

Gross, Theodore L. *Albion W. Tourgee.* New York: Twayne, 1963.

Olson, Otto H. "Albion W. Tourgee and Negro Militants of the 1890's." *Science and Society,* 28, 2 (Spring 1964): 183–207.

———. *Carpetbagger's Crusade: The Life of Albion Winegar Tourgee.* Baltimore: Johns Hopkins University Press, 1965.

*Andrew Smallwood*

## National Civil Rights Committee of the American Veterans Committee

Created in 1947 by black and white veterans of the American Veterans Committee (AVC), the National Civil Rights Committee (NCRC) emerged from the AVC's progressive platform that denounced racial and class discrimination following World War II. Established in spring 1944, the AVC, unlike many contemporary veterans' groups, had welcomed all ex-GIs regardless of race. The AVC had 106,000 members in forty-eight states.

In June 1947, members of the AVC's National Planning Committee, under the leadership of the prominent New York City parole commissioner and executive committee member Grant Reynolds and several noted African American political activists and scholars, such as the National Association for the Advancement of Colored People legal counsel Franklin H. Williams, the Lincoln University historian Ulysses G. Lee, and the Wisconsin Human Relations Committee chairman Theodore W. Coggs, first proposed the creation of the NCRC at a meeting in Chicago. Agreeing that the problem of racial prejudice constituted the direst threat to global and domestic peace, the eighteen-man governing body laid the foundations for a group to promote organizational strategies for social, political, and economic change and appointed Daniel James,

a white AVC rank-in-file member and former correspondent for the *Nation,* as its national chairman. Between 1947 and 1948, the organization attracted the interest of many AVC members who established area civil rights committees in many states throughout the country. Similar to the individuals who occupied cadre positions within the committee, its membership was interracial. In 1948, the antiracist sentiments espoused by the NCRC were translated into action when the committee launched a national campaign to demand improvements in American race relations and to promote a voter education program.

Almost from the beginning of its brief existence, however, the progressive activities of the NCRC were greatly hampered by the widespread reluctance of southern white veterans to embrace the AVC's interracial principles. Furthermore, the coming of the Cold War and the anti-Communist hysteria of the late 1940s contributed greatly to the committee's decline, producing deep political rifts among its leadership and ending in numerous suspensions of area chapters and members. By 1957, the organization had faded into oblivion as its core group of organizers—Coggs, Williams, Reynolds, and others—left to become more actively involved in local civil rights issues.

**FURTHER READINGS**

Bolte, Charles G. *Our Negro Veterans.* New York: Public Affairs Committee, 1947.

Milford, Lewis, and Richard Severo. *The Wages of War: When America's Soldiers Came Home—From Valley Forge to Vietnam.* New York: Simon and Schuster, 1989.

Minott, Rodney G. *Peerless Patriots: Organized Veterans and the Spirit of Americanism.* Washington, D.C.: Public Affairs Press, 1962.

Tyler, Robert L. "The American Veterans Committee: Out of a Hot War and Into the Cold." *American Quarterly* 18, 3 (Fall 1966): 419–436.

*Robert F. Jefferson*

## National Coalition of Black Meeting Planners

The National Coalition of Black Meeting Planners (NCBMP) represents the professional interests of African Americans employed in the meeting planning and convention industry. Founded in 1983 as the National Black Meeting Planners Coalition, the group adopted its current name in the following year. Its membership includes meeting planners working for business, civil rights, church, and fraternal organizations. Associate membership is available to individuals representing hotels, convention bureaus, city governments, and airlines and others working in the meeting and convention community.

The NCBMP is a clearinghouse for information about the meeting planning and convention industry. For this purpose, the NCBMP evaluates the needs of the industry and the participation of minority professionals. Moreover, the coalition seeks to enhance the skills and increase the number of minority professionals working in the hospitality industry. It helps members to prepare for the Certified Meeting Professional (CMP) examination and offers them the opportunity to earn credit toward certification by attending NCBMP conferences. The NCBMP's semiannual conventions, held in April and November, offer training sessions and open forums to discuss critical issues of common concern to meeting planners. Moreover, the gatherings provide minority meeting planners with opportunities for professional networking. In addition, the NCBMP staffs a speakers bureau and awards annual scholarships to minority students majoring in hospitality.

Headquartered in Silver Spring, Maryland, the NCBMP has currently eight hundred members and an annual budget of $250,000. It distributes an annual directory and a quarterly newsletter featuring information about the meeting planning industry, including articles on trends and new technologies as well as profiles of successful minority professionals.

**FURTHER READING**

"National Coalition of Black Meeting Planners." C. A. Fischer and C. A. Schwartz, eds. *Encyclopedia of Associations*, vol. 1, part 1. New York: International Publishing Company, 1995, 310.

*Barbara Buice*

# National Coalition of 100 Black Women

Founded in 1981 by Jewell Jackson McCabe, the National Coalition of 100 Black Women (NCBW) empowers black women through networking, leadership development, and mentoring. The advocacy group, with headquarters in New York City, attempts to increase the visibility and the economic and political leadership of African American women on local, state, and national levels.

The NCBW grew out of the Coalition of 100 Black Women (CBW), a New York City effort begun in 1970. The name represented the counterpoint to another New York group, 100 Black Men. Founders of CBW, political and corporate leaders such as Edna Beach, Cathy Connor,

Evelyn Cunningham, and Corien Davies Drew, met to assess the problems and opportunities facing African American women in the wake of the civil rights and women's movements. In 1977, when McCabe assumed the presidency, CBW included 127 members; by 1981, 890 New York women had joined. That year representatives from fourteen states and the District of Columbia responded to McCabe's call to form a national group— the NCBW—to address the personal and professional needs of black women and facilitate access to mainstream America. By 1997, the NCBW had sixty-three chapters in twenty-four states and the District of Columbia representing more than seven thousand members. Three women have served as the NCBW's presidents: McCabe (1981–1990); Barbara DeBaptiste of Connecticut (1990–1994); and Hattie Dorsey of Georgia. The coalition's sister organization—the NCBW/Community Services Fund, a tax-exempt organization—develops and designs the programs implemented by the NCBW. Shirley Poole has served as executive director of both the NCBW and the fund since 1991; McCabe has served as president of the fund since its founding in 1984 and as chair of the NCBW since 1990.

The NCBW publishes *Statement*, a biannual newsletter; conference proceedings; and biennial reports. It holds biennial conferences that address issues of concern to African American Women and their communities. In celebration of the diversity of black American women and their accomplishments, the NCBW bestows the annual Candace Awards (pronounced CAN-DAY-see, an ancient Ethiopian word meaning "empress" or "queen") on achievers such as the author Maya Angelou and the civil rights activist Rosa Parks. One prize, the Distinguished Service Award, honors both male and female leaders such as *Jet* and *Ebony* magazines publisher John H. Johnson and Coretta Scott King, the wife of slain civil rights leader Martin Luther King Jr.

The coalition attempts to link the organizational, corporate, and political sectors to garner national and local support and increase the visibility and power of black women. It focuses on economic, health, family, employment, education, housing, criminal justice, and urban life issues. In 1991 the NCBW carried out a national dialogue on reproductive health, with funding from the Ford Foundation. Many other organizations participated, including the National Black Women's Health Project. In recent U.S. presidential elections, the NCBW has held local and national voter registration clinics. Occasionally the group testifies in Congress, as in 1991 before Senate hearings on AIDS and women's health. From 1993 to 1994, the NCBW raised funds for the South African Free Election Fund. Corporations often support the NCBW's efforts. In 1992, with the support of the Maybelline cosmetic company, the NCBW began a pilot tutoring and mentoring project, "Literacy and Life Skills Development," in Georgia, Florida, Tennessee, Connecticut, New York, and other locations.

**FURTHER READINGS**

Brozan, Nadine. "Coalition of Black Women Goes National." *New York Times,* October 26, 1981.

McCabe, Jewell Jackson. "Black Women—Meeting Today's Challenges." *Crisis* 90, 6 (June/July 1983): 10–12.

Noel, Pamela. "New Battler for Black Women." *Ebony* 39 (February 1984): 43–44, 48, 60.

Wilkinson Meyer, Jimmy E. "National Coalition of 100 Black Women." In *U.S. Women's Interest Groups.* Westport, Conn.: Greenwood, 1995, 333–336.

*Jimmy Elaine Wilkinson Meyer*

# National Colored Labor Union

*See* Colored National Labor Union.

# National Colored Press Association

*See* Afro-American Press Association.

# National Colored Teachers Association

*See* American Teachers Association.

# National Colored Undertakers Association

*See* National Funeral Directors and Morticians Association.

# National Committee Against Discrimination in Housing

The National Committee Against Discrimination in Housing (NCDH) was founded in 1950 by an alliance of fifteen civil rights and human relations organizations. Throughout the 1950s, 1960s, and 1970s the Washington, D.C.–based NCDH was the leading educational, legal, and legislative force for open housing in America. During the 1950s the NCDH thrived, and by 1960 it had thirty-seven affiliated organizations. In 1990, the year

of the NCDH's demise, the organization boasted seventy-three local affiliates.

The NCDH originated in 1943 when the Metropolitan Life Assurance Company announced plans to build Stuyvesant Town, a massive housing complex to be located on an eighteen-city-block slum site on New York City's Lower East Side. Stuyvesant Town, arranged by Robert Moses, New York's parks chief and master builder, as a tax-exempt, pioneer redevelopment project, rejected federal aid to demonstrate that private enterprise could profitably clear slums and provide moderately priced housing. Stuyvesant Town excluded African Americans from occupancy, and agents steered black home seekers to Metropolitan's Riverton Homes project in Harlem. Stuyvesant Town's "Whites Only" stricture unleashed torrential protest and led to the formation of the New York State Committee Against Discrimination in Housing, which fought the exclusion of African American residents in the courts. In *Dorsey v. Stuyvesant Town* (July 19, 1949), the New York State Supreme Court ruled that tax-exempt projects could not discriminate. The decision attracted national attention, and in 1950 fifteen organizations whose concern for racial equality and fair housing had embroiled them in the Stuyvesant case joined to create the NCDH. Among the fifteen organizations were the American Civil Liberties Union, American Friends Service Committee, American Jewish Committee, American Jewish Congress, Anti-Defamation League of B'nai B'rith, Congress of Industrial Organizations, NAACP, and National Council of Churches of Christ.

From the outset the NCDH's goal was to establish nondiscrimination and nonsegregation as the rule in American housing. While its open-housing agenda involved a broad program of research, education, and consultation, the NCDH also focused on convincing federal agencies such as the Housing and Home Finance Administration and the Public Housing Administration to abandon discrimination and segregation in government-subsidized and -owned housing. In the 1950s the NCDH urged the Housing and Home Finance Administration to compel builders who received federal funds to state their preference for open housing. When William Levitt, the builder of giant Federal Housing Administration and Veterans Administration mortgage-insured suburbs, excluded African Americans from his "Levittowns," it was the NCDH that challenged him in court. In 1960, after eight years of litigation, Levitt grimly capitulated.

In 1960 the NCDH elected the esteemed federal housing expert, author, and future cabinet secretary Robert C.

Weaver as its president. Under Weaver's leadership the NCDH pressured President John F. Kennedy to sign Executive Order 11063, which abolished discrimination in federally subsidized housing in 1962. In the mid-1960s funding from the Ford Foundation and the U.S. Department of Housing and Urban Development (HUD) propelled the NCDH's budget to over $200,000. At the same time the committee's key publications such as *Trends in Housing* and the *Fair Housing Handbook* spurred the growth of local fair-housing groups across America. The NCDH also continued to lobby President Lyndon B. Johnson to extend the fair-housing order to private as well as public developments. The NCDH achieved its goal in 1968 with the adoption of the Fair Housing Act. Following the passage of that act, the NCDH opened dozens of local chapters throughout the nation to take advantage of the new law enforcing open housing.

During the 1950s and early 1960s the NCDH emphasized educational activities, using its *Fair Housing Handbook* and *Trends in Housing*, the committee's official record of progress in the fair-housing field, to goad federal and state agencies to enforce the law against housing discrimination. Between 1964 and 1970 the NCDH also sponsored twelve conferences in such cities as Chicago; Berkeley, California; Denver; Rochester, New York; and West Point, New York, to promote expanding housing opportunities for minorities. At the same time the NCDH linked fair housing to President Johnson's Great Society program, opening fair housing centers in hundreds of urban Anti-Poverty Program offices.

The NCDH's success in winning congressional approval of the 1968 Fair Housing Act, coupled with the publication in the same year of the Report of the National Advisory Commission on Civil Disorders (Kerner Commission), convinced the organization to shift its focus from cities to suburbs. A year earlier the NCDH had pioneered the "housing audit," a mechanism for surveying housing availability for minorities by employing pairs of prospective home buyers, one white and one black, to test the racial candor and, therefore, effectiveness of the suburban housing market. The NCDH unveiled survey findings in widely publicized forums. St. Louis hosted the first audit in 1969; thereafter the audit became a trademark of the NCDH's assault on fortress suburbia and an acceptable method for proving housing discrimination in court.

The NCDH's audit tactic complemented its legal barrage against discriminatory suburban zoning. During the mid-1970s the organization marshaled hundreds of class-action lawsuits against lily-white suburbia, including a celebrated 1974 lawsuit against twenty-three suburbs in Middlesex County, New Jersey. Despite such activity, the Washington, D.C.–based NCDH resided well within the capital establishment, and by the 1970s had lost the élan that drove it in the 1950s and early 1960s. Between 1971 and 1972 trouble plagued the organization as HUD and the Ford Foundation suspended financial support at the very moment a rival organization, National Neighbors, rose to challenge the NCDH's dominance. The Ford Foundation and HUD resumed funding after 1972, and the NCDH regained enough momentum to spearhead the protest against President Richard Nixon's 1974 moratorium on federal housing expenditures. However, in 1987 the NCDH again lost its HUD and Ford funding. By 1990 the NCDH faced bankruptcy and yielded its position in the open-housing arena to such organizations as National Neighbors and the National Fair Housing Alliance, the latter a successor organization.

Between 1950 and 1990 the NCDH mobilized liberal moral outrage against housing discrimination and strode the legal battlefield on behalf of open housing. The organization pioneered acclaimed antidiscrimination strategies such as the "housing audit" and won key housing victories over William Levitt in Pennsylvania as well as over New Jersey's real estate establishment. But as an established fair-housing bureaucracy composed of lawyers and housing experts, the NCDH lacked the verve and vitality to challenge the monolithic front put up by the real estate, banking, and housing industries that undergirded America's deeply embedded pattern of racial segregation. In *American Apartheid: Segregation and the Making of the Underclass*, Douglas Massey and Nancy Denton convincingly showed that despite manuals, fair-housing laws, audits, and litigation, the NCDH and similar organizations enjoyed only limited success in the open-housing field. Well into the 1990s, housing discrimination and segregation persisted.

**FURTHER READINGS**

Danielson, Michael N. *The Politics of Exclusion.* New York: Columbia University Press, 1976.

Graham, Hugh Davis. *The Civil Rights Era: Origins and Development of National Policy, 1960–1972.* New York: Oxford University Press, 1990.

Massey, Douglas, and Nancy Denton. *American Apartheid: Segregation and the Making of the Underclass.* Cambridge, Mass.: Harvard University Press, 1993.

Saltman, Juliet. *Open Housing: Dynamics of a Social Movement.* New York: Praeger, 1978.

———. *A Fragile Movement: The Struggle for Neighborhood Stabilization.* New York: Greenwood Press, 1990.

*John F. Bauman*

## National Committee for Fair Play in Bowling

*See* National Bowling Association.

## National Committee of Black Churchmen

*See* National Conference of Black Churchmen.

## National Committee of Negro Churchmen

*See* National Conference of Black Churchmen.

## National Committee of Negro Veteran Relief

African American soldiers, demanding medical care for disabled black veterans and employment opportunities for black professional medical personnel as a reward for their wartime services, founded the National Committee of Negro Veteran Relief (NCNVR) in the immediate aftermath of World War I. The federal government's decision to provide medical care for veterans was of particular importance to the estimated 385,000 African American troops who had served in the war. Most of the black soldiers lacked access to adequate health care facilities because public hospitals, particularly in the South, often refused to treat black veterans or provided only limited care.

In March 1921, Secretary of the Treasury Andrew W. Mellon appointed the Consultants on Hospitals, a committee of medical experts who were to advise him on the creation of a national veterans hospital system. Organized and financed by the federal government, these hospitals were to serve veterans with service-related diseases and injuries. While initial plans did not provide for the creation of segregated hospital facilities, the Consultants claimed that there was an "imperative demand for some separate provision in the South for the Negro soldier." Thus, in 1923, William Charles White, who chaired the Consultants, recommended the creation of a separate national hospital for black veterans in Tuskegee, Alabama.

The NCNVR opposed the construction of an African American veterans hospital in the South, claiming that it reinforced segregation. Moreover, the NCNVR feared that black men hospitalized in the North would be forced to transfer to Tuskegee, where they would be exposed to heightened racism. Finally, the NCNVR challenged the Tuskegee location because it was not near a recognized black medical school. Instead, NCNVR members urged that an all-black veterans hospital be built in Washington, D.C., in close proximity to Howard University's Medical School.

White, however, remained adamant, maintaining that the Tuskegee Veterans Hospital would provide southern black veterans with access to medical care. He vigorously defended the Consultants' decision, explaining that black veterans in the South had encountered great difficulties both in gaining admission to public hospitals and receiving adequate health care. While White supported the creation of a national black veterans hospital at Tuskegee, he reassured the NCNVR that black veterans hospitalized in the North would not be transferred to Tuskegee. White expressed hopes that the doors of veterans hospitals in the North would remain open to African Americans, yet he pointed out that his committee had no control over local hospital administrations, which set their own admissions policy. He further pointed out that it was "only a matter of administration" that separated black veterans from white ones in the northern facilities. After meeting with White, members of the NCNVR yielded to his decision, claiming that his reasoning had forced them to reconsider their stance. Unable to prevent the creation of a segregated veterans hospital, the NCNVR insisted that the hospital at least be staffed by African Americans. The group, however, also failed to achieve its second goal.

On February 12, 1923, Tuskegee's U.S. Veterans Hospital # 91 opened with an all-white staff, under the leadership of superintendent Colonel Robert H. Stanley. On June 15, 1923, the hospital started to admit the first group of black veterans. President of Tuskegee Institute Robert R. Moton continued to demand that the Veterans Hospital employ black medical professionals and lodged a protest with President Warren G. Harding. Despite opposition from the Ku Klux Klan, which staged protest marches to prevent the employment of black medical personnel, Moton's efforts were successful. By July 7, 1924, Tuskegee's Veterans Hospital operated with an all-black staff under the leadership of Colonel Joseph Henry Ward, the hospital's first black commanding officer.

**FURTHER READINGS**

Daniel, Pete. "Black Power in the 1920s: The Case of the Tuskegee Veterans Hospital." *Journal of Southern History* 36 (August 1970): 368–388.

Gamble, Vanessa Northington. *Making a Place for Ourselves: The Black Hospital Movement, 1920–1945.* New York: Oxford University, 1995.

Jakeman, Robert J. *The Divided Skies: Establishing Segregated Flight Training at Tuskegee, Alabama, 1934–1942.* Tuscaloosa: University of Alabama Press, 1992.

Rice, Mitchell F., and Woodrow Jones Jr. *Public Policy and the Black Hospital: From Slavery to Segregation to Integration.* Westport, Conn.: Greenwood Press, 1994.

Stevens, Rosemary. *In Sickness and in Wealth: American Hospitals in the Twentieth Century.* New York: Basic Books, 1989.

*David MacLaren*

# National Committee on Segregation in the Nation's Capital

Organized on October 14, 1946, the National Committee on Segregation in the Nation's Capital (NCSNC) exposed segregation in Washington, D.C., in an attempt to improve the living and working conditions of African Americans and to ameliorate race relations. Among the NCSNC's ninety-eight black and white founding members were top legislators and community leaders, including the liberal Democratic senator from Minnesota Hubert H. Humphrey and the former First Lady Eleanor Roosevelt.

In April 1946, the civil rights lawyer Charles Houston called a preliminary meeting to discuss segregation in Washington, D.C. Of primary concern were the implications that inequality in the nation's capital had for America's moral leadership in world politics during the Cold War. At the NCSNC's organizational meeting in October 1946, attendees gathered at the Washington, D.C., Young Women's Christian Association, elected Donald R. Young chairman, and proposed a study examining segregation in the nation's capital. George Schuster, the president of Hunter College, was later elected permanent national chairman of the NCSNC.

Administrators for the Julius Rosenwald Fund in Chicago were instrumental in gathering support for the NCSNC study. In the early stages, Rosenwald Fund president Edwin Embree and race relations directors Will Alexander and Charles Johnson worked extensively with Walter White, secretary of the National Association for the Advancement of Colored People. A research subcommittee conducted the official investigation of the causes and effects of segregation in the capital. The findings, published in 1949, generated widespread interest. Segregation, the study found, contributed to black poverty and had adverse effects on the housing conditions, quality of health care and education, and morale of African Americans. Moreover, the study concluded that segregation in the nation's capital had an adverse effect on U.S. foreign policy efforts as nonwhite foreign visitors and diplomats frequently became the victims of racial discrimination and segregation. The NCSNC condensed its study and distributed over twenty-five thousand copies of a booklet based on the report. In October 1949, the Psychological Study of Social Issues awarded the committee the Edward L. Bernays Intergroup Relations Award for Action-Research for its report.

Committee activity continued until 1952, when NCSNC members issued a final summary of their progress toward integration. The NCSNC report not only publicized the group's activities and achievements but also made the public aware of a set of antidiscrimination laws that had been passed in 1872 and 1873. Banning discrimination in restaurants and bars in the nation's capital, these laws had slipped into obscurity at the end of Reconstruction. The NCSNC's 1952 report resurrected the laws and in a subsequent ruling the District of Columbia Municipal Court of Appeals upheld them.

The NCSNC was significant because it called attention to segregation in the nation's capital and the negative impact of racial discrimination on African American residents as well as U.S. international relations.

**FURTHER READINGS**

Landis, Kenesaw M. *Segregation in Washington: A Report of the National Committee on Segregation in the Nation's Capital.* Chicago: National Committee on Segregation in the Nation's Capital, 1948.

Meier, August, and John Bracey, eds. "National Committee on Segregation in the Nation's Capital." *Papers of the National Association for the Advancement of Colored People.* Part 15, Series A, Reel 9; Part 15, Series B, Reel 8. Bethesda, Md.: University Publications of America, 1993.

*Katherine Kuntz Dill*

## National Committee to Abolish the Poll Tax

Formed in 1938, the interracial National Committee to Abolish the Poll Tax (NCAPT) lobbied for federal legislation to abolish the poll tax as a restrictive measure to voting rights. Established in the late nineteenth century in many southern states, poll taxes were intended to circumvent the Fifteenth Amendment, which granted blacks the right to vote. The NCAPT was mainly the brainchild of white southern liberals, including among its founding members Joseph Gelders, a professor at the University of Alabama, and Virginia Foster Durr, a civil rights activist. Durr served as vice chair for most of the committee's existence, while Jennings Perry, the white editor of the Nashville *Tennessean*, was the chair. The committee enjoyed the support of many influential individuals such as the black civil rights lawyer Thurgood Marshall and First Lady Eleanor Roosevelt. California congressman Lee Geyer, a founding member of the organization, sponsored bills and recruited congressional support for abolition of the poll tax.

By 1939, a few southern states had repealed or abolished the poll tax; however, Alabama, Arkansas, Georgia, Mississippi, South Carolina, Tennessee, Texas, and Virginia still imposed annual poll taxes ranging from one to twenty-five dollars, to prevent African Americans and poor whites from voting. The poll tax was but one of several devices employed by the white power structure to restrict voting rights. Other methods included property ownership and residency requirements, literacy tests, and intimidation.

The National Association for the Advancement of Colored People (NAACP) had been agitating for a number of years to abolish the poll tax. But the organization had many other issues on its agenda. Those who launched the NCAPT thought that a committee devoted solely to poll tax repeal would be more effective in achieving the goal. Rather than seeking to repeal each state's poll tax, the NCAPT lobbied for federal legislation. Between 1940 and 1948, the committee helped introduce several bills to abolish the poll tax in federal elections in one or both houses of Congress. The bills generally passed in the House of Representatives but were thwarted in the Senate, where opponents argued that only a constitutional amendment could override state election laws. To gain congressional support, the NCAPT organized mass letter-writing campaigns, issued press releases, and held a national conference in Washington, D.C., in March 1943. In addition to lobbying Congress, the NCAPT sought to educate and enlighten the public. For this purpose the committee published a newsletter, the *Poll Tax Repealer*, handbooks, fact sheets, and posters.

Despite its lobbying and public education efforts, the NCAPT failed to overcome congressional opposition, and by the summer of 1948 it ceased to operate, largely owing to lack of funding. While the NCAPT did not achieve its goal, it helped raise national awareness of voting discrimination, which became a target of civil rights activists in subsequent years. It was not until passage of the Twenty-fourth Amendment to the U.S. Constitution in August 1964 that state poll taxes were abolished.

### FURTHER READINGS

Durr, Virginia Foster. *Outside the Magic Circle: The Autobiography of Virginia Foster Durr*. Tuscaloosa: University of Alabama Press, 1985.

Lawson, Steven F. *Black Ballots: Voting Rights in the South, 1944–1969*. New York: Columbia University Press, 1976.

Ogden, Frederic D. *The Poll Tax in the South*. Tuscaloosa: University of Alabama Press, 1958.

*Papers of the National Association for the Advancement of Colored People*, part 4, *Voting Rights Campaign, 1916–1950*. August Meier and John H. Bracey Jr., eds. Frederick, Md.: University Publications of America, 1986.

Sullivan, Patricia. *Days of Hope: Race and Democracy in the New Deal Era*. Chapel Hill: University of North Carolina Press, 1996.

*Virginia M. Matthews*

## National Conference of Black Christians

*See* National Conference of Black Churchmen.

## National Conference of Black Churchmen

In 1966, the National Conference of Black Churchmen (NCBC) was founded as the National Committee of Negro Churchmen. In the following year the group became the National Committee of Black Churchmen, and in 1972 it adopted its current name. In the late 1970s, there was a movement to adopt the more inclusive name National Conference of Black Christians, because both women and men were active in the organization, but attempts to change the group's name failed. The NCBC, headquartered in Atlanta, was an interdenominational group that promoted Black Power and encouraged the influence of the movement on African American communities across the country.

While the NCBC, led by ministers such as Albert B. Cleage, was one of several interdenominational organizations that emerged in the later 1960s, the organization distinguished itself through bold public statements. On July 31, 1966, the group published a full-page advertisement in the *New York Times* demanding power, freedom, and justice from the leaders of America, the nation's white churches, and the media. On November 3, 1966, the group issued another statement at the Statue of Liberty in New York City, which was published three days later as "Racism and the Elections: The American Dilemma of 1966" in the *New York Times*. In this statement the group called for full manhood rights for African Americans and for public recognition of the truth of the African American experience. In the same year, the NCBC issued its statement "The Powell Affair—A Crisis of Morals and Faith," which challenged the decision of the U.S. Congress to exclude Adam Clayton Powell, an African American representative from New York accused of receiving checks designated for members of his staff. The NCBC argued that Congress had refused to seat Powell because he had gained an unacceptable level of power for a black man.

In November 1967, the NCBC held its first annual convention in Dallas, Texas, where it elected officers, created committees, and established annual conventions. On April 5, 1968, the NCBC's Board of Directors met in Chicago and issued a statement urging white churches to seek the advice of black churches to determine the allocation of resources for urban areas and to stimulate interest in race relations. In the following year, the NCBC once again challenged America's white churches when its Board of Directors supported James Forman's controversial "Black Manifesto." Forman, an outspoken civil rights activist, had issued a statement highly critical of white churches, insisting that they pay reparations to black Americans for their historical role in the subjugation of African Americans. On May 7, 1969, the NCBC's Board of Directors decided to support Forman's demand for reparations. Moreover, the board stated that the NCBC would play a central role in the process of interpreting the theological implications of the "Black Manifesto." In the same month, the NCBC launched a dialogue with African theologians. In September 1969, NCBC representatives attended the All-Africa Conference of Churches in Abidjan, Ivory Coast. A series of meetings between the NCBC and African church representatives following this conference led to the creation of a Pan-African Skills Project, which recruited African Americans to aid African countries.

On June 13, 1969, the NCBC issued a statement, drafted by the Committee on Theological Prospectus at the Interdenominational Theological Center in Atlanta, that defined Black Theology as a theology of black liberation. The NCBC adopted the statement later that year at its annual convocation in Oakland, California. The NCBC issued several more public statements including a Black Declaration of Independence on July 4, 1970.

While the late 1960s witnessed the creation of a number of black interdenominational organizations, the NCBC was distinctive because of its public proclamations that sought to influence the political discussions regarding the African American experience.

### FURTHER READINGS

Watts, Leon W., II. "The National Committee of Black Churchmen." *Christianity and Crisis* 30 (1970): 237–243.

Wilmore, Gayraud S. *Black Theology: A Documentary History, 1966–1979.* New York: Orbis, 1979.

*Julius H. Bailey*

## National Conference of Black Lawyers

The National Conference of Black Lawyers (NCBL), a progressive organization of lawyers, law professors, legal workers, and jailhouse lawyers, was founded in Virginia in 1968. Though at its height it may not have had more than two thousand members, its New York City headquarters was a beehive of activity as the organization came to play a prominent role in defense of the Black Panther Party, Angela Davis (an essayist who worked with the Student Nonviolent Coordinating Committee and the Black Panthers and joined the Communist Party in 1968), the Attica defendants (charged in connection with the 1971 seizure of control of the Attica State Prison in New York by approximately 1,200 black and Latino prisoners who demanded improvements in living conditions), and other prominent legal cases of the late twentieth century.

The moving spirit and first national director of the NCBL was W. Haywood Burns. A graduate of Harvard and Yale law schools, Burns initially came to prominence as a lawyer for the Southern Christian Leadership Conference (SCLC) during its attempt to establish Resurrection

City—a tent city of poor and minorities—in Washington, D.C., in 1968. This experience convinced him of the need to develop a corps of organized lawyers to defend the interests of those who traditionally lacked legal representation. He felt that the traditional bar—including the oldest and largest organization of this type among African Americans, the National Bar Association—was not capable of fulfilling this important task, hence the need for the NCBL.

Those who agreed with him included Margaret Burnham, a graduate of Tougaloo College in Mississippi and the law school at the University of Pennsylvania, who later became a judge in Boston and a defense attorney for Angela Davis. Subsequently, she worked in the New York City office as national director of the NCBL.

The NCBL was organized in chapters ranging across the country from New York City to Los Angeles. The organization also had members and chapters in the Virgin Islands and Toronto. In addition to working on high-profile cases, chapters also became involved in local activities, for example, defending anti-apartheid protesters, rent strikers, and the like. As their defense of anti-apartheid protesters suggested, the NCBL—unlike many African American organizations—intervened repeatedly in sensitive global questions, including taking pro-Palestinian positions in the 1980s in opposition to the government's pro-Israeli policy.

Born during an era of mass protest, the NCBL's fortunes waned as that era drew to a close. Ultimately, the organization was forced to abandon its Harlem headquarters, and as the 1990s dawned, the once vibrant NCBL maintained no permanent staff and consisted solely of volunteers. Still, its efforts continued to be felt on such important questions as reparations for African Americans, political prisoners (e.g., Geronimo Pratt and Mumia Abu-Jamal), and other matters that traditional organizations often avoided.

**FURTHER READING**

Ginger, Ann Fagan, and Eugene Tobin, eds. *The National Lawyers Guild.* Philadelphia: Temple University Press, 1988.

*Gerald Horne*

## National Conference of Black Policemen

*See* National Black Police Association.

## National Conference of Editorial Writers

The National Conference of Editorial Writers (NCEW), founded in 1947, serves as a central organization to address the needs of black editorial writers in the United States. Individuals who create opinion material for the print and broadcast media, college journalism teachers, and students who prepare editorials for campus newspapers or study journalism are eligible to join the NCEW. The conference merged with the National Broadcast Editorial Association in 1992, and all members can participate fully in the organization, vote at the annual convention, and attend professional workshops. The conference aspires to improve the quality of editorial writing, and in conjunction with the National Association of Black Journalists presents the annual Ida B. Wells award to noteworthy minority authors.

Members also benefit from the NCEW's job bank, meetings, and the quarterly *Masthead,* which distributes information to assist professionals in the field. The NCEW informs members about current national political news sources and offers issue briefings to provide accurate background information for editorial writers to use to form opinions. Collections of editorials are published in volumes entitled *Editorial Excellence.*

Keeping current with technology, the NCEW educates members about how to publish opinion pages on-line. The organization's Internet website and e-mail listserv connects members, alerting them about society news and professional opportunities. The Internet site contains information for members and the public about professional issues, scholarships, fellowships, educational programs, contests, and foreign and domestic travel planned for journalists. The conference's calendar, convention report, and directory of officers and members are also available on-line. A briefing section discusses potential editorial topics and offers editorial exchanges and critiques. Links to other sources including major wire services and members' Internet home pages are also provided on the website.

**FURTHER READING**

*Encyclopedia of Associations*, 33d ed. Detroit: Gale, 1998.

*Elizabeth D. Schafer*

## National Conference of Negro Methodists

*See* Black Methodists for Church Renewal.

## National Conference of Negro Youth

*See* National Council of Negro Youth.

## National Conference on the Problems of the Negro and Negro Youth

*See* National Council of Negro Youth.

## National Congress of Colored Parents and Teachers

The National Congress of Colored Parents and Teachers (NCCPT) was founded by Selena Sloan Butler (ca. 1872–1964) in Atlanta in 1926. The NCCPT was modeled after the National Association for Parents and Teachers (PTA), which had been organized in 1897. The NCCPT addressed the needs of African American children in states that legally mandated segregation, and it worked to improve their health, education, and welfare by linking home and school.

Butler, a woman of African, Native, and European American descent, graduated from Atlanta's Spelman Seminary (later Spelman College) at age sixteen with training in elementary school education. She taught English and speech in Georgia and Florida, married Henry Rutherford Butler, and had one son. When her son was of school age she began her lifelong involvement in community educational pursuits. Since there were no kindergarten facilities in her neighborhood, she established one in her home. When her son began public school, she initiated the first African American parent-teacher association in the country, modeled after the PTA. In 1920 Butler organized the Georgia Congress of Colored Parents and Teachers, and in 1926 she founded the NCCPT with headquarters in her Atlanta home. The NCCPT was composed of twenty southern state organizations.

The NCCPT maintained excellent relations with the PTA through Butler's efforts to coordinate the policies of both organizations. The PTA provided the NCCPT with resource materials, and together they formed a national advisory committee to assure uniform educational standards and objectives. Both organizations drew on their membership to influence legislation designed to improve the lives of children. Their efforts led to many federal, state, and local mandates, including the passage of the Federal Communications Commissions Act of 1934, a federally subsidized school lunch program in 1946, and creation of the Department of Health, Education, and Welfare in 1949. On the state level both organizations fought to provide adequate funding for public schools, and in school districts in forty-six states they launched Summer Round-Up of the Children, a program that provided health checkups between 1925 and 1950.

While the NCCPT and the PTA shared common goals and concerns, the NCCPT endured challenges beyond those it shared with its white counterpart. Facing discrimination and segregation as well as problems of severe poverty, hostility, violence, and economic oppression, the NCCPT fought for equal educational opportunities for black children. The NCCPT set standards for parents and teachers involved in the educational process and pressured school boards to provide literacy and adult education classes, quality textbooks, and safe recreational facilities.

By 1970, widespread school desegregation prompted the NCCPT to merge with the PTA. Because of her pioneering efforts in the NCCPT, the PTA named Butler one of the founders of the national organization.

FURTHER READINGS

"Selena Sloan Butler." In *Black Women in America: An Historical Encyclopedia.* Ed. Darlene Clark Hine. New York: Carlson, 1993.

"The National Congress of Colored Parents and Teachers." *Our Children* 21, 8 (May/June 1996): 16–17.

"The National PTA at 100: A Century of Commitment." *Our Children* 21, 8 (May/June 1996): 10–12.

*Julieanne Phillips*

## National Convention of Colored Newspaper Men

*See* Afro-American Press Association.

## National Council for a Permanent FEPC

The National Council was formed in 1943 to obtain a permanent Fair Employment Practices Committee (FEPC) to replace the wartime FEPC. Proponents of a permanent FEPC realized that its achievement, with adequate funding and authority, required majority acceptance of the principle of federal action to prevent discrimination in employment. The National Council, therefore, planned a campaign to educate the public about the necessity for equal employment opportunity. Further objectives of the National Council were to secure hiring on the basis of skills and experience; to obtain equal wages for the same work; and to secure the right to promotion within an industry regardless of race, creed,

The Girl Friends for the FEPC Fight present a $500 check to Asa Philip Randolph at the office of the Brotherhood of Sleeping Car Porters in New York City. January 7, 1950. *Library of Congress*

color, or national origin. The council's officers sought federal rather than state legislation to come under the constitutional authority of Congress, and they wanted the permanent FEPC to have jurisdiction over industries and unions engaged in interstate commerce as well as agencies of the national government. They anticipated that state legislation to carry the principle into intrastate enterprises would follow.

In response to the threat of A. Philip Randolph, head of the Brotherhood of Sleeping Car Porters (BSCP), to stage a march on Washington in 1941, the Roosevelt administration had agreed to issue executive order no. 8802, creating a wartime FEPC. But since the executive order creating the FEPC was designed to expire with the coming of peace, maintenance of the FEPC after the

war was a necessity if African Americans were not to be thrown out of their bitterly won, higher-status jobs to make room for returning white soldiers.

The idea of starting a movement for a permanent FEPC with strong enforcement powers was born at a Washington Conference to Save FEPC, in February 1943. The National Council for a Permanent FEPC was formally created at a second Conference to Save FEPC, held in September of that year and attended by one hundred delegates, representing fifteen organizations and states, who drew up a budget, drafted a constitution, and discussed the wording of permanent FEPC bills. Randolph and the Reverend Dr. Allan Knight Chalmers of the Broadway Tabernacle Church were elected cochairmen at an early meeting. Randolph, as the functioning chairman, wielded the most power in the National Council; Chalmers merely lent his name.

Since the National Council represented all minority groups, it was founded on an interracial basis and as a federation of civil rights groups. Because passage of permanent legislation would require votes from both Democrats and Republicans, the council endeavored to project a nonpartisan image, as well as rejecting support from the "extreme left wing." Projected as a clearinghouse for all organizational work on behalf of permanent FEPC legislation, the council hoped to avoid duplication of effort and coordinate lobbying activity.

In the beginning the National Council existed primarily on paper, operating out of the one-secretary BSCP office in New York. But Randolph realized the impossibility of conducting a successful lobbying campaign from New York. In January 1944, as soon as the FEPC bill was introduced into the House of Representatives, he took steps to establish a headquarters in Washington, D.C. He appointed Anna Arnold Hedgeman, who had been active in his earlier March on Washington Movement, as executive secretary. In February 1944, the National Council finally opened its Washington office after surmounting the problem of finding quarters for its racially diverse staff in the segregated capital.

Initially, the Washington office worked mainly through the council's cooperating organizations, but the council came to understand it needed to establish its own state and local chapters to apply pressure locally. The Washington staff aided communities in establishing state and local FEPC councils, helped with programming and education, distributed literature, and provided speakers. In theory the local councils were to be interracial, interfaith, and "truly representative of the community." The National Council suggested that a prestigious person in each community be made chairman and emphasized that the FEPC bill was "to be for the protection of all minorities and not just for the Negro." The local chapters were to make contacts with congressmen in their district, urging them to support the permanent FEPC bill. Moreover, they were to send delegations to Washington to secure commitments from individual congressmen to break filibusters and committee logjams. Most important, local chapters were to raise money for the National Council. Yet the National Council displayed contradictory attitudes about the role of the local chapters. It emphasized the importance of local branches but also tried to maintain tight control by setting up its own regional representative system, employing field representatives to do most of the local organizing by the late 1940s.

The drive for permanent legislation formally began at a Washington conference held January 20 and 21, 1944. The supporting groups, which had been broadened to include civic, church, liberal, educational, and even some labor organizations, pledged to work for action by Congress to attack discrimination. They argued that elimination of racism in the United States would provide a symbol to all oppressed peoples of the world. Randolph's plan to use the black vote as a lever in the 1944 elections to press for passage of a permanent FEPC law was thwarted, however, when the House Labor Committee voted to postpone completion of hearings on the bill until after the election. The stalling showed that a majority in the House did not favor the FEPC and was unwilling to face a vote on the issue.

Although President Harry S. Truman refused to meet with black leaders on the subject, he publicly expressed support for permanent FEPC legislation. But efforts to secure the approval of the Seventy-ninth Congress ended unsuccessfully when the bill was holed up in the House Rules Committee. In fall 1945, with the bill stalled in the House, the National Council decided on the unprecedented step of seeking an FEPC vote in the Senate first, but this strategy proved no more effective. Southern Senators subjected the bill to a filibuster, and a cloture vote failed.

After a National Council strategy conference, a Mass Rally to Save FEPC was held at Madison Square Garden in New York City on February 28, 1946. Although the president declined to speak at the rally, Truman indicated that he regarded FEPC as an "integral part" of his "reconversion program" and pledged to continue efforts to bring it before Congress. At the rally, Randolph called for a silent, nonviolent march in Washington if Congress failed to enact the FEPC by June 30, but by that time the National Council was in financial trouble, and the proposed march never materialized.

A congressional victory continued to elude the National Council, but Truman, in an attempt to woo the black vote, issued an executive order providing an FEPC for the federal government in 1948. The strategy worked; African Americans supplied an important component in Truman's unexpected reelection. With a Democratic majority in Congress again, when the president announced his Fair Deal in 1949, both he and civil rights proponents anticipated progress on the permanent FEPC bill, as well as other pro-minority measures. Nevertheless, in early February a Senate filibuster developed, this time over an effort to change cloture rules to make it easier to shut off debate, rather than over the FEPC. Liberals had decided that only by eliminating the filibuster could they get reform legislation past intransigent southern senators. The cloture vote lost by a narrow margin, however, demonstrating once again that neither Democrats nor Republicans had much interest in passing FEPC legislation.

While Randolph was working to get the Senate rules changed to abolish the use of the filibuster as an anti–civil rights weapon, the National Association for the Advancement of Colored People (NAACP) decided that the National Council was inadequate and, in November 1949, formed the National Emergency Civil Rights Mobilization. Although Randolph saw no need for another organization, he believed that passage of a federal FEPC bill was too important to obstruct with internecine strife and agreed to full cooperation. When Congress reconvened in January 1950, the new organization presented a petition for passage of FEPC legislation. Yet the bill failed again, a victim to postponement, in part because the European Recovery Program required quick action. Each time the FEPC bill was brought up between work on other business, it was greeted with a filibuster. By spring the mobilization no longer had illusions of victory. Stating that it considered itself only a temporary organization, it ended its brief life by merging with the National Council.

With the onset of the Korean War in June 1950, and despairing of passage of FEPC legislation, Randolph called on Truman to issue an executive order comparable to Roosevelt's creation of the FEPC in 1941. Still cognizant of the importance of the black vote, the president responded by ordering the creation of a Committee on Government Contract Compliance. Lacking enforcement provisions, and dependent solely on persuasion and conciliation, the order was largely ineffective.

Meanwhile, the National Council's executive committee unanimously approved the suggestion of the labor leader Walter Reuther to establish a committee to work for abolition of the Senate filibuster rule. Another new organization was developed for this purpose—the Leadership Conference on Civil Rights—which took as its slogan ABOLISH RULE 22 IN '52. This campaign also failed, and the FEPC issue lay dormant until the next spurt of civil rights legislative activism late in the decade. Proponents of equal employment opportunity realized there was little chance of government intervention in em-

ployment practices under the new Eisenhower administration. Devoted to free enterprise and against any form of "coercive" federal regulation, including integration of the military, Eisenhower was also aware that civil rights advocates bore the taint of being leftist. In the era of Senator Joseph McCarthy's Communist witch-hunt, champions of liberal causes found themselves vulnerable to accusations of disloyalty while their groups were smeared with charges of Communist domination. Despite their disclaimers and Randolph's anti-Communist credentials, the civil rights cause in general, and the National Council in particular, remained suspect.

During the ten years liberals had pushed for FEPC legislation, the House Rules Committee had never approved a bill for floor debate and a vote, and no FEPC bill had ever come to an actual vote in the Senate. Several factors account for the National Council's lack of success. For one, despite the council's assurance that it was only a temporary organization and would dissolve once its goal was achieved, a struggle for power and prestige developed between the cooperating organizations. In response, Randolph called for a "complete reorganization of the Council" at a board meeting in 1946. Elmer Henderson became executive secretary and the leadership became more representative, with the NAACP playing a larger role and Jewish agencies contributing financial support. Arnold Aronson, of the American Council on Race Relations, was named secretary of the executive committee, and Roy Wilkins, head of the NAACP, chairman. Since both were professional administrators, the council functioned more efficiently under their leadership, but greater efficiency had no noticeable effect on pushing through permanent FEPC legislation.

Inadequate financing was another factor in the National Council's poor showing. There was never enough money to mount an effective legislative campaign. Hedgeman had resigned in the summer of 1946 because of lack of funds to run the organization properly; her successor, Henderson, also complained that lack of financial resources reduced his effectiveness. Furthermore, Randolph's reluctance to share decision-making power with heads of the other groups meant that over time the constituent organizations began to actively contest for control. But after the broadening of leadership in 1946, the National Council still came no closer to its goal. Congress proved more resistant to pressure than the executive branch, and the postwar surplus of industrial labor power made the exclusion of African Americans from jobs seem more desirable than ever to many congressmen. In addition, the Cold War, with its concomitant domestic anti-Communist hysteria, did not provide a congenial atmosphere for reform legislation of any type.

The achievement of the wartime FEPC contributed to a reorientation wherein African Americans began to look first to the federal government, instead of, as formerly, to wealthy white patrons, on matters affecting their welfare. The constant agitation of the National Council helped educate white Americans to the need for greater fairness in hiring practices at the same time that the NAACP's victories in the courts began weakening the wall of legal segregation. The mass migration of African Americans to urban areas gave them political weight that politicians operating on the national level could no longer ignore. Although fair employment legislation would not be achieved until the Civil Rights Act of 1964, the efforts of the National Council, combined with the activities of other black leaders, laid the foundation on which the midcentury civil rights movement would build.

**FURTHER READINGS**

Kesselman, Louis. *The Social Politics of FEPC: A Study in Reform Pressure Movements.* Chapel Hill: University of North Carolina Press, 1948.

Maslow, Will. "FEPC—A Case History in Parliamentary Maneuver." *University of Chicago Law Review* (June 1946): 407–444.

Pfeffer, Paula F. *A. Philip Randolph, Pioneer of the Civil Rights Movement.* Baton Rouge: Louisiana State University Press, 1990.

Ruchames, Louis. *Race, Jobs and Politics: The Story of the FEPC.* New York: Columbia University Press, 1953.

*Paula F. Pfeffer*

## National Council for Black Studies

The National Council for Black Studies (NCBS) was established in 1975 to facilitate the study of the black experience and increase the number and quality of black studies programs and departments at universities and colleges. The NCBS was a response to the tremendous growth of black studies between 1966 and 1972. During those years five hundred universities and colleges established academic departments or programs in black studies. In 1975, Bertha Maxwell, chair of black studies at the University of North Carolina–Charlotte, concerned about this rapid growth, invited black studies scholars and administrators to her campus to discuss the future of black

studies programs. In the same year a follow-up meeting was held at the Educational Testing Service in Princeton, New Jersey. The NCBS grew out of these two meetings.

Those who served as NCBS presidents included Bertha Maxwell (1976–1978), William King (1978–1980), William Nelson (1980–1982), Carlene Young (1982–1984), Delores Aldridge (1985–1988), Selase Williams (1988–1992), and since 1992 William Little. The NCBS established a national office at Indiana University that was managed by Executive Director Joseph Russell. In 1991 the office moved to Ohio State University and Jacqueline Wade was appointed executive director. In 1996 the national office moved to its present site at California State University–Dominguez Hill, and Josiah A. M. Cobbah assumed the office of executive director.

The NCBS provides guidance for black studies programs, helps colleges to recruit black scholars, devises and implements educational programs for elementary, secondary, and postsecondary schools, promotes Afrocentric research, makes information about black life available to the public, serves as a consultant to policymakers, and encourages national and international linkages among scholars studying persons of African descent. In addition, the NCBS holds occasional conferences on curriculum development and in cooperation with the University of Ghana offers an African Language Institute. Finally, the NCBS evaluates black studies programs for colleges and facilitates international development of the discipline by holding meetings outside the United States in such countries as Guyana, Ghana, and South Africa. The NCBS meets annually, though regional and state affiliates may meet more often.

In the 1980s, the NCBS faced a crisis when many universities and colleges eliminated black studies departments by incorporating them into larger administrative units such as ethnic or multicultural studies. The number of black studies departments dropped precipitously as schools eliminated perhaps half the departments established in the 1970s. The NCBS tried to halt and reverse this trend by improving the quality of black studies programs. Between 1993 and 1996 the Ford Foundation provided the NCBS with a $300,000 grant to support the professional development of black studies. The grant provided funding for curriculum development and summer institutes in Accra, Ghana; Morgantown, West Virginia; and Dominguez Hills, California. NCBS summer institutes introduced junior faculty trained in one of the traditional disciplines to black studies and administrative workshops trained new black studies chairpersons. The

NCBS continues to provide support for alumni of these institutes and workshops.

The NCBS's newsletter, *Voice of Black Studies*, contains news from the national office, information on the history of the discipline, and job listings. In 1993, the NCBS began publication of a refereed scholarly journal, *Afrocentric Scholar*. But Afrocentricity has remained controversial among NCBS members. In the late 1980s and early 1990s, many members committed to black studies but unwilling to embrace Afrocentrism left the NCBS. Under the leadership of NCBS William Little, President 1994–1998, the organization compromised. It issued a statement welcoming all those interested in black studies, regardless of theoretical orientation or methodological approach, and renamed its journal *International Journal of Africana Studies*.

The NCBS has issued several publications discussing the discipline, including *Black Scholarship—Black Journals* and the *Organizational Handbook*. In 1995 the NCBS established its own publishing house, with Diedre Badejo serving as editor. Several regional NCBS affiliates also publish newsletters and journals, including the University of Washington's *Afro-Briefs* and the *New England Journal of Black Studies* and *Hantu*, published for the New England region.

**FURTHER READINGS**

Leonard, Carolyn M., and William A. Little. *National Council for Black Studies, Inc.: Organizational Handbook*. Bloomington, Ind.: National Council for Black Studies, 1988.

National Council for Black Studies. *Black Scholarship—Black Journals: Workshop Proceedings, Sixth Annual Conference of the National Council for Black Studies*. Bloomington, Ind.: National Council for Black Studies, 1982.

*Rhett S. Jones*

# National Council of Churches, Commission on Religion and Race

The National Council of the Churches of Christ in the U.S.A. (NCC) established the Commission on Religion and Race (CRR) on June 7, 1963. The CRR played an integral role in the civil rights movement by exerting considerable influence on federal legislation and public opinion through a network of major Protestant churches representing over fifty million members. The NCC, which serves as an umbrella organization for mainline Protestant denominations in the United States, created

the CRR in response to escalating racial confrontations in the South. The NCC (known as the Federated Council of Churches from 1908 to 1950) grew out of liberal Protestants' Progressive-era commitment to the social gospel. In 1921, this interchurch organization created a Department of Race Relations (known as the Department of Racial and Cultural Relations after 1950). The predominantly white organization believed that the sin of racism, particularly directed against African Americans, corrupted its work for a just society. Despite its antiracist position, the NCC upheld the racial status quo through the 1950s by restricting its efforts to nonpolitical, abstract denouncements of social evils.

The dramatic civil rights clashes of the late 1950s and early 1960s compelled the NCC leadership in New York City to reassess its tactics and take direct action. Particularly, Martin Luther King Jr.'s "Letter from the Birmingham Jail" sharply questioned the efficacy of liberal Protestant strategies, which avoided politics by conducting nonconfrontational, educational campaigns against racism. In response to recent events in the South, and anticipating violence in the North, the NCC created the CRR on June 7, 1963. The special body possessed emergency status, was well funded, and reported directly to the NCC board of directors. Robert W. Spike, a white United Church of Christ minister, became its first executive director.

Almost immediately, Spike and his staff reached out to the major civil rights organizations. The CRR played an important role in securing participation of forty thousand white Protestants in the August 28, 1963, civil rights March on Washington, D.C. Although not involved in most key arrangements, Spike and the commission chairman Eugene Carson Blake worked to integrate the previously all-black march. In addition, Blake helped persuade John Lewis of the Student Nonviolent Coordinating Committee (SNCC) to modify passages of his speech ridiculing the Kennedy administration's proposed civil rights bill. In summer 1964, the commission trained over eight hundred, mostly white, volunteers to teach "freedom schools" in Mississippi. Throughout "Freedom Summer," the NCC supported voter registration, raised bail money for jailed civil rights workers, and organized community centers. In September 1964, the NCC founded the Delta Ministry as a separate administrative body committed to long-range social and economic change in the region. The commission also lobbied for civil rights legislation in Congress, enlisting support, especially among Midwestern Republicans, for passage of the Civil Rights Act of 1964. The next year, the commission worked with the Johnson administration to enact the Voting Rights Act of 1965.

In December 1965, Executive Director Spike resigned from the CRR. The mostly white NCC—of eight full-time staff members on the commission in 1965, only three were black—hired African American Benjamin Payton as its executive director in 1966. Payton, a thirty-three-year-old Baptist minister with a Ph.D. in social ethics from Yale University, gained attention for critiquing a report on the black family by Assistant Secretary of Labor Daniel Patrick Moynihan. Payton's advocacy for systematic social and economic change beyond desegregation and voting rights represented a shift in NCC philosophy. The liberal Protestant organization now began addressing de facto segregation in the urban North. In summer 1964, the commission worked with the Southern Christian Leadership Conference (SCLC) in Rochester, New York. Community organizing efforts in Rochester, Detroit, and Cleveland proved less successful than earlier campaigns in the South.

In preparation for the White House Conference on Race, June 1–2, 1966, the CRR hosted a meeting on May 10, 1966, in New York City, attended by elected officials, ministers, and civil rights leaders. This preconference gathering recommended a comprehensive realignment of national priorities, but the Johnson administration's commitment to the Vietnam War precluded any significant changes. Executive Director Payton resigned in May 1967, and the NCC revoked the commission's emergency status. The NCC's inability to adequately address James Forman's 1969 "Black Manifesto," which called for reparations to African Americans from white churches, characterized the commission's diminished influence by the late 1960s.

**FURTHER READINGS**

Findlay, James F., Jr. *Church People in the Struggle: The National Council of Churches and the Black Freedom Movement, 1950–1970.* New York: Oxford University Press, 1993.

Pratt, Henry L. *The Liberalization of American Protestantism: A Case Study in Complex Organizations.* Detroit: Wayne State University Press, 1972.

*Social Action Collections at the State Historical Society of Wisconsin: A Guide.* Madison: State Historical Society of Wisconsin, 1983.

Spike, Robert W. *The Freedom Revolution and the Churches.* New York: Association Press, 1965.

*Timothy B. Neary*

**SEE ALSO**    Delta Ministry

## National Council of Churches, Department of Racial and Cultural Relations

*See* National Council of Churches, Commission on Religion and Race.

## National Council of Negro Women

Founded in 1935, the National Council of Negro Women (NCNW) is the nation's broadest-based organization of black women, often referred to as the black women's "organization of organizations." The NCNW is currently supported by 34 national affiliated organizations, 257 community-based sections chartered in forty-seven states, and 45,000 individual members. Because of its affiliation with a large number of diverse black women's organizations, including academic sororities, professional associations, and civic and social clubs, the NCNW reaches over four million women.

Since its inception, the organization has attempted to unify African American women's organizations in the struggle to end discrimination based on sex, race, creed, and national origin. Seeking to improve the quality of life of black women and their families and communities, the NCNW engages in a broad spectrum of activities. It serves as a clearinghouse for the dissemination of information about black women's activities; sponsors local, state, national, and international programs and conferences that provide minority women with a public forum to discuss their social, political, economic, and educational concerns; monitors racial discrimination and human rights violations; and engages in political lobbying and public education.

The NCNW was the brainchild of Mary McLeod Bethune, who hoped to unite black women's groups into a powerful unified force in the struggle to improve racial conditions in America and abroad. The daughter of newly emancipated slaves, Bethune overcame overwhelming odds to obtain a formal education and enter the teaching profession. In 1904, she founded the Daytona Educational and Industrial Training Institute for Negro Girls in Daytona, Florida. In 1923, a merger created the coeducational Bethune-Cookman College, making Bethune one of the first female college presidents in the nation. In the following year, Bethune became president of the National Association of Colored Women (NACW), a post she held until 1932. As a result of her efforts on behalf of black education and her leadership of the NACW, Bethune gained national and international recognition. Her status as one of the nation's most influential black women further increased, owing to her close personal relationship with President Franklin D. Roosevelt and First Lady Eleanor Roosevelt. During the 1930s, she frequently visited the White House and served as an informal presidential adviser on racial issues, leading to her appointment as head of the Negro Division of the National Youth Administration in 1936.

Bethune conceived the idea for the formation of the NCNW during her NACW presidency. The NACW, dominated by members of the educated and financial black elite, consisted of hundreds of local clubs that provided a variety of social welfare services in numerous cities and states. Bethune sought to centralize the NACW, hoping to provide the organization with a unified program that addressed national and international issues affecting black women and to open membership to all women of color regardless of national origin or economic status. Moreover, Bethune advocated that the NACW join with other women's organizations to achieve common goals and prevent the duplication of programs. NACW leaders, however, thwarted Bethune's centralization efforts. Unable to overcome NACW opposition, Bethune launched the NCNW in 1930.

For five years, Bethune courted prominent leaders of established black women's groups to gain their support for a national organization. On December 5, 1935, the leaders of twenty-nine of the most notable black women's organizations, including the NACW, met at New York City's 137th Street Young Women's Christian Association and inaugurated the NCNW. Speaking at the NCNW founding ceremony, Mary Church Terrell, former NACW president, articulated the reluctant support of the NACW. Terrell expressed doubts that the NCNW could achieve any more than had been accomplished by the NACW. Indeed, the NACW had done much to improve the quality of life of many black women through the establishment of kindergartens, day-care centers, playgrounds, and retirement homes in numerous black communities. But Bethune was convinced that a centralized organization that provided not only services to local black communities but also was national and international in scope and worked in conjunction with government agencies and other women's groups could achieve much more than the NACW had ever envisioned. The NCNW's potential to surpass the NACW as the most prominent black women's organization in America may have been the reason for the NACW's reluctant support of the NCNW.

As the first president-elect of the NCNW, Bethune set out to unite the organization's many affiliate groups into a cohesive force. She knew that bringing the varied organizations together to form the first national coalition of black women's associations would not be easy because of existing rivalries. As Bethune expected, members of several NCNW affiliate organizations were not pleased that their leaders had joined the NCNW. The election of several notable leaders as NCNW officers, including Charlotte Hawkins Brown, founder of North Carolina's all-black Alice Freeman Palmer Memorial Institute; Mary Church Terrell of the NACW; and Lucy D. Slowe, cofounder of Alpha Kappa Alpha, the first Greek-lettered black sorority, quelled some of the criticism and projected the image of a unified coalition of black women.

During the NCNW's early years, Bethune and a small volunteer staff worked out of her living room at 1318 Vermont Avenue in Washington, D.C. Under Bethune's direction, the NCNW began to locate volunteers in local communities to establish and supervise its programs. As the NCNW spread its base of operation, Bethune sought to establish the organization's credibility through affiliation with other associations. The NCNW's contacts soon included all major social, educational, governmental, and community organizations. Aided by its diverse contacts, media support, and publication of its *Aframerican Woman's Journal*, the NCNW sponsored adult education programs that sought to improve the conditions of black women in the areas of public affairs, family life, employment, citizenship, religion, consumer education, and rural life. While NCNW programs were geared toward black women, the organization also used its various contacts and resources to educate the general public about the conditions of black women.

During Bethune's fourteen-year presidency, which spanned the Great Depression and World War II, NCNW activism covered a broad spectrum. During the 1930s, the NCNW, in collaboration with the Young Women's Christian Association (YWCA) and labor unions, monitored the racial practices of New Deal agencies. It collected, analyzed, and distributed information about African Americans employed by New Deal agencies and publicized the exclusion of blacks from government training programs administered by local communities.

The NCNW's most notable effort during this time was the 1938 White House Conference on Governmental Cooperation in the Approach to the Problems of Negro Women and Children. The conference criticized the exclusion of black women from policy-making and management positions in social welfare programs. The absence of black female administrators, the conference claimed, was responsible for the minimal participation of black women and children in these government programs. NCNW members recommended the placement of competent black women in upper-level government positions. Although the conference did not force immediate change, it propelled the organization into the national limelight and marked the beginning of its almost annual White House visits, during which NCNW members continued to chip away at racial and gender discrimination.

The NCNW continued to be a vocal proponent of black women's rights during World War II. In 1941, after initially being barred, the NCNW became a member of the Women's Interest Section, an advisory council of the U.S. War Department's Bureau of Public Relations. It participated in and helped organize conferences initiated by Eleanor Roosevelt to discuss the role of black women in the war effort and the need for child-care facilities. Moreover, the NCNW documented black employment in defense industries and its findings, coupled with pressure from several other sources, resulted in the establishment of the Fair Employment Practice Committee. In addition, the NCNW fostered desegregation of the armed forces and fought to secure black women's participation in the Women's Army Corps (WACS) and the Women Accepted for Volunteer Emergency Service (WAVES). A series of conferences between Bethune and army leaders resulted in the admission of black women into the WACS in 1942 and their service overseas in the 688th Central Postal Battalion. Bethune personally oversaw this wartime campaign, recruiting many of the first black WACS, inspecting conditions in training camps, and lodging complaints about racial discrimination with the War Department. In its wartime fight to end racism and sexism, the NCNW joined forces with the League of Women Voters, the National Board of the YWCA, the National Association for the Advancement of Colored People (NAACP), and several national religious women's organizations. This collaboration resulted in the 1944 conference on the Position of Minorities in the United States.

While the NCNW attacked discrimination and segregation, it encouraged African Americans to demonstrate their patriotic support of the nation's war effort. It launched "Hold Your Job" campaigns, urging black workers in nationwide public meetings, newspaper articles, and pamphlets to improve their job skills and to maintain professional attitudes and appearances. At the local level, the NCNW's Metropolitan Councils sponsored special WACS programs to demonstrate black women's support of the war. As a further expression of black patriotism, the NCNW launched programs such as "We Serve America" and "Buy Bonds and Be Free."

Following World War II, the NCNW increasingly pursued a global agenda, seeking to improve the conditions of minority women throughout the world. The NCNW first ventured into the international arena in 1940, when it sponsored a conference of black Cuban women at the Association Feminia in Cuba, publicizing Cuban women's liberation struggle. Toward the end of World War II, the NCNW also demonstrated its growing concern about international racism and sexism through its participation in the United Nations. In 1945, Bethune attended the U.N. founding in San Francisco, inaugurating the NCNW's tradition of sending delegates as official observers to the General Assembly meetings.

By 1949, the NCNW had emerged as one of the most vocal and visible organizations advocating the rights of black women. In November of that year, Bethune stepped down as NCNW president and Dorothy Boulding Ferebee, the organization's treasurer, succeeded her. Ferebee was the grand niece of Josephine St. Pierre Ruffin, a founder of the NACW. In addition to her involvement in the NCNW, she had served as tenth national president of the Alpha Kappa Alpha Sorority and had founded the Southeast Settlement House in Washington, D.C.

Ferebee continued the NCNW's advocacy of black women's and human rights. Under her leadership, the NCNW endorsed the U.N. human rights charter and monitored and exposed discrimination against women and blacks in health care, education, housing, and the armed forces. In addition, Ferebee urged the NCNW's membership to play an active role in the emerging civil rights movement. Unlike Bethune, who had largely relied on public education and moral persuasion, Ferebee used the NCNW to challenge the legal system and to advocate black political participation. She introduced a Nine Point Program that initiated voter registration drives, lobbied for black appointments to strategic government positions, and promoted national legislation to abolish poll taxes, lynchings, and genocide. Moreover, the NCNW lobbied for women's rights legislation, federal aid to education, and establishment of a national health-care system and a permanent Fair Employment Practices Commission.

During Ferebee's administration, the NCNW's *Aframerican Woman's Journal*, published since 1940, was renamed *Women United*. Between 1949 and 1952, the journal publicized the accomplishments of black women and the activities of the NCNW. *Telefact*, a newsletter published from 1943 to 1963, continued to keep members and the public informed about national legislation, economic developments, and international affairs affecting black women.

In 1953, Vivian Carter Mason, who had worked closely with Bethune and Ferebee, was elected NCNW president. Mason, who had served as NCNW vice president under Ferebee, had been a vital force, often chairing meetings while Ferebee represented the organization at conferences and meetings in the United States and abroad. After Mason assumed the presidency, she used her considerable administrative skills to streamline the management of the NCNW's national headquarters. Located since 1943 at the second residence of Bethune on Pennsylvania Avenue in Washington, D.C., the national headquarters served as the NCNW's reception center for national and international dignitaries and provided space for the organization's social functions and meetings. Mason sent out program directives and postconvention materials such as board meeting minutes, budget reports, workshop summaries, and convention resolutions, keeping affiliates informed about the organization's activities.

Moreover, Mason imposed a centralized structure on the NCNW in an attempt to control the administration of local councils. Her decision to provide national supervision of local councils was sparked by a series of fact-finding studies that revealed that some local groups were soliciting funds and engaging in partisan politics—activities not sanctioned by the national office. While local affiliates were given the freedom to draft their own constitutions, they were required to conform to the legal guidelines of the national organization. To insure adherence to NCNW guidelines, local council manuals and regional director handbooks were revised and distributed to members. Mason also launched a series of publications that clearly explained the implementation of the NCNW's national program.

In addition to restructuring the NCNW, Mason's administration continued to foster civil rights activism and increasingly embraced interracial cooperation. Following the 1954 Supreme Court's *Brown v. Board of Education* decision, the NCNW started to collaborate with the NAACP to implement school integration. In 1956, the NCNW's twenty-first Annual Convention featured an Interracial Conference of Women, which explored how women of all colors and persuasions could work to "surmount barriers to human and civil rights." In the same year, the NCNW began sponsoring public programs in support of Rosa Parks and the nonviolent activists of the Montgomery, Alabama, bus boycott.

In 1957, Dorothy Irene Height became the NCNW's fourth president, a post she continues to hold in 2000. Height had held numerous NCNW positions since 1937. Moreover, she had served as president of the Delta Sigma Theta Sorority and had been a member of the YWCA National Board Staff. Under Height's direction, the NCNW explored new strategies to raise funds. For example, the NCNW developed revenue-producing materials and collaborated with businesses to raise funds. Prior to Height's administration, the NCNW relied on financial support from its members and a few white donors. In 1958, the NCNW hired a public relations firm to publicize its activities and created the Divisional Plan to recruit new members and expand its programs. By the early 1960s, the NCNW's expanding volunteer network had grown to approximately three million women.

While Height worked to increase the size and visibility of the NCNW, her organization's support of the civil rights movement remained largely concealed from the public. Although NCNW members launched voter registration drives in several locales, they did not participate in public protests such as sit-ins, pickets, or freedom rides. The organization, however, contributed to the movement behind the scenes. It sponsored Student Nonviolent Coordinating Committee volunteers, enabling the students to continue their education while donating their time to the struggle. Moreover, Height was often the only woman present at the meetings of the Big Six civil rights leaders, which included Martin Luther King Jr., of the Southern Christian Leadership Conference, John Lewis of the Student Nonviolent Coordinating Committee, James Farmer of the Congress of Racial Equality, Roy Wilkins of the NAACP, Whitney Young of the National Urban League, and A. Philip Randolph representing organized labor. Helping to guide the course of the civil rights movement, Height also utilized her position among the Big Six to advocate black women's rights.

Following passage of the 1964 Civil Rights and 1965 Voting Rights Acts, the NCNW turned its attention to economic problems affecting black women. Between 1965 and 1980, the NCNW initiated approximately forty national projects that sought to increase black women's employment opportunities and the availability of adequate and affordable housing and health care. Other NCNW programs aimed at improving the quality of black women's lives by supporting community volunteerism to reduce hunger, malnutrition, juvenile delinquency, and teenage pregnancies and parenthood.

Financial support for these programs came from a growing number of philanthropists and foundations who started to donate large amounts of money to the NCNW after the organization achieved tax-exempt nonprofit status in 1966. Since its inception, the NCNW had lacked a strong financial base, relying almost exclusively on the contributions of its members and a few white patrons. Hoping to increase the number and amount of philanthropic donations, Bethune had repeatedly attempted, but failed, to gain a tax-exempt status for the NCNW. Under Height's direction, the NCNW revised its Articles of Incorporation to broaden its educational and charitable programs and succeeded in meeting the federal guidelines for tax-exempt status. Grants from the Ford Foundation and the Department of Health, Education and Welfare allowed the NCNW to expand its headquarters staff from eight to nearly fifty. With the help of a larger support staff and a bigger budget, the NCNW aggressively recruited and trained black women for volunteer community service. As a result of these efforts, the number of NCNW volunteers grew to four million by 1979.

Drawing on this nationwide network of volunteers and increased financial resources, the NCNW launched several community service and social action programs. Many of the programs aimed at helping low-income black women, particularly female heads of household. The NCNW also initiated several programs that addressed the problems of black youth, such as teenage pregnancy and parenthood, lack of health care, and high unemployment and juvenile delinquency rates. One of the NCNW's most effective youth programs was Operation Sisters United Centers, which sought to provide a rehabilitation alternative to female juvenile detention. Funded by the Department of Justice's Law Enforcement Assistance Administration, Operation Sisters offered personal mentoring and career preparation and training to young female delinquents. Operation Sisters, which began as a pilot project in Washington, D.C., in 1972, was so successful that it was duplicated in more than ten American cities and the Virgin Islands.

Another NCNW initiative, Operation Daily Bread, aimed at alleviating the economic problems of black families. Launched in 1967, Operation Daily Bread distributed seeds and pigs to poor southern blacks in parts of rural Mississippi and Alabama. The NCNW's fight against hunger in the United States later served as a model

for similar programs that addressed poverty in South Africa. In addition to aiding rural black southerners, the NCNW launched "hunger" workshops in twenty American cities in 1967. During the workshops, NCNW volunteers gathered data, documenting the effectiveness of government-sponsored food programs. Using the data, the NCNW urged the Department of Agriculture to distribute food stamps to low-income families and to provide free school lunches to underprivileged children.

While the NCNW devoted much of its efforts to improving the quality of life of black families in the United States, it also remained active in the international arena. In 1975, the NCNW established an International Division, which formalized the organization's work in this area and enabled black American women to work with women in Africa, the Caribbean, and other Third World countries. The division, which had been financed by a grant from the Agency for International Development, arranged a "twinning" program that opened communications between the NCNW and national women's organizations of the African nations of Senegal and Togo.

While the NCNW's main objective was to assist black women in their struggle for legal, political, and economic equality, the organization also took an interest in preserving black history. Beginning in 1939, the NCNW collected historical materials for display at the 1940 American Negro Exposition in Chicago. Moreover, the NCNW utilized its quarterly publication to promote historical awareness and preservation. In 1974, after sixteen years of planning, the NCNW, in a tribute to its founder, erected the Bethune Memorial in the national capital's Lincoln Park. The statute, in close proximity to the U.S. Congress, the Supreme Court, and the Library of Congress, was the first memorial to a black American and a woman to be erected on public land in the nation's capital. In 1979, the NCNW established the Mary McLeod Bethune Memorial Museum and the National Archives for Black Women's History at 1318 Vermont Avenue, Bethune's last Washington residence and the organization's first national headquarters. The National Archives for Black Women's History was the first institution devoted solely to the documentation of black women's history. The archives now house the material gathered for the 1940 exposition, the personal papers of several black women, the records of the NCNW, and archival materials from other affiliated black and white women's organizations. The Mary McLeod Bethune Memorial Museum hosts exhibits that interpret the experience of black women and the black community in America and offers educational programs including lecture series, seminars, and films. In 1982 the building was designated a national historic site.

While preserving past achievements of black women, the NCNW has not lost sight of its long-standing commitment to community service and racial advancement. Under the leadership of Height, who continues to guide the NCNW as its president and chief executive, the organization has launched numerous new projects in the last two decades. The NCNW's Parents-Youth Groups Drug Abuse Prevention Program, for example, seeks to prevent and reduce alcohol and drug abuse among its more than 450,000 participants. The Eldercare Institute on Older Women, established under a cooperative agreement with the Federal Administration on Aging, encourages national women's organizations to include the concerns of seniors on their program agenda, disseminates information about older women, and provides technical assistance to eldercare coalitions. Honor Our Neighborhood's Older Residents Program is a community volunteer support network that promotes awareness of the needs of the elderly in five cities. In partnership with the Quaker Oats Company's Aunt Jemima Brand, the NCNW sponsors a A Tribute to Black Women Community Leaders, which recognizes black women's outstanding community services.

Among the NCNW's most popular recent projects is the annual Black Family Reunion Celebration, which drew over one million attendants in 1991. The celebration emphasizes the importance of heritage, traditional values, and historic strengths of African Americans and promotes education, hard work, and self-help. Since its inception in the late 1980s, the celebration has received the support of local governments, hundreds of volunteers, celebrities, and corporate sponsors including the Procter and Gamble Company, the Ford Motor Company, Coca-Cola, and Anheuser-Busch.

Recognizing the leadership of Height, who has been at the helm of the NCNW since 1957, thousands of women from across the nation attended the founding of the NCNW's National Centers for African American Women and the Dorothy I. Height Leadership Institute in Washington, D.C., on October 10, 1996. Participants at the opening ceremony included First Lady Hillary Rodham Clinton, the renowned author Maya Angelou, and the philanthropist Camille Cosby. In her closing remarks Height paid tribute to Bethune, proclaiming: "Never again shall we be left out, placed behind or allow someone else to speak for us."

**FURTHER READINGS**

"African-American Women Get It Done With the National Council of Negro Women, Inc." *Columbus Times* 38, 49 (October 29, 1996): A1.

Collier-Thomas, Bettye. *N.C.N.W., 1935–1980.* Washington, D.C.: National Council of Negro Women, 1981.

*Fact Sheet of the National Council of Negro Women, Inc.* Washington, D.C.: National Council of Negro Women, n.d.

McCluskey, Audrey Thomas. "Multiple Consciousness in the Leadership of Mary McLeod Bethune." *NWSA Journal* 6, 1 (Spring 1994): 69–81.

Smith, Elaine M. "Mary McLeod Bethune." *Black Women in America: An Historical Encyclopedia.* Ed. Darlene Clark Hine. Brooklyn: Carlson, 1993, 113–128.

*Karen Anderson*

**SEE ALSO** National Association of Colored Women's Clubs, Inc.

# National Council of Negro Youth

Mary McLeod Bethune founded the National Council of Negro Youth as the National Conference of Negro Youth in 1937. The organization maintained an impressive list of patrons and board members as well as an office in New York City. The conference met in 1937, 1939, and 1941 in Washington, D.C., to advise President Franklin D. Roosevelt on long-term domestic policies affecting black youth. Initial recommendations to the president included demands for increased employment opportunities, economic security, adequate educational and recreational facilities, improved health and housing conditions, security of life, and equal protection under the law. After its first meeting in 1937, the conference created a broader agenda at each subsequent gathering.

The 1939 report of the conference's second meeting evaluated the progress of African Americans in relation to a number of New Deal policies that had been enacted to bolster the security and stability of the nation. While many of the evaluations were positive, conference members criticized the federal government for supporting discrimination by failing to lift racial restrictions on voting, work relief, subsidized housing, civil service employment, and education for African Americans.

By 1941, the conference's program included An Evening of Negro Art and Culture, held at Dunbar High School Auditorium in Washington, D.C. The program featured musical performances, readings of literature and poetry, and presentation of a theatrical piece entitled "Sing Me A Song." Patrons of the event included McLeod Bethune; Alain L. Locke, the philosopher and first African American Rhodes scholar; Mary Church Terrell, the cofounder of the National Association for the Advancement of Colored People and first president of the National Association of Colored Women; Earl B. Dickerson, the first black assistant attorney general for Illinois and one of only two black members of President Roosevelt's Committee on Fair Employment Practices; and Ralph J. Bunche, the first African American to receive a Ph.D. in political science from an American university and first African American Nobel prize winner. Despite this impressive group of supporters, the conference also attracted the criticism of some African Americans. In 1941, for example, the Reverend Adam Clayton Powell, a powerful black minister and New York City council member, attacked many of the delegates and speakers. Powell charged that the conference was out of touch with the vast majority of young African Americans, most of whom were simply too poor to make the sojourn to attend the conference in the nation's capital.

By 1942, the conference appears to have made a dramatic change, precipitated by America's entry into World War II. At a meeting that year, delegates changed the organization's name to the National Council of Negro Youth. More important, though, they adopted an international agenda, linking the struggle for racial equality in the United States to the fight against fascism and racism overseas. The council, via its meetings, newsletters, and publications, compared the tyranny of Hitler to the system of racial segregation in the United States. Retreating from the conciliatory approach it had taken during the prewar years, the council now attacked white supremacy, domestic lynchings, segregation in the armed forces, and America's racially biased judiciary. Moreover, the council condemned the colonization of nonwhite peoples throughout the world, insisting that the racial oppression of African Americans and the economic exploitation of colonized people were forces that had to be treated simultaneously as different facets of the same illness. Instead of continuing in its advisory capacity, the council tried to mobilize the masses and launched grassroots efforts including letter writing, lobbying, and public awareness campaigns. U.S. involvement in the war effort, however, appears to have superseded the National Council and its work. The national government launched a second front, called for by the council, and provided thousands of African Americans with employment opportunities and military benefits, temporarily staving off protest.

**FURTHER READINGS**

National Conference of Negro Youth. *Agenda and Organization for the National Conference on Problems of the Negro and Negro Youth, January 18, 1937.* Washington, D.C.: Moorland-Spingarn Research Center, Howard University, 1937.

———. *Monthly Bulletin.* Washington, D.C.: Moorland-Spingarn Research Center, Howard University.

———. *Negro Youth Defends Democracy, November 14, 15, 16, 1941.* Washington, D.C.: Moorland-Spingarn Research Center, Howard University, 1941.

———. *Registered Delegates, The Second National Conference on the Problems of the Negro and Negro Youth. Washington, D.C., January 12, 13, 14, 1939.* Washington, D.C.: Moorland-Spingarn Research Center, Howard University, 1939.

———. *Reports.* Washington, D.C.: Moorland-Spingarn Research Center, Howard University, 1937.

———. *Summary Statement of the Evaluation Committees' Reports to the National Conference on the Problems of the Negro and Negro Youth, January 12, 1939.* Washington, D.C.: Moorland-Spingarn Research Center, Howard University, 1939.

White, Alvin E. "Rev. Powell Raps Urban League as 'Fifth-Columnist' Ridden." *Philadelphia Tribune,* November 22, 1941, 10.

*Julie S. Doar*

## National Defense Advisory Commission

*See* Office of Production Management, Minorities (or Minority Groups) Branch.

## National Democratic Party of Alabama

The National Democratic Party of Alabama (NDPA) represented a unique political organization created by southern African Americans. Established in 1968 to counter Alabama's segregationist state Democratic Party, the NDPA sought to end discrimination, guarantee the right to protest, insure equal legal protection of all citizens, and support selected candidates for public office.

During the twentieth century, Alabama's black population first secured the right to vote, then focused on how to vote. Although white northern Democrats had recognized the usefulness of black voters to defeat Republican candidates, southern Democrats passed segregation laws and disfranchised black voters in the 1920s by forbidding primary voting and implementing poll taxes.

As landmark federal civil rights legislation passed in the 1960s, activists in such groups as the Mississippi Freedom Democratic Party (MFDP) and the Lowndes County Freedom Organization publicized how blacks were denied the right to vote, though they wanted to exercise their constitutional rights. Alabama was a one-party state offering few political options in a segregated culture. Its exclusionary Democratic Party refused to compromise with black leaders.

African Americans attempted to secure prominent political offices as early as the 1950s when the Alabama Progressive Democratic Association, an African American wing of the National Democratic Party, supported candidates. The interracial Alabama Democratic Conference (ADC), established after the Supreme Court ruled against gerrymandering in Tuskegee, Alabama, helped elect the first black officials in that city since Reconstruction.

Inspired by the MFDP and frustrated by victories of racist white Democrats, John Logan Cashin Jr., a Huntsville dentist, and other ADC members founded the NDPA to give black voters a voice and to challenge the status quo. NDPA members wanted to be able to vote for the national Democratic presidential nominee, not the Alabama Democrats' choice, George Wallace. The NDPA desired an alternative democratic organization for blacks and progressive whites that represented national Democratic philosophy.

Receiving a state charter in January 1968, the first annual NDPA convention was held in Birmingham on July 20, 1968. Cashin was elected party chairman, and keynote speaker the Reverend Edwin King of the MFDP encouraged blacks to become politically empowered. The NDPA constitution and bylaws vowed to "provide an opposition voice to the political Lilliputianism of the conservative right."

With the motto To End Racism and Poverty and Bring Democracy to Alabama, the NDPA was the first political party in modern Alabama to adopt a platform. Striving to improve the standard of living, education, and the economy, the NDPA was also concerned with women's rights, pollution, tax reform, ending the draft, and services for the poor, elderly, and children.

Although the NDPA constituency was mostly black, prominent white members such as the civil rights activist F. Virginia Durr joined. Securing a Supreme Court ruling to place the NDPA on the ballot, the NDPA promoted the "Eagle Party" ticket, consisting of 170 candidates, mostly in the state's heavily African American–populated Black Belt. Cashin ran against George Wallace for governor in 1968.

In its newspaper, *The Eagle Eye*, the NDPA told black Alabamians to "Vote for yourself for a change!" and "Vote the Eagle to freedom!" Despite threats and bribes to withdraw, several candidates won their races in 1968, including congressional candidates in small districts. The NDPA's primary purpose, though, was to transform the state Democratic Party into a more progressive group friendly to black voters.

At the 1968 Democratic National Convention in Chicago, an NDPA delegation successfully challenged the state's Democratic delegation and was seated. Delegates proved to the national party that the state party did not represent the majority of voters. The NDPA repeated this action at the 1972 national convention.

One direct result of the NDPA was increased voter turnout both by blacks and by whites to counter black candidates and votes. By 1971, Wallace realized that he needed black voters to assure his political power, and he began to seek cooperation from NDPA leaders Fred Gray and Thomas Reed. The state Democratic Party became more racially moderate. As a result, many racist and conservative whites shifted from the Democratic to the Republican Party. By including black voters, the Democratic Party strengthened the candidacy of such politicians as Jimmy Carter in the 1976 presidential election.

By that time, the NDPA had ceased to exist. As an independent third party, it had minimal impact on national politics. The final NDPA convention was held in May 1972, and membership dwindled although candidates continued to run on the NDPA ticket. NDPA activity slowed after the November 1972 election. Having liberalized the state Democratic Party and secured control in rural counties predominantly populated by African Americans, the NDPA became inactive, and the state office in Huntsville closed.

## FURTHER READINGS

Frye, Hardy T. *Black Parties and Political Power: A Case Study.* Boston: G.K. Hall, 1980.

Garnett, Bernard E. "Dr. Cashin Leads Black Democrats." *Race Relations Reporter* 1 (October 16, 1970): 8–11.

———. "Wallace Contacts Key Black Leaders." *Race Relations Reporter* 2 (March 15, 1971): 7–8.

Oral History Interviews, 1972–1978, Collection. Interviews by Hardy T. Frye with NDPA leaders, Auburn University Archives, Auburn, Alabama.

Walton, Hanes, Jr. "The National Democratic Party of Alabama and Party Failure in America." In Kay Lawson and Peter H. Merkl, eds. *When Parties Fail: Emerging Alternative Organizations.* Princeton, N.J.: Princeton University Press, 1988, 365–388.

*Elizabeth D. Schafer*

## National Dental Association

The National Dental Association (NDA) was founded in 1913 by twenty-nine black dentists who had been denied membership in the major professional organization, the American Dental Association. Until the civil rights movement of the 1950s, African Americans were excluded from membership in many national professional organizations. Currently representing over seven thousand black dentists in the United States and abroad, the NDA is the largest organization of minority oral health and dental professionals in the world.

Although the U.S. population is approximately 12 percent black, only 4 percent of dentists are African Americans. Since its founding, the NDA has been dedicated to providing affordable dental care, education, and guidance to the poor and underserved, including racial and ethnic minorities, children, the elderly, and the disabled.

The NDA, headquartered in Washington, D.C., has approximately fifty state and local chapters in the United States and the Caribbean. It is the parent organization of the Student National Dental Association (SNDA), the National Dental Hygienists Association (NDHA), the National Dental Assistants Association (NDAA), and the Auxiliary of the National Dental Association. The NDA offers scholarships and other programs to encourage young African Americans to enter the field of dentistry and oral health care. The NDA also produces two publications, *Flossline*, a quarterly newsletter providing information on association activities, upcoming events, and conferences, and the *Journal of the National Dental Association*, a quarterly scientific journal covering research and advances in the field of dentistry and oral health.

The NDA holds an annual conference featuring technical papers, scientific courses, exhibits, and social programs for all its affiliated organizations. Held in Scottsdale, Arizona, the 1997 annual convention hosted a Minority Faculty and Administrators Forum, the fifth Anniversary Women's Health Symposium, and the NDA Leadership Institute, and commemorated the twenty-fifth anniversary of the Student National Dental Association. A special feature of each convention is the President's Symposium, which focuses on strengthening professional standards and ensuring the safety and health of patients. Some recent symposium topics have included voluntary HIV/AIDS testing, the efficacy of fluoride, infection control guidelines for practitioners, managed health care, amalgam/mercury toxicity, and the future of dentistry. Current and ongoing projects include fund-raising for scholarships, financial assistance for the recruitment of African American dental students, participation in the Head Start program, and the advancement of minority dental health professionals within the U.S. armed forces, federal government, health maintenance organizations, university health clinics, and dental schools. The organization also supports national health-care legislation.

The NDA works with the Howard University Dental School and the Meharry Medical College School of Dentistry—the professional schools that train the largest number of African American dentists. In 1976, the NDA founded the National Dental Association Foundation (NDAF) to improve the oral health of African Americans. The NDFA has cooperated with the Colgate-Palmolive Company to provide scholarship aid and sponsor research at the above-mentioned historically African American schools. Since 1990, approximately seven hundred students have received scholarship awards from these programs. Colgate-Palmolive also sponsored a multicultural program entitled "Bright Smiles, Bright Futures" to educate inner-city youths about the importance of oral hygiene. NDA members from local chapters have offered free dental screenings to children in day-care facilities, community centers, and schools. NDA volunteers have also provided professional care to developing countries, including Jamaica, Trinidad, and Guyana.

**FURTHER READINGS**

"Establishing a Dental Care Program." *Ebony* 51 (June 1996): 110–114.

"The National Dental Association celebrates 81st Anniversary." *Ebony* 49 (March 1994): 30.

*Donald Altschiller*

## National Domestic Workers Union

In 1968, Dorothy Bolden of Atlanta established the National Domestic Workers Union (NDWU) to organize the city's maids. The goal of the union was to improve the working conditions and wages of female domestics.

Born in 1923, Bolden began her own long career as a domestic worker at age seven. She and her husband, Abram

Thompson, were working and raising six children when Bolden became involved in the civil rights movement. "I marched with Dr. King every time he came to town," she recalled. While supporting King she realized that racial equality was difficult to achieve without equal economic opportunity. Thus, Bolden resolved that economic rights had to be an integral part of civil rights.

The idea for a domestic workers union emerged when Bolden "started talking with other maids on the bus on the way to work." The women were interested in a salary increase that reflected appropriate compensation for their work and respect for their skills. During the mid-1960s, Atlanta's female domestics, who cooked, cleaned, and took care of their employers' children, earned between three and ten dollars a day and were not covered by the minimum wage law.

In 1968, Bolden and seven other women held the first meeting of the NDWU at Perry Homes, a housing project in Atlanta. Martha Parker, the union's first president, soon resigned in favor of Bolden, who remained president thereafter. Each member of the NDWU was named organizer of those maids with whom she rode the bus to work. This grassroots organizing effort was successful, and within six months several hundred women had joined the union. Because NDWU members worked in separate households, they could not pursue traditional avenues of labor negotiation. Instead, each member was responsible for negotiating with her employer for NDWU-mandated wage rates and working conditions. The NDWU's strategy worked, and the average daily wage of Atlanta's domestic workers climbed quickly. In 1976 the women earned seventeen dollars per day, and by 1983 they were covered by minimum wage laws and Social Security, and some of them reported daily incomes of forty dollars.

As black women of Atlanta gained access to higher-status and better-paying jobs and immigrants began to pose a challenge to African American women's monopoly of domestic employment, the NDWU's concerns shifted. The group continued to defend members with grievances, but job placement and training became its most successful programs. The NDWU offered a six-month training program that included first aid, household budgeting, and early childhood education courses. When a potential employer called the NDWU's "hiring hall," Bolden, after certifying that the employer provided appropriate wages and working conditions, sent a trained member to apply for the position.

The membership rolls of the NDWU fluctuated during the 1970s, but two thousand core members and approximately eight thousand program participants made the union a potent political force as African Americans sought electoral offices and political power. The NDWU, which had declared in 1968 that its primary purpose was "to benefit the community," participated in voter registration drives and accepted only registered voters as members. Union members protested against bus fare hikes and worked for the election of sympathetic politicians. Dorothy Bolden also wedded her vision of black working-class activism to the burgeoning feminist movement of the 1970s. "My primary struggle is for women," she proclaimed, insisting that until "professional women unite with low-income women, we won't be as powerful as we should be." Bolden also served on the Georgia Governor's Commission on the Status of Women and on the U.S. Department of Health, Education, and Welfare's Advisory Committee on the Status of Women's Rights and Responsibilities.

During the Reagan years (1980–88), a federal grand jury launched an investigation of the NDWU's finances. Although the union and Bolden were vindicated, membership in the NDWU dropped precipitously. By 1990, the remaining NDWU members earned between fifty and eighty dollars daily and the union had trained and placed thirteen thousand women in jobs.

**FURTHER READINGS**

Laker, Barbara. "The Fighter." *Atlanta Constitution* 6 (January 1983).

Lutz, Christine. "Interview with Dorothy Bolden, August 1995." Voices of Labor Oral History Project, Southern Labor Archives, Pullen Library, Georgia State University, Atlanta.

Seifer, Nancy. *Nobody Speaks for Me*. New York: Simon and Schuster, 1976.

Tyson, Jean. "Dorothy Bolden Speaks for Herself, Others." *Atlanta Journal Constitution*, November 21, 1976.

Yancy, Dorothy Couser. "Dorothy Bolden, Organizer of Domestic Workers: She Was Born Poor, But She Would Not Bow Down." *Sage* 3 (Spring 1986): 53–55.

*Christine Lutz*

# National Economic Association

The National Economic Association (NEA) was founded in December 1969 as the Caucus of Black Economists. Marcus Alexis, Charles Z. Wilson, and Thaddeus Spratlen led the effort to found the caucus during that year's annual meeting of the American Economic Association.

Today, the NEA has members in the fifty states and the West Indies who work in government, business, and academe.

The NEA's main goals are to promote the professional life of minorities within the economics profession, to increase the number of black economists and improve their opportunities for career growth, and to advance the study of economic problems confronting the African American community. To help increase the number of minorities involved in the profession, the NEA operates a summer internship program that assists in the placement of African American students in paid summer internships. To promote the job opportunities of black economists, the NEA publishes the *Job Placement Bulletin* and keeps a directory of African American economists. The NEA publishes a monthly newsletter that serves as a forum for the exchange of ideas and provides commentary on current economic issues, as well as information on upcoming events within the economics profession. Since 1970 the NEA has published the *Review of Black Political Economy* to promote the study and analysis of the global black community and to serve as a vehicle for the exchange of ideas and further development of economics. Published in conjunction with the Atlanta University Center, the *Review* originated as part of the now defunct Black Economic Research Center in New York City's Harlem. Robert S. Browne, then director of the center, led the effort to launch the *Review* and became its first editor.

The NEA in partnership with the Allied Social Sciences Association organizes annual sessions at which economists present papers relating to economic issues affecting the African American community. During these meetings the NEA's national officers and board of directors are elected. The NEA's secretary-treasurer has an office at the University of Michigan Business School in Ann Arbor.

**FURTHER READING**

Browne, Robert. "The Origin, Birth, and Adolescence of the *Review of Black Political Economy* and the Black Economic Research Center." *Review of Black Political Economy* 23, 1 (Winter 1993): 9–23.

*Oscar Flores*

## National Emergency Committee Against Mob Violence

*See* American Council on Race Relations.

## National Equal Rights League

The National Equal Rights League (NERL) is the name of two civil rights organizations. The first was founded in 1864 at a meeting of the National Convention of Colored Men and sought full citizenship rights for slaves freed by the Civil War. The second was founded by the editor and militant civil rights activist William Monroe Trotter in 1908 in an effort to stop the educator and founder of Tuskegee Institute Booker T. Washington's accommodationism and gain equal treatment for African Americans.

By autumn 1864 it was clear that the Union would defeat the Confederacy and slavery would end. Leaders in the free black community, including Henry Highland Garnet, Frederick Douglass, and John Mercer Langston, worried that without effective pressure from blacks, the Union government would seek reconciliation with the South before it guaranteed rights to freedmen. Garnet called a meeting of his civil rights organization, the National Convention of Colored Men, to consider the course of the race. The convention agreed that a new, national organization, the NERL, was needed to press the media and government for full citizenship rights. Organizers also charged the NERL with supporting black self-improvement. Delegates at the meeting chose Langston to be the first president.

From the very beginning, disputes weakened the NERL. Delegates fought over where the organization should be headquartered, the cost of dues for its local branches, and its political orientation. Garnet claimed that Langston had won the presidency by promising Eastern delegates that the NERL offices would be in Philadelphia. Poor delegates complained that high dues would turn the organization into a tool of the wealthy. And speakers fought a long battle over the wisdom of emigration (Garnet's goal) versus remaining in the United States. Finally, in frustration, Garnet denounced the NERL as an instrument of "the milk and water-colored codfish aristocracy" and the meeting came to an end.

In spite of Langston's effort on behalf of the national organization, the NERL's local branches were always stronger than the national office. Langston had to cancel the first meeting of the Board of Directors because he could not assemble a quorum, and it took him months to publish the minutes of the organizing meeting, his first charge from the NERL's leadership. As president of the NERL, Langston met with Andrew Johnson April 18, 1865—only three days after he had replaced Abraham

Lincoln as president of the United States. Langston requested that Johnson support complete emancipation and equality before the law. The meeting apparently had little impact on the new president's policy.

Langston was more successful as an organizer of NERL branches. By the time of Lincoln's death, branches existed in North Carolina, Louisiana, Michigan, Pennsylvania, Massachusetts, Ohio, Missouri, and New York. Langston later helped form other branches in Tennessee and Kentucky. These local groups united freedmen in support of American democracy while challenging local leaders to accord them fair treatment based on their sacrifices during the Civil War. The branches in New Orleans and Wilmington, North Carolina, were particularly adept at winning and defending the freedom of the freedmen.

The first incarnation of the NERL died slowly during the years of Reconstruction. With the advent of Radical Reconstruction, the national office of the NERL seemed superfluous. With the rise of radical white power in the South, the local branches gradually lost the influence they once had. By the turn of the century, it was Booker T. Washington's quiescent voice, not the NERL's demands for equality, that dominated the world of black political rhetoric.

Perhaps no other black man took as much offence at Booker T. Washington as did William Monroe Trotter. Trotter left behind a prosperous real estate brokerage in Boston to battle Washington. In 1903 he founded the Boston *Guardian*, a weekly newspaper dedicated to rebutting Washington and promoting agitation in defense of black rights. Trotter and W. E. B. Du Bois led the group of young black intellectuals that founded the Niagara Movement. But when Du Bois and Trotter fell out over the administration of the Niagara Movement, Trotter formed his version of the National Equal Rights League to press the militant black position.

Trotter's NERL was, like Trotter himself, alternately brilliant and self-destructive. The NERL effectively used sit-ins to protest segregation in Boston, and Trotter's outspoken support for equality drew him a number of supporters in the central and western parts of the United States, including Ida B. Wells-Barnett. But Trotter's constant attacks on Washington made him and the NERL seem petty, while Trotter's fiery temper eventually offended most of his supporters. In one particularly public case, the NERL won hard-fought access to President Woodrow Wilson, only to have Trotter denounce him so angrily that Wilson later said that during his time as president he had never been "addressed in such an insulting fashion."

Washington's death in 1915 sapped much of the brio out of Trotter and the NERL; both quickly faded from view. Du Bois and the National Association for the Advancement of Colored People had drawn away most of Trotter's supporters, while Washington's disciples kept the Tuskegee machine running smoothly despite Trotter's increasingly cranky attacks.

**FURTHER READINGS**

Brisbane, Robert H. *The Black Vanguard: Origins of the Negro Social Revolution, 1900–1960*. Valley Forge, Pa.: Judson Press, 1970.

Cheek, William, and Aimee Lee Cheek. *John Mercer Langston and the Fight for Black Freedom, 1829–1865*. Urbana: University of Illinois Press, 1989.

Harding, Vincent. *There Is a River: The Black Struggle for Freedom in America*. New York: Harcourt Brace Jovanovich, 1981.

*Gary Daynes*

## National Extension Association of Family and Consumer Sciences

*See* National Association of Extension Home Economists.

## National Farm Labor Union

*See* Southern Tenant Farmers' Union.

## National Forum for Black Public Administrators

Founded in 1983, the National Forum for Black Public Administrators (NFBPA) is a professional membership organization dedicated to the advancement of black leadership in the public sector. Its membership is composed of more than three thousand public administrators employed by state and local governments, including city and county managers and assistant managers, chief administrative officers, agency directors, and bureau and division heads. Other members include managers and executives working in the corporate sector, as well as graduate students, deans, and faculty of public administration schools.

The NFBPA seeks to increase the number of blacks appointed to executive positions in public service organizations and to strengthen the position of blacks already employed in the field of public administration. For this purpose the NFBPA maintains a JOBS Hotline, with toll-free access to an up-to-date listing of public management positions in municipal, county, and state agencies, and helps prepare aspiring administrators for senior positions in the public administration sector. Moreover, the NFBPA has established a number of training programs that address the needs of both seasoned and emerging black public administrators in the United States and South Africa. The Executive Leadership Institute is an intense training program designed to polish the skills of black managers seeking executive appointments in public service. The Mentor Program partners junior public administrators with experienced executives who provide them with career planning assistance and skills enhancement.

In addition to fostering the recruitment and career advancement of black public administrators, the NFBPA conducts research on social and economic problems endemic to black communities. It sponsors national and regional forums to address the concerns of black communities and to further communication and collaboration among black public, private, and academic institutions. Moreover, the NFBPA encourages black public administrators to play an active role in building and maintaining viable black communities.

Headquartered in Washington, D.C., the NFBPA has more than forty-nine local affiliates, which it keeps informed with its quarterly newsletter, *The Forum*, a semiannual *Membership Directory*, and an annual *Resource Guide*.

### FURTHER READING

Jaszczak, S., and T. E. Sheets, eds. *Encyclopedia of Associations*, vol. 1, part 1. New York: Gale, 1997.

*Nancy Jean Rose*

## National Fraternal Council of Churches U.S.A., Inc.

*See* Fraternal Council of Negro Churches.

## National Freedmen's Relief Association

The National Freedmen's Relief Association (NFRA) was active in freedmen's relief efforts from February 20, 1862, until January 1, 1870. The NFRA, organized in New York City, was closely aligned and largely controlled by the American Missionary Association, a predominantly Congregationalist organization, until 1865. During those years it put most of its energy into relief and "experiments" in organizing ex-slaves as free laborers, particularly in the Port Royal, South Carolina, area. Subsequently, it shifted its emphasis to supporting schools and teachers among the freedmen.

From 1862 to 1865, the NFRA raised funds throughout the Northeast, competing with other secular freedmen's aid societies, most of which limited themselves to particular states, such as the Pennsylvania Freedmen's Relief Association and the New England Freedmen's Aid Society in Massachusetts. Beginning in mid-1865, however, the NFRA cooperated more closely with other secular societies, becoming a branch of the American Freedmen's Union Commission in 1866. After 1865, the association organized local auxiliary societies throughout New York State, relying on the local societies for fund-raising and the collection of supplies. At its height in 1867, the NFRA had over 550 auxiliary societies.

In 1863, to build public interest in the freedmen's aid movement, the association began publishing a brief, irregular *Monthly Paper*. In January 1864 it introduced a magazine-format journal, the *Freedmen's Advocate*, which was superseded by the association's *National Freedman*. Both the *Freedmen's Advocate* and the *National Freedman* were monthly publications that reported news regarding freedmen's education and relief. The *National Freedman* was discontinued after the American Freedmen's Union Commission began publication of the *American Freedman* in 1867.

Abolitionists were prominent among the officers of the association. Among them were Francis George Shaw, for several years its president; John Jay, Octavius B. Frothingham, Henry J. Fox, Norwood P. Hollowell, Edgar Ketchum, and James Miller McKim. McKim played a major role in organizing the Pennsylvania Freedmen's Relief Association as well, and was a leading light in the American Freedmen's Relief Association.

The association was the second largest of the secular societies. In its eight years of work it raised nearly one-half million dollars in cash and a quarter-million dollars in supplies for southern black relief and education. It supported no fewer than 625 individual teachers. As with all the freedmen's teachers, most of those who taught under the sponsorship of the NFRA were northern white women. However, at least 110 African Americans taught for the association, along with a handful of southern white teachers.

Northern abandonment of freedmen's aid struck the NFRA earlier than many of the other secular aid societies. Contributions dropped drastically in early 1868. By July 1868, the association entrusted its remaining assets and the remnant of its fund-raising activities to a group of trustees who continued to support its existing schools until 1870. In January 1870, the trustees gave its three southern normal schools, its teachers, and its remaining assets to the New England Freedmen's Aid Society and the Pennsylvania Freedmen's Relief Association.

**FURTHER READINGS**

Butchart, Ronald E. *Northern Schools, Southern Blacks, and Reconstruction: Freedmen's Education, 1862–1875.* Westport, Conn.: Greenwood Press, 1980.

————. "Recruits to the 'Army of Civilization': Gender, Race, Class, and the Freedmen's Teachers, 1862–1875." *Journal of Education* 172, 3 (1990): 76–87.

McPherson, James M. *The Abolitionist Legacy: From Reconstruction to the NAACP.* Princeton, N.J.: Princeton University Press, 1975.

Parmelee, Julius H. "Freedmen's Aid Societies, 1861–1871." Ed. Thomas Jesse Jones. In *Negro Education: A Study of the Private and Higher Schools for Colored People in the U.S.* U.S. Department of the Interior, Bureau of Education Bulletin No. 38, 1916. Washington, D.C.: Government Printing Office, 1917.

*Ronald E. Butchart*

# National Funeral Directors and Morticians Association

The National Funeral Directors and Morticians Association (NFDMA), originally called the Independent National Funeral Directors Association (INFDA), was founded on September 6, 1924. The INFDA's founder, R. R. Reed of Chicago, led the movement to organize licensed funeral directors who sought to maintain high professional standards in the business community. Prior to the INFDA's founding, black funeral directors had met in conjunction with the National Business League, an association of black business owners that sought to strengthen the African American business community. Funeral directors felt that they would not be able to develop and reach their full potential under the banner of the league. Although they continued to support the league, they sought their independence.

The first INFDA official meeting was held in Chicago on May 30, 1925. Following that meeting state associations were formed, and in 1926 the first national meeting was held in Indianapolis. At this meeting Lucas B. Willis of Indianapolis was named INFDA's first secretary and Reed became its national organizer. In the same year the INFDA unveiled the first edition of *The Colored Embalmer*, the official organ of the association. At the 1928 national meeting in Birmingham, Alabama, the INFDA, which was largely composed of urban funeral directors, merged with the National Colored Undertakers Association (NCUA), which represented largely rural and southern morticians. In the same year, the U.S. Department of Commerce recognized the INFDA as the official body of black funeral directors. In the following years the organization changed its name several times. In 1938 it became the Progressive National Funeral Directors Association, in 1940 the National Negro Funeral Directors Association, and in 1957 it adopted its present name, the National Funeral Directors and Morticians Association.

During the 1940s and 1950s the association expanded its work to include students of mortuary science and women. In 1945, the association organized Epsilon Nu Delta Mortuary Fraternity, which today has chapters throughout the United States. In 1952 at the national meeting in San Antonio, Texas, the Women's Auxiliary was formed, and Marguerite Purnell of Houston became its first duly elected president. In 1954 a new constitution and bylaws were written, and at the same time the association was divided into districts with eight governors who served as representatives to the body.

The objectives of the association have been consistent from its inception; it continues to foster research, conducts workshops and seminars, investigates funeral practices, develops and maintains standards of conduct among its members, and disseminates information to a much broader audience. The objectives are very similar to the activities of white funeral director and mortician associations throughout the United States.

The NFDMA today has an active membership of two thousand men and women organized into twenty-six chapters in the United States and the Caribbean. All members of state associations pay annual dues to the NFDMA as a condition for the granting and the annual renewal of each state's charter. All state associations are organized into districts, and their business is conducted by a district governor appointed by the president of the NFDMA. The state associations are grouped into nine geographical districts throughout the United States and the Caribbean. Principal officers are president, chairperson of the board of directors, corporate secretary, vice president, treasurer and clerk of the house, executive secretary, past presidents, and all life members who were life members on or before April 1986. The official organ of the NFDMA, *The National Scope*, is published quarterly at the association's national headquarters in Decatur, Georgia. In 2000, the president was Jimmie D. Boldien Jr. and the president-elect was Clarence E. Glover. The national convention of the NFDMA is held biannually in August in various locations throughout the United States.

During its history the association has provided important services not just to the black community. In 1978, for example, the U.S. government contracted Philadelphia NFDMA member Andrew W. Nix Jr. to recover the human remains of the victims of the Rev. Jim Jones's mass suicide in Guyana. Nix recovered and returned to the United States 913 bodies, including those of Jones and his family. In 1994 the Georgia Funeral Services Practitioners Association, an NFDMA affiliate, helped retrieve more than four hundred caskets that were displaced from cemeteries in Albany, Georgia, as a result of a flood. In 1995, the State Embalmers and Funeral Directors of Oklahoma, another NFDMA affiliate, coordinated their efforts with other morticians to recover victims in the Oklahoma City bombing that caused 168 deaths. More recently, NFDMA morticians representing the Washington, D.C., Funeral Directors traveled to Dover Air Force Base in Delaware to receive the remains of Commerce Secretary Ron Brown and others who perished in a plane crash in Croatia in 1996.

The NFDMA has remained faithful to its organizing principles by conducting workshops and seminars and representing the interests of its constituency before various federal, state, and local government bodies. For much of the twentieth century the association has enhanced the work of black funeral directors and morticians while it has provided dignity and comfort to relatives and friends of deceased African Americans.

**FURTHER READINGS**

Dorsey, Lois Lee. *Out of Our Past : History of the National Funeral Directors and Morticians Association.* Washington, D.C.: National Funeral Directors and Morticians Association, 1976.

Knox, George L. *Guide to Black Organizations*, 6th ed. New York: Phillip Morris Companies, 1992.

March, Erich. *The History of the African American Funeral Service—The African American Funeral Custom: Our 'Home Going' Heritage.* Nashville: Batesville Casket Company, 1997.

Tucker, Joyce B. *Black History Awareness—An Everyday Affair.* Decatur, Ga.: National Funeral Directors and Morticians Association, 1997.

*André D. Vann*

# National Health Circle for Colored People

The National Health Circle for Colored People (NHC) worked to improve health conditions in southern rural black communities following World War I. The NHC emerged from the Circle for Negro War Relief (CNWR), a service organization formed in 1917, whose board of directors was made up of prominent black and white citizens such as W. E. B. Du Bois, editor of *Crisis* magazine of the National Association for the Advancement of Colored People (NAACP); Tuskegee Institute's president, Robert R. Moton; Colonel Charles Young; the author Ray Stannard Baker; Grace Neil Johnson, wife of NAACP Executive Secretary James Weldon Johnson; and the white philanthropist George Foster Peabody. During the war the CNWR had worked to improve the health of black servicemen and their families through various programs. The CNWR, under the leadership of Adah Thoms, organized the Blue Circle Nurses to instruct blacks in impoverished communities about the importance of nutrition and sanitation. Moreover, in the first three months after its founding the CNWR raised $2,500 toward the purchase of an ambulance that it dispatched to the front in France. By the end of the war the CNWR claimed fourteen thousand members and reported that its female affiliates had done $50,000 worth of relief work during the war.

Determined to continue its health initiatives after the war, the CNWR appealed to the members of the black National Medical Association to help stimulate African American interest in public health and nursing and to assist in establishing black-staffed public health clinics in black communities. Thus, following the war, the CNWR was reorganized on a peacetime basis and dropped the reference to "war" from its name. The Circle for Negro Relief continued to raise funds for and organize public health and welfare programs in black communities. It worked to raise the health standards of African Americans by stimulating them to support public health nursing in communities where otherwise little or no such services were available. Moreover, the circle fostered recruitment, education, and placement of black public health nurses who operated under the guidance of state local and state health agencies. In 1920, the circle's letterhead revealed an extensive volunteer administration. In addition to an honorary president, president, treasurer, and executive secretary, the organization had twenty-two directors, six members on each of its executive and finance committees, and nine members on local advisory committees.

At some point during the 1920s the organization changed its name again, this time to National Health Circle for Colored People. From 1920 until at least 1929, Belle Davis served as the circle's executive secretary. A graduate of Fisk University and a former school teacher, Davis had established numerous personal contacts throughout the southern states and was instrumental in advancing the circle's work. A scholarship fund administered by Davis assisted in the training of the Blue Circle Nurses throughout the 1920s and early 1930s. The circle ceased to function during the Great Depression, likely owing to a lack of financial resources.

**FURTHER READINGS**

Hine, Darlene Clark. *Black Women in White: Racial Conflict in the Nursing Profession, 1890–1950.* Bloomington: Indiana University Press, 1989.

*Journal of the National Medical Association* 11, 4 (October-December 1919): 166–167.

Robert R. Moton Papers, Tuskegee Institute Archives, Tuskegee, Alabama.

Thoms, Adah B. *Pathfinders: A History of the Progress of Colored Graduate Nurses.* New York: Kay Print House, 1929.

*Dawn Nickel*

## National Home Demonstration Agents' Association

*See* National Association of Extension Home Economists.

## National Hospital Association

The National Hospital Association (NHA) was formed at the 1923 annual meeting of the National Medical Association (NMA) in St. Louis. Black physicians had launched the NMA in 1895 after unsuccessful attempts at joining the all-white American Medical Association (AMA). The NMA acted as an umbrella organization for national, regional, state, and local medical associations, including the NHA. The NHA's goal was to improve black medical facilities and the programs and status of black nursing schools. For this purpose the NHA created hospital standardization criteria, sponsored professional conferences, and produced and distributed educational literature.

At the time of the NHA's founding, hospital standardization and accreditation program criteria issued by the AMA and the American College of Surgeons threatened the survival of black hospitals. Between 1910 and 1923 a medical-education reform movement led initially by Abraham Flexner of the General Education Board had resulted in the closure of all but two of the country's black medical schools. Howard University's School of Medicine and Meharry Medical College and their affiliated hospitals were left with the task of training the majority of the country's black physicians. With the formation of the NHA, black physicians and nurses hoped to protect black hospitals essential not only to their own professional development but also to the well-being of the black patients whom they served.

The formation of the NHA was sparked by a controversy that erupted in Tuskegee, Alabama, in 1923. In February of that year, the Tuskegee Veterans Bureau Hospital was opened, and although the institution had been built specifically to serve black veterans, all the hospital employees except orderlies, laborers, and attendants were white. On July 1, after pressure from the NMA, the Veterans Bureau in Washington, D.C., agreed to employ some black physicians at the Tuskegee facility, but the hospital continued to be managed by whites. On July 3, 1923, hundreds of Ku Klux Klan members opposed to the appointment of African Americans as medical professionals demonstrated in the streets of Tuskegee. The NMA, supported by the National Association for the Advancement of Colored People (NAACP) and the National Negro Press Association, publicly demanded that the government keep its promise and do everything in its power to protect the black citizens and institutions of Tuskegee against any racially motivated violence. Black activists were particularly concerned about the safety of Tuskegee Institute. Founded by Booker T. Washington in 1892, it was one of the first black-controlled educational institutions in the United States. While the battle over Tuskegee's Veterans Hospital sought to ensure black physicians' access to a quality medical institution, it was also an effort to gain recognition of black contributions during World War I. Moreover, it was a test to determine whether racism or the federal government would ultimately reign over medicine in America. At Tuskegee, African Americans were successful. A year after the Klan march, black administrators were in charge of managing the hospital. The Tuskegee incident and the publicity it generated illuminated the plight of black physicians and hospitals and led to the creation of the NHA.

The NHA's charter group included physicians and a nurse. H. M. Green, a tireless advocate for black hospital reform, served as president of the NHA for its first eleven

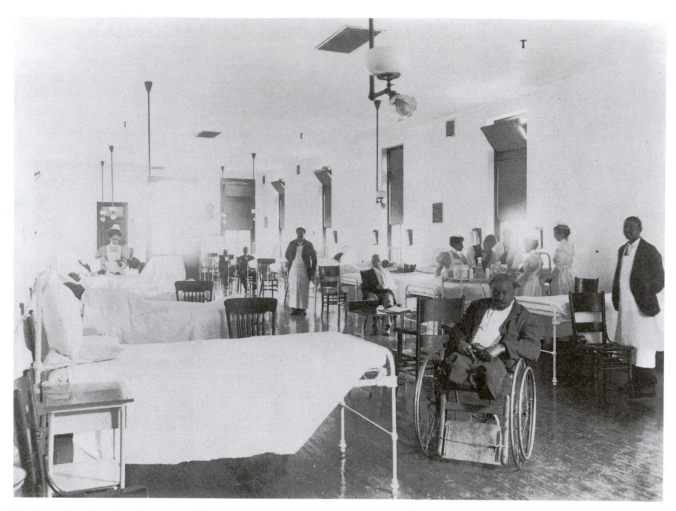

Men's ward at the Colored Home and Hospital, New York City, 1914. *Schomburg Center for Research in Black Culture*

years. He witnessed firsthand the impact of medical-education reform measures when his alma mater, Knoxville Medical College, was closed as a result of the 1910 Flexner Report. In addition to running a large private practice, Green was chief of the medical staff of a small black hospital in Knoxville and an assistant health officer for the Department of Public Health—the first African American to hold such a position. During his tenure as NHA president, Green traveled extensively and published numerous articles to promote the causes of the organization as well as the black hospital movement. Joseph H. Ward, vice president of the NHA, was a well-regarded physician from Indianapolis. On January 1924, less than a year after he assumed the NHA's vice presidency, Ward was appointed chief surgeon of the Tuskegee Veterans Hospital. John A. Kenney served as executive secretary of the NHA but was more influential as editor in chief of the *Journal of the National Medical Association*, a post

he held from 1916 to 1948. Kenney was a graduate of Leonard Medical College in Raleigh, North Carolina, a school that had also been closed as a result of Flexner's reform program. In 1923, Kenney became executive secretary of the NHA, after practicing medicine in Tuskegee for over twenty years. That year, Kenney and his family were forced to flee Tuskegee when whites threatened him because of his support of black administrative control of the veterans hospital. In 1927, frustrated with the limited access afforded black nurses and physicians, he opened the thirty-bed Kenney Memorial Hospital in Newark, New Jersey. Petra Pinn, treasurer of the NHA, was a nurse in West Palm Beach, Florida, at the time of her appointment. A 1906 graduate of Tuskegee Institute, Pinn worked as head nurse at Hale Infirmary in Montgomery, Alabama, and as superintendent of nurses of the Red Cross Sanitarium and Training School in Louisville, Kentucky. After a short stint as a nurse in Louisville's metropolitan nursing service, Pinn solicited the help of Kenney and was referred to a position as superintendent of nurses of Pine Ridge Hospital at West Palm Beach.

At the NHA's inaugural meeting, thirty-three black hospitals joined the association. Membership was open to individuals and any hospital that admitted black patients; however, only black-controlled hospitals joined the NHA. Annual membership fees of five dollars represented the NHA's primary source of income. Funds raised from dues, however, were insufficient because of the decreasing number of black hospitals. Thus, the NHA suffered financial hardship from the beginning. Between 1923 and 1931 the NHA's treasury peaked at only $300. At times, Green had to finance his own executive expenses, and there was never enough money either to employ a full-time executive director or to rent permanent office space. This weak financial position hampered the association's programs.

Members of the NHA believed that professional medical interests and the health of the country's black population would best be served by maintaining separate black hospitals. Although they condemned segregation, they accepted that racial discrimination was a strong force in medicine and one that they could not quickly or easily overcome. Thus, instead of challenging racial exclusion and discrimination, NHA members concentrated on reforming and refining medical and educational programs in black hospitals. Improving black medical facilities, they hoped, would benefit black health professionals because it would earn them the respect and attention they needed to gain entry into mainstream medicine. Thus, the NHA set out to create hospital standardization criteria, sponsor professional conferences, and produce and distribute educational literature. The goals of the association also included improving the programs and status of black nursing schools. Contrary to its claims, the NHA spent most of its energy promoting the professional interests of African American physicians and safeguarding black-controlled hospitals; it did little to improve the education of black nurses.

The NHA agenda was ambitious, given the association's lack of financial resources and the resultant weakening of its organizational structure. In addition the NHA suffered from its failure to arouse much enthusiasm among black physicians. Most black doctors who had joined the NMA were reluctant to join the NHA. Perhaps they expended so much mental and physical energy to promote and protect their professional status and that of their hospitals that they had little energy left to devote to an association that appeared to be fairly ineffective.

During the 1920s the NHA became an affiliate member of the all-white American Hospital Association (AHA), which did, however, very little to support the interests or efforts of the NHA. The AHA made only one attempt to address the problems that faced black hospitals. In 1929, it set up an ad hoc committee to study how the AHA could help the NHA in its hospital reform efforts. The committee recommended that the NHA hire a full-time executive secretary and suggested that the AHA help raise the necessary funds. But that assistance never materialized. In 1932, the NHA appealed to the Julius Rosenwald Fund, but that application was also unsuccessful. By the early 1940s, for reasons that are not clear, the NMA lost interest in supporting the NHA and the group ceased to function. The NHA was succeeded by the National Conference of Hospital Administrators, an organization whose members were professional hospital administrators, not physicians.

Although the NHA did not fulfill its ambitious mandate, it was an important forum for African American medical professionals. For nearly two decades the NHA provided them with the opportunity to discuss and consider the position of nurses and physicians in black hospitals. Perhaps even more important, the NHA initiated the African American "hospital renaissance."

FURTHER READINGS

Gamble, Vanessa Northington. *Making a Place for Ourselves: The Black Hospital Movement 1920–1945*. New York: Oxford University Press, 1995.

Hine, Darlene Clark. *Black Women in White: Racial Conflict in the Nursing Profession, 1890–1950*. Bloomington: Indiana University Press, 1989.

Price, Mitchell F., and Woodrow Jones Jr. *Public Policy and the Black Hospital: From Slavery to Segregation to Integration*. Westport Conn.: Greenwood Press, 1994.

Smith, Susan Lynn. *Sick and Tired of Being Sick and Tired: Black Women's Health Activism in America, 1890–1950*. Philadelphia: University of Pennsylvania Press, 1995.

*Dawn Nickel*

# National Institute of Science

On October 26, 1943, the National Institute of Science (NIS) was established at the twenty-first annual meeting of the Conference of the Presidents of Negro Land-Grant Colleges as the Association of Science Teachers in Negro Colleges and Affiliated Institutions. Renamed NIS in

1944, the institute was the culmination of a dream embraced by Hubert Branch Crouch, a biology teacher at Kentucky State College. In spring 1931, Crouch had attended the third annual meeting of the National Association for Research in Science Teaching. Interested in sharing the information he had obtained with some of his colleagues in the historically black colleges and universities, Crouch launched the NIS.

The objectives of the NIS were to stimulate interest in the field of science and improve the teaching of science; to make science more functional in general instruction and experimentation and in the core courses of historically black colleges and universities; to make institutional science function in the community; and to serve as an umbrella organization for other organizational and individual efforts in the sciences.

The NIS was preceded by the Physics Club of Richmond; the Alabama Association of Science and Mathematics Teachers, which published the *Morehouse Journal of Science;* Crouch's own Council of Science Teachers affiliated with the Kentucky Negro Education Association; and the Virginia Council of College Science Teachers. The NIS was formed to combat several problems, all caused to some extent by the reality of racial segregation in the early twentieth century. Owing to segregation and other discriminatory practices, black scientists were often unable to attend the meetings of major professional science organizations, particularly when those gatherings were held in the South, except in Texas. Whenever black scientists participated in professional conferences, as was the case to a limited extent in the activities of the Virginia Academy of Sciences, their white colleagues virtually ignored them. Another problem of black science teachers was that they worked in relative isolation from one another. Great distances between the historically black colleges and universities limited professional intellectual exchanges. Moreover, the paucity of trained black scientists frequently forced teachers to work in areas for which they had only minimal preparation. Science teachers also had to contend with a lack of resources aided and abetted by the attitudes of institutional administrators who placed most of their emphasis on undergraduate education. Support for science, especially research, was lukewarm at best, unless that work was in preparation for some other endeavor like medicine, dentistry, pharmacy, science teaching, home economics, or agriculture.

Confronting these obstacles, Crouch first presented his plan to organize black scientists at the 1939 meeting of the Virginia Conference of College Science Teachers, where he gave a paper titled "Science Organization in Our Colleges." It took four years, however, before Crouch's dream of an organization of black scientists materialized. In 1943, Crouch and his associates presented their organizational proposal to the Conference of the Presidents of Negro Land-Grant Colleges. Arguing that science would play an important role in American society after World War II, and seeking to emphasize the influence of blacks on advancing science and science education, they launched the NIS.

Since its founding in 1943, the NIS has remained committed to its initial objectives, while the number of its members and the variety of scientific specialties they represent has increased. In 1997, the NIS reported a membership of approximately 850 scientists. Members attend annual meetings, present papers, advocate the cause of science education, and pass the torch to younger scholars.

**FURTHER READING**

King, William M. "Hubert Branch Crouch and the Origins of the National Institute of Science." *Journal of Negro History* 79, 1 (Winter 1994): 18–33.

*William M. King*

## National Insurance Association

The National Negro Insurance Association (NNIA) (renamed the National Insurance Association in 1954) was founded at Durham, North Carolina, in 1921. Like a great many other African American trade and professional associations, the NNIA began in the South as part of a vast network of all-black institutions that owed their existence, on the one hand, to white discrimination and segregation, and on the other hand, to black pride and racial solidarity. This institution building had antebellum origins among free blacks, but it began in earnest with the emancipation of four million slaves.

By the turn of the twentieth century a full range of black businesses had come forward to meet the onslaught of Jim Crow and to provide goods and services for African American citizens. Indeed, in 1900, Booker T. Washington, following the lead of W. E. B. Du Bois in calling for "economic cooperation among Negroes," organized the National Negro Business League (NNBL). The NNBL, in turn, encouraged a broad array of trade associations, most notably the National Negro Bankers Association (1908) and the NNIA.

The early history of the NNIA is well documented. At the 1920 annual convention of the NNBL, George Washington Lee, vice president of Mississippi Life Insurance Company, announced the need to organize the growing number of black insurance companies. The NNBL acted on Lee's proposal at its 1921 convention in Atlanta, setting up a temporary committee to preside over the formal creation of the NNIA later that year in Durham.

It was no accident that the committee chose to meet in Durham, or that the delegates selected Charles Clinton Spaulding as the first president of the NNIA. Durham had gained the reputation as the "Black Wall Street of America." It was the headquarters of "the world's largest Negro business—the North Carolina Mutual Life Insurance Company—and Spaulding, its vice president and effective head, was well on his way to becoming the leading black businessman in the United States. Thirteen companies sent delegates to the meeting, but the NNIA counted forty-two black firms as eligible for membership (fraternal orders and benevolent societies that often provided insurance benefits to its members were excluded).

Given the relative size and importance of life insurance companies in the African American community, it is reasonable to agree with Merah S. Stuart, an NNIA president and custodian of its early history, that for much of the twentieth century the NNIA could claim to be the "most effective general economic organization of Negroes." But, of course, it was more than an economic organization; like all black institutions, its legitimacy ultimately lay in its larger commitment to racial uplift. This mixed identity encouraged a mixed agenda for NNIA annual conventions, which provided a forum for everything from technical papers on actuarial science, advertising, and business management to spirited sessions on community development, white competition, and civil rights. When the association launched National Negro Insurance Week in 1934, it did so to boost business; but it also did so to boost racial self-help and solidarity, not so different from the tradition expressed in National Negro Health Week or Negro History Week. Only in this transcendent context of race would it have made sense for Martin Luther King to give a major civil rights speech at the 1963 NNIA convention in Chicago. Or only in the context of *Brown v. Board of Education* can it be understood why in 1954 the NNIA became the National Insurance Association (NIA).

Desegregation was a double-edged sword for many black businesses, often undercutting their reason for being. In the meantime, the urban rebellions of the 1960s, followed by the call for Black Power and Black Capitalism, provided a reprieve for black life insurance companies, especially with a windfall of group insurance contracts granted to black firms by the federal government and major corporations. But this market proved to be only a temporary hostage at the same time the original captive market—millions of black policyholders—began to melt away into the mainstream or, in the case of a declining blue-collar class, the lifeblood of many of the companies, into oblivion.

In its post–World War II heyday, the NIA could claim as many as sixty-five members. In 1950 it established a national headquarters in Chicago, hired a permanent director and staff, and launched monthly training institutes and a bimonthly trade magazine, *The Pilot*. By 1998, the membership had dwindled to thirteen, the institutes and *The Pilot* had disappeared, and the national headquarters had relocated to Las Vegas, Nevada. For many of the same reasons that self-sufficient neighborhoods filled with mom-and-pop stores have passed from the scene, the NIA may not survive either. But the passing of African American institutions amounts to more than the impersonal process of history at work. For those generations of black Americans who lived and worked behind the veil of segregation, the legacy of otherwise mundane organizations like the NIA takes on an almost sacred quality, a hallowed reminder of how an entire people made bricks without straw by taking "advantage of the disadvantages" and daring to realize a dream that was never meant to include them.

**FURTHER READINGS**

National Insurance Association. "Golden Anniversary, Golden Opportunity." *Fiftieth Annual NIA Convention Program*, Richmond, Va., 1970.

Stuart, Merah Steven. *An Economic Detour: A History of Insurance in the Lives of American Negroes*. New York: Wendell Malliet, 1940.

Walker, Juliet E. K. *The History of Black Business in America: Capitalism, Race, Entrepreneurship*. New York: Macmillan, 1998.

Weare, Walter B. *Black Business in the New South: A Social History of the North Carolina Mutual Life Insurance Company*. Urbana: University of Illinois Press, 1973.

Weems, Robert E., Jr. *Black Business in the Black Metropolis: The Chicago Metropolitan Assurance Company, 1925–1985*. Bloomington: Indiana University Press, 1996.

*Walter B. Weare*

# National Interscholastic Basketball Tournament

Held annually between 1929 and 1942, the National Interscholastic Basketball Tournament (NIBT) was an athletic competition between black high schools primarily from the mid-Atlantic and Midwest regions. The NIBT was the brainchild of Charles H. Williams, director of physical education at Hampton Institute, who launched the national tournament to elevate the standards of African American high school athletic competition. Williams had been a central figure in the founding of the Colored Intercollegiate Athletic Association (CIAA), which had helped to raise the level of athletic competition between historically black colleges and universities since 1912. The NIBT, he hoped, would generate the same response among the nation's black high schools.

Prior to the creation of the NIBT, Edwin B. Henderson, physical education director of Washington, D.C.'s, high schools, had founded the Interscholastic Athletic Association (ISAA) to foster black high school sports. Beginning in 1905, the ISAA's efforts soon resulted in a proliferation of black high school athletic teams. By 1907, interscholastic competitions in track, baseball, and football thrived in Washington, D.C., Indianapolis, Baltimore, and Wilmington. The ISAA had its greatest impact on basketball, however, which was less expensive to play than football and more centrally positioned in the academic year than baseball. The work of the ISAA also stimulated the creation of state athletic associations. In 1924, for example, fourteen black high schools in West Virginia established the West Virginia Athletic Union, the first statewide black high school athletic association in the South. By 1948, every racially segregated Southern and Midwestern state had similar organizations, all of which sponsored state-wide basketball tournaments.

When Williams launched the NIBT in 1929, he envisioned a national tournament of all-black high school basketball teams. Initially, however, the NIBT failed to attract teams from the Midwest, Southwest, or Deep South. At the NIBT's 1929 inaugural tournament at Hampton Institute, teams from ten schools competed including three from Virginia, four from North Carolina, two from West Virginia, and Armstrong Technical High School from Washington, D.C. The tournament took place over the course of two days in a double-elimination format, with some teams playing three times on the first day. Armstrong, one of the country's first black schools with an indoor gymnasium, won the NIBT title over West Virginia's Douglas High School. The following year, the final match produced the same results.

In 1931, the tournament's national visibility increased with the addition of two Midwestern schools. That year, Chicago's city champion, Wendell Phillips, and the Roosevelt Panthers of Gary, Indiana, attended the NIBT. During the final match, Wendell Phillips beat West Virginia's Genoa High by twenty-five points. The 1932 tournament was cancelled because of extensive flooding in the mid-Atlantic region and in the following year, Hampton Institute, concerned about the tournament's cost, withdrew its sponsorship.

While 1933 witnessed an end to the NIBT's close relationship with Hampton, the year also marked the beginning of Midwest domination of the tournament. Following a Panther victory over North Carolina's Henderson Institute, the NIBT moved to the Panthers' home in Gary, where the tournament was run by Panther coach John Smith in 1934, 1935, 1937, and 1938. In its first year at Gary, the tournament reached a zenith when the NIBT introduced a victory trophy as well as a printed program containing sixty-eight pages of advertisements of local merchants. The tournament was held in Gary's seven thousand–seat Municipal Auditorium, while visiting teams stayed at Roosevelt High in cots supplied by U.S. Steel, one of the city's major employers. Local tournament organizers handed out free movie passes to players and arranged for a victory dance after the final game. That year Roosevelt beat Louisville's Central High, 30-24, and Smith became the nation's best-known black high school coach. In the following year, Roosevelt won its third straight title when the Panthers beat West Virginia's Kelley-Miller, 21-19, in front of twelve thousand fans. Roosevelt took six straight NIBT titles before losing in 1938 to West Virginia's Charleston Garnet High, 20-14. It was Smith's first loss in five years of playing in the tournament.

From 1936 to 1942, the tournament moved between various cities. During this period, interest declined, as the NIBT lost many of its teams to integration and to a new tournament created by Cleve Abbott, athletic director at Tuskegee.

**FURTHER READINGS**

Ashe, Arthur R., Jr. *A Hard Road to Glory: A History of the African-American Athlete.* New York: Amistad Press, 1988.

George, Nelson. *Elevating the Game: Black Men and Basketball.* New York: Harper Collins, 1992.

Henderson, Edwin B. "Physical Education and Athletics Among Negroes." *Proceedings of the Big Ten Symposium on the History of Physical Education and Sport.* Chicago: Athletic Institute, 1971.

*Amy Bass*

## National Lawyers Guild

Founded in 1936, the National Lawyers Guild (NLG) was the first racially integrated national bar association in the United States. From its inception the organization supported civil rights and prominently featured African Americans in leadership roles. Because of problems stemming from its leftist political orientation, however, it never attracted widespread membership from the black legal community.

The NLG emerged during a time of pronounced stratification within the American legal profession. Since 1878 the American Bar Association (ABA) had asserted itself as the representative organization of American lawyers, but it was dominated by corporate attorneys and graduates of elite law schools, and it had systematically excluded racial and ethnic minorities. During the Great Depression, when lawyers at the lower echelon of the profession experienced widespread unemployment and most Americans could not afford basic legal services, the ABA continued to espouse corporate interests. In December 1936 a group of lawyers met in New York City to form a progressive alternative to the ABA dedicated "to the end that human rights shall be regarded as more sacred than property rights." Over the next six months the guild attracted nearly three thousand members of diverse backgrounds—New Deal liberals, Communist Party members, government attorneys, labor lawyers, civil libertarians, and marginalized practitioners such as personal injury and criminal defense attorneys.

One of the primary ways that the NLG distinguished itself from the ABA was to welcome blacks as members. The guild's policy attracted several of the nation's most prominent black attorneys, including William H. Hastie, Raymond Pace Alexander, Thurgood Marshall, and Charles Hamilton Houston, who served on the NLG's first executive board. Several leaders of the National Bar Association (NBA), a professional organization for black lawyers, joined the guild, as did faculty from black law schools such as Howard University and Lincoln University. The nondiscrimination policy was not without its costs, however, as it prevented the guild from establishing chapters in the South.

Although the NLG attracted many of the nation's leading black attorneys, it never found widespread support among the rank and file of black lawyers. This may have stemmed from an understandable distrust of white bar organizations, but more likely it can be attributed to the position of civil rights in the guild's hierarchy of priorities. Leftists in the organization emphasized the rights of workers, while others concentrated on issues broadly related to economic inequality, rather than black civil rights specifically. Consequently black attorneys turned to organizations such as the NAACP and the NBA to implement their civil rights agenda.

The group's ability to accomplish meaningful civil rights reform was also thwarted by conflict within the organization. Political radicals warred with liberals over economic reform and foreign policy issues, and both factions clashed with members who believed that the guild should focus on strictly professional concerns. In 1940 it lost about two-thirds of its membership after extensive debate over the presence of Communists in the organization. Black members joined the exodus, either because they shared anti-Communist sentiments or because they feared that association with radicals would harm their reputations and hamper their efforts to build white liberal support for civil rights.

Despite these limitations, the NLG established a credible record of support for civil rights during the 1940s. It worked to desegregate the armed forces and promoted the hiring of black attorneys in the military and the federal government. It campaigned to strengthen the Civil Rights Section of the Justice Department and to establish the Fair Employment Practices Committee, successfully installing guild member Earl B. Dickerson as the only black lawyer on the committee. It filed amicus curiae briefs before the Supreme Court in cases dealing with voting rights, restrictive housing covenants, and segregated transportation. Guild-sponsored legal aid offices provided representation for poor blacks in civil and criminal cases. In 1951 Dickerson became the first black president of the NLG.

These initiatives were short-lived, however, as the guild came under increased scrutiny during the McCarthy era. It was vulnerable to attacks from anti-Communists not only because of the politics of some of its members but also because it was virtually the only organization to provide legal representation to Communists. In 1950 the House Un-American Activities Committee labeled the NLG the "legal bulwark of the Communist Party," and in 1953 Attorney General Herbert Brownell launched a campaign to place it on the Justice Department's list of subversive organizations. Although Brownell's successor dropped the effort in 1958, the anti-Communist crusade had a devastating effect on the organization. From 2,500 members in 1946, it shrank to 550 members by 1959. Its legal aid and civil rights programs also suffered as it devoted almost all its efforts to defending its members and pursuing protracted litigation to keep its name off the subversive list.

The civil rights movement of the 1960s sparked a temporary reorientation of the NLG's mission. In 1963 a new generation of guild leaders shepherded through the executive board a resolution that "the primary emphasis" of the guild would be the fight for racial equality. The organization established a Committee for Legal Assistance to the South to bolster the thin ranks of civil rights lawyers working in states such as Mississippi and Alabama. But by the end of the decade, the Vietnam War had diverted the guild's attention to the rights of draft resisters and antiwar protesters. It closed its southern offices, and black membership dwindled to about forty members, less than 2 percent of the total membership. Moderate blacks remained wary of its radical reputation, and activist black attorneys turned to the newly formed National Conference of Black Lawyers (NCBL). Since 1970 the guild's civil rights activities have emphasized cooperative efforts with the NCBL, particularly in support of affirmative action.

**FURTHER READINGS**

Bailey, Percival Roberts. "Progressive Lawyers: A History of the National Lawyers Guild, 1936–1958." Ph.D. diss., Rutgers University, 1979.

Ginger, Ann Fagan, and Eugene M. Tobin, eds. *The National Lawyers Guild: From Roosevelt Through Reagan.* Philadelphia: Temple University Press, 1988.

*Eric W. Rise*

## National Medical Association

The National Medical Association (NMA) protected the interests of the black medical profession and allied fields, including African American physicians, surgeons, dentists, and pharmacists. Founded in 1895, the NMA became one of the major organizations for the promotion of black rights in the United States. In the late nineteenth and early twentieth centuries, racial segregation forced black leaders to create separate and parallel professional medical bodies such as journals, medical and nursing schools, and hospitals.

The NMA was founded by twelve black doctors who gathered at the Cotton States and International Exposition in Atlanta. Concerned that racism and segregation restricted access to health services and health education, especially in the South, where most African Americans lived, the men launched the NMA to promote black health and combat racism. Among the founders were Robert F. Boyd of Nashville, Tennessee, who became the organization's first president, and Daniel Hale Williams of Chicago, who became its first vice president. African American physicians launched the NMA in response to their de facto exclusion from the American Medical Association (AMA). Black doctors were barred from joining the whites-only county and state medical societies recognized by the AMA. Denied access to the AMA, black physicians were forced to create their own medical organization.

Because of the small pool from which to draw recruits, membership in the NMA grew slowly. When the organization was founded in 1895 there were only about four hundred black doctors practicing in the United States. But by 1905 there were about fifteen hundred black doctors, about fifty of whom joined the NMA. At that point the organization began to hold annual meetings that attracted the attention of the black press. In 1910 the NMA boasted five hundred members, even as it criticized the black doctors who failed to join. By 1928 some four thousand black doctors were registered in the country and of those just under two thousand had joined the NMA.

Although most members of the black medical association were men, several black women participated in the organization. Among the early members were Matilda Evans of Columbia, South Carolina; Ionia Whipper of West Virginia; and Anna R. Cooper of Chicago. The presence of women was notable given that by 1920 there were still only sixty-five black women among the thirty-eight hundred black doctors in the country. By the 1930s another generation of black women doctors made their mark at NMA annual meetings, including Dorothy Boulding Ferebee of Washington, D.C., May Chinn of New York, and Lena Edwards of New Jersey. Women were particularly prominent among the pharmacists active in the organization, including J. P. H. Coleman of Virginia and Amanda V. Gray of Washington, D.C. Despite women's long presence within the organization, the NMA did not have a woman president until 1985, when Edith Irby Jones was elected.

The leaders of the NMA decided early on that the best way to promote the organization was through the publication of a journal. Thus, in 1909 the NMA launched the *Journal of the National Medical Association* to raise professional standards through continuing education for black doctors. Charles V. Roman of Nashville served as editor until 1918, when John Kenney of Tuskegee took over. Kenney kept the journal to a high academic standard and continued his role as editor until 1950, when Montague Cobb of Washington, D.C., assumed leadership. Each issue contained not only articles about medical practice but also updates about the status of the black health profession. For example, during the influenza epidemic of 1918–1919, the journal reported that black doctors and nurses earned increased recognition for their excellent skills. Apparently, racism was muted in the crisis of the epidemic as black health workers were called on more than ever before. At a time when many white health professionals were involved in the war effort, black health workers became essential to community health care for whites as well as blacks. The journal also promoted a sense of community among black health professionals as it reported on the activities of various members and provided biographical information. For a time, the journal even reported on the activities of the National Association of Colored Graduate Nurses, an organization that had at one point been interested in formal affiliation with the NMA.

The NMA played a significant role in the black health movement of the first half of the twentieth century. Together, black health professionals and layworkers struggled to draw government attention to black health needs. The NMA was eager to get state health boards and the U.S. Public Health Service to give greater attention to the health problems of African Americans, especially through the employment of black staff doctors.

The NMA also sought to provide the masses with health education. For example, its annual meetings always provided at least one session open to the public. Moreover, the NMA was active in public health work through the promotion of the annual National Negro Health Week observance during the interwar years. During that week, NMA members conducted free community health clinics in churches and schools. Although Negro Health Week was established in 1915 by Booker T. Washington at Tuskegee Institute, Roscoe C. Brown of the NMA led this health week campaign at the national level. A dentist by training, Brown gave up his private practice to pursue a career in public health. He became an active member of the NMA and headed the Dental Section of the organization during the 1910s. He also served

as associate editor of the journal. In the 1930s the NMA and other black leaders secured Brown a position in the U.S. Public Health Service in the new Office of Negro Health Work. He became the only black official in the Public Health Service during the 1930s and the only health official in President Roosevelt's "black cabinet."

In addition to public health, the NMA repeatedly addressed the need for black access to quality hospitals. By the 1920s the NMA launched a black hospital movement. Leaders of the organization argued that black doctors required access to hospitals to make a place for themselves in the medical profession. Thus, in 1923 the NMA established the National Hospital Association to improve black hospital standards. NMA leaders feared that as hospital accreditation required more rigorous qualifications, black hospitals would be at a disadvantage and face closure. The closing of black hospitals, they feared, would entail the near elimination of black doctors because hospitals had become essential to medical practice by the 1920s. Their fears were well founded, given the closure of most black medical schools. Between 1900 and 1923 eight of the ten black medical schools were forced to close. The solution, according to the NMA, was to improve black hospitals and therefore protect black professional interests. Thus, the organization urged black doctors to become active in hospital reform.

By the post–World War II era, members of the NMA joined other African Americans in the creation of a medical civil rights movement. Like many African Americans, most black doctors felt that integration was long overdue. As a result, the NMA launched several initiatives attacking segregation during the 1950s. First, it directly challenged the AMA's support of southern racial exclusion. Some county and state affiliates of the AMA in the South responded and started to accept black members. However, most southern chapters did not alter their white-only stance. Second, the NMA sought to remove racial barriers for admission to specialty boards, such as the American College of Surgeons. For too long Louis Wright had been the only black member of this esteemed body. Third, NMA leaders challenged segregation in nursing and medical schools at a time when the segregated education system in the South was under attack.

Finally, under the leadership of Montague Cobb, the NMA pushed for hospital integration. By the late 1950s most black leaders no longer supported separate black hospitals. Thus, the NMA sought equal access for black health workers and patients to white hospital facilities. As part of this civil rights effort, Cobb created the Imhotep conferences on hospital integration. These conferences were named after a famous Egyptian doctor from about 3000 B.C., who may have been the earliest known physician. Imhotep was an important symbol for the medical civil rights movement, according to Cobb, because his existence suggests that the medical profession may have been started by a nonwhite man. The Imhotep conferences began in 1957 and gained increasing support from white as well as black doctors.

Although formal legalized segregation was dismantled in the United States in the 1960s, equal access to health care did not become a reality. Over one hundred years after its founding, the NMA continues to play an important role in the promotion of black professional interests and quality health care for African Americans.

**FURTHER READINGS**

Beardsley, Edward H. *A History of Neglect: Health Care for Blacks and Mill Workers in the Twentieth-Century South.* Knoxville: University of Tennessee Press, 1987.

Gamble, Vanessa Northington. *Making a Place for Ourselves: The Black Hospital Movement, 1920–1945.* New York: Oxford University Press, 1995.

Morais, Herbert M. *The History of the Negro in Medicine.* New York: Publishers Company for the Association for the Study of Negro Life and History, 1967.

McBride, David. *From TB to AIDS: Epidemics Among Urban Blacks Since 1900.* Albany: State University of New York Press, 1991.

Smith, Susan L. *Sick and Tired of Being Sick and Tired: Black Women's Health Activism in America, 1890–1950.* Philadelphia: University of Pennsylvania Press, 1995.

*Susan L. Smith*

# National Negro Baseball Leagues

The National Negro Baseball Leagues provided opportunities for African American baseball players to learn the game and showcase their talent. Initiated in 1920, the Negro leagues lasted until 1960, though not always the same leagues or teams participated. After 1947, the leagues began to decline because of the integration of the Major Leagues.

Beginning in the 1880s, a gentlemen's agreement separated the races on the diamond. Adrian "Cap" Anson of the Chicago White Sox played a key role in creating this policy by refusing to play teams with African American players on their rosters. The agreement was an unspoken understanding that no one wanted to break. Nevertheless,

a number of African Americans did play in organized white clubs during the nineteenth century. In 1884, Moses and Welday Walker played for Toledo in the American Association, a major league at that time. Others like George Stovey, John Fowler, and Frank Grant performed on a number of different minor league squads before 1890. Jim Crow attitudes, however, helped push black players out of the white leagues, leading to unsuccessful early ventures such as the League of Colored Baseball Clubs. Another attempt to create a separate Negro league failed in 1910.

By the early decades of the twentieth century many amateur and semiprofessional African American teams flourished, such as the Indianapolis ABCs, the Chicago Union Giants, and the Homestead Grays. They built on the foundation laid in 1885 by the first African American professional team, the Cuban Giants. These teams provided the basis for the creation of a permanent league in 1920.

That year, Andrew "Rube" Foster, who had pitched for the Waco Yellow Jackets, the Philadelphia Giants, and a number of other baseball clubs during a career that spanned over twenty years, founded the Negro National League in Kansas City, Missouri. Foster organized the league to enable African American men to play baseball competitively. He called together a group of owners, lawyers, and news reporters to develop a constitution and a league schedule. Eight teams joined this new league, including Foster's Chicago American Giants, the Dayton Marcos, the Indianapolis ABCs, the Chicago Giants, the Detroit Stars, the Kansas City Monarchs, the Cuban Stars, and the St. Louis Giants. By the end of the first season, some problems surfaced that continued to plague the leagues throughout their existence. A key problem revolved around trying to find ways to keep players from jumping from one team to another. Fining them held no real threat because most players had no money and the league developed no system to collect the fines. Another problem the league tried to resolve was the lack of consistent newspaper coverage. Most African American newspapers could not afford to send reporters out with each team. Instead, they relied on teams calling in their own results, which happened sporadically. Most African American papers were published weekly, which also affected coverage. At various points throughout league history different methods were tried to encourage publication but none worked successfully. Securing umpires also posed problems. Initially, the league hired no regular umpires, but instead relied on teams to provide their own. Unfortunately, finding qualified African American men proved difficult, and often teams relied on local men who had enthusiasm but no real training. White umpires were also used at times, with varying degrees of success.

The 1921 season opened with most teams returning for their second year, though the Columbus Buckeyes replaced the Dayton club. Teams sometimes ran into financial troubles or scheduling problems that forced them to leave the leagues after only a short stint. This happened to the leagues throughout their history. At the same time teams such as the Kansas City Monarchs, the Chicago American Giants, and the Homestead Grays enjoyed long tenures.

By 1923 a major change took place with the creation of a second league known as the Eastern Colored League (ECL). Ed Bolden, its director, founded the league to cut down on travel costs for Eastern teams that were constantly forced to travel to the Midwest. As a result of the emergence of a second league, a Negro World Series began in 1924 and continued through 1927. Later an East-West Classic was added, to be played at Chicago's Comiskey Park, where thousands of spectators came to watch the stars.

The financial decline of the Depression years hurt the leagues, forcing both the ECL and the NNL to close their doors by the end of 1931. Foster had left the scene in 1926 to enter the hospital and died in 1930. By 1932, only one league, the East-West League, still operated. In 1933, however, a second Negro National League emerged, and in 1937 a Negro American League (NAL) was founded. The World Series was revived in 1942 and continued until 1955. The Kansas City Monarchs won the pennant seventeen times and the Series twice, followed by the Grays with twelve pennants and three Series victories. Foster's Chicago American Giants also won twelve pennants and two World Series between 1920 and 1949. In addition to these Major Leagues there were a number of smaller leagues, such as the Negro Southern League (NSL) and the Texas-Oklahoma-Louisiana (TOL) League. These leagues helped feed players to the Negro Leagues, acting much like a farm system.

Teams survived the worst years of the Depression by bringing in new money and adopting many new gimmicks to draw in the crowds. Numbers kings channeled their money into teams like the Cuban Stars and the Pittsburgh Crawfords. This enabled them to have a legitimate business that covered up many of their illegal business ventures and provided the opportunity for communities to have baseball squads.

The NAL and NNL took center stage during the 1930s, providing fans with great baseball. The All-Star game became an incredible success, with thousands of spectators coming out to see the best players from each league. Many major and minor league scouts came to watch as well. In addition to their league schedules, teams barnstormed across the country, playing opponents wherever they could find them. These nonleague games took place during the season as well as during spring training and in the winter months. Often black teams won against white Major Leaguers like Dizzy Dean, Babe Ruth, and Lou Gehrig.

In addition to playing in the United States, many black teams and players moved south of the border to play. Willard Brown, Josh Gibson, Willie Wells, and Ray Brown all became stars while playing for cities like Trujillo, Honduras; Ponce de Leon, Puerto Rico; and Caguas, Puerto Rico. While some players played in Latin America only during the off-season, others went during the season because the money was good and they were not treated as second-class citizens. There they were treated like heroes.

During the Second World War agitation increased toward racially integrating the Major Leagues. Many groups and individuals participated in this effort, leading to the signing of Jackie Robinson by the Brooklyn Dodgers in late 1945. Robinson played for the minor league Montreal Royals in 1946, then joined the parent club in 1947, cracking the color line that had existed since 1887. Robinson was chosen because of his educational background, his college career on integrated teams, and his character, even though Negro Leaguers believed that he was not the best player in their leagues. After Robinson joined the Dodgers, the Negro Leagues began a slow decline as more black players followed him and signed with white teams. Monte Irvin, Jim Gilliam, Don Newcombe, Roy Campanella, and Larry Doby joined the rosters of Major League clubs straight from the Negro Leagues. New stars like Henry Aaron and Willie Mays also began with short careers in the Negro Leagues before moving on to the big leagues. As the need for separate leagues lessened, teams folded and the schedule got smaller and smaller until only the Birmingham Black Barons were left in 1960.

For the Negro League owners, the desegregation of the Major Leagues created a dilemma. While they wanted their athletes to take advantage of the opening of the Major Leagues, they also recognized that this meant their teams would eventually fade away. Effa Manley, of the Newark Eagles, hoped to see whole teams incorporated into the farm system, but this never happened. It was not until 1959, when the Boston Red Sox finally brought up Pumpsie Green, that all the Major League teams had at least one African American player on their roster.

**FURTHER READINGS**

Clark, Dick, and Larry, Lester eds. *The Negro Leagues Book.* Cleveland: Society of American Baseball Research, 1994.

Riley, James A. *The Biographical Encyclopedia of the Negro Baseball Leagues.* New York: Carroll and Graf, 1994.

Rogosin, Donn. *Invisible Men: Life in Baseball's Negro Leagues.* New York: Kodansha International, 1995 (Original, 1983, Atheneum).

*Sol White's History of Colored Baseball with Other Documents on the Early Black Game, 1886–1936.* Introduction by Jerry Malloy. Lincoln: University of Nebraska Press, 1995.

Tygiel, Jules. *Baseball's Great Experiment: Jackie Robinson and His Legacy.* New York: Vintage Books, 1983.

*Leslie Heaphy*

**SEE ALSO**    Eastern Colored League; Negro American League; Negro National League; Negro Southern League

## National Negro Bowling Association

*See* National Bowling Association.

## National Negro Business League

*See* National Business League.

## National Negro Congress

During the 1930s the U.S. Communist Party (CP), as a result of its defense of the "Scottsboro 9" and the general ravages brought by the Great Depression, attained a foothold among African Americans that it did not have before or since. This was the era of the "popular front," when the party saw as a prime mission binding together disparate forces on behalf of a minimal political program. Perhaps the most significant example of the popular front in the African American community was the National Negro Congress (NNC).

The NNC had been preceded by other CP initiatives designed to attract African Americans, including the League of Struggle for Negro Rights (LSNR) and the American Negro Labor Congress (ANLC). These two organizations, however, were perceived as having agendas that were not sufficiently broad to attract adherents; while the LSNR and the ANLC were initiated by Communists, this was not true of the NNC—which, nonetheless, was influenced deeply by the party's radicalism.

The NNC emerged from a 1935 conference—organized by Ralph T. Bunche, chair of Harvard University's political science department, and John P. Davis, a civil rights activist and cofounder of the Joint Committee on National Recovery—at Howard University in Washington, D.C., on the Status of the Negro in the New Deal. There was much to complain about at this conference, for despite the liberal-sounding rhetoric of the New Deal, the fact that the administration of President Franklin D. Roosevelt was beholden to Southern Democrats made it difficult for the White House to move aggressively against lynching and other ills that plagued African Americans.

The NNC was formed in 1936 as a direct response to the crisis gripping African Americans that the Howard conference had detailed. The NNC brought under one roof a diverse array of ideologies, ranging from the liberalism of the National Association for the Advancement of Colored People leaders to the socialist orientation of labor leader A. Philip Randolph to the Marxism-Leninism of Communists. Also included in the ranks were religious leaders, heads of fraternal organizations, and entrepreneurs.

The NNC campaigned on behalf of the Scottsboro 9—the black youth from Alabama accused unjustly of sexually molesting two white females—and crusaded against lynching. In neighborhoods across the nation, the NNC pushed for an end to police brutality and for relief measures to alleviate the ravages brought by the Depression. It joined the Congress of Industrial Organizations in its attempt to organize workers in mass production industries into unions. NNC members were also involved in the effort to defend the republican government of Spain, which was under assault by the fascist forces of General Franco and the fascist powers of Germany and Italy, just as NNC members rose to the defense of Ethiopia after it was invaded by Italy.

Disagreements about foreign policy created rifts within the NNC. In 1939 the Soviet Union—after being rebuffed in its attempt to forge a collective security pact against fascism with, for example, Britain and France—signed a nonaggression pact with Hitler's Germany. This caused Communists within the NNC to soften their previous uncompromising, unyielding opposition to Germany. This, in turn, irked a number of non-Communists within the NNC who felt that this episode illustrated the unreliability of Communists. In their defense Communists argued that it was not necessary to reach total agreement on every point for disparate forces to work together—thus, atheists should not have to accept Jesus Christ in order to work with Christians on the question of lynching.

This position did not carry the day. By 1940 Randolph was denouncing the NNC for its alleged fealty to Moscow. This internecine squabbling weakened the NNC, and when the United States entered World War II in 1941, the NNC was weakened further as some members charged others with subordinating the struggle against racism to what was perceived as the larger goal: the struggle against fascism.

Hence, by the time the war ended in 1945, the NNC was a shadow of its former self. It was perceived that its goals could be better attained in a larger organization. Thus, in 1946 the NNC was folded into the Civil Rights Congress, which carried on the struggle for black rights in the broader context of a struggle against political repression brought by the nascent Red Scare.

Still, the practical lessons garnered by NNC members during its brief existence were applied and extended through the 1940s and 1950s as NNC members went on to play pivotal roles not only in struggling against the Red Scare but, as well, helping to bring the civil rights movement to fruition.

**FURTHER READINGS**

Egerton, John. *Speak Now Against the Day: The Generation Before the Civil Rights Movement in the South.* Chapel Hill: University of North Carolina Press, 1995.

Hughes, Cicero Alvin. "Toward a Black United Front: The National Negro Congress Movement." Ph.D. diss., Ohio University, 1982.

Naison, Mark. *Communists in Harlem During the Great Depression.* Urbana: University of Illinois Press, 1983.

*Papers of the National Negro Congress.* Frederick, Md.: University Publications of America, 1988.

Streater, John Baxter. "The National Negro Congress, 1936–1947." Ph.D. diss., University of Cincinnati, 1981.

Sullivan, Patricia. *Days of Hope: Race and Democracy in the New Deal Era.* Chapel Hill: University of North Carolina Press, 1996.

*Gerald Horne*

## National Negro Insurance Association

*See* National Insurance Association.

## National Negro Labor Council

William Hood, a member of the United Automobile Workers, and the labor organizers Coleman Young of the Amalgamated Clothing Workers and Ernest Thompson of the United Electrical Workers, founded the National Negro Labor Council (NNLC) in 1951. Until its demise in 1956, the NNLC sought to unite black workers in the struggle to improve their conditions. Headquartered in Detroit, the NNLC had twenty-three branches throughout the United States, the most active ones in Chicago, Detroit, and Louisville. NNLC campaigns varied from city to city; generally, though, the organization put pressure on companies to promote black employees and to hire additional black workers. It also leveled criticism at organized labor for not doing more to organize black workers. From its inception, government agencies and union leaders accused the NNLC of being infiltrated by Communists. In 1955, the NNLC was brought before the House Un-American Activities Committee (HUAC) and Hood, Coleman, and Thompson, with approval from NNLC members, decided to disband in 1956 rather than go through what they thought would be a futile effort to deny the charges. Though in existence for only five years, the NNLC offered an important critique of business and organized labor in the early Cold War years and paved the way for activists among its ranks to apply the lessons they had learned in other forums.

Black trade unionists first discussed establishing black labor councils at the National Trade Union Conference for Negro Rights in Chicago in 1950. Over nine hundred delegates came together to discuss the postwar displacement of black defense workers, race-based inequality in housing and education, the increase in murders of blacks, and the biased criminal justice system that tolerated "frame-ups" of black people. As trade unionists, conference participants decided to focus on obtaining what they called "economic democracy" while keeping a critical eye on developments in housing, education, and the criminal justice system. Thus, the agenda that emerged from the conference emphasized the need for economic security and called for the establishment of black labor councils to obtain better jobs for African American workers.

Just over one year later, this became a reality when the founding convention of the NNLC was held in Cincinnati in October 1951. Thompson gave a rousing address at the convention in which he likened the NNLC to a "new wind of freedom" that would sweep away exploitative imperialist business practices and racist labor unions. With Hood as president, Young as executive secretary, Thompson as director of organizations, and Octavia Hawkins as treasurer, the NNLC set up headquarters in Detroit. Branches were organized in Chicago, Louisville, New York, San Francisco, and other cities.

The NNLC set out to secure what it called economic democracy, which meant, first and foremost, expanded job opportunities for black workers. To this end, the NNLC pressured companies and labor unions to negotiate antidiscrimination clauses in employment contracts. Moreover, it called on federal and state government agencies to hire more black workers and pressured state legislatures to enact fair employment practices to make it illegal for businesses to discriminate on the basis of race.

In addition to working for expanded job opportunities for black workers, the NNLC also thought broadly about the causes of inequality among workers. At the root of the problem, argued the NNLC, was the existence of a cheap labor supply. As long as underpaid workers existed, the logic went, companies would continue to exploit them. Until the position of the most exploited worker was improved, no one's job was secure. Furthermore, the NNLC argued that business sustained the cheap labor supply by structuring wage rates according to racial and gender differences, thereby dividing the workforce. As long as business continued to draw on and maintain a cheap labor supply, argued the NNLC, workers would find it difficult to overcome the racism and sexism that employers used to justify differential wages and that ultimately enabled them to pay black workers poorly.

To eliminate the cheap labor supply, the NNLC developed a three-prong strategy. First, it fought the runaway shop—the process by which businesses moved from northern locations to the South, leaving union wages and benefits behind in an effort to find a new source of cheap labor. Second, it attempted to convince workers of the need for unity so that employers could not continue to exploit the differences among them and maintain the cheap labor supply. Finally, and perhaps its most unique accomplishment, the NNLC emphasized the need to organize black women to obtain better-paying jobs for them and more job security. Black women, the NNLC argued, were the most exploited segment of the working class. By raising their wages and their position within the labor force, the degree of inequality among workers would be reduced and a source of cheap labor would be eliminated.

Between 1951 and 1956, the NNLC organized campaigns in the electrical and railroad industries and in department stores to force companies like General Electric and Sears to hire African Americans as production workers or sales clerks rather than as janitors or matrons, a term that referred to women who performed janitorial duties. By exposing discriminatory hiring practices of businesses, the NNLC strove to produce sufficient public outrage to launch boycotts of companies until they hired black workers, improved existing work conditions, and/or upgraded jobs of black employees.

Although its campaigns were directed mostly at business practices, the NNLC was similarly critical of organized labor. Developments in the immediate postwar period left black trade unionists disillusioned with organized labor and prompted the creation of the NNLC. The NNLC felt it adhered to the goals of the original Congress of Industrial Organizations (CIO) of the late 1930s, whose mission had been to organize all the workers the American Federation of Labor (AFL) had refused to recognize, particularly unskilled workers, many of whom were black. Since the end of World War II, the NNLC had felt that the CIO had retreated from its original goal. Significant numbers of unskilled workers remained unorganized, particularly black workers and black women, and the CIO seemed less than eager to bring them into the fold. Black workers, despite their union membership, had been fired from their jobs after the war to make room for returning veterans. If black workers managed to remain in the factories, they often held the lowest-paid and most difficult and dangerous production jobs. More often, black workers were forced into low-paid and less respected service jobs. The Detroit branch of the NNLC was highly critical of the United Automobile Workers and its president, Walter Reuther, for not pressuring Ford, Dodge, and General Motors to upgrade the jobs of black production workers and provide more job security. According to the NNLC, the CIO "had joined the crowd of colonial oppression and exploitation and was running fast from its earlier position."

In 1952 the NNLC launched one of its most sustained efforts, the "Let Freedom Crash the Gateway to the South" campaign. Referring to the campaign as "the most important fight for economic democracy ever fought on behalf of the Negro people and the South," the NNLC found in it what it felt were the root causes of discrimination: the exploitation of black women, the runaway shop, and the exacerbation by businesses of racial differences among workers. In 1952, General Electric was in the process of opening a new plant in Louisville, Kentucky—the "Gateway to the South." Known as "Appliance Park," the plant created over thirty thousand new jobs in the Louisville area to be filled over the course of the summer and fall of that year. Although the NNLC applauded the creation of new industrial jobs in the South, it feared that General Electric was blazing a trail for other corporations to exploit the South as a "low-wage area" where big businesses could "run away" from unions and the high wages established in the North. To keep its employees from organizing, the NNLC anticipated that General Electric would pit white against black workers and inflame racial tensions. The NNLC was particularly worried about obtaining high-paying, stable jobs for black women, whom it deemed the most exploited members of the working class, and it planned to pressure the company to hire black women as production workers.

As General Electric constructed Appliance Park and began hiring workers, the Louisville NNLC traced the company's racial hiring practices and found that 50 percent of the first five thousand production workers hired were women but none were black. The Louisville branch of the NNLC, headed by Moses Sutton, issued pamphlets urging the public and General Electric to stop this "shameful policy." The NNLC found support among just a handful of organizations in the Louisville area and the campaign was limited to watchdog duties and public information.

By 1955, three years after the Gateway to the South campaign was launched, General Electric had hired only 156 African Americans, 10 of them women. All of the black women worked as matrons, performing janitorial services, rather than occupying the better-paid and more respectable jobs on assembly lines or as office clerks. The NNLC finally filed a complaint with the U.S. Department of Labor, citing General Electric's discriminatory hiring policies. The company, which hired 60 workers per day, responded by hiring one token African American woman to fill a production job. Sutton, executive secretary of the Louisville Area Negro Labor Council, insisted that a number of jobs should have been filled by black women, both on the production line and in the offices.

The NNLC's organizational tactics and philosophy, which emphasized pressuring companies to hire and provide good jobs to black women, who were the lowest-paid and most vulnerable members of the workforce, differentiated it from labor organizations associated with the Congress of Industrial Organizations (CIO) in the 1950s. Generally, unions organized workers after they had been hired by a company. Once organized, a union then tried to obtain higher wages, better working conditions, and job security for those employees. That strategy, however, did not help African Americans in Louisville, since Appliance Park did not even hire them. If a union managed to establish itself, which was difficult to do in the South in the 1950s, it represented only those workers General Electric had already hired. To stop the company's discriminatory practices, the NNLC attempted to organize prospective employees of General Electric and put pressure on the company to change its hiring policies.

For three years the NNLC kept pressure on General Electric in Louisville but ultimately failed in its goals of obtaining highly paid, secure jobs for black men and women. The key to the NNLC's success was garnering support from the general public in Louisville and from larger labor unions that might provide organizers and financial support. The NNLC, however, received neither. Organized labor seemed unable to develop strategies to overcome racial tension both among southern workers and within its own ranks.

To make matters worse, labor unions and the House Un-American Activities Committee accused the NNLC of being "Communist-dominated." Hood, Coleman, and Thompson were certainly influenced by labor organizers who were members of the Communist Party; however, it is unclear whether they ever joined the party. Yet during the 1950s the label "Communist-dominated" created suspicion of an otherwise bold attempt to improve the conditions of the black working class. The House Un-American Activities Committee and the Subversive Activities Control Board targeted the NNLC, claiming that the organization had given funds to and received financial support from the Communist Party. The most specific of the charges held that NNLC literature, leaflets, and newsletters "urg[ed] support of the CP leaders causes and objectives" and that NNLC conventions, meetings, and rallies were held "for the purpose of furthering and promoting the objectives of the CP." The Control Board labeled the NNLC's goals and objectives as Communist, stating that the organization "never knowingly has deviated from the positions taken and advanced by the Communist Party, as exemplified by, but not limited to the following facts: The NNLC has adopted the Communist Party's program concerning Negroes."

In denying the charges, Ernest Thompson and the NNLC reiterated their democratic goals and accused U.S. Attorney General Herbert Brownell and the Justice Department of violating the Constitution. The response by the NNLC, dated January 30, 1956, states that "the

Department of Justice, acting as the instrument and tool of the illegal and unconstitutional minority in the United States who desire to maintain and perpetuate Jim Crow and discriminatory practices, has instituted the present proceeding for the purpose of silencing the respondent, one of the effective instruments of the Negro people in its struggle for equality."

While the NNLC may not have succeeded in reaching its goals, it offered an important critique of organized labor and business in the early 1950s. The NNLC anticipated other black-led labor organizations like the Negro American Labor Council and the Revolutionary Union Movements, both active in the 1960s, that were concerned with organizing black workers in the South, raising wages, and forcing employers to hire black workers. Perhaps the NNLC's unique contributions were its initiatives on behalf of black women. The organization stood by its conviction that black women deserved more than service jobs and made "the right of Negro women to work anywhere and everywhere" central to its campaigns.

Members of the NNLC went on to work for economic democracy in other arenas. Coleman Young was elected mayor of Detroit and became a U.S. senator. Ernest Thompson was active in obtaining better housing standards in Newark, New Jersey. William Hood came to play an active role in the formation of the Revolutionary Union Movements in the Detroit area in the 1960s.

**FURTHER READINGS**

Foner, Philip. "The National Negro Labor Council, 1951–55." In Philip Foner, *Organized Labor and the Black Worker, 1619–1973*. New York: Praeger, 1974.

*The Freedom Train*. New York: Filmmakers Library, 1995.

Phillips, Lisa. "'A New Wind of Freedom': The National Negro Labor Council's 'Gateway to the South' Campaign, 1952–1954." Paper presented at the Columbia University Freedom Conference, October 12, 1996.

Thomas, Richard. "Blacks and the CIO." In Paul Buhle and Alan Dawley, eds. *Working for Democracy: American Workers from the Revolution to the Present*. Urbana: University of Illinois Press, 1985.

Ernest Thompson Papers. Rutgers University Special Collections. New Brunswick, N.J.

*Lisa Phillips*

## National Negro Press Association

*See* Afro-American Press Association.

## National Negro Race Conference

*See* Southern Society for the Promotion of the Study of Race Conditions and Problems in the South.

## National Newspaper Publishers Association

The National Newspaper Publishers Association (NNPA) represents black newspaper publishers nationwide. Since its 1940 inception, it has promoted blacks in the journalistic profession, facilitated advertising in black newspapers, fostered cooperation among its member organizations, and advanced the interests of the black community.

John H. Sengstacke of the Chicago *Defender* founded the organization, with eleven members, in 1940 as the Negro Newspaper Publishers Association. By 1945, fifty-three publishers had joined. The group was similar to the larger and all-white American Newspaper Publishers Association in promoting its own brand of journalism in the United States. During World War II, the NNPA assisted news publishers in adjusting to rationings and other wartime restrictions. It also advocated higher journalistic standards, helped to improve practices in the black press, and supported the issues and concerns of the black community. In 1943, for example, the NNPA met with President Franklin D. Roosevelt and presented him with a statement of black aspirations, which included a declaration of allegiance and an official deplorement of racial disunity during the war.

Also in 1943, the NNPA took over from Delta Phi Delta the observance of National Negro Newspaper Week, an event designed to elicit a favorable opinion of the black press while rallying aid and recognition for worthy publications and individuals. The event, later known as Black Press Week, has become a month-long activity and a time for editors to write and publish about their place and purpose in society.

During the 1940s, the NNPA launched its own news-gathering organization—the NNPA Press Service, which operated from 1947 to 1960 and was one of various black news services at the time. The service declined, however, as local coverage of the black community increased.

By 1953, NNPA membership dropped to twenty-eight publishers, due to rising operating costs and declining circulation. In 1955, as the Civil Rights Movement started to reach its stride, the Negro Newspaper Publishers Association changed its name to National Newspaper Publishers Association. Over time, the NNPA has weathered with resilience and resourcefulness such crises as the declining circulation of black newspapers and has remained a vital organization sponsoring a variety of activities.

In order to enlarge and promote the black press across the country and the journalistic profession in the black community, the NNPA sponsors a Merit Award Contest for black newspapers, which recognizes excellence in such areas as editorial, circulation, and advertising. It also sponsors Dollars for Black Scholars, which provides one-thousand-dollar scholarships for college juniors and seniors who seriously consider a journalism career with a black newspaper.

In 1989, the NNPA led a boycott of Japanese products after Japanese officials made disparaging remarks about blacks and other minorities. The boycott led to a meeting with Japanese officials which resulted in an increase of Japanese corporate advertising in the black press. In 1992, in conjunction with the Sears, Roebuck Foundation, the NNPA launched a study of the black press, focusing on reader markets and black press advertising. Today, the NNPA, headquartered in Washington D.C., has over two hundred members and supports a nonprofit foundation.

**FURTHER READINGS**

Pride, Armistead S., and Clinton C. Wilson II. *A History of the Black Press.* Washington, D.C.: Howard University Press, 1997.

Wolseley, Roland E. *The Black Press, U.S.A.* Ames: Iowa State University Press, 1990.

*Angel R. Rivera*

## National Office for Black Catholics

The National Office for Black Catholics (NOBC) was established in 1970 as a central agency for black Catholics, and was intended to stimulate full participation of the African American faithful in the life of the church.

The NOBC was the product of protests launched by a group of black Catholic priests, later known as the National Black Catholic Clergy Caucus. In April of 1968, inspired by the development of black Protestant liberation theology, the presentation of the Black Manifesto (calling on white churches and synagogues to pay reparations to blacks for slavery and racial oppression), the radicalization of the Black Power movement, and the emergence of a new black Catholic consciousness, this Caucus met in Detroit to force the church to respond to charges of racism and of being a "racist institution." Leveling nine demands against the church, the militant clergy insisted on a greater voice in decision making, spe-

cial programs for African American Catholics, the recruitment of more black clergy, sensitivity training for white priests working among African Americans, the appointment of black bishops, and a central office for black Catholics in the church's administrative bureaucracy.

When it opened, the NOBC temporarily functioned as an umbrella organization for other black Catholic groups in an attempt to represent the black Catholic community with a clear and unified voice. Today the NOBC represents over one million black Catholics and wields considerable power within the National Conference of Catholic Bishops.

**FURTHER READINGS**

Davis, Cyprian, O.S.B. *The History of Black Catholics in the United States.* New York: Crossroad, 1991.

Davis, Joseph, S. M., and Cyprian Rowe, F.M.S. "The Development of the National Office for Black Catholics." *U.S. Catholic Historian* 7 (Summer 1988): 265–289.

*A. J. Scopino Jr.*

## National Optometric Association

Founded in Richmond, Virginia, in 1969, the National Optometric Association (NOA), primarily composed of African American optometrists practicing in the United States, strives to enhance the delivery of eye and vision care services in both underserved and unserved communities. Currently headquartered in East Chicago, Indiana, the organization, which has more than three hundred members, actively recruits minority students for optometry schools and colleges and assists graduates in finding employment.

The NOA is also dedicated to improving the delivery of eye and vision care to the African American community. Recognizing the high frequency of glaucoma and diabetic eye disease among elderly blacks, the NOA works with the National Eye Health Education Program of the National Eye Institute to educate African Americans over the age of forty about the importance of early detection of these diseases. Membership fees and corporate sponsors provide funding for the NOA.

The organization has a board of directors, a newsletter, regional trustees, and a part-time executive director, currently Dr. Linda Johnson. NOA members are involved in all aspects of the optometric profession, including work in health clinics, private and group practice, teaching, and research.

FURTHER READING

National Optometric Association. *Organizational Summary—National Optometric Association.* East Chicago, Ind.: National Optometric Association, ca. 1996.

*Donald Altschiller*

## National Organization for the Professional Advancement of Black Chemists and Chemical Engineers

Incorporated in 1975 under the laws of the state of Georgia, the National Organization for the Professional Advancement of Black Chemists and Chemical Engineers (NOBCChE) was established to maintain and support regional programs that assist black scientists in achieving their academic and professional potential, introduce science and technology as viable professional goals to elementary and high school students, and encourage college students to pursue higher education in technical and scientific disciplines.

The group was originally organized in Philadelphia in April 1972—with funding from the Haas Community Fund and Drexel University—as an ad hoc committee that surveyed black professionals in chemistry and chemical engineering. Enthusiastic response to the committee led to an organizational meeting in December 1973 and the launching of the NOBCChE at a national gathering in New Orleans in March 1974.

In 1995, the NOBCChE developed a five-year plan that included objectives in the areas of educational initiatives, organizational effectiveness, personal and professional development, national and international affairs, and financial resources. The plan guides local chapters and national headquarters in developing programs, improving services, providing scholarships and other forms of support, and exercising a voice in national and international affairs of interest to chemists and chemical engineers.

The organization sponsors an annual Outstanding Teacher Award and the Percy L. Julian Award in Pure and Applied Research in Science and Engineering. It also administers fellowships to black students who have successfully completed at least one year of study in an accredited Ph.D. program in chemistry or chemical engineering, as well as cosponsors with various industries a number of science programs to increase black student interest in pursuing chemistry or chemical engineering careers. Many local chapters provide free tutoring and complete science curricula, and NOBCChE members regularly visit K–12 classrooms with significant percentages of African American children to encourage them to pursue careers in chemistry or chemical engineering.

The annual proceedings of the organization's national conference are published by the NOBCChE's national headquarters, at Howard University in Washington, D.C.

FURTHER READINGS

Brennan, Mairin B. "Black Chemists' Conference Stirs up Debate on Affirmative Action." *Chemical & Engineering News* 73, no. 19 (May 8, 1995): 44–48.

Johnson, Rita E. "Minority Chemists, Chemical Engineers Gather to Celebrate Accomplishments." *Chemical & Engineering News* 74, no. 20 (May 13, 1996): 46–48.

*Dennis W. Cheek*

## National Organization of Black County Officials

The National Organization of Black County Officials (NOBCO), which is private, nonpartisan, and not-for-profit, offers to its members technical assistance, project management, program planning, contract services, and information about economic development issues, transportation, hospitals, telecommunications, and housing. It is also committed to collecting data and organizing archival and historical information about its own growth and development.

Established in 1982 by the National Association of Black County Officials (NABCO), NOBCO consists of over two thousand six hundred black elected and appointed county officials in forty-seven states. Its board consists of members from various regions in the United States who have made significant contributions in the field of economic development, health care planning, and public services delivery.

NOBCO facilitates information exchange among its members, and it provides economic development assistance and program planning to its constituents. NOBCO coordinates its activities with other organizations, such as the National Policy Institute, an umbrella group composed of the seven national organizations of black elected officials.

An important program sponsored by NOBCO is Minority AIDS Information Network (MAIN). Started in Atlanta, Georgia, in 1987, this project is aimed at the elimination of HIV (Human Immunodeficiency Virus) among children and young adults. The project provides HIV/AIDS education, information, and technical assistance to minority youth, municipal organizations, health departments, and other national organizations around the country. In Atlanta, NOBCO MAIN conducts HIV/STD (Sexually Transmitted Disease) education sessions and safer-sex workshops in middle and high schools, colleges, youth detention centers, recreation and summer programs, and at community health fairs. In collaboration with social service organizations in the metropolitan Atlanta area, NOBCO MAIN also conducts HIV/AIDS forums for the community at large.

To assist in the consolidation of democratic institutions and organizations, NOBCO provides leadership and management training to various countries outside of the United States, including Cape Verde, Malawi, Liberia, Senegal, South Africa, Tanzania, Mexico, Guyana, Honduras, Uganda, Bosnia, and Croatia. NOBCO also coordinates international trade delegations and conducts studies and conferences abroad.

Headquartered in Washington, D.C., NOBCO publishes newsletters, conducts studies, and produces videos on a variety of public service issues. Since its founding it has conducted twelve major conferences on economic development and has served as a catalyst for heightened minority awareness and participation in a wide range of public policy initiatives, including international trade and market access.

**FURTHER READINGS**

*A Guide to Black Organizations.* New York: Phillip Morris, 1997.

Jaszczak, Sandra, ed. *Encyclopedia of Associations.* Detroit: Gale, 1997.

Oakes, Elizabeth H., ed. *Minority Organizations.* Chicago: Ferguson, 1997.

Spohn, Lein, ed. *The Kaiser Index to Black Resources 1948–1986.* Brooklyn, N.Y.: Carlson, 1992.

*Andrew Smallwood*

# National Pan-Hellenic Council, Inc.

The National Pan-Hellenic Council, Inc. (NPHC), a nonprofit social service organization, was founded at Howard University, in Washington, D.C., in May of 1930. The NPHC seeks to coordinate the social and political activities of predominantly black college-affiliated fraternal and sororal organizations, to establish unanimity of thought and action in the conduct of Greek-lettered groups, and to foster these groups' involvement in communities outside the college campus. Throughout its history, the NPHC has confronted problems common to its member organizations and coordinated its affiliates'

work on important issues confronting African Americans, including segregation, civil rights, antilynching legislation, voter registration, and illiteracy. Despite the broad-ranging missions and purposes of each of its member organizations, the NPHC continues to strive for the common goal of community uplift.

African Americans have established fraternal organizations based on religious or occupational affiliation since the revolutionary period. It was not, however, until the twentieth century, when large numbers of African Americans began attending colleges, that fraternal and sororal organizations with admission based specifically on educational standards began to emerge.

Interfraternity networking in the United States had begun as early as 1909. That year, former Brown University president W. H. P. Faunce invited all "known" fraternities to a meeting in New York City. Faunce, however, did not invite the two existing black student organizations, which later joined the NPHC, Alpha Phi Alpha Fraternity, Inc. (founded 1906), and Alpha Kappa Alpha Sorority, Inc. (founded 1908). Much like other African Americans, their existence was not formally acknowledged and their presence was not requested.

Excluded, then, from the interfraternity efforts of whites, African American students launched the NPHC. Since 1937, the NPHC has served as the umbrella organization for eight Greek-letter fraternities and sororities founded between 1906 and 1922: Alpha Kappa Alpha Sorority, Inc., Alpha Phi Alpha Fraternity Inc., Delta Sigma Theta Sorority, Inc., Kappa Alpha Psi Fraternity, Inc., Omega Psi Phi Fraternity, Inc., Phi Beta Sigma Fraternity Inc., Sigma Gamma Rho Sorority, Inc., and Zeta Phi Beta Sorority, Inc. Not surprisingly, five of the eight member organizations of the NPHC were also founded at Howard University.

The NPHC and its eight black fraternities and sororities function similarly on both the national and local level. The NPHC is composed of local chartered councils made up of representatives from each of its member groups. Officers are elected and regular meetings are held to discuss national policy as well as local events and initiatives. The locally chartered councils are governed by an executive committee, which consists of national representatives who are chosen primarily from the graduate membership of the fraternities and sororities.

Since its founding, the NPHC has not increased its membership beyond the original eight founding groups. Although expansion has been under consideration for approximately two decades, the absence of standards for membership has been a major stumbling block. Having been chartered by five of its present member organizations and having accepted three additional groups without much discussion, the NPHC has given little thought to the possibility of enlarging its constituency to include new organizations that are seeking membership. Moreover, many other, predominantly white, fraternal organizations, as well as umbrella associations of student groups, now admit black students and organizations. One such umbrella group is the National Interfraternity Conference, whose membership includes NPHC affiliate Kappa Alpha Psi Fraternity, Inc., and a much younger black organization whose mission and purpose closely mirrors that of the NPHC's Iota Phi Theta Fraternity, Inc.

In 1990, the eight member organizations of the NPHC collectively abolished traditional, highly unregulated, and sometimes extremely dangerous, pledge processes. Under NPHC direction, the eight affiliates created membership intake processes that retained many of the ceremonial rituals but allowed each group to develop additional service and educational requirements. Crucial to the abolition of practices such as hazing were not only legal and civil actions taken against some of the organizations, but also moral debate about such practices as initiate branding, which became a reminder of the oppression of African Americans during slavery.

The NPHC has been vital to organizing college-trained African American men and women. It serves as an advocate of black student interests and provides its members with a network of support that they have used to unite and mobilize.

FURTHER READINGS

Floyd, James T. "In My Opinion: The Need for Black Fraternities and Sororities." *The Crescent: The Official Publication of Phi Beta Sigma Fraternity, Inc.* 76, no. 1 (Winter 1995–1996): 13.

Ploski, Harry A., and James Williams. *The Negro Almanac: A Reference Work on the African American.* 5th ed. Detroit: Gale, 1989, p. 1362.

Riley, Marc C. "Phi Beta Sigma and the Interfraternity Conference (NIC): Should We Join?" *The Crescent: The Official Publication of Phi Beta Sigma Fraternity, Inc.* 76, no. 1 (Winter 1995–1996): 30–31.

Talbert, Charles H. "NPHC Expansion! The Debate Continues . . ." *The Crescent: The Official Publication of Phi Beta Sigma Fraternity, Inc.* 76, no. 1 (Winter 1995–1996): 42–45.

*Julie S. Doar*

## National People of Color Student Coalition

*See* United States Student Association.

## National Pharmaceutical Association

Originally the pharmaceutical section of the National Medical Association, which was founded in 1895, the National Pharmaceutical Association (NPhA) became a separate entity in the late 1940s. Headquartered in Cary, North Carolina, the association represents the professional views and interests of minority pharmacists "on critical issues affecting health care and pharmacy."

The NPhA is subdivided into regional zones to facilitate the dissemination of professional information. Each region, with its own elected officers, sponsors meetings and educational activities. The NPhA's annual national meeting as well as the regional meetings offer members a wide variety of lectures, panel discussions, and networking opportunities, as well as more than twenty hours of continuing pharmaceutical education courses each year.

The vast array of NPhA programs are designed to enhance professionalization of the group's membership, to promote good public health, and to encourage young people to pursue careers in the pharmaceutical industry. Following its pledge to serve as a role model for minority youth, and to support their recruitment into the profession, the NPhA provides scholarships for matriculating pharmacy students who are active members of the Student National Pharmaceutical Association. As part of its community service agenda, the NPhA members work to provide pharmaceutical care in underserved communities, and provide patient care through participation in local health fairs. The political activities of the organization are aimed at advancing legislative and regulatory interests of the NPhA and its members at the local, state, and national level.

The NPhA began publishing the *Journal of the National Pharmaceutical Association* in 1954, and now offers numerous educational and resource materials to professional and lay persons via the Internet, including information about topics such as diabetes care and advances in cancer research. Links to major medical organizations, disease-specific foundations, registration materials for nursing, medical, and pharmaceutical meetings are available on-line, as is the newly proposed strategic plan of the NPhA. As an associate of GlaxoWellcome pharmaceutical company, NPhA is able to provide several Internet hotlines, including a drug database and patient education resources. The NPhA also offers on-line courses such as the "Frontiers in Biomedicine Lectures" and the "Harvard School of Public Health Lectures," which provide continuing education credits. Moreover, the NPhA offers computer-accessible audio lectures about the prevention of medication errors and about HIV/AIDS.

The NPhA is a multifaceted organization that emerged in response to the exclusion of black pharmacists from white professional associations at the turn of the twentieth century. The organization today continues to represent and advance the professional interests of minority pharmacists.

**FURTHER READING**

Low, W. Augustus, and Virgil A. Clift. *Encyclopedia of Black America*. New York: Da Capo, 1990.

*Peggy Hardman*

**SEE ALSO** National Medical Association

## National Political Congress of Black Women

The National Political Congress of Black Women (NPCBW) promotes African American women's involvement in the political process. The NPCBW was created on August 2, 1984, at the headquarters of the National Alliance of Postal Workers, after C. DeLores Tucker called a meeting of over thirty African American women leaders to discuss ways of promoting black women's influence on politics. The women launched the NPCBW partially in response to the 1984 Democratic National Convention's failure to appoint African American women to important positions and to adopt various minority planks. This first meeting of the NPCBW lasted approximately four days and resulted in the election of Shirley Chisholm as the organization's first Chair.

The NPCBW has launched various activities that promote its primary objective of enhancing the political power of African American women. For example, the organization supports the education of black female teenagers, hoping to inspire them to become active in the political process at an early age. The NPCBW also works to increase the number of African American women nominated and elected to political as well as administrative government positions. The NPCBW also fosters voter registration drives among African American women.

At least partially due to the NPCBW's efforts, increasing numbers of black women have entered American politics.

In 1983, before the organization's existence, African American women held 1,223 elected government positions. By 1993, that number had nearly doubled to 2,332. Furthermore, the NPCBW has been active in influencing appointments of African American women to government offices. The organization's Commission for the Presidential Appointment of African-American Women presented the administration of Bill Clinton with names of black women qualified for positions within the executive branch. A reflection of these efforts is that, in the 1990s, more African American women were appointed to influential executive branch positions than during any other decade. In 1993–1994, Dr. M. Joycelyn Elders served as surgeon general and, in 1997, Alexis M. Herman was sworn in as secretary of labor. Other Clinton appointments of black women include Gail W. Laster, who became general counsel, and Gloria R. Parker, who was appointed chief information officer in the Department of Housing and Urban Development.

In addition to its efforts to increase black women's political participation and representation, the NPCBW has challenged violent rap music and its sometimes misogynist lyrics. C. DeLores Tucker has represented the NPCBW in Senate hearings investigating these lyrics and the NPCBW succeeded in changing the typical practices of promotion and marketing of such music.

Since 1984, the NPCBW has played an active role in helping to enhance black women's participation and representation in the political process. It has effectively attacked racial and gender inequities at the electoral, legal, and cultural level. The organization, which is funded by membership fees and donations, hosts a biennial convention.

**FURTHER READING**

Catherine Sheader. *Shirley Chisholm: Teacher and Congresswoman*. Hillside, N.J.: Enslow, 1990.

*Joseph S. Townsend*

## National Rainbow Coalition

The origins of the National Rainbow Coalition lie in Martin Luther King's Poor People's Campaign of 1967. The campaign was conceived as an interracial alliance of the poor and disadvantaged, an alliance that would mount a nonviolent crusade against persisting poverty and discrimination in America. In his campaigns for the Democratic party's presidential nomination in 1984 and 1988, Jesse Jackson, King's most prominent disciple, attempted to invoke a similar spirit by forming the Rainbow Coalition, an alliance of potential voters who were disillusioned with the conservatism of the administrations of Ronald Reagan and George Bush, as well as the established Democratic party leadership. Announcing his first candidacy in October 1983, Jackson placed a large emphasis on voter registration, and he called upon human rights activists and such disadvantaged groups as Hispanics, women, farmers, and industrial workers to form a coalition with African Americans to force the Democratic party to include their concerns in its platform.

Yet, despite the inclusive rhetoric of the Rainbow Coalition, and despite his support from many blue-collar, unemployed, and liberal whites, Jackson did not make any specific appeals to white voters. In fact, he seemed to do the opposite. He publicly welcomed the support of the Muslim leader Louis Farrakhan, widely viewed as anti-Semitic. Following a public outcry over an off-hand remark in which Jackson referred to New York City as "Hymie Town" Jackson publicly broke with Farrakhan, but he then aroused further controversy by conferring with Yasir Arafat, leader of the Palestine Liberation Organization, about a Palestinian homeland in Israel.

Nevertheless, Jackson and the Rainbow Coalition made significant progress. During his 1984 campaign, he distributed to Hispanic voters leaflets printed in English and Spanish that called for bilingual educational programs and the strict application of the 1965 Voting Rights Act to remedy the lack of informed voting by Hispanics. In New York State's primary, he gained 34 percent of the Puerto Rican vote.

Jackson was also the only candidate to attend the annual conference of the National Congress of American Indians, where he asserted that America's treatment of Native Americans was a "litmus test" of the "country's character." A Native American journalist wrote that Jackson was a "national minority leader who has captured the imagination of people of color other than blacks."

The platform of the Rainbow Coalition included demands for cuts in the national defense budget (with billions of dollars to be reallocated to domestic welfare programs), a bilateral nuclear freeze, the removal of Cruise and Pershing missiles from Europe, the normalization of diplomatic relations with Cuba, and opposition to U.S. military intervention in the Middle East and Central America. On all counts, Jesse Jackson and the Rainbow Coalition platform of 1984 represented "the left-wing of Democratic party opinion" (Marable, 276).

Throughout the 1984 campaign, Jackson reiterated his contention that "red, yellow, brown, black and white— we're all precious in God's sight." Despite an impressive

showing in the primaries, however, Jackson's Rainbow Coalition did not gain him the Democratic nomination. One opinion poll showed that African American Democrats preferred Walter Mondale over Jackson as the party's nominee by a margin of five to three, and the black mayors of Los Angeles, Detroit, Atlanta, and Birmingham supported Mondale. At the 1984 Democratic national convention in San Francisco, Jackson had about three hundred total delegates, but Mondale had two hundred black delegates alone and was the party's choice, with Geraldine Ferraro as his running mate.

In his address to the convention on July 17, Jackson reprised his campaign theme of a "rainbow coalition" which embraced Arab Americans who "know the pain and hurt of racial and religious rejection," Native Americans, "the most exploited people of all," Asian Americans, "now being killed in our streets, scapegoats for the failures of corporate, industrial, and economic policies," as well as "small farmers, lesbians, gays, and disabled veterans."

With the reelection of Ronald Reagan in 1984, Jackson, who had been a less than enthusiastic supporter of the Mondale–Ferraro ticket, began to refashion his projected interracial political alliance. In April 1986, at the National Rainbow Coalition's first annual convention in Washington, D.C., which was attended by hundreds of whites, Jackson stressed issues such as health care and unemployment and he stipulated a new multiethnic coalition, to include teachers and members of labor unions. This new approach, and the enlargement of the Rainbow Coalition's putative constituency, brought Jackson increased support from both whites and blacks. A 1986 survey showed that he was the first choice for president of 48 percent of black respondents, and 1 percent of whites. In the fall of 1987, a new survey showed him as the choice of 67 percent of African Americans, and 9 percent of whites. In the March 1988 Democratic presidential primaries in twelve Southern states Jackson won 10 percent of the white vote, and black mayors who had opposed him in 1984 rallied to his support.

In his second bid for the Democratic presidential nomination, Jackson agreed to abide by the rules of the National Democratic Committee for choosing delegates, and promised not to seek the nomination by running against the party if he failed to win its endorsement. During his campaign, Jackson addressed not only farmers, unemployed workers, and other disaffected groups, but also spoke in conciliatory terms to Jewish audiences, dispensing entirely with the services of Louis Farrakhan.

In 1988, Jackson won over seven million votes and seven state primaries, and he conducted the most serious bid ever mounted by an African American for the presidency. Jackson's appeared to address the concerns of many voters, regardless of race, on a wide range of domestic and international issues. Although Michael Dukakis was to receive the party's nomination, only to be defeated by Vice President George Bush, Jackson's second candidacy as the spokesman for the Rainbow Coalition revealed his ability to mobilize millions of voters, across the color line. His two presidential campaigns also inspired the enormous growth of African American participation in politics during the 1980s and 1990s.

The Rainbow Coalition was based on the premise that the multicultural nature of American society and the interests of disadvantaged minority groups could best be served by the politics of pluralism and inclusion. As Jackson informed the 1984 Democratic convention, "America is not like a blanket—one piece of unbroken cloth, the same color, the same texture, the same size. It is more like a quilt—many patches, many pieces, many colors and many sizes, all woven and held together by a common thread."

**FURTHER READINGS**

Carson, Clayborne et al., eds. *The Eyes on the Prize Civil Rights Reader: Documents, Speeches, and Firsthand Accounts from the Black Freedom Struggle, 1954–1990.* New York: Viking Penguin, 1991.

Frady, Marshall. *Jesse: The Life and Pilgrimage of Jesse Jackson.* New York: Random House, 1996.

Fuchs, Lawrence H. *The American Kaleidoscope: Race, Ethnicity, and the Civic Culture.* Hanover and London: The University Press of New England, 1990.

Marable, Manning. *Black American Politics From the Washington Marches to Jesse Jackson.* London: Verso, 1985.

Stone, Eddie. *Jesse Jackson.* Los Angeles: Holloway House 1979.

White, John. *Black Leadership in America: From Booker T. Washington to Jesse Jackson.* 2nd ed. London and New York: Longman, 1990, pp. 173–189.

*John White*

# National Society of Black Engineers

Established in 1975, the National Society of Black Engineers (NSBE) is one of the largest student-managed organizations in the nation. Its mission is to increase the number of black engineers who excel academically, pro-

fessionally, and culturally, and who positively affect their communities.

The NSBE originated at a national conference of the Society of Black Engineers at Purdue University in April 1975. A group of American and Canadian engineering students who attended the conference launched the NSBE to foster mutual academic and professional support and to help students interact with professors, managers, and other professionals crucial to their career advancement. Incorporated in 1976, the NSBE has more than ten thousand members who are organized in 368 college and university chapters and 150 alumni extension chapters. All NSBE officers are either students or alumni who are employed as professional engineers.

The NSBE raises its annual three-and-a-half-million-dollar budget from membership dues, foundation awards, and corporate sponsors who donate fixed sums each year to provide a core of programming dollars and organizational support.

The NSBE sponsors an annual National Leadership Institute and honors academic achievement and leadership. It provides tutorials, group study sessions, precollege outreach programs, technical seminars and workshops, and a national communications network (NSBENET), and it publishes two magazines (*NSBE Magazine* and *NSBE Bridge*), two newsletters, and resume books. The NSBE organizes career fairs, banquets, and an annual national conference attended by over six thousand students, professionals, and corporate representatives.

*Dennis W. Cheek*

# National Society of Black Physicists

The National Society of Black Physicists (NSBP), established at Morgan State University in Baltimore in 1977, seeks to "promote the professional well-being of African American physicists within the scientific community and within society at large." Founders and cochairs of the NSBP were Dr. Walter Massey, former dean of faculty and professor of physics at Brown University, and Dr. James Davenport, chair of the department of physics at Virginia State University.

The NSBP originated in 1973 when Fisk University honored three African American physicists, Donald Edwards, John McNeil Hunter, and Halston V. Eagleston. Those present at the ceremony discussed establishing a society to provide black physicists with mutual support and to arouse the interest of black students in careers in physics.

Since the NSBP's founding a number of its members have won international renown in physics. The association has been particularly active in stimulating the creation of and providing intellectual support for graduate degree programs and scientific research facilities at universities in sub-Saharan Africa.

Current activities include the appointment each year of a science "ambassador" to represent the NSBP before audiences of precollege and university students, the award of two undergraduate scholarships in physics (with Lawrence Livermore National Laboratory and Argonne National Laboratory), and confering a number of professional honors.

The more than one hundred NSBP members have established six local chapters in Atlanta; Los Angeles; Nashville; Greensboro, North Carolina; Grambling, Louisiana; and Jackson, Michigan. An annual conference, a newsletter, and a website facilitate communication between the members.

**FURTHER READINGS**

Beardsley, Tim. "Scientist, Administrator, Role Model." *Scientific American* (June 1992): 40–41.

*Notable Twentieth-Century Scientists*, S.V. "Walter E. Massey."

*Dennis W. Cheek*

## National Student Association

Founded in 1947, the National Student Association (NSA) was the dominant confederation of student governments in America for three decades after the end of World War II. African American students were always a significant constituency within the association, and issues of race and racism were prominent among its concerns.

In the 1940s and 1950s, NSA's cautious liberalism won it powerful allies and ensured its continuing popularity on a substantial number of American campuses. In 1967, however, the group's existence was threatened when a fifteen-year secret Central Intelligence Agency (CIA) subsidy was revealed. But the NSA survived by refashioning itself as a center of radical activism. In 1978, it merged with the National Student Lobby (NSL) to create the United States Student Association (USSA), under which title it has enjoyed something of a resurgence as a multicultural advocacy organization.

At the end of World War II, American veterans, under the GI Bill of Rights (1944), arrived on the nation's campuses eager to make contacts with other students, both domestically and internationally. The national student organizations to which they might have turned and which had thrived in the 1930s, however, had collapsed as the U.S. Communist Party toned down its radicalism. And the incipient Cold War now served as a spur to the creation of a more broad-based group as the students struggled to regroup and centrists found the United States government eager to help them enhance their national and international profile.

In 1946, two dozen American students attended the Prague World Youth Congress, from which the left-leaning International Union of Students emerged. After their return to the United States, these Americans gathered students from two hundred American colleges for a planning meeting that December. During the meeting they laid the groundwork for the NSA's constitutional convention in Madison, Wisconsin, the next summer.

The issue of racial discrimination dominated the convention in Madison and threatened to split the association. The delegates ultimately agreed on compromise language supporting the "eventual elimination" of discriminatory education, but few white Southern students were placated. Thus, for years afterward, the bulk of the NSA's southern membership came from black colleges.

In 1948, the NSA held its first congress, or annual membership meeting, and Ted Harris, an African American student from Philadelphia, was elected president. Although he was the only person of color to hold the association's top position until after the NSA merged with the NSL in 1978, blacks occasionally filled other national posts.

From the early 1950s until 1967, the NSA secretly received much of its funding from the CIA, which saw the association as both a force opposing global Communism and a potential conduit for information about foreign activists. Although CIA money eventually found its way to most of the NSA's endeavors, the agency's interest was primarily in the association's international wing, which operated independently of the national office. The subsidy was conducted with the support of the association's top leadership, and CIA-linked alumni were influential in setting NSA policy. However, students who worked solely on domestic issues knew nothing of the relationship.

The introduction of CIA money and influence had no obvious effect on the NSA's civil rights stance. The association's liberal majority was emboldened when the Supreme Court's 1954 *Brown* decision officially sanctioned its antisegregationist position. Yet it still took the NSA three years before it developed a commitment to civil rights activism. In 1957, Ray Farabee, a white Texan, was elected NSA's president. Farabee secured support from the Marshall Field Foundation for the creation of the Southern Student Human Relations Project (SSHRP), which conducted conferences and other activities in the field of race relations. SSHRP's centerpiece was its annual seminar, which brought together white and black student leaders from the South for several weeks of intensive discussion. The seminars, conducted in northern states, culminated in the annual NSA Congress.

It took some time for the seminar participants to settle on a clear activist agenda. The first few seminars were dominated by white participants and advisors. Students favoring segregation were invited, and a substantial amount of time was devoted to debating whether schools should integrate, rather than how.

In 1959, after the second seminar, the NSA was able to obtain funding for a year-round human relations office for the SSHRP in Atlanta. The association hired Constance Curry, a young white NSA alumna from North Carolina, as the project's new director. Curry intended to devote most of her energy to educational efforts and conference planning, but events quickly thrust her into a more activist role. In February 1960, just two months after the SSHRP office opened, the first wave of lunch counter sit-ins swept the South. Curry had already begun to make connections within the civil rights community, and her project's funding base, national contacts, and logistical expertise made it a natural resource for a movement that was quickly outstripping its infrastructure. That spring, Curry attended the founding meeting of the Student Nonviolent Coordinating Committee (SNCC) and shortly thereafter was named to its executive committee as an adult advisor. SSHRP provided the SNCC with financial support at a time when the newly formed group had few sources of revenue, and, through NSA's national office, built support for the civil rights movement on northern campuses.

The SSHRP seminars also took on a more activist orientation. In 1960, Curry recruited Sandra Cason, later known as Casey Hayden, from the University of Texas, and a Cason speech on the necessity of civil disobedience galvanized the NSA Congress that year. The delegates elected African American law student Timothy Jenkins to the NSA's national vice presidency and Jenkins went on to play a significant leadership role in SNCC's early development.

For several years, the NSA was a direct, though cautious, participant in the student civil rights movement, and the Congress became a place for activists to form ties and convert new adherents. Movement figures like Chuck McDew and Bob Zellner participated in the SSHRP seminars, and NSA recruits were well represented among 1964's Freedom Summer volunteers. By then, however, the civil rights struggle was moving beyond NSA's willingness or ability to follow.

In early 1964 Curry left SSHRP. The annual seminars were discontinued the following year, as their personalized, integrationist approach came to be seen as outdated. The project turned to direct organizing efforts, but suffered from rapid turnover in leadership and an inability to articulate an agenda distinct from other groups working in the South. It lost the financial support of the Field Foundation, and was dissolved in 1968.

As SSHRP was disintegrating, the NSA was undergoing a profound crisis. The association's relationship with the CIA was revealed in February 1967, provoking a firestorm of criticism from across the political spectrum. Many students who had not been privy to the secret felt betrayed, and some called for the group to be disbanded. As CIA-linked alumni fell out of favor, the NSA lurched sharply to the left, taking newly radical stands in opposition to the Vietnam war and in favor of educational reform.

At the 1969 NSA Congress, following bitter debate and substantial disruption of the meeting from several quarters, a group of students of color won support for a resolution declaring the fight against racism the student movement's "prime focus" and earmarking $50,000 of NSA's depleted funds for the struggle. In the 1970s, African American participation in the NSA swelled as black college enrollment rose and association mainstays like the City University of New York were transformed by new open admissions policies. At mid-decade NSA established a Third World Coalition, giving students of color formal representation within the organization for the first time.

In 1971, frustrated with the NSA's emphasis on the Vietnam war and other issues of broad social concern, a faction within the association broke away to form the National Student Lobby (NSL), an organization devoted to advocacy of educational issues. The end of the war brought with it a renewed emphasis on campus and educational issues, and the changing demographics of American colleges bred a new concern with economic access to higher education. As the 1970s wore on, the NSA and the NSL found themselves with increasingly similar agendas. In 1978, the two groups merged and created the

United States Student Association (USSA), ushering in an era in which African American students would take on increasingly central roles in the organization.

*J. Angus Johnston*

## National Technical Association

Founded on December 10, 1925, and incorporated in Illinois in 1926, the National Technical Association (NTA) organizes African American engineers, architects, mathematicians, and natural scientists. The NTA seeks to increase minority input in technology and science, awareness of minority technical contributions, access to and equity in technical careers, and career-building opportunities.

Charles S. Duke, founder and first president of the NTA, was the first African American to be awarded an engineering degree from Harvard University. In 1913, after a stint as chief engineer for an engineering firm and completion of a master's degree in civil engineering at the University of Wisconsin, Duke was hired by the city of Chicago as its first African American engineer.

The NTA now has fifteen hundred members organized in sixty chapters and ten regional groups. The organization maintains a speakers' bureau, compiles and disseminates statistics, conducts national precollege scientific and technical career awareness programs, sponsors technical symposia for students, grants scholarships and awards that recognize achievement and potential, and conducts a national mentor program. The NTA's national headquarters in Philadelphia publishes a quarterly journal and newsletter. Michael A. Chapman, computer engineer at NASA Langley Research Center, now serves as the organization's president and Dr. Mildred Fitzgerald-Johnson as executive director.

### FURTHER READING

Sammons, Vivian Ovelton. "Charles Sumner Duke, 1879–1952." In *Blacks in Science and Medicine*. New York: Hemisphere, 1990.

*Dennis W. Cheek*

## National Urban League

The National Urban League was formed in 1910 when the National League for the Protection of Colored Women (NLPCW), the Committee for Improving the Industrial Conditions for Negroes in New York (CIICN), and the Committee on Urban Conditions Among Negroes in New York (CUCANNY) merged their activities. The Urban League helped African Americans acculturate themselves to urban lifestyles and it sought to expand their employment, housing, healthcare, and educational opportunities.

Americans are less familiar with the Urban League's contributions to racial advancement and civil rights causes than they are with the work of the better-known National Association for the Advancement of Colored People (NAACP), Congress of Racial Equality (CORE), and Student Nonviolent Coordinating Committee (SNCC), yet few organizations have matched the Urban League's efforts to narrow the socioeconomic gap between African Americans and the white majority.

What have been the Urban League's distinguishing features? As the journalist Nat Hentoff wrote in 1961, "The Urban League is a nonpolitical, interracial social work and community planning agency that emphasizes—and often initiates—the expansion of equality of opportunity for Negroes in all phases of the national economy in our cities." A more contemporary portrait reads that the Urban League "works to eliminate institutional racism, and provides direct service to minorities in the areas of employment, housing, education, social welfare, health, family planning, mental retardation, law and consumer affairs, and community and minority business development" (*Black American Information Directory, 1992–93*, 391). Untold numbers of African American migrants who came to the cities and found themselves in need of employment in order to support themselves turned to the Urban League for help and assistance.

The Urban League was not the first racial advancement organization to call for equality before the law and equality of opportunity. T. Thomas Fortune, a newspaper editor, founded the Afro-American League in 1890. He and one hundred other African Americans pledged themselves to fight any and all forms of racial segregation and discrimination. The National Federation of Colored Men, composed exclusively of attorneys, was founded in 1895 in Detroit, and its members called for social, political, and economic justice for all Americans. African American women's contributions to the cause of racial advancement and civil rights also need mentioning. Begun in 1896, the National Association of Colored Women, primarily a group of civic-minded professionals, operated welfare programs, ran reformatories for troubled youths, held classes in the domestic arts, sponsored day-care nurseries for working mothers, and provided other community services.

National Urban League official Whitney Young Jr. (center) meets with President Kennedy and Henry Steeger (right) at the White House. 1962. *Library of Congress*

Other organizations promoting racial advancement were formed after 1900. The National League for the Protection of Colored Women (NLPCW), begun in 1905 by Miss Frances Kellor, a lawyer, and Mrs. William H. Baldwin Jr., the wife of a railroad magnate, worked to steer African American women who had migrated from the rural south to safe employment in cities like Norfolk, New York, Baltimore, and Philadelphia and away from the possible danger they could fall victim to.

In 1906, industrial discrimination practiced against black men and women led to the formation of the Committee for Improving the Industrial Conditions for Negroes in New York (CIICN). William L. Buckley was its chief architect. A graduate of Syracuse University with a doctorate in ancient and foreign literature, Buckley, like William E. B. Du Bois and a growing number of other black intellectuals, called for complete political and economic equality. CIICN's staff monitored the activities of the New York State legislature, and those of unions, whenever incidents of racial discrimination in housing and employment occurred. Some of its successes included the admission of qualified African American students to vocational schools in Harlem and Brooklyn and a pledge from the City and Suburban Homes Company, a construction firm, that African American mechanics, bricklayers, and carpenters would be hired on all of its work sites. CIICN's successes in breaking down established patterns of discrimination and segregation in education and employment were the result of its skill at persuading whites to end discrimination and segregation, rather than of public protests. This tactic remains a hallmark of the Urban League.

Some individuals who promoted political solutions to the migrants' problems were critical of the CIICN's decision to concentrate only on industrial advancement. They believed that winning political rights would speed up the migrants' acculturation to urban lifestyles, and was the surest way for African Americans to attain full equality in America. These complaints, however, did not slow the CIICN's progress.

While studying for a Ph.D. in the School of Philanthropy at Columbia University, George E. Haynes, an African American, conducted a study of the black population in New York City. His conclusions led to the formation of the Committee on Urban Conditions Among Negroes in New York (CUCANNY) in 1910, whose principal focus was employment and whose staff worked to open craft union membership, skilled occupations, and vocational education to African Americans.

It was only a matter of time before efforts to coordinate and merge the activities of the three bodies would be attempted, and on October 11, 1910, the CUCANNY did merge with the NLPCW and CIICN to form the National League of Urban Conditions Among Negroes, which name was later shortened to the National Urban League. The Urban League laid the groundwork at the national level for a scientific examination of problems spawned by social unrest, systematic racial discrimination, and racial and class conflicts, all of which affected society as a whole.

Social work became the Urban League's means for addressing problems facing migrants to cities across America. A staff of trained social workers and other professionals sought ways to expand employment, housing, health-care, and educational opportunities for the Urban League's clients and all who were in need of assistance in adjusting to urban lifestyles. Throughout its history, the Urban League's leadership, its board of directors, and its social work staff have all rejected the long-held belief that poverty is caused by a defect in an individual's character. Instead, the Urban League's programs have been based on the premises that solutions to urban problems can be found by trained social scientists, that intergroup cooperation among disparate groups is achievable if meaningful bonds are established, and that persuasion and winning the cooperation of the white elite will lead to improved opportunities for African Americans in every aspect of American society. These ideas have guided the Urban League's chief policy makers George E. Haynes (1910–1917), Eugene K.

Jones (1917–1941), Lester B. Granger (1941–1961), Whitney M. Young Jr. (1961–1971), Vernon E. Jordan (1971–1982), and John E. Jacobs (1982–1994), and they remain the pillars of Hugh B. Price's efforts to close the socioeconomic gap between African Americans and whites.

From its inception in 1910 until 1971, the Urban League's chief policy makers were African Americans who carried the title of executive secretary or executive director. In 1971, executive secretary Vernon E. Jordan, Jr. won the board of director's approval to have the position's title changed to president. Although until 1971 the Urban League already had a position carrying the title of president, it was largely a representative office occupied by wealthy whites, which served to underscore the interracial character of the Urban League and provide a link between the Urban League and white economic, political, and social elites.

George E. Haynes, the Urban League's first executive secretary, established three goals for the organization: Change the interracial status quo, establish a social work program at Nashville's Fisk University to train African Americans as social workers, and convince whites "to work with African Americans for their mutual advantage and advancement."

Launching a social work program at Fisk University occupied much of Haynes's time and effort. Eugene K. Jones, a graduate of Cornell University, was hired as the Urban League's field secretary, but he and Haynes shared the Urban League's leadership until the latter resigned from the organization in May of 1918 after being named director of Negro economics with the title of special assistant to the U.S. Secretary of Labor.

Jones's tenure as executive secretary spanned the 1920s, the Great Depression, and the onset of World War II, and his accomplishments were significant. Following World War I, when cities along the east coast, in the south, and the midwest launched Urban League branches, Jones helped secure financial support for their work from local community chests. Community-based funders, such as the United Way, supported the Urban League in its work among immigrant and migrant groups who needed help in adjusting to urban life. Moreover, Jones fostered a spirit of cooperation with the NAACP, and he convinced Urban League leaders of the importance of cultivating urban black leadership through vocational guidance.

Vocational guidance steered Urban League affiliates along new paths. Some mistakenly equated the Urban League's emphasis on it with industrial training, a type of education associated with the Tuskegee Institute and its accommodationist and gradualist founder Booker T.

Washington. Yet the Urban League's leadership believed that proper vocational guidance, if connected to industrial education, was as useful in directing inclinations for architectural drawing and medicine as it was for blacksmithing and cabinetmaking. The Urban League also sought to eliminate traditional restrictions against African American workers by advocating an integrated work force and to remove the lingering vestiges of a slave psychology from the minds of the migrants, but it met only limited success in both areas under Jones' leadership.

Jones' most notable success was his use of publicity to present factual data on African American life to businessmen, government officials, labor leaders, and organized and unorganized white workers. For this purpose the Urban League launched *Opportunity* magazine in 1925.

Jones retired from the Urban League at the end of 1941 because of ill health, after having left his imprint on the organization's policies and programs. Lester B. Granger replaced Jones as the Urban League's executive secretary. After graduating from Dartmouth College, Granger served in the 92nd Division of the U.S. Army during World War I, was industrial secretary of the New Jersey Urban League, organized the Los Angeles Urban League branch, and was a member of the staff of *Opportunity* magazine. His support of a number of left-wing causes led his enemies to refer to him as a "weekend Communist." Granger denied he was a Communist, but it is safe to say that his political views were left of center.

Granger wasted little time in putting his imprint on the Urban League by identifying what he referred to as "high priority challenges": the inequalities of opportunity, which were responsible for the economic and social lag imposed upon America's black urban population, had to be removed; press facilities, radio, and television had to be employed more widely in speeding up the pace of adjustment, assimilation, and acculturation of the urban black population into the mainstream of American society; the speed of urban decay had to be arrested; and "all possible ways must be explored toward speeding up the integration of the in-migrant into an orderly multiracial society in which a free flow of knowledge, training, and opportunity can be assured for all racial components along avenues that will provide the most good for the greatest number in modern urban America."

Between 1941 and 1961, Granger also gave the Urban League a highly visible role in civil rights causes. He was not above going it alone rather than cooperating with NAACP officials, choosing to ignore the 1911 Urban League–NAACP agreement not to duplicate each other's

efforts and steering clear of civil rights issues, as Jones had done during his tenure.

As efforts to end segregation in the armed forces intensified, Granger urged the Department of the Navy to conduct a thorough investigation into conditions facing black personnel after three hundred of them were charged with insubordination when they refused to return to work following an explosion on July 17, 1944, at an ammunitions depot at Port Chicago, California, which claimed the lives of 323 sailors, 203 of whom were black. Secretary of the Navy James Forrestal named Granger his civilian Negro advisor. In this capacity, Granger toured naval bases across the Pacific and interviewed scores of African American sailors. Upon completion of the tour, Granger charged the Navy with discrimination against African American sailors.

Granger's role as advisor to Forrestal was, in his eyes, his crowning achievement in the civil rights arena. Although Granger unquestionably exaggerated his and the Urban League's role in the desegregation of the armed forces and in other areas, notably in the housing and public school desegregation initiatives during the Dwight D. Eisenhower presidency, he nonetheless made lasting contributions to civil rights and racial advancement.

Perhaps Granger's biggest disappointment was that African Americans did not make remarkable strides in civil rights during the Eisenhower presidency. He was hostile toward President John F. Kennedy, which put him at odds with untold numbers of African Americans. Granger's unwillingness to combine direct action and confrontation with the Urban League's traditional program of friendly persuasion and social work led to sustained criticism from people working both inside and outside the Urban League. In 1961 Granger left the Urban League, having reached the mandatory retirement age of 65 years.

The Urban League's president, Henry Steiger, informed the news media that Whitney M. Young Jr. would become the organization's executive director effective October 1, 1961. A graduate of Kentucky State College and the University of Minnesota's School of Social Work, Young had served as director of industrial relations and vocational guidance for the St. Paul, Minnesota, Urban League, and had been dean of the Atlanta University School of Social Work. The Urban League Board of Trustees chose Young because of his belief that unity within diversity was possible and desirable. One executive secretary of a local Urban League branch noted that he and others were drawn to Young because he encouraged them to adopt a more aggressive style of confronting society than was acceptable during the Granger era.

The change in executive directors and the expectation of new accomplishments ushered in a new phase of Urban League history. Historian Nancy J. Weiss characterized Young as "the civil rights leader whom contemporaries described as the 'inside' man of the black revolution, the man who served as bridge and interpreter between black America and businessmen, foundation executives, and public officials who comprised the white power structure." Young's defining quality was his ability to express black America's anger over entrenched patterns of racism, segregation, and racial discrimination and at the same time win the white economic and political elite's endorsement of the changes in American society that he sought.

Indeed, Young fulfilled Granger's dream of the Urban League rivaling the NAACP in the civil rights arena. He is also responsible in large measure for the affirmative action initiatives that were put in place during the 1960s. Repeatedly, Young expressed to economic and political leaders that without special treatment, through service and opportunities, African Americans could not be expected to compete with those who had not been subjected to exclusion for over three hundred years.

Tragically, Young drowned off the coast of Lagos, Nigeria, on March 11, 1971. Vernon E. Jordan Jr., the executive director of the United Negro College Fund, was named to succeed him. Prior to his appointment, Jordan had served as NAACP field secretary in Georgia where he had led a boycott of stores in Augusta that refused to hire African Americans. As the Urban League's chief executive officer, Jordan was an advocate for African Americans in housing, family issues, civil rights, equal educational opportunity, desegregation initiatives, community organization in urban areas, and improved health care for the poor. Unlike his immediate predecessor, who had championed integration as the vehicle that would usher African Americans and other minorities into the American mainstream, Jordan promoted cultural pluralism as the goal of African Americans.

His departure through resignation in 1982 led to the appointment of John E. Jacob, who had been the Urban League's executive vice president since 1979. Jacob did not follow Granger, Young, and Jordan in the tradition of promoting the Urban League as a major civil rights body. Jacob seemed to look back to the Jones era for inspiration. He popularized the need for equality of opportunity in housing and employment as the way to resolve explosive racial tensions in urban America.

In May of 1994, Hugh B. Price succeeded Jacob as president. After earning a law degree at Yale Law School, Price was appointed executive director of New Haven's Black Coalition, which focused on restoring neighborhood vitality and cooperation between disparate groups in a city torn by ethnic and racial strife. Price's strengths are in the areas of human resources, management, financing, the evaluation of community development, public education, telecommunications, welfare, criminal justice, and interracial cooperation—all areas that the Urban League has historically addressed.

Urban League executive secretaries or presidents have guided the organization along a path established by the founding members—as a nonpolitical, interracial social work and community planning agency that has both initiated and emphasized the expansion of equality of opportunity for black Americans in all phases of the national economy in the nation's urban areas.

**FURTHER READINGS**

*Black Americans Information Directory, 1992–93.* Detroit: Gale, 1990.

Haynes, George Edmund. "Conditions Among Negroes in the Cities." *Annals of the American Academy of Political and Social Sciences 49* (September 1913): 105–19.

Lee, B. F. Jr., "Negro Organizations." *Annals of the American Academy of Political and Social Sciences 49* (September 1913): 129–37.

Moore, Jesse T., Jr. *A Search for Equality: The National Urban League 1910–1960.* University Park, Pa.: Penn State University Press, 1981.

*The Urban League Story: Golden Anniversary Book.* New York: National Urban League, 1961.

Weiss, Nancy J. *The National Urban League, 1910–1940.* New York: Oxford University Press, 1974.

———. *Whitney M. Young, Jr., and the Struggle for Civil Rights.* Princeton, N.J.: Princeton University Press, 1989.

*Jesse T. Moore Jr.*

# National Welfare Rights Organization

In May 1966, George Wiley, a former professor of chemistry and civil rights activist, along with four others, opened the Poverty/Rights Action Center in Washington, D.C. Following requests from women leaders of several local welfare rights groups across the nation, one of its objectives was to form a national welfare rights organization. In June 1966, forty welfare recipients and their supporters led a march from Cleveland to Columbus, Ohio, demonstrating against the state's welfare system. When the marchers reached Columbus, they were joined by two thousand protestors led by Wiley, who denounced Ohio's welfare program. Similar demonstrations were held in fifteen other cities, including New York, Baltimore, Washington, Trenton, and San Francisco.

The demonstrations received extensive press coverage, and shortly thereafter Wiley called a national meeting of organizers to lay the groundwork for a national organization. In August 1967, the National Welfare Rights Organization (NWRO) was formed, with Wiley as its chief executive and a membership composed mainly of poor women of color who were welfare recipients. Key women leaders in the NWRO included Johnnie Tillmon, Beulah Sanders, Jackie Pope, Ruby Duncan, Edith Doering, Geraldine Smith, and Etta Horn. Through disruptive protests NWRO members demanded increased welfare benefits and jobs, sought the right to obtain credit cards, pursued special grants for clothing and furniture, and fought for the removal of a host of statutes that prevented them from receiving benefits. NWRO members also recognized the need for permanent legislation on behalf of the urban poor. At its first national meeting, which attracted representatives from seventy cities and twenty-six states, the NWRO drafted a legal program to present to Congress demanding increased benefits, jobs, and a guaranteed annual income for the working poor. At its peak in 1969, the NWRO had twelve thousand members.

The immediate impact of the NWRO was tremendous; there was an increase in welfare benefits for poor women and a rise in the number of eligible recipients. For example, the number of families who received Aid to Families with Dependent Children (AFDC) nearly tripled from 1,127,000 in 1966 to 3,312,000 in 1974. State procedures for fair hearings were established, residence requirements were eliminated, and most home visits were abolished. Claiming a right to material resources enabled many women to find honor and self-esteem in a system that degraded them.

Ultimately, however, the NWRO failed to generate permanent changes. In 1967 Congress enacted several amendments, designed to slow the rise in AFDC recipients, to the Social Security Act. The amendments established work requirements for employable welfare recipients and froze federal reimbursements to states. The tightening of federal regulations slowed the momentum of the NWRO, as did public hostility to rising welfare rolls. Wiley's resignation in 1972, a decrease in financial support, in-fighting

among new leaders, organizers, and welfare recipients, and the withering of grassroot groups also contributed to the demise of the NWRO. By the fall of 1974 the NWRO went bankrupt and the national office closed.

**FURTHER READINGS**

Piven, Frances Fox, and Richard A. Cloward. *Poor People's Movements: Why They Succeed, How They Fail.* New York: Random House, 1979.

Quadagno, Jill. *The Color of Welfare: How Racism Undermined the War on Poverty.* New York: Oxford University Press, 1994.

*Catherine Fobes and Jill Quadagno*

# National Women's Committee for Civil Rights

The National Women's Committee for Civil Rights (NWCCR) was established in 1963 to assist in the implementation of President John F. Kennedy's civil rights program. Knowing that the 1963 Civil Rights bill would not pass through Congress quickly, President Kennedy requested Attorney General Robert Kennedy and the Justice Department to take the necessary steps needed to avert massive noncompliance with the proposed law. To build a consensus in favor of the Civil Rights bill, Robert Kennedy began a series of White House conferences, attended by seventeen hundred participants, including women's groups, prominent lawyers, business executives, labor and religious leaders, governors, mayors, and various government officials. Those who participated in these White House meetings organized several new alliances, including the Mayor's Community Relations Service, the Lawyer's Committee for Civil Rights Law, and the NWCCR.

Given official sanction by White House Resolution, the NWCCR consisted of various women's coordinating councils. It was composed of state affiliates in Maryland, Minnesota, Pennsylvania, southern California, and Washington; city branches in Akron, Chicago, Cleveland, Denver, Louisville, Mt. Vernon, Philadelphia, Portland, and Selma; and independent groups such as Louisville's Women United for Social Action, the Kansas City Women's Planning Committee, the Greater New Orleans Women's Intergroup Council, and Atlanta's Partners for Progress. Based in Washington, D.C., the NWCCR operated through a steering committee of eleven women, representing the various state and city groups, and an executive council consisting of executive director Shirley B. Smith and two cochairs, Mrs. Douglas Horton and Mrs. William B. Harris. The

NWCCR was funded through membership dues, contributions, and the Taconic Foundation, founded by philanthropists Stephen and Audrey Currier and known for its support of civil rights organizations.

On the state and city level, NWCCR members worked to stimulate civil rights activities and participation in the programs of the state Councils on Human Relations. The NWCCR also launched efforts to reduce the number of high school dropouts and establish leadership training for women through intergroup cooperation. The NWCCR supported passage of and compliance with the 1964 Civil Rights Act by lobbying legislators and joining Operation Compliance, a civil rights project initiated by the Southern Regional Council and the Potomac Institute. Throughout the 1960s, the NWCCR often collaborated with the National Council of Catholic Women, the National Council of Jewish Women, the National Council of Negro Women, the United Church Women, and the Young Women's Christian Association in support of other civil rights issues such as housing, employment, and education. Several of the local coordinating councils affiliated with the NWCCR continued their work into the 1970s.

**FURTHER READINGS**

Fleming, Harold C. Papers. Manuscript Division, Library of Congress, Washington, D.C.

Southern Regional Council Papers. Special Collections, Robert W. Woodruff Library, Atlanta University Center, Atlanta, Georgia.

*Kimberly E. Nichols*

# National Youth Administration, Office of Negro Affairs

Created in 1935, the National Youth Administration (NYA) Office of Negro Affairs (known as the Office) facilitated more equitable participation of African Americans in that agency's program than in any other New Deal program. At a time of legal segregation and discrimination, the Office promoted democratic principles on matters pertaining to both black youth and the general black populace. Notably, the Office gained NYA sponsorship of two national conferences on the problems of blacks and black youth in 1937 and 1939. These conferences were the first government-initiated meetings to solicit counsel from black leaders on federal responsibilities in the civil rights struggle.

Mary McLeod Bethune and Eleanor Roosevelt speak before an NYA meeting. Between 1935 and 1943. *Library of Congress*

On June 26, 1935, President Franklin D. Roosevelt issued Executive Order 7086, creating the NYA. The agency was designed to assist youth between the ages of sixteen and twenty-five with job placement, vocational training, and work-relief programs. NYA programs also supported students in their efforts to continue their high school and college education. While justifying the NYA primarily in terms of improving young people's abilities to find work and increasing their chances of staying in school, the agency's planners also wanted to instill in youth a greater understanding of and respect for democracy. Between 1935 and 1943, the NYA, under Executive Director Aubrey Willis Williams, spent more than half a billion dollars assisting almost five million people. It operated virtually autonomously within three larger, successive organizations, the Works Progress (Projects) Administration, the Federal Security Administration, and the Manpower War Commission.

In planning the NYA, Williams and his associates anticipated the creation of a unit whose goal would be to help African Americans counter pervasive institutionalized racism. Still, representatives of the black community had to lobby vigorously for the appointment of an African American to the national staff. The person who took this job was Juanita Saddler, student field secretary for the Young Women's Christian Association in New York

City. Saddler reported to work on December 2, 1935, as the Negro liaison officer, a title soon discarded in favor of administrative assistant in charge of Negro affairs.

Six months later, Mary McLeod Bethune, one of two blacks on the thirty-five member NYA National Advisory Committee, and the founder and president of Bethune–Cookman College and the National Council of Negro Women, displaced Saddler as the chief specialist in the Office. With enthusiastic endorsements from Williams and First Lady Eleanor Roosevelt, President Roosevelt made Bethune head of the NYA's black unit. In part, he expected her to forestall the embarrassing situations that had plagued the flagrantly racist Civilian Conservation Corps, the other federal agency designed to reach out to Depression-era youth. On January 16, 1939, the Civil Service Commission officially recognized the Office as a division and Bethune as a director rather than an assistant. At that time, Bethune occupied the highest federal post any black woman had held and one of the roughly twenty top appointed positions held by women in the New Deal administration.

Bethune relied on well-educated, highly motivated personnel. Waxing and waning with the fortunes of the NYA, a staff of three in 1936 expanded to seven by 1941, consisting of an assistant director, an administrative assistant, a section chief for Negro relations, two stenographers, and two secretaries. Four successive, stellar assistant directors worked in the office. Two hailed from academia: Frank Horne of Fort Valley Normal and Industrial Institute in Georgia and R. O'Hara Lanier of Florida A & M College in Tallahassee. T. Arnold Hill came from the National Urban League in New York and Charles P. Browning transferred from the NYA in Illinois. Executive Secretary Arabella Denniston, an early graduate of Bethune's school, provided continuity and competence.

Under Bethune's leadership, the Office aggressively integrated blacks into the agency's program. In large measure, it achieved this by publicizing NYA programs among African Americans and then interpreting the needs of black youth to white Americans, particularly NYA administrators in Washington and the state capitals. Whereas white NYA personnel everywhere could ignore the more administratively oriented Saddler, they could not act similarly with the high-profile and charismatic Bethune. In numerous localities, whites who had never before been required to acknowledge the authority of an African American, male or female, much less obey one, now treated Director Bethune as an envoy of a commanding general.

And her ability to work with white government officials yielded positive results. By 1941, African Americans sat on all state NYA advisory committees in the South and served as administrative assistants to state directors in twenty-seven states, New York City, and Washington, D.C. Wherever black administrative assistants served, typically more black youth enrolled in NYA projects and received upgraded benefits. The assistants and other black administrative and supervisory personnel constituted the Office centerpiece for enhanced black involvement in the NYA.

The Office increased benefits to blacks within each component of the NYA program. In work-study aid at the secondary and college levels, the Office worked out resourceful ways to further the education of students who failed to receive aid through normal channels. It administered a Special Fund for Higher Education totaling $609,930, and assisted 4,118 students.

But while the Office initially achieved marked success in the school-aid program, it was only during the exigencies of World War II that it could reap comparable results in vocational training. In keeping with NYA policies, it facilitated the shift of blacks from recreational, agricultural, and personal service projects, in which they had been disproportionately enrolled, to state-of-the-art vocational training in construction, mechanical, and metal-working projects. In 1943, such NYA training was the most visible means by which young black women acquired skills to obtain work in war industries.

The war also breathed life into efforts of the Office to find jobs for African Americans. Greatly assisted in 1941 by Executive Order 8802, which barred discriminatory practices in government and defense industries, the NYA placed thousands of blacks in jobs that had previously been denied them. It also worked to ensure that black and white youth were allowed to advance together. In 1942–1943, through its interstate transfer plan, the agency transported more than three thousand trained African Americans to areas of labor shortages and temporarily housed them in regional induction centers until they found other living quarters.

The Office ceased operations on July 27, 1943, when Congress denied the NYA's appropriation and thus abolished it. Congress rejected the agency's argument that despite ever-rising youth employment, blacks and others who faced job market prejudices continued to need the NYA. While African American leaders bemoaned the agency's demise, black America took it in stride. Allowing a three-million-dollar liquidation fund, Congress demanded that the NYA terminate all activity in January 1944. Staying until that time, Division Director Bethune compiled a copious final report and helped to ensure that NYA vocational equipment would not be moved from educational institutions.

Despite the Office's achievements, institutional racism prevented it from realizing the full integration of blacks into the NYA. While the agency's regional program, instituted in 1942, was relatively satisfactory to blacks, the state-based program, established in 1935 and run by powerful white state directors, was less sufficient. Black youths generally failed to receive a fair share of funds according to their percentage of the young population, their percentage of youth from families certified for relief, or their need regardless of certification. Moreover, blacks received inferior vocational training and only negligible job placement.

Yet, the Office became a symbol of the promise of American democracy. It succeeded in assuring that the NYA was fairer to African Americans than any other New Deal establishment. Its cadre of black assistants to state directors was the first quasi–field staff of a black federal bureaucrat and its Special Higher Education Fund was the first federal affirmative action program and the first federal money administered by an African American government official.

Finally, the Office came to serve as the federal headquarters for black America. It functioned as such because Bethune utilized the services of members of the Federal Council of Negro Affairs, known as the Black Cabinet, an informal group she organized on August 7, 1936. Black America and the federal bureaucracy, including the White House, turned to the Office for information and counsel on racial affairs far beyond youth issues. Inevitably, the Office accelerated the shift of African Americans from the Republican to the Democratic Party. Bethune had transformed this ostensibly small federal niche into a potent force that affected millions of Americans.

**FURTHER READINGS**

Kirby, John B. *Black Americans in the Roosevelt Era: Liberalism and Race.* Knoxville: University of Tennessee Press, 1980.

Reiman, Richard. *A New Deal and American Youth: Ideas and Ideals in a Depression Decade.* Athens: University of Georgia Press, 1992.

Ross, B. Joyce. "Mary McLeod Bethune and the National Youth Administration: A Case Study of Power Relationships in the Black Cabinet of Franklin D. Roosevelt." *Journal of Negro History* 60 (January 1975): 1–28.

Salmond, John A. *A Southern Rebel: The Life and Times of Aubrey Willis Williams, 1890–1965.* Chapel Hill: University of North Carolina Press, 1983.

Smith, Elaine M. "Mary McLeod Bethune and the National Youth Administration." In *Clio Was a Woman: Studies in the History of American Women.* Eds. Mabel E. Deutrich and Virgina C. Purdy. Washington, D.C.: Howard University Press, 1980, pp. 149–177.

Weiss, Nancy J. *Farewell to the Party of Lincoln: Black Politics in the Age of FDR.* Princeton, N.J.: Princeton University Press, 1983.

*Elaine M. Smith*

## Negro Actors Guild of America

The Negro Actors Guild of America, Inc. (NAG), based in New York City, was founded in 1937 and liquidated in the early 1970s. NAG worked to increase job opportunities for black performers in theater, radio, and television, while challenging racist castings. It promoted good fellowship and spiritual welfare among actors and musicians in all branches of the theatrical profession; it developed better understanding between the public and theater professionals; it rendered service throughout the country to actors and musicians in time of illness and distress; and it offered sympathetic interest and, when necessary, confidential assistance to the members of the profession. Moreover, the NAG furnished legal advice to black actors who were often unfamiliar with terms of contracts and therefore more likely to be exploited by their employers. NAG relied on volunteers to provide its varied services, which were organized into several subdivisions, including membership, legal, medical, social service, sick and visiting, publications, and memorial standing committees.

The founders of NAG included Bill "Bojangles" Robinson (1878–1949), perhaps the most famous of all African American tap dancers; Noble Sissle (1889–1975), who helped influence a generation of musical comedy through *Shuffle Along* (1921); the actress Fredericka Carolyn "Fredi" Washington (1903–1994), who vigorously supported black civil rights and worked against discrimination in theater and film; Rosetta Olive Burton LeNoire (1911–), a performer who brought dignity and self-worth to often demeaning domestic roles and a theater executive who helped sponsor many outreach programs designed to take theater into communities where it was rarely seen previously; and Charles "Honi" Coles (1911–1992), a tap dancer who founded the tap dancers' fraternity The

Copasetics in 1949, and whose films include *The Cotton Club* (1984) and *Dirty Dancing* (1987). NAG received initial support from Alan Corelli, executive secretary of the Federal Theater Authority, who helped Noble Sissle find prominent cofounders, and Judge Jonah Goldstein, who arranged for the Grand Street Boys Association to house the group's annual meetings.

Among NAG's first elected officers were Sissle, who served as the group's president until 1957 when he was succeeded by Leigh Whipper, and "Fredi" Washington, who became the organization's executive secretary. Other officers elected in 1937 included Robinson, Whipper, Muriel Rahn, William C. Handy, Cab Calloway, J. Rosamond Johnson, and the Reverend Adam Clayton Powell Jr. In later years, other well-known black Americans served with NAG, including James Brown, Duke Ellington, Louis Armstrong, Paul Robeson, and Frederick O'Neill, who succeeded Whipper as president in 1961, and in 1964 became the first black performer to be elected to the presidency of Actors Equity. NAG officers assisted producers, directors, and agents in securing black talent for radio, television, and Broadway shows.

Prior to the 1937 creation of NAG no organization promoting the interests of black actors existed. Many black actors, even those who had been in top salary brackets for years, found themselves in financial straits. They had to spent money for good grooming and well-made clothes, union dues, agents' commissions, and publicity fees. While performers tried never to accept less than their established salary, they were often lucky to work three or four months out of the year. Besides these general problems faced by all actors, black performers found that their employment opportunities were limited.

At the time NAG was organized, several other unions, including the Jewish Theatrical Guild, the Catholic Actor's Guild, and the Episcopal Actors Guild, existed to serve actors. These religiously based unions, however, excluded African Americans. Even when the government provided some employment, for example, through the Federal Theater Project (1935–1939), many talented black actors were forced to give up their professions and seek other means of employment. Often, NAG became the sole source of support for black entertainers, providing medical care, rescued musical instruments, weekly allotments to those who were destitute, railroad tickets for those who were stranded, and funeral arrangements, among other things. Funding for NAG's work came from the Federal Theater Authority as well as various fundraising activities, such as benefit performances.

Shortly after its founding, NAG secured a 15 percent profit share for African American actors who participated in benefit performances on Broadway. Bill "Bojangles" Robinson spearheaded the benefits, which also provided funds to assist destitute black actors. (Robinson performed in many NAG benefits in the course of his career and made generous contributions to NAG.) Early on, NAG also took an active part in union activities, demonstrations, and mass meetings, and sent letters and telegrams to Washington, protesting cuts in federal funds that affected black actors, such as the Works Progress Administration.

By the late 1930s, NAG had more than seven hundred members, a large percentage of which were lay people of all races and religions who wanted to support black performers. Among NAG's lifetime members were Ethel Waters and Lena Horne. Members of NAG's Hall of Fame included Florence Mills, a singer and dancer who became a Broadway star with *Shuffle Along*; Charles Gilpin, the star of Eugene O'Neill's *The Emperor Jones* (1920); Ira Aldridge, the first black Shakespearean star acclaimed throughout Europe; Bert Williams, star of *Ziegfeld Follies*; and George Walker, who formed with Williams the first popular black Vaudeville team. NAG's newsletter provided lists of active members, personal news, as well as information about meetings, awards, sick members, memorial services, and black-operated theaters.

During the early 1970s, NAG gradually faded away. Perhaps the reason for its demise was that the union had reached its aim of integrating black performers into the arts; however, some sources report that internal fights about the organization's direction and money preceded its demise.

**FURTHER READINGS**

Dewsberry, Jonathan. "Black Actors Unite: The Negro Actors Guild of America." Ph.D. diss., New York University, 1988.

Hay, Samuel A. *African American Theatre: A Historical and Critical Analysis.* Cambridge, England: Cambridge University Press, 1992.

*Thomas Leuchtenmüller*

## Negro Airmen International

Established in 1967, the Negro Airmen International (NAI) promotes the participation of African Americans in aviation through a variety of initiatives and programs.

The NAI was the brainchild of Edward A. Gibbs of New York City. Born in 1919, Gibbs began his aviation career as a student in Hampton Institute's Civilian Pilot Training

Program, a federally sponsored program begun in late 1939. After Gibbs was certified as a flight instructor, he taught for a time at the Coffey School of Aviation near Chicago and then joined the aviation program at Tuskegee Institute. During World War II, he was part of the cadre of black civilian instructors who worked at Tuskegee, Alabama, to provide Army Air Forces primary flight training for the men who formed the all-black Army Air Forces flying units, known today as the Tuskegee Airmen.

For several years after the war, Gibbs struggled to make aviation his vocation, but racial discrimination thwarted his ambitions. Consequently, he began a career as a public housing administrator, first in North Carolina and then in New York City. But despite his frustrated career ambitions, Gibbs organized the NAI to "further Negro participation and advancement in the field of aviation [and] to encourage broader job opportunities for Negroes in all phases of aviation."

The NAI was the first major African American aviation organization of the post–World War II era. Its nineteen charter members included several prominent African American pilots who had managed to break the color line and forge aviation careers for themselves, including Perry H. Young (New York Airways) and Spann Watson (United States Air Force). From the outset the NAI sought to foster an interest in aviation among African American youth. In 1973 the organization began offering summer flight academies, two-week programs aimed at introducing teenagers to aviation.

A decentralized organization consisting of local chapters in the United States and the Caribbean, the NAI is governed by a board of directors. The organization holds annual conventions and an annual Memorial Day "fly-in." Membership is limited to licensed pilots, and has never exceeded one thousand. The organization publishes a quarterly newsletter and maintains a website.

In 1997 another organization was formed that traces its origins to the NAI—the Black Pilots of America (BPA). The circumstances that led to the establishment of the BPA are unclear. The BPA's home page maintains that "a large number of the present members were former long-term members of the Negro Airmen International," a comment that suggests that a leadership dispute within the NAI may have prompted the formation of the BPA.

**FURTHER READINGS**

"Edward A. Gibbs," *New York Times*, 5 January 1973, p. 28. Obituary.

"Negro Airmen Inc. Granted Approval," *New York Amsterdam News*, 4 March 1967, p. 24.

*Robert J. Jakeman*

## Negro American Labor Council

The Negro American Labor Council (NALC) was founded in 1960. A. Philip Randolph, president of the Brotherhood of Sleeping Car Porters (BSCP), and Cleveland Robinson, secretary-treasurer of New York City's District 65 of the Retail, Wholesale, and Department Store Workers Union, spearheaded the organization. The formation of the NALC was precipitated by a growing feeling on the part of black workers and trade unionists that the AFL-CIO, the voice of organized labor, was not responsive to its black members. Despite the fact that the AFL-CIO pledged to fight racial discrimination, it allowed some of its locals to maintain separate white and black organizations. Tension between black workers and the AFL-CIO's executive board, headed by George Meany, had been building throughout the late 1950s and came to a head at the 1959 annual AFL-CIO convention, where Randolph challenged Meany to put an end to Jim Crow unionism and introduced a resolution that required that all segregated locals "be liquidated and eliminated." Meany wondered how Randolph could be certain that those locals wanted to be desegregated, and he brashly asked Randolph, "Who in the hell appointed you as guardian of the Negro members in America?" Every resolution that the BSCP introduced, including the one calling for desegregation, was defeated. Later that year, at the 1959 convention of the National Association for the Advancement of Colored People (NAACP), Randolph introduced a resolution that called for the formation of a national black labor committee "to fight and work to implement the civil rights program of the AFL-CIO."

On July 18–19, 1959, Randolph invited seventy-five black labor leaders to New York, where they agreed to hold the founding convention of the NALC in May 1960. The delegates to the founding convention elected Randolph president of the NALC and Robinson vice-president. Delegates contended that the AFL-CIO, "despite its good faith, good will, and splendid pronouncements against racial discrimination, cannot be expected to move voluntarily and seriously to take positive and affirmative action for the elimination of race discrimination unless they are stimulated, prodded, and pressured to do so, both from within and without." They pledged to organize to apply that pressure.

The same month the NALC was organized, Randolph presented the AFL-CIO with detailed charges of discrimination within organized labor and again called for the elimination of segregated locals. The AFL-CIO rejected the charges and its executive board, of which Randolph was a member, voted to censure Randolph and blamed his association with "militant groups" for causing the "gap that has developed between organized labor and the Negro community." Martin Luther King Jr. and the Southern Christian Leadership Conference (SCLC), Roy Wilkins and the NAACP, and other black leaders quickly chastised the AFL-CIO for censuring Randolph. Soon thereafter, the NAACP released its second report on discrimination within the AFL-CIO, charging that the union had again failed to eliminate wide-ranging racist practices. Meany countered that the critical tone of the report interfered with labor's organizing drives. Organized labor and the black community had reached an impasse.

When the NALC was initially organized, it attracted more than ten thousand members. Chapters formed in industrial cities such as Chicago, New York, Pittsburgh, Youngstown, and Detroit. The Detroit chapter, called the Trade Union Leadership Council, claimed the single largest membership—two thousand. By 1962, however, only two years after its founding convention, NALC membership had dropped to four thousand nationwide. While Randolph attributed the decline to a lack of funds, NALC members said they found it difficult, if not impossible, to retain official union posts within their AFL-CIO locals and to be at the same time active in the NALC.

Despite the drop in membership, for the first few years of its existence the NALC remained critical of the AFL-CIO's position on race and sought to draw attention to discriminatory employment practices. The NALC was particularly critical of the AFL-CIO's organizing drives in the South, arguing that it could have done much more to stop the Ku Klux Klan and end Jim Crow unionism. The fact that the South remained unorganized, Randolph claimed at the NALC's second annual convention in 1961, was the AFL-CIO's fault, for it had never "come to grips with the racial problem in the South." Instead, it adopted a policy of "appeasement, compromise, and defeatism" that included the AFL-CIO's acceptance of Jim Crow unions, separate promotion and seniority policies for white and black workers, racial job-typing that resulted in "white men's" and "black men's jobs," and racially

segregated AFL-CIO state conventions in southern cities. Again, the AFL-CIO responded by accusing the NALC and its supporters of dividing and weakening the labor movement by creating a condition of "dual unionism" and practicing "racism in reverse."

One of the NALC's best-known accomplishments was the 1963 March on Washington for Jobs and Freedom. The NALC initiated plans for the march at its annual convention in 1962 and solicited support from Martin Luther King Jr., the SCLC, the Congress of Racial Equality (CORE), the Student Nonviolent Coordinating Committee (SNCC), and the NAACP. Initially organizers wanted the march to highlight employment discrimination, but white trade union leaders criticized the march's call for a "Jobs-for-Negroes" program as preferential treatment for blacks. Despite efforts of Whitney Young, secretary of the Urban League, and Cleveland Robinson, who insisted that the program did not amount to preferential treatment, the controversy prompted the march's organizers to downplay the economic aspect and refocus on agitation for the passage of President John F. Kennedy's civil rights bill. Although the AFL-CIO did not officially endorse the march, its Industrial Union Department, headed by Walter Reuther, supported it and the labor movement was well represented during the August 28 demonstration.

By 1965, Randolph began, almost inexplicably, to make amends with Meany and the NALC took a less critical stand against organized labor. Historians have explained Randolph's change of heart as a reaction to the emerging black power movement that rejected class-based, interracial movements. While the NALC was making amends with Meany, black workers in Detroit were organizing the Dodge Revolutionary Union Movement (DRUM) which, like the early NALC, formed as a result of dissatisfaction with the United Auto Workers and the larger organized labor movement. Robinson, who took over as president of the NALC in 1966, continued to reject compromise and tokenism and the NALC joined the SCLC in organizing workers in Memphis and Baltimore. By 1966, however, that agenda appeared mainstream compared to Stokey Carmichael's calls for black power. African American workers who had been attracted to the NALC now looked to the black power movement and more radical groups like the Revolutionary Union Movements to exact change. As a result, the NALC lost its base of support and Robinson redirected his energies into the Coalition of Black Trade Unionists, founded in Chicago in 1972.

FURTHER READINGS

Foner, Philip S. *Organized Labor and the Black Worker, 1619–1981.* New York: International Publishers, 1982.

Manning, Marable. "Black Insurgency." In *Working for Democracy: American Workers from the Revolution to the Present*, edited by Paul Buhle and Alan Dawley. Urbana: University of Illinois Press, 1985.

Robinson, Cleveland. Papers. Tamiment Library, New York University, New York, New York.

*Lisa Phillips*

## Negro American League

Established in 1937 and lasting until 1959, the Negro American League (NAL) was essentially a league of midwestern and southern baseball teams. In 1948, after the Negro National League (NNL) closed operations, a number of eastern clubs joined the NAL.

In 1942, the NAL and the NNL revived the Negro League World Series, which led to the establishment of an East-West Classic or All-Star game. This became one of the most popular of all Negro league games, attracting thousands of fans to Comiskey Park in Chicago each season. Major league managers, scouts, and owners often attended these games. The money generated by this annual contest helped many of the black ball clubs meet their annual expenses.

The NAL enjoyed over two decades of operation because of the leadership of a number of key individuals who brought money to the league. Tom Baird of the Kansas City Monarchs, who had been with that club since 1920, bought out the previous owner J. L. Wilkinson, a white businessman, to become the sole owner of the team in the 1950s. Baird became a prominent figure in the league and well respected by players and management alike. Baird, who owned a number of bowling alleys and much real estate, including a flower shop, an apartment building, and an office building, invested a lot of his own money in the Monarchs. Wilbur Hayes and Ernie Wright, local Cleveland businessmen and sports promoters, played key roles in the success of the Buckeyes in the 1940s. They used their financial resources to put together a solid roster of players, who then brought the World Series crown to their city in 1945. Other victorious teams in the 1940s were from Indianapolis and Birmingham.

In addition to the skills of those in management, the NAL enjoyed the services of a number of fine ball players, such as Buck O'Neil, Willard Brown, Artie Wilson,

Theolic Smith, and future major leaguers like Junior Gilliam and Joe Black. Black and Gilliam both played for the championship Baltimore Elite Giants in 1949. In 1951 Willard Brown helped out his Kansas City teammates by leading the league in hitting with a .417 average. Theolic Smith provided Chicago with some solid pitching by compiling a league-leading 1.81 Earned Run Average and a fifteen to two record in 1951. Buck O'Neil provided some flashy fielding for the Monarchs by only making five errors at first base in 1951. O'Neil went on to become a player and manager for Kansas City and later a scout for the Chicago Cubs, helping to mold the careers of a number of young stars like Ernie Banks and Lou Brock. Artie Wilson helped Birmingham achieve success by playing at all-star level from 1946 through 1948. In 1951, Wilson's achievements led to a short stint with the New York Giants.

Eight teams from Kansas City, Cincinnati, Chicago, Indianapolis, St. Louis, Memphis, Birmingham, and Detroit joined the NAL. Kansas City won the first league pennant, one of nine such victories for the team during the existence of the NAL. Kansas City's success was matched by the long tenure of the Birmingham Black Barons, who ended seven years of independent playing by joining the NAL in 1937. During the 1940s the Barons won three division titles, but lost each World Series appearance to the Homestead Grays of the NNL.

Not all NAL clubs enjoyed the success of the Monarchs and the Barons. For example, the Cincinnati Tigers, under the leadership of former Olympian DeHart Hubbard, entered the league in 1937 and folded shortly thereafter. The club, consisting of local Cincinnati men such as Marlin Carter and Porter Moses, enjoyed a third place standing for the first half of the 1937 season. When it folded, many of the players joined the Memphis Red Sox for the 1938 season. The St. Louis Stars also spent time in the NAL and the NNL and operated as an independent club in an effort to meet daily expenses. The team, however, did not mobilize big crowds of spectators as did the clubs in Chicago or Kansas City. Moreover, the city lacked the support of national black newspapers, such as the *Chicago Defender* or the *Pittsburgh Courier*. The *St. Louis Argus* covered the team's home games, but often did not carry news of the Stars when they played out of town. This made it difficult for fans to remain loyal to their team, since they did not know what the players were accomplishing and whether the team was winning.

Other teams involved in the NAL included the Jacksonville Red Caps, the Cleveland Bears, the Toledo Crawfords, the New Orleans Stars, the Cincinnati Clowns, the

Houston Eagles, the Philadelphia Stars of the NNL, the Louisville Clippers, the Detroit Stars, the Raleigh Tigers, and the Cleveland Buckeyes. The Buckeyes finally gave Cleveland a team that lasted more than a single season in the Negro leagues and in the 1940s it was one of the most successful clubs, winning the pennant in 1945 and 1947.

Cleveland won the 1945 World Series over the Homestead Grays in four games, but in 1947 the team lost in five games to the New York Cubans of the NNL. The Buckeyes played one more season after their Series loss before closing operation for the 1949 season. Birmingham also won the NAL crown three times and the Indianapolis Clowns retained this honor twice in the 1950s.

Starting in 1949 the NAL changed its structure and created an East and West division. Each division operated with five clubs (which could afford the franchise fee). By 1952 only six teams remained, those from Kansas City, Chicago, Philadelphia, Memphis, Birmingham, and Indianapolis, and the league returned to a single division. These remaining entrants had been playing almost since the beginning of the Negro leagues in 1920. The Indianapolis team had not always enjoyed the support of its city, and it occasionally tried its hand at playing in Cincinnati in hopes of generating larger crowds at its league contests.

Beginning in 1947 the NAL had new concerns to worry about, with the signing of Jackie Robinson to the Brooklyn Dodgers. The loss of black players to the major leagues presented a serious dilemma for the NAL and the NNL. While the Negro leagues welcomed the major leagues's recruitment of black players, entailing better pay and public exposure of black athletes, they also realized that this meant the inevitable decline of their own teams and leagues. Not surprisingly, the NNL folded after the 1948 season. The NAL continued to operate but by the early 1950s was struggling to stay afloat. By 1959 all major league teams had at least one African American player on their roster and a year later the Birmingham Black Barons were the only remaining Negro league team.

In response to the desegregation of the major leagues, the NAL sought to attract fans with new players. The Barons, for example, tried to sign white pitcher Eddie Klep to their roster, only to experience reverse discrimination when Birmingham city officials informed them that racially mixed teams were not allowed to play in the city.

The Indianapolis Clowns added three women players to their roster in the mid-1950s. Toni Stone, Peanut Johnson, and Connie Morgan played in the Negro leagues, partly because the All American Girls Professional Baseball League (1943–1954) excluded African Americans. All three women signed contracts with Indianapolis because they were good ball players, though many fans came out to see them play simply out of curiosity. Toni Stone joined Indianapolis first, playing the infield and hitting in the .250s. Stone also received enough votes to play in the All-Star game in 1954.

The NAL finally folded in 1960 when the last-remaining black team, the Birmingham Black Barons, had no league opponents left. Financial obligations became too difficult to meet as fans followed the exploits of Jackie Robinson, Roy Campanella, Monte Irvin, Larry Doby, and Don Newcombe instead of the Homestead Grays, Kansas City Monarchs, Newark Eagles, and Chicago American Giants.

**FURTHER READINGS**

Baird, Tom. Papers. Spencer Research Library, University of Kansas, Lawrence.

Clark, Dick, and Lester, Larry. *The Negro Leagues Book.* Cleveland: Society of American Baseball Research, 1994.

Heaphy, Leslie. "Shadowed Diamonds: The Growth and Decline of the Negro Leagues." Ph.D. diss., University of Toledo, 1995.

Holway, John B. *Blackball Stars, Negro League Pioneers.* Connecticut: Meckler Books, 1988.

Riley, James A. *The Biographical Encyclopedia of the Negro Baseball Leagues.* New York: Carroll and Graf, 1994.

*Leslie Heaphy*

# Negro Christian Student Conference

Between May 14th and the 18th, 1914, 595 black and 70 white delegates from eighteen states and four continents gathered in Atlanta, Georgia, for the Negro Christian Student Conference (NCSC). Attendees included students, community leaders, ministers, teachers, and editors. Dr. John R. Mott, chairman of the Continuation Committee of the World Missionary Conference and general secretary of the World Student Christian Federation, presided over the conference.

The NCSC sought to improve church programming and religious activities in African American communities. Moreover, the conference encouraged black spirituality and reminded young African Americans of their evangelical Christian responsibilities both in America and Africa. In addition, conference leaders hoped to stimulate better race relations by encouraging attendees to propagate the conference's cooperative and Christian spirit. Conference speakers explained that interracial efforts to improve social conditions were effective methods of generating cooperative feelings that would benefit both races. They urged African Americans and whites to cooperate on community improvement projects and recommended that churches and colleges offer classes addressing the conditions of the needy and residents of rural areas.

But along with their call for interracial cooperation, conference speakers reminded African Americans that racial advancement also depended on their personal conduct and demeanor. Thus, they encouraged African Americans to display racial pride, to strengthen their families, and to practice mutual respect. The group did not discuss how to correct negative portrayals of African Americans, believing that such problems would be solved once the black community established a more solid Christian foundation.

In addition to exchanging information about methods for community uplift, black conference attendees also hoped white participants would reexamine their definition and practice of Christianity. Black speakers criticized southern white churches for excluding African Americans, insisting that Christian brotherhood was racially inclusive.

The NCSC united black and white religious and lay leaders in an effort to improve the plight of African Americans. Moreover, the conference encouraged participants to broaden their vision of black mission work to include America as well as Africa. However, while the NCSC may have inspired some delegates to embrace the idea of a racially inclusive Christian brotherhood, interracial cooperation was apparently limited to the conference and did not result in any concerted efforts following the 1914 gathering.

**FURTHER READING**

Trawick, A. M., ed. *The New Voice in Race Adjustments: Addresses and Reports Presented at the Negro Christian Student Conference, Atlanta, Georgia, May 14–18, 1914.* New York: Student Volunteer Movement, n.d.

*Katherine Kuntz Dill*

## Negro Conventions

*See* Colored Conventions.

## Negro Equity League of San Francisco

The Negro Equity League of San Francisco (NELSF) was a small, chronically underfunded organization committed to the fight for full equality for black San Franciscans.

The NELSF was led by the colorful San Francisco businessman and attorney Edward D. Mabson, a native of Columbus, Ohio, who settled in San Francisco at the turn of the century. Mabson held a number of menial jobs before becoming head of shipping for a major publishing company, where he gained notice for entering a burning building to retrieve the company's account books. Mabson studied law in night school and in 1919 was admitted to the California State Bar.

The NELSF gained prominence in 1915 when it joined the National Association for the Advancement of Colored People (NAACP) and two other Bay Area organizations, the Negro Welfare League and the Equal Rights League, to protest the showing of the racist epic *Birth of a Nation*.

Of greatest concern to the NELSF was the growing residential segregation in the city. The organization was convinced that having a separate branch of the NAACP in San Francisco would counter this trend. Since 1915 the Northern California branch of the NAACP resided in Oakland. Mabson met with Robert Bagnall, NAACP director of branches, to persuade him to approve the NELSF's request to charter a branch in San Francisco. The national office approved their application and in 1923 black San Franciscans founded their own NAACP branch. While the new branch sometimes dealt with discrimination cases, most of its time and efforts were consumed in fund raising and membership recruitment.

**FURTHER READINGS**

Broussard, Albert S. *Black San Francisco: The Struggle for Racial Equality in the West, 1900–1954.* Lawrence: University of Kansas Press, 1993.

Crouchett, Lawrence P., Lonnie G. Bunch III, and Martha Kendall Winnacker. *Visions Toward Tomorrow: The History of the East Bay Afro-American Community, 1852–1977.* Oakland: Northern California Center for Afro-American History and Life, 1989.

*Shirley Ann Wilson Moore*

## Negro Fellowship League

The Negro Fellowship League (NFL) was a Chicago-based social service organization founded by Ida B. Wells-Barnett in 1908. Between then and 1920, when it was disbanded, the NFL provided education, entertainment, job placement, and lodging to young black men living in Chicago's South Side. The league struggled during its entire existence. Funding was scarce, and membership remained small. After 1913 the League faced competition from the black branch of the Chicago Young Men's Christian Association (YMCA), and by 1917 it had also to compete with the efforts of the National Urban League. Nonetheless, the NFL is significant both as an early African American settlement house and as an outgrowth of Ida B. Wells-Barnett's mature social thought.

The lynching of three black men in Springfield, Illinois, in 1908 provoked Wells-Barnett to form the NFL at her Chicago Presbyterian church. Between 1908 and 1910 the League met weekly to discuss the treatment of African Americans in urban Illinois. It quickly focused its attention on the plight of young men newly arrived in Chicago. Without jobs or family support, many of these men fell victim to the vices of the big city—drinking, gambling, and crime. Help, in the form of settlement houses and the YMCA, already existed for white newcomers, but no similar organizations served the needs of new black Chicagoans.

In 1910, the NFL began to minister to this constituency. With funding provided (at the time anonymously) by Mr. and Mrs. Victor F. Lawson, owners of the *Chicago Daily News*, the League leased a building at 28th and State Street and opened the NFL Reading Room and Social Center. The League hosted debates, classes, and lectures. In 1911, it began publishing a newspaper, the *Fellowship Herald*, edited by Wells-Barnett. Shortly thereafter, the League opened the second floor of the Social Center for lodgers and began a job placement service. By 1913, the Reading Room and Social Center had become a complete settlement house, modeled on Jane Addams's Hull House.

Though the League managed to expand its offerings, it failed to become a stable organization. The League's secretaries were reluctant to seek out the needy in neighborhood bars and pool halls, and members of the black middle class were unwilling to leave their more comfortable environs to volunteer at the settlement house. While funding from the Lawsons lasted, Wells-Barnett made up for the flaws of the secretaries and volunteers by canvassing the neighborhood for young men who could be helped by the League. Then in 1913, Mrs. Lawson died and Mr. Lawson withdrew his money in order to support the YMCA's new black branch.

From 1913 to 1916, Wells-Barnett kept the Social Center open with money she earned working as a probation officer. During these years the League, free from the Lawsons' control, became more active politically, and it invited William Monroe Trotter, head of the National Equal Rights League, to speak in Chicago just after his well-publicized shouting match with the president of the United States had made him a pariah in much of America. The League was also able at this time to pay lawyers to defend African Americans unjustly accused of crime.

But the years of independence ended in 1916 when Wells-Barnett lost her job and the League had to move its headquarters to a smaller storefront on State Street. It never found funding to replace Wells-Barnett's salary, and after the Urban League and the Methodist Church rejected an NFL appeal for money, it disbanded in 1920.

**FURTHER READINGS**

Duster, Alfreda M., ed. *Crusader for Justice: The Autobiography of Ida B. Wells.* Chicago: University of Chicago Press, 1970.

Sterling, Dorothy. *Black Foremothers: Three Lives.* New York: The Feminist Press, 1988.

Thompson, Mildred I. *Ida B. Wells-Barnett: An Exploratory Study of an American Black Woman, 1893–1930.* Brooklyn, N.Y.: Carlson, 1990.

*Gary Daynes*

## Negro Industrial and Clerical Alliance

Sufi Abdul Hamid, an American-born black nationalist orator and organizer who claimed Egyptian ancestry, organized the Negro Industrial and Clerical Alliance in Harlem in 1934 to demand white-collar and clerical jobs for African Americans in white-owned neighborhood stores. He had earlier been part of a similar movement in Chicago, where his efforts helped produce three hundred such jobs. But black nationalist and anti-white rhetoric alienated others in the Chicago campaign, and his provoking strategies and divisiveness followed him to Harlem.

Harlem became the site of a national effort, often called "Don't Buy Where You Can't Work" or "Jobs for Negroes" campaigns, during the Great Depression to win employment opportunities for African Americans. At first, the Alliance worked alongside the Citizens' League for Fair Play, which launched an effort to win jobs for local black residents. But differences soon emerged. The Citizens' League was not nationalist in orientation and, according both to nationalists within the League and to Hamid, its success in winning employment extended only to skilled and light-skinned women. Hamid insisted that jobs ought more properly to go to darker-skinned blacks, and to members of his own organization. Nationalists within the Citizens' League then broke away and formed their own organization, the Harlem Labor Union, which made the same demands.

The Alliance then launched its own picket lines around businesses, demanding they hire Hamid's people or face a renewed boycott. Clashes with other groups, including the Harlem Labor Union and the Universal Negro Improvement Association, and confrontations with store owners and would-be patrons were frequent, provoking condemnation by the black press and the Citizens' League, and occasionally police intervention and arrests. Several store owners complained of bribery attempts by the Alliance, and they reported virulent anti-white and anti-Semitic invective from Hamid and his lieutenants. A few black employees reported that Hamid threatened them if they did not join his group and pay membership dues. These charges, many confirmed by the *Amsterdam News* and other Hamid opponents, were firmly denied by Hamid and his supporters, and, despite the controversy and accusations, the Alliance continued its pickets and protests. Finally, one target, A. S. Beck Shoe Company, won a state court injunction at the end of 1934 forbidding pickets on the ground that there was no formal labor dispute.

Hamid then reorganized the Alliance into the Afro-American Federation of Labor, hoping the title suggested a union whose picket might therefore survive legal scrutiny. But the court rejected this argument and Hamid left the organization and the jobs campaign in 1935 to marry Madame Stephanie St. Clair, a successful "policy" or numbers banker, and he founded the Temple of Tranquility. He died in a plane crash in 1938, the same year the Supreme Court overturned the antipicketing injunction and others like it. The decision permitted race-based picketing to protest racial discrimination in hiring. A new campaign, this time under the direction of Reverend Adam Clayton Powell Jr. of Harlem's Abyssinian Baptist Church, rejoined the battle and won employment concessions from local and municipal businesses.

**FURTHER READINGS**

Greenberg, Cheryl Lynn. *"Or Does It Explode?" Black Harlem in the Great Depression.* New York: Oxford University Press, 1991.

Greene, Larry. "Harlem in the Great Depression." Ph.D. diss., Columbia University, 1979.

Hunter, Gary. "Don't Buy From Where You Can't Work: Black Urban Boycott Movements During the Depression, 1929–1941." Ph.D. diss., University of Michigan, 1977.

McKay, Claude. *Harlem, Negro Metropolis.* New York: E. P. Dutton, 1940.

Muraskin, William. "The Harlem Boycott of 1934 and Its Aftermath." M.A. thesis, Columbia University, 1966.

Naison, Mark. *Communists in Harlem During the Depression.* Urbana: University of Illinois Press, 1983.

*Cheryl Greenberg*

**SEE ALSO** Afro-American Federation of Labor

# Negro Labor Committee

On July 20, 1935, an interracial group of twenty-five labor leaders met in Harlem to create the Negro Labor Committee (NLC). The NLC sought to organize black workers in the New York City area to help them advance from menial, racially typed jobs, such as dishwasher, porter, and cook, to better-paid unionized factory, shop, mine, mill, and transport jobs. The NLC tried to convince labor unions of the benefits of organizing African Americans, and to convince black workers of the benefits of joining a union. The NLC gained the support of the International Ladies Garment Workers Union (ILGWU), the American Federation of Labor (AFL), the Socialist Party, and unions affiliated with the newly created Congress of Industrial Organizations (CIO). Until the 1950s, the NLC remained active largely in the New York City area. Following the 1965 death of Frank Crosswaith, the organization's longtime president, the NLC started to disintegrate and in 1969 it ceased to function. By that time, the Negro American Labor Council, also headquartered in New York City, was actively promoting a similar agenda for black workers.

The NLC was created as a result of discussions that took place at "The First Negro Labor Conference," held under the auspices of the Harlem Labor Committee. The July 1935 conference, attended by white and black trade unionists from 110 labor unions, proclaimed that the organized labor movement offered the best vehicle for black workers to improve their economic situation. Conference participants realized, however, that before they could organize African Americans, they had to overcome the animosity and suspicion white labor unions and black workers harbored for each other. In the past, the labor movement had viewed black workers as a threat to organized labor because African Americans often worked for less money than unionized workers. Similarly, many black workers were suspicious of labor unions, which had traditionally excluded African Americans. Conference attendees were determined to rectify organized labor's image of black workers and to convince African Americans of the necessity of unionization. For this purpose, the group established a Labor Center in Harlem to act as a coordinating unit where labor unions and black workers could meet and learn to cooperate.

The delegates named a committee of twenty-five individuals to establish the NLC and map out an agenda. Frank Crosswaith, general organizer for the ILGWU, served as president; A. Philip Randolph of the Brotherhood of Sleeping Car Porters, Thomas G. Young of the Building Services Employees' Union, Julius Hochman of the ILGWU, Abraham Miller of the Amalgamated Clothing Workers, and Morris Feinstone of United Hebrew Trades all became vice chairmen; Philip Kapp of the Dressmakers' Union served as treasurer; Winifred Gittens of the ILGWU became financial secretary; and Noah A. Walter Jr. of the Laundry Workers' Union served as organizer. While the founders of the NLC reiterated their intention to organize African Americans and to educate black workers and organized labor of the benefits of working together, they nevertheless blamed the labor movement for the dearth of black unionized workers. Black workers, they admitted, were apt to befriend their employer and not their union. However, the NLC argued that in most instances this was due to the fact that organized labor "both by sins of omission and commission, has driven the Negro worker into the open and welcome arms of the employers with the result that the Negro has developed an unfriendly attitude toward the labor movement and a corresponding affection for the employers of labor." Despite organized labor's pronouncements to the contrary, some unions openly barred black workers from membership and others "covertly discriminated against the Negro worker" by establishing discriminatory practices.

The NLC's first accomplishment was the establishment of the Harlem Labor Center, or "Labor's Home in Harlem," at 312 West 125th Street. Then, at the Center's dedication on December 15, 1935, the NLC announced plans for a mass organizing drive and education campaign. To organize black workers, the NLC sought the affiliation of numerous unions in New York City, those with and without black members. Moreover, the NLC offered assistance to unions that were organizing black workers or staging strikes that involved African Americans. To educate white and black workers, the NLC set up the Negro Labor News Service, which provided nationwide coverage of information related to the black labor movement.

The NLC's efforts reached a peak in the 1930s and 1940s, when the number of black unionized workers increased dramatically. This surge was largely due to the 1935 creation of the CIO, which sought to organize unskilled workers regardless of race, and to greater attempts by the labor movement to organize black workers in World War II defense industries. Yet, the NLC itself also played an important role in increasing the number of organized black workers. At its peak, it represented over 250,000 black and white workers and "was widely acknowledged and respected as the voice of black labor" (Negro Labor Committee, "Introduction," 21). In 1941, for example, the NLC played an active role in the March on Washington Movement headed by A. Philip Randolph. The protest movement pressured President Franklin D. Roosevelt to enact wartime legislation banning racial discrimination in defense industries and to set up a Fair Employment Practices Commission (FEPC) for the duration of the war. After World War II, the NLC joined other organizations in lobbying Congress for a permanent FEPC.

The 1950s were a tumultuous decade for the NLC. In 1951, a group of black trade unionists challenged the leadership of the NLC and created the National Negro Labor Council (NNLC). The NNLC, many established union leaders in the CIO and American Federation of Labor (AFL) claimed, was a "communist-front" organization. Crosswaith, a Socialist and graduate of the Rand School, held long-standing disagreements with Communists and the Communist Party. He and other prominent black trade unionists felt that the Communist Party, which had made the plight of black Americans a central part of its critique of American democracy, was "merely using the grievances of black people for cheap political propaganda." Thus, Crosswaith, Randolph, and other prominent black leaders joined the CIO and the AFL in opposing the NNLC and other efforts by Communist-led groups to organize workers. Crosswaith and Randolph agreed with Philip Murray, president of the CIO, that Communists exploited the grievances of workers, particularly black workers, to gain new party members.

In March of 1952, Crosswaith called a conference to discuss the growing threat that the newly created NNLC posed to black workers nationwide. The six hundred delegates attending the conference decided to counter the efforts of the NNLC by expanding the NLC into a national organization. A 1952 press release announcing the reorganization of the NLC reported that the new Negro Labor Committee, U.S.A. (NLC, U.S.A.), condemned "Ku Kluxism and Communism as enemies of Democracy" and pledged "to devote its energies and resources to the true democratic principles of justice and equality and the advancement of the Negro workers' welfare."

The creation of the NLC, U.S.A., however, proved to be problematic for Crosswaith and the CIO, one of the NLC's main sponsors. A dispute arose between Crosswaith and fellow NLC member Benjamin McLaurin over the use of funds for the new national organization. According to Crosswaith, McLaurin, who had presided over the March 1952 conference and made Crosswaith "honorary chairman" of the NLC, U.S.A., had used funds collected at a testimonial dinner in honor of Crosswaith without the proper authority and without Crosswaith's knowledge. The internal friction drew negative attention to the NLC, U.S.A. and the CIO withdrew its support in the wake of the controversy, claiming that it could no longer be sure of the NLC, U.S.A.'s intentions. Crosswaith tried valiantly in a series of letters to Walter Reuther, president of the United Automobile Workers (UAW-CIO), to appeal the decision of the CIO's Civil Rights Committee, but the CIO stood firm.

The controversy surrounding the formation of the NLC, U.S.A., apparently resulted in the organization's gradual demise. While the NLC continued to operate until the late 1960s, it ceased to be a crucial force in African American labor relations. Crosswaith, however, remained politically active in the New York City area and he was involved in the civil rights movement as it gained momentum in the late 1950s and early 1960s. In 1963, for example, he joined Randolph and Cleveland Robinson of the Negro American Labor Council in organizing the March on Washington for Jobs and Freedom. Crosswaith also remained involved in the New York City Housing Authority until his death in 1965. Following Crosswaith's death, the NLC lost much of its organizing capability and political force, leaving only scattered records by 1969.

**FURTHER READINGS**

Foner, Philip. *Organized Labor and the Black Worker, 1619–1973.* New York: Praeger, 1974.

Negro Labor Committee. *Finding Aid.* "Introduction," Negro Labor Committee Record Group, 1925–1968, Schomburg Center for Research in Black Culture, New York Public Library, New York, New York.

———. "Letter," Frank Crosswaith to Benjamin McLaurin, 30 September 1952, reel 1, box 1, folder a14.

———. "Letter," Frank Crosswaith to Walter Reuther, 15 October 1953, reel 1, box 1, folder a15.

———. "Minutes," Negro Labor Assembly, 11 March 1953, reel 1, box 1, folder a15.

———. "Press Release," Negro Labor Committee, 5 March 1952, reel 3, box 5, folder b32.

*Lisa Phillips*

# Negro Medical Association of Virginia

Black physicians founded the Negro Medical Association of Virginia (NMAV) in the late nineteenth or early twentieth century. Barred from membership in white local, state, and national medical societies, black physicians organized their own professional associations beginning with the establishment of the National Medical Association (NMA) in 1895. State affiliates like the NMAV offered further avenues for socializing and exchange of new medical information and techniques.

Virginia hospitals, like those in all southern communities, denied staff privileges to doctors not affiliated with the all-white American Medical Association (AMA) and the Medical Society of Virginia (MSV). Hospital practice provided one of the most important means of postgraduate medical education, but black physicians, denied membership in the white national and state associations, could not access this training ground. In an effort to break down the racial barrier, the NMAV asked the white MSV to sponsor its cause. Although white physicians denied the NMAV's appeal, they did direct the black doctors to contact the Medical College of Virginia, which had demonstrated an interest in the care and treatment of African Americans. Collaborative efforts between the NMAV and the Medical College of Virginia did not end segregation, but they did result in expanded educational opportunities for black physicians.

By the 1930s Virginia's black doctors were able to attend two-week postgraduate medical education courses at Richmond's St. Philip Hospital. The hospital, sponsored by the Medical College of Virginia, served black patients and provided continuing medical education for black physicians, even while it adhered to Jim Crow rules and denied black physicians staff privileges, a feature of Virginian medical practice that remained in effect until the 1960s.

In the 1940s, the NMAV apparently adopted a new name. At that time the original name disappeared from use and records thereafter refer to the Old Dominion Medical Society. Despite this name change, the group continued to serve as the state medical association for black physicians and maintained its affiliation with the NMA.

The NMAV fought for decades to enhance the professionalization of black physicians and to win their full acceptance in the medical establishments of the state. Like similar all-black state medical societies, it provided important networking and professional advancement opportunities. By the 1960s, when white medical societies opened their doors to physicians of color, many of the black societies disbanded.

**FURTHER READINGS**

Gamble, Vanessa Northington. *Making a Place for Ourselves: The Black Hospital Movement, 1920–1945*. New York: Oxford University Press, 1995.

Garavati, Charles M. *Medicine in Richmond, 1900–1975*. Richmond, Va.: Richmond Academy of Medicine, 1975.

*Peggy Hardman*

## Negro National League

In 1920, after more than thirty years of exclusion from white organized baseball leagues, African Americans formed the Negro National League (NNL) in Kansas City. Andrew "Rube" Foster, a pitcher and manager of the Chicago American Giants, was the "Father of the Negro Leagues." Foster brought together a group of businessmen, reporters, and attorneys to establish this first successful all-black league.

Foster's league succeeded where previous attempts had failed because he provided leadership, secured financial backing from black and white businessmen, and generated publicity by inviting reporters to help create the league. Most important, his efforts were aided by a black population shift that had brought large numbers of African Americans from the rural South to the urban North during World War I. These black city residents provided sufficient numbers of spectators to support the league. Foster became president of the NNL, serving in that capacity until he became terminally ill in 1926. He died in 1930.

The new league included eight entrants, mainly from the midwest. In addition to Foster's Chicago American Giants, the league was composed of the Indianapolis ABCs, the Dayton Marcos, the Kansas City Monarchs, the St. Louis Giants, the Detroit Stars, the Chicago Giants, and the traveling Cuban Stars. The Stars, who had no ball park to call home, stayed on the road for all their contests.

Each entrant had to pay a franchise fee to join, and they were required to abide by the decisions of the league regarding fighting, contract disputes, umpires, and sta-

dium rentals. Failure to follow these stipulations resulted in fines and suspensions. Booking agents, who received a percentage for securing opponents and a place to play, were essential to establishing a workable schedule for all teams. Special arrangements were also made for the inclusion of associate members, those who could not afford the full franchise fee but wanted some of the benefits of being affiliated with a league. The inaugural season ended with Foster's American Giants in first place, followed by the Detroit Stars (the other Chicago club trailed the league leaders by nearly twenty games by season's end).

As the clubs readied themselves for a second season there were some changes made. The Bacharach Giants joined the fold as an associate member, while the Cincinnati Cubans replaced the Cuban Stars and the Columbus Buckeyes took over the franchise for the Dayton Marcos. These changes were typical in the league's history, since some teams left the league after only a short time, while others, such as the American Giants and the Monarchs, enjoyed long, successful tenures. The Kansas City Monarchs, for example, won seventeen pennants and two World Series during their existence, while the Chicago American Giants won twelve league titles. Other clubs with short tenures included the Cleveland Tate Stars, the Pittsburgh Keystones, the Toledo Tigers, the Milwaukee Bears, the Cleveland Browns, the Cleveland Elites, the Cleveland Hornets, and the Louisville White Sox.

In 1923 the NNL received some competition with the creation of the Eastern Colored League (ECL) under the direction of Ed Bolden. This league was formed in part to reduce the travel expenses of clubs on the East coast. As a result of the existence of two leagues, black teams launched their own World Series, which took place from 1924 to 1927.

Foster played a key role in the growth and success of the NNL, but he was not the only important figure. White businessman J. L. Wilkinson of Kansas City became a well-respected owner and supporter of the NNL. In addition to the Monarchs, Wilkinson owned other local teams and traveled with his clubs regularly. Joining Wilkinson was C. I. Taylor, the owner of the Indianapolis ball club and a player himself. Taylor owned a pocket billiard hall in Indianapolis that grew from a small venture into a successful city landmark. He came from a family of brothers who all played and managed in the Negro leagues.

Despite this support and the achievements of a number of fine athletes such as Satchel Paige, Biz Mackey, Oscar Charleston, Cool Papa Bell, and Judy Johnson, the

NNL did not survive the financially troubled times of the Depression. By 1932 the NNL folded, with only the Negro Southern League and the East–West League operating that season.

**FURTHER READINGS**

Clark, Dick, and Larry Lester. *The Negro Leagues Book.* Cleveland, Ohio: Society of American Baseball Research, 1994.

Heaphy, Leslie. "Shadowed Diamonds: The Growth and Decline of the Negro Leagues." Ph.D. diss., University of Toledo, 1995.

Holway, John B. *Blackball Stars, Negro League Pioneers.* Westport, Conn.: Meckler Books, 1988.

Riley, James A. *The Biographical Encyclopedia of the Negro Baseball Leagues.* New York: Carroll and Graf, 1994.

Whitehead, Charles E. *A Man and His Diamonds.* New York: Vantage, 1980.

*Leslie Heaphy*

# Negro Newspaper Publishers Association

*See* National Newspaper Publishers Association.

# Negro Railway Labor Executives Committee

Formed in early 1948, the Negro Railway Labor Executives Committee (NRLEC) brought together five organizations of African American railroad workers to coordinate legal struggles against discrimination by employers and trade unions and to advance a common agenda for civil rights. Four of the groups were composed of independent southern railroad operating craft workers, such as locomotive firemen and brakemen, which remained outside of the American Federation of Labor (AFL) and the Congress of Industrial Organizations (CIO). The oldest was the Association of Colored Railway Trainmen and Locomotives Firemen (ACRT), initially based in Tennessee and by the 1940s, centered in Roanoke, Virginia, which was founded as the Colored Association of Railroad Employees in 1912. The other three were the Colored Trainmen of America (CTA), representing black railroaders in eastern Texas and Louisiana, chartered in 1918; the International Association of Railway Employees (IARE), originally designed as a federation of small associations of

black railroaders, founded in 1934; and the Savannah, Georgia-based Southern Federation of Colored Locomotive Firemen's Union, established in 1939. The one northern service workers' union, the Chicago-based Dining Car and Railroad Foodworkers Union (DCRFU), was founded by Communist members of the Joint Council of Dining Car Employees, which was affiliated with the AFL's Hotel and Restaurant Workers Union. In 1947, the Joint Council's founder, Solon C. Bell, led a breakaway faction to form the new DCRFU after the Hotel and Restaurant Employees leadership removed leftists from their elected positions in the Joint Council.

The NRLEC brought together black activists who, voluntarily and involuntarily, stood outside the national labor movement. The four southern independent associations had rejected efforts by A. Philip Randolph and the Brotherhood of Sleeping Car Porters (BSCP) to unite in a single association, the BSCP-controlled Provisional Committee to Organize Colored Locomotive Firemen. The independents valued their autonomy, resented what they called the AFL's racist policies, and resisted Randolph's efforts to dominate organizing efforts in their crafts. Until the 1960s, the independents and the Provisional Committee repeatedly clashed over allegiance of the several thousand remaining southern black firemen.

In terms of strategy, though, both the independents and the NRLEC and the Provisional Committee focused their energies primarily on the courts, in an effort to challenge legally discriminatory practices and preserve black firemen's seniority and jobs, which were under constant threat from white firemen. Furthermore, with the founding of the NRLEC, the independents worked closely with another of Randolph's opponents—members of the Communist Party. Exposure to the Communist-influenced DCRFU led leaders of some of the black independents to participate in broader, northern civil rights conferences, and gained them national exposure through the DCRFU's and the Communist Party's publications.

The impetus for the formation of the NRLEC came from African American civil rights attorney Charles Hamilton Houston, who had once served as dean of the Howard Law School and as special counsel for the National Association for the Advancement of Colored People (NAACP). In the 1930s and 1940s, Houston and his law firm represented the ACRT, the IARE, and the CTA, waging a series of legal battles that ultimately resulted in the successful *Steele* and *Tunstall* decisions in 1944. The landmark cases established that white railroad unions could not legally negotiate contracts that discriminated against blacks. To start the NRLEC, Houston initially proposed, in the fall of 1947, a committee composed of the presidents of the various black railway unions. On March 6, 1948, the first meeting of the new NRLEC was held.

The NRLEC's goals included the protection of black railroaders' seniority and the opening up to black workers of all jobs in the highly discriminatory railroad industry. It sought to collect, formulate, and disseminate information about black railroaders. To accomplish this end, it periodically published a newsletter, the *Negro Railway Labor News*, from 1948 to 1950. Its legal counsel, Houston and his partner, Joseph Waddy, also testified on its behalf for fair employment legislation and against discriminatory aspects of the Railway Labor Act before Congress. Houston and Waddy used NRLEC meetings to foster greater cooperation among the independent associations and to raise funds to pursue the numerous legal cases they were bringing against southern railroads and the white firemen and brakemen's brotherhoods. With Houston's death in 1950, the NRLEC lost its momentum, but its constituent associations remained intact, at least until the 1960s, and continued to pursue a strategy of litigation against discrimination in employment.

**FURTHER READINGS**

Houston, Charles Hamilton. "Foul Employment Practice on the Rails." *Crisis* 56, no. 9 (October 1949): 269–271, 284–285.

McNeil, Genna Rae. *Groundwork: Charles Hamilton Houston and the Struggle for Civil Rights.* Philadelphia: University of Pennsylvania Press, 1983.

*Negro Railway Labor News.* Colored Trainmen of America Papers, Houston Metropolitan Archives, Houston Public Library.

*Blacks in the Railroad Industry Papers, 1946–1954.* Wilmington, Del.: Scholarly Resources, 1995.

*Eric Arnesen*

## Negro Rural School Fund

In 1907, Anna T. Jeanes, a Quaker philanthropist from Philadelphia, founded the Negro Rural School Fund, also known as the Jeanes Fund, when she directed that the income from her estate, valued at about one million dollars, be used to assist rural schools for blacks. James H. Dillard became the fund's first president and served in that capacity until Arthur D. Wright replaced him in 1931.

The fund's plan to allocate money was originated by Virginia E. Randolph, the daughter of former slaves, who had graduated from high school and begun a teaching career at age sixteen. In her Mountain Road School in Henrico County, Virginia, Randolph emphasized industrial arts—such as cooking, sewing, and gardening—suffused with moral values such as cleanliness and orderliness. When Jackson Davis, the school superintendent of Henrico County, received a Jeanes Fund grant to implement new teaching methods in black schools, he adopted Randolph's model. Impressed by Randolph's work, the fund appointed her as its first Supervising Industrial Teacher in 1908. Within less than three years, the fund, at a cost of $44,250, appointed 129 additional Jeanes teachers, most of whom were black women.

These dedicated and skilled teachers traveled throughout the South to increase interest in and support of rural schools for southern blacks. Although the fund paid the salaries of these traveling teachers, it insisted that school superintendents and boards recognize them as regular employees of the local school systems. The Jeanes teachers urged members of both races to take an interest in school activities and the problems of rural residents. Their pedagogical model blended formal and nonformal education. They stimulated support for schools by organizing improvement leagues and mothers' clubs and occasionally they attended Sunday services at local churches to address congregations on school-related issues. Emphasizing a connection between home, school, and community improvement, they also provided outreach services by teaching needlework, health care, nutrition, and homemaking skills in the homes of rural residents. Moreover, they encouraged children to grow or manufacture at home many of the products ordinarily purchased from stores. Children in domestic arts classes canned and preserved garden products grown by students in agriculture classes and constructed new equipment for their schools.

By 1936 the fund employed 426 teachers in fourteen southern states. While the first group of Jeanes teachers had no collegiate training, 45 percent of those in the field during the mid-1930s had obtained a bachelor's degree, primarily by attending summer courses at Hampton Institute, paid for by the fund. The work of the Jeanes teachers complemented that of other programs, most notably the county training schools established by the Slater Fund. Dedicated to an industrial curriculum, the county training schools helped to compensate for the lack of teaching expertise displayed by many of the teachers whose schools were visited by the Jeanes teachers.

As the demand for teachers grew, the fund was unable to meet its expenses and began to accept financial assistance from other educational foundations. The General Education Board, which made its first donation to the Negro Rural School Fund in 1914, continued to make periodic grants toward the teachers' salaries until 1949. Between 1920 and 1940, the Phelps–Stokes Fund successfully garnered the support of other philanthropic funds in an effort to transfer the Negro Rural School Fund model of industrial education to English-speaking Africa. By 1950, there were approximately five hundred fund supervisors, assigned mainly to southern counties with large black populations.

After the Supreme Court's 1954 ruling in *Brown v. Board of Education* declared segregation in public education unconstitutional, the number of fund teachers began to decrease. Other factors relegated teachers to a minor role, including school consolidations and passage of the Smith–Hughes Act, which provided federal funding for vocational courses at rural high schools. Moreover, by the 1950s the civil rights movement had gained momentum and industrial training for African Americans had become an anachronism, and the work of the fund teachers effectively ended in 1968.

**FURTHER READINGS**

Caliver, Ambrose. *Rural Education Among Negroes Under Jeanes Supervising Teachers.* Washington, D.C.: United States Government Printing Office, 1933.

Chapman, Bernadine Sharpe. "Northern Philanthropy and African-American Adult Education in the Rural South: Hegemony and Resistance in the Jeanes Movement." Ph.D. diss., Northern Illinois University, 1990.

Clarke, Vernon F. *The Jeanes Supervisors: Striving to Educate.* Atlanta, Ga.: Breaking Ground Productions, 1995.

Dale, Lily Farley Ross. "The Jeanes Supervisors in Alabama, 1909–1963." Ph.D. diss., Auburn University, 1998.

Wright, Arthur D., and Edward E. Redcay. *The Negro Rural School Fund, Inc. [Anna T. Jeanes Foundation] 1907–1933.* Washington, D.C.: The Rural School Fund, 1933.

Anna T. Jeanes Fund. Papers. Southern Education Foundation, Inc., Atlanta, Georgia.

*Jayne R. Beilke*

**SEE ALSO**   Southern Education Foundation

# Negro Service Committee of the United Service Organizations

The Negro Service Committee (NSC) was formed on September 4, 1941, after members of the Colored Work Department of the Young Men's Christian Association (YMCA) protested the dearth of social services provided for black soldiers and the lack of African American representation in the United Service Organizations (USO). The USO Executive Committee established the NSC to assist in the creation of services for black troops, their families, and black defense production workers; to recommend policies; and to review the scope and quality of USO programs.

The NSC was composed of representatives of various social service organizations, including Dr. Channing H. Tobias and Jay A. Urice of the YMCA, Helen Thatcher and Gladys Pullum Ervin of the Young Women's Christian Association, Walter Hoving of the Salvation Army, James Norris of the National Catholic Community Service, Louis Kraft of the Jewish Welfare Board, and S. J. Rosensohn of the National Travelers Aid Association. With the exception of Tobias and Ervin, all members of the NSC were white. During the war, however, the NSC's leadership cadre was joined by various African American luminaries such as noted entertainer Noble Sissle, Olympian Ralph Metcalfe, Howard University president Mordecai Johnson, and Fisk University sociologist Charles S. Johnson. To further bolster the committee's standing among African Americans, the USO asked Hubert T. Delany, national director of the National Association for the Advancement of Colored People (NAACP), to serve as NSC Director-at-Large.

Despite the creation of the NSC, the USO did not adopt an official segregation policy; however, it did practice de facto segregation. Thus, throughout the war the NSC operated without clearly defined racial guidelines. While the NSC did not challenge the exclusion of African Americans from white USO clubs, the committee refused to foster segregation and encouraged black soldiers to make use of white service centers whenever possible.

Of the more than three thousand USOs operating in America during the war, 109 clubs staffed by white personnel provided services for black troops. Nearly all of the USOs on the West Coast and Hawaii and some of the clubs in the north, particularly those that catered to a relatively small black soldier population, admitted blacks. While the West Coast and Hawaiian USOs admitted members of both races without restrictions, many of the other clubs only served black soldiers on separate nights.

Resenting, then, the lack of complete integration, many black soldiers favored the construction of separate black clubs. The NSC, however, was unwilling to acknowledge or endorse segregation and discouraged the establishment of separate black USOs whenever white clubs catered to African Americans in any way.

Reluctantly, the NSC finally recommended creation of separate USO clubs, staffed with black personnel, only when local laws and customs made the operation of racially inclusive clubs virtually impossible. In the South, white USOs excluded African Americans and in some cases white southern communities even opposed the construction of separate black clubs. While the NSC was usually able to overcome this opposition to separate clubs, white resistance often delayed their opening. Most white southerners, however, supported the construction of black service clubs to maintain segregation. By the end of the war the NSC operated 375 USOs specifically designed for the use of black soldiers. None of the black clubs excluded white servicemen.

Likewise, the NSC insisted on racially inclusive training of USO personnel and encouraged black USO workers to attend all of the organization's official functions. Yet, African Americans who attempted to attend USO functions in the South frequently encountered white hostility and abuse. In response, the NSC, in collaboration with the Colored Work Department of the YMCA, conducted a separate training institute for black USO workers in Bordentown, New Jersey.

While the NSC did not challenge racial exclusion and discrimination in the USO, it helped to prevent the further entrenchment of segregation and paved the way for integrated services following World War II.

**FURTHER READINGS**

Lancaster, Richard C. *Serving the U.S. Armed Forces, 1861–1986: The Story of the YMCA's Ministry to Military Personnel for 125 Years.* Schaumburg, Ill.: Armed Services YMCA of the USA, 1987.

Hopkins, C. Howard. *History of the YMCA in North America.* New York: Association Press, 1951.

Mjagkij, Nina. "The Negro Service Committee and African American Soldiers." Unpublished manuscript, 1995.

———. *Light in the Darkness: African Americans and the YMCA, 1852–1946.* Lexington: The University Press of Kentucky, 1994.

*Robert F. Jefferson*

# Negro Society for Historical Research

Founded in 1911, the Negro Society for Historical Research (NSHR) was one of several organizations that emerged around the turn of the century to preserve, study, and disseminate black history. The NSHR set out to gather books, pictures, letters, manuscripts, artifacts, and other historical data pertaining to blacks' contributions to world history. By encouraging the study of these documents the organization sought to counter blacks' erasure from mainstream histories and the widespread anti-black propaganda prevalent in American popular culture in the early twentieth century. Moreover, the Society sought to instruct African Americans in their own history of achievement. Reflecting a viewpoint common to many white and black intellectuals of the period, the Society's motto proclaimed that "race is the key to history."

Based in Yonkers, New York, the NSHR emerged from a group of five amateur historians who held regular, informal meetings at the home of outspoken journalist and activist John Edward Bruce. A former slave who for decades had used his acerbic pen to agitate for black rights, Bruce was the driving force of the group and served as its president. The most prominent and active of the other founders was Puerto Rico–born bibliophile Arthur A. Schomburg, who served as secretary-treasurer and whose personal collection of materials greatly augmented the Society's holdings. Schomburg and Bruce shared a close friendship, a passion for books and history, and active membership in the Order of Freemasons. They also were both dedicated Pan-Africanists, who emphasized the importance of connecting black peoples throughout the Diaspora with their African roots and with each other. The NSHR held that a broad, international perspective was crucial to a full appreciation of black history, an attitude that was reflected in a diverse membership, which included individuals from several Caribbean and African nations.

The organization was greeted enthusiastically by black scholars and received numerous inquiries for historical information. The NSHR loaned materials, sponsored public lectures, published occasional papers, and in 1924 cosponsored Alain Locke's official presence at the reopening of the Egyptian tomb of King Tutankhamen. Schomburg and Bruce hoped to establish branches across the nation and to publish a journal to further publicize the Society's activities, but these plans never came to fruition, largely due to a lack of funds. The NSHR cooperated with organizations like Carter G. Woodson's Association for the Study of Negro Life and History (ASNLH), though Society leaders bristled at Woodson's superior abilities in attracting outside financial support, particularly for his respected *Journal of Negro History*. Moreover, many of Woodson's associates criticized the NSHR for being too racially chauvinistic and unscholarly in its approach to black history. Society members' active support of the controversial programs of Marcus Garvey by the early 1920s exacerbated these tensions. By mid-decade, as the ASNLH grew in prominence, the NSHR faded from existence. Thanks, however, to Schomburg's sale of his extensive collection of historical materials to the New York Public Library in 1926, the work of the organization continues to contribute to the understanding of African and African American pasts.

### FURTHER READINGS

Meier, August. *Negro Thought in America, 1880–1915: Racial Ideologies in the Age of Booker T. Washington.* Ann Arbor: The University of Michigan Press, 1963.

Sinnette, Elinor Des Verney. *Arthur Alfonso Schomburg, Black Bibliophile and Collector: A Biography.* Detroit: Wayne State University Press and The New York Public Library, 1989.

*Mitchell Kachun*

## Negro Southern League

In 1920, African American businessmen, led by F. W. Purdue of Birmingham, Alabama, founded the Negro Southern League (NSL), which lasted until the mid-1950s. The NSL developed because white baseball leagues, beginning in the 1880s, excluded African American teams. Teams such as the Monroe Monarchs, the Nashville Elite Giants, the Memphis Red Sox, and the Birmingham Black Barons belonged at various times to the NSL. Every club had to pay a franchise fee to join the league and a percentage of the gate receipts went into a special fund to help with general league expenditures, such as umpires, equipment, and publicity.

NSL clubs often served as a training ground for players who moved into the major Negro leagues, the Negro National League (NNL), the Eastern Colored League (ECL), and the Negro American League (NAL). In 1932, the NSL itself joined the ranks of the black major leagues, but only after other leagues folded as a result of the depression. That year, Cole's American Giants beat the Nashville club and the Monroe Monarchs for the crown.

Much of the economic survival of the NSL depended on the black major leagues. During the spring many teams of the NAL, NNL, and ECL traveled south for spring training, stopping in NSL cities for barnstorming (unofficial) games. Similarly, after the baseball season ended in September and northern clubs traveled south to keep playing in the warmer weather, they staged games against NSL teams.

Leading figures in the NSL included the prominent brothers B. B., John, and William Martin, who owned, respectively, funeral homes, dentistry practices, and real estate in Tennessee. The Martins also owned several clubs and served the league in various capacities. For instance, B. B. Martin was secretary of the NSL, while John and William each served terms as president. John even built a stadium for Memphis, one of the few owned by African American management. The stadium attracted many black clubs to the city because of its seating capacity and because the money for renting the park went back into the African American community. John Martin also owned a hotel near the park where teams could stay while in the city, thus avoiding racial humiliations African Americans often encountered when seeking public accommodation.

In addition to the Martin brothers, other businessmen played key roles in the NSL. Fred Stovall, the white owner of the Monroe Monarchs and proprietor of a large plantation and casino, had a steady cash flow to put into the venture. J. C. Claybrook of Arkansas owned the Claybrook Tigers, a successful team that won two NSL pennants and paid regular salaries to players, such as Ted "Doubleduty" Radcliffe. Thomas T. Wilson, owner of the Nashville Elite Giants, ran a night club, a railway business, and a gambling operation in Nashville. Wilson developed a strong sporting network in the city, sponsoring teams in various local leagues before creating his own team in 1918. Wilson also built Wilson Park for his team in 1928. The park seated eight thousand people and was in the center of the African American community. In 1934, businessman Pat Riley spurred competition in the NSL when his Indianapolis Monarchs joined the league, mostly because they were winning too easily everywhere else.

Many teams had trouble paying their expenses, and membership in the NSL changed frequently. In 1932, for example, the Louisville Black Caps only lasted half a season before pulling out of the league. The Columbus Turfs replaced the Louisville franchise for the rest of that season. In the same year, the Atlanta Black Crackers joined the NSL, marking one of only two seasons they spent in an organized league. The rest of the years they barnstormed as an independent ball club, playing all over the country. The Crackers played most of their games outside of Atlanta due to the city's blue laws and segregation laws. Not all NSL clubs had short runs in the league, however. For example, the Birmingham Black Barons, the Nashville Elite Giants, and the Memphis Red Sox enjoyed many seasons in the NSL.

In 1947, after Jackie Robinson joined the Brooklyn Dodgers and a growing number of black players started to follow him into the major white leagues, the NSL declined, like other all-black leagues. Although the NSL, like all black baseball leagues, was the product of segregation, its clubs provided important services for the African American community and black athletes. The NSL provided entertainment for many African Americans and a source of income for its players. Moreover, it served as a training ground for black athletes, some of whom moved into the major Negro leagues and eventually into the major white leagues. One of the most important contributions of the southern teams was the discovery of Willie Mays in Chattanooga. Mays had a short-lived Negro league career before becoming a Hall of Fame player in the major white leagues.

**FURTHER READINGS**

Joyce, Allen E. "The Atlanta Black Crackers," M.A. thesis, Emory University, 1975.
"Marlin Carter: Texas Gold." *Black Ball News*, vol. 4 (Dec. 1992) pp. 2–11.
Peterson, Robert. *Only the Ball Was White*. New York: McGraw Hill, 1970.
Riley, James A. *The Biographical Encyclopedia of the Negro Baseball Leagues*. New York: Carroll and Graf, 1994.
"Southern Stars, Dixie's Contributions to the Negro Leagues." *Black Ball News* (May–June 1992), p. 9.

*Leslie Heaphy*

## Negro Theatre Guild

The Negro Theatre Guild was a short-lived organization that produced two all-black plays—*Louisiana* and *How Come, Lawd?*—during the Great Depression.

Involving close to fifty black actors, *Louisiana* opened February 27, 1933, for eight shows at the 48th Theatre in New York City. Directed by Samuel John Park and produced by George L. Miller for the Guild, *Louisiana* depicted a community's ability to use a mix of Baptist faith and residual voodoo practices to punish the town's bad man,

a lecherous blackmailer who victimizes a former convict turned preacher and his niece. J. Augustus Smith, who wrote the play, played the part of Preacher Amos Berry.

*How Come, Lawd?*, written by Donald Heywood, produced by the Guild, and directed by Charles J. Adler with sets by Stagecraft Studios, opened October 30, 1937, for two shows at the 49th Street Theatre. A folk drama like *Louisiana*, the play portrays the efforts of union organizer Aloes, played by Leigh Whipper, and black Alabama sharecroppers to battle an oppressive white system. It also tells the story of a worker caught up in the labor struggle who turns his back on God and falls into dissipation, with tragic consequences. When an angry boyfriend tries to kill him, his protective girlfriend (Hilda Rogers) dies instead. Citing amateurishness and confusion, the reviews for both plays were negative.

**FURTHER READINGS**

Bronner, Edwin. *The Encyclopedia of the American Theatre, 1900–1975*. San Diego: Barnes, 1980.
Leiter, Samuel L. *The Encyclopedia of the New York Stage, 1930–1940*. New York: Greenwood, 1989.

*Stephen Davenport*

## New England Anti-Slavery Society

Founded in January 1832, in Boston's African Baptist Church, the New England Anti-Slavery Society (NEASS) was the first significant racially integrated antislavery society in the United States. Under William Lloyd Garrison's inspired, if controversial, leadership, the NEASS opened a new salvo in the American crusade against slavery, and within four years, over five hundred antislavery associations had been established throughout the North. The NEASS called for an immediate end to slavery, an aim not realized until the Thirteenth Amendment prohibited any form of involuntary servitude in 1865. Although dominated by white abolitionists, the NEASS was unique in antebellum American society because it was a racially integrated organization through which African Americans denounced the "peculiar institution" of slavery and all forms of racial discrimination.

Although British abolitionists provided some impetus to American antislavery efforts before 1832, the NEASS developed out of causes indigenous to the United States. A key component lay in the Second Great Awakening, when waves of religious revivals swept the nation and convinced many Americans that they could perfect themselves and their society. Slavery was thus viewed as a sin, which had to be eradicated. In addition, the NEASS grew out of anticolonization and antislavery protests by black activists who had established the Massachusetts General Colored Association (MCGA) in Boston in 1826. One of the MGCA's founders, David Walker, published *Walker's Appeal* in 1829, calling for an end to slavery and discrimination against free blacks. Although the white abolitionist William Lloyd Garrison decried some of Walker's extreme language, he was certainly swayed by Walker's powerful call to arms.

Upon moving to Boston from Baltimore in 1830, Garrison joined forces with local blacks when he began to publish the nation's first significant antislavery newspaper, the *Liberator*, on January 1, 1831. Within its first half year of publication, this magazine drew nearly five hundred subscribers, most of them black, with African American agents spread throughout the northeast. By 1834, three-fourths of the *Liberator's* twenty-three hundred subscribers were black, and African American leaders, such as James Forten of Philadelphia and James Barbadoes of Boston, kept afloat Garrison's publishing venture with crucial subsidies. Garrison claimed in 1834 that his publication "belongs especially to the people of color—it is their organ." Although the *Liberator* undercut efforts to create a black-owned newspaper in Boston, it served the African American community until Garrison ceased publishing at the end of the Civil War.

Following its founding in 1832, the NEASS published newspapers, tracts, and convention proceedings; it sponsored speakers and circulated petitions; and it provided a moral and organizational basis for the burgeoning antislavery movement. The organization grew quickly in numbers and stature, prompted by the attention-getting *Liberator* and its editor, whom the NEASS sponsored on a trip to England in 1833.

By 1835, the emergence of the national American Anti-Slavery Society (AASS) and the development of state antislavery organizations in Maine, New Hampshire, and Vermont compelled the NEASS to narrow its scope to antislavery agitation within Massachusetts. Renamed the Massachusetts Anti-Slavery Society (MASS), the group remained a preeminent organization until after the Civil War, and it was significant for its continued embrace of radical causes, including nonviolent resistance to slavery, women's rights, and racial equality.

MASS expanded its efforts through the 1840s and 1850s. In 1841, John Collins, the general agent for MASS, extended an invitation to an ex-slave named Frederick Douglass to become a paid lecturer on the antislav-

ery circuit. Douglass later emerged as the foremost black leader of the nineteenth century. Two years later, in 1843, MASS garnered headlines for its Garrison-inspired denunciation of the United States Constitution as a "covenant with death and an agreement with hell." Garrison's support of "disunionism"—urging the North to withdraw from a nation that protected slavery—and other radical issues created much dissension among activists, yet African Americans in Boston and Philadelphia generally remained loyal to Garrison.

MASS survived its internal conflicts, tensions endemic to the antebellum antislavery movement, but in May 1839, a conservative faction split off to form the short-lived Massachusetts Abolition Society, and this schism foreshadowed a significant national conflict in 1840, when the New York-based Tappan brothers created the more conservative American and Foreign Anti-Slavery Society (AFASS). This new wing of the antislavery movement embraced political abolitionism, including affiliation with the Liberty and Free Soil parties, while the older, more radical AASS under Garrison's leadership continued to eschew participation in the "corrupt" political system that protected slavery. Some African Americans throughout the North began to turn away from the integrated but fractious organization, including Frederick Douglass, who defected from the Garrisonian camp to establish his own antislavery newspaper in the late 1840s.

In the 1850s, MASS continued to denounce slavery and attacks on blacks, including the infamous 1857 Supreme Court decision, *Dred Scott v. Sanford*, that stripped African Americans of basic citizenship rights. When the Civil War erupted in April 1861, antislavery societies promoted their own causes while championing the rights of black men to enlist in their country's military service. Abolitionists later remained active in reconstructing the war-torn South, advocating measures such as the Fourteenth and Fifteenth Amendments to the Constitution. When the latter was adopted in 1870, giving black men the right to vote, the AASS officially disbanded, nearly five years after Garrison published his last issue of the *Liberator*.

The NEASS stood out for its radical antislavery stance and for its commitment to racial equality. Although the organization was dominated by white Americans, Garrison's own strong ties to Boston's African American community promoted interracial cooperation that was unique in antebellum American society. In the United States, the NEASS was the first significant integrated antislavery organization committed to an immediate end to slavery; it was the first organization to bring together white and black activists who shared elected leadership positions; and it was the first antislavery group to hire an African American as a paid agent. Most importantly, the NEASS set the tone and agenda for an uncompromising assault on slavery that persisted for over thirty years.

**FURTHER READINGS**

Horton, James Oliver, and Lois E. Horton. *In Hope of Liberty: Culture, Community, and Protest Among Northern Free Blacks, 1700–1860.* New York: Oxford University Press, 1997.

————. *Black Bostonians: Family Life and Community Struggle in the Antebellum North.* New York and London: Holmes & Meier, 1979.

Jacobs, Donald M., ed. *Courage and Conscience: Black & White Abolitionists in Boston.* Published for the Boston Atheneum. Bloomington: Indiana University Press, 1993.

Quarles, Benjamin. *Black Abolitionists.* New York: Oxford University Press, 1969.

Ripley, C. Peter, ed. *The Black Abolitionist Papers, Volume III, The United States, 1830–1846.* Chapel Hill, N.C.: The University of North Carolina Press, 1991.

Zorn, Roman J. "The New England Anti-Slavery Society: Pioneer Abolition Organization." *Journal of Negro History* 43 (July 1957): 157–176.

*Earl F. Mulderink III*

# New England Freedmen's Aid Society

The New England Freedmen's Aid Society (NEFAS) was a leading organization among the phalanx of Northern missionaries, educators, and reformers who moved to the South to aid ex-slaves during and after the Civil War. Centered in Boston, the NEFAS sought to educate freed slaves through the instruction and example offered by skilled, committed northerners, most of them white and many of them women.

The NEFAS was founded in February 1862 as the Boston Educational Commission for Freedmen. Under the direction of Edward L. Pierce, seventeen individuals pledged themselves to "the industrial, social, intellectual, moral and religious elevations of persons released from Slavery in the course of the War for the Union." Massachusetts Governor John Andrew, an antislavery stalwart, served as the group's first president, and he was joined by abolitionists and liberal business leaders, including Henry Bowditch, George B. Emerson, Edward Everett Hale,

Samuel Cabot, and Edward Atkinson. Their strong desire to assist the former slaves was both moral and practical, for they believed that New England teachers and values could best oversee the ex-slaves' transition to freedom and free labor.

In March 1862, these Bostonians pledged cooperation with the New York-based National Freedmen's Relief Association to operate a mission of mercy, uplift, and education in Port Royal, South Carolina. By early March, Pierce and others in Boston had chosen, from a group of one hundred and fifty applicants, twenty-nine men and six women to head South as "evangels of civilization." These educational missionaries were well-schooled, young, earnest, and relatively free of racism. They were successful from the outset, for within one year some five thousand African Americans were enrolled in schools associated with the "Port Royal experiment." Each of the teachers was sponsored by a NEFAS branch in a New England town, and collectively they proved that ex-slaves could learn, earn wages, and adapt to their new-found freedom. The NEFAS and its allied organizations provided an impetus for the creation of the Freedmen's Inquiry Commission in 1863, which led ultimately to passage of the Freedmen's Bureau Act on March 3, 1865.

The Boston-based NEFAS also collaborated with the American Freedmen's Union Commission (AFUC), established on March 16, 1865. The AFUC was a large private umbrella organization composed of freedmen's aid societies from New England, Pennsylvania, Baltimore, and New York. It sought to assist "in adjusting, on a better basis, the civil, social, and industrial relations of Southern society," mainly by helping African Americans learn to read and write. This nondenominational organization became formidable competition for the large evangelical American Missionary Association and for other societies created by Methodist Episcopal, Presbyterian, and American Baptist denominations.

Although the federally chartered Freedmen's Bureau became the major institution to implement Reconstruction policies in the South after 1865, private organizations such as the NEFAS continued their educational efforts despite waning support. Between 1871 and 1874 the number of NEFAS-sponsored southern schools dropped from seventy to seven and the society decided to retain only two normal schools for teacher training in Georgia and Virginia. At their last meeting in 1874, members of the NEFAS, which outlived the AFUC by five years, recognized their group's diminished effectiveness in the face of improvements in public education and of southern blacks' efforts to help themselves. Begun by whites in Boston, the NEFAS was a pioneer organization in the education of African Americans in the South.

**FURTHER READINGS**

McPherson, James M. *The Abolitionist Legacy: From Reconstruction to the NAACP.* Princeton, N.J.: Princeton University Press, 1975.

Morris, Robert C. *Reading, 'Riting, and Reconstruction: The Education of Freedmen in the South, 1861–1870.* Chicago: The University of Chicago Press, 1976; 1981.

Richardson, Joe M. *Christian Reconstruction: The American Missionary Association and Southern Blacks, 1861–1890.* Athens: The University of Georgia Press, 1986.

Rose, Willie Lee. *Rehearsal for Reconstruction: The Port Royal Experiment.* New York: Bobbs-Merrill, 1964. New York: Oxford University Press, 1976.

*Earl F. Mulderink III*

SEE ALSO   American Freedmen's Union Commission; American Missionary Association; National Freedmen's Relief Organization

# New Negro Alliance

Founded in 1933, the Washington, D.C.-based New Negro Alliance (NNA) used direct-action protests, such as pickets and economic boycotts, to promote civil rights. It mobilized Washington's black residents to challenge the discriminatory hiring practices of white businesses operating in the city's black neighborhoods and sought to increase employment opportunities for African Americans, particularly in white-collar positions. The NNA was not the first group to advocate or launch direct-action protests. Since 1929 similar organizations had emerged in cities such as New York, Cleveland, Los Angeles, and Chicago. In the period prior to 1941, however, the NNA was arguably the largest and most successful local organization to use economic boycotts as its primary weapon. Although the number of NNA supporters is impossible to discern, its membership consisted of a sizeable percentage of Washington's black population, especially the city's middle-class leadership.

The NNA began to take form on August 28, 1933, after the Hamburger Grill, a white-owned business located in a black neighborhood, fired its only three black employees and replaced them with white workers. The next day twenty-one-year-old John Aubrey Davis, a recent black graduate of Williams College, gathered a group of black neighborhood men to organize a picket and boycott of the restaurant. By August 30, the protest had the desired effect and the Hamburger Grill rehired the three black workers.

Emboldened by their success, those involved in the boycott launched the NNA. Under the leadership of the recent college graduate Davis, the lawyer Belford Lawson, and M. Franklin Thorne, who in the late 1930s managed Langston Terrace, Washington's first New Deal housing project, the NNA mobilized blacks as well as whites to challenge discriminatory hiring practices, demand promotion of black workers, and fight other forms of discrimination. Davis in particular had given a great deal of thought to issues of civil rights, concluding that economic empowerment was the only way for African Americans to make strides in other areas.

Davis hoped that larger, well-established civil rights groups, such as the National Association for the Advancement of Colored People (NAACP), would endorse and join the NNA's efforts. The NAACP, however, shunned direct-action campaigns, afraid that pickets and economic boycotts would heighten hostility to the advancement of civil rights in the white community and thus prove detrimental.

But the group forged ahead. It launched Don't Buy Where You Can't Work and Jobs for Negroes campaigns. To mobilize protestors and publicize its efforts, the NNA published a weekly newspaper, *New Negro Opinion*, between December 1933 and 1937. Between 1933 and 1935, the NNA scored several victories over white-owned businesses, including the A & P Grocery chain, the *Evening Star* newspaper, and numerous small businesses. NNA-initiated campaigns succeeded, at least in part, because the organization picked its targets wisely and only used protests as a last resort, after negotiations broke down.

Another crucial factor contributing to the NNA's successes was the inability of white business owners to stop the protests. The 1932 Norris-LaGuardia Anti-Injunction Act, which forbade injunctions against picketing during labor disputes, provided NNA activists with legal protection. Nevertheless, businesses unwilling to accede to NNA demands sometimes obtained court injunctions against picketing. The first two businesses that used the courts to curb NNA protests were Kaufman's department store and High's ice cream store. In 1935, both establishments gained injunctions against the NNA because of rulings that the Norris-LaGuardia law did not protect those protests. Upon challenge, both the District Court and the district Court of Appeals upheld the injunctions in 1936, arguing that the NNA's pickets were not protected by the Norris-LaGuardia law, since the group represented neither employees nor a competitive business that could be harmed by the hiring practices of Kaufman's or High's.

While the NNA failed to convince the appeals court to overturn these injunctions, it scored a victory against the Sanitary Grocery Company, which had also obtained an injunction against NNA-picketing in 1936. The NNA challenged the legality of that injunction and, with the help of the lawyer Thurgood Marshall, managed to take the case to the Supreme Court. On March 5, 1938, the Supreme Court heard arguments in *New Negro Alliance v. Sanitary Grocery Company, Inc.* and decided in favor of the NNA. Chief Justice Charles Evans Hughes, leading a six to two majority, ruled that "those having a direct or indirect interest" in matters of employment have the freedom to take action against discrimination and "peacefully persuade others." The Court's decision sparked the formation of numerous "Don't Buy Where You Can't Work" groups across the country and resulted in a growing number of pickets and economic boycotts.

The Supreme Court victory strengthened the NNA. Many white-owned businesses in the nation's capital agreed to negotiate settlements rather than face economic losses sure to ensue from protracted boycotts and pickets. The NNA, however, did not always succeed in securing acceptable agreements. In 1939, after sixteen months of protests, the NNA was unable to reach an agreement with People's Drug Stores to stop segregating lunch counters and to hire more black workers and provide them with opportunities for promotion. People's, which had forty stores in the Washington area and could absorb the financial losses generated by pickets of one or several of its stores, had proved intransigent to NNA demands. The NNA was also unable to finally reach an agreement with Sanitary Grocery Company, which changed its name to Safeway following the 1938 Supreme Court decision. In 1941, after staging three months of unsuccessful protest activities targeting Safeway, the NNA folded.

But the NNA's failure to secure concessions from People's Drug Stores and Safeway was not the only reason for the organization's demise in 1941. That year, President Franklin D. Roosevelt's Executive Order 8802 established the Fair Employment Practices Committee, which investigated employment discrimination, obviating the need for the kind of campaigns launched by the NNA. Roosevelt's pronouncement, though certainly the result of a great number of forces, clearly stood as a victory for the nation's growing civil rights movement. Furthermore, increased employment opportunities, as a result of World War II defense production and a general belief that the wartime situation rendered protests inappropriate, helped facilitate the NNA's demise. Finally, many of the NNA leaders took on positions in government and in the private sector, generating a leadership vacuum that was accompanied by a dwindling membership.

In 1948, Rolandus H. Cooper tried to revive the NNA, but after a few struggling years the organization folded again. By then, the NAACP had adopted a more vigorous civil rights agenda, attracting those who had previously supported the direct-action campaigns of the NNA. Indeed, in 1952 Eugene Davidson, the last administrator of the NNA, became president of the Washington NAACP.

**FURTHER READINGS**

Meier, August, and Elliott Rudwick. *Along the Color Line: Explorations in the Black Experience.* Urbana: University of Illinois Press, 1976.

Pacifico, Michelle. "Don't Buy Where You Can't Work: The New Negro Alliance of Washington." *Washington History* 6, no. 1 (1994): 66–88.

*Derek C. Catsam*

# New York African Clarkson Association

Organized in 1825 and named in honor of the celebrated English cleric and abolitionist Thomas Clarkson, the New York African Clarkson Association (NYACA) was an antislavery society that reflected the changing consciousness of the North's black middle class during the first years of the nineteenth century. Hardening racism, colonization schemes aimed at removing African Americans from the United States, and growing legal and social repression motivated an increasing number of free blacks to deemphasize their efforts to achieve individual and class advancement in favor of working toward the complementary interests of abolishing slavery and achieving full equality for all black Americans. NYACA played a crucial role in this effort.

The association appeared to be little more than a typical African American benevolent organization inaugurated to provide sick, death, and survivors' benefits to members and their families. By design the organization was to consist of "free persons of moral character" formed into "an association for the benevolent purpose of raising funds to be exclusively appropriated to aid and assist the widows and orphans of deceased members, and for improvement in literature." Some of the crusading zeal that launched the group, however, surfaced in the charge to "increase its members and extend its influence by all just and honorable means."

Living in an era when the Missouri question had only recently elevated the issue of slavery to the national political stage, members of NYACA nevertheless sought to acknowledge their dual identity as Americans with obvious links to Africa. During this period numerous African Americans used the term "African" in the names of the organizations they created. Some continued proudly to refer to themselves as Africans even though they were born in the United States.

NYACA members illustrated their belief in America's democratic institutions and constitutional government by framing a constitution for their association. They then proceeded, on the basis of democratic principles, to admit new members only with the approval of a majority vote. To remain a member in good standing, individuals had to pay dues faithfully and read and sign the organization's constitution.

Perhaps more properly understood as part of a new era in black assertiveness, NYACA was but one of almost fifty black antislavery organizations in existence by 1830, to be found in cities such as New Haven, Boston, and Philadelphia. NYACA, like other groups with a similar purpose, used much its influence and resources to help African Americans achieve self-reliance. One of the surest ways to accomplish this was to help abolish slavery. Thus, groups like NYACA provided a springboard for black entrance into the antislavery fray during the 1830s. Those who joined NYACA often embraced and participated in the growing antislavery movement.

**FURTHER READINGS**

*Constitution of the New York African Clarkson Association.* New York: E. Conrad, 1825.

Horton, James O. *Free People of Color: Inside the African American Community.* Washington, D.C.: Smithsonian Institution Press, 1993.

Wright, Donald R. *African Americans in the Early Republic, 1789–1831.* Arlington Heights, Ill.: Harlan Davidson, 1993.

*Norman C. McLeod Jr.*

# New York City: Civic, Literary, and Mutual Aid Associations

New York City's black communities have a long tradition of uniting to meet their common needs and to fight for their political rights. The earliest organizations black city residents established were the African associations of the late eighteenth century. The New York African Society was founded in the 1780s and engaged in philanthropy and uplift work within the black community. A number of African associations then formed in the following decades, though most were ephemeral and only addressed the immediate needs of black Manhattanites. These organizations were closely tied to local African churches, especially Mother Zion, which was Manhattan's first black church. They were particularly effective in tightening the bonds of a community that often incorporated people from places as divergent as the Caribbean and Africa. In the Early National period (ca. 1783–1820), these societies answered the needs of New York's growing free black community and communicated its political vision. They raised money through initiation fees, monthly dues, occasional membership taxes, and general subscriptions for major undertakings.

The New York African Society for Mutual Relief (NYASMR), founded on June 6, 1808, was foremost among the early black associations. Led by William Hamilton, the founders determined that "the most efficient method of securing ourselves from the extreme exigencies to which we are liable to be reduced is by uniting ourselves in a body, for the purpose of raising a fund for the relief of its members." Mutual Relief initiates were particularly concerned with their public personality. In 1810 they decided to incorporate under New York State law to secure their investments and to demonstrate their citizenship. The NYASMR was very popular and attracted more than one hundred members during its first two years. Later, the society pioneered benevolent work by investing its funds in real estate and securities.

NYASMR's success sparked similar ventures in the early nineteenth century. In 1810 the Brooklyn African Woolman Benevolent society came together under the leadership of Peter and Benjamin Croger. They used the NYASMR constitution as a model and declared the woolman's aims to be mutual assistance, burial aid, and the support of widows and orphans. In addition to offering mutual aid to its members, the Woolman society funded the construction of Brooklyn's first independent black school. In 1810, another mutual aid group, the African Marine Fund, was established in Manhattan by the Reverends

June Scott and Abraham Thompson. The city's first black unisex society, African Marine allowed black women and men to hold membership and office. The pastors of Zion Church were, however, the ultimate authorities in Fund decisions. The ministers were also permitted to draw from the account to assist blacks who were suffering hardship even if they were not members. Another relief society, which included some of Manhattan's leading black men, the Wilberforce Philanthropic Association formed in 1812 as a regular mutual aid organization and developed a style all its own. It became known particularly for its participation in New York's early African parades, during which its members sported colorful uniforms, ribbons, and banners. The parades served to unite black city residents and publicized political issues that affected them.

These early associations, which operated as political and social extensions of the black church, dominated the cultural and public life of black New Yorkers and Brooklynites in the first decades of the nineteenth century. Other important additions to the broad spectrum of mutual relief societies were the New York African Clarkson Association (1825), the New York Union African Society (1830), and the Brooklyn African Tompkins Association (1845). These associations were men's mutual relief societies that kept funds to aid the sick and for burial, widow, and orphan assistance. Like the city's other African societies, these groups engaged in public charity and viewed themselves as the moral stewards of the black community. Another important venture launched by black men was the Colored Sailor's Home. William Powell, the sailor and abolitionist, founded the Home in 1839 to provide lodging for black men who passed through Manhattan while working on commercial ships.

By the 1830s numerous African organizations, including a growing number of women's groups, labored to meet the needs of black New Yorkers. The women of the African Dorcas Association, founded in 1827, clothed and assisted destitute children at African schools, in the hope of increasing attendance. Through the Female Mite Society, established in 1830, black women provided for the needs of the community's ministers. Black women were also key players in the 1833 formation of Manhattan's famous Colored Orphan Asylum and its equally well-known Home for Aged Colored People, established in 1845 as the Society for the Relief of Worthy Aged, Indigent Colored Persons. But the era's premier black women's society was the Abyssinian Benevolent Daughters of Esther Association, organized in April 1839, in which women were members and officers (two men were ap-

pointed as "guardians," a formality that protected Abyssinian's property and purse). The organization was the only African relief association to provide sick and burial aid for male spouses. It owned a cemetery in which members were assigned plots and husbands and children were buried for a small fee.

Black literary associations were also plentiful during the early nineteenth century. Most of the city's African societies included provisions for the education of their members or their children and supported educational institutions. In addition to schools, which were operated by various African organizations, the New York Manumission Society, and black community leaders and preachers who taught black residents in their homes, African Americans established numerous associations for the purpose of intellectual stimulation. The African Mutual Instruction Society, founded in 1827, encouraged young men to study literature and science, while the Philomathean Literary Society, established in 1829, acted as a debating club and hosted weekly lectures. Beginning in 1833, the Phoenix Society encouraged young men and women to attend school, provided job training, and fostered the formation of moral societies. Founded by leading black Manhattanites in 1847, the Society for the Promotion of Education Among Colored Children was yet another important group that supported black education prior to the Civil War.

There was a peculiar overlap between these organizations. Relief associations regularly sponsored educational and civic campaigns, and civic and literary societies often incorporated mutual relief features. More striking, though, is the moral reform aspect of these organizations. Virtually all of New York's early African associations policed the morality and behavior of their members. Not surprisingly, black men were key figures in the creation of Manhattan and Brooklyn's earliest temperance societies. For instance, the Reverend Benjamin Croger of the Brooklyn African Woolman Society also served as president of the Brooklyn Temperance Association.

With the coming of the Civil War, the African associations in Manhattan and Brooklyn slowly disappeared. (NYASMR was the only traditional African organization that survived the war; in fact, its impressive financial and property holdings allowed it to continue to operate until 1945, despite its declining membership and ultimate programmatic blandness.) Prior to the war the associations had not only provided mutual aid and social services for the city's black residents, but they had also played an active role in the fight to end slavery in New York. When the state of New York abolished slavery in 1827, the groups then joined the national abolitionist struggle. They participated in local conventions advocating suffrage for free black men and countering the agenda of the American Colonization Society, which proposed to relocate black Americans to Africa. New York's African societies were indeed so successful at local political organizing that their members were consistently chosen to represent the black communities of Manhattan and Brooklyn at the national Colored Conventions (a series of gatherings of free blacks held between 1830 and 1861 to develop strategies for combating racism). Chosen members included black New York's leading abolitionists, such as Charles Ray, Henry Highland Garnet, James McCune Smith, Samuel Cornish, and William Hamilton. Following the Civil War, however, in the absence of the need for abolition, African societies became much less effective at addressing the needs of black people. Black churches assumed many of their relief and benevolent functions, and as political associations they were unprepared to organize a rapidly expanding black community with marked class and cultural divisions.

The decline of New York's African associations, however, did not mean the end of the tradition of cooperation among black New Yorkers. The 1866 founding of the Howard Colored Orphan Asylum, a product of the hard work and ingenuity of Brooklyn's black community and its pastors, exemplifies continued black efforts to provide African American residents with important social services. Another important cooperative venture was the 1864 founding of the Coachmen's Union League by a group of black workers, who borrowed from NYASMR's constitution to form a society geared to the needs of free black men in the aftermath of slavery. The league, unlike earlier black societies, emphasized bourgeois goals such as industry, thrift, and material prosperity. By the twentieth century, the Coachmen had over twelve hundred members, owned an impressive Harlem building, hosted meetings of other black associations, and were fighting for the political unity of black community organizations.

Civic and literary societies also flourished in the decades following the Civil War. Black churches sponsored many literary associations, as well as essay contests, oratorical competitions, and debates. The Henry Highland Garnet Club (1898) offered lectures and forums on conditions in the South, the League's Forum (1912) worked to sustain appreciation for the nation's best black authors, and the Citizens' Club (1914) operated as a civil

rights watchdog group. Important religious, social, recreational, and educational programs were also provided by the city's black branches of the Young Men's Christian Association (YMCA) and the Young Women's Christian Association (YWCA). In 1901, a committee headed by Dr. William L. Bulkley, a Syracuse University doctorate and the black principal of a predominantly white public school, organized a "Colored YMCA" in Manhattan and Brooklyn. Similar efforts led by Addie W. Hunton and Eva Bowles resulted in the opening of a black YWCA branch in Manhattan in 1905. Three years later, black women, under the leadership of Dr. Verina Morton Jones, also spearheaded the creation of Brooklyn's Lincoln Settlement House.

In the late nineteenth century, the growth of New York's black migrant population stimulated the formation of state clubs (formed with others from their home states) and inspired the clannishness of black New Yorkers. In the 1880s black city residents founded the Society of the Sons of New York and soon thereafter a Daughters association. The Sons of North Carolina (1895) was likely the first club formed by black southern migrants, and certainly one of the more prominent associations that provided sick aid and burial funds as well as lectures and other opportunities for socializing. Other black southerners who migrated to the city during World War I established the South Carolina Club (1918), the United Sons and Daughters of Georgia (1920), the Sons and Daughters of Virginia (1920), and the Sons and Daughters of Florida (1920s). The Georgia club was rumored to be the richest of these state associations.

Similarly, black Caribbean immigrants organized various national associations in New York City. The Bermuda Benevolent Association (1897), the earliest group formed by immigrants from the West Indies, owned a Manhattan property with meeting rooms and a library, offered scholarships to students, and extended mortgages to its members. In 1915 a group of women from the Danish West Indies formed a separate association, later named the American West Indian Ladies Aid Society. In 1917, the newly formed Danish West Indian Benevolent Society joined other Caribbean and African American organizations in Manhattan's famous Silent Parade Against Lynching. Through the St. Vincent Benevolent Association (1920), black West Indians in Brooklyn sent supplies and assistance to the island in times of need and formed a relationship that continues to exist today. In 1925 the Montserrat Progressive Society counted over seven hundred members and owned a sizable Manhattan hall. By the 1930s the Grenada Benevolent Association, the Sons and Daughters of Barbados, the Trinidad Benevolent Association, and the St. Lucia United Association were operating in Manhattan. The Barbuda Progressive League and the Jamaica Progressive League helped immigrants find housing and jobs. The politically oriented Caribbean Union sought to maximize the strength of the black community. These Caribbean-American associations helped black immigrants adjust to the city while maintaining important cultural, commercial, and social links to the West Indies.

After World War I New York's black associations moved beyond community benevolence toward a greater focus on civil rights. This transformation began in the late nineteenth century, when New York's black women's organizations expanded their activities to embrace social and political work and attached themselves to emerging national organizations. In 1892, Maritcha Remond Lyons, an assistant principal in Brooklyn, and Victoria Earle Matthews, who became national organizer for the National Association of Colored Women (NACW) after its founding in 1896, organized the Women's Loyal Union (WLU) of New York and Brooklyn. The WLU became the city's first black association specifically organized to fight for civil rights. In 1897 Matthews and Lyons also established the White Rose Association to offer employment services, charitable assistance, and educational programs to black migrant women entering New York City. Sarah Garnet and her sister Dr. Susan Smith McKinney organized the Equal Suffrage League of Brooklyn. Both sisters also served as officers in the NACW during the early twentieth century.

During and after World War I, New York City's black women also used the experiences they had gained in social service and political associations to play an active role in organizations like the National Association for the Advancement of Colored People (1910) and the National Urban League (1911). The National Urban League and its local chapters proved to be most effective at documenting, politicizing, and responding to the plight of black New Yorkers during the economic crisis of the 1930s.

With the onset of the Great Depression black associations moved again to address immediate community needs. The Women's Fund Committee to Provide Relief for Unemployed Single Women and Girls used volunteers from black churches to staff charitable programs. Similarly, the church-based Society of St. Monica provided relief to needy black families. One of the most innovative responses to the economic crisis emerged in Brooklyn in 1932. That year, a group of men of Barbadian ancestry formed the Paragons Progressive Community Association and Federal Credit Union, a financial institution that sought to empower the black community by taking deposits and providing loans at reasonable rates. Begun with an initial investment of two hundred twenty-five dollars, the Paragons had loaned over seventy-five million dollars when they finally disbanded in the 1970s. In 1934, Harlem saw the rise of the Citizens' League for Fair Play, a coalition of organizations that coordinated protests against the discriminatory hiring practices of Manhattan department stores.

Following the outbreak of World War II, which brought an end to the economic crisis, black organizations intensified their demands for civil rights and launched attacks on discrimination and segregation. In the 1960s, several groups emerged to challenge the existence of de facto segregation in New York's public schools. In 1964 a coalition brought together the Parents' Workshop for Equality, the Citywide Committee for Integrated Schools, the Harlem Parents Committee, the Congress of Racial Equality, the NAACP's local branches, the National Association for Puerto Rican Civil Rights, and the Urban League of Greater New York for a series of protest campaigns that crippled the public school system. The campaigns sought to reduce the insularity of the board of education and change the demographic composition of the city's schools.

Since the late eighteenth century, black New Yorker's have organized a wide variety of associations to serve the social, economic, educational, and political needs of the city's African American residents. Mutual aid societies provided funds for decent funerals and aided widows, orphans, and other destitute black residents. Literary and civic clubs provided the black community with intellectual stimulation, education, and opportunities for social interaction. Migrant and immigrant clubs enabled blacks of diverse ethnic backgrounds to express, preserve, and celebrate their cultural heritage while adapting to urban life. Moreover, New York's black associations served as public forums for political protest and their members played active roles in the struggle for the abolition of slavery, racial advancement, and civil rights.

**FURTHER READINGS**

Brown Hamilton, Tulia. "The National Association of Colored Women, 1896–1920." Ph.D. diss. Emory University, 1978.

Foner, Philip S. *History of Black Americans: From the Emergence of the Cotton Kingdom to the Eve of the Compromise of 1850.* Westport, Conn. Greenwood, 1983.

Greenberg, Cheryl Lynn. *"Or Does it Explode?": Black Harlem in the Great Depression.* New York: Oxford University Press, 1991.

Osofsky, Gilbert. *Harlem: The Making of a Ghetto. Negro New York, 1880–1930.* New York: Harper & Row, 1963

Perlman, Daniel. "Organizations of the Free Negroes in New York City, 1800–1860." *Journal of Negro History.* 56, no. 3 (July 1971): 181–197.

Thomas, Bert J. *"Historical Functions of Caribbean-American Benevolent/Progressive Associations." Afro-Americans in New York Life and History* 12, no. 2 (July 1988): 45–58.

Toney, Joyce. "The Perpetuation of a Culture of Migration: West Indian American Ties With Home, 1900–1979." *Afro-Americans in New York Life and History* 13, no. 1 (January 1989): 39–55.

Waisenfeld, Judith. *African American Women and Christian Activism: New York's Black YWCA, 1905–1945.* Cambridge, Mass.: Harvard University Press, 1997.

Watkins-Owens, Irma. *Blood Relations: Caribbean Immigrants and the Harlem Community, 1900–1930.* Bloomington: Indiana University Press, 1996.

Wilder, Craig Steven. "The Rise and Influence of the New York African Society for Mutual Relief, 1808–1865." *African-Americans in New York Life and History* 22, no. 2 (1998): 7–18.

*Craig Steven Wilder*

## New York City Commission on Human Rights

Organized in 1961, the New York City Commission on Human Rights was, according to political scientist Gerald Benjamin, "the largest and most powerful city human rights agency in the country." The Commission on Human Rights emerged from the New York Commission on Intergroup Relations, which had superseded the New York's Mayor's Committee on Unity in 1955. Largely dominated by liberal Jewish groups, the Commission on Intergroup Relations soothed racial confrontations in the city, which had been exacerbated by the removal of African American and Puerto Rican tenants for Title I urban renewal and the 1956 fair-housing initiative, the Open Cities Program. With passage of the Sharkey-Brown-Isaacs Fair-Housing Law of 1958, the commission handled individual complaints of bias in private housing. The commission also assisted the school integration movement known as "open enrollment," and it reviewed contract compliance on fair employment among municipal vendors.

After a 1960 crisis in confidence, which stemmed from charges by the Puerto Rican Community that African Americans had monopolized Commission membership, the Commission on Intergroup Relations was reorganized into the New York City Commission on Human Rights. By and large, the commission's black leadership replaced Jews and adopted a direct response to the issue of school integration. But after it took sides in a 1963 school boycott and intervened in favor of employment quotas at the construction sites of Harlem Hospital and Downstate Medical Center, Mayor Robert F. Wagner Jr., pulled back on the commission's efforts, chiefly by allowing staff positions to remain unfilled.

The late 1960s brought a more combative stance from which the Commission on Human Rights never quite recovered. Under Mayor John V. Lindsay and commission chairman William Booth, an African American, the commission replaced conciliation with "immediate enforcement," encouraged by neighborhood field offices and telephone hotlines. The commission soon became a victim of the animosity between Jews and blacks that flared during the 1967 New York City teachers' strike and the controversy over school decentralization at Ocean Hill-Brownsville in Brooklyn. Amid the rancor, Jewish members on the commission charged Booth with "whipping up animosity" toward their community. Under Lindsay's successor, Mayor Abraham D. Beame, the commission returned to a routine of investigation, neighborhood conciliation, and quiet enforcement. Still in existence, the Commission on Human Rights guide books, legal digests, and reports deal with a wide array of biases based on race, gender, sexual preference, age, and HIV status.

**FURTHER READING**

Benjamin, Gerald. *Race Relations and the New York City Commission on Human Rights.* Ithaca, N.Y.: Cornell University Press, 1974.

*Joel Schwartz*

**SEE ALSO**    New York's Mayor's Committee on Unity

## New York City's People's Committee

*See* Greater New York Coordinating Committee for Employment.

## New York Commission on Intergroup Relations

*See* New York City Commission on Human Rights.

## New York Mayor's Commission on Conditions in Harlem

The Mayor's Commission on Conditions in Harlem, appointed by New York City Mayor Fiorello LaGuardia to explore the causes of the 1935 Harlem riot, thoroughly investigated the Harlem riot's proximate causes as well as its deeper roots, and issued a far-reaching and hard-hitting report documenting discrimination, racism, and poverty. The report, never officially released, was nonetheless printed and disseminated widely, and provided an important legitimizing voice to black protest efforts of the Great Depression and beyond.

On March 19, 1935, Harlem erupted into riot. A sixteen-year-old youth, Lino Rivera, detained for shoplifting at Kress's Store on 125th Street in Harlem, was falsely rumored to have been killed by police. This grievance, quickly publicized by leaflets and soapbox orations, confirmed for many a pattern of white disregard for black people. Police brutality, employment and educational discrimination, poorer city services in black neighborhoods, and the collapse of local political efforts to win white-collar jobs for Harlem residents (the first phase of Harlem's "Don't Buy Where You Can't Work" campaign) had been long-standing issues of concern, which the false rumor again raised. Thousands took to the streets, shouting, marching, breaking windows, and looting. Rioters seemed to come from every age and class. The riot, directed primarily against property rather than persons, caused extensive physical damage, sixty-four casualties, including seven police officers, and seventy-five arrests.

Although initial reports in the press blamed "hooligans" and Communists for fomenting the disorder, Mayor Fiorello LaGuardia appointed a distinguished commission of black and white leaders to investigate the riot's causes more fully: Dr. Charles Roberts (Chairman), the lawyers Eunice Carter (Secretary), Morris Ernst, Hubert Delany (later a judge in New York City's Domestic Relations Court), and Arthur Garfield Hays, the publisher Oswald Villard, the poet Countee Cullen, Dr. John Grimley, William McCann, the labor leader A. Philip Randolph, John Robinson, the Tuskegee trustee William Schieffelin, Judge Charles Toney, and the sociologist Dr. E. Franklin Frazier, the Commission's technical expert. These fourteen Commission members and a staff of thirty held hearings on virtually every aspect of black public life in the city, including employment, health, housing, crime, relief (the then-contemporary term for public welfare services), and education. Over one hundred local residents and scholarly experts testified before the Commission in both public and closed hearings, and the Commission accumulated thousands of pages of materials documenting its extensive investigations, ranging from health and mortality statistics to arrest records to labor union and public works hiring data to housing, population, and business surveys.

Rejecting both the Communism and hooligan theories as explanations for the riot, the Commission blamed what it concluded was a widespread and long-standing pattern of discrimination and inequity in employment, housing, municipal services, relief policies, and education. Such conditions, the Commission found, led to higher mortality and morbidity, lower educational achievement, overcrowding, less access to city services, inadequate recreational facilities, lower incomes, higher levels of malnutrition, higher rents, police brutality, and inadequate institutional care for the ill and dependent. The 1935 riot had been the "spontaneous, unpremeditated" response of these aggrieved and frustrated Harlemites. "The blame [for the riot] belongs to a society . . . that tolerates unemployment [and] discrimination in industry and the public utilities," the report concluded. The Commission also linked racial discrimination to its class implications, noting that "the citizens of Harlem understand that the invasion of their rights and the slight regard that is shown for their lives is due not only to the fact that they are Negroes but also to the fact that they are poor and propertyless and therefore defenseless." It warned that such conditions must be altered if the city hoped to forestall further violence.

The Mayor's Commission issued its strongly worded and thoroughly documented conclusions at the end of 1935, consisting of a summary report, "The Negro in Harlem: A Report on Social and Economic Conditions Responsible for the Outbreak on March 19, 1935," and detailed subcommittee reports on each of the areas of investigation. Mayor LaGuardia, who had not only created the Commission but encouraged it to cast its reach broadly, nonetheless refused to release the reports to the public, given their highly critical tone, although he did distribute the reports to various city departments and demand responses. Those reports reached the broader public only when Harlem's black newspaper, the *Amsterdam News*, obtained copies and published them in its issue of July 18, 1936. Despite the mayor's attempts to keep the report quiet, the Commission's well-documented findings and forceful recommendations did bring some improvement in municipal and social services as city departments responded to the report's sharp criticisms.

Perhaps more importantly, the stature of the Commission and the unequivocal nature of its findings provided an important intellectual sanction for later protest efforts to improve economic, housing, and health conditions in Harlem and to combat the pervasive racism and neglect that made such conditions possible. Nevertheless, similarly damning investigative reports, issued in 1938 and 1939 by the New York State Temporary Commission on the Condition of the Urban Colored Population (whose mandate, on a statewide scale, was similar to that of the Mayor's Commission), and a second riot in Harlem on August 1, 1943—again provoked by alleged police brutality and again causing millions of dollars of damage, several casualties, and numerous arrests—reveal how slowly improvement came to Harlem and how deeply entrenched patterns of racism and discrimination prove to be.

**FURTHER READINGS**

Greenberg, Cheryl Lynn. *"Or Does It Explode?" Black Harlem in the Great Depression*. New York: Oxford University Press, 1991.

Greene, Larry. "Harlem in the Great Depression." Ph.D. diss., Columbia University, 1979.

Mayor's Commission on Conditions in Harlem. "The Negro in Harlem: A Report on Social and Economic Conditions Responsible for the Outbreak of March 19, 1935." LaGuardia, Fiorello. Papers. Municipal Archives, New York, New York. Reprinted in *Amsterdam News*, July 18, 1936.

Naison, Mark. *Communists in Harlem During the Depression*. Urbana: University of Illinois Press, 1983.

*Cheryl Greenberg*

# New York State Commission Against Discrimination

The New York State Commission Against Discrimination emerged from Governor Herbert H. Lehman's 1941 appointment of a Temporary State Committee on Discrimination in Employment, which sought to ensure state cooperation with federal wartime fair-employment initiatives. In 1944, the Temporary State Committee recommended its continuation as a permanent body, based on public reaction to the August 1, 1943, Harlem Riot, along with revulsion at anti-Semitism and the lobbying

activities of the American Jewish Committee and the Anti-Defamation League of B'nai B'rith. In 1944, Governor Thomas E. Dewey, trying to establish liberal credentials for his presidential campaign, appointed an ad hoc commission against discrimination. In March of the following year, the New York State Legislature passed the Ives-Quinn Anti-Discrimination Law, which declared equal employment "a civil right" and set up the State Commission Against Discrimination to carry out provisions of the 1938 New York State Constitution, which barred "discrimination of rights" by race, color, creed, or religion. The New York commission was the nation's first state-level antidiscrimination enforcement body.

While the Ives-Quinn Law had far-reaching theoretical implications, the State Commission, under Dewey's leadership, moved cautiously in enforcement, largely relying on private and informal conciliation. In its first two years of operation, the commission handled about one thousand complaints of discrimination, largely from African Americans, Jews, Italians, and other ethnic groups. The commission also conducted investigations and studies of employment practices.

Under the vigorous leadership of chairman Charles Abrams from 1955 to 1959, the commission extended its writ to include discrimination in housing and issues of public accommodations connected with private clubs and volunteer fire companies. It produced varied studies, including one that pinpointed the economic costs of segregation and another that documented entrance exclusions to medical schools faced by Jews and other minorities. The state agency's work was aided by numerous private groups, notably the National Association for the Advancement of Colored People, the New York Urban League, the State Committee Against Discrimination, and the American Jewish Committee, which lobbied vigorously for fair housing and employment.

In 1962, the commission's name was changed to the State Commission for Human Rights, and in 1968 it became a gubernatorial line agency, the State Division of Human Rights, which carried on the fair housing and employment effort. In the 1980s and 1990s, it expanded its jurisdiction, handling cases of discrimination against the aged, challenging sexual harassment, and responding to those facing discrimination because of HIV/AIDS.

**FURTHER READINGS**

Bonfield, Arthur Earl. "The Origin and Development of American Fair Employment Legislation." *Iowa Law Review* 52 (1967), 1043–1092.

Higbee, Jay Anders. *The Development and Administration of the New York Law Against Discrimination.* Tuscaloosa: The University of Alabama Press, 1966.

Moreno, Paul D. *From Direct Action to Affirmative Action: Fair Employment Law and Policy in America, 1933–1972.* Baton Rouge: Louisiana State University Press, 1997.

State Commission Against Discrimination. *Annual Report for 1996.* Albany, N.Y.: State Commission Against Discrimination, 1997.

*Joel Schwartz*

## New York State Commission for Human Rights

*See* New York State Commission Against Discrimination.

## New York State Division of Human Rights

*See* New York State Commission Against Discrimination.

## New York's Mayor's Committee on Unity

In the wake of the August 1, 1943, Harlem Riot, New York City Mayor Fiorello H. La Guardia hurriedly organized the New York's Mayor's Committee on Unity to provide a moral voice for race relations in the wartime city. La Guardia appointed an independently funded private group of prominent New Yorkers, including the liberal author Fannie Hurst and Dr. Henry Sloane Coffin of Union Theological Seminary, along with representatives of interracial organizations such as the Urban League and the Young Men's Christian Association. Under chairman Charles Evans Hughes Jr., and with New York University sociologist Dan W. Dodson as executive secretary, the Committee was expected to produce high-level, authoritative studies on race relations.

Under Mayors William O'Dwyer and Robert F. Wagner Jr., the Committee soon applied itself to the task of quieting racial confrontations and improving minority housing. It recommended the creation of community councils in neighborhoods undergoing racial turnover, advised on educational issues, particularly racial incidents in high schools, and handled flagrant cases of racial discrimination, including the entertainer Josephine Baker's complaint in 1951 that she had been denied service at the Stork Club, a famous Manhattan night spot, because she

was black. In the early 1950s, the Committee did a series of investigations, which led to some policy changes, of municipal services in minority neighborhoods. In 1955, the Committee on Unity was superseded by an executive agency, the New York City Commission on Intergroup Relations, which, in 1961, became the New York City Commission on Human Rights.

**FURTHER READING**

Benjamin, Gerald. *Race Relations and the New York City Commission on Human Rights.* Ithaca, N.Y.: Cornell University Press, 1974.

*Joel Schwartz*

**SEE ALSO**   New York City Commission on Human Rights

## Niagara Movement

A civil rights organization dedicated to public protest, the Niagara Movement was founded in 1905 by W. E. B. Du Bois and others who were unhappy with Booker T. Washington's gradualist approach to racial uplift, and his domination of organizations designed to further African American Status in Society. The organization ceased functioning in 1910 when most of its membership joined the National Association for the Advancement of Colored People (NAACP). Although historians generally consider the Niagara Movement to be the forerunner of the NAACP, the organization never officially affiliated with it.

The history of the Niagara Movement is inextricably intertwined with the debate between Washington and Du Bois over methods of racial uplift and their subsequent personality conflicts. Its roots lay in the 1903 publication of Du Bois's book *Souls of Black Folks*, in which he criticized Washington by name for his domination of patronage (specifically, his control over funds given by white philanthropists to black causes) through the Tuskegee Institute and for his failure to speak openly against Jim Crow laws and black disenfranchisement.

The rift was aggravated by the "Boston Riot" in late July, 1903. Washington was scheduled to speak before the Boston chapter of the National Negro Business League but was heckled by William Monroe Trotter, editor of the Boston *Guardian*, and several other Trotterites, who then were attacked by Washington supporters. A brawl broke out, and in the aftermath Trotter was arrested. Washington was appalled at the first public show of opposition to

Tuskegee, and he used the black newspapers he subsidized to persecute those involved in the attack. When Du Bois then wrote a letter to the *Guardian* on Trotter's behalf, Washington became convinced that Du Bois had planned the whole affair.

Washington began to aggressively use his patronage power to punish those on his blacklist, and he began to wage a major campaign in the black press against Du Bois, Trotter, and other opponents. He also attempted to co-opt his opponents into a new organization, which he would control. To this end he called a conference at Carnegie Hall in January 1904 to discuss current race matters and plan future strategies. Washington carefully manipulated the invitation list to pack the conference with largely pro-Tuskegee men, who then created the equally Tuskegee-dominated Committee of Twelve for the Advancement of the Negro Race. But Du Bois, in disgust, almost immediately resigned his position on the Committee, and the Committee itself was largely ineffectual save for the publication of sporadic pamphlets.

The lack of any organization to protest segregation and racial injustice, combined with Du Bois's frustration with trying to negate Washington's influence, led to the creation of the Niagara Movement. Du Bois secretly gathered a group of Tuskegee opponents in Buffalo, New York, in July 1905. Facing segregated accommodations, the group moved to the Canadian side of Niagara Falls, thus inadvertently eluding a spy Washington had sent to Buffalo on hearing of the meeting. Of fifty-five men who had signed a call for the creation of an organization dedicated to public protest, twenty-nine attended the Niagara Falls conference, including Trotter; J. Max Barber, editor of *The Voice of the Negro*; former Du Bois Harvard classmate Clement Morgan; and other representatives of the Talented Tenth (educated black elite) from around the country.

Du Bois was elected general secretary, and the group proposed that each state have its own chapter, with chairmen of these chapters serving as an executive committee. The group issued a list of demands, including manhood suffrage, equal employment opportunities, universal common education, and an end to Jim Crow. The group challenged, albeit indirectly, the Tuskegee-subsidized press and its efforts to silence Tuskegee opponents. Above all, the Niagara Movement demanded public protest and action.

By the end of 1905, despite Washington's attempts in the press to block all accounts of the organization's activities, the Niagara Movement claimed one hundred and fifty members, and Du Bois noted the existence of seventeen "strong" state branches. Washington increasingly employed spies to monitor Niagara Movement activities, subsidized the printing of unflattering reports of the Movement, and attempted to have some Niagarites removed from their government positions. While *The Voice of the Negro*, under editor J. Max Barber, printed favorable accounts of the organization, Barber naively accepted help from Tuskegee, and was forced from his editorial position and hounded out of journalism due to Washington's vindictiveness.

Du Bois countered with the establishment of two pro-Niagara publications, neither of which long survived. The first, *The Moon*, lasted from 1905 to 1906; the second, *The Horizon*, from 1907 to 1910. Both suffered from lack of funds and low readership, and caused Du Bois and his investors great financial losses.

Initially, the Niagara Movement did little were than cooperate with the Constitution League, an interracial organization founded in 1904 to "enforce the mandates of the Constitution," and exchange speakers with various New England suffrage organizations. Lack of action prompted criticism at the organization's second conference, at Storer College in Harper's Ferry, West Virginia, in August 1906. But the organization did unite to condemn Theodore Roosevelt and Secretary of War William H. Taft for their role in the dishonorable discharge of an entire company of black soldiers in the aftermath of a racially motivated riot in Brownsville, Texas. By the end of 1906, local chapters reported successful campaigns. In Massachusetts, the organization lobbied against a bill in Congress to segregate rail cars, and opposed state funding of the Jamestown Exposition unless African Americans were allowed to attend. In Illinois, the state chapter protested the performance of the play *The Clansman*, and helped block a movement for segregated schools in Chicago.

In the aftermath of the August 1906 Atlanta race riot, the Niagara Movement began active lobbying for state civil rights laws, new trials for blacks convicted by all-white juries, and an end to segregation on trains. In this last matter, the Niagara Movement sponsored test cases, pushing itself into debt in the process.

By 1907, when the Niagara Movement met for its third annual conference in Boston, it was clear that the group was not achieving its goals. It had raised less money than it had spent, and divisions, especially between Trotter and Clement Morgan, were developing within the movement. Du Bois sided with his old classmate Morgan, earning Trotter's enmity. By the time of the fourth conference in Oberlin, Ohio, attendance had dropped and there were reports of demoralized state and local chapters. Washington had effectively persecuted many Niagarites and exploited the rift between Trotter and Du Bois. In 1908, Trotter split from the movement to head a rival organization that evolved into the National Equal Rights League.

In the same year, Du Bois advised blacks to support the Democratic Party due to increasing Republican hostility to black interests. But Du Bois himself was complaining that Niagara Movement affairs were keeping him from his scholarly work, and the 1909 meeting in Sea Island, New Jersey, was the organization's last. Meanwhile, Du Bois was involved with the 1909 conference that established the NAACP, and he was appointed its executive director. In 1910 he cancelled the annual meeting of the Niagara Movement and advised its members to join the NAACP, thus ending the organization's existence.

The Niagara Movement was the first civil rights organization to oppose Booker T. Washington, and one of the first to articulate an increasingly radical program for racial uplift, including public protest. Although its challenge to Tuskegee dominance was unsuccessful, it provided an alternative power base for the disaffected, and made a clear statement that blacks did not accept their segregated and disfranchised existence.

**FURTHER READINGS**

Broderick, Francis L. *W. E. B. Du Bois: Negro Leader in a Time of Crisis.* Stanford, Calif.: Stanford University Press, 1959.

Harlan, Louis H. *Booker T. Washington: The Wizard of Tuskegee, 1901–1915.* New York and Oxford, England: Oxford University Press, 1983.

Lewis, David Levering. *W. E. B. Du Bois: Biography of a Race, 1868–1919.* New York: A John Macrae Book, Henry Holt, 1993.

Marable, Manning. *W. E. B. Du Bois: Black Radical Democrat.* Boston: Twayne Publishers, 1986.

Rudwick, Elliott. *W. E. B. Du Bois: Voice of the Black Protest Movement.* Urbana, Chicago, and London: University of Illinois Press, 1960.

*Jacqueline M. Moore*

# Norfolk, Virginia: Civic, Literary, and Mutual Aid Associations

Founded in 1680, Norfolk, Virginia, virtually an island, developed alongside English plantation agriculture in the Lower Tidewater and Eastern North Carolina regions.

By 1790, 1,335 African Americans lived in the town of 2,957, and in the years to come the black population would continue to constitute a significant portion of the total populace, ranging from 35 to 49 percent.

Despite the size of Norfolk's African American population, the development of a distinct black community did not begin until approximately 1830, when free blacks comprised 25 percent of the total black population. The founding of First Baptist Church on Bute Street in 1830, Bank Street Baptist Church in 1840, and St. Johns Methodist Episcopal Church in 1848 began to afford opportunities for socialization, literacy programs, and burial and charity societies. During the antebellum years free and enslaved blacks also organized benevolent societies, such as the Norfolk Lyceum, the Sons of Liberty, the Bible Stars, the Daughters of St. Luke, the Pilgrims, Sons of Adam, Zion's Sons, Humble Sons of God, and Good Samaritans. These societies laid the groundwork for black self-help organizations in the post–Civil War era.

In the years following the Civil War, numerous African American churches rendered innumerable services to the black community, including Queen Street Baptist Church and St. Joseph's Catholic Church, and, after 1930, African Methodist Episcopal Zion and the Church of Christ. Committed to self-help, the churches' benevolent and mutual aid societies served as agencies for the improvement of social and moral conditions among African Americans, primarily by promoting education and encouraging members to become Bible readers. Along with auxiliary religious organizations such as the Norfolk Association of Colored Women, the women's auxiliary of Lott Carey, the black National Nurses Association, and the Colored King's Daughters, many church groups established missions in the slums and jails, founded and supported homes for the aged and orphans, and generally contributed to the overall improvement of black living conditions in Norfolk.

Norfolk's black women also launched several self-help organizations in the aftermath of the Civil War. These clubs provided orphanages, retirement homes, nursery schools, kindergartens, educational assistance, and day-care centers. The Grand United Order of Tents, the oldest women's lodge in Virginia, offered sick and death benefits and a retirement home for its members. Two enslaved women founded the Tents and secretly cooperated with abolitionists during the antebellum period; however, they did not formally organize their activities until 1867, nor incorporate until 1883. In 1893 several of Norfolk's prominent blacks formed the Colored Women's League

A group of Norfolk, Virginia, schoolchildren hold signs protesting the Norfolk School Board's treatment of African American teachers. 1939. *Library of Congress*

for the moral, financial, and material advancement of women. This group, headed by Laura E. Titus, created the Old Folks Home to care for the aged and infirm. In addition to supporting charitable community work, black women's organizations catered to the interests and needs of their female constituents. Founded in 1902 under the leadership of Emma V. Kelley, the Daughters of the Independent, Benevolent, Protective Order of the World was the female auxiliary of the Eureka Lodge, Inc., the first organization of African American Elks in the world, formed in 1897. Despite initial opposition from Elks members, its first formal meeting with women (forty) in attendance was held in St. John African Methodist Episcopal Church. In 1910 the Daughters published *The News and Recorder* to document and disseminate the history of this African American women's

organization. They also worked to establish numerous other branches of the Daughters of the Elks nationally and in the West Indies, fostering charity, justice, sisterly love, and fidelity to husband and family and raising thousands of dollars for charity, sick benefits, scholarships, and child welfare. Another organization specifically catering to the needs of the city's black women was the Phyllis Wheatley Branch of the Young Women's Christian Association (YWCA). Established in 1908, the black-controlled YWCA provided religious, recreational, social, and educational programs.

Similarly, Norfolk's black men launched several organizations that served the city's black male populace and the general needs of the black community. In 1888, they organized the oldest continuously operating all-black Young Men's Christian Association (YMCA) in the United States.

The Hunton YMCA, under the leadership of the Reverend William A. Hunton, offered religious study, literary and debating societies, educational classes, recreational programs, and athletics. Founded in 1914, the Sons of Norfolk Fraternal and Charitable Association assisted the needy in the community by feeding and housing the poor and providing burial funds. In 1922, the Bachelor Benedict Social Club, a fraternal society founded by Walter Fulford, a teacher at Booker T. Washington High School, also promoted charitable work. Moreover, the Bachelors, whose membership was initially restricted to single men, sponsored annual debutante balls.

Another manifestation of the desire of African Americans to become socially self-sufficient was the growth of local chapters of fraternal orders and benefit associations during the late nineteenth century. These organizations provided insurance for their members and were active in supporting antilynching legislation and voting rights. The black chapters of the Masons (originally established in Boston in 1775), the Odd Fellows (originally chartered in New York City in 1843), the Knights of Pythias (originally founded in Richmond, Virginia, in 1869), and the Knights of Tabor (originally founded in Independence, Missouri, in 1871) competed for membership among black men (the Order of Eastern Star and Sisters of Calanthe sought black women's membership). These groups offered health and life insurance, aided widows and orphans of deceased members, and provided opportunities for social intercourse. By 1897, the Supreme Lodge Knights of Gideon had expanded that charge by promoting racial unity, economic advancement, education, and political activism.

By the turn of the twentieth century, African Americans in Norfolk had launched numerous organizations that provided important religious, educational, recreational, entrepreneurial, and social services for the city's black community. In an ambitious effort to integrate the activities of black associations in Norfolk and other cities in Virginia into a single force promoting racial improvement, Booker T. Washington and Robert R. Moton founded the Negro Organizational Society of Virginia (NOS) in 1912. Washington, founder and principal of Alabama's Tuskegee Institute and graduate of Virginia's Hampton Institute, and his protégé Moton formed the statewide NOS, an interracial organization with local chapters in every major city in Virginia, including Norfolk. The NOS advocated Washington's racial advancement philosophy based on self-reliance, economic prosperity, and interracial goodwill and tolerance. It proposed to build better schools and educational programs, improve the health of African

Americans, create cooperatives among black farmers, and campaign for improved morals and standards of citizenship. At a conference in 1914, with three thousand blacks and one thousand whites in attendance, the NOS in Norfolk reiterated the challenges of Washington to stay in the South, cooperate with whites, and institute a program of self-help. But the NOS, which was confined to rural communities in the South, experienced limited success primarily because of racial restrictions inhibiting skilled employment, political power, education, and the economic advancement of blacks. Nonetheless, the NOS established the idea that opportunities existed in agricultural education, leadership, and rural life by stimulating vocational programs in agricultural development.

Despite the NOS's plea for interracial goodwill, racism and segregation continued to force Norfolk's African Americans to rely on their own resources in an effort to build a strong, socially self-sufficient community. Segregation also forced the benevolent and self-help societies to expand and form the nucleus of African American businesses, which included insurance companies, banks, retirement homes, unemployment insurance companies, food and clothing stores, and funeral homes. The Knights of Gideon Bank (1905), Brown's Saving and Banking Company (1909), the Tidewater Bank and Trust Company (1919), the Norfolk Home Building and Loan Association (1917), the Community Building and Loan (1928), and the Berkley Citizens Mutual Building and Loan Association (1928) worked to establish a stable economic base in the black community.

To further facilitate the growth and continued expansion of black-owned businesses, two hundred African Americans formed the Norfolk Negro Chamber of Commerce in the early 1920s. Its leadership consisted of prominent business and professional men who outlined a program covering every phase of community service, combined with chamber of commerce objectives. Perhaps due to the efforts of the Negro Chamber of Commerce, by 1922 Norfolk boasted twenty-five black-owned insurance companies, each maintaining a reserve of at least $1,000. These companies provided essential services for the black community because many established white-owned insurance companies refused to insure African Americans. Yet many of the black-owned insurance companies were plagued by a lack of capital and poor management. By 1926, only eight of the companies were still operating, among them the Norfolk branch of the North Carolina Mutual Life Insurance Company, which also owned the city's Attucks Theatre Building on Church Street.

Perhaps Norfolk's most important black-owned business was the city's weekly newspaper, the *Journal and Guide*. In 1908, the Knights of Gideon fraternal society, under the leadership of Plummer B. Young, had launched the paper as the *Lodge Journal and Guide*. For two years the paper served as the official organ of the Knights of Gideon, until P. B. Young purchased it in 1910. Young reorganized the paper as an independent weekly and renamed it the *Journal and Guide*. Within a short time, the *Guide* became the largest circulating weekly African American newspaper in Virginia, sending correspondents to Europe during the First and Second World Wars, and advertising the activities of the area's fraternal, sororal, political, educational, and mutual-aid societies. Although its circulation has been drastically reduced, it continues to thrive as a weekly newspaper.

Undoubtedly, the existence of the *Guide* facilitated the emergence of Norfolk's civic leagues, including the Colored Civic Welfare Association (1917), the Monroe Ward Citizen's League (1920), a branch of the Virginia United Civic League (1923), the Norfolk Civic and Welfare League (1923), the Civic Club (1925), and the Norfolk Civic Association (1932). The primary goal of the civic leagues was to improve the living conditions of Norfolk's black residents, most of whom were confined to a small area of the city with inadequate sanitation and other conveniences. The civic leagues sought to improve street conditions and schools in the African American neighborhoods of Titustown, Oakwood, Lamberts Point, Berkley, and Brambleton. Similarly, the Citizen's Club (1923), organized by young black professionals from the Berkley section of Norfolk, and the Commercial Thrift Club (1925) initiated a voter registration drive, encouraging African Americans to pay poll taxes and participate in politics. In the early years, the leagues found that their voices were often muted, if not ignored, yet their persistence eventually paid off, as the city of Norfolk capitulated and dedicated funds to pave streets, construct parks, and build or remodel schools in black neighborhoods. In 1928, under considerable pressure from a few prominent whites, the city consented to build Barraud Park, specifically for African Americans. These concessions, however, were not nearly enough and the city's black community continued to receive little municipal assistance. Undaunted, the black civic leagues expanded their activities and new groups emerged in the Huntersville, Lindenwood, and Young's Park neighborhoods. The Depression temporarily offset the momentum, as poll taxes kept blacks from voting and white city officials insisted that the poor economy prevented them from designating funds for the improvement of black neighborhoods. Nevertheless, some New Deal programs and the new-found power of blacks during World War II provided for the building of schools and neighborhood improvement and expansion.

While efforts to improve the quality of life of Norfolk's black population continued to be dominated by local groups, the city also witnessed the arrival of national organizations. In 1917, the National Association for the Advancement of Colored People (NAACP) and the National Urban League established branches in Norfolk. During the early years, however, Norfolk's NAACP chapter remained relatively inactive, largely due to internal discord sparked by chapter president P. B. Young's decision to pursue an accommodationist strategy rather than to challenge racism, discrimination, and segregation. Refusing to embrace the NAACP's protest strategy, Young sought racial advancement through diplomatic negotiations with white southerners, utilizing such established institutions of the early 1910s as the NOS, the Negro State Teacher's Association, the National Negro Business League, and the Federation of Colored Women's Clubs.

During the 1930s and 1940s, the Depression and the Second World War triggered a shift in Norfolk's race relations. The economic distress caused by the Depression forced thousands to seek employment in the North. While some blacks, who sought refuge in the escapism of entertainment, ritual, and spirituality joined organizations such as Sweet Daddy Grace's House of Prayer, others started to repudiate the policies of accommodationism and the racial status quo, which they believed had led to the Depression. No doubt the accommodationist posture of the city's black leadership and the conditions of the Depression swayed many in the black community, especially the poor and working classes, to support Marcus Garvey's new Universal Negro Improvement Association (UNIA). In 1938, a group of Norfolk blacks received a charter for the Berkley branch of UNIA, which advocated colonization to Liberia as the only hope for African Americans.

While some African Americans embraced UNIA's escapist rhetoric, others were determined to fight racial discrimination. In 1938, the Norfolk Teacher's Association (NTA), the Virginia Teacher's Association (VTA), and the NAACP challenged Norfolk's practice of paying black teachers lower salaries than whites. The groups particularly resented pay inequity at Booker T. Washington High School, where the white school custodian received a higher salary than the black principal or any of the teachers. In 1938, Aline Black, with the assistance of the

NAACP, initiated a law suit, challenging the city's wage discrimination. NAACP attorney Thurgood Marshall spearheaded Black's legal defense. The case went to the Circuit Court, where Judge Allan Hanckel ruled that the court lacked the power to determine personnel policy because Black had entered a contractual arrangement with the city. Black then filed an appeal for writ of error with the Virginia State Court of Appeals; but the school board terminated Black's contract before the court date was set. Protests against the school board's decision were swift. Twelve hundred individuals signed a petition demanding Black's reinstatement, while the *Journal and Guide* and the *Virginian Pilot* wrote protest editorials. NTA President Melvin Alston agreed to be a second litigant with the NTA, serving as coplaintiff. In March 1939, *Aline Black & Melvin O. Alston v. The City of Norfolk* was heard by the courts and met the same fate as Black's previous attempt. The plaintiffs appealed to the U.S. Court of Appeals, which then ruled that the city's unequal pay policy violated the Fourteenth Amendment. The court ordered the city of Norfolk to equalize teacher salaries and to reinstate Black, who then continued teaching chemistry at Booker T. Washington High School until her retirement in 1969. Despite the legal victory, some of Norfolk's black leaders, afraid that the city would delay implementation of the court order and hoping to maintain good relations with whites, agreed to compromise with the city on the issue of equal pay. Thurgood Marshall, critical of the lack of courage of the city's black leadership, complained that the compromise set the efforts of Norfolk's African Americans back by seventy-five years.

Perhaps emboldened by the World War II "Double V" campaign, which demanded a victory for democracy overseas and a victory for racial democracy in the United States, African Americans in Norfolk pressured the city in 1942 to provide a United Service Organizations (USO) club for black servicemen. Despite protests, the city located the black USO in its worst slum, on Smith Street. The efforts of the USO to provide recreational opportunities for black servicemen were supplemented by the Hunton YMCA, which opened a dormitory and sponsored weekly dances for the soldiers at Booker T. Washington High School.

Following World War II, school desegregation became a volatile issue in Norfolk. On June 7, 1958, U.S. District Judge Walter E. Hoffman directed Norfolk's school board to admit 151 African American students who had applied to white schools. The city tried to oppose and then delay the order, but on August 29, seventeen black applicants were admitted. Governor J. Lindsay Almond, Jr., who had championed school segregation as the state's attorney general and in his 1957 gubernatorial race, closed Norfolk's six white high schools on September 8 rather than see them integrated. While Norfolk's ten thousand white students did not attend school as a result of the closings, the city's black schools remained open, since no white students had applied for admission. Challenging the governor's decision to close the white schools, the Reverend John Henderson filed a lawsuit on behalf of the seventeen black students in October. Norfolk's city council, eager to avoid a legal conflict, tried to pressure the black community to drop the lawsuit by withdrawing funding for the city's black schools. Ironically, Governor Almond intervened, calling the move "vicious and retaliatory." However, on January 19, 1959, the issue became moot when the Federal District Court and the Virginia Supreme Court declared Virginia's massive resistance policy unconstitutional. On February 2, 1959, seventeen black students entered Norfolk's previously all-white schools, facing prejudice and discrimination but paving the way for citywide integration by the 1970s.

The school crisis sparked increased interracial efforts to improve race relations in Norfolk. A coalition of black and white citizens, including business leaders and politicians, had first emerged during World War II. The Women's Council for Interracial Cooperation, formed in 1945 and continuing until 1969, was among the first interracial groups operating in Norfolk. Vivian Mason, who spearheaded the organization, suggested that the group meet at the Ohef Sholem Temple in Norfolk and invited the most prominent women of the black and white communities. The group launched a campaign to hire black policemen, distributed shoes to impoverished children, sponsored an interracial nursery school, lobbied for an antisegregation bill, and fought for the appointment of an African American to the city's school board. The coalition achieved perhaps its most momentous victory in the struggle against discrimination and racism when Joseph A. Jordan Jr., a black attorney, was elected to Norfolk's City Council in 1968. Jordan became the first African American to win a seat on the council during the twentieth century. In 1972, he became the city's Vice Mayor and in 1976 he was appointed to serve as judge on Norfolk's General District Court. Other black Virginians were equally successful in the political arena. In 1968, Dr. James E. Holley III became the first African American elected to the Portsmouth City Council. In 1980, he became Portsmouth's first African American mayor, an office to which he was reelected in 1984 and again in 1996. Dr. William P. Robinson, a Norfolk State University professor, was elected to the Virginia House of Delegates in 1969, becoming the first African American to win that seat in the twentieth century. These elections, combined with the appointments of prominent African Americans to the school board and the city planning commission, heralded the beginnings of changes for African Americans in Norfolk. They did not, however, signal an end of the struggle.

With the onset of the civil rights movement during the decades following World War II, Norfolk slowly desegregated. In 1960, Norfolk won the National Municipal League's All-American City Award in recognition of the Norfolk Redevelopment and Housing Authority's (NRHA) efforts to improve the city's housing and living conditions. NRHA projects replaced the city's slums with low-rent housing, wider streets, boulevards, and controlled business and industrial development.

Despite the housing changes wrought by the NRHA, Norfolk's African Americans still lacked a voice in politics, due to voter registration discrimination. In 1960, only 23 percent of the city's eligible black voters were registered; yet blacks made up 25.8 percent of Norfolk's population. Following the 1964 adoption of the Twenty-fourth Amendment, which abolished the poll tax, and the 1965 Voting Rights Act, the number of registered black voters started to expand. The lingering effects of voting restrictions, however, resulted in the continuation of widespread inequities.

In the 1960s, civil rights activists challenged continued racial discrimination in public accommodation and launched a series of protests. Students who formed the Student Nonviolent Coordinating Committee played a leading role in the struggle for racial reform. In 1961, they staged numerous sit-ins, resulting in the successful desegregation of many southern lunch counters. African Americans in Hampton Roads, for example, organized sit-ins at Norfolk's Woolworths, Portsmouth's Mid-City Roses, and numerous other stores. In most cases, the protests remained peaceful, yet on occasion violent clashes resulted. In addition to demands for equality in public accommodation, civil rights activists staged protest marches and demonstrations to challenge racial discrimination in education, employment, politics, and housing.

While desegregation provided African American residents with access to better housing, education, and economic opportunities, it drained the black community's

racial solidarity. Today, many of the elementary and middle schools in Norfolk have been electively resegregated, under the auspices of creating neighborhood schools. The Church Street area, which served as a vital business district for the black community, has been gutted and the street widened to provide easy access from the downtown district to other locations, and only a few of the historic black social organizations, in weakened condition, remain.

Among them is the Eureka Lodge, which was established in 1897. The lodge is the oldest black-controlled chapter of the Improved Benevolent and Protective Order of Elks. Built as an extension of the Free African Society (1787), the first formal African American society founded by Richard Allen and Absalom Jones, the black Elks faced a prolonged court battle when the white Benevolent and Protective Order of Elks tried to prevent the black group from using the Elks name. Beginning in 1906, the black Elks successfully fought a ten-year battle, winning the right to function as Elks, and thereafter making charitable contributions to the community and providing a facility for community banquets, receptions, and educational needs. In recent years, its membership, which once surged to over four hundred, has severely declined as many younger black men have joined fraternities rather than lodges.

The Sons of Norfolk, a fraternal organization drawing its members largely from the city's black professional community, suffered a similar fate. Formed in 1914, the Sons of Norfolk attracted large numbers of members, reaching a peak during the 1940s, 1950s, and 1960s. During those decades thousands of Sons of Norfolk often marched in Christmas, Independence, Emancipation, and Memorial Day parades. Today, the organization has only a handful of members, due in part to the decision of some of the prominent older members not to initiate new members, fearing that their admission would lead to the introduction of new ideas.

Unlike the Sons of Norfolk, the United Order of Tents continues to thrive. In 1995 it opened a forty-unit multistory Senior Citizens Apartment Complex. Similarly, the Bachelor-Benedict Club endures and continues to stage elaborate annual debutante balls.

While Norfolk's African American community has seen the demise of many of its post–Civil War organizations, several fraternal, sororal, church, social, political, and economic institutions have survived, including branches of national organizations such as the Links, the Jack and Jills, and numerous Greek fraternities and sororities. These organizations continue to serve the long-standing traditions of self-help and social independence that have characterized the African American community in Norfolk since the Civil War.

**FURTHER READINGS**

Bogger, Tommy L. *Free Blacks in Norfolk, Virginia, 1790–1860: The Darker Side of Freedom.* Charlottesville: University Press of Virginia, 1997.

Fields, Norma. "Blacks in Norfolk, Virginia During the 1930s." M.A. Thesis, Old Dominion University. Norfolk, Virginia, 1979.

Lewis, Earl. *In Their Own Interests: Race, Class and Power in Twentieth Century Virginia.* Berkeley: University of California Press, 1991.

Parramore, Thomas, et. al. *Norfolk: The First Four Centuries.* Charlottesville: University Press of Virginia, 1994.

Schmidt, Alvin J. *Fraternal Organizations.* Westport, Conn.: Greenwood, 1980.

Suggs, Henry Lewis. *P. B. Young, Newspaperman: Race, Politics, and Journalism in the New South, 1910–1962.* Charlottesville: University Press of Virginia, 1993.

Workers of the Writers' Program of the Works Projects Administration in the State of Virginia. *The Negro in Virginia.* Winston-Salem, N.C.: John Blair, 1994. Originally published New York: Hastings House, 1940.

*Cassandra Newby-Alexander*

## North Carolina Council on Human Relations

This interracial civil rights association grew out of the North Carolina Commission on Interracial Cooperation (NCCIC). Founded in 1921, the NCCIC sought to influence state and local policies toward African Americans in the fields of education, public health, and civil rights. Prominent members included sociologist Howard W. Odum and Wake Forest College president William L. Poteat. The NCCIC also named several North Carolina governors honorary chairmen in recognition of their support. In 1946, the group became affiliated with the Southern Regional Council, but by then the NCCIC was plagued by internal divisions. By 1950, facing declining membership and decreased funding, the NCCIC was no longer a vocal and influential advocate for the civil rights cause.

In 1954, the NCCIC was renamed the North Carolina Council on Human Relations (NCCHR). The new name reflected a renewed spirit of civil rights activism that surfaced in North Carolina after the Supreme Court's *Brown v. Board of Education* decision. This activist spirit was personified by the NCCHR's new executive secretary, Harry S. Jones. Under his leadership, the group moved its organizational headquarters to Charlotte and began to forge alliances with local civil rights organizations. Within two years, Jones increased the Council's membership from sixty to three hundred and fifty. Despite this growth in membership, the group's activities were hampered by the racial paternalism of some of its white members.

Nevertheless, the NCCHR attempted to improve the socioeconomic conditions of North Carolina's black residents. In the early 1960s, it organized sit-ins, and it was a vocal champion of school desegregation. In the 1970s, the NCCHR splintered into several different organizations.

**FURTHER READINGS**

Allred, William Clifton, Jr. "The Southern Regional Council, 1943–1961." M.A. Thesis, Emory University, 1966.

Burns, Merrimon Augustus, III. "North Carolina and the Negro Dilemma, 1930–1950." Ph.D. diss., University of North Carolina, Chapel Hill, 1969.

Sosna, Morton. *In Search of the Silent South: Southern Liberals and the Race Issue.* New York: Columbia University Press, 1977.

*Richard D. Starnes*

## Northern California Center for Afro-American History and Life

*See* East Bay Negro Historical Society.

## Northern Student Movement

The Northern Student Movement (NSM) emerged out of the wave of southern sit-ins during the early 1960s. It supported civil rights efforts in the South as well as developed programs to address northern racial injustice.

The NSM emerged from the work of a committee formed at a conference sponsored by the New England Student Christian Movement in June of 1961. At a meeting in October 1961, this committee proposed, to students from twenty colleges, a structure for a new organization. Peter Countryman, a Yale undergraduate, was a leading spirit behind this effort, becoming the first executive director of the NSM, which initially was headquartered in New Haven, Connecticut.

Early on, the NSM mobilized student support for the southern struggle. It raised money for the Southern Voter Registration Program of the Student Nonviolent Coordinating Committee (SNCC) and supervised the donation of ten thousand books from northern campuses to Miles College in Birmingham, Alabama.

The NSM also focused, however, on the difficulties faced by minority groups in the North. In the spring of 1962, it brought together students, leaders, and field workers active in the northern civil rights struggle for a conference at Sarah Lawrence College. It encouraged direct-action protests as well. It helped send students to stage sit-ins against segregation on Maryland's Eastern Shore. And its members protested housing discrimination in Rye, New York.

But educational initiatives were the NSM's forte. In the summer of 1962, it organized tutorials for seventy-five students in New York City, one hundred and fifty students in Prince Edward County, Virginia, and nearly four hundred high school students, most of whom were black, from distressed Philadelphia neighborhoods.

The NSM developed a flexible and fluid organizational structure consisting of three parts: a central office, city projects, and campus affiliates. The central office raised funds, conducted research, and handled administrative matters. A Congress, composed largely of delegates from the projects and project staff, a student executive committee, and an advisory board determined the general direction of the organization, while individual project staffers had the most latitude in developing specific programs. In terms of salaries, NSM staffers lived, in the words of one member, from "hand-to-mouth."

By 1965, the NSM, like the Students for a Democratic Society and the northern chapters of the Congress of Racial Equality, turned to community organizing in the inner cities. It now described itself as a "non-profit, tax-exempt interracial organization committed to ending the economic, political, and social inequities which have created and maintain racial ghettos in the North." Its headquarters shifted from New Haven to New York City, and William Strickland, a black activist, replaced Countryman as executive director. The new primary aim of the NSM was "to build community organizations so that the deprived can use their power for change." Among other efforts, NSM activists tackled discriminatory hiring policies of the United Parcel Service in Hartford, protested police brutality in Detroit, and created a Freedom Library in Philadelphia.

The tone of the NSM reflected new race relations. NSM staffers debated the appropriate role for whites in the organizing effort. By 1966, Strickland declared that the NSM sought "to build a movement on *our* experience, on the black reality, a movement which is ours, a movement which is dedicated to our needs and objectives."

But NSM did not outlast the 1960s. After 1965, many of its staffers became heavily involved in the work of other organizations, like SNCC.

**FURTHER READINGS**

*Freedom North: A Publication of the Northern Student Movement, 1964–1966.*

*Students for a Democratic Society Papers, 1958–1970.* Reel 9. Glen Rock, N.J.: Microfilming Corp. of America, 1978.

*James Ralph*

# Northwestern Freedmen's Aid Commission

The Northwestern Freedmen's Aid Commission (NFAC) was a relatively short-lived secular voluntary aid association intended to raise funds for the relief and education of the freedmen. Organized in Chicago in January 1864, the NFAC was most active in Illinois and Iowa. Like other western freedmen's aid societies such as the Michigan Freedmen's Aid Commission, the Indiana Freedmen's Aid Commission, and the Cleveland Freedmen's Aid Commission, the Northwestern commission lost many members to missionary organizations, particularly the American Missionary Association and the Freedmen's Aid Society of the Methodist Episcopal Church, which lured away the association's teachers and its sources of philanthropic support. It began to lose teachers and schools in the South beginning in 1866; two years later it was dissolved.

Although grandiose claims were made for the organization in its early years, it is unlikely that it raised more than about $175,000 in its four years of service. It sponsored over a hundred teachers during those years, mostly from northwestern states. However, in contrast to its eastern co-laborers, who supported many African American teachers, the NFAC appears to have included no African Americans in its corps of teachers. At its height, the commission was sponsoring schools in Alabama, Louisiana, Mississippi, Tennessee, Kentucky, Missouri, and Arkansas.

The commission did not publish a monthly journal as did many other aid societies. It raised money primarily through subscriptions and voluntary church offerings. Apparently unique among aid societies was its "Great North-Western Fair for the Benefit of the North-Western

Freedmen's Aid Commission," which it held in late 1864 and which reportedly netted nearly ten thousand dollars.

From its beginning, the NFAC took a more racially conservative stance than did the eastern secular aid societies. Reflecting the greater racism of the northwestern states as contrasted with the eastern and northeastern states, the association initially opposed the plans of the American Freedmen's Union Commission and its constituent organizations to provide relief and education through interracial programs for both black and white southerners after the Civil War. It did not join the American Freedmen's Union Commission until late in 1867, after it had lost most of its schools and teachers to denominational societies. Then, despite the efforts of James Miller McKim, the secretary of the American Freedmen's Union Commission and indefatigable freedmen's aid worker, the NFAC closed in July 1868. The commission was effectively destroyed by denominational rivalry for control of southern black education and by northwestern hostility toward the freed slaves.

**FURTHER READINGS**

Butchart, Ronald E. *Northern Schools, Southern Blacks, and Reconstruction: Freedmen's Education, 1862–1875.* Westport, Conn.: Greenwood, 1980.

———. "Perspectives on Gender, Race, Calling, and Commitment in Nineteenth-century America: A Collective Biography of the Teachers of the Freedpeople, 1862–1875." *Vitae Scholastica* 13 (Spring 1994): 15–32.

———. "Recruits to the 'Army of Civilization': Gender, Race, Class, and the Freedmen's Teachers, 1862–1875." *Journal of Education* 172, no. 3 (1990): 76–87.

*Ronald E. Butchart*

# Oblate Sisters of Providence

The Oblate Sisters of Providence was the first Catholic religious order for African American women. Founded in Baltimore in 1829, it began its ministry among black Catholics who fled Haiti for the United States in the first decades of the nineteenth century. The organization provided a religious home to African American women and a Catholic education for thousands of students who attended Oblate-run schools across the United States.

The Oblate Sisters began as a collaboration between James Joubert, a French-born Catholic priest, and Elizabeth Lange and Marie Balas, Haitian women living in Baltimore. In 1818 the women began a school for free black girls in an effort to help them learn the catechism. They ran the school out of their home until 1828, when Joubert promised the backing of his religious order, the Sulpicians. With this support the women founded St. Frances Academy. The following year, Lange, Balas, and two others took their vows as the first members of the Oblate Sisters of Providence.

Though the education of black girls in Baltimore was the Oblates' primary goal, they quickly extended their service to other areas. The Oblates worked as nurses during the cholera epidemic of 1832, opened their doors to orphans and widows in need, and started schools for boys and adults across the United States. Their educational efforts were the basis of the creation of two black parishes, St. Frances Xavier in Baltimore, and St. Ann in Washington, D.C.

But their successes did not come without struggle. Anticatholicism, poverty, and racism all impeded the Oblates' work. During the 1830s, the Oblates' novitiate stood under constant threat from anticatholic rioters in Baltimore. Then after Joubert's death in 1843, the Oblates lost the support of the Sulpician order, though they made ends

meet by doing washing and sewing. During this time, Baltimore's archbishop, Samuel Eccleston, urged the Oblates to disband, and only the timely support of St. John Neumann and the Redemptorist order enabled the Oblates to continue their work. Still, poverty forced the closure of several Oblate schools in the mid-nineteenth century. And during the Civil War racism as well as poverty threatened the survival of the Oblates. The sisters had to briefly go into hiding in 1864, and during the 1870s Oblate-run schools in New Orleans had to close when the archbishop de-emphasized education for blacks.

In this century, Oblates and their supporters have been active in urging the Catholic church to pay greater attention to black Catholics in the inner cities. In 1970, the principal and faculty of St. Frances Academy picketed the archdiocese of Baltimore to demand more financial support for Baltimore's black parishes. Their protests were successful, and the Oblates' educational and religious efforts continue in Baltimore and elsewhere in the United States and in Costa Rica.

## FURTHER READINGS

Davis, Cyprian. *The History of Black Catholics in America.* New York: Crossroad, 1990.

Gerdes, Sister M. Reginald. "To Educate and Evangelize: Black Catholic Schools of the Oblate Sisters of Providence, 1820–1880." *U.S. Catholic Historian* 7 (Spring/Summer 1988): 183–199.

Morrow, Diane Batts. "Outsiders Within: The Oblate Sisters of Providence in 1830s Church and Society." *U.S. Catholic Historian* 15 (Spring 1997): 35–54.

Spalding, Thomas W. *The Premier See: A History of the Archdiocese of Baltimore, 1789–1994.* Baltimore: Johns Hopkins University Press, 1995.

*Gary Daynes*

## Odd Fellows

*See* Grand United Order of Odd Fellows.

## Office of Federal Contract Compliance Programs

The Office of Federal Contract Compliance Programs (OFCCP) was created by Executive Reorganization Plan Number 1 in 1978 as a federal agency to monitor government contractors' compliance with affirmative action provisions. The OFCCP is the successor to a number of executive branch antidiscrimination programs that date back to 1941 when President Franklin D. Roosevelt created the President's Committee on Fair Employment Practices to monitor and eliminate racial discrimination in defense industries. Roosevelt's committee dissolved in 1946, and in 1951 President Harry S. Truman created the President's Committee on Government Contract Compliance to succeed it. In 1953 President Dwight D. Eisenhower replaced Truman's committee with his own version, the President's Committee on Government Contracts. Similarly, President John F. Kennedy in 1961 began the President's Committee on Equal Employment Opportunity, with an executive order which for the first time required government contractors to take "affirmative action" to prevent discrimination. Heretofore executive committees had adopted a low-key, conciliatory approach to promoting minority employment opportunities. The stage, however, was set for vigorous efforts to implement affirmative action.

In 1965, President Lyndon B. Johnson replaced Kennedy's committee with the Office of Federal Contract Compliance (OFCC), housed in the Department of Labor. President Nixon left the OFCC in operation, and authorized what was known as the Philadelphia Plan, whereby government contractors were compelled to specify "goals and timetables" for the employment of minority workers. When challenged by contractors as an illegal system of preferential treatment based on race, the federal courts upheld the OFCC's power to require such racial quotas. Despite the fact that Nixon and the Republican party claimed to be opposed to racial preferences, the President intervened to preserve the Philadelphia Plan when a powerful movement in Congress, beginning in 1972, sought to eliminate the system.

President Carter strengthened the government contract affirmative action program by creating the Office of Federal Contract Compliance Programs in 1978. Although President Ronald Reagan campaigned vigorously against affirmative action in 1980, and could have abolished the system by revoking the executive orders that created it, the Reagan administration was deeply divided on the issue and did not scale back the program in any significant way.

**FURTHER READINGS**

Belz, Herman. *Equality Transformed: A Quarter-Century of Affirmative Action.* New Brunswick, N.J.: Transaction Press, 1991.

Blumrosen, Alfred W. *Modern Law: The Law Transmission System and Equal Employment Opportunity.* Madison: University of Wisconsin Press, 1993.

Graham, Hugh Davis. *The Civil Rights Era: Origins and Development of National Policy, 1960–1972.* New York: Oxford University Press, 1990.

Wolters, Raymond. *Right Turn: William Bradford Reynolds, the Reagan Administration, and Black Civil Rights.* New Brunswick, N.J.: Transaction Press, 1996.

*Paul D. Moreno*

## Office of Minority Business Development

*See* Minority Business Development Agency.

## Office of Production Management, Minorities (or Minority Groups) Branch

Established in January 1941, the Minorities (or Minority Groups) Branch of the Office of Production Management (OPM) was devoted to increasing the number of African Americans and other minorities, including the physically handicapped, working in defense industries during World War II.

Prior to the United States' entry into the war, American defense spending began to pull America out of the Great Depression as more and more people found employment. Despite the urgent need for workers, however, most employers were unwilling to hire African Americans, who continued to make up a disproportionately large number of the unemployed. The president of the North American Aviation Company, for example, announced that "regardless of their training as aircraft workers, we will not employ Negroes in the North American plant. It is against company policy." Similarly, many labor unions who were organizing workers in defense industries excluded African Americans from membership. African Americans protested their exclusion through several organizations, including the Committee on Negro Americans in Defense Industries.

In 1940, Sidney Hillman, cochairman of the National Defense Advisory Commission (NDAC), the forerunner of the OPM, and a vice-president of the Congress of Industrial Organizations, responded to black pressure. Hillman announced the creation of the NDAC's Minorities Branch to promote the employment of African Americans in defense industries. The Minorities Branch investigated discriminatory hiring practices in defense industries and negotiated with corporate employers and personnel directors urging them to hire black workers on defense related construction and production sites. Concurrently, Hillman created the Negro Employment and Training Branch to provide African Americans with necessary job skills. The Minorities Branch then encouraged defense contractors to hire black workers trained by the OPM. Dr. Will W. Alexander, a liberal white Southerner who had headed the Inter-Racial Commission, was in charge of the Minorities Branch and Robert C. Weaver, an African American economist and member of President Franklin D. Roosevelt's "black cabinet," headed the Negro Employment and Training Branch.

But the OPM's Minorities Branch was not very successful in increasing the number of African Americans employed in the nation's defense industries, largely because it lacked the power to enforce its dictates. Except in menial, low-paying jobs, it failed to overcome the opposition of white workers who often refused to labor alongside blacks. The failure of the OPM's Minorities Branch then increased African American doubts in the government's commitment to equality and led many to support A. Philip Randolph's proposed March on Washington, which resulted in the creation of the more powerful President's Committee on Fair Employment Practice on June 25, 1941.

**FURTHER READINGS**

Foner, Philip S. *Organized Labor and the Black Worker, 1619–1981.* New York: International Publishers, 1982.

Granger, Lester B. "Barriers to Negro War Employment." *Annals of the American Academy of Political and Social Science* 223 (September 1942): 72–80.

Reed, Merl E. *Seedtime for the Modern Civil Rights Movement: The President's Committee on Fair Employment Practice.* Baton Rouge: Louisiana State University Press, 1991.

Ruchames, Louis. *Race, Jobs, and Politics: The Story of FEPC.* New York: Columbia University Press, 1953.

U.S. Committee on Fair Employment Practice. *Minorities in Defense.* Washington, D.C.: Government Printing Office, 1941.

Weaver, Robert C. "Defense Industries and the Negro." *Annals of the American Academy of Political and Social Science* 223 (September 1942): 60–66.

*Peter Cole*

## Ohio Commission for Fair Employment Practices Legislation

The Ohio Commission for Fair Employment Practices Legislation formed in January 1945, shortly after the defeat of the state's first fair employment practices bill, which had been cosponsored by white Democrat Howard M. Metzenbaum of Cleveland and black Republican David D. Turpeau of Cincinnati. The Commission was composed of twenty-four local councils scattered throughout the state and was supported by the Anti-Defamation League of B'nai B'rith, the Consumers' League of Ohio, several branches of the National Association for the Advancement of Colored People (NAACP) and the National Urban League, the Ohio Pastors' Council, and the state councils of the American Federation of Labor and the Congress of Industrial Organizations. The Commission was led by black activists, in particular Theodore M. Berry, a lawyer and a Cincinnati NAACP official. Its mission was to organize support and lobby for an Ohio Fair Employment Practices law.

The Commission conducted its most intensive campaign during and immediately following the 1948 state elections. It lobbied both political parties to adopt fair employment planks in their platforms. Although both Democrats and Republicans proclaimed support for a Fair Employment Practices Act, only the Democrats actively campaigned on the issue. But because Ohio Democrats gained majorities in both houses of the General Assembly and Democrat Frank J. Lausche became governor, Commission leaders believed that their chances for a strong state fair employment practices law were good. They drafted a bill that laid the ground for powerful administrative agency capable of levying heavy fines for violators.

Although the bill passed the House in March 1949, it stalled in the Senate. During the Senate debates, the Ohio Chamber of Commerce, one of the groups opposing the proposed law, invited Donald Richberg, a one-time New Deal liberal, to speak against the creation of a state fair employment agency. Before the state Senate, Richberg redbaited the supporters of fair employment and claimed that such a powerful state agency would attack freedom. The Commission countered by bringing the NAACP's Thurgood Marshall to Columbus. But despite Marshall's intelligent and forceful plea for the legislation, the Ohio Senate voted down the bill.

From 1949 until 1959, over thirty fair employment practice bills were introduced into the Ohio General Assembly. All were defeated, owing much to the Commission's opponents, namely the American Council of Christian Churches of Ohio, the Ohio Bankers' Association, the Ohio Chamber of Commerce, the Ohio Manufacturers' Association, and the state Republican Party. In 1959, however, the Commission was given a boost by a renewed effort to pass fair employment legislation by state Democrats, who had captured control of the General Assembly and the governor's office. Soon after the Governor's Advisory Commission on Civil Rights issued a statement recommending fair employment legislation, an Ohio fair employment practice bill, which set up a weak administrative agency but which nevertheless had the support of the Commission, was passed by the General Assembly and signed into law by Governor Michael V. DiSalle on April 29, 1959.

**FURTHER READINGS**

Bowman, John Hemphill. "Fair Employment Practice Legislation: An Evaluation of the Ohio Experience, 1959–1964." M.A. Thesis, Ohio State University, 1965.

Kersten, Andrew E. "Fighting for Fair Employment: The FEPC in the Midwest." Ph.D. diss., University of Cincinnati, 1997.

Norgen, Paul and Samuel Hill. *Toward Fair Employment.* New York: Columbia University Press, 1964.

*Andrew E. Kersten*


## Old Dominion Medical Society

*See* Negro Medical Association of Virginia.


## Old North State Medical, Dental, and Pharmaceutical Society

In 1887, three black North Carolina physicians trained at the Leonard Medical School at Shaw University in Raleigh and one black medical student formed the Old North State Medical, Dental, and Pharmaceutical Society. The society provided the state's black physicians with professional networking opportunities and a forum to exchange information about advances in medical science. It also lobbied to increase the number of black practitioners, desegregate medical and dental schools, and improve the health care of North Carolina's black population.

After the Civil War, African Americans in North Carolina took advantage of expanded opportunities to engage in occupations traditionally practiced exclusively by whites. Black doctors, lawyers, teachers, and clergymen made up an educated elite, often providing black political leadership. These professions, however, were more than mere stepping stones to political careers. Black professionals cared very deeply about their communities and their chosen professions. The founding of the Old North State Medical, Dental, and Pharmaceutical Society is an example of the professional dedication of these black leaders.

In the early 1880s, Dr. L. A. Rutherford, a prominent African American physician in North Carolina, attempted to muster interest in forming a medical society for black practitioners. Such a society, he hoped, would provide a professional, collegial environment for black physicians, keep black doctors abreast of the latest developments in medical science, and address the health concerns of blacks in North Carolina. However, a shortage of African American physicians hampered Rutherford's efforts.

In 1881, the American Missionary Association established the Leonard Medical School at Shaw University in Raleigh. Dedicated to producing capable black physicians, this school also provided the cadre to fulfill Rutherford's vision. In 1887, three Leonard Medical School graduates and one medical student formed the Old North State Medical, Dental, and Pharmaceutical Society. One of the founders was Lamar Andrew Scruggs, the first valedictorian of Leonard Medical School.

While initially a small organization, the society extended its influence in the early twentieth century. It successfully promoted professional interaction between black and white physicians and was instrumental in the establishment of postgraduate education for black doctors at Duke University. In the 1930s, the society became a vocal advocate of public health reform and lobbied to improve health care for black North Carolinians. It also played a key role in the desegregation of medical and dental schools in North Carolina. In the 1970s, it called for more blacks to be appointed to medical accreditation boards. Claiming to be the oldest professional organization for black doctors in the world, the society continues to address the specific issues facing African American physicians and their patients in North Carolina.

**FURTHER READINGS**

Logan, Frenise A. *The Negro in North Carolina, 1876–1894.* Chapel Hill: University of North Carolina Press, 1964.

McConnell, Roland Calhoun. "The Negro in North Carolina Since Reconstruction." Ph.D. diss., New York University, 1944.

Savitt, Todd L. "The Education of Black Physicians at Shaw University, 1882–1918." In *Black Americans in North Carolina and the South.* Ed. Jeffrey J. Crow and Flora J. Hatley. Chapel Hill: University of North Carolina Press, 1984.

*Richard D. Starnes*

## Omaha, Nebraska: Civic, Literary, and Mutual Aid Associations

In Nebraska, only Omaha and Lincoln have attracted sufficient African American migrants to establish lasting, vibrant community associations. According to the 1910 census 1,192,214 people lived in the state, 7,689 (0.6 percent) of whom were black; 124,096 people resided in Omaha, 4,426 (3 percent) of whom were black. That geographic concentration intensified throughout the twentieth century: by 1990, 75 percent of Nebraska's 57,000 African Americans called Omaha home. Thus, a rich variety of African American community associations has existed and continues to flourish in Omaha, while a smaller assortment has also developed in Lincoln. The few associations that have existed in the less populous towns usually maintained a tenuous link with their big city brethren.

Omaha blacks took the lead in Nebraska beginning in the 1870s, by organizing music and literary societies, many associated with particular church parishes. Subsequently, they also established sports clubs, merchants' associations, business cooperatives, ministerial alliances, social services groups, women's clubs, partisan political organizations, and local segregated affiliates of national fraternities such as the Odd Fellows, Knights of Pythias, Elks, and the American Legion. All these groups received brief but frequent mention in the black weeklies that have existed in Omaha since the 1890s. None, however, have attracted scholarly attention nor left public records that illuminate their history.

By contrast, the Prince Hall Masons have documented their development. The first lodge opened in Omaha in 1875 and by World War I affiliates had taken root in Alliance, Grand Island, Hastings, and Lincoln. In 1919, they joined the existing five Omaha lodges to form the Prince Hall Grand Lodge of Nebraska. The other bodies associated with black masonry, such as the Order of the Eastern Star (OES) and the Shriners, swiftly affiliated with the new sovereign Grand Lodge. Prince Hall Masonry in Nebraska attracted upstanding blue-collar workers and members of the small number of black middle-class professionals and entrepreneurs. Membership peaked in the 1920s, retreated severely during the Great Depression, revived significantly after World War II, and has declined precipitously since the late 1970s. Today it consists of one lodge and one OES chapter in Lincoln, plus seven lodges, nine OES chapters, and the Shriners' Zaha Temple #72 and Zaha Court #52 in Omaha. But a revolution in race relations has produced encouraging results in the 1990s. The white Masons in Nebraska overturned two centuries of segregation and discrimination by signing an official joint resolution recognizing the legitimacy of both the white and black grand lodges, which then began to cooperate in fraternal exercises.

Prince Hall Masons played an instrumental role in the founding of another civic group—the National Association for the Advancement of Colored People (NAACP). The first Nebraska affiliate originated in Lincoln in 1913, but soon disbanded. The Omaha branch commenced in 1918 and remains active today, though it has had a checkered history, marred by recurrent lapses in activity and by frequent leadership controversies. Individual members or its youth affiliate sometimes provided yeoman service in advancing civil rights, but other organizations often had to direct the efforts. During the 1950s, for example, the interracial De Porres Club, founded by Denny Holland, a white Creighton University student, and a Jesuit faculty member, Fr. John Markoe, S.J., led marches and boycotts that desegregated some places of employment and recreation. Similarly, in the 1960s two black ministers, the Revs. Rudolph McNair and Kelsey Jones, founded the Citizens Coordinating Committee for Civil Liberties (the 4CL in local parlance) which continued the protests in the era of black power. Activists enjoyed significant success, but only national civil rights statutes achieved comprehensive change.

Finally, the Omaha Urban League, established in 1928, has maintained a more consistent record of community leadership. In 1933, it merged with the Mid-City Community Center, and during the Great Depression and World War II it dispensed a wide variety of social services to African Americans who otherwise would not have received them because of poverty and increasing discrimination and segregation. Also in 1933 it helped to organize a Lincoln Urban League that followed the same program, until its demise in 1955. In that year, the Lincoln Urban League reorganized as the independent Malone Community Center, severing its affiliation with the Urban League because the national office demanded a more militant program of civil rights advocacy. The Omaha Urban League, however, under the leadership of Whitney Young, who went on to become executive director of the National Urban League, became one of the principal examples of the "new directions" philosophy. In 1967, the affiliate changed its name to the Urban League of Nebraska to signify its growing role as an advocate for African Americans throughout the state. The League survived debilitating controversy associated with race riots and the black power movement and today it remains a vital civic organization.

### FURTHER READINGS

McMahon, David. "The Origins of the NAACP in Omaha and Lincoln, Nebraska, 1913–1926." M.A. thesis, Creighton University, 1993.

Mihelich, Dennis. "World War II and the Transformation of the Omaha Urban League." *Nebraska History* 60 (Fall, 1979): 401–423.

———. "The Formation of the Lincoln Urban League." *Nebraska History* 68 (Summer, 1987): 63–73.

———. "The Origins of the Prince Hall Mason Grand Lodge of Nebraska." *Nebraska History* 76 (Spring, 1995): 10–21.

Smith, Jefferey Harrison. "The Omaha De Porres Club." M.A. thesis, Creighton University, 1967.

*Dennis N. Mihelich*

## 100 Black Men of America, Inc.

Initially organized in New York City in 1963 as One Hundred Men, this group consisted of businessmen, professionals, public officials, and other men who pooled their resources and skills to improve the lives of African Americans and other minorities. Among the group's founders are David Dinkins, Andrew Hatcher, and Livingston Wingate. The group inspired the formation of One Hundred Black Men of New York, founded by J. Bruce Llewellyn in 1967, and One Hundred Black Men of New Jersey, founded by Dr. William Hayling in 1976.

In 1986, Hayling, with the help of Oliver Lofton, founded 100 Black Men of America, Inc. (BMoA), and became the first president of the nonprofit organization.

BMoA's stated mission is "to improve the quality of life of our citizens and enhance educational opportunities for African-Americans and minorities, through its chapters, in all communities—with a particular emphasis on young African-American males." On May 27, 1987, in Atlanta, Georgia, delegates from chapters in Atlanta, Indianapolis, Los Angeles, Nassau/Suffolk, New Jersey, Pittsburgh, Sacramento, San Francisco/Oakland Bay Area, and St. Louis held the first annual conference and established a confederation that now includes at least sixty-eight chapters in twenty-four states and the District of Columbia.

In 1995, at the national convention in Jackson, Mississippi, National President Thomas W. Dortch Jr., reasserted the original vision of BMoA, in a plan he called "Four for the Future." Dortch named antiviolence, youth mentoring, education, and economic development as the four areas critical to a healthy future for black America's youth and community. In February 1997, BMoA, which is funded solely by private and corporate donations, signed a deal with the Nike Corporation that promised to raise $3 million in cash, goods, and services over three years for BMoA's youth programs. BMoA has mentored over sixty thousand children and young adults across the nation and plans to send some of its young adults to Nike's summer intern program. Nike will use its considerable experience to advise BMoA in areas such as advertising and marketing.

Those who volunteer to serve as BMoA mentors must undergo training and certification. Student selection varies by chapter, but generally recommendations from schools, churches, and other community entities improve a student's chances of being selected for participation in one of the chapter's various programs.

The organization's national headquarters are in Atlanta. The board of directors of BMoA consists of the national president, four vice presidents (finance, operations, development, programs), three members-at-large, and all of the chapter presidents. At the annual convention in June, new chapters are presented with charters and although requirements vary from chapter to chapter, membership is typically open to anyone.

*Stephen Davenport*

## One Hundred Men

*See* 100 Black Men of America, Inc.

## Operation Breadbasket

This program, initiated by the Southern Christian Leadership Conference (SCLC), was based on the assumption that, since African American consumers contributed six billion dollars to the national economy, they could exercise considerable economic muscle in the use of their purchasing power. Operation Breadbasket grew out of the Selective Patronage Program, conceived by Philadelphia Reverend Leon Sullivan in 1960 and successfully developed by the Reverend Fred Bennette in Atlanta in 1962, where the Ford Motor Company, following representations by black ministers who threatened a boycott, agreed to hire black workers at its new assembly plant.

The aim of Operation Breadbasket was to pressure corporations and businesses located in African American communities into providing jobs for blacks at all levels, marketing products produced by black enterprises, and depositing the profits in black-owned banks. It organized black consumer boycotts, pickets, and "selective buying campaigns" targeting businesses that did not meet these demands, with notable successes in Chicago under the inspired leadership of SCLC staffer Jesse Jackson, who declared that "we are the margin of profit of every major item produced in America from General Motors on down to Kellogg's Cornflakes" (Stone 76).

Jackson, starting in 1966, with the support of Chicago's black clergy and David Wallace, a white minister at Chicago Theological Seminary, secured agreements from four local grocery companies to stock the products of black businesses, and he subsequently obtained 2,200 jobs for African Americans in white-owned firms. Employment agreements were obtained from the Pepsi, Coca-Cola

Donald S. Perkins, President of Jewel Co., with ministers of Operation Breadbasket, left to right: Strom Freeman, Martin Luther King Jr., Jesse Jackson. *Library of Congress*

and Seven-Up corporations, as well as from A&P, which pledged 770 additional jobs for African Americans. A&P also agreed to stock black products, including Joe Louis Milk, Mumbo Barbecue Sauce, and Staff of Life Bread. Red Rooster Markets, a food chain with a large presence of black neighborhoods and notorious for its health violations and inferior produce, was boycotted by Operation Breadbasket and eventually went out of business. In less than two years, Time magazine reported that Operation Breadbasket had increased the annual income of Chicago's South Side blacks by $22 million.

On July 20, 1967, more than one hundred and fifty black ministers from forty-two cities gathered at Chicago Theological Seminary and launched Operation Breadbasket as a national program covering twenty cities, with Jackson as head of the project. Ministers were to examine the employment of African Americans in firms operating within black communities and then recommend how to increase the number of black employees to reflect the proportion of the city's African American population. If negotiations failed to produce agreement, then boycotts and other forms of non-violent direct-action protest would be used.

Martin Luther King, who initially saw Operation Breadbasket as moving the SCLC "into the economic area with greater thrust," came to criticize Jackson for failing to realize that jobs would ultimately have to be provided by the public rather than the private sector. But in Andrew Young's recollection, Jackson remained obsessed with "the image of Breadbasket," since it provided him with an organizational power base (Young 444). Yet outside of Chicago, Operation Breadbasket existed only on paper. After King's assassination in 1968, and Jackson's subsequent split with SCLC, Operation Breadbasket became independent and was retitled Operation PUSH.

**FURTHER READINGS**

Marable, Manning. *Black American Politics From the Washington Marches to Jesse Jackson*. London: Verso, 1985.

Massoni, Gary. "Perspectives on Operation Breadbasket." *In Chicago 1966: Open Housing, Marches, Summit Negotiations, and Operation Breadbasket*. Ed. David J. Garrow. Brooklyn, N.Y.: Carlson, 1989, pp. 181–344.

Ralph, James R. *Northern Protest: Martin Luther King, Jr., Chicago, and the Civil Rights Movement*. Cambridge, Mass.: Harvard University Press, 1993.

Stone, Eddie. *Jesse Jackson*. Los Angeles: Holloway House, 1979.

Young, Andrew. *An Easy Burden: The Civil Rights Movement and the Transformation of America*. New York: HarperCollins, 1996.

*John White*

## Operation Crossroads Africa

In 1957 Reverend James H. Robinson founded Operation Crossroads Africa (OCA) to introduce Americans to the rich and varied cultures and peoples of Africa, while at the same time introducing Africans to Americans. Robinson launched OCA to send a select group of young Americans with leadership potential to conduct volunteer work in Africa. Their work, he believed, would build bridges of friendship and understanding between Americans and the people of the emerging African nations. Moreover, Robinson hoped that their experience would encourage the volunteers to pursue African studies or to work in Africa to provide the necessary manpower for the increasing engagement between the United States and Africa.

OCA sent groups of young volunteers to work on specific projects in African countries. Volunteers spent six weeks working on a development project while living with members of the local community. This arrangement reflected Robinson's belief that sharing living quarters and working on a common project would provide the crucible for a better mutual understanding.

As a way to ensure a commitment to the program, OCA expected each volunteer to pay a part of the cost. Initially OCA tried to avoid all connections to the American government, but increasing costs in the early 1970s made it difficult to maintain the organization solely through private funding. The death of Robinson in 1972 made this even more problematic.

The initial group that went to Africa in 1958 consisted of sixty volunteers. By the mid-1960s that number reached a peak of approximately three hundred and fifty volunteers per year. OCA continues to the present its efforts to promote sustainable development and to help local communities. It annually sends groups of volunteers to Africa, and has expanded its operations to the Caribbean and Brazil. In the forty years of its operation it has sent more than ten thousand volunteers overseas.

Much of OCA's thinking effected the subsequent establishment of the Peace Corps. Sargent Shriver, the first Peace Corps director, solicited the advice of OCA veterans, including Robinson. Thus, as a direct forerunner of the Peace Corps, OCA stands as a progenitor of the idea, important to the Peace Corps, that ultimately volunteers learn as much about themselves and their culture as about the new, host culture.

**FURTHER READINGS**

Cato, John David. "James Herman Robinson: Crossroads Africa and American Idealism, 1958–1972." *American Presbyterians* 68, 2 (Summer 1990): 99–107.

Isaacs, Harold. *Emergent Americans: A Report on "Crossroads Africa."* New York: The John Day Company, 1961.

Robinson, James H. *Africa at the Crossroads.* Philadelphia: The Westminster Press, 1962.

*Jim Meriwether*

# Order of Moses

*See* Grand United Order of Moses.

# Order of St. Luke

*See* Independent Order of St. Luke.

# Order of the Eastern Star

On August 10, 1874, Thornton Andrew Jackson, grand patron of the District of Columbia's Prince Hall Masons, founded and chartered the Order of the Eastern Star (OES) for the protection of the black Masons's "wives, widows, mothers, sisters, and daughters." Each OES chapter was placed under the guardianship of a Masonic Lodge to foster close ties between the male and female members of the Masonic family.

On December 1, 1874, the order's Queen Esther Chapter No. 1 was founded in the home of Georgiana Thomas at 708 O Street, N.W., Washington, D.C. Thomas had been a supporter of the Underground Railroad and served as deaconness at Plymouth Congregational Church in Washington, D.C. The chapter's first officers included Worthy Matron Sister Martha Welch and Worthy Patron Brother Thornton A. Jackson. In 1875, Pythagoras Lodge No. 9 presented the officers of Queen Esther Chapter No. 1 with their first badges, known as Rosettes. Jackson admonished the officers to wear the Rosettes with dignity, keeping before them the memory of the five biblical heroines: Adah, Ruth, Esther, Martha, and Electa. By 1876, nine OES chapters had emerged in various cities in the East, including Baltimore, Philadelphia, and Alexandria, Virginia. In

1880, the OES established its first grand chapter in Washington, D.C., and between 1892 and 1894, Thomas served as the chapter's grand matron. In 1955, in honor of Thomas, the Grand Order of the Eastern Star for the District of Columbia adopted the name Georgiana Thomas Grand Chapter.

Although several early OES groups ceased to exist, the number of members and chapters increased steadily during the 1890s. To foster unity among the work of the chapters, the International Conference of the Grand Chapters of OES was founded in 1907. By 1925, the OES had more than 100,000 members active in 3,500 local chapters throughout the United States, Canada, and Liberia. These chapters had a combined treasury of approximately $500,000, and several chapters owned property. Many OES chapters used the funds not only to support their work for black women but also to assist free and accepted colored Masons in maintaining Masonic temples.

Since its inception in the late nineteenth century, the OES has provided numerous services for its members as well as the black community. OES chapters founded homes for widows and orphans, established youth programs, and raised money to build Masonic halls, which functioned not only as the organization's meeting places but often provided African Americans with urban "leisure" spaces that offered film screenings and bowling, rental spaces for black businesses, gymnasiums, and auditoriums. Moreover, several OES chapters established dormitories, where youth were instructed in domestic science and agriculture. Chapters also operated burial funds, which upon the death of a member, paid a sum ranging from $25 to $500. The group raised revenues, in part, through membership dues and the sale of bonds.

The organization has also been visible in the arenas of civil and women's rights. In the 1920s, the OES encouraged its members to exercise their suffrage right. Of particular concern to OES members was the passage of the federal Dyer Anti-Lynching bill, which had twice failed passage in Congress. The Dyer bill, backed by the National Association for the Advancement of Colored People (NAACP), the National Association of Colored Women, and other civil rights groups, drew support from OES members who raised $200 for the antilynching fund of the NAACP. The group also submitted, along with a hundred other men and women of all races, a brief statement for publication by the antilynching committee. Despite these efforts, the group failed to secure adoption of the bill.

Along with the OES's long-standing commitment to racial advancement, members have found themselves combating sexism in their own ranks. As part of the Ninth Biennial Conference (biennial conferences began in 1908 and were held in conjunction with the male organization) held in Philadelphia in 1924, some OES leaders observed a lack of cooperation between grand matrons and grand patrons and were critical of the men's patronizing.

OES chapters today continue to be active in their communities, donating thousands of dollars annually to charitable and nonprofit organizations. Since 1954, OES members have contributed a total of approximately $1.5 million to various causes. Recipients of OES donations include the United Negro College Fund and the NAACP and its Legal Defense Fund. Other causes that have generated consistent financial support in the twentieth century include kindergartens and student scholarships. For example, the Arkansas chapter has over a period of forty years contributed approximately $200,000 to $300,000 to a four-year partial scholarships fund, while the Washington, D.C., chapter has donated $100,000 a year to religious colleges. In addition, OES chapters have raised funds for orphanages, retirement homes, and shelters for battered women.

Today, the OES has 3,600 local chapters and approximately 180,800 members in the United States and Canada, 42 grand chapters in the United States, and two grand chapters in Canada and the Bahamas. Worldwide, the number of OES chapters is more than 1.2 million. While OES chapters are autonomous, the secretary of the Conference of Grand Chapters, Virginia Vauls, maintains a membership roster and corresponds with the various branches, which are organized into regional groups. The Conference of Grand Chapters operates with a budget of approximately $25,000 to $30,000, supporting office expenses as well as charitable enterprises. The entire OES body meets once a year.

**FURTHER READINGS**

Brown, S. Joe. *The History of the O.E.S. Among Colored People.* Des Moines: Bystander Press, 1925.

Macoy, Robert. *General History, Cyclopedia and Dictionary of Freemasonry.* New York: Masonic Publishing, 1872.

*Prince Hall Masonic Directory*, 4th ed., 1992.

*Angela Hornsby*

## Oregon Civil Rights Advisory Committee

*See* Oregon Fair Employment Practices Advisory Committee.

## Oregon Fair Employment Practices Advisory Committee

The 1949 Oregon Fair Employment Practices Act guaranteed all state residents employment practices based on individual merit without regard to race, color, religion, or national origin. The law also provided for the creation of the Oregon Fair Employment Practices Advisory Committee to study discrimination in the state and to find ways of eliminating it. The original committee was composed of seven members appointed by the commissioner of labor. Committee members included David Robinson, C. Herald Campbell, Mrs. J. H. Thomas, Albert L. McCready, Francis J. Kern, Ulysses G. Plummer Jr., and S. P. Stevens.

The committee made recommendations to the commissioner of labor based on its investigations. The law provided two methods for achieving this purpose. The complaint procedure aimed to correct specific cases of discriminatory practices, while educational programs attempted to prevent discrimination by improving inter-group relations. Complaints filed with the state Bureau of Labor were investigated by the deputy commissioners. Commissioners attempted to resolve complaints through conferences and conciliation and, if necessary, the commissioner of labor called public hearings. If the review of a case uncovered unlawful practices, a cease and desist order was issued.

The committee served as mediator and adviser, informing individuals when they were in violation of state laws and advising employees, employers, and labor organizations about their legal rights and obligations. The committee also revised employment application forms that directly or indirectly asked applicants to reveal their race, skin color, religion, or national origin. In 1949, employment agencies, employers, and labor organizations submitted over 260 job application forms for review. The committee found that 166 of them violated the state's Fair Employment Practices Act.

The committee's educational programs were designed to inform state residents—particularly employers, employment agencies, and labor organizations—about the provisions of the law and the committee's duties. For this purpose, the committee produced the *Intergroup Relations Resource Book*, which contained pamphlets on inter-group education, civil rights, race relations, and fair employment practices. The book was distributed to students, teachers, and other state residents. The committee also produced kits containing summaries and copies of the Oregon Fair Employment Practices Act and a pamphlet explaining the law's implications. The kits were distributed to over 3,500 employment agencies and labor organizations throughout the state. Moreover, the committee arranged for the display of posters and distributed pamphlets in schools, libraries, and business establishments.

In addition to its publications, the committee organized meetings with local business people, minority groups, union leaders, and employment agency personnel, as well as civic, social, and religious groups to explain the stipulations and implications of the law. In February 1950, the committee met with the Washington State Board Against Discrimination in Employment to facilitate intra-regional cooperation. Moreover, the committee sought and maintained working relations with the Fair Employment Practices commissions in other states.

In 1955 an amendment to the state law deleted the mandatory nature of the committee, introducing language into the statute suggesting that the commissioner of the Bureau of Labor could create such advisory and inter-group relations councils as he or she deemed appropriate. The committee continued to exist under various names for a number of years. In 1959, its name changed to Civil Rights Advisory Committee and in 1971 to Human Rights Advisory Council, a name it retained until 1974.

**FURTHER READINGS**

Oregon, Fair Employment Practices Division. *A Law in Action: Oregon's Fair Employment Practices Act—1949–1950; First Report of the Oregon Fair Employment Practices Advisory Committee.* Salem: State of Oregon, Bureau of Labor, 1950.

———. *Intergroup Relations Resource Book: An Educational Project of the Employment Practices Advisory Committee and the Fair Employment Practices Division, Bureau of Labor.* Salem: State of Oregon, Bureau of Labor, 1951.

Oregon, Office of the Secretary of the State. *The Oregon Blue Book 1949–1950.* Salem: State of Oregon, Office of the Secretary of the State, 1950.

———. *The Oregon Blue Book 1950–1960.* Salem: State of Oregon, Office of the Secretary of the State, 1960.

———. *The Oregon Blue Book 1973–1974.* Salem: State of Oregon, Office of the Secretary of the State, 1974.

*Colin A. Beckles*

## Oregon Human Rights Advisory Council

*See* Oregon Fair Employment Practices Advisory Committee.

## Organization of Afro-American Unity

The first black militant nationalist organization to unite against black oppression and discrimination in the United States, the Organization of Afro-American Unity (OAAU) became Malcolm X's main organizational base from its founding on June 28, 1964, until his death on February 21, 1965. The OAAU was modeled on the Organization of African Unity, which Malcolm X had founded in May of 1963 in an effort to unite Africans around the world and to demand protection of their human rights. The OAAU strived to create a sense of common cause between African nations, the African diaspora, and African Americans. The organization followed a nationalist agenda, yet it engaged in various reform and social activities that appealed to many segments of the black community.

Malcolm X established the black nonsectarian nationalist organization after he left the Nation of Islam, disillusioned with its leader Elijah Muhammad's teachings. Malcolm X had already established the Muslim Mosque, Inc., a religious organization; he then established the OAAU for expressly political purposes. In 1964, Malcolm

Malcolm X addresses a national convention of Black Muslims in Chicago, February 26, 1963. *AP/Wide World Photos*

X announced the founding of the organization at the Audubon Ballroom in Harlem, an event that signaled his willingness to work more directly with the civil rights struggle. It also indicated Malcolm X's increased interest in human rights. The organization would go on to establish a working relationship with various elements of the civil rights movement.

The OAAU had strong community roots. Based in Harlem, it was active in working to improve conditions in the black ghetto. It was an advocate of black empowerment and sought to combat blacks' internalization of oppression. For this purpose, the organization mobilized communities, using voting as a tool to gain social and political power. It promoted voter registration in an effort to elect black leaders to office and to expand black political influence, and fought economic oppression by promoting rent strikes and supporting tenant organizations in their demands for better living conditions.

The OAAU also created self-defense, educational, and cultural institutions in black communities. Malcolm X and the OAAU advocated the formation of rifle clubs as part of self-defense structures for the black community, a position that distanced them from other Black Muslims. The OAAU also fought for better education for blacks. It organized school boycotts to push for quality education and created alternative schools that served not only as educational institutions but also as community cultural centers. For example, the OAAU Liberation School, modeled on southern freedom schools, taught African and African American history, political education, consumer information, and other practical skills. Both children and adults were able to enroll in classes. But even though the OAAU utilized black resources, it did not believe such measures meant the loss or renunciation of the community's right to government services and entitlements. As part of its community service, the OAAU sought to ensure that blacks received what they were entitled to from the government as citizens of the United States.

Malcolm X hoped that the OAAU would be instrumental in bringing together the diverse elements of the African unity movements. The OAAU continually struggled to gain recognition from Africans, the United Nations, and other members of the international community. International recognition, the OAAU hoped, would enable it to expose United States human rights violations to a global audience.

The OAAU also worked to unite all Africans and African Americans through information. To this end, it established an Information Bureau in Ghana, which was designed to keep Africans informed about the African American struggle against white oppression. Moreover, the Information Bureau supplied information about events and issues in African states to the African American press.

The OAAU worked to show that there was a common cause in the struggles and lives of Africans and African Americans. Despite the OAAU's efforts to foster a pan-African alliance, however, the group failed to gain international recognition and did not succeed in pressuring the United States to deal with its racial problems.

From the start, the organization suffered from internal dissensions, and it was strongly dependent on Malcolm X's leadership and charisma. Its wide-ranging goals appealed to black militants, but they alienated more traditional Muslims. As Malcolm X increasingly adopted an anticapitalist philosophy, he garnered the support of white radicals, but many African Americans were critical of him and his organization for their failure to lead a forceful attack against racial oppression. And, while the organization attempted to unite middle- and working-class blacks to work for civil and human rights without gender bias, it was unable to bring these diverse groups together; instead, it attracted the fear of the upper classes. Thus, the organization came under attack.

Its most visible target was Malcolm X, who was assassinated in 1965. Although three Black Muslims were convicted of the killings, suspicion arose that a government conspiracy existed to destroy militant black organizations. Malcolm X's death effectively ended the OAAU, since members quickly became demoralized. Ella Mae Collins, Malcolm X's sister, assumed the group's leadership after a conflict with Malcolm X's wife, Betty Shabazz. Collins, however, was unable to keep the organization alive, as members quietly left, many unwilling to work with a female leader.

The OAAU was the only group operating within the black community that sought to unite the working- and middle-class of both genders (though imperfectly), to work for human rights. Malcolm X was a strong advocate of women's involvement and he recruited Lynn Shifflet, a black producer at NBC television, to work for the OAAU. Shifflet had chaired OAAU meetings in 1964 and helped to unify the group. While the OAAU had strong pan-African links, it remained based in Harlem fighting for reform and civil rights at home and abroad until it disbanded soon after Malcom X's death.

**FURTHER READINGS**

Sales, William W., Jr. *From Civil Rights to Black Liberation*. Boston: South End Press, 1994.

Williams, Michael W., ed. *The African American Encyclopedia*. New York: Marshall Cavendish, 1997.

*Angel R. Rivera*

## Organization of Black Airline Pilots

The Organization of Black Airline Pilots (OBAP) promotes the participation of African Americans and other minorities in the commercial aviation industry, through meetings with airline industry leaders, congressional lobbying initiatives, scholarship programs initiatives, job placement services, and the compilation of statistics on airline hiring practices.

For two decades after World War II, African American pilots struggled with little success to enter the commercial air transport industry, though a handful did manage to obtain positions, such as Perry H. Young Jr. and James O. Plinton. In 1956 New York Airways, a scheduled helicopter airline, hired Young as a pilot. A year later Plinton began a career as an airline executive, and he held key positions with Trans World Airlines and Eastern Air Lines until his retirement in 1979. But despite these advances, most African American pilots met stubborn resistance when they sought employment with commercial air carriers. After pilot Marlon D. Green won an employment rights suit against Continental Airlines in the mid-1960s, major airlines began to hire qualified black pilots. Still, the number of African American commercial pilots remained disproportionately small.

In 1976, thirty-seven black airline pilots met in Chicago to address the problem. Under the leadership of Benjamin Thomas, an African American pilot with Eastern Air Lines, they formed the OBAP and dedicated themselves "to advancing and enhancing the participation of blacks and other minorities in the aviation industry, especially as pilots." Working cooperatively with other groups interested in promoting wider African American participation in aviation, such as the Tuskegee Airmen, Inc., and the Negro Airmen's Association, the OBAP initiated several programs aimed at encouraging young African Americans to prepare themselves for careers in commercial aviation.

Since its establishment, membership in the OBAP has never exceeded one thousand. The organization, headquartered in Atlanta, holds semiannual conferences and publishes a bimonthly newsletter.

**FURTHER READINGS**

Hardesty, Von, and Dominick Pisano. *Black Wings: The American Black in Aviation*. Washington, D.C.: Smithsonian Institution, 1983.

Ho, Rodney. "Pilot Inspires Others to Follow Her Lead." *Atlanta Constitution*, 25 January 1995 sec. D, p. 3.

Thurston, Scott. "Blacks Are Still Rare in the Cockpit." *Atlanta Constitution*, 20 August 1993.

U.S. House Committee on Appropriations. *Departments of Labor, Health and Human Services, Education, and Related Agencies Appropriations for 1994: Hearings before a Subcommittee of the Committee on Appropriations, Part 7, Testimony of Members of Congress and Other Interested Individuals and Organizations*. 103rd Congress, 1st session, 1993.

U.S. House Committee on Government Operations. *Discrimination Against Blacks in the Airline Industry: Joint Hearing before Certain Subcommittees of the Committee on Government Operations*. 99th Congress, 2nd session, 30 September 1986.

*Robert J. Jakeman*

**SEE ALSO**    National Airmen's Association of America; National Black Coalition of Federal Aviation, Negro Airmen International

## Organization of Black Episcopal Seminarians

In 1968 a group of black seminarians met for fellowship and prayer at the Episcopal Theological Seminary in Cambridge, Massachusetts. Such meetings offered them a unique opportunity to share their experiences as black seminarians and to discuss ways to improve their position in the church. Given the racial uneasiness in the Episcopal Church at the time, which expressed itself that same year in the founding of the Union of Black Clergy and Laity (UBCL), the seminarians decided they would benefit from continued meetings.

It was not until 1986, however, that black seminarians institutionalized their meetings and founded the Organization of Black Episcopal Seminarians (OBES) at Yale University's Berkeley Divinity School. Instrumental in the founding of OBES was Reverend Franklin Turner, now suffragan bishop of Pennsylvania. In 1975, Turner had become the first officer of the Episcopal Church's newly established Black Ministries Program, also known as the Black Desk or the Office of Black Ministries.

OBES's membership has remained small, ranging from twenty-five during its initial years to eighteen in 1998. OBES makes scholarship help available to postulants and candidates for holy orders through the trust fund generated by the Task Force for the Recruitment, Training, and Deployment of Black Clergy. Annually, scholarships are funded by the interest accumulated by the fund and not the principal. In 1997, over $51,000 in scholarship funds were distributed to black seminarians.

At an OBES meeting at the Berkeley Divinity School in April 1989, the group drafted its original mission statement: "In keeping with its founding principles, the mission of OBES continues to be advocacy for and support and training of black postulants and candidates. The group exists to encourage its members in the ordination process of this church; to affirm the black religious expression and its witness to the larger Church; to foster collegiality; and to strengthen the Christian faith of its members through prayer, study and worship."

**FURTHER READINGS**

*Mission Statement for the Organization of Black Episcopal Seminarians.* New York: Office of Black Ministries, 1989.

Rodman, Edward. *Let There Be Peace Among Us: A Story of the Union of Black Episcopalians.* Boston: n.p, 1989.

*Stephen Davenport*

**SEE ALSO** Union of Black Episcopalians

## Organization of Black Screenwriters, Inc.

Established in 1988 in Los Angeles, California, the Organization of Black Screenwriters, Inc. (OBS) is an interracial group of screenwriters devoted to increasing the number of black authors working in the Hollywood entertainment industry. The OBS assists black screenwriters in the creation of film and television scripts and helps them present their works to studio executives.

The OBS conducts an annual script competition, offers script development assistance, and maintains an agent outreach program. Its annual script competition is a national writing contest, open to full-length feature film, sitcoms, and one-hour television episode scripts. Winning scripts are circulated to top industry agents and studio executives. For a nominal fee, the OBS's script development assistance program provides black screenwriters with the opportunity to obtain professional evaluations of their manuscripts prior to studio submission. The OBS also works for writers as a referral service to the industry. Through its Agent Outreach Program, the OBS offers new and seasoned writers the opportunity to connect with more than twenty literary agencies. In addition, the OBS conducts workshops designed to guide aspiring screenplay authors through the process of writing and marketing their scripts.

Headquartered in Los Angeles, the OBS conducts bimonthly meetings and hosts an annual Brunch and Griot Awards honoring successful members. Past honorees included Charles Burnett, Spike Lee, Euzhan Palcy, and Richard Wesley for their work in film, and Yvette Lee-Bowser, Ralph Farquhar, Michael Moye, Vida Spears, and Sara Finney for their television work.

*Barbara Buice*

## Palmetto Medical, Dental, and Pharmaceutical Association

*See* Palmetto State Medical Association.

## Palmetto State Medical Association

Established in 1896 as the Palmetto Medical, Dental, and Pharmaceutical Association, the Palmetto State Medical Association was one of the first late nineteenth-century professional societies founded by black doctors, dentists, and pharmacists. The association offered its members opportunities for socializing and sharing information on new medical discoveries and techniques.

After the American Medical Association voted to exclude black physicians from membership, black doctors formed the National Medical Association in 1895. This organization extended membership to pharmacists and dentists holding professional degrees. The inclusiveness, common also in state and local black medical societies, helped build membership at a time when black medical practitioners of any kind were scarce. Segregation practices, limited numbers of medical schools that admitted blacks, and low-income potential often prevented black physicians and others in the various fields of medicine from gaining essential postgraduate education.

South Carolina medical societies barred blacks from membership. In response, Dr. C. C. Johnson of Columbia, South Carolina, encouraged the creation of an association for black medical professionals. Black doctors, R. Levy, L. A. Earle, and A. C. McClennan assisted in the creation and promotion of the Palmetto Medical, Dental, and Pharmaceutical Association. The new society divided along the state's prominent geographic regions: Piedmont, Pee Dee, and the Congaree. The various chapters held their own monthly meetings, and all met annually in April for a three-day conference sponsored by the association.

It is not known when the group simplified its name, but records indicate it continued to meet monthly until the 1960s. The organization eventually divided into four regional societies: Charleston County, the Congaree, Piedmont, and the Inter-County. A 1971 South Carolina Medical Association publication reported an approximate membership in the Palmetto State Medical Association of fifty physicians, fifty dentists, and twenty-five pharmacists. The small enrollment likely reflects changes encouraged by the integration of medical societies in the state.

### FURTHER READINGS

Gamble, Vanessa Northington. *Making a Place for Ourselves: The Black Hospital Movement, 1920–1945.* New York: Oxford University Press, 1995.

Waring, Joseph Ioor. *A History of Medicine in South Carolina, 1900–1970.* Charleston: South Carolina Medical Association, 1971.

*Peggy Hardman*

## Pan-African Conference

*See* Pan-African Congress.

## Pan-African Congress

Pan-Africanist ideals emerged in the late nineteenth century in response to European colonization and exploitation of the African continent. Pan-Africanist philosophy held that slavery and colonialism depended on and encouraged negative, unfounded categorizations of the race, culture, and values of African people. These destructive beliefs in turn gave birth to intensified forms of racism, the likes of which Pan-Africanism sought to eliminate.

As a broader political concept, Pan-Africanism's roots lie in the collective experiences of African descendants in the New World. Africa assumed greater significance for some blacks in the New World for two primary reasons. First, the increasing futility of their campaign for racial equality in the United States led some African Americans to demand voluntary repatriation to Africa. Next, for the first time the term *Africans*, which had often been used by racists as a derogatory description, became a source of pride for early black nationalists. Hence, through the conscious elevation of their African identity black activists in America and the rest of the world began to reclaim the rights previously denied them by Western societies.

In 1897, Henry Sylvester-Williams, a West Indian Barrister, formed the African Association in London to encourage Pan-African unity, especially throughout the British colonies. Sylvester-Williams, who had links with West African dignitaries, believed that Africans and those of African descent living in the Diaspora needed a forum to address their common problems. In 1900, Sylvester-Williams organized the first Pan-African meeting in collaboration with several black leaders representing various countries of the African Diaspora. For the first time, opponents of colonialism and racism gathered for an international meeting. The conference, held in London, attracted global attention, placing the word "Pan-African" in the lexicon of international affairs and making it part of the standard vocabulary of black intellectuals.

The initial meeting featured thirty delegates, mainly from England and the West Indies, but attracted only a few Africans and African Americans. Among them was black America's leading intellectual, W. E. B. Du Bois, who was to become the torchbearer of subsequent Pan-African conferences, or congresses as they later came to be called. Conference participants read papers on a variety of topics, including the social, political, and economic conditions of blacks in the Diaspora; the importance of independent nations governed by people of African descent, such as Ethiopia, Haiti, and Liberia; the legacy of slavery and European imperialism; the role of Africa in world history; and the impact of Christianity on the African continent. Perhaps of even greater significance was the formation of two committees. One group, chaired by Du Bois, drafted an address "To the Nations of the World," demanding moderate reforms for colonial Africa. The address implored the United States and the imperial European nations to "acknowledge and protect the rights of people of African descent" and to respect the integrity and independence of "the free Negro States of Abyssinia, Liberia, Haiti, etc." The address, signed by committee chairman Du Bois as well as its president Bishop Alexander Walters, its vice president Henry B. Brown, and its general secretary Sylvester-Williams, was published and sent to Queen Victoria of England. The second committee planned for the formation of a permanent Pan-African association in London with branches overseas. Despite these ambitious plans, the appeals of conference participants made little or no impression on the European imperial powers who controlled the political and economic destiny of Africa.

It was not until after World War I that Du Bois revived the Pan-African congresses. Following the war, European and American politicians gathered for a peace conference in Versailles, France. Du Bois, who attended the conference as a special representative of the National Association for the Advancement of Colored People (NAACP), appealed to President Woodrow Wilson. In a letter to Wilson, he urged the American government to initiate a comprehensive study of the treatment of black soldiers. Moreover, Du Bois expressed hope that the peace treaty would address "the future of Africa" and grant self-determination to the colonized peoples. President Wilson subsequently released a Fourteen Point memorandum, which suggested the formation a League of Nations and called for "an absolutely impartial adjustment of all colonial claims, based on the principle that the interests of the population must have equal weight with the equitable claims of the government." Although historians have questioned the impact Du Bois's request had on Wilson's Fourteen Point memorandum, it was apparent that the loudest voice on behalf of oppressed blacks in the New World and colonized Africa belonged to the participants of the Pan-African Congress.

Galvanized by the gathering of world leaders and the discussion of colonial Africa's future, Du Bois proposed the formation of a Pan-African Congress. In 1919, as the Versailles Peace treaty deliberations ran their course, Du Bois, with the support of Blaise Diagne, a member of the French Parliament from the West African colony of Senegal, and funding from African American civil rights and fraternal organizations such as the NAACP, the Elks, and the Masons, convened a Pan-African Congress in Paris. The Congress, attended by approximately sixty representatives from sixteen nations, protectorates, and colonies, however, was more "pan" than African since most of the delegates had little, if any, first-hand knowledge of the African continent. Prominent American attendees included black members of the NAACP such as John Hope, president of Morehouse College, and Addie W. Hunton, who had served with black troops in France under the auspices of the Young Men's Christian Association (YMCA), as well as white NAACP members, such as the Columbia University professor Joel Spingarn, the socialist William English Walling, and the socialist muckraking author Charles Edward Russell. Among the other delegates from the United States were Roscoe Conklin Simmons, a well-known black orator; Rayford W. Logan, who had served with the U.S. Army in France; black women's rights activist Ida Gibbs Hunt; and Dr. George Jackson, a black American missionary in the Congo.

Conference participants adopted a resolution calling for the drafting of a code of law "for the international protection of the natives of Africa." Other demands called for direct supervision of colonies by the League of Nations to prevent economic exploitation by foreign nations; to abolish slavery and capital punishment of colonial subjects who worked on the plantations of European colonial powers in Africa, especially in the Belgian Congo; and to insist on colonial peoples' right to education. Moreover, the gathering stressed the need for further congress meetings and suggested the creation of an international quarterly, the *Black Review*, which was to be published in several languages. While congress attendees insisted that African natives should be allowed eventually to participate in their own government, they did not demand African self-determination. Despite the moderate nature of the demands, the European and American powers represented at the Versailles Peace Conference remained noncommittal.

The Pan-African Congress reconvened in London in August 1921 and a month later in Brussels. Both meetings featured representatives from the Americas, the Caribbean, Europe, and Africa who echoed earlier Pan-Africanist reformist ideas, denouncing imperialism in Africa and racism in the United States. Moreover, the delegates demanded local self-government for colonial subjects and Du Bois stressed the need for increased interracial contacts between members of the black intelligentsia and those concerned about the political and economic status of colonial peoples.

In 1923, the Pan-African Congress met in two separate sessions in London and in Lisbon. Noted European intellectuals such as H. G. Wells and Harold Laski attended the London session. Several members of previous meetings participated in the deliberations that addressed the conditions of the African Diaspora as well as the global exploitation of black workers. While some scholars argue that the 1921 and 1923 congresses were effective only in keeping alive the idea of an oppressed people trying to abolish the yoke of discrimination, others claim that the international gatherings laid the foundation for the struggle that ultimately led to the political emancipation of the African continent.

Delegates reconvened for a fifth Pan-African Congress in New York in 1927. The congress featured 208 delegates from twenty-two American states and ten foreign countries. Africa, however, was represented only sparsely by delegates from the Gold Coast, Sierra Leone, Liberia, and Nigeria. The small number of African delegates was due in part to travel restrictions that the British and French colonial powers imposed on those interested in attending the congress, in an effort to inhibit further Pan-African gatherings. Most of the delegates were black Americans and many of them were women. The congress was primarily financed by Addie W. Hunton and the Women's International League for Peace and Freedom, an interracial organization that had been founded by opponents of World War I in 1919. Similar to previous Pan-African congresses, participants discussed the status and conditions of black people throughout the world.

The financial crisis induced by the Great Depression and the military exigency generated by World War II necessitated the suspension of the Pan-African Congress for a period of fifteen years. In 1945, the organized movement was revived in Manchester, England. It is unclear whether Du Bois or George Padmore, a West Indian Marxist, provided the initiative for this meeting. Recognizing Du Bois's historic contribution to the Pan-African movement, delegates named him president of the 1945 congress. The Manchester meeting marked a turning point in the history of the gatherings. For the first time representatives of political parties from Africa and the West Indies attended the meetings. Moreover, the conservative credo of the forum gave way to radical social, political, and economic demands. Congress participants unequivocally demanded an end to colonialism in Africa and urged colonial subjects to use strikes and boycotts to end the continent's social, economic, and political exploitation by colonial powers.

While previous Pan-African congresses had been controlled largely by black middle-class British and American intellectuals who had emphasized the amelioration of colonial conditions, the Manchester meeting was dominated by delegates from Africa and Africans working or studying in Britain. The new leadership attracted the support of workers, trade unionists, and a growing radical sector of the African student population. With fewer African American participants, delegates consisted mainly of an emerging crop of African intellectual and political leaders, who soon won fame, notoriety, and power in their various colonized countries.

The final declaration of the 1945 congress urged colonial and subject peoples of the world to unite and assert their rights to reject those seeking to control their destinies. Congress participants encouraged colonized Africans to elect their own governments, arguing that the gain of political power for colonial and subject peoples was a necessary prerequisite for complete social, economic, and political emancipation. This politically assertive stance was supported by a new generation of African American activists such as the actor and singer Paul Robeson, the minister and politician Adam Clayton Powell, and the educator and political activist William A. Hunton Jr. who took an increasing interest in Africa.

While the Pan-African congresses lacked financial and political power, they helped to increase international awareness of racism and colonialism and laid the foundation for the political independence of African nations. African leaders such as Kwame Nkrumah of Ghana, Nnamdi Azikiwe of Nigeria, and Jomo Kenyatta of Kenya were among several attendees of congresses who subsequently led their countries to political independence. In May 1963, the influence of these men helped galvanize the formation of the Organization of African Unity (OAU), an association of independent African states and nationalist groups.

### FURTHER READINGS

Esedebe, Olisanwube P. *Pan-Africanism: The Idea and the Movement.* Washington, D.C.: Howard University Press, 1982.

Geiss, Immanuel. *The Pan-African Movement.* London: Methuen and Co., Ltd., 1974.

Langley, J. Ayodele. *Ideologies of Liberation in Black Africa, 1857–1970: Documents on Modern African Political Thought from Colonial Times to the Present.* London: R. Collings, 1979.

Legum, Collin. *Pan Africanism: A Short Political Guide.* New York: Frederick Praeger, 1962.

Lewis, David Levering. *W.E.B. Du Bois: Biography of a Race, 1869–1919.* New York: Henry Holt and Co., 1993.

Plummer, Brenda Gayle. *Rising Wind: Black Americans and U.S. Foreign Affairs, 1935–1960.* Chapel Hill: The University of North Carolina Press, 1996.

Von Eschen, Penny M. *Race Against Empire: Black Americans and Anticolonialism, 1937–1957.* Ithaca, N.Y.: Cornell University Press, 1997.

*Saheed A. Adejumobi*

## Pan-Hellenic Council

*See* National Pan-Hellenic Council, Inc.

## Partners for Progress

This Atlanta-based biracial women's committee was organized in March 1964 to support equal opportunity in business, government, and community affairs through cooperative activities of women's civic, cultural, professional, and religious groups. Affiliated with the National Women's Committee on Civil Rights, Partners for Progress focused primarily on encouraging compliance with the provisions of the 1964 civil rights bill through the auspices of Operation Compliance, a civil rights project sponsored by the Southern Regional Council of Atlanta, Georgia, and the Potomac Institute of Washington, D.C. Prior to the passage of the Civil Rights Act, Partners for Progress organized visits, letters, and telephone calls to places of public accommodation, urging a voluntary open-door policy. The group launched various projects including a letter-writing campaign to administrators of hospitals, urging the desegregation of medical facilities and services, and a court visitation program investigating discrimination in the legal system. Moreover, Partners for Progress appealed to colleges and universities urging schools to increase their course offerings on human relations and to make them available to community residents. As part of the Georgia Women for Progress, the group also helped secure signatures for a testimonial presented to Governor Sanders, applauding his support of programs designed to provide Georgians with equal opportunity. Partners for Progress also investigated preschool educational opportunities for underprivileged children and published newsletters to inform its members about progress in education, housing, employment, and community relations. The group apparently ceased to function by the late 1960s.

FURTHER READING

Southern Regional Council Papers, Special Collections, Robert W. Woodruff Library, Atlanta University Center, Atlanta, Georgia.

*Kimberly E. Nichols*

## Peabody Education Fund

George Peabody, a New England merchant and banker, established the Peabody Education Fund in 1867. The Fund was the first of several educational philanthropic foundations established by northern industrialists and entrepreneurs between 1867 and 1917. Convinced that education was instrumental to reconciling the North and South during the Reconstruction period, Peabody chartered the fund to encourage "intellectual, moral and industrial education" in the South and Southwest by stabilizing the public education system and fostering the growth of common schools. The fund's ultimate goal of increasing the number and contributing to the effectiveness of southern normal schools culminated in the establishment of Central Normal College of the South, later renamed Peabody Normal College, in Nashville, Tennessee, in 1875.

Peabody's original charge to the board of trustees, accompanied by an initial gift of bonds worth more than $1 million, directed that the benefits be distributed "among the entire population without other distinction than needs and opportunities of usefulness." The fund's interest in African American schooling, however, was incidental to its support of public schools in general. Unconcerned with issues of racial equality, the fund's initial priorities included the support of a permanent system of public education that was to be organized, controlled, and supervised by the individual southern states; the granting of scholarships to students who were preparing to be teachers; and the promotion of the Hampton-Tuskegee program of industrial education for blacks. During the first year of the fund's activity, the trustees expended $4,000 in support of schools "for colored children" in North Carolina and Georgia. By 1871, the fund had adopted a differential pattern of assistance of public schools based on school population and racial composition. Operating under the assumption that it cost less to maintain schools for African Americans than for whites, the fund allocated to black schools two-thirds of the amount of aid given to white schools.

During the 1880s, the fund turned its attention to the establishment of normal schools and the training of teachers. Barnas Sears, who served as the fund's first general agent from 1868 to 1880, had previously worked as secretary of the Board of Education of Massachusetts. Convinced that effective teaching necessitated pedagogical training, he recommended that the fund support normal schools, particularly those that provided training for female teachers in primary schools. In cooperation with the state departments of public instruction, the fund assisted black normal schools and provided scholarships for students enrolled in teacher-training programs at historically black colleges. Moreover, the fund subsidized Teachers' Institutes to provide training for practicing teachers. The work of the fund was enhanced by its association with other educational, philanthropic funds such as the General Education Board and the John F. Slater Fund, the latter of which was devoted solely to the support of black education. Jabez L. M. Curry, who succeeded Sears as the general agent in 1881, assumed the role of field agent for both the Peabody and Slater Funds after 1890.

In 1911, the General Education Board assumed support of the fund's various state agents. The Peabody Fund's last direct activity in the field of black education occurred in 1914, when it contributed $350,000 to the Slater Fund.

FURTHER READINGS

Bane, E. B. *The Administration of the Peabody Education Fund from 1880–1905.* Nashville, Tenn.: George Peabody College for Teachers, 1936.

Curry, J. L. M. *A Brief Sketch of George Peabody and a History of the Peabody Education Fund through Thirty Years.* 1898; rpt., New York: Negro Universities Press, 1969.

Dillingham, George A. *The Foundation of the Peabody Tradition.* Lanham, Md.: University Press of America, 1989.

Leavell, Ullin W. *Philanthropy in Negro Education.* 1930; rpt., Westport, Conn.: Negro Universities Press, 1970.

Peabody Education Fund, Inc., Papers, Southern Education Foundation, Atlanta, Georgia.

Taylor, Hoy. *An Interpretation of the Early Administration of the Peabody Education Fund.* Nashville, Tenn.: George Peabody College for Teachers, 1933.

*Jayne R. Beilke*

**SEE ALSO**   Southern Education Foundation

## Peabody Fund
*See* Peabody Education Fund.

## Peace and Freedom Party

The Peace and Freedom Party (PFP) was established by Robert Scheer in the San Francisco Bay Area in 1966. It was the product of a union between white anti–Vietnam War protestors and the Black Panther Party. The PFP was dedicated primarily to ending the war in Vietnam but, as a result of its alliance with the Panthers, it also advocated black liberation.

In November 1967, a sound truck promoting the PFP's ideals caught the attention of the Black Panther Eldridge Cleaver. On December 22, 1967, he announced a coalition between the Black Panther Party and the PFP. First and foremost, the Panthers wanted to create a broad base of support for one of their leaders, Huey Newton, who had been jailed on October 28, 1967, on charges of shooting one police officer and killing another. Cleaver recognized that the PFP, largely composed of whites, had the administrative, publicity, and fund-raising skills necessary to help defend Newton. The PFP was to provide money for Newton's defense, which it did, raising at least three thousand dollars. In exchange the Panthers agreed to help the party register for elections by collecting signatures in predominantly black neighborhoods.

Key to the agreement between the two radical organizations was the understanding that the Black Panthers would control all aspects of the party's platform that affected African Americans. The Panthers refused to serve what they viewed as white interests, in part because they regarded themselves as the vanguard of a coming socialist revolution. The Panthers also insisted that the alliance with the PFP would cease, once it no longer furthered the cause of black liberation. White party members agreed not to campaign in black ghettos and left Cleaver in charge of the party's position on black issues.

PFP founder Scheer supported Cleaver's conditions, hoping that the publicity gained from running Panther members for office would increase the party's following. The coalition was successful and gathered enough signatures to get the party on the ballot. At the party's 1968 convention in Chicago, the PFP decided to run Cleaver as its write-in presidential candidate in California and other large states. Cleaver, who had promised to paint the White House black and burn it, did not appeal to all PFP members. Supporters of the activist and comedian Dick Gregory broke with the PFP, founded the Freedom and Peace Party, and nominated Gregory as their presidential candidate. Meanwhile, the PFP also ran the Freedom Summer veteran Mario Savio for the California State Senate, two Black Panthers—Kathleen Cleaver and Bobby Seale—for the California Assembly, and the imprisoned Huey Newton for California's Seventh Congressional District. Although Newton polled an amazing 7 percent of the vote, none of the PFP candidates were elected.

The electoral failure led the Black Panthers to turn away from working with radical white organizations. While the coalition between the Panthers and the PFP lasted only from 1967 to 1969, the party continues to be active in California.

**FURTHER READINGS**

Heath, G. Louis. *Off the Pigs: The History and Literature of the Black Panther Party.* Metuchen, N.J.: Scarecrow Press, 1976.

Newton, Michael. *Bitter Gain: The Story of the Black Panther Party.* Los Angeles: Holloway House, 1980.

*Bryan Bartlett Jarmusch*

**SEE ALSO**    Black Panther Party (for Self-Defense); Freedom and Peace Party

## Peace Mission Movement

The Peace Mission Movement (PMM), an interracial religious organization based on a philosophy of spiritual, economic, and social uplift, provided work relief and assistance during the Great Depression of the 1930s. Led by African American minister Father Divine, the PMM drew predominantly blacks but also whites from a variety of backgrounds into an organization devoted to social and political change. During its heyday in the 1930s, the movement attracted at least 50,000 core members and a much larger number of sympathizers who maintained an interest in its programs and leader.

An outgrowth of the evangelical activities of Father Divine, the PMM is best understood in relationship to his career and unique theology. Born George Baker in 1879 in the town of Rockville, Maryland, he left home and his struggling family just before 1900 to embark on a ministry in the storefront churches of Baltimore. Before long he fashioned a syncretic theology based on a variety of American religious trends including black religious traditions, Catholicism, Protestantism, Pentecostalism, and New Thought, an ideology advocating God's internal presence and positive thinking. Blending these elements, he articulated a belief system based on the idea that God's spirit dwelled within all persons and that by channeling His presence one could overcome all adversity and secure health, wealth, and success. He also advocated racial equality, contending that positive thinking eradicated racial discrimination. But what made his beliefs so controversial was the notion that he actually was God. Determined to spread his teachings, he departed Baltimore in 1912, preaching in the South for several years. Despite various brushes with the law and some close calls with lynch mobs, he attracted a small group of black followers, marrying one of them, Peninnah. This group formed the original core of the PMM.

In 1917, he settled with his flock in New York City. Two years later, members of the group pooled their earnings and purchased a home in a white neighborhood in the town of Sayville on Long Island. There the band lived collectively, supplying the local community with inexpensive, honest, and hardworking domestics and laborers and, as a result, securing the respect of their neighbors. This harmonious relationship continued until word of Father Divine's teachings spread, drawing increasing numbers of followers to his home by the early 1930s. His worship service, consisting of banquets with endless courses, drew many, while others, including a significant number of white New Thought adherents, came to learn about his philosophy. Father Divine's ability to provide jobs, food, and clothing during the depths of the Depression, combined with his alleged capacity to heal the sick, brought the destitute, the suffering, and the curious. Interestingly, he consistently refused to proclaim publicly that he was God, insisting that it was his followers who recognized him as divine. And many African American followers happily celebrated the concept of a black God.

In 1932, neighbors, alarmed by the growing crowds in his home and the interracial nature of his following, launched a campaign against Father Divine that culminated in his arrest and a jail term for maintaining a public nuisance. After his incarceration, he relocated to Harlem, and the PMM rapidly grew benefiting in part from the publicity generated by the Long Island clash.

Yet, the group's practices induced many, both black and white, to view the movement with suspicion and contempt. Disciples organized hostels for followers in many of the large cities in the United States. The devout relinquished familial ties, changed their names, and moved into quarters that were racially integrated but segregated by gender. Father Divine demanded that followers practice celibacy; he claimed that his marriage was purely spiritual. Disciples adhered to strict linguistic codes, substituting "Peace" for "Hello" and never referring to individuals by race. Father Divine demanded they abstain from alcohol, smoking, and drugs. He taught that a healthy lifestyle and positive thinking led to immortality. Finally, followers were expected to work and many joined together to open cooperative businesses, hotels, and restaurants.

While Peace Mission enterprises were popular for their excellent service and prices, the movement found itself frequently under attack, especially by those opposed to racial equality. Father Divine's teachings on race, based on the notion that race was a construct not of reality but of negative thinking, disturbed many whites. Undaunted by threats from white supremacists, followers campaigned for federal antilynching legislation, demonstrated against segregation and discrimination, and organized a nationwide voter registration drive targeting disfranchised African Americans. In 1936, they organized the Righteous Government Department that sponsored voter education and registration and several conventions that were unsuccessful in compelling politicians to endorse Father Divine's social, political, and economic programs and recognize his divinity.

Late in the decade, scandals rocked the PMM. Several key followers defected, one writing an exposé claiming that Father Divine engaged in debauchery, others filing court cases seeking monetary damages from him. A wealthy white follower, charged with kidnapping and transporting a minor across state lines for sexual purposes, brought a barrage of unflattering attention from the national media which viewed the PMM predominantly as a dangerous religious cult. In an effort to protect the movement, Father Divine consolidated extensions and businesses of the PMM under the Unity Mission Church, Palace Mission Church, and the Circle Mission Church, and he required that all branches report directly to him. Additionally, he required followers to join one of three orders each with distinctive uniforms and rigid requirements for admission.

In 1942, to escape a judgment against him by the New York courts, Father Divine relocated his headquarters to Philadelphia. The public scandals, the end of the Depression, and the institutionalization of the movement induced a decline in membership. The movement downsized its social relief programs and focused increasingly on maintaining its businesses and studying Father Divine's philosophy. In the late 1950s and early 1960s, Father Divine's public appearances became increasingly infrequent, and in September 1965 he passed away. Followers denied his death, explaining that he surrendered his physical body but remained present spiritually. The PMM continued under the leadership of his second wife Edna Rose Ritchings (know as Sweet Angel), a white woman whom he claimed was the reincarnation of his first wife who had died in the 1940s. Despite diminishing membership numbers in the 1990s, the movement continued to hold worship services and maintain properties and businesses in the northeastern United States.

### FURTHER READINGS

Burham, Kenneth. *God Comes to America: Father Divine.* Boston: Lambeth Press, 1979.

Watts, Jill. *God, Harlem U.S.A.: The Father Divine Story.* Berkeley: University of California Press, 1992.

Weisbrot, Robert. *Father Divine and the Struggle for Racial Equality.* Urbana: University of Illinois Press, 1983.

*Jill Watts*

## Pennsylvania Freedmen's Relief Association

The Pennsylvania Freedmen's Relief Association operated from March 5, 1862 to mid-1871 to assist the freed slaves of the American South during and after the Civil War. The association provided food, clothing, medicine, and other relief supplies during the war, but most of its efforts throughout its existence were aimed at providing teachers and schools for the freed people.

Organized originally as the Port Royal Relief Committee, the association initially focused its efforts on the Sea Islands around Port Royal, South Carolina. It changed its name to the Pennsylvania Freedmen's Relief Association (PFRA) in July 1862. James Miller McKim, a prominent Garrisonian abolitionist, was instrumental in organizing the association. Stephen Colwell and Matthias W. Baldwin, wealthy manufacturers from Philadelphia, were among its principal financial supporters, and Colwell served as its president for much of its existence.

The PFRA was an entirely voluntary organization, dependent upon benevolent donations for its work. To assist with fund-raising, the organization began publishing the *Pennsylvania Freedmen's Bulletin* in 1865. Published irregularly, the last number appeared in early 1868. The association was consistently a leader in the effort to forge a national organization of secular freedmen's aid associa-

tions, resulting in 1866 in the creation of the American Freedmen's Union Commission. It encouraged the formation of the Baltimore Association for the Moral and Educational Improvement of the Colored People and the Pittsburgh Freedmen's Relief Association. It was the first freedmen's aid society to create normal schools (teacher training institutions) in the South for African American students.

By 1865, the PFRA had moved well beyond its initial work in South Carolina. In that year it supported over sixty teachers in four states and the District of Columbia. By 1869 the number of PFRA-sponsored teachers had grown to 150, primarily working in Maryland and Virginia, along with fewer in the District of Columbia, North and South Carolina, Tennessee, Alabama, and Mississippi. In total, the association supported nearly 280 teachers, at least fifty of whom were African Americans. Between 1862 and 1869 the association raised over $268,000 to support southern black education.

The best known of the schools supported by the association was the Penn School on St. Helena Island, South Carolina. In 1865, the association sent a prefabricated schoolhouse to the island in which Laura M. Towne and Ellen Murray (both white) were to teach for the next three and a half decades. With the demise of the PFRA, a handful of benevolent patrons and Towne's family continued to support the school. After the deaths of Towne and Murray in 1901 and 1908, respectively, the school shifted its focus from academic education to industrial training, continuing to educate African Americans until 1948.

Like many of its counterparts, particularly among the secular freedmen's aid societies, the PFRA declined rapidly after 1869, and it dissolved sometime in 1871. Northern benevolent support for freedmen's education peaked in 1866 and 1867, declining quickly thereafter; some support shifted to the ecclesiastical freedmen's aid societies with their more racially conservative practices and ideas. When relatively generous support from the Freedmen's Bureau ended in 1870, the PFRA could no longer sustain its efforts.

### FURTHER READINGS

Butchart, Ronald E. *Northern Schools, Southern Blacks, and Reconstruction: Freedmen's Education, 1862–1875.* Westport, Conn.: Greenwood Press, 1980.

———. "Recruits to the 'Army of Civilization': Gender, Race, Class, and the Freedmen's Teachers, 1862–1875." *Journal of Education* 172, 3 (1990): 76–87.

Holland, Rupert Sargent, ed. *Letters and Diary of Laura M. Towne, Written from the Sea Islands of South Carolina, 1862–1884.* Cambridge, Mass.: Riverside Press, 1912.

Parmelee, Julius H. "Freedmen's Aid Societies, 1861–1871." In *Negro Education: A Study of the Private and Higher Schools for Colored People in the U.S.* Ed. Thomas Jesse Jones. U.S. Department of the Interior. Bureau of Education Bulletin No. 38, 1916. Washington, D.C.: U.S. Government Printing Office, 1917.

*Ronald E. Butchart*

# People United to Save Humanity

People United to Save Humanity, later known as People United to Serve Humanity (PUSH), was a black economic rights movement founded by Jesse Jackson in 1971. Jackson launched PUSH after the Southern Christian Leadership Conference (SCLC) had suspended him for sixty days from his post as director of Operation Breadbasket for organizing Chicago's "Black Expo," a black trade fair, under a separate corporation rather than under the aegis of the SCLC. Jackson subsequently resigned from both organizations and launched Operation PUSH, which grew to comprise about seventy chapters with over 80,000 members. Concerned that civil rights, without economic advancement, would be worthless, PUSH was initially formed to impress on the business and financial communities the need for economic parity for African Americans.

On December 18, 1971, Jackson addressed an audience of 4,000 blacks at the Metropolitan Theater on Dr. Martin Luther King Drive in Chicago and announced that Operation PUSH would be "officially born" on Christmas Day, when it would be "delivered by the soul saint." He declared: "Santa Claus delivers gifts on Christmas and leaves you in debt for the rest of the year. The soul saint's gift [PUSH] will help get us out of debt." More specifically, Jackson noted that "the problems of the seventies are economic, so the solution and goal must be economic." He also described the new organization as a "rainbow coalition" of whites and blacks that would "push for a greater share of economic and political power for all people in America in the spirit of Dr. Martin Luther King, Jr." (Fishel and Quarles, p. 577).

Continuing and expanding on his earlier Operation Breadbasket role as self-appointed ambassador to corporate America, Jackson threatened that PUSH would boycott selected firms if they did not provide economic opportunities for African Americans. Within a remarkably short time, Operation PUSH, under Jackson's charismatic leadership, developed into a nationally known and widely respected civil rights organization. Two years after the formation of PUSH, Jackson toured the country and mobilized a demonstration in Memphis to mark the sixth anniversary of Dr. King's assassination. In an article entitled "Completing the Agenda of Dr. King", which he wrote for *Ebony* magazine, Jackson asserted: "We in PUSH are about the serious business of resurrecting the agenda for which Dr. King gave his life—to 'Save the Worker' (Fishel and Quarles, pp. 578–579). The threefold goal of our movement . . . is to secure the jobs of those already working (that has to be where we hold the line), to get the unemployed employed, and to get those working but not making a livable wage organized. That has to be the three-pronged thrust of our Civil Economics Movement."

Jackson also anticipated his later National Rainbow Coalition with the statement that "the enlightened strategy" for building a mass movement required the formation of "coalitions at the local community level around issues, regardless of ethnicity." He envisioned "blacks in cooperation with Mexican Americans (Chicanos), Puerto Ricans, 'American Indians,' [and] Asian Americans," all of whom had "also experienced much of the 'benign neglect' that has been our experience, and who seek a constructive way out of the present crisis . . . . The multi-ethnic coalition we propose must mobilize around a New Agenda of economic rights." Operation PUSH, Jackson promised, would not be a "one-issue organization."

The preamble to the original Operation PUSH platform stated: "We, the People United to Save Humanity, believe that humanity will be saved and served only when justice is done for all people. We believe that we must challenge the economic, political, and social forces that make us subservient to others; and that we must assume the power (of being) given us by the Power of God. We believe that our worth as humane people is expressed in our united efforts to secure justice for all persons." The fifteen declared goals of Operation PUSH included "a comprehensive economic plan for the development of Black and poor people"; "human alternatives to the welfare system"; "the revival of the labor movement to protect organized workers and to organize unorganized workers"; "a survival Bill of Rights for the aging, guaranteeing adequate food, clothing, shelter, medical care and meaningful programs"; and "quality education regardless of race, religion or creed." Point fifteen of the platform announced the overall aim of "PUSH for black excellence," an aim later incorporated in the "self-help" PUSH-Excel program of 1975, which attempted to instill a sense of pride and purpose in young high school students, encourage disciplined study, and promote parent teacher cooperation. By the late 1970s, PUSH-Excel had been adopted by several major metropolitan school districts, including Buffalo and Rochester, N.Y., Chattanooga, Kansas City, Chicago, and Denver. In 1981, *Newsweek* magazine praised Jackson and PUSH-Excel for reaching into inner-city schools and motivating their pupils.

Like Operation Breadbasket, PUSH deployed the strategies of negotiations directed at affecting the policies of major corporations and of organized mass consumer boycotts mounted against offending companies. Its main tactic was to conclude "corporate covenants" by which defaulting companies pledged themselves to remedial action. In 1972, PUSH signed an agreement with the Schlitz Brewing Company stipulating that African Americans would constitute 15 percent of its work force, and black businesses would receive 15 percent of the company's advertising, construction, and insurance expenditures. Another agreement with the General Foods Corporation increased the company's employment of African Americans and contracts with black businesses. In 1981, the Coca-Cola Company signed a "covenant" agreeing to spend $14 million with minority vendors. Within a year the company exceeded its goal by more than 22 percent. Coca-Cola also sold thirty-two fountain-syrup franchises to African Americans and promised to increase its black management staff from 5 percent to 12.5 percent. When the CBS-TV affiliate in Chicago replaced an African American anchor man with a white anchor who had been working in New York, Jackson and PUSH organized a successful boycott of the station, which also appointed a black manager in 1986.

In June 1982, PUSH persuaded the 7-Up Corporation to sign a $61 million "covenant" to invest capital in black business enterprises. The agreement stipulated that the corporation would invest $10 million in black-owned 7-Up franchises, $5 million in black-owned life insurance companies, and $4.35 million in advertisements to be carried by black-owned radio stations and newspapers. The following year, the Burger King Corporation signed a covenant worth $450 million, under the terms of which it agreed to hire more African American employees and managers, to upgrade its restaurant facilities in black neighborhoods, and to deposit funds in black-owned banks.

Despite their wide publicity, PUSH's "covenants" did little to reduce the black urban unemployment of the 1970s and 1980s, and some of the companies involved either reneged on their agreements or repudiated them entirely. Not unlike the African American leader Booker T. Washington who, earlier in the century, had attempted to promote black capitalism as a solution to the "race problem," Jackson sought accommodation with rather than the destruction of the free enterprise system. Thus the response of PUSH to job losses by African American workers in the automobile industry was to purchase one hundred stock shares in Chrysler, General Motors, American Motors, and Ford. Jackson argued that the investment would "assure us the right and platform to voice our concerns" within the auto industry.

By the mid-1970s, PUSH was in financial difficulties, with debts of $400,000, and was facing an Internal Revenue Service investigation. Following the election of Ronald Reagan, the fortunes of PUSH began to decline even further. A federal audit of PUSH's finances resulted in a demand for the repayment of over $56,000, and the administration released a report, commissioned by the Department of Education, which was highly critical of PUSH-Excel's efforts to revive inner-city schools. The investigation also revealed that PUSH-Excel had accepted payments totaling $200,000 from the Arab League and that PUSH itself had received $10,000 from a Libyan diplomat in 1979.

During its twelve years of operations, PUSH had received over $17 million in grants and subsidies from private and corporate donations. Government agencies had awarded PUSH-Excel over $6 million in grants and contracts for its programs in African American communities but the organization had failed to account adequately for the disbursement of funds. Eventually, PUSH was forced to pay a $500,000 fine, imposed by the Reagan administration, as settlement of a claim for $1.4 million.

In 1984, Jackson resigned from his leadership of PUSH as he launched his first presidential campaign, and the organization declined rapidly in membership and influence. As Marshall Frady suggests, PUSH had been essentially "a reconstitution of [Operation] Breadbasket's program of economic militancy widened into a more general social ministry," and was "a curious montage of assorted ad-hoc social initiatives with churchly inflections." Despite its elaborate structure, PUSH was an organization geared to the promotion of Jackson's political ambitions and presidential aspirations. Conceived as a multiracial coalition that would mobilize the political and economic power of America's poor, PUSH became a vehicle for Jackson's campaigns against violence, drugs, teenage delinquency, and "underachievement." Despite its successes, charges of financial irresponsibility cast shadows on Jackson's involvement with PUSH and its predecessor, Operation Breadbasket.

**FURTHER READINGS**

Colton, Elizabeth O. *The Jackson Phenomenon: The Man, the Power, the Message.* New York: Doubleday, 1989.

Fishel, Leslie H., Jr. and Benjamin Quarles, eds. *The Black American: A Documentary History,* 3d edition. Glenville, Ill.: Scott, Foresman, and Co., 1970.

Frady, Marshall. *Jesse: The Life and Pilgrimage of Jesse Jackson.* New York: Random House, 1996.

Reynolds, Barbara A. *Jesse Jackson: The Man, the Movement, the Myth.* Chicago: Nelson-Hall, 1975.

*John White*

## People United to Serve Humanity

*See* People United to Save Humanity.

## Phelps-Stokes Fund

The Phelps-Stokes Fund was established in 1911 when Caroline Phelps Stokes, granddaughter of Anson Green Phelps who had been president of the New York State Colonization Society and instrumental in the establishment of the Republic of Liberia, bequeathed $800,000 for the education of African Americans, native Americans, poor whites, and Africans. During the first decade of the fund's existence, it concentrated on financially aiding black schools and colleges and improving race relations in the southern United States. By the early 1930s, the fund's initiatives had broadened to include black education and race relations in Africa. While the fund's financial resources were relatively modest, compared to other philanthropic funds established during the early twentieth century, its impact on American education was disproportionate to its resources.

The fund's influential role stemmed from its sponsorship and publication of landmark educational studies conducted by white scholars, including the field work of Thomas Jesse Jones, the fund's education director. Jones conducted a survey of 791 black educational institutions in the South that was published by the federal government in 1916. The survey documented the per capita amount of public funds spent on black and white educa-tion in every county south of the Mason-Dixon line. Many African Americans found the report to be highly objectionable because Jones concluded that on the basis of his findings only three historically black institutions—Howard University, Fisk University, and Meharry Medical College—merited the designation of "college." Black intellectuals also criticized Jones's report for advocating industrial, agricultural, and moral education rather than academic education for African Americans. Despite this criticism, the fund concurred with Jones's conclusions and sought to implement his recommendations. Following a policy of gradualism and accommodation, the fund aided black colleges and high schools that were patterned after the Hampton-Tuskegee model while working through the southern white political system. The fund supported similar educational goals in Africa following the publication of *Education in Africa* (1922) and *Education in East Africa* (1924). Although only partially funded by the Phelps-Stokes Fund, Lewis Meriam's *The Problem of Indian Administration* (1928) extended the fund's educational philosophy to include Native Americans. Meriam, who was affiliated with the Institute for Government Research, conducted a comprehensive survey of Indian reservations, agencies, hospitals, schools, and communities. Similar to Jones, Meriam recommended that educational efforts emphasize vocational training, with the goal of preparing Native Americans for assimilation into white society.

Not until after World War II did the fund retreat from its emphasis on industrial training. In 1946, the fund contributed nearly $18,000 toward the publication of the *Encyclopedia of the Negro,* whose editorial board included some of America's leading black scholars such as Monroe Work, W. E. B. Du Bois, and Alain Locke. Perhaps this policy shift was due to a change in the fund's leadership, as a growing number of African Americans were elected to its board of trustees during the 1940s. In 1945, Dr. Channing H. Tobias became the fund's first black director and the first African American to serve in such a position in any white philanthropic fund. He left the fund in 1953 to become chairman of the board of the National Association for the Advancement of Colored People (NAACP). Tobias was succeeded by Frederick Douglass Patterson, who was instrumental in the formation of the United Negro College Fund.

During the turbulent 1960s, the fund held largely to its original objectives of educational improvement for African Americans, Africans, and Native Americans and the publication of reference works. In 1966, the fund published the *American Negro Reference Work*, which celebrated the accomplishments of African Americans. By 1970, now under the leadership of Franklin H. Williams, the fund's educational agenda included seminars, scholarships for African scholars, lecture series that featured black intellectuals, and scholar exchange programs. The fund also provided staff development for Head Start trainers, financed the production of documentary television programs focusing attention on social problems such at-risk children, and granted emergency loans to African scholars studying in the United States.

Since 1989, the fund has been guided by a commitment to "Education for Human Development" and supports programmatic initiatives, the Center for Human Development, and the Phelps-Stokes Institute. Programmatic activities include the African Student Advisory Project that provides financial support for unsponsored African undergraduates who are attending U.S. colleges; postsecondary scholarship programs for students from South Africa and Namibia; the Bishop Desmond Tutu Southern African Refugee Scholarship Fund; and the Intervention Exchange Program for international scholars. The Center for Human Development concentrates on education for minorities, including the dispensation of grants-in-aid which provide scholarship support to the twenty-six institutions of the American Indian College Fund that was begun with the fund's assistance in 1987. The Phelps-Stokes Institute, the research division of the fund, conducts studies of African, African American, and American Indian education and disseminates its findings through conferences, symposia, and seminars. After Williams's death in 1990, the fund was headed by Wilbert J. Lemelle. Headquartered in New York City, the Phelps-Stokes Fund is a nonprofit foundation governed by a volunteer board of trustees.

**FURTHER READINGS**

Berman, Edward H. "Education in Africa and America: A History of the Phelps-Stokes Fund, 1911–1945." Ed. D. diss., Teachers College, Columbia University, 1970.

Phelps-Stokes Fund Papers. The Foundation Center Historical Foundation Collection. Ruth Lilly Special Collections and Archives, University Library, Indiana University–Purdue University at Indianapolis, Indiana.

Stokes, Anson Phelps. *Negro Status and Race Relations in the United States, 1911–1946: The Thirty-Five Year Report of the Phelps-Stokes Fund.* New York: Phelps-Stokes Fund, 1948.

*Jayne R. Beilke*

# Phi Beta Sigma

On January 9, 1914, A. Langston Taylor, Leonard Morse, and Charles Brown founded Phi Beta Sigma Fraternity, Inc., at Howard University in Washington, D.C. Sigma is an international social and service organization, committed to academic excellence as well as service to the black community. The group's motto, "Culture for Service and Service for Humanity," reflects this dual function.

Like other African American Greek-lettered fraternities and sororities, Sigma has a wealth of successful and inspired professionals among its members, including Kwame Nkrumah, the first president of Ghana; Alain Leroy Locke, the first African American Rhodes scholar; Huey P. Newton, founder of the Black Panther party; Blair Underwood, actor and producer; Dr. George Washington Carver, scientist; Reverend Benjamin Chavis, organizer of the Million Man March; James Weldon Johnson, poet and author of the *Negro National Anthem*; Walter Turnbull, founder and director of the Harlem Boys Choir; Edolphus Towns, Democratic representative from New York; and the late William Tolbert, president of Liberia.

Sigma is the only predominantly African American fraternity with official ties to a sister organization, Zeta Phi Beta Sorority, Inc. This organizational framework provides members with greater opportunities for networking and service as well as access to greater financial resources to implement the civic agendas of both groups. In addition to its affiliation with Zeta, the fraternity has maintained membership in the National Pan-Hellenic Council, Inc. (NPHC) since 1931. In keeping with the ideals expressed by the NPHC, Sigma recently launched a program called OAKS, which is designed to increase partnerships among fellow fraternal members of Omega Psi Phi, Alpha Phi Alpha, Kappa Alpha Psi, and Phi Beta Sigma.

While the primary focus of Sigma's social action agenda is to improve the plight of African American men, the fraternity's civic plan historically focuses on three areas. Sigma's Bigger and Better Business program promotes minority-owned businesses, its Social Action program addresses social problems that affect the African American community, and its Education program supports minority youth education through mentoring partnerships and financial support. One of its most important programs, the Sigma-Beta Club, provides role models, mentors, and scholarships to boys and young men ages six through nineteen.

Sigma also supports the initiatives of other organizations. In the past the organization has supported the

March of Dimes through a program entitled SATAP (Sigmas Against Teenage Pregnancy); Africare, to lobby for African Aid in Washington, D.C.; the National Association for the Advancement of Colored People (NAACP); the National Urban League (NUL); Head Start; and the National Boys Club of America. Most recently, it hosted the headquarters for the Million Man March at its own International Headquarters in Washington, D.C. Other initiatives sponsored by local chapters include health forums, fundraisers for local charities, hands-on assistance such as soup kitchens for the homeless and renovations of buildings, and campaigns to increase awareness and support of social issues.

Sigma is a lifetime membership organization that hosts over 300 graduate and undergraduate chapters throughout North America, Africa, Europe, and the Caribbean. A private, nonprofit organization, it is governed by a national board of elected and appointed officials. The organization is managed by a national executive director with the assistance of a paid staff who work at the international headquarters in Washington, D.C. The organization is multitiered with local, state, regional, and national chapters. Members conduct business and engage in social activities at annual regional conventions and biannual national conventions.

Sigma, like other predominantly African American Greek-lettered organizations, provides social, financial, and educational support to its members and the African American community. In the absence of efficient and fully funded social service agencies that address problems relevant to African Americans, these organizations fill a huge void and prevent the further degradation of black communities.

### FURTHER READINGS

"Spotlight." *The Crescent: The Official Publication of Phi Beta Sigma Fraternity, Inc.* 76, 1 (Winter 1995–96): 2–4.

Whitaker, Charles F. "Phi Beta Sigma: Seventy-eight-year-old Brotherhood Builds on its Legacy of Academic Excellence and Community Service." *Ebony* 47, 5 (March 1992): 54–56.

———. "Black Greek-Lettered Organizations: Cross-Roads of Existence?" *The Crescent: The Official Publication of Phi Beta Sigma, Inc.* 76, 1 (Winter 1995–1996): 35–38.

———. "Phi Beta Sigma: Brothers of the Dove." *Houston News Pages,* February 9–15, 1995, 5.

*Julie S. Doar*

## Philadelphia: Civic, Literary, and Mutual Aid Associations

African Americans took collective steps to improve their condition early, and nowhere was this more apparent than in Philadelphia. Although there are earlier instances of group activity, a notable event occurred in 1786 when a group of African Americans petitioned for a portion of public space to be set aside and established as a burial place for their people. At that time there were no black churches in Philadelphia, and few white churches permitted African Americans to be interred in their burial grounds. Consequently, the final resting places of most people of color were in unmarked, public burial grounds.

Attempts of African Americans to care for their own in a number of ways is evidenced by the proliferation of civic, literary, and mutual aid societies that were established in Philadelphia as early as 1787 with the founding of the Free African Society. This society, composed of African Americans and a few whites, was a multipurpose organization. Its primary purpose was to establish a place of worship for African Americans; mutual aid and social organization were secondary. Some members of the society were part of the group, which had petitioned for the private burial ground a year earlier.

Philadelphia's first black church, the African Church (now St. Thomas's Episcopal) was formed shortly after the Free African Society and dedicated in 1794. The second black church, Bethel Methodist Church (now Mother Bethel African Methodist Episcopal [AME]) was dedicated the same year. In 1796, another black church, African Zoar Methodist Church (now Mother Zoar United Methodist) was dedicated. Subsequently, more churches came into existence that provided African Americans with their own schools, burial grounds, and meeting places. As a result, two early beneficial societies emerged, the Friendly Society of St. Thomas established in 1795 and the Female Benevolent Society of St. Thomas formed in 1796. The former assessed members twenty-five cents dues a month and made disbursements to orphans and widows of deceased members, those in need, and other charitable causes.

Many organizations had multiple purposes. For example, civic concerns were part of the agenda not only of churches, but also of a number of literary societies. In 1800 a group of African Americans at the urging of Absalom Jones, the pastor of St. Thomas's Episcopal Church, presented a petition to the legislature opposing the slave trade. Jones and Richard Allen, pastor of Bethel Methodist Church, the second black church established in Philadelphia, were members of the Free African Society, the Masons, and other associations.

Literary societies, such as the Philadelphia Library Company, provided not only a forum for debates and discussions of issues such as colonization, slavery, and emigration, but also classical concerts, a library, readings, and lectures. Several literary societies provided a forum for discussion and offered library services. Libraries were especially needed since African Americans were not permitted to use public libraries. Education was another focus for organization. The Pennsylvania Augustine Education Society was founded in 1818 for the purpose of establishing a school where black children would be taught the arts and sciences. In 1820 the seminary was established. In addition to mutual financial aid, self-help took shape in other forms of associations. In 1810 the African Insurance Company was established as a stock company with $5,000 in capital. There was an attempt to form an African Fire Association in 1818. The only names that have survived from this association are those of its president, Derrick Johnson, and its secretary, Joseph Allen. At the urging of several prominent black Philadelphians, this association did not pursue the venture.

As more churches came into existence, so too did other associations including the Daughters of Noah of Bethel Church (1822), Sons of St. Thomas (1823), Female Beneficial Philanthropic of Zoar (1826), and Female Methodist Assistant Society (1827). Aside from religious denomination and gender, shared occupation was another reason for African Americans to come together for mutual aid, as indicated by the Coachman's Benevolent Society (1825), Humane Mechanics (1828), and African Porter's Benevolent Society (1828). The names of many black societies also reflected the members' desire to remember and acknowledge their heritage. A testimony to that are the Angola Beneficial Society (1808), Sons of Africa (1810), African Benevolent (1819), Female African Benevolent (1821), and Daughters of Zion Angolian Ethiopian Society (1822). Names chosen also demonstrated an appreciation of the efforts of whites who aided African Americans, for example, the Rising Sons and Daughters of Lucretia Mott, the [Dr. Benjamin] Rush Beneficial Society, and the [Anthony] Benezet Philanthropic Society founded in 1812. Although a few societies were racially integrated, most restricted membership to people of color.

Between 1820 and 1829, black Philadelphians established more than twenty mutual aid associations whose primary purpose was: "the relief of such of its members, as through sickness or misfortune, may be unable to work: to the interments of deceased members, and to the relief of their widows and orphans." Prospective members, upon meeting membership requirements, were charged an initiation fee of $1 to $8. Thereafter, the societies assessed dues ranging from twelve and one-half to twenty-five cents a month. The societies provided members and their orphans and widows with funds for proper burials as well as financial help, food, clothing, and shelter in times of distress.

Associations also exerted social control by stipulating acceptable and unacceptable behavior of members. For example, most associations expelled members who engaged in fraud, frequented "taverns, brothels, or gambling houses," brought court action against another member, or were convicted of any crime. The Brown Beneficial Society, whose members were "descendants of the natives of Africa," emphasized moral character and stipulated that burial benefits would only be paid if the deceased member had resided with his spouse prior to death. Still another association concerned with principles and conduct was the Society for Suppressing Vice and Immorality established in 1809. Its members gave religious instruction and engaged in discourse with residents in the city and county.

Many of Philadelphia's black associations considered how dispersed their members were and made allowances for those who were not always in close proximity and therefore could not regularly attend meetings. Several organizations accommodated distant members by making an exception to the timely payment of dues for those who lived outside the city or were away for an extended period of time. Although black seamen were excluded from membership in a few societies, they were given special consideration in others. The Brown Beneficial Society was one that allowed one year for urban residents to pay dues, eighteen months for those who lived fifteen miles from the city, and two years for those residing over fifty miles from Philadelphia. One association, the United Daughters of Bethlehem City and County of Philadelphia established in 1835, reflects this residential dispersion in its name.

As with other separate institutions that they sought to establish, African Americans in Philadelphia found it necessary to justify the formation of beneficial societies. In 1831, in order to demonstrate the "utility of these institutions," they published a list of incorporated male and female beneficial societies. The notice, which appeared in the *Philadelphia Gazette*, disclosed founding dates of thirty-four male and female societies and reported that their charitable disbursements totaled $5,819 for the year 1830.

From 1830 to 1837, approximately thirty-one additional associations were organized in the city and county. This number does not include those literary, secret, and civic associations for which no organizational records have survived. By 1837, Philadelphia's eighty beneficial societies reported 7,448 members. Their annual dues totaled $18,851, and expenditures were $14,172. An 1837 survey conducted by the Pennsylvania Abolition Society shows that of those black households surveyed in the city and county, nearly 59 percent reported that at least one member belonged to at least one society. African Americans residing in the city of Philadelphia reported the highest percentage of association members. The results of the study were published in 1838 as *The Present State and Condition of the Free People of Color in the City of Philadelphia, as Exhibited by the Report of a Committee of the Pennsylvania Society for Promoting the Abolition of Slavery*. Black association membership was examined again a decade later when the Society of Friends conducted a survey of black households in the city and county of Philadelphia. The Friends' survey was published in 1849 as *A Statistical Inquiry into the Condition of the People of Colour in the City and Districts of Philadelphia*. Of those surveyed in the city and county districts, 63 percent indicated that at least one person belonged to a society, whereas in the city of Philadelphia, nearly 68 percent indicated the same. Between 1837 and 1847 black association membership in the city and county increased, perhaps because during those years African Americans in Pennsylvania were disfranchised and subjected increasingly to attacks by whites both on their persons and their institutions.

The decade of the 1830s was violent and turbulent. White Philadelphians attacked and killed African Americans and white mobs destroyed several black churches, a Masonic hall, a beneficial hall, and a home for black children. Those who analyzed the violence during this period attribute it to the myriad of black institutions, which had become visible symbols of black economic success.

Among those organizations dedicated to improving the economic and political conditions of black Philadelphians were the American Society of Free People of Colour, the American Moral Reform Society, the Philadelphia Association for the Mental and Moral Improvement of People of Colour, and the Agriculture and Mechanics stock company. Led by Richard Allen, African

Americans established the American Society of Free People of Colour in 1830. Between 1830 and 1835 the society encouraged blacks to pursue "mechanical and agricultural arts" hoping to elevate the moral and political standing of African Americans. The meetings of the society crystallized in the convention movement, which brought groups of African Americans from many counties together to address the loss of suffrage in 1838. In 1837 the American Moral Reform Society was organized to foster "education, temperance, economy and universal liberty." The Philadelphia Association for the Mental and Moral Improvement of People of Colour, formed in 1838, advocated immigration to Canada and urged African Americans to pursue agriculture and education, which it hoped would encourage moral and intellectual improvement. Moral concerns persisted, and in 1839 the Agriculture and Mechanics, a shared stock company, was founded. Members paid $10 for $100 shares of stock and twenty-five cents a week for dues.

In 1848 black Philadelphians came together from a number of counties and petitioned for the right to vote. Black suffrage, however, was not reinstated until 1870, after the Pennsylvania Equal Rights League, a black association, successfully lobbied the state legislature to restore the black vote. Other organizations with civic concerns were the Philadelphia Young Men's Anti-Slavery Society, the Young Men's Vigilant Society, the Philadelphia Anti-Slavery Society established in 1834, the Philadelphia African Institution founded in 1807, a branch of the Friendly Society of Sierra Leone, and the Haitian Immigration Society. The former advocated trade with and immigration to Sierra Leone; the latter emphasized immigration.

Black exclusion from cemeteries was one of many precipitating events that caused African Americans to establish their own institutions. By 1899 there were three black cemeteries in Philadelphia: Olive, Lebanon, and Merion. In addition, black Philadelphians owned and operated schools, businesses, a Home for Aged and Infirmed Colored Persons, the Douglass Hospital and Training School, a Home for the Homeless, the Institute for Colored Youth (now known as Cheyney State University), and many other institutions.

At the end of the nineteenth century, black scholar W. E. B. Du Bois, referring to the existence of black associations, concluded "how intimately bound together the Negroes of Philadelphia are." There were still numerous associations for mutual aid. Secret societies flourished. Civil societies still existed but not in significant numbers.

Critical of these black institutions, Du Bois failed to recognize then the historical interaction between churches and societies and their respective roles, not only in community formation and development, but also in sustaining the existence of African Americans in Philadelphia and elsewhere. Black associations served as tools that enabled African Americans to cope with prejudice, racism, and exclusion. The proliferation of societies, their interrelated concerns, and the various functions they performed demonstrate how the needs of the black community were being met and how community members responded to dominant legal, political, economic, religious, and social control.

The tradition of voluntary associations in Philadelphia continued throughout the twentieth century. This continuance can be attributed to the large number of churches and their support for relief, literary, social, civic, and economic organizations. Thus, African Americans continued to come together collectively for the purpose of improving their conditions. For example, twenty-seven years after its founding, Enon Baptist Church established not only a literary society for young people, but also an industrial school, an employment bureau, and a women's home missionary society.

A number of Philadelphia's churches had women's societies, which, instead of concentrating on foreign missions, focused their efforts on local initiatives. For example, the Malinka Missionary Society of Shiloh Baptist Church in addition to local charitable work had a special focus on the "oversight of colored servant girls." Black church women also came together outside of their respective denominations to form the Woman's Union Missionary Society of Philadelphia, an interdenominational organization that operated a day nursery to care for children between the ages of two months and ten years.

The need to care for the young had been recognized years earlier by the members of the Chapel of St. Simon the Cyrenian. Founded as a Protestant Episcopal Mission for African Americans, St. Simon's established a kindergarten in 1849 that was still functioning twenty-five years later. In addition to a sewing class, a Women's Guild was formed that sought not only to "foster a higher standard of sociability," but also to teach its members to become efficient church workers.

Another reason for the persistence of voluntary associations were the periods of mass migration of African Americans. The percentage of increase of blacks from the South between 1860 and 1900 was 93.4, while in the North it was 164.3. As a result of the large numbers of migrants coming into the city, many churches focused

specifically on helping those newcomers from the South. For example, in addition to operating a bureau of information that helped newcomers find respectable lodgings, Metropolitan Baptist Church also operated a night school. In 1894 Enon Baptist Tabernacle Church established the Tabernacle Home Missionary and Independent School for Women with the purpose of training "colored women for domestic service in the North, especially those coming from rural districts in the South." It also served as a home for young, single women.

In addition to beneficial, educational, secret, and literary societies, black Philadelphians formed the Philadelphia Branch of the Afro-American Council. Established in 1899, the council was a multipurpose organization which, among other things, focused on the investigation of lynchings "and other outrages perpetrated upon" African Americans. Particularly, the council tested the constitutionality of laws that it deemed oppressive to African Americans. The council encouraged both industrial and higher education and urged using federal funds to educate those who had been denied an education.

The Colored Women's Business League of Philadelphia was formed in 1901. Focusing on the intellectual stimulation and moral development of its members, the league also sought to strengthen their individual efforts for humanity by efficient organization. Another worthwhile purpose of the organization was to unite African American women in business enterprises. Similarly, the Philadelphia branch of the National Negro Business Men's League established the same year sought to foster and encourage business enterprises among African Americans "by organization and acquaintance."

Among the major African American institutions in Philadelphia at the turn of the century were the Home for Aged and Infirmed Colored Persons, the Douglass Hospital and Training School, and various other institutions of learning. Many of these and a multitude of other organizations and institutions crucial to Philadelphia's black community originated among the black churches. The tradition of self-help begun so early in the history of African Americans in Philadelphia continued throughout the twentieth century with many organizations owing their beginning, existence, and continuation in whole or in part to the black churches.

## FURTHER READINGS

The Civic Club. *Directory of the Philanthropic, Educational and Religious Associations and Churches of Philadelphia.* 2nd ed. Lancaster, Pa.: Press of The New Era Printing Company, 1903.

Du Bois, W. E. B. *The Philadelphia Negro: A Social Study.* 1899; reprint, New York: Schocken Books, 1967.

Lapsansky, Emma Jones. "'Since They Got Those Separate Churches': Afro-Americans and Racism in Jacksonian Philadelphia." *American Quarterly* 32 (1980): 54–78.

Nash, Gary B. *Forging Freedom: The Formation of Philadelphia's Black Community, 1720–1840.* Cambridge, Mass.: Harvard University Press, 1988.

Shannon, Janet H. "Community Formation: Blacks in Northern Liberties, 1790–1850." Ph.D. diss., Temple University, 1991.

Ulle, Robert F. "A History of St. Thomas' African Episcopal Church, 1794–1865." Ph.D. diss., University of Pennsylvania, 1986.

Winch, Julie P. *Philadelphia's Black Elite, Activism, Accommodation, and the Struggle for Autonomy, 1787–1878.* Philadelphia: Temple University Press, 1988.

*Janet Harrison Shannon*

## Phoenix: Civic, Literary, and Mutual Aid Associations

African Americans in Phoenix, Arizona, have had a long history of organizing civic, literary, and mutual aid associations to improve their social, economic, and political status.

In 1868 African Americans began to migrate to Phoenix, and by 1900 they constituted nearly 33 percent of the city's total population of 11,134. During the early years of black settlement the needs of the city's African American community were primarily cared for by the black churches. The arrival of larger numbers of African Americans in the early twentieth century, however, sparked the formation of a variety of secular associations. By 1900, Phoenix blacks had created the Horseshoe Literature Club, the Colored Lecture Forum, black auxiliaries of the Young Men's and the Young Women's Christian Association, the Colored Republican Club (CRC), the Black Women's Republican Club (BWRC), and the McKinley and Republican Club (MRC). The CRC and the BWRC were two of the most prestigious black organizations, attracting the membership of the city's leading black residents, including William P. Crump, Ayra Hackett, Richard Rosser, and Ella S. White. As the number of black residents continued to grow, so did the organizational activities of African Americans. By 1910, Phoenix blacks had established local chapters of the Colored Odd Fellows, the Colored Knights of Pythias, the Black Veterans of Foreign Wars, the Black Elks, and the Colored Masons, and an African American branch of the American Legion. These organizations provided cultural camaraderie as well as opportunities for civic activism.

Between 1897 and 1920, African American women's associations in Phoenix consisted of missionary societies that were tied to the black churches. In 1897, Idonica Jones, superintendent of the Department of Colored Work of the Women's Christian Temperance Union of Phoenix, began organizing local black youth programs. In 1915 the Arizona Federation of Colored Women's Clubs (AFCWC), which supervised the activities of many of the state's smaller black women's organizations, started to hold meetings in Phoenix. In March 1927 the AFCWC erected the Phyllis Wheatley Community Center on the corner of 14th and Jefferson Streets to host black political meetings, concerts, and guest lecturers. Hallie Q. Brown (1845–1949), a noted African American educator and national president of the Colored Federation of Women's Clubs, lived in Phoenix in the winters and assisted local members of the AFCWC.

In an effort to battle segregation and the bigotry perpetuated by separate but unequal policies, Samuel Bayless, C. Credille, and R. D. Simpson founded the Phoenix Advancement League (PAL) in 1919. The PAL, forerunner of the Phoenix branch of the National Association for the Advancement of Colored People (NAACP), fought discrimination and segregation as well as African American unemployment. The NAACP, established in late 1919, and the Phoenix branch of the National Urban League (NUL) also assisted the city's black population during this period. Between 1919 and 1940 the PAL, the NAACP, and the NUL helped construct the pillars of the local civil rights movement that attacked white supremacy and sought to end legal segregation during the 1950s and 1960s.

The stock market crash of October 29, 1929, propelled Phoenix and the rest of the United States into the most catastrophic economic disaster in American history. In response blacks formed the Phoenix Protective League (PPL) in 1931, which organized food drives and distributed meals and clothing to indigent blacks. Furthermore, the PPL launched a job register for unemployed blacks and through contacts with other agencies secured funds to provide small indemnities to blacks who suffered financially.

Between 1940 and 1990 African Americans continued to seek racial advancement and equality through protests. Older associations such as the PAL, the PPL, the NAACP, and the NUL, were joined by more militant organizations such as local chapters of the Congress of Racial Equality (CORE), the Student Non-Violent Coordinating Committee (SNCC), and the Black Panthers. As legal segregation was dismantled, equal employment economic opportunity and political power became critical issues for African Americans in Phoenix. Groups such as the Black Women's Task Force and 100 Black Men of Phoenix were created to tend to the social, economic, and political needs of Phoenix's growing black community.

**FURTHER READINGS**

Harris, Richard E. *The First 100 Years: A History of Arizona Blacks.* Apache Junction, Ariz.: Relmo Publishers, 1983.

Luckingham, Bradford. *Phoenix: The History of a Southwestern Metropolis.* Tucson: University of Arizona Press, 1989.

———. *Minorities in Phoenix: A Profile of Mexican American, Chinese American, and African American Communities, 1860–1992.* Tucson: University of Arizona Press, 1994.

Rothschild, Mary Logan, and Pamela Claire Hronek. *Doing What the Day Brought: An Oral History of Arizona Women.* Tucson: University of Arizona Press, 1992.

Whitaker, Matthew C. "In Search of Black Phoenicians: African American Culture and Community in Phoenix, Arizona, 1868–1940." M.A. thesis, Arizona State University, 1997.

*Matthew C. Whitaker*

## Phyllis Wheatley Women's Clubs and Homes

Phyllis Wheatley Women's Clubs and Homes, named after the inspirational slave poet Phillis Wheatley, engaged in a wide range of charitable, social, and political activities on behalf of black women. They provided lodging for women, settlement house work, homes for the elderly, and job referral services, and they also sponsored educational and recreational programs for youth. The first clubs were independent organizations that arose spontaneously in several cities in the late nineteenth century, but after 1912 many segregated black branches of the Young Women's Christian Association (YWCA) also adopted the name of Phyllis Wheatley.

By the turn of the twentieth century African American women had established a plethora of clubs and organizations that engaged in a wide range of self-help, benevolent, social, religious, literary, and cultural activities. In addition to the specific projects that these clubs supported and the pressing social needs that they attempted to fill, black women's clubs served to defend African American womanhood in an increasingly hostile social environment. Contemporary racial ideologies portrayed African American women as devoid of morality, sexually wanton, and incapable of upholding marital and family responsibilities. Through their club activities African American women sought to appropriate for themselves the Victorian image of proper womanhood as bearers of culture, morality, and social uplift. Club women, largely members of the African American elite, sought the elevation of all black women and worked tirelessly on behalf of those less fortunate. Phyllis Wheatley clubs were a vital part of this much larger club movement.

The first Phyllis Wheatley clubs emerged in the last decade of the nineteenth century. Representatives from the Phyllis Wheatley Club of Nashville, Tennessee, attended the 1895 Atlanta Congress of Colored Women. The following year Phyllis Wheatley clubs from Chicago, New Orleans, and Jacksonville, Florida, were listed in attendance at the first meeting of the National Association of Colored Women (NACW). In 1897 Detroit clubwomen established the first-known Phyllis Wheatley Home for Elderly Women. Although other clubs also supported homes for the elderly, such as those in Nashville and Buffalo, most of them focused on serving the needs of young African American women.

In Chicago a Phyllis Wheatley Club was formed in 1896. Its early activities included the establishment of a nursery school, but by 1906 concern had shifted to the provision of lodging and employment for the thousands of young African American women migrating to Chicago who were not served by white-run settlement houses or social service agencies. The club began fund-raising for a home to protect young women "from the human vultures ever ready to destroy young womanhood." Chicago's clubwomen sought to rescue and protect young women from urban vices, foster racial uplift, and provide training in domesticity. Within a year they purchased a building and opened the first Phyllis Wheatley Home for Young Women in the nation. In 1915 a new and larger home was purchased, capable of housing forty-four girls at one time. The success of the home was due, in part, to the support of several of Chicago's leading African American women's clubs. The motto of the home was "Help our Own," and members took great pride in the fact that it was financed and managed entirely by African American women. In 1926 a far larger building was purchased, and the directors claimed that 1,286 young women were helped annually.

The Phyllis Wheatley Club in Buffalo, New York, founded by a social worker from Chicago, followed a similar model. Buffalo women were similarly concerned with the negative racial stereotypes that dominated press coverage of the African American community. Between 1899 and 1930 the club engaged in a wide variety of social, political, and benevolent reform work. In its early years club members donated large quantities of food and clothing to the needy and joined with other women's clubs to provide a monthly "pension" for Underground Railroad leader Harriet Tubman, who was then living in a nursing home. In 1905 the club established a settlement house that sponsored mothers' clubs and offered counseling and job referrals for women. The club later established a home for the elderly. In 1910 the club invited the newly formed National Association for the Advancement of Colored People (NAACP) to establish a branch in Buffalo and campaigned for an end to police toleration of vice in the African American community. In the 1920s the club donated books by leading African American authors, including Phyllis Wheatley, to the local library.

After 1900 Phyllis Wheatley Clubs and Homes followed two models: some, such as in Chicago and Buffalo, remained independent, local organizations, often affiliated with the NACW. Others, however, comprised the official "colored branches" of the YWCA. In 1870 African American churchwomen in Philadelphia had founded the first Colored Women's Christian Association. Soon black women in other cities established similar groups. The American YWCA, however, did not recognize these African American associations until after 1906, when a new national board first encouraged the affiliation of separate "colored" branches.

In 1911, the St. Louis Phyllis Wheatley Club became an affiliate of the city's YWCA, which was the world's largest branch and offered a full range of services, but had extended no welcome to the growing black population. That year a group of 150 prominent African American women appealed directly to the YWCA's national board, which pressured the St. Louis branch to designate the Phyllis Wheatley Club as its black affiliate. The white leadership of the St. Louis YWCA did so reluctantly and only after voting to reserve to themselves the right of supervision. Despite white oversight, the national board sent Mary Belcher, a dedicated African American YWCA worker, to direct the new Phyllis Wheatley branch. Soon the branch developed the largest membership of any black YWCA affiliate and offered a full range of services for women, including a lodging house.

In Cleveland black women started a fight for a black YWCA in 1906, but they were not successful until 1912. Cleveland's African American elite, raised with hopes of integration, was wary of establishing segregated institutions. It took a generation of "newcomers" from the South, lead by Jane Edna Hunter, a young nurse who had experienced personally the plight of young black women unable to find decent lodging, to champion a separate institution. As racial tensions mounted with the increased migration of African Americans to Cleveland, the city's black elite gradually came to accept the pressing need for a segregated institution. Meanwhile, Hunter proved adept at winning financial backing in the white community. Whites, however, would support a home for black women only if a group of white women was selected to oversee its operations. Hunter acquiesced, and a majority white board was elected. In 1912 the Phillis Wheatley Association of Cleveland was established, and by 1917 it offered the largest facility for African American women in the country, composed of an eleven-story building and several separate centers. The association provided lodging, job placement, and classes in cooking, sewing, nutrition, hygiene, and scientific home-making while sponsoring a wide range of social and recreational activities for neighborhood residents. Hunter successfully resisted formal YWCA branch affiliation for the next thirty-six years of her leadership, thereby preserving a greater degree of autonomy for both herself and the organization. While whites technically retained control of the black associations in St. Louis and Cleveland, African American women staffed and managed them. Black women tolerated white supervision and in exchange gained access to white funds and, in the case of the St. Louis association, to the resources of a powerful national organization.

World War I expanded and enlarged the work of black YWCAs and Phyllis Wheatley homes. The war created a large-scale demand for African American female domestic workers while fueling black migration northward. The national board of the YWCA received $4 million from the government for work with women, and one-tenth of the amount was earmarked for black women's work. During the war, the number of "colored" YWCA affiliates increased from sixteen to forty-nine, and at least seventeen of these took the name of Phyllis Wheatley. In Washington, D.C., for example, the Colored Women's Christian Association, founded in 1905, had struggled for years to provide services for migrants. After the war the national YWCA provided $20,000 for the establishment of an official Phyllis Wheatley branch. New Phyllis Wheatley clubs and homes continued to emerge during the 1920s and 1930s. In Minneapolis, a Phyllis Wheatley settlement house was created in 1924 under a white board although its head resident, Gertrude Brown, was African American. Brown, a college-educated woman with broad experience in settlement house work, served with the association for thirteen years.

The paternalism of the YWCA, along with its limited facilities for African American women, however, continued to generate dissatisfaction. In 1931 the NACW formed its own Phillis Wheatley Home Department to provide services for young women in cities that did not have YWCA branches and selected Jane Edna Hunter of Cleveland as its head. Her motto was "A Phillis Wheatley in every city where there is not a branch of the YWCA," and she boasted that the NACW had aided in the establishment or expansion of nine independent Phyllis Wheatley homes and numerous clubs during the 1930s. Although these clubs received support and advice from the NACW, they were locally funded and governed by independent boards of directors, thereby avoiding white control.

In 1946 the national YWCA adopted an interracial charter and began a desegregation effort. Today the legacy of these pioneering Phyllis Wheatley clubs and homes endures. Several branches of the YWCA continue to bear the name of Phyllis Wheatley. The Phyllis Wheatley settlements founded in Cleveland and Minneapolis continue to serve as African American community centers while over two dozen black women's clubs associated with the NACW still bear the name of Phyllis Wheatley.

**FURTHER READINGS**

Jones, Adrienne Lash. *Jane Edna Hunter: A Case Study of Black Leadership, 1910–1950*. Brooklyn, N.Y.: Carlson Publishing, 1990.

———. "Phyllis (Phillis) Wheatley Clubs and Homes." In *Black Women in America: An Historical Encyclopedia*. Ed. Darlene Clark Hine. Brooklyn, N.Y.: Carlson Publishing, 1993.

Karger, Howard Jacob. "Phyllis Wheatley House: A History of the Minneapolis Black Settlement House, 1924 to 1940." *Phylon* 47 (1986): 79–90.

Knupfer, Anne Meis. *Toward a Tenderer Humanity and a Nobler Womanhood: African American Women's Clubs in Turn-of-the-Century Chicago*. New York: New York University Press, 1996.

Salem, Dorothy. *To Better Our World: Black Women in Organized Reform, 1890–1920*. Brooklyn, N.Y.: Carlson Publishing, 1990.

Spratt, Margaret. "To Be Separate or One: The Issue of Race in the History of the Pittsburgh and Cleveland YWCAs, 1920–1946." In *Men and Women Adrift: The YMCA and the YWCA in the City*. Ed. Nina Mjagkij and Margaret Spratt. New York: New York University Press, 1997.

Williams, Lillian S. "And Still I Rise: Black Women and Reform, Buffalo, New York, 1900–1940." In *"We Specialize in the Wholly Impossible": A Reader in Black Women's History*. Ed. Darlene Clark Hine, Wilma King, and Linda Reed. Brooklyn, N.Y.: Carlson Publishing, 1995.

*L. Mara Dodge*

**SEE ALSO** Young Women's Christian Association, Council on Colored Work

# Pittsburgh: Civic, Literary, and Mutual Aid Associations

Historically, African Americans in the greater Pittsburgh region have established social institutions that were multi-faceted and flexible. Organizations that primarily served the social needs of the city's black residents often provided social welfare programs and engaged in civil rights protests and political activism. Civic, literary, and mutual aid associations proved an integral part of black community building both in the city and in the surrounding mill towns.

Prior to the Civil War, Pittsburgh was a frontier town and only beginning to build its industrial economy. By the 1830s, Pittsburgh's small but thriving black community started to develop social institutions dedicated to abolition and racial uplift. In 1832, for example, African Americans in Pittsburgh formed the African Education Society to raise the level of education of the city's black residents. Another civic group, the Philanthropic Society, was established by the city's leading African American citizens in 1837. Besides providing for the social welfare of the black community, the society was engaged in antislavery activities. In the same year, two other groups, the Theban Literary Society and the Young Men's Moral Reform Society, merged and combined intellectual pursuits with temperance.

Pittsburgh's black social institutions produced outstanding community leaders such as John Peck, John and

George Vashon, the Reverend Lewis Woodson, and most notably, the "Father of Black Nationalism," Martin R. Delany. In 1845, Delany, a leader of the Philanthropic Society, launched his newspaper *The Mystery*. While Delany left Pittsburgh in 1856, the region's black population continued to establish social organizations in the years prior to the Civil War.

By the late 1850s, several new community institutions emerged, such as the Avery Institute, an all-black college. Black militia units such as the Hannibal Guards and the Fort Pitt Cadets provided young men with military training and opportunities to socialize. At the outbreak of the Civil War, both units volunteered their services and eventually a number of blacks from the Pittsburgh region joined the Union cause.

Following the Civil War, greater Pittsburgh's African American community experienced a dramatic increase in population. Between 1870 and 1910 the city's black community increased from 1,996 to 25,623. This dramatic population growth was largely the product of black migration. Southern rural blacks, attracted to the region's industrial economy, came to Pittsburgh in search of employment. Industrial jobs, however, proved elusive. African Americans found race discrimination to be a potent barrier to industrial work during the late nineteenth and early twentieth centuries. Yet, the arrival of the migrants added vitality to the black community, which continued its tradition of using social institutions for a myriad of purposes.

In 1883 black women stepped to the fore when Mary Peck Bond and several friends organized the Home for Aged and Infirm Colored Women. Now known as the Lemmington Home, it remains Pittsburgh's longest continuously operating black institution. The home for aged women symbolized black women's expanded civic activities at the turn of the century. By 1910, black women alone had established over thirty social clubs. The Aurora Reading Club, founded by Rachel Jones in 1894, emphasized literary pursuits and social welfare and later became a member of the National Association of Colored Women's Clubs. Its twenty-five members represented the region's most notable black elite women, including Anna Posey and Virginia Procter. Similar women's organizations devoted to literary, cultural, and social pursuits included the Ladies Magnolia Society and the Narcissus Literary and Musical Club. Another women's organization, the Hawthorne Club of Sewickely, initiated in 1914, stressed educational achievement and charity. The Lucy Stone Civic League, founded by Daisy Lampkin in 1915, pursued suffrage and was the most politically active black women's club in Pittsburgh.

In addition to women's clubs, black city residents established numerous branches of national clubs and mutual aid societies in the late nineteenth and early twentieth centuries. The Odd Fellows, True Reformers, and Galilean Fishermen all thrived in the city and the surrounding mill towns. By 1910, at least five national mutual aid societies operated in the city of Pittsburgh, and additional branches of these groups existed in many of the region's mill towns. The buildings of these organizations, such as the Odd Fellows' Hall on Arthur Street in the Hill District, frequently served as headquarters for a variety of community groups and provided space for many community functions. Another important community center was the Young Men's Christian Association (YMCA) that the small African American community in Sewickely established in 1913.

While the Sewickely YMCA was the product of community effort and cohesion, other institutions illustrated the rapidly increasing class stratification of the city's black population. The Loendi Club organized in 1897, for example, was an exclusive club of the black elite, catering to the black business and professional class. Headed by Attorney William Maurice Randolph, the Loendi owned a large and commodious building in the Lower Hill District of Pittsburgh. The Frogs, composed of the Loendi's twenty-five most elite members, was the most aristocratic of the African American clubs.

While upper-class blacks enjoyed the conviviality of the Loendi and the Frogs, newer institutions such as the Soho Settlement House served the working class. Founded in 1906, the Soho Community House was significant for its interracial programs, staff, and clientele. Although the Soho Community House looked toward an interracial future, Pittsburgh's blacks continued to establish groups that catered to the specific needs of the African American community.

Political strength emerged in the community's numerous ward and political clubs such as the Afro-American Central Club of Duqusne. The Afro-American Republican League of Pennsylvania formally represented all associated black political clubs in the state between 1895 and 1913. Former league members helped establish the Pittsburgh branch of the National Association for the Advancement of Colored People (NAACP) in 1915. Three years later Pittsburgh's African Americans also founded a branch of the National Urban League (NUL) to respond to the needs of the rapidly expanding black population brought on by World War I.

The World War I marked the entry of large numbers of blacks into Pittsburgh's industrial work force. Factory jobs and the accompanying higher wages also triggered an increase of social institutions. Blacks in the steel towns of the greater Pittsburgh region launched a variety of new organizations in the 1920s and 1930s. Branches of national associations such as the Elks, the Odd Fellows, and Marcus Garvey's Universal Negro Improvement Association emerged in the bustling black communities of steel towns like McKeesport, Homestead, Coraopolis, and Beaver Falls. The Communist-backed National Minority Union also enjoyed popularity in some of the mill towns and in the 1930s the Congress of Industrial Organizations (CIO) became an important source of community support. Many of these organizations featured mutual aid programs and all provided blacks with opportunities for socializing and civic activism.

In addition to the rise of associations, clubs, and societies, the Pittsburgh region became famous for its black baseball teams in the years following World War I. The Homestead Grays and Pittsburgh Crawfords, which originated as neighborhood sports clubs, became rivals for the hearts of regional baseball fans. In addition to professional sports, branches of the YMCA provided athletic and recreational activities for black city residents. The YMCA on Center Avenue in the Hill District was the most famous institution to emerge during this period. Constructed in 1923, the YMCA provided many important services for its members and the black community. The YMCA, for example, operated eighty dormitory rooms, which were used by members as well as black travelers who could not find accommodation in the city's white hotels. These dorms also served as alternative housing for black students of the University of Pittsburgh who were barred from campus housing because of their race. Renowned scholar Alain Locke, Olympic track star John Woodruff, and long-time *Pittsburgh Courier* reporter Frank Bolden all boarded at the Center Avenue YMCA while they were students at the University of Pittsburgh.

During the 1940s, YMCA alumnus and local NAACP leader Judge Homer S. Brown, along with Daisy Lampkin and others, advocated civil rights legislation and encouraged African Americans to build institutions that served their needs. Lampkin, in particular, illustrates the number and range of social and civic groups that African Americans supported during the 1940s and 1950s. She became a high-ranking official in the national NAACP, organized the LINKS, Inc. Project in 1956, and served on the board of the *Pittsburgh Courier* and the Pittsburgh chapter of the American Red Cross. Lampkin's and Brown's tireless crusade for equal rights helped set the stage for the institutions that emerged in the subsequent decades.

In the 1970s, the United Black Front, a black action group, offered Pittsburgh's African American community economic programs and opportunities for political leadership. Another group, the Homewood Poetry Forum, provided a structured outlet for local poets and writers. The Pittsburgh branch of the LINKS promoted African American art through well-publicized exhibitions. These newer groups joined the efforts of the older civic, literary, and mutual aid associations that have served Pittsburgh's black community since the nineteenth century.

Although deindustrialization has left the region's African American community economically disadvantaged, its multifaceted social institutions continue to thrive. While African Americans in Pittsburgh have launched numerous new organizations to address issues of contemporary concern, they have also remained committed to longstanding organizations such as the Aurora Reading Club and the Hawthorne Club. These black community institutions have provided a broad range of services and programs. Moreover, they have served as a training ground for numerous dedicated men and women who will lead African Americans of the greater Pittsburgh region into the twenty-first century.

**FURTHER READINGS**

Blackett, R. J. M. "'. . . Freedom, of the Martyr's Grave': Black Pittsburgh's Aid to the Fugitive Slave." *Western Pennsylvania Historical Magazine* 61 (1978): 118–134.

Dickerson, Dennis C. *Out of the Crucible: Black Steelworkers in Western Pennsylvania, 1875–1980.* Albany: SUNY Press, 1986.

Donaldson, Al. "The Blacks." *Pittsburgh Press: Roto Magazine* (September 1989).

Glasco, Laurence. "Double Burden: The Black Experience in Pittsburgh." In *City at the Point: Essays on the Social History of Pittsburgh.* Ed. Samuel P. Hays. Pittsburgh: University of Pittsburgh Press, 1989.

Historical Society of Western Pennsylvania. *Blacks in Pittsburgh: A Chronology.* Pittsburgh: Historical Society of Western Pennsylvania, n.d.

*Charles Franklin Lee*

# Poor People's Campaign

The Poor People's Campaign (PPC) was launched by Martin Luther King Jr. and other leaders of the Southern Christian Leadership Conference (SCLC) in 1967. In the wake of what appeared to be the civil rights movement's diminishing momentum, King and his followers sought to invigorate the nonviolent protest movement by extending the civil rights agenda to include broad-based demands for economic and social justice.

In early December 1967, King announced that the SCLC intended to bring poor people of all races to Washington, D.C., the following April. These poor were to stay in the nation's capital until the government responded to the demands of the PPC. The PPC's main objectives were to secure federal legislation ensuring full employment and promoting the construction of low-income housing to raise the quality of life of America's poor. The centerpiece of the campaign was the creation of Resurrection City, or Tent City, which demonstrators planned to build in Washington, D.C.,

and where they intended to remain until their demands were met. Everything was set to begin on April 22, 1968, when King was assassinated in Memphis, Tennessee, on April 4.

In spite of King's assassination, plans for the PPC continued. Under the new leadership of Reverend Ralph Abernathy, waves of demonstrators from different sections of the country started to arrive in Washington on April 28, 1968. They came in cars, buses, trucks, and mule drawn wagons to symbolize the plight of the rural poor. On fifteen acres of land in West Potomac Park between the Washington Memorial and the Lincoln Memorial, the protestors constructed Resurrection City, a collection of plywood huts that housed between 2,500 and 3,000 people at its peak occupancy. Most of the residents of Resurrection City were black, 200 were Native Americans, 100 were white, and a few dozen were Hispanics. The protestors also erected a dining room and several other buildings to provide spaces for dentists, doctors, and a nursery.

"Resurrection City" after rainfall. June 22, 1968, Washington, D.C. © *Bettmann/Corbis*

A wide range of people from different racial, ethnic, and socioeconomic backgrounds joined the campaign in Washington, D.C. They participated in demonstrations and disrupted life in the nation's capital in an effort to force the federal government to respond to their demands. At a brief dedication service on May 13, 1968, Abernathy declared the group's insistence to remain in Washington until it achieved its goals.

In the beginning SCLC leaders believed that their efforts had successfully brought together a diverse group of people who were determined to rid the country of poverty. Yet, a multitude of problems arose that challenged the resolve of the protestors. During the month of May the nation's capital experienced an unusual amount of rainfall that turned the soil in Resurrection City into mud. The rickety constructed buildings weakened under the force of the rain. Donated clothing stacked in piles on dirt floors in one building was immersed in mud. The school that the local chapter of the American Federation of Teachers had planned to operate had to be drastically scaled down and eventually abandoned completely. Moreover, Resurrection City was plagued by violence, assaults, and interracial conflicts. Even the demonstrations at the federal agencies and offices were attended poorly.

Not only were there problems among the rank and file, but also among the PPC's leadership. Bayard Rustin, a long-time civil rights activist, organizer, and strategist, left the PPC because of a dispute about strategy. His departure came nearly two weeks before the "Day of Solidarity" scheduled for June 19. Various others followed Rustin. By the first week of June 1968, only about 300 of the nearly 3,000 protestors remained in Washington. Another event that demoralized the residents of Resurrection City was the loss of a powerful ally—Robert Kennedy. He was fatally shot on June 5, after winning the California Democratic primary, and pronounced dead the following day. Reverends Andrew Young, Hosea Williams, Jesse Jackson, and James Bevin were some of the stalwarts who remained at the side of Abernathy. They faced growing criticism of their efforts, as the media, members of Congress, other civil rights leaders, and President Lyndon Johnson expressed concern and skepticism about the PPC. After King's assassination, the city of Washington had experienced one of the most devastating riots ever and as a result many city leaders, residents, and black mayor Walter Washington were uneasy about the growing lawlessness in Resurrection City.

Despite these concerns and criticisms, Abernathy proclaimed June 19, 1968, as Solidarity Day and urged protestors to come once more to the nation's capital. Between 50,000 to 100,000 persons followed Abernathy's call and gathered on the Washington mall to demand the eradication of poverty in the United States. Sterling Tucker, the local head of the National Urban League (NUL), and actor Ossie Davis organized the major portion of the day's events that included speeches, entertainment, and marches. The main speaker was Abernathy who reiterated the PPC's demands: "That no child go hungry. . . . That no family lack good housing. . . . That no man be without a job . . . that no citizen be denied adequate income. . . . That no human being be deprived of health care. . . . That every American be educated to the limit of his hope and talent. . . . That no more of our people be murdered by the violence that torments America."

Solidarity Day was the last big rally of the PPC; within five days police removed the protestors and the city they had erected. On June 24, 1968, hundreds of demonstrators were arrested on the grounds of the U.S. Capitol for trespassing. Meanwhile at Resurrection City about 1,500 police, clad in crash helmets and carrying gas guns and pistols, closed down the encampment because its permit to occupy federal land had expired. Police announced that all who needed bus fare home could get it from the Traveler's Aid Society. When word of the police action reached some of Washington's poor black neighborhoods, rioting broke out in parts of the city. Mayor Washington declared a curfew and called in the National Guard to restore order.

While the PPC failed to achieve its goals, campaign leaders claimed one lasting victory when the government eliminated the policy of distributing commodities as sole sustenance for the poor, replacing it with food stamps. The introduction of food stamps liberated the poor from receiving foods chosen by the government and empowered them to chose their own groceries.

**FURTHER READINGS**

Abernathy, Ralph David. *And the Walls Come Tumbling Down.* New York: Harper and Row, 1989.

Fager, Charles. *Uncertain Resurrection: The Poor People's Campaign.* Grand Rapids, Mich.: Erdmans, 1969.

Garrow, David. *Bearing the Cross: Martin Luther King Jr. and the Southern Christian Conference 1955–1968.* New York: William Morrow, 1986.

McKnight, Gerald D. *The Last Crusade: Martin Luther King, Jr., the FBI, and the Poor People's Campaign.* Boulder, Colo.: Westview Press, 1998.

*Betty Nyangoni*

## Port Royal Relief Committee

*See* Pennsylvania Freedmen's Relief Association.

## Potomac Institute

Between 1961 and 1987 the Potomac Institute served as a think tank for the advancement of civil rights and the improvement of race relations in the United States. It was established by philanthropists Stephen and Audrey Currier of the Taconic Foundation in response to the racial violence of the early 1960s. The institute brought together representatives of the public and private sectors to discuss race relations and formulate civil rights policies and programs. At the request of the Curriers, Harold C. Fleming, former executive director of the Southern Regional Council, organized and directed the Potomac Institute as a nonprofit, tax exempt corporation, headquartered in Washington, D.C.

Between 1961 and 1964, the Potomac Institute served as an unofficial advisory agency to the president. When John F. Kennedy issued Executive Order 10925 on March 6, 1961, mandating that government contractors and federal agencies provide equal employment opportunities, the Defense Department asked the Potomac Institute to recommend mechanisms, staffing patterns, and procedures to help implement the presidential order. The institute performed a detailed study of Air Force employment practices and presented its recommendations in 1962. The study, the first in a series of policy studies conducted by the institute at the request of federal agencies, set the standard for equal employment practices for the U.S. government. The institute's other studies included investigations of antipoverty programs, equal housing opportunities, and treatment of minority civil service employees on military installations.

In 1963, President Kennedy proposed a comprehensive civil rights bill to ensure the right of every American to vote, attend school, find employment, and be served in public places without arbitrary discrimination. Of the bill's ten provisions, Title II—prohibiting discrimination in public accommodations including retail and service establishments—was the most controversial. Mindful of the massive white southern resistance that erupted following the 1954 *Brown v. Board of Education* decision, civil rights activists feared renewed turmoil. Therefore the Potomac Institute and the Southern Regional Council of Atlanta cooperated with the Justice Department to increase compliance with the public accommodations section of the civil rights bill. In March 1964, the institute launched Operation Compliance to convince the southern business community to desegregate public facilities voluntarily and to encourage support for the bill among the people of the South. In July 1964, after President Lyndon B. Johnson signed the bill into law, the Potomac Institute was employed to help design two federal agencies created by the act—the Community Relations Service and the Equal Employment Opportunity Commission (EEOC).

After 1967, the Potomac Institute focused on equal opportunity in housing, education, and employment. Among the most important of its contributions was forcing the federal government to comply with Title VI of the 1964 Civil Rights Act, which stipulates that "no person may be subjected to discrimination in any federally-financed program on the ground of race, color, or national origin" and "federal agencies may terminate assistance to the particular program or activity in which the discrimination is taking place." Paralleling this effort, the Potomac Institute also encouraged private citizens to sue the federal government when it failed to enforce civil rights legislation. Throughout the 1970s and 1980s, the Potomac Institute worked closely with other civil rights agencies to protect legislative and administrative gains. The most important of these struggles was its fight to preserve Affirmative Action during the Reagan administration.

As Potomac president Fleming neared his retirement, the board of directors decided to close the institute rather than seek new leadership, mainly due to the changing nature and direction of civil rights in the mid-1980s. The institute closed its office in 1987. Throughout its existence, it remained true to its initial vision as a small, independent center for the advancement of public policy and private practices affecting race relations. For three decades, the institute was an important behind-the-scenes, civil rights agency that became a model for small activist "think tanks" that developed in later years.

**FURTHER READINGS**

Fleming, Harold C., with Virginia Fleming. *The Potomac Chronicle: Public Policy and Civil Rights from Kennedy to Reagan.* Athens: The University of Georgia Press, 1996.

Harold C. Fleming Papers, Manuscript Division, Library of Congress, Washington, D.C.

*Kimberly E. Nichols*

# Presbyterian Afro-American Council of the North and West

*See* National Black Presbyterian Caucus.

# Presbyterian Church Committee on Missions to Freedmen

The Presbyterian Church Committee on Missions to Freedmen began in 1864 as northern Presbyterianism's answer to the crisis of abolition. That year the Reverend S. C. Logan, future leader of the Presbyterian mission to the South, suggested that abolition necessitated the creation of a separate church agency devoted solely to the freedmen's religious, social, and educational needs. In response the Presbyterian Church established the Committee on Missions to Freedmen to rebuild the free South and reshape the freed slaves according to Yankee industrialism and Presbyterian moralism.

The committee, headquartered in Philadelphia and Indianapolis, commissioned white and black Presbyterians to build churches and schools for the freedmen and to train race leaders. Ordained ministers led the committee's church-building efforts. Assisted by black catechists, they founded churches among freedmen who had abandoned southern Presbyterianism, seeking ultimately to gather them into independent presbyteries and synods. Presbyterianism, however, made few inroads among southern blacks. Aside from southern hostility and northern ambivalence, the missionaries' greatest obstacle was Presbyterianism's lack of appeal among southern black churchgoers due to its disdain for religious emotionalism and its demand for theological training.

But while the church gained few black converts, its schools provided the southern field with black ministers and teachers. In 1870, the committee's focus and funding turned from churchbuilding to educational expansion. The committee's greatest success lay in its educational legacy. Its primary and secondary schools helped form the basis for southern public education and its universities, such as Lincoln University in Pennsylvania and Biddle University in North Carolina, trained a generation of race leaders including Daniel Sanders. Born a slave, Sanders earned after gaining his freedom a degree from Western Theological Seminary, traveled internationally to raise funds for the committee, and, through his newspaper *Afro-American Presbyterian*, became the voice of black Presbyterianism in the South.

Beginning in the 1880s, this voice grew increasingly critical of the committee's conservative racial policies. Faced with accusations of paternalism and disrespect by its black ministers and teachers, the committee, renamed the Board of Missions to Freedmen in 1883, integrated administration and faculty at its schools earlier than other southern mission societies. For example, Biddle University appointed Sanders as its first black president in 1891 and recruited an all-black faculty by 1894. Southern black ministers, however, remained at odds with the board. Because only a fraction of its southern black churches were self-supporting, the board maintained fiscal and, therefore, political control over black presbyteries and synods.

With the rise of race consciousness in the early twentieth century, the Freedman's Board became for African American Presbyterians a symbol of black dependence. Black ministers urged the church to integrate the southern mission into the church's regular missionary work rather than manage it as a separate agency, which smacked of segregation. Such membership pressure, coupled with falling numbers of black converts in the southern mission field, prompted Presbyterian mission boards to reorganize in 1923. That year the Presbyterian Church dissolved the Freedman's Board, created a Department of Work for Colored People within its new Board of National Missions, and integrated its missionary efforts among southern blacks into its regular churchwide mission work. In 1932, the church afforded African Americans a greater degree of agency when the department became the Unit of Work with Colored People, and Reverend Albert B. McCoy was appointed first black field secretary.

**FURTHER READINGS**

McPherson, James M. *The Abolitionist Legacy: From Reconstruction to the NAACP.* Princeton: Princeton University Press, 1975.

Murray, Andrew E. *Presbyterians and the Negro—A History.* Philadelphia: Presbyterian Historical Society, 1966.

*Jennifer J. Wojcikowski*

# President Clinton's Initiative on Race

*See* President's Initiative on Race.

# President Eisenhower's Committee on Government Contracts

*See* President's Committee on Government Contracts.

## President Eisenhower's Committee on Government Employment Policy

*See* President's Committee on Government Employment Policy.

## President Hoover's Colored Advisory Commission

*See* Hoover's Colored Advisory Commission.

## President Kennedy's Committee on Equal Employment

*See* President's Committee on Equal Employment Opportunity.

## President Kennedy's Committee on Equal Opportunity in Housing

*See* President's Committee on Equal Opportunity in Housing.

## President Kennedy's Committee on Equality of Treatment in the Armed Forces (The Gesell Committee)

*See* President's Committee on Equality of Treatment in the Armed Forces (The Gesell Committee).

## President Nixon's Commission on Campus Unrest

*See* President's Commission on Campus Unrest.

## President Roosevelt's Committee on Fair Employment Practice

*See* President's Committee on Fair Employment Practice.

## President Truman's Committee on Civil Rights

*See* President's Committee on Civil Rights.

## President Truman's Committee on Equality of Treatment and Opportunity in the Armed Forces (The Fahy Committee)

*See* President's Committee on Equality of Treatment and Opportunity in the Armed Forces (The Fahy Committee).

## President Truman's Committee on Government Contract Compliance

*See* Government Contract Compliance Committee.

## President's Commission on Campus Unrest

On June 13, 1970, President Richard M. Nixon appointed the President's Commission on Campus Unrest to study the causes of and solutions to recent unrests and violence on college campuses. The commission was established approximately one month after National Guardsmen fired on white students at Ohio's Kent State University, killing four and wounding nine students, and police fired on black students at Jackson State College in Mississippi, killing two and leaving twelve others wounded. In his executive order establishing the commission, Nixon asked the commission to identify the sources of campus violence and propose "specific methods though which grievances can be resolved." The commission's impact on ending campus unrest was nominal due to the president's defensive reaction to the commission's findings and unrealistic expectations about the scope of its mission.

Former Pennsylvania governor William W. Scranton chaired the commission. The other eight members included university faculty and administrators, an attorney, a police chief, and a newspaper editor. The commission conducted its work between June and September 1970, holding public hearings at four locations across the nation, including Kent, Ohio, and Jackson, Mississippi. Fifteen executive sessions were held, and the commission's staff visited various universities, interviewing faculty, students, and administrators. On September 26, 1970, the commission delivered its 537-page report to the president.

The scope of the commission's report was comprehensive. Subjects covered included the sources of black and white student protest in the 1960s, the responses of universities and law enforcement agencies to campus protests and student movements, the role of the federal government in addressing the grievances of students, and the incidents at Kent State and Jackson State. The commission identified the sources of campus unrest as the Vietnam War, racism, and repression. According to the commission, black and white student protest was not identical, though the two groups shared the goal of ending racism. While ending racism and improving the socioeconomic status of all African Americans were the primary aims of black students, white students sought to reform the system that created and perpetuated racism and repression.

The commission tried to present the shootings at Kent State, a predominantly white campus, and the shootings at Jackson State, a historically black college, as separate manifestations of the white and black student movements. Protests against the Vietnam War and the American military and the actions of the National Guardsmen had led to the violence at Kent State, but the motives of the black students at Jackson State were not so easily described. The gathering of students at Jackson State that eventually brought police to campus was caused by angry black students who had thrown rocks at white motorists. The commission vacillated between presenting the violence at Jackson State as the result of black student protest against racism or the antagonism of the Mississippi Highway patrolmen and the Jackson police. The commission characterized the rock-throwing as "spring fever" and noted the lack of an organized protest movement at Jackson State, claiming that "[s]outhern black people as a group still believe that the American system will respond to their demands" without the use of protest.

The commission's difficulty in categorizing the incident at Jackson State points to the enormity of the commission's mission. Recommendations for quelling campus unrest also required suggesting fundamental changes in American society, government, and public policy. In reference to Jackson State, for example, the Commission proposed integration of the National Guard, increased federal financial aid to black colleges, and preparation of legislation giving the federal government the authority to integrate state and local police forces. In short, the commission urged the federal government to do more than it was doing to ensure equal opportunities and fair treatment of black Americans.

The final recommendations of the commission were even more sweeping than those included in the special report on Jackson State. The recommendations were tailored for the principal parties involved in campus unrests, including students, universities, law enforcement agencies, the president, and the American government. Though presented separately, the recommendations had a common theme: all stressed the importance of peaceful and respectful dialogue between the parties. To achieve this end, the commission urged the president to "exercise his reconciling moral leadership" to make it clear that confrontation and backlash were counterproductive. In its recommendations to the president, the commission also emphasized the need to end the Vietnam War and renew "the national commitment to full social justice."

President Nixon, however, regarded such suggestions as personal criticism. In his reply to the report, he rejected the need to exert moral leadership, contending that "[r]esponsibility for disruption of a university campus rests squarely on the shoulders of the disrupters." Vice President Spiro Agnew publicly denounced the commission's report, and during the fall of 1970, it became apparent that Nixon was not going to answer the report's call for active presidential leadership to help end campus unrest.

Nixon's handling of the report aside, the commission itself had a nearly impossible mission. For the commission to meet its mandate, it not only had to identify the sources of campus unrest, but also provide specific proposals for rectifying the problems causing unrest and the sort of violence that ensued at Kent State and Jackson State. Considering the sources of this discontent, such as the Vietnam War, racism, and students' perception of the United States as a repressive government, the commission was being asked to "fix America." As David Flitner Jr. has observed in his study of presidential commissions, such unrealistic expectations are commonly placed on the commissions and help explain their nominal impact in solving the problems or issues they are asked to study.

**FURTHER READINGS**

Flitner, David, Jr. *The Politics of Presidential Commissions.* Dobbs Ferry, N.Y.: Transnational Publishers, Inc., 1986.

O'Neil, Robert M., et al. *No Heroes, No Villains: New Perspectives on Kent State and Jackson State.* San Francisco: Jossey-Bass, Inc., 1972.

U.S. President's Commission on Campus Unrest. *The Report of the President's Commission on Campus Unrest.* Washington, D.C.: U.S. Government Printing Office, 1970.

*David F. Krugler*

## President's Committee on Civil Rights

Created by Harry S. Truman in 1946, the President's Committee on Civil Rights grew out of the racial violence that plagued the United States during World War II. Ideas for a presidential committee to investigate civil rights violations circulated during the later years of Franklin Roosevelt's administration as racial tensions escalated across the country, but, claiming that the war was his overriding concern, Roosevelt rebuffed such appeals. Tragically, violence against African Americans continued once the war ended. On February 13, 1946 Isaac Woodard, a black veteran, was savagely blinded by the police chief in Batesburgh, South Carolina, following a disagreement with a bus driver. Woodard had been discharged from the army only a few hours before the vicious assault. Accepting the officer's argument that he had only acted in self-defense, a local jury soon acquitted the police chief. Later that month members of the Ku Klux Klan, local police, and National Guard troops attacked African American residents of Columbia, Tennessee. Twenty-eight African Americans were arrested on charges of attempted murder; two others were killed in jail. On July 25, 1946, Klan members near Monroe, Georgia, killed two African American couples. Once again, the perpetrators were acquitted.

These incidents outraged civil rights advocates, who brought pressure on Truman. Many reiterated longstanding demands that the president back antilynching legislation that had stalled in Congress since the 1930s and insisted that he order the Justice Department to investigate developments in the South. Though Truman directed the Justice Department to look into the Monroe murders, there was little that Washington could do because laws only authorized federal prosecution against civil rights violations committed by state or local officials, not private citizens. Such limitations on federal power heightened the determination of civil rights proponents to fight for legal reforms. On September 19, 1946, leaders from the National Emergency Committee Against Mob Violence, which included outspoken liberals such as Eleanor Roosevelt and Dr. Channing H. Tobias, met with Truman. They detailed the deplorable conditions in the South and urged the president to call a special session of Congress to pass antilynching legislation. "My God!," a stunned Truman replied. "I had no idea it was as terrible as that! We have to do something." Presidential aide David Niles then suggested the creation of a presidential committee to examine civil rights issues and outline possible solutions. Truman concurred and indicated that he would establish such a body by executive order if necessary to avoid antagonism in Congress. Though the offer seemed spontaneous, the president and his staff had planned in advance to make such a suggestion.

Truman signed the executive order creating the President's Committee on Civil Rights on December 5, 1946. The committee would "inquire into and determine whether and in what respect current law enforcement measures . . . may be strengthened and improved to safeguard the civil rights of the people." The president also authorized it to make "recommendations with respect to . . . more adequate and effective means and procedures for the protection of civil rights."

The president's decision stemmed from personal and political motivations. Having grown up in the border state of Missouri, Truman harbored racist views personally, but violence against African Americans genuinely repulsed him and offended his beliefs in equal opportunity and fair play as bedrock principles of American life. The committee seemed to offer certain political advantages as well. On the one hand, it presumably would shore up the Democratic party's sagging position among northern liberals and African Americans, who believed that the president had done too little to promote racial justice. Conversely, Truman was not yet committing to any specific legislative program, and thus he hoped that southern opposition would be minimal.

The fifteen-member committee met for the first time on January 15, 1947. "I want our Bill of Rights implemented in fact," the president instructed them. "We have been trying to do this for 150 years. We are making progress, but we are not making progress fast enough." Truman appointed Charles Wilson, president of General Electric, as chair. Other members were drawn from the ranks of labor, law, business, education, and religion. Two African Americans, including Dr. Channing H. Tobias of the Phelps-Stokes Fund and Sadie Alexander, an attorney from Philadelphia who also served on the board of directors of the National Urban League (NUL), sat on the committee. Over the next ten months, the committee heard testimony from approximately forty witnesses, corresponded with 250 private organizations and individuals, and obtained information from dozens of federal, state, and local government agencies regarding the status of African Americans across the country.

The committee submitted its report, *To Secure These Rights*, in October 1947. Consisting of four parts, the report sounded a clear and forceful call for racial equality and provided a detailed examination of the numerous difficulties confronting African Americans. The committee affirmed the right of all citizens to personal safety, free expression, and equal citizenship as it offered numerous examples of how whites had denied these basic rights to African Americans, including lynching, police brutality, segregation, lack of equal employment opportunity, and inadequate housing and health care. Contending that state and local action would be insufficient to remedy these injustices, the committee urged the federal government to assume a much greater role in promoting racial equality. The most important section of the report, however, was a list of thirty-five specific recommendations for federal action. Some, such as the creation of a civil rights division in the Justice Department and the establishment of a Civil Rights Commission, would strengthen federal monitoring of civil rights violations. Others targeted specific areas of discrimination. The committee, for instance, endorsed legislation that would make lynching a federal crime, create a federal Fair Employment Practices Commission, guarantee voting rights through the abolition of the poll tax and other reforms, prohibit segregation in interstate transportation, end segregation in the armed forces, and eliminate Jim Crow laws in Washington, D.C. Reaction to the report predictably broke down along sectional and racial lines. White southerners denounced it, but Walter White of the National Association for the Advancement of Colored People (NAACP) called it "the most uncompromising and specific pronouncement by a governmental agency on the explosive issue of racial and religious bigotry which has ever been issued."

The report put Truman on the spot politically, for he had to decide whether to support or repudiate it. The president emphatically indicated where he stood by calling *To Secure These Rights* "an American charter of human freedom . . . [and] a guide for action." He followed up this endorsement with a message to Congress early in 1948 that urged enactment of a number of civil rights bills that the committee had favored. When Congress refused to act on civil rights, Truman moved to implement some of the report by issuing executive orders creating the President's Committee on Equality of Treatment and Opportunity in the Armed Services and guaranteeing equal employment opportunity within the federal government.

Though the President's Committee on Civil Rights existed for only a brief time, it exerted a powerful and lasting influence on the growing debate over civil rights during the 1940s and 1950s. Congress did not pass a civil rights bill during the Truman administration, but it did adopt many of the committee's recommendations when the legislative logjam finally did break during the late 1950s and early 1960s. Numerous state and local governments took a cue from the committee as they adopted civil rights reforms. More broadly, the committee helped arouse public awareness of racism as a national problem. It provided more than 25,000 copies of *To Secure These Rights* to the press. Many radio stations held discussions on the issues raised, and the American Jewish Congress distributed 200,000 copies of a summary of the report. In the end, therefore, the committee helped sow the seeds of the Second Reconstruction.

**FURTHER READINGS**

Berman, William C. *The Politics of Civil Rights in the Truman Administration.* Columbus: Ohio State University Press, 1970.

Hamby, Alonzo. *Man of the People: A Life of Harry S. Truman.* New York: Oxford University Press, 1995.

McCoy, Donald R., and Richard Ruetten. *Quest and Response: Minority Rights and the Truman Administration.* Lawrence: University Press of Kansas, 1973.

*Timothy N. Thurber*

## President's Committee on Equal Employment Opportunity

On March 6, 1961, President John F. Kennedy issued Executive Order 10925, creating the President's Committee on Equal Employment Opportunity (PCEEO). The twelve-member PCEEO, appointed by the president, was chaired by Vice-President Lyndon B. Johnson until Kennedy's assassination, when Secretary of Labor W. Willard Wirtz succeeded him as acting chair. The PCEEO was the successor to a number of executive branch antidiscrimination programs that dated back to 1941 when President Franklin D. Roosevelt established the President's Committee on Fair Employment Practice to monitor and eliminate racial discrimination in defense industries. Roosevelt's committee expired in 1946, and in 1951 President Harry S. Truman created the President's Committee on Government Contract Compliance to succeed it. In 1953 President Dwight D. Eisenhower replaced Truman's committee with his own version, the President's Committee on Government Contracts.

President John F. Kennedy, depending on the support of southern Democrats in Congress, was reluctant to pursue civil rights legislation when he came to office. Rather than push for a fair employment statute in Congress, he issued an executive order that created the PCEEO and imposed explicit and stringent requirements on government contractors. It mandated a compliance reporting system to compile a statistical profile of the nation's racial employment patterns and provided for explicit sanctions on government contractors who violated the order, including the threat of contract termination. The PCEEO was empowered to initiate investigations into discriminatory employment practices without waiting for an individual complaint. Despite the executive order's emphasis on enforcement, it did not provide any new standards for proving discrimination, which had been a crucial problem in making fair employment requirements "enforceable" in the past. Instead it stipulated that contractors not only cease discrimination, but also take "affirmative action" to ensure equal employment opportunity.

An important obstacle, though, remained the absence of a clear definition of "affirmative action." The term had originated with the National Labor Relations Act of 1935, which had created the National Labor Relations Board (NLRB). The NLRB had been empowered to order employers and labor unions to cease and desist from unfair labor practices. Moreover, the act had authorized the NLRB to order employers and labor unions to hire, reinstate, and promote minorities and take other appropriate affirmative action, including implementation of remedies negotiated by state antidiscrimination and executive committees. The administration likely meant affirmative action to mean aggressive recruitment, training, and encouragement of minority groups, to build on the gains made in the 1950s in hiring and to extend the steps taken in this direction by its predecessors. While affirmative action eventually became the symbol of a radical departure from the color-blind, individual rights, procedural model of antidiscrimination, this potential was not apparent in 1961.

The PCEEO operated under the same limitations as its predecessors. Unwilling to impair the national defense program, the PCEEO did not cancel large numbers of government contracts to combat discrimination. Moreover, it failed to confront racially exclusive labor unions and did not have the means to produce large numbers of qualified minorities for employment in technical and supervisory positions. Instead, the PCEEO advocated voluntary compliance, since it did not devise a standard of fair employment that could meet legal scrutiny. In order to achieve the desired results, it sponsored a program of voluntary racial preference known as the Plans for Progress. The PCEEO's program sought to induce prominent government contractors to devise their own plans for increasing minority group hiring and employment upgrading. Using statistical profiles of the work force, the program did not devise any new definition of discrimination or identify particular discriminatory policies of employers. It was concerned only with an increase in the number and level of minority group employment. It implied the use of preferential treatment based on race, although it prescribed no openly preferential policies or quotas.

After a year of operation the PCEEO was torn by internal conflicts and drew criticism from a number of quarters outside of the organization. Within the agency there was a dispute between moderates like Robert Troutman, engineer of the voluntary Plans for Progress program, and activists like John G. Field, who favored enforcement rather than voluntarism. In addition, the PCEEO faced attacks from southern Democrats in Congress as well as civil rights activists like Herbert Hill, labor secretary of the National Association for the Advancement of Colored People (NAACP), who took an increasingly critical view of the PCEEO. While NAACP executive secretary Roy Wilkins upbraided Hill for providing ammunition for opponents of equal employment opportunity, the Reverend Martin Luther King Jr. of the Southern Christian Leadership Conference (SCLC) thought Hill's observations were on target, indicating the impatience of the newer, more militant civil rights groups.

In 1962, Vice President Johnson, who chaired the PCEEO, recruited Theodore Kheel as an outside consultant to monitor the committee's work. Kheel had been a labor consultant for the National Urban League (NUL) and a critic of the voluntary, conciliatory approach to equal employment opportunity. He assumed that the affirmative action provision meant that the PCEEO would go beyond cases of overt discrimination. Discrimination in the past, Kheel argued, had made such a lasting impression on minority group workers that it was necessary to "encourage employers to seek out Negroes who will be able to qualify" for employment and job upgradings. The lack of qualified minority group members, he argued, should no longer excuse an employer's lack of minority employees. He urged the PCEEO to add more enforcement power to its conciliation and voluntary compliance program and suggested that the committee discard the individual-complaint process and replace it with a pattern-centered procedure.

The PCEEO also promoted innovative responses to discrimination in areas that were outside of its formal jurisdiction. PCEEO special counsel N. Thompson Powers, for example, set out to devise regulations to increase the representation of minorities in the construction industry apprenticeship system through the Bureau of Apprenticeship and Training in the Department of Labor. Since the principal route to admission to the building trades was familial sponsorship, the Department of Labor required that contractors either abolish nepotism and adopt a strict merit system, or keep the privilege of nepotism but set aside a special quota for minorities. This proposal was not a radically new one; the previous executive committee had experimented with a similar plan, several New Deal agencies had used specific quotas, and preferential treatment was at least implied in the "Plans for

Progress" program. The Department of Labor, however, retreated from its support of racial quotas when the issue generated controversy during the 1963 drafting of the Civil Rights Act of 1964.

Trying to avoid the difficult task of devising a standard of proof of discrimination that would make a color-blind antidiscrimination policy legally enforceable, the PCEEO attempted to encourage employers to demonstrate voluntary racial preference for minority group members. At that time, however, total blue-collar employment was declining, and it is unlikely that in the absence of preferential treatment minority blue-collar employment by government contractors would have increased.

The Labor Department's Bureau of Apprenticeship and Training program tried to combine preferential treatment with enforcement by getting craft unions to set aside places for minorities. This effort, however, ran quickly into the thicket of racial quotas, and the administration retreated from it, afraid to alienate white southern democrats. Thus, the PCEEO faced a serious dilemma; its attempt to rely on voluntarism did not achieve the desired results, while any efforts to enforce nondiscriminatory hiring practices could not avoid the issue of racial quotas.

Despite its best efforts, the PCEEO failed to satisfy the demands and expectations of civil rights advocates. While the PCEEO was probably more successful than its predecessors in gaining employment for minority workers and preparing employers for affirmative action, it achieved only "token" results, perhaps because its program was limited to government employment. Continuing the policies of the Eisenhower committee, the PCEEO foundered on the same rocks as its predecessors. Its decision to rely on voluntarism and its reluctance to resort to sanctions reflected the fact that the PCEEO had a no more satisfactory formula for proof of discrimination than its predecessors. Without legally satisfactory proof, however, no enforcement effort could survive a court challenge. The PCEEO was able to experiment with color-conscious remedies to discrimination only because no color-blind statute defined discrimination, but this same lack of statutory authority also forced the committee to rely on voluntary compliance.

After this unsuccessful foray into affirmative action, the PCEEO was soon eclipsed by the congressional creation of a fair employment statute in Title VII of the Civil Rights Act of 1964. While President Kennedy had proposed that the PCEEO be given statutory authority to implement fair employment practices, Congress decided to create the Equal Employment Opportunity Commission (EEOC) as a separate agency to enforce antidiscrimination in employment. Following the passage of the Civil Rights Act of 1964, the PCEEO retained its jurisdiction over federal contracts, however, it had only a limited budget. Operating in the shadow of the newly created EEOC, the PCEEO floundered for another year. In 1965, President Johnson appointed Vice President Hubert H. Humphrey to head a committee to review federal antidiscrimination programs. Humphrey's investigation resulted in the September 1965 abolition of the PCEEO and its replacement by the Labor Department's Office of Federal Contract Compliance.

**FURTHER READINGS**

Belz, Herman. *Equality Transformed: A Quarter-Century of Affirmative Action*. New Brunswick, N.J.: Transaction Press, 1991.

Brauer, Carl. *John F. Kennedy and the Second Reconstruction*. New York: Columbia University Press, 1977.

Gelber, Steven. *Black Men and Businessmen: The Growing Awareness of a Social Responsibility*. Port Washington, N.Y.: Kennikat Press, 1974.

Graham, Hugh Davis. *The Civil Rights Era: Origins and Development of National Policy, 1960–1972*. New York: Oxford University Press, 1990.

Moreno, Paul D. *From Direct Action to Affirmative Action: Fair Employment Law and Policy in America, 1933–1972*. Baton Rouge: Louisiana State University Press, 1997.

*Paul D. Moreno*

**SEE ALSO** National Council for a Permanent Fair Employment Practices Committee; President's Committee on Fair Employment Practice

## President's Committee on Equal Opportunity in Housing

President John F. Kennedy created the President's Committee on Equal Opportunity in Housing (PCEOH) in 1962 to monitor the enforcement of Executive Order 11063, which ended discrimination in federally funded housing. The PCEOH, chaired by David L. Lawrence, pressed for an end to all housing discrimination in the public and private sector. The committee operated until 1968 when the Fair Housing Act absorbed its mission.

During the 1960 presidential campaign Kennedy charged that his opponent, Richard M. Nixon, led a party that had ignored racial discrimination in federally aided and funded housing, and he promised that, if elected, he would end housing discrimination "with the stroke of a pen." Following the election a host of civil rights groups, including the U.S. Civil Rights Commission and the National Committee Against Discrimination in Housing, joined prominent black leaders and activists such as Bayard Rustin, Roy Wilkins, and A. Philip Randolph, in decrying Kennedy's failure to put his proverbial pen to paper. Finally, on November 20, 1962, Kennedy signed Executive Order 11063. The order, called "Equal Opportunity in Housing," prohibited housing discrimination on the basis of race, color, creed, or national origin, and directed federal agencies to "take every proper and legal action to prevent discrimination in the sale or leasing of housing that was owned or operated by the federal government; housing that was constructed or sold through loans which were made, insured, or guaranteed by the federal government; and housing which was made available through slum clearance or urban renewal programs." Builders and owners of housing that violated the order might be barred from further participation in federal aid programs. Executive Order 11063 affected approximately 225,000 units of public housing plus the sizable stock of housing constructed under the Veterans and Federal Housing Administration programs. The order, however, only applied to dwellings built after 1962 and did not affect the huge stock built in previous years.

To enforce the provisions of this executive order President Kennedy created the PCEOH and appointed the former mayor of Pittsburgh and ex-governor of Pennsylvania, David L. Lawrence, to chair the committee. The eight-member committee included four cabinet officers and the heads of the Veterans Administration, the Housing and Home Finance Administration, and the Federal Home Loan Bank Board. Among those who served on the committee were Jack T. Conway, Alexander Fuller, Theodore Jones, Ferdinand Kramer, Roland Sawyer, and Lewis Weinstein.

Although the PCEOH existed primarily to enforce Executive Order 11063 by monitoring and reporting racial progress in housing, the committee also launched "activities promoting the abandonment of discriminatory practices in housing provided by federal assistance." Ultimately, this educational mission overshadowed the committee's enforcement task. Indeed, Lawrence launched an educational crusade to end housing discrimination and with the support of the U.S. Civil Rights Commission and the National Committee Against Discrimination in Housing lobbied to have Kennedy's order extended to all housing, not just federal assisted units. PCEOH encouraged an end to housing discrimination mainly through a series of conferences held in cities nationwide. At these conferences interested persons discussed the problems of housing discrimination and unveiled successful efforts to eliminate racial barriers and to secure compliance with the executive order. Between 1962 and 1965 PCEOH conferences took place in Boston; Washington, D.C.; Cincinnati; San Francisco; Des Moines; Kansas City; Baltimore; Atlanta; Memphis; Nashville; Savannah; and Miami. To further press its case, the committee published a booklet entitled "How the President's Order Can Help You Acquire a Home of Your Choice."

While PCEOH under Lawrence's leadership vigorously pursued its educational agenda, it proved feeble as an arm of enforcement. Since the executive order only regulated federally assisted housing built after 1962, implementation rested in the hands of agencies such as the Veterans Administration, and the Housing and Home Finance Administration, which administered public housing programs. These agencies, however, frequently shared the values and interests of those being regulated and their staffs were overwhelmed by the task of monitoring compliance with the executive order.

Almost immediately civil rights leaders criticized the order as inadequate and "piecemeal" and urged the president to extend open housing to the private sector, a position fervently endorsed by Lawrence. After Kennedy's assassination in 1963 Rustin and Wilkins beseeched President Lyndon Baines Johnson to extend Executive Order 11063 to include private housing. Wary of igniting a politically explosive issue and with an election one year away, Johnson heeded the advice of Attorney General Nicholas Katzenbach and Robert C. Weaver, administrator of the Housing and Home Finance Administration, and tried to defuse the criticism by appointing a study committee headed by Hubert H. Humphrey. Yet, neither Lawrence nor the U.S. Civil Rights Commission slackened their pace. In March 1965 Lawrence hand-carried a petition to Johnson asking the president to extend Executive Order 11063 to include commercial banks, mutual savings banks, and savings and loans. Lawrence's petition triggered an avalanche of national support. Advocates included the Urban League (UL), the American Civil Liberties Union (ACLU), and the National Association for the Advancement of Colored People (NAACP) as well as the conservative National Association of Real Estate Boards. White House Aid Joseph Califano added his personal plea and in April 1966 Johnson, in a speech to

Congress, declared for a "national policy against racial discrimination in the sale and rental of [all] housing." A lengthy congressional filibuster in 1966 delayed passage of the "fair housing bill" until 1968. After 1968 the issue of prohibiting housing discrimination resided in congressional hands. Lawrence returned to Pittsburgh, and the PCEOH ceased operation.

### FURTHER READINGS

Citizens Commission on Civil Rights. "The Federal Government and Equal Opportunity: A Continuing Failure." In *Critical Perspectives on Housing*. Ed. Rachael G. Bratt, Chester Hartman, and Ann Myerson. Philadelphia: Temple University Press, 1986.

Dulles, Foster Rea. *The Civil Rights Commission, 1957–1965.* East Lansing: The Michigan State University Press, 1968.

Harvey, James C. *Black Civil Rights During the Johnson Administration.* Jackson: University and College Presses of Mississippi, 1973.

United States Commission on Civil Rights. *Twenty Years After Brown: Equal Opportunity in Housing/A Report of the United States Commission on Civil Rights.* Washington, D.C.: The Commission, 1975.

Weber, Michael P. *Don't Call Me Boss, David L. Lawrence: Pittsburgh's Renaissance Mayor.* Pittsburgh: University of Pittsburgh Press, 1988.

*John F. Bauman*

## President's Committee on Equality of Opportunity in the Armed Forces (The Gesell Committee)

The President's Committee on Equality of Opportunity in the Armed Forces, known as the Gesell Committee after its chairman, Gerhard A. Gesell, an attorney in the District of Columbia, was not a revival of the President's Committee on Equality of Treatment and Opportunity in the Armed Forces, the Fahy Committee, even though Executive Order 9981, which authorized the earlier group, remained in effect. On June 24, 1962, President John F. Kennedy announced the creation of the Gesell Committee to generate information and make recommendations assisting Secretary of Defense Robert S. McNamara, rather than the president, in his evaluation and modification of racial policy within the military establishment. The title, which McNamara later described as "windowdressing," and the fact that the president appointed the members, did not signal a resurrection of the Fahy Committee

but nonetheless underscored the importance attached by the Kennedy administration to equal opportunity in the armed services.

The Gesell Committee included one veteran of the Fahy Committee, the African American newspaper publisher of the *Chicago Defender*, John Sengstacke. The other blacks selected by President Kennedy were Whitney M. Young Jr., executive director of the National Urban League (NUL), and Nathaniel S. Colley, a California attorney affiliated with the National Association for the Advancement of Colored People (NAACP). Besides Gesell, the white members were Benjamin Muse, an official of the Southern Regional Council, a civil rights organization, and attorneys Abe Fortas and Louis Hoctor. Another white, Lawrence I. Hewes III, of the Yale school of law, served as the committee's general counsel.

The Gesell Committee set about discovering how racial policy affected the efficiency and effectiveness of the armed forces. To gather the necessary information, the panel and its staff of four obtained statistics from the armed services and from the U.S. Commission on Civil Rights, conferred with senior military and naval commanders, and dispatched interracial teams to various bases, where team members talked with senior and junior officers, members of the enlisted force, and local businessmen. The investigation revealed failures in the application of Department of Defense racial policy. African Americans rarely served on promotion boards, for example. Moreover, they tended to dominate certain less desirable occupational fields while being excluded from other more challenging ones, like serving as pilots. Race also seemed to affect officer training, for the other services lagged behind the army in commissioning African Americans. Despite these flaws, the Gesell Committee insisted that the armed forces set the pace for equal treatment and opportunity, leaving other elements of American society far behind. Indeed, as far as the armed services were concerned, the worst examples of racial discrimination occurred where military and civilian life interacted, specifically in the housing and public accommodations available to uniformed men and women in communities near military and naval bases.

The Kennedy administration asked the committee to report within a year, and in June 1963, the panel issued an interim statement. The Gesell Committee found that racism beyond the perimeter of a base undermined military morale as disastrously as racism on the installation itself and recommended holding the commanding officer responsible for making sure that local civilians, who rented houses or otherwise provided services to uniformed personnel, did not discriminate on the basis of race. In carrying out this responsibility, the commander, the committee believed, should be able to declare a business off-limits to his personnel in the same way that he might bar them from one that posed a danger to health or safety.

Although the services acknowledged the importance to morale of equal treatment and opportunity, on the base or off, they feared that an overzealous commander, aggressively wielding the power to declare businesses off-limits, could damage the relationship between an installation and the nearby communities serving it. In addition, making the commander responsible for this broadened definition of race relations raised the possibility that a civil rights agency within the Department of Defense might rate individual commanders, and the armed services jealously guarded the right to evaluate their own officers. Moreover, the Kennedy administration became concerned that an intrusion of military authority into the local business community might jeopardize congressional progress toward civil rights legislation.

The Department of Defense chose July 26, 1963, the fifteenth anniversary of President Truman's Executive Order 9981, to issue a policy statement reflecting the first year's work of the Gesell Committee as modified by the concerns voiced within the military establishment. The new policy, for example, directed commanders to oppose racial discrimination and promote equal treatment and opportunity in nearby communities but reserved to the secretaries of the army, navy, and air force the ultimate authority to punish offenders by declaring their businesses off-limits. Moreover, the statement confirmed the right of the armed services to rate their officers on carrying out racial policy, subject to a review by a new civil rights bureaucracy under the assistant secretary of Defense for Manpower.

The power to declare an activity off-limits contributed little to extending equal treatment and opportunity into communities near military and naval bases. Legislation replaced the initiative of commander and service secretaries. The Civil Rights Act of 1964 outlawed discrimination in public accommodations, and the Civil Rights Act of 1968 addressed fairness in the sale and rental of housing.

Having provided the information on which Secretary McNamara based the 1963 directive, the Gesell Committee turned to two remaining problems—ensuring equal treatment and opportunity overseas and in the National Guard. Although the committee was without the services of Nathaniel S. Colley, who resigned, it continued its

work after the assassination of John F. Kennedy and the succession of Vice President Lyndon B. Johnson. In addressing racial discrimination overseas, the panel recommended that commanders assume the same responsibility for race relations as in the United States but recognized that the Department of State and the foreign nations involved would have to help negotiate the lowering of racial barriers, which some of them had raised at America's insistence during the era of segregation.

Time-consuming and delicate negotiations with the National Guard Bureau finally resulted in the acceptance of African Americans by the National Guards of all the states, even the ten that as late as 1963 had refused to admit blacks. As the Gesell Committee suggested in its final report, sent to the president on November 20, 1964, the decisive factor in obtaining compliance by the recalcitrant states was the Civil Rights Act of 1964, which authorized cutting off federal funds supporting activities that practiced racial discrimination.

**FURTHER READINGS**

MacGregor, Morris J., Jr. *Integration of the Armed Forces, 1940–1965.* Washington, D.C.: Center of Military History, 1981.

President's Committee on Equal Opportunity in the Armed Forces. *Initial Report: Equality of Treatment and Opportunity for Negro Military Personnel Stationed Within the United States* and *Final Report: Military Personnel Stationed Overseas and Membership and Participation in the National Guard.* In *Blacks in the United States Armed Forces: Basic Documents,* vol. 13. Ed. Morris J. MacGregor Jr. and Bernard C. Nalty. Wilmington, Del.: Scholarly Resources, 1977, items 10 and 14.

*Bernard C. Nalty*

SEE ALSO   President's Committee on Equality of Treatment and Opportunity in the Armed Forces (The Fahy Committee)

# President's Committee on Equality of Treatment and Opportunity in the Armed Forces (The Fahy Committee)

President Harry S. Truman's Executive Order 9981 of July 26, 1948, provided for a President's Committee on Equality of Treatment and Opportunity to examine how the armed forces were complying with the directive, which in effect integrated the races throughout the military establishment. The panel came to be called the Fahy Committee in deference to Charles Fahy, the attorney who headed it. A white native of Georgia, Fahy held liberal views on race relations. When his committee met on January 12, 1949, for its first session, it had six members besides the chairman. Two members were African Americans: John Sengstacke, publisher of the *Chicago Defender*, and Lester Granger, an official of the Urban League and during World War II an advisor to James V. Forrestal, then secretary of the Navy. The remaing four members were white: William Stevenson, the president of Oberlin College, and three men prominent in business or industry, Alphonsus J. Donahue, Dwight Palmer, and Charles Luckman. Neither Donahue nor Luckman contributed much to the deliberations of the committee.

James Forrestal, the first secretary of Defense, and his successor, Louis A. Johnson, balked at having the Fahy Committee unilaterally establish a racial policy for the armed services. Instead they turned to the Personnel Policy Board within their department. The board failed, however, to meld the policies of the air force, which had begun to integrate the races, the navy, which had abandoned its wartime experiments with integration, and the army, which clung to segregation, despite the existence of a policy calling for greater racial equality. Instead of adopting a plan for carrying out Executive Order 9981, the board merely endorsed the objective of equal treatment and opportunity, in effect abandoning the field to the Fahy Committee.

Whether dealing with the Personnel Policy Board or reviewing the plans of the services, Fahy sought to persuade rather than to invoke the authority of the commander in chief. During its negotiations, his committee had fewer problems with the air force than with the navy or the army.

As early as the spring of 1948, before President Truman issued the integration order, the air force had begun laying the foundation for a program to find useful employment for its black airmen, training and assigning them according to the needs of the service rather than solely according to race. Opposition within the service yielded to pressure from Secretary of the Air Force Stuart Symington and to the arguments of Lieutenant General Idwal Edwards, the deputy chief of staff, personnel, who sought to promote the efficient use of manpower. The Fahy Committee received the air force plan in January 1949, reviewed it, and insisted on the elimination of a suggested racial quota. The policy, modified accordingly, went into effect in May of that year, as the air force con-

tinued to carry out the presidential directive by transferring individual African Americans from their segregated units to previously all-white organizations. By year's end, the service had created a racially integrated force that was 6 percent black, compared to the 2 percent that Edwards had expected.

The navy posed a greater challenge to the committee than did the air force. Although dependent on trained specialists from yeomen to gunners, the navy included a large number of African American stewards, who could not be transferred easily in grade to other duties. The marine corps, a component of the naval establishment, had similarly diverted the few African Americans it accepted into limited duty as stewards or security guards. During May and June 1949, Secretary of the Navy Dan A. Kimball and his successor, Francis P. Matthews, approved a series of reforms that the committee found acceptable. The Navy Department endorsed the principle of equal treatment and opportunity regardless of race throughout the navy and marine corps, specifically integrating recruit training for marines. The navy also decided to open the stewards branch to whites, enhance the prestige of that specialty by making chief stewards full-fledged chief petty officers, and attract more African Americans into the enlisted and commissioned ranks. In addition, the service studied the feasibility of making use of sailors, a number of them black, with lower test scores than presently required, and it tapped this source of manpower after the Korean conflict, when so many wartime enlistments expired, and again during the Vietnam War.

The Fahy Committee encountered its greatest difficulty in persuading the army to ensure equal treatment and opportunity regardless of race. The army, which accepted recruits—many of them African Americans—whose test scores would have disqualified them from the navy or air force, adhered to a racial quota that restricted the number of black recruits, excluded them from most training courses, and prevented the mingling of the races except for attaching small black tactical units to much larger white ones. The army seemed to be trying to postpone indefinitely genuine racial integration by arguing that the assignment of individual African Americans to fight alongside whites in the same unit would undermine combat efficiency.

In trying to persuade the army to abandon segregation, the Fahy Committee accepted the service's claim that some African American units had performed poorly during World War II, but the panel argued that segregation, far from being a solution to the problem, might have caused it by destroying morale and crippling efficiency. E. W. Kenworthy, the committee's white executive secretary, recommended emphasizing the link between equal treatment and opportunity and military efficiency, but his tactics might have failed had it not been for an African American personnel specialist employed by the army, Ray Davenport. Along with Major James D. Fowler, a black graduate of the U. S. Military Academy, Davenport explained to the committee that the army had no minimum quota for blacks in 81 percent of the training courses available upon completion of basic training. Also closed to African American soldiers were 198 of 490 military occupational specialties. Race, rather that individual ability or the needs of the service, determined how black soldiers would train and where they would serve, regardless of the impact on morale and effectiveness. The army, moreover, refused to assign individual African Americans to white units, and it had established no deadline for assigning smaller black units as segregated components of larger white ones, for example, African American companies within battalions or regiments.

The army in December 1949 addressed the problem of assimilating the large number of African Americans with low test scores into a racially integrated force, a task made all the more difficult by their eagerness to reenlist, thus monopolizing much of the racial quota. That same month, Fahy succeeded in persuading Secretary of the Army Gordon Gray, who had replaced a diehard segregationist, Kenneth C. Royall, and General J. Lawton Collins, the Army chief of staff, to start the service along the road to racial integration. In January 1950 the army issued a special regulation calling for equal treatment and opportunity and requiring that vacancies in certain critical specialties be filled promptly without regard to race. The service further satisfied the Fahy Committee by agreeing to accept an unlimited number of higher-scoring African Americans while excluding those with the lowest scores, even though they had successfully completed a previous enlistment. In March 1950, the army agreed to scrap the racial quota, provided it could be revived if the racial balance became "disproportionate," and on the March 27 recruiting began without regard to race. The expansion of the army to fight the Korean War and the need to make the most efficient use of manpower, rather than this new policy, doomed the racial quota.

Even though the committee convinced the armed forces to adopt a series of specific reforms that reflected the spirit of President Truman's executive order, Fahy and his colleagues remained concerned that equality of treatment and opportunity might not prevail. The panel considered including in its final report, published as *Freedom to Serve*, a formal recommendation that the president retain the committee to oversee compliance with the agreements it had forged. Under pressure from the White House staff, the committee decided to offer the suggestion orally at its final meeting with the chief executive in May 1950. In July, Truman thanked Fahy for his service and told him that Executive Order 9981, with its provision for a presidential oversight panel, would remain in effect.

**FURTHER READINGS**

Dalfiume, Richard M. *Desegregation of the U. S. Armed Forces: Fighting on Two Fronts, 1939–1953*. Columbia: University of Missouri Press, 1969.

Gropman, Alan L. *The Air Force Integrates, 1945–1964*. Washington, D.C.: Office of Air Force History, 1978.

MacGregor, Morris J., Jr. *Integration of the Armed Forces, 1940–1965*. Washington, D.C.: Center of Military History, 1981.

President's Committee on Equality of Treatment and Opportunity in the Armed Forces. *Freedom to Serve: Equality of Treatment and Opportunity in the Armed Services*. Washington, D.C.: Government Printing Office, 1950. In *Blacks in the United States Armed Forces: Basic Documents*, vol. 11. Ed. Morris J. MacGregor Jr. and Bernard C. Nalty. Wilmington, Del.: Scholarly Resources, 1977, item 37.

*Bernard C. Nalty*

**SEE ALSO**    President's Committee on Equality of Opportunity in the Armed Forces (The Gesell Committee)

## President's Committee on Fair Employment Practice

The President's Committee on Fair Employment Practice (FEPC) was created by President Franklin D. Roosevelt in June 1941. Roosevelt established the FEPC after A. Philip Randolph, of the Brotherhood of Sleeping Car Porters, organized the March on Washington movement and vowed to lead a protest of 100,000 African Americans to expose job discrimination in the nation's defense industries and segregation in the armed forces. To halt such embarrassing activity, Roosevelt reluctantly issued Executive Order 8802, which established the FEPC as an independent agency under the executive branch. The FEPC received authority to investigate racial, ethnic, and religious bias in defense industries and federal agencies,

Bertha Stallworth inspects a 40mm artillery cartridge case during World War II, ca. 1943. *Archive Photos*

but the president declined to deal with the issue of military segregation. Nevertheless, Randolph called off the march.

FEPC appointees included a southern editor, Committee Chairman Mark Ethridge of the *Louisville Courier-Journal;* an industrialist, David Sarnoff of the Radio Corporation of America; two African Americans, Milton Webster of the Brotherhood of Sleeping Car Porters and Chicago alderman Earl B. Dickerson; and two representatives from organized labor, John Brophy of the Congress of Industrial Organizations (CIO) and later, Boris Shishkin of the American Federation of Labor (AFL). A full-time executive secretary, Lawrence Cramer, and an assistant executive secretary, black Howard Law School dean, George M. Johnson, ran the committee and carefully recruited an interracial staff. The FEPC became the first federal agency in history to deal exclusively with minority employment problems and to place African Americans in policy-making positions.

During the first year, Executive Secretary Cramer established vital written agreements with other, sometimes hostile, federal agencies that dealt with manpower (U. S. Employment Service, War Manpower Commission), procurement (Army, Navy and Maritime Commission), and personnel (Civil Service Commission, War Department). Federal law required the inclusion of nondiscrimination clauses in the contracts that government agencies negotiated with defense and war industries. With mixed results, Cramer and his successors sought the cooperation of these bodies in investigating and dealing with contract violations that involved job discrimination.

Eschewing race-conscious quotas used by New Deal agencies, such as the Public Works Administration, the FEPC accepted and investigated the complaints of thousands of individuals in the belief that a color-blind approach to employment could eliminate discrimination. Especially important was the attention given to the quality of the job. The committee insisted that an applicant's training and qualifications should determine the level of employment, from the unskilled worker to the professional. No federal agency had ever pursued seriously such a goal for minority job-seekers.

Under determined prodding from Earl Dickerson, the FEPC undertook widespread investigations and conducted public hearings in Los Angeles, Chicago, and New York. In the aircraft industry, Boeing of Seattle, citing its contract with the International Association of Machinists (IAM), refused to hire skilled minority workers. After the FEPC referred this difficult case to the president, the IAM agreed to permit minority employment without union membership. Vultee Aircraft in Los Angeles also had serious problems. Its officers admitted that the company routinely excluded non-Caucasians, including Japanese, Mexican, and African Americans. Elsewhere, many defense contractors preferred only Protestant employees and used job application forms requiring religious and racial identification. Nearly all AFL unions barred African Americans from membership except in separate, inferior auxiliary unions. Almost without exception, the nation's newspapers carried employment ads that specified race and religion. In the South, such notices were segregated by race. Following each hearing, the committee issued findings of discrimination and monitored compliance with its orders.

Meanwhile, the FEPC also investigated bias in defense training. In administering this important program, the U.S. Office of Education established broad guidelines, but it left their implementation to state and local education officials. Various forms of discrimination against different minority groups occurred nationwide, but in the deep South, education officials refused to provide practically any training skills for African Americans because, they argued, employers would not hire them. Although Congress mandated that training be provided without discrimination, most federal funds and resources went to facilities for southern whites. Forbidden to air publicly charges of discrimination against a federal agency, the FEPC in April 1942 conducted a secret hearing that forced the U.S. Office of Education to issue orders against discrimination. Nevertheless, the administration forbade the FEPC to publish these findings.

In June 1942, the FEPC took its activity to Birmingham in the heart of the deep South, where it exposed bias in nearly every war-related industry. The committee, including its black members, publicly interrogated and sat in judgment on southern employers, union leaders, and state officials in a manner unfamiliar to the segregated society. The Birmingham hearing stirred up such a storm of protest, particularly from southern politicians, that Roosevelt took hostile action. Faced with an off-year election in which southern voters could be crucial, he tried to weaken the FEPC by transferring it to the powerful War Manpower Commission (WMC). This move ended the FEPC's independence and placed its financing, hitherto derived from the president's contingency fund, in the hands of a Congress with bitter FEPC enemies. But the agency also had influential opponents within the administration, and Roosevelt abolished the original FEPC ten months later.

Though the "old committee" had been weak and underfunded, its staff established sound administrative procedures as well as an agenda involving moral issues that could not be ignored. Its active cases included charges of discrimination against Gulf and West Coast shipyards and the boilermakers union, mining interests in the southwest, several railroads and their brotherhoods, numerous midwestern defense contractors, and public transportation companies and their unions in several cities, including the nation's capital. Meanwhile, the FEPC had attracted impressive support from African Americans, liberals, religious groups, and CIO unions. Their outraged protests led Roosevelt in May 1943 to issue Executive Order 9346, creating a second, independent FEPC attached to the Office of Emergency Management.

Monsignor Francis Haas, of the National Labor Relations Board (NLRB), headed the new committee. While Milton Webster, John Brophy, and Boris Shishkin stayed on, the militant Earl Dickerson reluctantly departed. His elderly successor, the conservative black editor, P. B. Young of the *Norfolk Journal and Guide*, served only briefly. He was replaced by the brilliant black attorney, Charles Hamilton Houston, a Harvard Law School graduate who had served on the legal staff of the National Association for the Advancement of Colored People (NAACP). Sarah Southall of International Harvester Company, whose background included work with the Chicago Urban League, also joined the committee.

In recruiting his two top administrators from the NLRB, Chairman Haas demoted George M. Johnson, FEPC's highest-ranking African American staff member. The arrival of Deputy Chairman Malcolm Ross and Director of Operations Will Maslow, both Caucasians with limited experience in race relations, led critics derisively to label these and other alleged race experts in the administration, some of them liberal southerners, as the "white cabinet." After heated protests, Haas appointed Johnson as a co-equal of Ross, with the title of assistant chairman. As such, he attended and participated in committee meetings. Johnson kept this position after Haas's October resignation and Ross's elevation to chairman. Significantly, the staff went through little change, and the new committee picked up virtually all of the old committee's agenda.

With nearly $500,000 in funding, the FEPC expanded their Washington headquarters and authorized regional offices. Its ten functioning regions utilized mixed racial staffs, half of them headed by African Americans. Region IV in Washington, D.C., was directed by Joseph H. B. Evans, a University of Michigan Phi Beta Kappa graduate who had served previously in the Resettlement Administration and the WMC's Minorities Branch. Edward Lawson left the WMC's Negro Branch to preside over New York's Region II. G. James Fleming III, a contributor to the Swedish economist Gunnar Myrdal's racial study, took over Region III in his native Philadelphia, where his Republican family was prominent. Milo Manly, an industrial relations expert, handled the FEPC's suboffice in Pittsburgh, where discrimination in the steel mills threatened war production. In the Midwest, William T. McKnight, previously an Ohio assistant attorney general, guided the Region V office in Cleveland. Chicago's Region VI was directed by Elmer Henderson, a social anthropologist from Dillard University in New Orleans.

Although these positions proved challenging, African American field investigators in the deep South and the Southwest could face real danger. In 1942, after sending G. James Fleming III to El Paso on a temporary assignment investigating the mining industry, the central office became so concerned about his safety that it considered seriously ordering him to leave. John Hope II, who handled cases out of the Region VII office in Atlanta, his home town, approached many of his tasks with fear. Sometimes followed during his travels, he stopped visiting friends, who might be compromised. L. Virgil Williams, a Dallas native, served only a short time in that city before accepting a transfer to Chicago.

Other minorities who served in the FEPC also experienced job discrimination. The Mexican American scholar, Carlos Castaneda, directed Region X's Dallas office. On the old committee, David Sarnoff considered himself a representative of the Jewish community as well as business. Will Maslow also had close ties to Jewish groups. Ethnic and racial organizations provided important, unofficial assistance by locating victims of job discrimination, helping them file complaints, scouting for biased employers, and finding minority job applicants willing to set up test cases. Branches of the NAACP and the National Urban League (NUL) as well as Jewish groups engaged in such activity. In 1942, the Jewish Coordinating Committee even proposed that the FEPC deputize representatives from private agencies as investigators.

As one of the most controversial agencies in history, the FEPC endured constant attacks from politicians, especially southerners, while many employers and AFL unions ignored its directives and blamed each other for noncompliance. After assaulting the FEPC for months with subpoenas and hearings, the House of Representative's Smith Committee, finding no violations of the law, adjourned without issuing a report. Georgia's senator Richard B. Russell damaged the FEPC most seriously with legislative amendments that mandated congressional financing. Moreover, he opened the FEPC to court attacks, weakened its already inadequate enforcement powers, and reduced the chairman's salary to that of a second-class agency. Despite such harassment, the FEPC still had widespread support, and Congress maintained its customary level of funding for 1944–45. In a presidential election year, however, attempts to create a permanent FEPC foundered partly for lack of administration support.

With the war winding down in 1945, a southern Senate filibuster, although failing to kill the FEPC outright, succeeded in reducing its appropriation to $250,000. As the agency dismantled regional offices and reduced personnel, it lost all hope of participating in the reconversion process and protecting minority workers from discrimi-

natory layoffs. While bias against minorities continued unabated in the American work-place, the ending of the national emergency left few war industries for the FEPC to oversee. Meanwhile, the committee's coalition of supporters began to disintegrate. A short Senate filibuster against a permanent FEPC early in 1946 assured the agency's demise the following June.

While most historians agreed that the creation of the FEPC provided African Americans with an important victory, many questioned the agency's effectiveness. Wartime labor shortages eased job discrimination, they maintained, not the weak and poorly funded FEPC. Undoubtedly, in the full employment economy, untold numbers of unskilled and low-paying jobs became available to minorities, but the FEPC demanded more. Its concentration on the quality of employment became one of its most important contributions. As some historians have noted, the FEPC also helped establish the precedent that job bias constituted a denial of civil rights. In its activities, the agency achieved both symbolic and long-term significance, and in some respects it served as a precursor of the upcoming civil rights movement.

**FURTHER READINGS**

Daniel, Cletus E. *Chicano Workers and the Politics of Fairness: The FEPC in the Southwest.* Austin: University of Texas Press, 1991.

Moreno, Paul D. *From Direct Action to Affirmative Action: Fair Employment Law and Policy in America, 1933–1972.* Baton Rouge: Louisiana State University Press, 1997.

Neuchterlein, James A. "The Politics of Civil Rights: The FEPC, 1941–1946." *Prologue* 10 (1978): 171–91.

Reed, Merl E. *Seedtime for the Modern Civil Rights Movement: The President's Committee on Fair Employment Practice, 1941–1946.* Baton Rouge: Louisiana State University Press, 1991.

Ruchames, Louis. *Race, Jobs & Politics, The Story of FEPC.* New York: Columbia University Press, 1952.

*Merl E. Reed*

**SEE ALSO**   National Council for a Permanent Fair Employment Practices Committee

## President's Committee on Government Contract Compliance

*See* Government Contract Compliance Committee.

## President's Committee on Government Contracts

On August 13, 1953, President Dwight D. Eisenhower signed an executive order creating the President's Committee on Government Contracts (PCGC). Established to oversee equal employment opportunity in firms with government contracts, the nine-member body was headed by Vice President Richard Nixon and included prominent labor, business, and political leaders such as Walter Reuther of the United Auto Workers (UAW), George Meany of the American Federation of Labor (AFL), Fred Lazarus of the American Retail Federation, and Congressman James Roosevelt of California. J. Ernest Wilkins, an attorney who would later become an assistant secretary of labor under Eisenhower, was the group's lone African American member and became a vice chair.

The committee emerged in part out of the failed struggle for a federal Fair Employment Practice Committee (FEPC) during the late 1940s and early 1950s. Rebuffed on Capitol Hill by a strong coalition of southern Democrats and conservative Republicans, civil rights advocates had turned to the White House for action to promote equal employment opportunity. President Harry Truman had responded by forming his Committee on Government Contract Compliance. That body, however, was not fully staffed until April 1953. A month later, Eisenhower directed aide Maxwell Rabb, his chief advisor on minority issues, to draft a plan for a new committee in this area.

The committee reflected Eisenhower's narrow vision of federal involvement in civil rights matters. During the 1952 campaign he had opposed FEPC legislation that would give a federal employment board enforcement powers and would apply to nearly all employers as an inappropriate extension of federal power, yet he did vow to fight for equal opportunity in areas under direct federal control. Fair employment practices in firms with government contracts thus became part of a civil rights program that included combating discrimination in the military, the denial of voting rights across the South, and segregation in the District of Columbia. Holding grave doubts about the power of laws to solve racial problems, Eisenhower considered moral exhortation and education as better approaches than the threat of legal action. Committee members thus gave numerous speeches outlining the social, political, and economic benefits of equal employment opportunity, and the group undertook promotional efforts through the production of brochures, films, and television and radio spots. It also sponsored several educational conferences for business, labor, and civil rights leaders. Equal employment opportunity, Vice President Nixon typically observed, was "good business, good citizenship, and plain, good sense."

Several features severely hampered the committee's effectiveness. Most important, it lacked enforcement powers, which were reserved for individual government agencies. The committee could investigate complaints of discrimination in firms with government contracts, but if problems were found members could only appeal to an employer's goodwill. Convinced that its conciliatory approach would improve race relations in the long run, the administration often assured irate southern leaders that the committee was not another FEPC and that it would not seek to expand the body's enforcement powers. Few agencies, moreover, showed much inclination to pursue reports of discrimination vigorously, and in no case was a contract canceled. Several large industries enjoyed exemptions from the nondiscrimination rule. Even submitting a complaint proved to be an arduous, time-consuming process, and relatively few African Americans chose to do so. Five years after its creation, the committee had received only 644 complaints. More than 40 percent of those lay beyond the committee's jurisdiction. Unions and businesses had little to fear as the committee conducted only perfunctory of investigations in most cases. Conflicts with several state fair employment agencies also limited the committee's impact. Finally, its initial annual budget of $125,000 was far too small for the enormous scope of its assignment. Herbert Hill of the National Association for the Advancement of Colored People (NAACP) aptly summed up the committee's shortcomings by noting in 1957 that in four years it had produced "mainly ritual and rhetoric with little substance."

The committee attempted to remedy some of these problems during Eisenhower's second term. Regional offices opened in Chicago, Los Angeles, Atlanta, and Dallas. By 1961 the committee had a twenty-four member staff and a budget of $375,000. The committee hoped to increase its profile and its effectiveness through persuading Congress to enact legislation making the body permanent, but southern intransigence on Capitol Hill and a reluctance by Eisenhower to fight vigorously for the proposal doomed the measure in 1959 and 1960. President Kennedy would take up the issue through his President's Committee on Equal Employment Opportunity (PCEEO), with the matter of equal employment in firms with government contracts eventually falling under the jurisdiction of the Office of Federal Contract Compliance Program (OFCCP).

**FURTHER READING**

Burk, Robert. *The Eisenhower Administration and Black Civil Rights.* Knoxville: University of Tennessee Press, 1984.

*Timothy N. Thurber*

SEE ALSO    National Council for a Permanent Fair Employment Practices Committee; President's Committee on Fair Employment Practice; President's Committee on Government Employment Policy

## President's Committee on Government Employment Policy

In 1953, President Dwight D. Eisenhower established the President's Committee on Government Employment Policy (PCGEP) to ensure merit employment in the federal government. The PCGEP was the successor to several executive agencies devoted to the elimination of racial discrimination in employment. The first of these was President Franklin D. Roosevelt's Committee on Fair Employment Practice, which prohibited discrimination in defense industries during World War II. Roosevelt's committee expired in 1946 due to the lack of congressional funding. In 1948 President Harry S. Truman issued Executive Order 9980, creating the Fair Employment Board (FEB) within the U.S. Civil Service Commission to investigate complaints of discrimination in government service.

When Eisenhower became president, the FEB caused the new administration considerable embarrassment that led officials to call for its abolition. Rather than abolish the FEB, however, Eisenhower issued Executive Order 10590, which prohibited discrimination in government employment and replaced the FEB with the PCGEP. The PCGEP's first five committee members were Maxwell Abbell, president of the United Synagogues of America; Archibald J. Carey of Chicago; Charles H. Kendall of the Office of Defense Mobilization; J. Ernest Wilkins of the Labor Department; and Civil Service Commissioner W. Arthur McCoy. In 1955, the committee expanded to seven members. It had a three-person staff that had to rely on government agencies for information on discrimination charges.

The PCGEP had essentially a policy-promulgating agenda, promoting self-policing of agencies. Procedural fairness, not racial proportionalism, was its animating goal. As was the case with other Eisenhower administration agencies, notably the President's Committee on Government Contracts, the PCGEP drew criticism from some sectors of the civil rights movement. In particular, Herbert Hill, labor secretary of the National Association for the Advancement for Colored People (NAACP), attacked the committee for lassitude. According to Jacob Seidenberg, executive director of the President's Committee on Government Contracts, Hill provided the principal source for William Peters's *The Southern Temper.* Published in 1959, the book presented a misleadingly biased and critical view of the administration's civil rights record. Peters's work, though, remains the principal source of information on the committee; no original research has been done.

The PCGEP is generally regarded as having done little to change the racial employment patterns in the federal bureaucracy, evincing a neglect of civil rights issues typical of the Eisenhower years.

**FURTHER READINGS**

Burk, Robert Frederick. *The Eisenhower Administration and Black Civil Rights.* Knoxville: University of Tennessee Press, 1984.

Mayer, Michael S. "Eisenhower's Conditional Crusade: The Eisenhower Administration and Civil Rights, 1953–1957." Ph.D. diss., Princeton University, 1984.

Schlundt, Ronald Alan. "Civil Rights Policies in the Eisenhower Years." Ph.D. diss., Rice University, 1973.

*Paul D. Moreno*

SEE ALSO    National Council for a Permanent Fair Employment Practices Committee; President's Committee on Fair Employment Practice; President's Committee on Government Contracts

## President's Initiative on Race

On June 13, 1997, President William Clinton issued Executive Order 13050, which established the President's Initiative on Race (PIR). The PIR was charged with formulating recommendations designed to improve race relations in the twenty-first century. For this purpose, the PIR sought to engage the American public in an examination of and dialogue about race, racism, and racial tolerance. The organization met with controversy early in its inception and questions regarding its purpose, usefulness, advisory board composition, and subject matter continued to plague it throughout its year-long existence.

The PIR's seven-member advisory board was chaired by John Hope Franklin, renowned scholar and author of numerous books on American history and racial politics. Other board members included Linda Chavez-Thompson, executive vice president of the AFL-CIO; Reverend Dr. Suzan D. Johnson Cook, author, pastor of Bronx Christian Fellowship, and civil rights activist; Angela E. Oh, lawyer and civil rights activist; Thomas H. Kean, author, president of Drew University, and former governor of New Jersey (1982–1990); William F. Winter, author, lawyer, and former governor of Mississippi (1980–1984); and Bob Thomas, executive vice president for Strategic Marketing of Republic Industries and former chief executive officer of Nissan Motor Corporation, U.S.A. The PIR was aided by a staff of more than fifty, headed by Executive Director Judith Winston. It received additional support from three consultants and members of the president's staff.

From the beginning, advisory board members as well as the entire board conducted numerous public meetings throughout the country. These gatherings usually highlighted specific areas in which barriers of discrimination continue to prevent the full inclusion of racial minorities in American society. Several hundred thousand people of diverse educational, racial, religious, age, geographical, and occupational backgrounds participated in conferences, seminars, workshops, lectures, and town meetings. These gatherings, focusing on education, employment, economic opportunity, health care, and criminal justice, culminated in a list of recommendations that the board presented to the president. In addition, President Clinton conducted several national town hall meetings across the United States, in an effort to engage the American public in a dialogue about the activities of the advisory board and to provide a forum for those who wanted to share their experiences with discrimination and racial intolerance.

Moreover, board and staff members organized a conference on hate crimes, held at the White House in November 1997; identified "Promising Practices" and 300 community organizations that addressed actively issues of race and racism; participated in numerous newspaper, television, and magazine interviews; suggested and aired two national public-service announcements; created a "guide book" to stimulate conversations about racial tolerance; and initiated a "Campus Week of Dialogue on Race" on over 600 college campuses.

Finally, the advisory board recommended enhancing the ability of civil rights organizations to enforce civil rights laws and strengthening hate crime laws and their enforcement as well as the collection and dissemination of information about such crimes. Additional recommendations included improving teacher preparation, encouraging high school students to attend college, endorsing diversity in grades K-12, providing education and job training for immigrants who lack language and job skills, and implementing and ensuring a comprehensive Native American and Alaskan Native education policy that is outlined in Executive Order 13096. Other recommendations included the creation of a commission to examine American Indian economic development, an increase of minimum wages and federal funds for urban revitalization, support of the right of working people to engage in collective bargaining, assistance of community development corporations, promotion of American Indian access to affordable housing, reduction and elimination of drug sentencing disparities, diversification of law enforcement, and advocacy of broad-based expansions of health insurance coverage. Moreover, the board urged Congress to appropriate funding for the Race and Ethnic Health Disparities Initiative and to increase funding for existing programs that target underserved populations of people of color. Finally, the board advocated antidiscrimination measures on behalf of every racial and ethnic group.

During its existence, the advisory board was the subject of much criticism. Many newspapers, including the *New York Times* and *Washington Post*, criticized the board for not having a large enough staff or for getting a slow start, while conservatives and opponents of affirmative action complained about their lack of representation on the board. Although the advisory board meetings never focused on affirmative action but on educational access, it was a criticism that gained steam throughout the term of the board. The most aggressive and long-lasting criticism, however, came from Native Americans who had no representatives on the advisory board. The board attempted to address the criticism by appointing a Native American consultant and meeting with Native Americans and their leaders. These efforts, however, did little to alleviate Native American concerns that advisory board members were ill-equipped to discuss or respond to the specific forms of discrimination experienced by Native Americans.

After formulating its policy recommendations, the PIR and its advisory board officially disbanded in September 1998. A permanent "Office for One America" continues the PIR's efforts to create "One America for the 21st Century" and bridge the racial divide.

**FURTHER READING**

Report of the Advisory Board. *One America in the 21st Century: Forging a New Future, The President's Initiative on Race.* Washington, D.C.: U.S. Government Printing Office, September 1998.

*Nishani Frazier*

## Prince Hall Masons

The Prince Hall Masons are an African American fraternal organization dedicated to promoting brotherhood, community service, and a positive black identity as well as to combating racism. The group emerged during the American Revolution. It is aligned with Scottish Rite rituals and grants mastery to the thirty-third degree. Its relationship to white Freemasonry, however, remains problematic because some whites refuse to accept Prince Hall Masons as legitimate.

Prince Hall Masonry was born in mystery and controversy. The organization derived its name from Prince Hall, its eighteenth-century founder. Hall was born in Barbados in 1748, the son of an English leather merchant and a free black woman of French descent. No records verify this and fragmentary evidence suggests Hall might have been born as early as 1735. By 1765 Hall was living in Boston, however, his legal status, like his birth date, remains ambiguous. Some sources indicate that Hall was not of free-born origins, but the slave of leather-dresser William Hall, who taught him the trade and freed him some time around 1770.

Harry A. Williamson (standing, far right) and five fellow members of the Barthaginian Lodge No. 47 (Prince Hall), 1907. *Schomburg Center for Research in Black Culture*

By 1773 Hall had acquired real estate and as a result his name was listed on the city's voting roll. During this time Hall may have become a minister of an African Methodist Episcopal (AME) Church, in Cambridge, but no extant evidence verifies this. On January 13, 1777, Hall's name appeared on a petition to the Massachusetts General Court calling for the abolition of slavery.

By then, the American Revolution was underway, and Hall used the conflict to his advantage. In 1775, just after colonial militia battled British soldiers at Lexington and Concord, Hall addressed the Massachusetts Committee of Safety in hopes of wrangling a commitment to black emancipation. That year, Hall and fourteen other African Americans petitioned to become members of Boston's St. John's Lodge, the first Freemasons who received a charter, or "warrant," in the American colonies. When the black men under Hall's leadership were rebuffed by Boston area Masons, they obtained a charter from a British regiment stationed at Castle Williams in Boston harbor. They were initiated into Lodge 441, Irish Constitution, which was attached to the Thirty-Eighth Regiment of Foot, British Army. This became the basis for Prince Hall Masonry. Though the British garrison retreated from Boston in 1776, it left behind a permit for Hall's group to assemble as African Lodge No. 1. After the war the Grand Lodge of England officially chartered the Boston group as African Lodge 459 on September 29, 1784.

Hall adroitly exploited the American Revolution to obtain a charter for black Freemasons and pressured both sides for greater racial justice by implying that African Americans would assist whichever side most supported black rights. The British actively recruited African Americans and held out vague promises of emancipation. Hall also represented a delegation of freedmen who offered their services to George Washington during the war. Hall may have served in the army, however, his military participation is difficult to determine because colonial records list three men by the same name. Hall's ambiguous military status notwithstanding, his efforts bore fruit. In 1783, Massachusetts chief justice William Cushing, pressured by various groups and individuals, including Hall, ruled that the commonwealth's 1780 constitution had abolished African slavery in the state.

Hall was less successful in getting white Freemasons to accept his organization as legitimate. African Lodge 459 was not granted its charter until 1784, a year after the Treaty of Paris, and it did not arrive in the United States until 1787. This led many white Masons to consider null and void the charter that the English had granted in 1784.

The situation was further complicated when the British Masons dropped African Lodge 459 from the list of recognized lodges in 1813, after the Grand Lodge of England healed a rift with rebellious factions and agreed to a policy of racial exclusion. In 1827, Prince Hall Masons issued a Declaration of Independence from England's Grand Lodge.

African Americans continued to meet, despite their uncertain status within the world of Freemasonry. A 1789 sermon delivered by the Reverend John Marrant before African Lodge 459 is reputed to be the first published speech by an African American. In 1791, Prince Hall was appointed Grand Master over all black lodges, a capacity in which he served until his death in 1807. The year Hall became Grand Master, Absalom Jones, an Episcopal minister from Philadelphia, requested permission to extend black Masonry to Pennsylvania. By the late 1790s African Americans had established new lodges in Philadelphia, New York, and Providence, Rhode Island. In 1808, the African Grand Lodge formed to oversee the practices of what was already informally dubbed "Prince Hall Masonry."

Black Masonry was not immune to the anti-Masonic hysteria following the disappearance of exposé writer Thomas Morgan, who was allegedly abducted by Masons in 1826. The anti-Masonic climate of the 1830s made recruitment of black Masons both difficult and dangerous. Nonetheless, nineteenth-century black Masons continued their recruitment, cooperated with the abolitionist movement, and made attempts to cultivate a positive public image of African Americans. Most early members came from the upper strata of black society. They were reformers, ministers, and skilled artisans who came to the lodges to meet in secrecy and safety. The latter group was especially drawn to black Masonry for physical protection and emotional support. Black artisans were frequently assaulted by white workers who resented their competition. In Cincinnati, for example, white workers protesting the employment of black workers rioted in 1829. Here, as elsewhere, Prince Hall Masonry offered fraternal solace as well as physical protection, providing patrols for black neighborhoods. Masonic membership also became an important element in securing work for traveling black artisans.

The existence of slavery in the South and racism in the North naturally led Prince Hall Masons to take up the question of race in American society. Some Masons, like Hall, supported the creation of an African colony for manumitted slaves, while others supported the abolitionist movement. Absalom Jones, who had established Masonic lodges in Pennsylvania, for example, helped underwrite William Lloyd Garrison's *Liberator*. By 1847, Prince Hall Masonic lodges existed in most states north of the Mason-Dixon line and in Liberia.

During the Civil War, Prince Hall Masons actively supported the Union cause and Grand Master Lewis Hayden assisted Massachusetts governor John Albion Andrew in establishing the famed Fifty-fourth Regiment commanded by Robert Boone Shaw. Hundreds of Prince Hall Masons served in the Union Army, including Martin Delany who was the first African American to rise to the rank of captain. Not surprisingly, several black Civil War regiments established Prince Hall lodges.

Prince Hall Masons were active in the Freedmen's Bureau during Reconstruction. Several Masons held posts with the bureau while others were elected to political offices, including Hiram Revels of Mississippi, the first African American elected to the U.S. Senate. The post-Civil War period also saw an expansion of lodges established by the members of the regular black army units, the Ninth and Tenth Cavalry and the Twenty-Fourth and Twenty-Fifth Infantry. Many of the black soldiers served on the western frontier, making up the fabled "buffalo soldiers." Several Prince Hall Masons won Congressional Medals of Honor, including Harry Williamson, later a noted historian of black Masonry. Prince Hall Masonry also established itself in the former Confederacy, and several of its members were active in the National Colored Labor Union. Black lodges often served as protective fronts for labor organizing. Several local assemblies of black Knights of Labor, for example, operated publicly as Masonic lodges to dissuade the violence of racist organizations like the Ku Klux Klan.

With the battle for emancipation won, Prince Hall Masons turned their attention to securing civil rights for African Americans. Prince Hall ranks included former Grand Master Richard Gleaves, the lt. governor of South Carolina during Reconstruction, as well as Hiram Revels. Famed social reformers Booker T. Washington and W. E. B. Du Bois were Masons, as was editor T. Thomas Fortune. By 1896, there were Prince Hall lodges in thirty-two states, the District of Columbia, Canada, and Liberia.

The end of Reconstruction exacerbated tensions between white and black Masons, especially in the South where white Masonry was occasionally linked to white supremacy groups. Many whites refused to accept Prince Hall Masons as legitimate, including Masonic historian Albert Pike who later recanted his position. In 1908, several white southern Grand Lodges severed ties with New Jersey Masons for allowing black initiates.

The establishment of Jim Crow systems once again made Prince Hall Masonry a physical as well as intellectual refuge. Not surprisingly, black intelligentsia often gravitated toward Freemasonry, as did cultural icons such as Eubie Blake, Bert Williams, Duke Ellington, and Count Basie. A. Philip Randolph, founder of the Brotherhood of Sleeping Car Porters (BSCP), was a Prince Hall Mason, and he drew upon that network for financial and logistical support.

In the twentieth century, Prince Hall Masons have been more overtly political than white Masons, whose bylaws often forbid political debate. Thurgood Marshall, the lawyer who argued the *Brown v. the Board of Education* case in 1954 and later became the first black Supreme Court justice, was a Prince Hall Mason. So too were civil rights leaders such as Medgar Evers, Benjamin Hooks, and Andrew Young; and prominent politicians such as Tom Bradley, Charles Rangel, and Carl Stokes.

Only since the 1970s has Prince Hall Masonry had the luxury of being primarily a fraternal organization. Today it is involved in community projects, mutual aid, morality building, and the promotion of positive images of black Americans. The organization has over 4,500 lodges worldwide and claims jurisdiction over more than 300,000 initiates. A national journal, *Phylaxis Magazine*, was established in 1974.

## FURTHER READINGS

Dumneil, Lynn. *Freemasonry and American Culture*. Princeton: Princeton University Press, 1984.

Stevens, Albert. *The Cyclopedia of Fraternities*. New York: E. B. Treat, 1907.

Walkes, Joseph. *Black Square & Compass: 200 Years of Prince Hall Freemasonry*. Richmond, Va.: Macoy Publishing, 1979.

Weir, Robert E. *Beyond Labor's Veil: The Culture of the Knights of Labor*. University Park: The Pennsylvania State University Press, 1996.

Williams, Loretta. *Black Freemasonry and Middle-Class Realities*. Columbia: University of Missouri, 1980.

*Robert E. Weir*

## Progressive Farmers and Household Union

*See* Arkansas Commission on Race Relations.

# Progressive National Baptist Convention

The Progressive National Baptist Convention (PNBC) was founded by a dissatisfied faction of the National Baptist Convention, U.S.A., Inc. (NBC) in 1961. The dissension began in 1957 when the NBC expelled ten pastors for challenging in court the leadership of the organization's president, Dr. Joseph H. Jackson of Chicago. Jackson had declared invalid a 1952 NBC rule that limited presidential terms to a four-year tenure, claiming that it had been passed in a manner that was procedurally unconstitutional. Jackson's position was upheld by a federal court but it did not pacify his opponents. Disagreement over procedure, however, was not the only reason for the rift between the PNBC and the NBC. The schism also reflected differences about the involvement of black religious leadership in the civil rights movement. Among those who challenged Jackson was one of the nation's most powerful black leaders, Dr. Martin Luther King Jr. In 1958, King, a Baptist minister, was elected vice president of one of the NBC's large auxiliary bodies, the National Sunday School and Baptist Training Union Congress. Jackson, a conservative Republican, contested King's direct action thrust of the civil rights movement, claiming that it would retard race relations in America.

At the 1960 NBC convention in Philadelphia, Jackson's opponents, disgusted with what they perceived as autocratic rule, tried to unseat him. King and other clergy in favor of social change, including Martin Luther King Sr., Ralph D. Abernathy, and Benjamin Mays, supported the candidacy of Dr. Gardner C. Taylor. The NBC's nominating committee, however, unanimously presented Jackson's name for another term and when he received the necessary vote declared his reelection. The Taylor team contested the results of the election and demanded a roll call by states. The NBC ignored the demands of Taylor's supporters and declared the convention adjourned. In response, some disgruntled delegates conducted a mock election that Taylor won. When the Jackson supporters refused to acknowledge the results of that election, the Taylor team conducted a spontaneous sit-in. Throughout the following year the Taylor faction proclaimed that Taylor was the duly elected president of the NBC, but again the courts ruled in favor of Jackson.

In 1961, when NBC delegates gathered for their annual convention in Kansas City, Missouri, the groundwork for disunion had been laid. The Taylor delegates, who were meeting in separate session, were barred from admission to the larger assembly. A brief period of physical violence

erupted as Taylor supporters moved to gain control of the platform. Later, a court-supervised election was held and Jackson again was declared the winner. Taylor was defeated by a vote of 2,732 to 1,321, and Jackson once again was proclaimed the head of the six million member body. Taylor and King accepted the results and called for unity among the delegates. Before the convention adjourned, however, King, his father Martin Luther King Sr., D. E. King, Marshall L. Shepard, C. C. Adams, and others who had supported Taylor were removed from all NBC offices.

In 1961, Reverend L. Venchael Booth, pastor of Cincinnati's Zion Baptist Church, one of Taylor's supporters, and leader of the "Volunteer Committee for the Formation of a New National Baptist Convention," called for a meeting to form a new organization. In November 1961, thirty-three delegates representing fourteen states met at Booth's church in Cincinnati. They voted to form the Progressive National Baptist Convention (PNBC) and adopted the motto "Unity, Service, Fellowship, and Peace." In 1962, at its first annual meeting in Philadelphia, the Reverend T. M. Chambers was elected president of the PNBC. He was succeeded by the Reverend Gardner Taylor in 1967.

The PNBC supported the civil rights and black power movements and was among the first groups to publicly oppose the Vietnam War. In recent years the PNBC has advocated black political and economic development, education, job training, and the strengthening of black families. Today, many PNBC churches maintain affiliations with one of the white conventions; they exchange pastors and pool money.

The PNBC, unlike the other two black Baptist conventions, the NBC and the National Baptist Convention of America, Inc., is organized into four geographic regions that meet annually. Each of the regions has thirty-five departments including Women, Laymen, Youth, Ushers and Nurses, Moderators, the Congress of Christian Education and Publication, Home Mission Board, Foreign Mission Bureau, Vocation Placement Center, Progressive Pension Plan Board, and Chaplaincy Endorsing Agency. In addition, there are various committees and commissions in charge of Programs, Convention Arrangements, Internal Affairs, Cooperative Christianity, Civil Rights, and Community Economic Development.

Since the formation of the convention in 1961, PNBC presidents have been limited to two consecutive one-year terms. In 1990, the constitution was amended to raise the tenure of all officers to three consecutive terms. The PNBC consists of a sixty-member executive board, which directs the business of the convention when not in session.

In 1996 the PNBC was composed of more than 1,800 churches with a total membership of 2.5 million. The annual meeting of the PNBC is held each August. National headquarters, with a permanent staff, are located in Washington, D.C., where a full-time general secretary coordinates the activities of the convention's program. The current president of the PNBC is Dr. Bennett W. Smith Sr., and the general secretary is Dr. Tyrone S. Pitts.

The PNBC regularly supports such educational institutions as the Nannie Helen Burroughs School and Howard University School of Religion in Washington, D.C.; Morehouse School of Religion in Atlanta, Georgia; Virginia Union University in Richmond, Virginia; Shaw University in Raleigh, North Carolina; and Morris College in Sumter, South Carolina. Moreover, the PNBC contributes annually to the National Association for the Advancement of Colored People (NAACP), National Urban League (NUL), Southern Christian Leadership Conference (SCLC), Operation PUSH, and the Martin Luther King Jr. Center for Non-Violent Social Change. In 1991, the PNBC purchased the NBC's publishing house and took control of *The Worker* (1934), a missionary and educational quarterly, and *Inteen* (1973), an award-winning magazine aimed at urban youth.

The illustrious roll of PNBC ministers include Dr. Howard Thurman, Dr. William A. Jones, Dr. Gardner Taylor, Dr. William Holmes Borders, Dr. Martin L. King Jr., Dr. Jesse Jackson, Dr. William Gray III, Dr. Benjamin Hooks, and Dr. Thomas Kilgore.

**FURTHER READINGS**

Garrow, David J. *Bearing The Cross: Martin Luther King, Jr., and the Southern Christian Leadership Conference.* New York: Vintage Books, 1988.

Lincoln, C. Eric, and Lawrence H. Mamiya. *The Black Church in the African American Experience.* Durham, N.C.: Duke University Press, 1990.

Melton, J. Gordon. *Religious Leaders of America: A Biographical Guide to Founders and Leaders of Religious Bodies, Churches, and Spiritual Groups in North America.* Detroit: Gale, 1991.

Progressive National Baptist Convention, Inc. *1996 Yearbook.* Washington, D.C.: Progressive National Baptist Convention, Inc., 1996.

Wilmore, Gayraud S. *Black Religion and Black Radicalism: An Interpretation of the Religious History of Afro-American People.* 2nd ed. Maryknoll, N.Y.: Orbis Books, 1983.

*André D. Vann*

## Provisional Committee to Organize Colored Locomotive Firemen

The Provisional Committee to Organize Colored Locomotive Firemen was founded in March 1941 in Washington, D.C., by A. Philip Randolph and other organizers of the Brotherhood of Sleeping Car Porters (BSCP) in an effort to unify black firemen and formulate an effective strategy to resist the employment and union discrimination they faced. Until the 1950s and 1960s, African American firemen confronted a stark system of racial discrimination on the nation's railroads. In the northern states, white unions and railroad managers agreed that no black man would be permitted to work as a fireman. In contrast, it was not uncommon for southern railroads to employ slaves, prior to the Civil War, and free black men, after the war, as firemen. But nowhere were black firemen permitted to climb the occupational ladder to become locomotive engineers, as white firemen did. By the early twentieth century, southern members of the all-white Brotherhood of Locomotive Firemen and Enginemen (BLFE) intensified their campaign to eliminate, or at least reduce the number of, black firemen by resorting to strikes and violence.

While these methods proved largely unsuccessful, white firemen finally achieved their goal of reducing the percentage and number of their black counterparts after World War I. Southern railroad companies, either openly in contract negotiations, or secretly, through unwritten "gentlemen's agreements," accepted restrictions on black employment. By the 1930s, few southern railroads were hiring new black firemen or placed "non-promotable men"—a euphemism for black firemen—on new diesel engines. To ensure that no blacks would ever work on a diesel engine, the white firemen's brotherhood negotiated the Southeastern Carriers Conference Agreement of 1941, which reserved all diesel jobs for whites and aimed at eventually eliminating blacks altogether. Although the numbers are not precise, one estimate of black employment revealed that black firemen had fallen in number from almost 6,500 in 1924 to just over 2,250 in 1940, and contemporaries reported that the 1941 agreement further decimated their ranks. In the years between World War I and World War II, African American firemen confronted a crisis of unprecedented proportions.

A. Philip Randolph sought to stem the tide of job losses and to protect the seniority rights of black firemen. The BSCP, the organization he led, was the most prominent black trade union in the United States. Following the BSCP's victories over the Pullman Company in the mid-1930s, Randolph extended his organization's assistance to black railroad station redcaps, dining car waiters, and train porters. In 1941, the BSCP sponsored a gathering of some fifty delegates, largely from the south Atlantic states, to form a single association of black firemen, called the Provisional Committee to Organize Colored Locomotive Firemen. The Provisional Committee elected Randolph its chairman, accepted without modification the structure proposed by BSCP organizers, and formally affiliated with the BSCP.

The Provisional Committee, however, did not win the unanimous support of black firemen. Two other organizations—the Association of Colored Railway Trainmen and Locomotive Firemen (ACRT), founded in 1912 as the Colored Association of Railroad Employees, and the International Association of Railway Employees (IARE), founded in 1934—were already active in the field and resented the intrusion of the BSCP into their jurisdiction. Both the ACRT and the IARE were autonomous associations that rejected affiliation with either the American Federation of Labor (AFL) or the Congress of Industrial Organizations (CIO), instead pursuing an independent course outside of the larger labor movement. More than organizational jealousies separated these rival bodies. The independent associations expressed little interest in joining the all-white firemen's brotherhood and advocated "minority representation" before federal railroad labor agencies, in which workers excluded from white unions could be represented legally by their own distinct organizations. Under the Amended Railway Labor Act of 1934, a union representing a majority of a "craft or class" possessed exclusive bargaining rights for all members of that craft or class; in the case of the firemen, the BLFE excluded blacks from membership yet negotiated contracts on their behalf. Those contracts often contained highly discriminatory clauses that deprived blacks of their seniority. The independent associations advocated a different system, one that would grant workers excluded from the powerful white unions a right to represent themselves before managers and government officials alike.

In contrast, Randolph and the Provisional Committee believed that the committee's ultimate goal was to eliminate all forms of Jim Crow in their craft, which meant the eventual destruction of the BLFE's ban on black membership and the integration of the union. The committee also rejected minority representation as opening the door to the wholesale fragmentation of labor representation and the weakening or even destruction of railroad unions. Rather than accept racial exclusion through the advocacy of "minority representation," Randolph insisted that the Provisional Committee had to become strong enough to bargain with the BLFE, force its integration, and win for blacks equal rights in the union. To achieve such strength, unity was absolutely necessary; standing in the way of that unity was the existence of multiple organizations with few accomplishments or members. Contemptuous of the independents, Randolph invited the IARE and the ACRT to join the Provisional Committee under his leadership. While many delegates at the founding conference enthusiastically embraced Randolph's and the BSCP's leadership, the independents, not surprisingly, rejected his overture and maintained their separate existence. Despite their differences, the independents and the Provisional Committee pursued somewhat parallel strategies and competed for members through the early 1960s.

The Provisional Committee publicized the plight of black firemen and mounted numerous legal challenges to discriminatory contracts during the 1940s and 1950s. As a result of Randolph's threat to bring 100,000 blacks to a March on Washington to protest discrimination in war industries and the military, President Franklin D. Roosevelt created a Committee on Fair Employment Practice (FEPC) in 1941. Weak, understaffed, and underfunded, the FEPC relied heavily upon organizations of black workers to provide evidence of the discrimination they suffered. The Provisional Committee, as well as the IARE and the ACRT, collected affidavits from their members, provided extensive documentation of specific discriminatory practices, and sent firemen to the formal hearings on railroad industry discrimination that the FEPC conducted in September 1943. Although the FEPC upheld black firemen's claims and ordered railroad companies and unions to cease their discrimination, little changed. The wartime agency possessed no power to compel compliance, and the stark defiance of white managers and trade unionists promised to disrupt transportation in a time of national emergency. Faced with the prospect of labor upheaval, President Roosevelt chose to do nothing, leaving the racial status quo on the railroads intact.

Black firemen fared better in the courts. In two related path-breaking cases—*Steele* and *Tunstall*—brought by the ACRT and the IARE, the Supreme Court ruled in 1944 that the white firemen's brotherhood could not negotiate contracts that discriminated on the basis of race against minority members of the craft or class. The court did not order the BLFE to admit blacks to union membership, but it did find that the law imposed upon the union a "duty of fair representation." Suddenly, overtly discriminatory contracts negotiated by the BLFE were held to be illegal. The landmark *Steele* ruling was less a panacea than a legal opening. Over the course of the next decade, the Provisional Committee and the independents would file dozens of legal suits to overturn the 1941 Southeast Carriers Conference Agreement and other discriminatory contracts.

By the mid-1950s, black firemen had won a number of impressive victories. Legal defeats and the cost of litigation brought a reluctant BLFE to the bargaining table. In December 1951, the Provisional Committee and the BLFE reached an agreement that stipulated that the various injunctions against discriminatory contact provisions be made permanent and that the white union pay monetary damages to the Provisional Committee. An internal study commissioned by the Provisional Committee in 1954 found that the "anti-discrimination injunctions" secured through the courts were "effective in practice." Although individual cases of discrimination existed, it could identify no overall patterns of discrimination. Black firemen had succeeded in preserving their jobs and their seniority. But black firemen and the Provisional Committee proved unable to remove all barriers confronting African Americans in their craft. While they preserved their own positions, they did not succeed in opening up firemen's jobs to new black workers. In an era of reduced railroad employment, few companies were hiring at all, and those that were first rehired furloughed whites before next turning to other whites.

The Provisional Committee also failed to force the integration of the white BLFE. In the case of *Lee Oliphant et al. v. Brotherhood of Locomotive Firemen and Enginemen et al.* (named after Lee Oliphant, a black fireman and local chairman of the Provisional Committee in Macon, Georgia), the Provisional Committee's attorneys argued that continued discrimination by the BLFE demon-strated that the white union could not carry out its "duty of fair representation" while it barred blacks from union membership. The courts disagreed. In 1958, the Sixth Circuit Court of Appeals declared the BLFE to be a "private association, whose membership policies are its own affair," and the following year the Supreme Court refused to hear the appeal of the case. Only with the passage of the 1964 Civil Rights Act would racial exclusion by unions become illegal. With union integration assured and with the railroad companies in the North and South finally hiring new black workers as firemen by the late 1960s, the Provisional Committee largely had accomplished its goals. Although discrimination by unions and management by no means disappeared, it fell to a new generation of black workers to protest individually and collectively through the courts and the Equal Employment Opportunity Commission (EEOC).

**FURTHER READINGS**

Arnesen, Eric. "'Like Banquo's Ghost, It Will Not Down': The Race Question and the American Railroad Brotherhoods, 1880–1920." *American Historical Review* 99, 5 (December 1994): 1601–1633.

"FEPC Fight to Save Colored Locomotive Firemen Jobs." *Black Worker* 9, 1 (January 1943).

"The Negro Rail Worker Gets a Hearing." *Black Worker* 9, 10 (October 1943).

Northrup, Herbert R. *Organized Labor and the Negro.* New York: Harper & Brothers, 1944.

Randolph, A. Philip. "The Crisis of Negro Railroad Workers." *American Federationist* 46, 8 (August 1939).

*Eric Arnesen*

# PUSH

*See* People United to Save Humanity.

## Railway Men's International Benevolent Industrial Association

Founded in Chicago in 1915, the Railway Men's International Benevolent Industrial Association (RMIBIA) was part of a general upsurge in working-class organization and black militancy in the World War I era. The RMIBIA enlisted in its ranks black locomotive firemen, brakemen, switchmen, train porters, machinists and helpers, Pullman porters, and dining car cooks and waiters; it also united a number of already existing southern associations of black firemen and brakemen. During and after the war, black railroaders faced systematic discrimination in promotion, pay, and access to certain higher paying jobs. Excluded from the powerful white railroad brotherhoods and in many cases from the American Federation of Labor (AFL), black railroaders formed their own organizations to press for improvements in wages and working conditions. In its decade-long existence, the RMIBIA represented black workers before railroad managers and especially before federal agencies like the Railway Labor Board to argue for wage increases, which it sometimes won. Association leaders lobbied Republican party politicians on behalf of legislation prohibiting discriminatory contracts, testified before congressional and state legislative committees to publicize the plight of their members, and initiated lawsuits over wages, job security, and working conditions. Although membership figures are not verifiable, the RMIBIA claimed 15,000 members at its height in 1920, with seventeen chapters with 1,200 members in Chicago alone in 1922.

Throughout its existence, the RMIBIA remained an all-black organization. Shortly after its founding, however, its leader, dining car waiter Robert L. Mays, pursued affiliation with the AFL. Mays' proposal to create a single industrial union of all-black railroaders ran afoul of the AFL's staunch commitment to craft unionism, as well as its members' reluctance to sanction an officially all-black union, although they rarely hesitated to sanction officially all-white unions. Operating outside of the AFL, Mays and the RMIBIA publicly and aggressively denounced the racism of the AFL and the white railroad brotherhoods, calling on black railroaders to stand together to resist white efforts to remove them from their jobs and to win higher pay and better conditions. RMIBIA organizers repeatedly rejected white union officials' efforts to enroll blacks in "federal" labor unions under AFL control, arguing that only after organized white labor abandoned its exclusionary practices and embraced full racial equality would the need for independent black associations end.

The RMIBIA entered a period of decline in the early 1920s. Wartime labor policies that aimed at reducing labor turnover and unrest had provided wage increases to railroad and other workers, recognized workers' right to organize, and generally improved working conditions. Following the war, however, changes in federal policy put an end to prolabor rulings. Dependent upon favorable government rulings, the RMIBIA had no strategy for dealing with the new, hostile political environment. In its final years, the RMIBIA advocated insurance and banking schemes and promoted, with little success, black business along with the Tuskegee Institute and the National Urban League (NUL). Internal craft divisions surfaced within the association, and opposition to Mays' somewhat dictatorial leadership style grew. By mid-decade, the RMIBIA had ceased to function as an effective organization.

Failure was by no means unique to the RMIBIA, for the era following World War I witnessed tremendous clashes between organized labor and capital that set back even the strongest AFL unions. Similarly, the black radicalism of the war and postwar years faded by the mid-1920s, as governmental repression and internal divisions took their toll. But the collapse of the RMIBIA did not spell the end of black trade unionism on the railroads, for black railroaders continued to organize along craft lines. It was only with the dramatic changes brought by the New Deal during the 1930s that some black railroad workers, particularly those in the service sector, managed to achieve the organizational breakthroughs that had eluded the RMIBIA.

**FURTHER READINGS**

Arnesen, Eric. "Charting an Independent Course: African American Railroad Workers in the World War I Era." In *Labor Histories: Class, Politics, and the Working-Class Experience.* Ed. Eric Arnesen, Julie Greene, and Bruce Laurie. Urbana: University of Illinois Press, 1998.

Chicago Commission on Race Relations. *The Negro in Chicago: A Study of Race Relations and a Race Riot.* Chicago: The University of Chicago Press, 1922.

*Eric Arnesen*

# Rainbow Coalition

*See* National Rainbow Coalition.

# Readjusters

In the early 1880s, Virginia African Americans, especially urban workers, participated in a political movement called "Readjusterism." This gave them a second bite at the apple of Reconstruction, which had officially ended in Virginia in 1870, and provided a foretaste of Populism.

In the aftermath of the deep and prolonged economic depression of 1873–1878, "independent" politics grew in popularity across the nation. "Workingmen's," "Greenback," "farmers'," and "reform" parties mushroomed. Virginia, its state treasury nearly exhausted, its school system in chaos, its economy faltering, was no exception. There, former Confederate general and railroad baron William Mahone galvanized frustrated small businessmen and farmers together with white workers and urban African Americans to forge a new political party, the "Readjuster party," which challenged both the Conservatives and the Republicans.

During the 1870s Virginia's debt had grown, its amortization made all the more difficult by the depression. Rather than raise taxes or scale down the debt, the politically dominant Conservative regime opted for austerity.

In 1877, when $526,000 intended for education was used for debt repayment, some cities closed schools and shortened the school year. Both white and African American working-class families had long seen access to public education as a priority, and the impact of the debt crisis on the schools pushed them in the direction of General Mahone and his Readjusters.

Urban working-class activists led the African American community into the Readjuster movement. They broke with the white and black Republican leadership, which had long held sway over the black electorate, delivering little more than lip service and a few symbolic patronage appointments. African American workingmen and women had faced the prolonged depression with little help from the national or the state GOP. While some officeholders still expressed their loyalty to the "Party of Lincoln," most black Virginians were ready for a change.

Leaving the "Republican ark" meant more than jumping into an uncertain political sea. Working-class activists promoted a complex strategy that relied both on strengthening independent black political organization and building upon tenuous but still evolving ties with white labor reformers. Nowhere in the Old Dominion did this process go further than in Richmond, where black activists who had come of age since the Civil War rose to leadership, challenged the older generation and its strategies, and set the stage for the biracial, class-based alliances of the Knights of Labor and the Populists, which would shake the social order of the South in the mid-1880s and the early 1890s.

The significance of the Readjuster party did not only lie in the foundation it established for future activism. Between 1879 and 1883, Virginia African Americans built new political organizations from a ward to a statewide level and experienced renewed political power. This power enabled them to make some impressive gains, including the abolition of the whipping post as a form of legal punishment, the expansion of free speech rights, scaling down the state debt, funneling resources into black schools, and hiring black principals and teachers.

This long-forgotten movement was an important chapter in the black political history of Virginia, the birthplace of Washington and Jefferson as well as the capital of the Confederacy.

**FURTHER READINGS**

Blake, Nelson. *William Mahone of Virginia.* Richmond, Va.: Garrett & Massie, 1935.

Moore, James Tice. *Two Paths to the New South.* Lexington: University of Kentucky Press, 1974.

Pearson, C. C. *The Readjuster Movement in Virginia.* New Haven: Yale University Press, 1917.

Rachleff, Peter. *Black Labor in Richmond, Virginia, 1865–1890.* Urbana: University of Illinois Press, 1989.

*Peter Rachleff*

## Reformed Church in America, Black Council

*See* Black Council, Reformed Church in America.

## Reparations Committee of Descendants of U.S. Slaves, Inc.

*See* Universal Association of Ethiopian Women.

## Richmond, Virginia: Civic, Literary, and Mutual Aid Associations

With limited resources and in an atmosphere of continual social conflict, African Americans built a rich, cohesive community in Richmond, Virginia. The roots of this community took hold during slavery, but its most impressive advancement came after the Civil War and in the years of Reconstruction, Redemption, and Jim Crow. This long-standing community provided the foundation for the civil rights movement, which emerged in the 1950s and 1960s to challenge the traditional restrictions and strictures that had been imposed upon it by the white elite.

Racism, discrimination, limited opportunity, and material poverty created the need and set the parameters for this community. Few African Americans could thrive through the practice of individualism, which was so widely touted in American society. At the same time, they drew upon their own cultural traditions and legacies to forge a complex collectivism that offered them hope of economic and emotional survival. It also provided a human soil from which movements for social change arose.

Richmond African Americans wove together the formerly free and the ex-slave, the city native, and the "country negro," dark skinned and light skinned, literate and illiterate, skilled and unskilled. The initial building block was the extended family. Linked with it was the church. Built on this foundation, a broad network of social organizations called "secret societies" fulfilled a multiplicity of purposes: funerals and death benefits, trade organization, collective self-education and self-improvement, religious advancement, charity, political expression, social life, and the like. Woven together, and interwoven with extended families and church congregations, these secret societies served as the circulatory system of the black community. The information, material assistance, and moral support that flowed through this system nourished the members of this community for generations.

These organizations provided an institutional framework through which black people could help each other and seek help beyond familial and churchly ties. There were many different kinds of societies, though they shared an ethos of mutuality and occasionally overlapping membership. They also typically shared a common internal social practice involving rituals, passwords, symbols, and the election of leadership. These internal practices conveyed values and ideologies and supported relationships that could assume an importance beyond the express purpose of the organization itself.

Mutual aid societies provided a "safety net" of sorts for people who had scant resources. They were a form of collective insurance. Meager dues were accumulated into treasuries that made possible the payment of funeral expenses and survivor benefits to families. Members buried fellow members with a dignity and respect that affirmed community ties. Rituals expressed these ties and elevated them to the level of principles.

Trade-based societies, some of which called themselves "unions," were another sort of organization. They offered some of the same benefits as the mutual aid societies and added sickness and out-of-work benefits. Typically male, the members and officers in these societies worked in the same occupation. These societies provided a mechanism to pass on skills and knowledge from older to younger workers and to provide some sense of solidarity. In some cases, they sought to protect or expand black employment in their line of work, or even to raise wages or reduce hours. In a few instances, they organized strikes and community support for strikers. These trade societies were rarely linked to white unions, although they did have relationships with wider labor organizations like the National Labor Union, the Industrial Brotherhood, and the Knights of Labor in the nineteenth century, and the American Federation of Labor (AFL) and the Congress of Industrial Organizations (CIO) in the twentieth century.

Societies that promoted self-education and self-improvement were widespread within black Richmond. "Literary and debating" societies, "chatauqua" societies, and musical and dramatic clubs heard speakers, read and discussed books, and encouraged the performance as well as appreciation of the arts in black Richmond. Women as well as men, and wage earners as well as professionals and businessmen, participated in these organizations. They did not only look inward; at times, they provided a foundation for community efforts to improve public education and brought these subjects to children as well as adults.

Many societies were organized around Richmond's impressive array of African American churches, and they functioned not only to support these institutions but also to extend charitable work into the black community. Including women and men, these societies made fund-raising a high priority, and they spawned a steady stream of bazaars, bake sales and the like, bringing their members together in preparing these functions as well as staging them. They were an important vehicle for the ethos of collectivism and mutuality that invigorated black Richmond.

These values were often articulated in more material forms by political societies, from the "Union Leagues" of Reconstruction to the Congress of Racial Equality (CORE), the Student Non-Violent Coordinating Committee (SNCC), and the National Association for the Advancement of Colored People (NAACP) of a century later. While some of these societies were linked to particular political parties, such as the Republicans and the Democrats, most drew their legitimacy from their bases in the community. They included members and leaders from the city's other societies, and they provided a focus, strategy, and vehicle for the realization of such values as dignity, respect, equality, and fairness. Through them the Richmond black community fought to advance its interests.

Together, these organizations shaped the social fabric of black Richmond. Not only were they based on extended families and the church, but they, in turn, served as the soil that nourished these institutions. Through their activities, single men and women met their potential spouses. Husbands and wives developed networks of friends who, with their families, sustained them over the years. Children made friendships that lasted throughout their lives.

This social system enabled African Americans to survive in the midst of virulent racism and discrimination by providing material and moral support for the community's members. It also made it possible for them to launch oppositional movements to challenge the social and political status quo, time and time again.

**FURTHER READINGS**

Brown, Elsa Barkley. "Womanist Consciousness: Maggie Lena Walker and the Independent Order of St. Luke." *Signs* 14, 3 (spring 1989): 610–633.

Greenbaum, Susan. "A Comparison Between African American and European-American Mutual Aid Societies in 19th Century America." *Journal of Ethnic Studies* 19 (fall 1991): 95–119.

Rachleff, Peter. *Black Labor in Richmond, Virginia, 1865–1890.* Urbana: University of Illinois Press, 1989.

———. "Richmond, Virginia." In *Encyclopedia of African-American History and Culture,* vol. 4. Ed. Jack Salzman, David Lionel Smith, and Cornel West. New York: Macmillan Library Reference, 1996.

*Peter Rachleff*

# Richmond Medical Society

*See* Negro Medical Association of Virginia.

# Robert Tanner Freeman Dental Society

*See* Negro Medical Association of Virginia.

## St. Louis: Civic, Literary, and Mutual Aid Associations

Civic, mutual aid, and literary associations are an integral aspect of St. Louis's African American history. While these associations provided an opportunity for social interaction, they also served as benevolent organizations, facilitated civic involvement, and stimulated intellectual development. Denied access to white-only charitable, social, and political institutions, African Americans created their own associations to meet the needs of their community.

One of St. Louis's earliest African American organizations that offered mutual aid services was the First African Baptist Church. Established in 1822, it was the city's first all-black church. In 1825, John Berry Meachum, a former slave, became the congregation's first minister. Under his leadership the church expanded its services to the community and launched a Sabbath school, a temperance society, and a school. By 1860, there were five black congregations in St. Louis with a membership of approximately 1,500 African Americans. While meager financial resources and a restricted legal status created obstacles to social interactions between slaves and free African Americans, these churches became important social institutions. They not only offered spiritual comfort to their members, but also became centers for leadership and educational training. Moreover, they assumed the responsibility of taking care of the old, the poor, the orphaned, and the infirm.

On January 11, 1865, the Missouri General Assembly granted freedom to all slaves but made no concessions to racial equality and denied African Americans the right to vote or hold public office. In October of that year, concerned citizens responded and established the Missouri Equal Rights League, the first African American political organization in the state. Members of the league appointed a committee to tour the state to present lectures on the unequal treatment facing African Americans. James Milton Turner, the league's secretary, became one of its best-known lecturers. Four thousand African Americans and whites petitioned the Missouri General Assembly to extend full rights of citizenship to African Americans. Despite these efforts, black men in Missouri did not receive the right to vote until the ratification of the Fifteenth Amendment in 1870.

The end of the Civil War saw a surge in the development of social and mutual aid organizations in the city's African American community. In 1866, Prince Lodge, the first African American Ancient Free and Accepted Masons lodge, opened in St. Louis. In 1872, Reverend Moses Dickson founded another social and benevolent organization, the International Order of Twelve Knights and Daughters of Tabor. This society was an offshoot of the Knights of Liberty, a secret society Dickson had organized in St. Louis in August 1846 in hopes of abolishing slavery through an armed insurrection. However, by 1857 when a civil war and the end of slavery appeared imminent, Dickson concentrated his efforts on assisting fugitive slaves on the Underground Railroad.

Following the Civil War the St. Louis black population continued to assist African Americans on the run. In the 1870s, the city's black residents launched a unique charitable effort when southern blacks who were fleeing oppression and Jim Crow laws passed through St. Louis on their way to Kansas. Poverty stricken, many of these so-called "exodusters" became stranded in the city without any assistance. In 1878 Charleston H. Tandy and other African American community leaders created the Refugee Relief Board to aid the refugees. The board provided the destitute exodusters with money, clothing, and food that had been donated primarily by the city's African American churches. The generosity of the community and the board's effectiveness allowed thousands of exodusters to continue their journey west.

Denied access to the all-white Young Men's Christian Association (YMCA), John Boyer Bashon, principal of Colored School Number Ten, advocated the establishment of an African American branch. As a result of his efforts the YMCA for Colored Men opened in 1887. Women's clubs campaigned for their own Young Women's Christian Associations (YWCA) and successfully founded the Phyllis Wheatley branch in 1911. The YMCA and the YWCA offered recreational, educational, and athletic facilities for the city's African American youth, as well as opportunities for leadership training. The clubs also provided meeting rooms for the city's varied social and civic associations.

Women's groups also became involved in social welfare efforts in the city. In 1888, a group of African American women, led by Sarah Newton, established the St. Louis Colored Orphans Home, which later became the Annie Malone Children's Home. Another notable group was the Wednesday Afternoon Sewing Club. Its members concentrated their efforts on providing health care for the city's elderly and offered home care for those financially unable to pay for medical treatment. As a direct consequence of the club's efforts the Colored Old Folks Home opened in 1906.

By 1900 approximately 36,000 African Americans lived in St. Louis, but they remained excluded from many public accommodations such as hotels, restaurants, swimming pools, and tennis courts. Most black city residents could find employment only in unskilled jobs as domestics or laborers. Furthermore, in 1916, the city enacted a segregated housing ordinance that effectively prevented African Americans from buying white-owned property. The ordinance virtually ensured that they remained crowded into all-black neighborhoods, such as the "Ville." Despite these injustices, the turn of the century was a time for significant achievements. Among these was the founding of Poro Beauty College in 1917 by businesswoman and social activist Annie Turnbo Malone. The college provided educational and employment opportunities to African Americans, but more importantly, it opened its doors to the community, hosting a variety of events from theatrical productions to public lectures. Mal-

one often provided meeting rooms free of charge to social and civic organizations.

The turn of the century also saw the creation of many literary associations. These clubs promoted intellectual development and served as forums for discussions on current social and political issues. In 1907, Carrie K. Bowles, after a visit to the Kansas City Booklovers' Club, founded the St. Louis Booklovers' Club. For over ninety years its exclusive membership of twenty-five women has met to review books and engage in discussions on a variety of topics, often concentrating on issues that affect women and African Americans. In 1915, Bowles and Georgiana Dickson helped to organize the Prudence Crandall Club, whose original members were young, unmarried teachers employed in the St. Louis public schools. They met regularly to discuss literary events. As part of the club's program designated members often led discussions or lectured on outstanding literary figures. The Informal Dames, while primarily a social club, also hold meetings to review contemporary literature. Another prominent group was the Twentieth Century Social Club. Established in 1917, this all-male social and civic club counted St. Louis' black doctors, lawyers, and businessmen among its members. The club's guest speakers often included prominent African American civic, literary, and social leaders. James E. Cook, director of the Pine Street YMCA, established a weekly literary and study group known as the Y Forum. Other literary associations that the city's black residents established included the Tuesday Poetry Group, the Friday Literacy Society, the Arsania M. Williams Reading Club, and the Harriet Tubman Literary Club. Many of these associations funded educational scholarships and supported local civic and social activities.

Essentially ignored by the Republican and Democratic parties, African American civic leaders sought equality by creating their own political organizations, such as the Citizens Liberty League and the Negro Jefferson Club. These organizations campaigned for African American political candidates and tried to encourage higher black voter turnout. In 1910 St. Louis' black voters achieved a major political victory when Charles Turpin was elected city constable, thus becoming the first African American in the state to be elected to a public office. One of the most powerful national civic associations to be established in St. Louis was the National Association for the Advancement of Colored People (NAACP), which opened a chapter in the city in 1914.

The 1920s proved to be a time of disillusionment for African Americans throughout the United States.

Despite their active participation in World War I, African Americans could not attain full political and civil rights in their own country. In St. Louis, African Americans remained barred from trade unions and jobs in skilled positions. Black construction workers were even denied jobs on building sites in their own neighborhoods. In response, African Americans took action by increasing their political activities. Labor unions, including the Brotherhood of Sleeping Car Porters and Maids, established by labor leader A. Philip Randolph, attempted to organize black workers. The African American newspapers the *St. Louis Argus* and the *St. Louis American* were part of a driving force in the St. Louis campaign for equal rights, fair housing practices, and better schools. The *St. Louis Argus*, established in 1912 by brothers Joseph and William Mitchell, is the oldest continuously operating African American business in the city. Its editors campaigned against the 1916 Segregation Ordinance and continue to be leading advocates of civil rights and equal access to education. The *St. Louis American*, founded in 1928 by A. N. Johnson and his son-in-law, John Procope, has also contributed to the struggle against racial discrimination. One of the newspaper's more successful campaigns was led by publisher Nathan Sweets when he encouraged community members to patronize only those businesses that hired African Americans. While the black newspapers became a political force, they also represent a major literary achievement of the city's African American community. Both newspapers continue to publish articles on current social issues, community events, education, and African American history. Moreover, they feature poetry, essays, and short stories written by African American authors.

Throughout the 1940s, 1950s, and 1960s, St. Louis' African Americans continued to strive actively for racial equality. Foremost in this effort were organizations like the National Urban League (NUL), the NAACP, and the League of Women Voters who successfully filed lawsuits against businesses with discriminatory practices. Of notable importance was the seven-month–long demonstration in 1963–1964 against the Jefferson Bank & Trust Company because of its refusal to hire black clerical workers. Members of the St. Louis chapter of the Congress of Racial Equality (CORE) and another more militant group called ACTION demonstrated against the bank until March 1964 when its management finally agreed to hire African American tellers. Encouraged by this success, these advocacy groups expanded their efforts by boycotting other businesses with discriminatory hiring

practices. As a result, substantial gains began to be made in the fight for civil rights in the city.

Despite the formidable obstacles posed by discrimination, economic disparity, and racial inequality, the St. Louis African American community throughout its history has created a rich cultural life based on a variety of mutual aid, literary, and civic associations. These organizations provided St. Louis' African Americans the opportunity to create a normal cohesive community in a white society that attempted to degrade and segregate them.

**FURTHER READINGS**

Corbett, Katherine T. "Missouri's Black History: From Colonial Times to 1970." *Gateway Heritage* (Summer 1983): 16–25.

Greene, Lorenzo J., Gary R. Kremer and Antonio F. Holland. *Missouri's Black Heritage.* St. Louis: Forum Press, 1980; 2nd ed., Columbia: University of Missouri Press, 1993.

Pearson, Thomas A., and Anne Watts. *St. Louis African-American Resource Book. Vol. 1, Biographical Sketches of St. Louisans.* St. Louis: St. Louis Public Library, 1996.

———. *St. Louis African-American Resource Book. Vol. 4, Events and Places.* St. Louis: St. Louis Public Library, 1996.

St. Louis Association of Colored Women's Clubs Collection, 1901–1980. Western Historical Manuscript Collection, St. Louis, Missouri.

*Linda Brown-Kubisch*

# San Francisco: Civic, Literary, and Mutual Aid Associations

African American organizations in the Bay Area date from the formation of two San Francisco churches in 1851 and 1852 that housed meetings, staged benefits, and nurtured community leaders. The denial of rights led blacks to form a Franchise League and to launch a series of California Colored Conventions from 1855 to the 1880s. Though mostly held in Sacramento, the conventions were led by San Francisco men who petitioned for an end to racial discrimination such as barring blacks from testifying against whites. They set up a state black newspaper and an executive committee in San Francisco. The Civil War sparked the formation of several military orders, especially the Brannan Guards, which, along with fraternal orders that emerged in the 1850s, projected a sense of dignity and self-worth. Women in the 1860s established benevolent societies to aid the sick and handle funeral expenses. They also set up literary societies, such as the Amateur Literary & Drama Association.

Oakland formed a black church in 1858, but community growth in the East Bay came largely after 1869, when the completion of the transcontinental railroad and Pullman sleeping cars brought black railroad workers to the city. By 1880, Oakland had several black lodges and clubs. Women formed social service groups, including a Literary and Aid Society set up in 1876, a beneficial society in the 1880s, and the Fannie Jackson Coppin Club in 1899, which served as the "mother club" for the black women's club movement in the state. During the 1890s Oakland's black population also established a Home for Aged and Infirm Colored People and several black churches. In the early 1900s, the emerging role of women in Oakland's black organizations culminated in the formation of an Arts & Industrial Club, a Women's Charity Club, and other educational and cultural organizations.

Black reliance on the Republican party was challenged by San Francisco's Equal Rights League in 1874 and Oakland's Black Independent League in 1878. But it was reaffirmed with the formation of the African American League in San Francisco in 1891 and a women's Afro American League the next year. San Francisco's African American League established branches in other communities, and held statewide Afro American congresses. Initially, these groups petitioned for equal rights, but by the early 1900s they placed greater emphasis on education and the formation of "general merchandise businesses." By 1910, the African American League had become ineffectual, and its demise marked the end of San Francisco's leadership among African Americans in the Bay Area.

The shift of black organizational activity from San Francisco to the East Bay reflected an increase in the black population of that area. African Americans in Oakland formed a black Young Men's Christian Association (YMCA) in 1920 and a separate branch of the Young Women's Christian Association (YWCA) in 1927. Local businessmen joined in an African American Cooperative Association, which evolved into an East Bay Negro Business League in 1919. Women set up the Fannie Wall Children's Home in 1918. Adjacent cities began establishing similar groups. By 1920 African Americans in Berkeley had founded two churches and black women had launched the Phyllis Wheatley Club, a service and charitable organization. Richmond's black population also supported a black church and two women's groups, the Chlora Hayes Sledge Club and the Richmond Self-Improvement Club.

Oakland formed the region's first branch of the National Association for the Advancement of Colored People (NAACP) in 1913. Its early activities included protests against the showing of D. W. Griffith's racist film *Birth of a Nation* and the city's attempts to adopt segregation ordinances. In 1923, the San Francisco–based Negro Equity League established a separate NAACP branch for that city, and Oakland's branch subsequently divided into several chapters that served various East Bay cities. In 1920, Garveyites organized divisions of the Universal Negro Improvement Association (UNIA) in Oakland and San Francisco. Less elite in membership than the NAACP, they were similar in many functions. San Francisco's UNIA chapter disappeared before the end of the decade, but Oakland's remained active into the 1930s.

African American political organizations in the 1920s included Berkeley's Appomatox Club, which supported candidates and served as a black public forum for several decades, and the Alameda County and San Francisco Leagues of Colored Women Voters. Community service was highlighted by San Francisco's Booker T. Washington Community Service Center. The creation of this multipurpose educational and social center during World War I indicates that secular organizations were beginning to displace churches as black community institutions. More elite in membership but also stressing "social elevation" was San Francisco's Cosmos Club.

The Great Depression broadened Bay Area black associations to include interracial alliances, especially with labor unions. A major influence was C. L. Dellums, who established a branch of the Brotherhood of Sleeping Car Porters (BSCP) in Oakland in the late 1920s. His election to the Alameda County Central Labor Council and the vice presidency of the local NAACP symbolized the growing liaison between legal protest and unionism. Some blacks went even further to the left. In Richmond, for example, several Communists assumed leadership positions in the city's NAACP branch. Oakland's NAACP and a Citizen's Employment Council set up in 1939 pushed "Don't Shop Where You Can't Work" campaigns to reduce unemployment. Federal relief programs produced the Oakland Colored Chorus sponsored by the Works Progress Administration (WPA), a notable example of the cultural activities that Bay Area black communities continued through the depression.

World War II brought an enormous population increase for the Bay Area, especially San Francisco and Richmond, which spawned associations committed to procuring equal rights. The Bay Area Council Against Discrimination was an interracial body that worked to open jobs in transportation and shipbuilding. Another interracial group, the Committee Against Segregation and Discrimination, was composed of black shipyard workers and white civic leaders. This group, under the leadership of Joseph James, who was also head of the San Francisco NAACP, succeeded in abolishing Jim Crow unions in shipyards. Richmond's United Negro Labor Committee conducted similar activities, while the Berkeley Interracial Council protested public housing discrimination. During and after World War II interracial unity was also promoted by San Francisco's Church for Fellowship of All People, founded in 1943, and the city's Council for Civic Unity, established in 1944. The council and a similar state organization studied and tried to end discrimination, as did the branches of the National Urban League (NUL) set up in San Francisco and Oakland in 1946. East Bay African Americans formed political coalitions with unions and liberals but realized few victories and by the 1950s gave way to mainstream associations.

The 1960s brought to the Bay Area other civil rights organizations, particularly the Congress of Racial Equality (CORE), which set up chapters in Berkeley and San Francisco. CORE picketed department stores and other businesses to open jobs to African Americans, and it campaigned for school desegregation in Berkeley. Token victories led to CORE's decline and a shift to black nationalism after 1964. During the early 1960s the Bay Area witnessed a growth in black nationalist groups such as the Black Muslims and the Afro-American Association, which promoted African culture and self-help. The most celebrated group was the Black Panther party, formed in Oakland in 1966. Advocating black nationalism and Marxism, it initially focused on exposing and fighting police harassment. After growing rapidly and contributing to such movements as the Third World Liberation Front at San Francisco State University in 1969, the Panthers suffered repression by federal authorities. By the early 1970s the Panthers had retreated from political action and become a community service organization. Their previous political activities, however, were instrumental in helping Oakland blacks win several local elections.

By the 1970s and 1980s Oakland's growing number of black elected officials gained access to public programs, which lessened the need for race associations. One casualty of this trend were black women's clubs, which virtually disappeared throughout California by the late 1960s. Despite increased black political participation in city government, equal employment opportunity remained a major problem and spawned several associations. In 1973,

for example, the Oakland Black Fire Fighters Association was formed to procure a fairer share of those jobs. In the same decade San Francisco and Oakland set up Black Chambers of Commerce, which pushed "Buy Black, Get It Back" campaigns. In 1983, African American women in Oakland formed the Women's Economic Agenda to develop skills and leadership among low-income blacks. The large number of Oakland's black community groups demonstrated their viability during the 1989 earthquake and fire. In response to the emergency, many of the city's several hundred black churches offered assistance and housing to the victims, while groups like the Citizens Emergency Relief Team were formed to use the disaster to promote jobs, low-income housing, and better public transportation.

## FURTHER READINGS

Broussard, Albert S. *Black San Francisco: The Struggle for Racial Equality in the West, 1900–1954.* Lawrence: University Press of Kansas, 1993.

Crouchett, Lawrence P., Lonnie G. Bunch III, and Martha Kendall Winnacker. *Visions of Tomorrow: The History of the East Bay Afro-American Community, 1852–1977.* Oakland: Northern California Center for Afro-American History and Life, 1989.

Daniels, Douglas Henry. *Pioneer Urbanites: A Social and Cultural History of Black San Francisco.* Philadelphia: Temple University Press, 1980.

McBroom, Delores Nason. *Parallel Communities: African Americans in California's East Bay, 1850–1965.* New York: Garland Publishing, 1993.

*Lawrence B. de Graaf*

## Savannah: Civic, Literary, and Mutual Aid Associations

Like its southern neighbors Charleston and New Orleans, Savannah's fraternal and benevolent associations were largely initiated and controlled by mulattos. They were the city's aristocrats of color, "the children or descendants of well-known whites. . . . Fair in complexion and 'naturally clannish,' they 'thought and felt differently', from the ignorant, brutalized lower-class blacks of slave origins" (Perdue, 89). Typical of other southern cities with large mulatto communities, Savannah's free people of colored owed their manumission to their white parents, which most often meant their white fathers. Thus, one historian explained the reason for the creation of these clubs: "Freed from the restraints of slavery and excluded from white organizations, Negroes tried to establish a social life similar to that of their formal masters" (Perdue, 89). The members of these fraternal, benevolent, and literary associations shared commonalities. Many members adopted the cultural accoutrements of the white affluent. One historian wrote that Savannah's colored aristocrats "affected graces, traditions, and manners that bore a striking resemblance to their upper-class class relatives across the color line" (Gatewood, 91). White blood gave one social elevation over any dark-skinned black. Blood, not race, was the common denominator among many of these racial hybrids. Class, not color, determined who was eligible for club membership. The racial heterogeneity of Savannah's mulatto class was due to a substantial influx of West Indians. Therefore, Savannah's black Creole population differed from that of New Orleans. As one recent history of Savannah surmised: "The number of French-speaking free persons of color in Savannah was too small to support cultural events and civic clubs" (Johnson, 109). Whatever modicum of interracial accord existed between blacks and whites, nothing approaching racial felicity ever existed. Whites in Savannah adopted a "new determination to relegate blacks to an inferior and fixed position in society. Blacks and whites were neighbors[; however], only occasionally were they friends" (Johnson, 133).

By the end of the nineteenth century, Savannah had approximately two hundred black fraternal clubs, literary associations, and benevolent societies. Activities of these groups ranged from parades and picnics to musical recitals and lectures. Members of Savannah's several Masonic halls routinely paraded in full regalia. Contemporary civil rights activist W. W. Law speculates that the penchant for colorful dress among Savannah's ante-bellum African American clubs likely had its ancestral roots in the status Africans posited in regal attire for important ceremonies and celebrations. The propensity for pomp and circumstance did not end with the Civil War; in fact, in the summer of 1876, Savannah's Masons lavishly entertained the Grand Lodge of Georgia for two days. Yet Savannah's fraternal organizations and mutual aid societies also "offered economic relief in times of sickness and provided a decent burial" (Perdue, 99). These cultural organizations concerned themselves with every aspect of racial uplift and "focused on areas that the other world-oriented black churches normally did not" (Perdue, 99).

Savannah's fraternal and benevolent organizations sought to address certain exigencies that plagued the black community. Perhaps the two direst problems at the end of Reconstruction were unsanitary living conditions and inadequate health care. Because many of the city's indigent blacks lived in dank and windowless homes, tuberculosis spread rapidly among the black population. The efforts of the Lincoln Freedman's Hospital and the Georgia Infirmary to dispense medical care to African Americans were augmented by the black physician George McKane, who in 1893 opened the McKane Hospital for the Care of Negroes. Similar services were provided in the asylums and homes for the aged, such as the Grand Lodge of Georgia's Colored Orphan Asylum. At the end of the nineteenth century, African Americans used self-help to address the epidemiological issues facing the city's black population.

When the Union General William T. Sherman captured Savannah on his historic march from Atlanta to the Atlantic, blacks were freed from slavery. But to be free from the yoke of slavery, blacks needed to educate themselves. Prominent blacks from Savannah's fraternal, benevolent, and literary clubs formed the Savannah Education Association to educate freedpersons. When northern white missionaries could no longer meet the demand for black teachers, the Beach Institute was established to train black teachers. As with many cities in the South following the Civil War, colleges for blacks came into being slowly. Black colleges augmented the rise of the black middle-class, which itself gave rise to black fraternal and benevolent organizations as well as literary clubs. Since Savannah's black Georgia State Industrial College did not open until 1891, there was a paucity of black professionals, unlike in Atlanta, where the burgeoning black professional class was directly linked to the city's four black liberal arts colleges.

One prominent Savannah group that touted its college-educated members was the Savannah Sunday Men's Club. It was incorporated on April 16, 1905, and its members were described by one historian as "the kind of college-educated professional men whom [W. E. B.] Du Bois had labeled The Talented Tenth" (McMurry, 38). Before he became the famed black statistician and creator of the *Negro Year Book*, Monroe Nathan Work served as the Sunday Men's Club's first president.

### FURTHER READINGS

Gatewood, Williard B. *Aristocrats of Color: The Black Elite 1880–1920*. Bloomington: Indiana University Press, 1990.

Hines, Linda O., and Allen W. Jones. "A Voice of Black Protest: The Savannah Sunday Men's Club, 1905–1911." *Phylon* 35 (June 1974): 193–202.

Johnson, Whittington B. *Black Savannah, 1788–1864.* Fayetteville: University of Arkansas Press, 1996.

McMurry, Linda O. *Recorder of the Black Experience: A Biography of Monroe Nathan Work.* Baton Rouge: Louisiana State University Press, 1985.

Perduc, Robert E. *The Negro in Savannah, 1865–1900.* New York: Exposition Press, 1972.

Porter, Dorothy B. "The Organized Educational Activities of Negro Literary Societies, 1828–1846." *Journal of Negro Education* 5 (1936): 555–576.

*Derryn E. Moten*

## Savannah Education Association

The Savannah Education Association (SEA) was a black-controlled organization that funded, organized, staffed, and superintended schools in Savannah, Georgia. Founded shortly after Union forces captured Savannah, SEA opened its first schools in January 1865. SEA hired only black teachers, raised money by donations from the black community, and resisted northern white control. Within six months it enrolled over 700 students.

Black ministers and the governing boards of black churches initiated SEA and appointed a nine-man board to administer its schools. Its first principals were James D. Porter, a free black from Charleston, and Louis B. Toomer, a Savannah native. Both had taught slaves clandestinely before the war; both went on to political careers in Georgia. At its height, SEA employed twelve teachers.

While Freedmen's Bureau general superintendent John W. Alvord staunchly supported SEA, the American Missionary Association (AMA) opposed it. In debt by March 1866, SEA sought a grant from the Freedmen's Bureau. The assistant superintendent of the bureau in Georgia, himself a former AMA agent, awarded the grant instead to the AMA in Savannah, forcing SEA to turn to the AMA. SEA lost control of its schools, and its black teachers became assistants to white AMA teachers.

Although in existence less than two years, SEA was emblematic of the black community's thirst for education, its desire for autonomy and independence, and its organizational ability. Ultimately, however, Savannah's African American community lacked the economic foundation to support through donations a system of free schools.

### FURTHER READINGS

Butchart, Ronald E. *Northern Schools, Southern Blacks, and Reconstruction: Freedmen's Education, 1862–1875.* Westport, Conn.: Greenwood Press, 1980.

Jones, Jacqueline. *Soldiers of Light and Love: Northern Teachers and Georgia Blacks, 1865–1873.* Chapel Hill: University of North Carolina Press, 1980.

Morris, Robert C. *Reading, 'Riting, and Reconstruction: The Education of Freedmen in the South, 1861–1870.* Chicago: The University of Chicago Press, 1981.

*Ronald E. Butchart*

## Save Our Schools

*See* Southern Regional Council.

## Seattle: Civic, Literary, and Mutual Aid Associations

At the turn of the twentieth century, an "ethos of community" was emerging among Seattle's African American population. This ethos was manifested by a growing number of black religious, social, educational, and recreational organizations. The early endeavors of black churches, fraternal groups, social service organizations, and mutual aid associations facilitated the development of this new African American community in the Pacific Northwest.

As in most African American communities across the nation, the primary institution buttressing Seattle's black community was the church. From the turn of the century to the mid-1960s, the black church formed an integral part of the lives of African Americans in Seattle. It served as a spiritual center as well as a meeting and gathering place for newcomers and established residents alike. Moreover, the black church had an important political function. Controlled by African Americans, it represented a vital source of community power. Seattle's first black church was the First African Methodist Episcopal (AME) Church, established in 1886. While Mount Zion Baptist, established in 1890, was not quite as old, it claimed the largest membership. The black church served the spiritual needs of the congregation and the community, while also functioning as a center for the literary, artistic, musical, and oratory expressions of the black community.

Black churches also provided limited necessary social outreach programs. The AME Church, for example, sponsored an Educational Endowment Day to assist black colleges, while their associated Widows Mite Missionary society raised funds to help widows and orphans. Other groups, most notably the Frances Ellen Harper branch of the Women's Christian Temperance Union (WCTU), assisted the city's black homeless and transient population. Founded in 1891 by Emma Ray, an African American, the branch organized fifteen female members of the Jones

Street AME Church to aid prostitutes, petty criminals, and drug addicts who frequented Seattle's red light district. Members assisted these people regardless of their religious affiliation, sitting with them, washing their clothes, visiting with and speaking to King County Jail inmates and performing various tasks with the hopes of showing the downtrodden a new way of life. The work of the Harper branch was highly visible, albeit controversial.

By the 1920s, Seattle's black churches spanned the breadth of African American denominational needs, including St. Phillips Chapel for Episcopalians, Grace Presbyterian, and the Full Gospel Pentecostal Mission. Even Father Divine's Temple of Peace operated in the city by the 1930s. Black churches in particular became fountainheads for the teaching of African American history and the discussion of socio-political issues. Indeed, churches such as First AME, Mount Zion, and Ebenezer AME Zion opened their doors for rallies against police brutality and job discrimination. Moreover, they provided space for Seattle's African American community to enjoy nationally renowned visiting black speakers such as W. E. B. Du Bois, A. Philip Randolph, Congressman Oscar De Priest, and the white socialist Mary White Ovington. Finally, some of Seattle's black churches also served the recreational needs of the city's African American residents. First AME, for example, launched a men's and a women's basketball program.

By 1940, at least ten churches served the myriad needs of Seattle's African American community. First AME swelled to six hundred members, representing close to 15 percent of Seattle's African American population. First AME and Mount Zion remained integral parts of Seattle's African American community. They provided much of the leadership during the 1960s civil rights movement and continue today to be primary spiritual, social, and political institutions for Seattle's black community.

Like the church, black fraternal organizations served a multitude of functions in Seattle's African American community. Black fraternal organizations existed in Seattle since the early 1890s. Their sacred rituals, elaborate pageantry, grand balls, temples, and large memberships were proud manifestations of black-controlled social organizations. Whereas African Americans were denied status and respect outside Seattle's Central District, within the lodges they held community-based positions of power. Fraternal organizations boasted the second-largest number of members, rivaled only by the churches. They functioned as social clubs and insurance companies, provided burial benefits and financial lending services, and served as a training ground for the city's black leadership. Moreover,

fraternal organizations served the cultural needs of the African American community. Groups such as the Sons of Enterprise organized Seattle's first "Juneteenth" celebration on June 19, 1890, commemorating the day when the news of emancipation finally reached all African Americans. Thus, blacks in Seattle joined African American communities nationwide in commemorating African American Independence Day. Finally, because of their nationwide scope, the fraternal orders also provided a familiar transition and rest points for lodge members venturing to Seattle for the first time.

Complementing the work of the black churches and fraternal orders were a plethora of African American social service and relief organizations. Committed to community uplift, they sought to raise the general condition and status of the African American community. Among the most active groups were women's organizations such as the Dorcus Charity Club, the Phyllis Wheatley Young Women's Christian Association (YWCA), and the Sojourner Truth Home.

The Dorcus Charity Club, founded by Susie Revels Cayton in 1906, initially assisted a set of abandoned twin girls who were stricken with rickets. After being contacted by the King County Hospital, Cayton and three other African American women—Letitia A. Graves, Alice S. Preston, and Hester Ray—organized the Dorcus Charity Club to help place the children in an appropriate home. For three years the club provided support for the children until they were placed. The club also provided services for others in need. It paid for the medical expenses of a destitute girl for twenty months, financed rent payments for widows, provided Christmas toys for orphaned children, and made donations to hospitals. The Phyllis Wheatley YWCA, established in 1919, flourished under the leadership of African American women. It offered recreational facilities for the community through various programs and provided shelter for homeless black women. Another institution catering to the particular needs of destitute women was the Sojourner Truth Home. Created in 1918 by members of the Sojourner Truth Club, the home was named after the great black woman orator and "conductor" on the Underground Railroad. Located at 1622 23rd Avenue, the home provided shelter for unwed mothers, single women, the destitute, and the "friendless." By 1927, the home had eighteen members, including Amanda Jackson, who held the position of corresponding secretary.

The number and programs of Seattle's black volunteer organizations further expanded during World War II. Attracted by wartime defense industry jobs, 45,000 African Americans migrated to the city in search of employment.

While this population influx contributed to a growth in black association activities and strengthened the political power of Seattle's black community, it also exacerbated racial tensions. African Americans in Seattle, emboldened by their wartime contributions, increasingly demanded social and political equality. Their determination to end segregation and discrimination was evident in the rapidly growing number of African Americans who joined the Seattle branches of the National Association for the Advancement of Colored People (NAACP) and the Urban League in the decades following World War II. Local organizations that advocated integration, such as the Christian Friends for Racial Equality, also attracted large numbers of members and wielded considerable political influence during the post-war years.

In the 1960s, as the Black Power movement swept across the nation, Seattle too was affected. Black nationalist, separatist, and radical organizations, such as the United Black Front, Nation of Islam, and Black Panthers, gained popularity and political influence throughout the late 1960s and early 1970s. Today, members of Seattle's black community continue to find institutional support among the city's various black churches, fraternal organizations, social clubs, and mutual aid groups, as well as the local chapters of the NAACP, Congress of Racial Equality, and Urban League.

**FURTHER READINGS**

Debow, Samuel, and Edward A. Pitter. *Who's Who in Religious, Fraternal, Social, Civic, and Commercial Life on the Pacific Coast*. Seattle: Searchlight, 1927.

Hayes, R., and Joe Frank. *Northwest Black Pioneers: A Centennial Tribute*. Seattle: Bon Marché, 1994.

Mumford, Esther Hall. *Seattle's Black Victorians: 1862–1901*. Seattle: Ananse Press, 1980.

Taylor, Quintard. *The Forging of a Black Community: Seattle's Central District from 1870 Through the Civil Rights Era*. Seattle: University of Washington Press, 1994.

*Colin A. Beckles*

## Seattle Civic Unity Committee

*See* Washington State Fair Employment Practices Committee.

## Secretariat for Black Catholics

The Secretariat for Black Catholics was created in 1988 as a service agency for the Committee on African American Catholics and is the officially recognized office for issues regarding the black Catholic community's ministry, evangelization, and worship.

The establishment of the secretariat was a response to the growing number of black Catholics and increasing concern about racism in the church. By the end of the 1980s the number of black Catholics had risen to 1.3 million. This was a dramatic increase compared to the previous century when black Catholics were largely confined to scattered, rural parishes in the lower South. In 1979, American bishops had issued a pastoral letter condemning racism in all its forms. In 1984, they issued another pastoral letter entitled "What We Have Seen and Heard," which called upon the church to be more responsive to the needs of African American Catholics.

The secretariat gives black Catholics a voice in the U.S. Catholic Bishops Conference which, in turn, affects the entire life of the church. In addition, the secretariat focuses on evangelization of unchurched African Americans. It also functions as a clearinghouse of ideas that affect the black community and maintains a network with non-Catholic agencies and institutions such as the National Association for the Advancement of Colored People (NAACP) and the National Urban League (NUL). Finally, it serves as the liaison between the U.S. Catholic Bishops' Conference and the National Black Catholic Caucus, the National Black Catholic Sisters' Conference, the National Black Catholic Administrators and the Knights and Ladies of St. Peter Claver.

**FURTHER READINGS**

Davis, Cyprian, O.S.B. *The History of Black Catholics in the United States*. New York: Crossroad Publishing Company, 1991.

Secretariat for Black Catholics. *Plenty Good Room: The Spirit and Truth of African American Catholic Worship*. Washington, D.C.; Secretariat for Black Catholics, 1991.

*A. J. Scopino Jr.*

## Secretary for Negro Work, Episcopal Church

*See* American Church Institute for Negroes, Episcopal Church.

## Sickle Cell Disease Association of America, Inc.

In 1971, Dr. Charles Whitten, the "Father of Sickle Cell Disease Research," founded the National Organization for Sickle Cell Disease. The name was changed in 1994 to the Sickle Cell Disease Association of America, Inc.

(SCDAA). The SCDAA, headquartered in Culver City, California, strives to inform and assist those living with the disease or the sickle cell gene trait. The organization is community based, offering direct services to its seventy chapters in the United States and Canada.

Committed to early detection, the SCDAA distributes information about sickle cell disease, operates mobile testing units, and counsels those affected by the disease as well as their families. Testing for the sickle cell trait is provided free of charge, and today the SCDAA also offers genetic counseling to prospective parents carrying the trait. Rounding out its ambitious agenda is an aggressive fund-raising program supporting research, improved treatment methods, and discovery of a cure.

The prevalence of sickle cell disease among African Americans prompted physicians and concerned lay persons to demand that the government fund a program of testing in black communities. In 1963, Congress responded by enacting the Sickle Cell Anemia Control Act establishing ten national treatment centers. The legislation also prompted a public education campaign and research programs dedicated to finding a cure. Howard University became one of the original research sites under the direction of Dr. Roland Scott.

Named for the sickle shaped red blood cells carried by those with the disease, the trait is inherited. The disease originated in several places in Africa and the Indian–Saudi Arabian subcontinents; thus, it exists throughout the world, wherever Africans migrated. The trans-atlantic slave trade carried the sickle cell trait gene to the Americas and the Caribbean. The disease is far more prevalent in West and Central Africa, but about 1,000 babies with the disease are born annually in the United States. The global scope of sickle cell disease makes the mission of the SCDAA an immense challenge.

Today, the SCDAA finances publication of educational materials; offers training and technical support programs; serves as an advocate for those affected; sponsors a national convention, workshops, and international symposiums; and awards research scholarships. Individual assistance is provided through home nursing care, psychosocial counseling, support groups, transportation programs, and summer camps for children with sickle cell disease. Many of the individual SCDAA chapters offer information, support, and medical contacts through sites on the Internet.

**FURTHER READINGS**

*African Americans: Voices of Triumph. Leadership.* Alexandria, Va.: Time-Life Books, 1993.

Sickle Cell Disease Association of America, Inc. *Sickle Cell Disease: A Global Health Challenge, A United World Effort.* Culver City, Calif.: Sickle Cell Disease Association of America, Inc., ca. 1998.

*Peggy Hardman*

## Sigma Gamma Rho

Sigma Gamma Rho was founded by seven black women on the campus of Butler University in Indianapolis, Indiana, on November 12, 1922. The founders were Mary Lou Gardner Little, Nannie Mae Johnson, Vivian White Marbury, Bessie Martin, Cubena McClure, Hattie Mae Dulin Redford, and Dorothy Henley Whiteside. Sigma Gamma Rho was the first sorority established by black women on a predominantly white campus. Three other sororities for black women had been established previously at Howard University. Sigma Gamma Rho embraced social service and community outreach and adopted the motto "Greater Service, Greater Progress" and royal blue and gold as the sorority's colors. At first the seven founding sorors, who were all aspiring teachers, envisioned Sigma Gamma Rho as a sorority for teachers. But they soon agreed to admit other students. In 1925, the group held its first meeting, the Boulé. They elected one of the seven founders, Mary Little, to serve as the first president or Grand Basileus.

During the 1920s and 1930s, the sorority targeted the expansion of its membership by setting up chapters throughout the Midwest and beyond. The group was especially interested in reaching historically black colleges and universities. During this expansion period Rubye Peake established the first West Coast chapter in Los Angeles on July 30, 1939. A charter member of Los Angeles's Sigma Sigma chapter was Hattie McDaniel, who was the first black recipient of an Academy Award for her much acclaimed performance in the 1939 classic movie *Gone with the Wind*. At the last Boulé of the 1920s, the members made a sweeping effort to increase scholarships and required each alumnae chapter to establish a scholarship fund.

During the 1930s, the sorority supported a wide range of social, cultural, and educational activities. It established Sigma Gamma Rho's Employment Aid Bureau to assist in finding jobs for the unemployed. It established libraries on wheels and sponsored literary contests, lectures, book exhibits, and so-called book showers for historically black colleges. The work of Sigma Gamma Rho also extended to Africa, where the sorority assisted women and children nearly forty years before the groundswell of interest in Africa took hold of many African Americans. The sorority sent books to school children in West Africa and launched the project "Linens for Africa," providing African women with bed sheets and towels.

During World War II, Sigma Gamma Rho—like many other groups and organizations—put its sorority work on hold and supported the war effort. Sorority members joined the Women's Army Corps, the Red Cross, and the United Service Organization.

Following the war, the sorority launched the project "Teen Towns" to provide for the recreational and educational needs of the growing number of black teenagers in America's inner cities. Teen Towns sought to create a positive and nurturing environment by offering art, music, literature, games, and other enrichment activities.

During the 1960s and 1970s, when the country experienced turmoil as a result of civil rights, women's liberation, and antiwar protests, the sorority increased its financial support of the National Association for the Advancement of Colored People (NAACP), the National Urban League (NUL), and the United Negro College Fund. The sorority also helped sponsor a young soror who was a member of the first group of American college students who went to Nyasaland (now Malawi) under the auspices of Operations Crossroads Africa in 1962.

In the ensuing years Sigma Gamma Rho initiated "Project Reassurance," which addressed the rising concern about teenage pregnancy and "Project Mwanamugimu," an essay contest, that seeks to educate black youth about Africa and African cultures. At the same time, the sorority continued to focus on providing scholarships and assisting its members to reach their highest potential through the distribution of information and the organization of workshops, conferences, and the annual boules. In 1984, for example, the sorority established the National Education Fund to finance continuing support for education and health programs.

Currently Sigma Gamma Rho's commitment of service is manifested in several national programs including a partnership with the March of Dimes to help single mothers; a New York–based Vocational Guidance and Workshop Center; Wee Savers, a financial seminar for black youth between the ages of sixteen and eighteen; the Gift of Life Membership Club that provides resources for the Judie Davis Marrow Donor Recruitment Program; work with Habitat for Humanity International to build housing for low-income Americans; and a joint effort with Africare to purchase grain grinders for African women.

At the end of the twentieth century, Sigma Gamma Rho had a membership of 72,000 college-trained women in various professions living throughout the United States, Bermuda, the Virgin Islands, and parts of Africa. Members are organized into more than 400 chapters in five geographical divisions: Central, Northeastern, Southeastern, Southwestern, and Western. Sigma Gamma Rho's headquarters in Chicago, Illinois, publishes the quarterly *Aurora*, a membership directory, and the proceedings of the biennial Boulé. The sorority is active in the National Pan-Hellenic Council and currently supports the National Council of Negro Women, the Association for the Study of Afro-American Life and History, the Leadership Conference on Civil Rights, the National Urban League, and the Sickle Cell Foundation. The national sorority and its alumnae and campus chapters continue to support scholarships, grants, awards, and training programs for its members and other deserving youth and adults.

## FURTHER READINGS

Brown, Annie Lawrence, et al. *The Legacy Continues*. Chicago: Sigma Gamma Rho Sorority, Inc., 1994.

Brown, Roxanne. "Sigma Gamma Rho." *Ebony* (February 1991).

Hine, Darlene Clark, ed. *Black Women in America: An Historical Encyclopedia*. Brooklyn, N.Y.: Carlson Publishing, 1993.

Jaszczak, Sandra, ed. Encyclopedia of Associations; *An Association Unlimited Reference. Vol. 1, National Associations of the U.S. Part 2*. Detroit: Gale, 1996.

Sigma Gamma Rho. *Sigma Gamma Rho Up Close*. Chicago: Sigma Gamma Rho, n.d.

White, Pearl Schwartz, et al. *Behind These Doors—A Legacy. The History of Sigma Gamma Rho*. Chicago: Sigma Gamma Rho Sorority, Inc., 1974.

*Betty Nyangoni*

## Sigma Pi Phi

Sigma Pi Phi is a Greek-lettered organization of black professionals that emphasizes an elegant lifestyle and social activism. Six black professionals in Philadelphia founded Sigma Pi Phi, commonly called The Boulé, on May 15, 1904. The organization was the brainchild of Dr. Henry M. Minton, a dentist. He was joined by five other medical men, Dr. Algernon B. Jackson, Dr. Edwin C. Howard, Dr. Richard J. Warrick, Dr. Eugene T. Hinson, and Dr. Robert J. Abele. All of the founders were successful professionals; however, they were painfully aware that racism excluded them from the mainstream of America's cultural life. Thus, they came together to seek the good life and to forge a sacred and fraternal union.

The fraternity is organized into local chapters known as Subordinate Boulés. At the national level, the organization meets biennially in what is called the Grand Boulé. These national meetings, held in cities with a large black population, feature a public session.

From its inception, Sigma Pi Phi held brotherhood as its highest ideal, and for nearly a century the fraternity has sought to achieve this ideal by inducting into its ranks the most prestigious black men in America. Its roster contains illustrious members such as the historian, educator, minister, and dean of Howard University's graduate school Charles Wesley; the minister, educator, and president of Morehouse College Benjamin Mays; the minister and civil rights leader Martin Luther King Jr.; Virginia's first black lieutenant governor, L. Douglas Wilder; artists such as Ulysses Kay and Hale Woodruff; twenty-one Spingarn medalists, numerous college presidents, bankers, economists, and other professionals. The list is so impressive that some African Americans have accused the fraternity of being an elite group that exists to satisfy creature comforts in the most elegant venues.

During the first fifty-odd years, the Boulé's members, called Archons, wrestled with the dilemma of whether to remain a purely social fraternity or to focus on social activism. During the civil rights era of the 1950s and 1960s, the controversy came to a head when Archon Percy L. Julian, the eminent chemist, urged the fraternity "to do something." In 1964 at the national meeting Julian challenged Sigma Pi Phi at the twenty-seventh Grand Boulé to help "fellow-human beings who are struggling to free themselves." Julian's stirring address proved to be a turning point in the history of the fraternity. Following his speech, Sigma Pi Phi became more active in civic affairs. In 1978 it established The Boulé Foundation, which annually awards ten $4,000 scholarships to aspiring African American undergraduates. Through the foundation the fraternity also pledges annual financial support to organizations such as the National Association for the Advancement of Colored People (NAACP) and its Legal Defense Education Fund, the United Negro College Fund, and the Association for the Study of Negro Life and History. An Archon who makes a $1,000 contribution to the foundation is designated a Minton Fellow in honor of Henry M. Minton, one of the founders of Sigma Pi Phi. Other social action programs sponsored by the Boulé support youth development activities and encourage voter registration, political participation, and the celebration of African American history.

Sigma Pi Phi places great importance on family and regards the wives of members as full-fledged partners in its program of cultural uplift. While there is no formal organization of a women's auxiliary, each wife is called an Archousa and collectively, wives are known as Archousai. When Sigma Pi Phi considers a man for membership his wife's character is also taken into consideration. At Christmas time, the Subordinate Boulés sponsor elaborate social gatherings at which the Archousai are guests of honor, and they are celebrated at the Grand Boulés. The Archousai, renowned in their own right, number among themselves college professors, administrators in various fields of endeavor, attorneys-at-law, research scientists, judges, Phi Beta Kappa members, and homemakers. Each June, the fraternity holds a picnic, which brings Archons, Archousai, and children together for a celebration of the family.

Since 1912 Sigma Pi Phi has published the quarterly *Boulé Journal*. The magazine chronicles the many social and civic activities of the fraternity and contains inspirational and scholarly articles written by Archons and Archousai as well as an abundance of pictures of fraternity leaders and their wives.

In 1996, the Grand Sire Archon (president) was Mr. Eddie N. Williams, president of the Joint Center for Political and Economic Studies in Washington, D.C. That year Sigma Pi Phi had 3,700 members enrolled in 105 Subordinate Boulés.

**FURTHER READINGS**

Franklin, Robert V. "The Report of the Boulé Foundation to the 43rd Grand Boulé." *Boulé Journal* 60, 2 (Summer 1996): 16–17.

Jarrett, Hobart S. *History of Sigma Pi Phi: First of the African American Greek-Letter Fraternities*, vol. 2. Philadelphia: Quantum Leap Publishers, Inc., 1995.

Williams, Eddie N. "Black Politics in the 21st Century." *Boulé Journal* 60, 4 (Winter 1996): 3–7.

*Joseph T. Durham*

## Sisters of the Blessed Sacrament for Indians and Colored People

The Sisters of the Blessed Sacrament (SBS) is a Catholic order of nuns founded by Katharine Mary Drexel (1858–1955) in 1891. Born into Philadelphia's elite society, Drexel enjoyed the benefits of education, wealth, culture, and travel. These advantages, however, did not prevent her from cultivating a sense of social justice and becoming a fervent spokesperson for oppressed minorities.

Following a visit from two Catholic missionaries who had worked among the western tribes and after reading Helen Hunt Jackson's *A Century of Dishonor*, a compelling indictment of the federal government's treatment of Native Americans, Drexel took her first vows in 1889. Two years later she founded the Sisters of the Blessed Sacrament for Indians and Colored People in Philadelphia. She served as the order's superior for the next forty-four years.

Believing that education was the best means to serve humankind, Mother Drexel proceeded to build, staff, and support a national network of schools for African Americans and Native Americans. Often her efforts were hampered by white resistance including threats, vandalism, and legal obstacles. Mother Drexel died in 1955; however, the Sisters of the Blessed Sacrament continue to administer to African Americans and Native Americans. They also provide health care, education, catechetics, pastoral, and spiritual care to others in need.

**FURTHER READINGS**

Baldwin, Lou. *A Call to Sanctity: The Formation and Life of Mother Katharine Drexel.* Philadelphia: The Catholic Standard and Times, 1988.

Hanley, Boniface, O.F.M. *A Philadelphia Story.* Paterson, N.J.: St. Anthony Guild, 1984.

*A. J. Scopino Jr.*

## Sisters of the Holy Family

The Sisters of the Holy Family is a religious order of Catholic nuns with the mother house located in New Orleans, Louisiana. Founded in 1842, this congregation is the second oldest Catholic order for women of color in the United States. The order has a history of providing services for black people in Louisiana, Texas, California, Oklahoma, and in the Central American country of Belize. These services have focused upon religious education for slaves and, after the U.S. Civil War, continued academic training for African Americans. In addition, the sisters have provided a home for the aged, orphanages, and in modern times, a day-care center for the working poor.

Henriette Delille (1813–1862), the founder of the congregation, was born in New Orleans. She was an educated free woman of African and European descent. A feminist, social worker, and educator, Delille rebelled against the gendered conventions of the quadroon women of her family who became concubines of wealthy white men during slavery. She and the women who joined with her to organize the order challenged the prevailing belief that women of color were not capable of practicing celibacy and being nuns. Despite racial prejudice and discrimination, Delille and her cohorts made three attempts between 1825, the year their charitable work began, and 1842, before the congregation was recognized by the church and officially founded.

Inspired by the Ursuline Sisters, Delille and a friend, Cuban-born Juliette Gaudin (1808–1888), began to teach religion to slaves. The young women soon became interested in dedicating their lives to this work and sought to become a branch of the Ursuline Sisters. Unfortunately, their plans were not well received by the all-white order. Nonetheless, throughout the 1830s, Delille and Gaudin worked in the slave communities of New Orleans. In 1835, Delille was declared of legal age. She sold all of her property with hopes of founding a community of nuns, separate from the all-white Ursulines, and started to teach in a school for free girls of color. However, a campaign waged by civil authorities against those who sought to educate black people thwarted the effort.

Finally, in November 1842, with support from other quadroons, Delille and Gaudin obtained permission from the Catholic dioceses to begin their new order in St. Augustine's Church. A year later the novices were joined by Josephine Charles, another quadroon woman. When in 1847 the state legislature passed an incorporation act that required the sisters to form an association, several prominent quadroons came to their assistance. The Association of the Holy Family was organized with Delille as president. In 1849 financial and moral support made it possible for the association to build a home for the sick, aged, and poor black residents of New Orleans. The home was called the Hospice of the Holy Family.

The first three novices who led the order from 1842 to 1882 were Delille (1842–1862), Gaudin (1862–1867), and Charles (1867–1882). They are considered the founders of the congregation, which initially focused on providing education for black people. Between 1852 and 1898 the sisters opened six schools in New Orleans and six in other Louisiana communities, Texas, and Belize. In addition to schools, the sisters administered other agencies during the nineteenth and twentieth centuries. Continuing their mission to meet the needs of black people, the sisters have operated asylums and orphanages for children and homes for the aged, and they have provided services to assist working poor families.

**FURTHER READINGS**

Detiege, Sister Audrey Marie. *Henriette Delille, Free Woman of Color.* New Orleans: Sisters of the Holy Family, 1976.

Hart, Sister Mary Frances Borgia. *Violets in the King's Garden: A History of the Sisters of the Holy Family of New Orleans.* New Orleans: By the Author, 1976.

Terborg-Penn, Rosalyn. "Sisters of the Holy Family." In *Black Women in America: An Historical Encyclopedia,* vol. 2. Ed. Darlene Clark Hine, et al. Bloomington: Indiana University Press, 1994.

*Rosalyn Terborg-Penn*

## Slater Fund

*See* John F. Slater Fund.

## Social Workers' Club

In 1915, the first black social work organization was established in New York City, the Social Workers' Club. Black social workers engaged in several activities to accomplish their goal of becoming professionals early in the twentieth century. The Social Workers' Club was one of the major vehicles that black social workers initiated to establish themselves as noted professionals. Eugene Kinckle Jones, executive secretary of the National Urban League (NUL) (1916–1940) was a founding member and first president of the organization. In 1918, Jones as president of the Social Workers' Club invited prominent African American sociologist Dr. W. E. B. Du Bois to join the group. Du Bois accepted the invitation, and by 1918 the organization boasted a roster of eighty members. The group's objective was "To furnish means of friendly intercourse between members of the profession." Most African Americans who considered themselves social workers during this era were not necessarily trained in the traditional social work manner. Accompanying Jones as officers of the Social Workers' Club in 1918 were Mrs. C. L. Anderson, vice president; Miss Carita V. Owens, secretary; and Mrs. Adah B. Thoms, a noted leader of the black nursing profession, as treasurer. By 1921, Jones and other African American social workers became involved actively in the American Association of Social Workers. Jones also went on to become the first African American elected to the executive board of the National Conference of Social Work in 1925. Social work is the only professional group within the United States that allowed African American and white professionals to co-exist within its ranks early in the

twentieth century. As a result of African American social reformers working within the larger social work establishment, it appears that the Social Workers' Club ceased to exist by 1921. Certainly no documentation exists of its activities in the following years.

**FURTHER READING**

Armfield, Felix L. "Eugene Kinckle Jones and the Rise of Professional Black Social Workers, 1910–1940." Ph.D. diss., Michigan State University, 1998.

*Felix L. Armfield*

## Society for the Collection of Negro Folk Lore, Boston

The Society for the Collection of Negro Folk Lore was a short-lived institution organized in 1890 by several members of Boston's black elite. The prime mover of the society was probably Josephine St. Pierre Ruffin, who is better known for her pioneering work in the colored women's club movement during the 1890s. Other members included Ruffin's daughter, Florida Ruffin Ridley, and W. E. B. Du Bois, who was pursuing his Ph.D. in History at Harvard. Not much is known about the activities of the society. It appears to have faded from existence by 1894 when Ruffin and Ridley became active in founding Boston's Women's Era Club.

The society reflected the growing interest in the United States in folk history and culture in general, and in the history and folklore of Africans and African Americans in particular. The American Folklore Association was founded in 1888; various black and white writers were involved increasingly in recording or interpreting African American folk tales and songs; and Hampton Institute established a Department of Negro Folklore in 1895. Black Americans were becoming more active at both national and local levels in the preservation, interpretation, and dissemination of black history. They formed several literary and historical societies including the Bethel Literary and Historical Association established in Washington, D.C., in 1881 and the American Negro Historical Society organized in Philadelphia in 1897. While the Boston society had negligible impact, it represents an expanding interest among African Americans after the 1880s in laying claim to their own history and culture.

**FURTHER READINGS**

Meier, August. *Negro Thought in America, 1880–1915: Racial Ideologies in the Age of Booker T. Washington.* Ann Arbor: The University of Michigan Press, 1963.

Moses, Wilson Jeremiah. *The Golden Age of Black Nationalism, 1850–1925*. Hamden, Conn.: Archon Books, 1978.

*Mitchell Kachun*

# Society for the Propagation of the Gospel in Foreign Parts

The Society for the Propagation of the Gospel in Foreign Parts (SPG), founded in 1701, served as the Church of England's missionary arm in North America and the Caribbean in the eighteenth century. Its founder, Thomas Bray (1656–1730), was a pietistic reformer who, after serving as the Church of England's representative in Maryland, recognized the need to expand the work of the church and reach out to the unchurched and dispossessed in colonial America. With contributions from British entrepreneurs and approval of the bishop of London, Bray established the SPG, which sent more than 300 missionaries, teachers, and catechists to the British colonies.

For nearly a century after its founding Bray's society pursued a variety of religious and political objectives in British North America. Using the Bible, the Book of Common Prayer, tracts, and sermons, society missionaries preached of both God and king to a predominantly white colonial audience. Their churches served as paragons of old world order amidst the new world's religious, social, and political disarray. They defended colonial Anglicanism against Puritans, Catholics, and Quakers, while they preached of the divine nature of social hierarchy. SPG missionaries also launched extensive missions to secure political allies among their Native American neighbors.

Preoccupied with these immediate mission demands, the SPG reserved limited resources for missionizing among the slaves. The society's first mission efforts were directed at slaves owned by missionaries and those working on the sugar plantation in Barbados that the SPG inherited from one of its supporters. The society's missionaries instructed their slaves in reading and religion and used them as models to demonstrate the benefits of Christian education to American plantation owners. More extensive efforts to reach larger numbers of slaves were launched by several missionaries, teachers, and catechists. In 1704, for example, Elias Neau founded a slave school in New York that, at its peak, catechized nightly over 200 slaves. Critical of the SPG's lack of outreach to the city's slave population, Neau demanded clerical support to teach the slaves. The Reverend Francis LeJau in South Carolina also lobbied the SPG to provide slaves with Christian education. Opening his church to slaves, LeJau decried their inhumane treatment and implored southern plantation owners to grant slaves time for Sunday worship.

Overall, however, the society's missionary work among slaves gleaned few converts. This was due only in part to its limited manpower. A more serious obstacle to slave conversion was Anglicanism's emphasis on literacy. Since the majority of slaves were illiterate, reading instruction had to precede conversions, which slowed down the work of the missionaries. Moreover, Bible readings and structured Anglican liturgy did not appeal to most slaves, many of whom believed in direct inspiration. SPG missionaries also faced the specter of slaveowner opposition. Slaveowners often prevented blacks from joining churches and prohibited their participation in the sacraments, fearing that biblical teachings would make slaves disobedient and baptisms would necessitate their manumission. To alleviate the fears of slaveowners, SPG missionaries, such as LeJau and Neau, made it clear that conversion did not affect the slave's legal status. For example, slaves who attended LeJau's church in South Carolina had to sign a baptismal waiver that stated that they were not seeking freedom as a result of their baptism. Similarly, Neau, who catechized hundreds of slaves in New York, supported legislation stipulating that Christianity had no relation to temporal liberty. These efforts did little to assuage the fears of slaveholders. When New York slaves staged a revolt in 1712, slaveowners accused Neau of fomenting the insurrection, charging that his teachings had inspired the slaves. While Neau's school remained open after the revolt, attendance dwindled and the school declined.

The importance of the society's slave mission, however, lies not in the number of slave conversions, but rather in its groundbreaking nature and its contribution to later historical research. Until the work of the SPG, no institutional attempt was made in British colonial America to confront the task of slave conversion. While massive conversions did not occur until the Second Great Awakening of the early nineteenth century, the SPG's initial efforts among the slaves set a mission precedent and planted among them the first seeds of Christian knowledge. SPG missionaries were also important because many of them visited slave quarters and in their letters have provided much of what scholars know today of slave life and religion.

**FURTHER READINGS**

Calam, John. *Parsons and Pedagogues: The S.P.G. Adventure in American Education*. New York: Columbia University Press, 1971.

Raboteau, Albert J. *Slave Religion: The "Invisible Institution" in the Antebellum South.* Oxford: Oxford University Press, 1978.

Woolverton, John Frederick. *Colonial Anglicanism in North America.* Detroit: Wayne State University Press, 1984.

*Jennifer J. Wojcikowski*

## Society for the Relief of Free Negroes Unlawfully Held in Bondage

The nation's first abolition society, formed by Philadelphia Quakers in 1775, initially called itself the Society for the Relief of Free Negroes Unlawfully Held in Bondage, and was composed mainly of white Quaker artisans and small shopkeepers. The Revolutionary War disrupted the organization, but it was reorganized in 1787 as the Pennsylvania Society for the Promotion of Abolition of Slavery, Relief of Free Negroes Unlawfully Held in Bondage, and for Improving the Condition of the African Race (PAS).

Other abolition societies organized along the PAS model, with Quakers often playing a founding role. Yet the PAS remained the largest and most active abolition society in the nation. Not all the members were Quakers. Benjamin Franklin served as president, and Dr. Benjamin Rush was also a member. Many of the members held public office. There were no black members.

The original objective of the PAS was the relief of free blacks who were kidnapped into slavery. The society kept manumission records and provided legal and financial assistance for freedom suits in court. The group also pressed for more stringent state antikidnapping legislation and petitioned the federal government for a national law opposing kidnapping. After 1787, the reorganized group also monitored the execution of the state's gradual emancipation law, petitioned the federal government for the complete abolition of slavery, distributed antislavery literature, and agitated against the slave trade. The society also assisted the free black community in a variety of ways, providing education and indentureships for black children and finding employment for black adults.

### FURTHER READINGS

Bacon, Margaret. *History of the Pennsylvania Society for the Promotion of Abolition of Slavery.* Philadelphia: Pennsylvania Abolition Society, 1959.

Needles, Edward. *An Historical Memoir of the Pennsylvania Society for the Promotion of Abolition of Slavery.* 1848; rpt., New York: Arno Press and New York Times, 1969.

Turner, Edward Raymond. "The First Abolition Society in the United States." *Pennsylvania Magazine of History and Biography* 36 (1912): 92–109.

Wilson, Carol. "'The Legitimate Offspring of Slavery': Kidnapping of Free Blacks and Abolitionists' Response." *Mid-America* 74 (April/July 1992): 105–124.

*Carol Wilson*

## Society for the Study of Black Religion

In February 1971, African American scholars of religion, most of whom were members of the American Academy of Religion, met at Atlanta's Gammon Theological Seminary to establish the Society for the Study of Black Religion (SSBR). The society promotes the study of African American Christianity as well as other black religions and seeks to strengthen the community of African American religious scholars. The SSBR publishes research reports and the proceedings of its annual meetings to foster increased scholarship in African American religions. Moreover, it encourages the teaching of the black religious experience at colleges, universities, and theological seminaries to increase the number of black students pursuing doctorates and to enhance awareness of the historic contributions of black religions.

The society emerged in the late 1960s, when black religious scholars expressed concern about the small number of African American educators who had assumed academic leadership positions, even in predominantly black schools. This concern was echoed by the Association of Theological Schools' Special Committee on the Black Religious Experience, which was particularly troubled by the lack of black faculty with doctoral degrees. The future of African American churches, the committee reasoned, depended on the work of black scholars at the postsecondary educational level. The committee asked Charles Shelby Rooks, Protestant minister and civil rights leader, to investigate the possibility of creating a professional support network and public forum for African American seminary professors. As associate director of the Fund for Theological Education, Rooks had been a pioneer in increasing the number of African Americans who pursued Ph.D.s in religion. In the summer of 1969 Rooks and other black religious scholars gathered at Atlanta's Gammon Theological Seminary to discuss preliminary plans for the formation of a professional organization. Two years later they reconvened and founded the SSBR as a fellowship and forum enabling African American scholars in the field of religion to discuss their work, explore research and writing possibilities, and stimulate each other intellectually. Rooks served as the SSBR's first president.

Much to the chagrin of its activist members, the SSBR was founded primarily as an academic society, designed to develop a professional and intellectual community among black faculty and administrators. Ardent civil rights proponents, including Gayraud S. Wilmore, SSBR founding member and dean of the Black Church Studies program at Colgate Rochester Divinity School, and James Cone, eminent black scholar and theologian, criticized the SSBR for emphasizing "scholarship for the sake of scholarship." They hoped that the society would make an effort to connect the scholarly study of African American religion to the black freedom struggle. Rooks argued that the SSBR could and should pursue both an activist and scholarly agenda. Yet, he stressed the need for an academic society that primarily addressed the needs of black scholars.

The SSBR is affiliated with the American Academy of Religion (AAR) and initially met annually in conjunction with the AAR. The society's exclusively black membership, however, felt uncomfortable excluding non-black members of the AAR from its proceedings and in 1972 started to hold separate meetings. The SSBR is headquartered in the office of the society's incumbent president and currently represents 115 members.

**FURTHER READINGS**

Rooks, Charles Shelby. *Revolution in Zion: Reshaping African American Ministry, 1960–1974.* New York: Pilgrim Press, 1990.

*Kurt W. Peterson*

## Society of Black Composers

In 1968, a group of young musicians founded the Society of Black Composers (SBC) in New York City to develop their composition skills, promote the work of black modern and classical composers, and enrich the cultural life of black communities.

SBC members had an eclectic musical and political vision. They agreed that black music, regardless of genre, served as a vehicle for community uplift. While some members believed that their music was black simply because it was composed by African Americans, others viewed "their works as mystic instruments of a political cultural liberation struggle."

The society presented a variety of concerts, colloquia, and lecture tours to perform and discuss the music of its members. The black composers worked within white tra-

ditions of musical composition, yet they also expanded them by incorporating other cultural traditions to create their own distinct sound.

The society's membership included composers Talib Rasul Hakim (né Stephen Chambers), William Fischer, Carman Moore, Dorothy Rudd Moore, John Price, Alvin Singleton, Roger Dickerson, Primous Fountain, James Furman, Adolphous Hailstork, Wendell Logan, and Olly Wilson. These composers represented a broad musical spectrum ranging from jazz and spiritual to classical concert music as well as varying levels of experience, including established composers as well as those who had only recently embarked on careers in composition. The society received a variety of grants, including Ford, Fulbright, Guggenheim, Whitney, National Endowment for the Arts, and National Endowment for the Humanities fellowships, which provided its members with the resources to study and perform in Europe and Africa.

The society ceased to exist in 1971. Like other short-lived cooperative efforts of black artists, creative projects and professional careers directed society members to different paths. Many members continued to perform while others pursued careers in higher education and joined university faculties. The society is best remembered for embracing and experimenting with all genres of African American music.

**FURTHER READINGS**

Moore, Carman. "Does a Black Mozart—Or Stravinsky—Wait in the Wings?" *New York Times*, September 7, 1969, sec. 2, 23, 28.

Southern, Eileen. *The Music of Black Americans: A History.* 3rd ed. New York and London: W. W. Norton & Company, 1997.

*Nichole T. Rustin*

## Society of the Divine Word

The Society of the Divine Word, founded by Father Arnold Jansen in Holland in 1875, adopted the creation of a black Catholic clergy as its missionary goal and started to train black priests in 1920. It has always been a policy of the Roman Catholic Church to establish an indigenous clergy to minister to the needs of native peoples. In the United States the creation of a native clergy to serve the African American Catholic community was frustrated by institutional racism and social conditions in the South. While a handful of black Catholic priests existed shortly after the turn of the twentieth century, the

Postcard depicting first communicants of the Society of the Divine Word mission in Vicksburg, Mississippi, with Rev. John Hoendrerop, S.V.D., 1910. *Schomburg Center for Research in Black Culture*

society's missionaries were the most dedicated and persistent in preparing the way for a black Catholic clergy.

In 1915 the society secured a tract of land in Greenville, Mississippi, and built a school, church, and rectory to serve as a training ground for black priests. On February 14, 1920, Sacred Heart Seminary opened its doors and eight black students registered for classes. Two years later, the school, renamed St. Augustine's, moved to Bay St. Louis along the state's gulf coast where more black Catholics lived. From this vantage point future missionaries would have greater access to the more numerous African American Catholic congregations of Louisiana and the scattered black parishes of Mississippi and Arkansas. Faced with the growing needs of the south's black Catholic population, the softening of southern bishops on racial issues, and pressure from Rome, four black candidates were ordained in 1934.

The work and success of the Divine Word missionaries is remarkable. They faced both internal and external opposition. They encountered vacillation and indifference from the Roman Catholic Church and endured threats and hostility from southern whites and non-Catholic forces. Nevertheless, the seminary at Bay St. Louis continues its mission today.

**FURTHER READINGS**

Davis, Cyprian, O.S.B. *The History of Black Catholics in the United States.* New York: Crossroad Publishing Company, 1991.

Ochs, Stephen J. *Desegregating the Altar: The Josephites and the Struggle for Black Priests 1871–1960.* Baton Rouge: Louisiana State University Press, 1990.

Simon, Joseph D., S.V.D. "The African American Apostolate and the Society of the Divine Word." Unpublished manuscript.

*A. J. Scopino Jr.*

## Sojourner Truth Citizens Committee

On January 17, 1942, the Sojourner Truth Citizens Committee (STCC) formed to secure black occupancy of 200 housing units named in honor of the famous abolitionist-feminist. It emerged from the controversy over federally financed public housing for defense workers in Detroit that began before the United States officially entered World War II and culminated several months after the Japanese attack on Pearl Harbor.

In mid-1941, federal officials authorized construction of 1,000 housing units in Detroit. At that time Detroit had become the "Arsenal of Democracy," producing more war work than any other city and, consequently, attracting thousands of migrants. Given segregation in public housing, federal officials earmarked 200 of the units for black workers, to be built in a northcentral neighborhood on one of the sites suggested by the Detroit Housing Commission (DHC). Black and white homeowners of the area feared that the project would provide housing for lower-class residents and as a result depreciate their property. However, once black proprietors realized that the units were intended for working-class families and that white homeowners opposed the project because of racism, federal representatives faced opposition only from white, mostly Polish residents and area realtors.

From June to December 1941, the recently formed Seven Mile–Fenelon Improvement Association, headed by realtor Joseph P. Buffa and supported by Reverend Constantine Dzink of St. Louis King Parish Church, pressured federal authorities to reassign the nearly completed homes to whites. On January 15, 1942, Buffa with the assistance of DHC director Charles Edgecomb and Congressman Rudolph G. Tenerowicz, persuaded government spokesmen to promise African Americans another housing project.

Blacks and liberal whites, who thus far largely challenged the Seven Mile–Fenelon Improvement Association through DHC commissioner Reverend Horace A. White, organized the STCC. They elected Reverend Charles A. Hill of Hartford Avenue Baptist Church as chairman and attorney LeBron Simmons as treasurer. They activated citizens by rotating weekly meetings among black churches, mobilized community leaders through daily luncheons at the Lucy Thurman YWCA, and selected "We Shall Not Be Moved" as their battle hymn. They appointed a biracial steering committee to determine strategy, including Reverend White, newsman Louis E. Martin, Civil Rights Federation of Michigan executive secretary Jack Raskin, and National Association for the Advancement of Colored People (NAACP) officers Dr. James J. McClendon and Gloster B. Current.

The committee also reached beyond the black community, which provided most of its supporters. For thirty days, committee members mobilized residents and groups across racial and religious, union and nonunion, and ideological and class lines. Through a series of mass meetings, pickets, phone calls, letters, and conferences with municipal authorities and housing officials in Franklin D. Roosevelt's administration, they forced the latter to reverse their decision. The Sojourner Truth Homes would be occupied by blacks on February 28, 1942, the date set by DHC commissioners despite continued opposition from Buffa's association.

On that day, disorder erupted, as whites secured the project and its perimeter, refusing black renters entry to their homes. Police separated the rioters while local and federal officials postponed the move-in, which incited another outburst between blacks and police. Forty persons were injured and 200 arrested, most of them black, sparking further controversy. Thereafter, supporters of the Seven Mile–Fenelon Improvement Association and members of the STCC blamed the other for the bloodshed and pressed authorities anew. The STCC expanded its efforts, including publication of *Sojourner Truth Daily News*. Ultimately, Mayor Edward J. Jeffries Jr. and federal officials sided with black citizens and, with the assistance of 3,100 local police, state police, and Michigan Home Guardsmen, placed the first families in the housing project on April 29. Afterward local judges released all prisoners save two black rioters, while federal agents investigated Communist presence in the STCC and Ku Klux Klan presence in the Seven Mile–Fenelon Improvement Association.

FBI inquiries brought no formal charges against either "reds" or klansmen. Federal grand jurors, however, indicted the Seven Mile–Fenelon Improvement Association's vice president and two officers of the neo-fascist National Workers League for promoting the riot, though they never came to trial. One year later, in April 1943, Jeffries persuaded Common Council to adopt the position that racial characteristics would not be altered in future projects under municipal jurisdiction, essentially ending wartime construction of defense housing for blacks in Detroit.

The STCC revealed the shift in race relations generated by wartime circumstances and democratic principles. It prefigured the biracial coalitions, religious foundations, and nonviolent, direct action tactics that characterized the later civil rights movement. It revealed the leadership, institutional development, and community building in black Detroit. Finally, it indicated the limitations of government officials and policies, which intensified racial competition and, unwittingly, contributed to greater collective violence the following year.

**FURTHER READINGS**

Capeci, Dominic J., Jr. *Race Relations in Wartime Detroit: The Sojourner Truth Housing Controversy of 1942.* Philadelphia: Temple University Press, 1984.

Clive, Alan. *State of War: Michigan in World War II.* Ann Arbor: University of Michigan Press, 1979.

Meier, August, and Elliott Rudwick. *Black Detroit and the Rise of the UAW.* New York: Oxford University Press, 1978.

Sugrue, Thomas J. *The Origins of the Urban Crisis: Race and Inequality in Postwar Detroit.* Princeton: Princeton University Press, 1996.

Thomas, Richard W. *Life for Us Is What We Make It: Building Black Community in Detroit, 1915–1945.* Bloomington: Indiana University Press, 1992.

*Dominic J. Capeci Jr.*

## South Carolina Committee on Interracial Cooperation

*See* South Carolina Council on Human Relations.

## South Carolina Council for Human Rights

*See* South Carolina Council on Human Relations.

## South Carolina Council on Human Relations

The South Carolina Council on Human Relations (SCCHR) emerged in 1954 from the South Carolina Committee on Interracial Cooperation, which had been active since 1919. The interracial SCCHR fostered civil and human rights through public education campaigns that sought to improve "educational, economic, civic, and racial conditions in the state in an endeavor to promote greater unity in South Carolina." The SCCHR was a state affiliate of the Southern Regional Council until 1963 when it became an independent agency. It was renamed the South Carolina Council for Human Rights in 1973, and ceased operations in 1975. Its demise was perhaps due to the establishment of the State Human Affairs Commission in 1972. This state-supported agency with a mandate to enforce civil rights took on much of the work of the SCCHR.

The SCCHR conducted numerous studies of issues affecting African Americans in South Carolina, including welfare, school desegregation, prison parole, old-age assistance, voting rights, and health care, and published various reports to disseminate its findings. Headquartered in the state's capital in Columbia, the SCCHR operated chapters in various South Carolina communities and on college campuses throughout the state. At the peak of its existence, the SCCHR boasted nearly 3,000 members, many of them well known South Carolinians including the black lawyer and civil rights activist Marion Wright, the white educator and writer James McBride Dabbs, the white director of the Penn Center (St. Helena Island, S.C.) Courteney Siceloff, the black attorney Mordecai Johnson, the attorney and South Carolina state senator Theo Mitchell, and the black history professor Ed Beardsley, each of whom served as SCCHR president. Some other prominent members were John McCray, a black newspaper editor from Columbia, and Mojeska Simkins, a pioneer of the South Carolina civil rights movement. Between 1968 and 1972/1973, the SCCHR provided its membership with a newsletter, *Council Currents,* which contained letters and speeches, descriptions of chapter activities, and lists of resources and informational pamphlets. The council had only three executive directors, Alice Norwood Spearman Wright (1955–1967), Paul Matthias (1967–June 1974), and Lawrence J. Toliver (1974–1975).

The SCCHR promoted racial harmony at a time when many southern states were torn by racial conflict. Thanks in large part to the efforts of the SCCHR and, later, the State Human Affairs Commission, South Carolina enjoyed an almost trouble-free desegregation era.

**FURTHER READINGS**

Bicentennial Project Editorial Board. *South Carolina's Blacks and Native Americans, 1776–1976.* Columbia, S.C.: The State Human Affairs Commission, 1976.

Quint, Howard H. *Profile in Black and White: A Frank Portrait of South Carolina.* Washington, D.C.: Public Affairs Press, 1958.

South Carolina Council on Human Relations Records, South Caroliniana Library, University of South Carolina, Columbia, South Carolina.

*Virginia M. Matthews*

## Southern Christian Leadership Conference

The Southern Christian Leadership Conference (SCLC) was formed at a meeting of about sixty black activists held at Ebenezer Baptist Church, in Atlanta, Georgia, on January 10–11, 1957. SCLC was, in essence, an effort to

Martin Luther King Jr. speaks at a rally of marchers in Selma waiting to start a march to Montgomery. March 1965. © *Flip Schulke/Corbis*

replicate on a wider scale those elements of organization, leadership, and philosophy that had brought success to the Montgomery (Alabama) bus boycott of 1955–56. Like the Montgomery Improvement Association, the organizational vehicle of the bus boycott, the SCLC was led by Martin Luther King Jr., wedded to the philosophy of nonviolence, and based upon the black church. Under King's leadership, the SCLC became a dynamic force within the emerging civil rights movement. It played a crucial part in abolishing legalized segregation, ending the disfranchisement of black southerners, and making the issues of segregation and discrimination matters of national political urgency. After 1965, the SCLC also tackled the issues of war and poverty.

Its founders disclaimed any intent to supplant or even compete with the National Association for the Advancement of Colored People (NAACP). Still, the SCLC was designed to offer black southerners an alternative leadership to that of the NAACP. The NAACP contended that

the outcome of the Montgomery bus boycott had actually underlined the effectiveness of its own litigation tactics, for NAACP lawyers had won the crucial court decision, *Gayle v. Browder*, that integrated the buses in Montgomery, Alabama. To King and many others, however, the Montgomery bus boycott had illustrated the efficacy of independent, local black organization, the moral force of the black church, and the power of mass nonviolent direct action. The boycott had also showcased the inspirational leadership of King himself. Very early on in the bus boycott, therefore, some civil rights activists suggested to King that the Montgomery movement, and his own leadership, might form the basis for a new, southwide, civil rights organization.

Although the basic impetus for the SCLC's mass nonviolent direct action came from the Montgomery bus boycott, three New York–based activists and intellectuals played a key role in creating and guiding the new organization. Bayard Rustin, then executive director of the War

Resisters League, helped King to clarify his ideas about nonviolence. More important, Rustin, who had a wealth of contacts in labor, pacifist, and civil rights organizations, became a key advisor to King, writing speeches for him, ghostwriting articles, raising funds, and counseling him on strategy and tactics. With two political friends, Ella Baker and Stanley Levison, Rustin drew up the plans for the SCLC and persuaded King to lead it. Baker, a black woman who had been the NAACP's director of branches in the 1940s, and Levison, a Jewish attorney and businessman, shared Rustin's view that the NAACP had become too conservative, too bureaucratic, and too wedded to legalism. They hoped that the SCLC would reinvigorate the flagging civil rights struggle in the South through the power of mass direct action.

The SCLC's opponents sometimes claimed that King was manipulated by Communists—or was even a Communist himself. Rustin, Baker and Levison were veterans of the "Old Left," a loose political movement of the 1930s and 1940s in which Communists had considerable influence; Levison, in particular, was once "close" to the Communist Party. By 1957, however, none of them had any ties to the party, which was virtually defunct. In any case, King was a man of great independence and was hardly susceptible to manipulation. Nevertheless, the FBI used King's association with Rustin and Levison (Baker became disillusioned with King and left SCLC in 1960) as a pretext to tap King's phones, bug his hotel rooms, label him a threat to national security, and wage a surreptitious campaign of blackmail, disruption, and character assassination.

During its early years, the SCLC benefited from the fact that state authorities across the South were attempting to destroy the NAACP through legal harassment. In Alabama, for example, a state court banned the NAACP altogether. In many communities, ad hoc local organizations emerged more or less spontaneously to replace the NAACP. These organizations had no formal membership, possessed the loosest of structures, and were often led by ministers, all characteristics that made them less vulnerable to official persecution. Many of these groups became local "affiliates" of the SCLC, an umbrella organization that also had no formal membership.

Although the SCLC had a board of directors that in theory set policy, the organization was, in effect, a loose network of black ministers and churches that had gathered around King. These ministers included C. K. Steele of Tallahassee, Joseph E. Lowery of Mobile, Fred L. Shuttlesworth of Birmingham, and Ralph D. Abernathy of Montgomery, who became King's closest associate and friend.

The SCLC's motto, "To Redeem the Soul of America," reflected its strong Christian commitment. However, King's efforts to mobilize the black church behind the civil rights struggle were strongly opposed by Joseph H. Jackson, president of the National Baptist Convention, the largest and most influential black denomination. Only a small minority of black ministers actively supported King and the civil rights movement.

During its first few years, the SCLC struggled to survive. When the Montgomery bus boycott failed to ignite a wave of similar protests, the SCLC shifted its attention to voter registration. With little money and only one full-time staff member, however, it accomplished little. The SCLC did, on the other hand, give King a platform, and his meetings with Vice President Nixon in 1957 and President Eisenhower in 1958 confirmed his status as a black leader of national stature.

The student sit-in movement of 1960 and the Freedom Rides of 1961 helped to invigorate the SCLC. They confirmed the efficacy of nonviolent direct action, introduced new tactics, and mobilized members of a younger generation. Significantly, however, when black students in the South formed an organization, the Student Non-Violent Coordinating Committee (SNCC), it chose to remain completely independent of the SCLC. King, in fact, seemed somewhat cautious during these years. He was jailed in a sit-in, but not until October 1960. He supported the Freedom Rides, but refused to go on one himself. Although a source of inspiration and a symbol of unity, King's leadership was hardly decisive.

Nevertheless, under Executive Director Wyatt T. Walker, who replaced Ella Baker in 1960, the SCLC began to acquire organizational substance. It received a foundation grant to take over the Highlander Folk School's Citizenship Education Project, which was run by Septima P. Clark, a schoolteacher from South Carolina. Andrew J. Young joined the SCLC to administer the program, and Dorothy Cotton helped Clark to teach it. The SCLC also added to its staff two veterans of the student sit-in movement, Bernard S. Lee and James L. Bevel. Along with other civil rights organizations, the SCLC received foundation money to finance voter registration work. In New York, Stanley Levison developed a direct mail fund-raising program. The SCLC suffered, however, from the departure of Bayard Rustin in 1960, after Congressman Adam Clayton Powell Jr. threatened to embarrass King by "exposing" Rustin's homosexuality. Rustin returned to King's circle of advisors in 1963, after his success in organizing the March on Washington.

In December 1961 the SCLC became embroiled in its first full-scale campaign of nonviolent direct action when King heeded an invitation to speak in Albany, Georgia, where the Albany movement, a local civil rights coalition led by Dr. William G. Anderson but guided by SNCC, had begun a series of marches to protest against segregation and discrimination. Over the next eight months the SCLC focused most of its energies on Albany, and King went to jail there three times. However, the SCLC's involvement suffered from lack of planning, tensions, and rivalries with SNCC, lack of sympathetic action by the federal government, and the hard-line resistance of local whites. The ostensibly "nonviolent" tactics of Albany police chief Laurie Pritchett, who knew full well that open police brutality would only arouse sympathy for the civil rights movement, also proved frustrating. Albany was widely perceived as a major defeat for the SCLC.

The Birmingham, Alabama, protests of early 1963 were the breakthrough the SCLC had been looking for. The assertion that the SCLC picked Birmingham in the hope that its demonstrations would provoke a violent white response has not been proven conclusively, although the organization was certainly aware that violence from the police and the Ku Klux Klan was a strong possibility. The SCLC also knew that because Birmingham was regarded as the most racist city in the South, a victory there would have repercussions far beyond Birmingham itself.

Eventually, after a month of demonstrations, the SCLC succeeded in "filling the jails" by mobilizing thousands of black schoolchildren. The dramatic confrontations between demonstrators and police gained worldwide publicity and prompted the Kennedy administration to seek a negotiated settlement. While the agreement that the SCLC signed with local business leaders signified only modest steps toward desegregation, the mere fact that concessions had been won at all inspired blacks across America. Birmingham sparked off a "long hot summer" of demonstrations and convinced Kennedy to introduce a Civil Rights Bill. Eventually passed under President Lyndon Johnson, the 1964 Civil Rights Act outlawed segregation in public accommodations, banned employment discrimination, and gave the federal government more authority to enforce school integration.

Birmingham greatly enhanced King's reputation. King's "Letter From Birmingham City Jail" became the classic defense of nonviolent protest. King's address to the March on Washington, "I Have A Dream," delivered on August 28, 1963, is the most famous speech of the civil rights movement. In 1964 King received the Nobel Peace Prize and was named "Man of the Year" by *Time* magazine. The success of Birmingham, however, was not due to King alone: credit should be shared with Fred L. Shuttlesworth, the courageous leader of the SCLC's Birmingham affiliate, with the staff members of the SCLC, particularly Wyatt Walker, James Bevel, Andrew Young, and Dorothy Cotton, and with the thousands of ordinary men, women, and children who marched and went to jail.

In 1964 the SCLC organized demonstrations against segregation in St. Augustine, Florida, and played a minor but supportive role in the Freedom Summer project in Mississippi. Partly because 1964 was a presidential election year, however, it did not undertake a major campaign of nonviolent direct action. Indeed, after rioting broke out in New York and other northern cities, the SCLC agreed to suspend demonstrations for the duration of the election. Although officially nonpartisan, it openly campaigned for presidential candidate Lyndon B. Johnson. In matters of political strategy, as well as in matters of tactics and fund-raising, King came to value the advice of his "Research Committee," a group of intellectuals whom he met with regularly in New York and frequently consulted over the telephone. The principal members of this informal "think tank" were Stanley Levison, Bayard Rustin, Harry Wachtel, and Clarence Jones.

In 1965 the SCLC orchestrated a series of protests in Selma, Alabama, in cooperation with SNCC and local black leaders, to dramatize the continuing scandal of black disfranchisement. As with Birmingham, the choice of Selma suggests that the SCLC realized that a brutal response from the white authorities would further its cause. The heavy-handed tactics of Sheriff Jim Clark ensured sympathetic news coverage, but the worst violence took place in Marion, Alabama, where a state trooper killed Jimmie Lee Jackson, a young black man. At the beginning of a planned march from Selma to Montgomery to protest Jackson's slaying—a protest that SNCC opposed—state troopers and Clark's deputies, instructed by Governor George Wallace to prevent the march, violently attacked the demonstrators. The resulting television pictures shocked the world and played an important part in persuading President Johnson to initiate, and Congress to pass, the Voting Rights Act of 1965, the SCLC's crowning achievement.

Its successes in Birmingham and Selma greatly enhanced the SCLC's ability to attract financial support, much of it in the form of small donations from members of the public. By 1965 the SCLC's annual income exceeded $1.5 million, and it had a full-time staff of about

200 people, including many northerners and a few whites. The SCLC had field secretaries in every southern state except Florida and Tennessee, as well as unpaid regional representatives outside the South, and a representative in Washington, D.C., the Reverend Walter Fauntroy. The number of local affiliated organizations, most of them churches, grew to well over 200, although the relationship between the affiliates and the SCLC remained tenuous. In its heyday, the SCLC also initiated new programs such as Operation Dialog (to promote interracial understanding) and Operation Breadbasket (to increase black employment by threatening employers with "selective buying" campaigns). "SCOPE," the SCLC's 1965 voter registration project, directed by Hosea Williams, covered about fifty southern counties.

The Watts, Los Angeles, riot of August 1965 prompted a major shift in the SCLC's orientation. Despite opposition from within the SCLC, King accepted James L. Bevel's plan to take the organization to Chicago to dramatize urban poverty and segregation. Working with a local civil rights coalition, and basing itself in Chicago's West Side ghetto, the SCLC eventually focused on the issue of housing segregation. Its campaign peaked in the summer of 1966 with marches into white neighborhoods that evoked violent reactions from white residents. However, the "Summit Agreement" that the SCLC negotiated with Mayor Richard J. Daley and representatives of Chicago's business community had virtually no impact on segregated housing patterns. Outmaneuvered by Daley, and overwhelmed by the enormity of the urban problems they encountered, the SCLC found Chicago a demoralizing experience.

In 1966 the SCLC had to contend with other discouraging developments, notably the spread of ghetto rioting, the escalation of the war in Vietnam, and the split in the civil rights movement caused by SNCC's turn toward black nationalism. With a strong commitment to participatory democracy, and a method of working that stressed grass-roots organizing, SNCC had always been critical of King's autocratic style and SCLC's "hit-and-run" tactics. More important, SNCC had become disillusioned with white liberals and regarded the Johnson administration as an enemy rather than an ally. During a march through Mississippi in 1966 (the Meredith March), SNCC's new leaders, notably Chairman Stokely Carmichael, openly challenged King's leadership, rejecting his principles of nonviolence and integration. The slogan "Black Power" was roundly denounced by the NAACP. King disliked the slogan, but his efforts to dissuade SNCC from embracing black nationalism failed. No longer able to function as a unifying force in the civil rights coalition, King saw his influence further diminish with the spread of ghetto rioting in 1966–1967, an intensification of the "white backlash," and America's growing involvement in the Vietnam War.

In 1967 King, impelled by both conscience and tactical considerations, denounced America's actions in Vietnam and began to campaign actively for an immediate end to the war. While his stand enjoyed the support of colleagues like James L. Bevel and James Lawson, who were already involved in the peace movement, it angered many friends and supporters, was criticized by the *New York Times*, and infuriated President Johnson, who now regarded King as a political enemy. Nevertheless, King's commitment to the peace movement added strength and respectability to the antiwar forces, which by 1968 came to dominate public opinion. The SCLC's failure in Chicago, however, and the lack of a major campaign in 1967 contributed to a decline in morale and discipline within the SCLC.

The Poor People's Campaign (PPC), launched in late 1967, marked a major shift for the SCLC. In an effort to head off further rioting, bridge the growing chasm between blacks and whites, and directly address the problem of poverty, the SCLC proposed to build an interracial alliance of poor people in order to put pressure on the federal government to divert money from the Vietnam War to domestic reform. For King, the campaign marked a turn toward socialism, framed in terms of the Social Gospel. Always sympathetic to Marx's critique of capitalism, his firsthand experience of Chicago's ghetto had convinced him that the United States ought to move in the direction of European-style social democracy. Colleagues such as Hosea Williams and Jesse Jackson, however, remained committed to free-market capitalism, while James L. Bevel and others believed that the SCLC should make the war in Vietnam its overriding priority. Other colleagues, among them Bayard Rustin, feared that the SCLC's plans for nonviolent protests in Washington, D.C., would not only fail, but might provoke further backlash and repression. The FBI made strenuous efforts to disrupt the SCLC's plans.

In the midst of these uncertainties, King committed the SCLC to backing a strike by Memphis sanitation workers. After a demonstration King led resulted in violence, he doubted his ability to maintain nonviolent discipline even within his own ranks. On April 4, 1968, while planning a second march, King was assassinated by James Earl Ray.

The SCLC never recovered from King's death, and its rapid decline revealed how completely the organization had depended on King's ability, influence, and integrity. The Reverend Ralph David Abernathy, whom King had nominated as his successor in 1965, was sincere and well meaning, but he lacked King's intellect, tactical skill, and moral authority. Personal rivalries, checked under King, became debilitating, and organizational discipline, never strong, quickly disintegrated. The Poor People's Campaign, mounted in the summer of 1968, turned out to be an embarrassing fiasco, with the SCLC leaving Washington virtually empty-handed. The SCLC continued to engage in valuable voter registration work, especially in the South, and it won a morale-boosting victory in Charleston, South Carolina, in 1969, when it aided striking hospital workers in their struggle for union recognition and better pay. By 1972, however, key staff members had quit the organization, notably Andrew Young, James L. Bevel, and Jesse Jackson. Jackson launched the Chicago-based Operation PUSH as a direct rival to the SCLC. In 1973, after its income had plummeted, SCLC's staff diminished to seventeen people. Abernathy soldiered on as president until 1977. The Reverend Joseph L. Lowery served as the SCLC's president for the next twenty years. King's son, Martin Luther King III, is the current president. Not since the Poor People's Campaign, however, has the SCLC been a strong force in the South and in the nation.

Harnessing the moral strength of the black church, and utilizing hard-headed and politically astute tactics, the SCLC proved brilliantly effective in mobilizing black southerners for short-lived but dramatic confrontations. By awakening national concern, the SCLC helped to desegregate public accommodations and win the right to vote. It proved less successful in tackling poverty and de facto segregation in the North, although it is fair to add that those systemic problems have defeated every other effort at reform.

**FURTHER READINGS**

Branch, Taylor. *Parting the Waters: America in the King Years, 1954–63*. New York: Simon & Schuster, 1988.
———. *Pillar of Fire: America in the King Years, 1963–65*. New York: Simon & Schuster, 1998.
Fairclough, Adam. *To Redeem the Soul of America: The Southern Christian Leadership Conference and Martin Luther King, Jr.* Athens: University of Georgia Press, 1987.
Garrow, David J. *Bearing the Cross: Martin Luther King, Jr. and the Southern Christian Leadership Conference.* New York: Williams Morrow, 1986.

Young, Andrew. *An Easy Burden: The Civil Rights Movement and the Transformation of America.* New York: HarperCollins, 1996.

*Adam Fairclough*

## Southern Coalition for Educational Equity

Founded by Winifred Green in 1978, the Southern Coalition for Educational Equity (SCEE) is an advocacy group that seeks to increase educational opportunities and eliminate racism and sexism in public schools in the South. Composed of parents, students, teachers, and school administrators, the SCEE works to make public schools "truly effective learning institutions" of academic excellence and equal opportunity. The SCEE operates in Alabama, Arkansas, Florida, Georgia, Louisiana, Mississippi, North Carolina, South Carolina, Tennessee, Virginia, and West Virginia.

Headquartered in Jackson, Mississippi, the SCEE has launched many successful programs, including Project MiCRO (Minority Computer Resources Opportunity), which provides poor and disadvantaged students with the opportunity to learn critical thinking skills through the use of computers, and the New Orleans Effective Schools Project, which fosters reading comprehension skills. SCEE funding is provided by private foundations, corporations, and individual donors.

**FURTHER READINGS**

Apple, Michael W. "The Politics of Curriculum and Teaching." *National Association of Secondary School Principals Bulletin* 75, 532 (February 1991): 39–50.
Jaszcsak, Sandra, ed. *Encyclopedia of Associations.* Detroit: Gale, 1997.
Southern Coalition for Educational Equity. *Annual Report 1986.* Jackson, Miss: Southern Coalition for Educational Equity, 1986.

*Virginia M. Matthews*

## Southern Commission on the Study of Lynching

In July 1930, the Commission on Interracial Cooperation (CIC), a group of prominent white Southerners concerned about improving race relations, founded the Southern Commission on the Study of Lynching (SCSL) to study and expose the underlying socioeconomic causes of lynchings in an effort to stop the racial violence. The SCSL was an interracial group composed of academics, journalists, and other professionals. White members included CIC founder Will W. Alexander, *Atlanta Constitution* news editor Julian Harris, and Furman University president W. J. McGlothlin. African American members included John Hope, president of Atlanta University, and Robert R. Moton of Tuskegee Institute.

The SCSL was founded in response to the growing number of lynchings that occurred in 1930. A wave of lynchings had first swept the nation in the late nineteenth century. Between 1884 and 1900, more than 2,500 lynchings occurred in the United States, five out of six in the South. Lynchings primarily victimized African Americans who were accused of offenses ranging from murder and rape to violations of "racial etiquette." The phenomenon of mobs spontaneously executing black suspects continued during the early twentieth century, claiming more than 1,100 victims prior to World War I. In the decade following the war, the number of lynchings declined. By 1929, lynching neared extinction, with only ten recorded cases that year, the lowest number since reliable statistics were kept. In 1930, however, the number more than doubled perhaps due to the Great Depression, which heightened economic competition between blacks and whites.

Alarmed by this dramatic increase and appalled by two highly publicized lynchings that year in Ocilla, Georgia, and Sherman, Texas, Will W. Alexander founded the SCSL. The commission launched a case-by-case study of racial violence in the South and published its findings in a number of pamphlets and books. Two sociologists, Arthur F. Raper, a white graduate of the liberally inclined University of North Carolina, and Walter R. Chivers, a black professor at Morehouse College, conducted the field research.

In October 1931, the SCSL published Raper's analysis of the causes of lynchings in the pamphlet *Lynchings and What They Mean*. The SCSL published a second pamphlet, *The Mob Murder of S.S. Mincey*, which presented a detailed case study of a lynching. Both pamphlets refuted the claim of white southerners that lynchings were necessary tools to punish and prevent rape and other sexual transgressions by African Americans. Raper and Chivers' research demonstrated that fewer than one-fifth of all lynchings were preceded by accusations of rape. Lynchings, Raper and Chivers concluded, were not manifestations of chivalrous attempts to defend the virtue of white womanhood, but the product of economic and political competition. *Lynchings and What They Mean* found that most lynchings happened in poor, thinly populated counties with relatively small African American populations.

Typically, poverty marked both lynchers and their victims. Poor whites, the SCLS's findings indicated, used lynchings as a means to assert their economic and political power. Moreover, the pamphlet presented conclusive proof that two of the individuals lynched in 1930 were innocent, and Raper expressed "grave doubts" about the guilt of eleven other victims.

Much of what Raper and Chivers concluded echoed earlier studies of lynchings conducted by black newspaper editor Ida B. Wells-Barnett and Walter White of the National Association for the Advancement of Colored People (NAACP). Unlike these earlier studies, however, the SCLS report generated considerable public attention in the South. Perhaps the authors' academic credentials and the involvement of white southern liberals who sponsored the SCSL study provided the report with increased credibility among the region's progressive whites.

While SCSL research suggested that poverty was an important factor contributing to the racial violence, poor education was equally responsible. SCSL member Howard W. Odum, head of the University of North Carolina's Institute for Research in Social Science, argued that lynching was a "southern folkway" resistant to change through legislation. "Education, publicity, civic appeal and courageous leadership" provided by white southern elites, he suggested, could transform those folkways. With this objective in mind, the SCSL aimed its public education efforts at elite southern audiences, hoping to stimulate a racially progressive spirit in the South. In 1933, the SCSL published the book *The Tragedy of Lynching*, an expanded version of Raper's *Lynchings and What They Mean*, and James Chadbourn's *Lynching and the Law*. Both books became definitive works on the subject and were influential among southern liberals.

Although the SCSL largely sought to abolish lynchings through public education, it also plunged into political controversy in 1931. That year, the SCSL conducted an investigation of the Scottsboro case in which nine black Alabama youths were accused of raping two white women. While SCSL researchers concluded that the defendants were innocent, they attacked the defense attorneys provided by the Communist International Labor Defense (ILD) organization, accusing them of exploiting the case for political purposes. The SCSL's criticism of the ILD indicated the commission's commitment to liberal reform. Education, not a radical restructuring of the southern economy and political system, remained the SCSL's focus.

The work of the SCSL concluded with the publication of Raper and Chadbourn's books. The SCSL, the CIC, and similar organizations dominated by white liberals, such as the Association of Southern Women for the Prevention of Lynching led by Jessie Daniel Ames of Texas, represented a new current of regional self-criticism grounded in reformist politics. While lynching declined throughout the 1930s, the leaders of the SCSL may have put too much faith in the power of white southern liberals to reform the region without assistance of federal law. The efforts of the SCSL primarily inspired other southern white elites, such as newspaper editor Hodding Carter of the *Delta Democrat Times,* to criticize mob violence and political demagogues who inspired such hysteria in the South. The SCSL, however, avoided direct attacks on segregation, black poverty, or the ideology of white supremacy that was at the heart of southern racial violence. This prevented the SCSL from articulating a clear program to end the poverty and political alienation researchers like Raper identified as the cause of lynching. Despite this shortcoming, the SCSL represented a rare case of southern opinion leaders examining a regional evil rather than insisting that the problem was a figment of northern propaganda.

**FURTHER READINGS**

Brundage, W. Fitzhugh. *Lynching in the New South: Georgia and Virginia, 1880–1930.* Urbana: University of Illinois Press, 1993.

Chadbourn, James. *Lynching and the Law.* Chapel Hill: University of North Carolina Press, 1933.

Hall, Jacquelyn Dowd. *Revolt Against Chivalry: Jessie Daniel Ames and the Women's Campaign Against Lynching.* New York: Columbia University Press, 1993.

Kneebone, John T. *Southern Liberal Journalists and the Issue of Race, 1920–1944.* Chapel Hill: The University of North Carolina Press, 1985.

Raper, Arthur Franklin. *The Tragedy of Lynching.* Chapel Hill: The University of North Carolina Press, 1933.

*Michael Phillips*

**SEE ALSO**    Commission on Interracial Cooperation

# Southern Conference Educational Fund

The Southern Conference Educational Fund (SCEF) emerged in 1946 as the educational wing of the Southern Conference for Human Welfare (SCHW), an interracial organization formed in 1938 that attacked economic, social, and racial injustice in the South. When the SCHW ceased to exist in 1948, the SCEF continued as an independent entity. Between 1948 and 1975 the SCEF oper-

ated in southern states to end segregation. Throughout its existence, the SCEF continued publication of the SCHW journal, *The Southern Patriot,* which served as a crucial communication medium for the southern civil right movement. By the 1960s the *Patriot* evolved into a monthly eight-page tabloid newspaper with a circulation of 20,000. Today the *Patriot* files are a valuable and unique source of contemporary reporting on that period, providing on-the-scene coverage of local and regional movements, usually written by active participants.

The SCEF's direction was set by the vision of James A. Dombrowski, a white southerner from Tampa, Florida, who had been strongly influenced by the social gospel teachings of Christian theology. In 1948, Dombrowski decided that while the SCHW addressed many important issues, none of them could be addressed adequately as long as racial segregation rendered the South a police state. He saw a need for an organization that would unite African American and white activists around a single-point program of eliminating Jim Crow. He pulled together an interracial board that eventually grew to over seventy persons. Among the early members were Dr. Herman Long, director of the Race Relations Institute at Fisk University and later president of Talladega College; Dr. Albert Barnett, distinguished professor at Candler School of Theology, Emory University; John Wesley Dobbs, legendary African American leader in Atlanta; Dr. Alva Taylor, theologian who was forced out of Vanderbilt School of Religion for his activism; Dr. Charles Gomillion, who organized the voting rights movement in Tuskegee, Alabama; and E. D. Nixon, one of the organizers of the Montgomery bus boycott. There was also an advisory committee of more than 100 leading citizens and activists, including Daisy and L. C. Bates, newspaper publishers who led the school desegregation battle in Little Rock, Arkansas; A. G. Gaston, African American owner of Birmingham's Gaston Motel, which was a center of civil rights activities in the 1960s; Reverend Ben Wyland, white church leader in St. Petersburg, Florida; Charlotte Hawkins Brown, black educator in North Carolina; and Reverend W. W. Finlator, of the Southern Baptist Convention. While the SCEF's only real members were its board members, the organization built a loose network of supporters across seventeen southern and border states and organized groups of friends throughout the nation who provided financial and political aid.

The SCEF's headquarters were in New Orleans until 1966, when the organization moved to Louisville, Kentucky, where it remained until its demise in 1975. Dombrowski served as first executive director of the SCEF until his retirement in 1966. That year, the post was assumed jointly by the husband-wife team of Carl and Anne Braden, Louisville activists who had joined the SCEF staff as field secretaries in 1957. The SCEF's first president was Aubrey Williams, a noted white liberal from Alabama, who served throughout the 1950s. In the 1960s and early 1970s, the post was held successively by Bishop Edgar A. Love, African American leader of the Methodist Church; Reverend Fred L. Shuttlesworth, black organizer of the civil rights movement in Birmingham, Alabama; and Modjeska Simkins, African American dean of civil rights activities in South Carolina. Supported entirely by individual donors, the SCEF operated on a meager budget, with a tiny staff. In the 1960s, staff members included John Salter, a white activist who emerged in the Jackson, Mississippi, movement; and Ella Baker, an African American activist who mentored and nurtured the emerging student movement in the South and worked for five years part-time for the SCEF.

From its beginning, the SCEF defied southern tradition and challenged racial segregation in the South. In the late 1940s and early 1950s, for example, the SCEF held conferences on segregation in education, conducted a campaign against racially discriminatory hospitals, and supported campaigns for black voting rights. In the mid-1950s, as a surge of African American protest sparked by the Montgomery bus boycott began to sweep the South, the SCEF—although remaining interracial in its leadership—focused primarily on encouraging southern whites to become active in the struggle against segregation and racism. In the late 1950s, the SCEF assisted whites who supported school desegregation but also worked closely with the newly formed Southern Christian Leadership Conference (SCLC). In the early 1960s, the organization also aided the interracial Student Non-Violent Coordinating Committee (SNCC) and its effort to maintain autonomy from all adult organizations (e.g., the National Association for the Advancement of Colored People, SCLC, and the Congress of Racial Equality). Moreover, the SCEF helped white students who, inspired by African American activism, formed the Southern Student Organizing Committee (SSOC) in 1964. Although the SCEF counseled against the creation of a separate white student organization, the SSOC succeeded in launching a social justice movement among white southern youth over the next five years.

Beginning in 1963, when SNCC and the SCLC started to focus on fostering economic justice, the SCEF initiated programs designed to unite working-class whites and African Americans. The SCEF, for example, set up a Southern Mountain Project, which encouraged working-class whites to organize against economic injustice in their own communities and link their work with the African American movement then sweeping the South. For example, Appalachian whites joined the Poor People's Campaign (PPC) led by African Americans in Washington, D.C., in 1968. The Southern Mountain Project continued until the SCEF began to break up in 1973. The SCEF also set up the Grass Roots Work project (GROW) in the Deep South under the leadership of Robert Zellner, a white former SNCC activist. GROW operated from 1967 until the SCEF break-up in 1973. It succeeded in forging some tenuous alliances between African American and working-class whites, including some former Ku Klux Klan members, who collaborated while trying to save a union in Laurel, Mississippi, and initiate a woodcutters union in Mississippi and Alabama.

Not surprisingly, the SCEF's struggle for racial, social, and economic justice made the organization a frequent target of southern segregationists who labeled it a Communist front. Mississippi senator James Eastland's Senate Internal Security Subcommittee (SISS), the House Un-American Activities Committee (HUAC), and southern state committees modeled after HUAC repeatedly investigated and harassed SCEF's staff and activities. In 1963, the Louisiana Un-American Activities Committee, for example, raided the SCEF headquarters in New Orleans, confiscated its files, and arrested its leaders, charging them with violating the state's anti-Communist law. The SCEF fought back in the court of public opinion as well as the federal courts. In 1965, the SCEF won a landmark victory in the *Dombrowski* case, when the U.S. Supreme Court dismissed all charges and acknowledged the SCEF's right to exist.

Despite repeated attacks by red baiters, the SCEF steadfastly refused to adopt a policy barring communists from its ranks. This position, as well as anti-Communist attacks, however, led many other civil rights groups to distance themselves from the SCEF, especially in the 1950s and early 1960s. Government harassment and the lack of cooperation with other civil rights organizations apparently did little to undermine the efforts of the SCEF. Indeed, the SCEF emerged stronger after each anti-Communist attack because it used skillfully the assaults to publicize its vision of a joint interracial movement for justice in the South. The SCEF also mounted a major counterattack against the

HUAC and similar state committees, succeeded in linking individuals who worked for civil liberties across the nation with those seeking civil rights in the South, and thus played a key role in the campaign that eventually abolished the HUAC in 1975.

In the early 1970s, having survived repeated external attacks, the SCEF succumbed to internal dissension. In the late 1960s, when SNCC urged whites to organize other whites against racism, large numbers of young whites flocked to the SCEF as "volunteer staff," gradually overwhelming its previously interracial board. The large numbers of young volunteers brought with them a broad range of competing ideologies for social change that turned the SCEF into an ideological battleground. Many former SCEF activists later came to believe that the resulting dissension was encouraged by the FBI's counterintelligence program (Cointelpro), which was targeting black activist organizations. While this allegation remains unproven, the ideological dissension split the SCEF in 1973. In 1974, some SCEF members formed the Southern Organizing Committee for Economic and Social Justice to carry on the work of the "Southern Conference movement" through a multiethnic force, seeking true democracy in the South. Following the 1973 division, the SCEF continued for approximately four more years, but two other splits followed, and by 1977 the SCEF ceased to exist.

**FURTHER READINGS**

Adams, Frank. *James A. Dombrowski: American Heretic, 1897–1983.* Knoxville: University of Tennessee Press, 1992.

Carl and Anne Braden Collection, State Historical Society of Wisconsin, Madison, Wisconsin.

Klibaner, Irwin. *Conscience of a Troubled South: The Southern Conference Educational Fund, 1946–1966.* Brooklyn, N.Y.: Carlson Publishing, 1989.

Krueger, Thomas. *And Promises to Keep: The Southern Conference for Human Welfare, 1938–1948.* Nashville: Vanderbilt University Press, 1967.

Morris, Aldon. *The Origins of the Civil Rights Movement: Black Communities Organizing for Change.* New York: Free Press, 1984.

Reed, Linda. *Simple Decency and Common Sense: The Southern Conference Movement, 1938–1963.* Bloomington: Indiana University Press, 1991.

Southern Conference Educational Fund Papers, Tuskegee University Archives, Tuskegee, Alabama.

*Anne Braden*

# Southern Conference for Human Welfare

Inspired by the democratic activism of the New Deal, black and white southerners founded the Southern Conference for Human Welfare (SCHW) in 1938. The SCHW played a leading role in the voting rights movement of the 1940s and helped organize black and white opposition to segregation until the organization's demise in 1948.

On Thanksgiving weekend of 1938, more than 1,000 black and white southerners met in Birmingham, Alabama, to publicize the positive impact the New Deal had on the development of the region's human and economic resources and to organize political support for continued reform. Those attending the SCHW's founding represented a broad cross-section of southern life, including labor organizers, business executives, students, college professors, sharecroppers, textile workers, elected officials, and New Deal policymakers. Founding members of the SCHW included New Deal officials such as Clark Foreman and Mary McLeod Bethune, civil rights leader John P. Davis, labor organizers Joseph Gelders and Lucy Randolph Mason, voting rights activist Virginia Durr, and first lady Eleanor Roosevelt. It was, sociologist Arthur Raper recalled, "one of the most exaggerated expressions of change in the South up to that time."

The interracial group mixed freely until Birmingham's police commissioner Eugene "Bull" Connor insisted on enforcing a municipal segregation law. Under the threat of arrest, the participants decided to accommodate the order rather than break up the meeting. Organizers of the SCHW, however, vowed never to meet again in a place where racial segregation could be enforced. First Lady Eleanor Roosevelt waged a symbolic protest by placing her chair in the middle of the aisle separating the two races. The protest generated by the enforcement of segregated seating led white southerners who favored segregation to avoid further involvement with the SCHW, leaving the organization free to pursue a racially egalitarian agenda.

From the start, the SCHW was primarily concerned with broadening the political base of support for New Deal reform in the South. A variety of state-mandated voting restrictions—such as literacy tests, the all-white primary, and poll taxes—kept most blacks and a large number of whites southerners from voting. During its early years, the SCHW focused its scant resources on a campaign to eliminate the poll tax. SCHW founding members Durr and Gelders led this effort, which culminated in the establishment of the National Committee to Abolish the Poll Tax, a coalition of labor and civil rights groups, which sponsored a major lobbying effort for federal anti–poll tax legislation. In 1942, the national committee sponsored the Pepper-Geyer bill barring poll taxes in federal elections, which passed the House of Representatives, but southern senators tabled the legislation with a filibuster, a pattern that would be repeated during the 1940s.

Despite continued southern resistance to anti–poll tax legislation, World War II transformed the political landscape in America and made race an issue of national consequence. As racial tensions rose in the South and the urban North, the SCHW embraced the "Double V" campaign launched by the *Pittsburgh Courier* to promote the struggle for democracy at home and abroad. The SCHW's third national meeting in Nashville in 1942 focused on employment discrimination and its detrimental effect on the war effort. Robert Weaver of the War Labor Board and SCHW member Ira De A. Reid, who served as an investigator for the Fair Employment Practice Committee (FEPC), reported on the persistence of racial discrimination in defense-related industries and urged continued pressure on the Roosevelt administration for fair treatment.

While the SCHW agreed on working to eliminate defense employment discrimination, the Communist leanings of some of its members created controversy during the Nashville meeting. Socialist SCHW board member Frank McAllister and a handful of other socialists demanded that singer and actor Paul Robeson be censured when he appealed to the SCHW on behalf of Communist Party leader Earl Browder, who was in prison for a passport violation. They also called for the dismissal of National Negro Congress (NNC) head, John P. Davis, from the board of the SCHW, charging that the NNC was a Communist front organization. While the SCHW had passed a resolution barring individuals who advocated the violent overthrow of the government, its leadership refused to adopt a blanket anti-Communist policy that would have required a "purge" of the organization. Such tactics, SCHW chairman Foreman warned, were divisive and destructive. Moreover, he observed that Davis understood better than any of his critics that if the economic conditions of the South were to be improved, blacks and whites would have to put aside their differences and work together "toward the common end."

The SCHW entered its most active and expansive period following Roosevelt's reelection in 1944. With the financial support of the Congress of Industrial Organizations (CIO) and the endorsement of the National Association for the Advancement of Colored People (NAACP), the SCHW launched an ambitious campaign to organize southerners for progressive political action. These efforts were enhanced by the Supreme Court's ruling in *Smith v. Allwright*, which struck down all-white primaries, thus removing the most effective barrier to black voter participation. In response to the 1944 ruling SCHW supporters organized state committees in nearly every southern state as well as chapters in major southern cities. In addition, a New York chapter worked to publicize conditions in the South and raise support for SCHW's organizing efforts.

Political scientist V. O. Key described the SCHW as "one of the most conspicuous agencies in exciting the electorate" in the immediate postwar years. Tapping into labor groups, civic leagues, student organizations, and NAACP chapters, the SCHW provided a base for organizing black and white southerners around a common program of political action. In 1946, SCHW field organizer Osceola McKaine traveled throughout the South promoting and supporting black voter registration. McKaine, a seasoned NAACP activist from South Carolina, had helped organize South Carolina's Progressive Democratic party (PDP) in 1944 and became the first African American to run for statewide office since Reconstruction when he ran for the U.S. Senate on the PDP ticket.

The efforts of organizations like the SCHW, the NAACP, and the CIO–Political Action Committee, working in tandem with local groups, contributed to a dramatic rise in black voter registration and to several liberal victories at the polls in 1946. Yet nationally, a Republican sweep in the midterm elections signaled the end of the New Deal era. Early in 1947, the Truman administration enacted the Truman Doctrine and a federal loyalty program that made the drive against Communists a national priority. In response, SCHW board member Durr articulated a view shared by the majority of SCHW members. She acknowledged that Communists represented "the extreme left of the political circuit" and admitted that she often disagreed "with their program and methods." Yet, her experiences in the South illustrated the dangers inherent in an anti-Communist campaign and she warned that "when one group of people are made untouchable the liberties of all suffer, and our democracy is on the way to ruin. I see and feel so clearly how it has crippled the lives and hopes of both the Negro and the white people of the South." While the SCHW had very few Communist Party members in its ranks, the organization's refusal to adopt an anti-Communist policy made it a target of federal investigation.

During 1947, the SCHW continued its efforts in the South while working with other progressive groups and labor organizations to provide an alternative candidate to Truman in the 1948 election. Many SCHW officials and members joined the Progressive party in 1948 and campaigned for Henry Wallace for president. In the South, Wallace's campaign expanded upon the SCHW's movement for full democracy and racial justice. Black and white candidates ran for office on the Progressive party ticket, and Wallace became the first presidential candidate to tour the South, speaking only to nonsegregated audiences.

The democratic political coalitions born at the high tide of the New Deal could not survive the growing repression of the Cold War. After the November 1948 elections, the SCHW disbanded. However, the Southern Conference Educational Fund (SCEF), established in 1946 as SCHW's educational arm, continued, and provided critical support for the desegregation movements of the 1950s and 1960s.

**FURTHER READINGS**

Key, V. O. *Southern Politics in State and Nation.* New York: Alfred A. Knopf, 1950.

Reed, Linda. *Simple Decency and Common Sense: The Southern Conference Movement, 1938–1963.* Bloomington: Indiana University Press, 1994.

Sullivan, Patricia. *Days of Hope: Race and Democracy in the New Deal Era.* Chapel Hill: The University of North Carolina Press, 1996.

*Patricia Sullivan*

## Southern Conference on Afro-American Studies

The Southern Conference on Afro-American Studies (SCAAS) was established at Texas Southern University in 1979. That year the university hosted the first annual Texas Conference on Afro-American History. Howard Jones, a professor of American Studies, and other faculty members, encouraged by the success of the conference, hoped to make it a recurring meeting and worked to expand it beyond Texas. They noted that while a sizable number of African Americans resided in the South, most of the organizations and intellectual activities concerned with black history and culture were located elsewhere. Thus, they founded the SCAAS to provide support and offer a forum for those interested in interpreting and preserving African American history and culture, particularly in the South.

The founders pledged to hold the annual meetings of SCAAS in the former Confederate and slave-holding border states and whenever possible on the campuses of the historically black colleges. Since 1979, SCAAS has met at thirteen black institutions in nine states, including Texas Southern University, Dillard University, Tougaloo College, Alabama State University, Morehouse College, Jackson State University, North Carolina A & T State University, Southern University, LeMoyne-Owen College, Virginia State University, Clark-Atlanta University, Paul Quinn College, and Florida A & M University. While historically black colleges have hosted SCAAS conferences, faculty and students from traditionally white southern colleges, such as the University of Alabama-Birmingham, Clemson University, University of Maryland, University of Miami, University of Mississippi, Oklahoma State University, University of Tennessee-Chattanooga, Texas A & M University, University of Texas, University of Virginia, and Washington University, have also contributed to its work.

Despite its southern orientation the conference is a national organization with a national membership. *The Griot: The Journal of Black Heritage*, SCAAS's refereed journal, edited by Andrew Baskin since 1985, is supported by Berea College and published twice a year. Howard Jones, secretary-treasurer of SCAAS since its inception, edits the conference's newsletter, the *Grapevine*.

The conference encourages and rewards undergraduate research on the black experience in the American South. The Lillie Newton Hornsby Memorial Collegiate Essay Award is presented to the authors of the three best undergraduate papers on the annual theme of the SCAAS's convention. The Reanitsa K. Butler Memorial Scholarship recognizes collaborative efforts and is awarded to the best paper delivered by a group of undergraduates at the annual meeting. The Yvonne Ochillo Memorial Award is given to the author of the best article published in *The Griot* in the year preceding the SCAAS's annual meeting.

In addition to its annual conferences in the United States, SCAAS has twice held joint meetings abroad with the Association of Caribbean Studies. The two groups met in Dakar, Senegal, in 1991 and in Cairo, Egypt, in 1993.

*Rhett S. Jones*

## Southern Education Foundation

The Southern Education Foundation (SEF) was established when four foundations had provided financial support for black education in the South consolidated their efforts in 1937. That year, the SEF assumed the remaining assets of the Negro Rural School Fund, also known as the Anna T. Jeanes Fund (1907–1937), the

John L. Slater Fund (1882–1937), and the George Peabody Fund (1867–1914). The fourth foundation to join the SEF was the Virginia Randolph Fund, which had been created in 1937 by Mayme Copeland, a Jeanes teacher (a teacher who worked for the Anna T. Jeanes Fund) in Kentucky, to honor the memory of the first Jeanes teacher. The SEF's objective was "to cooperate with public and private school officials and others in improving educational and living conditions" of African Americans. Between 1937 and 1978, the SEF's leadership ranks were dominated by whites. Arthur D. Wright served as the SEF's first president from 1937 until 1946. That year, Wright was succeeded by J. Curtis Dixon, the SEF's first executive director, who remained at the helm of the organization until 1964 when John A. Griffin assumed his post. Griffin served as executive director until 1978, when Elridge W. McMillan became the SEF's first African American chief executive officer (a post he continues to hold).

Between 1937 and 1950, the SEF concentrated on improving the quality of education in southern rural schools by supporting financially the work of the Jeanes teachers. As the southern states assumed greater responsibility for the financial and administrative support of public schools, the SEF's funds were disbursed for other purposes such as the professional enhancement of black elementary and secondary school principals. During the 1950s and 1960s, guided by associate director Robert Cousins, "the father of kindergartens in the South," the SEF spearheaded the establishment of kindergartens in southern schools and held regional and state conferences on early childhood education. It also provided technical assistance to historically black colleges and universities and promoted equal education for southern African Americans.

During the 1960s and 1970s, under the leadership of Executive Director John A. Griffin, the SEF continued to advocate state funding for kindergartens, monitored and analyzed the actions of states involved in desegregation litigation, and established an internship program in southern education that placed seventy-five teachers in a variety of educational settings. The SEF also promoted minority participation in higher education, supported black teachers, and contributed to the public policy agenda for educational reform in the United States.

The SEF, headquartered in Atlanta, Georgia, operated as a private foundation until 1988, when it was designated a tax-exempt nonprofit organization by the U.S. Internal Revenue Code. Financed by an endowment of approximately $10 million along with individual and corporate contributions, the SEF actively raises funds and manages programs for larger foundations that directly affect educational equity in the South such as placing minority teachers in low-income public schools. Through the formation of partnerships with other foundations such as the Pew Charitable Trusts and the Ford and Rockefeller Foundations, the SEF conducts research, convenes periodic conferences of educational experts, and launches programs to eliminate socioeconomic and racial inequalities that affect educational opportunity.

The SEF also commissions research on a wide variety of educational issues. In 1995, the organization published the report *Redeeming the American Promise: A Report of the Panel on Equal Opportunity and Postsecondary Desegregation*, an investigation into the impediments to student achievement and access to higher education in nineteen southern states. The report articulated the lingering effects of legal segregation and determined that educational achievement at the postsecondary level was highly dependent upon school reform at the elementary and secondary level. In particular, the report recommended standards-based accountability at the K-12 level and a move toward student-centered, comprehensive, and accountable systems of public higher education.

The SEF continues to sponsor a broad range of educational initiatives. It supports the improvement of libraries at historically black universities and colleges, early childhood education projects, programs designed to encourage community involvement in schools, and summer programs for gifted elementary and secondary students. Moreover, the SEF organizes conferences and symposia on higher education, makes contributions to the Children's Defense Fund, and sponsors studies that explore the plight of the black male. The SEF has addressed the national shortage of black elementary and secondary teachers. Other SEF initiatives include the award of start-up funds and technical assistance for the improvement of schools in southern rural communities and teacher recognitions. The SEF disseminates information about its activities in a quarterly newsletter, *Southern Education Foundation News*.

Currently, the fund operates programs in the following areas: Teacher Preparation, which supports and encourages minorities who want to pursue a teaching career; Student Opportunity and Performance, which aids historically black colleges and universities in maintaining and improving their academic resources; Educational Equity and Opportunity, which sponsors research and public policy initiatives that study and challenge systemic racism in the school systems; Socio-Economic Factors Affecting Equity, which seeks to improve intergroup relations and create equal opportunities through the reduction of racial inequalities; and Community Enrichment, which supports a variety of programs designed to strengthen community life.

Although the SEF has made programmatic adjustments over time, it has adhered to its original mission, promoting educational equity for southern African Americans and disadvantaged southerners and serving as a catalyst for school reform.

**FURTHER READINGS**

Conley, Darlene Joy. "Philanthropic Foundations and Organizational Change: The Case of the Southern Education Foundation (SEF) during the Civil Rights Era." Ph.D. diss., Northwestern University, 1990.

Southern Education Foundation. *Annual and Biennial Reports of the Southern Education Foundation.* Southern Education Foundation, Atlanta, Georgia.

*Jayne Beilke*

**SEE ALSO**   John F. Slater Fund; Negro Rural School Fund; Peabody Education Fund

## Southern Legislative Research Council

*See* Southern Regional Council.

## Southern Negro Youth Congress

The Southern Negro Youth Congress (SNYC) was a significant harbinger of the civil rights movement. The idea for a SNYC arose coincident with the founding of the National Negro Congress, which was founded in 1936. It was felt that African American youth had special problems—and special insights and energies—that could be addressed more effectively in their own organization. Hence, in February 1937 in Richmond, Virginia, the first All-Southern Negro Youth Conference was held, which drew more than 500 delegates. Communist Party members James E. Jackson and Ed Strong played a pivotal role in bringing these forces together, which included religious, fraternal, and a broad assemblage of political organizations.

In Chattanooga in 1938 and in Birmingham in 1939 two more well-attended conferences were held, focusing on southern black youth. Like the original gathering in Richmond, these meetings too focused on the plight of young black workers, the case of the "Scottsboro 9"—black youth from Alabama accused unjustly of sexually molesting two white females—antilynching laws, and other

issues reflected in their slogan: "Freedom, Equality and Opportunity." By 1939 the leadership of Jackson and Strong had been supplemented with the arrival of Esther Cooper, Thelma Dale, and Louis and Dorothy Burnham.

In 1940 this grouping met in New Orleans and decided to start a crusade focused on the right to vote, coupled with a campaign against police brutality. By 1941 SNYC had published its first issue of *Cavalcade: The March of Southern Youth*, an effective publication that was the initial voice of this still growing organization.

During this period, much of SNYC's activity was centered in Birmingham and New Orleans. There the group collaborated closely with National Association for the Advancement of Colored People (NAACP) youth and others with like concerns. Reflective of this broad approach was the SNYC's attempt to incorporate diverse cultural expressions within its publication and conferences. Playwrights like Langston Hughes and poets like Owen Dodson often were to be found at SNYC gatherings. At the SNYC's initiative, puppet shows traveled throughout the rural south bringing both entertainment and political education.

After the United States entered World War II, SNYC fought mightily against racial discrimination within the armed forces, while continuing its ongoing efforts on behalf of black labor and voting rights. In 1942, meeting in Tuskegee, Alabama, the SNYC came up with a new slogan: "Fight Fascism Abroad and K-K-K-ism at Home." Though its critics later charged that Communists and the organizations they led, for example, SNYC, abandoned the struggle for racial equality during the war, this was not an accurate assertion. Indeed, the Reverend Martin Luther King Sr. saw fit to attend the SNYC's annual meeting in Atlanta in 1944.

The SNYC's meeting in Columbia, South Carolina, in 1946 may have been its most famous conference. This was the occasion when the educator and writer Dr. W. E. B. Du Bois gave his heralded "Behold the Land" speech that counseled an intense focus on democratizing the South as a precondition to democratizing the nation. Just as the amity of the war was being replaced by the discord of the early Red Scare, the SNYC too accelerated its militance, calling for independence of colonized lands, an end to Jim Crow, and banning nuclear weapons.

However, the SNYC's opponents proved to be stronger. In 1948 when the group met in Birmingham, the city's Public Safety commissioner Eugene "Bull" Connor harassed participants and several were arrested, including the senator from Idaho, Glenn Taylor. The 1948 meeting proved to be the "last hurrah" for the SNYC. Many of its members moved to work for the third party presidential campaign of Henry Wallace, while others were intimidated by the incipient Red Scare and abandoned the organization altogether.

However, the SNYC's legacy continued beyond 1948 as many of its members went on to play instrumental roles in the post–*Brown v. Board of Education* civil rights movement.

**FURTHER READINGS**

Egerton, John. *Speak Now Against the Day: The Generation Before the Civil Rights Movement in the South.* Chapel Hill: The University of North Carolina Press, 1995.

Hughes, C. Alvin. "We Demand Our Rights: The SNYC, 1937–1949." *Phylon* 48, 1 (1987): 38–50.

Kelley, Robin D. G. *Hammer and Hoe: Alabama Communists During the Great Depression.* Chapel Hill: The University of North Carolina Press, 1990.

Richard, Johnetta. "The Southern Negro Youth Congress: A History." Ph.D. diss., University of Cincinnati, 1987.

Strong, Augusta. "Southern Youth's Proud Heritage." *Freedomways* 4, 1 (1964).

Sullivan, Patricia. *Days of Hope: Race and Democracy in the New Deal Era.* Chapel Hill: The University of North Carolina Press, 1996.

*Gerald Horne*

# Southern Organization for United Leadership

In 1965, New Orleans civil rights activists founded the Southern Organization for United Leadership (SOUL) to open elective offices to black and progressive white candidates. Among the founding members was Robert Collins who became the first African American serving as a federal judge in the South during the Carter administration.

SOUL was launched following the passage of the 1965 Voting Rights Act, which sparked a major increase in black voter registration in New Orleans. SOUL sought to transform this growing black electorate into a powerful force in city and state politics. Building support among lower-middle and middle-class African Americans in New Orleans's Lower Ninth Ward, SOUL registered voters and campaigned for liberal white and African American candidates in subsequent elections. In 1970, a coalition including SOUL, the Community Organization for Urban Politics (COUP), headquartered in New Orleans's Seventh Ward, and the city's National Association for the Advancement of Colored People (NAACP), mobilized the black vote for white moderate liberal Moon Landrieu during his successful mayoral campaign. Landrieu repaid the support of SOUL and its allies by ending discrimination in public accommodations and rewarding members of SOUL and COUP with city patronage, including jobs connected with the construction of the Superdome sports arena.

The perception of economic favoritism for African Americans and an increase in black migration to the city contributed to white flight, turning New Orleans into a black-majority city between 1970 and 1980. The political coalition that dramatically reformed municipal politics in the early 1970s fragmented toward the end of the decade. Former NAACP chief Ernest N. "Dutch" Morial won the mayor's race in 1978, despite a lack of support from SOUL and COUP. This split, partly a result of past personal differences, deepened over Morial's hiring policies as mayor, which he described as "merit-based," but SOUL and COUP leaders felt it perpetuated discrimination. In spite of frequent controversy, SOUL leaders continued to hold prominent positions in state and local government. SOUL activist Nils Douglas, who was black, won appointment by Governor Edwin Edwards to the Louisiana Board of Highways in the 1970s and also served as a magistrate commissioner in the Orleans Parish Criminal Court System.

SOUL became Louisiana's largest black political organization and again demonstrated its influence in state elections in the early 1990s. The group's campaign efforts on behalf of former three-term governor Edwards against former Ku Klux Klan leader and neo-Nazi David Duke proved decisive in Louisiana's 1991 gubernatorial race. A thousand SOUL volunteers canvassed New Orleans's black neighborhoods on election day in a door-to-door effort to prevent a Duke victory. Statewide, an amazing 80 percent of black voters cast ballots, and the African American turnout was particularly strong in New Orleans. The black turnout exceeded the total number of white ballots cast in a statewide race for the first time in Louisiana history, as Edwards carried 61 percent of the vote. In 1994, Edwards appointed Douglas to the five-member state Board of Ethics for elected officials amid charges that Edwards was trying to stack the board with supporters to impede an investigation of ethics violations.

**FURTHER READINGS**

Nicholas, Peter, and James Varney. "House Vote Ousts McCall From State Ethics Board." *New Orleans Times-Picayune,* June 28, 1994, sec. B, 3.

Rogers, Kim Lacy. *Righteous Lives: Narratives of the New Orleans Civil Rights Movement.* New York: New York University Press, 1993.

Turque, Bill, Ginny Carroll, Vern E. Smith, Peter Annin, Howard Fineman, and Eleanor Clift. "Saying 'No' To Duke." *Newsweek*, November 25, 1991, 18.

*Michael Phillips*

## Southern Organizing Committee for Economic and Social Justice

Founded in 1975, the Southern Organizing Committee for Economic and Social Justice (SOC) is an interracial and multiethnic network of southerners working against racism, war, economic injustice, and environmental destruction. The SOC emerged following the demise of the Southern Conference Educational Fund (SCEF), an interracial group that had fought for racial equality and economic and social justice since 1948. When the SCEF disintegrated due to ideological dissension, several of its members were determined to carry on the organization's goals of establishing racial, economic, and social democracy in the South.

For fifteen years, the SOC built mutual support systems among local activist groups, led regional actions against resurgent racism and racist violence, supported southern workers who were trying to organize, launched resistance against attacks on voting rights, and sparked a national "Housing, Not Bombs" campaign led by southern public housing tenants. The SOC often served as a catalyst for broad coalitions and played key roles in launching the National Anti-Klan Network (later the Center for Democratic Renewal), the Southern Rainbow Education Project, and the People's Institute for Survival and Beyond, a training program for community organizers, both people of color and whites, which stresses antiracist values, historic perspective, and respect for cultural traditions.

In the early 1990s, SOC turned its attention to campaigns against massive toxic pollution of southern communities by waste sites, industry, and military bases, which soon became the centerpiece of its work. The SOC worked with poor communities of color and working-class whites to set up a Health and Environmental Justice Project that aided emerging local leaders in the creation of viable local, state, and regional organizations. As a result of the project's work, a southern grass-roots environmental justice movement emerged that was instrumental in making the U.S. Environmental Protection Agency (EPA) more responsive to the needs of the nation's black and poor

people. There were soon more clean-ups in progress in the EPA's Region IV, which covers eight southern states, than anywhere else in the country. Moreover, local people collaborated with government officials in planning the revitalization of their communities. In 1993, the SOC also launched a Youth Task Force, which became independent, and in 1996 set in motion a regional African American Environmental Justice Action Network.

Through its Environmental Justice work, the SOC broadened its outreach to include Latinos, Native Americans, and Asian Americans. Increased ethnic and racial minority participation diversified the organization's constituency and board, which consisted of about sixty individuals. By 1995, the SOC was composed of 70 percent people of color and 30 percent Caucasians and had become one of the few multiracial organizations in the country that is essentially led by people of color. In the same year, the SOC began restructuring to become a membership organization, opening the way for involvement of more grass-roots activists.

The SOC's headquarters were in Birmingham, Alabama, from 1975 until 1993, when it moved its office to Atlanta. The SOC's first co-chairs were Anne Braden of Kentucky and Reverend Ben Chavis of North Carolina. In the 1980s, Chavis became co-chair emeritus when Reverend Fred Shuttlesworth of Ohio assumed the post. Between 1976 and 1984, SOC's only staff member was Judy Hand, a white woman from Birmingham. She was succeeded by Scott Douglas, an African American from Birmingham who held the position until 1989. From 1989 until 1993, the SOC carried on its program entirely with volunteers. In 1993, because its environmental justice work had increased rapidly its constituency, the SOC created the post of executive director. This position was filled by Connie Tucker, who had been an activist in Florida's Black Liberation movement during the 1960s. Under her leadership, the organization's grass-roots work continued to expand.

**FURTHER READING**

Papers of the Southern Organizing Committee for Economic and Social Justice, State Historical Society of Wisconsin, Madison, Wisconsin.

*Anne Braden*

## Southern Poverty Law Center

The Southern Poverty Law Center (SPLC) is a nonprofit organization that has put most of its resources into advocating racial equality and monitoring hate groups such as the Ku Klux Klan. Two young white southern lawyers, Morris Dees and Joseph Levin, founded the organization in Montgomery, Alabama, in 1971. Since its founding, the SPLC has witnessed a tremendous membership growth. In 1973, the center had approximately 3,000 members. In 1996, it reported a membership of 300,000. The organization's membership growth was accompanied by an increase in funds as well as staff.

In the 1970s, the SPLC's litigation efforts resulted in electoral changes that enhanced the chances of African Americans who were running for various state offices in Alabama. Moreover, as a result of SPLC pressure the Alabama state troopers were integrated and living conditions in the state's prisons improved. In 1979, the SPLC launched its first major civil suit against a Klan group when Klansmen attacked a civil rights gathering on May 26. The attack also resulted in the 1981 formation of the SPLC's Klanwatch, which monitors organized hate groups throughout the country.

In the mid-1980s the SPLC initiated a new strategy to combat Klan activities. In an effort to undermine the economic power of Klan groups, the SPLC sued hate organizations, claiming that they were legally responsible for violence committed by their members. This strategy forced Klan groups to engage in expensive litigation battles resulting in the depletion of their financial resources. In 1987 and 1990, the SPLC achieved its most noteworthy courtroom victories. In 1987, the SPLC represented Beulah Mae Donald, whose son was lynched by Klan members, in a suit against the United Klans of America. The court ruled in favor of the SPLC, garnishing the wages of several Klan members and forcing the Klan to close its Anglo-Saxon Club outside of Tuscaloosa, Alabama. In 1990, the SPLC represented the family of an Ethiopian man who was beaten to death by a member of the White Aryan Resistance. The SPLC won the case, and the court fined the defendant, Californian Tom Metzher, $12.5 million.

Suspecting links between white supremacists and militia groups, the SPLC's Klanwatch formed the Militia Task Force in 1994. The task force monitors and compiles data on the activities of over 600 militia organizations and provides information to law enforcement authorities. In 1995, Klanwatch began to distribute a bimonthly newsletter, the *Intelligence Report*, which seeks to inform law enforcement personnel about hate crimes and the activities of militia groups.

In addition to its courtroom and monitoring activities, the SPLC has developed an education program to combat hate crimes and to teach tolerance. For this purpose the SPLC provides teachers with teaching kits and the magazine *Teaching Tolerance*.

The SPLC, headquartered in Montgomery, Alabama, has been a forceful opponent of racism and hate groups during the last three decades. It has served as a watchdog agency that monitors and publicizes the activities of hate groups and informs law enforcement officials about civil rights violators. The SPLC's litigation efforts have challenged significantly the economic power of some Klan groups. Advocates for racial equality have recognized the SPLC as a major force in the struggle against racism and hate crimes.

**FURTHER READINGS**

Dees, Morris. *A Season for Justice: The Life and Times of Civil Rights Lawyer Morris Dees.* New York: Charles Scribner's Sons, 1991.

Southern Poverty Law Center. *SPLC Report: Special 25th Anniversary Issue.* Montgomery, Ala.: Southern Poverty Law Center, 1996.

Wilkie, Curtis. "Lawsuits Prove to Be a Big Gun in Anti-Klan Arsenal." *Boston Globe*, June 17, 1993, 1.

*Joseph S. Townsend*

## Southern Regional Council

Established in 1944, the Southern Regional Council (SRC) grew out of a series of meetings between black and white members of the Commission on Interracial Cooperation (CIC) who were searching for an alternative approach to remedying the ills of southern society. The CIC was founded in 1919 by "southerners of good will" who wanted to end racial violence and create racial harmony in the South in light of post–World War I racial tensions. Waning in popularity and support among white liberals and black moderates, the CIC was on the verge of collapse by the early 1940s until its executive director, Jessie Daniel Ames, set forth a plan to reconcile the different agendas and demands of southern blacks and whites in order to revitalize the organization. The result was the creation of the SRC, an interracial council devoted to "regional" research and development. Taking over the CIC's financial assets and its headquarters in Atlanta, the SRC was headed by a president and four vice presidents as well as two governing bodies, a board of directors, and an executive committee. In contrast to the CIC, the SRC attempted to divide equally the membership of the board of directors and the executive committee between blacks and whites in order to demonstrate its commitment to interracial activism. SRC also continued the tradition of being financed by northern foundations and the contributions of its members.

Under the leadership of Executive Director Guy B. Johnson and President Howard Odum, white sociologists at the University of North Carolina; Executive Committee Chairman Charles S. Johnson, a black sociologist and president of Fisk University; and Associate Director Ira De A. Reid, a black sociology professor at Atlanta University, the SRC worked to solve "southern" problems without casting them in terms of race. As Odum noted, the SRC's aim was to administer programs that would benefit the disadvantaged classes of the South rather than just African Americans, in the hopes of building consensus for racial reform in the process. Taking this regional approach, the SRC incorporated most of the CIC's programs including the support of state and local interracial committees, the cooperation and assistance of church and women's groups, the continuation of publications such as *The Southern Frontier*, and the adoption of educational programs for improving race relations. But more significantly, the SRC also adopted the CIC's position on segregation. Believing that social equality was a long-term goal, the leaders of the organization recognized that the New Deal and World War II had strengthened white southerner's commitment to the separation of the races and that the immediate goal of the SRC should focus attention on what it could do immediately to improve the lives of all the region's people.

However, just as in the CIC, the issue of segregation proved divisive for the SRC. Within a month after its founding, the SRC was bombarded with dissenting voices concerning its ideology and approach to the racial situation in the South. Among those who spoke out against the SRC were novelist Lillian Smith and English Professor J. Saunders Redding, arguing that the organization's attempts to conciliate the white power structure made its actions suspect and that the SRC needed to set an example by publicly denouncing segregation. At the same time that the SRC was criticized for not being liberal enough to eliminate segregation, the organization was under attack by white conservatives like David Clark, editor of *The Textile Bulletin*, who believed that the SRC was fomenting subversive activity by promoting interracial cooperation. Heeding these outside pressures, the SRC chose to reexamine its policies as early as 1947. However, it was not until 1951 that the board of directors adopted a resolution that clearly outlined the organization's intentions to work for an American society free of racial discrimination. Accordingly, segregation was no longer an acceptable prac-

tice and every individual deserved the opportunity to "enjoy a full share of dignity and self-respect."

One of the SRC's main purposes was the gathering and dissemination of information as part of its goal to educate private citizens and public officials on a wide range of issues including civil rights, segregation and desegregation, police brutality, violence, unemployment, housing, suffrage, and racism. The SRC's Information and Research Departments collected materials such as newspaper articles and literature about the South, conducted surveys of southern communities, and drafted reports on their findings. Closely tied to the Information and Research Departments was the Publication Department through which the SRC disseminated the information and data it collected. The SRC's main publication was *The Southern Frontier*, first published by the CIC, which experienced several name changes throughout the 1960s and 1970s but remained the primary source of information on the organization's activities and programs. In addition to its serial publications, the SRC published a wide range of pamphlets, leaflets, brochures, and special reports to publicize the findings of the Information and Research Departments. Another significant publication was the SRC's series of *Leadership Reports*, produced and distributed between 1959 and 1964. These reports dealt almost entirely with school desegregation and overall problems of race relations in the South during that period.

Though serving as a clearinghouse of information remained vital to the SRC's goals, the organization also continued to support the work of the state and local interracial committees first established by the CIC. Under the leadership of the SRC, these state and local groups changed their names to Councils on Human Relations, a transformation that helped to emphasize the SRC's commitment to regional development of all peoples of the South. Maintaining their original purpose, these councils encouraged individuals to join interracial activities and create specific programs to alleviate problems in their communities. The work of the state and local Councils on Human Relations proved vital to the success of the SRC in carrying out its goals and programs on the local level.

The Veterans Services Project, which operated between 1944 and 1951, was the first large-scale program initiated by the SRC. Recognizing that postwar racial tensions could destroy any hope of racial conciliation in the South, the SRC launched this project to gather statistics and other information pertinent to the reintegration of returning World War II veterans, especially African American veterans. Through this project, the SRC investigated possibilities for employment, job training, resumption of high school and college education, housing, and financing of small businesses for ex-military personnel. Furthermore, by documenting the number of black and white veterans who were taking advantage of these opportunities, the SRC could assist federal, state, and private agencies in redirecting their programs to include more eligible veterans.

One of the most important lessons learned from the Veterans Services Project was the extent of labor problems in the South. Addressing the issues of workmen's and unemployment compensation, protective legislation, job discrimination, job training, and unions through various means, the SRC decided that it was essential to initiate a program that specifically focused on labor issues. Therefore in 1965, in cooperation with the National Institute for Labor Education and the American Federation of Labor–Congress of Industrial Organizations (AFL-CIO), the SRC established the Labor Education Program. Working until 1973, the Labor Education Program volunteers struggled to expand southern labor unions to make them more inclusive of minorities and women and promoted the economic development of the South, best exemplified in the creation of the Federation of Southern Cooperatives in 1968.

In the field of civil rights, the SRC took great strides after 1951 to redress racial inequalities in southern society. Apprehensive of direct action, the SRC decided to focus on eliminating the barriers to African American suffrage and investigating the impact of segregation on African American education. Under the auspices of its Councils on Human Relations, the SRC embarked on a campaign to survey the extent of desegregation of southern schools after the Supreme Court's 1954 *Brown v. Board of Education* decision. Reporting their findings to local, state, and federal agencies, the SRC was able to assist in the evaluation of the progress of desegregation efforts in southern communities. Given the violent reaction among southern extremists to the *Brown* decision and the slow course of desegregation, many local and state Councils on Human Relations launched petitions to endorse immediate or gradual adoption of federal school desegregation policy. Because so many public school systems opted to close schools rather than desegregate them, the SRC supported the 1958 Help Our Public Education (HOPE) program, initiated by the parents of black Atlanta school children who sought to keep Georgia's public schools open. In 1959, the SRC expanded its support of local desegregation efforts and conceived the Save Our Schools campaign for other southern states to be carried out by local and state Councils on Human Relations.

Turning to the extension of voting rights for African Americans, the SRC joined with the Student Non-Violent Coordinating Committee (SNCC), the Congress of Racial Equality (CORE), the National Urban League (NUL), and the National Association for the Advancement of Colored People (NAACP), in the creation of the Voter Education Project (VEP) in 1962. With the expressed purpose of educating poor and black southerners about their voting rights and assisting them in registering to vote, the VEP helped to increase voter rolls in the South by 11 percent by April 1963. The SRC served as a clearinghouse for information gathered during the project and provided strategy-planning and administration for the organizations involved. After the initial voter registration campaign of 1963, the VEP expanded its efforts to include citizenship training, educational conferences, support of black candidates, and the publication of voter registration materials. The VEP continued as part of the SRC until 1970, when federal law prohibited voter registration organizations from receiving more than 25 percent of its funding from a single source. After separating from the VEP, the SRC continued its commitment to voter equality through a number of campaigns including the Southern Legislative Research Council, which provided aid to black elected officials throughout the South; a 1979 redistricting project, which sought to improve voter participation in more than 2,000 jurisdictions in the South; and a 1982 voter education project, which led to the extension of the 1965 Voting Rights Act.

In the late 1960s, the SRC came under fire again as critics condemned the council for challenging civil rights organizations that purged whites from their ranks and for rejecting the violent tactics of some black power activists. Many southern black leaders believed that the SRC had become little more than a sounding board for white progressivism and believed that its policies no longer reflected a true commitment to racial equality. These charges were symptomatic of the country's changing racial climate and created tensions between the SRC's black staff members and white administrators. The SRC's response was to step away from the front lines of racial reform and refocus attention on its role as a clearinghouse of information in order to achieve its goal of promoting racial justice, protecting democratic rights, and broadening civic participation in the South.

The SRC expanded its range of concerns, collecting information and publishing a variety of reports on issues such as hunger, public health, migrant labor, and prison and urban conditions. In the 1970s, the SRC initiated a "governmental monitoring project" to study the social impact of federal laws and political agendas. In the 1980s, the SRC became an avid critic of the Reagan administration's federal policies on welfare, voting rights, and affirmative action. Throughout the 1990s, the SRC sponsored a number of programs including Community Fellows for Public School Change and the Mississippi Delta Principals Institute, which promoted education reform, and Experts-in-Training, which sought to preserve minority voting rights. Moreover, the SRC provided leadership training and technical assistance to AmeriCorps, the volunteer organization established in 1993 by President Bill Clinton that incorporated Volunteers in Service to America and National Civilian Community Corps. In 1994, the SRC launched a landmark civil rights radio documentary project titled "Will the Circle Be Unbroken?" as part of an educational program to assist the American public in understanding civil rights issues of the past and the future. Debuting in 1997 on Public Radio International, this award-winning radio documentary series traced the civil rights movement of five southern cities through first-person narratives.

From its inception, the SRC has remained true to its policy of regional development by helping southerners confront the fundamental social and economic problems that have plagued their region since the Second World War II. The SRC remains a viable organization, dedicated to correcting social injustices and creating opportunities for all people of the South.

**FURTHER READINGS**

Allred, William C., Jr. "The Southern Regional Council, 1943–1961." M.A. thesis, Emory University, 1966.

Egerton, John. *Speak Now Against the Day: The Generation Before the Civil Rights Movement in the South.* New York: Alfred A. Knopf, 1994.

McDonough, Julia Anne. "Men and Women of Good Will: A History of the Commission on Interracial Cooperation and the Southern Regional Council, 1919–1954." Ph.D. diss., University of Virginia, 1993.

Plowman, Edwin Lee. "Analysis of Selective Strategies Used by the Southern Regional Council in Effecting Social Change in the South." Ph.D. diss., Boston University, 1976.

Southern Regional Council Papers, Special Collections, Robert W. Woodruff Library, Atlanta University Center, Atlanta, Georgia.

*Kimberly E. Nichols*

**SEE ALSO**    Alabama Council on Human Relations; Arkansas Council on Human Relations; Commission on Interracial Cooperation; Florida Council on Human Relations; Georgia Council on Human Relations; Louisiana Council on Human Relations; Mississippi Council on Human Relations; North Carolina Council on Human Relations; South Carolina Council on Human Relations; Tennessee Council on Human Relations; Virginia Council on Human Relations; Voter Education Project

## Southern Society for the Promotion of the Study of Race Conditions and Problems in the South

In May 1900, Edgar Gardner Murphy, minister and Progressive from Montgomery, Alabama, organized the Southern Society for the Promotion of the Study of Race Conditions and Problems in the South. Murphy invited a group of influential white citizens of Montgomery and other cities across the country, including educators, politicians, ministers, and journalists, to discuss the plight of blacks in the South and formulate solutions for their many problems. While the group sought to prevent lynchings and hoped to improve the educational and political status of African Americans, it did not challenge segregation.

Hoping to include blacks among the initial group of participants, Murphy sought the counsel of fellow Alabamian and leading black spokesman Booker T. Washington, who suggested several white speakers, including William MacCorkle, former governor of West Virginia, and Chauncey M. Depew, as well as the Reverend H. H. Proctor, an African American minister from Atlanta. Yet, Murphy decided to forego the convening of an interracial meeting, afraid it would alienate southern whites. Instead, Murphy invited MacCorkle and asked Washington to organize an all-black counterpart to the Southern Society proceedings. When the all-black National Negro Race Conference met in 1900, Washington chose not to attend, fearing that such a meeting would inflame whites. Despite the exclusion of blacks from the society's founding, African Americans were allowed to sit in the balcony on the final day of the proceedings, and among them was Washington.

Between May 8 and 10, 1900, southern whites, representing a broad political spectrum, gathered for the largest meeting ever assembled in Montgomery. Participants discussed the conditions of African Americans in the South and argued whether black progress was desirable or even possible. Murphy proposed educational efforts to end lynch mobs and thereby quell northern criticism of the South. Moreover, he advocated black suffrage; however, he insisted on limiting the right to vote to the intelligent men of both races. Finally, Murphy suggested providing greater educational opportunities for whites and blacks in the South. Murphy had high hopes that the "better class" of whites would support his moderate proposals, which did not advocate racial equality but conceded black rights under the law. Yet, not all conference participants agreed with Murphy. Several speakers insisted that segregation was the only solution to the race problem and suggested to disfranchise blacks through repeal of the Fifteenth Amendment. These included Alfred Moore Waddell, mayor of Wilmington, North Carolina; John Temple Graves, editor of the Atlanta *Constitution*; and Paul B. Barringer, chairman of the faculty of the University of Virginia. Blacks, they believed, would eventually disappear from the United States as a result of natural extinction. More enlightened men, such as J. R. M. Curry, head of the Peabody and John F. Slater Funds, presented industrial education programs as the best way to assist southern blacks. Yet, even men in the latter category endorsed a repeal of the Fifteenth Amendment. Only Washington supporter MacCorkle and a handful of other participants demanded that blacks receive their full constitutional rights.

Following the initial meeting of the society, Murphy published the proceedings in late 1900 and made plans for the publication of a journal dedicated to the race problem in the United States. Murphy's ambitious plans, however, never materialized. When no southern city offered to host the second meeting of the society, Murphy lost interest in racial issues and turned his attention to other social problems such as child labor.

While the society met only once, its deliberations on black suffrage affected Alabama's black population for years to come. The majority of influential southern whites, including racial liberals, who had attended the society's Montgomery conference had voiced opposition to black voting rights. In 1901, this overwhelming support for the disfranchisement of blacks apparently helped to legitimize the decision of Alabama's Constitutional Convention to deny blacks the right to vote.

**FURTHER READINGS**

Bailey, Hugh C. *Edgar Gardner Murphy: Gentle Progressive.* Coral Gables, Fla.: University of Miami Press, 1968.

Chappell, David L. *Inside Agitators: White Southerners in the Civil Rights Movement.* Baltimore: The Johns Hopkins University Press, 1994.

Harlan, Louis R., and Raymond W. Smock, eds. *The Booker T. Washington Papers.* 5 vols. Urbana: University of Illinois Press, 1976.

Luker, Ralph. *A Southern Tradition in Theology and Social Criticism, 1830–1930: The Religious and Social Conservatism of James Warley, William Porcher Dubose, and Edgar Gardner Murphy.* New York: Mellon Press, 1984.

Sosna, Morton. *In Search of the Silent South: Southern Liberals and the Race Issue.* New York: Columbia University Press, 1977.

*Robin B. Balthrope*

## Southern Sociological Congress

The Southern Sociological Congress (SSC) was a regional organization that helped promote social reform and the study of social problems in the South between 1912 and 1919. The SSC first met in Nashville, Tennessee, on May 7, 1912. Its purpose was to gather social welfare workers, social reformers, and sociologists to organize and study the means of solving some of the South's problems.

The SCC originated in 1911 when Kate Barnard, the Oklahoma commissioner of Charities and Corrections, suggested to the Republican governor of Tennessee, Ben W. Hooper, to organize the first SCC conference. During the group's first meeting, participants discussed prohibition, child welfare, crime, penal reform, public health, Christian charity, and race relations. Most of the conference participants, speakers, and session chairs came from the ranks of the Christian ministry, educational institutions, and social work, but various sessions were open to the public.

During its first meeting, conference participants decided to launch a permanent organization and to draft a constitution. The group adopted a series of social reform measures and resolved to focus on practical applications of sociological thought rather than academic discussions. The SSC sought to modernize the South's penal system, demanding the elimination of the convict-lease system and an increase in the size and quality of juvenile reformatories. Moreover, the organization opposed the use of child labor by southern industry, promoted compulsory school attendance, and supported temperance as well as the abolition of prostitution. Furthermore, the SSC demanded that state governments provide funding for services for those with physical and mental disabilities. The SSC also urged southern states to create family courts and adopt standardized marriage laws that would make divorce more difficult. Finally, the SSC resolved to improve race relations in the

South. It challenged racism in the judicial process and opposed lynchings, race-based political campaigns, and the economic exploitation of black sharecroppers. Although SSC members voiced their opposition to racial injustices in the South, they did not challenge racial segregation. Critics charged that the racists and paternalistic views of many SSC members accounted for the group's accommodationist policy.

The SSC reflected the social reform zeal of the progressive era and inspired many southern reformers to launch lobbying groups that sought to implement the SSC's agenda. Some of these groups successfully lobbied for the creation of state boards of charities and corrections. Yet, the SSC neither eliminated racial injustices in the legal system nor improved the economic conditions of African Americans in the South. The SSC disbanded soon after its May 1919 meeting; however, many of its members continued to remain active in the various state reform associations that they had helped to create.

**FURTHER READINGS**

Grantham, Dewey W. *Southern Progressivism: The Reconciliation of Progress and Tradition.* Knoxville: University of Tennessee Press, 1983.

McCulloch, James E., ed. *The Call of the New South: Addresses Delivered at the Southern Sociological Congress, Nashville, Tennessee, May 7 to 10, 1912.* Nashville: Southern Sociological Congress, 1912.

*Joseph S. Townsend*

## Southern Student Human Relations Project

*See* National Student Association.

## Southern Tenant Farmers' Union

Founded in 1934, the Southern Tenant Farmers' Union (STFU) was an interracial labor organization dedicated to protecting southern sharecroppers from socioeconomic discrimination. The STFU was unique because it was a racially integrated organization at a time when other agricultural groups were not. During the Depression when agricultural prices plummeted because of federal regulations, the STFU brought national attention to the plight of tenant farmers in the South.

African American agrarians had organized as early as the 1880s, allying with white members of the Farmers Alliance and People's Party. In 1886, the Colored Farmers' Alliance was established in Houston, Texas, and had about 600,000 members by 1890. The group promoted land ownership, but an agricultural depression forced many members into tenancy. A cotton pickers' strike during the summer of 1891 demanded payment of $1 per 100 pounds of cotton picked, but local whites reacted violently. Similar protests occurred in the twentieth century. The 1919 Elaine race riot in Arkansas was sparked by black farmers requesting itemized statements of cotton sales and demanding higher payments.

In the 1920s, another agricultural depression devastated southern agriculture, which became based on farm tenancy, sharecropping, and debt peonage, exploiting labor as prices rapidly decreased. Landowners suffered bankruptcy and absentee owners, such as lumber companies, stripped forests and planted cotton fields. President Franklin D. Roosevelt and the federal government tried to mitigate the farm price crisis by limiting production, which caused the displacement of tenant farmers. New Deal programs, such as the 1933 Agricultural Adjustment Act (AAA) (which called for destruction of cotton in an attempt to raise prices), encouraged mechanization, and distributed subsidy and parity payments to reward landowners for taking these actions. These programs did not stop the suffering of southern tenant farmers but only made it worse. As a result of reduced cotton planting, planters evicted tenants from the land, causing high unemployment. Black tenant farmers joined groups such as the Communist-supported Alabama Sharecroppers Union to seek relief from miserable and unjust conditions.

By 1934, African Americans and poor whites competed for agricultural employment as cotton prices continued to fall. That year, an estimated 60 percent of Arkansas farms were farmed by tenants, while the tenancy rate in the Mississippi Delta rose to 80 percent. Harry Leland Mitchell, a sharecropper from Tennessee and founding member of the STFU, moved to Arkansas where he decided to manage a dry cleaning store instead of farming poor land. He soon realized that sharecroppers in the area lacked employment opportunities and cash to spend in his business. In 1934, when plantation owner Hiram Norcross evicted twenty-three tenant families, Mitchell joined forces with Henry Clay East, who owned the gas station next to his dry cleaning store. Mitchell and East, who embraced socialism, met with socialist Norman Thomas who encouraged them to organize a tenant farmers' union. Local sharecroppers had heard Thomas speak and began meeting in barns to discuss his ideas. They invited Mitchell and East to attend a meeting on July 13, 1934, at the Fairview plantation schoolhouse near Tyronza, Arkansas.

Eighteen men—eleven whites and seven blacks—decided to form the STFU to aid disfranchised tenant farmers and challenge agricultural landowners. The men agreed that interracial cooperation was necessary for success because if whites and blacks organized separately planters could easily counter their divided efforts. Mitchell believed that the organization could secure government help so that farmers would have bargaining power with landlords. He was named executive secretary of the STFU, and East was elected president. The STFU was incorporated according to state laws with its headquarters at Tyronza. The union eventually secured resources and help from powerful individuals, including Memphis physician Dr. William R. Amberson, radical clergyman Howard Kester, and Gardner Jackson, who had been ousted from his AAA position in the Roosevelt administration because of his liberal views. Jackson served as the STFU's representative in Washington, D.C.

Using the slogan "Land for the Landless," members asserted that the "sole purpose in building the Southern Tenant Farmers' Union is to secure better living conditions by decent contracts and higher wages for farm labor and help build a world wherein there will be no poverty and insecurity for those who are willing to work." The STFU specifically wanted to acquire an equitable share of government resources for tenant farmers. "We maintain that the earth is the common heritage of all, that the use and occupancy of land should constitute the sole title there-to," the STFU constitution declared, affirming "that this organization is dedicated to the complete abolition of tenantry in all its forms, and to the establishment of a new order of society wherein all who are willing to work shall be given the full products of their toil."

Promising to secure and protect the rights of its members through collective action, the STFU welcomed male tenant farmers eighteen years or older and their wives. While the STFU organized farmers who worked for landowners, it specifically barred those who made a "living off the labor of others." STFU members paid a $1 initiation fee and $2 annual dues that were divided among the community and the central and executive councils. Some of the dues were designated for an emergency fund to aid farmers. Each STFU local had a business agent who sought better contracts, working conditions, and adjusted wages for members. Members could be expelled and ostracized for divulging STFU secrets to outsiders and had to promise not to usurp other members' jobs.

The STFU's goals were farm labor representation on federal agricultural boards and agencies, enforcement of government contracts awarded to tenants and sharecroppers, cessation of evictions, distribution of federal payments when land was removed from cultivation, and "the right of all farm workers to organize without fear of terrorism and violence being done them by planters and their retainers." Members sought model contracts with fair wages according to the cost of living, loans at legal interest rates, and the right to sell cotton at market prices "to whom we please." They wanted planters to recognize the STFU as the farmer's agency for collective bargaining. The STFU also hoped to improve the quality of life, securing decent housing, rent-free land for gardens and livestock, and free schools, buses, hot lunches, and textbooks for children.

Ten thousand individuals joined the STFU in its first year, including radical southern clergymen and college students. Arkansas was the center of membership, yet farmers in Missouri, Oklahoma, Texas, Alabama, and Mississippi also joined, including blacks, whites, Native Americans, and Mexican Americans. STFU meetings were sometimes held in churches to confuse enemies. Secrecy became important as planters threatened to lynch STFU members. Black members, for example, often carried chickens when visiting white union members so that they could explain to outsiders that they had only been trying to sell poultry. Spirituals were used as signals for members to meet. The STFU carefully issued various publications—*The Sharecroppers Voice* with "The Voice of The Disinherited" printed on its banner, *The S.T.F.U. News*, and *The Farm Worker*—to spread news through poems and articles.

The STFU's legal defense fund assisted evicted members. In November 1934 attorney C. T. Carpenter filed a test case in federal court on behalf of sharecroppers and tenants evicted from Hiram Norcross's plantation. Carpenter wanted the judge to determine if the farmers could be evicted without just cause. Moreover, he hoped that the case would set a legal precedent. While white landowners protested the case, a delegation of STFU leaders traveled to Washington, D.C., to meet with Henry A. Wallace, secretary of Agriculture. Wallace, however, did not support the sharecroppers, and the case was dismissed. Another trial, involving a STFU member who was arrested as an agitator, fueled white hostilities toward the union. In response, the STFU moved its headquarters to a safer location in Memphis, Tennessee, in 1934.

One year later, the STFU scored its first victory. In the fall of 1935, cotton pickers went on strike demanding that they be paid $1 per 100 pounds of cotton instead of the usual 40 and 60 cents. The average cotton picker generated 200 pounds per day and received between 80 cents and $1.20 for ten to twelve hours of work. Five thousand workers refused to pick cotton for ten days until the STFU settled for 75 cents per hundred pounds. Although STFU members were threatened and arrested, thousands of farmers joined the union. In response to the strike, the state of Arkansas and the federal government began to investigate the working conditions of cotton pickers. A 1936 STFU strike asked for $1.50 per 100 pounds and a union contract. This time, however, the STFU failed to achieve its goals. During the strike, John Handcox began composing protest songs such as "Roll the Union On," which became the STFU's official song. Music played an important role in the history of the union because many STFU members were members of fundamental religions and used gospel songs to voice their protests.

Despite the failure of the 1936 strike, the sharecropper movement gained national strength. Advocates in Washington, D.C., helped STFU leaders speak to politicians, lobbied and testified to Congress, raised funds, and publicized the poverty of southern sharecroppers. The STFU received additional attention when 2,000 Missouri tenants were evicted and camped on highways until state troopers forcibly removed them. In 1937, the STFU initiated the annual Sharecroppers' Week and well-known residents of large cities led week-long fund-raising campaigns. Leading African Americans such as educator Mary McLeod Bethune were members of the National Sharecroppers' Fund national board, and the National Association for the Advancement of Colored People (NAACP), the National Negro Congress, and the American Civil Liberties Union (ACLU) publicly supported the STFU. In 1938, STFU membership peaked at 31,000 members of which 80 percent were African Americans.

As the STFU gained strength, southern planters increasingly viewed its members as a threat to their labor system and initiated brutal terror tactics to undermine the work of the union. STFU members were arrested, attacked, and lynched; union leaders endured assassination attempts; and the churches and homes of members were shot at and burned. Deputies stopped STFU meetings, and planters evicted tenants whom they suspected of supporting the union. Afraid to escalate the violence, the STFU maintained a nonviolence policy.

During its early years, the STFU enjoyed racial harmony as black and white members worked together. The union's president was usually white, while the vice president was black. Henry Clay East served as the STFU's first president until he was replaced by J. R. Butler who held

the post from 1935 to 1942. E. B. McKinney, a prominent black Baptist minister, served as the STFU's first vice president. Many African Americans who respected and trusted McKinney joined the STFU because of his endorsement of the union. Moreover, African American activists and labor leaders such as Walter White, A. Philip Randolph, and Roy Wilkins addressed STFU conventions.

By the late 1930s, however, as a recession worsened the conditions of black tenant farmers, Communist and socialist factions within the STFU divided its membership. On March 11, 1939, after the STFU affiliated with the Congress of Industrial Organizations (CIO), McKinney left the union in protest. Charging that affiliation with the CIO would result in white domination, McKinney attempted to organize an all-black agricultural group. Mitchell, one of the STFU founding members, also broke with the union, claiming that the CIO was influenced by Communists and used dues for political activities that neither he nor the STFU supported. Following his departure from the STFU, Mitchell worked for the National Youth Administration and the International Ladies' Garment Worker's Union (ILGWU). He returned to the STFU in 1941 and was elected president in 1944.

The controversy generated by the STFU's affiliation with the CIO obscured the union's mission to secure civil rights for farmers. As a result, black members became increasingly disillusioned with the STFU. This trend continued during World War II, when the STFU ceased to address the socioeconomic and racial concerns of farmers and instead transported agricultural workers to the North to help them find employment in defense industries.

Following the war, the STFU continued its efforts to assist agricultural workers. In 1947, the STFU helped launch a strike at DiGiorgio Farms outside Bakersfield, California, which laid the foundation for organizing migrant workers into the United Farm Workers of America. The STFU, however, was unable to regain its prewar strength and officially ceased to exist by 1948. That year, its work and leadership was absorbed by the National Farm Labor Union (NFLU) with headquarters in Washington, D.C. Mitchell continued to guide the union through its 1960 transformation into the National Agricultural Workers Union, which had limited success because gas tractors and mechanized cotton pickers started to displace farm laborers.

Encouraging scholars to study the contributions of the STFU to American labor history, Mitchell donated the papers of the organization to the University of North Carolina in the early 1970s. Moreover, he supported the production of the documentary film *Our Land Too: The*

*Legacy of the STFU* and lectured at colleges and universities until the year prior to his death in 1989. The STFU was an important participant in the twentieth-century southern labor movement, proving that interracial cooperation could protect laborers' rights.

**FURTHER READINGS**

Grubbs, Donald H. *Cry from the Cotton: The Southern Tenant Farmers' Union and the New Deal.* Chapel Hill: The University of North Carolina Press, 1971.

Kester, Howard. *Revolt Among the Sharecroppers.* Introduction by Alex Lichtenstein. New York: Covici, Friede, 1936; rpt., Knoxville: University of Tennessee Press, 1997.

Mitchell, Harry Leland. "The Founding and Early History of the Southern Tenant Farmers Union." *Arkansas Historical Quarterly* 32 (Winter 1973): 342–369.

———. *Mean Things Happening in This Land: The Life and Times of H. L. Mitchell, Co-Founder of the Southern Tenant Farmers Union.* Montclair, N.J.: Allanheld, Osmun, 1979.

———. *Roll the Union On: A Pictorial History of the Southern Tenant Farmers Union as told by its Co-founder H. L. Mitchell.* Introduction by Orville Vernon Burton. Chicago: Charles H. Kerr Publishing Co., 1987.

*Our Land Too: The Legacy of the STFU.* Huntsville, Ala.: Kudzu Film Productions, Inc., 1987.

*Elizabeth D. Schafer*

# Special Committee on Negroes and Economic Reconstruction

*See* Commission on Interracial Cooperation.

# State Council for a Pennsylvania Fair Employment Practices Commission

The State Council for a Pennsylvania Fair Employment Practices Commission was established by the Philadelphia Committee on Equal Job Opportunity (CEJO) in 1948. In the years immediately following World War II, the council lobbied the state government to establish a fair employment practices commission (FEPC). It took seven years to attain that goal.

The need for a state FEPC had been demonstrated during the war years. The wartime federal Fair Employment Practice Committee spent much of its scant resources in Pennsylvania to adjust numerous discrimination complaints and to integrate essential war industries such as the Philadelphia Transit Authority. After the federal FEPC was dismantled by Congress in 1946, Pennsylvania's civil rights leaders tried to recreate the agency at the state level. Their efforts were hampered not only by well organized political resistance but also by competition among the groups fighting for a state FEPC.

After the war, two organizations, the moderate Philadelphia CEJO, founded in 1943, and the more radical Bi-Partisan Committee for a Pennsylvania FEPC, established in 1944, led the movement to create a Pennsylvania fair employment practices commission. These two organizations did not work together, and without coordinated efforts, the state's first two fair employment practice bills died in legislative committee. Soon after, in late 1945, the most influential groups pushing for a state FEPC, including the Philadelphia National Association for the Advancement of Colored People (NAACP), the Bi-Partisan Committee for a Pennsylvania FEPC, and the Philadelphia CEJO, formed the Pennsylvania Committee for a Permanent FEPC. The Committee, under the leadership of Goldie Watson of the Philadelphia NAACP, was generally considered "leftist." Because of its direct action approach, which included a sit-down protest on the floor of the Pennsylvania House of Representatives, the Committee lost its support among moderate groups and politicians. In 1948 the Philadelphia CEJO created a rival organization, the State Council for a Pennsylvania FEPC, which used traditional political methods to accomplish its goal.

The leaders of the State Council, Nathan Agran of the Philadelphia CEJO, Robert J. O'Donnell of the National Conference of Christians and Jews, and Harry Boyer of the United Steelworkers of America, focused their lobbying efforts on Republican Governor John S. Fine, his successor, Democratic Governor George M. Leader, and Democrats in the General Assembly. The opposition to a state FEPC consisted largely of business leaders, particularly G. Mason Owlett, president of the Pennsylvania Manufacturers Association, and many Republicans. The turning point came in 1954 when Democrats won the statehouse and took control of the legislature. In 1955, the General Assembly passed and Governor Leader signed a law creating the Pennsylvania Fair Employment Practices Commission.

**FURTHER READINGS**

Gray, Gibson. "The Lobbying Game: A Study of the 1953 Campaign of the State Council for a Pennsylvania Fair Employment Practices Commission." Ph.D. diss., Columbia University, 1967.

Kersten, Andrew E. "Fighting for Fair Employment: The FEPC in the Midwest." Ph.D. diss., University of Cincinnati, 1997.

Norgen, Paul, and Samuel Hill. *Toward Fair Employment.* New York: Columbia University Press, 1964.

Reed, Merl E. *Seedtime for the Modern Civil Rights Movement: The President's Committee on Fair Employment Practice, 1941–1946.* Baton Rouge: Louisiana State University Press, 1991.

*Andrew E. Kersten*

## Student National Pharmaceutical Association

*See* National Pharmaceutical Association.

## Student Nonviolent Coordinating Committee

At a meeting in April 1960 at Shaw University in Raleigh, North Carolina, African American college students who were participants in the 1960 sit-in movement to desegregate southern lunch counters agreed to establish the Student Non-Violent Coordinating Committee (SNCC). The principal organizer of the gathering was Ella Baker, a veteran civil rights organizer and an official of the Southern Christian Leadership Conference (SCLC). Baker invited representatives of other organizations to the meeting, but she also encouraged the more than 120 student attendees to remain autonomous rather than to affiliate with SCLC or one of the other existing civil rights groups. The students admired SCLC leader Martin Luther King Jr., who addressed the gathering, but were generally reluctant to compromise the autonomy of their local protest groups and gave only tentative support to the idea of creating a permanent regional organization, even if under student leadership. They voted to establish a temporary coordinating body, with Fisk University student Marion Barry to serve as chairman. Vanderbilt University theology student James Lawson, whose workshops on nonviolence served as a training ground for many of the Nashville student protesters, wrote an organizational statement of purpose, which reflected the strong commitment to Gandhian nonviolence that would pervade SNCC during its early years: "We affirm the philosophical or religious ideal of nonviolence as the foundation of our purpose, the presupposition of our faith, and the manner of our action. Nonviolence as it grows from Judaic-Christian traditions seeks a social order of justice permeated by love."

After the Raleigh conference, a small group of volunteers worked with Baker at the SCLC headquarters to maintain channels of communications among the assertively independent local student protest groups. In June 1960 the first issue of SNCC's newspaper, the *Student Voice*, appeared, and during the summer SNCC representatives delivered statements calling for civil rights reform at the Democratic and Republican national conventions. As a result of a second conference of 138 students on October 14–16 in Atlanta, SNCC acquired a more defined organizational structure. Student representatives agreed to establish a policy-making Coordinating Committee to be composed of one representative from each state and the District of Columbia. Kentucky State student Edward King became SNCC's Executive Secretary. After Barry resigned to return to graduate school, Charles McDew of South Carolina State College was selected to replace him as chair.

As SNCC "freedom fighters" became deeply involved in an expanding social movement in the South, they developed a distinctive style of protest and of community organizing that inspired many black southerners and stimulated mass movements under indigenous leadership. A brash willingness to challenge powerful institutions and their experimental approach to life made SNCC organizers particularly effective in the most racially repressive regions of the Black Belt where blacks saw SNCC's militancy as an alternative to cultural and political conformity. As SNCC workers came together to form an activist community in the midst of a politically awakening black populace, they were transformed by their experiences. They became role models for a generation of young activists, inside and outside the South, who challenged many of the assumptions that made possible the continued existence of injustice and oppression in American society. SNCC's militancy particularly influenced the early development of the predominantly white New Left group, Students for a Democratic Society (SDS).

SNCC's emergence as a significant force in the southern civil rights movement came largely through the involvement of students in the 1961 Freedom Ride campaign, which was designed to bring about desegregation of eating facilities at southern bus terminals. The Congress of Racial Equality (CORE) organized the initial Freedom Ride in May, but after this CORE's effort was stymied by violent assaults on Freedom Riders traveling through Alabama. Students from Nashville, under the leadership of Fisk University student Diane Nash, resolved to continue the rides. Once the new group of Freedom Riders demonstrated their determination to continue the rides into Mississippi, other students joined the movement. The resulting threat of major racial violence in Birmingham and Montgomery forced President John F. Kennedy and other members of his administration to become involved. During June hundreds of student protesters were jailed in Mississippi, but by the fall of 1961 the campaign had produced a cadre of highly committed student activists who were willing to become full-time SNCC workers.

As SNCC acquired a staff of organizers and full-time protesters, the group established major projects in those areas of the Deep South where segregationist resistance was greatest. The Albany, Georgia, campaign, which soon expanded to the nearby rural areas of southwest Georgia, was one of the most sustained of these efforts. Former Virginia Union theology student Charles Sherrod initiated voter registration and desegregation programs in Albany during the fall of 1961. He worked close with local students and older black residents who formed a group called the Albany Movement, which invited King and other SCLC officials to participate in major protests during December 1961 and the summer of 1962. These protests, which brought in few concessions from white officials, highlighted SNCC workers' increasing disillusionment with King's top-down leadership style and with the Kennedy administration's reluctance to intervene forcefully on behalf of the civil rights movement.

The most extensive of SNCC's organizing efforts occurred in Mississippi, the state with the lowest proportion of registered voters in the black population and the highest level of white resistance to racial integration. After participating in an unsuccessful voting rights project in McComb, Mississippi, during the fall of 1961, former Harvard University graduate student Bob Moses moved to Jackson and began recruiting young Mississippi residents to serve as field secretaries, mainly in the Mississippi Delta region. Moses, who eventually became voter-registration director of Mississippi's Council of Federated Organizations (COFO), which included SNCC as well as other civil rights groups, epitomized SNCC's nonhierarchical, grassroots organizing approach. Despite confronting considerable racist violence and intimidation, the Mississippi voter registration effort created conditions for racial reform by bringing together three crucial groups: dynamic and determined SNCC field secretaries, influential civil rights leaders from Mississippi (most notably Amzie Moore of Cleveland, Mississippi, Aaron Henry of Clarksdale, and Fannie Lou Hamer of Ruleville), and white student volunteers who participated in the Freedom Vote

mock election of October 1963 and the Freedom Summer campaign of 1964. Early in 1964 SNCC supported the formation of the Mississippi Freedom Democratic Party (MFDP) in order to challenge the legitimacy of the all-white regular Democratic Party of the state. After one black and two white civil rights workers were murdered by white segregationists in June 1964, the Federal Bureau of Investigation (FBI) stepped up its investigation of anti-black violence, and the voter registration effort garnered unprecedented press coverage. Yet, although violent attacks against voter registration workers declined after the summer, many SNCC workers were disturbed by the failure of President Lyndon B. Johnson and other Democratic leaders to support the MFDP challenge to the seating of the regular delegates at the August 1964 national Democratic convention. Moreover, racial tensions within SNCC became more evident after the summer as many of the white volunteers in Mississippi sought to join SNCC's staff.

By this time, SNCC began a period of internal ideological ferment, as staff members began to question some of the assumptions underlying their previous activities. During intense and extended debates, staff members challenged not only SNCC's interracial composition but also its guiding ideals. Initially dominated by advocates of Christian Gandhianism, during the period after 1961 SNCC increasingly became a secular community of organizers devoted to the development of indigenous black leaders and local institutions. As the focus of the southern black struggle changed from desegregation to political and economic concerns, SNCC's radicalism was increasingly influenced by Marxian and black nationalist rather than religious ideals, although a theme of moral outrage remained evident in SNCC's public criticisms of the federal government and of Cold War liberalism. Having shifted its focus from nonviolent desegregation protests to long-term voting rights campaigns in the deep South, SNCC policies and direction were increasingly determined not by the coordinating committee, which rarely met, or by its officers, but by its field secretaries, who worked for nominal salaries and insisted on a great degree of autonomy. John Lewis' controversial speech at the 1963 March on Washington, which questioned the adequacy of the Kennedy administration's civil rights activities, only hinted at SNCC workers' growing sense of disillusionment with conventional liberalism and their identification with the emergent sense of racial pride and potency that had resulted from the southern struggle.

The crucial series of voting rights demonstrations that began early in 1965 in Selma, Alabama, stimulated increasingly bitter ideological debates within the group, as some SNCC workers openly challenged the group's previous commitment to nonviolent tactics and its willingness to allow the participation of white activists. In addition to these bitter conflicts over racial issues, SNCC was also divided by conflicts between "hardliners" favoring greater organizational discipline and "floaters" emphasizing the freedom of staff members to direct their own activities. Distracted by such divisive issues, the day-to-day needs of the group's ongoing projects suffered from neglect. In many deep Southern communities where SNCC had once attracted considerable black support, the group's influence waned.

Nevertheless, some SNCC workers were buoyed by their success in challenging SCLC's more cautious leadership during the Selma voting rights campaign and the resulting march to the state capitol in Montgomery. During the spring of 1965, SNCC organizers entered the rural area between the two cities and helped black residents launch the all-black Lowndes County Freedom Organization (LCFO), soon known as the Black Panther party. Meanwhile, a few SNCC workers established incipient organizing efforts in volatile urban black ghettos.

These new initiatives, designed to capture the support of previously unorganized but discontented blacks, strengthened support for racial separatism. In addition, the gulf between SNCC and its former liberal allies enlarged. Early in 1966 the lack of a federal response to the killing of Tuskegee Institute student Sammy Younge when he attempted to use a segregated filling station restroom prompted other SNCC workers to overcome their previous reluctance to take a stand opposing United States involvement in the Vietnam war. SNCC's opposition to the Vietnam war generated further controversy when the Georgia legislature refused to allow newly elected representative Julian Bond of SNCC to take his seat due to Bond's support of the antiwar stand. The following summer SNCC's relations with the Johnson administration reached a low point when the group refused to attend a presidential conference on civil rights.

In May 1966, a new stage in SNCC's history began with the election of SNCC's chair Stokely Carmichael, who had helped establish the Lowndes County project. Because Carmichael identified himself with the trend away from nonviolence and interracialism, his election over the more moderate John Lewis damaged SNCC's relations with more moderate civil rights groups, such as the National Association for the Advancement of Colored People (NAACP) and the SCLC, and with many of its

white supporters. During the month following his election, Carmichael publicly expressed SNCC's new political orientation when he began calling for "Black Power" during a voting rights march through Mississippi. The national controversy surrounding Carmichael's black power speeches brought increased notoriety to SNCC, but the group remained internally divided over its future direction. SNCC's staff did not determine how militant racial consciousness could be used to achieve tangible gains and thereby provided an opportunity for more moderate leaders to exploit black power rhetoric for their own purposes. As the ambiguous black power slogan became linked with programs ranging from the election of black politicians and the development of black capitalism to the creation of a new black value system and the fostering of a black revolution, Carmichael's most sophisticated statement on black power failed to provide a coherent and radical set of ideas for future black struggles. Co-authored by political scientist Charles V. Hamilton, *Black Power: The Politics of Liberation in America* (1967) eclectically drew ideas from Third World nationalist movements and Western scholarly studies of those movements. The book, which they described as "a political framework and ideology which represents the last reasonable opportunity for this society to work out its racial problems short of prolonged destructive guerrilla warfare," contained only vague references regarding the need for blacks to reject existing political rules and to adopt "new political forms." Carmichael's attempt to provide an intellectually defensible basis for the black power slogan soon gave way to a willingness on the part of many SNCC workers to allow black people to define the slogan through their militancy.

In addition, Carmichael himself found that his support within SNCC was tenuous once he became a highly visible leader in a group previously characterized by distrust of leaders. Even as he emerged as the preeminent national symbol of black power, other SNCC workers questioned his commitment to the ideal of racial separatism. Carmichael's opposition came mainly from members of SNCC's Atlanta Project, who saw themselves as disciples of Malcolm X. While the Atlanta organizers achieved only modest success in organizing blacks in the Vine City ghetto, they succeeded in pressing Carmichael and other SNCC officers to confront the issue of the continued presence of whites in SNCC. Racial separatists from the Atlanta Project and elsewhere hoped for a final resolution of the "white" question at a December 1966 staff meeting. After several days of rancorous debate that led some staff members to leave in disgust, the staff members who remained narrowly passed a resolution excluding whites. Through their single-minded determination, the Atlanta Project staff dominated the December staff meeting, but their effort to expel whites was followed soon afterward by their own expulsion on grounds of insubordination.

Even after the dismissal of the Atlanta separatists, SNCC was weakened by continued internal conflicts and external attacks, which not only hampered its projects but also contributed to the loss of northern financial backing. To provide funds for payroll expenses, SNCC began to rely almost totally on speechmaking and its New York office, manned by professional fundraisers and veteran staff members. When these sources proved insufficient, staff members were forced to skip paychecks, prompting some to leave the organization in order to support themselves and their families. The selection in June 1967 of Hubert "Rap" Brown as SNCC's new chair was meant to reduce the notoriety the group had acquired as a result of Carmichael's speeches, but Brown sought to encourage the militancy of leaderless urban blacks and soon became as much of a firebrand as Carmichael had been. Although he announced that SNCC was moving from rhetoric to program, Brown soon became caught up in national controversy when he accepted an invitation from the Cambridge Action Federation, composed of former members of SNCC's affiliate in Cambridge and black youngsters reacting to an upsurge in anti-black activities by members of the Ku Klux Klan and the States Rights Party. Against a background of news reports of incipient black guerrilla warfare, Brown was blamed for the racial violence that erupted after his speech. Recently elected Maryland governor Spiro T. Agnew quickly became a leading symbol for law and order (and a successful candidate for the vice presidency) after he publicly condemned Brown and criticized black leaders who refused to join in his denunciation.

The subsequent federal campaign against black militancy severely damaged SNCC's ability to sustain its organizing efforts. The FBI's Counterintelligence Program (Cointelpro), for example, targeted SNCC as part of a concerted effort at all levels of government to crush black militancy through overt and covert means and through the more subtle techniques of cooptation and timely concessions. Having survived attacks by southern racists, SNCC withered under the assault of opponents with access to the enormous power of the federal government. SNCC executive director Ruby Doris Robinson's death from illness further weakened the organization.

Although severely weakened by police repression, loss of white financial support, and internal dissension and disarray, SNCC workers tried to establish close ties to revolutionary groups outside the United States. At the May 1967 meeting when staff members elected Rap Brown as chairman, they also declared SNCC a "Human Rights organization" and announced that they would "encourage and support the liberation struggles against colonialism, racism, and economic exploitation" around the world. Proclaiming a position of "positive non-alignment" in world affairs and indicating a willingness to meet with Third World governments and liberation groups, SNCC applied for nongovernment organization status on the United Nations Economic and Security Council. After being replaced by Brown as SNCC's chair, Carmichael traveled extensively to build ties with revolutionary movements in Africa and Asia. During his 1967 tour of Third World nations, Carmichael portrayed black urban rebellions in the United States as part of the international socialist movement.

Upon his return to the United States, Carmichael participated in an abortive effort to establish an alliance between SNCC and the California-based Black Panther party. The FBI exploited the tensions that existed between Carmichael, who advocated racial unity, and Panther leaders, who stressed the need for class-based alliances that included white revolutionaries. Although Carmichael, Brown, and SNCC executive director James Forman believed that an alliance with the urban-based Black Panthers could bring new vitality to SNCC, the alliance foundered during the summer of 1968 due to ideological differences and misunderstandings resulting from anonymous letters sent by FBI agents.

The spontaneous urban uprisings that followed the assassination of Martin Luther King in April 1968 indicated a high level of black discontent, but by then SNCC had little ability to mobilize the discontent into an effective political force. Its most effective community organizers had left the organization, which became known as the Student National Coordinating Committee. Although the increasing popularity of black militant rhetoric gave the appearance of racial unity, black communities were divided by serious conflicts between self-defined cultural nationalists, who urged blacks to unite around various conceptions of an African cultural ideal, and self-defined political revolutionaries who advocated armed struggle to achieve political or economic goals. SNCC's dwindling staff included adherents of each of the two major trends, but by 1968 both factions had begun to doubt whether SNCC would remain the principal vehicle to reach their goals. Although individual SNCC activists played significant roles in African American politics during the period after 1968, and many of the controversial ideas that once had defined SNCC's radicalism had become widely accepted among blacks, the organization disintegrated. By the end of the decade, FBI surveillance of SNCC's remaining offices was discontinued due to lack of activity.

## FURTHER READING

Carson, Clayborne. *In Struggle: SNCC and the Black Awakening of the 1960s.* Cambridge, Mass.: Harvard University Press, 1981.

*Clayborne Carson*

## Tennessee Council on Human Relations

The Tennessee Council on Human Relations (TCHR) was one of twelve state Councils on Human Relations established by the Southern Regional Council of Atlanta, Georgia. The TCHR was chartered by the state of Tennessee in 1954 as a nonpolitical, nondenominational, interracial organization. Its goal was to help improve human relations in Tennessee during the 1950s and 1960s. For this purpose the TCHR gathered information about racial problems and discussed solutions with those concerned. Employing educational methods, the TCHR worked to improve economic, civic, and racial conditions. As an incorporated nonprofit organization, the TCHR derived its financial support from membership dues, contributions, and grants from the Fund for the Republic and the Field Foundation.

The TCHR advocated the formation of biracial committees to build community understanding and provide leadership for the solution of local problems. TCHR members operated on the assumption that once a community is aware of its human relations problems and their causes, it will attempt to find solutions. Compiling information and statistics from fact-finding surveys conducted by local chapters, the TCHR identified human relations problems and made recommendations to local, state, and federal government officials. The TCHR concluded that "action" was the most effective route for communities to challenge human and race relations problems. Therefore, the TCHR supported various programs designed to improve equal opportunity in education, housing, health facilities, public accommodations, employment, welfare, and voter registration. The council ceased to function during the 1960s.

FURTHER READING

Southern Regional Council Papers, Series IV: State Councils on Human Relations, 1946–1968, Reels 147–148, Special Collections, Robert W. Woodruff Library, Atlanta University Center, Atlanta, Georgia.

*Kimberly E. Nichols*

## Theater Owners Booking Association

The Theater Owners Booking Association (TOBA), a booking organization for black performers, was founded sometime after 1920 and went into eclipse by the end of the decade. Over thirty theater owners, none from the black metropolises of New York and Washington, united to form this circuit. One of the main investors was Sherman Houston Dudley (1872–1940), who began his career in a medicine show and later helped form the Colored Actors Union. TOBA's members sold shares of stock at $100 each, at a three-share minimum. At its peak the TOBA brought to more than eighty theaters in the South and Midwest various forms of entertainment, including blues, jazz, gospel, musicals, and vaudeville. The organization was known for its tight contracts, small salaries, and the bad performing conditions it offered. Thus, black performers sometimes translated the acronym TOBA as "Tough on Black Actors," or "Tough on Black Asses." Most performers had seasonal contracts, and only headliners like blues singers Bessie Smith and Ma Rainey secured work twelve months out of the year.

TOBA was also called the "Chitlin Circuit" because some of its artists performed in blackface, and critics accused the organization of enhancing racial stereotypes. Apart from presenting female blues stars, as well as jazz musicians like Louis Armstrong and Duke Ellington, many vaudeville stars, such as Bill "Bojangles" Robinson and Bert Williams, toured the country with the help of TOBA. To the large group of TOBA theaters belonged the Walker Theater in Indianapolis and the Lyric Theater in New Orleans. The growing attraction of sound films at the end of the 1920s seems to be the chief reason why the circuit declined.

**FURTHER READINGS**

Gates, Henry Louis, Jr. "The Chitlin Circuit." *The New Yorker*, February 3, 1997.

Riis, Thomas L. *Just Before Jazz: Black Musical Theater in New York, 1890–1915*. Washington, D.C.: The Smithsonian Institution Press, 1989.

van Valkenburgh, Carole Doyle, and Christine Dall, prods. *Wild Women Don't Have the Blues*. San Francisco: California Newsreel, 1989.

*Thomas Leuchtenmüller*

## Topeka, Kansas: Civic, Literary, and Mutual Aid Associations

African Americans have been present in Topeka since the New England Emigrant Aid Company founded the city in 1854 as part of its antislavery campaign in the Kansas Territory. Topeka's black community was small when Kansas became a free state in 1861, and association activities were limited to informal kinship networks. The Freedmen's Congregational Church, the only black church in Topeka before 1865, was the product of white missionary efforts. After the war, however, the African American population steadily increased from eighty-three residents in 1865 to 724 in 1875. Churches established within the community replaced white missionary endeavors, and black Topekans began to demand their full citizenship rights.

In 1866 the legislature legally segregated public schools in Topeka, and black people began organizing to voice their concerns over this and other forms of racial discrimination. Moral outrage about segregation first surfaced in the black churches, which served as the community centers of Topeka's African American residents. In the early 1870s initial calls for desegregation emerged in the St. John AME (African Methodist Episcopal) Church and the Second Baptist Church. By the mid-1870s black fraternal orders such as the Great Western Lodge and the Occidental Lodge became centers for social activity and community discussion.

After 1875, migrations of African Americans from the upper South to the West helped spark black interest in Kansas that peaked in the Great Exodus of 1879 and 1880. As a result Topeka's black population increased dramatically. By 1880 the city had 3,648 black residents, and within a decade that number had grown to 5,024. The new arrivals were activists who contributed their organizational skills to the existing community and reinforced desires for civil rights reform.

Mutual aid associations to assist the new migrants were among black Topekans' foremost concerns. Created in 1879, the Colored State Emigration Board was one of the earliest groups founded to help the newcomers. The board had no funding to provide relief on its own but did advise the white-controlled Kansas Freedmen's Relief Association, which did have money for relief efforts. After 1880, most African American associations remained autonomous, which reflected both the independence of Topeka's black community and the growing problem of segregation. Black civic groups like the Young Ladies Charitable Union (YLCU) and the Colored Juvenile Benevolent Society (CJBS) were active in the late 1880s and reflected the community's concerns about poverty and delinquency. The YLCU worked to find homes for orphaned children and others in need of shelter while CJBS members addressed the causes of crime by advocating proper home training for children. The United Colored Links (1881) was a semipolitical organization that urged a united front to develop and support black-owned businesses and industries. The group urged separation from the Republican party, arguing that it had betrayed African Americans, and considered fusion with the Greenback party. The group was powerful enough that Greenback party presidential candidate James B. Weaver came to court its members in August 1881. Others like the Afro-American League and the Colored League were active from the late 1880s to the early 1900s. They were political groups that responded to race violence and the disfranchisement of African Americans.

Blacks in Topeka viewed education as an important measure of racial progress and furthered that goal by actively supporting literary and cultural societies. The Interstate Literary Association (1892), for example, sponsored discussions, lectures, musical concerts, and art exhibits for the benefit of the African American community. Association members actively supported public education and firmly opposed segregated schools. Fine arts and literary discussions, however, did not appeal to all black city residents. Many African Americans preferred to watch the games of Topeka's black baseball team, the Mascots.

Members of all classes, however, agreed on the importance of combating segregation in public and private facilities.

Discrimination in the workplace was a major concern for both skilled and unskilled black workers. In the twentieth century the Commercial Club and the Topeka chapter of the National Negro Business League worked to gain a larger market share for African American businesses and to end prejudicial hiring practices in local industries. The Sunflower State Agricultural Association, which met at the Kansas Industrial and Educational Institute in Topeka, addressed progressive farming techniques and other issues affecting black farmers.

The Topeka affiliate of the National Association for the Advancement of Colored People (NAACP) became an important twentieth-century medium for the advancement of civil rights. Although the highest ranking officials of Topeka's NAACP were white, many of the city's black residents supported its fight against segregation, particularly in the schools. Closely aligned with the NAACP was the Young Men's Educational Association, an African American–led society that challenged segregated education. The efforts of these groups successfully integrated Topeka's junior and senior high schools by the 1940s. The city's elementary schools, however, remained segregated until the 1954 landmark decision in *Brown v. Board of Education* declared racial segregation unconstitutional.

Discrimination in urban renewal programs became an issue for black Topekans in the early 1960s. African Americans united to preserve affordable housing in deteriorating historic black neighborhoods like Tennesseetown, an old Exoduster community. Exodusters were black southerners who migrated to rural Kansas in the late nineteenth century, following Reconstruction. Groups like the Neighborhood Improvement Association took the lead in saving these neighborhoods and refurbishing housing.

For more than a century Topeka's civic, literary, and mutual aid associations sought to provide for the needs of the city's black population and in the process forged a sense of community identity. In 1968 local black leaders responded to the assassination of Martin Luther King Jr. by establishing the Coordinating Committee of the Black Community to promote community concerns and to coordinate various African American organizational activities.

**FURTHER READINGS**

Athearn, Robert G. *In Search of Canaan: Black Migration to Kansas, 1879–80.* Lawrence: The Regents Press of Kansas, 1978.

Cox, Thomas C. *Blacks in Topeka, Kansas, 1865–1915: A Social History.* Baton Rouge: Louisiana State University Press, 1982.

Gordon, Jacob U. *Narratives of African Americans in Kansas, 1870–1992: Beyond the Exodust Movement.* Lewiston, N.Y.: The Edwin Mellon Press, 1993.

Painter, Nell Irvin. *Exodusters: Black Migration to Kansas after Reconstruction.* New York: Knopf, 1977.

Wilson, Paul E. *A Time to Lose: Representing Kansas in Brown v. Board of Education.* Lawrence: University Press of Kansas, 1995.

*Gary R. Entz*

## Trade Union Education League

*See* Trade Union Unity League.

## Trade Union Leadership Council

In 1957, black members of the United Auto Workers (UAW) founded the Trade Union Leadership Council (TULC) to address the lack of African American representation on the executive board and to combat discrimination in labor. During World War II, a left-wing caucus of the UAW—Congress of Industrial Organizations (CIO)—had demanded black representation on the International Executive Board (IEB). Yet, African Americans still had no representation on the twenty-two–member executive board in the late 1950s. The UAW's Fair Employment Practices Department, formed in 1944, did little to address issues of either representation on the IEB or discrimination against black workers in skilled positions in UAW plants. To fill the void, Horace Sheffield, an activist who had played a major role in mobilizing support in the black community of Detroit for the strike against Ford Motor Company at the River Rouge Plant in 1941, was an organizer of the TULC in the Detroit area. Similar organizations were formed in other northern cities by black workers during this time. Black steel workers in the Pittsburgh area organized a Fair Share Group of Steel Workers to lobby for concrete action on black problems and conditions in the steel industry.

The issue of black representation was raised at the 1959 UAW convention, but it was three more years before Walter Reuther, president of the UAW, bowing to public exposure of racism within the UAW, organized factories. The persistent voice coming from the TULC finally expanded the board and designated one seat for an African

American. Despite the TULC's desire that Sheffield fill the African American slot, the executive board elected Nelson Jack Edwards.

The TULC opened its membership to white unionists as well as black nonunionists. It served as a liaison between the black community and the union movement, recognizing that discrimination had to be attacked within the community as well as within the labor union. By 1962 the TULC had established a communitywide Educational Center. The center established a school in an old hardware store that offered classes in secretarial and clerical skills, business English, remedial reading, business math, leadership training, and preapprenticeship electrical training.

The TULC's strength as a community institution was tested when Jerome Cavanagh challenged to defeat a conservative candidate for mayor of Detroit. Cavanagh was backed by the TULC, which successfully mobilized thousands of campaign workers from the National Association for the Advancement of Colored People (NAACP) and black churches and clubs to defeat the conservative candidate, who was backed by UAW leaders and the white business community. By 1962, the efforts of the community education project and Cavanagh's political campaign broadened the TULC's base to around 10,000 members. By turning the TULC into a social movement, the organization gained considerable control over the direction of black politics in Detroit for a few years.

By the mid-1960s, however, the TULC's position within the black community of Detroit was challenged by a rival black community organization created by Edwards. It was an association that gained influence both at the local level and within the power structure of Michigan's Democratic party. Internal strife, combined with the emergence of more militant forces within the black community, diluted the power and influence of the TULC. One group that competed for influence was composed of black ministers; another group consisted of the younger generation of African Americans who entered the auto shops in large numbers during the tight labor market of the mid-1960s. By 1967 Sheffield threw his influence behind Edwards and worked as his administrative assistant on the IEB. By the late 1960s, the TULC had declined to relative ineffectiveness.

**FURTHER READINGS**

Boyle, Kevin. *The UAW and the Heyday of American Liberalism, 1945–1968*. Ithaca, N.Y.: Cornell University Press, 1995.

Foner, Philip S. *Organized Labor and the Black Worker, 1619–1981*. New York: International Publishers, 1974.

Geschwender, James A. *Class, Race, and Worker Insurgency: The League of Revolutionary Black Workers*. New York: Cambridge University Press, 1977.

Jacobson, Julius, ed. *The Negro and the American Labor Movement*. New York: Anchor Books, 1968.

Lichtenstein, Nelson. *Walter Reuther: The Most Dangerous Man in Detroit*. New York: HarperCollins, 1995.

Ross, Arthur M., and Herbert Hill, eds. *Employment, Race, and Poverty*. New York: Harcourt, Brace and World, 1967.

UAW Fair Practices Department. United Auto Workers Papers. Walter P. Reuther Library. Archives of Labor and Urban Affairs. Wayne State University, Detroit, Michigan.

*Beth Tompkins Bates*

# Trade Union Unity League

The Trade Union Unity League (TUUL), a Communist labor federation aimed at establishing a revolutionary interracial working-class movement, was founded in Cleveland, Ohio, in September 1929. The TUUL succeeded the Trade Union Education League (TUEL), both of which were affiliated with the Communist Party of the United States of America (CPUSA). The TUEL, founded in 1920 by William Z. Foster, sought to amalgamate craft unions into industrial unions. Upon orders from the Soviet-led Red International of Labor Unions, the TUEL was abandoned and the TUUL created in its stead, with Foster as secretary. The TUUL practiced "dual unionism." It attempted to establish independent, revolutionary unions to draw workers away from the American Federation of Labor (AFL), the largest body of organized workers in the United States. The TUUL sought to organize the tens of millions of American workers, in particular blacks, who had been excluded from the AFL.

The TUUL maintained constituent unions in the railroad, textile, mining, maritime, garment, auto, and steel industries. The constitutions of these TUUL unions mandated absolute racial equality within their ranks and pledged to fight for equality in the workplace and throughout American society. Unlike other American labor organizations, which sought to improve wages and reduce work hours, TUUL trade unions advocated the revolutionary overthrow of the capitalist system.

A number of the TUUL-affiliated unions organized in industries with large numbers of African American workers. These unions attacked their AFL counterparts for practicing racial discrimination and urged black workers to join the Communist unions. The National Miners' Union (NMU), for example, attempted to compete with the United Mine Workers of America (UMWA). The NMU elected William Boyce, a black miner from Indiana, as national vice president. Boyce led the NMU's drive to attract black miners, arguing that although the UMWA technically opposed racism, in practice it blatantly discriminated against African Americans. Black miners were among the most active members of the 1931 NMU strikes in West Virginia and Pennsylvania; 6,000 of the 42,000 striking miners were black. Even when black miners were few in number, the NMU insisted on strict racial equality. In 1931, for example, during the famous strike of Kentucky miners in Harlan County, the NMU refused to tolerate segregation within its ranks. Later that year in Birmingham, Alabama, the NMU and the Steel and Metal Workers' Industrial Union organized hundreds of black workers who were disillusioned with the AFL's racism and antiquated craft tactics.

The TUUL, much like the TUEL, did not fare very well. In the harsh antilabor and antiradical climate of the late 1920s and early 1930s, militant left-wing unions did not attract much support. With the onset of the Great Depression, however, more Americans, including many African Americans, became attracted to Communism and Communist-led trade unions. The TUUL ceased to exist when the Soviet Union changed its stance on dual unionism in 1935. That year, the Soviet Union and Communist parties around the world, including the CPUSA, ordered their members to abandon their unions and join mainstream labor organizations to forge a Popular Front. In the United States, CPUSA members joined the AFL and later the CIO and played influential roles in the successes of the American labor movement during the late 1930s.

**FURTHER READINGS**

Bernstein, Irving. *The Lean Years: The American Worker in 1920–1933.* Boston: Houghton-Mifflin, 1960.

Foner, Philip S. *Organized Labor and the Black Worker, 1619–1981.* New York: International Publishers, 1982.

Kelley, Robin D. G. *Hammer and Hoe: Alabama Communists During the Great Depression.* Chapel Hill: The University of North Carolina Press, 1990.

*Peter Cole*

## TransAfrica

TransAfrica is a private Washington, D.C.–based organization that advocates a progressive U.S. foreign policy toward the world's predominantly black nations, including those in Africa, the Caribbean, and, to some extent, Latin America.

TransAfrica was founded in 1977 with financial support from the National Council of Churches and the United Methodist Church. Randall Robinson, Herschelle Challenor, and Willard Johnson played important roles in securing initial funding and creating an organizational design. Actor Ossie Davis and tennis star Arthur Ashe were other early TransAfrica supporters. The need for an international affairs lobby grew out of a Black Leadership Conference, sponsored by the Congressional Black Caucus in 1976. Conference participants lamented the general absence of African Americans from high-level foreign policy positions and agreed that TransAfrica's creation would be one way to focus the American government's attention on African, Caribbean, and Latin American issues. In 1977, Randall Robinson was named TransAfrica's executive director and has served in that capacity ever since.

TransAfrica lobbies the U.S. government and monitors legislative activities on matters pertaining to the economic, political, and social concerns of many of these developing and underdeveloped countries. TransAfrica also works to assess the status of human rights and democracy in these countries. Finally, TransAfrica sponsors programs aimed at creating closer ties among African Americans, Africans, and Caribbeans by promoting their political awareness and increasing their involvement in foreign affairs.

Much of TransAfrica's success in the past two decades has rested upon its inexorable ability to help raise the profile of foreign policy issues that might otherwise go unnoticed, or overlooked, by American policymakers. TransAfrica has organized or initiated letter-writing campaigns, hunger strikes, and protest marches to highlight what it believes to be important, unresolved foreign policy issues. TransAfrica also publishes policy statements, conducts press conferences, testifies at congressional hearings, and meets with members of Congress. Through such actions, TransAfrica has helped to change the foreign policy priorities and policies of the American government.

One of the most important chapters in TransAfrica's history has been its effort to oppose apartheid in South Africa. In 1984, Randall Robinson and other TransAfrica supporters arranged a meeting in Washington, D.C., with the South African ambassador. They refused to leave the embassy until the ambassador agreed to release political dissident Nelson Mandela from jail and to take immediate steps to dismantle apartheid. The incident helped initiate the Free South Africa movement, which eventually resulted in the arrests of some 5,000 people for protesting in front of the South African Embassy. TransAfrica's actions helped ensure the passage of the 1986 Anti-Apartheid Act, which imposed economic sanctions on South Africa. Congressional support for the act was so strong that it was passed despite President Ronald Reagan's veto—the first time in the twentieth century that a president's foreign policy veto was overridden.

More recently, TransAfrica has protested human rights violations in Ethiopia, Kenya, Liberia, Nigeria, and Zaire. In 1994, Randall Robinson endured a twenty-seven–day hunger strike to protest President Bill Clinton's policy of forcible return of Haitian refugees who were fleeing their country's political dictatorship.

TransAfrica currently boasts some 15,000 members and an annual budget in excess of $1 million. Recent corporate sponsors of TransAfrica include the Reebok and Coca-Cola Corporations.

*Scott W. Webster*

## Tri-State Dental Association of DC, VA, MD

Founded in 1913, the Tri-State Dental Association (TSDA) was the product of a merger of various black dentists' organizations that were active in Washington, D.C., Maryland, and Virginia. The TSDA provided a forum for the advancement of dental science and techniques and promoted the adoption of ethics and professionalization in the field of dentistry. Black dentists organized to overcome numerous racial barriers, including limited access to dental colleges and postgraduate professional development. Moreover, black dentists suffered from low incomes, due to the limited funds of most of their black clients, as well as negative public perception, which was frequently expressed by fears that black dentists lacked the competency of white practitioners. Black dentists hoped to overcome their problems by forming dental societies to promote professionalization.

Whites who founded professional medical organizations in the late nineteenth and early twentieth centuries excluded black dentists and physicians. Denied membership in the American Medical Association (AMA), black physicians formed the National Medical Association (NMA) in 1895. The NMA welcomed those with dental degrees, but it was concerned primarily with physicians' needs and proved unable to advance the agenda of black dentists. Thus, black dentists launched their own local, state, and regional dental groups.

In 1900, black dentists in the District of Columbia formed the Washington Society of Colored Dentists, hoping that their group would become the nucleus of a national dental organization. Between 1901 and 1905 black dentists in Virginia and Maryland also organized. In 1905, Richmond, Virginia, dentist D. A. Ferguson called a meeting of black dentists to discuss the creation of a National Association of Negro Dentists. The group met at the Dental College of Howard University and elected Ferguson president of the proposed association. Various committees organized to canvas black dentists across the country and to disseminate information about the benefits of membership in a national organization. Despite the group's enthusiasm, however, the effort failed.

While Ferguson's efforts to establish a national organization failed, local and state organizations continued to emerge and grow. The Washington Society sponsored annual meetings where black dentists could hear papers explaining the latest scientific developments in dentistry and attend demonstrations of new dental techniques. Moreover, the society's membership policy reflected its continued interest in establishing and leading a national organization for black dentists. While membership in the society was limited to D.C. dentists, nonresidents could apply for associate membership. In 1907, the group relinquished some local identity when it became the Robert Tanner Freeman Dental Society, in honor of the first black who received a D.D.S. from Harvard University.

Similar activities occurred in Maryland and Virginia dental organizations. In 1905, black dentists in Maryland joined forces to create the Maryland Dental Society. In Virginia, Dr. Ferguson spearheaded campaigns to increase membership in state and local dental organizations and to educate the public about dental health and the role of black dental professionals.

In 1912, the Washington Society invited black dentists from Virginia and Maryland to attend the group's annual banquet and to discuss plans for a merger. Agreeing to the idea, the dentists chose Dr. Ferguson to initiate the scheme. In January 1913, Ferguson called for a formal planning session and a first meeting of the newly created TSDA on July 19, 1913. The roster of those convening at Buckroe Beach, Virginia, included the names of black pioneers in American dentistry. Among the TSDA founding members were John E. Washington, who, in 1905, became the first black licensed by the District Board of Dental Examiners in Washington, D.C.; George H. Butler, the first member of the Washington Society; and A. O. Reid and O. D. Jones, founding members of the Maryland Dental Society. The TSDA dedicated itself to elevating the status of professional black dentists, recruiting new practitioners, advancing and disseminating dental knowledge and techniques, and ensuring the maintenance of ethical behavior and standards among its membership.

After only five years, the TSDA outgrew its local identity and changed its name to the Interstate Dental Association (IDA). Membership expansion generated demands for program changes, including the addition of clinics at yearly conferences. New members also represented their profession in states beyond D.C., Virginia, and Maryland. When the IDA disbanded after the 1930s, the National Dental Association took its place.

**FURTHER READINGS**

Dumett, Clifton O. "The Negro in Dental Education: A Review of Important Occurrences." *Phylon Quarterly* 20 (December 1959): 379–388.

Kidd, Foster, ed. *Profile of the Negro in American Dentistry.* Washington, D.C.: Howard University Press, 1979.

Lewis, Stephen J. "The Negro in the Field of Dentistry." *Opportunity* 2 (July 1924): 207–212.

*Peggy Hardman*

**SEE ALSO**    National Dental Association

## True Reformers

*See* Grand United Order of True Reformers.

## Truman's Committee on Civil Rights

*See* President's Committee on Civil Rights.

## Tuskegee Conference

The Tuskegee Conference served as an educational forum for rural residents in the Deep South. The reformer and educator Booker T. Washington established the Tuskegee Normal and Industrial Institute in 1881, hoping to improve the quality of life for Alabama African Americans through reform and revitalization. He stressed that economic independence was the key to success and political and social freedom.

Washington promoted his philosophy of the "Tuskegee Ideal," emphasizing that educated blacks should teach all African Americans in their communities, helping them improve their daily lives. He believed that education should extend beyond classrooms. Aware that land-grant colleges hosted farmer institutes and short courses, Washington began planning a conference at Tuskegee to improve agricultural and rural conditions.

In January 1892, he issued a circular inviting seventy-five area residents to "an interesting and somewhat unique Negro Conference." Instead of selecting politicians and prominent leaders, he chose "representatives of the masses—the bone and sinew of the race—the common, hard working farmers with a few of the best ministers and teachers." At the conference, he hoped to determine the "actual industrial, moral and educational condition of the masses" and decide how Tuskegee Institute students could "use their education in helping masses of the colored people to lift themselves up."

African American farmers in Alabama's Black Belt faced a variety of problems. Despite erratic markets, most farmers focused on cotton planting, living in debt and mortgaging their meager possessions for supplies, clothes, and food. Tenant farmers rented land and lived in one-room cabins. Children attended schools for less than three months each year. Poverty and ignorance dominated.

The first Tuskegee Conference began on February 23, 1892. Washington's circular had passed through communities, and approximately 500 people, both black and white, arrived on campus to listen to Washington's "live at home" gospel. He stressed that farmers must own their own homes and land and grow ample food to feed their families. Only by becoming self-sufficient, Washington warned, could African Americans advance.

Conference lectures also urged farmers to diversify their crops by investing in livestock and orchards in addition to cotton. Farmers were encouraged to learn trades to supplement their incomes. Urging a "partial reconstruction of life and manners," Washington demanded that farmers strengthen their schools and churches. Farmers participated in informal sessions, sharing experiences and setting goals. Authors recited stories of adversity to inspire participants, who repeated the information to neighbors, an early form of extension work.

In the *Declarations of the First Tuskegee Negro Conference*, a group statement assured that "we believe we can become prosperous, intelligent, and independent where we are" and that "we urge that all strive in every way to cultivate the good feeling and friendship of those about us in all that relates to our mutual elevation." Enthusiastically, Washington wrote his Hampton mentor, Samuel

Chapman Armstrong, about the farmers: "they wanted light, and they all realized that education was their only salvation."

Although many rural residents were suspicious of the annual conference, by 1894, 1,000 participants attended, touring the campus and listening to lectures about health, sanitation, and parasites by experts, such as George Washington Carver, with whom they could consult on individual concerns. The conferences also addressed racial issues, including discrimination faced by black railroad passengers and lynching, and compiled statistics of such incidents.

Women farmers spoke at the conferences and also met separately, and black leaders encouraged them to improve their homes while their husbands worked in the fields. Satellite conferences and special meetings for teachers and businessmen were developed, and African American leaders in other states modeled conferences after the Tuskegee example.

After Washington's death in 1916, the Tuskegee Conference remained the "same potent agency." Community leaders assured farmers that the conference would continue "so that rural life may be richer, finer, more remunerative and satisfying. This spirit of the conference is permanent." The fiftieth Tuskegee Conference occurred in 1940, the same year that the first All Institute Conference was held. World War II interrupted agricultural and educational programs, which were resumed eventually. Based on the tradition of the Tuskegee Conference, Tuskegee University currently hosts a variety of conferences, discussing such topics as agricultural extension, veterinary medicine, and biotechnology.

**FURTHER READINGS**

Crosby, Earl William. "Building the Country Home: The Black County Agent System, 1906–1940." Ph.D. diss., Miami University, Oxford, Ohio, 1977.

Du Bois, W. E. B. "Results of the Ten Tuskegee Conferences." *Harper's Weekly* 45 (June 22, 1901): 641.

Harlan, Louis R., ed. *The Booker T. Washington Papers.* 14 vols. Urbana: University of Illinois Press, 1972–1981.

Neverdon-Morton, Cynthia. *Afro-American Women of the South and the Advancement of the Race, 1895–1925.* Knoxville: University of Tennessee Press, 1989.

Tuskegee Institute News Clipping File, Tuskegee University Archives.

Washington, Booker T. "How I Came to Call the First Negro Conference." *A.M.E. Church Review* 15 (April 1899), 802–808.

*Elizabeth D. Schafer*

## Twelve Knights of Tabor

The Twelve Knights of Tabor was an all-black fraternal organization that provided benevolent and financial programs for African Americans living in the South and Midwest after the Civil War. The Knights of Tabor officially began in 1872 in Independence, Missouri, when founder Moses Dickinson called together friends and family committed to building an African American institution that cared for members in sickness and distress. The organization grew quickly and boasted a membership of over 20,000 by the 1910s; its numbers dropped soon thereafter, though, as black insurance companies and banks offered similar financial benefits. Still, during the decades of legal segregation after Reconstruction, the Knights of Tabor, along with other black fraternal orders, offered black men and women distinctive opportunities for social and material advancement.

The rise of the Twelve Knights of Tabor depended on the lifelong work and vision of Moses Dickinson. Dickinson was born a free man in 1824 in Cincinnati, Ohio. One of nine children, he grew up as a member of the AME (African Methodist Episcopal) Church and as a boy was christened by Paul Quinn, a future bishop of the church. He learned to read and write by attending the local public grammar school. Because both of his parents died before his thirteenth birthday, Dickinson was forced at a young age to support himself and his siblings. He quickly learned the trade of the barber and became quite successful at it. Yet his real talents lay in organizing.

During the antebellum era, as a frequent traveler on the steamboats that ran the Mississippi River, Dickinson saw firsthand the widespread cruelties of slavery and dreamed of someday abolishing them. In his twenties and thirties, Dickinson apparently formed the Knights of Liberty, a loosely structured club composed of small, secret groups of black men throughout the free and slave states who were bent on ending the practice of human bondage. Wherever he visited, he clandestinely gathered men willing to aid runaways and, when the day came, to fight for freedom for all blacks. When that day came, in April 1861, Dickinson and his colleagues enlisted in the Union effort.

After the Civil War, Dickinson extended his knack for organizing and emerged as a leader of African American Republicans in Missouri. He served as a delegate to every Republican state convention from 1864 to 1878 and as Elector-at Large on the Grant ticket in 1872. He also rose to prominence as a civic leader. In the late 1870s, when thousands of blacks fled the post-Reconstruction South for the port city of St. Louis, Dickinson was president of the Refugee Relief Board based in that city. He secured and distributed thousands of dollars in supplies and provisions to the wayfarers, enabling many to continue their journey into Kansas, Nebraska, and Colorado.

Building on his experience in politics and local government, Dickinson founded the Twelve Knights of Tabor as an institution to enhance liberty and opportunity for ex-slaves. In choosing the name of the new organization, he meant to recall the original twelve Knights of Liberty and their commitment to racial achievement. The name also reflected the religious sensibilities of Dickinson and his followers. Dickinson earned his license to preach in the AME Church in 1867 and pastored a church throughout the postbellum era. He saw the Twelve Knights of Tabor as an extension of his work as a church leader dedicated to ameliorating the needs of his flock. Indeed, he chose the name Tabor to evoke the courage displayed by the soldiers of Israel battling the army of Sisera in the Old Testament. The Israelites, despite being outnumbered twenty to one, won the fight and their freedom from bondage.

As in his own AME church, Dickinson set the bar high for membership in the Knights of Tabor. Candidates were required to join a local Evangelical church, forswear alcohol, secure a basic education, and buy property, if financially possible. The act of acquiring property, counseled Dickinson, made a man or woman a frugal and temperate citizen. The organization was open to both sexes, though each typically met apart from the other.

No doubt a major attraction of the Knights of Tabor was its rich life of pageantry and ritual. During the late nineteenth and early twentieth centuries, when the politics and terror of white supremacy were at their zenith, the Knights of Tabor offered a world of symbolic meaning to members. Holidays of particular importance to African Americans, such as Emancipation Day, were celebrated with public parades and picnics. Members marched in uniforms ablaze with medals indicating rank and role within the local lodge and often performed drills with military precision. Events of a less festive nature, such as a monthly meeting or a funeral of a member, were organized with an equal degree of ritual drama. Guidebooks outlined the particular uniform and ceremony according to the event and left no detail to the imagination. The greeting, handshake, prayer, and seating assignments all were tightly regulated by custom.

Knights also enjoyed special opportunities for financial security and advancement. Membership dues underwrote a general fund that acted as a type of insurance policy: Sick members and the family of deceased members drew on the fund for their own support. Dues also supported small loans to members in need of financial backing. The attraction of the material advantages offered by the Knights of Tabor, and its overall total membership, however, lessened in the face of competition from new black financial institutions that mushroomed in the 1920s. But during its peak years, from 1875 to 1920, the Twelve Knights of Tabor was a popular avenue for the development of African American society.

**FURTHER READINGS**

Dickinson, Moses. *A Manual of the Knights of Tabor, and Daughters of the Tabernacle, including the Ceremonies of the Order, Constitutions, Installations, Dedications, and Funerals, with Forms and the Taborian Drill and Tactics.* St. Louis, Mo.: G. I. Jim, 1871.

———. *Internal 777—Order of Twelve—333 of Knights and Daughters of Tabor: Taborian Constitution of the Several Departments.* St. Louis, Mo.: A. R. Fleming & Co., 1896.

———. *Manual of the International Order of Twelve of Knights and Daughters of Tabor, Containing General Laws, Regulations, Ceremonies, Drill and a Taborian Lexicon.* 3rd ed. St. Louis, Mo.: A. R. Fleming & Co., 1903.

Du Bois, W. E. B. *Economic Cooperation Among Negro Americans.* Atlanta: The Atlanta University Press, 1907.

Palmer, Edward. "Negro Secret Societies." *Social Forces* 23 (December 1944): 207–212.

*John M. Giggie*

# U

## Union League

The Union League, created in 1863, was the first African American–mass-based political organization. It originated in the border slave states among white unionists at the outset of the Civil War and then spread north during the war and south during Reconstruction. The league encouraged freed people to use political action to achieve economic and social improvement. It met violent resistance from conservative whites, spurring its relatively rapid decline after 1868.

In 1861, white unionists in Missouri, Kentucky, Maryland, and eastern Tennessee, hoping to counter the efforts of secessionist public officials, formed secret, oath-bound societies to aid the Union cause. Although not Republicans, they supported Lincoln during the war and generally endorsed radical war measures such as emancipation and the creation of African American regiments. In 1862, a Tennessee member introduced the league to Republicans in Pekin, Illinois. It spread slowly until midwestern newspaper editors and governors, in the wake of Republican losses in the midterm elections of 1862, adopted it as a way to reenergize the party. Meanwhile in eastern cities such as Boston, Philadelphia, and New York, patriotic members of the elite abandoned social clubs patronized by war critics and founded Union League clubs, which raised money for new regiments and the publication of prowar pamphlets. A meeting in Cleveland in May 1863 adopted a common constitution and ritual, creating the Union League of America. James M. Edmunds, a friend of Lincoln from Illinois who held a patronage appointment in the Land Office, became president, operating the organization from his Washington office. The league distributed copies of the ritual, constitution, and Republican literature, but its pleadings for chapter reports reveals

a decentralized organization that could not enforce ideological consistency. Leagues formed among soldiers and sailors, African Americans, and ethnic groups such as Germans and, in some instances, moved beyond Lincoln's positions on confiscation of rebel property and race relations. Some leagues opposed colonization, encouraged the vigorous confiscation of slaves, and favored the use of black officers; other units took less radical positions. The league claimed over 700,000 members representing 4,554 councils in late 1863.

Secretary of the Treasury Salmon P. Chase, a radical who favored franchisement of African Americans, sent numerous treasury agents who were league members to the South during the war. Their efforts to establish new, usually segregated leagues among southern loyalists in anticipation of Reconstruction were assisted by military officers, black soldiers, missionaries, and agents of the newly established Freedmen's Bureau. Particularly in southern cities, African Americans adopted the leagues as a way to promote equal rights. White loyalists, however, often preferred disfranchisement of Confederates and military occupation to African American voting. The level of league organization varied considerably among states. In April 1867 with new legislation franchising freedmen passing in Congress, the league sent Thomas Conway, a New Yorker and longtime freedman's advocate, south with the goal of introducing the league to every southern county. Arguing that the league would promote intelligent voting, respect for laws, and middle-class virtues of order and sobriety, league leaders hoped to blunt white opposition.

Paid agents, black and white, blanketed the South. The league mushroomed in rural areas among the African American population. Assembling secretly at member's homes, churches, or even outdoors under the protection of armed guards, members prayed, sang patriotic songs, and took oaths to support the constitution and vote for candidates loyal to the union and the constitution. Leaders read aloud from Republican publications, inviting discussion of party principles. Members raised issues of concern to them: the building of schools and churches, raising money for the sick, acquiring land, securing a fair division of crops, suing employers, preventing economic retaliation against political activists, and securing fair treatment from the courts. They circulated petitions, organized strikes and boycotts, recommended candidates for office, and planned campaign rallies. Although most local black leagues had white leaders, increasingly African Americans, both from the North and the South, assumed these roles. A few groups were integrated racially and shared leadership roles.

The league's secrecy enabled its opponents to spread false and inflammatory reports about its activities. White terrorist organizations such as the Ku Klux Klan targeted league members during the 1868 presidential election. Newly established Republican state governments considered party, not league, meetings preferable and safer. Although local leagues continued for years, their heyday was past. With the resignation of Edmunds as president in 1869, the national league moved to Pennsylvania. No longer a needed organizational base for Republicans, it declined rapidly in membership. A few local groups, most notably the exclusive urban social clubs, survived. The league's contribution to ending plantation agriculture through organized resistance outshines its efforts at political mobilization as its legacy in the South.

**FURTHER READINGS**

Abbott, Richard H. *The Republican Party and the South.* Chapel Hill: University of North Carolina Press, 1986.

Fitzgerald, Michael W. *The Union League Movement in the Deep South: Politics and Agricultural Change During Reconstruction.* Baton Rouge: Louisiana State University Press, 1989.

*Phyllis Field*

# Union of Black Clergy and Laity

*See* Union of Black Episcopalians.

# Union of Black Episcopalians

Founded in 1968 as the Union of Black Clergy and Laity (UBCL), and given its present name in 1971, the Union of Black Episcopalians (UBE) continues the race work of earlier Episcopalian organizations like the Protestant Episcopal Society for Promoting the Extension of the Church Among Colored People and its female auxiliary, the Good Angels; the Convocation of Colored Clergy, which later became the Conference of Church Workers Among Colored People; and the Episcopal Society for Cultural and Racial Unity. Almost from the inception of the Episcopal Church in 1789, black Christians have provided active leadership in the church's daily life and mission. The UBE is the latest, most visible incarnation of the strong black Episcopalian presence that began with Absalom Jones, who established the St. Thomas African Episcopal Church of Philadelphia in 1792 and became the first black ordained Episcopalian priest in 1804. By the late 1960s, the growth of black consciousness and the emergence of black nationalism was also reflected in rising separatist sentiments within the church.

African American members began to hold their own meetings to air grievances, map strategies, and organize for a fuller involvement in Episcopal life. Affronts like the 1967 General Convention failure of white clergy and laity to seek the advice and participation of their black counterparts in addressing urban justice issues spoke to the second-class status and low visibility of black efforts within the church. That year, the General Convention Special Program, urged into existence by the presiding bishop to express the church's concern for social justice, gave money to secular self-help organizations instead of the African American ministries working in urban settings. In response, a small group of blacks within the church formed the UBCL in 1968. The UBCL's primary goal was to increase black involvement in the Episcopalian Church, especially in decision-making positions. For example, it attempted to place a black priest on the staff of the General Convention Special Program and in 1973 was instrumental in the creation of the Black Desk (Episcopal Commission for Black Ministries).

With over forty-five chapters and interest groups, the UBE maintains a strong presence throughout the United States and the Caribbean and is working to strengthen its membership base in Latin America and Africa. One of the primary ways in which the UBE demonstrates its interest in youth development is through its ongoing efforts to secure support for three predominantly black Episcopal colleges: St. Paul's in Lawrenceville, Virginia; St. Augustine's in Raleigh, North Carolina; and Voorhees in Denmark, South Carolina. The UBE holds its annual three-day meeting in late June. Every three years the location of the National Executive Office changes when a new president is elected. The current coordinator of the Office of Black Ministries is Reverend Lynn A. Collins in New York City.

**FURTHER READINGS**

Office of Black Ministries. *The Union of Black Episcopalians: Seeds of Healing, Signs of Hope.* N.p.: n.d.

Randolph, Michael P. G. G. *Absalom Jones.* N.p.: Union of Black Episcopalians, n.d.

Rodman, Edward. *Let There Be Peace Among Us: A Story of the Union of Black Episcopalians.* Boston: n.p, 1989.

*Stephen Davenport*

## United African Nationalist Movement

*See* Universal African Nationalist Movement.

## United Auto Workers: Fair Practices and Anti-Discrimination Department

In 1944, the executive board of the United Auto Workers (UAW)–Congress of Industrial Organizations (CIO) created the Fair Practices and Anti-Discrimination Department, also known as the Fair Employment Practices Department (FEPD), to investigate charges of racial discrimination on the shop floor in UAW locals. Divisive racial politics came to the fore within the UAW during World War II. A black caucus proposed that the UAW create a "Minorities Department" headed by a black worker, who would also become a member of the board of directors of the UAW International. The department grew out of these grievances and became an arena for UAW's black activists under the guidance of its first director, George Crockett.

When Walter Reuther became president of the UAW in 1946, he replaced Crockett with William Oliver, who had no political influence within the black community. Oliver directed the department for over twenty-five years, focusing the efforts of the FEPD in two specific directions. The department operated as the representative of the UAW to the national civil rights community—the National Association for the Advancement of Colored People (NAACP), the National Urban League (NUL), and liberal politicians. It also was responsible for gathering complaints about job discrimination from black UAW members. However, the department did not have much authority to correct or even address grievances. The FEPD could not initiate its own investigations and could only act on formal complaints brought by the rank and file. After a complaint was processed by the FEPD, it was transferred to the regional director for investigating antidiscrimination. The only way the FEPD could carry out its own investigation was if the regional director did nothing. Thus, there were limitations to policy changes that the FEPD could implement due to the department's structure. The department continued to exist into the late 1960s, serving as a means to process African American grievances.

**FURTHER READINGS**

Boyle, Kevin. *The UAW and the Heyday of American Liberalism, 1945–1968.* Ithaca, N.Y.: Cornell University Press, 1995.

Foner, Philip S. *Organized Labor and the Black Worker, 1619–1981.* New York: International Publishers, 1974.

Geschwender, James A. *Class, Race, and Worker Insurgency: The League of Revolutionary Black Workers.* New York: Cambridge University Press, 1977.

Jacobson, Julius, ed. *The Negro and the American Labor Movement.* New York: Anchor Books, 1968.

Lichtenstein, Nelson. *Walter Reuther: The Most Dangerous Man in Detroit.* New York: HarperCollins, 1995.

Ross, Arthur M., and Herbert Hill, eds. *Employment, Race, and Poverty.* New York: Harcourt, Brace & World, 1967.

UAW Fair Practices Department. United Auto Workers Papers. Walter P. Reuther Library. Archives of Labor and Urban Affairs. Wayne State University, Detroit, Michigan.

*Beth Tompkins Bates*

## United Black Christians, United Church of Christ Inc.

*See* Ministers for Racial and Social Justice.

## United Black Churchmen, United Church of Christ Inc.

*See* Ministers for Racial and Social Justice.

## United Brothers of Friendship and Sisters of the Mysterious Ten

The United Brothers of Friendship and Sisters of the Mysterious Ten began as a local benevolent society in Louisville, Kentucky, in 1861; or, according to a less persuasive alternative account, in 1854. Both slaves and free blacks participated, most of them young. After the interruption of the Civil War, the society was reorganized in 1868 under the leadership of a new recruit, William H.

Gibson. A Maryland-born free black, Gibson had taught many of the early members of the United Brothers of Friendship in the day and night schools sponsored by the AME (African Methodist Episcopal) Church. Subsequently he was active in Republican politics and held patronage positions such as mail agent. Gibson was the first Grand Master of the grand lodge of Kentucky, established in 1871, which incorporated other previously separate societies. After considerable controversy over the wisdom of converting a benevolent society into a secret ritual society and squabbles between the grand lodges in Kentucky and Missouri, a national grand lodge was organized in 1876. Gibson was elected Grand Master. In 1878 a fourth degree in the United Brothers' hierarchy of honors was created, the Knights of Friendship. Its ritual was based on the Old Testament story of David and Jonathan. The Knights of Friendship operated quasimilitary "camps," with drill exercises and uniforms.

Also in 1878, the United Brothers created a women's auxiliary, the Sisters of the Mysterious Ten, superceding earlier unofficial auxiliaries. To supervise the sisters three males belonged to each "ladies' temple." The woman heading a temple was styled a "princess." Although contrary to the constitution of the United Brothers, men and women sometimes were mixed in the lodges of the male organization. Gibson recognized that in northern cities such as Indianapolis, Cincinnati, and Chicago "our greatest support was derived from the women." In 1892 the order established a widows' and orphans' home in Kentucky.

Although a few whites allegedly belonged to the order, its official history boasted that the United Brothers of Friendship was "a Negro Order" unrelated to any white organization. Despite the fact that Gibson was himself both a Mason and an Odd Fellow, he implicitly criticized these prestigious black fraternal orders for their white connections. Gibson also acknowledged criticisms that religious people raised against fraternal societies in general, that lodge meetings kept members out too late and that Sunday funerals, accompanied by bands, were unseemly. He went on to claim that the Sons of Friendship were solving the "Negro Problem" through "education, wealth, moral and Christian influence."

By 1892 the United Brothers of Friendship and the Sisters of the Mysterious Ten claimed 100,000 members; 30,000 were in the original grand lodge of Kentucky. In the early twentieth century Texas stood out as a stronghold that produced many national officeholders. The *Negro Year Book* for 1913 reported that the Texas grand lodge had over $40,000 in its treasury and that the Texas lodges collectively owned $200,000 in property. The United Brothers published several newspapers such as the Sedalia, Missouri, *Searchlight*. The United Brothers of Friendship and the Sisters of the Mysterious Ten seem to have been a casualty of the Great Depression and World War II. No lodges are known to exist today.

**FURTHER READINGS**

Gibson, William H. *History of the United Brothers of Friendship and Sisters of the Mysterious Ten.* Louisville: Bradley & Gilbert, 1897; rpt., Freeport, N.Y.: Books for Libraries, 1971.

Stevens, Albert C. *Cyclopaedia of Fraternities.* Rev. ed. New York: E. B. Treat, 1907; rpt., Detroit: Gale, 1966.

*David M. Fahey*

## United Colored Democracy

United Colored Democracy (UCD) was a late nineteenth-century political club allied with the Democratic party in New York City. Black New Yorkers had long supported the Republican party in the city, but the Republican hierarchy did not reciprocate, assuming that blacks would always vote Republican in gratitude for the party's role in ending slavery. In 1897, James C. Carr, a lawyer, and Edward Lee, a bellman, founded UCD to prove the Republican party wrong. Carr had expected an appointment as assistant district attorney for his work on behalf of the GOP in the 1896 elections. When the appointment was not forthcoming, Carr and Lee approached Tammany Hall and pledged UCD's support of the city's Democratic party. Tammany responded by making UCD the party's official representative to New York's black citizens.

While most of Tammany Hall was organized by voting precinct, UCD was responsible for the entire black population of the city. As a result, the leaders of UCD obtained significant jobs through the party machine. Carr got his appointment as assistant district attorney, and Tammany appointed Carr's successor at UCD, Ferdinand Q. Morton, to the city's Civil Service Commission. But while UCD worked well for its leaders, its citywide organization kept rank-and-file members out of the precinct and district level jobs that were Tammany's most common form of patronage.

UCD's broad role in city politics also kept it from effectively serving the parts of the city where blacks resided. In the 1920s, black activists tried to increase the number of black doctors and nurses at Harlem Hospital, the source of health care for most of the city's black residents. The hospital stood in an area controlled by a white Tammany district leader, who would not support the proposed changes. UCD was powerless to sway Tammany's decision. Nor was the UCD more effective than the Republican party at getting blacks elected to office. Few blacks, Republican or Democratic, won any elections until the 1920s. Then, both parties had some success, though the Democrats were limited by the fact that most blacks continued to vote Republican at the national and state levels, even if they supported Democrats in the city.

Ferdinand Q. Morton was responsible for much of UCD's success in the 1920s. Morton was an ambitious man, an excellent organizer, and a good speaker. Under his leadership black Democrats won spots on the council of aldermen and the state assembly. But Morton was mercurial and authoritarian, a fact many black Democrats resented. State-led corruption investigations weakened Tammany in the 1920s. Morton saw that power in the city was moving toward the Republicans. When Fiorello La Guardia was elected mayor in 1932, he promised Morton reappointment to the Civil Service Commission if he switched parties. Morton agreed, and with his defection, UCD ceased to be an effective voice on behalf of New York City's black Democrats. That there were black Democrats at all, though, was a result of the efforts of United Colored Democracy.

**FURTHER READINGS**

Hamilton, Charles V. *Adam Clayton Powell, Jr.: The Political Biography of an American Dilemma*. New York: Atheneum, 1991.

Osofsky, Gilbert. *Harlem: The Making of a Ghetto, Negro New York, 1890–1930*. Chicago: Ivan R. Dee, 1996.

*Gary Daynes*

## United Golfers Association

Golfers from Washington, D.C., organized the United Golfers Association (UGA) as the Colored Golfers Association in Stowe, Massachusetts, in 1925. One year later, the group adopted its current name. Dr. George Adams was the UGA's first permanent president.

Beginning in the late eighteenth century, when golf came to America, African Americans were virtually excluded from the game, a pattern that continued well into the twentieth century. Because of Jim Crow laws and the "apartheid-like structures" that existed in most sports during the first decades of the twentieth century, many

black golfers were forced to travel to the North to have a chance to play golf. In light of these difficulties, UGA organizers staged many of the group's initial competitions in New England, hoping to provide African Americans with an increased opportunity to play and participate in tournaments in a less racially restrictive environment. Organized through regional groups and competitions, the UGA quickly became both a sporting and social venue for many middle-class blacks.

In 1925, the first UGA championship took place at the Shady Rest Country Club in New Jersey. While women were allowed to compete in UGA events at this time, the organization's membership was initially all male. The winners of the first competition were Henry Jackson of Washington, D.C., and Marie Thompson of Chicago, Illinois. The UGA championship grew into the Annual Negro Open, which was the most popular of all UGA activities and attracted golfers from throughout the United States. Other early players included Robert "Pat" Ball, Walter Speedy, Laura Osgood, Lucy Williams, Ella Able, Melanie Moye, and Cleo Ball.

While the UGA opened its doors to all golfers, the golf world was not as gracious. Initially, the Professional Golfers Association (PGA), founded in 1916, did not officially discriminate against blacks. In the 1920s, Dewey Brown became the first black member of the PGA. In 1943, however, the PGA amended its constitution to exclude African Americans. This helped to strengthen the UGA as black golfers sought to play without discrimination. The UGA was an all-male club until the late 1930s when several women, led by Anna Mae Robinson, requested membership in the group. These women, members of the Chicago Women's Golf Club, were successful and sent representatives to the 1939 UGA national meeting in Los Angeles. A year later, the women hosted the annual UGA championship. However, the UGA was unable to assist women in breaking gender barriers at local clubs. Women also remained at the periphery of the organization.

The UGA was most prosperous between 1946 and 1961, when several UGA stars were at the top of their games. For example, Charlie Stifford, who was the first African American to win a major PGA event at the 1967 Hartford Open, won five consecutive National Negro Open titles from 1952 to 1956. UGA clubs tried to maintain the UGA's popularity by attracting proathletes from other sports. Joe Louis, the heavyweight boxing champion, played golf for the UGA and helped finance the career of golfer Ted Rhodes. However, when the PGA relaxed its racial discrimination policy, the UGA began to falter as black golfers opted to play in the newly opened tournaments. UGA membership continued to decline as both the PGA and golf courses across the nation relaxed their segregationist practices. By 1975, the UGA no longer sponsored professional competitions. Throughout its existence the UGA provided a sense of racial solidarity, protected black golfers from "the hostility of mainstream golf," and assisted in the goal of putting an end to racial discrimination in the game.

**FURTHER READINGS**

Ashe, Arthur R., Jr. *A Hard Road to Glory: A History of the African-American Athlete Since 1946*, vols. 2 and 3. New York: Amistad Press, Inc., 1988.

Londino, Lawrence. "United Golfers Association." In *Encyclopedia of African-American Culture and History*, vol. 5. Ed. Jack Salzman et al. New York: Simon & Schuster, 1996.

"Remembering the Old UGA Tour." *Ebony* (September 1997): 138.

Sinnette, Calvin H. *Forbidden Fairways: African Americans and the Game of Golf.* Chelsea, Mich.: Sleeping Bear Press, 1998.

*Alexandra Epstein*

## United Lutherans for Black Concerns

*See* African American Lutheran Association.

## United Negro and Allied Veterans of America, Inc.

Composed largely of black and white ex-GIs, the United Negro and Allied Veterans of America, Inc. (UNAVA) was founded in Chicago, Illinois, in 1946, under the auspices of the Provisional Committee for a National Veterans' Organization. The UNAVA was a collective response to the growing activism among black veterans and the social, economic, and political discrimination they faced during the immediate postwar period. Organized by former soldiers and members of the Communist Party, the UNAVA employed a wide array of tactics including mass mobilization, protest politics, and legal strategy to assist black veterans in their demands for equal housing, employment, medical care, and educational opportunities under the GI Bill of Rights.

The UNAVA first convened on April 6–7, 1946, at Dusable High School on Chicago's South Side under the leadership of white organizers such as Bertram Alves, a

former *PM* magazine reporter; Walter Bemstein, a former *Yank* correspondent; and Alan Morrison, a *Stars and Stripes* staff writer; as well as black luminaries including George B. Murphy Jr., former secretary of the National Negro Congress; Mercer Ellington, son of the famous musician Duke Ellington; and Jacob Lawrence, a noted New York City visual artist. Over 500 black and white veterans representing various organizations, including trade unions, church groups, fraternal organizations, and political factions, gathered for the opening session. Among the prominent black political, civic, and religious figures who were elected to regional leadership positions were Kenneth Kennedy of the Southern Negro Youth Congress; Chicago lawyer Ulysses S. Keys; Chicago AME (African Methodist Episcopal) Church minister Charles T. Watkins; ex-Women's Army Corps officers Ruth Freeman and Catherine Godfrey; and former Ninety-second Infantry Division veteran Howard Johnson. The UNAVA pledged to advance racial equality and work for economic democracy and lasting peace.

A year later, the UNAVA held its first constitutional convention in New York City, passing resolutions that called for federal legislation to help facilitate the filing of claims of black veterans returning to the South, the termination of Veterans Administration policies that prevented black veterans from securing full benefits under the GI Bill, and permanent federal fair employment practices legislation. A part of the UNAVA resolutions was implemented when Congress, at the behest of Representative Vito Mercantonio of New York, passed legislation extending by an additional year the filing deadline for thousands of veterans who had not yet applied for their terminal leave pay under the Armed Forces Leave Act.

In its few years of existence, the UNAVA, headquartered on New York City's Lenox Avenue, claimed more than 10,000 members organized in forty-one chapters in twenty-one states, including South Carolina, Texas, Alabama, Georgia, and Louisiana. By the end of 1946, the organization had attracted national attention as a result of its efforts to assist African American veterans in their fight against housing and employment discrimination and cases involving the abrogation of their civil rights and the denial of veterans benefits. In September, hundreds of UNAVA members traveled to Washington, D.C., to stage public demonstrations demanding anti-lynching legislation, the repeal of the poll tax, and the removal of Mississippi Democratic senator Theodore Bilbo. Perhaps the most prominent UNAVA campaigns were the organization's demonstrations in front of Chicago mayor Edward Kelly's office, requesting an end to the white mob violence that black veterans and their families faced when they attempted to move into the Airport Homes Housing Project, and its collaborative work with Illinois Democratic congressman William Dawson to secure federal housing fair practices legislation for the state.

However, the anti-Communist hysteria and state repression of the postwar period severely crippled UNAVA's protest strategies. In late 1947, a loyalty board, created by President Harry S. Truman, placed the veterans' group on its list of subversive organizations. As a result, UNAVA members found it increasingly difficult to carry out the organization's program. By 1949, the UNAVA had folded; however, much of its membership remained active participants in the modern civil rights movement.

### FURTHER READINGS

Horne, Gerald. *Black and Red: W. E. B. Du Bois and the Afro-American Response to the Cold War, 1944–1963.* Albany: State University of New York Press, 1986.

Jefferson, Robert F. "Making the Men of the 93rd: African American Servicemen in the Years of the Great Depression and the Second World War, 1935–1947." Ph.D. diss., University of Michigan, 1995.

Johnson, Howard. "The Negro Veteran Fights for Freedom!" *Political Affairs* 26, 5 (May 1947): 429–440.

Kelley, Robin D. G. *Race Rebels: Culture, Politics, and the Black Working Class.* New York: Free Press, 1994.

Record, Wilson. *The Negro and the Communist Party.* Chapel Hill: University of North Carolina Press, 1951.

*Robert F. Jefferson*

## United Negro Bus Strike Committee

*See* Greater New York Coordinating Committee for Employment.

## United Negro College Fund

In 1944, the presidents of twenty-seven historically black colleges and universities founded the United Negro College Fund (UNCF) to combine their fund-raising efforts and to dispense funds equitably. Based in New York, the UNCF initially raised funds for the schools' operating expenses, including teacher salaries, scholarships, and educational equipment. Today, the organization also manages endowment funds and finances the construction, expansion, and maintenance of physical plants of its forty-one member institutions.

Most black colleges and universities were founded in the late nineteenth and early twentieth centuries in response to black exclusion from white schools and as a result of black efforts to define their own educational destiny. They provided African Americans with access to postsecondary education at a time when Jim Crow laws and customs severely limited their educational opportunities. These institutions depended heavily on charitable donations from African American supporters, white philanthropists, and black institutions such as churches. By the early 1940s, however, the Great Depression and wartime shortages had reduced the schools' financial resources so drastically that most black institutions were on the brink of collapse.

In 1943, in response to the financial crisis, the president of Tuskegee Institute, Frederick Douglass Patterson, published an article in the *Pittsburgh Courier*, a leading black newspaper. Patterson, who received his Ph.D. in agriculture from Cornell University in 1932, had joined the faculty of Tuskegee Institute in 1928, and became its president in 1935. Concerned about the depletion of funds, Patterson called for a meeting of the presidents of the nation's black colleges and universities to discuss joint efforts to ensure the schools' continued operation. Patterson argued that a central charitable organization was needed to conduct fund-raising campaigns in order to provide financial support for the schools. The presidents of twenty-seven historically black colleges and universities responded to Patterson's call for action and founded the UNCF. Donations from the Julius Rosenwald Fund and the Rockefeller-based General Education Board assisted the founders in their initial organizational efforts.

In 1944, the UNCF's first executive director, William Trent, a manager trained at the University of Pennsylvania's Wharton School, inaugurated the group's first national campaign. Exceeding all expectations, the campaign raised $765,000, considerably more than all of the black colleges combined had raised during the previous year. Within a few years, the organization grew rapidly and hired a permanent staff to oversee operation of the fund. In 1951, the UNCF began to expand its efforts to address the need for endowment funds, new campus buildings, and maintenance of existing structures. Over the next four years, a separate capital campaign, the National Mobilization of Resources, raised $18 million with the help of John D. Rockefeller. In 1963, with the backing of President John F. Kennedy and the Ford Foundation, the UNCF launched another capital campaign, raising $30 million in a single year.

Despite the tremendous successes of the UNCF's fund-raising efforts, black colleges faced another severe financial crisis during the 1960s. By 1964, implementation of the Supreme Court's 1954 decision to desegregate all educational institutions forced black colleges to compete with predominantly white universities for students. As growing numbers of African American students entered schools that previously had denied them admission, black colleges and universities lost revenues generated by tuition. Moreover, the turbulence created by civil rights protests frightened away many potential donors and funding levels plummeted. Finally, as white schools not only began to admit black students but also started to recruit black faculty, many contemporaries began to question the continued need for black colleges and universities.

In the face of school desegregation and the resulting decline of enrollments and diminished budgets of UNCF member institutions, Trent resigned and the organization embarked on an effort to redefine its mission. Under the leadership of Patterson, who served as UNCF president from 1964–1966, and his six successors—Steven J. Wright (1966–1969), Henry V. Richardson (1969–1970), Vernon E. Jordan (1970–1972), Arthur A. Fletcher (1972–1973), Christopher Edley (1973–1990), and William Gray III (1991– )—the organization launched an aggressive campaign to raise funds and promote the continued need for black colleges. In 1972, the UNCF became a member of the Advertising Council and started to utilize television and radio advertisements to appeal for funds and to emphasize the importance of maintaining black schools despite the desegregation of public education. Beginning in 1980, for example, the UNCF launched "The Lou Rawls Parade of Stars," an annual fund-raising telethon. The television and radio campaigns increased public awareness of the UNCF and helped popularize its now famous slogan, "A mind is a terrible thing to waste."

While the desegregation of American schools threatened the existence of historically black colleges and universities, the UNCF succeeded in maintaining and strengthening black educational institutions. UNCF president Patterson designed a College Endowment Funding Program to reduce college dependence on federal funding for permanent expenses such as maintenance of grounds and buildings, equipment, and salaries. Determined to fight for their survival, many of the black schools joined the UNCF during the 1970s and 1980s, increasing the organization's membership to forty-one colleges. Under the guidance and leadership of Christopher Edley, who served as UNCF president from 1973 until 1990, the

UNCF's annual income rose from $11.1 million to $48.1 million. In addition, the UNCF's 1978 Capital Resources Development Program raised over $60 million for its member institutions. After the 1990 departure of Edley, U.S. House majority whip William Gray III left his seat in Congress to assume the UNCF presidency in 1991. In the same year, the UNCF initiated a drive to raise $250 million by the year 2000. In the first year alone, the "Campaign 2000" raised $86 million with the support of President George Bush and a $50 million gift from media magnate Walter Annenberg.

For more than fifty years, the UNCF has provided many black educational institutions with financial stability, ensuring the survival of most of them. While the UNCF continues to be the major source of outside funding for historically black colleges, its appeals to donors across the political spectrum has garnered criticisms from several quarters. UNCF supporters, however, argue that black colleges are an important educational alternative to students seeking higher education. While some of the UNCF member schools have developed sufficient endowments to place them on solid financial ground, many of the institutions continue to be plagued by a lack of financial resources. Whether they are financially weak or stable, the UNCF has been a key factor in the survival of historically black colleges and universities.

**FURTHER READING**

Patterson, Frederick Douglass. *Chronicles of Faith: The Autobiography of Frederick Douglass Patterson.* Tuscaloosa: University of Alabama Press, 1991.

*Tiffany Ruby Patterson*

## United Slaves

*See* US.

## United States Commission on Civil Rights

Since its creation in 1957 the United States Commission on Civil Rights has served as a watchdog of the federal government to ensure implementation and enforcement of civil rights laws. As one former staff director noted, the commission has been "the duly appointed conscience of the nation." The commission has published more than 40 statutory reports and approximately 160 other studies on racial matters. During the early years of the civil rights movement, the commission proved to be a valuable ally to African Americans as it helped expose discrimination and prodded federal leaders to take decisive action against Jim Crow laws. Once those victories had been won, however, the commission's effectiveness diminished and it became the source of intense partisan fighting.

Though the commission was created by the 1957 Civil Rights Act, its origins lay in the Truman administration. In 1946, following several incidents of racial violence in the South, President Harry S. Truman had formed the President's Committee on Civil Rights. In the following year the committee issued its report *To Secure These Rights*, which included a call for the creation of a civil rights commission. In 1949, led by Senator Hubert Humphrey of Minnesota, liberals in Congress introduced a bill that provided for the establishment of such a commission. Civil rights advocates hoped that the agency would gather facts about the extent of racial injustice and pave the way for more substantive civil rights legislation. Meanwhile, southern Democrats objected on grounds that a commission represented unwarranted federal intrusion into "local" matters. The bill attracted little support on Capitol Hill because a coalition of southern Democrats and Republicans kept it bottled up in committee. Prospects for the legislation improved by the mid-1950s, when white southerners waged a "massive resistance" campaign to defy the Supreme Court's school desegregation ruling in *Brown v. Board of Education* and increased efforts by African Americans to register to vote. President Dwight D. Eisenhower endorsed the commission proposal in 1956, and Congress included it in the civil rights law it passed the following year.

The commission had limited powers. A bipartisan, independent agency that was to operate only for two years, it originally consisted of six members chosen by the president and confirmed by the Senate. Congress authorized the commission to investigate allegations that citizens were being denied the right to vote, to gather information on denial of equal protection of the law, and to evaluate the civil rights policies of the federal government. It also had the power to subpoena witnesses, issue reports, and make recommendations. However, the commission lacked any enforcement powers. Eisenhower's nominees included two northern Republicans, three southern Democrats, and one independent. The first chair of the commission was John Hannah, president of Michigan State University, and the first African American member was Ernest Wilkins. In 1958, shortly after members had been confirmed, the commission set up an advisory committee in each state. Composed of prominent

individuals, the committees were designed to enable the commission to keep a close watch on local developments.

The commission initially focused on issues related to voting rights and desegregation of education in the South. In December 1958, at the commission's first hearing held in Montgomery, Alabama, African Americans testified that they encountered delays, complicated procedures, and confusing forms when they tried to register to vote. Although the commission did not have the power to initiate a lawsuit to gain access to the records of local voting registrars, it compiled substantial evidence documenting widespread discrimination against African Americans. The commission encountered stiff resistance from local officials regarding another hearing in Louisiana, but there, too, it was eventually able to demonstrate flagrant violations of the Fifteenth Amendment. The commission's early investigations into educational matters focused solely on the upper South. Hearings in Nashville in 1959 revealed that most districts refused to admit black students to white schools, while others offered only token integration. Moreover, testimonies disclosed that southern school districts used pupil placement laws, tuition grants for students who attended private schools, and other means to delay compliance with the *Brown* decison.

Initially African American leaders doubted that the commission would be very effective because none of its members had been involved extensively in the civil rights movement. The commission's investigations into the denial of voting rights in the South, which constituted the focus of its first report, erased much of the skepticism. There were sixteen counties in the South, the commission revealed, where blacks were a majority of the population yet not one African American was registered to vote. In forty-nine other counties, African Americans comprised the majority of the population but less than 5 percent had registered. The commission concluded that these and other instances of discrimination signaled that the voting sections of the 1957 Civil Rights Act urgently needed strengthening. Thus, the commission proposed that the federal government appoint special voting registrars and dispatch them to troubled areas of the South to administer state election laws, register voters, and monitor polling sites during elections. Civil rights advocates from both parties hailed the commission's report and sponsored legislation to implement the registrar plan, but Congress included only moderate voting provisions in the 1960 Civil Rights Act.

The commission did not ignore racial matters in the North during its early years. Hearings in New York and in

Chicago in 1959 showed that many African Americans lived in deteriorating housing in segregated neighborhoods. Two years later, the commission investigated black life in Detroit and in Los Angeles. Unemployment, poverty, juvenile delinquency, discrimination in home buying and labor unions, police brutality, and drug addiction, the commission noted, were common features of African American urban life in the North. In its five-volume 1961 report, the commission predicted that African Americans would "swell the ranks of the unemployed as technological changes [eliminated] the unskilled or semiskilled tasks they once performed." To prevent such an economic catastrophe, the commission urged the federal government to expand job training programs. However, President John F. Kennedy and Congress largely ignored these suggestions. Nevertheless, the commission's investigation of social and economic conditions of African Americans in the urban North foreshadowed issues that would come to the fore a few years later.

As the civil rights movement gained momentum in the early 1960s, the commission adopted a more advocatory stance, due in part to the appointment of two new members in 1961. Whereas the commission initially had been evenly balanced between northern liberals and southern conservatives, the two Kennedy appointees were much more sympathetic to the African American cause than the members they replaced. Chair John Hannah, meanwhile, had also become a more outspoken supporter of racial justice. These changes were evident in the recommendations included in the commission's 1961 report. It called upon Congress to outlaw literacy tests and other restrictions hindering African Americans from registering to vote. Moreover, the commission recommended that Congress require school boards that allowed segregation to file a desegregation plan with the federal government within six months and empower the attorney general to take action to implement such plans. Finally, the commission called upon lawmakers to limit federal aid to those areas that continued to practice segregation and urged the president to issue an executive order banning discrimination in federally assisted housing programs. Though a few liberals in Congress introduced legislation based on some of the commission's suggestions, most legislators, as well as President Kennedy, paid little attention to the 1961 report.

By 1963, however, it was evident that the commission exercised greater influence in the federal government. In 1962 Kennedy issued a housing executive order that drew heavily on the commission's recommendations, and he included some of the group's proposals in civil rights legislation that he endorsed. Indeed, the commission's plan to cut off federal funding of programs that discriminated on the basis of race formed the basis of Title VI of the 1964 Civil Rights Act. Likewise, during the mid-1960s the Department of Health, Education, and Welfare adopted several of the commission's recommendations, while numerous federal agencies followed its suggestions in crafting equal employment policies.

During the early 1960s relations between federal agencies and the commission improved, but there were important instances when the commission clashed with the Kennedy administration. The president rebuffed attempts by commission members to broaden their powers to include enforcement of civil rights laws. Attorney General Robert F. Kennedy on three separate occasions rejected commission plans to hold voting hearings in Mississippi, where violence and discrimination against African Americans and their white allies was common. President Kennedy asked the commission to refrain from releasing a report that presented a harrowing picture of the conditions facing African Americans in the Magnolia State. The commission, however, published the report, which included a recommendation that the president "seriously consider" withholding all federal money from Mississippi. The president refused to do so. Despite these conflicts, Kennedy saw the commission as a valuable part of the civil rights struggle and preserved its independence by resisting appeals to let it expire or replace its members with individuals less sympathetic to the civil rights struggle.

By the fall of 1963, though, the commission was pessimistic about its future. The commission's very existence was uncertain because it was due to expire within the year, if Congress failed to extend its life, as it had done twice before. Sensing that the commission had fulfilled its original mandate of gathering information, members grew dispirited over an apparent lack of direction and worried about losing political influence. Changes in staff personnel and the resignation of two commission members further added to the sense of disarray. Meanwhile, southerners on Capitol Hill had grown more critical of the commission's work on behalf of civil rights. Senator Lister Hill of Alabama, for instance, charged that commission members had "invaded our communities and [had] incited action and animosity where none existed before they came."

Enactment of the 1964 Civil Rights Act buoyed the spirits of commission members considerably. Not only did the far-reaching law include many commission proposals, it also extended the life of the commission for four years and broadened its role by empowering it to serve as a clearinghouse of civil rights information for the federal government. Soon after Lyndon B. Johnson became president, the commission saw a dramatic increase in its budget and in the number of staff assistants. As the Johnson administration oversaw implementation of the new law, the commission worked closely with federal agencies, including the Equal Employment Opportunity Commission and the Community Relations Service, to establish nondiscrimination guidelines. Moreover, the commission sponsored numerous regional conferences to foster discussion among local residents about enforcement of the 1964 Civil Rights Act, and it prepared several reports that informed citizens of their rights. At the same time, however, the commission retained its independent voice by issuing several reports criticizing the Johnson administration's enforcement of Title VI in areas such as education, welfare programs, and health-care facilities.

Despite the advances ushered in by the 1964 Civil Rights Act, commission members knew that racial problems continued to plague the South, especially Mississippi. In the spring of 1965, despite objections of the Justice Department, the commission finally held hearings in the Magnolia State to examine voting rights abuses and unequal treatment of African Americans by law enforcement personnel. White officials predictably argued that there was no racial problem in Mississippi. Black witnesses, however, told of bombings of homes and churches, police brutality, and widespread use of literacy tests, poll taxes, and other devices to prevent African Americans from voting. The commission's report about racial conditions in Mississippi, as well as its broader account of law enforcement across the South, attracted widespread attention and helped raise awareness of the daily horrors African Americans encountered. The abuses uncovered in Mississippi also helped lead the commission to endorse unanimously Johnson's voting rights bill. Enacted during the summer of 1965, the Voting Rights Act contained many of the commission's earlier proposals, including those related to the poll tax and voting registrars, and represented the peak of the commission's influence on Congress. Commission data showing the denial of voting rights in the South also played an integral part in the Supreme Court's decision to reject a challenge to the constitutionality of the Voting Rights Act. By the mid-1960s, however, the commission had begun to focus more closely on civil rights problems in the North. There the chief issues continued to be housing, employment, and law enforcement. The 1965 riots in Watts, California, as well as other incidents of mass violence, led the commission to hold several on-site hearings in the North. The commission tried to work closely with federal agencies and local organizations to remedy urban ills, but it enjoyed few successes.

The commission's ability to influence civil rights policy diminished considerably during the early 1970s. It provoked strong hostility from policymakers after the release of a 1970 study alleging a "major breakdown" in federal civil rights enforcement during the Nixon administration. Additional reports accused the administration of "foot-dragging" on school desegregation efforts, trying to dilute the Voting Rights Act, and "retreating" in the field of open housing enforcement. In 1973, the commission issued another study indicating that there had been no improvement in the administration's effort. Many federal agencies simply would not cooperate with the commission's investigations. Agencies frequently lost commission letters, canceled appointments with members, refused to acknowledge discriminatory practices, or delayed implementing compliance regulations. Following the 1972 election, President Richard M. Nixon severely undermined the autonomy of the commission when he forced the resignation of its chairman, Father Theodore Hesburgh, who had criticized the president's opposition to busing as a remedy for school segregation. In 1974 hostility to the commission also mounted on Capitol Hill when it raised the possibility of investigating charges of discriminatory hiring practices by Congress. Angry legislators threatened budget reductions and dilution of commission authority. The days of exerting influence over major civil rights legislation were gone.

Partisan fighting over the role and authority of the commission intensified during the Reagan administration. Throughout the 1970s the commission continued to press the federal government for vigorous enforcement of the civil rights laws and staunchly advocated busing and affirmative action, including quotas, in areas such as employment and college admissions. The Reagan administration firmly opposed such policies. In 1983, when the commission was up for renewal, President Reagan announced that he would fire three Democratic members who had been critical of his civil rights policies and replace them with conservatives. Two of the three Democrats immediately sued the president and were eventually reinstated. Reagan's move prompted howls of protest on Capitol Hill, where Democrats accused him of undermining the commission's autonomy. That November, however, the administration and Congress temporarily resolved their differences by reaching an agreement that extended the life of the commission for six years and, more important, fundamentally reorganized it. Under the new terms, the commission was to be enlarged from six to eight members, four of whom were to be appointed by the president and the other four members would be determined by Congress. Neither the president nor Congress had to approve the other's nominees.

President Reagan quickly used the new format to shift the ideological orientation of the commission in a more conservative direction. He named former San Diego Urban League chief Clarence Pendleton as chair and Linda Chavez as staff director. Pendleton quickly proved to be a source of controversy. He announced that the commission was a part of the Reagan administration and characterized African American leaders who favored racial quotas as "divisive, unpopular, and immoral." Pendleton exacerbated tensions between the commission and civil rights leaders by accusing them of promoting a "new racism" and suggesting that the commission investigate the effects of affirmative action on white males. Chavez, meanwhile, outlined program reforms that included reversing longstanding commission positions on affirmative action, quotas, busing, and Title VI. Further changes occurred on the State Advisory Committees when white males started to replace minorities in many top positions. Reflecting its optimistic view of the state of race relations, the commission during the Reagan years promoted a color blind ideal of racial justice and attempted to remove questions of economic power from the debate over equality.

Civil rights leaders and their allies in Congress mounted an aggressive counterattack. Following a 1986 report by the General Accounting Office that charged the commission with gross financial mismanagement and improper personnel policies, Democrats in Congress led a successful effort to cut the commission's budget by one-third and reduce its staff by nearly half. The commission also closed seven of its ten regional offices. Disturbed by the conservative tone of the commission, some lawmakers joined forces with prominent civil rights groups, including the National Association for the Advancement of Colored People (NAACP), to call for the elimination of the commission altogether. The House of Representatives voted to do so in 1987, but the Senate refused. Nevertheless civil rights activists remained critical. NAACP leader Benjamin Hooks called the commission "a sham and a national disgrace," while liberal members Mary Frances Berry and Blandina Cardenas Ramirez regularly criticized the scholarship on which the conservative majority based its reports. Even black Republicans, alarmed at Pendleton's opposition to minority "set-aside programs" in the federal

government, called for his resignation. To many civil rights leaders, the commission had become a captive of the Reagan administration. Ironically, groups that had once been among the commission's strongest backers now proved to be its harshest critics.

The commission continued to conduct investigations of civil rights issues during the 1990s. It examined the small number of minorities in management positions in Wall Street investment firms, the bombings of black churches in the South, federal enforcement of Title VI, and racial unrest in major urban areas. The commission's importance, however, remained limited. In 1997 President Bill Clinton indirectly acknowledged this when he bypassed the commission and as part of his "national conversation on race" appointed a new body, the Advisory Board for the President's Initiative on Race. In the same year the General Accounting Office reported that the commission was "an agency in disarray" and criticized it for poor financial recordkeeping, lax management of projects, and unnecessary delays in completing its work. A decade of partisan squabbling, budget and staff reductions, internal divisions, and ideological transformation had diminished the commission's autonomy and relevance.

**FURTHER READINGS**

Amaker, Norman C. *Civil Rights in the Reagan Administration.* Washington, D.C.: Urban Institute Press, 1988.

Baker, Robert Stephen. "The Impact of the United States Commission on Civil Rights in the Struggle for Racial Equality in America: The Problems in Urban Housing, Employment, and Criminal Justice (1965–1974)." Ph.D. diss., Michigan State University, 1989.

Dulles, Foster Rhea. *The Civil Rights Commission: 1957–1965.* East Lansing: Michigan State University Press, 1968.

Frye, Jocelyn C., Robert S. Gerber, Robert H. Pees, and Arthur W. Richardson. "The Rise and Fall of the United States Commission on Civil Rights." *Harvard Civil Rights–Civil Liberties Law Review* 22 (Spring 1987): 449–505.

Walton, Hanes. *When the Marching Stopped: The Politics of Civil Rights Regulatory Agencies.* Albany: State University of New York Press, 1988.

*Timothy N. Thurber*

## United States Student Association

Founded in 1978, the United States Student Association (USSA) is the largest confederation of student governments in the United States, with a membership of more than 300 campuses. Based in Washington, D.C., the USSA lobbies the federal government on issues of concern to its members and serves as a clearinghouse for information on higher education policy. The association is the hub of a national network of activists and student government leaders and conducts frequent training sessions for young activists. As the demographics of American higher education have shifted, African American students have become a dominant constituency in the USSA, an ascendancy that has been increasingly reflected in the association's leadership.

The USSA was the product of a 1978 merger between the United States National Student Association (NSA) and the National Student Lobby (NSL). The NSL had broken with the association at the height of the NSA's activism against the Vietnam War in order to pursue a more education-oriented agenda. At the end of the war, as the NSA turned back to the problems of students on campuses, the two groups reunited as the USSA.

Breaking with both NSA and NSL tradition, the delegates to the USSA's constitutional convention established affirmative action rules mandating that all but the smallest conference delegations include women and people of color. This new mandate resonated with the politics of the time, but it also reflected an ongoing shift in NSA/USSA membership, as predominantly white elite schools were replaced by public colleges with more diverse student bodies and some longtime members instituted more inclusive admissions policies.

The USSA's affirmative action rules helped to bring a new group of students into the association—members of the ethnic and cultural student unions that were springing up on campuses across the nation. As schools with largely white student governments struggled to meet the USSA's new requirements, many turned to the leadership of local black and Latino student organizations and women's centers. In the early 1980s when campaigns for South African divestment by academic institutions gained momentum, the links forged by such recruitment strategies helped to raise that struggle and others to a national level.

In 1985, the NSA's and the USSA's longstanding commitment to training student leaders to be more effective advocates gained a new focus when the association and several of its allies launched the Grass Roots Organizing Weekend (GROW) program. During these weekends experienced student activists provided small groups of selected students with intensive leadership instruction. By 1995, more than a thousand students had received GROW training at campuses across the country.

By the late 1980s, NSA/USSA's Third World Coalition, which had been established in the mid-1970s to give students of color representation in the organization, had become a powerful institutional force. Renamed the National People of Color Student Coalition (NPCSC), it was dominated by African American students. The NPCSC held an annual conference in advance of the USSA Congress and maintained enough delegate discipline to constitute a powerful voting bloc each year. But despite this prominence, African Americans were underrepresented in the leadership ranks of the USSA. Students of color were sometimes elected to regional and at-large positions, but the NPCSC controlled only two seats on the forty-eight–member board of directors. This situation created tensions not only because of the perceived slight, but also because of growing pains within the NPCSC, which now housed subcaucuses of students of African, Arab, Asian, Latino, and Native American descent.

In 1989, at the USSA Congress at the University of California at Berkeley, the NPCSC proposed to raise its representation on the board from two to five seats, reflecting the internal structure of the caucus. The proposal received strong support from the membership, but the peculiarities of the USSA's constitutional amendment procedures created a situation in which a small dissenting minority was able to block the change.

The vote threw the conference into disarray, sparking a mass walkout of students of color from the plenary floor. There was talk of a split in the organization, even of disbanding, as the Congress ground to a halt, and the NPCSC met behind closed doors to prepare a response to the rebuff. When the conference reconvened, the NPCSC introduced a dramatically more formidable proposal, calling for ten caucus seats instead of five and a guarantee that half the seats on the board of directors would be filled by students of color. After some last-minute horsetrading, the strengthened proposal passed easily. Although African Americans filled many seats on the newly reconstituted board, the structure of the body and the USSA's ethnic diversity made it impossible for any one racial group to gain a majority. Thus, every decision made by the new board that year and afterward depended on a multiracial coalition, imparting a new dynamic to the association and codifying a transition to multiculturalism that had been years in the making.

A year after the Berkeley conference, the USSA and the NPCSC instituted a new project devoted to the recruitment and retention of students of color in higher education. This project, directed by a full-time staff member in the association's national office and accountable to the NPCSC, compiles and disseminates information to students on member campuses, and serves as a resource for the USSA's advocacy efforts in the nation's capital.

Today the USSA claims a membership of several hundred campuses—fewer than at the NSA's peak, but far more than any similar organization active today. Its staff of half a dozen is well below the scores its predecessor employed in its headiest years, but substantially more robust than the skeleton crew of the early 1980s. The association's leadership, once overwhelmingly white and male, is now dominated by women and students of color. While the USSA retains a commitment to such ostensibly race-blind issues as academic freedom, financial aid, and disciplinary due process, it now approaches them from a new perspective. At the same time, the association provides the nation's African American students with a diverse array of resources and experiences, from networking and training as activists to advocacy within the federal government.

*J. Angus Johnston*

## United Transatlantic Society

Benjamin "Pap" Singleton (1809–1892), a former Tennessee slave and fugitive abolitionist, established the United Transatlantic Society (UTS) in Kansas City in 1885. The society encouraged African Americans to oppose race prejudice by repudiating white America and immigrating to Africa. The UTS held several conventions and remained active for two years, but it never had the funding to send immigrants across the Atlantic. Throughout its brief lifespan the organization provided a public forum for proponents of a separate black national existence.

Singleton had long pressed for black economic independence, and during the 1870s he founded two African American colonies in Kansas. The 1879 Great Exodus of blacks from the South propelled Singleton into the national spotlight, and he hoped that public sympathy for the Exodusters would lead to racial equality in America. When no meaningful reforms emerged, Singleton altered his nationalist rhetoric to call for complete separation from the United States.

The UTS was a fraternal organization that accepted only African American males above the age of eighteen into its fellowship, and society leaders expected members to uphold the integrity of the association by pledging to a temperate lifestyle. Membership dues for immigration were an unrealistic ten cents per month, but Singleton hoped that all African Americans would voluntarily con-

tribute their talent and finances in a united effort. While the idea of an African Fatherland served as a rallying point, society representatives also worked to establish true social justice wherever descendants of Africans lived. The society remained small and after a September 1887 gathering disappeared from the public record.

**FURTHER READINGS**

Entz, Gary R. "Image and Reality on the Kansas Prairie: 'Pap' Singleton's Cherokee County Colony." *Kansas History* 19 (Summer 1996): 124–139.

Fleming, Walter L. "'Pap' Singleton, the Moses of the Colored Exodus." *American Journal of Sociology* 15 (July 1909): 61–82.

Garvin, Roy. "Benjamin, or 'Pap,' Singleton and His Followers." *Journal of Negro History* 33 (January 1948): 7–23.

Hicky, Joseph V. "'Pap' Singleton's Dunlap Colony: Relief Agencies and the Failure of a Black Settlement in Eastern Kansas." *Great Plains Quarterly* 11 (Winter 1991): 23–36.

Painter, Nell Irvin. *Exodusters: Black Migration to Kansas after Reconstruction.* New York: Knopf, 1977.

*Gary R. Entz*

## United Transport Service Employees of America

The United Transport Service Employees of America (UTSEA), a trade union international, was founded in Chicago as the International Brotherhood of Red Caps (IBRC), by black and some white red caps in 1937. It changed its name in 1941. The job of the red cap, the railroad station worker who carried rail passengers' baggage to and from trains and provided directions and other information, came into being in the 1890s. Unlike Pullman porters or dining car cooks and waiters, red caps were often treated as "independent concessionaires" by station managers, who refused to negotiate with them. In most cases, red caps worked for tips, not wages. During the Great Depression of the 1930s, red caps took inspiration from the New Deal era upsurge in black trade unionism, especially that of the Brotherhood of Sleeping Car Porters, and organized their own small unions during the mid-1930s. In 1937, representatives of these black—and some white— red cap unions united and formed the IBRC. The new union was led by Willard Saxby Townsend (1895–1957), a Cincinnati-born, college-educated red cap from Chicago's North Western station. Shortly after the union's formation, however, many white red caps expressed their opposition to membership in a black-dominated organization by withdrawing from the IBRC and instead affiliating with the all-white Brotherhood of Railway Clerks (BRC).

In its first significant step, the IBRC withdrew from the American Federation of Labor (AFL) in 1937 to pursue an independent course until it affiliated with the Congress of Industrial Organizations (CIO) in 1942. Originally a "federal" local with little influence or representation within the AFL, the IBRC also objected to efforts by the white BRC to claim jurisdiction over the red caps' craft. As an independent union, the IBRC next initiated a nationwide organizing drive to bring unorganized red caps and unaffiliated red cap unions into its ranks. In 1937, it launched a "March Forward to Job Legality" campaign that aimed at winning government recognition of its members' right to organize. Red caps were not legally employees under the terms of the 1934 amendments to the Railway Labor Act and hence were excluded from the benefits of New Deal labor legislation. That is, as "privileged trespassers" on railroad property, they had no legal access to the complex labor relations machinery of the National Mediation Board. Unable to call upon the government to oversee union elections, the IBRC was powerless to compel employers to recognize the union and negotiate with it. The union succeeded in convincing the Interstate Commerce Commission by 1938 that the red caps' independent status was fictitious and that red caps, like Pullman porters and dining car workers, were genuine railroad employees, subject to the conditions of the Railway Labor Act. With their legal status officially recognized, the IBRC called upon the National Mediation Board to conduct union representation elections at stations across the country; the union proceeded to win the overwhelming number of them. By 1940, the IBRC boasted over 3,500 members.

Unionization of the red cap labor force brought significant changes to the station porters. By 1941, the IBRC/UTSEA had established seniority rights, a reduction in working hours, the elimination of the seven-day week, and a grievance procedure that offered substantial protections to union members. On monetary issues, rail managers only grudgingly accepted small wage increases (required by federal minimum wage legislation), but they also undercut red caps' autonomy by charging passengers a fee for red cap service. High fees, along with the decline in railroad passenger service after World War II, contributed to the long-term decrease in the red caps' trade. By the 1950s and 1960s, stations employed few red caps,

and the IBRC, financially and organizationally weak, eventually merged with its former rival, the Brotherhood of Railway Clerks.

The IBRC/UTSEA addressed not only its members' on-the-job concerns but larger racial issues as well. In the late 1930s and 1940s, union leaders publicly attacked the AFL's racist policies, and membership in the CIO afforded them a platform to attack racism in the railroad industry, the labor movement, and in American society generally. When UTSEA president Willard Townsend was appointed to the CIO's executive board in 1942, he became that organization's highest ranking African American. In addition to serving on the CIO's Anti-Discrimination Committee, Townsend and other leaders were active in promoting civil rights in the national political arena. From 1937 to 1944, the union published at least two journals—*Bags and Baggage* and the *CIO News* (UTSEA edition).

**FURTHER READINGS**

Calloway, Ernest. "The Red Caps' Struggle for a Livelihood." Part 1. *Opportunity* 18, 6 (June 1940).

Calloway, Ernest, ed. *The Birth of a Union: What the Press of the Nation Has to Say About the New Red Cap.* Chicago: Educational Department, UTSEA, October 1, 1940.

Drake, St. Clair, and Horace R. Cayton. *Black Metropolis. Vol. 1, A Study of Negro Life in a Northern City.* 1945; rpt., New York: Harcourt, Brace, & World, 1970.

Johnson, Reginald A. "Red Caps Seek a Living Wage." *Opportunity* 17, 4 (April 1939).

Romero, Patricia W. "Willard Townsend and the International Brotherhood of Red Caps." M.A. thesis, Miami University, Oxford, Ohio, 1965.

"This Is the Story." *Eighth Biennial Convention of the United Transport Service Employees Convention Journal.* June 22–25, 1952. Cincinnati, Ohio: n.d.

Yancey, John L. "Our Right to Live." *American Federationist* (March 1939).

*Eric Arnesen*

## Universal African Nationalist Movement

The Universal African Nationalist Movement (UANM), also known as the United African Nationalist Movement, originated in the 1940s following a factional dispute in Marcus Garvey's Universal Negro Improvement Association (UNIA). The UANM was an outgrowth of the Garveyite wing of the UNIA. Leading members of the UANM included Benjamin Gibbons, who was the group's president general in the late 1940s and early 1950s, and

Benjamin W. Jones, who served as its executive secretary during those years. Carlos Cooks, whose black nationalist career spanned the 1930s to the 1960s, was also associated briefly with the UANM in the late 1940s.

Based in New York, the UANM promoted African American immigration to Liberia. For this purpose the UANM sought alliances with other organizations that supported repatriation for quite different reasons. The UANM, for example, established ties with the black-controlled Peace Movement of Ethiopia as well as white Mississippi senator Theodore Bilbo, whose Greater Liberia bill sought federal funding to support the repatriation of African Americans. Bilbo, who originally introduced the bill in 1939, kept reintroducing the proposed legislation until his death in 1947. Following Bilbo's death, the UANM turned to Senator William Langer of North Dakota to solicit his support for a repatriation bill. Between 1949 and his death in 1959, Langer continually reintroduced the bill but it was never reported out of committee.

The UANM also promoted the memory of Garvey and his role as a race patriot. It supported recognition of August 1 as Marcus Garvey Day, in honor of the opening of the first Garvey convention of the Negro Peoples of the World in 1920. Despite such public efforts, however, the UANM was never able to expand its membership to sustainable levels.

**FURTHER READING**

Hill, Robert A., ed. *The Marcus Garvey and Universal Negro Improvement Association Papers.* 8 vols. Berkeley: University of California Press, 1983–1995.

*Jim Meriwether*

# Universal Association of Ethiopian Women

Audley Moore, known as "Queen Mother Moore," founded the Universal Association of Ethiopian Women (UAEW) in Louisiana in the mid-twentieth century. Taking its name from the presence of Ethiopian women in the Bible, the UAEW fought for civil and human rights of African Americans, Africans, and members of the African Diaspora around the globe. A nationalist black liberation organization, the UAEW advocated welfare and prisoners' rights and fought against lynchings and interracial rape.

Moore, born in New Iberia, Louisiana, in 1898, first began fighting for black rights during World War I, when she and her sisters sought to provide supplies and entertainment for black soldiers. In the 1920s she participated in Marcus Garvey's Universal Negro Improvement Association and fought for African Americans to recognize their African heritage. Moore also was a member of the Communist Party in the 1930s, founded the Ethiopian Coptic Church of North and South America in the 1960s, and traveled to Africa many times.

Few records of the UAEW remain. Moore recalled that she and her sister Eloise, Mother Langley, and Dara Collins, founded the UAEW to combat rape cases against African American men. Allegations of rape often resulted in black men's execution or castration, while African American women were not protected from rape by white men. UAEW women tried to persuade white women who had accused black men of rape to recant their testimony and visited jails to pray with some of the imprisoned men. The group was successful in preventing the execution of several black men. The UAEW also fought to secure the release of a black Alabama woman who had been charged with perjury and sentenced without a trial to 218 years in prison.

In addition to prisoners' rights, the UAEW also became an advocate of welfare rights. The group lobbied the Louisiana legislature to change welfare legislation after the state cut welfare payments to over 20,000 families in need. Moreover, UAEW women argued that whites owed African Americans payment for the suffering that they had experienced during slavery. In the early 1960s, Moore founded the Reparations Committee of Descendants of U.S. Slaves, Inc., to demand that the federal government pay reparations to the descendants of slaves in compensation for their oppression.

Moore believed that black women needed to fight for rights for the race as a whole and refused to ally herself with the white feminist movement of the 1970s. She argued that although white women felt oppressed by white men, black women needed to help black men who were themselves persecuted.

Records are unclear as to the fate of the association after Moore left Louisiana in 1957.

**FURTHER READINGS**

Bair, Barbara. "Moore, Audley (Queen Mother)." In *Black Women in America: An Historical Encyclopedia.* Ed. Darlene Clark Hine. Brooklyn, N.Y.: Carlson Publishing Company, 1993.

"The *Black Scholar* Interviews: Queen Mother Moore." *Black Scholar* 4 (March-April 1973): 47–55.

Lanker, Brian. "Queen Mother Audley Moore." In *I Dream a World: Portraits of Black Women Who Changed America.* New York: Stewart, Tabori & Chang, 1999.

Moore, Audley. Oral History interview by Cheryl Townsend Gilkes. In *The Black Women Oral History Project*, vol. 8. Ed. Ruth Edmonds Hill. Westport, Conn.: Meckler, 1991.

*Joan Marie Johnson*

## Universal Negro Improvement Association and African Communities League

The Universal Negro Improvement Association and African Communities League (UNIA) was the first Pan-African organization to attempt to attract the black masses in the United States, the Caribbean, and Africa. Founded in 1918 by Marcus Garvey in New York, the UNIA was a fraternal organization. Officers in New York, called the Parent Body, established divisions throughout the black world, but the UNIA's greatest success was in the United States. Annual conventions ratified projects, like the Black Star Line (BSL), but they were often independent entities, chartered separately.

Experiences similar to those of its creator animated the UNIA. Garvey was born in St. Ann's Bay, Jamaica, in 1887. He became a printer and moved to Kingston in 1904. Like other Jamaicans, suffering from the lack of economic opportunity on the stagnating island, Garvey sought work and experience in various Caribbean and Central American countries. Everywhere he saw black people exploited and powerless. Garvey's travels continued in London in 1912. There, he joined an international black community and encountered an ideology, Pan-Africanism, that explained what he had experienced and observed.

Pan-Africanism was a response to the new imperialism in Africa and Jim Crowism in the United States. Meeting in London in 1900, elites from Africa and the Americas feared that new racial proscriptions threatened the universal progress promised during the Era of Emancipation. The defeat of popular resistance to imperialism in Africa, and the ending of African American involvement in Republican and Populist politics in the American South, led to profound changes in black thought and organization. Although the Pan-Africanists eventually protested mass grievances, like land alienation in Africa and Jim Crow and disfranchisement in the United States, they believed that strengthening racial bonds and creating institutions similar to those triumphing in the West was the appropriate route to progress. Thus, they became nationalists. Yet they also became Pan-Africanists because they saw identical forces at work in the United States, the Caribbean, and Africa. Although Pan-African organization was

Marcus Garvey on his way to a Madison Square Garden rally for the Universal Negro Improvement Association, wearing "Provisional President of Africa" uniform, New York City, 1922. *Archive Photos*

impermanent, the core ideas of creating racial institutions such as schools, businesses, newspapers, and perhaps nations, became common, and sometimes linked, in each region of the black world.

When Garvey returned to Jamaica in 1914, he created UNIA, a black self-help organization that proclaimed Pan-African aspirations. His immediate goal was to establish a school for blacks in Jamaica. He had little success, and in 1916 he went to the United States, a growing destination for other islanders. In contrast to black Jamaicans, African Americans had already created racial organizations, businesses, and schools. A new black migration from the rural South to northern cities invigorated urban life. Garvey was impressed and incorporated the UNIA as a fraternal organization and the African Communities League as a business corporation in Harlem.

Initially, Garvey had attempted to raise money in the United States for a Jamaican school. Such a project was tame fare in the changing environment of World War I. During the war the American government tried to marshal the nation behind the war effort and as a result African Americans won positions in the federal government and in local communities. National goals to increase production and sell Liberty Bonds carried the war propaganda of democracy into the most isolated and backward areas of the nation. The success of the Bolsheviks in Russia, the growth of unionism in the United States, and the rise of nationalist movements throughout the world further enhanced popular expectations. The progress produced by migration and high cotton prices escalated black demands for change.

Garvey too became more radical. While he had earlier appealed to elite whites and blacks for support, he now attempted to harness the new mass assertions to Pan-African goals. Still, throughout 1918 and 1919, the UNIA was a small organization centered in New York, with satellites in a few cities along the eastern seaboard. Garvey had started a newspaper, *The Negro World*, which was supportive of the new radicalism. His indictment of racial injustice and imperialism in Africa and delineation of a prosperous and powerful alternative for blacks earned the cheers of enthusiastic UNIA audiences. He celebrated the Russian Revolution, Irish independence, and many of the other popular successes of the day. However, Garvey called upon blacks "to evolve a national ideal," to prepare for the future, not to act now.

From the beginning, Garvey talked as much about economic opportunities as political changes. The combination of politics and business would prove to be a fatal mix, but from the beginning, Pan-Africanism had assumed that racial businesses were crucial routes to black freedom. Garvey said the basis of "racial greatness was becoming a commercial and industrial people." Still, his only business, a UNIA restaurant, was a frail instrument to effect the "redemption and regeneration of Africa."

Garvey obtained an appropriate vehicle in May 1919 when he announced plans to create the Black Star Line. According to the conventional wisdom of the day, great nations possessed shipping lines, which secured markets, power, and prestige. During World War I the American government had awarded ship building the highest priority and shippers had reaped enormous profits. With the launching of the BSL Garvey embraced a project that he believed could unite the Pan-African world.

Garvey had wanted the BSL to be owned and controlled by the UNIA but because ships were costly, financial appeals to the black public became necessary. Thus, the BSL became an independent corporation financed largely by the black urban masses. UNIA organizers, selling $5 shares, fanned out all over the country, but did especially well in the cities that had attracted large numbers of migrants during the war. Blacks, like other Americans, had purchased Liberty Bonds, and it was not difficult for UNIA organizers to replace the patriotism of race for that of nation.

Many critics and skeptics became converts when Garvey bought his first ship in October 1919. Older nationalists, like the Yale graduate William Ferris and the journalist John Bruce, added their prestige and influence to the enterprise. Even W. E. B. Du Bois, who subsequently became a critic, was thrilled: "What he [Garvey] is trying to say and do is this: American Negroes can be accumulating and ministering their own capital, organize industry, join the black centers of the South Atlantic by commercial enterprise and in this way ultimately redeem Africa as a fit and free home for black men. . . . It is feasible."

In August 1920, the BSL's three ships drew 25,000 people to New York's Madison Square Garden, where UNIA delegates elected Garvey provisional president of Africa and president-general of the UNIA. The delegates also published a Declaration of Negro Rights, an eloquent bill of racial complaint that ranged from protesting discrimination in public hotels to decrying the treatment of Africans under imperialist rule. The declaration, however, was vague about methods and priorities and merely restated traditional black demands and strategies for racial progress. Since the UNIA lacked a unified political strategy, increasing its membership depended upon Garvey's ability to conquer the marketplace.

From the beginning Garvey's mixture of politics and business made operations of the BSL difficult. When the postwar depression turned the shipping boom of the war and immediate postwar period into a shipping glut, it became easy to obtain ships, but it became also more difficult to operate them profitably. Garvey's attempt to establish a base in Liberia posed yet another problem.

In the nineteenth century there were many "back-to-Africa" movements, motivated in part by the land hunger of African American farmers in the South. Garvey's African plans, however, stemmed from a modern Pan-African vision. UNIA vice president William Sherrill told blacks in Gary, Indiana, that "the UNIA is not a 'Back to Africa' movement, it is a movement to redeem Africa. The Negro in America has had a better opportunity than any other Negro." Like other blacks in Western society, Garvey assumed that African Americans were the most advanced segment of the black race. They possessed the expertise and capital to modernize Africa, and with their help the UNIA promised to strengthen the economic position of West African elites. Trade fluctuations, currency scarcities, and shipping shortages that occurred during the war revealed the strength of foreign firms and the reliability of colonial economies. West Africans enthusiastically greeted Garvey's BSL plans and other investments. The independent black republic, Liberia, offered the greatest opportunity.

Created by the American Colonization Society in 1822, Liberia became an independent republic in 1847. In 1920, 5,000 descendants of the nineteenth-century African American emigrants ruled about 500,000 indigenous Africans. During World War I, the expulsion of Germans, who had controlled Liberia's foreign trade, and the shipping shortage threatened Liberia's delicately poised economy and independence. In 1918, the United States, which had pressured Liberia to declare war against Germany, extended a loan to the republic. Garvey, refusing to make a distinction between European and American aid, proposed to raise money to free Liberia from foreign, white control. For this purpose the UNIA sent Elie Garcia, a Haitian, to Liberia in May 1920. Garcia's report did not promise a warm Pan-African partnership. He told Garvey that the Liberians were devious, parasitic, and unreliable. The Liberians were equally suspicious of the Garveyites. Nevertheless, Garvey sent a UNIA delegation to Liberia in 1921. However, the UNIA's financial difficulties and its implicit challenge to Liberian authority ended the partnership amidst mutual recriminations.

The ambitions of 1919 and 1920, manifested in the BSL and the Liberian project reflected Garvey's growing confidence. The subsequent recession and the Republican ascendancy, however, caused Garvey to adopt a more defensive posture. This was also true of other black movements in the United States. American government and business repulsed the new labor movement, and A. Philip Randolph's plans to unionize the new black working class became inevitable casualties. Members of the insurrectionary African Blood Brotherhood transferred their allegiance to the Communist Party. Many of the new southern chapters of the National Association for the Advancement of Colored People (NAACP), created during the war, did not survive the postwar retreat. The business route to racial progress was as dependent upon wartime conditions as the political movements. Garvey searched in vain for a new project to unite the hundreds of UNIA locals. He attempted to resurrect the past by purchasing another ship, and he tried to repair the relationship with Liberia by sending another expedition. Both efforts were fruitless.

Other difficulties exacerbated troubles within the UNIA. Garvey had attracted the applause of prominent figures in the African American world, but his autocratic manner made it difficult for talented men and women to work with him. The UNIA was both strengthened and weakened by its architect and prime mover. Without success Garvey became vulnerable, and his opponents attempted to wrest control from him at the annual convention in 1922. Lacking alternative plans, however, their efforts were no match for his charisma. Most dissidents simply left the UNIA.

In 1922 Garvey won a new round of opponents after an infamous meeting with Edward Clarke, head of the Ku Klux Klan. Garvey had wanted to expand the UNIA into the South, where a majority of African Americans lived. However, Garvey's racial appeals and militant speeches brought swift retribution in the South. In response, Garvey toned down his rhetoric when he was below the Mason and Dixon line. In New Orleans, he even praised Jim Crow, which caught Clarke's attention. Clarke, in line with his new strategy to eradicate the violent image of the Klan, proposed a meeting with the UNIA president. While the talk was probably just that, Garvey's opponents, A. Philip Randolph, Chandler Owen, and NAACP officials Robert Bagnall and William Pickens, feared the worst. The roasting Garvey received when he returned to New York damaged his reputation and kept UNIA's Parent Body on the defensive.

Local chapters of the UNIA often had little to do with Garvey's debates with socialists, communists, and other critics in New York. Perhaps one million people at one time or another joined one of the UNIA divisions. Originally offshoots of BSL fund-raising campaigns, the locals often proceeded independently, providing many services for members and their communities. It took a minimum of seven persons to set up a division. Ten cents of the thirty-five cents monthly dues were sent to the Parent Body in New York, from which branches purchased copies of the UNIA constitution, songbooks, photographs, flags, uniforms, and the *Negro World.*

The rituals of the Parent Body and local divisions were like those of fraternal orders. Thus, the UNIA bound members with solemn oaths, honored racial service with degrees of chivalry, such as the Cross of African Redemption, and created an auxiliary Ladies' Division, with its own president. Because women as well as men were eligible for membership, the auxiliary simply was a vehicle for traditional, female organizational work. Both of Garvey's wives, Amy Ashwood, whom he divorced in July 1922, and Amy Jacques, whom he married a month later, were powerful figures in the UNIA. Henrietta Vinton Davis, the UNIA's international organizer, was part of the inner sanctum of leadership. But the top leaders of the UNIA, like those of the NAACP and the Republican party, were male, and for the same reasons.

Traditional black expectations forced the Parent Body to offer sickness and death benefits although few members received the promised aid. Because so many of the activities of the Parent Body were voluntary, local chapters had considerable leeway to shape their own programs. Nevertheless, the affiliation with the UNIA often gave ordinary people their first taste of modern politics and culture. The *Negro World* transmitted knowledge of the broader world and black intellectuals and leaders from all parts of the Pan-African world addressed local chapters. Yet UNIA locals interpreted Garveyite language on the basis of their own experiences. To Garvey, independence meant big business and national self-determination. To members of the UNIA in Miami, Florida, it was home ownership, the traditional goal of working-class Americans.

Urban locals of considerable size, like those in Detroit, Cincinnati, and Chicago, did not create new politics, but reflected the new ethnic politics of the 1920s. Because the UNIA was only one embodiment of the new race consciousness, it necessarily shared the stage with other racial groups. In Cleveland, where the NAACP better protected black workers and more aggressively took advantage of electoral opportunities, the UNIA was never able to obtain a secure place in the city. In Detroit, where an axis of the Ford Motor Company, the Detroit Urban League,

and ministers who led the NAACP dominated politics, the UNIA, composed mostly of autoworkers, represented some dissent, but not enough to change politics.

The problem of self-interest and racial interest plagued local chapters as well as the Parent Body. The UNIA in Gary, Indiana, for example, supported the building of an all-black high school in 1931, which the NAACP and most members of the black community opposed. Led by F. C. McFarlane, the future principal of the school, the UNIA's endorsement merged personal and racial interest. Whatever position they took, local UNIA leaders were usually new persons challenging traditional black elites. UNIA branches in the Caribbean, Central America, and Africa were similar to those in the United States. Their leaders were the same aspiring businesspersons and professionals who dominated the American chapters.

Many locals survived Garvey's deportation to Jamaica in 1927. The UNIA president was indicted for mail fraud in 1922, tried and found guilty in 1923, and imprisoned in Atlanta in 1925 after his appeal failed. In 1919 Garvey had gained the animosity of J. Edgar Hoover, head of the Justice Department's newly created General Intelligence Division. Although the General Intelligence Division targeted predominantly alien Communists, the International Workers of the World, and the Socialist party, Hoover's persistence reaped dividends on January 12, 1922, when the Justice Department indicted Garvey and three other BSL officers for mail fraud. The government had discovered a BSL flyer, which, agents claimed, implied that the company owned and operated a ship capable of going to Africa when it was only attempting to purchase one. Although the purposes of the indictment were political and the case was weak, the dissension caused by the declining BSL convinced many former supporters that the charges were true. Irregular business procedures, lax bookkeeping, and Garvey's imperious manner all worked against him.

When Garvey returned to Jamaica, he tried but failed to resurrect the UNIA and run the organization first from Kingston and then London. Until his death in 1940, Garvey persistently sought to regain the power and influence that he had tasted briefly during the 1920s. However, the Great Depression destroyed those dreams and placed jobs not businesses at the top of the racial agenda. Many UNIA leaders transferred their hopes and devoted their talents to building new working-class institutions with the help of the Democratic party and trade unions. At the far end of the social spectrum, the UNIA lost its poorest, least-educated members to various cults that flourished as a result of the Depression. In 1934, Charles

James, head of the Gary UNIA deplored the fact that "simple-minded Negroes were turning Moors, Arabs, Abyssinians. . . . They were growing beards and refusing to cut their hair . . . and have even gone the length of changing their names." The diverse classes that the UNIA had once united went their separate ways in the 1930s. Remnants survived and some loyalists kept the faith, but the UNIA's size and significance never returned.

In the end, the UNIA could not combine an elite model of racial progress with a black mass base. The establishment of the UNIA in the United States, the Caribbean, and Africa was possible because the black middle classes chose a strategy of business enterprise that required minimal political organization. While the UNIA's Pan-African consciousness reflected the experiences of many of its leaders, who had lived and worked in various black communities, these commonalities were not enough to sustain the organization. This was also evident at the Pan-African conference of 1945. The gathering did not appeal to the "enlightened western nations or humanity," as the first one did in 1900. The conference demanded racial independence through the mass organizations of workers and peasants, yet it dissolved into regional and national groups to achieve nationhood. Yet the class that created Pan-Africanism was able to dominate the process of independence as well as the black politics created by the civil rights movement in the United States. As with the UNIA, the social question was the persistent dilemma of Pan-Africanism.

**FURTHER READINGS**

Cronon, E. David. *Black Moses: The Story of Marcus Garvey and the Universal Negro Improvement Association.* Madison: University of Wisconsin Press, 1955.

Hill, Robert A., ed. *The Marcus Garvey and Universal Negro Improvement Association Papers.* 8 vols. Berkeley: University of California Press, 1983–1995.

Stein, Judith. *The World of Marcus Garvey: Race and Class in Modern Society.* Baton Rouge: Louisiana State University Press, 1986.

Vincent, Theodore. *Black Power and the Garvey Movement.* Berkeley, Calif.: Ramparts Press, 1972.

*Judith Stein*

# University Commission on Southern Race Questions

On May 24, 1912, white southern college professors representing each of the eleven state universities in Alabama, Arkansas, Florida, Georgia, Louisiana, Mississippi, North Carolina, South Carolina, Tennessee, Texas, and Virginia, gathered in Nashville to form the University Commission on Southern Race Questions. The commission's purpose was to conduct scholarly studies of the problems facing African Americans and whites in the South in an attempt to improve race relations. The group investigated the status of religion, education, hygiene, economics, and civic conditions in the South and utilized its findings to educate white southerners, particularly college students. On at least three occasions the commission issued "Open Letters to College Men of the South." The letters, published widely by the southern press, were designed to arouse sympathy among southern whites for the conditions of African Americans. The first letter, dated January 5, 1916, addressed the topic of lynchings; the second, issued in September 1916, focused on education; and the third, published in 1917, discussed the mass migration of rural southern blacks to the urban North.

Between 1912 and 1917, the commission met at least eight times at various locations throughout the South. While the group was composed entirely of whites, commission members sought the cooperation of African Americans. They conducted several meetings at black educational institutions and invited representatives from the African American community as guests or speakers. The commission, for example, held part of its second meeting at Hampton Institute in Virginia and, in May 1915, it gathered for its fifth meeting in Montgomery as well as at Tuskegee Institute, where Dr. Booker T. Washington addressed the group. In 1916, the commission invited a number of African American civic leaders to present their views and opinions on race relations at the group's seventh meeting in Asheville, North Carolina.

The commission's efforts to improve race relations in the South also attracted the attention of the president. In December 1914, Woodrow Wilson addressed the group's fourth meeting in Washington, D.C., assuring the members of his personal interest and support. Despite the president's endorsement, the commission failed to accomplish much beyond conducting studies, writing reports, and publicizing its findings. Nevertheless, the commission helped to raise public awareness of the conditions of African Americans in the South and drew attention to racial problems in that region. In 1917, the commission ceased its activities following the entry of the United States into World War I.

**FURTHER READINGS**

Morse, Josiah. "The University Commission on Southern Race Questions." *The South Atlantic Quarterly* 19, 4 (October 1920): 302–310.

University Commission on Southern Race Questions. *Minutes of the University Commission on Southern Race Questions.* Lexington, Va.: The Commission, n.d.

*Virginia M. Matthews*

## Urban League

*See* National Urban League.

## US

Founded in 1965, US (United Slaves) was a cultural nationalist group based in Los Angeles and headed by Maulana Ron Karenga. US espoused the doctrine of racial pride and the value of learning about and strengthening African American culture. Best known for their traditional African garb and the creation of the African American holiday, Kwanzaa, US collapsed in the 1970s under the pressures of conflict with the Black Panther party and the Federal Bureau of Investigation (FBI).

During the 1960s, the Los Angeles–based group US was the quintessential "cultural nationalist" "Black Power" organization. Embracing the idea of an "African American" identity, US called for a cultural rebirth among black Americans as the first step in creating a more just society and a more independent black America. US emphasized the uniqueness of black culture, claiming that it had evolved separate from white society, and held that a strong African American culture was the real source of black power. Adopting African dress codes (dashikis and bubas) and languages (especially Swahili), US members were the West Coast's cultural vanguard in the African American freedom movements of the late 1960s.

Born Ronald McKinley Everett in Parsonburg, Maryland, in 1941, Maulana Ron Karenga became one of the leaders of the African American cultural nationalist movement. In 1965, following the California Watts riots, Karenga established US on the principles of black cultural unity and a "back to black" worldview that drew from African and African American roots. Karenga, whose Swahili name meant "keeper of the tradition," formulated the core of US philosophy on the basis of the seven points of the Nguzo Saba: Umoja (unity), Kujichagulia (self-determination), Ujima (collective work and responsibility), Ujamaa (cooperative economics), Nia (purpose), Kuumba (creativity), and Imani (faith). US also created new African American holidays, such as Uhuru Day (August 11, the anniversary of the Watts riots), Kuzaliwa (May 19,

to honor the birthday of Malcolm X), and Kwanzaa (first celebrated December 26, 1966–January 1, 1967, an alternative to Christmas). The seven points of the Nguzo Saba, the new holidays, and US's traditional African garb were all symbolic representations of the ideology of Kawaida, which held that cultural revolution preceded political and economic change and that blacks could only free themselves by first rejecting white values and strengthening their own culture. US grew quickly and became a leading militant organization in southern California. Among its African American admirers was the black poet-playwright LeRoi Jones, who embraced the tenets of Kawaida and adopted the Swahili name Imamu Amiri Baraka.

US's cultural nationalist beliefs also attracted their share of critics and led to violent clashes with police and the revolutionary nationalist Black Panther party. Conflicts between US and the Black Panthers arose out of struggles over control of the Black Congress, a collection of Los Angeles' black radical groups. Tensions flared between Karenga and the Panthers, and shoot-outs between the Panthers and US's paramilitary security force, the Simba Wachanga (Young Lions), resulted in numerous casualties, including the deaths of Panther captains John Huggins and Alprentice "Bunchy" Carter. The Panther-US conflict made headlines across the country, and the FBI's Counterintelligence Program (COINTELPRO), manipulated the splits between the two groups in the hope that the black power movement would destroy itself. Ultimately, the violence that ignited between the Black Panthers and US, fed by the FBI's actions, perverted the cultural nationalist movement in the eyes of many African Americans, and as a result US splintered and disintegrated by the mid-1970s.

**FURTHER READINGS**

Brown, Elaine. *A Taste of Power: A Black Woman's Story.* New York: Pantheon, 1992.

Horne, Gerald. *The Fire This Time: The Watts Uprising and the 1960s.* Charlottesville: University Press of Virginia, 1995.

Karenga, Maulana Ron. "From *The Quotable Karenga.*" In *The Black Power Revolt: A Collection of Essays.* Ed. Floyd B. Barbour. Boston: Extending Horizons Books, 1968.

Van Deburg, William L. *New Day in Babylon: The Black Power Movement and American Culture, 1965–1975.* Chicago: The University of Chicago Press, 1992.

*Daniel E. Crowe*

## Veterans Services Project

*See* Southern Regional Council.

## Virginia Council on Human Relations

The Virginia Council on Human Relations (VCHR) was one of twelve state Councils on Human Relations established by the Southern Regional Council of Atlanta, Georgia. Organized in 1955 as a nonpolitical, nondenominational, nonprofit, interracial organization, the VCHR used fact-finding, education, communication, negotiation, and persuasion to improve human relations in Virginia. The VCHR tried to prevent human relations conflicts and solve existing problems by organizing local residents in numerous communities. During the 1950s and 1960s the VCHR supported thirty-two local chapters. These local groups provided forums for community leaders and interested citizens to discuss methods of building better community relations and avoiding conflicts, tensions, and misunderstandings among the citizenry. Recognizing the importance of youth as future leaders, the VCHR also created several youth Councils on Human Relations as well as the Virginia College Council on Human Relations.

As an advocate of equal employment opportunity, the VCHR was instrumental in convincing Virginian businesses to adhere to a policy of employment based on merit. This resulted in 1963 in the establishment of the Virginia Equal Job Opportunity Bureau (VEJOB). Funded by a grant from the Field Foundation, the VEJOB was a private, nonprofit consulting service for Virginian businessmen who wanted to comply with federal requirements for equal employment opportunities. The VCHR was also committed to equal opportunity in public accommodation, housing, transportation, health, and law enforcement, and it supported school desegregation, antipoverty programs, and voter registration projects. The council ceased to function during the 1960s.

**FURTHER READING**

Southern Regional Council Papers, Series IV: State Councils on Human Relations, 1946–1968, Reels 149–50, Special Collections, Robert W. Woodruff Library, Atlanta University Center, Atlanta, Georgia.

*Kimberly E. Nichols*

## Visions Foundation

The Visions Foundation, founded in 1983, seeks to increase awareness of and educate the public about the contributions of African Americans to American culture. Supported by the Smithsonian Institution, the foundation publishes a monthly magazine, *American Visions: The Magazine of Afro-American Culture,* which explores the uniqueness of the African American experience. The foundation also supports the publication of books, including local and national guides to places of historic and cultural interest with African American ties. The foundation is headquartered in Washington, D.C., and has currently approximately 60,000 members.

**FURTHER READINGS**

Jaszcsak, Sandra, ed. *Encyclopedia of Associations.* Detroit: Gale, 1994.

*Minority Organizations: A National Directory.* Garrett Park, Md.: Garrett Park Press, 1992.

*Virginia M. Matthews*

## Voluntary Committee on the Federation of Negro Religious Denominations in the United States of America

*See* Fraternal Council of Negro Churches.

## Voter Education Project

A major effort to extend the franchise to Southern blacks during the 1960s, the Voter Education Project (VEP) was the product of an intersection of the interests of civil rights groups and the Kennedy administration. After the Freedom Rides crisis of 1961, the Kennedy administration sought to direct civil rights activists away from dramatic confrontations with white segregationists and toward the less inflammatory, yet important, work of increasing southern black participation in politics. This desire dovetailed with a long-standing drive by African Americans for the ballot. Once liberal foundations, encouraged by Kennedy officials, offered to fund a project to register black voters, the major civil rights groups, including the National Association for the Advancement of Colored People (NAACP), the Southern Christian Leadership Conference (SCLC), the Congress of Racial Equality (CORE), the Student Nonviolent Coordinating Committee (SNCC), and the National Urban League (NUL), agreed to launch a voter registration drive.

SNCC and the NAACP had the greatest reservations about this initiative. Some SNCC activists feared that the project was an effort by the Kennedy administration and civil rights moderates to defuse the growing momentum of the movement. The NAACP had its own fears, which were relieved only gradually. It worried that the young firebrands were likely to lose sight of their mission as they succumbed to the temptation of dramatic demonstrations and that its long-standing efforts to extend the franchise would be eclipsed by the new initiative.

The Southern Regional Council (SRC), a nonprofit organization headquartered in Atlanta, Georgia, with a long history of support for racial justice, became the dispenser of funds from the Field Foundation, the Taconic Foundation, and the Stern Family Fund. Over its first two-and-a-half years, the VEP spent nearly $900,000, ostensibly to "research" the causes of low black registration in the South, a mission that helped it gain a tax-exempt status. Wiley Branton, a black lawyer from Arkansas, who had been the legal advisor to the teenagers who integrated Little Rock High School in 1957, was tapped to direct the project, which began in April 1962.

Branton supervised the initiative with skill, but the real work fell on the civil rights groups. Each was given specific regions on which to focus its work. CORE tackled northern Louisiana and South Carolina, while SCLC and SNCC targeted southwest Georgia and Mississippi. The NAACP and the National Urban League focused on other parts of the South. In Mississippi, VEP funds helped energize the Council of Federated Organizations, a union of civil rights groups.

As some activists predicted and to the dismay of the Kennedy administration, voter registration work, just like direct action, could produce a violent white response. Nowhere was this more true than in Mississippi, where Bob Moses and courageous young activists sought to overcome the fears of local African Americans about the dangers of registering. White supremacists turned to threats, arrests, and violence to stifle insurgency.

The lack of a strong federal response angered insurgents who believed that Kennedy officials had promised to protect civil rights workers and blacks who attempted to register. For many activists, this abandonment greatly deepened their doubts about the allegiances of the federal government.

Branton exercised a strong hand as the director of the VEP. He temporarily suspended funds for SCLC's program when that organization could not properly account for its expenditures. And in late 1963, Branton halted funding for the voter registration projects in Mississippi because the hostile climate there ensured little gain in the number of black registrants. When the VEP's first suffrage campaign ended in late 1964, it had helped register tens of thousands of new black voters. Along with litigation by the Justice Department, the project helped to increase the proportion of African American registrants in the South from less than 30 percent to 43 percent.

Ultimately, it would take the Voting Rights Act of 1965 to fully mobilize black voters in the South. But the first VEP project had helped to raise consciousness about the voting rights issue and, as important, it helped to empower oppressed southern blacks to take action.

The SRC revived the voter education project in 1966. Under the direction of Vernon Jordan, a rising young black attorney, the second VEP subsidized hundreds of suffrage programs. From 1970 to 1977, John Lewis, the well-known civil rights activist, guided the effort with success, despite a small staff and limited funding. The VEP continued until 1992, but it never again matched the importance of its first fifteen years.

**FURTHER READINGS**

Lawson, Steven F. *Black Ballots: Voting Rights in the South, 1944–1969.* New York: Columbia University Press, 1976.

———. *Running for Freedom: Civil Rights and Black Politics in America Since 1941.* New York: McGraw-Hill, 1991.

Payne, Charles M. *I've Got the Light of Freedom: The Organizing Tradition and the Mississippi Freedom Struggle.* Berkeley: University of California Press, 1995.

Watters, Pat, and Reese Cleghorn. *Climbing Jacob's Ladder: The Arrival of Negroes in Southern Politics.* New York: Harcourt, Brace & World, 1967.

*James Ralph*

## Voter Registration Project

*See* Voter Education Project.

# War Manpower Commission, Negro Manpower Service

Established on April 18, 1942, the Negro Manpower Service of the War Manpower Commission (WMC) led the federal initiative to ensure the efficient utilization of African American workers during World War II. By the spring of 1942, the level of unemployment in America began a rapid decline. The massive production increase in support of the Allied war effort, combined with the millions of American men who joined the military, not only ended unemployment but resulted in labor shortages, particularly in defense industries. In response, President Franklin D. Roosevelt established the WMC under the chairmanship of Indiana Democrat Paul McNutt.

The WMC regulated manpower in areas that suffered from acute labor shortages, established policies to maximize labor utilization, and assisted private industries in finding workers. It determined when workers were allowed to change jobs and, in collaboration with the Selective Service, granted deferments to men employed in vital military production. The WMC's Negro Manpower Service was created to ensure that industries did not discriminate against African American job applicants and that black workers were treated fairly.

The WMC was often at odds with the War Production Board (WPB), which was controlled by "dollar-a-year" men, executives on loan to the federal government from private corporations for the duration of the war. The WPB resisted WMC efforts to implement Executive Order 8802 and end racial discrimination in defense industries. The WPB's willingness to tolerate violations of the president's fair employment mandate reflected the attitudes of many employers who failed to comply with Executive Order 8802 and only hired black workers when particularly dire labor shortages left them no other choice.

While the WMC had little power to enforce equal treatment of African American workers, on occasion it was successful. In 1944, for example, the WMC, in cooperation with the President's Committee on Fair Employment Practice (FEPC), ordered the Philadelphia Transportation Company to promote eight African Americans to streetcar drivers. When the company complied, the white workers belonging to the Transit Workers' Union protested and launched a strike that shut down the entire public transportation system. The strike stopped production in Philadelphia's many war-related factories because workers were unable to get to work. When the war effort was affected, the federal government dispatched 8,000 troops to break the strike and enforce the WMC and FEPC's dictates. Subsequently, more defense industry positions were available to the city's large African American population.

FURTHER READINGS

Fairchild, Byron, and Jonathan Grossman, *The Army and Industrial Manpower. Vol. 7, United States Army in World War II*. Ed. Kent Roberts Greenfield. Washington, D.C.: Government Printing Office, 1959.

Hill, Herbert. *Black Labor and the American Legal System: Race, Work, and the Law*. Washington, D.C.: Bureau of National Affairs, 1977.

King, Desmond. *Separate and Unequal: Black Americans and the US Federal Government*. Oxford: Clarendon Press, 1995.

Lichtenstein, Nelson. *Labor's War at Home: The CIO in World War II*. New York: Cambridge University Press, 1982.

Poster published by the War Manpower Commission, 1943.
*Library of Congress*

Winkler, Allan M. "The Philadelphia Transit Strike of 1944." *Journal of American History* 41, 1 (June 1972): 73–89.

*Peter Cole*

## War Production Board, Negro Employment and Training Branch

In January 1942, the War Production Board (WPB), Negro Employment and Training Branch (NETB), succeeded the Minorities Branch of the Office of Production Management. The NETB, headed by Robert C. Weaver, an African American economist and member of President Franklin D. Roosevelt's "Black Cabinet," was to provide African Americans with job skills necessary for employment in World War II defense industries.

Roosevelt assigned primary responsibility for mobilizing American industries to the military and the nation's corporations. Thus, business leaders dominated the ranks of wartime government agencies. Daniel Nelson, a vice president of Sears, Roebuck & Company, headed the WPB and most of the agency's key positions were held by "dollar-a-year men," executives on loan from their corporations, whose companies continued to pay their salaries while they worked for the government. The armed forces determined production requirements based on military necessity, and the WPB decided what types of products companies were allowed to produce. Thus, the WPB exercised considerable power over the nation's economy.

The purpose of the WPB's NETB was to ensure that private employers effectively utilized black workers for wartime production. The need for African American workers was obvious, since a simultaneous increase in production and flight from civilian jobs into the military had created a massive labor shortage. The NETB tried to help black workers take advantage of the wartime labor shortage by providing vocational classes designed to prepare African Americans for industrial employment. The NETB offered these classes in industrial centers and black technical institutions and colleges.

Despite the dramatic need for workers and the NETB's efforts to train African Americans for employment in defense industries, white employers continued to discriminate against blacks. Weaver complained that the continuing discrimination of black workers was due to the lack of coordination between employers and the government. Yet Weaver also insisted that the WPB was at least in part to blame for the racial discrimination black workers continued to encounter in the industrial sector. The WPB, he lamented, had failed to propose a detailed plan for the utilization of African Americans in the burgeoning defense industry. Moreover, Weaver criticized the agency for operating segregated training programs and thereby enabling prospective employers to request only white workers trained by the WPB. Using information gathered by the NETB, the President's Committee on Fair Employment Practice (FEPC) repeatedly cited incidents of white employers refusing to hire black workers, claiming that they were not trained adequately. The southern shipbuilding industry in particular strongly resisted efforts to increase the number of black workers at its shipyards, even when black workers had the necessary skills. Finally, in many locales, especially in the South, employers and government officials purposefully delayed implementing plans to train black workers for war-related employment.

Throughout the war, the NETB worked to combat discriminatory job requests as well as the government's lack of commitment to provide adequate training for African Americans.

FURTHER READINGS

King, Desmond. *Separate and Unequal: Black Americans and the US Federal Government.* Oxford: Clarendon Press, 1995.

Lichtenstein, Nelson. *Labor's War at Home: The CIO in World War II.* New York: Cambridge University Press, 1982.

Smith, R. E. Berton. *The Army and Economic Mobilization. Vol. 5, United States Army in World War II.* Ed. Kent Roberts Greenfield. Washington, D.C.: Government Printing Office, 1958.

*Peter Cole*

# Washington, D.C.: Civic, Literary, and Mutual Aid Associations

Washington, D.C.'s civic, literary, and mutual aid associations have a long tradition, although most African American associations came into being after the Civil War. Washington was primarily a center for slave trading rather than a slave holding area in the nineteenth century. As the nation's capital it was also a focus for abolitionist activity and was home to several stops on the Underground Railroad. As such, the District became home to a sizable population of free blacks. By 1840 there were twice as many free blacks as slaves, and by 1860 the ratio of free to slave was over three to one.

Free blacks faced severe restrictions and the District government forbade any meetings except for fraternal and religious purposes. The major antebellum black associations in Washington therefore came under these headings. Fraternal organizations spread quickly among free blacks after the founding of the first Prince Hall Mason lodge in 1787. By 1825 District black masons had established Lodge #7, and in 1848 three District lodges formed a Grand Lodge. Freemasonry, with its emphasis on equality for all citizens, appealed to free blacks ideologically, and socially it provided a further basis for distinction between middle- and working-class free blacks. In 1855 John A. Simms and other members of the black elite helped to establish a District lodge of the Odd Fellows named for prominent educator and Odd Fellow John F. Cook. The District Odd Fellows purchased a hall on Fifteenth Street and hosted the Ninth Annual Convention in 1863.

Both organizations opened other lodges in the District and attracted leading free blacks to their ranks. Among those attracted was Thomas H. Wright, who served on the Board of Trustees of Union Bethel African Methodist Episcopal (AME) Church. In 1889, Wright sponsored the drive to build the new Odd Fellows Hall, which became a center for fraternal activity in the city.

The other major black association created by free blacks in antebellum Washington was a local branch of the Young Men's Christian Association (YMCA), founded in 1853 by Anthony Bowen, a clerk in the Patent Office. This branch had the honor of being the first black YMCA in the country. Unfortunately the group survived only a few years and was not revived until the late nineteenth century.

While not producing formal organizations in other areas, free blacks were active in creating private schools such as that established in 1834 by John F. Cook. Free blacks also established successful businesses, particularly in the fields of catering, livery, taverns, and hotels. It was this class of teachers and businessmen that would provide later associational leadership.

During the Civil War and Reconstruction, Washington's black population increased significantly. Refugees headed for the capital following the Emancipation Proclamation in hopes that Lincoln could also find them work or a new home. Black regiments were mustered out in Washington, and many of the soldiers stayed in the nation's capital. The new arrivals drastically changed the nature of the black population, which by 1880 was roughly one-third of the total District population. Before 1867 most blacks had owned real estate and held regular jobs or ran businesses. The new arrivals were, for the most part, indigent, and were shunted into squalid alley dwellings such as Hell's Bottom and Goose Level. The Freedmen's Bureau was active in establishing a public school system for blacks and also founded Freedmen's Hospital in 1862 and Howard University in 1867.

Ultimately these new institutions and the promise of government appointments made Washington a mecca for educated and professional blacks. These elite newcomers combined with the older inhabitants in an attempt to separate themselves both physically and socially from the working classes and indigent. By the 1880s black Washington had become segregated along race and class lines.

Following Emancipation, blacks began association building in earnest. In 1867, in the wake of the creation of the public schools, John F. Cook helped to found an organization for black teachers, designed to bring the curriculum of the black schools in line with that of the white schools. The establishment of the Freedmen's Bank in

1865 helped to fortify a new class of black government appointees. Loosely associated with this group of men was a social group known as the Lotus Club. Widely criticized for its clique mentality and its overemphasis on light skin, the Lotus Club was typical of many late nineteenth-century social organizations in that it tried to segregate the black elite from the masses.

Despite social exclusivity, black leaders worked to enhance the African American community. Business leaders formed the Union Joint Stock Association in 1867 in order to create a black daily newspaper in Washington. Leading blacks such as George T. Downing and Lewis Douglass figured prominently in the black labor movement. Others formed the Colored Union Benevolent Association in the 1860s to provide assistance for the sick, needy, and destitute.

By the 1880s it was becoming clear that whites did not accept blacks as equals, and the realization spurred a host of black literary and professional organizations. In 1882 John W. Cromwell, editor of the *People's Advocate*, and clubwoman Rosetta Coakley, among others, founded the Chatauqua Literary Scientific Circle to discuss issues of contemporary concern. In the late 1880s the Friday Night Literary met frequently at the home of Frederick Douglass and discussed women's suffrage and temperance.

By far the leading literary association at the turn of the twentieth century was the Bethel Literary and Historical Association, founded in 1882. From its inception the organization discussed racial issues and studied black history. The group attracted some of the leading black intellectuals to its meetings. It instilled race pride and furthered the sense of connection between the black elite and the rest of the black community. It inspired other turn-of-the-century groups such as the Second Baptist Lyceum and the Congressional Lyceum to address issues of concern to the black community and to debate methods of racial uplift.

Other groups founded in the 1890s fostered elite connections with the black community. In keeping with Progressive Era sentiments, black associations began to focus on reform of the black working class. In the process they began working for racial uplift. Biracial charitable organizations often segregated black and white workers and African Americans often found all-black organizations more capable of effecting racial uplift.

The rise of the black women's club movement was particularly important in this respect. Initially associated with church groups, black club women turned to quasi-independent associations to bring about scientific reform.

In Washington a group of women emerged who were prominent in most of the city's reform organizations at the turn of the twentieth century.

Mary Church Terrell was president of the Phyllis Wheatley Young Women's Christian Association (YWCA), established in 1905, founder of the Colored Women's League, and Trustee of the Colored Social Settlement Centre. Helen Appo Cook served on the Board of Managers for the National Association for the Relief of Destitute Colored Women and Children and was president of the Women's Protective Union. Anna Evans Murray started a campaign to create a kindergarten system and was a delegate to the interracial Congress of Mothers in 1898. Josephine Bruce was the first president of the National Association of Colored Women (NACW) and a YWCA worker. Nannie Helen Burroughs was a member of the NACW and founded the National Training School for Women and Girls. Amanda Bowen was president of the Sojourner Truth Home for Working Women and founder of the Teacher's Benefit and Annuity Association.

Washington's black club women, in association with others, established the Stoddard Baptist Home for the Elderly in the 1890s, sponsored Fresh Air campaigns for underprivileged children, ran day-care programs for working mothers, and lobbied for playgrounds in alley neighborhoods. In 1908, they created the Alley Improvement Association to improve housing and sanitary conditions for alley dwellers. The Anthony Bowen YMCA re-formed in 1895 and worked toward building a new home, a feat accomplished in 1912. The YWCA established traveler's aid programs and opened a reading library. Charitable organizations blossomed during the Progressive Era, and although in the 1930s New Deal agencies took over many of their programs, private associations have continued to maintain a social welfare aspect.

Fraternal organizations also blossomed. For the newcomers, fraternal organizations provided insurance features and death benefits. For black professionals and businessmen they offered a chance to establish a clientele through connections with the broader black community. They also offered a chance for valuable legal and financial experience handling insurance funds and lawsuits initiated by white orders challenging their legitimacy. Some lodges remained elite in orientation, providing a measure of social segregation.

Professional organizations increased with the rise of segregation in the 1890s. After repeated rejections of black applicants to the white medical society, a group of doctors associated with Freedmen's Hospital, including John R.

Francis, Daniel Hale Williams, and Arthur W. Tancil, established the Medico-Chirurgical Society in 1895. The group attempted to gain recognition by the American Medical Association (AMA) but was denied and became a leading force in the National Medical Association that African Americans had formed in 1870. The organization exists to this day, with prominent past presidents including William Montague Cobb and Edward Mazique. Ultimately professional organizations found themselves in the forefront of the movement against racial discrimination. At the turn of the century black lawyers formed a black bar association, black dentists joined the Tri-State Dental Association of DC, VA, MD and the Robert T. Freeman Dental Society, and black pharmacists joined the Colored Druggists Association. All of these associations were dependent on black patronage, and all had to fight community stereotypes of black professionals as being inferior to whites in the same professions.

The rise of national organizations in the twentieth century meant that local branches often took on the work of smaller local organizations. The local NACW succeeded in raising funds to purchase and preserve Frederick Douglass's home in Anacostia in 1916. The Washington branch of the National Association for the Advancement of Colored People (NAACP) led a "Don't Buy Where You Can't Work" campaign in the 1930s. In addition, increasing government bureaucracy during the New Deal meant increasing attention paid to the needs of blacks after the Depression.

Nonetheless, black professional groups such as the Howard University Women's Club experienced increases in membership in the 1920s and 1930s. The NACW added a Washington and Vicinity Federation of Women's Clubs to its original branch in 1924. National sororities such as Alpha Kappa Alpha, Phi Delta Kappa, and Zeta Phi Beta established local alumnae chapters in the 1920s. In the 1930s the Medico-Chirurgical Society and the Robert T. Freeman Dental Society created women's auxiliaries that focused on fund-raising for scholarships. In 1931, the Ionia R. Whipper Home for Unwed Mothers was the first of its kind in Washington to open its doors to blacks.

Beginning in the 1940s, associations such as the Consolidated Parents Group focused on accomplishing school desegregation, while new elite social groups like the Links and the Paragons focused on charity work combined with social activities, a pattern that continues today. In the 1950s when many black professional organizations were dissolving in other cities as a result of increasing desegregation, Washington's black professionals continued to create separate associations such as the Capitol City Educators Club, Women In Government Service, and the Women's Auxiliary of Howard University Hospital. National groups such as Jack and Jill and National Tots and Teens opened Washington branches to care for the city's black children. The Capitol Press Club, founded in 1943, aimed to introduce black media colleagues to leading political and community figures. In the 1970s the club began publishing the "In Book," a comprehensive register of black civic, social, and community organizations.

Beginning in the 1960s and 1970s, Washington's population, partly as a result of white flight to Virginia and Maryland suburbs, became majority black. This has led to all-black chapters of national organizations that are not specifically aimed at African Americans. For example a 1983 register of black women's associations lists the District of Columbia Democratic Women's Club and the District of Columbia Citywide Welfare Rights Organization. Such organizations mirror what would be biracial organizations in other cities.

In the 1970s black women's organizations such as the Black Women's League, the National Black Women's Political Caucus of Washington, D.C., and Black Women for Social Action reflected the national trend for women's rights organizations. Most of these organizations also incorporate traditional club women's agendas including child care and education.

In the 1980s, black men's groups arose in response to the men's movement, including the Black Men's Forum, and Concerned Black Men. In 1986, Assistant Principal Cleo Davis Jr. formed the Alpha Omega Young Men's Association of H. D. Woodson Senior High. The group worked to counteract negative stereotypes of black males and to develop positive leadership roles. The association soon spread to include other high schools and one junior high school.

With the city's historically large and varied African American population, it is not surprising that Washington's black associational activity has been lively. Limited to religious and fraternal activities, free blacks established a foundation for future associations. Overwhelmed by the influx of refugees during Reconstruction, the black elite attempted to segregate themselves socially while still working for the community. With the rise of segregation they created separate professional and charitable organizations that tied them closer to the rest of the black community, as did the lessons in race pride they learned in literary associations. National organizations such as the NAACP took over many racial uplift efforts as government agencies took on more in the 1930s, but women's and professional organizations continued to flourish beyond World War II. Black social groups maintained charitable goals and gender-oriented groups followed patterns in the white community. The rise of a black majority population in Washington has made it harder to identify race-oriented organizations, yet black associations still play an important role in Washington at the beginning of the twenty-first century.

**FURTHER READINGS**

Federal Writers Project. *The Negro in Washington.* 1937?: rpt., New York: Arno Press and the *New York Times,* 1969.

Gatewood, Willard B. *Aristocrats of Color: The Black Elite, 1880–1920.* Bloomington and Indianapolis: Indiana University Press, 1990.

Green, Constance McLaughlin. *The Secret City: A History of Race Relations in the Nation's Capital.* Princeton, N.J.: Princeton University Press, 1967.

Moore, Jacqueline M. *Leading the Race: The Transformation of Washington D.C.'s Black Elite, 1880–1920.* Charlottesville: University Press of Virginia, 1999.

Wesley, Charles Harris. *The History of the National Association of Colored Women's Clubs: A Legacy of Service.* Washington, D.C.: National Association of Colored Women's Clubs, Inc., 1984.

*Jacqueline M. Moore*

# Washington Society of Colored Dentists

*See* Tri-State Dental Association of DC, VA, MD.

# Washington State Board Against Discrimination in Employment

In 1949, the Washington State Law Against Discrimination in Employment made discrimination in employment and public accommodations a state concern and a violation of state law. The act mandated the creation of a permanent five-member board, appointed by the governor. The Washington State Board Against Discrimination in Employment (WSBAD) monitored discrimination based on "race, creed, color or national origin" in the job and housing markets and served as a clearinghouse for discrimination complaints.

The original board included Chairman David E. Lockwood, Richard W. Axtell, the Reverend Fountain W. Penick, Mrs. Robert M. Jones, the Reverend Jerome L. Toner O.S.B., and Glen E. Mansfield, who served as the first executive secretary for the board. Over the years, African American board members included the Reverend Penick, Ola Browning, Roberta Byrd, and Calvin Johnson.

The board operated on the assumption that the eradication of discriminatory practices could most effectively be attained "by reason [rather] than by force." Board members believed that any form of intimidation of employers, unions, and employment agencies as well as increasing tensions between whites and minority groups would only disrupt the normal order of business and not produce the intended results. Thus, board members decided to appeal to the "sense of justice" of both employers and the employees.

In its early years, the board's primary goal was to disseminate information about the state's antidiscrimination law and the board's role in implementing it. Thus, board members spent much time and effort meeting with employers, labor organizations, employment agencies, religious leaders, civil rights groups, schools, and other members of the public. During the board's first year of operation, its members spoke to approximately two thousand high school students. As part of this public education campaign, the board distributed copies of the law, proposed rules and regulations, and issued pamphlets and other resource materials. Moreover, board members organized luncheons, speaking engagements, and conferences throughout the state and met with representatives of various organizations, including the Civic Unity Committee, Yakima Chamber of Commerce, Anti-Defamation League of Seattle, Seattle Urban League, and Central Labor Councils of Bremerton. Finally, the board organized a conference in conjunction with the Oregon State Fair Employment Practices Committee. On February 1, 1950, participants gathered in Portland, Oregon, to facilitate intraregional cooperation. Board members also sought to connect with similar groups in other parts of the country and corresponded with organizations such as the New York State Fair Employment Practices Commission. In its first year of operation, the board received forty complaints, twenty-nine of which were filed by African Americans. The board dismissed twenty-seven of those complaints and settled nine by conciliation.

Throughout the 1950s and 1960s, the board continued its public education campaign through meetings, conferences, publications, public speaking engagements, and radio and television programs. Between June 1968 and July 1969, board members participated in 4,892 public speaking engagements and received fifty-four discrimination complaints. During the late 1960s, the board also attempted to work with other agencies such as the Equal Employment Opportunity Commission to promote affirmative action. Technical studies of discrimination also became part of the board's agenda, resulting in the publication of reports such as *A Study of Racial Tension in Tacoma* in 1970.

Despite the board's efforts, it had only limited success in ending discrimination in employment and public accommodation. Insufficient funding as well as the board's nonconfrontational approach may help explain its lack of effectiveness. By the 1960s, a number of direct-action protest groups challenged the board's approach and took the lead in the state's struggle for civil rights.

In 1971, a state law changed the board's name to Washington State Human Rights Commission. The commission continues to implement the board's original mandate, while extending its scope to include the prevention of discrimination based on sex, age, or mental or physical handicap.

## FURTHER READINGS

Taylor, Quintard. *The Forging of a Black Community: Seattle's Central District from 1870 Through the Civil Rights Era.* Seattle: University of Washington Press, 1994.

Washington State Board Against Discrimination. *State Board Against Discrimination: 1966–67 Annual Report.* Seattle: Washington State Board of Discrimination, 1967.

———. *A Study of Racial Tension in Tacoma.* Seattle: Washington State Board of Discrimination, 1970.

Washington State Board of Discrimination in Employment. *First Semi-Annual Report of the Washington State Board of Discrimination in Employment.* Seattle: Washington State Board of Discrimination in Employment, 1949.

———. *Thirteenth Report to the Governor.* Seattle: Washington State Board of Discrimination in Employment, 1956.

*Colin A. Beckles*

**SEE ALSO**  Washington State Fair Employment Practices Committee

## Washington State Committee Against Discrimination in Employment

*See* Washington State Fair Employment Practices Committee.

## Washington State Committee for Legislation Against Discrimination in Employment

*See* Washington State Fair Employment Practices Committee.

## Washington State Fair Employment Practices Committee

The Washington State Fair Employment Practices Committee was established in Seattle in 1946 when the U.S. Congress ended the national Fair Employment Practices Committee. At that time the Civic Unity Committee (CUC) in Seattle, a predominantly white civil rights organization, lobbied for civil rights laws and attempted to use persuasion to stop racial discrimination. When the CUC turned its attention to securing passage of a state anti–job discrimination law, it created the committee as a sister organization specifically designed for that purpose.

Sponsors of the committee included Roy Atkinson, regional director of the Congress of Industrial organizations and executive board member of the National Association for the Advancement of Colored People; F. B. Cooper, an African American dentist on the board of Seattle's Urban League and a member of the CUC; and William Devin, mayor of Seattle. Remaining sponsors included attorneys, other CUC members, physicians and students, as well as members of the Seattle school board and the business and labor communities. Original committee members held prominent positions in Seattle. Chairman Frank Haley was an attorney and state chairman of the American Veterans Committee. Vice chairmen included Arthur Barnett of the American Friends Service Committee, Harold Barde of the Seattle Federated Jewish Fund, and the Reverend Benjamin Davis, an African American minister. The treasurer was Sidney Gerber, president of Anderson and Thompson Ski Company.

Committee members attended meetings of the state legislature, giving much attention to national currents, such as the 1947 publication of *To Secure These Rights*—the report of President Truman's Committee on Civil Rights. With the help of the report, the committee persuaded Washington's Governor Monrad C. Wallgren to select a nonpartisan commission of responsible citizens to study the need for state civil rights legislation. Members of the committee served on that commission.

In December 1947, the committee started to reorganize. In July 1948, it was renamed Washington State Committee for Legislation Against Discrimination in Employment.

Structural changes included the creation of a legislative committee responsible for drafting a state anti–job discrimination bill, the appointment of a treasurer to conduct fund-raising campaigns, and the formation of a membership committee responsible for enlisting members and securing small contributions.

In November 1948, the committee, now known as the Washington State Committee Against Discrimination in Employment, met to discuss the proposed bill drafted by its legislative committee and send fund-raising letters to various agencies. Committee members also made plans to contact personally potential donors to secure large contributions for the struggle to implement the bill. Moreover, the committee made plans to contact Governor-elect Arthur B. Langlie to ascertain his position on the legislative proposal. The group also established a public relations committee to aide in designing a pamphlet about the proposed legislation.

On March 19, 1949, the legislative drafting and lobbying efforts of the committee and it allies succeeded as the Washington State Law Against Discrimination in Employment was signed into law by the governor. The law declared that equal opportunity to work without discrimination based on race, creed, color, or national origins was a matter of state concern and recognized it as a civil right.

**FURTHER READINGS**

Taylor, Quintard. *The Forging of a Black Community: Seattle's Central District from 1870 Through the Civil Rights Era*. Seattle: University of Washington Press. 1994.

University of Washington Libraries. *Civic Unity Committee of Seattle: Guide*. Seattle: University of Washington Libraries, Manuscripts and Archives Division, 1997.

*Colin A. Beckles*

**SEE ALSO** Washington State Board Against Discrimination in Employment

## Washington State Human Rights Commission

*See* Washington State Board Against Discrimination in Employment.

## West Coast Baseball Association

In 1946, Eddie Harris and several other members of Berkeley's all-black High Marine Social Club organized the West Coast Baseball Association (WCBA). Abe Saperstein, the owner of the Harlem Globetrotters basketball team, was named president of the league, and Jesse Owens, owner of the franchise in Portland, Oregon, served as vice president.

The WCBA included six teams; Seattle Steelheads, Portland Rosebuds, Oakland Larks, San Diego Tigers, Los Angeles White Sox, and San Francisco Sea Lions. Initially, the league outlined a schedule of 110 games. Home games were to be played in the ballparks of the Pacific Coast League (PCL) while its team was traveling. Games were also scheduled in nearby locations. The WCBA disbanded about two months into its schedule. At that time, Oakland was in first place and Seattle in second.

The Seattle Steelheads were Saperstein's Harlem Globetrotters baseball team, which had debuted in 1944. By 1946, most of the Globetrotters baseball players appeared for the Seattle Steelheads, but in the following year, the team started using its Harlem Globetrotters name again. Some of the better-known Steelhead/Globetrotters players were Sherwood Brewer, Nap Gulley, Paul Hardy, Everett Marcel, Rogers Pierre, and Ulysses Redd.

After the league disbanded, the Oakland Larks played several barnstorming games in the state of Washington, including a three-game series against the State Semi-Pro Champions, the Bellingham Bells. The Bells prevailed, 2–1. The pitcher for the Larks in the first game in the series was Lionel Wilson. Wilson would soon forsake baseball for law school, and after a long career as a practicing attorney and judge, he became the first black mayor of the City of Oakland, California.

Starting to play as early as 1920, the Los Angeles White Sox was probably the oldest organization in the WCBA. The team played in White Sox Park, owned by Joe Pirrone. Hall of Fame inductee "Bullet" Rogan was one of the early stars of the White Sox.

The San Francisco franchise also had a history that preceded the West Coast league and continued after its demise in 1946. Playing under various nicknames, including the Sea Lions, Tigers, and Cubs, the team traveled extensively throughout the western part of the United States and Canada and in 1948 visited the Philippines. Among the team's illustrious alumni are Bill Bruton, who later played in the Major Leagues, and Toni Stone, one of the few females who played professionally in the Negro Baseball Leagues.

With such good franchises, the WCBA should have had greater success. After all, the teams had good players, and the games were well attended. The teams, however, were underfunded and the league started at a time when the Major and Minor Leagues began to admit black players, eventually contributing to the demise of all organized Negro baseball leagues.

**FURTHER READINGS**
*Bellingham Herald,* June-September 1946.
*Chicago Defender,* January-May 1946.
*Mariners Magazine* 6, 3 (1995).
*San Francisco Chronicle,* February 23, 1993.
*Seattle Times,* September 9, 1995.

*Lyle K. Wilson*

## Western Freedmen's Aid Commission

The Western Freedmen's Aid Commission (WFAC) was one of over fifty secular and ecclesiastical organizations that worked among the freed slaves of the American South during and after the Civil War. The WFAC, whose work was confined largely to southern Ohio, was wracked by dissension and subterfuge throughout its eight-year life. Like other voluntary freedmen's aid organizations in the states of the Old Northwest, the WFAC was briefly successful in raising funds, but lost support quickly after the end of the war.

The commission was formed in January 1863 when some members of the Cincinnati Contraband Relief Commission withdrew to create an organization that would put more emphasis on education for the freedmen. The Quaker abolitionist Levi Coffin, Methodist ministers John M. Walden and Richard S. Rust, and Congregationalist minister Charles B. Boynton were prominent in the commission's early years. In 1864, the WFAC sent Coffin to England where he raised over $100,000 for freedmen's relief, relying primarily upon his connections with wealthy Quaker abolitionists. The commission reported that it employed nearly 125 teachers by mid-1865 as a result of Coffin's work. Fund-raising within Ohio never approached that level, however, and the organization's teacher corps dropped to fewer than fifty by early 1866.

Throughout 1865 and early 1866, officers of the WFAC sought to influence the national freedmen's aid movement, insisting on a much larger voice in the movement than its size warranted. For a brief time one of its officers, the Reverend Jacob Shipherd, managed to designate the commission as the western division of the American Freedmen's Aid Commission, with himself as the western secretary with a large salary. Meanwhile, in February 1866 the Methodist members of the commission, led by Walden, attempted to turn the WFAC into the nucleus of a new Methodist freedmen's aid association. Failing that, Walden, Rust, and others withdrew in the summer of 1866, taking with them most of the commission's officers and many of its teachers and schools and creating the Freedmen's Aid Society of the Methodist Episcopal Church. When the American Freedmen's Union Commission abolished the western division and the western secretaryship, reducing the WFAC to a status equal to others in the national association of secular aid societies, the WFAC withdrew from the national body. In October 1866, Shipherd and other Congregationalist members of the WFAC merged the commission into the American Missionary Association, the Congregationalist Church's missionary society. The WFAC maintained a separate identity within the American Missionary Association until March 4, 1870, though the officers of the two organizations were identical and their work was indistinguishable. The commission published the *Freedmen's Reporter* irregularly in 1867 and early 1868.

Like other secular aid societies in the western states, the WFAC was far less successful in raising funds than its eastern counterparts and adopted more racially conservative policies regarding the distribution of aid and the form of schooling for freed slaves. It survived longer than other western aid societies, but did so only by attaching itself to the highly effective American Missionary Association.

**FURTHER READINGS**
Butchart, Ronald E. *Northern Schools, Southern Blacks, and Reconstruction: Freedmen's Education, 1862–1875.* Westport, Conn.: Greenwood Press, 1980.
Holliday, Joseph E. "Freedmen's Aid Societies in Cincinnati, 1862–1870." *Bulletin of the Cincinnati Historical Society* 22 (1964): 169–185.
Richardson, Joe M. *Christian Reconstruction: The American Missionary Association and Southern Blacks, 1861–1890.* Athens: University of Georgia Press, 1986.

*Ronald E. Butchart*

## Will the Circle Be Unbroken?

*See* Southern Regional Council.

## Wisconsin Governor's Commission on Human Rights

*See* Governor's Human Rights Commission, Wisconsin.

# Women Wage Earner's Association

The Women Wage Earner's Association (WWEA) was organized by middle-class African American club women in Washington, D.C., during World War I. WWEA president Jeanette Carter, secretary Julia F. Coleman, and treasurer Mary Church Terrell attempted to form a proto-union for exploited domestic service and tobacco industry workers in Washington, D.C., and Virginia. The purpose of the WWEA was to assist these women, who were organized by neither the American Federation of Labor (AFL) nor the Women's Trade Union League, in securing higher wages and better working conditions.

Throughout much of the twentieth century, African American women performed some of the most laborious and menial jobs for the lowest wages in the American work force. Domestic service, for example, was often the only available employment outside of farming, and black women dominated the domestic service industry until the mid-1920s. Yet, domestic service work was virtually unregulated. During World War I black female domestics often worked as many as sixty, seventy-two, or even eighty-four hours per week for a monthly wage of no more than $12.50. Black women employed in the Virginia cigar and cigarette-making industry, who were hired to stem tobacco leaves during World War I, earned seventy cents a day, for a ten-hour work day, and usually worked a fifty-five–hour work week. Moreover, African American women were subject to prosecution under "work or fight" laws enacted by numerous states during World War I. Thus, black women had no choice but to work at these below subsistence wages, if they were not already forced to work by economic necessity. Although wartime compulsory work laws exempted white women with family obligations who had economic support, black women were not so exempted.

Recognizing the severe hardships that black women faced in race- and gender-segregated workplaces in an unapologetically racist society, African American club women in Washington, D.C., founded the WWEA. These reform-minded, middle-class black women, who were engaged in racial uplift projects and programs, counseled their less fortunate working-class sisters in the virtues and benefits of unity of purpose through membership in the WWEA. In September 1917, the WWEA branch in Norfolk, Virginia, organized 600 black women workers to call on their employers in private households, restaurants, laundries, and in the tobacco industry to improve working conditions and to adjust wages to meet the rising cost of living that resulted from wartime price inflation. Three hundred WWEA members employed as tobacco stemmers at the American Cigar Company in Norfolk, pleaded their case with their employers and with the general public in the pages of the *Norfolk Journal and Guide*. WWEA tobacco stemmers explained that the most basic living expenses for one week added up to $7.25 and demanded raises in wages from seventy cents to $1.50 per day to cover the weekly expenses. When the American Cigar Company refused to raise wages, black women workers went on strike. Other members of the Norfolk WWEA, including domestic servants, waitresses, and laundresses, staged simultaneous strikes and demanded pay raises to meet a minimum wage of $1 per day.

Although their wage demands were conservative, the black women strikers were considered to be radically subversive for not supporting sufficiently the nation's wartime labor needs, as defined by U.S. government authorities. Norfolk police arrested the strikers, who were labeled "slackers," and charged them with violating "work or fight" laws. Moreover, the federal government investigated the WWEA to determine whether it had interfered with the war effort and had violated the 1917 Espionage Act. Under the dual forces of government pressure and employer resistance, the Norfolk branch of the WWEA dissolved in the fall of 1917, and the "national" WWEA soon ended its efforts to unionize black women workers. Although the short-lived WWEA achieved few of its immediate goals, it brought black women together in highly visible public activism in and around the nation's capital and raised expectations for economic and social progress for all African American women workers in the postwar period.

## FURTHER READINGS

Foner, Philip S. *Women and the American Labor Movement, From World War I to the Present.* New York: The Free Press, 1980.

Hunter, Tera. *To 'Joy My Freedom: Southern Black Women's Lives and Labor after the Civil War.* Cambridge, Mass.: Harvard University Press, 1997.

Neverdon-Morton, Cynthia. *Afro-American Women of the South and the Advancement of the Race, 1895–1925.* Knoxville: University of Tennessee Press, 1989.

Salem, Dorothy. *To Better Our World: Black Women in Organized Reform, 1890–1920.* Brooklyn, N.Y.: Carlson Publishing, Inc., 1990.

*Karen Garner*

# Women's Christian Temperance Union, Department of Colored Work

The Department of Colored Work of the Women's Christian Temperance Union (WCTU) was established in 1883 to promote temperance among African Americans. The department organized African American women who supported the WCTU's goals to prohibit alcohol and instill Christian morality. The group sought to influence public policies by attacking social, political, and economic inequalities that its members believed were related to alcohol consumption and abuse. Joining the WCTU allowed African American women to enter the political arena under the auspices of the most broadly based women's organization of the nineteenth century, which fought to change fundamentally a society that discriminated against and oppressed its nonwhite members.

African American women demonstrated a long-running interest in temperance, which they linked with their general concern for racial uplift throughout the nineteenth century. While they challenged racial conditions and attitudes, they supported popular nineteenth-century gender expectations that relegated women to a special role as protectors of society's morals. Linking weakness and torpidity with alcohol abuse, black women joined local African American–led temperance and mutual aid societies through their churches and within male-led fraternal organizations during the antebellum and post–Civil War eras.

When the WCTU formed in 1874 as an exclusively female temperance organization, some African American women saw a rare opportunity to advance a cause that they believed in within a national, Christian, and multiracial movement while developing their political and leadership skills. The WCTU, led during its heyday in the 1880s and 1890s by white president Frances Willard, was engaged in a moral crusade to "Do Everything" to combat social, political, and economic "evils" that stemmed from, or were exacerbated by, alcohol abuse. African American women who joined the crusade were already involved in wide-ranging attacks on social inequalities and had been searching for "social purity" when the WCTU formed a "Department of Colored Work" in 1883.

The WCTU grew rapidly as a national organization. In the late 1870s the WCTU had 27,000 members organized in 1,000 local chapters in twenty-four states. By 1900 the number of members had increased to 168,000 enrolled in 7,000 local chapters that provided some representation in every state. The overwhelming majority of WCTU members were native-born, Protestant white women. African American women made up 0.9 percent of the total membership in 1874, and only 1.7 percent in 1894. From the WCTU's inception separate black local chapters were formed that usually reported to regional committees of white women. When the WCTU organized a Department of Colored Work at the national level, black women saw this as an opportunity not only to promote temperance but also to promote racial advancement by fostering self-help and social improvement among African Americans.

In 1883, the WCTU appointed Frances Ellen Watkins Harper to the post of superintendent of the Department of Colored Work. She was the first and only African American woman to hold a position on the executive committee or the board of WCTU superintendents. Harper, who had grown up in a free black family in slave-holding Maryland, became involved in the abolitionist movement in the 1850s as a writer, public speaker, and active member of the Underground Railroad. During the 1870s Harper joined the temperance movement and served as superintendent of Colored Work for the Philadelphia and Pennsylvania chapters of the WCTU. Emphasizing personal integrity, Christian service, and social equality in all her public and private activities, Harper believed that African Americans should strive for assimilation rather than separation from white society. Yet she recognized the difficulties of working within a white-run organization. Thus, Harper helped African American women who resented the racism expressed by white WCTU members to organize separate local chapters, while advocating the importance of building coalitions with all women who shared Christian reform goals.

Sarah Jane Woodson Early succeeded Harper, according to some sources in 1888 and according to others in 1890. Woodson Early learned to value black separatism and self-help during her childhood, when her family joined other free blacks in forming an economically self-sufficient black farming community in Berlin Crossroads, Ohio. Inducted into the Christian reform tradition in the African Methodist Episcopal (AME) Church where her three brothers were clergymen, she continued her Christian education at Oberlin College, where she studied to become a teacher. In 1866 she became the first black woman college faculty member when she joined the faculty of Wilberforce University. She continued to teach after she married the Reverend Jordan Winston Early in 1868. In the 1880s, Woodson Early assumed a public leadership role when she joined the WCTU. She embraced the temperance movement because she believed that alcohol abuse weakened African American communities. Moreover, she hoped to encourage black women to assume leadership roles in their communities' self-help efforts.

Lucinda "Lucy" Thurman, became the national superintendent of the Department of Colored Work in 1893. Thurman had been involved in the temperance movement in the Midwest as a popular public lecturer since 1873. She served as leader of the WCTU's work among African Americans until 1908, when she became president of the National Association of Colored Women (NACW) and continued her temperance advocacy in that organization. It was during Thurman's tenure as superintendent that the antilynching activist and journalist Ida B. Wells Barnett criticized WCTU president Frances Willard for remarks she made during her 1893 tour of southern states. In one of her speeches Willard had alluded to "great dark-faced mobs" that threatened the safety of southern (white) women and their homes. Barnett demanded that Willard apologize to all African American males for perpetuating the pervasive myth that black men desire to rape white women. Although Thurman remained active in the WCTU as the Willard-Barnett controversy continued during the following two years, other African American women stopped joining white-run organizations.

The popularity of the WCTU declined in the early twentieth century as the suffrage movement appealed more strongly to reform-minded black and white women activists. The link between the social purity sought by the WCTU and what was increasingly thought of as an "outdated" Victorian morality also eroded the WCTU's popularity—even as prohibition gained converts in the early twentieth century, culminating in the passage of the Eighteenth Amendment (the "prohibition amendment") in 1919. National organizations of African American social reformers, such as the NACW organized in 1894, also provided national public forums for black women reformers who had formerly joined the WCTU. The full story that explains why small but significant numbers of African American women joined the WCTU's Department of Colored Work in the late nineteenth century awaits further scholarly research.

**FURTHER READINGS**

Bordin, Ruth. *Women and Temperance: The Quest for Power and Liberty, 1873–1900.* New Brunswick, N.J.: Rutgers University Press, 1990.

Epstein, Barbara Leslie. *The Politics of Domesticity: Women, Evangelism and Temperance in Nineteenth-Century America.* Middletown, Conn.: Wesleyan University Press, 1981.

Hunter, Tera. *To 'Joy My Freedom: Southern Black Women's Lives and Labor after the Civil War.* Cambridge, Mass.: Harvard University Press, 1997.

Lawson, Ellen N. "Sarah Woodson Early: 19th Century Black Nationalist 'Sister.'" *UMOJA* 2 (1981): 815–826.

Salem, Dorothy. *To Better Our World: Black Women in Organized Reform, 1890–1920.* Brooklyn, N.Y.: Carlson Publishing, Inc., 1990.

Terborg-Penn, Rosalyn. "Discrimination Against Afro-American Women in the Women's Movement, 1830–1920." In *The Afro-American Woman: Struggles and Images.* Ed. Sharon Harley and Rosalyn Terborg-Penn. Port Washington, N.Y.: Kennikat Press, 1978.

*Karen Garner*

# Women's Day Workers and Industrial League

The Women's Day Workers and Industrial League (WDWIL) was a domestic workers' union during the Great Depression of the 1930s. The league's purpose was to protect African American women from exploitative working conditions and to increase their low wages. It had little immediate impact on the terms of domestic service work.

Traditionally, American women have been responsible for the unpaid household-based work inside their own homes, while African American women, and other women of color, including recent immigrants, have dominated paid housework positions in other people's homes. Throughout the 1920s and 1930s, over 50 percent of African American women working outside their homes were employed as domestic workers in jobs that required long hours and paid low wages. By the 1930s, most domestics were employed as day workers, rather than "live-ins" within their employers' homes. This development allowed domestic workers to reduce their isolation from one another and to develop new types of relationships with their employers. It also facilitated the organization of domestic workers into unions such as the WDWIL.

In the 1930s young left-wing activists, such as Ella Josephine Baker, became involved with the league's unionization efforts and challenged some of the worst aspects of the domestic labor system. President Franklin D. Roosevelt's New Deal administration favored the unionization of workers. The 1933 National Industrial Recovery

Act and the 1935 Wagner Act encouraged workers to bargain collectively for higher wages and safer working conditions and protected unionized workers from employer discrimination. In 1933 only 6 percent of the workforce was unionized; by 1939, 17 percent of the workforce had joined unions. In spite of the growth of union membership and the advances workers made under the provisions of the Democratic New Deal, domestic workers did not fare as well. Paid household labor was virtually unregulated by government agencies throughout the Great Depression and would remain unregulated until the late 1940s. The 1935 Social Security Act and the 1938 Fair Labor Standards Act excluded domestic workers. Consequently, there were no provisions for unemployment benefits, nor were there maximum hours or minimum wage standards.

During the first and most severe years of the Depression, black domestic workers often lost their jobs when their white female employers resumed responsibility for household labor in order to economize. Moreover, wages for black domestic workers dropped, as did wages for all paid employment. By 1935, wages for black domestic workers, who often worked from seven in the morning until nine o'clock in the evening, averaged four dollars for a six-day work week. In addition, domestic workers had to pay for their transportation to and from the workplace out of their four-dollar salaries. Often these exploitative terms of employment were fixed by the white middle-class women who ran the household. They expected dedicated, selfless, often unrewarded, and personalized service from their domestic help, as society expected all women to display these "female" characteristics.

In spite of the efforts by unions such as the WDWIL to improve wages and reduce hours for domestic servants, domestic service conditions did not change until after World War II. During the war the increased demand for labor in war production industries offered black women new employment opportunities, and they left domestic service jobs in significant numbers. Approximately 20 percent of black women previously employed as domestic workers moved into factory and other jobs where overt racism that affected working conditions and wages for African Americans were checked by the Fair Employment Practices Commission.

### FURTHER READINGS

Clark-Lewis, Elizabeth. "'This Work Had a End': African-American Domestic Workers in Washington, D.C., 1910–1940." In *"To Toil the Livelong Day": America's Women at Work, 1780–1980*. Ed. Carol Groneman and Mary Beth Norton. Ithaca, N.Y.: Cornell University Press, 1987, 196–212.

Kessler-Harris, Alice. *Out to Work: A History of Wage-Earning Women in the United States*. New York: Oxford University Press, 1982.

Palmer, Phyllis. "Housewife and Household Worker: Employer-Employee Relationships in the Home, 1928–1941." In *"To Toil the Livelong Day": America's Women at Work, 1780–1980*. Ed. Carol Groneman and Mary Beth Norton. Ithaca, N.Y.: Cornell University Press, 1987, 1792–195.

*Karen Garner*

## Women's Home and Foreign Missionary Society, African Methodist Episcopal Church

*See* Women's Missionary Society, African Methodist Episcopal Church.

## Women's International League for Peace and Freedom

Established in 1919, the Women's International League for Peace and Freedom (WILPF) is the oldest women's antiwar group in the United States. The WILPF grew out of the women's suffrage movement, the Women's Peace Party, and a 1915 meeting in The Netherlands at which women from belligerent nations proposed an immediate end to World War I. This meeting led to the 1919 Second International Congress of Women, held in Switzerland, at which the WILPF was established. Members of the WILPF were present at the founding of the League of Nations and the United Nations. Today, the WILPF has fifty chapters around the world and holds official UN consultative status.

The WILPF advocates universal disarmament; political solutions to international conflicts; economic and social justice; an end to discrimination and exploitation; international recognition of fundamental human rights; and gender equality. The WILPF has always attempted to speak to the particular concerns of African American women and has linked its antiwar campaigns to demands for racial justice. Several African Americans have served in leadership positions in the organization's American section and have helped to keep a commitment to social justice at the forefront of the international group's programs.

The involvement of African American women in this majority-white organization had its roots in the post–World War I internationalism of black feminists and social activists. Their desire for international peace seemed inseparable from their wish for social justice, and this drew them to the WILPF. Among the WILPF founding members was Mary Terrell, president emeritus of the National Association of Colored Women. In 1904, Terrell had spoken at the First International Congress of Women in Germany and following World War I the Women's Peace Party, of which Terrell was a member, asked her to attend the 1919 congress, along with Jane Addams, Emily Balch, Florence Kelley, Jeanette Rankin, and several other American feminists. Terrell was responsible for summarizing the discussions of the American delegates and turning them into resolutions to present to the international body. She wrote and convinced the U.S. delegation to present a resolution proclaiming, "We believe no human being should be deprived of an education, prevented from earning a living, debarred from any legitimate pursuit in which he wishes to engage, or be subjected to humiliations of various kinds on account of race, color, or creed." Terrell, speaking in German, also delivered the American delegation's speech to the convention. She told the fledgling WILPF, "You may talk about permanent peace 'til doomsday, but the world will never have it 'til the dark races are given a square deal." Although Terrell remembered this founding meeting as "illuminating and gratifying," she was disappointed to be "the only delegate who gave any color to the occasion at all." During the next two years, while serving on the WILPF's board of directors, Terrell encountered racism in the organization but also some white women who demonstrated "grit" when grappling with segregation.

In the years following World War I the international organization lobbied on issues of particular concern to women of color. As early as 1921, the WILPF protested "the military use of natives by foreign countries." The WILPF lobbied for withdrawal of U.S. Marines from Haiti and enforcement of the League of Nations' antislavery convention in Africa. Moreover, the women intervened against the use of slave labor by American corporations in Ethiopia and Liberia.

During the 1920s thousands of American women joined the WILPF's campaign for a "permanent peace," including black women such as Bertha McNeill, Charlotte Atwood, and Addie W. Hunton, a leading figure in the International Council of Women of the Darker Races. In 1926 Hunton participated in the league's investigation of the American occupation of Haiti. Following the three-week trip, she contributed an essay on the con-

dition of Haitian women to the delegation's book, *Occupied Haiti*, insisting that "interracial cooperation is necessary for peace." Hunton directed the league's Inter-Racial Committee, was active in its New York City chapter, lectured on peace work at black colleges, and spoke about "race relations" to peace activists at the American section's summer school and at the WILPF's Sixth International Congress. By 1935, however, Hunton was discouraged by the reluctance of rank-and-file members to confront racism and, although she praised the organization's national leaders and programs, she stepped away from the WILPF into other areas of activism.

Despite Hunton's withdrawal from the organization, African American women such as Helen Curtis and Alice Dunbar-Nelson continued to speak under the auspices of the WILPF in the years between the wars. Some league members demonstrated against segregated public facilities, and the organization published educational literature such as *Achievements of Negro Women*, and its summer schools, which began in 1922, included lectures and discussions about "Cooperation Among Races." When black women such as the educator Mary Bethune protested against racism within the league, national leaders attempted to resolve such problems.

The WILPF's national leadership, with at least the token approval of its rank-and-file members, consistently lobbied against racial violence and legal discrimination. Emily Balch, the WILPF's director of policies, publicly condemned "the stupidities and the cruelty of race prejudice" in a league-endorsed statement on racial and ethnic prejudice. In the 1930s, after the WILPF resolved that "lynching and the burning of the bodies of Negroes is a blot on our civilization," the organization repeatedly urged Congress to pass antilynching legislation. Lynching drew the league's attention to the South. The American WILPF proposed that Congress investigate the status of southern sharecroppers and allowed the Southern Tenant Farmers Union to share its Washington, D.C., headquarters. Moreover, the league condemned the "terrible display of racial and social prejudice" in the Scottsboro case (eight black teenagers who had been convicted of raping two white women) and in 1937 urged the governor of Alabama "to issue a full pardon to the defendants." The Ninth World Congress of the WILPF also called for pardons for the Scottsboro boys, whose imprisonment had become symbolic of the racial injustices of the American legal system.

After World War II, the WILPF's central concerns were to end the arms race of the cold war and to forestall the accumulation of nuclear weapons. The league's 1983 "Stop the Arms Race" campaign, for example, mobilized over 50,000 women and helped pave the way for an international nuclear test ban. The cold war's "red-baiting" in the United States, however, reduced the influence of the league in the post-war years. During the 1950s black women leaders such as Bertha McNeill risked being charged with subversion when they insisted that "peace and economic justice" were interrelated. And in the 1960s and 1970s, league chapters risked assault when they expressed sympathy for militant African American groups.

The WILPF stalwarts in the United States responded to political slander and violence by stepping up their engagement with the civil rights and the antiwar movements of the 1960s. League members invited civil rights leader Bayard Rustin to be the keynote speaker at the WILPF's Sixteenth Congress, and they lobbied in Congress for passage of the Civil Rights Act and federal action against racial violence in Mississippi. The group also launched a consumer boycott of goods manufactured in Mississippi, including the products of companies such as Kraft, Pet, Borden, and Hunt. In addition, dozens of league members participated in numerous civil rights activities, including the 1965 Selma to Montgomery march. Following the protest march some league members remained in Alabama for almost two years to assist civil rights activist Amelia Boynton. By 1966, the league's American section had assigned a staff person to work for the Poor People's Campaign of the Southern Christian Leadership Conference (SCLC). Prominent black women such as Fannie Lou Hamer, Coretta Scott King, Lucy Diggs Slowe, Velvalea Rogers, Erna Prather Harris, and Enola Maxwell continued to join the WILPF, although black members remained a small minority in the league's American section. In 1968, Coretta Scott King helped to lead 5,000 women, known as the Jeanette Rankin Brigade, to the U.S. Congress to demand an end to America's involvement in the Vietnam War.

Most recently, the American section of the WILPF has sponsored a 1979 Conference on Racism, participated in the 1983 March for Jobs, Peace, and Freedom, and designated "racial justice" as one of its three priorities for 1988–1990. The international body has stepped up its work with African and Asian peace activists, most notably through the UN's Third World Conference on Women in Kenya, the Fourth World Conference on Women in the People's Republic of China, and through its own Peace Train, which carried 200 women representing forty-two nationalities across Eurasia in 1995.

**FURTHER READINGS**

Adams, Judith Porter. *Peacework: Oral Histories of Women Peace Activists.* Boston: Twayne, 1990.

Alonso, Harriet Hyman. *Peace as a Women's Issue: A History of the U.S. Movement for World Peace and Women's Rights.* Syracuse, N.Y.: Syracuse University Press, 1993.

Foster, Carrie A. *The Women and the Warriors: The U.S. Section of the Women's International League for Peace and Freedom, 1915–1946.* Syracuse, N.Y.: Syracuse University Press, 1995.

Foster, Catherine. *Women for All Seasons.* Athens: University of Georgia Press, 1989.

Terrell, Mary Church. *A Colored Woman in a White World, 1940.* Rpt., New York: G. K. Hall & Co., 1996.

*Christine Lutz*

## Women's Missionary Society, African Methodist Episcopal Church

The Women's Missionary Society (WMS) of the African Methodist Episcopal (AME) Church, was the product of the 1936 merger of the Women's Parent Mite Missionary Society (WPMMS) and the Women's Home and Foreign Missionary Society (WHFMS).

The WPMMS, founded on May 8, 1874, was the AME's first women's missionary organization. It held its first convention in Philadelphia on August 11. Between 1874 and 1878, President Mary A. Campbell created local societies and performed missionary work in Haiti, Santo Domingo, and West Africa, while focusing the domestic efforts of the organization in the North. From 1878 to 1883, Harriett Wayman served as president. In 1888, the WPMMS sent its first missionary, Sarah Gorham, to Sierra Leone, West Africa. Other late nineteenth-century ventures included Charlotte Manya's trip to South Africa, where she established an AME Church. In 1895, President Sarah E. Tanner founded Conference Branch Societies.

The WHFMS held its organizational meeting in 1893. The society primarily sent missionaries and resources to South Africa and lent support to African American preachers and communities in the South. In 1912, the society established the newspaper the *Women's Christian Recorder* with Laura L. Turner as editor. In 1927, the society elected Lucy Medorah Hughes of Cameron, Texas, as president and sent financial support to build the Bethel AME Church in Capetown, South Africa.

In the 1930s, because of financial difficulties and increasing regional tensions, leaders of the AME Church began a movement to unite the WPMMS and the WHFMS. In 1932, the General Conference of the AME Church called for a merger of the two missionary branches. Representatives of both women's organizations met to discuss the logistics of the merger at Chicago's Quinn Chapel. While WPMMS president Christine Smith raised some objections, WHFMS president Lucy Hughes apparently favored the merger. The AME Church called an additional meeting at the Pearl Street Church, Jackson, Mississippi, which was presided over by Senior Bishop H. B. Parks.

After extensive discussion during the AME's 1936 General Conference in New York, the merger of the two organizations was finalized, creating the WMS. The WMS established its headquarters in the Allen Building in Philadelphia. The AME Church elected Lucy Hughes as the first president of the new organization and appointed Christine Smith as General Secretary. After the death of Hughes in an automobile accident, Vice President Anne E. Heath of St. Petersburg, Florida, assumed the presidency. At the First Quadrennial meeting of the new society in Union Bethel, New Orleans, Christine Smith retired. In 1944, the society established the Missionary Education Department in Philadelphia, and in 1954, it created the Canadian Women's Missionary Society. The AME Church also launched the *Women's Missionary Recorder*, edited by Mrs. A. B. Williams, to keep the church abreast of the work of the society. The WMS continues to be a vital part of the missionary work of the AME Church.

**FURTHER READINGS**

Dandridge, Octavia W. *Eleven Decades of Historical Events: Featuring the Women's Missionary Society African Methodist Episcopal Church, 1874–1984.* N.p.: Women's Missionary Society A.M.E. Church, 1985.

———. *A History of the Women's Missionary Society of the African Methodist Episcopal Church, 1874–1987.* N.p.: Women's Missionary Society A.M.E. Church, 1987.

Peck, Dorothy Adams, ed. *Women on the Way: African Methodist Episcopal Women Maximizing Their Human and Spiritual Potential.* N.p.: Women's Missionary Society A.M.E. Church, 1983.

Singleton, George A. *The Romance of African Methodism: A Study of the African Methodist Episcopal Church.* New York: Exposition Press, 1952.

*Julius H. Bailey*

# Women's Parent Mite Missionary Society, African Methodist Episcopal Church

*See* Women's Missionary Society, African Methodist Episcopal Church.

# Women's Volunteer Service League

The Women's Volunteer Service League was one of many black women's volunteer organizations that operated under the aegis of the Women's Division of the Council of National Defense during World War I.

World War I involved American women nationwide in a variety of volunteer activities in support of the nation's domestic war efforts. Activities included conserving food while developing higher nutritional standards and better health care for Americans in general and women and children in particular. Women raised funds and knitted for soldiers and other Americans in need. They built and operated recreational facilities for families and for veterans. They advocated the creation of federal working standards for women workers who had entered the industrial labor force in large numbers to replace male workers enlisted in the armed services.

African American women participated enthusiastically in all these activities because they recognized the particular benefits these services could provide for black communities. For example, in Florida they formed the Negro War Relief organization and in Colorado they established the Negro Women's Auxiliary War Council. Nationally, black women's organizations raised approximately $5 million in support of the war effort. The government and national volunteer organizations, such as the Red Cross and the Young Women's and the Young Men's Christian Association, actively sought the volunteer services of black women.

Following the entry of the United States into World War I, the American government organized the Women's Division of the Council of National Defense. According to its national field representative, Alice Dunbar-Nelson, the Women's Division "made the best attempt" at organizing African American women, compared to the many other wartime volunteer service agencies. During the war, the Women's Division helped to register the American female population, gathered statistics on births and birth weights, distributed government-issue milk to mothers and children, established health and community recreation centers, and supervised industrial labor conditions of women factory workers.

In some states, black women worked side by side with white women in local Women's Division activities. In other states, such as New Jersey, black women organized a separate branch of the Women's Division, the Women's Volunteer Service League (WVSL). The president of Newark's WVSL, Amorel Cook, and other African American club women, including Mary E. Cary Burrell, opened and managed a canteen and rest home for black soldiers. The canteen provided a welcoming and wholesome atmosphere for black soldiers who were training near and passing through the Newark area. The facility also provided industrial training for local black women. Burrell earned the U.S. government's distinguished service badge for her participation in these volunteer activities.

As a result of their volunteer wartime activities, African American women's contributions to the improvement of black communities and to the work and social life of the whole nation became more visible.

FURTHER READINGS

Dunbar-Nelson, Alice. "Negro Women in War Work." In Emmett J. Scott, *Scott's Official History of the American Negro in the World War*. New York: Arno Press, 1969.

"Women's Volunteer Service League," in *Black Women in America: An Historical Encyclopedia*. Ed. Darlene Clark Hine. Brooklyn, N.Y.: Carlson Publishing Inc., 1993.

*Karen Garner*

# World Community of Al-Islam in the West

*See* Nation of Islam.

## Young Men's Christian Association, Colored Work Department

The Young Men's Christian Association (YMCA), Colored Work Department, provided religious, social, recreational, entertainment, and educational programs for African Americans in cities and on college campuses. Despite the YMCA's segregation, African Americans joined the YMCA in large numbers. They organized their own black-controlled branches, raised funds to purchase buildings, and recruited and trained black men to staff their associations. After establishing control over their associations, African Americans challenged the YMCA's decision to desegregate all of its facilities in 1946.

The YMCA was founded in 1844 in London, where Americans first encountered the association during the 1851 World's Fair. In the following year several North American cities established associations, and in 1854 American and Canadian branches organized the Confederation of North American YMCAs. The confederation, afraid to alienate southern members, avoided any discussion of slavery and did not encourage free blacks to join the YMCA.

Nevertheless, African Americans had already established a separate black association in 1853. Anthony Bowen, a former slave who had purchased his freedom and then became the first black clerk in the U.S. Patent Office, founded the first black YMCA in Washington, D.C. The association, though limited by lack of funds and restrictive laws regulating the personal freedom of African Americans, offered Bible study meetings to free blacks throughout the 1860s.

During the Civil War the Confederation of North American YMCAs disintegrated, but associations in the North continued to operate. They disbanded regular activities and organized the U.S. Christian Commission to provide relief work for soldiers. Following the war those who had been active in the Christian Commission rebuilt the North American YMCA and dominated the association's leadership ranks. Hoping to christianize the former slaves, white association leaders encouraged freedmen to join the YMCA in separate associations. During the 1860s and 1870s, several black associations emerged, but they were short-lived due to local white opposition, lack of financial resources, and the YMCA's failure to provide any type of assistance.

Following Reconstruction the North American YMCA started to promote association work for African Americans in response to pressure from three groups: those hoping to recruit African Americans for missionary work in Africa, former abolitionists who were concerned about the condition of the freedmen, and white southerners who worried about maintaining racial harmony. In 1876, the North American YMCA appointed its first International Secretary for black association work. Between 1876 and 1891 two white men, George D. Johnston and Henry Edwards Brown, served successively in the post. Johnston visited southern communities soliciting white support for black association work while trying to arouse African American interest in the YMCA. Johnston, a former Confederate general, was unable to gain the trust and confidence of African Americans, and black YMCA work therefore made little progress. In 1879 Henry Edwards Brown, a former abolitionist, succeeded Johnston. Brown visited black colleges and introduced students to association work in the hope that after graduation they would return home and establish YMCAs in their local communities. Brown's strategy was successful, and by 1887 African

Group of boys receiving first membership cards, Hackensack, New Jersey, not dated. *YMCA of the USA Archives, University of Minnesota Libraries*

Americans operated twenty-six YMCAs on college campuses and ten associations in cities. In the same year Brown convinced the North American YMCA to allocate a permanent budget for African American association work and to recruit a black man to work as full-time secretary for the black YMCA in Norfolk, Virginia.

In 1888, Canadian-born William A. Hunton became the first black employee of an African American YMCA, and in 1891 he succeeded Brown as International Secretary for black association work. Hunton's appointment marked the shift from white supervision for black YMCAs to African American leadership. During the 1890s Hunton laid the foundation for the emergence of a nationwide network of black YMCAs. He helped establish seventeen city and forty-three college branches, published a monthly newspaper to facilitate communication between local asso-

ciation leaders, and consolidated black YMCAs by organizing them into regional conferences. The North American YMCA was impressed with Hunton's achievements and employed an additional black International Secretary. In 1898, Jesse E. Moorland, a Howard University graduate and former minister, became Hunton's assistant.

Under the leadership of Hunton and Moorland, black YMCA work flourished during the early twentieth century. Between 1900 and 1920 the number of black associations in cities grew from 21 to 44, college branches increased from 53 to 113, and African American membership rose from 5,100 to nearly 26,000. Members of the black educated urban elite were particularly eager to join the association. At a time when white society refused to recognize black men fully as men, the YMCA's programs provided African Americans with a unique opportunity to develop their manhood. Indeed black branches served as sanctuaries that preserved African American manhood and prepared men and boys for their leadership in the struggle for racial equality that lay ahead. Although black YMCA members resented segregation, they believed that serving the men and boys of their race in separate branches was better than depriving them of the association's services.

As memberships in African American YMCAs grew, black association leaders struggled to improve existing facilities. By 1900, only five black associations owned buildings specifically designed and constructed for YMCA use while the remaining city branches either rented rooms, apartments, or buildings or purchased residences that were ill-suited for the association's programs. During the first three decades of the twentieth century several black branches acquired modern buildings with the support of white philanthropists. George Foster Peabody, John D. Rockefeller Sr., and especially Julius Rosenwald contributed matching funds to black YMCA fund-raising campaigns, which resulted in the construction of twenty-six buildings equipped with swimming pools, gymnasia, cafeterias, reading rooms and classrooms, employment bureaus, and dormitories. Some critics charged that the contributions of white philanthropists perpetuated segregation in the YMCA, but most African Americans welcomed the financial support.

While the acquisition of buildings allowed black YMCAs to expand their programs and services, it also generated a growing demand for full-time staff. Hunton and Moorland tried to recruit association secretaries from the college graduates who had been members of campus branches. Attracting competent and reliable men, however, was difficult. The YMCA secretaryship was a new profession that offered little pay and no job security but required hard work and long hours. Those who entered professional association work had to serve as janitors, librarians, teachers, preachers, counselors, accountants, fundraisers, athletic instructors, and song leaders, and assist men in finding housing and employment.

The professional training of secretaries presented yet another problem. While the recruits were college graduates who had been members of campus YMCAs, they lacked any expertise in association work. In the 1890s the North American YMCA had established secretarial schools in Chicago and Springfield, Massachusetts. Both schools admitted African Americans but high tuition fees and hostile work environments virtually excluded them.

In response Hunton and Moorland established the Chesapeake Summer School in 1908. The school, which operated in various locations throughout the late 1940s, offered black secretaries instruction in YMCA work during their summer vacation and helped foster racial solidarity. Through the efforts of Hunton and Moorland the number of black secretaries increased steadily. Between 1900 and 1944, the number of black YMCA secretaries rose from 6 to an all-time high of 149.

While the Chesapeake Summer School trained black secretaries for work in city associations, it did not prepare them for the YMCA's military work. During World War I approximately 400 black secretaries accompanied the nearly 400,000 African American soldiers to the military camps in the United States and France, providing them with religious, recreational, and educational programs in segregated Y-huts. YMCA secretaries also staffed and managed two military vacation resorts for black soldiers in France. In 1918 and 1919 nearly 20,000 black troops spent their seven-day furloughs in the YMCA Leave Areas at Challes-les-Eaux and Chambéry.

Following World War I black YMCA work reached new heights. In 1925, African Americans operated 51 associations in cities and 128 branches on college campuses. Local YMCAs employed 132 full-time secretaries and 8 black men served as International Secretaries, replacing Hunton, who had died in 1916, and Moorland, who retired in 1923. By the end of the decade most associations had acquired property, thirty-six branches owned modern buildings specifically designed for YMCA use, and memberships rose from almost 26,000 in 1920 to nearly 34,000 by 1930.

The onset of the Depression brought an end to the decade's prosperity, and black YMCAs struggled for survival. As unemployment skyrocketed, fewer African Americans were able to pay association membership fees or contribute to YMCA fundraisers. Meanwhile, attendance at the associations increased as growing numbers of unemployed sought the services of the YMCA. Reduced budgets and large groups of nonpaying patrons forced local black associations to dismiss staff and cut salaries in order to continue operating. Similarly, the national YMCA was forced to reduce its staff from eight to three black men. Between 1932 and 1946 Channing H. Tobias, Robert B. DeFrantz, and Ralph W. Bullock supervised all African American association work in the United States. Despite financial problems most black associations survived the Depression with the help of the federal government. New Deal agencies assigned personnel to black branches, provided educational and work project programs, and helped to renovate YMCA buildings.

While black association leaders were fighting for their survival they started to attack segregation in the YMCA. During the 1930s, Tobias, who had succeeded Moorland as black senior secretary, used the World's Conference of YMCAs as a forum to expose segregation in the American association. Although the World's Conference repeatedly condemned discrimination, it was not until World War II that the American YMCA examined its racial policy in response to growing black protest. African American association leaders, inspired by the rhetoric of the war, demanded the elimination of segregation and challenged the YMCA to live up to the democratic ideal black soldiers were defending around the world. White YMCA officials, concerned about the discrepancy between the association's policy of racial exclusion and the nation's defense of democracy, decided to desegregate the association. In 1946, the American YMCA dissolved the Colored Work Department, abolished all racial designations from its publications, and urged white associations to end their racist practices. Many white branches in the South refused to desegregate, insisting on local autonomy. Similarly, African Americans were faced with the dilemma of surrendering their control over black associations.

Despite segregation the YMCA provided many African American communities with facilities and programs no other urban institutions offered. The association's recreation and physical exercise programs launched the careers of many nationally known athletes, including Jesse Owens and Jackie Robinson. The educational programs provided many men with opportunities to enhance their vocational and professional training, while the reading rooms offered access to newspapers and books at a time when most public libraries did not admit black patrons. YMCA dormitories provided affordable, clean, and safe housing for travelers and newcomers to the cities, and the associations' employment bureaus helped locate jobs. Unlike the churches and fraternal orders, associations catered to men of all religions and professions and provided space for social interaction, professional networking, and male bonding. For many black secretaries, the YMCA also served as a steppingstone to a more prestigious career. Several secretaries went on to become college presidents, including Mordecai W. Johnson of Howard University and Benjamin E. Mays of Morehouse College. Others like George E. Haynes, Ralph W. Bullock, Campbell C. Johnson, and Channing H. Tobias attained high government positions.

**FURTHER READINGS**

Mjagkij, Nina. "A Peculiar Alliance: Julius Rosenwald, the YMCA, and African-Americans, 1910–1933." *American Jewish Archives* 44, 2 (Fall/Winter 1992): 584–605.

———. *Light in the Darkness: African Americans and the YMCA, 1852–1946.* Lexington: The University Press of Kentucky, 1994.

———. "True Manhood: The YMCA and Racial Advancement, 1890–1930." In *Men and Women Adrift: The YMCA and the YWCA in the City.* Ed. Nina Mjagkij and Margaret Spratt. New York: New York University Press, 1997.

*Nina Mjagkij*

## Young Women's Christian Association, Council on Colored Work

The Young Women's Christian Association (YWCA), Council on Colored Work was the division of the national organization that directed the work of its African American staff, proposed policy regarding racial issues, and advised paid staff members and volunteers in African American city associations and on college campuses.

Middle-class Christian women organized the YWCA in America in the decade following the Civil War. Concerned with the moral ambiguity and physical danger that young, single women workers confronted in the growing industrial urban areas of the country, early association founders sought to provide a Christian, homelike atmosphere for women adrift in the evil and impersonal city. Attempting to impose middle-class values on their working-class sisters, board members of local YWCA associations bought or built residences, hired matrons, instituted regulations regarding residency and behavior, and offered religious instruction and classes in the domestic arts.

Although the majority of city and campus associations in the nineteenth century attracted white, native-born Protestant women, a handful of associations founded by African American women existed before 1900. In Philadelphia, a Colored Women's Christian Association established two residencies for African American working women, but they struggled with few financial resources and never affiliated with the national movement. Meanwhile, in Dayton, Ohio, a sewing club founded by a group of African Methodist Episcopal church women incorporated its own Women's Christian Association in 1893. Seven years later, the organization bought a building, which it maintained until 1918 when it affiliated with the white YWCA of that city. The Dayton group claims to have the oldest branch for African American women in the United States.

As the association movement spread throughout the cities and college campuses in the latter decades of the nineteenth century, a major problem of organization arose. Local associations could affiliate with one of two loosely organized umbrella groups—the International Board or the American Committee. This caused great confusion and after much negotiation, the two groups united in 1906 under the leadership of Grace Dodge, a wealthy New York philanthropist. Those local associations affiliated with either of the two umbrella groups, as well as those that were conducting their work independently, were asked to join the new YWCA of the United States of America. The list of 608 member associations included four African American city associations located in Washington, D.C.; Baltimore; Brooklyn; and New York City and three student associations operating on the campuses of Spelman College, Tuskegee Institute, and the Agricultural and Mechanical College at Normal, Alabama.

In June 1907 southern white members, called together by the National Board, met in Asheville, North Carolina, to discuss the future of the YWCA's "colored work." The conference did not involve any African American women and concluded that no new work to establish independent African American associations should be undertaken. However, the women suggested that black student associations that had already been organized be helped by "headquarters." Apparently, southern white participants of the Asheville meeting were concerned that they be forced to attend national conventions with African American women.

Following the Asheville conference, the National Board hired Addie Waite Hunton, club woman, teacher, and wife of the administrative secretary of the Colored Men's Department of the International Young Men's Christian Association, William Hunton, to survey African American college associations. Hunton soon realized that many more student groups existed than the National Board was aware of and that a permanent staff needed to be hired to work with the college associations. In 1908 the National Board established the Council on

Colored Work, and Elizabeth Ross Haynes was appointed to be the special worker for colored students and made a member of the national staff. Haynes and Hunton, retained by the board as a special consultant, traveled to cities and campuses throughout the South and East. Confronted by a myriad of questions and issues regarding national YWCA policy (or lack thereof) governing the affiliation of black associations, the two women were nonetheless convinced that African American associations could succeed in communities where the white association membership was cooperative and the black membership was active and financially solvent.

Faced with the constant dilemma of reconciling common racial practices of the time with YWCA Christian principles, the National Board outlined an administrative plan for the establishment of African American associations in 1910. Although the National Board allowed that an independent African American association could be established in a city with no white YWCA in place, it also required that the independent African American association become a branch as soon as a white association was established in the community. Independent African American city associations were to be supervised by a national staff member and affiliated directly with the National Board.

Hunton continued to work toward affiliating new African American associations, concentrating her work in the cities after the National Board hired a second student worker to aid Haynes. The National Board sponsored its first Summer Training School for African American students in 1911. The following year, Hunton oversaw a survey investigating industrial conditions for African American women in Winston-Salem, Durham, and Fayetteville, North Carolina, and she organized the first Conference of Volunteer and Employed Workers in Colored YWCAs. Hunton reported on her work at the YWCA's national convention in 1912 and aroused interest among the membership, who decided to place "emphasis on colored work, where conditions [were] favorable for model Associations." However, for personal reasons, Hunton and her co-worker, Haynes, resigned their positions around the same time, and the National Board, encouraged by the membership's action at the national convention established the Subcommittee for Colored Work and appointed a full-time staff member to work with the African American city associations. Although originally disappointed by philanthropist Julius Rosenwald's (supporter of the YMCA's Colored Work Department) rejection of application for funding of this new position, the National Board moved ahead by appointing Eva D. Bowles to hold the first national staff position for supervision of colored city work.

Eva del Vakia Bowles came to the national office well prepared for the work that lay ahead. Born and raised in Ohio, Bowles, following the examples of her father and grandfather before her, became a teacher and held positions in schools in Kentucky, North Carolina, and Virginia. In 1905, she became the first African American YWCA secretary overseeing the Colored YWCA of New York, later known as the 137th Street YWCA in Harlem. After a short stint as a social caseworker in her hometown of Columbus, Ohio, Bowles returned to the YWCA to assume her most important position—secretary to the National Board Subcommittee for Colored Work. Bowles's position was housed in the Department of Method, but she worked specifically with African American local associations and strove to integrate "colored work" into the mainstream of the national organization.

The Subcommittee on Colored Work organized a conference for southern women, held in Louisville, Kentucky, in 1915. Unlike the 1907 Asheville conference, both African American and white women participated. The group agreed upon three principles that would have a long-lasting effect on the national organization and its general membership. First, the National Board appointed an interracial committee. Second, training for African American staff and volunteers was to be provided by the National Board. Third and most important, African American associations were required to affiliate as branches of local white associations. This policy of branch status for African American local associations was the focus of much controversy in the YWCA for years to come. However, Bowles and the other African American national staff members supported it, advising that the local white central association appoint a committee to oversee the black branch, which continued to have its own committee of management. Both the city's white association and the African American branch appointed representatives to a committee on colored work. African American national staff members as well as the committee on colored work assisted the branch, but local branch staff were employed by the white central association. The National Board also formed regional interracial committees that extended the work of the local committees on colored work and organized regional training workshops, camps, and conferences. Although the Louisville recommendations supported an uneven distribution of power between central associations and black branches, they did

explore ways for African American and white women to work together on local and regional levels, creating a highly unusual situation in an era characterized by tight segregation.

World War I provided an opportunity for the national Council on Colored Work and its African American staff to extend its influence in American society. During the war, the U.S. government allocated $1 million to the YWCA to be used for the benefit of women and girls. The organization formed the War Work Council (disbanding the Council on Colored Work) and designated $200,000 for "colored work." Bowles and her staff seized this unprecedented opportunity to mobilize volunteers and local staff to establish "Hostess Houses" at sixteen locations to serve African American soldiers stationed at segregated army camps with few if any recreational facilities. Cooperating with affiliated clubs of the National Association of Colored Women (NACW), the YWCA hired forty-six new staff members for the project. The Hostess House provided a refined environment for soldiers and their families to congregate under the supervision of middle-class, college-educated African American YWCA members. Thus, the Hostess House served an additional purpose—to act as an arena for racial uplift activities.

The War Work Council also aided African American industrial workers, who were often unskilled and unprepared for the changes that city dwelling and wartime caused. The YWCA hired a special Industrial Secretary for Colored Work, Mary E. Jackson, a clubwoman and former employee of the Rhode Island Department of Labor. She conducted numerous investigations of industrial and living conditions and directed YWCA regional field workers in their search to identify potential local industrial secretaries. By war's end, Jackson and her staff had established forty-five Colored Industrial Work Centers in twenty-one states and the District of Columbia.

The War Work Council also attempted to address the recreational needs of younger women. Under the auspices of local associations, girls under eighteen joined "Patriotic Leagues" and engaged in sporting activities, camps, and other leisure activities. Not only did these groups help to assure future organizational members, but they also gave opportunities to young African American women to develop leadership skills.

World War I provided Bowles and the other national staff with an unprecedented opportunity to increase their visibility within the organization and to attract a large base of support among the growing African American constituency. The Hostess Houses closed in October

1919, and the African American national staff members were dispersed throughout the YWCA's organizational structure.

Following World War I, Bowles and her staff, striving to include African American women and race issues in all phases of association life, worked to convince the National Board to sponsor regional and national meetings only in cities and facilities that catered to members of both races. In 1920, for instance, forty-four African American delegates attended the YWCA's national conference in Cleveland. That year, the relationship between black branches and white central associations and the status of African American members within the YWCA once again caused controversy. At the 1920 national conference in Cleveland, a group of nationally prominent African American club women presented a list of demands to the YWCA. The women demanded representation of African American members on the National Board, a reinterpretation of the 1915 Louisville decree concerning the establishment of independent associations and branches of central associations (which were always assumed to be white), the reestablishment of a national Bureau of Colored Work, and greater representation on local boards of directors.

Unwilling to deal with the issue at the Cleveland conference, the YWCA organized a meeting in Richmond, Virginia, chaired by Bowles. Once again, however, the women were unable to work out their differences, and the National Board called a second Louisville conference on Colored Work to be held in 1921. Meanwhile, the national staff reorganized a council on colored work, an unofficial division or department, and Bowles continued to integrate additional African American women into the national structure by appointing new regional field committee and staff members. At the 1921 Louisville conference, the National Board appointed Charlotte Hawkins Brown, founder of Palmer Memorial Institute in North Carolina, as a member-at-large of the YWCA's Southern Regional Committee.

The Bureau of Colored Work, called the Council on Colored Work before World War I, was to "take up matters of moment to the whole of the colored work and the race problem." Bowles continued to support the 1915 decision, which had stipulated that only one association was to operate in each city and that black association work

was to be conducted in a separate branch. Yet, Bowles insisted that black branches be represented on the central association board and an African American presence be felt in all levels of the organizational structure. Ultimately, Bowles believed, the YWCA should be a true interracial organization and she energetically opposed the establishment of a permanent "colored department." In 1931, the Bureau of Colored Work was disbanded.

The complexities of black-white relationships on the local association level, however, continued to plague the national organization for decades to come. Throughout the twentieth century the YWCA engaged in interracial work through the establishment of various committees, held numerous meetings, and collaborated with other groups such as the National Urban League (NUL), the National Association for the Advancement of Colored People (NAACP), and the NACW. In the annals of the organization's history, Bowles and her Council of Colored Work represented the energy and hope of many in an organization that provided a place for African American and white women to meet on common ground. It was not until 1946, however, that the YWCA adopted its "Interracial Charter," which called for the desegregation of all local branches.

**FURTHER READINGS**

Bell, Juliet O., and Helen J. Wilkins. *Interracial Practices in Community Y.W.C.A.'s.* New York: The Woman's Press, 1944.

Jones, Adrienne Lash. "Struggle Among Saints: African American Women and the YWCA, 1870–1920." In *Men and Women Adrift: The YMCA and the YWCA in the City.* Ed. Nina Mjagkij and Margaret Spratt. New York: New York University Press, 1997.

Sims, Mary S. *The Natural History of a Social Institution—The Young Women's Christian Association.* New York: The Woman's Press, 1936.

———. *The YWCA—An Unfolding Purpose.* New York: Woman's Press, 1950.

Weisenfeld, Judith. *African American Women and Christian Activism: New York's Black YWCA, 1905–1945.* Cambridge, Mass.: Harvard University Press, 1997.

*Margaret A. Spratt*

**SEE ALSO** Phyllis Wheatley Women's Clubs and Homes

# Z

## Zeta Phi Beta

Zeta Phi Beta Sorority, Inc., a private, nonprofit organization, was founded at Howard University in Washington, D.C., in January 1920. The five founders, or "Pearls," as they are more commonly referred to—Pearl Anna Neal, Arizona Cleaver Stemons, Viola Tyler Goings, Myrtle Tyler Faithffil, and Fannie Pettie Watts—strove to charter an organization that focused on the ideals of scholarship, service, sisterly love, and finer womanhood. A founding member of the National Pan Hellenic Council, Inc., Zeta is also the only African American Greek-lettered sorority that is constitutionally bound to a brother organization, Phi Beta Sigma Fraternity, Inc. Sharing the official colors of royal blue and white, both organizations have their national headquarters in Washington, D.C.

Zeta is also proud of its other "first" accomplishments. It was the first black sorority that chartered international chapters in West Africa and Germany, formed both adult and youth auxiliary groups, and employed the first paid staff to administer both its national and international affairs from its central office in Washington, D.C. Like other African American Greek-lettered organizations, Zeta's membership hosts a variety of impressive and accomplished women, including the actresses Janet DuBois and Esther Rolle, the singers Sarah Vaughn and Dionne Warwick, the author Zora Neale Hurston, and Dr. Deborah Wolfe, former educational chief of the House of Representatives.

Zeta, like the other eight major black Greek-lettered organizations, is a life-time membership organization. With official membership criteria tied to post-secondary education, many of its projects provide college and community service at the local, national, and international level. Zeta maintains a list of traditional initiatives such as Stork's Nest, a program that provides goods and services to young mothers. In recent years Zeta also organized relief programs in response to national disasters. In the aftermath of Hurricane Andrew, for example, the organization called upon members to send money and other donations to the victims of the storm.

Preparing for the approaching millennium, Zeta has encouraged local chapters to sponsor young people at the NASA Space Camp. Zeta chapters also support voter registration campaigns and efforts of local charities. At the beginning of each new calendar year, Zeta salutes its founders with Salute to Finer Womanhood activities and luncheons. Zeta is supported financially through dues and gifts of members, or "Sorors."

In the United States, all national initiatives and administrative work are managed by the national headquarters. National policy and program initiatives are dictated by an executive board that oversees state chapters and eight regional divisions: Midwestern, Great Lakes, Atlantic, Eastern, Southeastern, South Central, Southern, and Pacific. Chapters in Germany are supervised by the Atlantic region and those in the Caribbean are directed by the Southeastern region. Information about Zeta's programs is distributed during local chapter meetings, annual regional conferences, and biannual national conferences and through the organization's official publication, *The Archon*. Local chapters are represented on the local councils of the National Pan-Hellenic Council (NPHC). Through its affiliation with the NPHC, Zeta Phi Beta also works with other black Greek-lettered organizations, pooling resources and sponsoring joint service projects and program initiatives to assist African American communities.

Zetas have supported the efforts of their fellow members and aided black communities through charity events conducted in churches, schools, and other community organizations. Moreover, Zeta's members provide scholarships, education, health and wellness programs, and financial advice to members of the African American community. Zeta works with women of various ages and varied educational backgrounds through its auxiliary organizations, Archonettes, for youth, and Amicae, for adults.

The broad reach of Zeta Phi Beta has contributed to its longevity as well as its many successes. Until public policy and national legislation provide equal access for all, organizations such as Zeta will continue to play an important role in fostering scholarship, service, sisterly love, and finer womanhood.

**FURTHER READINGS**

Ploski, Harry A., and James Williams. *The Negro Almanac: A Reference Work on the African American.* 5th ed. Detroit: Gale, 1989.

Walker, Cecily. "Zeta Phi Beta Sorority, Inc." *Ebony* (May 1991): 58–60.

———."Examples of Finer Womanhood: Zeta Phi Beta Sorority, Inc." *The Houston News Pages,* February 9–15, 1995, 4.

———. *The Archon* 44, 1 (Spring 1993): i, 4, 16, 22–27.

*Julie S. Doar*

# Zora Neale Hurston Society

In 1984, a group of scholars, journalists, educators, folklorists, historians, and students, under the leadership of Dr. Ruthe T. Sheffey, professor of English and former chair of Morgan State University's English Department, founded the Zora Neale Hurston Society (ZNHS).

Founding members included the novelists Paule Marshall and Toni Cade Bambara, the literary critics Haki Madhubuti and Henry Lewis Gates, the art historian Richard A. Long, and the professor of literature Mary Helen Washington.

The society seeks to promote appreciation for the life, works, and legacy of Zora Neale Hurston, a multitalented black anthropologist, dramatist, and novelist, who attended Morgan State University in 1917 and 1918. Moreover, the society is dedicated to the preservation of the works of other authors of the African Diaspora, particularly those of the first half of the twentieth century. The ZNHS was the first scholarly and literary society named for a notable African American female.

In 1986, the society launched publication of the *Zora Neale Hurston Forum.* The journal contains scholarly articles, critiques of black authors, and original poetry and prose, with a particular emphasis on women and their contributions to the literature of the African Diaspora. While the *Forum* serves largely as an outlet for African American academics, it has featured articles by Japanese, East Indian, German, and Jewish scholars, and a special issue has explored Afro-Canadian female writings. Many of the journal's essays are based on papers presented at the society's annual three-day international meeting, usually held on the first weekend in June. The preselected conference papers represent the best of the scholarly submissions. Originally published biannually, the *Forum* is now published annually.

The journal's broad range of literary coverage as well as the society's annual conference has attracted a large following. The society, headquartered at Morgan State University in Baltimore, Maryland, has currently over 100 members. Although most of the society's members are women, at least one-fourth of them are male.

*Ruthe T. Sheffey*

# Addendum

## National Association of Black Scuba Divers

The National Association of Black Scuba Divers (NABS) is an organization of African American divers interested in promoting awareness and providing education about scuba diving and aquatic environments in the black community. This national organization brings together individuals and local diving clubs to address interests and concerns of black divers as well as to promote fellowship and exchange of skills and experiences.

The NABS was established in January of 1991 by Dr. José Jones and Ric Powell. Members of Jones' Underwater Adventure Seekers—a club with over thirty years of diving experiences and a distinguished history, founded by Jones in Washington D.C.—provided the initial support and core charter membership for the NABS. Jones is an avid diver and spearfisher as well as a distinguished marine biologist. He constantly competes and places in scuba events. As a marine scholar, he has published in his field and has produced various slide and video series. He is also a widely respected diving instructor with certifications from the Atlantic Skin Diving Council (ASDC), Confédération Mondiale des Activités Subaquatiques (CMAS), and the Professional Association of Diving Instructors (PADI). He has trained over two thousand divers worldwide and is often referred to as the "black Jacques Costeau." NABS co-founder Ric Powell is also an active and dedicated scuba diving instructor with certifications from the National Association of Underwater Instructors (NAUI) and PADI. He has been an instructor at various academic institutions including the California State University and the University of South Florida in Tampa. His efforts have provided many students who might not have had the opportunity otherwise with scuba diving instruction and experiences. Powell has been especially recognized for his work with inner-city youth.

In 1991 Jones, Powell, and the Underwater Adventure Seekers organized a conference in Washington, D.C., on the Martin Luther King Jr. holiday to charter the NABS. The conference attracted divers and interested individuals from California, Florida, Maryland, New York, New Jersey, Ohio, Pennsylvania, Virginia, and the District of Columbia. The PADI headquarters and the Diving Equipment and Marketing Association (DEMA) provided financial support to the NABS.

Since its inception, the NABS has organized over fifty diving clubs nationwide. The organization is dedicated to providing networking opportunities for divers and clubs. For instance, the NABS sponsors an annual Dive Summit to foster interaction and cooperation between clubs. The Summit is an opportunity for NABS members to participate in a variety of diving trips and learning experiences. Past summits have been held in Ft. Lauderdale, Nassau, and Cozumel.

The NABS is a strong promoter of scuba diving awareness in the African American community. To this end, the NABS sponsors various activities. It develops and implements educational programs and provides a clearinghouse for safety and technical information. The NABS, through its annual Dive Summit and other events, sponsors trips and overseas excursions that individual clubs very often would not be able to undertake on their own. The NABS also provides scholarships for students interested in marine and environmental sciences. Overall, NABS members find in the organization a national network of fellow divers with whom they can share skills and experiences though various symposia, conferences, diving trips, and activities.

*Angel R. Rivera*

## National Association of Minority Contractors

The National Association of Minority Contractors (NAMC) is a nonprofit business trade association that seeks to provide education and training to minority contractors in the construction industry. As part of its mandate, the NAMC seeks to promote the economic and legal interests of its members through the advocacy of laws and government actions that benefit minority contractors. The NAMC was founded in 1969 to address the needs and concerns of minority contractors operating in the United States. As a liaison for minority contractors, the NAMC monitored the policies of government agencies affecting minority contractors.

The NAMC is headquartered in Washington, D.C., and has a membership base that extends over forty-seven states. The membership of the NAMC is diverse and reflects a wide variety of professions related to the construction industry. Membership consists of general contractors, subcontractors, manufacturers, suppliers, and local minority contractor associations. The NAMC offers four types of membership in its organization which relate to the occupational background of the prospective member. These are regular, associate, affiliate, and golden life memberships. Currently, NAMC membership consists of over 3,500 members.

In its role as an advocate for minority contractors, the NAMC disseminates to its members information concerning the construction industry, and publishes an assorted network of news bulletins in addition to a quarterly newsletter. Along with its advocacy role, the NAMC works with policy makers in Congress to meet the interests of minority contractors. The NAMC also conducts seminars and workshops to help minority contractors compete in the government and private sectors.

The NAMC's accomplishments are varied. Through its Major Corporation Program the NAMC has fostered relationships between major corporations and contractors and minority-owned businesses. Under the auspices of the Small Business Administration, the Minority Business Development Agency, and the Department of Labor, the NAMC has provided construction management training programs to minority contractors. In its capacity as advocate, the NAMC has testified before numerous congressional committees on behalf of minority contractors concerning issues such as prompt payment, bonding, construction financing, and government set asides.

*Opolot Okia*

### FURTHER READING

*National Association of Minority Contractors.* Washington, D.C.: National Association of Minority Contractors, n.d.

## National Bankers Association

The National Bankers Association (NBA) was founded as the National Negro Bankers Association in Durham, North Carolina, in 1927. Instrumental in laying the groundwork for the organization were Richard R. Wright of the Citizens Bank and Trust Company of Philadelphia and C. C. Spaulding of the Mechanics and Farmers Bank of Durham. Concerned about the exclusion of African Americans from the American Bankers Association, Wright and Spaulding met with representatives of nineteen black banks in Philadelphia in 1926, and in the following year launched the NBA.

The NBA seeks to strengthen and promote the general welfare and development of minority- and women-owned banks and the communities they serve. The NBA serves as an advocate of legislative and regulatory matters that concern and affect its members. The association also provides information to member banks with the objective of enhancing sound and profitable operations.

To be eligible for membership in the association a bank must share the common interests and concerns of the NBA and its members. Currently there are forty-six member banks in sixty-one cities, thirty states, and two territories. Member banks serve more than three million depositors, have a combined asset base of over $31 billion dollars, and provide employment for approximately 25,000 people. Banks not owned and operated by minorities and their staffs can join the NBA as "affiliate" members. There are now seven affiliate members as well as twelve individual or "associate" members of the NBA. The association has an operating budget of $60,000. Revenues generated by the membership, including dues, represent a substantial portion of the association's annual revenues. Dues are based on local assets and range from $2,000 to $15,000.

The U.S. government has cited the NBA and its Corporate Advisory Board (CAB), consisting of representatives from fourteen corporations, for their efforts to increase the number of Fortune 500 companies that do business with minority financial institutions and other minority businesses. Currently over two hundred of the Fortune 500 companies are doing business with NBA member banks. These relationships have generated over $30 million in lines of credit and $10.3 billion in non-credit services.

In addition to the CAB, the NBA has a member board of twelve officers. All positions, with the exception of the President, are elected positions. Elections take place at the NBA annual business meeting. Headquartered in Washington, D.C., the NBA provides its members with the semiannual magazine *NBA Today*.

*Maria Elena Raymond*

FURTHER READING

Henderson, Alexa Benson. "Richard R. Wright and the National Negro Bankers Association: Early Organizing Efforts Among Black Bankers, 1924–1942." *Pennsylvania Magazine of History and Biography* 117 (1993): 51–81.

"The National Bankers Association: What's It all About?" *Black Business Digest* 2 (December 1971): 31–32.

## National Black Media Coalition

Founded in 1973, the nonprofit National Black Media Coalition (NBMC) promotes the interests of African Americans in the communications industry. As an advocacy group, it seeks to broaden black employment opportunities in the media professions and to promote the inclusion of African Americans in the policy decisions of the communications industry.

Headquartered in Silver Spring, Maryland, the NBMC hosts regional and annual conferences to foster networking and to assess progress. The NBMC also sponsors training seminars for participating companies, which focus on human resource development, multicultural and diversity training, and media relations. The NBMC maintains an Employment Resource Center, which acts as a job bank and referral center. To attract young African Americans to the communications industry, the NBMC offers college students internships in various branches of the industry such as journalism, marketing, and public relations. The NBMC's quarterly newsletter, *Media Line*, contains information about the communications industry that is pertinent to African Americans, while its monthly, *Career Moves*, provides a listing of employment opportunities in the media. In addition, the NBMC pub-

lishes the *Career Makers Directory*, which lists hundred of internships, training programs, and fellowships.

The NBMC has negotiated pioneering affirmative action agreements with at least eighty leading media organizations. These agreements have increased minority employment and led to the appointment of African Americans to the boards of corporations with substantial media interests. One of the accomplishments of the NBMC has been the creation of a Minority Ownership Investment Fund, which has generated increased investments in minority-owned banks. The NBMC has also been instrumental in awarding more than $2.5 million designated for grants, scholarships, and internships at predominantly African American post-secondary educational institutions such as Clark Atlanta University, Texas Southern University, Johnson C. Smith University, and Howard University. In part as a result of the NBMC's efforts, minority employment in the media industry increased by 10 percent and minority ownership increased fourfold by 1998.

*Opolot Okia*

FURTHER READING

*National Black Media Coalition*. Silver Spring, Md.: National Black Media Coalition, n.d.

## National Black Youth Leadership Council

The National Black Youth Leadership Council (NBYLC) was founded in 1983 with a five-member staff. This organization provides educational opportunities—including workshops, skills training, and personal development and enrichment programs—to groups working with black youth. The NBYLC is particularly concerned with reducing the number of black high school dropouts. Moreover, it seeks to improve school and community relationships, reduce racism and bigotry, and prevent drug abuse. The NBYLC provides training and support to parents, teachers, and administrators in the areas of multiculturalism and diversity issues.

*Thalia M. Mulvihill*

## National Caucus and Center on Black Aged

The National Caucus and Center on Black Aged (NCBA) is a housing, employment, and advocacy organization for the African American aged community. Its goal is to improve the lives of the African American and low-income elderly. The NCBA advocates policy changes in economic, health, and social conditions of low-income senior citizens at the local, state, and national levels. Through its educational and community programs, it helps to promote awareness of issues affecting the elderly community.

Hobart C. Jackson of Philadelphia, a home nursing professional, established the NCBA with a group of concerned citizens in 1970. Initially, the organization was interested in assuring that the 1971 White House Conference on Aging would address the specific needs and concerns of the African American elderly. The NCBA continued to operate as an advocacy group until 1973. At that time, the organization received a grant from the Administration on Aging to conduct research on the African American elderly population, to train personnel to work with the elderly, and to serve as an information resource center. In 1978, the organization expanded its scope further when it began to operate the Senior Community Service Employment Program in five states with a grant from the U.S. Department of Labor. Currently, the NCBA's employment program involves about two thousand senior citizens in fourteen states.

Since 1977, the NCBA has been active in providing housing for low-income elderly and disabled citizens. In conjunction with the Housing and Urban Development (HUD) Department's Section 202 Program, the organization has developed twelve housing projects for low-income elderly and disabled persons. The NCBA created a subsidiary corporation, the NCBA Housing Management Corporation (HMC), to oversee its housing development activities. The HMC provides housing management services as well as health and social services to residents of housing projects. Currently, the NCBA-HMC manages Section 202 properties in Florida, Maryland, and Washington, D.C. The organization has been recognized for consistently implementing housing standards above those established by HUD in terms of maintenance, income, cost-control, and accounting. Among its social and health services, the NCBA-HMC develops and implements programs in disease prevention and wellness promotion, public benefits counseling, alcohol and drug abuse awareness, and recreational activities. These programs are provided free of charge. In addition, the HMC trains senior citizens as aides in support of the projects. This program provides meaningful employment for senior citizens and offers support for the program staff, without adding costs to the overall project operations.

In addition, the NCBA conducts training and internships for those pursuing careers in nursing home administration, long term care, housing management, and commercial property maintenance. The NCBA also offers a graduate fellowship in gerontology. To further its goal of raising awareness of issues affecting the elderly community, the NCBA publishes the *Golden Page*, a newsletter that reports on issues of concern to the elderly and provides a legislative update.

*Angel R. Rivera*

### FURTHER READING
Sheets, Tara E., ed. *Encyclopedia of Associations.* Detroit: Gale, 1999.

## National Coalition of Black Lesbians and Gay Men

In 1979 a small band of black activists formed the National Coalition of Black Gays in Washington, D.C. This group soon worked in conjunction with African American lesbians and adopted the name National Coalition of Black Lesbians and Gay Men (NCBLGM). The NCBLGM is a political activist group that seeks to improve the legal status and the perception of black lesbians and gay men. It challenges homophobia and racism and seeks to establish a sense of cultural and political unity among African American gays and lesbians. The Coalition also cooperates with other gay and lesbian organizations to coordinate protests against homophobic legislation and to influence public opinion.

Its initial and most active chapter, the D.C. Coalition of Black Lesbians, Gay Men, and Bisexuals, has conducted most NCBLGM activities. In the 1990s when gay issues and concerns became part of many public debates, the Coalition lobbied on behalf of black lesbians and gay men in the nation's capital. In July of 1991, the D.C. chapter pressed district council members to amend the district's sodomy laws by decriminalizing oral and anal sex between consenting adults over the age of sixteen. While Jim Nathanson, a Democratic D.C. Council member, supported the measure, it ultimately failed to become law because the council claimed it was too busy to consider the amendment.

Moving beyond the realm of local politics, the D.C. chapter of the NCBLGM also challenges homophobia in African American communities nationwide. In 1994, for example, black gay and lesbian demonstrators celebrated the silver anniversary of the Stonewall riot, which gave birth to the gay rights movement in New York City's Greenwich Village in June of 1969. In commemoration, they participated in a parade that proceeded past the United Nations building.

The NCBLGM has also struggled to gain the political and social recognition of the African American community. When the Nation of Islam announced plans for its 1995 Million Man March in Washington, D.C., the Coalition protested sexist and homophobic comments made by Nation of Islam leader Louis Farrakhan and other organizers of the march. In opposition to the event, the D.C. chapter staged a counter-protest at the Carnegie Library on Mount Vernon Square, and was the only gay and lesbian organization to do so.

Through protests, lobbying efforts, and public education, the NCBLGM seeks to overcome prejudices and discrimination that black homosexuals experience by virtue of their race, gender, and sexual orientation.

*Stephanie Gilmore*

FURTHER READING

Dewey, Jeanne, and Brian Blomquist. "Black Foes of March Schedule Visible Events in Opposition." *The Washington Times*, 15 October 1995.

"How D.C. Makes Felons out of Honest Citizens." *The Washington Post*, 21 July 1991.

Wheeler, Linda. "Honoring Stonewall: Hundreds Join Gay Rights March in N.Y." *The Washington Post*, 26 June 1994.

# National Coalition on Black Voter Participation

Founded in 1976, the nonpartisan National Coalition on Black Voter Participation (NCBVP) seeks to increase the number of registered minority voters. Its membership is small, consisting of approximately ninety individuals who are active in religious organizations, sororities, fraternities, government and political groups, labor organizations, and black caucuses. In addition to increasing black voter registration and participation in elections, the NCBVP conducts training programs and collects and analyzes data, including statistics on the black voting age population. Headquartered in Washington, D.C., the group also provides guidance, informational pamphlets, teaching tools, and funding for local independent coalitions to help increase black voter participation. For its

members, the NCBVP issues the bimonthly *Operation Big Vote Newsletter* and sponsors an annual seminar to update skills and increase community awareness. At the time of its founding, the organization also created and funded Operation Big Vote (OBV), which targets specific communities that have large black populations or histories of low black voter participation. OBV provides onsite training and funding for local nonpartisan coalitions that seek to enhance black voter participation and supports community-based programs in thirty-one states. In 1983, the NCBVP also started to provide funding for the Black Women's Roundtable on Voter Participation (BWRVP), which focuses on voter registration and education as well as empowerment programs specifically designed to increase the number of black women voters. Moreover, the BWRVP provides black women with the opportunity to exercise their leadership skills.

*Maria Elena Raymond*

FURTHER READING

Jaszczak, Sandra, ed. *Encyclopedia of Associations: An Associations Unlimited Reference, National Organizations of the U.S.*, 32nd ed., vol. 1. New York: Gale, 1997.

# National Colored Spiritual Association of Churches, Inc.

The National Colored Spiritual Association of Churches (NCSAC) was founded as an auxiliary of the National Spiritual Association (NSA) of Churches in 1925. Since 1893, the NSA had operated as an integrated organization mainly in northern cities. During the racial unrest that erupted in the aftermath of World War I, the NSA started to discuss forming a separate black wing. In response, the NCSAC was formed at the Labor Temple on Euclid Avenue in Cleveland, Ohio, on April 21, 1925. Among the black founders were the Reverend John R. White, president; Sara Harrington, vice president; and Mrs. C. W. Dennison, secretary.

The NCSAC charters member churches, ordains ministers, and licenses healers. The NCSAC, like the NSA, believes in communicating with the dead through the use of spiritual mediums. According to the NCSAC, mediumship demonstrates the principles of prophecy and the survival of individuals after death. The organization believes that happiness can be achieved by obeying the natural and spiritual laws of nature. Women, who have assumed leadership positions in the NCSAC, have launched a subsidiary which is headquartered in Phoenix,

Arizona, and administered by the Reverend Nellie Mae Taylor. To facilitate communication between its members, the NCSAC launched publication of the newsletter the *National Spiritualist Reporter* in 1926.

*Sherry Sherrod DuPree*

**FURTHER READING**

DuPree, Sherry Sherrod. *African-American Holiness Pentecostal Movement: An Annotated Bibliography.* New York: Garland Publishing, Inc., 1996.

## National Conference of Black Mayors

The National Conference of Black Mayors (NCBM) was founded in 1974. The NCBM, headquartered in Atlanta, is a nonprofit organization that serves as a support network for black mayors throughout the United States. It provides its members with management skills and technical assistance and serves as a lobbying group advocating equity in employment, health care, education, and voter participation. The NCBM compiles and disseminates information about the status of African Americans and maintains task force committees on Economic Development, Energy, Black and Minority Health, and Environment and Public Policy. The NCBM also examines systemic patterns of racism and inequality in the employment sector and in the admission policies of colleges and universities.

The NCBM objectives are to improve the executive management capacity and efficiency of member municipalities; to create viable communities in which normal government function can be performed efficiently; to provide the basis upon which new social overhead investments in the infrastructure of municipalities can utilize federal, state, local, and private resources to encourage new industry and increase employment; and to assist municipalities in stabilizing their population (Jaszczak, 566).

The NCBM has approximately four hundred members who are either mayors or hold other elected positions in city governments. The majority of black mayors has served in cities—such as New York City; Atlantic City; and Gary, Indiana—that have faced severe economic problems, racial tensions, and physical deterioration. Among the NCBM's more illustrious members are the late Harold Washington of Chicago; Marion Barry of Washington, D.C.; and Andrew Young and Maynard Jackson of Atlanta.

The NCBM has five full-time secretaries and administrators and chapters in nineteen states that discuss public policies and issues of administrative concern affecting African American constituencies. In 1988, the NCBM established a Black Women Mayors Caucus (BWMC) to enhance the role of black women mayors; to focus national attention on the needs of black women elected officials; to expose young black women to the challenges of elected offices; and to examine issues that are of particular concern to women. In 1990 Unita Blackwell, who was elected mayor of Meyersville, Mississippi, in 1976, became the first black woman to serve as president of the NCBM.

The NCBM conducts annual leadership institutes for fifty black mayors to assist with management, financial planning, human resources, and personnel issues. Moreover, the NCBM holds an annual convention which provides networking opportunities and serves as a communication forum for black mayors. The NCBM has played a crucial role in fostering social networks, group solidarity, and the coercive capacity for African Americans to examine systems and patterns of government, public policy, economics, health care, and critical social issues that address race, gender, and class.

*James L. Conyers Jr.*

**FURTHER READINGS**

Estell, Kenneth, ed. *The African American Almanac.* Detroit: Gale, 1994.

Jaszczak, Sandra, ed. *Encyclopedia of Association.* Detroit: Gale, 1997.

Williams, Michael W., ed. *The African American Encyclopedia*, vol. 4. North Bellmore, N.Y.: Marshall Cavendish Corporation, 1993.

## National Conference of Black Political Scientists

In 1969 faculty and administrators from Southern University, Atlanta University, and Howard University founded the National Conference of Black Political Scientists (NCOBPS) at Southern University in Baton Rouge, Louisiana. The NCOBPS was the product of the 1960s black power movement, which "unleashed the desire for an indigenous scholarship of Black peoples," "challenged the hegemony of white scholarship," promoted Pan-Africanism, and advocated a call for African Americans to organize (Walters, 365). This was reflected in the NCOBPS's motto "Seeking the key to African unity."

The NCOBPS's goal was to develop "a new, a different political science, a black political science, and . . . an organization that would be a part of that interrelated network of self-defining and self-directed black organizations involved in the struggle for black liberation" (Jones 1990, p. 4). The NCOBPS sought to define and direct African American intellectualism, autonomous social thought, political behavior, and action. Thus, the founding members of the NCOBPS made the conscious decision not to become a caucus of the American Political Science Association (APSA), which they believed marginalized black scholars, but to remain an autonomous organization.

Initially, the NCOBPS focused on the dissemination of information and the application of social science research to address social and political problems confronting African Americans. Moreover, the organization sought to "encourage research, publication, and scholarship by black Americans in political science; and improve the political life of black Americans" (*Encyclopedia of Associations*, p. 730). For this purpose, the NCOBPS launched in 1989 the *National Political Science Review* (*NPSR*) to provide a scholarly forum for alternative research perspectives on black politics.

The NCOBPS is governed by a president, a president elect, a secretary, a treasurer, a membership secretary, a parliamentarian, historians, and a ten-member council including the editor of the *NPSR* and the *NCOBPS Newsletter*.

Currently, the NCOBPS has approximately four hundred members, most of whom are university faculty and administrators with cognitive areas of study in political science, social science, law, and related professional areas of interest. The NCOBPS sponsors graduate assistantships, compiles data on black political behavior, provides service to High School students, publishes the annual journal *NPSR* and the *NCOBPS Newsletter*, and holds an annual conference at which it presents Annual Service Awards to members who have demonstrated excellence in teaching and research.

The NCOBPS continues to pursue its aims and objectives. Some of the founding members, however, have acknowledged that the organization has made an ideological transition from activism to formal politics. Nevertheless, the NCOBPS's effort to examine and interpret political science from an African American perspective has generated new research as well as alternative analytical frameworks.

*James L. Conyers Jr.*

### FURTHER READING

Jaszczak, Sandra, ed. *Encyclopedia of Associations*, vol. 1. Detroit: Gale, 1997.

Jones, Mack H. "Responsibility of Black Political Scientists to the Black Community." In Shelby Lewis Smith, ed. *Black Political Scientists and Black Survival: Essays in Honor of a Black Scholar*. Detroit: Balamp Publications, 1977.

———. "NCOBPS: Twenty Years Later." *National Political Science Review* 2 (1990): 3–12.

Pinderhuges, Diane M. "NCOBPS: Observations on the State of the Organization." *National Political Science Review* 2 (1990): 13–21.

Walters, Ronald W. *Pan Africanism in the African Diaspora: An Analysis of Modern Afrocentric Movements*. Detroit: Wayne State University Press, 1993.

## National Congress of Black Faculty

The National Congress of Black Faculty was founded in 1988 to serve African American faculty, administrators, and graduate students. The members of the National Congress provide resources and services to assist black professionals in higher education with problems such as academic freedom, tenure issues, and racial or gender discrimination. Furthermore, this organization has a broad mission to support the professional development of African Americans working in the field of higher education. It publishes the *National Congress of Black Faculty Newsletter* three times per year and holds an annual conference for its approximately 250 members.

*Thalia M. Mulvihill*

## National Hook-Up of Black Women

Founded in 1975, the National Hook-Up of Black Women serves as a nationwide communication and political network for African American women. Its goal is to improve the quality of life of the African American community while advancing the status of black women by eliminating racism as well as sexism. For this purpose, the organization encourages African Americans to exercise their right to vote and familiarize themselves with the political process. The National Hook-Up has its roots in the Congressional Black Caucus (CBC), a group of black members of Congress that began meeting annually in 1970 to discuss the impact of politics on the African American community. While the first meetings of the CBC were formal dinners in celebration of African

Americans who had made a difference in the black community in the arena of politics, the social events soon grew into weekends filled with political meetings, receptions, and functions.

The National Hook-Up emerged in 1975 when a group of black women decided to retain and foster the contacts they had established while attending the CBC's annual meetings. Arnita Young Boswell became the group's first national chairwoman. Though the National Hook-Up never adopted an exclusively feminist agenda, it helped create a network of organizations dedicated to eliminating racism and groups concerned with sexism. In 1984, for example, the organization helped launch a nonpartisan coalition in Washington, D.C. to celebrate Susan B. Anthony's 164th birthday and to initiate a massive voter registration drive for that year's national election. The National Hook-Up also served as one of several organizations representing African American women in the Council of Presidents, an umbrella organization of over one hundred groups representing more than six million women. In 1996, through the Council of Presidents, the National Hook-Up joined forces with other women's groups in a successful effort to prevent the removal of the Lifetime cable television channel in favor of another news channel.

The National Hook-Up has also worked in African American communities to educate black voters. In 1982, it sponsored candidate forums in African American neighborhoods in the Washington, D.C., area enabling constituents to see, meet, and question political candidates. In 1990, the organization sponsored a "leadership tour" that brought inner-city black youth from Chicago to the nation's capital.

The National Hook-Up collaborates with other women's groups and works in African American communities to provide black women with a powerful political voice. It encourages political activism among Americans who have historically been marginalized in the political process, including youth, women, and people of color, and its members provide positive role models for black women.

*Stephanie Gilmore*

**FURTHER READINGS**

Karlovich, Janice. "Chicago Teens Bring Worries to Capital." *Chicago Tribune*, 30 September 1990.

Kleiman, Carol. "More Black Women Tied to Low-Wage Jobs." *Chicago Tribune*, 24 June 1991.

Krucoff, Carol. "Woman of the Moment: The Politics of Susan B. Anthony's 164th Birthday." *The Washington Post*, 15 February 1984.

Sauve, Frances. "Forums for State and County Candidates." *The Washington Post*, 8 September 1982.

Trescott, Jacqueline. "The Caucus and the Comet." *The Washington Post*, 26 September 1977.

"Women's Groups Call on TCI and Fox to Reconsider Their Decision to Drop Lifetime, Television for Women." *PR Newswire*, 19 September 1996.

## New Orleans: Civic, Literary, and Mutual Aid Associations

Perhaps no single southern African American community dramatized the racial and class rift often evident in black fraternal, benevolent, and literary societies more than nineteenth and twentieth century New Orleans. Because of the admixture of cultures, and intertwining blood, language, and religion, African Americans who formed New Orleans' social club elite were not simply mulattos, but rather were Creoles, that is, African Americans mixed with Spanish, French, English, and Native Americans. Perhaps an extreme example of the domination of culture involved the Franco-African New Orleans club, whose library contained only materials written in French and whose meetings were conducted entirely in French. Anyone who could not speak French could not become a member.

Early scholars tended to agree that among New Orleans' black and Creole organizations, class was conflated with culture and complexion. More recent scholars, however, refute such notions and contend that New Orleans never had a mulatto-defined organization such as the Brown Fellowship Society in Charleston, South Carolina. Franco-Africans in New Orleans, notwithstanding the aristocratic sentiments of a few, "did not neatly categorize themselves by color; and the city's black Anglo-Americans, with their own organizational network, similarly failed to replicate the Charleston experience" (Hirsch and Logsdon, 156). Instead, these scholars argue that when Crescent City Creole elites wished to express a sense of institutional exclusivity, they organized on the basis of class and profession, creating the Société d'Economie and Société des Artisans. Sheer numbers tell one story; black fraternal, benevolent, and literary clubs flourished in the late nineteenth century.

In his pioneering work, John Blassingame noted that between 1862 and 1880, there were more than 226

Negro societies listed in the Signature Books of the Freedmen's Bank. In addition to the usual assortment of fraternal societies such as the Odd Fellows, New Orleans boasted thirteen Negro baseball clubs by 1875, including one state champion. Despite the claim that many fraternal and societal groups lacked any business acumen, the value of real property owned by several black social organizations averaged about $12,000. Wealth and prestige accounted for the influence of clubs and their members in city and state politics. The coveted Americus Club was founded in 1874 to "cultivate literary tastes . . . and to sponsor debates and lectures." Many of its members were graduates of Straight University and several were prominent members of Louisiana's Reconstruction government. However much class divided Creoles and blacks socially, white prejudice behooved Creoles and blacks to work together to accomplish mutual political goals and racial progress.

Club life was center stage of New Orleans' black high culture. In a city known for its Mardi Gras parades and balls, the entire city lived up to its wanton reputation for *Laissez les bons temps rouler* (let the good times roll). White antipathy for black wealth and prestige was palpable, and this harassment included the sacred as well as the secular. Perhaps the worst case of such haranguing occurred in 1858, when white city officials endeavored to curtail the clandestine abolitionist activities of the African Methodist Episcopal (AME) Church. Eventually, the city passed an ordinance that "banned any black organization or church not under the control of whites." Besieged AMEs found refuge in the Congregational Churches around town and in Prince Hall Mason lodges. So enamored were the AMEs of the Prince Hall Masons that "the leadership of AME churches was almost identical to that of the Prince Hall Masons in New Orleans" (Hirsch and Logsdon, 214). Prince Hall Masonic lodges provided an important nucleus for political activism and harbingers for twentieth century political organizations.

The fiduciary care of New Orleans' black and Creole citizens was not left to that city's black and Creole secular benevolent associations. Churches played a large role also, particularly when the exigency concerned neglected and wayward youth. As with the case of the black Baptist sponsored Union Sisters Asylum, orphanage work became vital in the wake of the Civil War when large numbers of black children were rendered orphans because of the ravages of war. In some cases, a parent was not deceased but merely missing or had abandoned the family. Benevolent and fraternal secret orders shared one commonality, they refused to leave the well-being of the African American community to the kindness of strangers.

Unable to gain protection from its white guardians and benefactors, New Orleans' black and Creole clubs and societies found their protection in politics. The Louisiana Progressive Club was overtly political in its activities and boasted among its members P. B. S. Pinchback, Louisiana's first elected African American lieutenant governor who briefly served as governor in 1873. Indeed, the Louisiana Progressive Club fought to protect the very rights won during the hard scrabble of Reconstruction. Sometimes it was difficult for an outside observer to ascertain the true nature of a club's work. "In New Orleans, the Iroquois Literary and Social Club, which in the early twentieth century owned a building with 'spacious parlors,' appeared to be more social than literary but in fact was neither. Rather it was a Republican organization whose membership included politically active men of the city's social elite" (Gatewood, 214).

New Orleans' black clubs, societies, and benevolent associations were the most important agencies involved in organized efforts to solve community social problems. Savings institutions provided loans; sometimes receiving nothing more than pennies, these banks amassed considerable wealth. Insurance companies guarded against lost wages due to illness or death. They guaranteed financial assistance to widows as well as orphans. In addition, burial insurance policies provided for bands in funeral processions as well as arranged for special ceremonies and ceremonial attire. A few burial societies even fined members who failed to attend the wakes of deceased members. The Good Samaritans and the Union Benevolent Association both provided cemeteries for their members. Some benevolent societies were so complete in attending to their members' needs that *Les Jeunes Amis* recruited physicians and pharmacists into their organization ostensibly to care for its members. Similarly, *La Concorde* cared for its convalescent members out of a sense of "racial pride and *noblesse oblige*" (Blassingmae 169).

*Derryn E. Moten*

**FURTHER READINGS**

Blassingame, John W. *Black New Orleans, 1860–1880.* Chicago: The University of Chicago Press, 1973.

Gatewood, Willard B. *Aristocrats of Color: The Black Elite, 1880–1920.* Bloomington, Ind.: Indiana University Press, 1990.

Hirsch, Arnold R. and Joseph Logsdon. *Creole New Or-leans: Race and Americanization*. Baton Rouge, La.: Louisiana State University Press, 1992.

Porter, Dorothy B. "The Organized Educational Activities of Negro Literary Societies, 1828–1846." *The Journal of Negro Education*, 5 (1936): 555–576.

## New Orleans Community Relations Council

Formed in 1962, the Community Relations Council (CRC) was an interracial organization composed of black and white political leaders who banded together to redress police brutality and other manifestations of racial bigotry and Jim Crowism in New Orleans. The brainchild of its founding member, Helen Mervis, the CRC acted as a liaison between white city fathers and the black community in an effort to wrest civil rights from New Orleans' white leadership. Hence, black CRC members held leadership positions in other groups whose work was of vital interest to black city residents. The CRC was the same type of moderate, interracial coalition as the larger constituency-based National Urban League or National Association for the Advancement of Colored People. Black and white CRC members displayed so much racial decorum that some black city residents accused black CRC members of being too cozy with whites.

However, the CRC was a stalwart, and it showed no trepidation about taking city officials to court or about imposing economic boycotts of white businesses when its efforts at diplomacy failed. The CRC served as the cauldron of activists who did not capitulate in the heat of battle. The organization was also important because it provided women with the opportunity to test their political acumen in a civil rights movement that often privileged male leadership but counted on its sizeable women cohorts.

*Derryn E. Moten*

**FURTHER READING**

Rogers, Kim Lacy. *Righteous Lives: Narratives of the New Orleans Civil Rights Movement*. New York: New York University Press, 1993.

# Index

Entries with page numbers in **bold** indicate main entries. Entries with page numbers in *Italics* indicate illustrations.